Hockey Prospectus 2015-16

ANALYTICAL INSIGHTS INTO THE 2015-16 NHL SEASON

Tom Awad • Stephen Burtch • Matt Cane • Scott Charles
Wesley Chu • Matthew Coller • John Fischer • Lucas Friesen
Sam Hitchcock • Pat Holden • Matthew Kory • Jason Lewis
William Loewen • Micah Blake McCurdy • Dustin Nelson
Shane O'Donnell • Jack Ries • Benoit Roy • JH Schroeder
Ryan Schwepfinger • Timo Seppa • Ryan Stimson
Rob Vollman • Ryan Wagman • Ryan Wilson • Erik Yost

Edited by Timo Seppa and Matthew Coller
Cover by Amanda Bonner
Layout by Vince Verhei and Meredith Clark

Copyright 2015 Timo Seppa

ISBN-13: 978-1517518806

ISBN-10: 1517518806

All rights reserved

Without limiting the rights under copyright reserved above, no part of this publication may be reproduced, stored in or introduced into a retrieval system, or transmitted, in any form, or by any means (electronic, mechanical, photocopying, recording, or otherwise), without the prior written permission of both the copyright owner and the above publisher of this book.

Table of Contents

Foreword	v
Introduction to GVT and VUKOTA	vii
Introduction to Total Performance Charts	xiii
Introduction to Score-Adjusted and Goaltender Statistics	xix

NHL Teams

Anaheim Ducks	1
Arizona Coyotes	16
Boston Bruins	31
Buffalo Sabres	47
Calgary Flames	62
Carolina Hurricanes	78
Chicago Blackhawks	92
Colorado Avalanche	108
Columbus Blue Jackets	126
Dallas Stars	143
Detroit Red Wings	158
Edmonton Oilers	173
Florida Panthers	189
Los Angeles Kings	203
Minnesota Wild	216
Montreal Canadiens	232
Nashville Predators	247
New Jersey Devils	263
New York Islanders	279
New York Rangers	293
Ottawa Senators	308
Philadelphia Flyers	322
Pittsburgh Penguins	337
St. Louis Blues	352
San Jose Sharks	365
Tampa Bay Lightning	380
Toronto Maple Leafs	394
Vancouver Canucks	410
Washington Capitals	425
Winnipeg Jets	439

Fenwick vs. Estimated Possession from Play-by-Play	455
Microstat Tracking 2.0: Passes	458
Top 100 NHL Prospects	462
Player Tables	482
Biographies	506
Glossary	511
Appendix	520
Index	521

Foreword

To kick off *Hockey Prospectus 2015-16*, I would like to talk to you about the state of statistical analysis in hockey: where we have come from, and where we are now.

As a long-time, diehard baseball fan, I have often contrasted the baseball and hockey statistical analysis ("analytics") movements. While not perfectly overlapping, there are certainly a lot of similarities. The arguments against progression are strikingly similar, as is the drastic overhaul of an industry in a short period of time. If anything, once other sports had proved the concept's merit in their fields, and once the ball got rolling in hockey, the pace of its widespread acceptance has arguably occurred faster than it did in baseball.

These changes were not the result of analytics companies forming, or teams looking to experiment. While those things have been happening for a while, the analytics movements in both baseball and hockey were initiated and driven by a particular group of people. One could argue that their work ethic regarding the analysis was unreasonable given the complete lack of financial incentives, and the audience was incredibly small. These groups of bloggers and fans, who could also be called academics, lawyers, engineers, scientists, or just overall smart people, helped create a voice, and a demand, for quality statistical analysis in hockey. It was out of this demand that sites like *Hockey Prospectus* (and *Baseball Prospectus* before it) were born, and it was what drew me to them. It was easy to qualify this new group of people as a niche… until they started getting calls right.

While we can get bogged down on the everyday conversations of a player's Corsi, one would be misinformed if they were unaware of how hockey analysts have answered some big questions over the last decade. As a short example list: the value of outshooting opponents versus shooting percentage; the talent in shot quality; the amount of time needed to gain value from special teams; how long it takes for a goalie's save percentage to normalize; the impact of opponents, linemates, and zone usage on performance; the impact of scorer bias on a goalie's stats; the merit of adjusting stats for the score of a game; how to quantify a player's game in all aspects, and then turning that into a financial value relevant for a hard salary-cap world.

Some of the answers simply reinforced existing beliefs within the industry. However, many people aren't as informed as those within the industry and needed this insight to learn about the game. On the other hand, many discoveries ran contrary to the common beliefs of hockey people. For instance, there is still resistance within some corners of the NHL to the idea of shooting-percentage regression, and overreaction to a goalie's three-month performance. One could easily argue that without the diehard hockey analysts, like those at *Hockey Prospectus*, the ones who plug away for the love of the game, and for the love of knowledge, that these big debates would not have occurred over the previous 10 years.

Like baseball, and other sports, hockey is substantially better off as a community for being more knowledgeable. Now, arguments over evaluations are more precise, and detailed, not to mention many of the newer metrics are quite simple. Detractors can no longer get away with the excuse that the game is too hard to quantify, complaining that there are too many variables to account for. It may not be perfect, but the hit rate for those who make evaluations using a variety of numbers, and their acquired skill for interpreting those numbers, has gotten attention for a reason.

Of course, we have a ways to go. Like how the baseball statistical community still has questions to answer about defense, in hockey, we still have big questions to answer: isolating performance; how to properly evaluate goalies; and what are the ideal tactics for a team to implement. But maybe the answers aren't too far away with the advances of new technology. What we can be sure of is that the demand to have those questions answered hasn't gone away—it has grown exponentially, and people will continue to discover

FOREWORD

new, exciting revelations about the game we all love, and they will have the evidence to back it up.

I read *Hockey Prospectus* originally for the new and thoughtful insight about an area of the game I had a strong desire to learn more about. As with *Baseball Prospectus*, the talent, and the commitment created an appeal in an emerging field. *Hockey Prospectus* is one of the longest-standing institutions in a field that has shed the "emerging" label, and is now established, and important.

This book, *Hockey Prospectus 2015-16*, will cover the complexities of player projection in a manner you won't find in other places. It will statistically break down players for the casual and hardcore fan alike. It will carefully review last season and preview the upcoming one, not with a lazy opinion, but with reasoned analysis backed up by evidence. As I did in this space for four years, you will also see a group of up-and-coming scouts go into an excellent analysis on the top NHL prospects. You may not recognize every author's name, although some are already quite noteworthy in the field, but do know that they all smart, care a lot about this sport, and put a volume of work into this publication that may make you question their sanity.

So give this book a read. You might learn something.

Corey Pronman

Introduction to GVT and VUKOTA

Last summer, NHL general managers embraced analytics, naming several well-known analytics experts to positions within their organizations. This year, the NHL itself came on board, rolling out a new website that contains—and officializes—several of the metrics that have been used by the analytics community over the last several years. While the website itself may have had some growing pains, the message was clear: advanced statistics are here to stay.

This matters more than people think. Not only does the NHL's involvement formalize names for statistics, such as SAT (formerly Corsi), that had lived with informal monikers for years, but official NHL statistics are the only ones that can be used for official NHL processes, such as salary arbitration. As a consequence, good possession players will eventually start to be recognized at their fair value, and the NHL's salary structure will converge closer to the true value of players. Hockey analytics is having far-reaching effects on every aspect of the NHL.

This is not very surprising. The statistics revolution has taken over one sport after another, starting with baseball, followed by basketball, and now moving to hockey and soccer. It used to be the case that there was no objective way to analyze hockey. Hockey statistics were long laggards in North American professional sports, especially compared with baseball, and to a lesser extent, basketball. For decades, fans had to content themselves with Goals, Assists, Points, Penalty Minutes, and Goals Against Average. There was no way to know who had good numbers due to ice-time, linemates, or luck, and absolutely no way whatsoever to quantify defense. Because of this dearth of information, player reputations hinged on the success of their teams: if you played for the Montreal Canadiens, you were a superstar because, hey, look at all those Stanley Cups! Conversely, many players from the weaker teams of previous eras have faded into obscurity, lacking the validation that team success brings.

We have come a long way from that time. Today, there is an embarrassment of statistics, both available in raw form from the NHL and other outlets, as well as analytical statistics produced by a number of professionals, amateurs, and charlatans. Today, the challenge is not getting access to statistics but interpreting them, understanding what they mean, and figuring out which ones bode for future success and which ones are meaningless. At *Hockey Prospectus*, we take great pride in having knowledgeable hockey fans, and we take it seriously as our job to help them become even more knowledgeable. It is in this spirit that we present to you our latest offering, *Hockey Prospectus 2015-16*.

Each year, our job gets more challenging. Hockey fans are getting more knowledgeable about statistics by the day, as players' relative possession numbers and shooting percentage regression are now quoted in the mainstream media, and even casual fans may now be aware of statistics like Corsi. In a way, we are victims of our own—and the community's—success. Our mission has always been to bring awareness and statistical insight to hockey. Now that this awareness has blossomed, people are demanding more, better, deeper analysis. We are rising to this challenge.

This is our sixth annual, and once again our objective is to not only entertain but to explain. Herein, we expect that a hockey fan will find a complete recap of the 2014-15 NHL season, and an understanding: Why did things happen as they did? Was it a fluke? What can we expect in the future? In this book, you will find statistics and projections for every player who appeared in the NHL last season, as well as comments to help you get a better understanding of the players and teams involved. We recap each team's 2014-15 campaign, and explain whether they got the results they deserved or were the beneficiaries of good luck, or conversely, the victims of bad bounces. We also explain what you should expect from them in 2015-16, and why. We obviously don't limit our analysis to just statistics: that would be missing a significant part of the picture. But we do ground all of our opinions in facts.

While aiming to improve on traditional hockey statistics, we have developed a fair number of metrics of our own to measure hockey players' performance. One of our most fundamental statistics, one that you will be seeing a lot of in this annual, is GVT. GVT stands for Goals Versus Threshold: it is a measure of how much value a player contributes above what a replacement-level player would have contributed. For those of you who are familiar with baseball statistics, think of GVT as VORP applied to hockey.

"Replacement level" is an important concept in all player evaluation metrics. It means the next-best-available talent level. In other words, who gets called up if a player is injured? In the NHL, 13th forwards or seventh defensemen are considered replacement level, as are good AHL players. A replacement-level team would get outscored by 1.5 goals per game on average, or 123 goals over the course of an entire season. Replacement level explains why Pavel Datsyuk, who scored 65 points in 63 games, was as valuable offensively as Jiri Hudler, who scored 76 points in 78 games. However, it is even more essential that that.

GVT, as its name implies, is calculated in goals. This is fundamental: goals, not wins, are the currency of hockey games. While hockey is ultimately about winning or losing, players' contributions always come down to scoring goals and preventing them. A player cannot "win" a game, even though he may be put in a situation where scoring a goal or making a key save would create or conserve a win. Each player's role, no matter his position, is to try and increase the goal differential in favor of his team. An offensive player who scores a hat trick only to see his teammates allow four goals against has nevertheless done his job; a goaltender who stops 39 of 40 shots only to lose 1-0 has likewise performed well. Using this standard, all players can be compared by the same yardstick: how much did they help (or harm) their team's goal differential?

Because GVT is measured in goals, it has built-in accounting: teams also have GVT, which is simply their goal differential, and the sum of player GVTs on a team gives the team's GVT plus the replacement level. This makes it much easier to measure "How good would this team be replacing Player A with Player B?" It is also essential in that player success is correlated with team success, which after all is the entire point of the sport. Because GVT is measured in goals and not shots, this means that some lucky players—successful shooters, hot goaltenders—will have a correspondingly high GVT.

GVT has four distinct categories: Offense, Defense, Goaltending, and Shootout. Offensive GVT is extremely straightforward: it measures a player's contribution to scoring goals. Offensive GVT is based on goals and assists scored above what a replacement-level player would have done with the same ice-time. That last part is key: players who play more games or get more ice-time, especially power-play ice-time, are expected to score more, and should not get credit for inflated scoring totals. GVT also assumes that goals and assists are not of equal value, and assigns a weight of 1.5 to goals relative to assists.

This produces Offensive GVT numbers that do not exactly match point totals. Last season, Rick Nash finished sixth in Offensive GVT (16.1) despite finishing 20th in the points race because GVT was impressed that he managed to score 42 goals in 79 games despite getting only 2:41 per game on the power play and 17:27 per game overall. Conversely, Jakub Voracek, who was 16th among forwards in power-play ice-time, receiving 3:15 per game over 82 games, finished only 17th in Offensive GVT (13.4) even though he was fifth overall in points. Without GVT, it would be hard to see that Nash was more valuable offensively than Voracek in 2014-15. Yet here it is, crystal clear, and it helps explain why the Rangers offense was so much better than the Flyers' even though their stars got comparable headline numbers.

The distinction between defense and goaltending is finer: GVT defines the defense's job as preventing shots on goal, and the goaltender's job as stopping shots. Defense has always been the most difficult skill to quantify in hockey, and this is no different in GVT. GVT factors in the number of shots allowed by a player's team, his plus/minus, and his penalty-killing ice-time to obtain his Defensive GVT. While the inputs seem like a bit of a jumble, the results are not: last season, the top five NHL defensemen by Defensive GVT were Rob Scuderi, Paul Martin, Niklas Hjalmarsson, Jonas Brodin, and Hampus Lindholm, followed by

INTRODUCTION TO GVT AND VUKOTA

T.J. Brodie, Andrej Sekera, Ryan Suter, and Roman Josi. If you were looking to acquire a quality defensive defenseman for your team, these guys would almost certainly be near the top of your list. Because defensemen are more responsible for team defense than forwards are, they get more credit, and blame, for team defensive performance than forwards do.

The goaltending measurement is simple: stop the puck. This makes Goaltending GVT relatively easy to calculate: it is the expected number of goals allowed given the number of shots faced, minus the actual number of goals allowed by the goaltender. As a nod to shot-quality effects, the goaltender is only credited for 75% of the extra saves performed, while the defense gets the credit for the remaining 25%.

Lastly, Shootout GVT simply measures whether a player was good at capitalizing on his shootout chances, or preventing them if he is the goalie. For a skater, it is shootout goals minus shootout shots times 30%, which was the average shootout success rate in 2014-15, while for goaltenders, it is the opposite. Over a single season, the shootout is mostly luck, so some players' Shootout GVT will simply be a transient value. However, some good players, like Henrik Lundqvist and Jonathan Toews, have managed to be consistently successful in the shootout. Some non-elite players, like Frans Nielsen and Marc-Andre Fleury, have actually made the shootout one of their specialties, and to ignore this skill would be to ignore a portion of the value these players contribute.

GVT is simply the sum of Offensive, Defensive, Goaltending, and Shootout GVT. While these categories are coarse, they are intentionally so. When trying to figure out the details of a player's game, it is useful to have data that is broken down, but when gauging a player's overall value, you want a statistic that will quickly tell you what kind of player this really is. Roman Josi and Erik Karlsson are very different players, even if they both play a lot of minutes at the same position, and without GVT, it would be extremely difficult to quantify which one was more valuable to his team last season, and by how much. In this case, GVT tells us that Josi was the more valuable of the two, at 17.2 GVT to Karlsson's 15.0.

GVT is far from perfect, but it has the benefit of encapsulating a player's contribution in a nice, neat package that is easily comparable across positions and seasons. With GVT, there are far fewer caveats.

"Claude Giroux is an MVP player!" "No, he's terrible!" In fact, last year the Flyers captain was good offensively, with an 11.0 Offensive GVT (33rd in the league), average defensively (2.6 GVT, middle of the pack for a forward), and poor in the shootout (-2.3, worst among all league skaters), for a total GVT of only 11.3. Having Giroux on their roster instead of a fourth-line player made the Flyers better by about 11 goals in 2014-15. Giroux has had MVP-level seasons in the past: he put up 24.3 GVT in 2011-12 and 20.1 in 2013-14. But last year was not one of them.

Because GVT is calculated based on statistics the NHL has kept for over 40 years, we have a rich historical record of GVT values since 1967. This has allowed us to develop GVT's most powerful descendant: the VUKOTA projection system. VUKOTA is based on finding comparable players throughout hockey history and projecting, based on their results, what the player is likely to do next season.

VUKOTA is named after Mick Vukota, an enforcer for the New York Islanders for 10 seasons, who registered 17 goals but over 2,000 penalty minutes over the course of a 574-game career; amazingly, three of his goals came in a single game. Despite lending his name to our system, Vukota's career GVT of -12.7 puts him in the bottom 1% of NHL players all-time.

VUKOTA, fundamentally, is an individual player-projection system, not a team system, and thus it projects individual statistics, such as Goals, Assists, Save percentage, and GVT; it doesn't attempt to project statistics such as plus/minus and goaltender Wins that are more of a team than a player result. However, since team GVT is simply the sum of player GVTs, the sum of VUKOTA GVT values on a team becomes our projection for the team's goal differential, and consequently its win-loss record as well—since teams, on average, record one extra point in the standings for every three goals scored or prevented. One thing you will notice is how tightly bunched up our team projections are: all 30 teams project between 76 points (Arizona) and 99 points (Tampa Bay). What's more, the top is even more tightly packed than that, with the top 20 (!) teams between 92 and 99 points. Only at the bottom are there outliers: Arizona and Buffalo are much worse than everyone else, while New Jersey and Toronto are at 82 and 84 points respectively. Despite this, even these teams have a fighting chance. There is still a significant amount of luck involved even over the course of an entire season of hockey. Even if we are right that 76 points is the Coyotes' "true talent", this just means that they will likely finish somewhere between 67 and 85 points. 67 points will mean they will be drawing ping pong balls for the #1 or #2 draft pick in June 2016, while 85 points could leave them in the playoff hunt until February.

Remember that as you leaf though this annual: any projection in hockey must be taken with a grain of salt because of the nature of the game. Some team will end up at 70 points or below, as is the case almost every season, but this will be because they underachieved. Similarly, for some team, the stars will align and they will obtain over 110 points. We can't tell you who it will be, and for this coming season, it is even harder to narrow it down to a few challengers because they all have their issues. As dominant as Chicago seemed in the playoffs, they only finished fourth in the West during the regular season and have already lost one key player, Brandon Saad, from their Cup-winning roster. The Tampa Bay Lighting are good and young but very top-heavy, with a huge amount of their production coming from just six players. The New York Islanders look to be one of the league's future elite, but they haven't won a playoff series in over 20 years. The Los Angeles Kings won two Cups in three years but didn't even make it to the dance last year. Overall, there is a very even spread of talent among NHL teams. Parity is not just a buzzword, it is the reality. Whatever team finishes last overall will probably do so because of injuries and bad luck, not because it was far worse than the 29 other teams in the league. We did correctly pick Buffalo to finish last in 2014-15, but we were wildly optimistic about some teams with recent success, including Boston and Los Angeles, both of whom missed the playoffs in the last week of the season.

Because of the aspects of hockey that exist in neither baseball nor basketball, such as variable ice-time and special teams, VUKOTA relies more on interpolation and less on exact player comparables. For example, let's say we are trying to project a young player with a limited track record, like Jonathan Huberdeau. VUKOTA will utilize a large pool of historically-comparable players—say, all forwards who played the entire season at age 21—and see how they fared the next season, then adjust Huberdeau's numbers depending on where he fits on that curve. Mathematically, it is a combination of comparable player selection and multi-variable linear regression. This makes VUKOTA rougher than its baseball or basketball cousins, but that is both because of the limited nature of the statistics and the nature of the sport. Player profiles in basketball are far more defined: big men get a lot of rebounds, have poor free-throw rates, and take almost no three-pointers. Point guards who run the offense record many assists and many turnovers. In hockey, the best information we have on player types is ice-time and special-teams usage: after all, based on traditional statistics, what was the difference last season between Marian Hossa (82 games, 22 goals, 39 assists, 61 points) and Phil Kessel (82 games, 25 goals, 36 assists, 61 points)? Yet we know there are huge differences between these two players in age, style of play, and value. Hossa's better defensive play and penalty killing earned him a 15.0 GVT, compared to Kessel's 6.4.

Eventually, as advanced statistics continue to be recorded in the future, we will have a richer historical record on which to draw for them as well, and we will be able to integrate them into VUKOTA to produce even more reliable projections. Currently, with the lack of statistics that accurately reflect defense, both measuring and projecting defensive contributions is difficult.

There are still improvements to be made to VUKOTA, even with the data we have today: results from the AHL are not well incorporated and require a bit of hand-waving to include. This is important, as 5-10% of NHL players this season will have played in the AHL last year. Projecting games played is still fraught with risk: right now, the system can't distinguish non-recurring injuries, such as a torn biceps, from chronic conditions that represent a health risk going forward, such as groin or back problems; concussions are an even bigger problem (in every way). We are also learning as we go along, and mistakes in previous predictions have helped to inform this year's model. Despite all this, we still feel the current results make it the most reliable hockey projection system out there. VUKOTA understands that players age, that high shooting percentages are rarely sustainable, that goaltenders regress to the mean, and that breakout seasons for 30-year-olds are often mirages.

INTRODUCTION TO GVT AND VUKOTA

We now have six full seasons of VUKOTA projections under our belts. Overall, there have been more hits than misses, but as with any projection system there are always some embarrassments along the way. Last season, we did pretty well at the player level but less well at the team level: we predicted Pittsburgh and Boston as our top choices in the East, with Chicago and Los Angeles as the best teams in the West. Of those teams, only Chicago did not disappoint. The Kings lost one of their top-four defensemen, Slava Voynov, early in the season and never recovered, while Boston's roster finally creaked under the strain of age, David Krejci got injured, and Brad Marchand and Milan Lucic failed to maintain their offensive output. The Penguins once again suffered from their lack of wingers, and showed what happens when Sidney Crosby can't bail them out every single night.

However, most of the other teams we predicted near the top of the East did well. We foresaw that the Islanders would begin their ascent into the league's better teams, that the Rangers would be among the top three in the East, and that Tampa Bay would be near the top as well. The one team we didn't see coming was Montreal: we assumed that Carey Price's elite 2013-14 season would be a blip, and that he would be more like Jose Theodore than Patrick Roy. He proved us (and everyone else) emphatically wrong!

In the West, our record was mixed. We thought that St. Louis, San Jose, Colorado, Dallas, and Anaheim would all be competitive; it turned out that three of them missed the playoffs, although they were all respectable teams. We got the very bottom of the standings, with Edmonton and Arizona, also correct. Again, there was one big team we missed: Calgary, where Jiri Hudler had a career year at age 31, and where Mark Giordano, rookie John Gaudreau, and a bit of puck luck turned an unheralded group into a playoff team.

On the individual level, we picked Sidney Crosby to run away with the league lead in assists and points. He was among the top three in both, despite the worst full season of his NHL career. We had a pretty good handle on the top-five scorers, including Jamie Benn, who we had projected for 75 points, Alex Ovechkin, John Tavares, and even Jakub Voracek, who we saw having a career year with 66 points (he had 81). We obviously missed the more surprising scorers, including Hudler and Nick Foligno, who had never scored more than 18 goals or 47 points before exploding for 31 goals and 73 points last year.

We correctly tapered expectations for Joe Pavelski, who had scored 79 points in 2013-14; we projected 66 and he got 70. The same for Corey Perry, who we saw with "only" 70 points; injury limited him to 55 in 67 games.

On the flip side, we had Phil Kessel second overall in points with 83; instead, he and the Leafs fell apart and he scored only 61 to go with the league's second-worst plus/minus at -34. We thought Nathan MacKinnon could improve on his spectacular rookie year, but instead of ascending to 77 points, he regressed all the way back to 38. Same thing with Matt Duchene: we thought he could repeat his 70-point season, but instead he fell back to 55.

We correctly picked the obvious choice, Erik Karlsson, to lead the league in scoring among defensemen, and we almost hit his exact numbers. We also saw that P.K. Subban would be his main competition, although we thought that the next challengers would be Shea Weber and Alex Pietrangelo, instead of Dennis Wideman and Brent Burns. In the case of Burns, we weren't even sure what position he would be playing!

Goaltending is always unpredictable, so our picks often don't work out. This season in particular saw a number of goaltenders play unexpectedly, chief among them Devan Dubnyk. We predicted him as a replacement-level player, which he was until a mid-season trade to Minnesota, at which point he became the second coming of Jacques Plante. We had Braden Holtby, Carey Price, and Cory Schneider as the seventh, ninth, and 10th-best goaltenders in the league; they finished fourth, first, and third, while Dubnyk was second. The goaltenders we had the best projections for were Tuukka Rask, who had another excellent season with 23.7 GVT, Sergei Bobrovsky (17.1), Henrik Lundqvist (13.6), and Ben Bishop (10.1). All had good seasons, with Bishop having a memorable run in the playoffs.

The upcoming year's team predictions are even more inconclusive than usual, given the squeeze of parity in the league. Our top projections are between 97 and 99 points, but 97 points would not have even gotten you into the playoffs last season! This means that some teams will have to overachieve; there will be several 100+ point teams, we just don't know which ones they will be. If you take anything away from our projected standings, remember that there are only four or five teams that have little chance of making the playoffs, and close to a dozen teams that could win the Stanley Cup if everything breaks exactly in their favor next in 2015-16.

Among the few big changes we see to the standings: we think that Montreal won't be able to ride Carey Price as strongly for a second straight season. Not only will they not challenge for the Conference crown, they could even miss the top eight in the East. Despite their aging rosters, we think San Jose and Los Angeles will rejoin the ranks of the West's top teams. Only at the bottom are things unchanged: the bottom six from last year could well be the bottom six this year. Only Edmonton has the talent to begin a climb out, but VUKOTA has given up on them until they find a strategy to allow fewer than 283 goals against!

At the player level, we see Alex Ovechkin winning the goal-scoring race again, although Tyler Seguin and John Tavares's numbers are close enough that they could catch him if he stumbles. Tavares is the favorite for the point-scoring title, although Crosby, Seguin, or a Jamie Benn repeat aren't out of the question, either. Price is the favorite to keep the title of the league's best goaltender; he and Rask are the two safe bets; Bobrovsky, Holtby, and Semyon Varlamov round out the top five. The five best defensemen by GVT are predicted to be Karlsson, Burns, Josi, Weber, and Kevin Shattenkirk, but P.K. Subban and Kris Letang are close behind, and any of them could be the Norris Trophy winner.

The youth movement has now completely taken over the NHL. With the retirement of Martin St. Louis, all of the league's top scorers are 30 or younger, which means there shouldn't be any huge dropoffs among the elite. The biggest declines should come from those who had surprising 2014-15 seasons: we see Jiri Hudler falling back from 76 to 59 points... which would still be his second-best total! We also see Daniel Sedin regressing from 76 to 58 points, and Henrik from 73 to 54; as good as the Sedins are, they will be 35 in September, and they scored just 47 and 50 points back in 2013-14. The biggest potential rises are also the most uncertain: we see Nathan MacKinnon bouncing back to 58 points from 38, Taylor Hall jumping back from 38 points to 57, and David Krejci climbing back from 31 points in just 47 games to 43 points in 61 games. But it is always hard to know what we will see from promising young players like Gaudreau, Huberdeau, and Filip Forsberg.

Anyone who makes predictions is putting their reputation on the line, but we have confidence in VUKOTA. We hope this annual succeeds in its twin goals of entertaining and informing you, whether you simply aim to win your pool or you are gauging your team's chances to know if you should plan a day off for a Stanley Cup parade in June. Enjoy your hockey, and enjoy this book.

Tom Awad

Introduction to Total Performance Charts

They say a picture is worth a thousand words, but at *Hockey Prospectus*, we prefer to calculate the value of a replacement-level picture and measure a picture's value relative to that threshold…but any way you measure their value, pictures are a highly-efficient way to present information.

Our adoption of using charts instead of words and tables began in the 2011 offseason, when the Atlanta Thrashers franchise relocated to become the Winnipeg Jets. Local fans had not had the opportunity to watch their new team in the previous seasons, and they needed a quick way to learn about its players. Enter Player Usage Charts (or as they were first poorly named, OZ-QoC charts), which made their first appearance in print the following season in our *Hockey Prospectus 2012-13* book.

The following year, for *Hockey Prospectus 2013-14*, we introduced four sets of "Total Performance Charts", to help you better visualize the overall roles and abilities of players on a team.

After a (lazy) one-year hiatus of going back to just the Player Usage Charts, we are bringing the multiple charts back to you: Even-Strength Usage (i.e. Player Usage Charts, renamed once again) to visualize differences in deployment at even strength; Special Teams Usage to display even-strength, power-play, and shorthanded minutes; Offensive Profile to help you discern the passers from the shooters; and Cap Efficiency, showing Goals Versus Threshold (how good a player is), cap hit (how much they cost), and Goals Versus Threshold (the bang for the buck).

Even-Strength Usage

Following their creation by Rob Vollman, "Player Usage Charts" broke quickly into the mainstream. Their popularity was primarily based on how quickly and easily anyone can tell, at a glance, how a team's players are being used, which gives observers the proper context with which to evaluate both their traditional and non-traditional statistics. Consider, for instance, the chart for the Chicago Blackhawks (next page).

Using this Even-Strength Usage chart, you can see which players start their shifts primarily in the offensive zone (on the right side of the chart) or in the defensive zone (on the left side of the chart). Players above "the horizon" of neutral-level competition face top-six forwards and top-four defensemen, while those below the horizon are mostly lining up against depth players. This estimate of a player's average quality of competition is calculated based on their opponents' average attempted shot differential, which is why you sometimes find players below the line that you were not expecting to see there—like perhaps Patrick Sharp.

As for the bubbles, a dark-shaded bubble means the team has an advantage over their opponents in terms of attempted shots, while a light-shaded bubble indicates a disadvantage, the extent of which is measured by the size of the bubble. These so-called "possession bubbles" are calculated relative to their teammates (i.e. Relative Corsi), so players on particularly skilled teams will not be at an advantage.

One of the important things to look for on an Even-Strength Usage chart are players who are near one of the corners of the chart. Given the different number of shifts each team plays in the offensive zone, and the need to fit as many players as possible on a single chart, these corners are at a different scale for every team. Be sure to check the team scale when comparing players on different teams—and be mindful of players with asterisks. Those with an asterisk before their name (like Antoine Vermette) started the season with a different team, while those with the asterisk as a postfix (like Adam Clendening) ended it with a different team—and potentially one with a far different average offensive zone start percentage. Data for such players is for their entire season—not just the portion they spent with the featured team.

When you see a player near one of those corners, consider how their extreme usage may affect their statistics, or their position on another chart. For example, a player on the far-right side (like Brad Richards) is being used in a very offensive-minded role, and while that does not necessarily mean he is weak defensively, it does mean that he should have a big, dark-shaded possession bubble, and potentially great offensive totals. On the other hand, those on the far and upper left (like Marcus Kruger and Joakim Nordstrom) usually have the defensive talent to be trusted with lots of shifts in the defensive zone and against top opponents, but consequently, they may fare quite poorly by most statistical measures (and potentially, to the naked eye).

Watch out for players with out-of-place bubbles. Those with large light-shaded bubbles (like Daniel Carcillo or Johnny Oduya) are being dominated, and have potentially been given too aggressive of an assignment. Similarly, those with unusually large dark-shaded bubbles (like David Rundblad) are doing so well that they could probably help the team with more challenging responsibilities. Those with even modestly-sized dark-shaded bubbles in sections of the chart normally reserved for white ones are likely the undervalued gems that can quietly make all the difference.

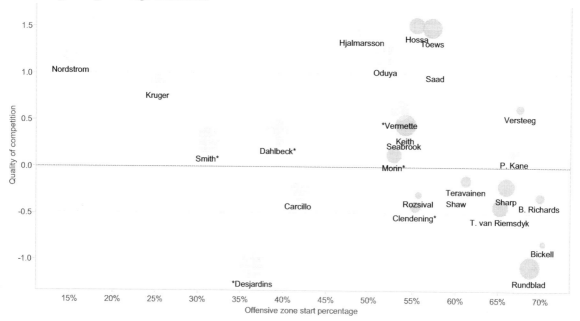

INTRODUCTION TO TOTAL PERFORMANCE CHARTS

Special Teams Usage

The Special Teams Usage chart fills in the gap left by Even-Strength Usage chart. This chart displays each player's average power-play ice-time per game (horizontal axis) and his average shorthanded ice-time per game (vertical axis). This time, the bubble's size indicates the player's even-strength ice-time (above a threshold of eight minutes).

While this chart does not say anything about the relative success of these players in these situations, it does reveal, at a quick glance, who has been used in a strictly offensive or defensive fashion, and which players have been trusted in both situations—a very important type of player. This is especially true for a team like the Montreal Canadiens that tends to specialize. Only Andrei Markov, P.K. Subban, and to a lesser extent, Tomas Plekanec and Max Pacioretty were used regularly in all man-power situations.

Be aware of the impact it may have on a team when players at either extreme of the chart change teams, retire, or go down to injury.

Otherwise, the key things to look for in Special Teams Usage are players whose scoring totals may have been boosted by significant time on the man advantage, and those whose ice-time bubbles are sized disproportionally to players around them.

When studying these charts, always make the distinction between forwards and defensemen, remembering that blueliners usually get much more ice-time. While it is not unusual for forwards to get through a season without killing penalties, only the weakest defensemen are generally excused from such assignments—like the 40-year-old Sergei Gonchar.

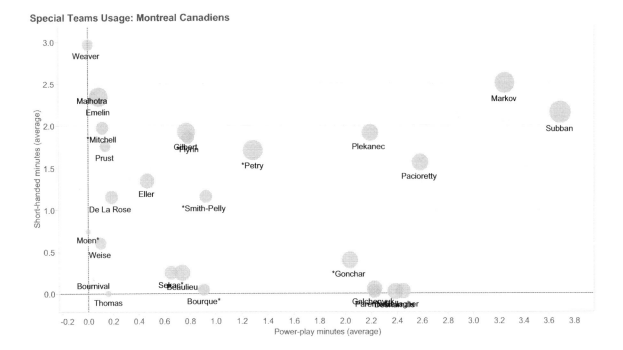

Offensive Profile

Trying to determine who is driving a team's offensive production? With one glance at the Offensive Profile chart, it is easy to see which players are taking the most shots (horizontal axis) and making the most passes that result in shots (vertical axis). Since both stats are being measured per 60 minutes of ice-time, players can be compared on equal footing.

This is another classic example of how the charts work together so nicely. Having reviewed the Player Usage Charts, we know which players have had more time in the offensive zone, and should therefore be at the top and/or the far right side of the Offensive Profile. Having also reviewed Special Teams Usage, we know which players have received the power-play ice-time required to boost those totals even further. Therefore, look for players who do not appear where you expect them to be.

Here, the bubbles represent a player's even-strength scoring rate (over the threshold of 0.75 ESP/60). You would therefore expect the bubbles to increase as you move to the top right-hand corner of the chart, but due to weak linemates and/or bad luck, that is not always the case. So, keep an eye out for players whose scoreboard results do not match the actual offense they have been generating, like Washington's Tom Wilson. Likewise, those with unexpectedly large bubbles may have had their traditional scoring totals artificially bloated by a particularly skilled linemate or a streak of favorable bounces.

The best part of this chart is seeing at a glance who are the team's primary shooters (Alex Ovechkin—no shock there) and big passers (Nicklas Backstrom—ditto), not to mention how various line combinations might perform. Remember to make a distinction for defensemen, who are responsible for a far smaller share of a team's offensive production.

One quick word on passes—they are just an estimate. As goals can be driven by luck, shots can be a more reliable indicator of whether or not a player is driving the offense. The same idea applies to playmakers, who can be judged on whether or not they are making the passes—that with decent luck, should be leading to primary assists.

Unfortunately, high-level estimates, like passes, quality of competition, or even GVT, make some

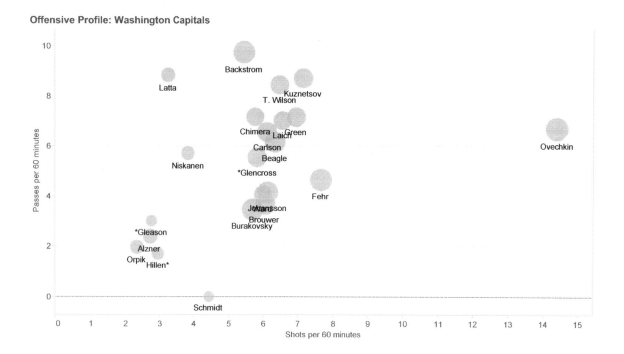

analysts absolutely blind with rage. For practical purposes, these charts are a great start; you can always dig deeper into their analytics and shift a player up or down if you think that a certain factor has been overestimated or underestimated. There is a prevalent fear that mainstream fans will walk away from analytics *en masse* if an estimate is not sufficiently accurate—which seems like an overreaction—but please keep the limitations of the top-level estimates in mind whenever they are being used.

Cap Efficiency

The Cap Efficiency chart pulls everything together. So far, the first three charts have provided a reasonably good idea of how players are being used, and how successful they are in those roles. Now, it is time to see how that measures up to their financial compensation.

Cap Efficiency seamlessly integrates a player's cap hit (horizontal axis) with an estimate of their overall contribution using Goals Versus Threshold (vertical axis). The charts are completed with bubbles that measure each player's total cap efficiency using Goals Versus Salary. A big dark-shaded bubble represents the kind of tremendous value that can help a salary cap era team to overachieve (like Tomas Tatar, Danny DeKeyser, and Gustav Nyquist), whereas a big light-shaded bubble indicates an anchor that is using up cap space that would be best invested elsewhere (like Jonathan Ericsson or Stephen Weiss).

On a well-managed team like Detroit, most players will be clustered close to a gently upward-sloping line. Being just a top-level estimate of a player's overall contributions, GVT can appear unkind to defensive players who endure difficult playing conditions. A glance at the Even-Strength Usage chart and Special Teams Usage chart will reveal which players may deserve a little slack, like perhaps Ericsson.

Of course, highly-paid players like Henrik Zetterberg and Pavel Datsyuk are not where NHL general managers will pinch pennies, so only expect the truly exceptional players (like Datsyuk) to actually provide positive value at the upper ranges of salary according to GVS.

Finally, players who missed part of the season due to injury may also look bad (like Johan Franzen), but

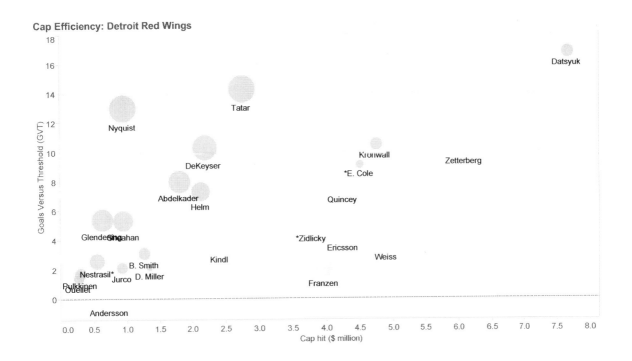

remember that an injured player is still using up cap space. It is not his fault, but even if he is placed on long-term injured reserve, a team does not get cap relief unless his replacement pushes the team over the limit.

Closing thoughts

While these four charts work well on their own, they work best when used together. Player Usage shows us how players are being used at even strength, Special Teams Usage shows us which way things are tilted on the power play and penalty kill, and the two together give us the information to properly interpret each player's Offensive Profile. Cap Efficiency then provides an idea of whether a team's cap space is being well invested.

In all of the charts, a cutoff of 18 games played was used, both to cut down on clutter and to avoid obscuring the overall picture with any small-sample miracles. Even then, some of the charts get crowded.

Always keep in mind that these charts are meant to reveal a high-level picture only. They are not an exact science, and often based on estimates, so use your own judgment when something appears unusual. Dig deeper by reading the player profiles and examining additional analytics more carefully. These charts are not intended to be the destination, but merely a shortcut to get most of the way there at a glance.

Finally, be mindful of different scales, of players who changed teams, and the distinction between forwards and defensemen. Defensemen get more icetime, do not get as big an offensive/defensive split in Even-Strength Usage, and are not responsible for as much offense.

Enjoy the charts.

Rob Vollman and Timo Seppa

Introduction to Score-Adjusted and Goaltender Statistics

Skater statistics

Score-adjusted metrics

Score-adjusted metrics hit the mainstream in 2014-15. Since being introduced by Eric Tulsky (now of the Carolina Hurricanes) in 2012, analysts across the hockey world have slowly been moving away from traditional all-situation or "close" (i.e. within one goal in first or second period, or tied in third period) metrics towards adopting score-adjusted metrics as a universal standard. The big breakthrough came this year when Micah Blake McCurdy published a seminal study showing that Score-Adjusted Corsi outperforms both all-situation and close metrics at predicting future goal differential.

We use score-adjusted metrics because of the changes that occur when teams are trailing or leading. Teams that are ahead tend to sit back and post worse possession numbers, while clubs that trail tend to take a greater proportion of the total shot attempts.

To account for this, we apply a weight to each event depending on the score. For example, when the home team is up by 1, they take roughly 48.2% of all missed shots, which translates to a weight of 1.035 for each missed shot they take. The less statistically likely a team (or player) is to take an attempt in a given situation, the more credit we give them.

We can create these weights for each score differential (down 1, down 2, down 3+, tied, up 1, up 2, up 3+) and shot-attempt type (goal, saved shot, miss, block). These weights can be totaled across a team or player to calculate percentage or rate statistics that provide us with a more context-neutral evaluation of the team's performance or player's performance.

Score-Adjusted Corsi-for percentage (CF%)

Traditional (raw, unadjusted) Corsi percentage is simply the number of even-strength shot attempts (including goals, saved shots on goal, misses, and blocked attempts) for a team or player divided by the total number of shot attempts for both teams. When we say for a player, we mean for the player's team while the player is on the ice.

Score-Adjusted CF% (simply shown as CF% in the player tables you will find in each chapter) is calculated using the same method as standard Corsi-for percentage; however, it uses the total of the weights described above rather than simply counting the events for and against. Score-Adjusted CF% utilizes the same scale as traditional CF%, with percentages above 50% being good, and anything above 55% being near the top of the league (though you will obviously want to take small-sample cases as just hints of how a player might perform over a longer stretch of games).

Individual Score-Adjusted Corsi attempts per 60 minutes (iCF/60)

Individual Score-Adjusted Corsi attempts per 60 minutes (shown as iCF/60 in the player tables) measures a player's individual offensive generation ability; it is one of the single-most consistent indicators of talent that exists today. iCF/60 totals the even-strength score-adjusted shot attempts a player takes themselves and divides by their total even-strength ice-time, to normalize for differences in opportunity. For reference, forwards posted an average iCF/60 of 12.0, with the best rate among full-time players belonging to Alex Ovechkin, at 25.2. The average for defensemen was, of course, lower at 8.5, with Brent Burns topping all point men at 16.6.

Goaltender statistics

Even-strength save percentage (ESSV%)

For years now, even-strength save percentage (shown as ESSV% in the player tables) has been a go-to measuring stick for goaltenders, due to its ability to even the playing field between goalies on different teams. Since netminders face a different number of shorthanded shots against depending on their teammates' relative propensity to head to the sin bin, traditional (overall) save percentage can be a misleading indicator of goaltending talent; special teams save percentages can also vary widely from season to season. As such, we look to ESSV% to get a better estimate of a goalie's true talent level. Over the course of the 2014-15 season, the average ESSV% was .922, with goalies above .933 ranking in the top 20%, and goalies below .900 landing in the bottom quintile. For reference, the average (overall, traditional) save percentage was .915, with the top 20% at .923, and the bottom 20% at .891.

Quality Start percentage (QS%)

Invented by analytics pioneer and founding *Hockey Prospectus* author Rob Vollman, Quality Start percentage (shown as QS% in the player tables) measures how frequently a goaltender does enough to give his team a good chance at winning. Modeled after the baseball statistic of the same name, a goaltender earns a Quality Start for posting a save percentage of .917 when facing 20 or more shots in a given game (or for a save percentage greater than .885 in the infrequent cases of facing less than 20 shots in a game). For 2014-15, the median QS% was 53.4%. Goaltenders below 50% have generally been poor starters, while those above 60% have been amongst the league's best.

Matt Cane

Anaheim Ducks

Since the 2012-13 lockout, few teams have been as dominant during the regular season as the Anaheim Ducks. In the past three regular seasons, no team has had more points than the Ducks (291). Only one team has had more wins, the Pittsburgh Penguins (Pittsburgh 136, Anaheim 135). That is fitting since the Penguins and the Ducks have run into similar pitfalls over the last few years. Ducks coach Bruce Boudreau has earned the tag of being "regular-season good" for several years. The former Caps coach took over in Orange County halfway through the 2011-12 season after failing to take a powerhouse Washington Capitals squad that dominated the regular season to the promised land. The question often asked is: How much of that is coaching and how much is the makeup of the team? Despite the trend of Boudreau teams failing to make deep playoff runs, the answer has more to do with the makeup of the squad.

The Ducks have made strides, especially in the most recent 2014-15 season, to round out their roster. During several of their quality years, they were a one or one-and-a-half line team. Fortunately for SoCal's former champion, that one line has two of the most potent players in the game: the dominant duo of Corey Perry and Ryan Getzlaf have terrorized defenses out West for the better part of a decade. Since 2010-11, only two players have more goals than Perry: Steven Stamkos and Alex Ovechkin. Over the same stretch, only four players have more assists than Getzlaf: Nicklas Backstrom, Joe Thornton, Claude Giroux, and Henrik Sedin. Not surprisingly, since 2010-11, Anaheim is one of only three teams to have two players among the top-15 scorers. The others are Vancouver, with the Sedin twins, and Pittsburgh, with Evgeni Malkin and Sidney Crosby. The parallel between Anaheim and Pittsburgh is there yet again: a team with not one, but two dynamic superstars, that unfortunately has struggled to win a championship in recent years. The same could be said about the Vancouver Canucks, who have failed to put a complete team around their top-end talent.

A simple representation of how dominant Perry and Getzlaf have been outside of their ridiculous point production is their Fenwick Close numbers. Perry and Getzlaf hold the highest Fenwick For relative to their team at 11.3% and 10.6%, respectively. With the pair on the ice, the Ducks have held a 56.7% Fenwick For over the last three years. However, when they are off the ice, it has been an entirely different story. Without Anaheim's star players on the ice, the team has put together a measly 45.5% Fenwick

DUCKS IN A BOX

Last Season
Goals For	236	t-10th
Goals Against	226	t-19th
GVT	10	17th
Points	109	t-3rd
Playoffs	Lost Conference Final	

The Ducks came within one game of the Stanley Cup Final, and were possibly the second-best team in the NHL last year.

Three-Year Record
GVT	89	6th
Points	291	1st
Playoffs	3 Appearances, 21 Wins	

VUKOTA Projection
Goals For	221	17th
Goals Against	215	7th
GVT	7	13th
Points	94	13th

With Kesler and Silfverberg, the Ducks finally have a strong second line. Expect another season near the top of the West.

Top Three Prospects
S. Theodore (D), N. Ritchie (F), N. Kerdiles (F)

For. But that has been changing.

Despite the ultimately disappointing final results, the 2014-15 campaign was far from the same ol' Ducks. Though the team still registers its worst Fenwick with the 29-year-old Perry off the ice, that figure is now 48.0%, up from 45.5%. Likewise, the team's Fenwick For without Getzlaf has risen to 49.5%. The addition of two-way center Ryan Kesler, and the emergence of players like Rickard Rakell, Matt Beleskey, and Patrick Maroon have lessened the reliance on the big boys up front.

If they improved in depth, why were the Ducks still unable to get to the Stanley Cup Final? In the postseason, matchups are highly scrutinized and no coach is capable of hiding a weak center. The Los Angeles Kings, the Chicago Blackhawks, and the Detroit Red Wings all had dominant playoff teams based around the depth of their lineups and their coaches' abilities to find weaknesses in their opponents' depth. In a world where general managers are constantly looking for sustainability from regular-season play to postseason play, the Ducks did not have a formula for it in the lineup or with their coach, who was run out of his home building in Game 7 against Chicago. But it is not entirely Bruce Boudreau's fault he was dominated in matchups during the Western Conference Final. Anaheim's addition of Kesler played a major role in the deep playoff run, but the Ducks' third- and fourth-line centers were still not good enough—no matter how you shuffled them around. When you pull up the worst Fenwick For percentage offenders for the Ducks since 2010-11, it is a who's who of Ducks bottom-line centers, both old and new: Nate Thompson, Todd Marchant, Saku Koivu, Andrew Cogliano, and others. In case anyone was wondering, the same exact trend carries out on the Penguins. Up top, the team has Crosby and Malkin as their top Fenwick performers, and on the bottom? Craig Adams, Max Talbot, Brandon Sutter, Joe Vitale. The Washington Capitals do the same dance with Ovechkin and Backstrom standing opposite of Boyd Gordon, Jeff Halpern, Jay Beagle, and Brooks Laich.

If the NHL and NHL general managers needed any evidence of how one-line teams and top-heavy teams do not work in this day and age, they need look no further than three of the most prominent regular season teams in recent memory: the Washington Capitals, Pittsburgh Penguins, and Anaheim Ducks. Even the best of the best cannot offset a roster that is not deep enough in its supporting cast. Come playoff time, when all eyes fixate on the biggest weapons, someone has to pick up the slack. Anaheim started to correct that deficiency in the 2014 offseason and were rewarded with their deepest playoff run since the 2007 Stanley Cup win. With plenty of promising young prospects, a couple of superstars, and a relatively young core, the Ducks may be poised for a long stay amongst the NHL's top teams.

Jason Lewis

ANAHEIM DUCKS

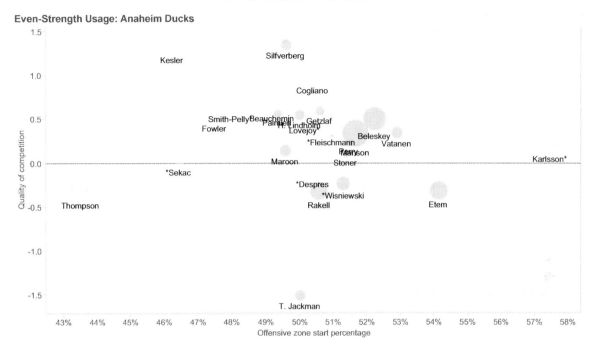

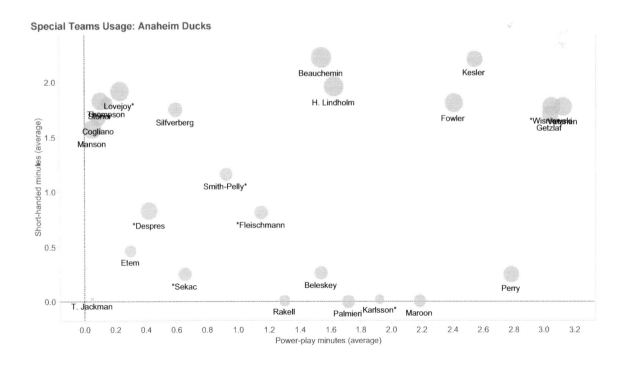

4 ANAHEIM DUCKS

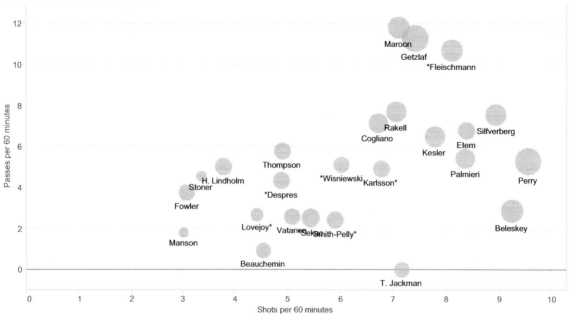

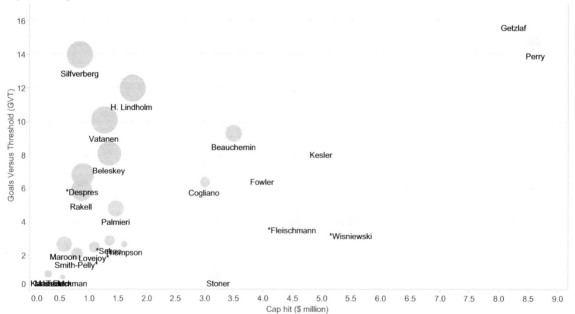

FORWARDS

Matt Beleskey							LW						BOS
Season	Team	Age	GP	G	A	Pts	+/-	ESP/60	AdjCF%	iCF/60	OGVT	DGVT	SGVT	GVT
2012-13	ANA	24	42	8	5	13	2	1.41	43.3%	13.6	1.2	1.1	0.0	2.4
2013-14	ANA	25	55	9	15	24	8	1.93	50.4%	19.9	3.0	1.3	-0.3	4.1
2014-15	ANA	26	65	22	10	32	13	2.04	54.0%	20.4	5.2	2.9	0.0	8.1
2015-16	BOS	27	62	19	16	35					4.3	1.6	0.0	5.9

If you tried to guess who the most effective possession players were on the Ducks, Matt Beleskey might not be the first name you would mention. Call it a contract year, call it luck, but Beleskey was a strong contributor to Anaheim's possession game. His 57.6 Corsi-for percentage was second on the team, and his Corsi-for per 60 minutes was tops. Unlike past years, Beleskey did not play the majority of his time with Perry and Getzlaf, but predominantly alongside Kesler and Palmieri—it is hard to say Beleskey rode any coattails during his first 20+ goal season. The Bruins took the risk of investing in the one-year wonder, though not at quite the big AAV that was expected; going out on a limb may pay off for Boston if he continues to be a strong complementary player.

Andrew Cogliano							LW/C						ANA
Season	Team	Age	GP	G	A	Pts	+/-	ESP/60	AdjCF%	iCF/60	OGVT	DGVT	SGVT	GVT
2012-13	ANA	25	48	13	10	23	14	1.93	52.2%	11.8	4.1	3.0	-0.3	6.9
2013-14	ANA	26	82	21	21	42	13	1.99	48.9%	13.3	8.4	3.9	0.0	12.3
2014-15	ANA	27	82	15	14	29	5	1.48	50.9%	12.2	3.3	3.1	0.0	6.4
2015-16	ANA	28	69	15	20	35					3.7	2.6	0.0	6.3

Given his role, Andrew Cogliano had a respectable year despite not duplicating his 40+ point output from 2013-14. With the departures of Saku Koivu and Daniel Winnik, the former Oiler most frequently suited up alongside Jakob Silfverberg and Nate Thompson. Perhaps as a consequence, he saw an increase in his possession stats, despite getting matched up against the opposition's top players. Only Silfverberg and Kesler faced tougher opponents.

Emerson Etem							RW						NYR
Season	Team	Age	GP	G	A	Pts	+/-	ESP/60	AdjCF%	iCF/60	OGVT	DGVT	SGVT	GVT
2012-13	ANA	20	38	3	7	10	7	1.23	45.3%	12.3	0.4	1.8	0.0	2.1
2013-14	ANA	21	29	7	4	11	3	1.67	49.0%	14.0	2.3	1.0	0.0	3.3
2014-15	ANA	22	45	5	5	10	-6	1.16	53.3%	15.3	0.3	0.4	0.0	0.7
2015-16	NYR	23	48	9	8	17					0.9	1.0	0.0	1.9

Fans are still waiting for Emerson Etem to live up to his first-round tag. If you look at his production, you will be disappointed—with just 10 points and five goals in 45 games, it is hard to imagine that he once put up 107 points for the OHL's Medicine Hat Tigers. However, there were incremental improvements in individual shots, Corsi, and Fenwick per 60 minutes from 2013-14 to 2014-15. Etem is outchancing opponents and possessing the puck more, yet is getting little in the way of production to show for it. At a 96.8 PDO, the Long Beach, California native had some of the worst luck on the team. The Rangers acquired him at the right time, when his value was low and there was a good chance he would see an improvement in puck luck.

ANAHEIM DUCKS

Tomas Fleischmann — LW — Free Agent

Season	Team	Age	GP	G	A	Pts	+/-	ESP/60	AdjCF%	iCF/60	OGVT	DGVT	SGVT	GVT
2012-13	FLA	28	48	12	23	35	-10	1.70	46.8%	12.4	5.7	1.5	0.0	7.2
2013-14	FLA	29	80	8	20	28	-18	1.11	49.3%	13.7	-1.4	1.3	0.3	0.2
2014-15	FLA, ANA	30	66	8	19	27	12	1.86	52.4%	14.4	1.2	3.8	-0.5	4.4
2015-16	Free Agent	31	62	8	17	25					0.7	2.2	0.0	2.9

Numerous teams have tried to ignite the untapped potential of 2002 second rounder Tomas Fleischmann. Despite a few quality offensive seasons, the Czech winger has never been able to produce year after year. His best statistical season came in 2011-12 with Colorado, when he potted 27 goals. Not surprisingly, when you glance at the Fleischmann's shooting percentage and where the goals come from, it is wildly inconsistent. His shooting percentage has run the gamut, swinging from highs in 2009-10 (15.5%), to lows in 2013-14 (4.7%), and everything in between. Some years, the lion's share of his goals come in the slot, other years the perimeter. He has never been able to repeat any sort of offensive style or success.

Max Friberg — LW/RW — ANA

Season	Team	Age	GP	G	A	Pts	+/-	ESP/60	AdjCF%	iCF/60	OGVT	DGVT	SGVT	GVT
2014-15	ANA	22	1	0	0	0	0	0.00	30.0%	6.6	0.0	0.0	0.0	0.0
2015-16	ANA	23	26	5	6	11					0.8	0.5	0.0	1.3

Max Friberg is on the cusp of making the Ducks roster in a bottom-line spot. However, at five-foot-eleven and with a limited offensive upside it remains to be seen if the young Swede can sustain utility in the NHL. Friberg has remained a consistent AHL scorer over two seasons, averaging about a point every other game. He also has decent defensive instincts, making him more than just a flashy, undersized, Euro-forward. Friberg may push for a roster spot to start 2015-16.

Ryan Getzlaf — C — ANA

Season	Team	Age	GP	G	A	Pts	+/-	ESP/60	AdjCF%	iCF/60	OGVT	DGVT	SGVT	GVT
2012-13	ANA	27	44	15	34	49	14	2.65	50.4%	10.4	9.2	2.5	1.2	12.9
2013-14	ANA	28	77	31	56	87	28	3.22	51.4%	12.3	18.7	4.3	-1.7	21.3
2014-15	ANA	29	77	25	45	70	15	2.79	51.7%	13.3	12.0	4.6	-0.5	16.1
2015-16	ANA	30	74	25	49	74					11.0	3.2	0.0	14.3

When you think about Ryan Getzlaf, the first thing that comes to mind is power. The six-foot-four center is a nightmare to defend because of his strength and viscious intensity. You also think of his powerful wrist shot and ability to keep the puck on his stick and shoot from all angles on the ice. However, one underappreciated element of his elite-level game is his playmaking. Linemate Corey Perry would attest that the 2003 first rounder is one of the best facilitating centers in the game: the 2007 Cup winner was 23rd in assists per 60 minutes, and even more impressively, 13th in first assists. As the total package and one of the top five centers in the NHL, the Ducks will always be competitive with Getzlaf in the lineup.

ANAHEIM DUCKS

Dany Heatley — LW/RW — Germany

Season	Team	Age	GP	G	A	Pts	+/-	ESP/60	AdjCF%	iCF/60	OGVT	DGVT	SGVT	GVT
2012-13	MIN	31	36	11	10	21	-12	1.51	47.6%	10.6	0.9	0.4	0.0	1.4
2013-14	MIN	32	76	12	16	28	-18	1.16	44.3%	8.9	-0.3	0.8	-0.3	0.2
2014-15	ANA	33	6	0	0	0	-3	0.00	41.5%	10.7	-0.6	-0.2	-0.3	-1.1
2015-16	Germany	34	43	6	9	15					0.5	0.9	0.0	1.3

Ostensibly, Dany Heatley was a low-risk, high-reward free agent signing, at a $1 million hit (though he did seem pretty done already). When the former 50-goal scorer did not pan out for the Ducks, it was not much of a loss. In his six games with Anaheim, he recorded no points and only eight shots, in a not-insignificant 12 minutes per night. Plus, the 33-year-old played 21 of his 64 even-strength minutes alongside Ryan Getzlaf—Heatley lined up with only Nate Thompson more than the Ducks' captain. So maybe not every upright mammal with a stick can score alongside Getzlaf.

Tim Jackman — RW — ANA

Season	Team	Age	GP	G	A	Pts	+/-	ESP/60	AdjCF%	iCF/60	OGVT	DGVT	SGVT	GVT
2012-13	CGY	31	42	1	4	5	-9	0.76	47.3%	12.2	-0.9	-0.2	0.0	-1.0
2013-14	CGY, ANA	32	36	4	1	5	-3	1.19	48.9%	15.0	0.0	0.2	0.0	0.1
2014-15	ANA	33	55	5	2	7	-4	0.92	50.7%	13.4	-0.2	0.4	0.0	0.2
2015-16	ANA	34	47	4	3	7					-0.7	0.6	0.0	-0.1

Tim Jackman led the Ducks in penalty minutes (including majors and misconducts) and he was eighth on the team in hits. This, for the most part, is what you would expect from a 33-year-old AAAA-type banger. As far as actual hockey goes, the Minot, North Dakota native was fairly average. Although he managed a subpar 41.7 goals-for percentage, his relatively low 1.82 goals-against per 60 minute rate and the roughly breakeven Corsi for made him a pretty low-risk play for eight minutes per night.

Ryan Kesler — C — ANA

Season	Team	Age	GP	G	A	Pts	+/-	ESP/60	AdjCF%	iCF/60	OGVT	DGVT	SGVT	GVT
2012-13	VAN	28	17	4	9	13	-5	2.05	49.9%	12.3	1.1	0.1	-0.9	0.3
2013-14	VAN	29	77	25	18	43	-15	1.26	52.4%	13.2	2.0	4.0	-1.1	5.0
2014-15	ANA	30	81	20	27	47	-5	1.66	50.9%	12.7	4.7	3.0	0.9	8.6
2015-16	ANA	31	72	21	25	45					4.7	2.4	0.0	7.1

Ryan Kesler was targeted in the 2014 offseason to strengthen the Ducks down the middle. Although Nick Bonino was young and promising, it became apparent in the 2014 playoffs that Anaheim needed a better shutdown option. Kesler did indeed face the toughest quality of competition, remaining at 51.5% Corsi despite the heavy minutes. As expected, he was typically excellent in the faceoff circle, at a 56.2% success rate. However, his penchant for dumb penalties can leave fans a bit frustrated at times, but overall, he was a worthwhile addition. The ex-Canuck showed his true value during the postseason when he was matched up with Jonathan Toews in the seven-game Western Conference Final. He performed admirably—which is a lot more than most who face Toews can say.

ANAHEIM DUCKS

Patrick Maroon — LW — ANA

Season	Team	Age	GP	G	A	Pts	+/-	ESP/60	AdjCF%	iCF/60	OGVT	DGVT	SGVT	GVT
2012-13	ANA	24	13	2	1	3	-1	1.48	45.4%	15.2	0.3	0.1	0.0	0.5
2013-14	ANA	25	62	11	18	29	11	2.29	54.6%	13.3	3.9	1.6	0.0	5.4
2014-15	ANA	26	71	9	25	34	-5	1.89	51.7%	11.5	1.9	0.8	0.0	2.7
2015-16	ANA	27	62	13	22	36					3.4	1.4	0.0	4.9

Six-foot-two power forward Patrick Maroon provided Anaheim with valuable scoring depth. While he potted just nine goals, he tallied a career-high 25 assists. The former London Knight did exactly what you want of power forwards: he got to the net. With Maroon on the ice, the Ducks have had very good shot-rate numbers (1.09 with, 0.97 without) and shot-rate differential numbers in the low slot (+1.48) over the past two seasons. If he is not scoring himself, the 2007 sixth rounder is putting himself in a position to create havoc in front. Plugged in with Perry and Getzlaf, that is all the duo needs from a complementary winger.

Stefan Noesen — RW/LW — ANA

Season	Team	Age	GP	G	A	Pts	+/-	ESP/60	AdjCF%	iCF/60	OGVT	DGVT	SGVT	GVT
2014-15	ANA	21	1	0	0	0	0	0.00	43.2%	8.3	0.0	0.0	0.0	0.0
2015-16	ANA	22	26	5	6	11					0.8	0.5	0.0	1.3

It is hard not to root for Stefan Noesen given his troubled injury history. Drafted in the first round by Ottawa in 2011, the Plano, Texas native came to the Ducks along with Jakob Silfverberg in the Bobby Ryan trade. Since then, he has missed the better part of two years with a season-ending knee injury in 2013 and a four-month Achilles injury in early 2014. He stormed back in the late stages of 2014-15, scoring 16 points in 26 games with the Norfolk Admirals, earning his first NHL call-up on April 3. At 22, there is plenty of time for him to display the offensive talent that saw him score back-to-back 30-goal seasons for the OHL's Plymouth Whalers.

Kyle Palmieri — RW — NJD

Season	Team	Age	GP	G	A	Pts	+/-	ESP/60	AdjCF%	iCF/60	OGVT	DGVT	SGVT	GVT
2012-13	ANA	21	42	10	11	21	2	2.35	49.6%	17.9	3.4	1.1	0.0	4.5
2013-14	ANA	22	71	14	17	31	9	2.46	48.5%	15.7	4.8	1.7	-0.5	6.0
2014-15	ANA	23	57	14	15	29	-2	1.53	51.4%	14.6	4.4	0.6	-0.3	4.8
2015-16	NJD	24	59	14	17	31					3.2	1.3	0.0	4.5

With good but not overwhelming numbers (51.1% Corsi for and 52.9% goals for), Kyle Palmieri doesn't jump out as an outstanding contributor in 2014-15. However, when you look at his usage, the stats are definitely positive. Saddled up at Kesler's wing, he received some of the toughest minutes on the team outside of Getzlaf and Cogliano. The 2009 first rounder put up fairly decent offensive numbers, but was relied on in a more defensive role than in previous years. Was it he or his linemates that did the real legwork, though? It feels like we are still trying to solve Kyle Palmieri.

Corey Perry — RW — ANA

Season	Team	Age	GP	G	A	Pts	+/-	ESP/60	AdjCF%	iCF/60	OGVT	DGVT	SGVT	GVT
2012-13	ANA	27	44	15	21	36	10	2.22	51.6%	15.2	5.1	2.0	1.7	8.8
2013-14	ANA	28	81	43	39	82	32	3.07	53.2%	17.6	18.7	4.0	1.3	24.0
2014-15	ANA	29	67	33	22	55	13	2.85	51.0%	16.7	11.5	3.0	0.3	14.7
2015-16	ANA	30	73	31	34	65					10.7	2.5	0.0	13.2

At this point in his career, Corey Perry has solidified himself as one of the NHL's most effective power forwards. The fifth 30+ goal season of his career came amidst a battle with the mumps and a knee injury that sidelined him for a combined 15 games. Nevertheless, he had the league's third-highest goals per 60 minutes rate at 1.71—only Alex Ovechkin and Rick Nash scored with more regularity. He can be a frustrating opponent for opposing teams and fans alike with his chippy style, but that is Corey Perry. You love to hate him, but no one can deny they would take him on their team in a heartbeat. Together with Getzlaf, the pair are capable of dominating entire games.

Rickard Rakell — C/RW — ANA

Season	Team	Age	GP	G	A	Pts	+/-	ESP/60	AdjCF%	iCF/60	OGVT	DGVT	SGVT	GVT
2012-13	ANA	19	4	0	0	0	-2	0.00	31.2%	5.9	-0.3	-0.1	0.0	-0.4
2013-14	ANA	20	18	0	4	4	-3	1.18	56.1%	15.7	-0.3	-0.1	-0.3	-0.7
2014-15	ANA	21	71	9	22	31	6	1.65	52.8%	12.1	3.8	1.5	0.6	5.9
2015-16	ANA	22	61	10	18	28					1.7	1.3	0.0	3.0

By almost all statistical accounts, Rickard Rakell had a marvelous rookie season. What was exceptional was his growth as the year unfolded. Of his 71 games, the 2011 late first rounder had 17 of his 31 points in the second half of his season.

Jiri Sekac — LW/C — ANA

Season	Team	Age	GP	G	A	Pts	+/-	ESP/60	AdjCF%	iCF/60	OGVT	DGVT	SGVT	GVT
2014-15	MTL, ANA	22	69	9	14	23	0	1.37	49.9%	10.5	1.6	1.3	0.0	2.9
2015-16	ANA	23	61	9	15	24					0.7	1.3	0.0	2.0

Jiri Sekac, amusingly known amongst fans by his semordnilap of "Cakes", was part of an interesting and altogether fruitful deal for the Ducks. GM Bob Murray moved away from power forward Devante Smith-Pelley, picking up the lanky and speedy Sekac from Montreal in a "hockey trade" of wingers. Aligned with Rakell and Etem, the Czech native and his linemates were able to use that speed to become one of the more dominant lines for the Ducks late in the season. Over the course of their collaboration, the trio amassed a whopping 73.1 Corsi for per 60 minutes, along with a 3.97 goals-for per 60. Yes, the group could be an adventure defensively, but the trade brought the Ducks impressive versatility. Sekac lost his place in the lineup entering the playoffs, but it is hard to imagine he will not be back.

Jakob Silfverberg														RW									ANA
Season	Team	Age	GP	G	A	Pts	+/-	ESP/60	AdjCF%	iCF/60	OGVT	DGVT	SGVT	GVT
2012-13	OTT	22	48	10	9	19	9	1.40	53.3%	18.2	1.1	1.9	1.2	4.2
2013-14	ANA	23	52	10	13	23	2	1.94	51.0%	14.8	3.0	1.2	0.0	4.3
2014-15	ANA	24	81	13	26	39	15	1.78	51.9%	16.8	5.4	4.1	4.5	14.0
2015-16	ANA	25	69	16	30	46					5.9	3.0	0.2	9.1

Jakob Silfverberg and Andrew Cogliano formed two-thirds of the Ducks shutdown line. Usually, their center rotated between Kesler and Thompson. "Cogs" and Silfverberg were together last year as well, but they were far less effective. This season was a different story: the duo were well positive in both Corsi for (52.7%) and goals for (57.1%). The 24-year-old Silfverberg faced a tall order from head coach Bruce Boudreau, receiving the most difficult minutes in terms of quality of competition. And when away from Cogliano, Silfverberg also got only 25% offensive zone starts. He was easily the Ducks most heavily-stressed defensive forward, but still managed one point shy of 40.

Nate Thompson														C									ANA
Season	Team	Age	GP	G	A	Pts	+/-	ESP/60	AdjCF%	iCF/60	OGVT	DGVT	SGVT	GVT
2012-13	TBL	28	45	7	8	15	-2	1.69	43.7%	11.2	1.3	1.8	0.0	3.1
2013-14	TBL	29	81	9	7	16	3	0.96	51.7%	10.8	-0.6	3.0	0.0	2.3
2014-15	ANA	30	80	5	13	18	0	1.12	48.1%	9.0	0.2	2.5	0.0	2.7
2015-16	ANA	31	62	7	11	18					0.3	2.0	0.0	2.3

The additions of Kesler and Nate Thompson gave the Ducks much-needed center depth, one of the key areas requiring improvement coming out of the 2014 playoffs when they were defeated by the Los Angeles Kings, a team with great center depth. Although by no means an offensive juggernaut, the former Lightning center was an underrated add. Thompson was the Ducks' second-best faceoff man (52.8%), a welcome addition to one of the weakest teams at the dot in 2013-14.

Chris Wagner														C/RW									ANA
Season	Team	Age	GP	G	A	Pts	+/-	ESP/60	AdjCF%	iCF/60	OGVT	DGVT	SGVT	GVT
2014-15	ANA	23	9	0	0	0	-2	0.00	46.1%	10.5	-0.6	-0.1	0.0	-0.7
2015-16	ANA	24	30	4	5	9					0.0	0.5	0.0	0.5

Chris Wagner has emerged as a nice little sleeper pick. The gritty Colgate University alum was on pace to shatter his AHL career highs before getting a brief call-up to the Ducks late in the season. Alas, he failed to really cash in on the opportunity. That being said, he has an outside shot of being a contributor to the Ducks' bottom lines in 2015-16. In a small sample, he was exceptional on the draw, winning 33 of 55 (60%) in nine games.

DEFENSEMEN

Francois Beauchemin — LD — COL

Season	Team	Age	GP	G	A	Pts	+/-	ESP/60	AdjCF%	iCF/60	OGVT	DGVT	SGVT	GVT
2012-13	ANA	32	48	6	18	24	19	1.10	49.6%	7.3	4.1	5.0	0.0	9.0
2013-14	ANA	33	70	4	13	17	26	0.66	49.5%	8.2	-1.3	6.5	0.0	5.2
2014-15	ANA	34	64	11	12	23	17	0.94	50.7%	7.8	4.2	5.0	0.0	9.3
2015-16	COL	35	61	5	18	23					2.4	3.7	0.0	6.1

11-year veteran Francois Beauchemin had a surprisingly strong year, putting up a career-high 11 goals and posting 23 points, which is excellent for a defender that some were expecting to drop off. Beauchemin's numbers were elevated by playing almost exclusively with dynamic youngster Hampus Lindholm, with the pair registering 2.47 even-strength goals for per 60 minutes and a 61.9 goals-for percentage. The wily 35-year-old provided solid positioning and stay-at-home skill to allow his cohort to take risks. It should come as no surprise he scored a large contract with Colorado, where Tyson Barrie will be the benefactor of his play. The biggest question is whether age will catch up with him over the next three years of the deal.

Simon Despres — LD — ANA

Season	Team	Age	GP	G	A	Pts	+/-	ESP/60	AdjCF%	iCF/60	OGVT	DGVT	SGVT	GVT
2012-13	PIT	21	33	2	5	7	9	0.79	53.3%	7.2	0.7	1.5	0.0	2.2
2013-14	PIT	22	34	0	5	5	4	0.46	53.3%	8.7	-0.4	1.6	0.0	1.3
2014-15	PIT, ANA	23	75	3	20	23	11	1.13	53.3%	10.5	3.1	3.9	-0.3	6.8
2015-16	ANA	24	64	3	15	18					1.2	2.9	0.0	4.2

Of all the deals on deadline day 2015, the swap of Ben Lovejoy and Simon Despres was perhaps the most perplexing. The 23-year-old got something with the Ducks he was not getting with Pittsburgh: more opportunity. The Quebec native saw his average ice-time go from 16 to almost 19 minutes per night. His strong even-strength Corsi numbers dipped, but he was getting more difficult minutes against better opponents with Anaheim. Moving forward, the Ducks hope the smooth-skating, offensively-gifted youngster rewards that sort of trust from the coaching staff.

Mark Fistric — LD — Free Agent

Season	Team	Age	GP	G	A	Pts	+/-	ESP/60	AdjCF%	iCF/60	OGVT	DGVT	SGVT	GVT
2012-13	EDM	26	25	0	6	6	6	1.09	46.2%	5.7	0.8	1.5	0.0	2.3
2013-14	ANA	27	34	1	4	5	9	0.52	49.1%	5.6	-0.3	1.6	0.0	1.3
2014-15	ANA	28	9	0	0	0	-3	0.00	47.1%	4.5	-0.7	-0.1	0.0	-0.8
2015-16	Free Agent	29	33	1	5	6					-0.3	1.2	0.0	0.8

For the majority of the past two seasons, Mark Fistric drew the ire of Ducks fans. When you look at his numbers, you cannot really blame them. Teams utterly demolished the 28-year-old defenseman. When the ex-Oiler was on the ice (GM Bob Murray seems to have a thing for former Oilers) opponents tallied 3.88 goals against per 60 minutes. They were able to get off shots at a higher rate in each of the high-, medium-, and low-danger varieties with Fistric on the ice.

Cam Fowler — LD — ANA

Season	Team	Age	GP	G	A	Pts	+/-	ESP/60	AdjCF%	iCF/60	OGVT	DGVT	SGVT	GVT
2012-13	ANA	21	37	1	10	11	-4	0.47	46.8%	7.7	0.6	0.3	0.0	0.8
2013-14	ANA	22	70	6	30	36	15	0.96	49.7%	6.4	5.1	3.4	0.0	8.5
2014-15	ANA	23	80	7	27	34	4	1.02	50.0%	5.4	4.0	2.9	0.0	6.9
2015-16	ANA	24	69	7	26	33					3.7	3.3	0.0	7.0

Cam Fowler came into the league with an emphasis on his offensive prowess. He put up exceptional numbers with the OHL's Windsor Spitfires and has done respectably for himself at the NHL level. Defense, however, has always been a concern. Since 2012, Fowler has seen modest progression in his Corsi- and Fenwick-for percentages, but it is time to start wondering if he has been surpassed by Lindholm as the Ducks' top defender.

Korbinian Holzer — RD — ANA

Season	Team	Age	GP	G	A	Pts	+/-	ESP/60	AdjCF%	iCF/60	OGVT	DGVT	SGVT	GVT
2012-13	TOR	24	22	2	1	3	-12	0.52	40.8%	5.3	-0.3	-0.8	0.0	-1.0
2014-15	TOR	26	34	0	6	6	3	0.72	43.3%	5.8	-0.2	2.4	0.0	2.1
2015-16	ANA	27	41	2	8	9					0.2	2.2	0.0	2.4

Since coming to North America from Germany in 2010-11, Korbinian Holzer has been a staple of the Toronto Marlies lineup. As an AHL defenseman, he brings good hockey sense and a steady presence alongside whichever Leafs defensive prospect happens to be in the minors. Along the way, he has commuted to 58 NHL games, including 34 in 2014-15, a career high. The results were not ideal. His big chance came as the Leafs were falling apart, but his numbers reflected that fact. He finished the season with a 43.7% Corsi despite playing more than half his minutes with Jake Gardiner.

Hampus Lindholm — LD — ANA

Season	Team	Age	GP	G	A	Pts	+/-	ESP/60	AdjCF%	iCF/60	OGVT	DGVT	SGVT	GVT
2013-14	ANA	19	78	6	24	30	29	1.18	51.6%	8.2	3.6	4.7	0.0	8.3
2014-15	ANA	20	78	7	27	34	25	1.18	51.6%	7.8	5.1	6.8	0.0	12.0
2015-16	ANA	21	74	8	27	35					4.2	4.6	0.0	8.8

The Ducks have an exceptional play-driving defenseman in the making. Hailing from Helsingborg, Sweden, Hampus Lindholm put together a great sophomore season, building on what was a tremendous rookie year in 2013-14. While Francois Beauchemin no doubt helped him on the defensive side of the ice, the the 20-year-old flashed dynamic offensive skill, beginning with explosive skating ability. When Lindholm is bringing the puck up the ice, dodging defenders in the neutral zone, he is in rare air. He is one of the few defenseman who can start transition offense simply by getting his hands on the puck. There is still room to grow defensively—and he will have to take more of the burden now that Beauchemin is gone—but look for his name amongst the elite soon.

Josh Manson — RD — ana

Season	Team	Age	GP	G	A	Pts	+/-	ESP/60	AdjCF%	iCF/60	OGVT	DGVT	SGVT	GVT
2014-15	ANA	23	28	0	3	3	1	0.38	54.2%	6.7	-0.7	1.1	0.0	0.4
2015-16	ANA	24	39	2	6	8					-0.1	1.6	0.0	1.5

The son of former NHLer Dave Manson, Josh has extremely limited offensive capabilities, but may be able to stick in the NHL as a stay-at-home defender to complement and potentially improve the play of more risk-taking puck movers. With size and enough skating ability to play at the highest level, the Northeastern product will need to prove he can be a consistent, smart, and reliable blueliner in order to see the ice every night. His work received strong reviews from management and it appears he will get a chance to take the next step soon.

Colby Robak				**LD**									**Free Agent**
Season	Team	Age	GP	G	A	Pts	+/-	ESP/60	AdjCF%	iCF/60	OGVT	DGVT	SGVT	GVT
2012-13	FLA	22	16	0	1	1	-1	0.28	49.1%	7.6	-0.6	0.8	0.0	0.1
2013-14	FLA	23	16	0	2	2	-4	0.24	46.2%	5.4	-0.4	0.0	0.0	-0.4
2014-15	FLA, ANA	24	12	0	1	1	2	0.38	51.3%	6.1	-0.4	0.7	0.0	0.3
2015-16	Free Agent	25	30	1	5	6					0.0	1.1	0.0	1.2

Colby Robak was a short-lived resident of the Ducks defensive carousel, which follows the pattern from his past with the Florida Panthers. After coming over from Florida, the 24-year-old spent four games up with Anaheim in December before logging a fifth in late January, which is only a few games under his career high of 16 in a single season. As with many AHL-caliber defensemen, he was infrequently utilized. Unless Robak magically becomes a much improved puck handler and skater, it is hard to imagine him having much impact on the Ducks blueline in the future, but he could have utility as a seventh or eighth defenseman.

Clayton Stoner				**LD**									**ANA**
Season	Team	Age	GP	G	A	Pts	+/-	ESP/60	AdjCF%	iCF/60	OGVT	DGVT	SGVT	GVT
2012-13	MIN	27	48	0	10	10	0	0.68	47.8%	6.9	0.2	2.9	0.0	3.1
2013-14	MIN	28	63	1	4	5	-6	0.40	47.3%	7.4	-1.3	1.6	0.0	0.3
2014-15	ANA	29	69	1	7	8	-2	0.44	50.9%	8.1	-1.4	2.3	0.0	0.9
2015-16	ANA	30	57	2	6	8					-1.1	2.4	0.0	1.3

Clayton Stoner held the Ducks bottom-pairing spot nearly all season, and inexplicably kept that spot when the team acquired quality offensive defenseman James Wisniewski. An unspectacular 17 minutes per night, with a few hits thrown in and barely above 50% possession numbers was apparently enough to gain ice-time over the former Blue Jacket in the playoffs. While he is a tick above the true stay-at-home bruisers of the past, the Ducks are an up-tempo, speed-through-the-neutral-zone team. It is difficult to see where Stoner fits in that system.

Sami Vatanen				**RD**									**ANA**
Season	Team	Age	GP	G	A	Pts	+/-	ESP/60	AdjCF%	iCF/60	OGVT	DGVT	SGVT	GVT
2012-13	ANA	21	8	2	0	2	3	0.57	50.7%	4.1	0.6	0.6	0.0	1.1
2013-14	ANA	22	48	6	15	21	9	1.18	54.4%	9.5	4.0	1.5	0.0	5.5
2014-15	ANA	23	67	12	25	37	5	1.03	51.7%	7.4	6.4	3.1	0.6	10.1
2015-16	ANA	24	65	9	28	37					5.3	3.1	0.0	8.4

One of the elite power-play defensemen in the NHL, the offensively-gifted Sami Vatanen posted eye-popping man-advantage numbers, ranking eighth in points per 60 minutes. He has proven to be the perfect compliment for Getzlaf and Perry with both solid puck-moving skills and a sniper's shot. One surprising element of his game, however, is that Vatanen was far and away the Ducks best shot blocker while still being a top-notch puck-possession defender. He was top-40 in the league in Fenwick-for percentage, finishing in the same range as

Dustin Byfuglien, Andrej Sekera, Zdeno Chara, and Niklas Hjalmarsson. With his mobility, offensive mindset, and developing defensive game, the 24-year-old Finn is becoming a dangerous second-pairing defenseman.

James Wisniewski								RD						CAR
Season	Team	Age	GP	G	A	Pts	+/-	ESP/60	AdjCF%	iCF/60	OGVT	DGVT	SGVT	GVT
2012-13	CBJ	28	30	5	9	14	-1	0.89	50.0%	8.3	1.8	1.0	-0.3	2.4
2013-14	CBJ	29	75	7	44	51	0	1.08	54.5%	10.2	9.4	3.0	0.0	12.4
2014-15	CBJ, ANA	30	69	8	26	34	-13	1.01	48.9%	10.9	4.7	-0.6	0.0	4.2
2015-16	CAR	31	57	6	24	30					3.7	1.5	0.0	5.2

30-year-old James Wisniewski struggled to get into the lineup after coming back West. The hard-shooting journeyman was expected to be a top-four addition for the postseason run, but quickly saw himself phased out of the lineup in favor of the likes of Clayton Stoner. "The Wiz" had a fairly good numbers by the end of the year, but it was quite clear that something was not right in Anaheim. He attempted to block a trade out of Columbus, which may have affected his attitude about being in Southern California. As a strong-skating, super-shooting blueliner, he should still have enough in the tank to make an impact on Carolina's blueline and power play.

GOALTENDERS

Frederik Andersen								G						ANA
Season	Team	Age	GP	W	L	OT	GAA	Sv%	ESSV%	QS%	GGVT	DGVT	SGVT	GVT
2013-14	ANA	24	28	20	5	0	2.29	.923	.928	54.2%	9.7	-0.1	1.1	10.7
2014-15	ANA	25	54	35	12	5	2.38	.914	.920	62.3%	7.1	0.7	-1.2	6.6
2015-16	ANA	26	46					.915			5.6	0.3	0.0	5.9

At this point, the starting role of Freddie Andersen is tenuous, at best. He still remains the best of the options available to the Ducks, but the shine of his good 2013-14 season has started to fade. The Danish goalie saw his save percentage decline from .923 in 2013-14 to .914 in 2014-15. With multiple numbers trending in the wrong direction, and young phenom John Gibson waiting in the wings, it is hard to imagine there would not be a goalie battle in Anaheim in 2015-16. That could end up as a "good problem to have" for the Ducks. Whether Andersen wins or loses the goalie battle, they will have a trade chip.

Ilya Bryzgalov								G						Free Agent
Season	Team	Age	GP	W	L	OT	GAA	Sv%	ESSV%	QS%	GGVT	DGVT	SGVT	GVT
2012-13	PHI	32	40	19	17	3	2.79	.900	.907	50.0%	-5.0	0.3	-1.4	-6.1
2013-14	EDM, MIN	33	32	12	9	8	2.68	.909	.923	53.3%	0.3	0.1	-1.3	-0.9
2014-15	ANA	34	8	1	4	1	4.19	.847	.882	33.3%	-7.8	0.1	-1.0	-8.7
2015-16		35	16					.907			-1.9	0.0	-0.2	-2.2

What can you say about Ilya Bryzgalov? He did exist this year, but that was about it. If "Mr. Universe" was somewhere in orbit before 2014-15, he came crashing back down to earth somewhere during his disastrous starts this season. Murray had reached out to the 34-year-old goalie when injuries plagued their men between the pipes. In his six starts as a Duck, he posted an awful 4.19 goals against and an equally dreadful .847 save percentage. When the era of Bryzgalov came to an end in Anaheim, it was best for everyone.

John Gibson — G — ANA

Season	Team	Age	GP	W	L	OT	GAA	Sv%	ESSV%	QS%	GGVT	DGVT	SGVT	GVT
2013-14	ANA	20	3	3	0	0	1.33	.954	.941	100.0%	3.3	0.0	0.0	3.4
2014-15	ANA	21	23	13	8	0	2.60	.914	.927	66.7%	2.9	-0.2	-0.1	2.5
2015-16	ANA	22	27					.916			4.3	-0.1	0.0	4.2

While a lot of noise came in the 2014 playoffs for John Gibson, his first true rookie season was in 2014-15. It did not go exactly as planned. While the 21-year-old had exceptional numbers at the AHL level when healthy, he dealt with his fair share of injuries and inconsistency at the NHL level. The promise is still quite high for Gibson, though, and learning NHL goaltending is extremely difficult. He will be fighting for the starting job in the near future.

Jason LaBarbera — G — PHI

Season	Team	Age	GP	W	L	OT	GAA	Sv%	ESSV%	QS%	GGVT	DGVT	SGVT	GVT
2012-13	PHX	32	15	4	6	2	2.64	.923	.925	50.0%	5.8	-0.7	0.1	5.1
2013-14	EDM	33	7	1	3	0	3.28	.870	.903	0.0%	-4.6	0.3	0.6	-3.8
2014-15	ANA	34	5	2	0	1	2.61	.909	.923	100.0%	0.0	0.0	-0.1	0.0
2015-16	PHI	35	12					.911			0.1	0.0	0.0	0.2

Jason LaBarbera was signed by Bob Murray over the summer as an insurance policy on both Frederik Andersen and John Gibson. It is safe to say that the Ducks had desperately hoped they would not have to use him, but the contingency came to pass in November. With Gibson shelved with a groin injury and Andersen dealing with a nagging leg injury, for a brief few games, he was the Ducks healthy number-one starter. All expectations were tossed out the window, and with good reason. He was strictly a worst-case scenario for the Ducks, much like Bryzgalov. Just goes to show that you are never quite out of a job in the NHL as a goaltender.

Jason Lewis

Arizona Coyotes

Last year, the hockey media made a lot of the "Tank for McDavid" run that the Buffalo Sabres appeared to be on. That said, Arizona made it a photo finish. The Coyotes were really bad, too. One could argue they seemed intentionally bad, just like the highly-criticized Sabres. The Coyotes were a poor team to begin with, but the moves they made sank them into more lottery balls. If only they had made some of these moves earlier—like trading Devan Dubnyk to Minnesota before he went 9-5-2—they might have beaten Buffalo in the footrace to 30th and guaranteed themselves at least Jack Eichel, a first-overall talent in most drafts.

In any normal year, with a measly 56 points in the standings, Arizona would have come in 30th. Give credit to their management for taking the right direction—selling—rather than trying to hang onto 10th place in the West. The Coyotes finished 29th in goals per game (2.01) and 28th in goals against per game (3.26), they had the league's 29th-ranked penalty kill (76.7%), they actually had a worse five-on-five goal differential than the pitiful Sabres (-68), they were 23rd in team Fenwick for, and they allowed the fourth-most shots per 60 minutes (32.7). Whew! (See table, next page.)

Another factor that helped them sink to the bottom was poor goaltending. It made the decision to trade off parts and promote replacement-level AHLers easy. If Arizona had a big year from their netminders—a la New Jersey—it would have been detrimental for their rebuild. Instead, the combination of Mike Smith, Dubnyk (in his limited run), and Louis Domingue posted the fourth-worst team save percentage (.902). True, it was a little better at even strength (.915), but that was still fifth worst in the league. One of the reasons the Coyotes just missed out to Buffalo for "McEichel" was that in close games, Arizona's save percentage rose to a .918, good enough for 11th overall in the league.

Making the decision to rebuild is one of the hardest a GM and organization can make. It has to go all the way up to ownership and be accepted by the fanbase and local media – otherwise it turns into a nightmare. Ideally, the decision should come before the season and carry through, despite inevitable hot stretches.

From our vantage point, the Coyotes made a mistake by not realizing earlier they could get to Buffalo-Edmonton territory, and by keeping a winning coach behind the bench. While they were losing the possession battle—46.1% Corsi for percentage in close games—they could have sunk lower under a less qualified bench boss than

COYOTES IN A BOX

Last Season

Goals For	170	29th
Goals Against	272	28th
GVT	-102	29th
Points	56	29th
Playoffs	Did not make playoffs	

What had been a competitive team for five years fell to pieces, as the Coyotes finished last in the West.

Three-Year Record

GVT	-123	27th
Points	196	27th
Playoffs	0 Appearances, 0 Wins	

VUKOTA Projection

Goals For	189	30th
Goals Against	236	29th
GVT	-48	30th
Points	76	30th

The lineup hasn't changed, and Yandle is gone for good. Arizona may not finish last again, but it won't be pretty.

Top Three Prospects

D. Strome (F), M. Domi (F), N. Merkley (F)

ARIZONA COYOTES

How bad were Arizona and Buffalo?			
Stat	Arizona	Buffalo	NHL Average
Goals per game	2.01 (29th)	1.87 (30th)	2.73
Goals against per game	3.26 (27th)	3.28 (29th)	2.53
Penalty-killing percentage	76.7% (29th)	75.1% (30th)	81.0%
5-on-5 goal differential	-68 (30th)	-67 (29th)	+5*
Shots against per 60	32.7 (28th)	35.1 (30th)	29.8
Standing points	56 (29th)	54 (30th)	97.5*

*Median

Dave Tippett, who had dragged a so-so team to the Western Conference Final back in 2011-12. Before they started sending dinged-up players like Martin Hanzal and Mikael Boedker to the IR and trading solid players like Keith Yandle and Zbynek Michalek, Arizona's Corsi for percentage was near 50% in January. Oddly enough, bad goaltending kept them in the race for last all along. With better goaltending, the Coyotes may have just stood pat and tried to compete for eighth.

However, the team's poor play was too much for their mediocre netminders. The Coyotes weren't going to get bailed out by Smith the way Carey Price made bad Canadiens performances turn into wins. While there has been a notable decline for the team since 2011, Arizona has generally remained a breakeven Corsi and Fenwick team over that stretch. This year, they saw a further dip. Scoring chances against rose slightly, shots against rose slightly, and high-danger scoring chances allowed stayed at the scary high level from prior years. It may have simply been a matter of time before Arizona had a season like 2014-15. All of their peripheral numbers had been in a small incremental decline until this season when everything collapsed.

After January 29, when Hanzal left the lineup, the Coyotes appeared to go into full-fledged tank mode (where they should have gone even earlier). They went 7-25-2 in the final 34 games without Hanzal and Boedker. The six-foot-six center, Hanzal, had paced the team with 2.04 points per 60 minutes prior to injury, while the Danish winger, Boedker, was second at 1.44. Boedker was also the highest-rated goal scorer at even strength for Arizona with a 0.96 goals per 60 minutes. Only two other players on Arizona cracked the 0.50 mark at five-on-five, Hanzal, and diminutive journeyman Marc Arcobello. In 2013-14 as well, Hanzal was the top player on Arizona in terms of production per 60 categories; Boedker was less productive but still an important top-six producer.

Joining the 28-year-old Hanzal at the top of the production chart in 2013-14 were two other key departed members: Mike Ribeiro and Radim Vrbata. Their contributions at even strength were simply never replaced. The Coyotes made little effort to fill in the gap of nearly 1.00 goals per 60 and 3.00 points per 60 lost from Vrbata and Ribeiro by only adding Oilers castoff Sam Gagner and young players like Lucas Lessio and Tobias Rieder. Also lost were the defensive contributions of Hanzal, Ribeiro, and Vrbata, who had been three of Arizona's better possession forwards in 2013-14. They walked to the edge, but couldn't quite jump until they finally saw 30th on the horizon.

It is hard to tell a team to trade or bench good players in the name of 30th place, but you don't have to take an in-depth look at high draft picks (see: Blackhawks, Chicago) to know the most direct way to rebuild a flailing team is to draft high. Unfortunately for 2014-15, Hanzal and Boedker were buoying the Coyotes slightly above Sabre-level. In the end, it cost them a future can't-miss star. The Coyotes did the right thing by going all-in after January, while their goalies helped the cause by being bad the entire year—but the path should have been obvious before then.

The overall positive? Despite the opportunity missed, Arizona is still in great shape for a rebuilding club. The Coyotes have a number of tremendous prospects—like Max Domi, Dylan Strome, Brandon Perlini, Christian Dvorak, and Anthony Duclair—waiting in the wings. It is hard to imagine most or all of them going bust.

However, this time around—despite no McDavid-caliber prospect available at the end of the rainbow—the Coyotes should make a conscious decision, before opening night, to continue a full-out rebuild. The goal should not be to only land a decent prospect. If they can select another future star to add to their current crop of prospects and young star defenseman Oliver Ekman-Larsson, it won't be too long before they are a solid playoff team or better. If they select in the middle of the first round because they waffled? Good luck, because history isn't on that side.

Jason Lewis

ARIZONA COYOTES

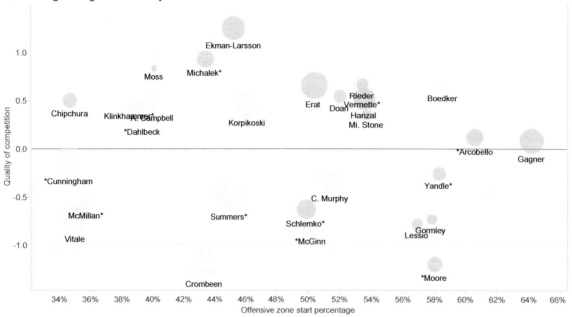

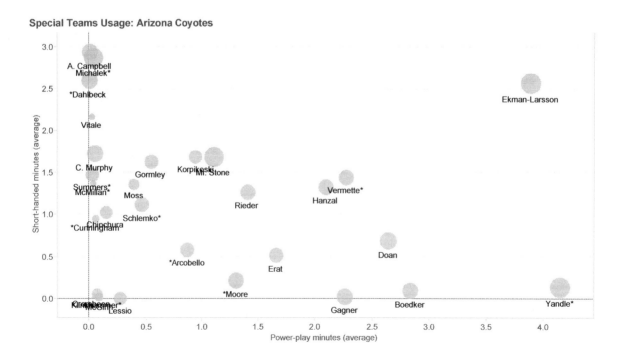

ARIZONA COYOTES

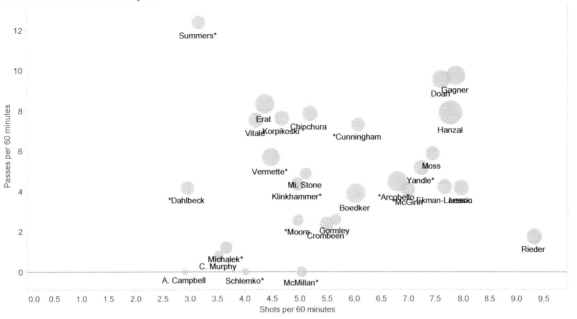

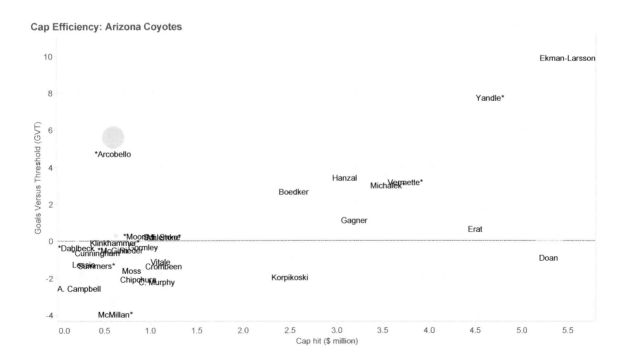

ARIZONA COYOTES

FORWARDS

Mark Arcobello							C/RW						TOR
Season	Team	Age	GP	G	A	Pts	+/-	ESP/60	AdjCF%	iCF/60	OGVT	DGVT	SGVT	GVT
2012-13	EDM	24	1	0	0	0	0	0.00	35.8%	0.0	-0.9	0.5	0.0	-0.4
2013-14	EDM	25	41	4	14	18	-7	1.79	46.5%	13.1	1.6	1.2	0.0	2.8
2014-15	EDM, NSH, PIT, ARI	26	77	17	14	31	-10	1.52	50.6%	12.1	3.8	2.4	-0.5	5.6
2015-16	TOR	27	64	12	16	28					2.3	1.8	0.0	4.1

It is hard to have a more unsettled season than the one Marc Arcobello had in 2014-15. In just five months, the 26-year-old played for four different teams in four different time zones. Just the four teams part is a lot. Arcobello stands as just the third player in history to play for four different NHL teams over the course of one season. Despite all of the moves, the former Yale Bulldog finished up with a respectable 31 points in 77 games, 16 of which came in the 27 contests with Arizona. He also recorded a positive GVT, which was hard to come by on the Arizona roster. Nevertheless, his cushy zone starts and usage, his diminutive size, and his high goals-against and scoring chances against numbers make him a questionable subject in terms of repeatable success. That said, he will look to build on 2014-15 in Toronto.

Mikkel Boedker							LW						ARI
Season	Team	Age	GP	G	A	Pts	+/-	ESP/60	AdjCF%	iCF/60	OGVT	DGVT	SGVT	GVT
2012-13	PHX	23	48	7	19	26	0	1.63	48.6%	9.4	1.7	1.0	-1.0	1.7
2013-14	PHX	24	82	19	32	51	-9	1.71	48.4%	11.6	6.3	1.8	0.8	8.9
2014-15	ARI	25	45	14	14	28	-10	1.47	46.4%	10.4	2.7	0.9	-0.4	3.2
2015-16	ARI	26	60	17	22	39					4.3	1.6	0.0	5.9

It was a difficult, injury-riddled year for Mikkel Boedker. The Danish winger had been on a run of 257 straight games before he was sidelined with a spleen injury in January that required removal of the organ (erk!). He lost a reported 20 pounds during his five-week recovery. On the ice, he continues to be a marginal possession forward with good offensive flash. He was one of Arizona's best five-on-five goal scorers, but also one of their worst defensive forwards. That kind of dichotomy can make the 26-year-old a frustrating player to value.

Alexandre Bolduc							C						KHL
Season	Team	Age	GP	G	A	Pts	+/-	ESP/60	AdjCF%	iCF/60	OGVT	DGVT	SGVT	GVT
2012-13	PHX	27	14	0	0	0	-4	0.00	47.5%	13.5	-0.9	-0.2	0.0	-1.1
2014-15	ARI	29	3	0	0	0	-1	0.00	38.4%	5.5	-0.2	0.0	0.0	-0.2
2015-16	KHL	30	24	4	5	8					0.5	0.5	0.0	0.9

Alexandre Bolduc played three uneventful games for Arizona in early February. Otherwise, he spent the majority of the year with their AHL affiliate, the Portland Pirates, where he put up an impressive 23 goals, 52 points, and 106 penalty minutes over 62 games. An excellent minor-league player, he was also captain of the Pirates. Despite the AHL success, the veteran played 11 minutes per night with the Coyotes, featuring a sub-40% Corsi. Those are not the greatest numbers, but it was not the biggest sample size, either. Seeing the writing on the wall as a fringe North American pro entering his thirties, Bolduc has headed to Russia where he will play for the colorful-sounding Traktor Chelyabinsk.

Kyle Chipchura — C/RW — ARI

Season	Team	Age	GP	G	A	Pts	+/-	ESP/60	AdjCF%	iCF/60	OGVT	DGVT	SGVT	GVT
2012-13	PHX	26	46	5	9	14	1	1.92	49.6%	8.1	1.3	1.0	0.0	2.2
2013-14	PHX	27	80	5	15	20	3	1.56	51.9%	6.7	0.5	2.2	0.0	2.7
2014-15	ARI	28	70	4	10	14	-23	0.91	48.7%	8.5	-1.4	0.0	0.0	-1.4
2015-16	ARI	29	57	5	9	15					-0.2	1.0	0.0	0.8

Kyle Chipchura was one of Arizona's least effective even-strength scorers, though he was slammed with difficult minutes and tough competition—he and Joe Vitale were easily the most strained forwards defensively. While the goals-for numbers were woeful, the 2004 eighth-overall draft choice nearly broke even in Corsi, better than could be said for many of his teammates. There was interest at the deadline from other clubs because of his solid faceoff (51.6%) and possession capabilities. If Arizona isn't in the playoff race (don't hold your breath), expect there to be interest in this depth center again.

B.J. Crombeen — RW — Free Agent

Season	Team	Age	GP	G	A	Pts	+/-	ESP/60	AdjCF%	iCF/60	OGVT	DGVT	SGVT	GVT
2012-13	TBL	27	44	1	7	8	4	1.17	46.2%	11.0	0.2	1.6	0.0	1.7
2013-14	TBL	28	55	3	7	10	-2	1.14	49.0%	13.1	0.1	1.3	0.0	1.4
2014-15	ARI	29	58	3	3	6	-6	0.77	42.0%	10.5	-1.3	0.6	0.0	-0.7
2015-16	Free Agent	30	48	4	5	8					-0.5	1.0	0.0	0.4

B.J. Crombeen has made his way in the league by combining tough physical play with a couple of surprising offensive seasons in St. Louis. However, his days of flirting with 20 points seem to be gone for good. While he has never been a truly effective player, he has remained a fringe fourth liner for several seasons. But Crombeen started to slip in 2014-15, as his possession stats dropped to career lows. If he could chip in double-digit goals again, he could be a tolerable option, but this last campaign may prohibit him from getting further chances.

Craig Cunningham — RW/C — ARI

Season	Team	Age	GP	G	A	Pts	+/-	ESP/60	AdjCF%	iCF/60	OGVT	DGVT	SGVT	GVT
2013-14	BOS	23	2	0	0	0	0	0.00	54.0%	14.0	-0.1	0.1	0.0	0.0
2014-15	BOS, ARI	24	51	3	4	7	-7	0.75	42.3%	8.7	-0.7	0.5	0.0	-0.2
2015-16	ARI	25	48	5	6	11					-0.4	0.9	0.0	0.5

Craig Cunningham, former Boston and Providence Bruin, was claimed off waivers by Arizona in March, instantly becoming one of Tippet's most-utilized defensive forwards. Cunningham suffered what most Coyotes players suffered this past season: low Corsi-for percentage, low goals for, high goals against. It is hard to really gauge the overall effectiveness of the 25-year-old, since he has just 53 games of NHL experience and was on a struggling roster near the bottom of the league. He is a perfect candidate for a wait-and-see approach on a rebuilding team.

Shane Doan — RW/LW — ARI

Season	Team	Age	GP	G	A	Pts	+/-	ESP/60	AdjCF%	iCF/60	OGVT	DGVT	SGVT	GVT
2012-13	PHX	36	48	13	14	27	6	1.99	51.6%	14.9	3.2	1.8	-0.3	4.8
2013-14	PHX	37	69	23	24	47	-7	1.52	50.7%	13.7	5.3	1.7	-0.6	6.4
2014-15	ARI	38	79	14	22	36	-29	1.27	48.3%	11.7	-0.8	0.9	0.1	0.1
2015-16	ARI	39	64	13	18	31					2.0	1.3	0.0	3.3

It took a while, but 2014-15 looked to be the year in which Shane Doan hit the wall; the Coyotes captain has been on a slow decline since 2009. The possible future Hall of Famer appeared to have lost a step, causing him to look very little like the explosive power forward he once was. It was the first time in six years that Doan posted sub-50% possession numbers, and it was also his lowest even-strength points per 60 minutes rate in memory. And he was a highly sought-after free agent just a few summers ago.

Anthony Duclair — LW/RW — ARI

Season	Team	Age	GP	G	A	Pts	+/-	ESP/60	AdjCF%	iCF/60	OGVT	DGVT	SGVT	GVT
2014-15	NYR	19	18	1	6	7	4	1.86	49.8%	9.4	0.9	0.6	0.0	1.5
2015-16	ARI	20	34	6	11	16					1.5	1.0	0.0	2.4

A third-round pick in 2013, Anthony Duclair shot up the prospect ranks by scoring 99 points in 2013-14 with Quebec of the QMJHL. Making the Rangers club out of camp proved the five-foot-eleven winger had taken a leap forward since his draft year. However, after a handful of games in New York, the team elected to send him back to juniors, but his stock remained high when the trade deadline came along. GM Glen Sather moved him as a major piece in the deal for Keith Yandle. While Duclair is a tad undersized, he has quickness, offensive instincts, and slick hands. He will get plenty of opportunity with the rebuilding Coyotes.

Martin Erat — RW/LW — KHL

Season	Team	Age	GP	G	A	Pts	+/-	ESP/60	AdjCF%	iCF/60	OGVT	DGVT	SGVT	GVT
2012-13	NSH, WSH	31	45	5	19	24	-7	1.46	47.5%	8.6	1.4	1.0	-1.1	1.2
2013-14	WSH, PHX	32	70	3	26	29	5	1.71	50.2%	6.5	2.2	2.5	0.0	4.7
2014-15	ARI	33	79	9	23	32	-16	1.44	52.0%	8.0	0.0	1.9	-0.3	1.6
2015-16	KHL	34	62	7	18	26					1.1	1.7	0.0	2.8

It seems like a long time ago that Martin Erat was an effective player in Nashville. Now, he is just the guy who was used to flim flam the Capitals for Filip Forsberg. In terms of puck possession and even-strength scoring, Erat wasn't that bad in 2014-15, but someone had to receive top-six minutes on a team sinking to the bottom. At this point in his career, the veteran brings very little to the table above a replacement-level player.

Sam Gagner — C — PHI

Season	Team	Age	GP	G	A	Pts	+/-	ESP/60	AdjCF%	iCF/60	OGVT	DGVT	SGVT	GVT
2012-13	EDM	23	48	14	24	38	-6	1.76	43.1%	11.9	6.0	0.9	0.2	7.0
2013-14	EDM	24	67	10	27	37	-29	1.69	43.0%	11.5	1.2	-0.2	0.0	1.1
2014-15	ARI	25	81	15	26	41	-28	1.44	50.5%	12.7	1.2	1.0	-0.4	1.9
2015-16	PHI	26	68	16	25	41					3.2	1.5	0.0	4.6

ARIZONA COYOTES

It is amazing to think that Sam Gagner, at age 26, has already been in the league for eight years. A long-time disappointment in Edmonton, based largely on his pedigree—sixth overall pick in 2007 after putting up a crazy 118 points in 53 OHL games—he saw little in the way of a positive change in Arizona. A rare Coyotes forward above 50% Corsi, he still had a scary-high goals-against number because he is virtually inept in his own zone. Another change of scenery is in the cards as he moves on to Philadelphia. This will likely only add to the list of clubs frustrated by his talent level versus what they receive from his overall play.

Tyler Gaudet							C							ARI
Season	Team	Age	GP	G	A	Pts	+/-	ESP/60	AdjCF%	iCF/60	OGVT	DGVT	SGVT	GVT
2014-15	ARI	21	2	0	0	0	-1	0.00	21.3%	3.3	-0.2	0.0	0.0	-0.2
2015-16	ARI	22	26	5	6	11					0.7	0.5	0.0	1.2

Do not kick yourself if you do not know the name Tyler Gaudet. The undrafted center from the Sault Ste. Marie Greyhounds was signed by Arizona back in 2013 during his overage season in the OHL. Last season, he appeared in 71 games for the Portland Pirates and only managed eight goals and 20 points. The 21-year-old got a brief call-up at the end of December for two games, averaging nine minutes per contest.

Martin Hanzal							RW/LW							ARI
Season	Team	Age	GP	G	A	Pts	+/-	ESP/60	AdjCF%	iCF/60	OGVT	DGVT	SGVT	GVT
2012-13	PHX	25	39	11	12	23	2	1.56	51.9%	14.6	2.4	1.0	0.0	3.3
2013-14	PHX	26	65	15	25	40	-9	1.70	50.0%	12.2	4.0	1.7	0.0	5.7
2014-15	ARI	27	37	8	16	24	-1	2.15	51.3%	12.7	2.0	2.0	0.0	4.0
2015-16	ARI	28	55	13	21	34					3.4	2.0	0.0	5.3

Like Boedker, Martin Hanzal had a lost year due to injury. The hulking six-foot-six center was playing with a bum back that required season-ending surgery in late January. It was the right move, given that Arizona was in no way pushing for a meaningful finish. The Coyotes missed his two-way play desperately, as the big Czech remains one of the better complementary two-way centers in the Western Conference. Six of his eight professional seasons have seen him register positive possession numbers, and even this season before his injury, he was a positive contributor. He was on pace for a career year in goals, assists, and points before being shelved. If his back is right, look for Hanzal to have a big bounceback season.

Justin Hodgman							C/RW							STL
Season	Team	Age	GP	G	A	Pts	+/-	ESP/60	AdjCF%	iCF/60	OGVT	DGVT	SGVT	GVT
2014-15	ARI	26	5	1	0	1	-2	0.00	52.2%	2.3	0.1	-0.1	0.0	-0.1
2015-16	STL	27	27	5	6	11					0.8	0.5	0.0	1.2

27-year-old Justin Hodgman from Brampton, Ontario was scoring with decent regularity in the KHL over the past two seasons. As a junior player with the Erie Otters, he had also posted some pretty respectable numbers. Thus, his summer signing with Arizona was intriguing. Hodgman played 62 games with the Portland Pirates of the AHL, logging 35 points. He was up with the Coyotes in late October and early November, and actually posted solid possession numbers. It was a small sample size, but he came away with a 53.8% Corsi and a cool

54.3% over 46 faceoffs. Maybe Arizona should have given the Metallurg standout more than five games to prove himself.

Lauri Korpikoski — LW — EDM

Season	Team	Age	GP	G	A	Pts	+/-	ESP/60	AdjCF%	iCF/60	OGVT	DGVT	SGVT	GVT
2012-13	PHX	26	36	6	5	11	-3	1.11	49.1%	15.9	-0.7	1.1	-0.3	0.1
2013-14	PHX	27	64	9	16	25	-7	1.42	46.3%	12.8	2.3	1.8	0.0	4.0
2014-15	ARI	28	69	6	15	21	-27	0.83	42.8%	9.0	-1.3	0.2	0.0	-1.1
2015-16	EDM	29	56	8	13	21					0.7	1.1	0.0	1.9

No two ways about it, Lauri Korpikoski had an awful season. There is bad luck, and then there is the luck that the Finnish winger had. In 2013-14, he posted an even-strength shooting percentage of around 8%. He had that same number in 2012-13. However, in 2014-15, the Turku native shot at a 1.6% clip and also had a career-low 94.9 PDO. Korpikoski had just one even-strength goal all season long. It was not all luck based, though. The former Ranger also saw marked downturns in almost every category, be it goals, points, shots, and everything else that anyone ever tracks. Some of it was beyond his control, but he coupled an unlucky year with a flat-out bad year. If he doesn't bounce back in Edmonton, his NHL career could be over.

Lucas Lessio — LW — ARI

Season	Team	Age	GP	G	A	Pts	+/-	ESP/60	AdjCF%	iCF/60	OGVT	DGVT	SGVT	GVT
2013-14	PHX	20	3	0	0	0	-2	0.00	42.5%	11.8	-0.3	-0.1	0.0	-0.4
2014-15	ARI	21	26	2	3	5	-10	0.92	47.5%	11.2	-1.1	0.1	0.4	-0.7
2015-16	ARI	22	38	6	7	13					0.2	0.7	0.0	0.9

When you look at Lucas Lessio's incredibly poor 29.2% goals-for percentage, it is hard to imagine him having a good year. Nevertheless, he was actually a fairly solid Corsi contributor, and the real underlying issue was an awful .895 on-ice save percentage behind him, fueling an ugly 93.8 PDO. With a glance at his -10 plus/minus and poor goals-for percentage, you could easily write off the 2011 second-round pick. However, he was actually pretty serviceable and could be a good depth forward in the future.

Jordan Martinook — LW/C — ARI

Season	Team	Age	GP	G	A	Pts	+/-	ESP/60	AdjCF%	iCF/60	OGVT	DGVT	SGVT	GVT
2014-15	ARI	22	8	0	1	1	-3	0.69	53.4%	13.8	-0.8	0.1	0.0	-0.7
2015-16	ARI	23	29	5	6	11					0.2	0.6	0.0	0.9

Similar to Hodgman, Jordan Martinook is another Arizona forward who probably could have gotten a longer look than eight games. In a common trend amongst Coyotes players, his goals-for percentage was outright terrible, but he too was let down by poor goaltending—they stopped a criminally-low 86.7% of shots while he was on the ice. However, the 2012 second rounder had a very good Corsi percentage. It is hard to know if that is repeatable.

Tye McGinn — LW — TBL

Season	Team	Age	GP	G	A	Pts	+/-	ESP/60	AdjCF%	iCF/60	OGVT	DGVT	SGVT	GVT
2012-13	PHI	22	18	3	2	5	0	1.51	55.3%	13.5	0.3	0.3	0.0	0.6
2013-14	PHI	23	18	4	1	5	-1	1.60	45.0%	9.5	0.2	0.2	0.0	0.4
2014-15	SJS, ARI	24	51	2	5	7	0	0.82	46.7%	13.8	-1.2	1.2	0.0	-0.1
2015-16	TBL	25	47	5	6	11					-0.4	1.2	0.0	0.8

Tye McGinn was a fill-in player for both the Sharks and the Coyotes in 2014-15. He provided little in the way of offense, and was a fringe to middling player in several analytics categories. However, he did have a fairly positive arc to his season. The former Flyer was losing the Corsi battle on a nightly basis from October through January, but saw a sharp increase from January through the remainder of the season.

David Moss — RW/LW — Free Agent

Season	Team	Age	GP	G	A	Pts	+/-	ESP/60	AdjCF%	iCF/60	OGVT	DGVT	SGVT	GVT
2012-13	PHX	31	45	5	15	20	3	1.76	52.5%	14.6	1.5	1.7	0.0	3.2
2013-14	PHX	32	79	8	14	22	-1	1.26	52.2%	15.9	-0.7	3.0	0.0	2.3
2014-15	ARI	33	60	4	8	12	-18	0.81	48.0%	12.9	-1.3	0.3	0.0	-1.0
2015-16	Free Agent	34	55	7	9	15					0.2	1.3	0.0	1.5

33-year-old David Moss was a breakeven player in most categories, which was actually not horrible considering the tough minutes he received and what a down year it was for the team. With that in mind, being in the 50% range in almost every important category is fairly impressive. Over his nine-year career, the University of Michigan product has been a highly-effective third-line winger, notching as many as 20 goals. While he still has the smarts and size to add some defensive presence to the Coyotes' bottom six, his goal-scoring days are numbered. Over the past three years, Moss has put 329 shots on goal and only 17 have gone in the net. Even for a fourth liner, that type of production is easily replaced.

Tobias Rieder — RW/LW — ARI

Season	Team	Age	GP	G	A	Pts	+/-	ESP/60	AdjCF%	iCF/60	OGVT	DGVT	SGVT	GVT
2014-15	ARI	21	72	13	8	21	-19	0.94	48.6%	16.5	-1.3	1.6	-0.3	0.0
2015-16	ARI	22	67	17	12	29					1.4	1.9	0.0	3.3

Tobias Rieder received plenty of opportunity with the struggling Coyotes, playing nearly 1,000 minutes in the desert. However, those minutes were rarely successful: the 22-year-old winger averaged less than one point per 60 minutes. A fourth-round pick of the Oilers in 2011, Rieder theoretically has a goal-scoring touch, but little else that would suggest he is an NHL-caliber talent. The German forward is on the small side at five-foot-ten, and not particularly fast or feisty. He may receive another shot on a rebuilding Coyotes team, but is likely to be a better fit in the AHL.

Henrik Samuelsson — RW/C — ARI

Season	Team	Age	GP	G	A	Pts	+/-	ESP/60	AdjCF%	iCF/60	OGVT	DGVT	SGVT	GVT
2014-15	ARI	20	3	0	0	0	-2	0.00	45.4%	8.5	-0.3	-0.1	0.0	-0.4
2015-16	ARI	21	26	5	6	10					0.6	0.5	0.0	1.1

The best thing about Henrik Samuelson's season is that he was not thrown into the fire in an altogether lost year. The 2012 first-round selection had a very good rookie AHL campaign and got two brief cups of coffee in the latter portion of the season. The son of former NHLer Ulf Samuelsson logged 13 minutes per game and totaled four shots in his three appearances. He was a positive possession player in two of his three games played. It is probably best he was left in the AHL to develop, as one of Arizona's promising young prospects.

Brendan Shinnimin						C							**ARI**
Season	Team	Age	GP	G	A	Pts	+/-	ESP/60	AdjCF%	iCF/60	OGVT	DGVT	SGVT	GVT
2014-15	ARI	23	12	0	1	1	-1	0.46	47.7%	10.1	-0.3	0.1	0.0	-0.2
2015-16	ARI	24	30	4	6	10					0.4	0.6	0.0	1.1

When a team is at the bottom of the standings, players who normally wouldn't see NHL ice get their chance to live the big-league dream for a while. Brendan Shinnimin was one of those cases. After three mediocre seasons in Portland, he produced at a career-high rate in the minors and was given a shot for a dozen games. The undrafted center scored 47 points in 64 AHL games and had one assist in Arizona. In the WHL, he was known as an undersized scorer with some grit, but he has not carried the scoring touch over to the professional level. At age 24, there is a chance he will see more NHL time, but not likely as a regular.

Jordan Szwarz						RW							**ARI**
Season	Team	Age	GP	G	A	Pts	+/-	ESP/60	AdjCF%	iCF/60	OGVT	DGVT	SGVT	GVT
2013-14	PHX	22	26	3	0	3	-6	0.92	49.5%	10.7	-0.5	0.1	0.0	-0.4
2014-15	ARI	23	9	1	0	1	-2	0.60	33.3%	5.8	-0.1	0.0	0.0	-0.1
2015-16	ARI	24	33	6	5	11					0.4	0.6	0.0	1.0

Jordan Szwarz got a late-season cup of coffee with Arizona, playing the last nine games with the big club. In the AHL, his scoring totals were uninspiring to say the least. Prior to his call-up, the 2009 fourth-round pick potted only nine goals in 45 games, adding 13 assists. Profiling as an "energy" winger, the 24-year-old has gotten several chances with the big club because of his skating ability, but has offered only four goals in 35 games. If he gets another shot, the right winger will have to produce more in order to stick around.

Joe Vitale						C/RW							**ARI**
Season	Team	Age	GP	G	A	Pts	+/-	ESP/60	AdjCF%	iCF/60	OGVT	DGVT	SGVT	GVT
2012-13	PIT	27	33	2	3	5	-7	0.97	42.6%	8.5	-0.5	-0.3	0.0	-0.8
2013-14	PIT	28	53	1	13	14	-1	1.43	45.7%	8.8	0.3	1.7	0.0	2.0
2014-15	ARI	29	70	3	6	9	-11	0.85	41.4%	8.3	-1.8	1.3	0.0	-0.5
2015-16	ARI	30	54	3	7	10					-0.9	1.4	0.0	0.5

The appeal of Joe Vitale must have been as a defensive specialist of sorts when he was brought on board by the Coyotes. The description of "specialist" when it comes to the 30-year-old is generous at best. He was never a breakeven possession or shot-suppression player when playing in Pittsburgh, and he did not generate the offense to be impactful on the other side of the puck. He saw a pretty skewed zone start differential, but overall, his quality of competition rankings were among the easiest on the Coyotes. Despite the reasonable circumstances, he experienced his worst-ever Corsi differential and shot differential, and a new high in his scoring chances against per 60 minutes rate. There were few things in his season that would instill confidence in his being an effective grind-line or two-way forward in the future.

DEFENSEMEN

Andrew Campbell								LD					TOR
Season	Team	Age	GP	G	A	Pts	+/-	ESP/60	AdjCF%	iCF/60	OGVT	DGVT	SGVT	GVT
2013-14	LAK	25	3	0	0	0	0	0.00	49.4%	12.2	-0.1	0.1	0.0	-0.1
2014-15	ARI	26	33	0	1	1	-13	0.12	45.1%	7.2	-1.3	-0.5	0.0	-1.9
2015-16	TOR	27	38	1	4	6					-0.5	0.7	0.0	0.1

Having seen the young talent and depth in front of him in Los Angeles, Andrew Campbell headed to Arizona for a better chance at seeing the ice. "Soupy", as every Campbell is apparently known, finally got his chance in late January and stuck with the team through the end of the season. However, his numbers were not much of a feel-good story, for instance, his allowing 64.1 Corsi-against per 60 minutes. The only silver lining was his difficult zone starts. Head coach Dave Tippett killed the former Soo Greyhound, utilizing him in a manner similar to Zbynek Michalek. We will be able to evaluate Campbell better when he has a more standard workload.

Klas Dahlbeck								LD					ARI
Season	Team	Age	GP	G	A	Pts	+/-	ESP/60	AdjCF%	iCF/60	OGVT	DGVT	SGVT	GVT
2014-15	CHI, ARI	23	23	1	3	4	-8	0.69	42.5%	9.1	0.0	-0.1	0.0	0.0
2015-16	ARI	24	35	2	6	8					0.2	0.8	0.0	1.0

Klas Dahlbeck was part of the swap that sent Antoine Vermette to the Chicago Blackhawks at the trade deadline, and he was immediately given a full-time spot in Arizona. While he was buried on the Chicago blueline, playing 9-10 minutes per game when he did appear, the Swedish rookie was frequently elevated to a 20+ minute-per-night defenseman with the Coyotes. His 23-game track record makes it difficult to evaluate him fully, but he can skate and handle the puck at the NHL level. He will have plenty of opportunity to get in on Arizona's squad as a decent bottom-pairing defenseman.

Oliver Ekman-Larsson								LD					ARI
Season	Team	Age	GP	G	A	Pts	+/-	ESP/60	AdjCF%	iCF/60	OGVT	DGVT	SGVT	GVT
2012-13	PHX	21	48	3	21	24	5	1.09	51.0%	9.8	3.0	2.5	-0.3	5.1
2013-14	PHX	22	80	15	29	44	-4	0.87	49.1%	10.1	7.0	2.9	-0.5	9.3
2014-15	ARI	23	82	23	20	43	-18	0.86	50.6%	13.3	7.9	3.0	-0.5	10.3
2015-16	ARI	24	78	16	34	49					7.8	3.7	-0.1	11.4

As might be expected, Oliver Ekman-Larsson was the lone bright spot for Arizona. In fact, he continues to be one of the most dynamic all-around defensemen in the NHL. "OEL" was just outside the top 20 in defenseman scoring, though he led all defensemen in power-play goals and game-winning goals, and was second in shots (264) behind only two-time Norris Trophy winner Erik Karlsson. The Swedish Olympic semi-snub was far and away the Coyotes' most effective player, coming up positive in possession, and nearly breaking even in goals-for percentage. Ekman-Larsson did all of this while playing some of the heaviest defensive-oriented minutes amongst Arizona blueliners.

Brandon Gormley — LD — ARI

Season	Team	Age	GP	G	A	Pts	+/-	ESP/60	AdjCF%	iCF/60	OGVT	DGVT	SGVT	GVT
2013-14	PHX	21	5	0	0	0	4	0.00	47.9%	9.1	-0.3	0.8	0.0	0.5
2014-15	ARI	22	27	2	2	4	-7	0.51	48.2%	11.0	-0.3	0.4	0.0	0.2
2015-16	ARI	23	38	3	7	10					0.4	1.4	0.0	1.8

Coyote fans had been waiting on Brandon Gormley, and this season, they got to see a little bit of their 2010 first-round selection. While the offensive-leaning defenseman has had his share of struggles with adjusting to the defensive aspect of the game, his brief appearance in 2014-15 was fairly positive. The Murray River, Prince Edward Island native had decent shot-suppression numbers, although marginally negative. However, his destiny is not in the desert, but in the mountains. Gormley was sent to the Colorado Avalanche over the summer for Stefan Elliot, in a hockey trade of two defensive prospects.

John Moore — LD — NJD

Season	Team	Age	GP	G	A	Pts	+/-	ESP/60	AdjCF%	iCF/60	OGVT	DGVT	SGVT	GVT
2012-13	CBJ, NYR	22	30	1	6	7	4	1.11	49.1%	10.0	1.0	1.7	0.0	2.7
2013-14	NYR	23	74	4	11	15	7	0.75	51.3%	11.7	1.1	2.9	0.0	4.0
2014-15	NYR, ARI	24	57	2	9	11	-4	0.50	50.0%	10.7	0.0	0.5	0.0	0.6
2015-16	NJD	25	57	3	10	14					0.5	2.1	0.0	2.5

A Blue Jackets first-round selection in 2009, six-foot-three defenseman John Moore will be going on his fourth team in five professional seasons. This is strange, considering Moore has been a pretty decent middle-pairing defenseman who can create scoring chances. His season took a tumble when he was moved at the deadline, going from a 54.7% Corsi player with the Rangers to a 43.1% Corsi player with the Coyotes. One common trend in his career, thus far, is that if he is not protected, he can be a bit of a liability. Hence, why Moore's tenure in Arizona was less than spectacular. New Jersey will look to fit him into their developing defense corps.

Connor Murphy — RD — ARI

Season	Team	Age	GP	G	A	Pts	+/-	ESP/60	AdjCF%	iCF/60	OGVT	DGVT	SGVT	GVT
2013-14	PHX	20	30	1	7	8	5	0.99	51.4%	8.5	0.8	2.2	0.0	3.0
2014-15	ARI	21	73	4	3	7	-27	0.38	43.9%	8.3	-2.0	0.5	0.0	-1.5
2015-16	ARI	22	61	3	8	12					-0.5	2.0	0.0	1.6

21-year-old Connor Murphy experienced a proverbial trial by fire in 2014-15. As the youngest member of the team's regular defensive corps, Murphy never settled on a regular partner. In fact, he split nearly even time with five different Coyotes defensemen. On top of that, Murphy came in last among his peers in nearly every possession category. A bottom-of-the-league team is never the ideal situation in which to develop youngsters; the 20th overall selection from 2011 definitely took his knocks because of it.

Dylan Reese — RD — ARI

Season	Team	Age	GP	G	A	Pts	+/-	ESP/60	AdjCF%	iCF/60	OGVT	DGVT	SGVT	GVT
2012-13	PIT	28	3	0	0	0	0	0.00	33.6%	3.9	-0.1	0.0	0.0	-0.2
2014-15	ARI	30	1	0	0	0	-1	0.00	61.4%	18.7	-0.2	0.0	0.0	-0.1
2015-16	ARI	31	23	1	4	6					0.3	0.8	0.0	1.1

ARIZONA COYOTES

After a season in Russia, veteran defenseman Dylan Reese was brought back to North America by the Coyotes. Back in the Western Hemisphere, he played nearly the entire season with the AHL's Portland Pirates. The Coyotes did throw him a bone in late February, one game with the big club, joining the season-long carousel of blueline guest stars in Arizona. When he stepped onto the ice, Reese became one of 13 different defensemen used over the course of the season—which is quite a few. The former Islander and Bridgeport Tiger played nearly 20 minutes in that appearance, before heading back across the country to Maine for the remainder of the campaign.

Philip Samuelsson					LD								ARI
Season	Team	Age	GP	G	A	Pts	+/-	ESP/60	AdjCF%	iCF/60	OGVT	DGVT	SGVT	GVT
2013-14	PIT	22	5	0	0	0	-1	0.00	49.0%	8.4	-0.1	-0.1	0.0	-0.2
2014-15	ARI	23	4	0	0	0	-3	0.00	40.3%	5.0	-0.2	-0.3	0.0	-0.5
2015-16	ARI	24	26	2	5	7					0.3	0.7	0.0	1.0

The older brother of teammate Henrik, Philip Samuelsson was in a similar situation. The 23-year-old was given a brief January call-up—in his case, to the ever-changing Arizona defense corps. The former Wilkes-Barre/Scranton Penguin was a negative possession player in three of his four games while averaging 17 minutes per night. When he suited up alongside Zbynek Michalek, though, they put up some decent shot-suppression numbers. Only when Samuelsson played alongside fellow youngster Brandon Gormley did things look dicey. Given the depth and youth of the Arizona blueline, this fringe NHLer is going to have to make an unexpected impact to earn more than an occasional fill-in game.

Michael Stone						RD								ARI
Season	Team	Age	GP	G	A	Pts	+/-	ESP/60	AdjCF%	iCF/60	OGVT	DGVT	SGVT	GVT
2012-13	PHX	22	40	5	4	9	2	0.73	50.7%	9.5	1.3	1.6	0.0	3.0
2013-14	PHX	23	70	8	13	21	-10	0.78	49.9%	11.3	2.6	2.0	0.0	4.5
2014-15	ARI	24	81	3	15	18	-24	0.53	48.0%	10.7	0.0	0.8	0.0	0.7
2015-16	ARI	25	66	6	15	21					1.7	2.3	0.0	3.9

Michael Stone may have been the third-best defenseman on Arizona last season—which is damning with faint praise. He benefited from being a regular partner of both OEL and Yandle, a decent complementary player to their puck-moving styles. Because of that, most of his possession stats remained fairly strong throughout the season. The former Calgary Hitman captain also stood head and shoulders above the rest of his Arizona blueline mates (and fifth in the NHL) in shot blocking, but as hockey analytics have taught us, that is not necessarily a positive stat.

GOALTENDERS

Louis Domingue														ARI
Season	Team	Age	GP	W	L	OT	GAA	Sv%	ESSV%	QS%	GGVT	DGVT	SGVT	GVT
2014-15	ARI	22	7	1	2	1	2.73	.911	.902	75.0%	0.3	-0.1	0.0	0.3
2015-16	ARI	23	15					.914			1.7	-0.1	0.0	1.6

Louis Domingue was pressed into NHL duty as a backup after spending the previous two years as a minor-league backup. The 22-year-old had only appeared 41 ECHL games and 38 AHL games prior to 2014-15. His numbers were never outstanding in the minors, even prior to his call-up. However, in his seven NHL games, the 2010 fifth-round pick performed better than expected, posting a .911 save percentage. While goalies tend to develop in their mid-to-late twenties, Domingue has not given any indication he will be a full-time NHLer any time soon.

Mike McKenna — G — FLA

Season	Team	Age	GP	W	L	OT	GAA	Sv%	ESSV%	QS%	GGVT	DGVT	SGVT	GVT
2013-14	CBJ	30	4	1	1	1	3.01	.904	.919	0.0%	-0.5	-0.1	0.0	-0.5
2014-15	ARI	31	1	0	1	0	5.00	.853	.862	0.0%	-1.6	0.0	0.0	-1.7
2015-16	FLA	32	11					.912			0.5	-0.1	0.0	0.4

Mike McKenna continued his amazing journeyman career in 2014-15, this time with the Coyotes organization. The 32-year-old has unbelievably suited up for Norfolk, Omaha, Milwaukee, Portland (on three separate stints), Lowell, Albany, Binghamton, Peoria, and Springfield in the AHL, as well as Tampa Bay, New Jersey, Columbus, and Arizona in the NHL…not counting Las Vegas in the ECHL and a full four years at St. Lawrence University. McKenna got into one game with the big club, giving up five goals on 34 shots. While he has not had a career of outstanding numbers or accolades, it has been remarkable in its own way.

Mike Smith — G — ARI

Season	Team	Age	GP	W	L	OT	GAA	Sv%	ESSV%	QS%	GGVT	DGVT	SGVT	GVT
2012-13	PHX	30	34	15	12	5	2.58	.910	.924	44.1%	3.3	-0.1	-1.4	1.8
2013-14	PHX	31	62	27	21	10	2.64	.915	.925	57.4%	9.7	-0.9	-2.6	6.2
2014-15	ARI	32	62	14	42	5	3.16	.904	.912	47.5%	-8.2	-2.1	0.1	-10.2
2015-16	ARI	33	36					.912			1.2	-0.8	-0.2	0.2

Mike Smith needed to be better than he was in 2014-15, but it was not entirely on him. The six-foot-four Canadian international faced the most shots of any starting goaltender in the league, at 33 per night. Smith had a rough year, but Arizona gave up the fourth-most scoring chances in the league, and third-most high-danger chances. Overall, it was an unhealthy combination of the 32-year-old netminder having a bad year along with a defense that didn't limit opposing opportunities. By the way, remember that huge season (.930, 35.0 GVT) he had in 2011-12?

Jason Lewis

Boston Bruins

For the first time in eight seasons, the Boston Bruins watched the playoffs from their couches. After finishing each of the previous four years with over 100 points, Boston—a preseason Cup favorite—ended the 2014-15 campaign with 96 points, placing them ninth in an Eastern Conference where point totals were inflated by tanking teams Buffalo, Carolina, and Toronto. The response from Bruins ownership was swift: 2011 Stanley Cup winning general manager Peter Chiarelli was fired only four days after season's end.

At first glance, this reaction to the end of the Bruins' streak seemed excessively harsh. While the B's possession numbers did drop—their five-on-five Corsi percentage of 51.7 was more than 2% lower than any of the previous three years—they still ranked 11th in the league. Missing the playoffs under those circumstances is uncommon: 80% of teams that finished in the top 11 in CF% over the past five years made it to the playoffs. Not only were the Bruins a strong possession club, but they received some of the NHL's best goaltending at five-on-five, with the Nordic tandem of Tuukka Rask and Niklas Svedberg coming in at eighth in the league. Although Boston struggled to convert on their opportunities—their even-strength shooting percentage was sixth worst of all clubs—the Bruins still marginally got the better of their opposition at five-on-five, scoring 50.5% of the goals.

Of course, even-strength performance doesn't tell the whole story of what happens on the ice. Although teams played with equal skaters roughly 83% of the time in 2014-15, only 74% of goals were scored during this time. During the power play/penalty kill, the scoring rate is nearly three times higher than it is for five-on-five play. Therefore, teams' abilities to draw penalties, and conversely, to avoid going down a man can make a significant impact on their point total – and this is exactly where the story of the Bruins starts to fall apart.

Boston posted the fourth-worst penalty differential, ceding a net 34 power-play opportunities to their opponents. The easy narrative is that the Bruins' trademark gritty style sent them to the sin bin far too frequently for a team with playoff aspirations. After all, noted pest Brad Marchand finished fourth in the league in penalties taken with 33 minors on his own. But if we dig a little deeper, it becomes clear that the problem for Boston lies less with the number of infractions they commit, and more with their inability to lure opponents into taking penal-

BRUINS IN A BOX

Last Season

Goals For	213	23rd
Goals Against	211	t-11th
GVT	2	18th
Points	96	17th
Playoffs	Did not make playoffs	

After a six-year run near the top of the league, Boston's aging roster finally caught up to them.

Three-Year Record

GVT	108	3rd
Points	275	5th
Playoffs	2 Appearances, 21 Wins	

VUKOTA Projections

Goals For	218	20th
Goals Against	210	3rd
GVT	8	12th
Points	94	12th

The Lucic trade indicates the Bruins know their time isn't now. They may squeeze into the playoffs in a weak Eastern Conference, but no more.

Top Three Prospects

J. Zboril (D), M. Subban (G), S. Griffith (F)

ties. Boston only managed to head to the power play roughly 2.5 times per game, placing them 29th in the league in penalties drawn – perhaps symptomatic of a lack of speed.

A hard-nosed, on-the-edge style has been a hallmark of the Bruins clubs that have had much recent success. Yet statistically, last season's Bruins weren't all that different from Julien's squads that have performed so well over the past half-decade. While the Cup-winning team from 2010-2011 actually managed to post an even penalty differential, for the two years prior to 2014-15, Boston was atrocious in this department, with their 2013 Cup finalist roster from the lockout-shortened year actually finishing last in the league in even-strength penalty differential. Just like this year's B's, the 2012-2013 team struggled in the same way: they drew far fewer penalties than most other clubs. Further, if we look at that team's other statistics, we see that the similarities to the 2014-15 team go beyond just penalty differential: both teams received top-tier goaltending at even strength (fourth in 2012-13 and eighth in 2014-15), both posted above-average possession numbers at five-on-five, and both struggled to convert those same even-strength scoring opportunities (7.3% shooting in 2012-13 versus 7.1% shooting in 2014-15).

So where did last year's Bruins differ from their more successful 2012-2013 counterparts? Quite simply, they just couldn't keep the puck out of their own net on the penalty kill. While both squads struggled to convert shots while up a man, ranking 26th last year and 29th in the lockout-shortened season, Bruins goalies were not the penalty-killing wizards they were in 2013, when they posted a top-five save percentage of .896 while down a man. Although Boston's goaltending duo put up top-10 results at five-on-five, on the penalty kill they were significantly more pedestrian, posting a middle-of-the-road .873 save percentage (15th). That drop in save percentage alone cost Boston eight goals, which probably would have pushed them over the top and into the last playoff spot in the East. (see table).

Make no mistake, the Bruins roster had some obvious flaws: they drew far too few penalties relative to the number they took, and their possession stats were headed in the wrong direction for a team so reliant on an aging Zdeno Chara. But Boston's last year was not as grim as their offseason might have suggested. Their most recent roster put up numbers remarkably similar to those posted by their Stanley Cup finalist squad from three years ago, and if it weren't for a bout of bad luck for one of the best goalies in the league, things might have turned out differently for Chiarelli and company. Unfortunately for Bruins fans, one year without a postseason run led to the departure of one of the league's top-tier executives and a potential future Norris Trophy winner in Dougie Hamilton. While it is too early to judge whether new GM Don Sweeney's plan will pan out in the long run, from where we sit right now, it is hard to see the Bruins' summer moves as anything other than a massive overreaction driven by only a minor departure from years of sustained success.

Matt Cane

Perception: Wasn't last season just like 2012-13?

Statistic	2012-13	2014-15
AdjCF%	54.3% (3rd)	51.7% (11th)
ES Sh%	7.3% (23rd)	7.1% (25th)
ESSV%	.932 (8th)	.929 (4th)
Penalty Differential/60	-1.2 (30th)	-0.5 (27th)
Penalty-killing save %	.896 (4th)	.873 (15th)
Result	Lost in Cup Finals	Missed playoffs

BOSTON BRUINS

33

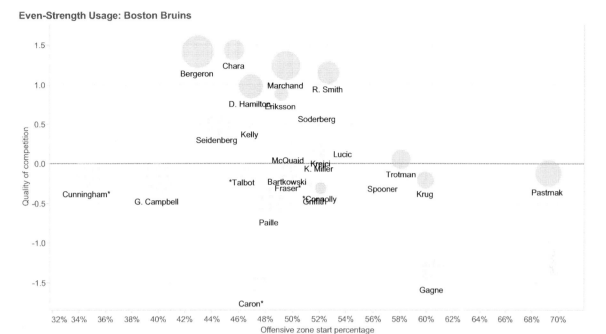

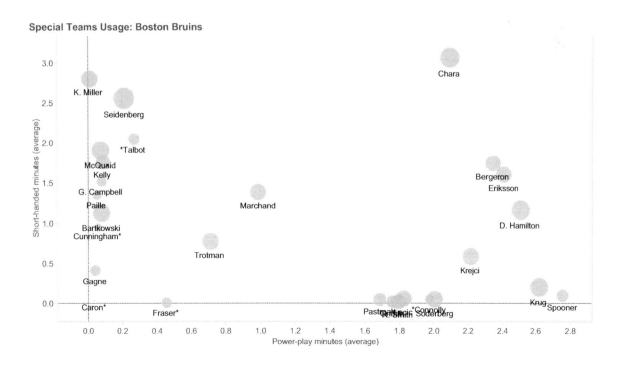

BOSTON BRUINS

Offensive Profile: Boston Bruins

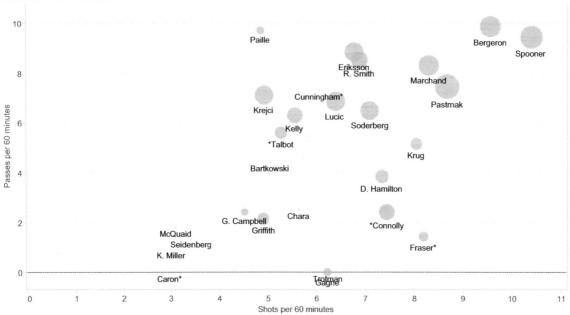

Cap Efficiency: Boston Bruins

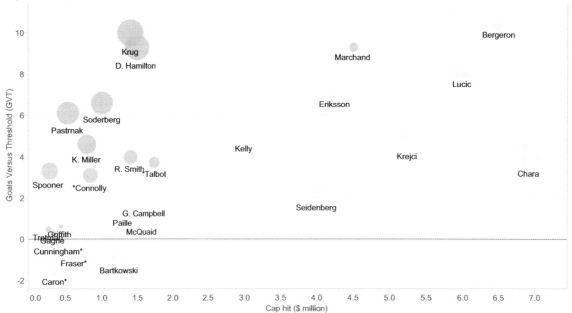

FORWARDS

Patrice Bergeron						C							BOS
Season	Team	Age	GP	G	A	Pts	+/-	ESP/60	AdjCF%	iCF/60	OGVT	DGVT	SGVT	GVT
2012-13	BOS	27	42	10	22	32	24	2.59	61.4%	17.1	5.7	3.7	0.4	9.7
2013-14	BOS	28	80	30	32	62	38	2.51	62.3%	18.7	12.1	5.5	0.7	18.2
2014-15	BOS	29	81	23	32	55	2	2.06	58.2%	16.5	7.4	3.6	-0.5	10.5
2015-16	BOS	30	74	24	31	54					7.2	3.1	0.0	10.3

Selke Trophy nomination? Check. 20-plus goals? Check. 30-plus assists? Check. Top three in the league in faceoff percentage? Check. Corsi percentage over 58%? Check. While reaching any of these milestones would be a good year for most players in the league, for Patrice Bergeron it was the fourth consecutive campaign that he hit each and every one of these marks (prorating the lockout-shortened season, of course). Need further proof that Bergeron is one of the game's best two-way forwards? Not once over those four seasons have his zone starts topped 50%. Simply put, Bergeron has been asked to take on his team's toughest minutes, yet he has consistently tilted the ice in the B's favor.

Gregory Campbell						C/LW							CBJ
Season	Team	Age	GP	G	A	Pts	+/-	ESP/60	AdjCF%	iCF/60	OGVT	DGVT	SGVT	GVT
2012-13	BOS	29	48	4	9	13	2	1.23	49.8%	10.8	-0.2	2.5	0.0	2.3
2013-14	BOS	30	82	8	13	21	1	1.33	47.5%	10.4	1.2	2.1	0.0	3.3
2014-15	BOS	31	70	6	6	12	1	0.89	41.8%	8.3	-0.6	2.3	0.0	1.7
2015-16	CBJ	32	58	6	7	13					-0.2	1.8	0.0	1.5

For the third time in four years, Gregory Campbell finished with one of the three worst Relative Corsi scores in the entire NHL. While his 40% zone start rate did not help his numbers, it is becoming increasingly apparent that his "defensive specialist" label is no longer justified. The lone bright spot for "Soupy" was his 53.6% faceoff percentage, which marked the first time since 2011-2012 that the veteran center was above par on the draw.

Paul Carey						C/LW							WSH
Season	Team	Age	GP	G	A	Pts	+/-	ESP/60	AdjCF%	iCF/60	OGVT	DGVT	SGVT	GVT
2013-14	COL	25	12	0	0	0	2	0.00	47.7%	7.6	-0.6	0.3	0.0	-0.3
2014-15	COL	26	10	0	1	1	2	0.76	48.2%	10.7	-0.3	0.3	0.0	0.0
2015-16	WSH	27	31	4	6	10					0.2	0.7	0.0	1.0

After four years at Boston College, Paul Carey has become a solid AHL player, playing as a defensive-minded center who can add offense on occasion. He topped out at 41 points in 72 games for the Lake Erie Monsters in 2012-13, and has earned calls to the NHL in each of the last two seasons. With well below-average offensive skill for that level, Carey's smarts, effort, and versatility have allowed him to get a chance as a fill-in player. That is likely his career ceiling. The 26-year-old joined the Bruins organization in the deal that sent Max Talbot to Boston.

Brett Connolly								RW						BOS
Season	Team	Age	GP	G	A	Pts	+/-	ESP/60	AdjCF%	iCF/60	OGVT	DGVT	SGVT	GVT
2012-13	TBL	20	5	1	0	1	-3	0.00	45.1%	22.4	0.0	-0.3	0.0	-0.3
2013-14	TBL	21	11	1	0	1	-5	0.50	49.9%	7.8	-1.2	-0.1	0.0	-1.3
2014-15	TBL, BOS	22	55	12	5	17	3	1.51	55.4%	12.9	2.3	0.8	0.0	3.1
2015-16	BOS	23	51	11	8	19					1.6	1.0	0.0	2.5

If it wasn't for bad luck, he would have no luck at all: only two days after being traded to a Bruins team that could desperately use his scoring touch, 2010 first rounder Brett Connolly fractured a finger in practice, keeping him out of the lineup until the very last days of the season. Even before that untimely injury, Connolly was not getting many bounces to go his way: his teammates abandoned him offensively all year long, shooting only 4.8% while he was on the ice, limiting him to four even-strength assists over 55 games. In spite of all this misfortune, the year had some bright spots for the one-time CHL Rookie of the Year, as he found both a stronger possession game (55.3% CF%) and his scoring touch, racking up 10 even-strength goals while shooting 14% at five-on-five. After getting into only 84 contests over his first three NHL seasons, it looks as if Connolly may finally be finding his game. At only 23 years of age, he still has time to develop into the top-tier prospect he once appeared to be.

Loui Eriksson								LW						BOS
Season	Team	Age	GP	G	A	Pts	+/-	ESP/60	AdjCF%	iCF/60	OGVT	DGVT	SGVT	GVT
2012-13	DAL	27	48	12	17	29	-9	1.48	50.6%	11.2	3.1	0.2	-0.6	2.8
2013-14	BOS	28	61	10	27	37	14	1.87	59.9%	10.9	5.0	2.4	-0.6	6.8
2014-15	BOS	29	81	22	25	47	1	1.79	53.1%	10.0	5.2	2.9	-1.1	7.0
2015-16	BOS	30	69	18	25	43					4.6	2.4	-0.1	6.9

To diagnose the offensive struggles that have plagued Loui Eriksson since coming to Boston in the Tyler Seguin deal, look no further than his linemates. While the skilled winger spent most of his last two seasons in Dallas skating next to Jamie Benn and a still-productive Michael Ryder, since moving to the East Coast, Eriksson's most common linemates have been Carl Soderberg and Chris Kelly. That magnitude of a talent drop helps explain why the veteran Swede has yet to hit the 2.0 ESP/60 mark that he managed four times while playing in Big D. And although the 2004 SEL Rookie of the Year has been a positive possession player in both of his years in Beantown, if his true talents are to be taken advantage of, the Bruins will need to provide him with a bit more complementary talent.

Brian Ferlin								RW						BOS
Season	Team	Age	GP	G	A	Pts	+/-	ESP/60	AdjCF%	iCF/60	OGVT	DGVT	SGVT	GVT
2014-15	BOS	22	7	0	1	1	0	0.98	48.1%	15.4	0.0	0.1	0.0	0.1
2015-16	BOS	23	28	5	6	11					0.7	0.6	0.0	1.3

One year removed from leading the Cornell Big Red in scoring, Brian Ferlin began his year with Boston's AHL affiliate Providence, where he set to work showing that he was not going to be pushed around, racking up 36 penalty minutes over his first 46 games as a professional. After getting called up in late February, Ferlin was a frequent healthy scratch, although the Florida native made a solid effort to maintain the Bruins hard-hitting reputation, posting a team-leading 19.6 Hits/60 in the seven games he suited up for. After being returned to Providence to finish out the year, the big winger seemed to settle his game down a bit, limiting himself to four PIM while scoring four of his 20 total points during his last seven AHL games.

BOSTON BRUINS

Simon Gagne								LW						Retired
Season	Team	Age	GP	G	A	Pts	+/-	ESP/60	AdjCF%	iCF/60	OGVT	DGVT	SGVT	GVT
2012-13	LAK, PHI	32	38	5	11	16	-1	1.43	48.8%	14.8	2.1	0.6	-0.3	2.4
2014-15	BOS	34	23	3	1	4	0	0.96	47.6%	11.0	-0.3	0.6	0.0	0.3
2015-16	Retired	35	33	5	5	9					0.3	0.8	0.0	1.0

It was the end of the line. After a career that included five appearances for Team Canada, including a gold medal at the 2002 Winter Games in Salt Lake City, Simon Gagne's final season ended with more of a whimper than a bang. Dressing for only 23 games with Boston, the smooth-skating winger was relegated to a support role when he was in the lineup, receiving next-to-no special teams time, and recording only four points while playing fourth-line minutes. Gagne took a personal leave from the Bruins in December, and was released from his contract in January.

Seth Griffith								RW						BOS
Season	Team	Age	GP	G	A	Pts	+/-	ESP/60	AdjCF%	iCF/60	OGVT	DGVT	SGVT	GVT
2014-15	BOS	21	30	6	4	10	-2	1.20	48.8%	9.8	0.8	0.3	-0.5	0.6
2015-16	BOS	22	41	9	9	18					1.4	0.8	0.0	2.1

The past season was another step forward for Seth Griffith, who got an extended look at the NHL level after finishing 2013-14 as runner-up on the Providence Bruins in scoring. Although he started the year back with the Baby B's, Griffith was quickly called up for a 30-game stretch starting in early October. While the small winger was primarily used in a top-six role alongside David Krejci and Milan Lucic, his 10 points in 30 games were not enough to warrant risking his development to have him play limited minutes further down the lineup. When he returned to the AHL, the London Knights alumnus picked up where he left off in the previous campaign, producing at a 0.79 point-per-game pace to finish fourth on the farm club in spite of playing in only 39 games. At only 22 years old heading into this season, the Wallaceburg, Ontario native should get another opportunity to prove that the Bruins found a late-round special in the 2012 fifth-round pick.

Chris Kelly								C						BOS
Season	Team	Age	GP	G	A	Pts	+/-	ESP/60	AdjCF%	iCF/60	OGVT	DGVT	SGVT	GVT
2012-13	BOS	32	34	3	6	9	-8	1.12	51.4%	8.6	0.0	0.8	0.0	0.9
2013-14	BOS	33	57	9	9	18	2	1.41	52.5%	9.5	0.5	2.0	-0.3	2.2
2014-15	BOS	34	80	7	21	28	6	1.47	51.9%	9.7	1.5	3.6	-0.3	4.8
2015-16	BOS	35	63	8	15	23					1.3	2.3	0.0	3.5

Always a laggard in the possession game at the start of his career in Ottawa, Chris Kelly also struggled to keep up in his first three full years in Boston, averaging a -4% Relative Corsi from 2011 to 2014. In 2014-15, he was nearly able to buck that trend, raising his rate to -0.1% on a team that finished in the top half of the league in Corsi percentage. To be fair, the Toronto native has been given tough assignments by the Bruins' coaching staff throughout his tenure. With a cap hit of $3 million per season, Kelly is a bit pricey for an aging third-line role player, but with his scoring pace remaining steady—topping 1.4 ESP/60 for the past two seasons—the Bruins will try to milk at least one more year out of their assistant captain.

Alex Khokhlachev — C — BOS

Season	Team	Age	GP	G	A	Pts	+/-	ESP/60	AdjCF%	iCF/60	OGVT	DGVT	SGVT	GVT
2013-14	BOS	20	1	0	0	0	0	0.00	36.6%	7.8	0.0	0.0	0.0	0.0
2014-15	BOS	21	3	0	0	0	-2	0.00	42.6%	2.5	-0.3	-0.1	0.6	0.2
2015-16	BOS	22	26	4	6	10					0.6	0.5	0.0	1.1

While his contributions were limited over three NHL games, it was another good year for Alexander Khokhlachev. For the second consecutive season, the Muscovite center led the Providence Bruins in scoring; although his AHL point totals were down year-over-year, his shots per game were up 30% to 2.7. Though Khokhlachev's stats certainly suggest that he may be ready for an extended shot in Boston, he will have to fight it out with a glut of young Bruins to win a spot on a club that already features David Krejci and Patrice Bergeron as fixtures down the middle.

David Krejci — C — BOS

Season	Team	Age	GP	G	A	Pts	+/-	ESP/60	AdjCF%	iCF/60	OGVT	DGVT	SGVT	GVT
2012-13	BOS	26	47	10	23	33	1	2.08	56.7%	12.2	3.5	0.8	-0.3	4.0
2013-14	BOS	27	80	19	50	69	39	2.36	53.8%	10.7	11.7	4.5	-1.4	14.8
2014-15	BOS	28	47	7	24	31	7	1.83	51.7%	8.3	3.2	2.0	-0.4	4.8
2015-16	BOS	29	61	13	30	43					4.9	2.4	0.0	7.3

The only number you need to know about David Krejci's season is 35: the number of games he missed to injury in a year where the Bruins fell short of the playoffs by two points. When healthy, Krejci was a critical cog in the offense, posting the highest power-play points per 60 minutes of any Boston skater who contributed at least 50 minutes on the man advantage. Fans in Beantown have little reason to fear that their highest-paid player will be nagged by any lingering pains: the 29-year-old pivot has been a model of durability, racking up the fifth-most total minutes of any forward between 2010 and 2014. With the Bruins missing the playoffs for the first time since 2006-2007, Krejci will get an extended break to rest and recover, which should help him to return to his dominant and durable self.

Matt Lindblad — C/LW — NYR

Season	Team	Age	GP	G	A	Pts	+/-	ESP/60	AdjCF%	iCF/60	OGVT	DGVT	SGVT	GVT
2013-14	BOS	23	2	0	0	0	0	0.00	31.1%	0.0	0.0	0.0	0.0	0.0
2014-15	BOS	24	2	0	0	0	0	0.00	78.0%	21.0	0.0	0.0	0.0	0.0
2015-16	NYR	25	26	5	6	11					0.7	0.6	0.0	1.3

Matt Lindblad only registered 15 NHL minutes in 2014-15, but the 24-year-old from Evanston, Illinois did everything he could to make his short opportunity count, recording five shot attempts over this brief tenure in Boston. However, down on the farm, his medicore minor-league stats showed no improvement, mired as a sub-0.5 point-per-game player on a fairly good AHL team. Given his age and standing on Boston's depth chart, Lindblad's chances of landing a full-time NHL role are slim.

Milan Lucic — LW — LAK

Season	Team	Age	GP	G	A	Pts	+/-	ESP/60	AdjCF%	iCF/60	OGVT	DGVT	SGVT	GVT
2012-13	BOS	24	46	7	20	27	8	2.19	58.2%	13.9	1.6	1.3	0.0	2.9
2013-14	BOS	25	80	24	35	59	30	2.35	55.0%	12.1	10.1	3.4	0.0	13.5
2014-15	BOS	26	81	18	26	44	13	1.84	51.3%	12.8	5.4	3.4	-0.5	8.2
2015-16	LAK	27	72	19	27	46					5.5	2.7	0.0	8.2

Is it possible that Milan Lucic shied away from some of the physical play that made him such a force in years past? With his Penalties Taken down nearly 50% since signing a three-year, $18 million contract two years ago—ostensibly, a good thing—Lucic has struggled to put up points at the same pace as before his new deal. While he has been far from bad, one has to wonder whether the Bruins thought they would be spending $6 million per year on a player producing roughly a point every other game. With free agency looming at the end of the upcoming season, the Bruins elected to trade Lucic to the Kings. It is hard to know whether he will continue to dip or bounce back in L.A.

Brad Marchand — LW — BOS

Season	Team	Age	GP	G	A	Pts	+/-	ESP/60	AdjCF%	iCF/60	OGVT	DGVT	SGVT	GVT
2012-13	BOS	24	45	18	18	36	23	2.87	60.1%	12.4	7.5	3.3	-0.1	10.7
2013-14	BOS	25	82	25	28	53	36	2.42	60.8%	12.1	11.2	5.7	-0.8	16.1
2014-15	BOS	26	77	24	18	42	5	1.98	56.8%	15.2	5.7	3.9	-0.4	9.3
2015-16	BOS	27	74	22	23	45					5.6	3.2	0.0	8.8

Has the rest of the league figured out Brad Marchand's pest routine? While the pesky winger has always employed a style that made him a frequent visitor to the sin bin, over the first three full seasons of his career he was at least able to draw his opponents into taking more penalties than he took. The last two years have been a different story: Marchand's penalty differential has gone far into the red, with his most recent total of 27 infractions ranking worst in the league for all forwards. While Marchand is still putting points up at a reasonable rate, if he wants to add value to the Bruins, he will need to ensure he keeps himself on the ice and out of the box.

Daniel Paille — LW — Free Agent

Season	Team	Age	GP	G	A	Pts	+/-	ESP/60	AdjCF%	iCF/60	OGVT	DGVT	SGVT	GVT
2012-13	BOS	28	46	10	7	17	3	1.68	51.2%	10.6	2.6	2.3	0.0	4.9
2013-14	BOS	29	72	9	9	18	9	1.50	49.6%	9.0	2.2	2.6	0.0	4.9
2014-15	BOS	30	71	6	7	13	-9	0.92	46.1%	9.0	0.0	1.3	0.0	1.2
2015-16	Free Agent	31	55	6	8	14					0.4	1.5	0.0	1.8

Although Boston only scored 35% of the goals with Dan Paille on the ice last year, when they did manage to get one past the opposing netminder, it was a pretty safe bet that Paille was involved. The Welland-born winger managed to record a point in 92% of Boston goals while he was over the boards, placing him third in iPP amongst skaters who played at least 500 minutes. While his ESP/60 of 0.92 was the lowest level of his career, the former Sabre remains a relative bargain for a solid third-line player, particularly one who has had past success in drawing penalties, on a team that is more used to taking them.

David Pastrnak — RW — BOS

Season	Team	Age	GP	G	A	Pts	+/-	ESP/60	AdjCF%	iCF/60	OGVT	DGVT	SGVT	GVT
2014-15	BOS	18	46	10	17	27	12	2.56	55.5%	16.7	5.0	2.2	-1.1	6.1
2015-16	BOS	19	53	15	21	36					5.1	2.0	-0.1	7.1

Despite playing in 28 fewer games, David Pastrnak had more points as an 18-year-old than Tyler Seguin did at the same age. With injuries forcing the Bruins to dig deep into their prospect pool, the rookie winger made the most of his opportunity, emerging as a genuine offensive talent on a team that sorely needed goals. While Pastrnak's 103.9 PDO may set off some regression alarms heading into next season, most of this "luck" was on the defensive side, where B's goalies stopped 95% of the shots they faced while he was on the ice. Make no mistake, young Czech pulled his weight, registering the highest total points per 60 minutes of any Bruin…with the majority coming at even strength.

Bobby Robins — RW — Retired

Season	Team	Age	GP	G	A	Pts	+/-	ESP/60	AdjCF%	iCF/60	OGVT	DGVT	SGVT	GVT
2014-15	BOS	33	3	0	0	0	0	0.00	35.0%	0.0	-0.1	0.0	0.0	0.0
2015-16	Retired	34	27	5	6	10					0.6	0.5	0.0	1.2

It may seem hard to believe, particularly given the depth of NHL-ready talent that the Bruins were able to summon from Providence when injuries struck, but Bobby Robins made Boston's opening day roster. Although Robins' presence was likely one of the last gasps of the enforcer in the modern NHL, he was almost entirely absent from the gamesheet when he did play, notching only six hits and a single fight in the three games he dressed for. After being sent back down to Providence, Robins only laced up twice more, with his season ending after a mid-October loss to Worcester.

Reilly Smith — RW — FLA

Season	Team	Age	GP	G	A	Pts	+/-	ESP/60	AdjCF%	iCF/60	OGVT	DGVT	SGVT	GVT
2012-13	DAL	21	37	3	6	9	0	1.54	53.8%	10.2	0.7	0.9	0.0	1.7
2013-14	BOS	22	82	20	31	51	28	2.07	59.7%	11.6	7.9	3.3	0.6	11.9
2014-15	BOS	23	81	13	27	40	7	1.58	55.1%	12.8	2.7	2.8	-1.5	4.0
2015-16	FLA	24	70	17	26	43					4.3	2.7	0.0	6.9

For the second consecutive season, Reilly Smith had a nearly perfect campaign for a second-line winger. Solid, and at times dominant, possession numbers, backed up by a respectable 1.6 ESP/60 and a second straight year of 10%-plus shooting took a bit of the sting off of the deal that sent Tyler Seguin to the Stars. Although some of Smith's success is no doubt due to the fact that he has played the majority of his even-strength minutes alongside Patrice Bergeron, he managed to hold his own even without the elite two-way center. His 1.6 ESP/60 with the perennial Selke candidate is actually lower than the 1.8 ESP/60 rate when lining up with any of the other centers. With two full NHL seasons under his belt, Smith seems to be finding the touch that had him in the top 10 in NCAA scoring for his last two years at Miami of Ohio.

BOSTON BRUINS

Carl Soderberg — LW — COL

Season	Team	Age	GP	G	A	Pts	+/-	ESP/60	AdjCF%	iCF/60	OGVT	DGVT	SGVT	GVT
2012-13	BOS	27	6	0	2	2	-2	1.63	46.8%	5.7	0.1	-0.1	0.0	0.0
2013-14	BOS	28	73	16	32	48	4	2.11	54.2%	13.8	8.6	0.8	-0.6	8.8
2014-15	BOS	29	82	13	31	44	10	1.78	51.7%	12.9	4.1	3.0	-0.5	6.6
2015-16	COL	30	67	15	27	42					4.5	2.3	0.0	6.8

After playing in Sweden until age 25, Carl Soderberg has demonstrated that for a talented player, it is never too late to make the move to the NHL. While his scoring rates dropped off in his second season as his ice-time increased, most of the slide was due to reasonable regression in both his individual shooting percentage (down to 7% from 9.8% at five-on-five) and his power-play rate (from 7.2 to 2.6 PPP/60). While he is a solid scorer, it was still surprising to see him rewarded by the Avalanche with a big-money, long-term contract. Jackpot.

Ryan Spooner — LW/C — BOS

Season	Team	Age	GP	G	A	Pts	+/-	ESP/60	AdjCF%	iCF/60	OGVT	DGVT	SGVT	GVT
2012-13	BOS	20	4	0	0	0	0	0.00	47.7%	16.0	-0.1	0.0	0.0	-0.1
2013-14	BOS	21	23	0	11	11	0	1.23	53.0%	13.3	0.8	0.1	-0.8	0.1
2014-15	BOS	22	29	8	10	18	2	2.30	50.8%	13.3	3.2	0.6	-0.5	3.3
2015-16	BOS	23	39	10	14	23					2.8	1.0	0.0	3.8

Ryan Spooner must really have wanted to make the postseason. With the Bruins locked in a battle with Ottawa and Florida for the final playoff spot throughout March, the 22-year-old center put up seven points in four games against the Senators and Panthers. While he only recorded 11 points over his 25 other games, the 2014-15 campaign demonstrated that the 2010 second rounder could be ready to make the jump to the NHL.

Max Talbot — LW/C — BOS

Season	Team	Age	GP	G	A	Pts	+/-	ESP/60	AdjCF%	iCF/60	OGVT	DGVT	SGVT	GVT
2012-13	PHI	28	35	5	5	10	2	1.31	44.7%	8.9	0.4	2.7	0.0	3.1
2013-14	PHI, COL	29	81	8	19	27	5	1.40	43.5%	9.9	1.6	3.3	0.0	4.9
2014-15	COL, BOS	30	81	5	13	18	-1	1.18	44.3%	8.9	-1.8	4.8	0.6	3.7
2015-16	BOS	31	64	5	12	17					-0.5	2.8	0.0	2.3

Max Talbot logged a lot of penalty-kill minutes. Unfortunately, Max Talbot did not play well in those minutes. Although he managed to earn enough trust from head coaches Patrick Roy and Claude Julien to get significant penalty-killing time, Talbot's shorthanded shot attempts against per 60 ranked third worst amongst all forwards who saw at least 100 minutes on the penalty kill—a disappointing result for a player who was once one of the more dependable shorthanded forwards. The trouble for Talbot is that his penalty-killing success was his main source of value; the two-time QMJHL playoff MVP has struggled to keep up at even strength for several years running, posting a negative Relative Corsi in nine of the past 10 seasons. Unless he can regain the shot prevention skill that earned him a five-year deal back in 2011, the aging Talbot may have trouble finding work past the end of this season.

BOSTON BRUINS
DEFENSEMEN

Matt Bartkowski								LD						VAN
Season	Team	Age	GP	G	A	Pts	+/-	ESP/60	AdjCF%	iCF/60	OGVT	DGVT	SGVT	GVT
2012-13	BOS	24	11	0	2	2	0	0.82	57.0%	11.8	0.1	0.1	0.0	0.2
2013-14	BOS	25	64	0	18	18	22	0.96	54.5%	10.9	1.2	4.4	0.0	5.6
2014-15	BOS	26	47	0	4	4	-6	0.32	50.0%	11.3	-1.8	0.8	0.0	-0.9
2015-16	VAN	27	51	2	9	11					0.0	2.4	0.0	2.3

Despite receiving a new contract in the summer of 2014, Matt Bartkowski was a frequent healthy scratch and saw his usage decrease significantly, with his TOI/game dropping over two minutes. Most of the blueliner's minutes shifted to Torey Krug, while his role on the penalty kill was primarily taken over by Dougie Hamilton. Part of this shift away from the former Buckeye is likely due to his inability to drive offense on his own. Bartkowski was the only player in the league to play over 2000 minutes since the start of the 2010 season without recording a goal (yikes!). Given Boston's preference for other options in the organization, it seems unlikely he will be given much of an opportunity in 2015-16.

Zdeno Chara								LD						BOS
Season	Team	Age	GP	G	A	Pts	+/-	ESP/60	AdjCF%	iCF/60	OGVT	DGVT	SGVT	GVT
2012-13	BOS	35	48	7	12	19	14	0.91	56.6%	12.1	2.4	4.4	0.0	6.9
2013-14	BOS	36	77	17	23	40	25	0.98	56.7%	11.1	8.0	5.3	0.0	13.3
2014-15	BOS	37	63	8	12	20	0	0.63	54.8%	10.5	1.1	3.3	-0.3	4.1
2015-16	BOS	38	60	7	19	25					3.0	3.4	0.0	6.4

Any human being who stands six-foot-nine and is forced to charge around a sheet of ice on 3-mm-wide pieces of steel is bound to eventually break down. For Zdeno Chara, it appears as if 2014-15 may have been the year that physics finally caught up to him, with the mammoth blueliner dropping below the 70-game mark for the first time in a decade and a half. Although Chara was still a plus-possession player, he was significantly buoyed by playing alongside budding superstar Dougie Hamilton for the vast majority of his minutes, with his CF% dropping over 10% when he was away from the youngster. Chara likely has another year or two of positive play left in him, but it looks as if we are entering the twilight years of one of the best defensemen in Slovakian—and Bruins—history.

Dougie Hamilton								RD						CGY
Season	Team	Age	GP	G	A	Pts	+/-	ESP/60	AdjCF%	iCF/60	OGVT	DGVT	SGVT	GVT
2012-13	BOS	19	42	5	11	16	4	1.15	56.7%	12.4	2.9	1.0	0.0	3.9
2013-14	BOS	20	64	7	18	25	22	1.08	57.5%	10.7	4.2	3.3	0.0	7.5
2014-15	BOS	21	72	10	32	42	-3	1.27	55.2%	12.9	6.8	2.8	-0.3	9.3
2015-16	CGY	22	69	10	30	41					6.1	3.4	0.0	9.5

If the Bruins fans were worried about finding a replacement for the aging Zdeno Chara, the emergence of Dougie Hamilton as a true top-pairing option must surely have put their mind at ease. Once again, Hamilton's even-strength scoring topped a point per 60 minutes, making him the only defenseman over the past 10 years to accomplish that feat three times before hitting age 21. Hamilton's role as a leader on offense has also steadily increased, with the blueliner now taking one in five of the shots the Bruins attempted while he was on the ice. Cornerstone of the organization, right? Maybe not, as new GM Don Sweeney traded the talented youngster to

Calgary at the 2015 NHL Entry Draft. Yes, the Bruins were cap strapped from the Chiarelli years, but it is highly questionable whether Hamilton was the right player to ship out.

Torey Krug							LD						BOS
Season	Team	Age	GP	G	A	Pts	+/-	ESP/60	AdjCF%	iCF/60	OGVT	DGVT	SGVT	GVT
2012-13	BOS	21	1	0	1	1	-1	0.00	49.8%	4.7	0.0	-0.2	0.0	-0.1
2013-14	BOS	22	79	14	26	40	18	1.08	56.6%	14.2	8.8	2.8	0.0	11.6
2014-15	BOS	23	78	12	27	39	13	1.15	53.2%	13.8	6.9	3.8	-0.7	10.0
2015-16	BOS	24	73	12	30	42					6.9	3.5	0.0	10.4

There was no sophomore slump for Torey Krug, as the former Michigan State Spartan posted a stat line nearly identical to his rookie season, with his 1.15 ESP/60 improving on his freshman mark of 1.08. Perhaps more impressive than his even-strength play, however, has been the five-foot-nine blueliner's contributions on the man advantage, where he is fourth amongst all defensemen with 4.91 power-play points per 60 minutes over the past three years. With the departure of Dougie Hamilton, it remains to be seen if the 2012 Hobey Baker finalist will continue to get favorable (even-strength) zone starts, but his power-play usage could increase, if anything.

Adam McQuaid							RD						BOS
Season	Team	Age	GP	G	A	Pts	+/-	ESP/60	AdjCF%	iCF/60	OGVT	DGVT	SGVT	GVT
2012-13	BOS	26	32	1	3	4	0	0.41	54.0%	8.7	-0.2	0.3	0.0	0.1
2013-14	BOS	27	30	1	5	6	12	0.84	51.0%	7.9	0.4	2.4	0.0	2.8
2014-15	BOS	28	63	1	6	7	-2	0.41	50.0%	7.4	-1.3	2.2	0.0	0.9
2015-16	BOS	29	54	2	7	9					-0.4	2.5	0.0	2.1

Despite playing the most minutes per game of any season in his career, 2014-15 was just another in a line of relatively unremarkable campaigns for Adam McQuaid. While he has never been confused for an offensive threat (his seven points were 16% of his career total), McQuaid put up respectable stats in his own end, finishing second on the team in even-strength shots blocked, and first on the team with a penalty-kill CA/60 rate of 93.2. With both Zdeno Chara and Dennis Seidenberg well on the wrong side of 30, McQuaid is in good position to take on more of their shutdown role.

Kevan Miller							RD						BOS
Season	Team	Age	GP	G	A	Pts	+/-	ESP/60	AdjCF%	iCF/60	OGVT	DGVT	SGVT	GVT
2013-14	BOS	26	47	1	5	6	20	0.50	52.7%	8.4	-0.5	3.6	0.0	3.1
2014-15	BOS	27	41	2	5	7	20	0.67	49.5%	8.1	0.0	4.6	0.0	4.6
2015-16	BOS	28	52	3	9	12					0.2	3.6	0.0	3.8

The season probably did not turn out the way that Kevan Miller had hoped. After playing his way up from an amateur tryout contract with Providence to a regular role with B's in the second half of 2013-14, Miller looked to be turning into a pillar of Claude Julien's penalty kill heading into the 2014-15 campaign. Instead, the ex-Vermont Catamount captain struggled through shoulder injuries, spending a 12-game stint on the IR in November before finally being shut down with 26 games left in the regular season. When he was healthy, Miller's performance was limited offensively, as he recorded 0.7 points/60 and a 49.8 CF% at five-on-five. Defensively, he benefited for the second straight year from goaltending that stopped more than 95% of the shots opponents took while he was on the ice. If his shoulder is good to go, Miller should remain a reasonable stay-at-home option capable of handling penalty-kill minutes for a Bruins blueline filled with more offensive-minded players.

Joe Morrow						**LD**								**BOS**
Season	Team	Age	GP	G	A	Pts	+/-	ESP/60	AdjCF%	iCF/60	OGVT	DGVT	SGVT	GVT
2014-15	BOS	22	15	1	0	1	3	0.25	49.8%	11.6	-0.2	0.8	0.0	0.7
2015-16	BOS	23	32	2	6	8					0.4	1.3	0.0	1.7

The last piece of the Tyler Seguin deal to make his big-league debut, Joe Morrow appeared in a 15-game stretch from late October to December, when he recorded his only NHL point—a goal—in a 3-2 loss to the team that drafted him, the Pittsburgh Penguins. After being sent back down, Morrow struggled to find the form that had him second in scoring amongst Providence defensemen in 2013-14, finishing with only 12 points in 33 games. Perhaps more concerning than his decline in point production was his drop in shot generation, from 2.3 to 1.4 shots per game. While the Bruins have no need to rush the former Portland Winter Hawk up to the NHL, they are hoping he finds the offensive touch that had him producing more than a point per game in his last WHL season.

Dennis Seidenberg						**LD**								**BOS**
Season	Team	Age	GP	G	A	Pts	+/-	ESP/60	AdjCF%	iCF/60	OGVT	DGVT	SGVT	GVT
2012-13	BOS	31	46	4	13	17	18	1.00	54.7%	11.1	2.2	5.5	0.0	7.6
2013-14	BOS	32	34	1	9	10	11	0.93	51.0%	10.1	0.6	2.1	0.0	2.7
2014-15	BOS	33	82	3	11	14	-1	0.53	48.4%	7.6	-1.6	3.9	0.0	2.3
2015-16	BOS	34	63	3	12	15					0.2	3.4	0.0	3.6

The only Bruins defenseman to suit up for every game, Dennis Seidenberg was the blueliner Claude Julien turned to most often when he needed to defend a lead, with the German veteran receiving nearly 40% of available ice-time. While his heavy defensive usage (-8% Relative Zone starts were the toughest on the team) limited his offensive contribution, Seidenberg remained a rock in his own end, leading the Bruins in blocked shots as he has in three of the past four seasons while receiving more than twice as many hits as any other Boston player. Although he is starting down the dicey part of the aging curve for defensemen, Seidenberg is signed at a reasonable $4 million AAV for the next two years, which should be more than enough time for the Bruins to find a pointman to take over his responsibilities.

Zach Trotman						**LD**								**BOS**
Season	Team	Age	GP	G	A	Pts	+/-	ESP/60	AdjCF%	iCF/60	OGVT	DGVT	SGVT	GVT
2013-14	BOS	23	2	0	0	0	0	0.00	55.7%	11.5	0.0	0.0	0.0	0.0
2014-15	BOS	24	27	1	4	5	-2	0.74	53.7%	13.9	0.1	0.4	0.0	0.5
2015-16	BOS	25	38	3	8	11					0.8	1.2	0.0	2.0

Following two years of continued improvement in the minors, Zach Trotman got a few shots to make his mark in the NHL, being called up to Boston for three separate stints with the big club. While the Lake Superior State alumnus struggled to generate much on the scoresheet during his time in Beantown, putting up only five points over 27 games, he managed to play a solid possession game, finishing with a 3.4% Relative Corsi, generally playing alongside Zdeno Chara or Torey Krug. As the last player taken in the 2010 NHL Entry Draft, expectations were not high for the Carmel, Indiana product, but Trotman has shown continued development over the past three seasons, suggesting he might have a future as a bottom-pairing defenseman.

David Warsofsky									LD					PIT
Season	Team	Age	GP	G	A	Pts	+/-	ESP/60	AdjCF%	iCF/60	OGVT	DGVT	SGVT	GVT
2013-14	BOS	23	6	1	1	2	1	1.47	57.1%	11.1	0.0	0.1	0.0	0.1
2014-15	BOS	24	4	0	1	1	1	1.04	58.0%	9.3	0.1	0.2	0.0	0.4
2015-16	PIT	25	27	2	6	8					0.6	1.0	0.0	1.6

At 25 years of age, has David Warsofsky missed his window to move into a full-time NHL role? While his minor-league career got off to a promising start, with the Boston University grad leading all Providence pointmen in scoring in his rookie season, his subsequent numbers have been inconsistent, capped by a career-low 15 points in 40 AHL games in 2014-15. Eclipsed on the depth chart by the younger Torey Krug—and Dougie Hamilton, prior to his trade to Calgary—and with Joe Morrow looking to take on a larger role, the best opportunities for Warsofsky may lie outside of the Boston organization.

GOALTENDERS

Tuukka Rask										G					BOS
Season	Team	Age	GP	W	L	OT	GAA	Sv%	ESSV%	QS%	GGVT	DGVT	SGVT	GVT
2012-13	BOS	25	36	19	10	5	2.00	.929	.938	76.5%	18.5	0.3	1.8	20.6
2013-14	BOS	26	58	36	15	6	2.04	.930	.941	69.0%	29.2	0.4	1.3	30.9
2014-15	BOS	27	70	34	21	13	2.30	.922	.930	62.7%	21.5	-0.2	2.4	23.7
2015-16	BOS	28	61					.920			18.0	0.1	0.4	18.5

After landing in the top three in five-on-five save percentage for the previous two seasons, it was a down year by Tuukka Rask's standards, with the Finnish netminder's .931 rate dropping him to eighth amongst goalies who made at least 30 starts. Part of this decline could be related to Rask's significant increase in workload, as his 70 appearances were 12 higher than he had achieved in any prior season. However, at 28, Rask is entering the prime of his career, and with a contract that runs through to the end of 2022, the Bruins are positioned to take advantage of the best years of one of the game's premier goaltenders.

Malcolm Subban										G					BOS
Season	Team	Age	GP	W	L	OT	GAA	Sv%	ESSV%	QS%	GGVT	DGVT	SGVT	GVT
2014-15	BOS	21	1	0	1	0	5.81	.500	.500	0.0%	-2.0	0.1	0.0	-1.9
2015-16	BOS	22	11					.913			0.6	0.0	0.0	0.6

Appearing in his first NHL game in February, Malcolm Subban received a rough welcome from the St. Louis Blues, surrendering three goals on six shots in just over 30 minutes. The former first-round pick spent most of his year with Providence, where he shared the starter's role with veteran journeyman Jeremy Smith. Subban's sophomore year in the AHL was statistically similar to his first season, with his save percentage remaining nearly constant at .921, from .920. With Niklas Svedberg heading to the KHL, Subban may begin the year in Boston's backup role, as he looks to re-establish his position as the heir apparent to the Bruins' crease.

Niklas Svedberg — G — KHL

Season	Team	Age	GP	W	L	OT	GAA	Sv%	ESSV%	QS%	GGVT	DGVT	SGVT	GVT
2013-14	BOS	24	1	1	0	0	1.97	.943	.938	100.0%	1.0	0.0	0.0	0.9
2014-15	BOS	25	18	7	5	1	2.33	.918	.926	64.3%	2.9	0.2	1.5	4.6
2015-16	KHL	26	23					.917			4.5	0.1	0.2	4.8

As Niklas Svedberg learned first-hand in 2014-15, playing behind one of the league's elite netminders leaves few opportunities, with the Swede getting only 14 starts and 18 appearances as Tuukka Rask's backup. Svedberg performed admirably in his limited opportunities, achieving a .925 save percentage at five-on-five, placing him sixth amongst backups who played in 15-25 games. As a free agent faced with the possibility of another year behind Rask on the depth chart, the Swede elected to leave North America, signing a one-year deal with the KHL's Salavat Yulaev Ufa.

Matt Cane

Buffalo Sabres

Boston Bruins winger Milan Lucic barreled toward a loose puck in the Sabres zone as Buffalo goalie Ryan Miller chased after it. Far out of his net, Miller leaned down to play the puck and Lucic—as you would expect—trucked over the lanky netminder. The Team USA goalie went down with a concussion. Slack-jawed Sabres players did little to hold Lucic accountable for his action; the NHL did not suspend him.

They didn't know it then, but that night in November 2011 laid out the course that led the Buffalo Sabres to draft Jack Eichel second overall in the 2015.

In the offseason prior to 2011-12, the Sabres had stocked up on high-priced free agents Ville Leino and Christian Ehrhoff and traded for stay-at-home defender Robyn Regehr in attempts to rekindle the magic of their runs to the Eastern Conference Final in 2006 and 2007. With new owner Terry Pegula willing to spend aggressively, the Sabres overhauled roster opened the season 10-6-0. Their star players Jason Pominville and Thomas Vanek started the season hot, flanking a promising prospect in center Luke Adam. Heading into the game against Boston, Buffalo fans saw an early-season test.

Instead, it turned into a nightmare. Miller was crushed by Lucic and missed several weeks, Ehrhoff and young defenseman Tyler Myers suffered injuries, and Adam's production fell off the map. By the middle of January, the Sabres were in last place in the Eastern Conference, losing 23 of their next 31 games following the Lucic incident.

Despite a hot streak at the end of the season, it was clear the window to win was over in Buffalo. Pegula gave a clear directive: the Sabres would go into full rebuild mode.

And they tore it down in spectacular fashion. The Sabres traded Pominville, Vanek, and Miller. They bought out Leino and Ehrhoff. They fired head coach Lindy Ruff. They fired general manager Darcy Regier. They hired and quickly fired Pat Lafontaine as team president. And they drafted eighth, second, and second overall in the 2013 through 2015 drafts.

The culmination of the Sabres rebuild came on draft night 2015, when they selected Boston University phenom Jack Eichel. The Boston native had won the Hobey Baker Award as an 18-year-old—virtually unheard of in NCAA hockey—and was widely considered the second-best prospect since Crosby...with only first-overall pick Connor McDavid thought of more highly.

While Eichel is expected to be the centerpiece of the rebuild—Buffalo's version of Jonathan Toews, John Tavares,

SABRES IN A BOX

Last Season

Goals For	161	30th
Goals Against	274	29th
GVT	-113	30th
Points	54	30th
Playoffs	Did not make playoffs	

Buffalo finished last overall, but failed to achieve the one thing they wanted, drafting Connor McDavid.

Three-Year Record

GVT	-222	30th
Points	154	30th
Playoffs	0 Appearances, 0 Wins	

VUKOTA Projections

Goals For	195	28th
Goals Against	239	30th
GVT	-44	29th
Points	77	29th

There is nowhere to go but up, but that is little comfort. The Sabres will once again be one of the worst teams in the league.

Top Three Prospects

J. Eichel (F), S. Reinhart (F), J. McCabe (D)

Steven Stamkos, and the like—new GM Tim Murray has completely turned over the roster, building up the prospect system, and then flipping several key young pieces for proven stars.

Very few times in NHL history has a team seen such massive change in its top-nine forwards. Eichel will join fellow second-overall pick (2014) Sam Reinhart, who spent nine games in Buffalo before being returned to junior in 2014-15, and recently-acquired forwards Evander Kane and Ryan O'Reilly.

After a bizarre incident involving a track suit, Kane and the Jets decided it was finally time to end their rocky relationship. The Sabres packaged a first-round draft pick, which had been acquired from the Blues in a deal for Ryan Miller, along with one of their most dynamic offensive prospects Joel Armia and future third-line grinder Brendan Lemieux. Myers was included in the deal that also saw former third-overall selection Zach Bogosian end up in Buffalo.

Armia is a boom-or-bust prospect, whose estimated time of arrival as an impact player is likely 2016-17, while Lemieux is maybe four years away from sniffing the NHL. The move sped up the Sabres rebuild significantly by placing a young, 30-goal-scoring, former fourth-overall pick on their first-line wing.

In the offseason, Murray took advantage of Colorado's unwillingness to pay center Ryan O'Reilly. Once again, Buffalo's general manager used his prospect system to grab a big fish. He dealt two former first rounders in Mikhail Grigorenko and Nikita Zadorov to the Avalanche in exchange for O'Reilly. You can trace the move back to the teardown, as Zadorov was picked with a first-round selection from Minnesota that came in the Pominville trade.

Murray wasn't done. He spent more rebuild currency to nab his future number-one goaltender. Buffalo traded a first-round pick from the New York Islanders—part of a deal for Vanek—to the Ottawa Senators to get 23-year-old goalie Robin Lehner.

Kane and O'Reilly join 14th overall selection from 2012 Zemgus Girgensons, whose pick was acquired in a deal for Paul Gaustad at the 2012 trade deadline. Girgensons was impressive in his first full season as a top-six center, scoring 15 goals and 15 assists in 61 games. He projects as either a power top-six winger or top-end third-line center, assuming Eichel, Reinhart, and O'Reilly ultimately end up in two of the top-three center spots.

Intriguing young forward Johan Larsson, who led the team in Relative Corsi and finished the season as the team's top center, was also a return on Buffalo's trade of Pominville to Minnesota. The hard-nosed Swede could play a top-nine role on the wing as a strong two-way possession player.

On the blue line, Rasmus Ristolainen has the promise to be Buffalo's Shea Weber. The eighth-overall pick in 2013 has blown away the organization with his fast development. The young Finn has the determination to put all his tools together and become a top-end defenseman.

Whether it all comes together to become the next dynasty a la the Chicago Blackhawks is yet to be determined. Plenty of things will have to go right in order for the Sabres rebuild to be a success. Expectations for 2015-16 should be tempered with so many young players in the mix. But make no mistake, the Sabres laid out the blueprint for how a team should rebuild by sinking to the bottom, gaining elite talents through the top of the draft, and moving other prospects for established stars.

And isn't it so darn ironic that they owe it all to Milan Lucic?

Matthew Coller

BUFFALO SABRES

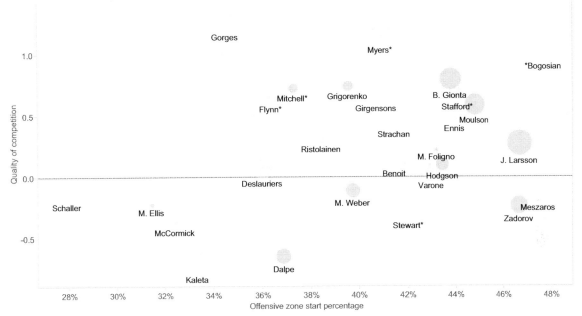

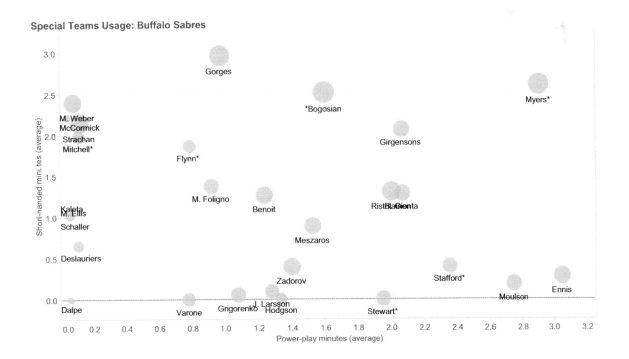

BUFFALO SABRES

Offensive Profile: Buffalo Sabres

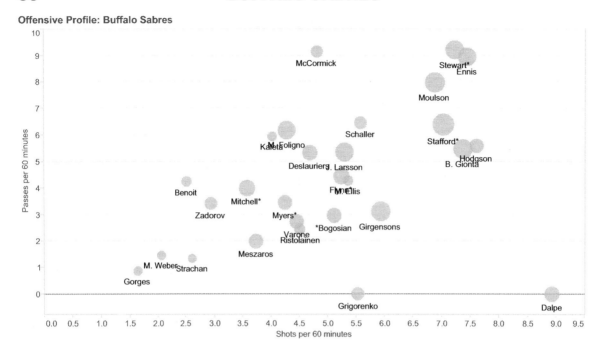

Cap Efficiency: Buffalo Sabres

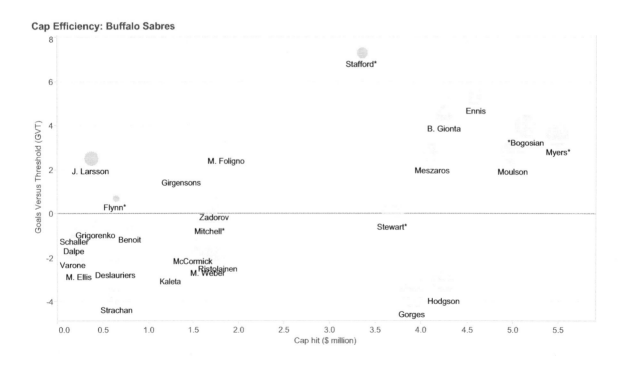

FORWARDS

Jerry D'Amigo — LW — BUF

Season	Team	Age	GP	G	A	Pts	+/-	ESP/60	AdjCF%	iCF/60	OGVT	DGVT	SGVT	GVT
2013-14	TOR	22	22	1	2	3	-1	1.17	37.0%	7.2	-0.3	0.3	0.0	0.0
2014-15	BUF	23	9	0	0	0	-4	0.00	38.4%	6.1	-0.9	-0.1	0.0	-1.0
2015-16	BUF	24	32	4	6	10					0.0	0.6	0.0	0.6

Hard-working, intelligent Jerry D'Amigo was targeted by the Sabres in a trade for 2008 second-rounder Luke Adam because of what he brings to the locker room and the AHL club. A member of several quality Toronto Marlies teams, D'Amigo adds defensive skill and speed that frustrates opponents. He isn't much of an offensive threat, though. The Binghamton, New York native has dressed for only 31 NHL games, potting one goal. But his smarts and skating ability make him a capable fourth-line call-up option.

Zac Dalpe — RW — MIN

Season	Team	Age	GP	G	A	Pts	+/-	ESP/60	AdjCF%	iCF/60	OGVT	DGVT	SGVT	GVT
2012-13	CAR	23	10	1	2	3	-7	1.57	52.3%	17.4	-0.3	-0.4	0.0	-0.7
2013-14	VAN	24	55	4	3	7	-7	0.95	44.7%	14.8	-0.7	0.3	-0.6	-1.0
2014-15	BUF	25	21	1	2	3	-11	0.93	38.8%	12.7	-0.7	-0.5	0.0	-1.2
2015-16	MIN	26	39	5	5	10					0.0	0.5	0.0	0.5

Quick-footed Zac Dalpe is an impact player at the AHL level, with speed that is virtually unmatched in the minor leagues. The Canes' second-round pick from 2008 scored 16 goals in 44 games for the Rochester Americans, but when he received significant NHL time, he demonstrated exactly why he will spend his days on buses: he does not have an NHL-level tool outside of speed. The Ohio State product cannot beat goaltenders or get to scoring areas in the NHL nor does he have enough hockey IQ or toughness to perform as a quality role player.

Nicolas Deslauriers — LW — BUF

Season	Team	Age	GP	G	A	Pts	+/-	ESP/60	AdjCF%	iCF/60	OGVT	DGVT	SGVT	GVT
2013-14	BUF	22	17	1	0	1	-10	0.31	44.0%	12.7	-1.3	-0.5	0.0	-1.8
2014-15	BUF	23	82	5	10	15	-24	0.92	32.9%	9.0	-2.3	0.1	0.0	-2.2
2015-16	BUF	24	64	6	9	15					-1.5	0.7	0.0	-0.8

A converted defenseman, Nicolas Deslauriers played his first full NHL season as a fourth-line bruiser with a little bit of skill. The former Manchester Monarch notched a few points despite playing with well below-average linemates on the 30th-place Sabres while making it clear that middleweight fist-throwers will want to avoid dropping the gloves with him. There will be a lot more competition for depth spots on the improving Sabres, so Deslauriers will have to demonstrate more offensive capability to keep a regular spot.

Matt Ellis — C/LW — BUF

Season	Team	Age	GP	G	A	Pts	+/-	ESP/60	AdjCF%	iCF/60	OGVT	DGVT	SGVT	GVT
2012-13	BUF	31	6	0	0	0	0	0.00	40.6%	15.2	-0.1	0.0	0.0	-0.1
2013-14	BUF	32	50	4	2	6	-6	0.90	42.0%	14.6	-1.0	1.1	0.0	0.2
2014-15	BUF	33	39	1	1	2	-12	0.43	36.9%	7.8	-2.0	-0.3	0.0	-2.3
2015-16	BUF	34	40	3	3	7					-0.6	0.6	0.0	0.0

BUFFALO SABRES

Matt Ellis, long-time member of the Sabres organization, has been harder to kill off than Jason Voorhees. Despite scoring a meager 21 goals in 356 games, the undrafted centerman has continued to receive significant NHL time, seeing time in 89 games over the past two seasons despite producing eight points. There are few players who set a better example for up-and-comers, which is exactly why Buffalo brought him back on an AHL deal. Ellis will act as a form of player-coach for a club that is focused on the future.

Tyler Ennis							LW						BUF
Season	Team	Age	GP	G	A	Pts	+/-	ESP/60	AdjCF%	iCF/60	OGVT	DGVT	SGVT	GVT
2012-13	BUF	23	47	10	21	31	-14	1.50	45.6%	13.0	3.0	-1.2	-1.2	0.6
2013-14	BUF	24	80	21	22	43	-25	1.30	42.3%	12.6	1.4	1.0	-0.1	2.3
2014-15	BUF	25	78	20	26	46	-19	1.36	36.0%	10.7	3.4	0.6	1.2	5.3
2015-16	BUF	26	69	20	25	44					4.2	1.5	0.1	5.8

After back-to-back 20-goal seasons on the worst team in hockey, Tyler Ennis has to be thrilled to see the Sabres augmented by top-six forwards like Ryan O'Reilly and Evander Kane. As one of the NHL's best skaters, the 2008 first-round selection has made a name for himself despite standing at a modest five-foot-nine. His shiftiness, speed, creativity with the puck, and finishing skill around the net make him a scoring threat, but the jury is still out on whether he can become an above-average top-six winger. Inconsistencies in effort and serious defensive lapses have only marginally improved since his early days. If he is going to turn into a star, this year is the year.

Marcus Foligno							LW						BUF
Season	Team	Age	GP	G	A	Pts	+/-	ESP/60	AdjCF%	iCF/60	OGVT	DGVT	SGVT	GVT
2012-13	BUF	21	47	5	13	18	-4	1.39	50.6%	8.6	0.3	0.5	0.0	0.8
2013-14	BUF	22	74	7	12	19	-17	1.07	41.6%	7.1	-1.6	1.7	-0.6	-0.5
2014-15	BUF	23	57	8	12	20	-5	1.36	36.8%	6.7	1.5	1.5	-0.3	2.7
2015-16	BUF	24	58	9	13	22					1.0	1.6	0.0	2.6

Back in 2011-12, Marcus Foligno gave Sabres fans something to get excited about. The former Sudbury Wolf scored 13 points in 14 games and threw his body around like the next coming of Milan Lucic. Unfortunately, Foligno's subsequent production has been a serious downer, with a tepid 20 goals in 178 games since that unsustainable hot stretch. Even more frustrating to Sabres management is that the son of former Sabres captain Mike Foligno has been massively inconsistent with his physical play, more of a question of mindset for the six-foot-three 227 pounder than the athletic feat required to produce points. As a fourth-round pick, Foligno's best-case-scenario was always as a third liner, but if he does not make more of a—figurative and literal—impact in his all-around game, he may not stick with the Sabres for much longer.

Brian Gionta							RW						BUF
Season	Team	Age	GP	G	A	Pts	+/-	ESP/60	AdjCF%	iCF/60	OGVT	DGVT	SGVT	GVT
2012-13	MTL	33	48	14	12	26	3	1.64	52.4%	14.6	2.6	1.4	-0.6	3.4
2013-14	MTL	34	81	18	22	40	1	1.60	45.5%	14.9	5.3	2.7	0.0	8.0
2014-15	BUF	35	69	13	22	35	-13	1.48	39.4%	12.1	3.6	1.0	-0.1	4.5
2015-16	BUF	36	60	13	19	32					3.2	1.6	0.0	4.7

BUFFALO SABRES

Buffalo inked Rochester, New York native and Canadiens captain Brian Gionta to provide leadership for their young team, but the two-time Stanley Cup winner had plans of being more than a locker-room figurehead. The 35-year-old proved he can still play, scoring 35 points in 69 games. Gionta played so well, in fact, that the Sabres almost missed out on finishing 30th—risking losing out on second pick Jack Eichel—due to his torrid 16 points over the final 14 games. Buffalo also fell apart during his stint on IR, which gives a window into his leadership qualities and remaining on-ice ability. Gionta will slide into a third-line role as the club improves and will inevitably see a slip in play, but for all the overachieving he has done, we should never count him out.

Zemgus Girgensons														C											BUF
Season	Team	Age	GP	G	A	Pts	+/-	ESP/60	AdjCF%	iCF/60	OGVT	DGVT	SGVT	GVT
2013-14	BUF	19	70	8	14	22	-6	1.30	43.1%	10.8	-0.6	3.1	-0.2	2.2
2014-15	BUF	20	61	15	15	30	-16	1.51	34.2%	9.5	1.0	1.0	-0.4	1.7
2015-16	BUF	21	65	16	19	35					2.3	1.8	0.0	4.2

There is no question that Zemgus Girgensons was in over his head as the number-one center in his age-20 season, but 15 goals and 15 assists in 61 games from the two-way center was promising enough, given the team around him. As the 14th-overall pick in 2012, the biggest question mark was whether the Latvian native could produce enough offense to stick as a top-six forward. Girgensons demonstrated finishing skill with several highlight-reel goals, though his lack of passing and playmaking talent may ultimately result in a move to wing. His biggest future impact may come from his shutdown skills—a tireless worker, Girgensons frustrates opponents by tracking them down from behind and knocking them off pucks.

Mikhail Grigorenko														C											COL
Season	Team	Age	GP	G	A	Pts	+/-	ESP/60	AdjCF%	iCF/60	OGVT	DGVT	SGVT	GVT
2012-13	BUF	18	25	1	4	5	-1	1.25	45.0%	12.8	-0.3	0.3	0.0	0.0
2013-14	BUF	19	18	2	1	3	-3	0.64	37.0%	9.2	-0.5	0.2	0.0	-0.3
2014-15	BUF	20	25	3	3	6	-10	0.68	37.8%	8.2	-0.3	-0.2	0.0	-0.5
2015-16	COL	21	37	7	7	14					0.5	0.6	0.0	1.1

For the first time, Russian center Mikhail Grigorenko showed signs of the offensive talent that made him a first-round pick in 2012 (although he had slid down the draft board to #12 due to concerns about his makeup). Scoring 36 points in 43 games with Rochester gave GM Tim Murray reason to give him a shot in 25 NHL contests. However, once again Grigorenko looked well behind the pace of The Show, struggling at both ends of the ice. He posted just six points while showing very little progress in the defensive zone. As part of the Ryan O'Reilly trade, the Avalanche hope Grigorenko will rediscover his game under his former QMJHL coach Patrick Roy. If he does not take leaps forward this year, don't be surprised if he ends up in the KHL for the rest of his career.

Cody Hodgson														C/RW											NSH
Season	Team	Age	GP	G	A	Pts	+/-	ESP/60	AdjCF%	iCF/60	OGVT	DGVT	SGVT	GVT
2012-13	BUF	22	48	15	19	34	-4	2.33	46.1%	12.9	3.9	0.8	-0.3	4.5
2013-14	BUF	23	72	20	24	44	-26	1.43	40.8%	13.0	4.3	0.5	-0.5	4.3
2014-15	BUF	24	78	6	7	13	-28	0.80	37.3%	12.3	-3.2	-0.3	0.4	-3.1
2015-16	NSH	25	62	12	13	24					0.9	0.9	0.0	1.8

BUFFALO SABRES

The 10th-overall pick in 2008, Cody Hodgson had one of the most shocking dropoffs in recent memory, belly-flopping from 20 goals in 72 games to just six in 78. The 25-year-old has frustrated multiple coaches on multiple teams with dynamic offensive skill coupled with a complete lack of defensive awareness, but last season, even Hodgson's scoring deserted him. Head coach Ted Nolan took him off the power play—which unfortunately, may be the only place he can score. If his contractual situation had been better, general manager Tim Murray may have elected to wait and see, but signed for four more years at $4.3 million AAV, Buffalo wisely bought him out. Nashville will now be team #3 to hope the former World Juniors star comes around.

Patrick Kaleta					**RW**								**BUF**
Season	Team	Age	GP	G	A	Pts	+/-	ESP/60	AdjCF%	iCF/60	OGVT	DGVT	SGVT	GVT
2012-13	BUF	26	34	1	0	1	-4	0.21	42.2%	9.4	-1.5	0.2	0.0	-1.3
2013-14	BUF	27	5	0	0	0	-1	0.00	30.0%	1.7	-0.2	0.0	0.0	-0.3
2014-15	BUF	28	42	0	3	3	-11	0.37	31.1%	7.0	-2.3	-0.1	0.0	-2.4
2015-16	BUF	29	40	2	4	6					-1.1	0.5	0.0	-0.6

Once an effective fourth liner and agitator, veteran Patrick Kaleta seems to have lost the skills that once made him a helpful depth player. No longer can Kaleta skate at a high level, which hurts his ability to match up against top opponents, and contribute to the penalty kill. Further, with an eagle eye on him after multiple suspensions, the Western New York native no longer gets any benefit of doubt from referees. It would be surprising if Kaleta's NHL career isn't nearing its end.

Evander Kane					**LW**								**BUF**
Season	Team	Age	GP	G	A	Pts	+/-	ESP/60	AdjCF%	iCF/60	OGVT	DGVT	SGVT	GVT
2012-13	WPG	21	48	17	16	33	-3	2.13	48.9%	21.9	4.9	1.4	-0.6	5.7
2013-14	WPG	22	63	19	22	41	-7	2.00	51.0%	22.3	4.1	2.2	-0.8	5.4
2014-15	WPG	23	37	10	12	22	-1	1.37	54.6%	20.3	1.5	1.3	0.4	3.2
2015-16	BUF	24	56	17	20	37					4.0	1.9	0.0	5.9

For Evander Kane, 2014-15 was the year of the track suit. He was (reportedly) scratched after an incident involving wearing a track suit to the arena, and oddly enough, that turned out to be the straw that broke the camel's back in Winnipeg. After a number of silly "incidents" like Kane posting things on his Twitter account that the team (reportedly) didn't appreciate, the Jets elected to move the 24-year-old. While they received good return in defenseman Tyler Myers and top Sabres prospect Joel Armia, they gave away the best player in the deal. The fourth-overall pick in 2009 is a quality power forward with 30-goal capabilities. Kane fires shots from just about anywhere, resulting in one of the best shots per 60 minute rates in the NHL. Between 2011 and 2014, he was top 25 in goals per 60 minutes. In Buffalo, he joins a rising team that is thrilled to have him. Look out, Atlantic Division.

Johan Larsson					**C/LW**								**BUF**
Season	Team	Age	GP	G	A	Pts	+/-	ESP/60	AdjCF%	iCF/60	OGVT	DGVT	SGVT	GVT
2012-13	MIN	20	1	0	0	0	0	0.00	36.4%	9.0	0.0	0.0	0.0	0.0
2013-14	BUF	21	28	0	4	4	0	0.70	43.8%	6.1	-0.7	0.8	0.0	0.1
2014-15	BUF	22	39	6	10	16	0	1.41	40.6%	8.1	1.8	0.7	0.0	2.5
2015-16	BUF	23	43	7	11	18					1.4	1.1	0.0	2.5

When the Sabres traded for Johan Larsson from the Minnesota Wild, they hoped he would become a solid defensive third-line center. Since joining the organization, the Swedish forward has hinted at more scoring ability than once believed. In two seasons with AHL Rochester, Larsson has scored 81 points in 95 games. In the NHL, he had been given fourth-line minutes until the end of 2014-15, when he moved into a top-line center role with Girgensons hurt. Larsson shone, finishing the season as the Sabres' top Relative Corsi forward, second best in five-on-five scoring, and best in goals-for percentage. Where he fits in going forward is yet to be determined, but it is definitely in the NHL.

Cody McCormick														C					BUF
Season	Team	Age	GP	G	A	Pts	+/-	ESP/60	AdjCF%	iCF/60	OGVT	DGVT	SGVT	GVT
2012-13	BUF	29	8	0	0	0	-2	0.00	40.9%	13.3	-0.4	-0.1	0.0	-0.5
2013-14	BUF, MIN	30	43	2	5	7	-6	1.29	36.8%	7.6	-1.0	0.8	0.0	-0.2
2014-15	BUF	31	33	1	3	4	-9	0.58	33.3%	9.3	-1.5	0.1	0.0	-1.5
2015-16	BUF	32	41	3	5	8					-0.7	0.8	0.0	0.1

Veteran Cody McCormick was sidelined by blood clots after appearing in 33 games. At one time, the bruising center was a useful role player, providing goals here and there to go along with significant toughness. But the miles on his body have taken their toll. No longer can he play more than a few very sheltered minutes per game—and even then, he is a liability. The Sabres want to keep hard-nosed professionals around their rebuilding team, but they have to provide something more than work ethic. In McCormick's case, it makes more sense to have him in the AHL.

Matt Moulson														LW					BUF
Season	Team	Age	GP	G	A	Pts	+/-	ESP/60	AdjCF%	iCF/60	OGVT	DGVT	SGVT	GVT
2012-13	NYI	29	47	15	29	44	-3	2.34	52.3%	15.9	8.1	1.2	0.0	9.3
2013-14	NYI, BUF, MIN	30	75	23	28	51	2	1.72	45.4%	12.0	6.3	2.9	2.3	11.5
2014-15	BUF	31	77	13	28	41	-11	1.58	38.9%	10.4	2.2	1.4	-0.9	2.7
2015-16	BUF	32	65	14	23	37					3.1	1.8	0.0	4.9

Veteran goal scorer Matt Moulson had a down year in terms of production, largely due to playing on the worst power-play unit in the NHL. It is a long way down from having his buddy John Tavares on the man advantage to the cluster of forwards the Sabres ran out. Still, at five-on-five, Moulson was effective, leading the Sabres with 1.58 points per 60 minutes. At 32, the time left for the veteran winger to be a top goal scorer is running out, but he may transition into more of a playmaker and power-play specialist.

Sam Reinhart														C					BUF
Season	Team	Age	GP	G	A	Pts	+/-	ESP/60	AdjCF%	iCF/60	OGVT	DGVT	SGVT	GVT
2014-15	BUF	19	9	0	1	1	-1	0.65	33.6%	3.7	-0.2	0.1	0.0	-0.1
2015-16	BUF	20	29	4	6	11					0.5	0.6	0.0	1.1

In his first NHL action, 2014 second-overall pick Sam Reinhart proved to need more development before being ready for the big time; he was knocked off the puck easily and lacked the speed to keep up. When Reinhart returned to pro hockey in the AHL at the end of the season, he looked like a changed (young) man. He was stronger on the puck and showed the elite-level playmaking skill that had made him a top selection. There may be some question marks about his skating, but it didn't hurt that he was the best player at the World Juniors. As he likely heads into his first full NHL season, fans will find that Reinhart's playmaking, vision, and smarts will mitigate concerns about his feet.

Tim Schaller								C/LW						BUF
Season	Team	Age	GP	G	A	Pts	+/-	ESP/60	AdjCF%	iCF/60	OGVT	DGVT	SGVT	GVT
2014-15	BUF	24	18	1	1	2	-5	0.65	34.8%	7.8	-0.8	0.0	0.0	-0.8
2015-16	BUF	25	33	5	6	11					0.1	0.6	0.0	0.8

It doesn't happen too often that a player can develop offensive ability as a 24-year-old, but Tim Schaller proved it to be possible. Schaller was purely a defensive center at Providence University and in his first pro season. The undrafted free agent saw a jump in offense from 18 to 43 points with the Amerks and earned his first NHL call-up. As a quality north-south skater with hockey IQ and size to boot, there is a chance Schaller could become an NHL regular in a Paul Gaustad or Matt Hendricks mold.

Phil Varone								C/LW						BUF
Season	Team	Age	GP	G	A	Pts	+/-	ESP/60	AdjCF%	iCF/60	OGVT	DGVT	SGVT	GVT
2013-14	BUF	23	9	1	1	2	-3	1.18	49.1%	12.2	-0.1	0.0	0.0	-0.1
2014-15	BUF	24	28	3	2	5	-14	0.85	35.4%	7.2	-1.2	-0.3	-0.3	-1.8
2015-16	BUF	25	39	6	6	13					0.0	0.5	0.0	0.5

On a 30th-place team, a lot of players who would never otherwise see the NHL light of day get a chance to prove they belong. As a four-year contributor to the Sabres AHL affiliate, Phil Varone finally received that opportunity with 28 games in Buffalo. Unfortunately, there won't be a Disney Movie-ending here, as the undersized center failed to keep up with the big-league pace, physicality, and defensive requirements—and showed very little capability of scoring at the highest level. Expect him to have a long, solid minor-league career.

DEFENSEMEN

Andre Benoit								LD						STL
Season	Team	Age	GP	G	A	Pts	+/-	ESP/60	CF%	iCF/60	OGVT	DGVT	SGVT	GVT
2012-13	OTT	28	33	3	7	10	-3	1.03	56.4%	12.8	0.6	0.0	0.0	0.6
2013-14	COL	29	79	7	21	28	2	0.90	47.3%	8.4	3.0	1.5	0.0	4.6
2014-15	BUF	30	59	1	8	9	-19	0.45	35.7%	5.5	-1.0	0.3	0.0	-0.7
2015-16	STL	31	54	3	11	14					0.4	1.7	0.0	2.1

After a long tenure in the minors, the Colorado Avalanche gave Andre Benoit a shot as an NHL regular in 2013-14. The move paid off, as he scored 28 points and helped the Avs to the postseason. Benoit was a fit in Colorado as a talented offensive defenseman despite significant shortcomings in his own end. With Buffalo, those shortcomings were incredibly evident as he consistently turned pucks over, made soft plays in the corner, and was not quick enough to make up for mistakes. His production did not carry over to the brutal Buffalo team, either. It is hard to see the 31-year-old playing as an NHL regular again.

BUFFALO SABRES

Zach Bogosian								LD						BUF
Season	Team	Age	GP	G	A	Pts	+/-	ESP/60	AdjCF%	iCF/60	OGVT	DGVT	SGVT	GVT
2012-13	WPG	22	33	5	9	14	-5	1.03	48.2%	13.1	2.1	1.3	0.5	3.9
2013-14	WPG	23	55	3	8	11	3	0.57	49.1%	10.9	-0.9	2.8	0.0	1.8
2014-15	WPG, BUF	24	62	3	17	20	-6	0.89	46.8%	9.7	1.8	2.2	0.0	4.0
2015-16	BUF	25	58	4	15	19					1.4	2.8	0.0	4.2

After years of hoping and praying he would live up to his draft status—third overall in 2008—the Jets finally pulled the cord and traded Massena, New York native Zach Bogosian to Buffalo. The fact that he was a throw-in on the Evander Kane trade shows exactly where he stood in Winnipeg. Considering his tools—top-notch skating, physical play, a big shot—the 25-year-old should have been a star, but he never developed an NHL-caliber offensive game plus he makes a myriad of questionable decisions on the blue line. That said, Buffalo can make the most out of their new defender by simply putting Bogosian in the lower-expectation role of a quality fourth or fifth D-man.

Josh Gorges								RD						BUF
Season	Team	Age	GP	G	A	Pts	+/-	ESP/60	AdjCF%	iCF/60	OGVT	DGVT	SGVT	GVT
2012-13	MTL	28	48	2	7	9	4	0.64	52.2%	6.2	0.1	3.5	0.0	3.6
2013-14	MTL	29	66	1	13	14	6	0.62	45.5%	5.0	0.4	4.8	0.0	5.2
2014-15	BUF	30	46	0	6	6	-28	0.35	32.3%	3.8	-2.2	-1.5	0.0	-3.7
2015-16	BUF	31	47	1	7	8					-0.9	1.4	0.0	0.5

At one time, Josh Gorges was a force for the Canadiens, giving P.K. Subban a smart, hard-nosed partner who could cover up when the talented youngster's risks didn't pay off. However, in his final year in Montreal, Gorges began to show his age. Moving to Buffalo, the Sabres asked the Kelowna, British Columbia native to be on their top pairing and even the power play, which inevitably yielded disastrous results. His stat line featured the team's worst Relative Corsi along with a -28 in just 46 games before being shut down with a knee injury. With the defense corps still undermanned in Buffalo, new head coach Dan Bylsma will likely be looking for more from the veteran blueliner than he can manage these days.

Jake McCabe								LD						BUF
Season	Team	Age	GP	G	A	Pts	+/-	ESP/60	AdjCF%	iCF/60	OGVT	DGVT	SGVT	GVT
2013-14	BUF	20	7	0	1	1	-3	0.60	36.4%	2.9	-0.1	-0.1	0.0	-0.2
2014-15	BUF	21	2	0	0	0	0	0.00	48.5%	6.5	0.0	0.0	0.0	0.0
2015-16	BUF	22	26	2	5	7					0.3	0.8	0.0	1.1

Jake McCabe had his ups and downs in his first pro season, spent almost exclusively with the Rochester Amerks. The 2012 second-round pick impressed the organization with his work ethic, making big strides after a rough first few months; he earned a late-season call-up for his efforts. While the gold medal-winning Team USA WJC captain received power-play time in the AHL, he projects as a fourth or fifth defenseman who will bring more of a physical than offensive presence. The Wisconsin Badger may need another year in the AHL before his game is mature enough for the big leagues.

Andrej Meszaros — LD — Free Agent

Season	Team	Age	GP	G	A	Pts	+/-	ESP/60	AdjCF%	iCF/60	OGVT	DGVT	SGVT	GVT
2012-13	PHI	27	11	0	2	2	-9	0.36	36.5%	10.8	-0.1	0.0	0.0	-0.1
2013-14	PHI, BOS	28	52	7	15	22	5	1.46	49.0%	11.9	4.6	1.8	0.0	6.4
2014-15	BUF	29	60	7	7	14	-13	0.84	37.5%	6.4	1.0	1.6	0.0	2.7
2015-16	Free Agent	30	54	5	12	17					1.6	2.0	0.0	3.7

In the same way the NHL has moved on from fighters, they have also moved on from defensively-incapable defensemen who are good on the power play. Thus, it is tough for a player like Andrej Meszaros to get a job anywhere but on a team that is gunning for 30th place. The veteran Slovak scored more than any other Sabre defenseman, but was a complete liability on the defensive end. The six-foot-two, 225-pound Meszaros is not the most fleet of foot, which makes him incapable of tracking quicker opponents, and he does not make up for lack of speed with physical play. Add that to a heap of turnovers when trying to exit the D-zone and you have too many issues to make him valuable in the NHL anymore.

Mark Pysyk — RD — BUF

Season	Team	Age	GP	G	A	Pts	+/-	ESP/60	AdjCF%	iCF/60	OGVT	DGVT	SGVT	GVT
2012-13	BUF	20	19	1	4	5	-7	0.84	44.6%	7.3	1.0	-0.8	0.0	0.2
2013-14	BUF	21	44	1	6	7	-11	0.42	43.7%	7.1	-0.8	1.0	0.0	0.3
2014-15	BUF	22	7	2	1	3	4	1.53	36.3%	4.6	0.7	1.1	0.0	1.8
2015-16	BUF	23	38	3	8	11					0.7	1.8	0.0	2.5

As the Sabres aimed for last place, one of the victims of this apparent "direction" was Mark Pysyk. The 2010 first rounder was deserving of being on Buffalo's top pair, but was curiously kept in the AHL. This caused much frustration for head coach Ted Nolan, who openly criticized his GM several times for keeping Pysyk in the minors, declaring the young defenseman "ready for prime time". This season, the bright, smooth-skating Pysyk will get his chance to play on Buffalo's top four and show that his former coach was right. New head coach Dan Bylsma will come to appreciate his exceptional first pass and head-down demeanor.

Rasmus Ristolainen — RD — BUF

Season	Team	Age	GP	G	A	Pts	+/-	ESP/60	AdjCF%	iCF/60	OGVT	DGVT	SGVT	GVT
2013-14	BUF	19	34	2	2	4	-15	0.44	39.1%	6.8	-0.9	-0.4	0.0	-1.3
2014-15	BUF	20	78	8	12	20	-32	0.49	35.7%	7.2	0.1	-1.9	0.0	-1.8
2015-16	BUF	21	62	7	15	22					1.3	0.8	0.0	2.1

2014 World Junior championship hero Rasmus Ristolainen got his first shot as a full-time NHL defender and gave the Sabres plenty of reason to believe he will be their future #1 defenseman. The 2013 eighth-overall selection is the total package, with six-foot-four size, physical play, a big shot, top-notch skating, work ethic, and confidence. His emergence gave Buffalo the ability to part ways with 2013 16th-overall selection Nikita Zadorov in the O'Reilly deal. At 21, there is still a long way to go before Ristolainen can put his name amongst the best of the best, but he has all the tools to get there.

BUFFALO SABRES

Chad Ruhwedel — RD — BUF

Season	Team	Age	GP	G	A	Pts	+/-	ESP/60	AdjCF%	iCF/60	OGVT	DGVT	SGVT	GVT
2012-13	BUF	22	7	0	0	0	0	0.00	40.5%	8.5	-0.3	0.1	0.0	-0.2
2013-14	BUF	23	21	0	1	1	-3	0.00	43.1%	10.3	-1.2	0.4	0.0	-0.8
2014-15	BUF	24	4	0	1	1	3	1.22	43.8%	6.9	0.1	0.6	0.0	0.7
2015-16	BUF	25	30	2	6	7					0.3	1.3	0.0	1.5

UMass-Lowell blueliner Chad Ruhwedel was a highly sought-after unrestricted free agent at the end of his NCAA career, in 2013. The Sabres landed the smooth-skating righty, in part by offering him a chance to play in the NHL right away. Ruhwedel may have been in the plans of the previous regime under GM Darcy Regier, but current GM Tim Murray elected to keep him in the AHL for all but four games, despite boasting one of the poorest defense corps in the NHL. Murray pushed him farther down the depth chart with the additions of quality AHL defensemen Bobby Sanguinetti and Matt Donovan, giving the impression that Ruhwedel may not see much NHL ice unless he does it elsewhere.

Tyson Strachan — RD — MIN

Season	Team	Age	GP	G	A	Pts	+/-	ESP/60	AdjCF%	iCF/60	OGVT	DGVT	SGVT	GVT
2012-13	FLA	28	38	0	4	4	-13	0.37	49.1%	8.1	-1.2	0.7	0.0	-0.5
2013-14	WSH	29	18	0	2	2	-2	0.41	40.7%	5.8	-0.2	0.3	0.0	0.1
2014-15	BUF	30	46	0	5	5	-30	0.31	36.5%	5.5	-1.6	-2.1	0.0	-3.7
2015-16	MIN	31	40	1	5	6					-0.6	0.1	0.0	-0.5

Fans never would have expected newcomer Tyson Strachan to play the entire NHL season. At every stop, the 30-year-old has been a fill-in player, at best. It was painfully clear why the former Blue, Panther, and Capital had spent most of his time in the AHL, as his skating was far behind that of NHL regulars. The only positive Strachan brought to the Sabres was his character—active in the community, and taking a professional approach. If you are going to finish 30th, at least have good locker room and community guys.

Mike Weber — LD — BUF

Season	Team	Age	GP	G	A	Pts	+/-	ESP/60	AdjCF%	iCF/60	OGVT	DGVT	SGVT	GVT
2012-13	BUF	25	42	1	6	7	3	0.55	40.3%	5.2	0.3	1.6	0.0	1.8
2013-14	BUF	26	68	1	8	9	-29	0.45	39.0%	7.1	-1.7	0.7	0.0	-1.0
2014-15	BUF	27	64	1	6	7	-22	0.35	37.2%	6.1	-1.8	-0.2	0.0	-2.0
2015-16	BUF	28	52	1	6	7					-1.0	1.2	0.0	0.2

After showing some promise early in his career, Pittsburgh native Mike Weber had settled into a career as a third-pairing defenseman. However, over the past two seasons, he has been asked to play much more than he is capable of, averaging nearly 19 minutes per game. Back in 2010-11, on a playoff team, he was on the ice for just under 17 minutes against third and fourth lines. Until he gets back into a reasonable role, it will be hard to say whether Weber still belongs in an NHL lineup or not.

Nikita Zadorov — LD — COL

Season	Team	Age	GP	G	A	Pts	+/-	ESP/60	AdjCF%	iCF/60	OGVT	DGVT	SGVT	GVT
2013-14	BUF	18	7	1	0	1	-4	0.54	37.1%	4.4	0.1	-0.2	0.0	-0.2
2014-15	BUF	19	60	3	12	15	-10	0.63	37.9%	4.8	-1.0	1.3	0.0	0.4
2015-16	COL	20	56	3	13	16					-0.1	2.1	0.0	2.0

Nikita Zadorov showed up to camp out of shape and rode the pine for the first month. When he finally cracked the lineup, the six-foot-five blueliner demonstrated some serious potential, throwing wrecking-ball hits and exceptional skating skill for his size, while tossing in some offense to boot. He also developed quick chemistry with the Sabres' future number-one defenseman Rasmus Ristolainen. Unfortunately, Zadorov continued to show commitment issues, being suspended multiple times for showing up late to practice. Buffalo's management was concerned enough about the young Russian to part ways with him as part of the O'Reilly trade with Colorado. If he starts taking his job seriously, Zadorov could become a force for the Avs.

GOALTENDERS

Matt Hackett — G — ANA

Season	Team	Age	GP	W	L	OT	GAA	Sv%	ESSV%	QS%	GGVT	DGVT	SGVT	GVT
2012-13	MIN	22	1	0	1	0	5.08	.848	.909	0.0%	-1.7	0.0	0.0	-1.7
2013-14	BUF	23	8	1	6	1	3.10	.908	.912	50.0%	-0.2	-0.3	0.0	-0.5
2014-15	BUF	24	5	0	4	1	4.32	.884	.898	25.0%	-3.5	-0.3	0.0	-3.8
2015-16	ANA	25	13					.912			0.2	-0.2	0.0	0.0

It must be nice to have a name. The nephew of former Blackhawks goalie Jeff Hackett has never shown any capability to be an NHL goaltender, but he continues to get chances. Matt Hackett was one of the worst goalies in the AHL over the past two seasons, with a horrendous .898 save percentage in 2013-14 for the Rochester Americans, followed up by a .904 in 2014-15. Therefore, it should come as no shock that he was smoked by NHL competition over five games, giving up 4.32 goals against per contest. Yet, somehow, the Ducks signed him to a two-year contract. Hmmm.

Anders Lindback — G — ARI

Season	Team	Age	GP	W	L	OT	GAA	Sv%	ESSV%	QS%	GGVT	DGVT	SGVT	GVT
2012-13	TBL	24	24	10	10	1	2.90	.902	.903	47.6%	-2.8	-0.1	-0.2	-3.1
2013-14	TBL	25	23	8	12	2	2.90	.891	.911	38.9%	-8.2	0.6	1.1	-6.5
2014-15	DAL, BUF	26	26	6	16	2	3.11	.909	.914	40.9%	-1.0	-1.0	0.4	-1.6
2015-16	ARI	27	22					.910			-0.9	-0.2	0.1	-1.0

Potential, potential, potential. Every team that signs Anders Lindback believes he will finally figure it out under their tutelage. And every time, he disappoints. Except for a tiny stint in Buffalo in which he posted a .924 save percentage over 15 starts, the 27-year-old behemoth has statistically been one of poorest goalies in the NHL, including playing a major role in sinking the Dallas Stars' season, winning just two of his 10 starts. Because of his size, however, he will keep getting big-league jobs, including backstopping Arizona in 2015-16.

Andrey Makarov — G — BUF

Season	Team	Age	GP	W	L	OT	GAA	Sv%	ESSV%	QS%	GGVT	DGVT	SGVT	GVT
2014-15	BUF	21	1	0	1	0	3.00	.917	.939	100.0%	0.2	-0.1	0.0	0.1
2015-16	BUF	22	13					.915			1.5	-0.1	0.0	1.4

Young Russian Andrey Makarov got his first sniff of the NHL, though he didn't exactly earn it with his minor-league play. At 21, his youth was taken advantage of by opponents as he recorded a below-average .905 save percentage in Rochester. As an undersized goalie, he will have to make a ton of progress in technique in order to see NHL time again

Matthew Coller

Calgary Flames

The Calgary Flames have set themselves up for critical viewing. On the heels of a 2014-15 season in which they bucked virtually every analytical indicator, to not only make the playoffs but progress to the second round, expectations are raised for this young club in the future. Finishing the season ranked 24th in score-adjusted Corsi in all situations (46.6%), the Flames had the worst possession results of any playoff team, comparable to the 2013-14 Colorado Avalanche (47.0%) and the 2012-13 Toronto Maple Leafs (45.7%). Both the Avalanche and Leafs doubled down on the style of high-percentage, poor-possession hockey that they felt was leading to sustainable success...and both teams saw their shooting and save percentages regress heavily the following season on their way to a tumble down the standings. At least Calgary appears to be avoiding the trap of resting on its laurels, unconvinced that what worked this past season will work again in the future.

What most Flames followers should expect is a bit more balance to the team's results in 2015-16. Consider that the top eight scorers for Calgary all hit career highs in points. In the case of the under-25 crowd—Gaudreau, Monahan, Brodie, and Bouma—those numbers may presage future production. However, regression is likely for the squad's veterans, particularly those over the age of 30—Hudler, Wideman, and Giordano—all of whom have a significant track record that last season deviated from.

In net, Jonas Hiller compiled a solid rebound season as the main man for Calgary—following his departure from Anaheim as the primary starter—but he had the crease taken away from him in the playoffs by head coach Bob Hartley. His backup, Karri Ramo, was handed the reins despite struggling to produce replacement-caliber numbers in the postseason.

The Flames capitalized more than most on late-game heroics. Yet, they also had the second-best winning percentage when leading after the first period, and the fourth-best winning percentage when leading after the second period. This was a team that not only came back late but also managed to close out games when they had the lead. Despite their propensity for fantastic finishes, and good results in terms of holding leads, the Flames were ironically very average when the game was tied.

Stealing Hamilton?

It would appear the Flames are attempting to buck the trend of the anti-analytics fluke by beefing up their roster on the fly in the offseason. Their acquisition of young defen-

FLAMES IN A BOX

Last Season
Goals For	241	8th
Goals Against	216	t-14th
GVT	25	8th
Points	97	16th
Playoffs		Lost Conference Semifinal

The biggest surprise of 2014-15, Calgary took a hard-working lineup to an unexpected playoff berth.

Three-Year Record
GVT	-39	23rd
Points	216	23rd
Playoffs		1 Appearance, 5 Wins

VUKOTA Projection
Goals For	237	2nd
Goals Against	220	16th
GVT	17	4th
Points	97	4th

The Flames got lucky last year, but if they get Giordano for the whole year, they could be even better. The "wild card" team of 2015-16.

Top Three Prospects
S. Bennett (F), E. Poirier (F), M. Klimchuk (F)

seman Dougie Hamilton from Boston on draft day and the addition of veteran forward Michael Frolik as a pricey free agent on July 1 indicate that GM Brad Treliving is avoiding doubling down on the misconception that playing pond hockey is a sustainable method of long-term winning.

However, the additions do raise question marks around roster composition for the coming season. Hamilton becomes a highly-paid, highly-touted option on the blue line; the question is which of the incumbent top-four defenders' jobs he supplants. It won't be perennial Norris Trophy candidate and team captain Mark Giordano. That leaves one of T.J. Brodie, Dennis Wideman, and Kris Russell. Wideman and Russell played as a productive pair in the surprising stretch run while Giordano was out with injury, but Brodie has the most significant defensive impact of any skater and led the team in average ice-time.

Hamilton's impact is largely offensive, and his long-term contract sits in contrast to the soon-to-be-expiring deals of Russell and Wideman, who will be unrestricted free agents after the 2015-16 and 2016-17 seasons. Hamilton is a right-handed shot, and thus likely slots into the spot occupied by either Wideman or Brodie in the top four. Wideman is also right-handed, while Brodie is a left-handed skater playing the right side of the ice. Perhaps the best option would be to play Giordano and Hamilton on the left and right of the top pairing while shifting Brodie to the left to play his strong side with Wideman on the second unit. Playing Brodie and Giordano on separate pairs in the top four could also spread out their defensive impacts—sheltering their partners and improving Calgary's defensive game holistically by ensuring at least one of the two is on the ice for most of the game.

Hamilton averaged 21+ minutes with the Bruins while producing elite-level offense: 42 points in only 72 games, ranking in the top 20 defenders in points per game, alongside the likes of Shea Weber and Alex Pietrangelo. If we compare his expected shot-attempt results based on his usage, to those that actually took place with him on the ice, Hamilton outperformed his minutes to an absurdly high degree. Using multivariate regression, we can project that during five-on-five play, Hamilton should have been on the ice for 55.8 shot attempts per 60 minutes in 2014-15. In actuality, he was on the ice for 63.2 shot attempts per 60 minutes, a massive uptick in shot attempts with him present on the ice.

However, a word of caution is in order to those suggesting that Hamilton will be a panacea to the Flames possession woes. In comparing his results with and without Patrice Bergeron, his shot-attempt impacts become significantly muted in Bergeron's absence. The Bruins' Corsi For rate with Hamilton and Bergeron on the ice was 76.4 attempts per 60 minutes, yet when Hamilton was on the ice without Bergeron, it dropped to a much less impressive 55.2. While both values exceed expected results, the former does so to a massive degree (+22.4 attempts per 60) while the latter does so only marginally (+0.4 attempts per 60). The other reason for caution is the Hamilton-Bergeron synergy took place in a small segment of approximately 400 even-strength minutes.

Who's in goal?

The other major question mark for the Flames is in goal. In their Anaheim series, Hartley appeared to dissipate any remaining goodwill between himself and incumbent starter Hiller by pulling him and never returning to him in the series—despite poor play in the remaining games on the part of backup Karri Ramo—who Calgary has decided to bring back on a one-year, $3.9 million contract.

Essentially, the Flames are riding out one more year with the same duo that got them to round two of the playoffs, while banking on the development of prospect Joni Ortio for the future. Ortio has posted adequate AHL numbers, but his NHL results in brief showings don't indicate he is ready for an increased role yet.

The Flames need to see developmental progress from the youth on the roster, and would ideally like to see full, healthy seasons from possession linchpins like Mikael Backlund and Mark Giordano. If Calgary can improve their underlying play, particularly that of their top-six forwards and bottom-four defenders, they have the potential to consolidate their gains before making significant strides in the coming years.

Stephen Burtch

CALGARY FLAMES

Even-Strength Usage: Calgary Flames

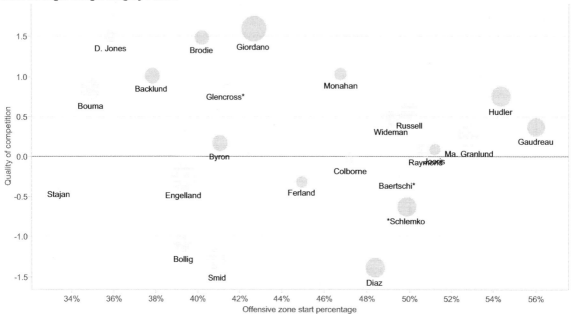

Special Teams Usage: Calgary Flames

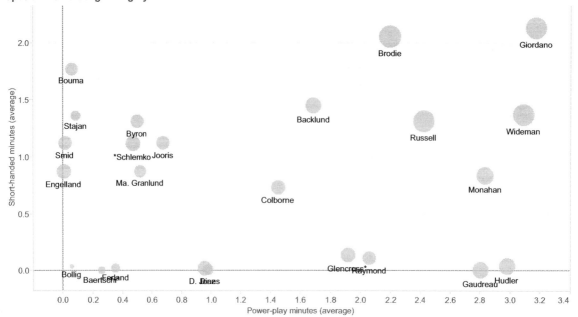

CALGARY FLAMES

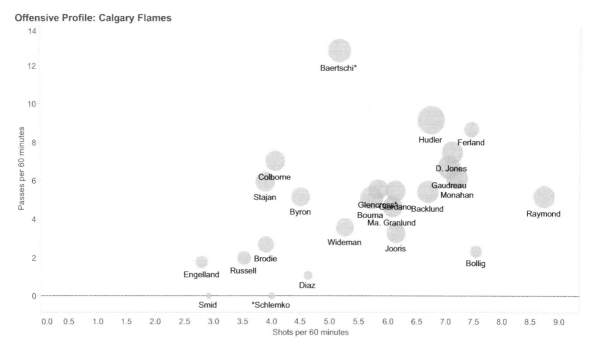

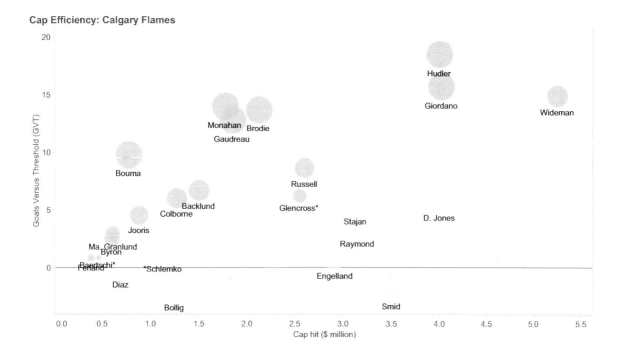

CALGARY FLAMES
FORWARDS

Mikael Backlund							C						CGY
Season	Team	Age	GP	G	A	Pts	+/-	ESP/60	AdjCF%	iCF/60	OGVT	DGVT	SGVT	GVT
2012-13	CGY	23	32	8	8	16	-6	1.69	50.4%	18.4	2.6	0.2	0.0	2.9
2013-14	CGY	24	76	18	21	39	4	1.29	51.1%	13.7	3.9	4.6	-0.6	7.9
2014-15	CGY	25	52	10	17	27	4	1.90	46.3%	13.2	4.0	2.7	0.0	6.7
2015-16	CGY	26	62	14	19	33					3.2	2.5	0.0	5.8

While he may no longer be the key to the future for Flames fans, Mikael Backlund's prodigious possession skills may be best served if he can fly under the radar a bit. Backlund's largest obstacle in his recent career has been staying healthy, missing a combined 93 games (32%) since the start of 2011-12. When the Vasteras product is on the ice, Calgary has been a far better possession side; since 2011, he has bumped up the team's Corsi percentage from 48.7% to 51.4% when on the ice. In fact, since entering the NHL as a rookie in 2009-10, Backlund has made a positive impact on possession in every season he has played. As an average offensive producer, he will never receive a Selke Trophy vote, but he is deserving.

Sam Bennett							C						CGY
Season	Team	Age	GP	G	A	Pts	+/-	ESP/60	AdjCF%	iCF/60	OGVT	DGVT	SGVT	GVT
2014-15	CGY	18	1	0	1	1	-1	3.97	59.3%	11.2	0.3	0.0	0.0	0.3
2015-16	CGY	19	31	6	8	14					1.1	0.4	0.0	1.4

The fourth-overall selection of the 2014 NHL Entry Draft, Sam Bennett had a chance at starting his first NHL season dashed when he needed surgery to repair a damaged shoulder. Having played through a shoulder separation for much of his draft year, Bennett reinjured the shoulder in a preseason game against Vancouver. Following his return to the OHL's Kingston Frontenacs, Bennett tallied an impressive 24 points in only 11 games, a rate better than any skater in the league except for super-phenom Connor McDavid. At the close of the year, Bennett got a shot at contributing to Calgary's playoff drive, suiting up for all 11 games of the Flames' surprising run to the second round. Based on his pedigree, performance, and skill level, Bennett will be in the NHL full time next season, likely in a sheltered scoring role.

Brandon Bollig							LW						CGY
Season	Team	Age	GP	G	A	Pts	+/-	ESP/60	AdjCF%	iCF/60	OGVT	DGVT	SGVT	GVT
2012-13	CHI	25	25	0	0	0	-1	0.00	59.0%	16.7	-1.5	0.2	0.0	-1.3
2013-14	CHI	26	82	7	7	14	-1	1.02	51.6%	13.6	-1.0	1.4	0.0	0.4
2014-15	CGY	27	62	1	4	5	-9	0.57	41.6%	13.0	-2.5	0.3	0.0	-2.2
2015-16	CGY	28	56	4	4	8					-1.5	0.9	0.0	-0.7

Added last offseason in a trade to clear cap space for the perennially-contending Blackhawks, Brandon Bollig was brought in to add some sandpaper and size to the bottom six. Possession-wise, Bollig exceeded expectations in tough minutes in Chicago, but failed to provide solid value in a similar role in Calgary. With two years remaining on his contract at an affordable $1.3 million cap hit, expect nothing more than replacement-level production from the veteran winger.

Lance Bouma — LW — CGY

Season	Team	Age	GP	G	A	Pts	+/-	ESP/60	AdjCF%	iCF/60	OGVT	DGVT	SGVT	GVT
2013-14	CGY	23	78	5	10	15	-4	1.04	43.0%	10.2	-1.8	3.6	0.0	1.8
2014-15	CGY	24	78	16	18	34	10	2.02	41.6%	10.6	5.1	4.7	0.0	9.8
2015-16	CGY	25	67	12	16	28					2.2	3.1	0.0	5.2

Entering the season, Lance Bouma's career shooting percentage was 5.1% on only 117 shots across three seasons. Out of nowhere, he suddenly started finding the twine, firing home 16 goals at 15.4% shooting on 104 shots. Even in the AHL with Adirondack, and WHL with the Vancouver Giants, he never broke the 14-goal plateau in a season, so to suggest he will reproduce those totals is a stretch to say the least. Unfortunately, his phantom breakout sets him up for increased expectations of offensive progress.

Paul Byron — C — CGY

Season	Team	Age	GP	G	A	Pts	+/-	ESP/60	AdjCF%	iCF/60	OGVT	DGVT	SGVT	GVT
2012-13	CGY	23	4	0	1	1	-2	1.57	37.9%	6.4	0.1	-0.1	0.0	0.0
2013-14	CGY	24	47	7	14	21	6	1.44	48.9%	8.2	2.7	2.6	0.6	5.9
2014-15	CGY	25	57	6	13	19	-2	1.33	45.8%	7.9	0.2	2.3	0.0	2.5
2015-16	CGY	26	54	8	14	22					1.2	2.1	0.0	3.3

Paul Byron is another piece in Calgary's underrated group of bottom-six forwards. An excellent skater who is dogged on the backcheck, Byron is extremely undersized at five-foot-seven and 155 pounds. Consequently, he will be a significant risk to miss time due to injury given his relatively physical style of play. Even with injury issues this past season, he played a career high 57 games, producing a modest six goals and 19 points. Considering that he is 26, contributes to possession very effectively on both sides of the puck, and is unlikely to ever eat up much cap space due to his third-line production level, Byron is an ideal fit in the bottom six.

Joe Colborne — C/LW — CGY

Season	Team	Age	GP	G	A	Pts	+/-	ESP/60	AdjCF%	iCF/60	OGVT	DGVT	SGVT	GVT
2012-13	TOR	22	5	0	0	0	-1	0.00	45.1%	6.8	-0.2	-0.1	0.0	-0.3
2013-14	CGY	23	80	10	18	28	-17	1.43	44.4%	7.1	0.6	1.5	1.0	3.2
2014-15	CGY	24	64	8	20	28	7	1.56	42.5%	7.0	3.3	2.9	-0.2	6.0
2015-16	CGY	25	62	10	18	27					1.8	1.9	0.0	3.8

Former Leaf Joe Colborne has recaptured the belief that he will one day develop into a top-six skater. In his second year with the Flames, Colborne received more opportunity in a consistent third-line role, and seemed to be discovering a physical edge in the playoffs to go along with his very impressive physical stature. Unfortunately, Colborne again seemed to be suffering ill effects from a prior wrist injury, leading him to seek out a specialist at season's end. Should the problems again hamper Colborne's offensive performance, his roster spot may be in called into question as other prospects climb up to challenge for it.

Micheal Ferland — LW — CGY

Season	Team	Age	GP	G	A	Pts	+/-	ESP/60	AdjCF%	iCF/60	OGVT	DGVT	SGVT	GVT
2014-15	CGY	22	26	2	3	5	1	0.91	45.2%	13.64	0.3	0.5	0	0.8
2015-16	CGY	23	42	8	9	17					1.4	1.0	0.9	2.4

Young winger Micheal Ferland is hoping to continue his development into a prototypical power forward. The 22-year-old rookie's rambunctious, physical style of play was extremely entertaining when paired with his natural gifts. His performance in the playoffs, particularly his 40-hit, burr-in-the-saddle showing against the Canucks in the opening round, teased fans with what he may provide over the long term. Defensively, Ferland was effective as an injury fill-in alongside Stajan and Jones, and unlike Bouma, his offense was not predicated on a bizarre inflation in shooting percentage. Ferland's 26 regular-season and eight playoff games showed he has significant potential as an energy player, and his offensive production at lower levels gives hope that his heavy shot and size will lead to more output at the NHL level.

Johnny Gaudreau — LW — CGY

Season	Team	Age	GP	G	A	Pts	+/-	ESP/60	AdjCF%	iCF/60	OGVT	DGVT	SGVT	GVT
2013-14	CGY	20	1	1	0	1	1	4.39	54.2%	8.4	0.4	0.1	0.0	0.5
2014-15	CGY	21	80	24	40	64	11	2.16	45.9%	11.2	8.9	3.7	0.2	12.8
2015-16	CGY	22	77	28	42	70					10.0	2.7	0.0	12.7

"Johnny Hockey" electrified the hockey world with his show-stopping, highlight-reel performances in college, and then he brought his act to the Big Show with the Flames, never missing a beat. Initial concerns around his size and ability to cope with physical play evaporated as the season wore on. Gaudreau only absorbed 44 recorded hits all season, plus another seven in the playoffs. If teams want to slow him down, they will likely have to find more success in tracking him down physically than 51 hits in 91 games, though his shifty skating makes that particularly difficult. Eventually, the Boston College Eagle found himself on the top line with Sean Monahan and Jiri Hudler, seeing his ice-time rise from an average of 14:29 in October to over 19 minutes per game in March and April. He proved to relish the primetime role, and will grow further into it moving forward. While his defensive performance was significantly below that of an average NHL skater, his unique offensive skillset and explosiveness more than compensate. Expect his scoring to increase next season.

Markus Granlund — C — CGY

Season	Team	Age	GP	G	A	Pts	+/-	ESP/60	AdjCF%	iCF/60	OGVT	DGVT	SGVT	GVT
2013-14	CGY	20	7	2	1	3	2	1.70	44.3%	8.0	0.7	0.4	0.0	1.1
2014-15	CGY	21	48	8	10	18	-4	1.67	40.6%	11.5	1.4	1.4	0.0	2.9
2015-16	CGY	22	53	11	14	25					2.0	1.6	0.0	3.6

Being the second Granlund was always likely to pin expectations on Markus. Older brother Mikael went ninth overall to Minnesota in the 2010 NHL Entry Draft, while Markus lasted until the 45th pick a year later for Calgary. Being the lesser of two extremely talented players isn't a bad thing, though. Markus has had to work harder to make his entry to the NHL, but finally, after two full seasons against men in Finland's Liiga and a full year in the AHL with Adirondack, Granlund suited up for 48 regular-season and three playoff games for Calgary. The main weaknesses in his game are defensive, and he put up abysmal numbers at the faceoff dot (36.8%). He was deployed largely in a sheltered third-line role, though he occasionally saw promotion due to injury. The knocks on Granlund's defensive play will likely continue, but given his offensive potential, he is worth developing.

CALGARY FLAMES

Jiri Hudler — C — CGY

Season	Team	Age	GP	G	A	Pts	+/-	ESP/60	AdjCF%	iCF/60	OGVT	DGVT	SGVT	GVT
2012-13	CGY	28	42	10	17	27	-13	1.90	46.6%	6.9	3.6	0.1	0.2	3.9
2013-14	CGY	29	75	17	37	54	4	2.09	45.7%	7.8	6.7	3.6	0.1	10.4
2014-15	CGY	30	78	31	45	76	17	3.08	46.4%	10.3	14.0	4.3	0.2	18.5
2015-16	CGY	31	71	23	37	59					8.1	2.7	0.0	10.8

Former Red Wing Jiri Hudler is unlikely to replicate his 2014-15 season ever again, though Flames fans live in the hope it wasn't a one-time show. The Lady Byng Memorial Trophy recipient lit up the hockey world with his awesome shoeless acceptance speech, in addition to producing impressively on the ice. The five-foot-nine Czech forward registered career highs in goals (31), assists (45), and points (76), leading the Flames in all three categories. His offensive production continued into the playoffs, where he produced four goals and eight points in the surprising 11-game run. Hudler's possession stats were the worst of his career, but given his elite offensive production, that can be taken with a grain of salt. At age 31, it is unlikely he will match last year's totals, but if his talented young linemates Monahan and Gaudreau trend upwards, Hudler could continue to generate impressive scoring totals in the top-line role.

David Jones — RW — CGY

Season	Team	Age	GP	G	A	Pts	+/-	ESP/60	AdjCF%	iCF/60	OGVT	DGVT	SGVT	GVT
2012-13	COL	28	33	3	6	9	-11	1.08	45.9%	11.6	-0.7	0.3	0.0	-0.4
2013-14	CGY	29	48	9	8	17	1	1.38	44.6%	13.6	0.9	1.9	0.0	2.8
2014-15	CGY	30	67	14	16	30	-3	1.88	44.0%	12.9	3.7	1.7	0.0	5.4
2015-16	CGY	31	59	13	15	28					2.6	1.7	0.0	4.2

David Jones had an admirably productive season in the bottom six. The Dartmouth College product and long-time Av faced exceptionally challenging usage, with the highest expected rate of even-strength shot attempts against for any regular NHL skater not playing for the Sabres (64.0 attempts per 60 minutes). Nevertheless, Jones managed to produce a solid 14 goals and 30 points in 67 games while averaging his lowest ice-time in the last six years. His 16 even-strength assists were a career high. His offense may not sustain as he enters his thirties, but his size and decent hands will continue to provide value in a third- or fourth-line role.

Josh Jooris — RW — CGY

Season	Team	Age	GP	G	A	Pts	+/-	ESP/60	AdjCF%	iCF/60	OGVT	DGVT	SGVT	GVT
2014-15	CGY	24	60	12	12	24	1	1.50	45.9%	11.1	1.9	2.2	0.4	4.5
2015-16	CGY	25	60	12	14	26					1.1	1.9	0.0	3.0

Suiting up for 60 regular-season and nine playoff games following an eye-opening preseason camp, Josh Jooris had a successful rookie season. The three-year Union College man had turned heads at his first camp prior to the 2013-14 season, but he followed that up with a relatively pedestrian rookie season in the AHL. His dogged determination doesn't appear likely to lead to high-level offense, but his possession impacts were positive at both ends of the ice. His versatility in being able to play both center and wing positions and win a reasonable number of faceoffs will also serve him in good stead.

CALGARY FLAMES

Brian McGrattan							LW						ANA
Season	Team	Age	GP	G	A	Pts	+/-	ESP/60	AdjCF%	iCF/60	OGVT	DGVT	SGVT	GVT
2012-13	NSH, CGY	31	21	3	0	3	-4	1.21	39.8%	12.5	0.2	0.0	0.0	0.2
2013-14	CGY	32	76	4	4	8	-4	0.95	37.8%	14.5	-1.2	1.2	0.0	-0.1
2014-15	CGY	33	8	0	0	0	-2	0.00	40.6%	16.3	-0.4	-0.1	0.0	-0.5
2015-16	ANA	34	40	4	4	7					-0.3	0.7	0.0	0.4

Veteran tough guy Brian McGrattan closed out his third consecutive year with the Flames organization plying his trade in Adirondack, suiting up for only eight games with Calgary, registering four penalty minutes. Regarded as one of the NHL's premier enforcers during his career, McGrattan's brand of rough-and-tumble play appears to have been in slow decline. Declarations of the death of the role may have been premature though, as Anaheim has signed him to a one-year contract for $600,000. Hoping to resuscitate his career in Southern California, McGrattan is likely to drop the gloves early and often to make a case for his value to his new team.

Sean Monahan							C						CGY
Season	Team	Age	GP	G	A	Pts	+/-	ESP/60	AdjCF%	iCF/60	OGVT	DGVT	SGVT	GVT
2013-14	CGY	19	75	22	12	34	-20	1.58	42.8%	11.8	2.8	1.2	2.2	6.1
2014-15	CGY	20	81	31	31	62	8	1.90	45.2%	12.1	10.1	3.7	0.2	14.0
2015-16	CGY	21	76	29	30	59					8.1	2.3	0.0	10.5

Boring Sean Monahan (it's a Twitter reference) has been anything but boring on the ice for the Flames since joining the club as a rookie two years ago. Tying for the Flames team lead in goals this past season at 31 and leading with 10 power-play markers, Monahan has cemented himself as a fixture on the top line between "Johnny Hockey" and Flames leading scorer Jiri Hudler. The The sixth-overall pick in 2013 has set a goal-scoring pace that is unlikely to dry up given his 16.0% shooting through a combined 156 career games at the NHL level. Assuming he can regularly generate around 200 shots in coming seasons, he should be good for 25 goals even in an off-year.

Emile Poirier							LW						CGY
Season	Team	Age	GP	G	A	Pts	+/-	ESP/60	AdjCF%	iCF/60	OGVT	DGVT	SGVT	GVT
2014-15	CGY	20	6	0	1	1	1	1.28	37.6%	8.0	0.1	0.2	0.0	0.3
2015-16	CGY	21	28	5	6	11					0.8	0.6	0.0	1.4

Emile Poirier, Calgary's first-round selection in the 2013 NHL Entry Draft, is a gifted scorer with a knack for finding seams in the offensive zone that allows him to get off an above-average shot. Poirier has produced offensively at every level, and last season was no different, when he made his full-time transition to the pro game, suiting up for 55 games with Adirondack. He earned selection to the AHL All-Star Game, after producing 19 goals and 42 points as a 20-year-old, and ranking second on Adirondack in scoring. Poirier was rewarded with a six-game promotion to Calgary, but is likely to continue to work on developing his play away from the puck in the AHL.

CALGARY FLAMES

Mason Raymond						RW							CGY
Season	Team	Age	GP	G	A	Pts	+/-	ESP/60	AdjCF%	iCF/60	OGVT	DGVT	SGVT	GVT
2012-13	VAN	27	46	10	12	22	2	1.66	49.4%	11.6	1.9	1.8	-0.1	3.6
2013-14	TOR	28	82	19	26	45	-6	1.67	43.6%	12.7	5.9	0.7	-0.2	6.5
2014-15	CGY	29	57	12	11	23	-8	1.83	42.7%	14.8	2.6	0.8	-0.3	3.2
2015-16	CGY	30	59	14	17	31					3.2	1.1	0.0	4.3

After joining the Flames, Mason Raymond's role was ratcheted back—he received less ice-time as a supporting veteran further down the lineup. The former Canuck and Leaf was also hampered by injury, missing 18 midseason games. Despite the upper-body injury, he produced well offensively at even strength, leading the team with 1.04 goals per 60 minutes. He also produced shooting opportunities at an elite rate (15.3 shots per 60 minutes), with Gaudreau the only Flame superior to Raymond in this regard. His late-season performance saw him sporadically shuffled off to the pressbox as a healthy scratch a couple of times in the playoffs. This may portend less of a role for Raymond in the future, particularly as the Flames attempt to inject more youth into the top half of their forward group.

Max Reinhart						C							NSH
Season	Team	Age	GP	G	A	Pts	+/-	ESP/60	AdjCF%	iCF/60	OGVT	DGVT	SGVT	GVT
2012-13	CGY	20	11	1	2	3	-3	0.87	43.5%	14.0	-0.1	0.1	0.0	0.0
2013-14	CGY	21	8	0	2	2	1	1.50	42.5%	11.2	-0.1	0.3	0.0	0.2
2014-15	CGY	22	4	0	0	0	-3	0.00	42.2%	20.2	-0.4	-0.2	0.0	-0.6
2015-16	NSH	23	26	4	5	9					0.4	0.5	0.0	1.0

Max Reinhart had three cups of coffee with Calgary, beginning in 2012-13. Coming into training camp, Reinhart was considered to be in the mix for an NHL roster spot, but a lower-body injury in preseason put a damper on that. Last season, he again only saw spot duty with the big club as an injury replacement, but his four games (each cup of coffee has gotten smaller) saw him held pointless. After a down year in the AHL, it seems the Calgary organization soured on his development as he was dealt to Nashville in exchange for a conditional fourth-round pick.

Devin Setoguchi						RW							Free Agent
Season	Team	Age	GP	G	A	Pts	+/-	ESP/60	AdjCF%	iCF/60	OGVT	DGVT	SGVT	GVT
2012-13	MIN	26	48	13	14	27	5	2.11	48.1%	13.0	4.0	2.2	0.0	6.2
2013-14	WPG	27	75	11	16	27	-7	1.45	48.5%	11.6	2.1	0.4	1.3	3.8
2014-15	CGY	28	12	0	0	0	-7	0.00	42.9%	8.8	-1.7	-0.4	0.0	-2.1
2015-16	Free Agent	29	43	6	8	15					0.4	0.6	0.0	1.1

The Devin Setoguchi experiment did not last long in Calgary. The long-time Shark played 12 games with the Flames at the start of the season and produced no points, finding himself as a healthy scratch on 11 other occasions. He was demoted to the AHL at the end of November and appeared in 19 games there over the remainder of a season marred by a sports hernia. With the way things have been going, Setoguchi was lucky to get a gig in Toronto.

Drew Shore — C/RW — CGY

Season	Team	Age	GP	G	A	Pts	+/-	ESP/60	AdjCF%	iCF/60	OGVT	DGVT	SGVT	GVT
2012-13	FLA	21	43	3	10	13	-10	0.90	53.5%	13.9	-0.8	1.0	0.0	0.2
2013-14	FLA	22	24	5	2	7	-1	1.34	49.5%	8.4	1.1	0.4	0.0	1.5
2014-15	CGY	23	11	1	2	3	-5	1.62	39.0%	11.3	0.1	-0.2	-0.3	-0.4
2015-16	CGY	24	32	6	6	12					0.8	0.5	0.0	1.3

Drew Shore was acquired in a January trade with Florida in exchange for Corban Knight. The 24-year-old AHL All-Star has had forays to the NHL level on three occasions, with his most effective year coming at age 21 in a half season of games as a bottom-six skater for the Panthers. His brief 11-game stint in Calgary showed that while his ability to drive offensive play followed him north, the significant uptick in defensive workload that came with playing in the Flames system was mildly overwhelming. His versatility to play both in the middle as a natural center, or on the right side where the Flames have more opportunity, will likely serve him in good stead.

Matt Stajan — C — CGY

Season	Team	Age	GP	G	A	Pts	+/-	ESP/60	AdjCF%	iCF/60	OGVT	DGVT	SGVT	GVT
2012-13	CGY	29	43	5	18	23	7	2.15	47.6%	6.3	1.7	4.4	0.0	6.1
2013-14	CGY	30	63	14	19	33	-13	1.73	46.4%	6.8	3.2	3.3	0.0	6.5
2014-15	CGY	31	59	7	10	17	7	1.54	44.3%	8.2	1.9	2.9	0.0	4.8
2015-16	CGY	32	55	8	13	21					1.4	2.0	0.0	3.3

Matt Stajan is one of the more underappreciated centers in the NHL. Handed some of the toughest minutes of any pivot in the league, he regularly outperforms defensive expectations and quietly generates a respectable level of offense for a bottom-six skater, regularly exceeding 1.50 even-strength points per 60 minutes. His PDO was an astronomical 1036, largely the result of an unsustainable .956 save percentage behind him, not unrealistic shooting on the part of him or his primary linemates. An affordable option just entering his thirties, Stajan will continue to be a useful—if often injured—supporting piece.

David Wolf — LW — CGY

Season	Team	Age	GP	G	A	Pts	+/-	ESP/60	AdjCF%	iCF/60	OGVT	DGVT	SGVT	GVT
2014-15	CGY	25	3	0	0	0	0	0.00	48.7%	8.0	-0.1	0.0	0.0	0.0
2015-16	CGY	26	27	5	6	10					0.5	0.6	0.0	1.1

David Wolf finally got a shot in the NHL after a number of years plying his trade in the German Elite League. The six-foot-three, 215-pound winger was productive in his initial foray into the AHL, tallying 20 goals and 38 points to go along with 168 penalty minutes in a rambunctious 59 games. They were good numbers, especially given Wolf's acknowledged difficulties getting out of the gate—due to a summer without much on-ice training along with adjusting to the smaller North American ice. Despite making a strong impression, Wolf elected to head back to his home country for next season.

CALGARY FLAMES

DEFENSEMEN

TJ Brodie — LD — CGY

Season	Team	Age	GP	G	A	Pts	+/-	ESP/60	AdjCF%	iCF/60	OGVT	DGVT	SGVT	GVT
2012-13	CGY	22	47	2	12	14	-9	0.58	49.7%	5.7	1.9	0.5	0.0	2.4
2013-14	CGY	23	81	4	27	31	0	0.80	50.8%	7.4	3.2	6.7	-0.3	9.6
2014-15	CGY	24	81	11	30	41	15	1.02	45.2%	7.3	6.9	6.8	0.0	13.7
2015-16	CGY	25	75	8	27	35					4.5	5.0	0.0	9.4

T.J. Brodie has done nothing but impress since entering the NHL full time in 2011-12. His ice-time, defensive responsibility, offensive production, and impacts on possession have increased consistently since his rookie season. He led all Flames skaters in ice-time, posted a career-high 11 goals and 41 points, and had the seventh-most significant shot suppression impact of all NHL defenders. Brodie faced challenging defensive minutes, but used his exceptional mobility and instincts to perform at a very high level. When playing alongside Mark Giordano, they are one of the elite pairings in the league.

Raphael Diaz — RD — NYR

Season	Team	Age	GP	G	A	Pts	+/-	ESP/60	AdjCF%	iCF/60	OGVT	DGVT	SGVT	GVT
2012-13	MTL	26	23	1	13	14	4	1.05	48.1%	6.7	2.9	1.4	0.0	4.3
2013-14	MTL, VAN, NYR	27	63	2	13	15	-2	0.66	50.3%	9.7	1.7	1.8	-0.3	3.2
2014-15	CGY	28	56	2	2	4	-3	0.29	45.2%	9.6	-1.3	0.7	0.0	-0.6
2015-16	NYR	29	50	2	6	8					-0.2	1.5	0.0	1.3

Signed late last offseason by the Flames on a cheap one-year deal to fill the role of seventh defender, Raphael Diaz eventually became a regular in the lineup due to injuries. In an odd shift for a right-shooting defender, he predominantly patrolled the left side on a pairing with Deryk Engelland, propping up a defensively-suspect partner with solid puck-handling and passing abilities that helped keep said partner out of trouble defensively. Diaz's distinct lack of physicality and the perception that he should produce more points than he did on a third pairing of one of the worst possession teams in hockey combine to give the perception that he is barely a replacement-level skater. His underlying performance definitely indicates otherwise.

Deryk Engelland — RD — CGY

Season	Team	Age	GP	G	A	Pts	+/-	ESP/60	AdjCF%	iCF/60	OGVT	DGVT	SGVT	GVT
2012-13	PIT	30	42	0	6	6	5	0.66	48.2%	6.4	-0.1	1.3	0.0	1.2
2013-14	PIT	31	56	6	6	12	-6	0.99	44.8%	7.9	2.1	0.9	0.0	3.0
2014-15	CGY	32	76	2	9	11	-16	0.58	40.0%	6.6	0.1	0.5	0.0	0.6
2015-16	CGY	33	55	2	7	9					0.0	1.2	0.0	1.2

Ex-Penguin Deryk Engelland was brought in to provide grit and toughness on the blueline in a bottom-pairing role similar to what the Flames were looking for up front from Brandon Bollig. Unfortunately, Engelland is paid significantly more than Bollig, over double the cap hit with an annual cost of almost $3 million. The six-foot-two, 216- pound Engelland also provides far less effective defensive performance. However, his role is limited and thus so is his negative impact.

CALGARY FLAMES

Mark Giordano								RD						CGY
Season	Team	Age	GP	G	A	Pts	+/-	ESP/60	AdjCF%	iCF/60	OGVT	DGVT	SGVT	GVT
2012-13	CGY	29	47	4	11	15	-7	0.70	46.6%	7.5	-0.2	3.3	0.0	3.1
2013-14	CGY	30	64	14	33	47	12	1.18	52.8%	13.8	9.8	6.5	0.0	16.3
2014-15	CGY	31	61	11	37	48	13	1.63	47.8%	12.0	10.4	5.4	0.0	15.7
2015-16	CGY	32	65	10	32	43					7.4	4.4	0.0	11.7

32-year-old Mark Giordano has been playing at a Norris-worthy level for the past two seasons. His main obstacle to being named the best defender in the NHL has been injury. In each of the past two seasons, he has provided some of the most significant possession impacts of any skater in the NHL while also providing elite-level offense, ranking second in points per game (0.76) amongst defenders, trailing only two-time Norris winner Erik Karlsson. Due to his age and potential decline, there are some concerns over his recently-signed contract that keeps him with the Flames through 2022. However, the remainder of his prime years will be worth every penny, even if there is a slip on the back end of the deal.

Brett Kulak								LD						CGY
Season	Team	Age	GP	G	A	Pts	+/-	ESP/60	AdjCF%	iCF/60	OGVT	DGVT	SGVT	GVT
2014-15	CGY	20	1	0	0	0	0	0.00	59.6%	3.4	0.0	0.0	0.0	0.0
2015-16	CGY	21	25	2	5	7					0.4	0.8	0.0	1.2

Brett Kulak spent the majority of his first year as a full-time professional in the ECHL with the Colorado Eagles. He was demoted in early November after only slotting into six AHL games through October and producing a single point, finding himself lower on the depth chart than fellow puck-moving defender and 2012 fourth-round draft pick Ryan Culkin. When Culkin went down with injury in February, Kulak got the return call and didn't waste the opportunity, producing six points in his first nine games back in the AHL. His solid offensive performance and decent defensive showing eventually earned him a single-game call-up to the big club in April.

Corey Potter								RD						Free Agent
Season	Team	Age	GP	G	A	Pts	+/-	ESP/60	AdjCF%	iCF/60	OGVT	DGVT	SGVT	GVT
2012-13	EDM	28	33	3	1	4	8	0.37	46.3%	8.7	-0.1	2.0	0.0	1.8
2013-14	EDM, BOS	29	19	0	5	5	-1	0.80	42.5%	6.7	0.2	0.4	0.0	0.6
2014-15	CGY	30	6	0	0	0	-1	0.00	52.5%	6.1	-0.1	-0.1	0.0	-0.2
2015-16	Free Agent	31	28	1	5	6					0.0	0.8	0.0	0.8

Corey Potter spent the majority of the campaign recovering from offseason shoulder surgery, then as a reserve blueliner, suiting up in only six regular-season and two playoff games. The 31-year-old journeyman has slotted in as a replacement-level defender for much of his nine years as a professional, with solid AHL production and limited showings at the NHL level.

John Ramage								RD						CBJ
Season	Team	Age	GP	G	A	Pts	+/-	ESP/60	AdjCF%	iCF/60	OGVT	DGVT	SGVT	GVT
2014-15	CGY	23	1	0	0	0	-1	0.00	55.3%	13.1	0.0	0.0	0.0	0.0
2015-16	CBJ	24	25	2	5	7					0.5	0.8	0.0	1.3

CALGARY FLAMES

Following a full four-year stint in the NCAA with the University of Wisconsin and playing most of two seasons in AHL Abbotsford, John Ramage finally got an NHL game. The son of former first-overall draft pick and member of the 1989 Stanley Cup champion Flames, defender Rob Ramage, John was the captain of a middling Badgers club for two years and captained the USA entry at the 2011 World Juniors tournament. He was at his most successful in college when he was using his physical defensive play to backstop the freewheeling tendencies of blueline partners like Brendan Smith. Ramage's leadership abilities and his game as a physical, shutdown-style defender mean he has value to teams in a depth role, but his lack of offensive upside limits his pro ceiling.

Kris Russell — LD — CGY

Season	Team	Age	GP	G	A	Pts	+/-	ESP/60	AdjCF%	iCF/60	OGVT	DGVT	SGVT	GVT
2012-13	STL	25	33	1	6	7	6	0.61	51.4%	9.1	0.2	2.5	0.0	2.7
2013-14	CGY	26	68	7	22	29	-11	0.73	43.0%	8.1	2.3	2.7	-0.3	4.7
2014-15	CGY	27	79	4	30	34	18	0.75	42.9%	7.7	2.2	6.4	0.0	8.6
2015-16	CGY	28	69	6	25	31					2.9	3.9	0.0	6.8

Kris Russell has turned the idea of a defensive defender who is perennially under siege into an art form. He earns regular plaudits for his shot blocking, but unlike many skaters who receive that sort of recognition, Russell's is well deserved. Last season, he led all regular defenders in proportion of shot attempts blocked at 14.0%, which was 1.3% higher than the next closest skater. He also ranked third in the NHL in shot-blocking contributions, as he was responsible for the third-largest percentage of blocks by his team while he was on the ice (44.0%). Unfortunately, blocking the puck means your team does not have possession of it. This reflects Russell's possession results, which were abysmal last season as they have been for his entire tenure in Calgary. With a pairing of Russell and Wideman in the top four, it seems unlikely the team will be able to stay above 50% possession in the near future.

David Schlemko — LD — Free Agent

Season	Team	Age	GP	G	A	Pts	+/-	ESP/60	AdjCF%	iCF/60	OGVT	DGVT	SGVT	GVT
2012-13	PHX	25	30	1	5	6	8	0.86	48.9%	8.7	0.2	1.9	0.5	2.6
2013-14	PHX	26	48	1	8	9	2	0.56	53.4%	9.8	-0.3	2.2	0.0	1.9
2014-15	ARI, DAL, CGY	27	44	1	3	4	1	0.20	49.2%	8.4	-1.6	2.0	0.4	0.7
2015-16	Free Agent	28	47	1	7	8					-0.8	2.2	0.0	1.4

David Schlemko finished his season with Calgary in respectable fashion as a consistent contributor to the team's third defensive pairing with solid possession results. After starting the season in Arizona, Schlemko was claimed on waivers twice, first by Dallas and then Calgary. The former Medicine Hat Tiger doesn't put up boxcar stats and is not known as an exceptional passer, but his teams tend to produce shot attempts at a higher than expected rate.

Lasdislav Smid — LD — CGY

Season	Team	Age	GP	G	A	Pts	+/-	ESP/60	AdjCF%	iCF/60	OGVT	DGVT	SGVT	GVT
2012-13	EDM	26	48	1	3	4	-1	0.22	44.3%	5.3	-1.7	2.0	0.0	0.3
2013-14	EDM, CGY	27	73	2	6	8	-10	0.41	40.5%	4.2	-1.5	3.4	0.0	1.9
2014-15	CGY	28	31	0	1	1	-12	0.15	41.3%	6.1	-1.3	-0.4	0.0	-1.7
2015-16	CGY	29	46	1	4	5					-0.9	1.4	0.0	0.5

CALGARY FLAMES

Ladislav Smid spent most of the past season recovering from a neck injury, only skating in 31 games for the Flames. Prior to his injury, he was utilized as a bottom-pair, shutdown defender, averaging the lowest ice-time (13:58) of his career in the process. He did a decent job defensively given what is expected in that role. Offensively, Smid has never been a contributor. His one point was not unusual; he hasn't broken the eight-point barrier for the past five seasons.

Dennis Wideman							RD							CGY
Season	Team	Age	GP	G	A	Pts	+/-	ESP/60	AdjCF%	iCF/60	OGVT	DGVT	SGVT	GVT
2012-13	CGY	29	46	6	16	22	-9	0.54	47.0%	9.4	2.5	2.1	0.0	4.6
2013-14	CGY	30	46	4	17	21	-15	1.14	44.8%	10.7	1.9	1.8	0.0	3.7
2014-15	CGY	31	80	15	41	56	6	1.30	42.8%	9.5	10.5	4.3	0.0	14.9
2015-16	CGY	32	69	10	33	43					6.6	3.4	0.0	10.0

At age 31, Dennis Wideman posted career highs with 15 goals and 56 points, followed by another seven assists in 11 postseason games. He also averaged his highest ice-time since his 25-year-old season in Boston (24:39), which was also the last time he produced 50 points. The question with Wideman has never been his offense, but he will go long stretches stuck in his own end defensively. As long as the rest of the team can shelter him, he can continue to be an effective point producer.

Tyler Wotherspoon							LD							CGY
Season	Team	Age	GP	G	A	Pts	+/-	ESP/60	AdjCF%	iCF/60	OGVT	DGVT	SGVT	GVT
2013-14	CGY	20	14	0	4	4	-3	1.28	39.7%	5.1	0.5	0.3	0.0	0.8
2014-15	CGY	21	1	0	0	0	-3	0.00	43.6%	10.8	0.0	0.0	0.0	0.0
2015-16	CGY	22	29	2	5	7					0.1	0.9	0.0	1.0

Only suited up for one regular-season game, 21-year-old Tyler Wotherspoon got to soak up the atmosphere in six playoff games through the Flames' unexpected run. His contributions at the AHL level significantly improved as a second-year professional: he recorded 24 points in 64 games with Adirondack. The former Portland Winter Hawk is noted for his mobility and defensively responsible play, and should see more opportunity as the Flames let unrestricted free agent defenders Diaz, Potter, and Schlemko walk. However, the addition of Dougie Hamilton means there aren't any obviously available roster spots on the blueline, so if Wotherspoon hopes to make the big club, he will have to steal a job.

GOALTENDERS

Jonas Hiller							G							CGY
Season	Team	Age	GP	W	L	OT	GAA	Sv%	ESSV%	QS%	GGVT	DGVT	SGVT	GVT
2012-13	ANA	30	26	15	6	4	2.36	.913	.936	64.0%	3.6	0.4	0.5	4.5
2013-14	ANA	31	50	29	13	7	2.48	.911	.925	58.0%	3.0	0.9	-1.4	2.5
2014-15	CGY	32	52	26	19	4	2.36	.918	.927	54.5%	7.6	0.7	-1.2	7.1
2015-16	CGY	33	37					.913			2.9	0.4	-0.2	3.1

CALGARY FLAMES

Forced out of Anaheim after several mediocre seasons, Jonas Hiller bounced back to provide stable goaltending for the Flames. The lefty netminder posted his highest save percentage since 2010-11 while starting 52 games. Entering the back end of a two-year contract, this season will be about Hiller playing for his next deal, which may or may not work out in the Flames' favor. The team's chances of a repeat playoff appearance may hinge on Hiller's performance. However, the Swiss goalie is about to hit the age where even the best begin to fall off, meaning Calgary would be wise to move on to their next netminder even if Hiller does have a solid year.

Joni Ortio														G							CGY
Season	Team	Age	GP	W	L	OT	GAA	Sv%	ESSV%	QS%	GGVT	DGVT	SGVT	GVT
2013-14	CGY	22	9	4	4	0	2.51	.891	.879	44.4%	-2.8	0.6	0.0	-2.2
2014-15	CGY	23	6	4	2	0	2.52	.908	.902	50.0%	-0.3	0.2	0.0	-0.2
2015-16	CGY	24	15					.912			0.5	0.1	0.0	0.6

In his two seasons in North America, Joni Ortio has played primarily as an AHL starter with Adirondack. He was named first to the AHL's All-Rookie team in 2013-14, and then to the AHL All-Star Game in 2014-15. Oddly, his save percentage dropped from .926 in his rookie season to .912, ranking 31st amongst regular AHL goaltenders. His brief showings in the NHL have consisted of largely adequate strings of play for a young goalie, ending in abysmal showings preceding his demotions back to the minors. With the return to Calgary of incumbent backup Karri Ramo, Ortio's status will be in limbo entering this season, as his waiver status will require him to clear before demotion to the AHL.

Karri Ramo														G							CGY
Season	Team	Age	GP	W	L	OT	GAA	Sv%	ESSV%	QS%	GGVT	DGVT	SGVT	GVT
2013-14	CGY	27	40	17	15	4	2.65	.911	.919	48.6%	1.3	0.1	-2.1	-0.7
2014-15	CGY	28	34	15	9	3	2.60	.912	.916	46.9%	0.4	0.2	1.9	2.5
2015-16	CGY	29	28					.913			1.5	0.1	0.0	1.6

Karri Ramo has proven to be an adequate backup, showing in the playoffs he was capable of stepping in when Hiller had a rough outing against the Ducks. Internal politics and second guessing may have been at play as Ramo was never forced to hand back the reins despite a relatively poor showing as the Flames exited the post-season. The Finn remains the inferior option to the incumbent starter Hiller, but was shockingly re-signed at the hefty price tag of $3.8 million for 2015-16. We can't figure it out.

Stephen Burtch

Carolina Hurricanes

When Rasmus Ankersen took over as chairman of Denmark's FC Midtjylland football club, he sought to infuse the entire organization with a new way of thinking about the game of soccer. Team management developed its own model of evaluating the club, dismissing league standings as "vulgar and imprecise".

No NHL team fell more victim to the vulgarity and imprecision of league standings in 2014-15 than the Carolina Hurricanes. The standings say this team is in dire straits and in serious need of a new direction. But dig a little deeper, and this is a hockey team that is more competitive than the standings suggest.

The Hurricanes finished with 71 points, the second-lowest total in franchise history—the worst since they relocated from Hartford. The 30-41-11 record left Carolina in the basement of the Metropolitan Division. Captain Eric Staal's 54 points was his lowest output of any non-lockout-shortened season since his rookie campaign. His brother Jordan fared even worse, posting just 24 points, the lowest total of his career, in a season cut short by injuries. The team's second-highest-paid player, Alex Semin, recorded a measly six goals and 19 points, which relegated him to the press box as a healthy scratch for extended periods throughout the season. And in goal, Cam Ward registered his lowest five-on-five save percentage since 2006-07.

Yet, Ankersen might say that things aren't nearly as bad as they seem in Raleigh.

On the possession front, the Hurricanes finished ninth in the league with a 52.4% Corsi. Only one other team that made the top nine missed the playoffs, while 70% of teams in the top 20 qualified for the postseason. At five-on-five, the Hurricanes' process was strong, but they were betrayed by the often finicky and random results.

So where is the disconnect?

The Hurricanes were the most unfortunate team in the league when it came to puck luck, finishing 30th with a 97.1 PDO (shooting percentage plus save percentage). Their shooting percentage ranked 29th at 6.2%. A lucky deflection here, or the back of the net instead of a post there, and the standings may have more appropriately reflected their solid approach on the ice.

Carolina's five-on-five team save percentage of .909 also ranked 29th in the NHL. Say what you will about the quality of netminding the team received in 2014-15, but a lucky save here or a fortuitous bounce there would have gone a long way towards making the situation appear less dis-

HURRICANES IN A BOX

Last Season

Goals For	188	27th
Goals Against	226	t-19th
GVT	-38	26th
Points	71	26th
Playoffs	Did not make playoffs	

A good possession team, the Hurricanes had the fourth-worst percentages of any team in the league, which left them near the bottom of the East.

Three-Year Record

GVT	-93	26th
Points	196	26th
Playoffs	0 Appearances, 0 Wins	

VUKOTA Projections

Goals For	207	27th
Goals Against	223	23rd
GVT	-17	26th
Points	86	26th

They got an upgrade with Eddie Lack, and their shooting percentages should naturally bounce back, but Carolina is still one of the weaker teams.

Top Three Prospects

N. Hanifin (D), L. Wallmark (F), R. McKeown (D)

mal. That, or a better goaltender than Cam Ward, who hasn't been better than average in a long, long time.

The Hurricanes were also unlucky in their record in one-goal games. They finished the season 13-16-11 in games decided by one goal, a winning percentage that…wait for it…also ranked 29th in the league.

However, Carolina was a solid special-teams squad. The process matched the results fairly well when up a man, as they were 17th in generating shot attempts on the man advantage and finished 15th in power-play percentage. The Hurricanes also saw more deserved results when down a man. They limited shot attempts better than every team except the New York Rangers, and finished fourth in the league in penalty-killing percentage, stifling 84.7% of all short-handed opportunities.

Despite the modicum of good news within a season of bad results, it is not all sunshine and rainbows in Raleigh. The Hurricanes franchise finds itself at a crossroads.

Head coach Bill Peters didn't come into his rookie season as an NHL coach hoping to win the consolation prize of being better than his team's record shows. If the Hurricanes come out of the gate in 2015-16 as poorly as they did this past season—in which they dropped their first eight games—will his job be at risk?

Team captain and franchise player Eric Staal is entering the final year of his contract and is coming off an underwhelming season in terms of production. If he doesn't bounce back, does the team move on without him? Once a Stanley Cup hero, Ward is entering the final year of his deal as well. Will he be able to hold on to the starting role all season or will he be pushed aside by Eddie Lack?

Alex Semin was bought out over the summer—so that crossroads was already crossed.

The team also dealt away a couple of the pieces that made them such a solid puck-possession team for much of the year: Andrej Sekera and Jiri Tlusty were both dealt during the season. The question of how well second-year general manager Ron Francis—now assisted in the front office by stats whiz (and former Hockey Prospectus contributor) Eric Tulsky—can replace these losses and fill in other existing voids in the lineup looms large in determining how the 2015-16 season will go.

If Carolina struggles to accumulate points again, the direction of the franchise will be altered significantly. Staal and Ward could be moved during the season, Peters could be let go, and a full-on rebuild would likely be underway. But if Francis pulls the right strings and the team's puck luck turns in the right direction while the solid process from 2014-15 stays in place, the Hurricanes could very well compete for a playoff spot in 2015-16.

Pat Holden

CAROLINA HURRICANES

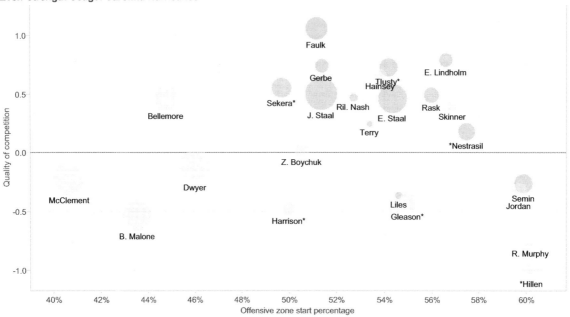

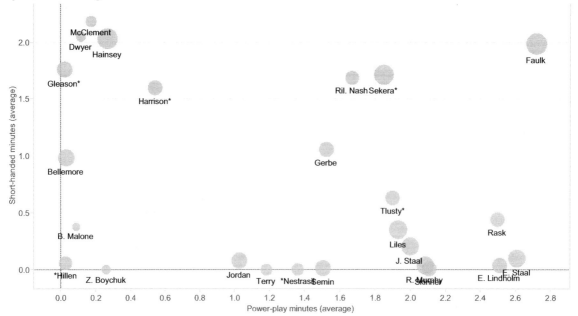

CAROLINA HURRICANES

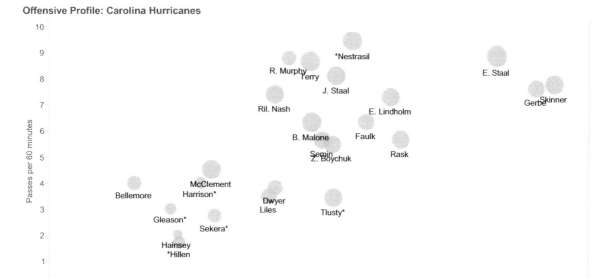

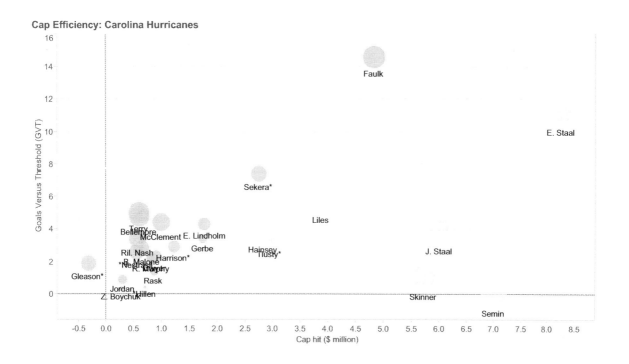

CAROLINA HURRICANES

FORWARDS

Zach Boychuk					LW								CAR
Season	Team	Age	GP	G	A	Pts	+/-	ESP/60	AdjCF%	iCF/60	OGVT	DGVT	SGVT	GVT
2012-13	CAR, PIT, NSH	23	13	1	1	2	-1	0.76	54.8%	10.6	-0.7	0.2	0.0	-0.5
2013-14	CAR	24	11	1	3	4	2	2.35	47.1%	12.6	0.8	0.4	0.0	1.2
2014-15	CAR	25	31	3	3	6	0	1.12	47.9%	10.4	-0.6	1.2	-0.3	0.3
2015-16	CAR	26	39	6	7	13					0.4	1.2	0.0	1.6

Fully two seasons removed from a harrowing journey through the waiver-wire cyclone, Zach Boychuk has come full circle. Unfortunately for the 2008 first rounder, that only means that he is still mediocre. It also means that when the Hurricanes placed him on waivers in 2014-15, no other team claimed him. Despite the unremarkable campaign, his 31 NHL games played tied his career high. Boychuck re-signed with the Hurricanes on a one-year deal, but he is unlikely to garner more than spot duty.

Patrick Brown					RW								CAR
Season	Team	Age	GP	G	A	Pts	+/-	ESP/60	AdjCF%	iCF/60	OGVT	DGVT	SGVT	GVT
2014-15	CAR	22	7	0	0	0	-4	0.00	42.6%	9.0	-0.8	-0.1	0.0	-0.9
2015-16	CAR	23	28	4	5	10					0.2	0.5	0.0	0.7

Signed as an undrafted free agent out of Boston College, Patrick Brown is a mediocre offensive forward, but he plays with good awareness and smarts in his own end. A sluggish skater, the Michigander managed only 13 points in 80 games in his first three seasons with the Eagles before exploding as a senior with 30 points in 40 games. Perhaps his professional career will mirror his collegiate exploits, as he has gotten off to a similar start, with 10 points in 60 games with the Charlotte Checkers.

Patrick Dwyer					RW								Free Agent
Season	Team	Age	GP	G	A	Pts	+/-	ESP/60	AdjCF%	iCF/60	OGVT	DGVT	SGVT	GVT
2012-13	CAR	29	46	8	8	16	-7	1.41	51.3%	15.2	1.1	1.0	0.0	2.1
2013-14	CAR	30	75	8	14	22	-2	1.25	48.2%	13.6	2.4	3.0	0.0	5.4
2014-15	CAR	31	71	5	7	12	-12	0.88	44.2%	9.7	-2.1	4.4	0.0	2.3
2015-16	Free Agent	32	60	7	9	16					0.0	2.6	0.0	2.6

While Patrick Dwyer always has poor possession numbers, he has almost always started the majority of his shifts in his own zone, against an above-average slate of opponents—until last year. For the first time since 2008-09, his average opponent was below par; he also started 5% more of his shifts in the offensive end. Yet instead of benefitting from the softer usage, his Corsi measures went from below grade to the bottom of a depthless pit. Only eight NHL players appeared in at least 40 games and had a worse Relative Corsi, and none of them started as frequently in the offensive end.

CAROLINA HURRICANES

Nathan Gerbe — LW — CAR

Season	Team	Age	GP	G	A	Pts	+/-	ESP/60	AdjCF%	iCF/60	OGVT	DGVT	SGVT	GVT
2012-13	BUF	25	42	5	5	10	-3	1.12	40.8%	12.0	0.4	0.4	0.2	0.9
2013-14	CAR	26	81	16	15	31	-6	1.19	51.2%	16.7	3.9	2.1	-0.6	5.5
2014-15	CAR	27	78	10	18	28	-14	1.11	53.1%	18.6	0.6	3.0	-0.2	3.4
2015-16	CAR	28	66	15	17	32					2.9	2.5	0.0	5.4

One of the shortest skaters in league history, Nathan Gerbe has proven over and over again that he can produce at the NHL level without needing to be sheltered from a heavy defensive load. In spite of playing an above-average level of opponent in six of the past seven seasons, the Michigan Mite has been a positive possession player more often than not. That said, his coaches have long recognized that a player of his stature needs some help to create space on the ice. As such, the ex-Sabre is lined up with larger teammates. Last year, those linemates usually included two of Victor Rask, Elias Lindholm, and Riley Nash, the smallest of whom is six-foot-one, 192 pounds. To Gerbe's credit, his own 178 pounds are more impressive on a five-foot-five body than they would be on most of his peers. He is also a slippery skater, but at his size, he needs to be.

Elias Lindholm — C/RW — CAR

Season	Team	Age	GP	G	A	Pts	+/-	ESP/60	AdjCF%	iCF/60	OGVT	DGVT	SGVT	GVT
2013-14	CAR	19	58	9	12	21	-14	1.21	48.7%	8.0	-0.1	0.2	-0.3	-0.2
2014-15	CAR	20	81	17	22	39	-23	1.28	52.9%	13.1	2.2	1.7	0.4	4.3
2015-16	CAR	21	71	18	23	41					3.4	1.7	0.0	5.2

After an understandably challenging rookie season as a 19-year-old, the still-teenaged Elias Lindholm took a huge step forward as a sophomore. The Swedish tyro has excellent vision and owns a strong and accurate snapshot. For Don Cherry fans, he also plays a very physical game, which he ramped up last season. But possession is where he really shone. The youngster went from a negative to a serious plus, as shots against dropped by nearly four per 60 minutes, while shots taken went up by two with him on the ice. Much of that was Lindholm's direct doing. As a rookie, he took 4.1 shots per 60 minutes at even strength. Last year, that rate jumped to 7.2 per 60 minutes. In summary, 2013 fifth-overall pick is good, and has only begun to scratch at the surface of his potential.

Brad Malone — LW/C — CAR

Season	Team	Age	GP	G	A	Pts	+/-	ESP/60	AdjCF%	iCF/60	OGVT	DGVT	SGVT	GVT
2012-13	COL	23	13	1	1	2	-7	1.09	46.6%	12.3	-0.7	-0.3	0.0	-1.0
2013-14	COL	24	32	3	2	5	-4	1.40	41.6%	8.9	0.3	-0.1	0.0	0.2
2014-15	CAR	25	65	7	8	15	-8	1.43	44.8%	11.0	0.0	2.8	0.0	2.8
2015-16	CAR	26	56	7	8	15					0.0	1.8	0.0	1.8

An early under-the-radar move by new general manager Ron Francis, Brad Malone was signed to a two-year, low-budget contract at the opening of free agency in 2014. Prior to that point, he was a yo-yo player, toggling back and forth between the Colorado Avalanche and their AHL farm club in Cleveland. His NHL career had amounted to 54 games across three seasons, with nine points. It took two months on the East Coast, but Malone earned the trust of his new coaching staff and became a lineup mainstay by early December. While the North Dakota grad will never become a top-six winger, his brand of hard-hitting, two-way play is endearing, which has a way of making fungibility appear irreplaceable.

Jay McClement — C — CAR

Season	Team	Age	GP	G	A	Pts	+/-	ESP/60	AdjCF%	iCF/60	OGVT	DGVT	SGVT	GVT
2012-13	TOR	29	48	8	9	17	0	1.84	36.6%	7.9	2.2	3.5	0.0	5.7
2013-14	TOR	30	81	4	6	10	-8	0.59	38.6%	8.2	-2.7	1.2	0.0	-1.5
2014-15	CAR	31	82	7	14	21	-7	1.37	43.0%	7.7	-2.3	6.9	-0.3	4.4
2015-16	CAR	32	66	6	10	16					-1.0	3.2	0.0	2.1

Jay McClement has won 52.1% of his draws over his career, finishing above 50% in every season but one of his eight in the league. On the other hand, the Brampton Battalion alum has always been a possession cipher, due in part to always starting shifts in his own zone (his 40% offensive zone start rate was his highest mark since 2009-10), as well as to simply never shooting the puck—he has averaged less than one shot per game in each of the past two seasons. Yet, his sins can be forgiven due to being the Hurricanes' most trusted forward of their upper-echelon penalty kill and for his low cap hit of $1.2 million, locked in place for two more years.

Riley Nash — C — CAR

Season	Team	Age	GP	G	A	Pts	+/-	ESP/60	AdjCF%	iCF/60	OGVT	DGVT	SGVT	GVT
2012-13	CAR	23	32	4	5	9	-4	1.44	51.1%	9.3	0.5	0.3	0.5	1.4
2013-14	CAR	24	73	10	14	24	0	1.48	50.2%	9.6	1.9	1.8	0.0	3.8
2014-15	CAR	25	68	8	17	25	-10	1.29	51.9%	9.1	-0.2	3.9	-0.3	3.4
2015-16	CAR	26	62	10	16	26					1.2	2.6	0.0	3.7

Once upon a time (in 2007), Riley Nash was considered promising enough to be selected with a first-round draft pick. Three years later, despite a point-per-game NCAA career with Cornell, his drafting team, the Edmonton Oilers, dealt him to Carolina for a second rounder. However, a close look at his five seasons in the professional ranks reveals some positives: an upward trend in his point production despite tougher assignments and a lousy PDO, and drawing more penalties than he takes. The Kamloops, British Columbia native may soon be recognized as a solid third liner.

Andrej Nestrasil — LW/RW — CAR

Season	Team	Age	GP	G	A	Pts	+/-	ESP/60	AdjCF%	iCF/60	OGVT	DGVT	SGVT	GVT
2014-15	DET, CAR	23	54	7	13	20	-1	1.39	55.0%	11.9	1.1	1.7	-0.3	2.6
2015-16	CAR	24	54	8	15	23					1.2	1.6	0.0	2.7

Andrej Nestrasil is the counterargument to Detroit's long-standing practice of keeping prospects down in the AHL until they are overripe. Teams can only send a player down so many times before they have to surrender their rights to him. At that point, the other 29 teams have the right to claim him. In his fourth professional season, the hulking Czech winger had only appeared in 13 games for the Red Wings before they risked waivers with him. The Hurricanes, whose head coach Bill Peters would have been very familiar with Nestrasil from his time in Detroit, took their chances and snatched up the potential second-line contributor for next to nothing. The 2009 third-round pick has already shown himself to be a fantastic possession player. Expect him to tap into some as-yet-hidden offensive upside this season.

Victor Rask — C — CAR

Season	Team	Age	GP	G	A	Pts	+/-	ESP/60	AdjCF%	iCF/60	OGVT	DGVT	SGVT	GVT
2014-15	CAR	21	80	11	22	33	-14	1.23	53.0%	12.4	-0.6	2.7	-0.7	1.4
2015-16	CAR	22	73	16	23	39					2.1	2.6	0.0	4.6

Knocked for a weak stride, Victor Rask was available in the middle of the second round when the Hurricanes called his name in the 2011 NHL Entry Draft—after being ranked very highly a year prior. Two solid seasons of North American acclimation in the WHL was followed by a decent rookie season in the AHL, where the Swedish center's scoring numbers (16 goals, 39 points in 76 games) served as fair warning for what he would do as an NHL rookie. While the scoring numbers do not pop, what did stand out was his Relative Corsi—only surpassed by four Carolina forwards. Like most of his teammates, Rask suffered from horrible puck luck (97.1 PDO), suggesting that there is a fair bit more in the tank.

Alexander Semin — RW — MTL

Season	Team	Age	GP	G	A	Pts	+/-	ESP/60	AdjCF%	iCF/60	OGVT	DGVT	SGVT	GVT
2012-13	CAR	28	44	13	31	44	14	2.80	50.0%	19.7	6.7	2.5	-0.3	9.0
2013-14	CAR	29	65	22	20	42	1	1.68	54.5%	20.1	5.8	2.6	-0.8	7.6
2014-15	CAR	30	57	6	13	19	-10	1.10	54.7%	12.9	-1.1	1.9	-0.8	0.0
2015-16	MTL	31	57	12	15	27					1.9	1.8	0.0	3.7

Through the first seven seasons of his career, Alexander Semin scored 197 goals on exactly 1,400 regular-season shots, for a 14.1 shooting percentage. In the past three seasons, the same man has fallen off the shooting-percentage cliff, scoring a paltry 41 goals on 453 shots (9.1%). The obvious contextual difference between the early, high-percentage shooting phase and the latter shooting-blanks phase is that he played with Washington when he was good and Carolina when he was not. Of course, we can dig a bit deeper. Oddly, Semin's even-strength scoring-chance rates remained stable over both phases, from 53.7% with the Capitals to 52.8% with the Canes. However, on a relative basis, those figures wash out. In the American capital, his quality of teammate was measured as a strong cumulative 51.9%, earning considerable ice-time with the likes of Nicklas Backstrom, Mike Green, and John Carlson. Since taking Peter Karmanos' money, his quality of teammates has dropped to 50.8%, still above average, but not exceptionally so. That could account for a marginal drop, but not the magnitude that has occurred. The decline in production still must be blamed on the prototypical enigmatic Russian. GM Ron Francis was right to swallow the sunk cost, buying out the remaining three years of his contract, though you can't blame Montreal GM Marc Bergevin for taking a flyer on him.

Justin Shugg — RW — CAR

Season	Team	Age	GP	G	A	Pts	+/-	ESP/60	AdjCF%	iCF/60	OGVT	DGVT	SGVT	GVT
2014-15	CAR	23	3	0	0	0	0	0.00	48.5%	14.4	-0.1	0.0	0.0	0.0
2015-16	CAR	24	26	5	6	10					0.7	0.6	0.0	1.3

A 2010 fourth-round pick from the Windsor Spitfires organization, Justin Shugg has a plus release on a hard, accurate wristshot. At the AHL level, he plays a smart game that allows him to find seams in coverage, making him available for passes from teammates. On the other hand, you should expect his smarts to stand out for an ostensibly offensive player in his fourth year in the bus league. It was the Niagara Falls native's finest professional season; his NHL cameo, replacing an injured Alexander Semin, was deserved. However, he will need to be more than just a minor-league triggerman to receive a sustained opportunity.

CAROLINA HURRICANES

Jeff Skinner — LW — CAR

Season	Team	Age	GP	G	A	Pts	+/-	ESP/60	AdjCF%	iCF/60	OGVT	DGVT	SGVT	GVT
2012-13	CAR	20	42	13	11	24	-21	1.38	51.6%	21.1	1.5	-1.3	0.5	0.7
2013-14	CAR	21	71	33	21	54	-14	2.04	51.0%	21.1	9.8	0.8	-1.1	9.5
2014-15	CAR	22	77	18	13	31	-24	1.34	50.8%	20.7	1.3	1.4	-1.6	1.0
2015-16	CAR	23	68	24	19	43					5.1	1.7	-0.1	6.7

Jeff Skinner still has the shot that made him a single-digit draft pick five years ago, one that subsequently won him the Calder Memorial Trophy. His possession rates are consistently strong, although he dipped (if only marginally) below water for the first time last year. What has been inconsistent, and wildly so, has been his puck luck. In his two 30-goal seasons, his shooting percentage was 13.1. In his other three campaigns, the former Kitchener Ranger scored on only 8.4 percent of his shots. Perhaps a third season with an improving Elias Lindholm and Victor Rask will enable the good Skinner to return to the ice. Or the rumors could come to fruition and Skinner could end up with a new team. At only 23 years of age, neither scenario would surprise.

Eric Staal — C — CAR

Season	Team	Age	GP	G	A	Pts	+/-	ESP/60	AdjCF%	iCF/60	OGVT	DGVT	SGVT	GVT
2012-13	CAR	28	48	18	35	53	5	3.31	49.0%	13.7	10.4	1.8	0.0	12.3
2013-14	CAR	29	79	21	40	61	-13	2.13	51.6%	14.1	6.9	2.5	0.6	10.0
2014-15	CAR	30	77	23	31	54	-13	1.79	56.5%	17.4	8.5	2.4	0.1	11.0
2015-16	CAR	31	69	22	31	52					6.8	2.3	0.0	9.1

On many shifts, on many nights, Eric Staal can still show off some of the skillset of a prototype power forward, with good speed and drive. Unfortunately, we will always compare these demonstrations to those that came in his peak years—and it is looking more and more like those peak years ended around 2012-13. From his sophomore campaign through that season, Staal had averaged between 0.85-1.22 points per game. His recent 0.74 average pales in comparison to his illustrious past. His power-play production will keep the former second-overall choice on everyone's mind, but with one year remaining on his massive contract, the eldest Staal brother will soon be forced to take a pay cut commensurate with his current skillset.

Jordan Staal — C — CAR

Season	Team	Age	GP	G	A	Pts	+/-	ESP/60	AdjCF%	iCF/60	OGVT	DGVT	SGVT	GVT
2012-13	CAR	24	48	10	21	31	-18	1.84	52.6%	12.1	2.4	0.1	0.0	2.5
2013-14	CAR	25	82	15	25	40	2	1.26	53.3%	11.6	4.6	4.2	0.0	8.8
2014-15	CAR	26	46	6	18	24	-6	1.36	59.0%	11.3	2.2	1.6	0.0	3.8
2015-16	CAR	27	59	12	22	34					3.4	2.3	0.0	5.8

Jordan Staal has many of the same physical tools and skills as his older brother Eric, but he mainly puts his to use facing the other direction. While his size, speed, and phenomenal reach can be offensive weapons, for the most part, he is viewed as a shutdown center, in the mold of Patrice Bergeron. A poor man's Patrice Bergeron, of course. A Patrice Bergeron who is oddly not used to kill penalties, as new coach Bill Peters instead preferred to use McClement, Dwyer, Nash, Gerbe, and others in that role. With eight years remaining on a contract that pays him $6 million annually, the Hurricanes rightfully expect more.

Brody Sutter — RW/C — CAR

Season	Team	Age	GP	G	A	Pts	+/-	ESP/60	AdjCF%	iCF/60	OGVT	DGVT	SGVT	GVT
2014-15	CAR	23	4	0	0	0	-2	0.00	40.3%	3.8	-0.3	-0.1	0.0	-0.4
2015-16	CAR	24	27	5	6	10					0.5	0.5	0.0	1.0

In some ways, entering the family business is the most natural thing in the world; after all, the scion was raised in the culture and language of the industry. And yet, in other ways, there is nothing more belittling than trying to follow in the footsteps of giants. Brody Sutter is, of course, among the second-generation Sutter family members, of which the first generation produced an incredible six NHLers, including Brody's father, Duane, a veteran of 731 NHL games (and currently a scout for the Oilers). Although the Sutter Six produced a plethora of hockey-playing children, Brody is only the third to make his way to the NHL. Massive and responsible in his own zone, young Brody lacks the scoring touch that would ensure a career rivalling that of his father.

Chris Terry — LW — CAR

Season	Team	Age	GP	G	A	Pts	+/-	ESP/60	AdjCF%	iCF/60	OGVT	DGVT	SGVT	GVT
2012-13	CAR	23	3	1	0	1	0	2.16	56.3%	9.1	0.3	0.0	0.0	0.3
2013-14	CAR	24	10	0	2	2	-4	0.00	50.3%	14.5	-0.4	-0.2	1.2	0.6
2014-15	CAR	25	57	11	9	20	-4	1.46	50.7%	10.2	2.5	1.7	0.8	5.0
2015-16	CAR	26	52	10	11	21					1.8	1.5	0.1	3.4

Chris Terry serves to remind us all of the folly of using the first few games of a season to glean insights. A veteran of 375 AHL games, Terry started the campaign in the NHL for the first time. He scored thrice and added two assists in his first five games. After 10 games, his point total stood at seven points. With strong minor-league numbers on his resume, there was some thought that the 2007 fifth rounder had officially arrived in the big time. Of course, he followed that scorching start with an 11-game pointless streak, not including nine games sitting in the pressbox. More inconsistency followed, and Terry finished the year with a modest 20 points in 57 games. While definitely a strong showing from a player many had thought was no better than an up-and-down guy, the fleeting hope that he could be a top-six performer has been extinguished.

Brendan Woods — LW — CAR

Season	Team	Age	GP	G	A	Pts	+/-	ESP/60	AdjCF%	iCF/60	OGVT	DGVT	SGVT	GVT
2014-15	CAR	22	2	0	0	0	-1	0.00	27.1%	18.8	-0.2	0.0	0.0	-0.2
2015-16	CAR	23	26	5	6	11					0.7	0.5	0.0	1.2

A strong passer with good vision, Brendan Woods showed greater comfort in the AHL in his second go-round after leaving the University of Wisconsin early. His health, as much as his relative success, earned the 2012 fifth-round draft pick a two-game cameo bookending Christmas as the Hurricanes waited for Jordan Staal to return from a preseason injury. Another AHL season awaits.

CAROLINA HURRICANES

DEFENSEMEN

Brett Bellemore								RD						Free Agent
Season	Team	Age	GP	G	A	Pts	+/-	ESP/60	AdjCF%	iCF/60	OGVT	DGVT	SGVT	GVT
2012-13	CAR	24	8	0	2	2	-2	1.28	50.8%	10.9	0.4	-0.1	0.0	0.2
2013-14	CAR	25	64	2	6	8	-1	0.49	48.2%	6.3	-0.2	2.4	0.0	2.2
2014-15	CAR	26	49	2	8	10	1	0.80	48.1%	4.8	0.9	4.0	0.0	4.8
2015-16	Free Agent	27	53	2	9	11					0.4	2.8	0.0	3.2

Brett Bellemore is a good litmus test. As far as basic analytics go, he is subpar. His Corsi marks are poor, but they are mitigated by intense usage—as the former Plymouth Whaler is often buried in his own end, facing upper-echelon opponents. He isn't a huge point producer, either. Among Hurricanes' blueliners over the past three seasons, he ranks 11th out of 14 in points per 60. What the Windsor native does is hit people. A lot. No one on the team threw more body checks over the past two seasons. What makes Bellemore a litmus test, too, is that he is a free agent. In spite of repeated statements by Ron Francis about wanting to get bigger and to play bigger, he let Carolina's biggest man walk away. Through the free-agent frenzy that entails the first few days of July, Bellemore was untouched. In a hockey world that is rapidly becoming more and more analytics friendly, Bellemore's eventual contract will tell us how much analytics has really sunk in.

Danny Biega								RD						CAR
Season	Team	Age	GP	G	A	Pts	+/-	ESP/60	AdjCF%	iCF/60	OGVT	DGVT	SGVT	GVT
2014-15	CAR	23	10	0	2	2	-5	0.75	54.8%	8.7	0.1	-0.2	0.0	-0.1
2015-16	CAR	24	28	2	6	8					0.5	0.7	0.0	1.2

Danny Biega and older brother Alex are in a race to be the first Biega to establish himself as a *bona fide* NHL journeyman. Kid brother Danny enters the 2015-16 season with a marginal edge, having already played in 10 games to Alex's seven. The Harvard grad is known for his smarts, but has to refine his defensive game to have a greater chance at prolonged NHL duties, with gap control a particular area of weakness. The offensive touch that accompanied his game in his sophomore and junior seasons with the Crimson has yet to be repeated in two professional seasons.

Justin Faulk								RD						CAR
Season	Team	Age	GP	G	A	Pts	+/-	ESP/60	AdjCF%	iCF/60	OGVT	DGVT	SGVT	GVT
2012-13	CAR	20	38	5	10	15	1	0.95	49.4%	7.5	1.9	1.7	0.0	3.6
2013-14	CAR	21	76	5	27	32	-9	0.96	51.4%	10.6	2.6	4.2	0.0	6.8
2014-15	CAR	22	82	15	34	49	-19	1.00	54.1%	12.0	8.3	6.3	0.0	14.6
2015-16	CAR	23	78	12	35	47					6.7	5.3	0.0	11.9

At the tender age of 23, having already experienced Olympic participation, Justin Faulk has emerged as one of the top young blueliners in the game. Any short list of future Norris Trophy winners has to have the former Minnesota-Duluth Bulldog's name on it. Much of his quality lies in a tremendously high panic threshold, allowing him to remain completely calm with the puck on the point or in transition, even when harried by opponents. He is a great skater and owns a terrific shot. An absolute possession driver, Faulk led all Hurricanes' blueliners in Relative Corsi despite heavy minutes. Among NHL rearguards who receive regular power-play time, only four contributed offensively at a higher rate than Faulk. He was top 30 in even-strength production as well. If that were not enough, the 2010 second-round pick led Hurricanes defenders in hits and finished six from the lead in blocked shots, giving Faulk old-school appeal in addition to his obvious analytic pluses. He is Carolina's greatest on-ice asset, and his team-friendly contract will look better and better as he continues to mature.

Ron Hainsey							LD						CAR
Season	Team	Age	GP	G	A	Pts	+/-	ESP/60	AdjCF%	iCF/60	OGVT	DGVT	SGVT	GVT
2012-13	WPG	31	47	0	13	13	-8	0.79	47.6%	7.0	0.5	1.9	0.0	2.4
2013-14	CAR	32	82	4	11	15	-9	0.55	50.6%	6.1	0.1	3.1	0.0	3.2
2014-15	CAR	33	81	2	8	10	-14	0.35	51.1%	6.4	-2.8	6.2	0.0	3.4
2015-16	CAR	34	63	2	10	12					-0.6	3.9	0.0	3.3

Perhaps the most remarkable factoid about Ron Hainsey, after 12 years and 754 games, is that he has never played in a one single playoff game. Now 34, with his skills diminished, he may never get that chance. While he can still log heavy minutes, the Connecticut native was sheltered in terms of offensive zone starts more than in any season since 2007-08, while his Relative Corsi has slipped into the red. However, as a prolific shot blocker, Hainsey will always look better through the eyes of Fenwick than Corsi. Carrying a cap hit of $2.8 million through the end of 2016-17, he is not a likely trade target for a contender, either. He lacks that ever-essential playoff experience, after all.

Jack Hillen							LD						Free Agent
Season	Team	Age	GP	G	A	Pts	+/-	ESP/60	AdjCF%	iCF/60	OGVT	DGVT	SGVT	GVT
2012-13	WSH	26	23	3	6	9	9	1.42	51.8%	9.3	2.2	1.8	0.0	3.9
2013-14	WSH	27	13	0	1	1	-4	0.28	42.3%	6.6	-0.3	-0.3	0.0	-0.6
2014-15	WSH, CAR	28	38	0	5	5	-1	0.62	48.7%	8.8	-0.5	0.9	0.0	0.4
2015-16	Free Agent	29	39	1	6	7					-0.2	1.2	0.0	1.0

If nothing else, Jack Hillen serves as irrefutable proof that a defenseman can be small—and not especially prolific at either end of the ice—but can still have a significant career. Recent employers may have hoped he could recreate his solid seasons with the Islanders in 2009-10 and 2010-11, but surely, by this point, those benefactors would have learned the folly of that line of thinking—the Colorado College grad has contributed 21 points in his last 129 games.

Michal Jordan							LD						CAR
Season	Team	Age	GP	G	A	Pts	+/-	ESP/60	AdjCF%	iCF/60	OGVT	DGVT	SGVT	GVT
2012-13	CAR	22	5	0	0	0	-2	0.00	50.3%	7.5	-0.1	-0.3	0.0	-0.4
2014-15	CAR	24	38	2	4	6	-7	0.43	50.2%	7.6	-0.4	1.3	0.0	0.9
2015-16	CAR	25	42	3	8	10					0.3	1.7	0.0	2.1

Recalled from Charlotte in late November with Brett Bellemore hitting the shelf, Michal "Air" Jordan endeared himself to new bench boss Bill Peters as he never had with the previous coaching staffs in his first four professional seasons. A 2008 fourth-round selection, the Czech rearguard has some intriguing tools that hint at a viable bottom-pairing defender. His strong possession rates suggest that he may already be there.

CAROLINA HURRICANES

John-Michael Liles — RD — CAR

Season	Team	Age	GP	G	A	Pts	+/-	ESP/60	AdjCF%	iCF/60	OGVT	DGVT	SGVT	GVT
2012-13	TOR	32	32	2	9	11	-1	1.17	45.9%	8.3	2.1	-0.1	0.0	2.1
2013-14	TOR, CAR	33	41	2	7	9	5	0.43	49.6%	7.1	-0.4	1.9	0.0	1.6
2014-15	CAR	34	57	2	20	22	-9	0.94	53.5%	9.6	3.3	2.0	0.0	5.3
2015-16	CAR	35	49	3	14	17					1.8	2.1	0.0	3.8

Evidence that small-framed blueliners could make it to The Show even in the days before analytics, John-Michael Liles and his five-foot-ten, 185-pound body have appeared in 719 regular season games over an 11-year career, scoring roughly one point every other game. Still quick and with a good hockey mind, time is otherwise catching up on the 34-year-old. Prone to playing the puck when a more physical defender might have stepped into his opponent, Liles can be a liability in his own zone. Further, his offensive game has seen a steady drop since leaving Colorado after 2010-11; last year's modest rebound was fortified by nine points on the man advantage. Despite his negative traits, Liles is still a good possession player; he has been the most effective Carolina defender at suppressing shots since joining the squad.

Keegan Lowe — LD — CAR

Season	Team	Age	GP	G	A	Pts	+/-	ESP/60	AdjCF%	iCF/60	OGVT	DGVT	SGVT	GVT
2014-15	CAR	21	2	0	0	0	-2	0.00	30.4%	8.0	0.0	0.0	0.0	0.0
2015-16	CAR	22	25	2	5	6					0.4	0.8	0.0	1.2

As last season wound down, the Hurricanes cycled through a few minor leaguers, looking to see if any had what it takes to play in the NHL. Not that two games is any real sample size, but Keegan Lowe did not impress in debut his unless you count two separate tangos with Vincent Lecavalier as impressive. Son of long-time Edmonton Oiler blueliner and executive Kevin Lowe, Keegan will receive additional chances on teams that value brawn over talent. Considering the demotion of Dear Ol' Dad from Oilers' GM to a more honorary role, there is one fewer decision-maker out there that values the type of game exemplified by young Keegan.

Ryan Murphy — RD — CAR

Season	Team	Age	GP	G	A	Pts	+/-	ESP/60	AdjCF%	iCF/60	OGVT	DGVT	SGVT	GVT
2012-13	CAR	19	4	0	0	0	-4	0.00	40.4%	10.4	-0.4	-0.5	0.0	-0.9
2013-14	CAR	20	48	2	10	12	-9	0.72	47.4%	11.1	1.1	0.3	0.0	1.4
2014-15	CAR	21	37	4	9	13	-11	0.80	50.2%	10.0	1.7	0.8	-0.3	2.2
2015-16	CAR	22	46	5	13	17					1.9	1.5	0.0	3.4

Undersized and lacking in functional hockey strength, Ryan Murphy was selected near the top of the 2011 draft due to his skating and offensive instincts. Although the former Kitchener Ranger spent a long chunk of last season in the minors, his NHL game improved by leaps and bounds under the tutelage of Peters. Despite no discernable change in his usage pattern from previous stints, Murphy's possession rates all shot upwards, indicating that he is catching up to the speed of the NHL game. Much of the difference was in the defensive zone, where opponents went from averaging 34.2 shots against Carolina with Murphy on the ice to only 26.6.

CAROLINA HURRICANES

Rasmus Rissanen — LD — CAR

Season	Team	Age	GP	G	A	Pts	+/-	ESP/60	AdjCF%	iCF/60	OGVT	DGVT	SGVT	GVT
2014-15	CAR	23	6	0	0	0	-5	0.00	47.0%	5.9	-0.4	0.2	0.0	-0.1
2015-16	CAR	24	27	2	5	6					0.1	1.0	0.0	1.1

A good skater who uses his mobility to maintain tight gaps on incoming attackers, Rasmus Rissanen is nevertheless not a highly touted prospect. On the other hand, the 2009 sixth rounder is a viable depth blueliner, capable of handling sheltered shifts in a pinch. Repeat opportunities with the Hurricanes will be as dependent on the readiness of blue-chip prospects Noah Hanifin and Haydn Fleury as Rissanen's own abilities.

GOALTENDERS

Anton Khudobin — G — ANA

Season	Team	Age	GP	W	L	OT	GAA	Sv%	ESSV%	QS%	GGVT	DGVT	SGVT	GVT
2012-13	BOS	26	14	9	4	1	2.32	.920	.916	57.1%	4.5	0.0	0.1	4.5
2013-14	CAR	27	36	19	14	1	2.30	.926	.934	64.7%	14.5	-0.3	0.8	15.0
2014-15	CAR	28	34	8	17	6	2.72	.900	.902	50.0%	-7.8	0.9	1.7	-5.2
2015-16	ANA	29	30								4.0	0.3	0.2	4.4

Like goalies often do, Anton Khudobin looked pretty good suiting up for Claude Julien's Boston Bruins. In parts of two seasons in Beantown, the five-foot-eleven netminder stopped 401 of 433 shots for a nifty .926 save percentage. Unlike many of those goalies, Khudobin looked even better in his first season away from New England, posting a .926 save percentage in 36 games for the relatively porous Hurricanes. Unfortunately for both the goalie and the Hurricanes, the bubble burst in 2014-15: his save percentage dropped to .900, well below par. Short, but quick and shifty in the crease, the 2004 seventh rounder was dealt to Anaheim on draft day in exchange for offensive blueliner James Wisniewski, in what was largely a cap-related move for the Ducks.

Cam Ward — G — CAR

Season	Team	Age	GP	W	L	OT	GAA	Sv%	ESSV%	QS%	GGVT	DGVT	SGVT	GVT
2012-13	CAR	28	17	9	6	1	2.84	.908	.917	43.8%	0.3	-0.3	0.0	0.1
2013-14	CAR	29	30	10	12	6	3.06	.898	.909	39.3%	-8.0	0.0	-0.4	-8.4
2014-15	CAR	30	51	22	24	5	2.40	.910	.914	56.0%	-0.6	1.7	0.2	1.2
2015-16	CAR	31	34								-0.7	0.6	-0.1	-0.1

One of our first lessons in the folly of signing (especially non-elite) goaltenders to big-money, long-term contracts, Cam Ward is finally entering the last season of what started out as a six-year, $37.8 million pact. In the first five years of that deal, Ward stopped 91.4% of all shots, placing him slightly below league average. Even less heartening is that his even-strength save percentages have steadily declined: starting at a solid .929 in 2010-11, down to .914 last year. Sensing a trend, the Hurricanes acquired Eddie Lack from Vancouver to complete with Ward in 2015-16, and to perhaps become the starter of the future.

Ryan Wagman

Chicago Blackhawks

It is not often that we agree with Gary Bettman, but what he said during the presentation of this year's Stanley Cup is correct: the Chicago Blackhawks are a dynasty. Chicago has been the league's dominant team for seven years—the entire time that *Hockey Prospectus* has been in business. Within these pages, our prognosis has never been for anything less than Stanley Cup contention.

The table on the next page summarizes the team's incredible achievements over that seven-year span as one of the league's most successful teams offensively, defensively, in terms of puck possession, and overall. Also note that Chicago has never relied on the fleeting nature of elite shooting, goaltending, or special teams for its success, areas in which the Blackhawks barely rank above average.

How has Chicago done it? Consider that the Blackhawks had made the playoffs only once in the preceding 10 seasons, when they were eliminated in five games. They cycled through nine different coaches during that long, cold stretch, and only two point-per-game players: Tony Amonte in 1999-00 and Martin Havlat in 2006-07.

Chicago's success is often attributed to drafting Jonathan Toews third overall in 2006 and Patrick Kane first overall in 2007, but there was much more to their rise to power than the two superstars. When this team is studied closely, a strategy for success is revealed—one that can be emulated with enough time and patience, the willingness to take a few risks, and more than a few good lucky breaks along the way. Let's examine each in detail.

Adoption of analytics

Every year, *ESPN the Magazine* ranks every franchise in the "four major sports" in regards to their adoption of analytics. Obviously, there are several baseball, basketball, and football teams that were awarded the distinction of being "All-In", but there was only one hockey team. Guess who?

Chicago isn't exactly the Oakland Athletics of hockey, because it took a long time for the secretive use of hockey analytics to take root, and to bear fruit. While the organization has always been tight-lipped about what it has done with analytics, we know that it goes back at least as far as the turn of the century, when Mike Smith was hired as the Manager of Hockey Operations—he received a quick promotion to general manager, in which capacity he served until seven games into the 2003-04 season, and yet it took another five more years for the Blackhawks dynasty to begin.

BLACKHAWKS IN A BOX

Last Season		
Goals For	229	16th
Goals Against	189	t-1st
GVT	40	4th
Points	102	7th
Playoffs	Won Stanley Cup	

After a ho-hum regular season, the Blackhawks looked nearly unstoppable in their drive for a third Stanley Cup in six years.

Three-Year Record		
GVT	140	1st
Points	286	2nd
Playoffs	3 Appearances, 43 Wins, 2 Cups	

VUKOTA Projection		
Goals For	228	8th
Goals Against	215	8th
GVT	14	6th
Points	96	6th

Cap issues will continue to hamper this team, which lost Saad, but the Blackhawks enter the season as the team to beat once again.

Top Four Prospects
T. Teravainen (F), M. Dano (F), A. Panarin (F)

CHICAGO BLACKHAWKS

Chicago Blackhawks, 2008-09 to present

Category	Value	Rank
Points	700	1st
Wins	317	2nd
Possession	54.9%	1st
Goals per game	3.09	1st
Goals allowed per game	2.52	5th
Share of all goals	55.1%	2nd
Shots per game	32.7	2nd
Shots allowed per game	27.8	4th
Share of all shots	54.0%	1st
Power play	18.4%	11th
Penalty kill	82.2%	12th
Shooting percentage	9.5%	10th
Save percentage	.909%	14th
Faceoffs	51.0%	6th
Fewest penalty minutes	5,324	4th

If you have never heard of Mike Smith, no, we are not talking about the Coyotes' goalie. This particular Mike Smith was the man who drafted Brent Seabrook, Duncan Keith, Dustin Byfuglien, Corey Crawford, and James Wisniewski over the course of two drafts, and was named Executive of the Year by the *Sporting News* after the 2001-02 season.

This is also the Mike Smith who co-founded Coleman Analytics way back in 2005, which provided hockey analytics to GMs and coaches. At the time, it was a small group of five to nine clients who each paid between $50,000 and $100,000 per year (so we have heard), which is amazingly affordable when you consider the value of one good draft pick, one good trade, or one good free agent signing—or the prevention of a bad one!

It is easy for *Hockey Prospectus* to argue that the adoption of hockey analytics is an important ingredient, but we are merely echoing what has been said by Chicago GM Stan Bowman himself. Frankly, there is no longer any excuse to spend millions on a department of 20 scouts, and maybe another million on a crew of trainers and equipment managers, and then invest no more than a few thousand for a blogger, grad student, or intern to count shot attempts. Chicago may be one of the shrewd teams that used analytics to get an early edge, but now it is a matter of avoiding falling behind.

Adoption of possession-based hockey

The importance of puck possession has been known for a very long time, but there was always some mystery about how it could be achieved. Even those in the mighty Detroit Red Wings dynasty of the 1990s admit that their highly-effective roster was constructed as much by sheer luck as it was by design.

Even if Chicago was one of the teams to get an early jump on the value of possession, it still took a few years to move the needle in the right direction. Once the pieces came together, the Blackhawks became the NHL's dominant puck-possession team, whether your preferred estimate is based on shots or the portion of faceoffs that occurred in the offensive vs. defensive zone. By either metric, no team can come close to Chicago's success, other than perhaps the Los Angeles Kings, or the Detroit Red Wings before them.

Chicago's dominance in puck possession, 2008-09 to present

Season	Share of shot attempts	Rank	Offensive zone start %	Rank
2008-09	54.5%	5th	54.3%	3rd
2009-10	56.9%	1st	55.5%	1st
2010-11	54.1%	2nd	53.7%	1st
2011-12	53.3%	6th	54.4%	2nd
2012-13	55.4%	2nd	53.7%	4th
2013-14	55.8%	2nd	54.9%	1st
2014-15	54.0%	2nd	55.2%	1st

How did they do it? Building a roster with the right players is essential, but it is no coincidence that Chicago's success began when head coach Joel Quenneville arrived in town.

Investing in a great coaching staff

We don't have much in the way of coaching analytics, but the method we introduced back in late 2009 has proven surprisingly insightful. It is calculated by comparing a team's year-end results to its preseason expectations—which is usually just how they performed the year before—regressed 35% back towards league average. That may not sound like a particularly clever approach, but coaches who started the season ranked in the bottom half have proven three times more likely to get fired that year, and the average preseason ranking of those coaches who wind up in the Conference Final is 6.5 out of 30. So, there is definitely some value to this perspective.

What does this coaching stat say about Quenneville? He ranks third all-time among active coaches, barely behind Anaheim's Bruce Boudreau. Among those with at least three full NHL seasons under their belts, Quenneville also ranks third among active coaches on a per-game basis. All-time, Quenneville ranks as the 10th-most accomplished NHL head coach, behind some of the sport's biggest names.

Points above expectations (all-time)		
Rank	Coach	Extra points
1	Scotty Bowman	291.6
2	Al Arbour	109.0
3	Glen Sather	102.0
4	Ken Hitchcock*	97.9
5	Dick Irvin	96.7
6	Jacques Lemaire	85.2
7	Toe Blake	83.8
8	Fred Shero	78.3
9	Bruce Boudreau*	73.9
10	Joel Quenneville*	71.7

Chicago's investment goes beyond just the head bench boss, to the entire coaching staff. Assistant coach Kevin Dineen, for instance, would be an upgrade at head coach for about half the league's teams. As a head coach, Dineen won the gold medal with the Canadian Olympic Women's hockey team in Sochi. In the NHL, his only full 82-game season as head coach of the Florida Panthers in 2011-12 resulted in the second-best record in franchise history, and the team's only playoff appearance since 1999-2000. Chicago has pursued quality throughout the entire organization, not just at the top.

Someone has been paying close attention. Toronto GM Brendan Shanahan turned a lot of heads when he invested $50 million over eight years in new head coach Mike Babcock, but it was the right idea. In Chicago, and on other successful teams, investing in the coaching staff has been proven to consistently move the needle in the standings by four or more points, and in a way that falls outside salary cap restrictions. If you have got the cash, spend it!

Build through the Draft

With notable exceptions like free agent Marian Hossa and trade acquisition Patrick Sharp, Chicago was built through the draft, where it has taken full advantage of the cost savings inherent to younger players. About 60 percent of the team was originally drafted by this organization, according to a study by local hockey analytics writer Jen Lute Costella, which ranks third in the NHL behind Detroit and Ottawa. In all, Chicago has 27 draft picks in the NHL right now, of which they have kept 14, also third in the NHL.

Acquiring players through trades requires sacrificing near-equal assets in exchange, and signing free agents requires paying a premium for players that are already on the decline, but players can be drafted at no cost. Furthermore, the current Collective Bargaining Agreement has built-in rules that significantly reduce what players on entry-level contracts and in restricted free agency are paid. That is why trades and free agency are meant for tuning the roster, but the best way to consistently improve a team long term is through the draft.

The only problem with building through the draft is it takes a lot of time and patience, and it is difficult to tell if a team is off track until it is too late. Most of today's top Blackhawks were drafted long before Bowman took the helm in 2009. As mentioned, Smith was responsible for drafting Keith and Wisniewski in 2002, and then Seabrook, Crawford, and Byfuglien in 2003. Then, his successor Bob Pulford landed Bryan Bickell, Dave Bolland, and Troy Brouwer in 2004, before Dave Tallon took over to draft Niklas Hjalmarsson in 2005, Jonathan Toews in 2006, and Patrick Kane in 2007. Bowman has continued this fine tradition since 2009, which is why we saw a dozen Chicago draft picks aged 24 or younger on the team this year, along with two more undrafted prospects in Kyle Baun and Trevor van Riemsdyk. Teams need to have a long-term view, and to remain loyal and consistent to the strategy even in the face of inevitable front-office turnover.

Manage the salary cap

In the salary cap era, draft success can lead to an interesting predicament when all those great players can't be kept in the organization. It is easy enough to fit players protected by the cost savings inherent to entry-level contracts and restricted free agency under the cap, but once players reach unrestricted free agency around age 27, and therefore need to be paid their full worth, some difficult decisions need to be made. Selecting which veterans to keep, and which ones to "recycle" for draft picks and prospects is one of an organization's most difficult decisions.

Chicago's current contracts and cap hits

Player	Age	Years remaining	Age in final season	Cap hit ($M)
Patrick Kane	26	8	34	10.5
Jonathan Toews	27	8	35	10.5
Corey Crawford	30	5	35	6.0
Patrick Sharp	30	2	35	5.9
Brent Seabrook	30	1	31	5.8
Duncan Keith	32	8	40	5.6
Marian Hossa	36	6	42	5.2
Niklas Hjalmarsson	28	4	32	4.1
Bryan Bickell	29	2	31	4.0

In the aftermath of winning their third Stanley Cup in six seasons, the Blackhawks had $57.6 million invested in nine players with an average age over 30. Next year's salary cap is $71.4 million, meaning there is just $13.8 million left to stock the remaining 14 active roster spots—less than a million dollars per player.

While individual circumstances can vary, players generally don't improve past age 25 or so. The team is getting old, and is locked in to these old or soon-to-be-old players. Unless the salary cap goes way up, the team won't have room for any more high-paid veterans—just prospects and depth NHLers. Even after letting one or more of these players go, Chicago will still be highly reliant upon low-cost players on ELCs or RFAs.

The good news is that Bowman has been through all of this several times before. After previous Stanley Cup runs, the Blackhawks had to shed players like Byfuglien, Andrew Ladd, Antti Niemi, Brian Campbell, Bolland, Kris Versteeg, Troy Brouwer, and Nick Leddy—usually in exchange for the draft picks or prospects they are relying on today. Similarly, it shouldn't be hard to move any of these nine players for the team's future stars of the 2020s.

What to expect this year

The Chicago Blackhawks have achieved enormous success by building their team through the draft, and with an emphasis on hockey analytics, coaching, puck possession, and salary cap management. In hindsight, it is easy to see how elements built upon each other and took advantage of market inefficiencies of the day, but will this model remain valid for the future? Absolutely.

Great coaches frequently become available, can achieve almost instant results, and have salaries that fall outside of salary cap restrictions. As for the rules that increase the contractual value of restricted free agents and players on entry-level contracts, they were extended in the 2013 CBA, and will continue to apply through the 2021-22 season. Perhaps most surprisingly, players who excel in puck possession are still an undervalued commodity, even years after their value was established by teams like Chicago.

More importantly, there are new market inefficiencies that warrant deeper exploration, but only teams that complement their existing scouting staff with an investment in a hockey analytics department are going to have the greatest odds of finding and exploiting them.

This is not the only successful team-building model in the NHL today, but it has certainly been the right one for Chicago, not to mention for teams like the Los Angeles Kings, Detroit Red Wings, and St. Louis Blues—to lesser extents. Chicago's next challenger could also involve teams on the rise who have adopted this approach more recently, like the Tampa Bay Lightning, Ottawa Senators, Nashville Predators, or Columbus Blue Jackets.

Rob Vollman

CHICAGO BLACKHAWKS

Even-Strength Usage: Chicago Blackhawks

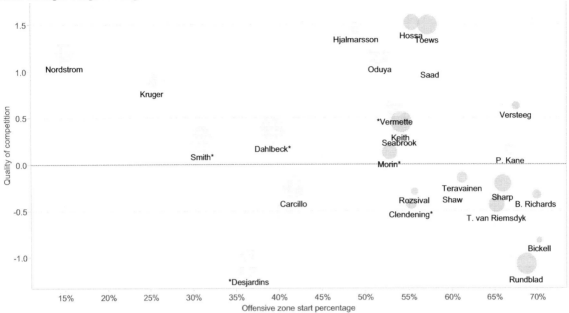

Special Teams Usage: Chicago Blackhawks

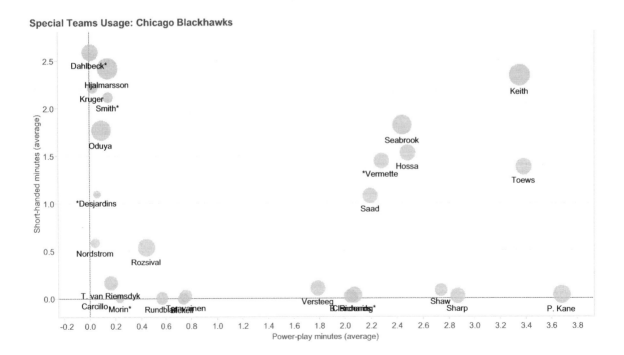

CHICAGO BLACKHAWKS

Offensive Profile: Chicago Blackhawks

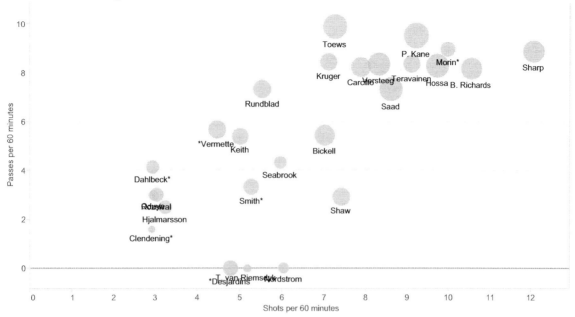

Cap Efficiency: Chicago Blackhawks

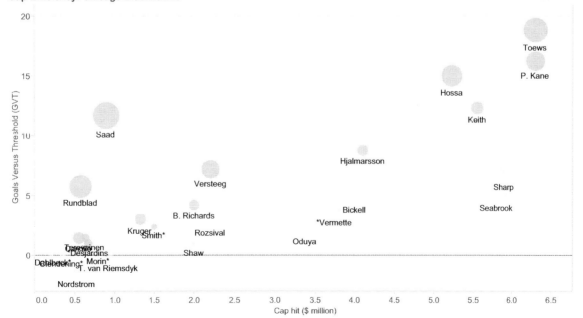

CHICAGO BLACKHAWKS

FORWARDS

Kyle Baun — RW — CHI

Season	Team	Age	GP	G	A	Pts	+/-	ESP/60	AdjCF%	iCF/60	OGVT	DGVT	SGVT	GVT
2014-15	CHI	22	3	0	0	0	-1	0.00	51.4%	12.5	-0.1	0.0	0.0	0.0
2015-16	CHI	23	26	5	6	11					0.7	0.6	0.0	1.3

Colgate University standout and grandson of famous Maple Leafs defenseman Bobby Baun, Kyle Baun signed with Chicago as a college free agent. He had accrued 14 goals and 15 assists in 38 games in the ECAC in his junior year. In his first three games at the NHL level, he failed to record any points or penalty minutes. The upshot is that it looks like the six-foot-two, 200-pound Baun will need to prove himself in the AHL to start.

Bryan Bickell — LW — CHI

Season	Team	Age	GP	G	A	Pts	+/-	ESP/60	AdjCF%	iCF/60	OGVT	DGVT	SGVT	GVT
2012-13	CHI	26	48	9	14	23	12	2.30	56.8%	15.0	4.9	1.8	0.0	6.7
2013-14	CHI	27	59	11	4	15	-6	1.41	58.7%	16.3	0.8	0.5	0.0	1.4
2014-15	CHI	28	80	14	14	28	5	1.65	54.4%	12.2	3.2	2.0	-0.3	4.9
2015-16	CHI	29	64	11	13	25					1.6	1.6	0.0	3.1

A playoff hero of seasons past, Bryan Bickell offered very little to Chicago's third Cup in six years. The six-foot-four, 223-pound power forward failed to record a goal in the playoffs while notching a modest five assists. During the regular season, he offered the type of production you would expect from an average third-line winger. The best argument for Bickell is that he can fit on a third line or occasionally pop up to the top line to add a spark. His physical play also adds a bit of value, but it is questionable whether Bickell justifies a $4 million cap hit.

Daniel Carcillo — LW — Retired

Season	Team	Age	GP	G	A	Pts	+/-	ESP/60	AdjCF%	iCF/60	OGVT	DGVT	SGVT	GVT
2012-13	CHI	27	23	2	1	3	1	0.87	55.6%	12.5	-0.8	0.4	0.0	-0.4
2013-14	LAK, NYR	28	57	4	1	5	-1	0.57	51.7%	11.3	-2.3	1.0	0.0	-1.3
2014-15	CHI	29	39	4	4	8	3	1.51	50.4%	13.8	0.6	1.0	0.0	1.5
2015-16	Retired	30	46	5	5	10					-0.1	1.1	0.0	1.0

Once known as one of the best pests in the league, Dan Carcillo's game has fallen significantly since his days in Philadelphia, where he could offer around 20 points, draw and kill penalties, and stand up for his teammates. While a lack of quickness has certainly played a role in his dropoff, the league simply is not putting up with players like Carcillo anymore. In particular, he has a reputation as a cheap-shot artist, making him a constant target of referees. The veteran winger can still offer a few even-strength points and maybe 8-10 minutes per night, but he may be more trouble than he is worth.

CHICAGO BLACKHAWKS

Phillip Danault						C/LW							CHI
Season	Team	Age	GP	G	A	Pts	+/-	ESP/60	AdjCF%	iCF/60	OGVT	DGVT	SGVT	GVT
2014-15	CHI	21	2	0	0	0	0	0.00	61.3%	15.2	0.0	0.0	0.0	0.0
2015-16	CHI	22	26	5	6	11					0.7	0.6	0.0	1.3

The Blackhawks spoke highly of Phillip Danault following training camp, saying the first-round pick from 2011 was starting to become comfortable at the pro level. While he does not have a tool that will make the casual observer notice him—much like Marcus Kruger—the 22-year-old has a strong defensive game that should give him a shot to be an NHL regular. He failed to tally any points in two games with the Blackhawks, but he registered a respectable 38 points in 70 AHL games with the Rockford IceHogs.

Andrew Desjardins						C							CHI
Season	Team	Age	GP	G	A	Pts	+/-	ESP/60	AdjCF%	iCF/60	OGVT	DGVT	SGVT	GVT
2012-13	SJS	26	42	2	1	3	-6	0.48	48.8%	14.1	-1.6	0.7	0.0	-0.8
2013-14	SJS	27	81	3	14	17	-8	1.28	51.2%	11.5	0.4	1.5	0.0	1.9
2014-15	SJS, CHI	28	69	5	5	10	-1	0.91	46.2%	8.4	-0.9	1.9	0.0	1.0
2015-16	CHI	29	58	4	7	11					-1.1	1.1	0.0	0.0

With the team holding a lead in the final minutes of Game 6 of the Stanley Cup Final, Andrew Desjardins did something no player ever wants to do: he took a penalty. Sitting in the penalty box as his teammates scrambled to keep the Lightning out of the back of the net must have been painful—and nobody was more relieved when the Blackhawks killed it off. Outside of his notable gaffe, Desjardins impressed the team enough to be re-signed in the Windy City. He will add depth to the bottom six, but little else as the 29-year-old has a career high of 17 points (recorded in his time in San Jose).

Ryan Hartman						RW							CHI
Season	Team	Age	GP	G	A	Pts	+/-	ESP/60	AdjCF%	iCF/60	OGVT	DGVT	SGVT	GVT
2014-15	CHI	20	5	0	0	0	-1	0.00	52.0%	15.1	-0.2	0.0	0.0	-0.3
2015-16	CHI	21	27	5	6	10					0.6	0.5	0.0	1.2

A late first-round pick by the Blackhawks in 2013, Ryan Hartman's AHL role points to what his NHL role will be: as a scrappy bottom sixer. The U18 and U20 WJC gold medalist does not have much in the way of puck skills, but could become an everyday energy player who dishes out some hits and kills penalties.

Marian Hossa						RW							CHI
Season	Team	Age	GP	G	A	Pts	+/-	ESP/60	CF%	iCF/60	OGVT	DGVT	SGVT	GVT
2012-13	CHI	33	40	17	14	31	20	2.46	59.5%	16.9	6.9	3.0	0.7	10.6
2013-14	CHI	34	72	30	30	60	28	2.43	58.5%	19.1	13.0	5.0	-0.8	17.2
2014-15	CHI	35	82	22	39	61	17	2.16	55.4%	17.9	9.4	5.9	-0.3	15.0
2015-16	CHI	36	72	20	33	53					6.7	3.2	0.0	9.9

Marian Hossa has continued to be one of the most dominant two-way wingers in the game at age 36, as he has maintained high-level skating ability and an unflappable work ethic. Not to mention offensive skill. The four-time Olympian and three-time Cup winner finished with 22 goals and 39 assists and demonstrated a prolific ability to control even-strength shot attempts by constantly pick pocketing and winning battles. His skill at disrupting opposing skaters with his indefatigable back pressure while stoking the Blackhawks' offense with his dynamic cross-and-drops enables him to remain a premier power forward.

Patrick Kane							RW						CHI
Season	Team	Age	GP	G	A	Pts	+/-	ESP/60	AdjCF%	iCF/60	OGVT	DGVT	SGVT	GVT
2012-13	CHI	24	47	23	32	55	11	2.84	52.5%	14.5	12.4	1.2	1.6	15.2
2013-14	CHI	25	69	29	40	69	7	2.35	55.9%	17.0	14.5	2.0	-2.2	14.3
2014-15	CHI	26	61	27	37	64	10	2.56	53.4%	15.1	11.4	2.2	2.7	16.3
2015-16	CHI	27	68	28	41	69					11.0	2.3	0.1	13.4

Injury derailed a Hart Trophy bid for Patrick Kane, though the 2007 first-overall pick was the only player who averaged one point per game during the regular season and playoffs. While he could be considered a one-dimensional scorer, that one dimension is probably the best in the NHL. Kane's puck-handling skill isn't just elite, it is all-time great. His finishing skill, creativity in passing, vision, and ability to slow the game down with the puck are nearly unprecedented since Gretzky. Amazingly, he hasn't even had to be on the same line with Toews to achieve his scoring prowess, often being shifted between different centers—he spent the most ice-time with Brad Richards. The only thing that could slow his career is off-ice issues, which have not seemed to disappear for the Buffalo native, even into his mid-twenties.

Marcus Kruger							C						CHI
Season	Team	Age	GP	G	A	Pts	+/-	ESP/60	AdjCF%	iCF/60	OGVT	DGVT	SGVT	GVT
2012-13	CHI	22	47	4	9	13	3	1.24	57.3%	8.0	0.4	2.9	0.0	3.4
2013-14	CHI	23	81	8	20	28	6	1.78	52.2%	9.3	3.5	4.4	-0.6	7.3
2014-15	CHI	24	81	7	10	17	-5	1.16	52.6%	12.3	0.1	2.9	0.0	3.0
2015-16	CHI	25	64	8	12	20					0.0	2.0	0.0	2.0

Marcus Kruger's influence on the Blackhawks is derived from his defensive play. The 2009 fifth-round selection has found a niche as more than just a glorified faceoff winner. Despite taking only a quarter of his faceoffs in the offensive zone and 52.0% in the defensive zone, he was still able to manage a Corsi above 50%. His relentless effort and positional smarts make him a solid bottom-line role player. One thing to his advantage, and all of the Blackhawks' advantage, is that he wins faceoffs to the brilliant Duncan Keith, which makes it easy to transition. His Corsi numbers might not be as impressive elsewhere.

Joakim Nordstrom							C/LW						CHI
Season	Team	Age	GP	G	A	Pts	+/-	ESP/60	AdjCF%	iCF/60	OGVT	DGVT	SGVT	GVT
2013-14	CHI	21	16	1	2	3	-2	1.07	51.2%	16.4	-0.2	0.3	0.0	0.1
2014-15	CHI	22	38	0	3	3	-5	0.46	50.5%	13.1	-1.6	0.3	0.0	-1.4
2015-16	CHI	23	43	4	6	9					-1.0	0.7	0.0	-0.3

2010 third-round pick Joakim Nordstrom saw his first significant NHL action, dressing for 38 contests. He stuck out in one category in particular: hits. Nordstrom racked up 73 in under 400 minutes. That was about all that the six-foot-one center racked up. He managed just three points and was under 50% Corsi, a rarity for any Blackhawk. In the playoffs, Nordstrom was a liability in his three games, with a -3 blemish in very limited duty. After reworking their bottom six, it would not be a surprise to see the Swede fit in where he is better suited: the AHL.

Peter Regin							C						KHL
Season	Team	Age	GP	G	A	Pts	+/-	ESP/60	AdjCF%	iCF/60	OGVT	DGVT	SGVT	GVT
2012-13	OTT	26	27	0	3	3	-4	0.69	55.3%	14.0	-2.1	0.4	0.5	-1.2
2013-14	NYI, CHI	27	61	4	7	11	-5	0.76	51.3%	10.0	-0.8	1.1	0.0	0.3
2014-15	CHI	28	4	0	1	1	1	1.86	57.6%	8.8	0.1	0.1	0.0	0.3
2015-16	KHL	29	38	4	6	10					0.0	0.9	0.0	0.9

After playing 243 games at the NHL level, Peter Regin's departure for Europe seemed inevitable; he played 69 games in Rockford and only four with the Blackhawks. Even when he posts decent Corsi numbers during his big-league time, he is too small and lacks the offensive skill to be an impact player. Next season, the former Senator and Islander will suit up for Jokerit of the KHL.

Brad Richards							C							DET
Season	Team	Age	GP	G	A	Pts	+/-	ESP/60	AdjCF%	iCF/60	OGVT	DGVT	SGVT	GVT
2012-13	NYR	32	46	11	23	34	8	2.11	53.8%	13.2	5.0	2.0	-0.9	6.1
2013-14	NYR	33	82	20	31	51	-8	1.56	53.9%	16.4	4.8	1.1	1.2	7.1
2014-15	CHI	34	76	12	25	37	3	1.85	54.8%	16.0	2.4	2.0	-0.3	4.2
2015-16	DET	35	64	13	24	37					3.4	1.7	0.0	5.1

Last offseason, the Blackhawks signed Brad Richards for one year and $2 million, and the return on their investment was a solid contributor who chipped in 37 points during the regular season while centering Patrick Kane. In the playoffs, Richards added three goals and eleven assists, one of which was the clinching helper to Kane in Game 6. The Blackhawks had reached out when Richards' value was low and made out like bandits. At 35, the 2004 Conn Smythe winner is not much of a defensive presence and his speed is receding, but he can still fire a hefty number of shots on goal (199 in 76 games) while adding some shooting and playmaking skill on the power play. However, the Red Wings may have missed their chance at grabbing his last valuable year. If Richards loses one more step, he could look a lot like the second coming of Stephen Weiss.

Brandon Saad							LW							CBJ
Season	Team	Age	GP	G	A	Pts	+/-	ESP/60	AdjCF%	iCF/60	OGVT	DGVT	SGVT	GVT
2012-13	CHI	20	46	10	17	27	17	2.13	58.5%	12.9	3.6	3.3	-0.3	6.5
2013-14	CHI	21	78	19	28	47	20	2.01	58.1%	13.7	7.1	4.2	-0.8	10.4
2014-15	CHI	22	82	23	29	52	7	2.20	53.8%	14.5	8.4	3.5	-0.3	11.7
2015-16	CBJ	23	74	23	29	51					6.7	2.9	0.0	9.6

As he heads to Columbus, we will find out whether Brandon Saad is one of the best young American forwards in the NHL or a product of playing on a team with a dynastic roster. His performance of the past two years lean us toward the former. His combination of power and finesse allows him to accelerate past inadequate defensive coverage, transporting the puck into the middle of the ice or button-hooking to buy extra time for Chicago's trailers. Just entering his prime, Saad's boxcar and advanced stats weren't equal to some of his superstar teammates, but the Pittsburgh native has exhibited a pronounced 200-foot game and is comfortable generating offense even when facing difficult usage. While he won't be with Kane anymore, Saad joins a Blue Jackets club on the rise. He will play a major role in whether they succeed or fail.

Patrick Sharp — C/LW — DAL

Season	Team	Age	GP	G	A	Pts	+/-	ESP/60	AdjCF%	iCF/60	OGVT	DGVT	SGVT	GVT
2012-13	CHI	31	28	6	14	20	8	1.88	53.1%	18.3	3.1	1.0	-0.6	3.6
2013-14	CHI	32	82	34	44	78	13	2.49	57.9%	19.2	15.5	3.0	1.7	20.2
2014-15	CHI	33	68	16	27	43	-8	1.84	55.6%	18.9	5.6	0.6	0.8	7.0
2015-16	DAL	34	64	19	29	48					6.2	1.5	0.1	7.8

Strong statistical evidence suggests that once a sniper reaches his thirties, his numbers decline, often precipitously. Patrick Sharp had avoided this gloomy fate in the first three seasons of his thirties; in fact, some of his best efforts have come during these years. But last season, Sharp's prolific scoring fizzled. His shooting percentage was in single digits, in part because his shots were coming from the perimeter, not the middle, as revealed in his shooting charts. That said, the Thunder Bay, Ontario native still posted robust possession numbers—his new team, the Dallas Stars, was in need of some speed and shooting on the wings. Sharp can still supply shot volume, but even if playing with the likes of Tyler Seguin or Jason Spezza, it is questionable if he can return to his point-per-game ways.

Andrew Shaw — C — CHI

Season	Team	Age	GP	G	A	Pts	+/-	ESP/60	AdjCF%	iCF/60	OGVT	DGVT	SGVT	GVT
2012-13	CHI	21	48	9	6	15	6	1.26	55.0%	9.2	0.9	0.9	-0.1	1.7
2013-14	CHI	22	80	20	19	39	12	1.75	57.3%	12.0	2.7	2.9	-0.6	5.1
2014-15	CHI	23	79	15	11	26	-8	1.25	54.0%	12.6	-0.2	0.8	0.6	1.2
2015-16	CHI	24	67	15	17	32					2.1	1.3	0.0	3.5

On contenders and especially Cup winners, players like Andrew Shaw are lauded for their role and pumped up despite mostly mediocre play. While he may be known as a hard-working, gritty center, his numbers sunk badly after being taken off a line with Brandon Saad. The 24-year-old saw his points drop by 13 and goals-for percentage sink to 40.3% despite facing bottom lines. While Shaw did contribute five goals to Chicago's playoff run, he is a replaceable bottom-line forward—one that may fit the mold of a classic sell-high trade chip for the savvy Blackhawks management.

Teuvo Teravainen — C — CHI

Season	Team	Age	GP	G	A	Pts	+/-	ESP/60	AdjCF%	iCF/60	OGVT	DGVT	SGVT	GVT
2013-14	CHI	19	3	0	0	0	0	0.00	51.5%	9.3	-0.2	0.0	0.0	-0.2
2014-15	CHI	20	34	4	5	9	4	1.18	54.8%	14.7	0.4	1.1	0.0	1.5
2015-16	CHI	21	48	10	13	23					1.8	1.2	0.0	3.0

For a team that has won the Stanley Cup three times in six years, their prospect pool always seems to produce the next young star to step in. Teuvo Teravainen played 34 games in the regular season, putting up four goals and five assists, and then took his play to the next level come postseason time. The offensively-gifted former first-round pick yielded more points in the playoffs than he did during his regular-season stint, showcasing the upside that has the Blackhawks so high on his future. A highway robbery-type steal at 18th-overall in 2012—blame the organizations choosing ahead of Chicago here—Teravainen represents a player from whom Chicago hopes to extract high value while he is still on his entry-level deal. The Helsinki, Finland native supplies valuable puck-handling and playmaking that help create space and shot opportunities for his teammates.

Jonathan Toews							C						CHI
Season	Team	Age	GP	G	A	Pts	+/-	ESP/60	AdjCF%	iCF/60	OGVT	DGVT	SGVT	GVT
2012-13	CHI	24	47	23	25	48	28	3.27	59.0%	16.1	10.9	3.9	0.8	15.7
2013-14	CHI	25	76	28	40	68	26	2.41	59.9%	11.0	11.4	5.2	2.5	19.1
2014-15	CHI	26	81	28	38	66	30	2.30	55.9%	9.8	11.0	5.8	2.1	18.9
2015-16	CHI	27	77	27	40	67					9.6	3.7	0.1	13.4

As if Jonathan Toews wasn't already solidified as a future Hall of Famer, he made sure there was no room for debate by winning his third Stanley Cup as Blackhawks captain. He does everything on the ice at a high level, from driving possession, to scoring highlight goals, to shutting down opponents. He is the consummate leader on and off the ice. His poise is palpable in crunch-time situations in the playoffs. While teammate Patrick Kane produced points at a higher rate in the regular season and postseason, Toews can dominate in all three zones and still be effective when his offense is diminished. Despite being beaten by Bruins center Patrice Bergeron for the Selke Trophy, Toews has a convincing argument for being the best player in the NHL.

Antoine Vermette							C							ARI
Season	Team	Age	GP	G	A	Pts	+/-	ESP/60	AdjCF%	iCF/60	OGVT	DGVT	SGVT	GVT
2012-13	PHX	30	48	13	8	21	-3	1.61	49.1%	11.0	1.7	1.5	-0.9	2.3
2013-14	PHX	31	82	24	21	45	0	1.46	48.3%	9.3	4.5	3.3	1.0	8.8
2014-15	ARI, CHI	32	82	13	25	38	-25	1.24	47.1%	7.6	0.3	1.6	2.0	3.9
2015-16	ARI	33	66	11	19	30					1.3	1.6	0.1	3.1

The Blackhawks added Antoine Vermette for his faceoff acumen and to strengthen their center depth. Following the trade, it took a quite some time for him to find his comfort level in Chicago, but the former Blue Jacket scored several huge playoff goals, making the first-round pick sent to Arizona well worth it. Once a solid second-line center, the veteran forward has seen his effectiveness in both ends fade to a third-line center at best. As he returns to the Coyotes, he may find himself overwhelmed once again by assignments that he simply cannot handle anymore. And the Yotes may look to trade him for a first-round pick again this deadline!

Kris Versteeg							LW							CHI
Season	Team	Age	GP	G	A	Pts	+/-	ESP/60	AdjCF%	iCF/60	OGVT	DGVT	SGVT	GVT
2012-13	FLA	26	10	2	2	4	-8	1.29	41.9%	10.5	-0.2	-0.2	0.0	-0.3
2013-14	FLA, CHI	27	81	12	24	36	0	1.67	53.8%	13.3	3.1	1.9	-0.6	4.5
2014-15	CHI	28	61	14	20	34	11	2.04	54.5%	14.4	5.2	2.3	-0.3	7.2
2015-16	CHI	29	62	13	19	32					2.9	1.9	0.0	4.7

In his second stint with Chicago, Kris Versteeg has been very capable in his role as a two-way, complementary winger. The 2004 fifth rounder does not factor in the power play as he did during his first run with the Blackhawks, so his points will not be in the fifties as they once were, but he can still be a significant contributor at even strength—Versteeg scored 10 goals and added 16 assists at five-on-five. It didn't hurt that Joel Quenneville played him more minutes alongside Patrick Kane than any other forward on the team. When playing on the other wing from Kane, the pair had an incredible 71.0 goals-for percentage.

CHICAGO BLACKHAWKS

DEFENSEMEN

Kyle Cumiskey						LD						Free Agent	
Season	Team	Age	GP	G	A	Pts	+/-	ESP/60	AdjCF%	iCF/60	OGVT	DGVT	SGVT	GVT
2014-15	CHI	28	7	0	0	0	-1	0.00	52.0%	7.4	-0.3	0.1	0.0	-0.2
2015-16	Free Agent	29	28	1	4	5					-0.5	0.7	0.0	0.2

A 2005 seventh-round pick who has played 154 NHL games, Kyle Cumiskey returned to the league at the perfect time after a two-year stint in Sweden. The five-foot-ten blueliner played seven games for Chicago in the regular season before filling in for nine games during the postseason, where Quenneville used him very sparingly. While the 28-year-old showed he can still skate with NHLers, being able to skate is not enough to be a regular. Cumiskey struggles badly in his own zone to gain position on bigger players and lacks the hockey IQ to make up for his disadvantage, meaning Chicago would prefer to have him in Rockford than playing playoff minutes.

Niklas Hjalmarsson						LD							CHI
Season	Team	Age	GP	G	A	Pts	+/-	ESP/60	AdjCF%	iCF/60	OGVT	DGVT	SGVT	GVT
2012-13	CHI	25	46	2	8	10	15	0.72	56.0%	7.2	0.5	4.6	0.0	5.2
2013-14	CHI	26	81	4	22	26	11	0.89	54.0%	8.1	4.0	5.3	0.0	9.4
2014-15	CHI	27	82	3	16	19	25	0.72	53.7%	8.8	1.2	7.5	0.0	8.8
2015-16	CHI	28	68	4	16	19					1.1	4.3	0.0	5.3

Niklas Hjalmarsson is one of the NHL's best players in his own zone and also one of the most underappreciated because of the surrounding star power in Chicago. Quenneville happily employs him against opposing superstars and watches their offense evaporate. Hjalmarsson's pokechecking ability to disrupt zone entries helps Chicago reclaim possession, and he dissipates offensive-zone pressure via blocked shots. His main struggle is in handling the puck and making clean exit passes, which can cost Chicago offensive opportunities. But that seems like nitpicking after watching him lock down star after star.

Duncan Keith						LD							CHI
Season	Team	Age	GP	G	A	Pts	+/-	ESP/60	AdjCF%	iCF/60	OGVT	DGVT	SGVT	GVT
2012-13	CHI	29	47	3	24	27	16	1.07	54.2%	8.3	4.1	4.3	0.0	8.4
2013-14	CHI	30	79	6	55	61	22	1.55	57.3%	12.2	11.2	6.1	0.0	17.2
2014-15	CHI	31	80	10	35	45	12	1.06	56.0%	10.5	6.5	5.8	0.0	12.3
2015-16	CHI	32	72	9	36	45					6.9	4.6	0.0	11.4

Two-time Norris Trophy winner Duncan Keith added a Conn Smythe Trophy to his sparkling resume, as he ignited the Blackhawks in their historic Cup run and proved himself as the man to beat for best D-man in the NHL. The capability to play 30+ minutes and still dominate possession is unheard of outside of the elites—Keith does so by being savvy with his stickwork in his own end, consistently breaking up passes and scoring chances. Once he gets a hold of the puck, he can drive it up ice or save energy with a first pass. And he is unstoppable in distributing the puck in the offensive zone. He also proved that he can play without Brent Seabrook and still perform at a high level, as the two were split up in the postseason.

Johnny Oduya							LD						DAL
Season	Team	Age	GP	G	A	Pts	+/-	ESP/60	AdjCF%	iCF/60	OGVT	DGVT	SGVT	GVT
2012-13	CHI	31	48	3	9	12	12	0.71	56.5%	8.1	1.4	3.6	0.0	5.0
2013-14	CHI	32	77	3	13	16	11	0.66	53.8%	6.9	0.9	4.8	0.0	5.7
2014-15	CHI	33	76	2	8	10	5	0.43	51.8%	8.4	-1.6	4.0	0.0	2.4
2015-16	DAL	34	59	2	10	12					-0.3	2.7	0.0	2.4

Johnny Oduya experienced some bumps in the road during the regular season as it appeared Father Time was finally starting to catch up to him. However, come playoff time, he battled through injury to provide terrific defensive play. While he has never scored more than 29 points, the former Devil and Jet is a +58 for his career and has been as reliable night in and night out as any defenseman in the NHL. With Chicago, he was a perfect fit with their skilled veteran defensemen. His new role in Dallas will offer a significant challenge as he joins an up-tempo Lindy Ruff system and group of up-and-coming blueliners.

Michael Paliotta							RD						CBJ
Season	Team	Age	GP	G	A	Pts	+/-	ESP/60	AdjCF%	iCF/60	OGVT	DGVT	SGVT	GVT
2014-15	CHI	22	1	0	1	1	0	4.71	48.3%	13.6	0.3	0.0	0.0	0.3
2015-16	CBJ	23	25	2	6	8					0.7	0.8	0.0	1.5

A third-round pick from 2011, Michael Paliotta chose to stay with the Blackhawks organization after finishing his career at the University of Vermont. The Westport, Connecticut native played in just one game in Chicago, but will see more action if he can transfer his offensive talent to The Show—as Paliotta scored an impressive 36 points in 41 games at Vermont.

Michal Rozsival							RD						CHI
Season	Team	Age	GP	G	A	Pts	+/-	ESP/60	AdjCF%	iCF/60	OGVT	DGVT	SGVT	GVT
2012-13	CHI	34	27	0	12	12	18	1.47	61.8%	5.0	2.3	3.2	0.2	5.8
2013-14	CHI	35	42	1	7	8	7	0.74	59.3%	6.7	0.1	2.3	0.0	2.3
2014-15	CHI	36	65	1	12	13	0	0.75	53.9%	7.4	-0.1	2.8	0.0	2.7
2015-16	CHI	37	51	2	9	11					-0.1	2.2	0.0	2.1

At 37, Michal Rozsival proved he could still offer solid minutes on a third pairing. The former Penguin, Ranger, and Coyote makes up for his lack of foot speed with positioning and simple play. A slow-skating, make-the-right-play defenseman may sound fairly replaceable, but when Rozsival went down before playoff time, the Blackhawks struggled to fill the role, barely giving their fill-in third pairing any ice-time in the postseason. Moving forward, it may be tough for the aging veteran to find a spot in the league as the Blackhawks move toward a more mobile blueline.

David Rundblad							RD						CHI
Season	Team	Age	GP	G	A	Pts	+/-	ESP/60	AdjCF%	iCF/60	OGVT	DGVT	SGVT	GVT
2012-13	PHX	22	8	0	1	1	-5	0.77	41.9%	10.6	-0.2	-0.5	-0.3	-0.9
2013-14	PHX, CHI	23	17	0	1	1	-4	0.00	54.4%	11.2	-0.7	-0.3	-0.6	-1.5
2014-15	CHI	24	49	3	11	14	17	1.30	56.4%	13.1	2.2	3.6	0.0	5.8
2015-16	CHI	25	52	3	11	14					1.0	2.6	0.0	3.5

CHICAGO BLACKHAWKS

Chicago traded for David Rundblad to help bolster its defensive depth, but he was mostly found on the bench or in the pressbox come crunch time. The young Swede's puck skills are admirable but his defensive ability and decision-making are serious concerns. Solid offensive output and an outstanding +17 should give the Blackhawks hope that he can eventually take bigger assignments, but he demonstrated in the playoffs he is not yet ready for the brightest lights. Defensemen like Rundblad usually take the next step to become effective possession defenders or bounce from team to team, frustrating each one along the way.

Brent Seabrook							RD						CHI
Season	Team	Age	GP	G	A	Pts	+/-	ESP/60	AdjCF%	iCF/60	OGVT	DGVT	SGVT	GVT
2012-13	CHI	27	47	8	12	20	12	0.95	53.3%	7.6	3.8	3.9	0.0	7.7
2013-14	CHI	28	82	7	34	41	23	1.24	57.4%	9.4	6.6	6.5	0.0	13.1
2014-15	CHI	29	82	8	23	31	-3	0.61	52.3%	10.9	2.5	2.9	0.0	5.4
2015-16	CHI	30	69	8	26	34					4.4	3.4	0.0	7.8

Brent Seabrook was separated from Duncan Keith for the first time in a long time during the playoffs, but still proved immensely valuable to Chicago. The Blackhawks essentially had no third pair, putting all the pressure on their top four. The 2003 first-round selection finished in the top 50 in regular-season points among defensemen and added a surprising seven goals in the playoffs. In addition, the stoutly-built Seabrook brings a necessary physical edge that the Blackhawks otherwise lack. The Richmond, British Columbia native can get overshadowed by Keith's star power, but he is very skilled at defending enemy forays and catalyzing Chicago's transition.

Kimmo Timonen							LD						Retired
Season	Team	Age	GP	G	A	Pts	+/-	ESP/60	AdjCF%	iCF/60	OGVT	DGVT	SGVT	GVT
2012-13	PHI	37	45	5	24	29	3	1.06	52.2%	9.1	5.2	3.5	0.0	8.7
2013-14	PHI	38	77	6	29	35	5	0.81	55.1%	9.9	4.6	3.7	-0.3	8.0
2014-15	CHI	39	16	0	0	0	-3	0.00	45.6%	5.0	-0.5	-0.3	0.0	-0.9
2015-16	Retired	40	44	2	9	11					0.2	1.5	0.0	1.7

The Blackhawks acquired long-time Flyer Kimmo Timonen to help solidify their defensive corps. The hope was that after missing most of the season with blood clots, the proud veteran could stabilize Chicago's bottom pairing. Unfortunately, he didn't. Timonen was a turnstile defensively and incapable offensively. His poor play, along with Michal Rozsival's playoff-ending injury, forced the Blackhawks to lean on their top-four defensemen to a startling degree. However, he provided a wonderful moment, taking the Stanley Cup handoff from Jonathan Toews, putting an exclamation point on a terrific career.

Trevor van Riemsdyk							RD						CHI
Season	Team	Age	GP	G	A	Pts	+/-	ESP/60	CF%	iCF/60	OGVT	DGVT	SGVT	GVT
2014-15	CHI	23	18	0	1	1	0	0.25	60.0%	9.9	-0.5	0.3	0.0	-0.2
2015-16	CHI	24	34	2	5	7					-0.2	1.0	0.0	0.8

Trevor van Riemsdyk was not the heralded prospect that his brother was when he turned professional. Unlike James, who went second overall in 2007, Trevor was never drafted, instead signing as a college free agent after spending three years at New Hampshire. The New Jersey native acclimated impressively in his rookie season, appearing in 18 games before suffering a regular-season-ending injury. While "TVR" only registered an assist for his efforts, his hockey IQ could help earn him a regular spot going forward.

GOALTENDERS

Corey Crawford — G — CHI

Season	Team	Age	GP	W	L	OT	GAA	Sv%	ESSV%	QS%	GGVT	DGVT	SGVT	GVT
2012-13	CHI	28	30	19	5	5	1.94	.926	.934	67.9%	12.1	0.8	-1.5	11.4
2013-14	CHI	29	59	32	16	10	2.26	.917	.925	58.9%	9.8	1.5	0.0	11.3
2014-15	CHI	30	57	32	20	5	2.27	.924	.931	68.4%	18.8	0.0	2.4	21.2
2015-16	CHI	31	49					.917			9.3	0.4	0.2	9.9

How history remembers Corey Crawford will be fascinating. When the hockey intelligentsia discusses his place in the Blackhawks' success, they should see a goaltender who consistently manned the nets well enough for Chicago to be a juggernaut and compete for the Stanley Cup on an annual basis. The Montreal native offered an impressive .924 save percentage during the regular season and rose to the occasion after being benched in favor of backup Scott Darling during the opening series against Nashville. However, there is no ignoring the fact that the Blackhawks make kings out of their goalies—and not just Cup-winning starters Antti Niemi and Crawford. Darling and Antti Raanta each had .936 save percentages in 2014-15. It is enough to make you wonder, even though he has won and performed well, if spending big to keep "Crow" long term was a mistake.

Scott Darling — G — CHI

Season	Team	Age	GP	W	L	OT	GAA	Sv%	ESSV%	QS%	GGVT	DGVT	SGVT	GVT
2014-15	CHI	26	14	9	4	0	1.94	.936	.947	76.9%	8.8	0.0	1.9	10.6
2015-16	CHI	27	29					.919			7.6	0.0	0.3	8.0

An Illinois native and sixth-round pick who fought against the odds to make it to the NHL, Scott Darling became the much-discussed Cinderella story after he performed spectacularly in a relief role for Corey Crawford during the first-round series against the Predators. Eventually, the magic wore off and Crawford replaced Darling permanently. However, Darling's .936 save percentage during the regular season and postseason—albeit in a small sample—suggests that the former Maine Black Bear is a very competent backup who may get a chance to start down the road.

Antti Raanta — G — NYR

Season	Team	Age	GP	W	L	OT	GAA	Sv%	ESSV%	QS%	GGVT	DGVT	SGVT	GVT
2013-14	CHI	24	25	13	5	4	2.71	.897	.896	59.1%	-6.2	0.8	-2.0	-7.3
2014-15	CHI	25	14	7	4	1	1.89	.936	.938	66.7%	8.2	0.1	-1.0	7.3
2015-16	NYR	26	23					.913			1.2	0.1	-0.2	1.1

Antti Raanta struggled during his first stint in 2013-14, but turned things around when given a second chance. The undersized Finn posted an outstanding .936 save percentage, which caught the attention of the New York Rangers, where he signed to back up Henrik Lundqvist for 2015-16. Known as an athletic but wild netminder, Raanta will have to perfect the art of staying ready to play despite getting starts only once or twice per month.

Sam Hitchcock and Matthew Coller

Colorado Avalanche

Every season, there is at least one team that makes the playoffs despite terrible underlying numbers, as Colorado did in both 2009-10 and 2013-14. As a rule, those teams experience regression...and feel the wrath of disappointed fanbases the following season. At *Hockey Prospectus*, we have been around long enough (since 2009!) to have seen this pattern repeat itself numerous times, in Colorado, Dallas, Minnesota, and Toronto—and maybe next season in Calgary (although VUKOTA is bullish on them). We have studied the concepts of random variation, sustainability, and regression in detail, and have the perspective to understand that there is more to projecting teams than pointing at one or two numbers and forecasting doom.

What is regression?

It was widely written that Colorado's success in 2013-14 was due to random variation, it was unsustainable, and their results were due for regression (or more precisely, reversion). But what does all of that really mean?

First of all, these are all statistical terms, not hockey terms. There is no rule in hockey that states that just because a player or team is doing well, that it is random, that it cannot last, and that performances will be closer to league average the following year. Similarly, a bad player or team won't necessarily get better (without a good reason).

However, in the world of analytics, the basic premise is that when past statistics are used to predict the future, you acknowledge that a portion of observed historical results are caused by random variation, and not the skill or talent being tracked and predicted. This concept applies to any future prediction for which stats are used, not just hockey.

We all know that every team's final position in the standings is some combination of its own combined talent along with breaks and bounces along the way. That random variation includes uncontrollable factors such as injuries, hot and cold streaks, difficulty of schedule, officiating, hitting goalposts and crossbars in close-game situations, and the shootout. When the portion of the observed outcome caused by random variation returns to normal, leaving only the reproducible, skill-based component, that is regression at work.

How can you determine what portion of the observed outcome was caused by random variation? The most popular method is to split the data in half, and to calculate the variation between the halves. Loosely speaking, two halves that are entirely skill-based will

AVALANCHE IN A BOX

Last Season

Goals For	219	21st
Goals Against	227	21st
GVT	-8	21st
Points	90	21st
Playoffs	Did not make playoffs	

After a breakout season in 2013-14, the Avalanche's percentages fell back to earth, and so did their position in the standings.

Three-Year Record

GVT	-14	19th
Points	241	16th
Playoffs	1 Appearance, 3 Wins	

VUKOTA Projection

Goals For	225	12th
Goals Against	215	9th
GVT	9	10th
Points	95	10th

The Avalanche remain one of the best young teams in the NHL. With just a slight improvement, they will be back among the playoff teams.

Top Four Prospects

M. Rantanen (F), B. Gormley (D), C. Bigras (D)

match exactly, while two halves that are entirely the result of random chance will have no relationship. Variation between the two halves is the result of random chance.

A second approach is to simulate performances entirely with random variation, and then calculate the extent to which the simulations match the actual, observed outcomes. Any relationship between the two is due to random chance, and whatever is left over is the skill-based component within the player's or team's control, with predictive value. This second method can be useful in its own right, or to verify conclusions reached with the split-halves approach.

What happened to the Avalanche?

Applying this approach to the 2013-14 Avalanche, the observed result was that they finished third overall with 112 points (largely a consequence of the second-best team shooting percentage of 10.1% and a fifth-best save percentage of .923), had a league-best 15-8 combined record in overtime and the shootout, and were 13-4 in one-goal games decided in regulation.

Each of these observed outcomes included a great deal of random variation, as opposed to persistent talent. If that random variation returned to league average, then there would not be enough of an remaining skill component to maintain Colorado's lofty position in the standings.

Although their save percentage remained high in 2014-15, the Avalanche finished with a league-average shooting percentage of 9.1%, a .500 overtime and shootout record (12-12), and they were slightly underwater in one-goal games decided in regulation (9-11). Consequently, Colorado finished with only 90 points, and tumbled all the way down to 21st place overall. That is regression.

It is not our intention to make this sound simplistic. A team is not destined to suffer from regression simply because its shooting-, save-, and close-game winning percentages are excellent. There are many reasons why such blind faith in a small set of numbers can lead an analyst astray.

First of all, it might actually be a great team. Not only do great teams have great shooting and save percentages, and great records in close games, but they also continue to win even when those particular strengths are failing them. That is why it is important to look at areas where there is far less random variation, such as puck-possession percentage, the most prominent and frequently-noted example.

Unfortunately for the Avalanche, their 2013-14 edition was one of the league's worst possession teams. In close-game, even-strength situations, Colorado ranked 25th in Corsi percentage (47.4%). If you prefer to base their possession estimate on the percentage of even-strength faceoffs taken in the offensive versus defensive zone, then they were 20th (49.5%). Even if your preference is "the eye test", it was still obvious that Colorado was often playing without the puck, especially relative to other teams at the top of the standings, like Boston, St. Louis, and Chicago.

Low possession numbers among playoff teams is one of the most reliable indicators of an upcoming tumble in the standings. As shown in the chart below, the average finish the following season for comparable teams is 23rd. Colorado finished 21st.

\multicolumn{4}{c}{**Top-10 worst possession teams in the playoffs, 2009 to 2015**}
Season	Team	Possession	Next year
2012-13	Toronto	44.0%	22nd
2014-15	Ottawa	45.6%	TBD
2010-11	Anaheim	45.7%	26th
2011-12	Nashville	46.1%	27th
2013-14	Colorado	46.8%	21st
2014-15	Calgary	46.8%	TBD
2009-10	Colorado	46.9%	29th
2008-09	Montreal	46.9%	20th
2012-13	Washington	47.7%	17th
2013-14	Philadelphia	48.2%	24th

However, even though Colorado was a poor possession team in 2013-14, there was no commandment that they had to remain that way. Every season, several teams make dramatic improvements in possession, because of new players and/or coaches, or the natural, age-related development of their existing rosters.

Unfortunately for the Avalanche, they lost two of their top possession players in Paul Stastny and P.A. Parenteau while acquiring 35-year-old stay-at-home defenseman Brad Stuart and a pair of 37-year-old forwards in Jarome Iginla and Daniel Briere. That did not represent a net improvement, even when the natural development of an otherwise young team was factored in. Unlike in Nashville, where there was a new coach, an influx of new players, and a new focus on puck possession, there was no reason to believe things would change in Colorado.

Blending in traditional analysis

Traditional analysis continues to play a leading role in team evaluation, despite the tremendous strides we have made in understanding the game through the lens of hockey analytics. Possession numbers are helpful, but that is where the job begins, not where it ends.

To make a prediction, it is not enough to calculate random variation, apply some regression, and place extra weight on persistent attributes like puck possession. If that were so, then a purely statistical model would consistently outperform hockey's foremost experts. And trust me: no one is more capable of developing such a system than our resident genius Tom Awad, and he would be the first one to stop you from taking his VUKOTA projections to the bank.

The most important service the analytics community can provide is to bridge the cold, dispassionate world of numbers and the realities we see with our own eyes. From this critical perspective, everybody saw Colorado's depth lines exposed by the Minnesota Wild in the opening round of the 2014 playoffs. Furthermore, it just simply didn't make sense that Erik Johnson could continue to single-handedly carry a blue line composed entirely of long-time AHLers, near-retirement veterans...and youngster Tyson Barrie.

While it is probably obvious why a two-way, tough-minutes defenseman like Erik Johnson is being singled out here, Barrie may be more of a surprise. Aside from his 10 games prior to the 2012-13 lockout, Barrie now has 104 points in 176 career games. That is just shy of 0.60 points per game, which ranks an impressive 13th among NHL defensemen over that span. And yet, he doesn't get the same attention as other relatively-sheltered puck-moving defensemen who produce at the same level, like Kevin Shattenkirk, Mike Green, and Keith Yandle. And he certainly doesn't get paid like them!

Barrie's even-strength scoring rate of 1.45 points per 60 minutes over that span is dead even with Kris Letang, and behind only Victor Hedman. And those are defensemen who get to play with Sidney Crosby and Evgeni Malkin, and Steven Stamkos and Tyler Johnson!

Leading defensemen scorers at even strength, post-2013 lockout		
Player	Team	ESP/60
Victor Hedman	Tampa Bay	1.51
Kris Letang	Pittsburgh	1.45
Tyson Barrie	Colorado	1.45
Erik Karlsson	Ottawa	1.35
Dustin Byfuglien	Winnipeg	1.29
Duncan Keith	Chicago	1.25
P.K. Subban	Montreal	1.22
Alex Pietrangelo	St. Louis	1.22
Mark Giordano	Calgary	1.22
Mike Green	Washington	1.18
Minimum 1500 minutes played		

This is not to ignore Colorado's impressive group of forwards. In old stars Jarome Iginla and Alex Tanguay, and young stars Gabriel Landeskog, Matt Duchene, and Ryan O'Reilly (now with the Sabres), the Avalanche had five forwards who scored 55 points or more. The Avs are the only team to accomplish this feat in back-to-back seasons since Buffalo and Carolina in 2005-06 and 2006-07. Even if Iginla or Tanguay slides in scoring, 20-year-old Nathan MacKinnon could help Colorado become the first team to accomplish this feat three seasons in a row since the mighty 1988-1989 to 1990-91 Oilers.

What to expect in 2015-16

While it is fair to say Colorado overachieved in 2009-10 and 2013-14, it is equally fair to say they underachieved in 2008-09, 2010-11, and 2012-13. Along with 2011-12, last year's performance was the truest representation of the team's abilities, and an excellent basis on which to project them going forward.

Given the incredible youth and two-way talent the team possesses up front, and how teams like the Islanders, Lightning, and Capitals have shown that weak blue lines can be repaired quickly, it is reasonable to put the Avalanche back in the wild-card picture...if the management team of Joe Sakic, Patrick Roy, and company plays their cards right.

As for all the statistical concepts like random variation, regression, and sustainability, they can all be summarized with the first three of Alan Ryder's 2008 "Ten Laws of Hockey Analytics." The first law is that winning is all that matters, the second law states that goals for and against are the only factors that affect winning, and the third law is that goals are random events.

To outscore opponents, teams have to generate more opportunities than their opponents, and/or capitalize on a greater share of them. Since that latter factor is largely a "random event", Colorado has to transform itself from a team that is being outplayed by 5.3 shots, 6.0 chances, and 13.4 shot attempts per night into one that no longer needs to rely on sharp shooting and hot goaltending. In a sense, it is really that simple.

Rob Vollman

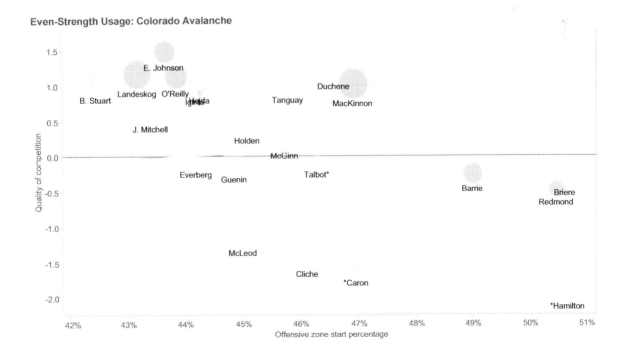

COLORADO AVALANCHE

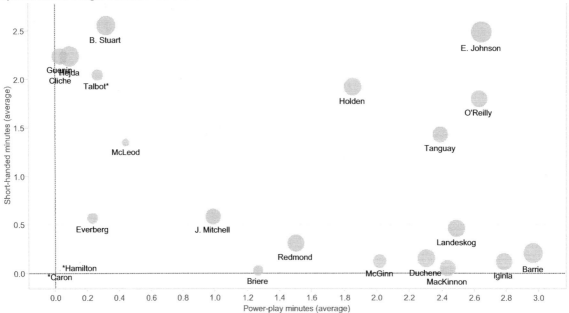

Special Teams Usage: Colorado Avalanche

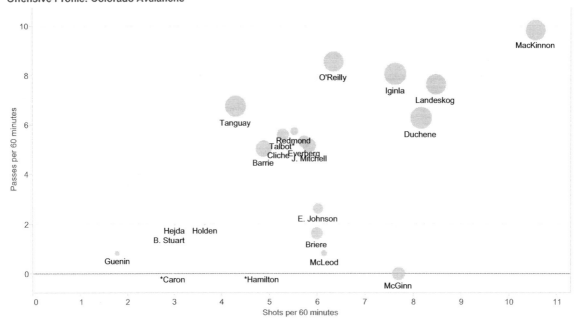

Offensive Profile: Colorado Avalanche

COLORADO AVALANCHE

Offensive Profile: Colorado Avalanche

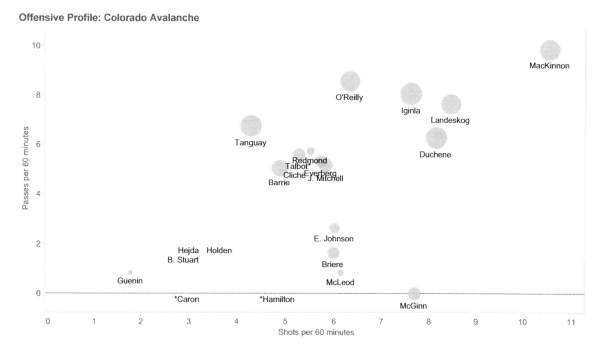

FORWARDS

Andrew Agozzino							LW							COL
Season	Team	Age	GP	G	A	Pts	+/-	ESP/60	AdjCF%	iCF/60	OGVT	DGVT	SGVT	GVT
2014-15	COL	23	1	0	1	1	1	6.15	30.8%	10.7	0.2	0.1	0.0	0.3
2015-16	COL	24	26	5	7	12					1.0	0.6	0.0	1.6

A small but skilled forward, Andrew Agozzino drew into his first NHL game and registered his first career point. Despite going undrafted, Agozzino has been a remarkably consistent offensive force throughout his young career, including setting all-time career scoring marks for the OHL's Niagara IceDogs. Over the course of four seasons, he amassed 159 goals and 306 points...concluding his career by winning the somewhat inauspicious Leo Lalonde Trophy as the OHL's best overage player, a list dominated by more unknowns than NHL regulars. Yet, his junior success has translated well to the professional ranks, as he carried the Lake Erie Monsters offensively in 2014-15, notching an impressive 30 goals and 64 points in 75 contests, 24 points beyond his closest teammate. Given the struggles the Avalanche faced filling out their bottom six in 2014-15, the team should be looking for talented newcomers, like Agozzino.

Patrick Bordeleau							LW							COL
Season	Team	Age	GP	G	A	Pts	+/-	ESP/60	AdjCF%	iCF/60	OGVT	DGVT	SGVT	GVT
2012-13	COL	26	46	2	3	5	-7	1.06	44.2%	8.1	-0.8	-0.1	0.0	-0.9
2013-14	COL	27	82	6	5	11	-1	1.17	42.6%	6.7	0.2	0.6	0.0	0.9
2014-15	COL	28	1	0	0	0	0	0.00	34.2%	0.0	0.0	0.0	0.0	0.0
2015-16	*COL*	*29*	*41*	*4*	*4*	*8*					*-0.2*	*0.7*	*0.0*	*0.4*

After years of toiling in the minors, Patrick Bordeleau emerged to provide the Avalanche with a physical, enforcer-like presence on their fourth line. After playing all 82 games in 2013-14, the six-foot-six Bordeleau was beset by injuries in 2014-15. The Montreal native missed the first three months recovering from back surgery, only to fracture his kneecap in his first game back, ending his season. When healthy, Bordeleau played a role that no longer brings value in the NHL as an enforcer, spearheading the Avalanche's never-have-the-puck strategy. He led the team in hits in 2012-13 and 2013-14, despite averaging just 6:53 per game.

Daniel Briere							RW							Retired
Season	Team	Age	GP	G	A	Pts	+/-	ESP/60	AdjCF%	iCF/60	OGVT	DGVT	SGVT	GVT
2012-13	PHI	35	34	6	10	16	-13	1.34	47.3%	14.0	0.8	-0.6	-0.3	-0.1
2013-14	MTL	36	69	13	12	25	1	1.49	47.3%	13.1	2.4	1.2	0.0	3.7
2014-15	COL	37	57	8	4	12	-7	1.17	41.1%	9.6	-0.3	0.0	0.4	0.1
2015-16	*Retired*	*38*	*50*	*7*	*8*	*15*					*0.7*	*0.8*	*0.0*	*1.5*

Acquired on June 30, 2014, the plan was for Daniel Briere to replace some of the scoring punch the Avs lost down the middle when Paul Stastny departed for St. Louis. The experiment was short lived as the veteran center was primarily stuck playing right wing on the fourth line. Despite sheltered minutes, including the luxury of the highest offensive zone start percentage of any Avalanche forward outside of Max Talbot, Briere generated scoring chances at a pedestrian rate. Worse, Briere and his linemates were consistently outplayed by opposing team's fourth lines, yielding almost 46 scoring chances per 60 minutes. Given his marked, steady decline since 2010-11, the time was right to call it a career for the 37-year-old former Sabre and Flyer.

Jordan Caron							LW							STL
Season	Team	Age	GP	G	A	Pts	+/-	ESP/60	AdjCF%	iCF/60	OGVT	DGVT	SGVT	GVT
2012-13	BOS	22	17	1	2	3	1	1.16	45.2%	11.4	0.1	0.3	0.0	0.3
2013-14	BOS	23	35	1	2	3	-8	0.51	50.6%	14.7	-1.8	-0.3	0.0	-2.1
2014-15	BOS, COL	24	30	0	0	0	-2	0.00	39.2%	7.0	-1.7	0.2	0.0	-1.5
2015-16	*STL*	*25*	*38*	*3*	*3*	*6*					*-1.0*	*0.6*	*0.0*	*-0.3*

Colorado dealt veteran center Maxime Talbot to Boston at the trade deadline, receiving 2009 first-rounder Jordan Caron in return. Caron had struggled to gain regular ice-time on the Bruins, but there was some optimism that he could recapture the scoring touch he had demonstrated both with Rimouski in the QMJHL and Providence in the AHL. Following his acquisition, the Avs debuted the young left wing on the second line alongside Matt Duchene and Jarome Iginla. Unfortunately, Caron struggled to make any kind of impact and quickly found himself in a fourth-line role. In his 19 games with the Avalanche, he managed to record a big goose egg in points, but more alarming is that his possession numbers were even worse. Even accounting for his time with Boston, the one-time prospect posted only 35.9 Corsi for per 60 minutes, among the worst in the entire league.

Marc-Andre Cliche — C — COL

Season	Team	Age	GP	G	A	Pts	+/-	ESP/60	AdjCF%	iCF/60	OGVT	DGVT	SGVT	GVT
2013-14	COL	26	76	1	6	7	-11	0.59	41.5%	8.9	-2.6	1.1	0.0	-1.5
2014-15	COL	27	74	2	5	7	-2	0.67	38.5%	8.4	-1.9	2.7	0.0	0.8
2015-16	COL	28	57	3	5	8					-1.4	1.8	0.0	0.4

Marc-Andre Cliche is one of several journeymen who finally found a regular NHL job under new head coach Patrick Roy in 2013-14. Cliche is well removed from any prospect luster attached to his second-round selection in the 2005 NHL Entry Draft, but he does possess a marketable skillset. Strictly a fourth-line center for the Avalanche, he led Avalanche forwards in penalty-kill minutes, and won 51.3% of his faceoffs. Offense does not appear to be Cliche's strong suit, due in part to abysmal 2.2% shooting over his two NHL seasons.

Matt Duchene — C — COL

Season	Team	Age	GP	G	A	Pts	+/-	ESP/60	AdjCF%	iCF/60	OGVT	DGVT	SGVT	GVT
2012-13	COL	21	47	17	26	43	-12	2.65	47.2%	12.6	6.1	1.2	0.7	8.1
2013-14	COL	22	71	23	47	70	8	2.89	49.7%	17.3	12.8	1.8	1.0	15.6
2014-15	COL	23	82	21	34	55	3	2.18	42.8%	13.3	8.3	2.0	1.6	11.9
2015-16	COL	24	72	24	38	62					9.1	2.4	0.1	11.7

The third-overall selection in 2009, Matt Duchene was expected to become a cornerstone of a rebuilding franchise. The Brampton Battalion star received plaudits for his skating and hockey sense with the anticipation he would blossom into an elite two-way center. The early returns on Duchene's career showed a player with dazzling offensive upside, averaging nearly a point per game in 2012-13 and 2013-14. Yet, Duchene's game took a major step backward in 2014-15. Despite seeing more sheltered minutes behind top center Ryan O'Reilly, Duchene notched only 55 points. Duchene will either need to bump his scoring back up or develop his two-way game to have a chance at elite status.

Dennis Everberg — RW — COL

Season	Team	Age	GP	G	A	Pts	+/-	ESP/60	AdjCF%	iCF/60	OGVT	DGVT	SGVT	GVT
2014-15	COL	23	55	3	9	12	-7	1.19	39.8%	10.2	-0.7	0.1	0.0	-0.6
2015-16	COL	24	51	6	11	17					0.3	0.8	0.0	1.1

Dennis Everberg, a native of Nicklas Lidstrom's hometown of Vasteras, Sweden, was signed as a 22-year-old free agent following the conclusion of the 2013-14 season. Originally intended to provide the team with organizational depth, the young Swede found himself a frequent fixture in the lineup due to a multitude of injuries. At six-foot-four with a strong skating stride, the Avalanche hope Everberg can develop into a third-line power forward with some scoring punch, who could fill a hole in the top six when called upon. Everberg created little offense in his first taste of NHL action, though he potted five goals in 12 AHL games with Lake Erie.

Freddie Hamilton — C/RW — COL

Season	Team	Age	GP	G	A	Pts	+/-	ESP/60	AdjCF%	iCF/60	OGVT	DGVT	SGVT	GVT
2013-14	SJS	22	11	0	0	0	-5	0.00	49.1%	13.6	-0.9	-0.3	0.0	-1.2
2014-15	SJS, COL	23	18	1	0	1	-2	0.46	39.4%	10.5	-0.8	0.0	0.0	-0.8
2015-16	COL	24	33	5	5	9					-0.1	0.5	0.0	0.4

The older brother of Bruins and Flames defenseman Dougie, Freddie Hamilton was acquired from San Jose at the 2015 trade deadline for defenseman Karl Stollery. Given the poor play of the Avs, Hamilton got what amounted to an extended tryout. Yet in 17 games, Hamilton scored just one goal, and like the rest of his Avalanche teammates, was dominated in terms of puck possession. Reason for hope? At 23 years old, the right-shooting centerman is only three years removed from an appearance on Team Canada's 2012 World Junior team. Furthermore, he has been moderately productive his past two AHL seasons, with 77 points in 121 games. Given his pedigree, Hamilton remains in contention for a depth role.

Joey Hishon — C — COL

Season	Team	Age	GP	G	A	Pts	+/-	ESP/60	AdjCF%	iCF/60	OGVT	DGVT	SGVT	GVT
2014-15	COL	23	13	1	1	2	-1	1.01	39.4%	13.0	0.1	0.0	0.0	0.1
2015-16	COL	24	31	5	6	12					0.8	0.6	0.0	1.4

Originally drafted in the first round of 2010, Joey Hishon had a long, arduous road to his NHL debut, including missing all of 2011-12 and most of 2012-13 with post-concussion syndrome. Hishon was a dynamic player in junior hockey, garnering recognition as the best playmaker and stickhandler in the OHL's Western Conference in 2010-11. While Hishon appeared in three playoffs games in 2014, he received his first extended look last season, playing in 13 games. The young center performed well in his debut, despite only tallying two points. Though he is already age 24, given his injury history, there should be some expectation of further growth, even if he never becomes a dynamic top-six talent as originally envisioned.

Jarome Iginla — RW — COL

Season	Team	Age	GP	G	A	Pts	+/-	ESP/60	AdjCF%	iCF/60	OGVT	DGVT	SGVT	GVT
2012-13	CGY, PIT	35	44	14	19	33	-5	1.88	48.7%	13.8	5.2	0.8	-0.3	5.7
2013-14	BOS	36	78	30	31	61	34	2.36	54.8%	14.7	11.5	4.0	-0.8	14.7
2014-15	COL	37	82	29	30	59	0	2.21	41.2%	11.5	10.4	1.7	1.0	13.1
2015-16	COL	38	68	21	26	46					6.0	1.8	0.0	7.9

When Paul Stastny departed via free agency, the Avalanche moved quickly, reallocating his money to Jarome Iginla, ostensibly to provide another veteran scoring presence. In theory, the move allowed the team to play O'Reilly and Duchene at center, with Iginla offering scoring and leadership on one of the team's top two right-wing positions. On the surface, the 37-year-old Iginla maintained his historically strong production level, notching 29 goals (16th in NHL) and 30 assists while dressing for every game. Signed for two more seasons, the Avalanche are hoping the aging forward will be able to keep up his scoring pace without being overmatched defensively. At the end of it all, Iginla will waltz into the Hockey Hall of Fame as an all-time great power forward.

COLORADO AVALANCHE

Gabriel Landeskog — LW — COL

Season	Team	Age	GP	G	A	Pts	+/-	ESP/60	AdjCF%	iCF/60	OGVT	DGVT	SGVT	GVT
2012-13	COL	20	36	9	8	17	-4	1.33	49.4%	15.9	1.5	0.6	-0.3	1.8
2013-14	COL	21	81	26	39	65	21	2.54	49.4%	15.4	11.2	3.2	0.0	14.4
2014-15	COL	22	82	23	36	59	-2	1.98	47.3%	13.1	8.0	2.2	0.1	10.3
2015-16	COL	23	73	25	35	60					8.1	2.4	0.0	10.6

At just 23 years of age, Gabriel Landeskog is emerging as one of the NHL's more complete young left wings. The team captain has recorded at least 50 points and 150 hits in each of his three full NHL seasons. Last year, Landeskog was again asked to do the heavy lifting for an overmatched Avalanche team—and he performed admirably. In addition to leading the team in on-ice scoring chances, Landeskog essentially played the opposition to a draw, surrendering just seven more scoring chances against than created. Despite Colorado's 29th-ranked power play, Landeskog set a new personal best with eight power-play goals, tied for the team lead with Iginla. The Kitchener Rangers product, in the midst of a seven-year extension, will be a fixture for many seasons to come.

Nathan MacKinnon — RW/C — COL

Season	Team	Age	GP	G	A	Pts	+/-	ESP/60	AdjCF%	iCF/60	OGVT	DGVT	SGVT	GVT
2013-14	COL	18	82	24	39	63	20	2.25	47.2%	15.6	10.5	3.1	-0.8	12.7
2014-15	COL	19	64	14	24	38	-7	2.00	48.3%	17.4	3.7	0.7	2.9	7.4
2015-16	COL	20	69	23	35	58					8.1	2.1	0.1	10.4

2013 first-overall selection and 2014 Calder Trophy winner Nathan MacKinnon can be an elite, game-breaking offensive talent, as evidenced by playoff runs with the Halifax Mooseheads during the Memorial Cup and the 2014 playoffs with the Avalanche. MacKinnon's top-end speed and puck skills helped him drive Colorado's attack. Despite finishing with a disappointing 38 points in 2014-15, the speedy right wing paced the Avs in Relative Corsi while finishing second in individual scoring chances—despite seeing action in only 64 games, his season ending on March 4 due to a broken foot.

Jamie McGinn — LW — BUF

Season	Team	Age	GP	G	A	Pts	+/-	ESP/60	AdjCF%	iCF/60	OGVT	DGVT	SGVT	GVT
2012-13	COL	24	47	11	11	22	-13	1.35	46.7%	14.6	0.0	0.2	0.0	0.2
2013-14	COL	25	79	19	19	38	-3	1.61	47.5%	14.6	3.8	1.0	0.0	4.8
2014-15	COL	26	19	4	2	6	-9	1.25	39.2%	9.7	-0.3	-0.5	0.0	-0.8
2015-16	BUF	27	49	12	12	24					2.1	0.7	0.0	2.8

A strong close to the 2011-12 season following his acquisition—eight goals in 17 games—has left Jamie McGinn permanently miscast. As a result, the ex-Shark has been deployed predominantly as a top-six left wing. In his shortened 2014-15 season—19 games due to season-ending back surgery—he was utilized almost exclusively in the top six. A product of head coach Brian Kilrea of the OHL's Ottawa 67s, McGinn is a fairly complete player who skates, shoots, and hits, but remains better utilized in a checking role.

Cody McLeod — LW — COL

Season	Team	Age	GP	G	A	Pts	+/-	ESP/60	AdjCF%	iCF/60	OGVT	DGVT	SGVT	GVT
2012-13	COL	28	48	8	4	12	4	1.24	47.1%	12.7	1.9	1.5	0.0	3.4
2013-14	COL	29	71	5	8	13	2	1.15	42.3%	10.1	0.3	1.6	0.0	1.9
2014-15	COL	30	82	7	5	12	-2	0.86	38.6%	9.1	-1.4	1.7	0.0	0.3
2015-16	COL	31	61	6	5	11					-0.7	1.4	0.0	0.7

The longest-tenured member of the Colorado Avalanche, Cody McLeod provides a physical element, leading the team in hits and fighting majors. In fact, the Manitoba native finished sixth in the NHL with 268 hits and led the league with 19 fighting majors. The pugilistic left winger is not one dimensional, though, as his 0.47 even-strength goals per 60 minutes is comparable to offensive talents like Jakub Voracek, Patrick Sharp, and Alexander Semin. McLeod has been a consistent source of goals throughout his career, averaging 8.5 per 82 games played, and never finishing with less than four in a season. Roy also deployed McLeod as one of the team's top penalty-killing forwards on what was the NHL's fourth-best penalty kill.

John Mitchell — C/LW — COL

Season	Team	Age	GP	G	A	Pts	+/-	ESP/60	AdjCF%	iCF/60	OGVT	DGVT	SGVT	GVT
2012-13	COL	27	47	10	10	20	5	1.58	48.3%	11.1	3.1	1.9	-0.3	4.7
2013-14	COL	28	75	11	21	32	13	1.67	46.4%	10.6	3.8	2.9	0.0	6.7
2014-15	COL	29	68	11	15	26	-9	1.30	42.0%	11.3	1.2	0.6	-0.5	1.3
2015-16	COL	30	59	11	15	26					2.0	1.4	0.0	3.4

A former castoff of the Toronto Maple Leafs, John Mitchell may be one of the more consistent depth scoring options in the NHL since his debut in 2007-08. With the exception of the 2010-11 season in which he was dealt by the Leafs, Mitchell has scored between 16 and 32 points, reaching his career high in 2013-14. Last year, the Waterloo, Ontario native played up and down the lineup, even closing the season as the left winger on Colorado's top line alongside Duchene and Iginla. Like McGinn, Mitchell is a little over his head in the top six, but possesses all the tools to be an efficient third-line center or winger.

Ryan O'Reilly — C — BUF

Season	Team	Age	GP	G	A	Pts	+/-	ESP/60	AdjCF%	iCF/60	OGVT	DGVT	SGVT	GVT
2012-13	COL	21	29	6	14	20	-3	1.93	53.1%	11.7	2.5	0.4	0.0	2.9
2013-14	COL	22	80	28	36	64	-1	1.97	48.9%	11.3	10.0	1.4	0.7	12.1
2014-15	COL	23	82	17	38	55	-5	1.96	45.7%	10.0	4.6	3.3	1.1	9.0
2015-16	BUF	24	74	21	36	57					6.6	2.8	0.1	9.5

The departure of Paul Stastny signaled Ryan O'Reilly's ascension to first-line center. Playing most of the season between budding stars Landeskog and MacKinnon, O'Reilly provided the team with two-way dependability and playmaking. The 2013-14 Lady Byng winner logged heavy minutes in all situations. O'Reilly is also an excellent faceoff man (53.2%); only seven other NHLers won more draws and at a higher rate than he did. An above-average playmaker, known for his hockey smarts, O'Reilly was also effective on the power play, despite the team's overall struggles. He isn't quite a franchise player, but the Sabres made a huge upgrade in their top six by trading for O'Reilly and locking him up long term.

Borna Rendulic							RW						COL
Season	Team	Age	GP	G	A	Pts	+/-	ESP/60	AdjCF%	iCF/60	OGVT	DGVT	SGVT	GVT
2014-15	COL	22	11	1	1	2	1	1.19	46.7%	6.3	-0.4	0.3	0.0	-0.1
2015-16	COL	23	31	5	6	11					0.4	0.7	0.0	1.1

After a breakout season in 2013-14 with HPK Hameenlinna in Finland (leading the team with 32 points), Borna Rendulic signed a two-way entry-level contract with Colorado. When he made his debut on December 9, 2014, Rendulic became the first Croatian to play in the NHL. The 23-year-old boasts good size, but he is more known for his offense than physicality, and the Avs did their best to employ him accordingly. In his 11 games with the big club, he saw the highest offensive zone start percentage (53.2%) of any Colorado forward who played 10+ games.

Colin Smith							C						COL
Season	Team	Age	GP	G	A	Pts	+/-	ESP/60	AdjCF%	iCF/60	OGVT	DGVT	SGVT	GVT
2014-15	COL	21	1	0	0	0	0	0.00	42.3%	8.9	0.0	0.0	0.0	0.0
2015-16	COL	22	26	5	6	11					0.8	0.5	0.0	1.3

Colin Smith has done much to elevate his prospect status following a seventh-round selection in 2012. Following his draft year, the speedy Smith exploded for 106 points in 72 games for the WHL's Kamloops Blazers. Despite being a little undersized for the center position, the Edmonton native has already established himself as durable, appearing in every game for Kamloops from 2010 through 2013, and in all 76 games for Lake Erie in 2013-14. This past season, Smith made his NHL debut, a sneak preview of one game for the injury-stricken Avalanche on November 30.

Ben Street							C						COL
Season	Team	Age	GP	G	A	Pts	+/-	ESP/60	AdjCF%	iCF/60	OGVT	DGVT	SGVT	GVT
2012-13	CGY	25	6	0	1	1	-1	0.00	49.7%	19.7	-0.2	0.1	0.0	-0.2
2013-14	CGY	26	13	0	1	1	-2	0.52	41.3%	14.2	-0.7	0.5	0.0	-0.2
2014-15	COL	27	3	0	0	0	0	0.00	38.4%	11.8	-0.4	0.1	0.0	-0.4
2015-16	COL	28	27	4	5	9					0.2	0.7	0.0	0.9

A former NCAA champion with the Wisconsin Badgers, Ben Street has proven himself to be an effective AHL center, with 216 points in 278 games across three organizations. Touted for his intelligence, both on and off the ice, the 28-year-old can no longer be considered much of a prospect, and while productive at the AHL level, he remains no more than organizational depth. Under contract for another season, he will continue to provide scoring punch and leadership for Lake Erie.

Alex Tanguay							LW						COL
Season	Team	Age	GP	G	A	Pts	+/-	ESP/60	AdjCF%	iCF/60	OGVT	DGVT	SGVT	GVT
2012-13	CGY	33	40	11	16	27	-13	1.70	46.4%	6.5	3.4	0.7	-0.1	4.0
2013-14	COL	34	16	4	7	11	7	2.20	50.4%	7.6	1.6	0.9	0.0	2.5
2014-15	COL	35	80	22	33	55	-1	2.09	42.5%	6.3	8.5	2.5	0.3	11.3
2015-16	COL	36	67	16	27	43					5.0	2.0	0.0	7.0

Alex Tanguay has carved out a long, successful career with his vision and playmaking ability. The 35-year-old continued to be productive at the offensive end of the rink, though like most of his Avalanche teammates, he performed poorly in the possession game. Tanguay spent most of the season on a line with Duchene and Iginla, and like his linemates, he put up some of the worst numbers in the league on shots allowed and chances allowed. Signed through 2015-16, the veteran still possesses a nice offensive skillset, but may require careful management, and more sheltered minutes, moving forward.

Tomas Vincour							RW						KHL
Season	Team	Age	GP	G	A	Pts	+/-	ESP/60	AdjCF%	iCF/60	OGVT	DGVT	SGVT	GVT
2012-13	DAL, COL	22	17	2	2	4	-1	1.62	46.9%	9.9	0.6	0.2	0.0	0.8
2014-15	COL	24	7	0	1	1	-1	1.19	44.8%	7.2	-0.1	0.0	0.0	-0.1
2015-16	KHL	25	27	4	6	9					0.5	0.5	0.0	1.1

The Avalanche acquired winger Tomas Vincour, a native of the Czech Republic, from the Stars for defense prospect Cameron Gaunce. Through four professional seasons, Vincour has struggled to establish himself at either the NHL or AHL level. He has decent size for a winger, and good hands, but he is not a great skater, and he struggles to get to the dirty areas in front of the net. Vincour received a brief opportunity with the big club when the team's forwards were racked with injuries. Skating primarily alongside Max Talbot in a fourth-line role, the former Edmonton Oil King saw just 7:10 minutes of ice-time per game.

Jesse Winchester							LW						COL
Season	Team	Age	GP	G	A	Pts	+/-	ESP/60	AdjCF%	iCF/60	OGVT	DGVT	SGVT	GVT
2013-14	FLA	29	52	9	9	18	-2	1.87	49.9%	14.8	2.5	1.6	0.0	4.2
2015-16	COL	30	15	2	3	5					0.7	0.5	0.0	1.2

Another of the Avalanche's depth forwards to be struck by injury was Jesse Winchester, who missed the entire campaign with post-concussion syndrome following a preseason hit by Dennis Wideman. That is a shame as Winchester can be an effective two-way depth forward. In 2013-14, playing for Florida, the Colgate University graduate was deployed on a team-low 43.2% of offensive zone draws yet still managed to post positive possession numbers. Had he been available, Winchester represented a clear upgrade over the experiments the Avalanche rolled out in their bottom-six forwards on a nightly basis.

DEFENSEMEN

Tyson Barrie							RD						COL
Season	Team	Age	GP	G	A	Pts	+/-	ESP/60	AdjCF%	iCF/60	OGVT	DGVT	SGVT	GVT
2012-13	COL	21	32	2	11	13	-11	0.84	50.3%	11.6	1.7	-0.6	0.0	1.0
2013-14	COL	22	64	13	25	38	17	1.68	50.4%	9.5	8.3	2.7	0.3	11.3
2014-15	COL	23	80	12	41	53	5	1.53	44.6%	8.7	9.3	1.5	-0.5	10.3
2015-16	COL	24	72	11	35	46					7.2	2.8	0.0	9.9

After breaking out in 2013-14, Tyson Barrie backed up his status as one of the game's best young offensive defensemen with a 53-point season. While a bit undersized, Barrie is an excellent skater who loves to join the rush and create from the point, whether at even strength or on the power play. In fact, Barrie tied for second amongst all NHL defensemen in five-on-five assists. Unfortunately, he can struggle in his own zone. The Avalanche did their best to mitigate that weakness by giving his pairing the easiest minutes.

Stefan Elliott — RD — ARI

Season	Team	Age	GP	G	A	Pts	+/-	ESP/60	AdjCF%	iCF/60	OGVT	DGVT	SGVT	GVT
2012-13	COL	21	18	1	3	4	-3	0.64	49.6%	13.2	0.4	0.0	0.0	0.4
2013-14	COL	22	1	1	0	1	0	3.80	48.3%	8.5	0.4	0.0	0.0	0.4
2014-15	COL	23	5	0	0	0	-2	0.00	44.9%	10.1	-0.2	-0.3	0.0	-0.5
2015-16	ARI	24	26	2	5	7					0.4	0.7	0.0	1.1

Considered to be the top prospect in Colorado's system at one point, Stefan Elliot has seen his star dim since winning the Bill Hunter Memorial Trophy as the WHL's best defenseman in 2010-11. Elliot possesses terrific offensive skills and instincts in quarterbacking the power play or jumping into the rush. The former Saskatoon Blade has appeared in a total of 63 NHL games across four seasons, but made significant progress playing almost exclusively for the Lake Erie in 2014-15; his 19 goals tied for best amongst AHL defensemen. Ideally, the right-shooting defender could improve enough on defense to provide NHL minutes in a sheltered role.

Nate Guenin — RD — COL

Season	Team	Age	GP	G	A	Pts	+/-	ESP/60	AdjCF%	iCF/60	OGVT	DGVT	SGVT	GVT
2013-14	COL	31	68	1	8	9	3	0.55	45.1%	5.9	-1.1	2.0	0.0	0.9
2014-15	COL	32	76	2	13	15	-1	0.81	39.5%	4.3	0.5	3.0	0.0	3.5
2015-16	COL	33	57	2	9	11					-0.1	2.4	0.0	2.2

An NCAA champion with Ohio State in 2003-04, Nate Guenin has solidified a role on Colorado's third defense pairing. He has left much to be desired on the offensive side, as the team created shots and scoring chances at a lower rate with him on the ice than any other regular on the Avalanche blue line. On a more positive note, Guenin was an effective part of Colorado's fourth-ranked penalty kill unit, in part due to his team-leading 162 blocked shots.

Jan Hejda — LD — Free Agent

Season	Team	Age	GP	G	A	Pts	+/-	ESP/60	AdjCF%	iCF/60	OGVT	DGVT	SGVT	GVT
2012-13	COL	34	46	1	9	10	-3	0.78	46.3%	8.7	0.7	1.4	0.0	2.1
2013-14	COL	35	78	6	11	17	8	0.68	45.1%	5.8	0.5	2.7	0.0	3.2
2014-15	COL	36	81	1	12	13	-12	0.49	43.3%	7.0	-1.5	2.1	0.0	0.6
2015-16	Free Agent	37	58	2	9	12					0.2	2.2	0.0	2.0

At his best, Jan Hejda was a reliable, stay-at-home defenseman with good size capable of handling top-four minutes. Now, at 37 years old, his performance has fallen off—he is a defenseman of limited offensive capability and physicality who struggles to control the play. The past two seasons, Hejda skated almost exclusively on Colorado's top pairing alongside Erik Johnson. Throughout his career, Hejda has been an effective player in the top-four role but he began showing signs of aging during this past season. The Czech still uses his reach and savvy to control the ice well in the defensive zone, particularly on the penalty kill, but he may be more suited to a defensive role on a bottom pairing at this point in his career.

Nick Holden — LD/LW — COL

Season	Team	Age	GP	G	A	Pts	+/-	ESP/60	AdjCF%	iCF/60	OGVT	DGVT	SGVT	GVT
2012-13	CBJ	25	2	0	0	0	1	0.00	49.6%	6.4	-0.2	0.2	0.0	0.1
2013-14	COL	26	54	10	15	25	12	1.23	48.5%	9.1	4.8	2.4	0.0	7.2
2014-15	COL	27	78	5	9	14	-11	0.38	41.8%	8.0	-1.1	0.5	0.0	-0.7
2015-16	COL	28	62	5	14	19					1.3	2.1	0.0	3.4

Originally an undrafted free agent with the Blue Jackets, Nick Holden was one of a number of players to successfully break into the NHL under Patrick Roy in 2013-14. Like many of his compatriots on the back end, Holden is probably more suited for a depth role despite seeing second-pairing ice-time for the majority of last season. The six-foot-four left-shooting defenseman actually saw his play decline so badly in the first half of the season that he found himself playing fourth-line left wing, covering for team injuries.

Erik Johnson — RD — COL

Season	Team	Age	GP	G	A	Pts	+/-	ESP/60	AdjCF%	iCF/60	OGVT	DGVT	SGVT	GVT
2012-13	COL	24	31	0	4	4	-3	0.47	47.5%	10.0	-1.9	1.5	0.0	-0.3
2013-14	COL	25	80	9	30	39	5	0.97	47.6%	9.2	5.9	1.2	0.0	7.1
2014-15	COL	26	47	12	11	23	2	1.06	45.9%	10.7	4.3	3.1	0.0	7.3
2015-16	COL	27	63	10	23	33					4.7	3.0	0.0	7.7

The St. Louis Blues' first overall selection in the 2006 NHL Entry Draft, Erik Johnson has emerged to become Colorado's *de facto* #1 option on the back end. The former Minnesota Golden Gopher has the impressive physical skillset you would expect of a number-one overall pick, but his play has often lagged behind his abilities. This season, Johnson again led Colorado's blue line, posting the best Relative Corsi percentage while pacing their defenders with 2.45 shots per game, a mark that ranked 15th among NHL rearguards. Furthermore, Johnson set a new career high with 12 goals in just 47 games prior to being sidelined with a season-ending knee injury.

Zach Redmond — RD — COL

Season	Team	Age	GP	G	A	Pts	+/-	ESP/60	AdjCF%	iCF/60	OGVT	DGVT	SGVT	GVT
2012-13	WPG	24	8	1	3	4	0	0.90	56.9%	8.5	1.0	0.2	0.0	1.2
2013-14	WPG	25	10	1	2	3	1	1.23	51.2%	12.2	0.6	0.3	0.0	1.0
2014-15	COL	26	59	5	15	20	-1	0.93	44.7%	9.7	2.8	0.7	-0.3	3.2
2015-16	COL	27	54	5	15	20					2.5	1.6	0.0	4.0

Offensively-minded Zach Redmond had flashes of brilliance in his first full NHL season. Frequently a healthy scratch early on for his defensive blunders, Redmond found himself a regular fixture for the team down the stretch due to injuries, managing to chip in 20 points in 59 games, in predominantly sheltered minutes. The former second-team All-American at Ferris State is particularly effective at filling open space in the offensive zone, creating scoring chances for himself. Surprisingly, given his reputation for defensive miscues, Redmond was the only Avalanche defenseman to have a positive giveaway to takeaway ratio. One of the few the Colorado blueliners not forced to play significantly over his head in 2014-15, Redmond showed his potential as a puck-moving third-pairing defenseman.

Duncan Siemens — LD — COL

Season	Team	Age	GP	G	A	Pts	+/-	ESP/60	AdjCF%	iCF/60	OGVT	DGVT	SGVT	GVT
2014-15	COL	21	1	0	0	0	0	0.00	45.5%	0.0	0.0	0.0	0.0	0.0
2015-16	COL	22	25	2	5	7					0.4	0.8	0.0	1.2

The fourth defensemen selected in the 2011 NHL Entry Draft, immediately behind budding stars Dougie Hamilton and Jonas Brodin, Duncan Siemens made his long-awaited NHL debut in Colorado's last game of the season. In fact, the former Saskatoon Blade was the last of 11 defensemen selected in the 2011 first round to make his NHL debut. Best known for his physicality, what makes Siemens unique is his combination of size and skating ability. His physical gifts likely portend a future as an intimidating, stay-at-home defender, but he has shown no indication he can develop into the two-way threat some pundits envisioned when he was selected 12th overall.

Brad Stuart — RD — COL

Season	Team	Age	GP	G	A	Pts	+/-	ESP/60	AdjCF%	iCF/60	OGVT	DGVT	SGVT	GVT
2012-13	SJS	33	48	0	6	6	4	0.35	47.8%	9.1	-1.7	5.0	0.0	3.2
2013-14	SJS	34	61	3	8	11	4	0.64	52.0%	9.2	0.3	4.0	0.0	4.4
2014-15	COL	35	65	3	10	13	-4	0.63	39.3%	6.2	0.6	1.9	0.0	2.5
2015-16	COL	36	52	3	9	12					0.5	2.2	0.0	2.7

After playing protected minutes in San Jose behind defensive stalwarts Justin Braun and Marc-Edouard Vlasic, the Avalanche acquired Brad Stuart to help shore up their own defense corps. Stuart, who has had a negative Relative Corsi each of the past six seasons, could have provided some physicality and leadership on a lower pairing, but instead was tasked with very difficult minutes on the undermanned Colorado blue line. Despite his calling card as a defensive defenseman, Stuart gave up more Corsi chances per 60 minutes than any other Av defenseman. The 36-year-old still contributes to an extent, pacing the blue line in hits and leading the team in shorthanded minutes. Stuart, and his shot blocking, were integral to the team's fourth-ranked penalty kill.

Ryan Wilson — LD — CGY

Season	Team	Age	GP	G	A	Pts	+/-	ESP/60	AdjCF%	iCF/60	OGVT	DGVT	SGVT	GVT
2012-13	COL	25	12	0	3	3	4	1.01	49.2%	13.3	0.3	1.5	0.0	1.7
2013-14	COL	26	28	0	6	6	1	0.97	45.2%	7.7	0.1	0.4	0.0	0.6
2014-15	COL	27	3	0	0	0	-3	0.00	41.3%	14.4	-0.2	-0.4	0.0	-0.6
2015-16	CGY	28	30	2	6	7					0.3	0.7	0.0	1.1

A former undrafted free agent, Ryan Wilson is a capable open-ice hitter who had entrenched himself in the lineup in the years preceding coach Roy's tenure. However, after purportedly showing up to 2013-14 training camp out of shape, Wilson had difficulty staying in the lineup due to inconsistent play and injuries. In 2014-15, the Windsor, Ontario native reported to camp back in the team's good graces and ready to lock down a spot with the team, yet injuries continued to plague his career. Wilson drew into only three games before requiring season-ending shoulder surgery in November.

COLORADO AVALANCHE

GOALTENDERS

Reto Berra — G — COL

Season	Team	Age	GP	W	L	OT	GAA	Sv%	ESSV%	QS%	GGVT	DGVT	SGVT	GVT
2013-14	CGY, COL	26	31	9	18	3	3.07	.893	.898	51.7%	-11.6	0.4	1.4	-9.7
2014-15	COL	27	19	5	4	1	2.65	.918	.926	41.7%	2.7	-0.3	0.2	2.5
2015-16	COL	28	22					.911			-0.3	0.0	0.1	-0.3

The fourth Swiss-born goaltender to make the National Hockey League, Reto Berra was acquired from Calgary at the 2014 trade deadline for a second-round pick. Considered an overpay for a rookie goalie struggling in his first big-league action, Berra's play in 2014-15 went a long way towards establishing himself as a reliable NHL goalie. The 27-year-old was particularly effective at even strength, posting a .926 save percentage. With his large frame and traditional butterfly style, Berra performs best when asked to make routine saves, but can look a little out of place when faced with high-quality scoring chances, or power-play situations.

Calvin Pickard — G — COL

Season	Team	Age	GP	W	L	OT	GAA	Sv%	ESSV%	QS%	GGVT	DGVT	SGVT	GVT
2014-15	COL	22	16	6	7	3	2.35	.932	.945	69.2%	9.1	-0.6	-0.1	8.3
2015-16	COL	23	25					.917			5.4	-0.4	0.0	5.0

Calvin Pickard, the third goalie selected in the 2010 NHL Entry Draft, made a strong first impression. His first NHL win came in relief of Berra on November 22, stopping all 17 shots he faced in relief. The former Seattle Thunderbird appeared in 16 contests and logged an impressive .932 save percentage, fifth among goalies to appear in at least five games. The younger brother of Nashville goalie Chet Pickard, Calvin is known for his smarts and instincts, but has shown the ability to be successful in scrambling situations, finishing with one of the league's best save percentages in high-danger situations. The combination of draft pedigree (Pickard was the top-ranked goalie by Central Scouting in 2010) and a commendable rookie performance give the Avalanche confidence in Pickard's adding to the organization's goaltending depth.

Semyon Varlamov — G — COL

Season	Team	Age	GP	W	L	OT	GAA	Sv%	ESSV%	QS%	GGVT	DGVT	SGVT	GVT
2012-13	COL	24	35	11	21	3	3.02	.903	.911	33.3%	-2.9	-0.8	0.1	-3.6
2013-14	COL	25	63	41	14	6	2.41	.927	.933	73.3%	30.0	-1.9	0.2	28.3
2014-15	COL	26	57	28	20	8	2.56	.921	.916	57.9%	16.7	-1.5	-0.1	15.1
2015-16	COL	27	52					.920			14.9	-0.9	0.0	14.1

A former first-round pick himself, many pundits considered it an overpay when the Avalanche pried Semyon Varlamov away from Washington for a first-round pick in July 2011. Years later, Colorado appears to have been prescient in their decision. In 2014, the Russian-born goaltender was a finalist for the Vezina Trophy, his strong play the single largest factor in Colorado's return to the postseason. This past year, Varlamov backed up his breakout season with another solid performance, including a league-best .941 save percentage while short-handed, fulfilling the old hockey cliche that a good penalty kill always starts with the goaltender. To put into context how special this number was, the only other regular goaltenders to finish over .900 while shorthanded were Marc-Andre Fleury (.911) and Ben Bishop (.909). Varlamov dealt with several nagging injuries over the course of the season, but his strong play has firmly established him as an above-average NHL netminder.

JH Schroeder

Columbus Blue Jackets

The 2013-14 season saw a return to the playoffs for the Columbus Blue Jackets after a four-year layoff. The last time Columbus had been in the postseason, Scott Howson was GM, Ken Hitchcock was head coach, and Rick Nash was captain and franchise player. They lost to defending champion Detroit in four games straight.

This time around, the Blue Jackets of GM Jarmo Kekalainen and head coach Todd Richards won their first two playoff games as a franchise. Columbus gamely pushed a strong Pittsburgh squad to a six-game series in round one.

The outlook was bright for 2014-15. However, promise quickly turned to despair as the talented, up-and-coming team ended up on the outside looking in for one reason, and one reason alone: injuries.

This is not to say that Columbus had been a beacon of health in their moderately successful 2013-14 campaign, but they had been able to overcome a ninth-overall ranking in man-games lost (297). Yet, that number was nowhere close to the carnage they experienced in 2014-15. Columbus led the league with a decimating 508 man-games lost, a significant portion of the injuries to key players. As shown in the chart on the next page, the combined contribution of Anisimov, Bobrovsky, Dubinsky, Horton, Jenner, Letestu, and Murray fell 24.5 GVT, equivalent to eight points in the standings.

It is next to impossible to overcome that volume of injuries within a hard-cap salary system. As a consequence, Columbus swooned from a solid 50.3% score-adjusted Fenwick to 46.7%, among the bottom six teams in the league.

When Columbus got healthier towards the end of the year, they started showing signs of the playoff-caliber team from 2013-14. From the beginning of the season until January 31, their score-adjusted Fenwick was 45.8%. That rate improved to 48.1% from February 1 until the end of the season. Why choose those particular date ranges? It is based on when Dubinsky and Anisimov returned to the lineup full time. Getting second- and third-line centers back will improve a team's chances of winning, and it did.

With the former Rangers back in the mix, Columbus ended the year on a 21-11-2 run, a huge improvement from the preceding 21-24-3 span. The strong finish helped the Jackets tally 89 points in the standings, amazingly only four points shy of their playoff-worthy total from 2013-14. If Columbus' point pace from February 1 to year end was extrapolated over

BLUE JACKETS IN A BOX

Last Season
Goals For	236	t-10th
Goals Against	250	25th
GVT	-14	22nd
Points	89	t-22nd
Playoffs	Did not make playoffs	

It was a small step backwards for the injury-plagued Jackets, who weren't bad, but missed the playoffs for the fifth time in six years.

Three-Year Record
GVT	2	15th
Points	237	17th
Playoffs	1 Appearance, 2 Wins	

VUKOTA Projections
Goals For	222	15th
Goals Against	223	22nd
GVT	2	20th
Points	92	20th

The acquisition of Saad shows this team is serious, but the blueline is still too thin for them to be truly competitive.

Top Three Prospects
Z. Werenski (D), O. Bjorkstrand (F), S. Milano (F)

COLUMBUS BLUE JACKETS

Impact of significant injuries, 2014-15

Player	2013-14		2014-15	
	Games played	GVT	Games played	GVT
Artem Anisimov	81	8.5	50	3.0
Sergei Bobrovsky	58	20.5	50	17.1
Brandon Dubinsky	76	10.0	45	10.0
Nathan Horton	36	1.2	0	0.0
Boone Jenner	72	6.3	29	2.1
Mark Letestu	82	7.1	54	1.7
Ryan Murray	66	5.4	11	0.6
Total		59.0		34.5

82 games, they would have totaled 106 points in the standings, good for second in the Metropolitan Division and fourth in the Eastern Conference.

Horton-Clarkson trade

While in most situations, a player can recover from an injury and return the following year, Columbus received some really bad news regarding one of their impact players. Nathan Horton's long-term future as an NHL player was—and still is—in serious doubt. Before 2013-14, Columbus signed the 2011 Stanley Cup champion to a seven-year, $37.1 million contract; Horton was supposed to be one of the centerpieces of the top-six forward grouping for years to come. The plan did not come to fruition as the ex-Panther and ex-Bruin was diagnosed with a degenerative back condition which will likely prevent him from ever playing NHL hockey again. Columbus is not a franchise that can afford to spend dead money on players that are unable to play, even if a majority is covered by insurance. Instead of placing the former six-time 20-goal scorer on long-term injured reserve (like Philadelphia had done with Chris Pronger), the Blue Jackets elected to trade him away for a player who is physically able to take the ice.

Columbus found a trade match with Toronto. Instead of paying Horton to not play hockey, they acquired former Devils' 30-goal man David Clarkson at a similar cap hit to suit up for the team. Toronto was a great fit for this kind of exchange because of the massive amounts of disposable cash they have available to them. Toronto was more than willing to remove Clarkson's ill-advised contract off of their active salary cap.

Signed through the 2019-20 season, Clarkson will need to do much better than in Toronto to not negatively impact Columbus in terms of value for the money. His career mark of 1.29 even-strength points per 60 minutes is at the lower end of a third-line production level, and he has typically been an average possession player.

Surprisingly Saad

In what may have been the surprise move of the summer, Kekalainen acquired Brandon Saad from the Stanley Cup champion Chicago Blackhawks. Instead of taking the risk of an offer sheet being accepted by Saad, Chicago GM Stan Bowman was proactive on the trade front, accepting an offer of Marko Dano, Artem Anisimov, Jeremy Morin, Corey Tropp, and a 2016 fourth-round pick for the prized youngster. Saad immediately signed a six-year extension worth $36 million dollars, making him the second-highest cap hit on the team behind Sergei Bobrovsky's $7.4 million.

The good news for Columbus is that they have invested in a young, highly-skilled player. It is a case of the Blue Jackets paying for future rather than past performance, unlike most big contracts in the NHL.

However, the deal does come with some risk. In his career to date, Saad has been surrounded by some of the best players in the world. By even-strength minutes, the top four skaters the Pittsburgh native has played with are Jonathan Toews (1,297), Marian Hossa (1,078), Duncan Keith (1,038), and Brent Seabrook (1,019). How much of his apparent value came from his teammates? A valid question. Can Saad continue to put up 2.20 ESP/60 with Ryan Johansen and Jack Johnson instead?

Ryan Wilson

COLUMBUS BLUE JACKETS

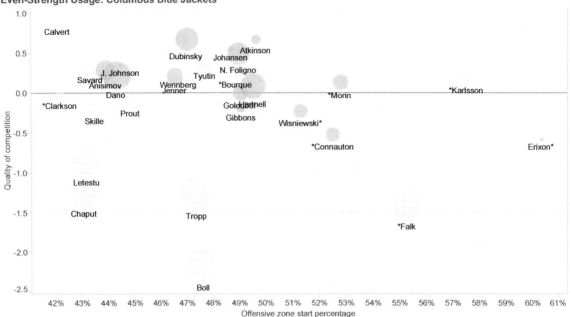

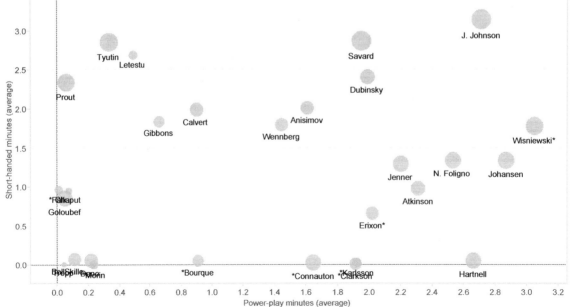

COLUMBUS BLUE JACKETS

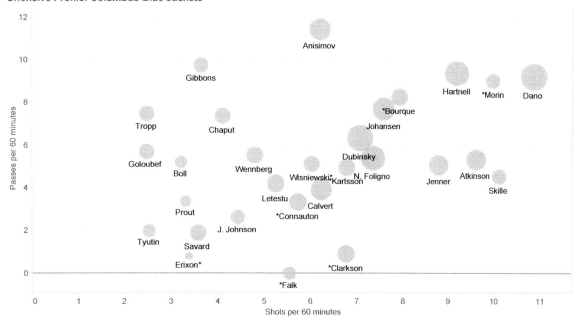

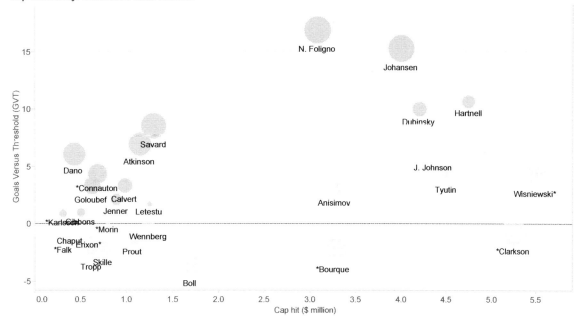

FORWARDS

Luke Adam								C/LW						NYR
Season	Team	Age	GP	G	A	Pts	+/-	ESP/60	AdjCF%	iCF/60	OGVT	DGVT	SGVT	GVT
2012-13	BUF	22	4	1	0	1	1	1.59	33.3%	7.0	0.1	0.2	0.0	0.3
2013-14	BUF	23	12	1	0	1	0	0.41	47.9%	13.1	-0.5	0.2	-0.3	-0.6
2014-15	CBJ	24	3	0	0	0	0	0.00	49.7%	2.6	-0.1	0.0	0.0	-0.1
2015-16	NYR	25	27	4	5	9					0.4	0.6	0.0	1.0

Luke Adam was an impressive goal-scoring center during his days in the QMJHL, lighting the lamp at a pace of 0.48 goals per game. The Sabres' second rounder from 2008 made the successful jump from juniors to the professional ranks when he potted 29 goals in his debut AHL season with Portland back in 2010-11. He transitioned to Buffalo in 2011-12, thriving for a few dozen games in Buffalo's top six—but that is when the progress came to a halt. Overall, Adam has 15 goals in 90 career games, but has been unable to earn extended stays at the highest level. With great hands but plodding speed and questionable makeup, Adam might still contribute as fourth-line depth scorer who can contribute on the second power-play unit. The problem is not many teams save room for that kind of player on their roster.

Josh Anderson								RW						CBJ
Season	Team	Age	GP	G	A	Pts	+/-	ESP/60	AdjCF%	iCF/60	OGVT	DGVT	SGVT	GVT
2014-15	CBJ	20	6	0	1	1	-1	0.74	50.4%	13.5	-0.5	0.0	0.0	-0.5
2015-16	CBJ	21	28	5	6	11					0.5	0.6	0.0	1.1

Former London Knight Josh Anderson was a 2012 fourth-round pick as well as a participant of the 2014 World Junior Championships for Team Canada. Anderson showed some offensive talent by putting up a solid 122 points in 191 games while playing for London. In his first professional season with Springfield, he found himself playing bottom-six minutes while registering a meager 17 points in 52 games. Given a six-foot-three, 218-pound frame, he has the potential to become an NHL depth player if he can hone his defensive and possession game at the AHL level.

Artem Anisimov								C/LW						CHI
Season	Team	Age	GP	G	A	Pts	+/-	ESP/60	AdjCF%	iCF/60	OGVT	DGVT	SGVT	GVT
2012-13	CBJ	24	35	11	7	18	-6	2.22	45.7%	12.9	2.0	0.9	1.5	4.4
2013-14	CBJ	25	81	22	17	39	-2	1.84	51.3%	14.1	5.0	3.5	0.0	8.5
2014-15	CBJ	26	52	7	20	27	-6	1.81	49.9%	11.9	2.8	1.0	-0.8	3.0
2015-16	CHI	27	60	14	21	34					3.6	1.9	0.0	5.4

Six-foot-four Artem Anisimov is one of the more underrated third-line centers in hockey, able to play in all situations, and at center and wing. Since coming over from New York, he has been placed in a shutdown role at even strength, yet has still put up solid possession numbers. The normally-durable Russian forward missed 30 games but maintained a 50.1% score-adjusted Fenwick while producing at a fringe top-six level at even strength. It will be interesting to see how those numbers jump as a member of the Blackhawks.

Cam Atkinson — RW — CBJ

Season	Team	Age	GP	G	A	Pts	+/-	ESP/60	AdjCF%	iCF/60	OGVT	DGVT	SGVT	GVT
2012-13	CBJ	23	35	9	9	18	9	2.02	53.8%	17.0	2.9	2.0	-0.3	4.5
2013-14	CBJ	24	79	21	19	40	-4	1.70	51.7%	16.5	5.4	1.2	0.4	7.0
2014-15	CBJ	25	78	22	18	40	-2	1.63	47.3%	14.5	5.8	1.1	-0.1	6.9
2015-16	CBJ	26	66	21	20	41					5.4	1.7	0.0	7.1

A national champion at Boston College, Cam Atkinson's size was a concern as he entered the professional ranks. Some wondered if his five-foot-seven, 173-pound frame could hold up to the rigors of NHL hockey. Yet more and more, we are finding out that size is an overrated variable if you have the work ethic and puck skills like Atkinson. His 22 goals were fourth best on Columbus and his 212 shots led the team. Clever and tenacious, Atkinson can overcome some of the difficulties shorter players face at the highest level.

Jared Boll — RW — CBJ

Season	Team	Age	GP	G	A	Pts	+/-	ESP/60	AdjCF%	iCF/60	OGVT	DGVT	SGVT	GVT
2012-13	CBJ	26	43	2	4	6	1	1.04	40.6%	6.7	-0.6	0.8	0.0	0.3
2013-14	CBJ	27	28	1	1	2	-6	0.56	41.0%	6.4	-0.9	-0.2	0.0	-1.1
2014-15	CBJ	28	72	1	4	5	-13	0.57	36.3%	6.1	-3.2	-0.5	0.0	-3.7
2015-16	CBJ	29	52	1	2	3					-2.2	0.3	0.0	-1.9

Rugged Jared Boll is a veteran of 488 NHL games. The six-foot-two, 219-pound right winger is more known for his physicality than his ability with the puck. In eight NHL seasons, he has 1,134 career penalty minutes but only 59 points. In the possession department, Boll is a black hole. He has a sub-40% score-adjusted Fenwick in each of the last three seasons. Inexplicably, Boll has two years left on his deal which costs Columbus $1.7 million per year. There is a reason most teams have moved on from enforcers like Boll: because he brings very little to the table in a league that has nearly eliminated fighting.

Rene Bourque — LW — CBJ

Season	Team	Age	GP	G	A	Pts	+/-	ESP/60	AdjCF%	iCF/60	OGVT	DGVT	SGVT	GVT
2012-13	MTL	31	27	7	6	13	-1	1.70	49.6%	16.4	1.8	0.4	-0.3	1.9
2013-14	MTL	32	63	9	7	16	-1	0.88	45.8%	15.0	0.5	0.7	0.0	1.2
2014-15	MTL, ANA, CBJ	33	51	6	8	14	-15	1.11	47.7%	15.5	-1.7	-0.6	0.0	-2.3
2015-16	CBJ	34	49	7	9	16					0.3	0.6	0.0	0.9

Rene Bourque was a perennial 20-goal scorer who has been limited to short outbursts of goal-scoring brilliance in recent years. Bourque only has 22 goals in his last three years of regular-season hockey. That said, he put on a show in the 2014 playoffs, scoring eight goals in 17 games for Montreal. Similarly, in his eight contests with Columbus in 2014-15, he tallied four goals. The twin issues with Bourque are that his production is no longer consistent and he carries an outsized $3.3 million cap hit—not a good combination.

Matt Calvert — LW — CBJ

Season	Team	Age	GP	G	A	Pts	+/-	ESP/60	AdjCF%	iCF/60	OGVT	DGVT	SGVT	GVT
2012-13	CBJ	23	42	9	7	16	-9	1.71	51.3%	12.8	0.3	1.0	-0.3	1.0
2013-14	CBJ	24	56	9	15	24	-1	1.65	52.8%	10.9	1.9	1.5	0.0	3.5
2014-15	CBJ	25	56	13	10	23	1	1.80	46.9%	10.9	2.9	1.2	-0.8	3.3
2015-16	CBJ	26	55	13	14	27					2.6	1.5	0.0	4.1

A regular in Columbus' lineup since the shortened 2012-13 season, Matt Calvert has taken on some of the tougher minutes among the forward ranks, both in zone starts and competition. Still, his possession numbers were right around the team average and his even-strength scoring was at a top-nine level. After Kekalainen's acquisition of Brandon Saad, Calvert may return to a less stressful role, which could translate into more five-on-five offense.

Michael Chaput — C — CBJ

Season	Team	Age	GP	G	A	Pts	+/-	ESP/60	AdjCF%	iCF/60	OGVT	DGVT	SGVT	GVT
2013-14	CBJ	21	17	0	1	1	0	0.41	36.1%	6.5	-1.0	0.3	0.0	-0.7
2014-15	CBJ	22	33	1	4	5	-8	0.99	36.4%	7.7	-0.7	0.1	0.0	-0.6
2015-16	CBJ	23	40	4	7	11					-0.3	0.7	0.0	0.4

A third-round selection by Philadelphia in 2010, Michael Chaput has been unable to stick at the NHL level. In 50 career games, the Montreal native has only registered six points. Worse, his Fenwick-for percentage over that stretch has been a woeful 38.7%. With limited offense and an inability to push play towards the other team's net, he finds himself unable to land consistent work in the world's best league. With a solid shot, he does contribute at the AHL level by scoring over a point every other game.

David Clarkson — RW — CBJ

Season	Team	Age	GP	G	A	Pts	+/-	ESP/60	AdjCF%	iCF/60	OGVT	DGVT	SGVT	GVT
2012-13	NJD	28	48	15	9	24	-6	1.43	60.9%	18.1	2.6	1.4	-0.3	3.7
2013-14	TOR	29	60	5	6	11	-14	0.64	41.7%	11.3	-2.0	-0.3	-0.6	-2.9
2014-15	TOR, CBJ	30	61	10	5	15	-12	1.16	45.3%	11.0	-0.9	0.1	0.0	-0.7
2015-16	CBJ	31	52	6	6	13					-0.5	0.5	0.0	0.0

A six-foot-one power forward from Etobicoke, Ontario, David Clarkson signed a seven-year $36.8 million contract with his hometown Maple Leafs in the summer of 2013. Unfortunately, the homecoming did not go as planned, to say the least. Clarkson's play was underwhelming and he became a target of fan frustration. Most of the frustration was based on his extreme lack of offensive production, but he was not a physical intimidator or two-way player he was in New Jersey. Instead of paying big money for poor production, Brendan Shanahan and company elected to trade Clarkson to Columbus for the injured Nathan Horton (ostensibly to bury him on the books). Perhaps this latest change of scenery will do Clarkson some good; he is better than than he has shown, though obviously worse than perceived two summers ago.

Sean Collins — LW — WSH

Season	Team	Age	GP	G	A	Pts	+/-	ESP/60	AdjCF%	iCF/60	OGVT	DGVT	SGVT	GVT
2012-13	CBJ	24	5	0	0	0	-2	0.00	40.0%	4.3	-0.5	-0.1	0.0	-0.6
2013-14	CBJ	25	6	0	1	1	1	1.23	46.7%	8.0	-0.1	0.2	0.0	0.1
2014-15	CBJ	26	8	0	2	2	0	1.46	45.4%	4.6	-0.1	0.1	0.0	0.0
2015-16	WSH	27	27	4	6	10					0.5	0.6	0.0	1.2

Cornell University graduate Sean Collins signed an entry-level contract with Columbus following the completion of his senior year in 2012. Most of his professional career has been spent in Springfield, where he has a respectable 113 points in 203 games. There, Collins has shown flashes of speed, initiative, and net-front presence. However, he has also demonstrated inconsistent effort; combined with an AHL-caliber skillset, you get a player that is an injury call-up at best. Since 2012, the former Big Red has appeared in 19 NHL games, registering three assists.

Ryan Craig — LW — CBJ

Season	Team	Age	GP	G	A	Pts	+/-	ESP/60	AdjCF%	iCF/60	OGVT	DGVT	SGVT	GVT
2013-14	CBJ	31	6	0	0	0	-3	0.00	29.8%	7.2	-0.4	-0.2	0.0	-0.6
2014-15	CBJ	32	2	0	0	0	0	0.00	40.6%	13.4	-0.2	0.0	0.0	-0.2
2015-16	CBJ	33	24	3	4	8					0.3	0.5	0.0	0.8

Ryan Craig is a veteran of 198 NHL contests, mostly long, long ago and far, far away with Tampa, following the 2004-05 lockout; he has not scored a big-league point since 2007-08. However, Craig has made a mark at the AHL level, captaining the Wilkes-Barre Scranton Penguins and the Springfield Falcons over a combined five seasons. As you would expect from such a resume, Craig brings plenty of heart and hustle combined with modest but clearly limited skill. The former Brandon Wheat Kings captain—yes, at that level, too—has tallied 248 points in 458 career AHL games.

Marko Dano — LW/C — CHI

Season	Team	Age	GP	G	A	Pts	+/-	ESP/60	AdjCF%	iCF/60	OGVT	DGVT	SGVT	GVT
2014-15	CBJ	20	35	8	13	21	12	2.77	53.9%	16.7	4.3	1.7	0.0	6.1
2015-16	CHI	21	41	13	18	31					6.8	0.9	0.0	7.7

Marko Dano made the most of his time with Columbus, flashing his incredibly high offensive upside. The slick Slovakian rookie made jaw-dropping plays with the puck and put up numbers as well, leading all Columbus forwards in Corsi and even-strength points per 60 minutes. He also put 84 shots on goal in 35 games, reflective of just how often the puck was on his stick. Dano may be the piece of the Brandon Saad trade that will come back to haunt Columbus, as he will be given a chance to earn a top-six slot right away and line up on the Chicago power play with the likes of Kane and Toews. Like many young offensive dynamos, he has much to learn about the NHL game. Joel Quenneville's patience will be tested by Dano's propensity to leave his position to chase the puck. But if he learns to properly take risks, watch out.

Brandon Dubinsky — C — CBJ

Season	Team	Age	GP	G	A	Pts	+/-	ESP/60	AdjCF%	iCF/60	OGVT	DGVT	SGVT	GVT
2012-13	CBJ	26	29	2	18	20	2	1.84	54.0%	10.1	1.8	1.5	0.0	3.3
2013-14	CBJ	27	76	16	34	50	5	2.03	52.7%	14.2	6.4	3.7	0.0	10.0
2014-15	CBJ	28	47	13	23	36	11	2.62	51.2%	11.6	7.3	3.0	-0.3	10.0
2015-16	CBJ	29	61	17	28	44					6.0	2.7	0.0	8.7

When NHL general managers talk about grit, they should be talking about players like Brandon Dubinsky. Grit absent skill can get you into trouble, but grit when combined with hockey IQ and puck skill is ideal for a two-way center. Dubinsky fits into the latter category, as a top-two center who epitomizes "tough to play against." His non-stop dogging of top players in the corners and in front of the net makes it difficult for top scorers to keep the puck on their stick or gain position to score. The former Ranger is also willing to bend the rules on away-from-the-puck spearing and jabbing, as was best evidenced during Columbus's 2014 playoff series against the Penguins, where Dubinsky battled and injured Sidney Crosby. The Jackets have a nice one-two punch with a tough defensive center in Dubinsky and a near-elite offensive center in Ryan Johansen.

Nick Foligno — LW — CBJ

Season	Team	Age	GP	G	A	Pts	+/-	ESP/60	AdjCF%	iCF/60	OGVT	DGVT	SGVT	GVT
2012-13	CBJ	25	45	6	13	19	6	1.48	46.9%	9.0	1.0	1.5	0.0	2.6
2013-14	CBJ	26	70	18	21	39	5	2.00	52.0%	10.3	5.6	2.4	0.0	8.0
2014-15	CBJ	27	79	31	42	73	16	2.39	49.7%	10.6	14.7	3.3	-1.1	16.9
2015-16	CBJ	28	72	25	35	60					8.8	2.5	0.0	11.3

The hockey world got to see some of Nick Foligno's personality when he was named a Team Captain for the 2015 NHL All-Star Game, hosted by Columbus. They also got to see what Foligno could do with a little more opportunity. The son of former Sabres captain Mike Foligno saw top-six and power-play minutes galore after a host of injuries slowed the Blue Jackets. Consequently, Foligno posted a career year, which resulted in a nice six-year, $33 million contract extension. While he reached career highs in goals (31), assists (42), points (73), and shots on goal (182), an absurdly high shooting percentage on the power play boosted his numbers significantly. Expect the former first-round pick of the Senators to come back to earth in scoring. However, as a solid two-way player and hard worker, Foligno will still be worth the cap hit even if he doesn't score 70 points again.

Brian Gibbons — LW/C — NYR

Season	Team	Age	GP	G	A	Pts	+/-	ESP/60	AdjCF%	iCF/60	OGVT	DGVT	SGVT	GVT
2013-14	PIT	25	41	5	12	17	5	2.01	50.8%	6.6	2.0	1.7	0.0	3.7
2014-15	CBJ	26	25	0	5	5	2	0.85	45.0%	7.3	0.6	0.4	0.0	1.0
2015-16	NYR	27	42	6	11	17					1.3	1.2	0.0	2.5

Small but speedy Brian Gibbons can be a quality asset to an organization, providing above-average AHL play while being a useful NHLer in reasonable doses. The two-time NCAA champion with Boston College was able to chip in offensively with Pittsburgh, but that was while getting spot duty with Sidney Crosby. Unfortunately, his transition to Columbus has seen his production rate and possession drop, in part due to a change in circumstances but also in bouncing back from injury. Gibbons can still contribute as an effective penalty killer as he is able to utilize his blazing speed to make life tough on the opposing power play. Cheap, effective depth is something all teams should strive for, and Gibbons has shown to be that.

COLUMBUS BLUE JACKETS

Scott Hartnell							LW						CBJ
Season	Team	Age	GP	G	A	Pts	+/-	ESP/60	AdjCF%	iCF/60	OGVT	DGVT	SGVT	GVT
2012-13	PHI	30	32	8	3	11	-5	0.87	51.2%	13.7	0.6	0.1	0.0	0.7
2013-14	PHI	31	78	20	32	52	11	1.82	54.3%	15.2	6.8	1.6	0.0	8.4
2014-15	CBJ	32	77	28	32	60	1	2.35	51.1%	13.5	9.5	1.2	0.0	10.7
2015-16	CBJ	33	67	21	28	49					6.2	1.6	0.0	7.8

Former Philadelphia fan favorite Scott Hartnell brought his offensive and physical prowess to Columbus after a trade that sent R.J. Umberger to the City of Brotherly Love. In Hartnell's first year with the Blue Jackets, he recorded 60 points, the second-best total of his career; the power forward showed little sign of slowing down, despite not having high-end speed. Under contract through 2018-19, he may not be the same by the end of the deal, but the Jackets have built up a solid group of young top-six forwards that will allow Hartnell to transition into more of a role player. However, until his game slips, the six-foot-two, 210-pound winger gives Blue Jackets play makers a go-to guy in front of the net, especially on the power play.

Boone Jenner							LW/C						CBJ
Season	Team	Age	GP	G	A	Pts	+/-	ESP/60	AdjCF%	iCF/60	OGVT	DGVT	SGVT	GVT
2013-14	CBJ	20	72	16	13	29	6	1.40	51.1%	12.3	4.4	1.9	0.0	6.3
2014-15	CBJ	21	31	9	8	17	-5	1.57	47.4%	14.6	1.5	0.2	0.4	2.1
2015-16	CBJ	22	55	16	17	33					4.0	1.3	0.0	5.2

Boone Jenner, the 37th-overall pick of Columbus in 2011, had his latest season put on hold by injuries after a solid debut in 2013-14. In 103 career games, the six-foot-two forward has managed 25 regular-season goals while adding three more in six games against the Penguins in his lone playoff action. As the Blue Jackets stock up talent, we can expect Jenner to slide into an appropriate role as a third-line center, where he can use his smarts and physical toughness to slow down opponents. In order to take on that role, he will have to see some improvement in the faceoff circle, where he is under 50% for his career.

Ryan Johansen							C						CBJ
Season	Team	Age	GP	G	A	Pts	+/-	ESP/60	AdjCF%	iCF/60	OGVT	DGVT	SGVT	GVT
2012-13	CBJ	20	40	5	7	12	7	1.21	44.5%	10.4	-1.7	0.3	-0.9	-2.4
2013-14	CBJ	21	82	33	30	63	3	2.20	51.2%	15.4	12.8	2.6	0.7	16.1
2014-15	CBJ	22	82	26	45	71	-6	2.06	47.1%	11.7	11.0	1.9	2.4	15.3
2015-16	CBJ	23	74	27	40	67					9.9	2.4	0.1	12.4

After an offseason contract dispute that lasted through training camp, Ryan Johansen proved his point to Columbus' management right out of the gate. The former Portland Winter Hawk opened the year tallying 13 points in 10 games. Johansen took a few years to develop, but the six-foot-three, 220-pound offensive monster has become the number-one center talent the Jackets were hoping for when they drafted him in fourth overall in 2010. There were once concerns about his motivation and whether he would work to hit his high ceiling, but those concerns are no more. As Johansen enters his prime and the Blue Jackets grow as a team, we could see him compete for a scoring title soon.

COLUMBUS BLUE JACKETS

William Karlsson — C — CBJ

Season	Team	Age	GP	G	A	Pts	+/-	ESP/60	AdjCF%	iCF/60	OGVT	DGVT	SGVT	GVT
2014-15	ANA, CBJ	21	21	3	2	5	3	1.11	49.3%	11.6	-0.3	0.6	0.6	0.9
2015-16	CBJ	22	36	6	7	14					0.6	0.9	0.0	1.5

The man known as "Wild Bill" saw his first NHL action, playing his first 18 games with Anaheim. William Karlsson was then involved in the mid-season trade that saw James Wisniewski move from Columbus to Anaheim. Subsequently, when he was assigned to Springfield of the AHL, it was bizarre to see him go scoreless over 15 games. Karlsson is known more for his speed than his hands, projecting as a third-line setup man at best. The WJC gold and silver medalist will have a chance to make the Blue Jackets out of camp, but will most likely start in the AHL, where he will need to do way better than he did in his first stint in the organization.

Mark Letestu — C — EDM

Season	Team	Age	GP	G	A	Pts	+/-	ESP/60	AdjCF%	iCF/60	OGVT	DGVT	SGVT	GVT
2012-13	CBJ	27	46	13	14	27	7	1.99	46.5%	11.0	5.1	2.7	1.2	9.0
2013-14	CBJ	28	82	12	22	34	1	1.31	49.4%	9.9	3.4	3.0	0.7	7.1
2014-15	CBJ	29	54	7	6	13	-9	1.20	42.1%	9.4	0.5	1.0	0.2	1.7
2015-16	EDM	30	55	9	11	20					1.1	1.2	0.0	2.3

Normally a reliable bottom-six center, Mark Letestu saw injuries take their toll. Abdominal surgery limited him to only 54 games, and he was understandably ineffective during that stretch. The former Penguin has been known as an above-average bottom-two center, but after posting a replacement-level year, the Jackets allowed him to sign with Edmonton. The Oilers are in dire need defensive-minded forwards, so they are putting their hopes in a bounceback season from the veteran, who still knows how to handle himself in the faceoff circle, where he won 52.9% of his draws.

Jeremy Morin — RW — CHI

Season	Team	Age	GP	G	A	Pts	+/-	ESP/60	AdjCF%	iCF/60	OGVT	DGVT	SGVT	GVT
2012-13	CHI	21	3	1	1	2	1	3.21	52.5%	16.1	0.5	0.1	0.0	0.7
2013-14	CHI	22	24	5	6	11	5	3.11	62.9%	20.9	1.9	0.9	0.0	2.8
2014-15	CHI, CBJ	23	43	2	4	6	1	0.84	53.2%	14.6	-1.0	0.7	0.6	0.2
2015-16	CHI	24	44	5	7	12					0.2	1.1	0.0	1.3

Caught up in Chicago's immense forward depth, Jeremy Morin was never able to crack an NHL lineup on a consistent basis. In need of a change of scenery, it was provided to him in his trade from Chicago to Columbus. The former 45th-overall selection of the Atlanta Thrashers has strong AHL numbers—118 points in 158 career games—all with Rockford, but only 22 points in 82 career NHL games. However, there are some encouraging signs in his underlying stats, which include a career score-adjusted Fenwick of 55.6%. Morin is big, drives hard to the net, is strong on his skates, checks and plays in the corners, and has a strong and quick wrist shot. He certainly has the tools to be a top-nine NHL power forward.

Kerby Rychel — LW — CBJ

Season	Team	Age	GP	G	A	Pts	+/-	ESP/60	AdjCF%	iCF/60	OGVT	DGVT	SGVT	GVT
2014-15	CBJ	20	5	0	3	3	3	3.40	45.3%	11.6	0.6	0.4	0.0	1.0
2015-16	CBJ	21	28	5	8	13					1.3	0.8	0.0	2.0

COLUMBUS BLUE JACKETS

Recent 19th overall pick Kerby Rychel wrapped up an exceptional junior career in which he accumulated 272 points in 256 contests, capped off by 32 points in 20 playoff games with Guelph in 2014. Last year, he made the jump to the AHL level and continued to show off his offensive ability by recording 33 points in 51 games with Springfield. His first five NHL games saw him register three points. As a workhorse power forward, the son of former NHLer Warren Rychel could make an impact soon. The question is whether he will be a highly-competitive role player or legit scorer. That will depend on his continued development.

Jack Skille — RW — Free Agent

Season	Team	Age	GP	G	A	Pts	+/-	ESP/60	AdjCF%	iCF/60	OGVT	DGVT	SGVT	GVT
2012-13	FLA	25	40	3	9	12	-9	1.50	45.3%	13.5	0.1	0.9	0.0	1.0
2013-14	CBJ	26	16	4	0	4	2	1.76	48.1%	16.2	0.8	0.5	0.0	1.3
2014-15	CBJ	27	45	6	2	8	-18	0.86	44.6%	15.2	-1.2	-1.0	0.0	-2.2
2015-16	Free Agent	28	43	8	5	13					0.4	0.3	0.0	0.7

Jack Skille is a former national champion at Wisconsin as well as the seventh-overall pick in the 2005 NHL Entry Draft. In other words, Skille has pedigree. However, he has struggled to live up to it. Projected by some to be a top-six power forward and by others to fill a checking-line role, he has succeeded at neither, with three organizations: Chicago, Florida, and Columbus. Not surprisingly for a top prospect who continues to receive chances, the Madison, Wisconsin native has raw tools—speed, skill, shot—but inconsistent effort and poor hockey IQ will likely scuttle any promise his career seemed to have.

Corey Tropp — RW — CBJ

Season	Team	Age	GP	G	A	Pts	+/-	ESP/60	AdjCF%	iCF/60	OGVT	DGVT	SGVT	GVT
2013-14	BUF, CBJ	24	53	2	9	11	3	1.42	47.1%	7.0	-0.8	1.5	0.0	0.7
2014-15	CBJ	25	61	1	7	8	-14	0.90	37.8%	5.1	-2.0	-0.6	0.0	-2.6
2015-16	CHI	26	49	2	7	9					-1.1	0.6	0.0	-0.5

Former Michigan State Spartan Corey Tropp is a strong skater with absolutely no fear. His presence on the ice is more noticeable in the energy department than it is in boxcar results. In his first year in Columbus, Tropp showed flashes of offensive ability, but for some reason his role changed. It appeared that head coach Todd Richards wanted the 25-year-old to play a simple dump-and-get-off-the-ice game—one that is usually fit for bruisers rather than a quick winger who can win battles in the corners. A trade to Chicago may be the best thing for him, if he can earn a chance to see the ice.

Dana Tyrell — C/LW — Free Agent

Season	Team	Age	GP	G	A	Pts	+/-	ESP/60	AdjCF%	iCF/60	OGVT	DGVT	SGVT	GVT
2012-13	TBL	23	21	1	3	4	-3	1.27	47.6%	9.5	-0.1	0.1	0.0	0.0
2013-14	TBL	24	7	0	0	0	0	0.00	30.7%	4.2	-0.2	0.1	0.0	-0.1
2014-15	CBJ	25	3	0	0	0	-1	0.00	27.4%	2.3	-0.2	-0.1	0.0	-0.2
2015-16	Free Agent	26	26	4	5	9					0.4	0.5	0.0	1.0

Early in his career, Tampa Bay used Dana Tyrell, their 2007 second rounder, as a regular fourth-line player; he appeared in 78 regular-season and seven playoff games in 2010-11 as a versatile depth forward. Since then, Tyrell has seen very little regular NHL time. Even with injuries galore in the Columbus lineup, he dressed for only three games, hinting that the remainder of his career will be played in the minors. While his above-average skating and speed once made the Lightning think he could be a solid third liner, Tyrell has never given any indication that he can produce points at the pro level.

Alexander Wennberg					C/LW								CBJ
Season	Team	Age	GP	G	A	Pts	+/-	ESP/60	AdjCF%	iCF/60	OGVT	DGVT	SGVT	GVT
2014-15	CBJ	20	68	4	16	20	-19	1.14	47.8%	8.4	-1.8	0.3	1.3	-0.1
2015-16	CBJ	21	59	7	16	23					-0.1	1.2	0.1	1.2

The Blue Jackets put Alex Wennberg on the Ryan Johansen Plan, throwing him into the fire prematurely and letting him work through tough times. And boy, were there tough times. The team struggled, and the 20-year-old posted only two points and a -14 over the first 15 games. But the 14th overall pick from 2013 started to get the hang of the NHL as the season went on, finishing the year with nine points in his final 11 games. If Wennberg reaches his potential, he can be an all-around forward, with the ability to skate at a high level, create with his vision, play on the defensive end, and penalty kill as well. Entering the big leagues at six-foot-one, 175-pounds, he will need to continue adding strength and size to reach his ceiling.

DEFENSEMEN

Kevin Connauton						LD								CBJ
Season	Team	Age	GP	G	A	Pts	+/-	ESP/60	AdjCF%	iCF/60	OGVT	DGVT	SGVT	GVT
2013-14	DAL	23	36	1	7	8	-6	0.69	50.1%	12.6	0.6	-0.1	0.0	0.5
2014-15	DAL, CBJ	24	62	9	12	21	5	1.20	47.9%	10.3	3.0	1.6	-0.3	4.4
2015-16	CBJ	25	59	5	14	19					1.6	1.9	0.0	3.5

Picked up through a shrewd waiver-wire move, Kevin Connauton flashed some of the offensive skill that made him a standout with the WHL's Vancouver Giants back in 2009-10. Injuries to Columbus' blue line afforded Connauton the opportunity to play in 54 games, in which he scored an impressive 0.97 points per 60 at even strength, the best by a regular Columbus defender. The Edmonton native is prone to big errors in his own zone, but if he is used judiciously, the Jackets could have an offensive weapon on their bottom pair.

Justin Falk						LD								CBJ
Season	Team	Age	GP	G	A	Pts	+/-	ESP/60	AdjCF%	iCF/60	OGVT	DGVT	SGVT	GVT
2012-13	MIN	24	36	0	3	3	-9	0.42	49.5%	9.3	-1.0	0.4	0.0	-0.7
2013-14	NYR	25	21	0	2	2	-5	0.51	45.0%	6.1	-0.2	-0.3	0.0	-0.5
2014-15	MIN, CBJ	26	18	1	1	2	-9	0.68	43.8%	9.7	-0.4	-0.9	0.0	-1.3
2015-16	CBJ	27	31	2	4	6					0.1	0.4	0.0	0.5

Hulking six-foot-five, 215-pound Justin "not that Faulk" Falk continued his journey around pro hockey, spending time with the Iowa Wild, Minnesota Wild, and Blue Jackets. As usual, he was little more than a spot-filler, eating up a few minutes while trying not to turn the puck over. The 2008 Memorial Cup champion may find it tough to even receive occasional duty going forward. With only two goals in 147 NHL games and a -42, most teams will opt for a more mobile defender, even if defensive mistakes are made.

Cody Goloubef — RD — CBJ

Season	Team	Age	GP	G	A	Pts	+/-	ESP/60	AdjCF%	iCF/60	OGVT	DGVT	SGVT	GVT
2012-13	CBJ	23	11	1	0	1	-3	0.37	48.0%	6.4	0.0	-0.1	0.0	-0.1
2013-14	CBJ	24	5	0	0	0	0	0.00	50.6%	6.1	-0.1	0.0	0.0	-0.1
2014-15	CBJ	25	36	0	9	9	12	0.91	49.9%	7.2	1.1	2.3	0.0	3.3
2015-16	CBJ	26	42	2	8	10					0.7	2.0	0.0	2.7

A native of Oakville, Ontario, Cody Goloubef was an early second-round selection of the Blue Jackets in the 2008 NHL Entry Draft. With its AHL affiliate in Springfield, Goloubef displayed promising skating, passing, and shooting skills along with good awareness and even physicality—though partially offset by the odd defensive-zone lapse. After a long minor-league apprenticeship, the six-foot-one, 198-pound defenseman played in a career-high 36 NHL games, nicely managing to end up breakeven in possession.

Jack Johnson — LD — CBJ

Season	Team	Age	GP	G	A	Pts	+/-	ESP/60	AdjCF%	iCF/60	OGVT	DGVT	SGVT	GVT
2012-13	CBJ	25	44	5	14	19	-5	0.77	45.3%	9.4	2.3	1.5	-0.3	3.5
2013-14	CBJ	26	82	5	28	33	-7	0.59	48.6%	8.2	1.9	2.9	0.0	4.8
2014-15	CBJ	27	79	8	32	40	-13	0.79	47.0%	8.5	5.0	0.6	0.4	6.0
2015-16	CBJ	28	67	8	27	35					4.1	2.7	0.0	6.8

Since coming over from Los Angeles via trade, Jack Johnson has led Columbus in ice-time per game in each of the last four seasons. He is also utilized in a shutdown role. Unfortunately—as any stats hack could have told you anytime over the past three or four years—this trust in Johnson does not yield positive results. The next time the one-time US Olympian registers a score-adjusted Fenwick above 50% will be the first in his career. However, that does not mean he cannot be an effective defenseman. As the Blue Jackets beef up their blueline, the offensively-capable Johnson should be dialed back in the amount of tough ice-time he receives. Then, the team will be able to utilize his playmaking and power-play skills without paying for his frequent mental mistakes while facing top lines.

Ryan Murray — LD — CBJ

Season	Team	Age	GP	G	A	Pts	+/-	ESP/60	AdjCF%	iCF/60	OGVT	DGVT	SGVT	GVT
2013-14	CBJ	20	66	4	17	21	4	0.74	52.2%	5.5	2.0	3.4	0.0	5.4
2014-15	CBJ	21	12	1	2	3	1	0.61	49.2%	3.9	0.2	0.5	0.0	0.6
2015-16	CBJ	22	45	3	12	15					1.0	2.1	0.0	3.1

2012 second-overall pick Ryan Murray has not had the start to his career that he or Columbus wanted. Injuries have played a major role to this point as he battled a shoulder problem in 2013-14 to start his professional career, followed by a knee injury and a high-ankle sprain limiting him to only 12 games in 2014-15. His small sample of play has been promising: Murray has an overall score-adjusted Fenwick of 51.4%. At 22, there is still plenty of time to right the ship. The former Everett Silvertips captain is an exceptionally bright defender with terrific skating ability and natural leadership qualities. He projects to be a big-minute, top-pairing blueliner if he can ever get healthy.

Dalton Prout — RD — CBJ

Season	Team	Age	GP	G	A	Pts	+/-	ESP/60	AdjCF%	iCF/60	OGVT	DGVT	SGVT	GVT
2012-13	CBJ	22	28	1	6	7	15	0.73	44.9%	6.0	1.3	3.0	0.0	4.3
2013-14	CBJ	23	49	2	4	6	-7	0.47	50.1%	8.3	-0.4	0.8	0.0	0.4
2014-15	CBJ	24	63	0	8	8	-14	0.48	46.2%	7.6	-1.0	-0.3	0.0	-1.3
2015-16	CBJ	25	52	2	7	9					-0.3	1.2	0.0	0.9

Almost every depth player on Columbus' roster ended up playing over their head; Dalton Prout was no different. The six-foot-three, 220-pound physical defenseman was often asked to take on bigger minutes than he is capable of, and in tough situations. However, the former Barrie Colt did not drown in his role, delivering possession numbers which were in the middle of the pack for the team. Not bad, all things considered. The 25-year-old will slide into a more fitting bottom-pairing role as the Jackets continue to improve, and he should be above average in that role.

David Savard — RD — CBJ

Season	Team	Age	GP	G	A	Pts	+/-	ESP/60	AdjCF%	iCF/60	OGVT	DGVT	SGVT	GVT
2012-13	CBJ	22	4	0	0	0	-3	0.00	33.3%	4.7	-0.2	-0.3	0.0	-0.5
2013-14	CBJ	23	70	5	10	15	2	0.59	48.4%	6.5	1.0	2.4	0.0	3.4
2014-15	CBJ	24	82	11	25	36	0	1.05	46.5%	7.9	5.9	2.5	0.0	8.5
2015-16	CBJ	25	70	7	22	29					3.6	3.0	0.0	6.6

There has been a lot to like about the offensive growth of David Savard. The former Moncton Wildcat joined up with Jack Johnson to form Columbus' top pairing, producing 36 points while playing in all 82 games. He completed the first step in his development by proving he can be a productive NHLer. Next season, we will get a feel for whether Savard is simply an average middle-pairing defender who can put up points, or if he can elevate his all-around game and become a quality top-four blueliner. After last year, the higher projection doesn't seem crazy, though the team should not expect him to score double-digit goals each year. A 9.8 shooting percentage is unsustainable for a defenseman.

Frederic St. Denis — LD — Germany

Season	Team	Age	GP	G	A	Pts	+/-	ESP/60	AdjCF%	iCF/60	OGVT	DGVT	SGVT	GVT
2014-15	CBJ	28	4	0	1	1	-1	1.16	45.1%	7.6	0.3	0.0	0.0	0.3
2015-16	Germany	29	24	1	5	6					0.5	0.7	0.0	1.2

Although undrafted, Frederic St-Denis was able to experience most Quebec kids' dreams by playing for the Montreal Canadiens, suiting up for 17 games in 2011-12. A skilled-enough AHLer with a mixed bag of good moments and poor lapses, it is not surprising the five-foot-eleven blueliner didn't receive additional NHL time until last season. After producing a solid 88 points in 263 AHL games, St-Denis heads to Germany's DEL for 2015-16 to skate for EHC Munchen.

Fedor Tyutin — D — CBJ

Season	Team	Age	GP	G	A	Pts	+/-	ESP/60	AdjCF%	iCF/60	OGVT	DGVT	SGVT	GVT
2012-13	CBJ	29	48	4	18	22	9	1.06	48.0%	6.4	3.0	4.4	0.0	7.5
2013-14	CBJ	30	69	4	22	26	6	0.77	49.6%	6.1	3.0	3.8	0.0	6.8
2014-15	CBJ	31	67	3	12	15	8	0.64	44.8%	6.6	1.0	3.4	0.0	4.3
2015-16	CBJ	32	57	3	13	16					1.2	2.9	0.0	4.1

Since signing a six-year deal in August 2011 the six-foot-two, Russian-born Fedor Tyutin has been a steady presence on Columbus' blueline. His 250 games played during this timeframe is only bested by Jack Johnson's 287. Formally a solid second-pairing blueliner, Tyutin showed signs of age as he watched his offensive production fade to its lowest level since his early days with the New York Rangers. Playing an average of 20 minutes per night, head coach Todd Richards would be wise to ease back on the heavy ice-time for the 32-year-old.

GOALTENDERS

Sergei Bobrovsky — G — CBJ

Season	Team	Age	GP	W	L	OT	GAA	Sv%	ESSV%	QS%	GGVT	DGVT	SGVT	GVT
2012-13	CBJ	24	38	21	11	6	2	.932	.941	73.0%	22.2	-0.2	1.8	23.8
2013-14	CBJ	25	58	32	20	5	2.38	.923	.931	58.6%	20.5	-0.6	0.7	20.5
2014-15	CBJ	26	51	30	17	3	2.69	.918	.925	57.1%	12.8	-1.8	6.1	17.1
2015-16	CBJ	27	49					.920			14.2	-0.5	0.6	14.3

Since coming over in a trade from Philadelphia, Sergei Bobrovsky has been one of the league's best goaltenders. He followed up his Vezina-winning campaign from 2012-13 with an impressive .931 even-strength save percentage the following year. Despite the 2014-15 season falling short of his recent play, a .925 even-strength save percentage for "Bob" was still above the league average of .921. There are very few goaltenders who justify a contract that eats up around 10% of their team's salary cap, but the Russian netminder is one of them. Amazingly, Bobrovsky is still just entering his prime at age 27, and should continue his high-level play for a long time to come.

Anton Forsberg — G — CBJ

Season	Team	Age	GP	W	L	OT	GAA	Sv%	ESSV%	QS%	GGVT	DGVT	SGVT	GVT
2014-15	CBJ	22	5	0	4	0	4.69	.866	.884	0.0%	-5.4	-0.2	0.0	-5.7
2015-16	CBJ	23	11					.909			-0.7	-0.2	0.0	-0.9

Anton Forsberg earned his first NHL opportunity in 2014-15. The former seventh-round pick out of Sweden achieved a .927 save percentage with Springfield, leading to his promotion. While the promotion had merit, it was not very successful. Forsberg made four starts and appeared in five games with Columbus—the Blue Jackets lost all five games in regulation. Even though it came in a very small sample, Forsberg's even-strength save percentage was a frightening .884. Maybe the bright lights got to him, or it was just a five-game fluke. Give the young goalie more time before passing judgement.

Curtis McElhinney — G — CBJ

Season	Team	Age	GP	W	L	OT	GAA	Sv%	ESSV%	QS%	GGVT	DGVT	SGVT	GVT
2013-14	CBJ	30	28	10	11	1	2.70	.909	.914	52.4%	0.3	0.0	0.5	0.9
2014-15	CBJ	31	32	12	14	2	2.88	.914	.917	46.4%	3.9	-1.2	-0.9	1.9
2015-16	CBJ	32	25					.914			2.2	-0.4	-0.1	1.8

A career backup, Curtis McElhinney put together his finest season to date. The Colorado College graduate received a career-high 28 starts due to Sergei Bobrovsky being out of action from January 22 through March 2. During that timeframe, McElhinney performed admirably. Starting in 16 games, McElhinney registered a .924 save percentage.

Ryan Wilson

Dallas Stars

Coming off of an impressive 2013-14 with new bench boss Lindy Ruff at the helm, it turned into a season to forget for the Dallas Stars. Their 2014 playoff appearance did not hint at an impending downturn. In fact, the Stars were commonly picked as an up-and-coming team in the Western Conference. While expectations were high entering the year, and their confidence was even higher, the Stars' lackluster performance warrants a closer examination, as they look for a crucial bounceback year.

High-paced, high-scoring and porous?

The Stars are one of the most offensively-talented teams in the league. The addition (aka "highway robbery") of Tyler Seguin and the arrival of rookie phenom Valeri Nichushkin pushed them into the playoffs in 2013-14, but this past year's numbers were even better. The Stars had the second-highest even-strength per 60 minutes scoring rate in the league (2.83), only trailing Stanley Cup finalist Tampa Bay (see table, next page). Dallas got their offensive by committee, with three players topping two points per 60 minutes at five-on-five, along with another seven forwards who recorded over 1.5 points per 60 minutes.

However, the cause for concern comes on the back end. While the Stars do have talented defensemen in their lineup, with the likes of Alex Goligoski and now Jason Demers, the team's overall defensive numbers have been less than stellar. They ranked second worst in terms of goals against per 60 minutes at even strength, offsetting their potent production at five on five. The Stars can score with the best of them, but they could not keep the puck out of their net. The combination led to missing the playoffs and finishing a disappointing 10th in the Western Conference, especially given the high expectations.

The fact that Dallas could not hold up defensively, allowing more goals per 60 minutes than the awful Buffalo Sabres, is indicative of a larger problem: the Stars play a high-paced, action-packed style of hockey that keeps fans on the edge of their seats. But a fast-paced, adrenaline-filled game is not always effective as far as wins and losses.

Games involving the Stars averaged 5.7 goals, a solid half-goal more than any other team in the league. But within that high-scoring environment, Dallas was being outscored at even strength.

Enter: Lindy Ruff

Arriving on the scene in Dallas in 2013 was longtime Sabres head coach Lindy Ruff. He was cred-

STARS IN A BOX

Last Season
Goals For	261	2nd
Goals Against	260	26th
GVT	1	19th
Points	92	19th
Playoffs	Did not make playoffs	

Dallas had the league's top one-two punch in Benn and Seguin, but a knee injury to the latter cost the team a playoff berth.

Three-Year Record
GVT	-4	17th
Points	231	21st
Playoffs	1 Appearance, 2 Wins	

VUKOTA Projection
Goals For	241	1st
Goals Against	229	27th
GVT	12	9th
Points	96	9th

With two of the top scorers in the league, both 26 and younger, the Stars should be able to grab one of the elusive bubble spots.

Top Three Prospects
D. Guryanov (F), J. Honka (D), B. Ritchie (F)

Best even-strength offenses and worst even-strength defenses, 2014-15					
Rank	Team	ESGF/60	Rank	Team	ESGA/60
1	Tampa Bay	2.94	30	Edmonton	3.04
2	**Dallas**	**2.83**	29	**Dallas**	**2.90**
3	NY Rangers	2.80	28	Toronto	2.86
4	NY Islanders	2.69	27	Arizona	2.84
5	Minnesota	2.69	26	Buffalo	2.80

Which teams played the highest-scoring games?		
Rank	Team	Total goals/60
1	**Dallas**	**5.70**
2	Vancouver	5.20
3	NY Islanders	5.20
4	Columbus	5.19
5	Toronto	5.13

ited for sparking the young Dallas squad, pushing them into the playoffs for the first time in six seasons. Fast forward one year later, and the Stars were already on the golf course come mid-April. Overall, Ruff has a fine coaching record, and his teams have made the playoffs five times since the 2004-2005 lockout.

In the past, Ruff had iced teams that relied less on strong possession numbers and more on their goaltending (aka "Ryan Miller"). But in 2014-15, the numbers were flipped from Ruff's old Sabre days. The Stars finished 10th in Corsi for at five-on-five (52.1%), yet the club ended the year 29th in even-strength save percentage (.910). (See chart, this page.)

Ruff utilized starting goaltender Kari Lehtonen much in the way he used to handle Miller: play him until he croaks. In each of the past two seasons, the

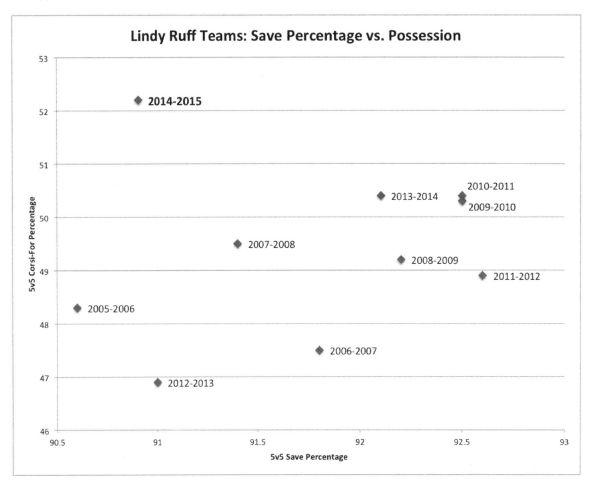

Finnish goalie has been tabbed for 65 games. Despite some of Lehtonen's struggles, Ruff was forced to run him out night after night because his backup, Anders Lindback, performed so poorly. The six-foot-six ex-Predator played in 10 games last season, losing eight while allowing 3.71 goals-against per game with a horrendous .875 save percentage.

During Ruff's time in Buffalo, he was often tabbed as a "defensive-minded coach". However, that is a misnomer. During his runs to the Eastern Conference Final in 2006 and 2007, he played an up-tempo style that led to a lot of goals but also a lot of Grade A scoring chances. Considering the roster he was given in Dallas, with offensive dynamos like Tyler Seguin, Jason Spezza, and Jamie Benn along with a mobile defense corps, it was appropriate to harken to the good old Sabre days, bringing back the boom-or-bust system.

That could be, in part, an explanation for why Lehtonen saw a drop in save percentage, but his win-loss record was nearly identical to 2013-14. To be exact, the Stars' starter won one more game and lost three fewer games last season as opposed to Ruff's first year. The run-and-gun could also be a reason why a mediocre netminder like Lindback couldn't handle the heat.

Just because the results weren't exactly what the Stars wanted doesn't mean that Ruff should go back to his Dominik Hasek days and try to win games 1-0. It means a tweak to the backup position could make all the difference.

When the Stars dealt for ex-Sabre Jhonas Enroth, they hoped for improvement behind Lehtonen and they received it. The Swedish goalie went 5-5-1 with a .906 save percentage. While that save percentage mark is far from Carey Price, it was good enough to gain points in six of 10 games, unlike Lindback's two-of-10 rate. Maybe if Enroth had been the backup all year, the Stars would have made up the five points they were short of for the playoffs.

General manager Jim Nill seems to see it that way, based on his offseason signing of former Blackhawks and Sharks goalie Antti Niemi. The Cup-winning goalie is 32 and may be at the tail end of his prime, but he brings much more reliability to the position than many of the other available goaltenders. He has posted save percentages of .913 and .914 over the past two seasons on offensive-minded, possession-strong Sharks teams. If he can carry over average play to the explosive Stars offense while giving Lehtonen some more nights off, Dallas should see a jump in the standings.

Another factor to consider is Nill's move to bring in defensive-minded blueliner Johnny Oduya and part ways with scoring defender Trevor Daley. Still a nifty skater and passer, Oduya brings more to the defensive end than Dallas has had in some time. His addition should make the Finnish netminders feel more at ease.

And Ruff will have to make a tweak. We rarely give credit to coaches for their ability to self-evaluate and adapt. Ruff has done it before and is likely to make changes to amend his mistakes. If he doesn't and the Stars slip again, he will certainly be on the hot seat.

Lucas Friesen

DALLAS STARS

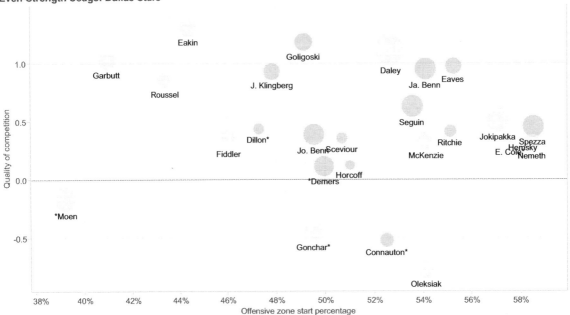

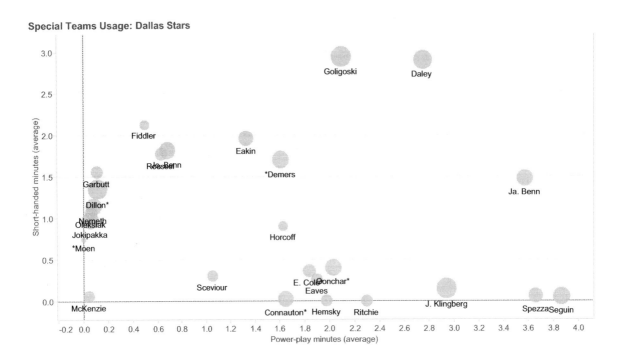

DALLAS STARS

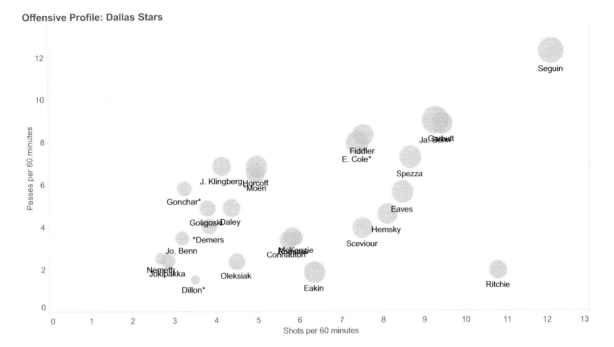

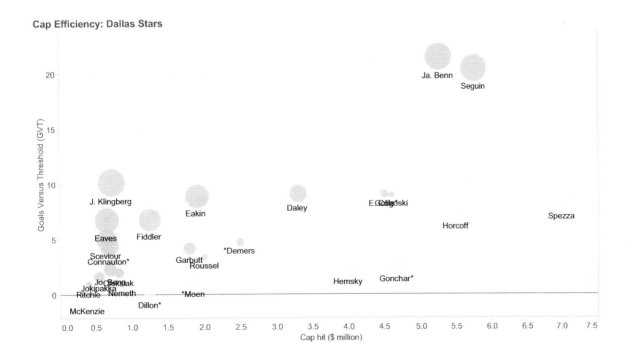

DALLAS STARS

FORWARDS

Jamie Benn								LW						DAL
Season	Team	Age	GP	G	A	Pts	+/-	ESP/60	AdjCF%	iCF/60	OGVT	DGVT	SGVT	GVT
2012-13	DAL	23	41	12	21	33	-12	2.08	49.2%	16.0	4.3	-0.5	0.0	3.8
2013-14	DAL	24	81	34	45	79	21	2.86	52.1%	19.4	14.8	4.3	0.0	19.0
2014-15	DAL	25	82	35	52	87	1	2.90	54.5%	17.4	18.5	3.1	0.0	21.5
2015-16	DAL	26	78	35	49	84					13.9	3.1	0.0	17.0

After a strong offensive campaign in 2013-14, Jamie Benn was able to follow it up with a season to remember. The hard-nosed winger picked up his Art Ross-winning assist with 9.5 seconds left in the Stars season. With Dallas attempting a late push toward the playoffs, Benn went on a tear with 20 points in his final 10 games. Benn's hybrid style of power forward and a sniper fit perfectly with Tyler Seguin's magnificent offensive talents. Holding constant his 12.1% career shooting, expect Benn to post many more 30+ goal seasons in the future.

Cody Eakin								C						DAL
Season	Team	Age	GP	G	A	Pts	+/-	ESP/60	AdjCF%	iCF/60	OGVT	DGVT	SGVT	GVT
2012-13	DAL	21	48	7	17	24	1	2.16	49.5%	10.4	3.2	1.8	0.0	5.1
2013-14	DAL	22	81	16	19	35	-9	1.51	51.6%	12.8	2.8	2.1	-0.3	4.6
2014-15	DAL	23	78	19	21	40	-1	1.83	50.6%	12.6	5.4	3.5	0.0	8.9
2015-16	DAL	24	70	18	22	41					4.5	2.6	0.0	7.2

The Stars have been able to find a strong two-way center in Winnipeg native Cody Eakin. Since coming over from the Capitals, the 2009 third-round pick has been able to bring energy and a grinding style of play to the lineup in addition to even-strength scoring at a fringe top-six level. Further, Eakin was given a lot of the big-minute opportunities to shut down opposing teams' top lines. The Stars were impressed enough with their well-rounded third-line center to sign him to a four-year contract extension worth $15.4 million.

Patrick Eaves								RW						DAL
Season	Team	Age	GP	G	A	Pts	+/-	ESP/60	AdjCF%	iCF/60	OGVT	DGVT	SGVT	GVT
2012-13	DET	28	34	2	6	8	-1	1.31	54.3%	14.0	-0.1	1.1	0.0	0.9
2013-14	DET, NSH	29	30	2	3	5	-7	0.44	50.0%	16.5	-0.8	-0.1	0.9	0.0
2014-15	DAL	30	47	14	13	27	12	1.99	54.8%	16.5	5.2	1.9	-0.3	6.8
2015-16	DAL	31	47	11	13	24					2.8	1.4	0.0	4.2

When healthy, Patrick Eaves fit better with this offensively-talented Stars group than he has with any NHL club since his first two seasons in the league with Ottawa. After struggling through the past few years with stints in Detroit, Nashville, and even the AHL, the veteran winger's "bounceback" had a lot to do with being given the opportunity to play with Seguin and Benn for nearly 50% of his total ice-time. However, the former Boston College Eagle was limited to only 47 games, as he was unable to stay healthy for very long, suffering an ankle injury in December and concussion later on. At age 31, a revitalization of his career could prove difficult, but Seguin and Benn both had better Corsi and goals-for percentages when playing with Eaves than with other wingers.

Vernon Fiddler — C — DAL

Season	Team	Age	GP	G	A	Pts	+/-	ESP/60	AdjCF%	iCF/60	OGVT	DGVT	SGVT	GVT
2012-13	DAL	32	46	4	13	17	3	1.82	45.3%	11.5	1.8	2.3	0.0	4.1
2013-14	DAL	33	76	6	17	23	3	1.43	48.7%	12.1	1.1	3.7	0.3	5.2
2014-15	DAL	34	80	13	16	29	-5	1.71	50.4%	13.6	4.1	2.6	0.1	6.8
2015-16	DAL	35	61	10	14	24					2.1	2.1	0.0	4.2

Typically touted for his toughness, Vernon Fiddler had one of his best offensive seasons. He was able to set a career high in goals while assuming a bottom-six role on most nights. With Lindy Ruff attempting to get his skilled scorers as much offensive zone time as possible, the 34-year-old pivot received far more defensive zone starts than most of his teammates, making his production numbers that much more impressive. However, in posting his highest shooting percentage since 2008-09 (9.6%), it is unlikely the former Predator and Coyote can repeat a double-digit-goal season.

Ryan Garbutt — RW — CHI

Season	Team	Age	GP	G	A	Pts	+/-	ESP/60	AdjCF%	iCF/60	OGVT	DGVT	SGVT	GVT
2012-13	DAL	27	36	3	7	10	1	1.84	48.4%	17.2	0.7	0.9	0.0	1.5
2013-14	DAL	28	75	17	15	32	10	2.07	52.1%	18.9	6.1	3.2	-0.3	9.1
2014-15	DAL	29	67	8	17	25	-9	1.81	50.4%	18.4	2.4	1.8	0.0	4.2
2015-16	CHI	30	60	12	16	28					3.1	2.0	0.0	5.1

Ryan Garbutt had assumed a significant role for the Stars on their third line with Cody Eakin and Antoine Roussel, bringing a shade of toughness with solid production. The past two seasons have been Garbutt's best offensively, staying solidly in the top-six range at even strength—pretty amazing for a guy who worked his way up from the Corpur Christi Icerays of the Central Hockey League to the NHL. However, Garbutt frustrated his coach by serving two suspensions for a total of five games. Following the suspensions, it seemed his relationship with Ruff deteriorated, as the scrappy winger found himself watching from the pressbox quite often through the Stars' playoff push. In Chicago now for the 2015-16 campaign, Garbutt could be an underrated part of the Patrick Sharp deal.

Ales Hemsky — RW — DAL

Season	Team	Age	GP	G	A	Pts	+/-	ESP/60	AdjCF%	iCF/60	OGVT	DGVT	SGVT	GVT
2012-13	EDM	29	38	9	11	20	-6	1.34	44.3%	12.3	1.4	-0.2	-0.1	1.2
2013-14	EDM, OTT	30	75	13	30	43	-15	1.79	48.8%	12.2	4.6	0.3	0.6	5.4
2014-15	DAL	31	76	11	21	32	-8	1.63	52.1%	15.1	2.8	0.6	-0.8	2.6
2015-16	DAL	32	60	11	20	31					2.9	1.1	0.0	4.0

After being shuffled around in the 2013-14 season, Ales Hemsky signed with Dallas, hoping to be another piece in the offensive juggernaut of the Stars. The two-time 20-goal scorer has not reached that mark since the 2008-09, and seems to be headed on a decline as he enters his thirties. Hemsky had been hotly debated in Edmonton because his Relative Corsi numbers were often positive, yet he fell short of expectations as a scorer and all-around forward. While the two-time Czech Olympian may be a touch overpaid and frustratingly inconsistent, he is better when out of the limelight, as he is in Dallas. Hemsky also had good chemistry with Jason Spezza, which adds to his value.

Shawn Horcoff — LW — ANA

Season	Team	Age	GP	G	A	Pts	+/-	ESP/60	AdjCF%	iCF/60	OGVT	DGVT	SGVT	GVT
2012-13	EDM	34	31	7	5	12	8	1.31	42.3%	7.8	0.3	1.9	0.0	2.2
2013-14	DAL	35	77	7	13	20	1	1.12	49.4%	7.1	0.7	1.8	-0.3	2.2
2014-15	DAL	36	76	11	18	29	9	1.81	53.0%	9.3	4.2	2.9	0.4	7.4
2015-16	ANA	37	58	8	14	22					1.8	1.8	0.0	3.6

If the Stars ignore the veteran winger's ridiculous $5.5 million cap hit, they should be fairly happy with Shawn Horcoff's production as a bottom-six forward. The former Michigan State Spartans captain played around 10 minutes per game, tallied 22 even-strength points, and several more on the power play. Horcoff will always be haunted by his 70-point season in 2005-06, which set unfair expectations for the rest of his career in Edmonton. At age 37, he has finally escaped the criticism of being a disappointment, and will hope to continue fitting into a depth role, now with the Anaheim Ducks.

Curtis McKenzie — LW — DAL

Season	Team	Age	GP	G	A	Pts	+/-	ESP/60	AdjCF%	iCF/60	OGVT	DGVT	SGVT	GVT
2014-15	DAL	23	36	4	1	5	-8	0.73	51.0%	11.4	-0.4	-0.2	0.0	-0.6
2015-16	DAL	24	42	7	5	12					0.2	0.5	0.0	0.7

Curtis McKenzie has been quite the surprise for the Stars' organization. The former Miami Redhawk was drafted in 2009, getting his first AHL action in 2012-13. A year later, McKenzie helped lead the Texas Stars to an AHL title by scoring 65 points in 75 games. This was good enough to earn a call-up to the big-league club last season, where he received mainly fourth-line minutes. On a team with high expectations and stocked with top-nine forwards, the question is whether the sixth-round pick can change his game to play only a few mistake-free shifts per game as opposed to getting big offensive minutes in the minors. He will either adapt and become a solid NHL depth player, or remain an AHL lifer.

Travis Moen — LW — DAL

Season	Team	Age	GP	G	A	Pts	+/-	ESP/60	AdjCF%	iCF/60	OGVT	DGVT	SGVT	GVT
2012-13	MTL	30	45	2	4	6	-4	0.87	48.1%	9.0	-0.9	1.4	0.0	0.4
2013-14	MTL	31	65	2	10	12	2	1.14	46.2%	8.9	-0.8	3.8	0.0	3.0
2014-15	MTL, DAL	32	44	3	6	9	0	1.42	44.8%	8.7	0.4	0.7	0.0	1.1
2015-16	DAL	33	47	4	8	11					-0.1	1.4	0.0	1.3

An early-season trade saw the Stars acquire long-time Habs grinder Travis Moen in exchange for aging blue-liner Sergei Gonchar. Moen has played his 12-year NHL career as a gritty, tough forward who can hold his own defensively. Unfortunately, one thing that goes along with toughness is injury, and his season was filled with stints out of the lineup. When he was dressed, his minutes were limited, and he received primarily defensive assignments for the third straight year. If the former Kelowna Rocket cannot stay in the lineup consistently, there is a stocked cupboard of depth forwards in the Stars system who will be clamoring for his position.

DALLAS STARS

Travis Morin — C — DAL

Season	Team	Age	GP	G	A	Pts	+/-	ESP/60	AdjCF%	iCF/60	OGVT	DGVT	SGVT	GVT
2013-14	DAL	29	4	0	1	1	2	1.47	55.2%	8.0	-0.1	0.3	0.0	0.2
2014-15	DAL	30	6	0	0	0	1	0.00	63.8%	19.2	-0.2	0.2	0.0	-0.1
2015-16	DAL	31	26	4	5	8					0.4	0.6	0.0	1.0

A ninth-round pick in 2004, Travis Morin has spent most of his professional hockey career in the minors. In his stints in the ECHL and AHL, he has always been able to produce at a high level, posting 54 goals and 97 assists in 129 games—big numbers—over the past two seasons for the Texas Stars, winning the AHL scoring title in 2013-14. Oddly, the success of this minor-league sniper hasn't transferred into serious NHL consideration. The 31-year-old forward has played 13 career NHL games without scoring a goal while only recording one assist. For the AHL level, Morin has a great shot and hockey sense, but at the NHL level, his skill would place him on the bottom six. Without a toughness or defensive element to his game, he brings very little to that role. Morin is a classic tweener.

Valeri Nichushkin — RW — DAL

Season	Team	Age	GP	G	A	Pts	+/-	ESP/60	AdjCF%	iCF/60	OGVT	DGVT	SGVT	GVT
2013-14	DAL	18	79	14	20	34	20	1.73	51.1%	11.1	4.2	3.7	-0.3	7.5
2014-15	DAL	19	8	0	1	1	-5	0.57	51.1%	11.2	-0.4	-0.3	0.0	-0.7
2015-16	DAL	20	49	10	14	23					2.0	1.4	0.0	3.4

Coming off a rookie season that showed flashes of brilliance, Valeri Nichushkin's sophomore campaign was basically erased by injury. After just four games, the power forward was forced out of the lineup until very late in the season after requiring hip surgery. Oozing with offensive talent, there will be high expectations for the six-foot-four, 210-pound winger. He is the total package offensively, with great instincts, a terrific shot, and the vision to make a pass that only top-level skill players can make. That said, he is kind of a man-child at only 20 years old, so Nichushkin still has to learn to use his size more often and pay attention to details in his own zone.

Rich Peverley — C/RW — Retired

Season	Team	Age	GP	G	A	Pts	+/-	ESP/60	AdjCF%	iCF/60	OGVT	DGVT	SGVT	GVT
2012-13	BOS	30	47	6	12	18	-9	1.09	52.2%	12.9	1.2	0.6	-0.3	1.5
2013-14	DAL	31	62	7	23	30	-3	1.98	49.8%	12.2	2.8	1.4	1.5	5.6
2015-16	Retired	32												

Rich Peverley was forced to retire after suffering a scary in-game cardiac event during the 2013-14 season. Known as a bright, hard-working player, the former Bruin has already been working towards finding a role with the Stars organization as a coach and mentor for younger players. The Kingston native and former NCAA student-athlete could pass along a few words of wisdom to some up-and-coming Stars players given his success as a depth forward for the majority of his career.

Brendan Ranford — LW — DAL

Season	Team	Age	GP	G	A	Pts	+/-	ESP/60	AdjCF%	iCF/60	OGVT	DGVT	SGVT	GVT
2014-15	DAL	22	1	0	0	0	0	0.00	56.4%	11.2	0.0	0.0	0.0	0.0
2015-16	DAL	23	26	5	6	11					0.8	0.5	0.0	1.3

Brendan Ranford got the call-up to play in one game with the big-league club. The Kamloops Blazers alum has spent the past two seasons with the AHL's Texas Stars, increasing his production from 33 to 51 points from his first to second year. He also made a strong impression during the Texas Stars' 2013-14 stretch run, posting 16 points in 21 games. The seventh-round pick of the Flyers in 2010 is a bit undersized at five-foot-ten, but may provide enough bottom-six grit to find a spot with the big club.

Brett Ritchie								RW						DAL
Season	Team	Age	GP	G	A	Pts	+/-	ESP/60	AdjCF%	iCF/60	OGVT	DGVT	SGVT	GVT
2014-15	DAL	21	31	6	3	9	-1	1.32	55.8%	19.3	0.6	0.3	0.0	0.9
2015-16	DAL	22	42	10	8	19					1.7	0.9	0.0	2.6

Big-bodied 2011 second rounder Brett Ritchie has spent time in the AHL in each of the past three seasons, working his way up to a midseason recall to Dallas. The 22-year-old power forward saw a jump in his goal-scoring rate from 22 markers in 68 AHL games to 14 in 33 AHL games, while adding six more in 31 NHL games. The Orangeville, Ontario native has put up impressive possession numbers, with the best Corsi-against rate among Dallas forwards, albeit in a small sample and in sheltered minutes. It has taken a while for Ritchie to be ready for the NHL, but he has a good chance to become a regular that plays defensive minutes and pots a few goals along the way.

Antoine Roussel								LW						DAL
Season	Team	Age	GP	G	A	Pts	+/-	ESP/60	AdjCF%	iCF/60	OGVT	DGVT	SGVT	GVT
2012-13	DAL	23	39	7	7	14	3	2.51	44.1%	11.9	2.3	1.1	0.0	3.4
2013-14	DAL	24	81	14	15	29	-1	1.74	52.6%	13.4	3.9	2.8	0.0	6.7
2014-15	DAL	25	80	13	12	25	-20	1.36	51.1%	11.5	1.4	1.3	0.6	3.4
2015-16	DAL	26	66	12	13	25					1.9	1.7	0.0	3.6

The Stars are thrilled they found Antoine Roussel. The undrafted Frenchman was brought into the organization after a few stints in the ECHL and AHL with the Bruins and Canucks affiliates. His 2013-14 season saw him succeed in the Dallas lineup, bringing physical play and flashes of offensive talent. However, Roussel plays on the edge, sometimes overstepping and taking bad penalties. His even-strength scoring rate has declined since he arrived in the league, but this regression was expected given his defensive usage.

Colton Sceviour								RW						DAL
Season	Team	Age	GP	G	A	Pts	+/-	ESP/60	AdjCF%	iCF/60	OGVT	DGVT	SGVT	GVT
2012-13	DAL	23	1	0	1	1	-1	12.37	27.0%	0.0	0.1	-0.1	0.0	0.0
2013-14	DAL	24	26	8	4	12	-3	1.83	50.4%	15.9	1.7	0.3	-0.3	1.7
2014-15	DAL	25	71	9	17	26	1	1.64	54.1%	15.6	2.4	1.6	1.0	5.0
2015-16	DAL	26	60	12	17	29					2.8	1.8	0.0	4.6

After spending five seasons in the AHL, Colton Sceviour worked like crazy to earn his first full season with the Stars. He proved that sometimes all a guy needs is a chance. At 1.64 even-strength points per 60 minutes, the 25-year-old was a quality producer amongst bottom sixers. The concerns from Sceviour's AHL days were based on his size and speed, whether he could keep up with the NHL pace. But it seems that playing a smart, hard game at both ends has garnered positive results, as he managed a positive Relative Corsi and goals-for percentage. With a crowded, quality bottom six and more depth players working their way through the system, the former Portland Winter Hawk and Lethbridge Hurricane will have to continue to fight for every day at the highest level.

Tyler Seguin — C — DAL

Season	Team	Age	GP	G	A	Pts	+/-	ESP/60	AdjCF%	iCF/60	OGVT	DGVT	SGVT	GVT
2012-13	BOS	20	48	16	16	32	23	2.19	60.7%	20.7	4.9	2.6	0.4	7.9
2013-14	DAL	21	80	37	47	84	16	2.85	52.5%	16.6	17.9	3.4	-0.2	21.1
2014-15	DAL	22	71	37	40	77	-1	2.59	54.4%	18.7	17.7	1.2	1.6	20.5
2015-16	DAL	23	72	37	45	82					14.6	2.3	0.1	17.0

Tyler Seguin has officially solidified himself as an elite talent. Teaming up with Jamie Benn on the first line for the Stars, the second-overall pick of 2010 was second in the NHL in points per game. If it weren't for a minor injury that had the winger miss time, Seguin may have been in contention with Benn for the Art Ross Trophy. Whether it is skating, shot, vision, or instincts, the tattooed 23-year-old is amongst the best in the NHL, making him an unstoppable force at five-on-five and on the power play. What might come as a surprise is that Seguin's defensive numbers are very good, despite the narrative that he is a one-dimensional player. Seguin is a superstar and will be for a long time.

Jason Spezza — C — DAL

Season	Team	Age	GP	G	A	Pts	+/-	ESP/60	AdjCF%	iCF/60	OGVT	DGVT	SGVT	GVT
2012-13	OTT	29	5	2	3	5	3	2.43	55.1%	9.6	1.0	0.3	0.5	1.8
2013-14	OTT	30	75	23	43	66	-26	2.45	51.9%	15.9	10.7	-1.6	-0.1	9.0
2014-15	DAL	31	82	17	45	62	-7	1.95	54.5%	16.7	8.4	0.8	-0.7	8.5
2015-16	DAL	32	67	20	37	57					7.4	1.2	0.0	8.7

The offseason acquisition of Jason Spezza was a move that GM Jim Nill hoped would take them over the top. Offensively, he did the trick, but some of the Senators' concerns showed up with the Stars. Spezza continues to produce points at a top-six rate, no doubt, and he was able to stay healthy for the Stars last year, but his regression is something to take note of. His shooting percentage over the past two seasons, at 10.3% and 8.5%, were career lows. Toward the end of the season, Ruff used Seguin on the wing with the 31-year-old at center. The results were impressive, as they averaged 3.86 points per 60 minutes together.

DEFENSEMEN

Jordie Benn — LD — DAL

Season	Team	Age	GP	G	A	Pts	+/-	ESP/60	AdjCF%	iCF/60	OGVT	DGVT	SGVT	GVT
2012-13	DAL	25	26	1	5	6	-4	0.83	50.0%	10.0	0.4	0.6	1.0	2.0
2013-14	DAL	26	78	3	17	20	16	0.78	51.0%	9.1	1.9	5.3	-1.6	5.6
2014-15	DAL	27	73	2	14	16	-5	0.74	55.0%	9.2	0.6	2.2	-0.4	2.3
2015-16	DAL	28	62	3	13	16					1.0	2.6	0.0	3.5

After working his way through the Stars organization, Jordie Benn has found his way into the regular defensive rotation of the big-league club. Some new arrivals to the defensive corps limited Jordie's minutes over the past season, but he has settled into a regular third-pairing role. Like his brother, Benn brings toughness to the ice, but adds a strong defensive presence. Among all Stars defensemen, the undrafted 27-year-old was on the ice for the fewest shot attempts against per 60 minutes.

Trevor Daley							LD							CHI
Season	Team	Age	GP	G	A	Pts	+/-	ESP/60	AdjCF%	iCF/60	OGVT	DGVT	SGVT	GVT
2012-13	DAL	29	44	4	9	13	1	0.74	47.3%	9.0	1.0	2.2	0.0	3.2
2013-14	DAL	30	67	9	16	25	10	1.07	51.3%	10.0	4.9	4.3	0.0	9.2
2014-15	DAL	31	68	16	22	38	-13	1.23	46.2%	8.6	7.8	1.5	-0.3	9.1
2015-16	CHI	32	61	9	23	32					5.1	2.5	0.0	7.5

Trevor Daley's scoring rate on the power play led the team's defensemen, while his even-strength production was second to super-rookie John Klingberg. However, the 31-year-old blueliner's scoring numbers were boosted by career-high 14.2% shooting, and his numbers beyond the scoring stats were abysmal. Daley's Corsi was four percent lower than the next-worst regular Stars defenseman, while his Corsi-against per 60 minutes was more than six shot attempts worse. Circumstances may have been partially responsible for the rough five-on-five numbers, as he was asked to play against top lines, which he is nowhere near capable of. An offseason trade to Chicago may be the best thing for Daley, as he can take on a protected, third-pairing role there.

Jason Demers							RD							DAL
Season	Team	Age	GP	G	A	Pts	+/-	ESP/60	AdjCF%	iCF/60	OGVT	DGVT	SGVT	GVT
2012-13	SJS	24	22	1	2	3	-4	0.51	49.9%	10.3	0.0	0.3	0.0	0.3
2013-14	SJS	25	75	5	29	34	14	1.19	56.2%	9.2	4.9	4.4	-0.3	9.1
2014-15	SJS, DAL	26	81	5	20	25	-3	0.94	55.6%	9.6	3.2	1.5	0.0	4.8
2015-16	DAL	27	65	5	18	23					2.5	2.4	0.0	5.0

In November, the Stars shipped out promising young defenseman Brendan Dillon in exchange for Jason Demers from the San Jose Sharks. While Dillon had size, Demers brings versatility to the Stars defensive group, with above-average puck skills and solid defensive poise. The seventh-round pick from 2008 has seen improving numbers over the past two seasons and looks to continue the trend as he settles into his role with Dallas. Demers and Jordie Benn made for a quality pair, combining the former's mobility with the latter's defensive approach.

Alex Goligoski							LD							DAL
Season	Team	Age	GP	G	A	Pts	+/-	ESP/60	AdjCF%	iCF/60	OGVT	DGVT	SGVT	GVT
2012-13	DAL	27	47	3	24	27	4	1.06	50.7%	11.1	3.9	1.5	0.0	5.5
2013-14	DAL	28	81	6	36	42	9	1.08	50.9%	8.0	6.0	4.5	0.0	10.5
2014-15	DAL	29	81	4	32	36	0	1.03	53.8%	9.3	4.7	4.4	0.0	9.0
2015-16	DAL	30	68	6	26	32					4.0	3.9	0.0	7.9

Since being acquired from Pittsburgh for James Neal in February 2011, Alex Goligoski has been arguably the best defenseman on the Stars roster. When Dallas promoted promising young blueliner John Klingberg, he was paired with Goligoski and the two had terrific chemistry. The duo posted a dominant 55.3% Corsi when together. With the plethora of well-known top-tier defensemen around the league, the five-foot-eleven rearguard hasn't gained as much recognition as other number ones around the league, but now that he has a skilled defenseman alongside, we will see his ceiling. Considering the ice-time he logs, Goligoski's $4.6 million cap hit is a steal.

Jyrki Jokipakka — LD — DAL

Season	Team	Age	GP	G	A	Pts	+/-	ESP/60	AdjCF%	iCF/60	OGVT	DGVT	SGVT	GVT
2014-15	DAL	23	51	0	10	10	-2	0.76	50.1%	7.7	0.4	1.1	0.0	1.6
2015-16	DAL	24	48	2	10	12					0.5	1.6	0.0	2.1

Rookie defenseman Jyrki Jokipakka demonstrated that Finnish players often adapt quickly to the NHL. Jokipakka jumped right into the Dallas defensive group after only one year in the AHL, having produced 21 points in 68 games for the Calder Cup winning 2013-14 Texas Stars. The 2011 seventh rounder has length, a booming shot, and surprising skating ability for his size. His minutes mainly came in the top four, paired with Trevor Daley, getting the nod against some fairly tough opponents. Once he gets comfortable with the team, look for him to play a larger role.

John Klingberg — RD — DAL

Season	Team	Age	GP	G	A	Pts	+/-	ESP/60	AdjCF%	iCF/60	OGVT	DGVT	SGVT	GVT
2014-15	DAL	22	65	11	29	40	5	1.38	53.5%	8.5	8.7	2.1	-0.5	10.2
2015-16	DAL	23	65	11	30	40					6.9	2.3	0.0	9.2

The arrival of rookie John Klingberg was one of the highlights of the season for the Stars. The 22-year-old Swede did something few rookies can do: he stepped right onto the top pairing and flourished. He and Alex Goligoski generated the best goals-for percentage of any pairing on the team (56.8%). Klingberg has great offensive skills and his skating abilities are toward the top of the league. The 2010 fifth rounder was called up after spending a season and 10 games in the AHL, and hasn't looked back since joining the big club. He led the Dallas defensive group in raw points, points per 60 minutes, and on-ice Corsi-for in all situations. For a rookie—even a slightly older rookie—it does not get much better than that. His numbers in only 65 games should have warranted Calder consideration, if only fellow freshman Aaron Ekblad wasn't breaking records in the Sunshine State.

Patrik Nemeth — LD — DAL

Season	Team	Age	GP	G	A	Pts	+/-	ESP/60	AdjCF%	iCF/60	OGVT	DGVT	SGVT	GVT
2013-14	DAL	21	8	0	0	0	-3	0.00	45.9%	3.8	-0.4	-0.3	0.0	-0.7
2014-15	DAL	22	22	0	3	3	0	0.55	54.2%	7.3	0.1	0.7	0.0	0.8
2015-16	DAL	23	34	2	6	7					0.1	1.1	0.0	1.2

After playing a role for the Stars late in the 2013-14 season and into the playoffs, Patrik Nemeth suffered a deep laceration on his arm early in the season and was held out for the majority of 2014-15. Although it was first thought that the 2010 second-round pick would miss the entire regular season, Nemeth slid back into the defense corps in early March. In what he has shown, the six-foot-four Swede can play at the NHL level as a bottom-pairing blueliner. Consistently offering a physical presence will keep him there because there isn't much offense to speak of.

Jamie Oleksiak — LD — DAL

Season	Team	Age	GP	G	A	Pts	+/-	ESP/60	AdjCF%	iCF/60	OGVT	DGVT	SGVT	GVT
2012-13	DAL	20	16	0	2	2	-5	0.54	50.1%	8.8	-0.3	-0.1	0.0	-0.4
2013-14	DAL	21	7	0	0	0	-3	0.00	49.1%	4.2	-0.6	0.0	0.0	-0.6
2014-15	DAL	22	36	1	7	8	0	1.09	49.8%	7.5	0.6	1.4	0.0	2.0
2015-16	DAL	23	42	2	8	10					0.6	1.6	0.0	2.2

As injuries and on-ice struggles plagued the Stars' defensive unit, Jamie Oleksiak was called up to drive to provide some production, and size; at six-foot-seven, the 2011 first rounder towers over anyone who comes his way. Oleksiak split time between the NHL and AHL, showing flashes of potential while with the big club. At age 23, plenty of patience will still be required as Oleksiak develops, as very few defensemen of his height are able to have success right away.

GOALTENDERS

Jhonas Enroth — G — LAK

Season	Team	Age	GP	W	L	OT	GAA	Sv%	ESSV%	QS%	GGVT	DGVT	SGVT	GVT
2012-13	BUF	24	12	4	4	1	2.60	.919	.931	77.8%	3.5	-0.4	-1.0	2.0
2013-14	BUF	25	28	4	17	5	2.82	.911	.918	53.8%	1.7	-0.5	0.0	1.1
2014-15	BUF, DAL	26	50	18	26	2	3.07	.904	.915	45.5%	-7.8	-1.0	5.5	-3.3
2015-16	LAK	27	35					.914			3.1	-0.4	0.5	3.3

Jhonas Enroth was shipped to the Lone Star State from Buffalo in exchange for disappointing but tall netminder Anders Lindback, in a move to support starting netminder Kari Lehtonen amidst his struggles. The 27-year-old is the smallest goalie in the NHL at five-foot-ten, but he has worked his way into being a reliable backup. His potential may not truly be known, as he has played on very bad Sabres teams over the past few seasons. The Swedish puck stopper got peppered in Buffalo, and while his underlying numbers did drop compared to the past, they should not be taken as is. Looking forward, Enroth will back up Jonathan Quick in L.A., where he will have limited duty behind a great defensive club.

Kari Lehtonen — G — DAL

Season	Team	Age	GP	W	L	OT	GAA	Sv%	ESSV%	QS%	GGVT	DGVT	SGVT	GVT
2012-13	DAL	29	36	15	14	3	2.66	.916	.924	57.1%	8.9	-1.0	0.5	8.3
2013-14	DAL	30	65	33	20	10	2.41	.919	.925	57.8%	16.0	0.0	1.6	17.6
2014-15	DAL	31	65	34	17	10	2.94	.903	.909	47.7%	-9.6	-0.5	0.3	-9.8
2015-16	DAL	32	40					.913			2.6	-0.1	0.1	2.6

After firmly securing his starting spot in the Dallas net, Kari Lehtonen let down many of his supporters. His numbers trended down from recent seasons, leading to the Finnish netminder taking a lot of the blame for the struggles of the Stars, thought to be on an upswing after their 2014 playoff promise. However, Lehtonen was not backed by a strong defensive squad, and Lindy Ruff utilized a high-risk system, which led to a great deal of odd-man rushes and turnovers. That said, Ruff used a similar system with a talented Buffalo team coming out of the 2004-05 lockout, and it did not destroy his goalies' numbers. Only four goaltenders with over 2,000 minutes played had a lower even-strength save percentage than the 2002 second-overall draft choice, which led the Stars to sign his countryman Antti Niemi as insurance.

Jussi Rynnas — G — KHL

Season	Team	Age	GP	W	L	OT	GAA	Sv%	ESSV%	QS%	GGVT	DGVT	SGVT	GVT
2012-13	TOR	25	1	0	0	0	0.00	1.000	1.000	0.0%	0.5	0.0	0.0	0.5
2014-15	DAL	27	2	0	1	0	4.57	.841	.861	0.0%	-2.5	0.0	0.0	-2.5
2015-16	KHL	28	11					.912			0.4	0.0	0.0	0.3

Dallas inked Jussi Rynnas prior to the 2014-15 season, looking to add depth in the crease and support down in the AHL. With the presence of Lindback, and then Enroth in the backup role, Rynnas never really got much of a shot at proving himself. While his numbers in Dallas were not flattering, he has been strong in his AHL stints: the six-foot-five Finn posted a .920 save percentage for the Texas Stars in 39 games played.

Lucas Friesen

Detroit Red Wings

Does it matter if a goaltender is a playoff rookie? Because it is frequently cited as a reason to pick their opponent to advance, particularly in mainstream media previews. It was a predominant theme as the Red Wings prepared to face eventual Stanley Cup finalist Tampa Bay in the first round. However, head coach Mike Babcock chose to start Czech rookie Petr Mrazek in goal over seasoned, well-paid veteran Jimmy Howard.

Why would playoff experience matter between the pipes? There are valid reasons why players with certain skillsets might fare better in the postseason—for instance, better even-strength performers, given fewer penalties called—but nothing obvious that would favor experienced netminders over playoff neophytes. One might note the lack of poor teams making the second season, leaving more above-average offenses to face. But it remains unclear how that contextual fact would place inexperienced goalies at increased peril over their graying brethren.

A glance at the starting goaltenders for all Stanley Cup finalists since 2005-06 shows that four out of the 20 starters (Cam Ward, Antti Niemi, Michael Leighton, Ben Bishop) were postseason rookies, a full 20% making the Stanley Cup Final with 10% raising the Cup (see Table 1, next page).

Expanding the study to more than just the Cup finalists, we can examine the 57 goalies who made their postseason debuts since 2004-05 (with a minimum of 60 minutes played). If postseason experience mattered, we would expect to see worse save percentages in a goalie's first playoff experience than in later years. Further, we would expect the postseason virgins to have save percentages less in line with their regular-season performances than the veterans.

To answer the first question, the pool was limited to goalies who have made multiple subsequent postseason trips, to compare their first exposure to their total body of work. Looking at 122 individual goalie postseasons, the sample consists of 1,967 even-strength goals allowed on 26,734 even-strength shots, for an overall even-strength save percentage of .926. In comparison, the 31 individual goalie seasons since 2005-06 where a goalie took the reins of a playoff team for the first time produced a .923 even-strength save percentage. That is essentially the difference between Semyon Varlamov and Kari Lehtonen, or Varlamov and Ryan Miller. There is a difference, but not much of one (see Table 2, next page).

We see an apparent sign of some truth to the old concern with inexperi-

RED WINGS IN A BOX

Last Season		
Goals For	235	12th
Goals Against	221	16th
GVT	14	15th
Points	100	t-11th
Playoffs	Lost Conference Quarterfinal	

The Red Wings exceeded expectations, to extend their league-best playoff streak to 24 seasons.

Three-Year Record		
GVT	15	13th
Points	249	12th
Playoffs	3 Appearances, 11 Wins	

VUKOTA Projections		
Goals For	222	14th
Goals Against	217	12th
GVT	4	16th
Points	93	16th

Even at ages 34 and 37, Zetterberg and Datsyuk are among the best, but if either is injured, Detroit will come crashing down.

Top Three Prospects
D. Larkin (F), A. Mantha (F), Y. Svechnikov (F)

Table 1: Playoff rookies in the Stanley Cup finals, 2005-06 through 2014-15

Season	Winner	Runner up
2005-06	Cam Ward*, CAR	Dwayne Roloson, EDM
2006-07	J-S Giguere, ANA	Ray Emery, OTT
2007-08	Chris Osgood, DET	Marc-Andre Fleury, PIT
2008-09	Marc-Andre Fleury, PIT	Chris Osgood, DET
2009-10	Antti Niemi*, CHI	Michael Leighton*, PHI
2010-11	Tim Thomas, BOS	Roberto Luongo, VAN
2011-12	Jonathan Quick, LAK	Martin Brodeur, NJD
2012-13	Corey Crawford, CHI	Tuukka Rask, BOS
2013-14	Jonathan Quick, LAK	Henrik Lundqvist, NYR
2014-15	Corey Crawford, CHI	Ben Bishop*, TBL

*No playoff experience prior to Cup-finalist postseason

Table 2: Do goaltenders fare worse in the rookie playoff season?

	Goalie-seasons	Goals allowed	Shots faced	ESSV%
All goalies with multiple postseasons	122	1967	26734	.926
First playoff experience	31	470	6138	.923

enced playoff goaltenders. However, correlation does not necessarily equate to causation. To ensure that the goalies were not simply young and inexperienced in general, we can compare how they fared in their first playoff tests compared to their regular season numbers in that same season, and then run the same comparison test in their subsequent playoff seasons (see Table 3).

We see that goalies in their first playoff experience performed nearly identically in the playoffs (in the aggregate) as they did during the corresponding regular seasons. If anything, their postseason play was marginally better.

Goalies that had previous postseason experience on their resume actually performed worse in the playoffs than during the regular season. Again, the difference is not large, but it is larger than the difference for the rookies, and in the opposite direction (see Table 4).

Overall, goaltenders should be expected to perform roughly as well in the playoffs as they had during the regular season. Instead of coaches worrying about choosing their playoff starter on the basis of having previous postseason experience or not, they should instead look to pick the netminder who had the current best season.

So did the Red Wings choose correctly? Considering the rookie Mrazek's .931 even-strength save percentage versus the incumbent Howard's .922 mark in 2014-15 tells us that Babcock made a wise choice. That Detroit was knocked out in the first round by Tampa Bay does not negate that wisdom. That Mrazek only stopped 90.3% of even-strength shots in that seven-game set does not make Babcock foolish by hindsight. It would ignore two shutouts of the dynamic Lightning as well as a Game 7 in which the rookie allowed only a single goal in a 2-0 decision. The fact that the Lightning scored at a higher clip against the likes of superstars Henrik Lundqvist and Carey Price in later rounds will be conveniently forgotten by pundits next year, when some team chooses to run with an inexperienced goalie in the first round again.

The Red Wings lost to Tampa Bay because they only scored 13 times in seven games.

Ryan Wagman

Table 3: Regular season vs. playoff performance – in the season of first playoff experience

	Goalie-seasons	Goals allowed	Shots faced	ESSV%
Regular season	31	2125	27653	**.9231**
Playoffs	31	470	6138	**.9234**

Table 4: Regular season vs. playoff performance – non-rookie playoff experiences

	Goalie-seasons	Goals allowed	Shots faced	ESSV%
Regular season	92	7442	103391	**.928**
Playoffs	92	1497	20596	**.927**

DETROIT RED WINGS

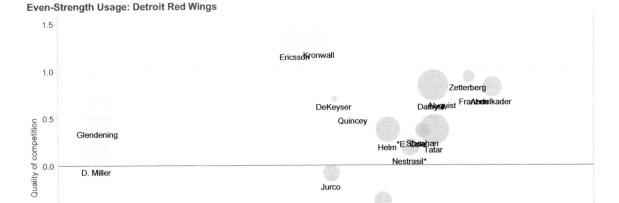

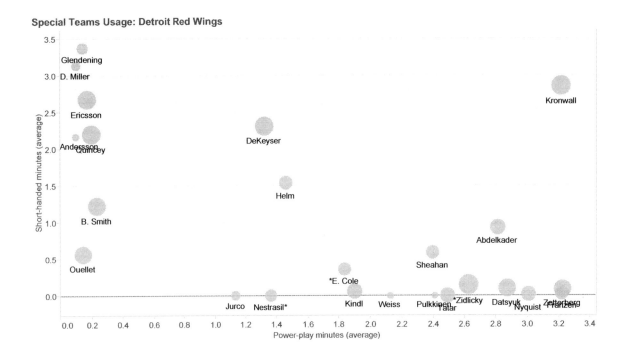

DETROIT RED WINGS

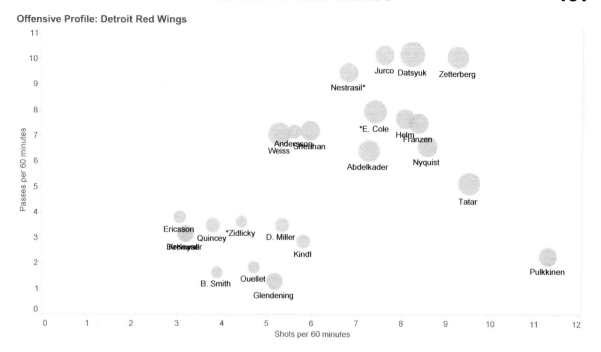

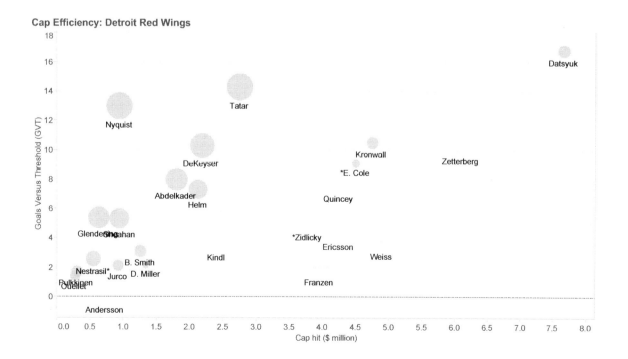

DETROIT RED WINGS

FORWARDS

Justin Abdelkader						LW/C							DET
Season	Team	Age	GP	G	A	Pts	+/-	ESP/60	AdjCF%	iCF/60	OGVT	DGVT	SGVT	GVT
2012-13	DET	25	48	10	3	13	6	1.19	56.2%	12.7	0.7	2.7	0.0	3.4
2013-14	DET	26	70	10	18	28	2	1.56	51.6%	13.1	2.0	2.2	0.0	4.2
2014-15	DET	27	71	23	21	44	3	1.79	56.3%	10.6	5.4	2.5	0.0	8.0
2015-16	DET	28	65	17	21	38					3.8	2.1	0.0	5.9

For many years, age 27 was widely viewed as the most common age for peak performance in baseball. Hockey, a much faster game, saw the average player peak in the 22-24 range, when athleticism is thought be higher. No one will ever call Justin Abdelkader average again. At 27 years of age, he simply exploded. Whenever any player takes this kind of leap, we need to look for probable causes of future regression. In his case, there is one big sign pointing to a return to career norms, and another suggesting an ability to repeat. The pessimist point of view comes from his 14.9% shooting, more than double his career rate entering the season, 6.6%. On the other hand, the rugged winger had never averaged even one minute of power-play time per game before, and last season saw him at 2:45. Entering the season with a single power-play goal to his name, he exited with nine. Should Abdelkader continue to receive power-play ice-time, the native Michigander will continue to produce.

Joakim Andersson						C							DET
Season	Team	Age	GP	G	A	Pts	+/-	ESP/60	AdjCF%	iCF/60	OGVT	DGVT	SGVT	GVT
2012-13	DET	23	38	3	5	8	2	1.05	57.8%	9.6	-0.8	1.5	0.0	0.7
2013-14	DET	24	65	8	9	17	-11	1.35	50.8%	9.0	0.0	2.4	0.0	2.4
2014-15	DET	25	68	3	5	8	-4	0.75	44.8%	8.6	-2.2	1.9	0.0	-0.3
2015-16	DET	26	57	6	8	14					-0.7	1.9	0.0	1.2

Sometimes, the Red Wings draft a Swedish player in the middle to late rounds and he turns into Henrik Zetterberg or Gustav Nyquist. We remember those players and forget the plethora of players who fit that basic criteria but never made it: guys like Daniel Larsson, Johan Ryno, Anton Axelsson, and Johan Berggren, among many, many others. Then there are the guys like Joakim Andersson, the guys who make it, but make it small, guys who fill depth-line roles, playing unglamorous minutes, often pegged in their own zone and struggling to make the scoresheet. It is not fancy, but it still marks as a draft success. It is fair to question whether Andersson can take on an expanded role, as he did show good AHL scoring touch in a half season under new Detroit head coach Jeff Blashill, promoted from Grand Rapids.

Daniel Cleary						LW/RW							DET
Season	Team	Age	GP	G	A	Pts	+/-	ESP/60	AdjCF%	iCF/60	OGVT	DGVT	SGVT	GVT
2012-13	DET	34	48	9	6	15	-6	0.88	53.9%	10.7	-0.4	1.1	0.0	0.7
2013-14	DET	35	52	4	4	8	-11	0.74	47.3%	9.4	-1.7	0.8	0.0	-0.9
2014-15	DET	36	17	1	1	2	-4	0.81	55.0%	11.4	-0.4	-0.1	0.0	-0.4
2015-16	DET	37	37	4	5	8					0.0	0.6	0.0	0.6

When you are a healthy scratch for 72 of 89 games, including all seven games of a playoff run, you should know that it is time to go. Dan Cleary, who has been an at-times critical component of the perennially contending Red Wings since the lost season of 2004-05, is at an age where most of his peers have long since given up the dream. Don't be fooled by his relatively high possession metrics. Between the tininess of the sample and his

DETROIT RED WINGS

extremely friendly usage pattern—when he was on the ice at all—nothing suggests a player who can continue to contribute to an NHL team. Oddly, not only did Cleary not recognize the end of his effective career, but neither has Detroit GM Ken Holland, who gave him $950,000 to return for one more season.

Erik Cole							LW						Free Agent
Season	Team	Age	GP	G	A	Pts	+/-	ESP/60	AdjCF%	iCF/60	OGVT	DGVT	SGVT	GVT
2012-13	MTL, DAL	34	47	9	4	13	-6	1.01	46.1%	14.0	-4.0	1.6	0.0	-2.4
2013-14	DAL	35	75	16	13	29	-17	1.39	49.7%	13.1	1.9	0.0	-0.3	1.6
2014-15	DAL, DET	36	68	21	18	39	2	2.07	50.6%	12.6	7.3	2.1	-0.3	9.1
2015-16	Free Agent	37	58	13	16	28					2.9	1.2	0.0	4.1

When Erik Cole finally hangs up his skates, few will remember his 11 games as a Red Wing. Acquired around the trade deadline for two promising Swedish talents plus a second-round pick, Cole was just getting the hang of the Babcock way when an upper-body injury knocked him out for the duration. Now in his late thirties, Cole can still be considered a plausible depth-scoring option, with a good shot and reasonable possession rates if his shifts can be sheltered. That said, his 17.2% shooting percentage, the Clarkson alum's best rate since 2006-07, should be expected to regress towards his more recent marks around 11-12%. Still good, but not nearly as exciting.

Pavel Datsyuk							C							DET
Season	Team	Age	GP	G	A	Pts	+/-	ESP/60	AdjCF%	iCF/60	OGVT	DGVT	SGVT	GVT
2012-13	DET	34	47	15	34	49	21	2.52	57.9%	14.1	8.5	4.0	-0.4	12.0
2013-14	DET	35	45	17	20	37	1	2.03	55.9%	13.9	4.9	2.0	-0.5	6.4
2014-15	DET	36	63	26	39	65	12	2.43	59.7%	12.7	13.8	3.3	-0.3	16.8
2015-16	DET	37	61	20	31	51					7.1	2.1	0.0	9.1

Of the eight players to appear in more than one game and score at least one point per game in 2014-15, no one was older than Pavel Datsyuk, who played the entire season at age 36. The runner up, Alex Ovechkin, was a sprightly 29. You might think of the magical Datsyuk as an ageless wonder, but there are signs of mortality. To start, the 1998 sixth rounder averaged only 19 minutes per game, the least since he was a mere child of 27. While that is more a remedy of a disease than a symptom, the real issue has been health. Whenever the Sverdlovsk native plays, he shines. But he plays less and less. Not just in terms of time per game, but sheer games. He has missed at least 12 games in his last four non-strike-shortened seasons, with last year's 63 contests played his second-highest total in that span. One may be inclined to take solace in the fact that he has not been sidelined by any one chronic malady, but that may not be any better than being pushed to the sidelines by different ones.

Landon Ferraro							C/RW							DET
Season	Team	Age	GP	G	A	Pts	+/-	ESP/60	AdjCF%	iCF/60	OGVT	DGVT	SGVT	GVT
2013-14	DET	22	4	0	0	0	0	0.00	34.5%	4.1	-0.1	0.0	0.0	-0.1
2014-15	DET	23	3	1	0	1	1	1.67	44.5%	10.3	0.5	0.0	0.0	0.5
2015-16	DET	24	30	5	5	10					0.2	0.5	0.0	0.7

Landon Ferraro will never pack the offensive punch of his father, Ray, who scored 408 goals in his NHL career. Of course, we knew that back when Papa Ray was still in the WHL, as he scored 108 goals in a single season for the Brandon Wheat Kings. In contrast, Landon scored 76 times combined in his four WHL seasons. That figure has almost been matched across his four AHL seasons. What the younger Ferraro can do is play hockey across

200 feet of ice. In spite of his middling offensive stats, Landon has the tools to succeed in the NHL, including a strong skating stride, soft hands, good instincts, and a sense of defensive responsibility. He should make the opening game roster for the first time this year.

Johan Franzen									RW					DET
Season	Team	Age	GP	G	A	Pts	+/-	ESP/60	AdjCF%	iCF/60	OGVT	DGVT	SGVT	GVT
2012-13	DET	33	41	14	17	31	13	1.96	53.3%	15.6	5.1	2.0	-0.3	6.9
2013-14	DET	34	54	16	25	41	6	1.85	51.8%	14.4	6.6	1.7	-0.6	7.8
2014-15	DET	35	33	7	15	22	-12	1.56	52.4%	12.4	2.7	-0.4	-0.3	2.1
2015-16	DET	36	45	11	18	28					3.1	0.8	0.0	3.9

"The Mule" is down. For the second year in a row, Johan Franzen missed a large chunk of the season to injury, this time a concussion followed by long-lasting post-concussion symptoms that kept him on the shelf from January 6 onward. Still a viable offensive producer—especially on the man advantage—when healthy, that latter qualifier is no longer a guarantee. Signed to a front-loaded contract when that tactic was still kosher, Franzen has four more years left with a cap hit of nearly $4 million. While his long-term health is far more important than extending his hockey-playing career, it must be noted that an inability to recover will put the Wings in a situation much like Philadelphia with Chris Pronger and Boston with Marc Savard. Let's hope for a return to health for the Mule.

Luke Glendening									C/RW					DET
Season	Team	Age	GP	G	A	Pts	+/-	ESP/60	AdjCF%	iCF/60	OGVT	DGVT	SGVT	GVT
2013-14	DET	24	56	1	6	7	-8	0.68	46.7%	7.0	-2.4	2.2	0.0	-0.2
2014-15	DET	25	82	12	6	18	5	1.11	44.6%	8.4	0.2	5.3	0.0	5.4
2015-16	DET	26	72	11	10	21					-0.2	3.3	0.0	3.1

The fact that Luke Glendening grew up in the shadow of Detroit's farm club in nearby Grand Rapids, Michigan is old news. The fact that he went from an undrafted free agent out of Michigan, through a brief tryout at the AHL level in the Bruins organization, and emerged three years later as the leading penalty-killing forward in the NHL (3:30) doesn't get nearly enough mention. If he can continue to contribute offense like he did last year, the 26-year-old will continue to play the role of hometown hero for many years to come.

Darren Helm									C/LW					DET
Season	Team	Age	GP	G	A	Pts	+/-	ESP/60	AdjCF%	iCF/60	OGVT	DGVT	SGVT	GVT
2012-13	DET	25	1	0	0	0	0	0.00	60.6%	28.5	0.0	0.0	0.0	0.0
2013-14	DET	26	42	12	8	20	2	1.97	53.6%	14.7	7.5	0.6	0.3	8.4
2014-15	DET	27	75	15	18	33	7	1.50	57.6%	14.6	3.3	3.6	0.4	7.3
2015-16	DET	28	64	15	19	34					3.8	2.3	0.0	6.2

Experiencing a rare healthy season, Darren Helm established new career highs in goals scored, points, power-play goals, and average time on ice. And those are just the traditional numbers. The former Medicine Hat Tiger also excelled via advanced analysis, with a career-best Relative Corsi (12.3). One of the fastest skaters on the team, and in the league, Helm has also long excelled at creating manpower-advantage situations for the Wings, as he drew 1.2 penalties per 60 minutes, among team leaders in what was actually a down year by that particular metric for the 2005 fifth rounder. If he can navigate a second healthy season in a row, Helm should find a very healthy market for his services when his contract expires next summer.

Tomas Jurco						RW							DET
Season	Team	Age	GP	G	A	Pts	+/-	ESP/60	AdjCF%	iCF/60	OGVT	DGVT	SGVT	GVT
2013-14	DET	21	36	8	7	15	0	1.73	56.2%	15.5	1.6	0.8	-0.6	1.8
2014-15	DET	22	63	3	15	18	6	1.47	55.6%	13.8	0.4	2.0	-0.3	2.1
2015-16	*DET*	*23*	*59*	*9*	*16*	*25*					*1.4*	*1.8*	*0.0*	*3.2*

More significant than any on-ice metric put up by Tomas Jurco in his first full NHL season is the fact that he graduated to the NHL with only one-and-a-half seasons of AHL time under his belt. For Detroit, an organization that has long prided itself on letting prospects marinate in the minors for as long as possible before earning their Winged Wheel jersey, Jurco's meager total of 106 games in the bus league says a great deal about their trust in his hockey intelligence. As a point of reference, high-scoring Gustav Nyquist had to put in 137 games with Grand Rapids before getting that chance. To take the next step, the young Slovakian will have to push his NHL shooting percentage (6.5%) up closer to his marks in the AHL (12.9%) or even the QMJHL (16.7% in his final two seasons).

Drew Miller						LW							DET
Season	Team	Age	GP	G	A	Pts	+/-	ESP/60	AdjCF%	iCF/60	OGVT	DGVT	SGVT	GVT
2012-13	DET	28	44	4	4	8	-8	0.84	47.5%	10.1	-0.9	1.3	0.0	0.4
2013-14	DET	29	82	7	8	15	-11	0.99	49.6%	11.5	-2.4	3.8	0.0	1.4
2014-15	DET	30	82	5	8	13	-3	0.79	43.4%	9.8	-2.2	4.3	0.0	2.1
2015-16	*DET*	*31*	*64*	*6*	*8*	*14*					*-0.9*	*2.6*	*0.0*	*1.7*

The prototypical fourth-line winger, Drew Miller has only once exceeded 20 points in a season over eight NHL campaigns. A prolific penalty killer, he breached 3:00 of penalty kill time per game for the first time. When not killing penalties, the Michigan State alum is still carrying a heavy load, leading all Red Wing forwards in defensive zone start rate for the second year in a row.

Gustav Nyquist						LW/RW							DET
Season	Team	Age	GP	G	A	Pts	+/-	ESP/60	AdjCF%	iCF/60	OGVT	DGVT	SGVT	GVT
2012-13	DET	23	22	3	3	6	0	1.00	54.5%	18.4	0.4	0.3	-0.6	0.2
2013-14	DET	24	57	28	20	48	16	3.02	54.9%	15.8	11.1	2.8	-0.8	13.1
2014-15	DET	25	82	27	27	54	-11	1.61	53.2%	14.2	8.7	0.9	3.4	13.0
2015-16	*DET*	*26*	*69*	*25*	*28*	*53*					*7.4*	*1.8*	*0.1*	*9.3*

As exciting as Gustav Nyquist is, his first full NHL season must be seen as somewhat of a disappointment coming off the wild exploits of 28 goals in 57 games in 2013-14. Having only scored on 13.7% of his shots in the AHL, it had to be expected that the 18.3% rate that drove his previous success would not be sustainable. In other words, while disappointing, he returned to his minor-league rate and rang the bell on 13.8% of his shots last year. The bottom line here is that former Maine Black Bear is very good and simply needs to up his shot rate in order to push above 30 goals. Good thing the Red Wings have two of the best playmakers of the past generation ready to give him the puck. Expect the goals to increase once the talented Swede embraces his role as trigger man.

DETROIT RED WINGS

Teemu Pulkkinen — RW — DET

Season	Team	Age	GP	G	A	Pts	+/-	ESP/60	AdjCF%	iCF/60	OGVT	DGVT	SGVT	GVT
2013-14	DET	21	3	0	0	0	0	0.00	61.1%	15.3	-0.1	0.0	0.0	0.0
2014-15	DET	22	31	5	3	8	5	1.28	56.2%	19.7	0.8	0.9	0.0	1.7
2015-16	DET	23	42	9	8	17					1.5	1.2	0.0	2.6

With great offensive instincts and a quick shot release, Teemu Pulkkinen was a force for the Grand Rapids Griffins. Finding holes in coverage and then pouncing on loose pucks with great closing speed, the slight Finnish dynamo scored a fantastic 34 goals in 46 AHL games. He even finished in the top 10 in AHL scoring despite playing 31 games up in the NHL. Therein lies the rub. Despite receiving very favorable shifts with Detroit, the 2010 fourth-round pick was unable to bring the goals at the highest level. While the skillset is evident, if Pulkkinen does not up the numbers this year, he risks being lumped in with the other little AHL scorers who could not play in the NHL, like Martin St. Pierre, Keith Aucoin, or Corey Locke. For some, opportunities are limited.

Riley Sheahan — C — DET

Season	Team	Age	GP	G	A	Pts	+/-	ESP/60	AdjCF%	iCF/60	OGVT	DGVT	SGVT	GVT
2012-13	DET	21	1	0	0	0	0	0.00	59.4%	8.6	0.0	0.0	0.0	0.0
2013-14	DET	22	42	9	15	24	8	2.20	56.2%	9.9	3.3	1.8	-0.3	4.8
2014-15	DET	23	79	13	23	36	-3	1.50	55.4%	10.8	2.9	2.1	0.4	5.3
2015-16	DET	24	66	14	22	36					3.1	2.1	0.0	5.2

For someone who elicited so many maturity concerns as an emerging prospect, Riley Sheahan has provided another reminder that teenagers who do stupid things do not always turn out to be adults who do stupid things. A grinder with Notre Dame, Sheahan now grinds in the NHL, with little to no degradation in his offensive production. Bearing in mind that Mike Babcock sheltered his young charge, showering him with an overabundance of offensive zone starts against bottom-six lines, the 24-year-old has taken full advantage of the opportunities afforded him, displaying a plus two-way game with fantastic possession numbers. If new coach Jeff Blashill plays him on the penalty kill, we will finally be able to call the St. Catharine's native a mature hockey player.

Tomas Tatar — LW/RW — DET

Season	Team	Age	GP	G	A	Pts	+/-	ESP/60	AdjCF%	iCF/60	OGVT	DGVT	SGVT	GVT
2012-13	DET	22	18	4	3	7	2	2.09	61.2%	15.7	1.1	0.7	0.0	1.7
2013-14	DET	23	73	19	20	39	12	2.25	56.4%	15.1	6.1	2.7	0.1	8.9
2014-15	DET	24	82	29	27	56	6	1.97	59.0%	17.0	11.5	2.5	0.3	14.3
2015-16	DET	25	71	25	27	52					7.8	2.2	0.0	10.0

Tomas Tatar is a prime example of why the Red Wings let their prospects spend more time learning and developing in the AHL than any other NHL organization does. Also, he is a prime example of why it pays to get draft picks right, even after the first round. A highly-skilled shooter with a nose for the net, the Slovakian spent nearly four full seasons in Grand Rapids before earning a full-time NHL gig in 2013-14. If there is an outlying statistic to be found in his breakout season, it is not obvious. Tatar has always been a high percentage shooter, partially due to putting himself into positions of high danger for opposing defenses. His 71 individual high-danger scoring chances was more than any other Red Wing in the past three seasons. Maintaining his current pace will see Tatar threaten to triple his current bargain-rate $2.8 million salary when his contract expires in two years.

DETROIT RED WINGS

Stephen Weiss — C — Free Agent

Season	Team	Age	GP	G	A	Pts	+/-	ESP/60	AdjCF%	iCF/60	OGVT	DGVT	SGVT	GVT
2012-13	FLA	29	17	1	3	4	-13	0.50	40.3%	6.0	-1.2	-0.4	0.0	-1.5
2013-14	DET	30	26	2	2	4	-4	0.55	42.9%	6.2	-0.9	0.2	0.0	-0.7
2014-15	DET	31	52	9	16	25	-2	2.00	52.5%	8.7	4.0	0.7	-0.8	3.9
2015-16	Free Agent	32	47	8	13	21					1.9	0.9	0.0	2.7

After eight years of prolific, yet obscure, scoring in the Sunbelt for the Florida Panthers, Stephen Weiss signed a big-money five-year pact with the Red Wings and immediately set about identifying with his new surroundings in the Rust Belt. In other words, look at that stat line from 2013-14. Unlike their neighbors, General Motors, Ford, and Chrysler, the Red Wings could not ask for a government bailout to cope with Weiss' anchor salary. To make matters worse, the 2001 fourth-overall pick hurt his groin early last season, limiting him to a total ice-time of 8:03 before November 24. He returned a changed man, putting up 10 points in his next seven games. Alas, 15 points in his final 44 contests had the good people of Detroit forgetting his brief glow. He was a healthy scratch for the final five games of the Red Wings' abbreviated playoffs for good reason. With three years remaining on his contract, Weiss was bought out at the start of the free agency period.

Henrik Zetterberg — C/LW — DET

Season	Team	Age	GP	G	A	Pts	+/-	ESP/60	AdjCF%	iCF/60	OGVT	DGVT	SGVT	GVT
2012-13	DET	32	46	11	37	48	2	1.96	55.3%	17.3	7.3	1.8	-0.6	8.5
2013-14	DET	33	45	16	32	48	19	2.51	53.8%	15.8	8.4	4.0	-1.1	11.2
2014-15	DET	34	77	17	49	66	-6	1.87	54.2%	15.1	9.5	1.7	-1.1	10.1
2015-16	DET	35	68	19	39	57					7.1	2.2	0.0	9.4

Although Henrik Zetterberg recovered nicely enough from the injuries that derailed his 2013-14 campaign to appear in 77 games for the Red Wings, his 0.86 points per game mark was his second lowest of the salary cap era. While the health is certainly nice, the latter point should strike a sad chord with Red Wings fans and management. Further adding fuel to that fire is the fact that the 34-year-old also had a higher percentage of offensive zone starts than at any point in his career. Having only scored on 6.4-8.2% of his shots on net in five of the past six seasons, Zetterberg's value now lies primarily in his exemplary passing skills. There may not be a fifth 30-goal season in his future, but continued ice-time with a natural goal scorer like Gustav Nyquist should ensure that he continues to rack up the helpers.

DEFENSEMEN

Danny DeKeyser — LD — DET

Season	Team	Age	GP	G	A	Pts	+/-	ESP/60	AdjCF%	iCF/60	OGVT	DGVT	SGVT	GVT
2012-13	DET	22	11	0	1	1	4	0.35	57.3%	8.7	-0.1	0.9	0.0	0.8
2013-14	DET	23	65	4	19	23	10	0.93	49.4%	7.6	3.2	4.8	0.0	8.0
2014-15	DET	24	80	2	29	31	11	1.08	54.0%	7.7	4.1	6.1	0.0	10.3
2015-16	DET	25	70	5	21	25					2.5	4.3	0.0	6.8

Emerging fully formed from the Western Michigan program, Danny DeKeyser practically stepped right into the Red Wings lineup—nearly unheard of for non-Europeans in the modern era—and has just as quickly become a staple of their top four. His presence is equally important for the Wings whether they are at even strength, playing a man up, or one down. The top scorer among Detroit blueliners at even strength, his points are heavily weighted to the category of second assists. This is appropriate, as it is reflective of his strengths: he is a good puck mover, whether skating with it or passing it to a more skilled player. A quality supporting player, you could almost say that DeKeyser is the Darren Helm of the blueline.

Jonathan Ericsson							LD						DET
Season	Team	Age	GP	G	A	Pts	+/-	ESP/60	AdjCF%	iCF/60	OGVT	DGVT	SGVT	GVT
2012-13	DET	28	45	3	10	13	6	0.97	54.0%	6.6	1.6	4.5	0.0	6.1
2013-14	DET	29	48	1	10	11	2	0.70	52.5%	8.4	-0.2	3.6	0.0	3.4
2014-15	DET	30	82	3	12	15	-5	0.61	50.4%	7.4	-0.5	4.9	0.0	4.4
2015-16	DET	31	66	3	13	16					0.4	3.9	0.0	4.3

Jonathan Ericsson is kind of big, kind of tough, kind of mobile, and kind of overpaid. A stay-at-home type, the large Swede has had his Relative Corsi in the red for the past four seasons, bottoming out at -11.4, dead last among Red Wing defenders. In fact, only 13 regular defensemen across the league were worse. It is a metric that equates Ericsson with the likes of Nate Guenin and Brett Bellemore. Back to that overpaid comment: it is bad enough that the 2002 ninth rounder will carry a cap hit of $4.3 million next year. It is worse that he will carry it for four more seasons after that. This isn't Stephen Weiss bad, but this contract will not be on Ken Holland's Greatest Hits album.

Jakub Kindl							LD						DET
Season	Team	Age	GP	G	A	Pts	+/-	ESP/60	AdjCF%	iCF/60	OGVT	DGVT	SGVT	GVT
2012-13	DET	25	41	4	9	13	15	0.93	55.6%	10.4	1.8	3.8	0.0	5.6
2013-14	DET	26	66	2	17	19	-4	0.72	51.9%	8.7	1.7	1.1	0.0	2.8
2014-15	DET	27	35	5	8	13	2	0.74	58.3%	11.0	2.1	1.2	0.0	3.3
2015-16	DET	28	50	4	13	18					1.9	1.8	0.0	3.7

Of the 53 games for which Jakub Kindl was not in the lineup, playoffs included, only 12 were due to injury. In the remaining 41, the 2005 first rounder was left in the pressbox due to former coach Mike Babcock not liking the cut of his jib. Never mind that his 0.74 even-strength points per 60 minutes was third among his blueline brethren and that he had a higher goal-scoring rate than all of them. A new coach may help instill confidence in the six-foot-three Czech defender, but despite having spent 239 games with AHL Grand Rapids, the last of them was two seasons before new Wings coach Jeff Blashill joined the organization. Kindl will need to prove that he can manage tougher assignments to keep ahead of youngsters like Ouellet, Sproul, and Marchenko in the coming years.

Niklas Kronwall							LD						DET
Season	Team	Age	GP	G	A	Pts	+/-	ESP/60	AdjCF%	iCF/60	OGVT	DGVT	SGVT	GVT
2012-13	DET	31	48	5	24	29	-5	0.90	54.1%	6.3	3.8	2.4	0.0	6.2
2013-14	DET	32	79	8	41	49	0	0.98	52.2%	5.9	6.9	4.4	0.0	11.3
2014-15	DET	33	80	9	35	44	-4	0.89	49.9%	5.5	6.3	4.8	-0.5	10.5
2015-16	DET	34	67	7	28	34					4.1	3.7	0.0	7.7

It is unfortunate that the last remnant of Niklas Kronwall's solid season was getting suspended for a borderline hit in Game 6 of the first round, forcing him to watch his Red Wings get eliminated by the Tampa Bay Lightning from the pressbox. Detroit didn't just miss his physical presence—most famous for his jarring hip checks—but also his offensive contributions. Not only was Kronwall the Wings' most prominent power-play quarterback, but only three Detroit forwards earned more points on the man advantage than the Stockholm native. The 34-year-old has missed only 10 games in the past five seasons and has the type of skillset—employing both physical talents and smarts—that should allow him to remain a force until the odometer nears 40.

Brian Lashoff							LD						DET
Season	Team	Age	GP	G	A	Pts	+/-	ESP/60	AdjCF%	iCF/60	OGVT	DGVT	SGVT	GVT
2012-13	DET	22	31	1	4	5	-10	0.63	47.1%	5.5	0.0	0.6	0.0	0.6
2013-14	DET	23	75	1	5	6	-2	0.40	50.7%	6.6	-1.9	3.5	0.0	1.6
2014-15	DET	24	11	0	2	2	4	0.92	51.1%	5.1	0.2	0.9	0.0	1.0
2015-16	DET	25	45	1	6	7					-0.4	2.1	0.0	1.7

Only 25 years old and with over 100 games of NHL action under his belt, Brian Lashoff is slowly carving out a career for himself as a solid enough depth defenseman. The former Kingston Frontenacs captain has never been much of a pro scorer, only hitting double digits in one season, 19 points for the 2011-12 Griffins in 76 games. Then again, some of the lack of production is from infrequent game action. If Lashoff cannot carve out more of a role for himself, he may eventually follow the footsteps of his older brother, Matt—who played in 74 NHL contests over five seasons for Boston, Tampa, and Toronto—heading over the pond, to play in Europe.

Alexey Marchenko							RD						DET
Season	Team	Age	GP	G	A	Pts	+/-	ESP/60	AdjCF%	iCF/60	OGVT	DGVT	SGVT	GVT
2013-14	DET	21	1	0	0	0	2	0.00	57.3%	0.0	-0.1	0.3	0.0	0.2
2014-15	DET	22	13	1	1	2	1	0.63	59.3%	6.2	0.2	0.5	0.0	0.7
2015-16	DET	23	32	2	6	8					0.2	1.1	0.0	1.3

Long searching for a highly-coveted right-shot defender, when the Red Wings struck out at the deadline on Jeff Petry, it had the potential to open the door for Alexey Marchenko to make his mark in Detroit. Instead, the Wings added Marek Zidlicky via trade, while sending the 2011 seventh-round draft pick back to Grand Rapids, where he would stay until the NHL playoffs were approaching. Known for his puck-moving abilities, Marchenko will fight for a spot on Detroit's third pairing, or as the seventh defenseman. He is one of many on the roster who new coach Jeff Blashill will know how to utilize, from experience.

Xavier Ouellet							LD						DET
Season	Team	Age	GP	G	A	Pts	+/-	ESP/60	AdjCF%	iCF/60	OGVT	DGVT	SGVT	GVT
2013-14	DET	20	4	0	0	0	0	0.00	65.3%	10.7	-0.1	0.0	0.0	0.0
2014-15	DET	21	21	2	1	3	4	0.55	58.5%	11.7	0.0	1.4	0.0	1.4
2015-16	DET	22	36	3	7	9					0.5	1.7	0.0	2.2

As is too often the case with young role players trying to make their mark in the NHL, one stinker of a game can sink the ship. For Xavier Ouellet, that stinker took place on January 29, the 21st game in a row that the Montreal native found a spot in Mike Babcock's lineup. On this night, paired with Brendan Smith, the 2011 second rounder was a -3 in a 5-1 loss to Tampa Bay. Ouellet would not wear the Red Wings game jersey again for the remainder of the season. A good skater who plays responsibly and tight in his own zone, he is nevertheless in rough to gain a regular blueline spot in Detroit next season.

Kyle Quincey — LD — DET

Season	Team	Age	GP	G	A	Pts	+/-	ESP/60	AdjCF%	iCF/60	OGVT	DGVT	SGVT	GVT
2012-13	DET	27	36	1	2	3	7	0.21	55.9%	8.6	-1.5	3.2	0.0	1.8
2013-14	DET	28	82	4	9	13	-5	0.53	50.4%	8.3	-0.7	4.3	0.0	3.6
2014-15	DET	29	73	3	15	18	10	0.82	53.2%	10.2	1.7	5.5	0.0	7.3
2015-16	DET	30	65	4	13	17					1.0	3.8	0.0	4.9

Kyle Quincey is the defender the Red Wings signed when they failed to entice more attractive options such as Matt Niskanen, Christian Ehrhoff, and Dan Boyle to take their money last offseason. While not bad, Quincey underwhelmed as much on the ice as the news of his re-signing did in July. The Kitchener, Ontario native had mediocre possession numbers in spite of starting a healthy number of shifts in the offensive end and facing off against generally middling competition. His total GVT looks sharp, but it was buttressed by an inflated PDO, the result of a .930 save percentage put up by Detroit netminders when Quincey patrolled the blueline.

Brendan Smith — LD — DET

Season	Team	Age	GP	G	A	Pts	+/-	ESP/60	AdjCF%	iCF/60	OGVT	DGVT	SGVT	GVT
2012-13	DET	23	34	0	8	8	1	0.66	56.1%	7.2	0.9	1.5	0.0	2.4
2013-14	DET	24	71	5	14	19	-2	0.87	54.3%	9.1	2.2	2.7	0.0	4.9
2014-15	DET	25	76	4	9	13	-2	0.53	55.5%	8.5	0.2	3.2	-0.3	3.1
2015-16	DET	26	64	4	11	15					0.6	3.0	0.0	3.5

Long considered a plus two-way defender from his amateur days up through his first few NHL seasons, the offense suddenly dried up for Brendan Smith. It is tempting to blame puck luck, as the Wisconsin Badger had a subpar 98.2 PDO. On the other hand, it was worse in 2012-13, when he contributed 13 points in 48 regular-season and playoff games. It wasn't usage, either, as the Toronto native was the most protected blueliner on the Wings, receiving a plethora of zone starts in the offensive end and generally against depth-line forwards. It wasn't his teammates, either, as two of his three most-frequent linemates were Henrik Zetterberg and Gustav Nyquist. Whatever it was, it isn't going to help Smith at the bargaining table this summer as the restricted free agent seeks a new contract.

Marek Zidlicky — RD — NYI

Season	Team	Age	GP	G	A	Pts	+/-	ESP/60	AdjCF%	iCF/60	OGVT	DGVT	SGVT	GVT
2012-13	NJD	35	48	4	15	19	-12	0.58	57.1%	10.7	2.2	2.2	-0.3	4.2
2013-14	NJD	36	81	12	30	42	-3	0.88	53.6%	7.0	6.7	4.9	-0.3	11.3
2014-15	NJD, DET	37	84	7	27	34	-9	0.55	50.2%	7.8	3.0	2.4	-0.5	4.9
2015-16	NYI	38	62	4	20	24					2.0	2.7	0.0	4.6

Not willing to part with the assets (a second-round pick) demanded by Edmonton for Jeff Petry, Detroit fulfilled their right-shot defenseman fetish by acquiring Marek Zidlicky from New Jersey for a 2016 third rounder. Now 38 years old, the ancient blueliner can still crush from the point, putting up production totals that do not fall out of line with anything he has done over the past decade. Now that his shifts are more protected in terms of quality of competition as well as the heavily offensive-tilted zone starts that are seemingly his birthright, the former Predator, Wild, and Devil is also a possession plus. An unrestricted free agent, Zidlicky should be able to stay in the NHL, but his next contract will fall short of his previous $3 million salary.

GOALTENDERS

Jonas Gustavsson														Free Agent
Season	Team	Age	GP	W	L	OT	GAA	Sv%	ESSV%	QS%	GGVT	DGVT	SGVT	GVT
2012-13	DET	28	7	2	2	1	2.92	.879	.891	50.0%	-3.2	0.3	0.9	-2.1
2013-14	DET	29	27	16	5	4	2.63	.907	.915	50.0%	-0.2	0.2	0.8	0.9
2014-15	DET	30	7	3	3	1	2.56	.911	.939	50.0%	0.4	0.0	0.0	0.4
2015-16	Free Agent	31	20								1.7	0.0	0.0	1.8

In parts of five campaigns, Jonas Gustavsson never once managed to get his save percentage up to NHL average. Between a left shoulder injury and a concussion last year (added to the litany of other maladies—including heart surgery—he has faced during his time in North America), the man once coined "The Monster" saw his contract end with Detroit after his successor had already been anointed. In other words, the two-time Swedish Olympian is not going to return to the Motor City. Also in question is whether the athletic, but generally poorly-positioned puck stopper will be able to find any job in North America.

Jimmy Howard														DET
Season	Team	Age	GP	W	L	OT	GAA	Sv%	ESSV%	QS%	GGVT	DGVT	SGVT	GVT
2012-13	DET	28	42	21	13	7	2.13	.923	.937	66.7%	16.0	0.4	-1.0	15.4
2013-14	DET	29	51	21	19	11	2.66	.910	.919	54.0%	2.8	-0.2	0.2	2.8
2014-15	DET	30	53	23	13	11	2.44	.910	.919	58.0%	2.8	0.9	-6.9	-3.3
2015-16	DET	31	35								0.6	0.1	-0.6	0.1

The goaltender who was given a six-year, $31.8 million contract extension in April 2013 was one who had put up a save percentage of .920 or better in three of his four full seasons. He was also in the midst of a season in which he stopped 93.7% of even-strength shots, a figure that easily clears the bar as his career high. That goalie, like this one, named Jimmy Howard, has since fallen on tough times, with two of his three worst seasons coming in the subsequent years, a turn of events which caused him to lose his starting job to rookie Petr Mrazek in the postseason. As the majority of his downturn last year was due to a career-worst .803 save percentage on shots defined as "high danger", there may be hope for a rebound if the team in front of him can minimize those Grade A chances. The Wings should be able to afford Howard one more year to turn things around. If he can't, they will have to make a decision next offseason, with Mrazek eligible for a new contract.

Tom McCollum														DET
Season	Team	Age	GP	W	L	OT	GAA	Sv%	ESSV%	QS%	GGVT	DGVT	SGVT	GVT
2014-15	DET	25	2	1	0	0	0.91	.960	.960	0.0%	1.1	0.1	0.0	1.2
2015-16	DET	26	13								1.7	0.0	0.0	1.7

In making an NHL appearance last January coming on in relief of Petr Mrazek and then repeating the feat 11 days later, Thomas McCollum has avoided the ignominy that comes with his initial NHL exposure, also a relief appearance, in which he allowed three goals on eight shots in 15 minutes of action. One day, McCollum will actually start a game in the NHL. Until then (and for long after), he will serve as a reminder that it is always better to wait until the second round or later to draft a goalie. In the 13 picks that followed his selection at the tail end of the 2008 first round, regular NHL blueliners Slava Voynov, Roman Josi, Patrick Wiercioch, and Justin Schultz were selected.

Petr Mrazek — G — DET

Season	Team	Age	GP	W	L	OT	GAA	Sv%	ESSV%	QS%	GGVT	DGVT	SGVT	GVT
2012-13	DET	20	2	1	1	0	2.02	.922	.935	50.0%	0.7	0.1	0.0	0.7
2013-14	DET	21	9	2	4	0	1.74	.927	.914	66.7%	3.0	0.4	0.0	3.4
2014-15	DET	22	29	16	9	2	2.38	.918	.930	57.7%	6.3	0.0	-0.5	5.8
2015-16	DET	23	32								4.4	0.1	-0.1	4.5

Before we get carried away with stereotypes about the Red Wings and European scouting, we should remember that new incumbent netminder Petr Mrazek was actually drafted out of the Ottawa 67s program in the OHL. Thankfully, we can still rely on the old trope about the Wings drafting well in the later rounds. In his fifth season after being selected in the fifth round, Mrazek was given the opportunity to do for the Red Wings what he did for his native Czech Republic at the 2012 WJC, lead his team to glory. As at that ill-fated tournament, the Ostrava native showed well in a losing cause. Back then, he was honored as the best goalie of the event. This time, he may well have walked away with the starting job in Detroit. With the best high-danger save percentage among Wings' goalies in 2014-15, at the very least, he has earned the right not to head back for a fourth go-round in the AHL.

Ryan Wagman

Edmonton Oilers

April 18th is a date that may very well "live in infamy" in Edmonton Oilers history. The Oilers won the 2015 NHL Draft Lottery (again!), giving them the opportunity to draft Connor McDavid, arguably the best player available through the draft since Sidney Crosby.

The lottery win kicked off a number of changes. The Oilers hired accomplished general manager Peter Chiarelli, who won a Stanley Cup and a President's Trophy with the Boston Bruins, and head coach Todd McLellan, who led the San Jose Sharks to six straight playoff appearances from 2008-2014 before having his roster gutted during the 2014-2015 season.

With a generational talent joining the team for 2015-16, Chiarelli decided to take immediate steps toward being a playoff contender and ending the decade-long cycle of rebuilding. The new general manager and president of hockey operations added quality players via free agency and trades in the hopes of making a leap in the standings.

Will it be enough for the team to make the postseason?

Time to step up for former #1 picks

While defense and goaltending took the brunt of the blame for the Oilers' failures in 2014-15, the talented centerpieces of the rebuild did not hold up their end of the bargain, either. 2010 first-overall selection Taylor Hall did not perform as expected, managing only 38 points in 53 games. The 23-year-old battled injury and distraction as he became part of trade rumors and accusations that he was not getting along with the coaching staff.

The Oilers should expect a huge bounceback from Hall. Between 2011-12 and 2013-14, the dynamic winger was the NHL's third-best even-strength scorer, only trailing Sidney Crosby and Evgeni Malkin. Hall scored 117 points at five-on-five over that stretch, at a rate of 2.63 even-strength points per 60 minutes, a shade higher than the production rate of Jamie Benn and Jonathan Toews. In 2014-15, Hall continued to average over three shots on goal per game, but had a career-low 8.9% shooting percentage. With his career rate at 11.1%, there is little doubt the point-per-game version of Hall will return.

We know that Hall can be an elite player when at his best, but the jury is still out on subsequent first-overall picks Ryan Nugent-Hopkins and Nail Yakupov. While Nugent-Hopkins has posted back-to-back 56-point seasons, there is still disappointment in his plateaued production, considering he scored 52 points in 62 games as a rookie. In addition, the Oilers expected RNH to put on weight and strength

OILERS IN A BOX

Last Season
Goals For	198	26th
Goals Against	283	30th
GVT	-85	28th
Points	62	28th
Playoffs	Lost Conference Semifinals	

The Oilers managed to post their very worst season of the last decade, getting outscored by 85 goals.

Three-Year Record
GVT	-161	29th
Points	174	29th
Playoffs	0 Appearances, 0 Wins	

VUKOTA Projection
Goals For	209	26th
Goals Against	221	17th
GVT	-12	25th
Points	87	25th

At some point, Edmonton's rebuild will help them turn the corner, but this won't be the year. Expect improvement, but the playoffs are still out of reach.

Top Three Prospects
C. McDavid (F), L. Draisaitl (F), D. Nurse (D)

as he entered his early twenties, and consequently, to improve his ability to win battles and gain position on defenders. That has not happened, as Nugent-Hopkins still stands at an unimposing six-foot, 190-pounds.

Improved circumstances, however, may help the 22-year-old to take the next step. From a very young age, Nugent-Hopkins was asked to be a top center in the tough Western Conference, where he regularly faced off against the likes of Jonathan Toews. The Oilers tried to protect him from defensive zone time, giving the youngster only 22.1% of his total faceoffs in the defensive zone—although he was still at the top of the Oilers' list in quality of competition faced. As McDavid grows into Edmonton's true number-one center, the Oilers can move RNH into a more fitting role of second-line center, where he will likely be more talented than his counterpart on a nightly basis.

But it is concerning that Nugent-Hopkins only managed a 50.0% Corsi when seeing so little defensive zone time, while playing the entire season with highly-skilled forward Jordan Eberle.

As for Yakupov, it appeared his career in Edmonton was over until he was saved by a coaching change and the acquisition of Derek Roy. Yes, Derek Roy. After bench boss Dallas Eakins was fired, there was an obvious change in the Russian winger, who was allowed to crack the team's system and use his offensive instincts and athleticism to track down pucks, even if it meant taking risks. He also started shooting more often—a novel concept for an elite talent.

Yakupov finished the season with only 33 points, but 20 of them came in the final 28 contests, giving hope to Oilers faithful and convincing the new management to give him a chance under McLellan. Yakupov was mostly matched up with Roy as his center, with whom he gained instant chemistry.

Like Nugent-Hopkins, there are still major concerns. Yakupov was at an ugly -35 plus/minus, the worst on the team, and was a poor possession player at a 46.3% Corsi percentage. He will have to find a happy medium of risk-taking and playing within McLellan's system, or he may end up back in the doghouse and on the trade block.

Despite worries for two of the three top picks, more signs point toward Yakupov and Nugent-Hopkins being good to very good players rather than complete failures. Sometimes we treat each player as if they played in a vacuum, but that is not the case in hockey.

The all-around improvement of the team will have a positive effect on both young forwards.

Improving defensively

With McDavid in the fold and skilled young centerman Leon Draisaitl (third-overall pick in 2014) on the way, the Oilers will no doubt have a talented offense. However, keeping pucks out of their own net will still be a challenge. The team added Andrej Sekera and his rising stock to the tune of a six-year, $33 million contract. While Sekera can bring strong puck possession at even strength along with improved power-play scoring, he is not a defensive stalwart, rather a player who impacts the defensive game positively by being a strong passer and puck carrier.

Beyond Sekera, there isn't much in terms of quality veteran defensemen on the roster. Mark Fayne can be a solid second-pairing defender, but not much more. Justin Schultz has proven to struggle mightily in his own zone, and Eric Gryba, Nikita Nikitin, and Andrew Ference are all close to being replacement-level players.

In order to be a playoff team, the Oilers will have to receive stellar performances from two quality young defensemen in Darnell Nurse and Griffin Reinhart. Both are top-10 draft picks, but there will be bumps along the way. And last season, Oscar Klefbom proved he is ready to be a top-four defenseman, another piece toward a much better looking blueline.

Goaltending

If there is one player who could have an even bigger impact on the standings than McDavid, it is Cam Talbot. The former Ranger backup—who stood in for Henrik Lundqvist for two months without a hiccup—takes over between the pipes for a team that had the NHL's last-ranked even-strength save percentage at .902; the next-worst team was at .910.

Talbot comes from darn good circumstances, playing behind a highly competitive Rangers team with an elite defenseman in Ryan McDonough. Therefore, he will need to cover up mistakes much more frequently in order to keep pucks out of his net, considering the number of one-dimensional and young players on the Edmonton roster.

However, the small-sample numbers suggest that Talbot could be up for the challenge. In 57 games as a Ranger, he had a .931 save percentage. Similar to what Jaroslav Halak did for the Islanders last season, even average goaltending could mean a huge drop in goals against and a jump in the standings.

But rein in your expectations a bit. Even with all the improvements, the West may be too strong for the Oilers to reach the postseason. That said, all signs point to Edmonton's rebuild finally resulting in a competitive team, and within a few years, into a possible Cup contender.

Matthew Coller

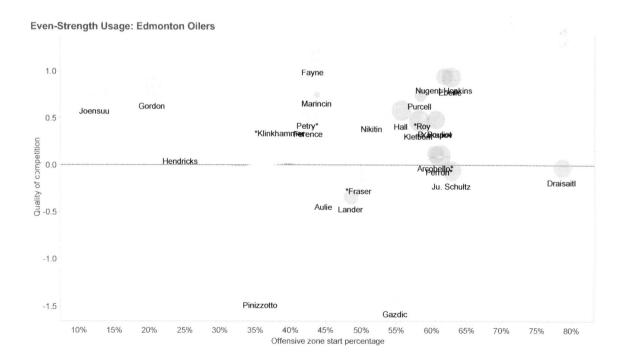

EDMONTON OILERS

Special Teams Usage: Edmonton Oilers

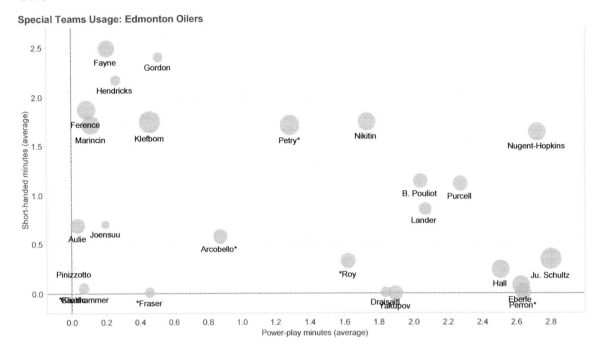

Offensive Profile: Edmonton Oilers

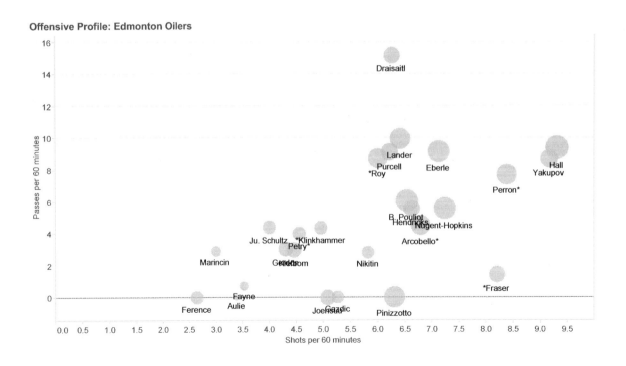

EDMONTON OILERS

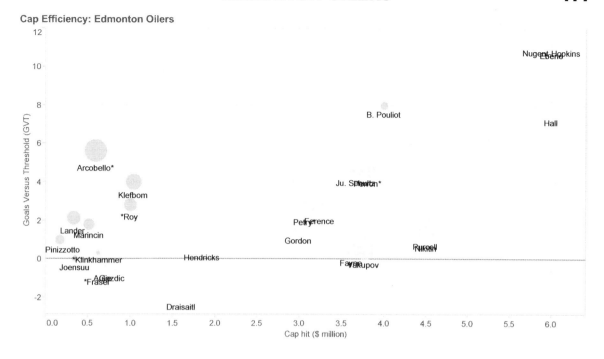

FORWARDS

Leon Draisaitl														C				EDM
Season	Team	Age	GP	G	A	Pts	+/-	ESP/60	AdjCF%	iCF/60	OGVT	DGVT	SGVT	GVT
2014-15	EDM	19	37	2	7	9	-17	1.05	50.7%	8.8	-1.5	-0.2	0.0	-1.7
2015-16	EDM	20	43	6	10	16					0.0	0.6	0.0	0.6

2014 third-overall pick Leon Draisaitl was mishandled by management in his first year. The Cologne, Germany native figures to be an important player in the Oilers' future, but he was nowhere close to ready for NHL action, even when head coach Dallas Eakins gave him the kid-gloves treatment, only utilizing him in very protected minutes. After scoring only a handful of points, he was returned to the WHL at midseason. Thereafter, Draisaitl impressively produced 53 points in 32 contests for Kelowna, plus 28 in 19 playoff games; he was named the Stafford Smythe Trophy winner as Memorial Cup MVP. Expect to see offensively-gifted top-six forward soon, at an NHL rink near you.

Jordan Eberle														RW				EDM
Season	Team	Age	GP	G	A	Pts	+/-	ESP/60	AdjCF%	iCF/60	OGVT	DGVT	SGVT	GVT
2012-13	EDM	22	48	16	21	37	-4	2.24	50.4%	13.0	5.4	0.4	1.0	6.8
2013-14	EDM	23	80	28	37	65	-11	2.09	44.9%	12.4	10.3	1.6	2.5	14.4
2014-15	EDM	24	81	24	39	63	-16	1.90	49.7%	10.5	9.9	2.6	-1.4	11.1
2015-16	EDM	25	73	26	38	63					8.9	2.4	0.0	11.3

Brushing aside trade rumors, Jordan Eberle continued as a leading offensive contributor for Edmonton. Though the 24-year-old sputtered out of the gate, he heated up in the latter half of the season, putting up an impressive 43 points in his last 45 games. While he is often labeled a defensive liability, Eberle only trailed Taylor Hall in relative goals-for percentage. As a gifted playmaker and sniper, there is a good chance his peak output hasn't yet reached a career high—especially as the 2008 first-round pick should reap the benefits of playing with generational talent Connor McDavid. Put the rumors to rest: it would be unwise to move Eberle.

Matt Fraser — LW — WPG

Season	Team	Age	GP	G	A	Pts	+/-	ESP/60	AdjCF%	iCF/60	OGVT	DGVT	SGVT	GVT
2012-13	DAL	22	12	1	2	3	0	1.36	52.9%	14.0	0.2	0.2	-0.3	0.1
2013-14	BOS	23	14	2	0	2	0	0.91	54.3%	9.3	-0.3	0.2	0.0	-0.1
2014-15	BOS, EDM	24	60	8	4	12	-16	1.02	45.8%	11.7	-0.3	0.1	-0.5	-0.7
2015-16	WPG	25	51	7	6	13					-0.1	0.7	0.0	0.6

Former Edmonton GM Craig MacTavish claimed Matt Fraser—who had demonstrated significant production on the AHL level with the Texas Stars and Providence Bruins—off of waivers in late December, hoping his finishing ability would develop and flourish at the NHL level. Fraser didn't exactly break out, but five goals in 36 games while averaging only 11 minutes wasn't disastrous output, either. Unfortunately, in March, he suffered a concussion from a Nazem Kadri elbow, which kept him out of service for almost two weeks. Don't count Fraser out of a bottom-six NHL career yet.

Luke Gazdic — LW — EDM

Season	Team	Age	GP	G	A	Pts	+/-	ESP/60	AdjCF%	iCF/60	OGVT	DGVT	SGVT	GVT
2013-14	EDM	24	67	2	2	4	-8	0.62	35.8%	7.5	-1.8	-0.1	0.0	-1.8
2014-15	EDM	25	40	2	1	3	-4	0.61	41.7%	9.1	-0.8	0.4	0.0	-0.5
2015-16	EDM	26	49	4	3	7					-1.2	0.7	0.0	-0.5

Racking up only half of the fights he was a part of in 2013-14 and only a third of the penalty minutes, Oilers enforcer Luke Gazdic had a relatively tame year. Enforcers are a dying breed, and there is little chance Gazdic can show the organization that he can play productive hockey otherwise. In the last year of his contract, we can expect a similar role and stat line, perhaps with even less playing time.

Boyd Gordon — C — ARI

Season	Team	Age	GP	G	A	Pts	+/-	ESP/60	AdjCF%	iCF/60	OGVT	DGVT	SGVT	GVT
2012-13	PHX	29	48	4	10	14	0	1.15	52.3%	10.1	0.2	1.7	0.0	1.9
2013-14	EDM	30	74	8	13	21	-15	1.06	41.4%	8.6	0.5	3.4	0.0	3.9
2014-15	EDM	31	68	6	7	13	-5	0.85	42.9%	8.5	-0.7	2.7	-0.3	1.7
2015-16	ARI	32	57	6	9	15					0.0	2.1	0.0	2.1

In his two years with the Oilers—as well as before—Boyd Gordon has been known as a defensive center. True to form, he received the most shorthanded minutes among Edmonton forwards, while at even strength, he was run out for a ridiculously high percentage of defensive zone faceoffs. Given the circumstances, Gordon put up expectedly low possession numbers. The 31-year-old is slipping from being the quality role player of his Coyote days, producing his lowest point totals since his 60-game season for Washington in 2010-11.

Taylor Hall — LW — EDM

Season	Team	Age	GP	G	A	Pts	+/-	ESP/60	AdjCF%	iCF/60	OGVT	DGVT	SGVT	GVT
2012-13	EDM	21	45	16	34	50	5	3.13	50.0%	18.8	10.3	1.3	0.0	11.6
2013-14	EDM	22	75	27	53	80	-15	3.01	43.3%	15.3	14.0	1.0	0.3	15.3
2014-15	EDM	23	53	14	24	38	-1	2.20	49.1%	15.3	5.5	3.0	-0.5	7.9
2015-16	EDM	24	65	23	35	57					8.1	2.5	0.0	10.6

It was a rough year all around for the Oilers, even for established offensive stars like Taylor Hall. The 2010 first-overall selection experienced his lowest points-per-game rate since his age-18 rookie season. Appearing in only 53 games due to injury, his 8.9 shooting percentage might have rebounded closer to his 11.1 career mark had he played the entire year. However, don't worry about the numbers. The 24-year-old may be the best passing winger in the NHL and he gets shots on net as well as any player in the league. While he may currently be the center of criticism over perceived leadership failings, those narratives often fade as teams improve.

Curtis Hamilton — LW — Free Agent

Season	Team	Age	GP	G	A	Pts	+/-	ESP/60	AdjCF%	iCF/60	OGVT	DGVT	SGVT	GVT
2014-15	EDM	23	1	0	0	0	0	0.00	19.1%	0.0	0.0	0.0	0.0	0.0
2015-16	Free Agent	24	26	5	6	11					0.7	0.5	0.0	1.3

Curtis Hamilton was so amped up for his sole game with the Oilers that received a five-minute major for boarding just two minutes after the puck dropped. The long-time Saskatoon Blade had a solid rest of the season down in OKC, racking up 32 points in 63 games with the Barons. Coming up to the Oilers, he was asked to improve upon his physical play and his coaches seemed to be pleased with his progress. The organization has time to see where he goes from here.

Ryan Hamilton — LW — EDM

Season	Team	Age	GP	G	A	Pts	+/-	ESP/60	AdjCF%	iCF/60	OGVT	DGVT	SGVT	GVT
2012-13	TOR	27	10	0	2	2	1	1.27	40.8%	6.4	0.0	0.2	0.0	0.2
2013-14	EDM	28	2	0	0	0	-2	0.00	35.6%	12.8	-0.2	-0.1	0.0	-0.4
2014-15	EDM	29	16	1	1	2	-8	0.31	40.4%	5.9	-0.9	-0.2	-0.3	-1.4
2015-16	EDM	30	30	4	5	8					0.0	0.4	0.0	0.3

Ryan Hamilton finally managed to score his first career NHL goal, after having appeared in 30 scattered games over the course of the past four seasons with the Leafs and Oilers. The bulk of his time has been in Oklahoma City since he left the Toronto Marlies—where he was captain in 2011-12 and 2012-13. Hamilton has always been a productive minor-league point producer; he netted 18 goals in 43 games for the Barons, true to form. The 30-year-old may not be able to shake the AAAA tag: a great AHLer, he was last on the Oilers in Corsi percentage, one of the league's poorest possession teams.

Matt Hendricks — C — EDM

Season	Team	Age	GP	G	A	Pts	+/-	ESP/60	AdjCF%	iCF/60	OGVT	DGVT	SGVT	GVT
2012-13	WSH	31	48	5	3	8	-6	1.01	47.1%	11.7	-0.4	0.3	-0.1	-0.2
2013-14	NSH, EDM	32	77	5	2	7	-11	0.47	40.9%	10.7	-2.0	2.1	-0.8	-0.8
2014-15	EDM	33	71	8	8	16	-14	1.10	44.2%	12.4	-0.5	2.1	-0.8	0.7
2015-16	EDM	34	58	7	6	13					-0.3	1.6	-0.1	1.2

Defensive specialist Matt Hendricks had a busy summer, captaining the USA at the IIHF World Championships after a 71-game campaign with the Oilers. The gritty 33-year-old veteran threw a bunch of hits (220) per usual, and was among the cadre of bottom sixers completely—utterly—buried in defensive zone starts by Dallas Eakins, who was following Alain Vigneault's Vancouver playbook, and then some.

Jesse Joensuu						**LW**							**KHL**
Season	Team	Age	GP	G	A	Pts	+/-	ESP/60	AdjCF%	iCF/60	OGVT	DGVT	SGVT	GVT
2012-13	NYI	25	7	0	2	2	2	1.69	51.0%	15.3	0.4	0.3	0.0	0.7
2013-14	EDM	26	42	3	2	5	-16	0.65	43.2%	10.5	-1.3	-0.8	0.0	-2.1
2014-15	EDM	27	20	2	2	4	-8	0.93	44.7%	8.8	-0.2	0.2	0.0	0.0
2015-16	KHL	28	37	5	5	10					0.1	0.5	0.0	0.6

Jesse Joensuu played 20 games for the Oilers from mid-October through late November before getting transferred to Bern of the Swiss Elite League. At age 28, his opportunities to break through and become a viable NHL forward may have run out, but he has returned from Europe to North America before—so who knows. Joensuu actually has gotten a bad rap in his time with the Oilers—deployed highly defensively (12.5% offensive zone starts!) by the Edmonton coaching staff, apparently management didn't get that memo in evaluating his performance. We see this a ton in the NHL: Brandon Dubinsky and Jussi Jokinen come to mind. Front offices throughout the league are often blind to evaluating performance in proper context.

Rob Klinkhammer						**LW**							**EDM**
Season	Team	Age	GP	G	A	Pts	+/-	ESP/60	AdjCF%	iCF/60	OGVT	DGVT	SGVT	GVT
2012-13	PHX	26	22	5	6	11	7	2.29	54.8%	12.6	2.7	1.1	0.0	3.7
2013-14	PHX	27	72	11	9	20	6	1.43	53.6%	12.9	1.7	2.5	0.0	4.1
2014-15	ARI, PIT, EDM	28	69	5	4	9	-4	0.71	47.3%	8.9	-1.9	1.6	0.6	0.3
2015-16	EDM	29	56	6	6	12					-0.6	1.5	0.0	1.0

An underappreciated contributor to possession and even-strength scoring in Arizona, the production didn't translate well in Edmonton for Rob Klinkhammer: he managed only one goal and two assists in a half-season for the sad-sack Oilers. Still, the man with the NHL's best name played adequately enough to be re-signed by the Edmonton brass. The 29-year-old hopes to return to doing what he is capable of: adding 20 points while playing an energetic game on the fourth line.

Anton Lander						**C**							**EDM**
Season	Team	Age	GP	G	A	Pts	+/-	ESP/60	AdjCF%	iCF/60	OGVT	DGVT	SGVT	GVT
2012-13	EDM	21	11	0	1	1	-4	0.00	47.3%	8.2	-0.5	-0.2	0.0	-0.8
2013-14	EDM	22	27	0	1	1	-10	0.21	42.8%	6.6	-2.5	0.1	0.0	-2.4
2014-15	EDM	23	38	6	14	20	-12	1.70	48.1%	8.6	2.4	0.3	-0.5	2.1
2015-16	EDM	24	42	8	13	20					1.5	0.8	0.0	2.3

Since 2011-12, Anton Lander has split time between the Oklahoma City Barons and the Edmonton Oilers. Finally receiving significant NHL ice-time, he made the most of it. After managing only eight points in his first 94 games, he netted six goals and 14 assists in only 38 games—more than a nice improvement. It is a good stepping stone for the 24 year-old Swede, but with additions to the roster, he will need to battle to stay in an improving top nine.

Andrew Miller — C/RW — EDM

Season	Team	Age	GP	G	A	Pts	+/-	ESP/60	AdjCF%	iCF/60	OGVT	DGVT	SGVT	GVT
2014-15	EDM	26	9	1	5	6	-2	2.91	44.9%	10.3	1.3	0.1	0.0	1.5
2015-16	EDM	27	30	6	10	16					1.9	0.7	0.0	2.6

Captain of the 2013 national champion Yale Bulldogs, Andrew Miller entered his second season in the Edmonton organization—his first NHL goal came on a penalty shot in late March against Dallas. Sent back to Oklahoma City after a pleasantly surprising six points in nine NHL games, Miller tore up the AHL to the tune of 60 points in 63 games. The five-foot-nine forward could be assigned to the team's new minor-league affiliate in Bakersfield to start the season, but Miller is making a great case for inclusion on the NHL roster.

Ryan Nugent-Hopkins — C — EDM

Season	Team	Age	GP	G	A	Pts	+/-	ESP/60	AdjCF%	iCF/60	OGVT	DGVT	SGVT	GVT
2012-13	EDM	19	40	4	20	24	3	1.25	49.9%	10.6	0.1	1.0	-0.3	0.8
2013-14	EDM	20	80	19	37	56	-12	1.67	43.6%	10.0	5.5	2.3	-0.3	7.5
2014-15	EDM	21	76	24	32	56	-12	1.99	49.0%	12.6	7.4	4.3	-0.4	11.2
2015-16	EDM	22	77	25	37	62					7.7	3.2	0.0	10.8

One of the concerns about Ryan Nugent-Hopkins has been his slight frame. At six-foot, 190-pounds, the 2011 first-overall selection still leaves much to be desired in terms of his defensive play and ability to win puck battles, which is keeping him from growing into more than a number-two center; the same goes for his 45.7% faceoff percentage. Yet, as Connor McDavid is expected to take the top center slot going forward, the pressure will soon ease off of Nugent-Hopkins.

Iiro Pakarinen — RW — EDM

Season	Team	Age	GP	G	A	Pts	+/-	ESP/60	AdjCF%	iCF/60	OGVT	DGVT	SGVT	GVT
2014-15	EDM	23	17	1	2	3	-4	0.38	46.7%	18.3	0.0	-0.1	-0.3	-0.4
2015-16	EDM	24	33	6	7	13					0.9	0.6	0.0	1.5

A strong winger with good speed, Iiro Pakarinen received a 17-game run in the big leagues. He was even a part of Edmonton's top line with Nugent-Hopkins and Eberle for a few games after making a nice first impression. Before his call-up, the Finnish winger put up 28 points in 39 games for the minor-league club, along with a +17 plus/minus—that is after breaking out with a 20-10-30 line in 60 games for HIFK as a 22-year-old. Size is on Pakarinen's side at a sturdy six-foot-one, 215-pounds, giving him an advantage in front of the net. If he can prove himself to be a consistent all-around player, he will see NHL ice more often.

Steven Pinizzotto — RW — Germany

Season	Team	Age	GP	G	A	Pts	+/-	ESP/60	AdjCF%	iCF/60	OGVT	DGVT	SGVT	GVT
2012-13	VAN	28	12	0	0	0	-6	0.00	39.9%	7.1	-0.9	-0.4	0.0	-1.3
2013-14	EDM	29	6	0	2	2	-1	2.08	41.0%	4.8	0.1	0.0	0.0	0.2
2014-15	EDM	30	18	2	2	4	1	1.74	44.0%	6.9	0.3	0.7	0.0	1.0
2015-16	Germany	31	32	4	6	10					0.6	0.8	0.0	1.3

At age 31, Steven Pinizzotto got another cup or two of coffee, though they may have been his last. He appeared 18 games for the Oilers, potting his first career goal (against Vancouver in November). No further strides were made in his time up or in his time down on the farm, where he posted 11 points in 25 games. Known for his aggressive play, Pinizzotto tallied 30 PIM in the NHL—taking a lot more minors than he drew—and 117 PIM in 25 AHL games. The Mississauga native heads to play for Germany's EHC Munchen in 2015-16.

Tyler Pitlick						C/RW							EDM
Season	Team	Age	GP	G	A	Pts	+/-	ESP/60	AdjCF%	iCF/60	OGVT	DGVT	SGVT	GVT
2013-14	EDM	22	10	1	0	1	-2	0.67	39.3%	10.5	-0.1	-0.1	0.0	-0.1
2014-15	EDM	23	17	2	0	2	-3	0.58	49.3%	11.6	-0.5	0.3	0.0	-0.3
2015-16	EDM	24	33	6	5	11					0.3	0.7	0.0	1.0

Recently signed to a one-year contract, the oft-injured Tyler Pitlick needs to continue to progress to demonstrate that he should be in the team's future plans. The 23-year-old managed only 17 NHL games and 14 AHL games (with three goals, six assists). He may have the makings of an everyday NHLer, as evidenced by his above-average possession numbers, but he will need to prove his long-term health first. With a deep forward group ahead of him, Bakersfield—the new home of the AHL affiliate—will be the platform to showcase his versatility and scoring skill.

Benoit Pouliot						LW							EDM
Season	Team	Age	GP	G	A	Pts	+/-	ESP/60	AdjCF%	iCF/60	OGVT	DGVT	SGVT	GVT
2012-13	TBL	26	34	8	12	20	8	2.63	49.9%	13.3	3.3	1.2	0.0	4.5
2013-14	NYR	27	80	15	21	36	10	1.83	55.1%	12.0	4.6	2.7	0.0	7.3
2014-15	EDM	28	58	19	15	34	-1	2.00	49.7%	10.9	5.8	2.7	-0.5	8.0
2015-16	EDM	29	63	17	19	36					4.2	2.3	0.0	6.5

Having played for six teams in six years, the Oilers were pleasantly surprised to see Benoit Pouliot garner the most goals he has ever had in a single season (19). The 2005 fourth-overall pick found his way onto the top line with his excellent puck-possession skills and added scoring punch. On a team where 16 players had a plus-minus of -11 or worse, Pouliot was tied for first with Taylor Hall with a -1 (out of all players who appeared in 20+ games). The bad news for Edmonton was that a broken foot prevented the former Sudbury Wolf from appearing in more than 58 games. Though that should improve, on the flip side, Pouliot was scoring at a higher clip than could be expected over the long term, blessed with a 18.1 shooting percentage in 2014-15.

Teddy Purcell						RW							EDM
Season	Team	Age	GP	G	A	Pts	+/-	ESP/60	AdjCF%	iCF/60	OGVT	DGVT	SGVT	GVT
2012-13	TBL	27	48	11	25	36	-1	2.16	47.9%	11.8	4.7	0.2	-0.1	4.9
2013-14	TBL	28	81	12	30	42	-3	1.38	54.0%	11.7	2.6	1.5	-0.8	3.3
2014-15	EDM	29	82	12	22	34	-33	1.17	48.2%	11.4	1.0	0.5	0.2	1.6
2015-16	EDM	30	64	12	20	33					2.4	1.3	0.0	3.7

On a team littered with injury-prone players, only Teddy Purcell played all 82 games for the copper and blue. As a pass-first forward, his role—coming over from Tampa Bay—was to create additional scoring opportunities for the Oilers' talented forwards. Instead, his point totals dropped to their lowest since 2009-10 (a common theme on the squad). At 30, there isn't much hope for a return to days of scoring 65 points, but the undrafted winger should fit a third-line role as a positive possession player.

Derek Roy — C — Free Agent

Season	Team	Age	GP	G	A	Pts	+/-	ESP/60	AdjCF%	iCF/60	OGVT	DGVT	SGVT	GVT
2012-13	DAL, VAN	29	42	7	21	28	4	1.89	52.7%	11.2	3.7	1.6	-0.6	4.7
2013-14	STL	30	75	9	28	37	-1	1.50	52.5%	11.3	4.2	1.0	0.3	5.5
2014-15	NSH, EDM	31	72	12	20	32	-13	1.52	48.4%	9.9	2.3	1.6	-1.1	2.8
2015-16	Free Agent	32	59	10	19	28					2.0	1.4	0.0	3.4

Hitting the extreme journeyman phase of his career, Derek Roy performed adequately after coming over from Nashville. His added value was as mentor to struggling 2012 first-overall pick Nail Yakupov (though role that could cause some smirks and muffled laughs in Buffalo). Overall, Roy put up unimpressive numbers, but had natural chemistry with the young Russian, giving the Oilers good reason to continue to play him despite being only a shell of a high-scoring center. With limited speed, and no size or extra effort to speak of, Roy does not fit in any competitor's top-six anymore, nor does he bring any of the elements usually possessed by bottom-six forwards. He may have to call it a career soon.

Bogdan Yakimov — C

Season	Team	Age	GP	G	A	Pts	+/-	ESP/60	AdjCF%	iCF/60	OGVT	DGVT	SGVT	GVT
2014-15	EDM	20	1	0	0	0	-1	0.00	56.2%	4.8	-0.1	-0.1	0.0	-0.2
2015-16	EDM	21	26	5	6	11					0.7	0.5	0.0	1.2

In his first season of experience as an NHLer, Bogdan Yakimov saw 11 minutes of action. However, the big Russian received ample playing time with Oklahoma City, when he was healthy. He appeared in 57 games for the Barons before an injury ended his season with a month to go. Nevertheless, he tied for seventh on the team with 12 goals. At six-foot-five and 230 pounds, Yakimov uses his size to outmuscle the opposition, and as an added bonus, he has great puck-handling skills in his toolbox.

Nail Yakupov — RW

Season	Team	Age	GP	G	A	Pts	+/-	ESP/60	AdjCF%	iCF/60	OGVT	DGVT	SGVT	GVT
2012-13	EDM	19	48	17	14	31	-4	2.17	42.0%	11.3	5.6	0.3	0.0	5.9
2013-14	EDM	20	63	11	13	24	-33	1.41	43.7%	12.4	0.2	-1.3	0.0	-1.1
2014-15	EDM	21	81	14	19	33	-35	1.26	45.2%	14.1	1.5	-0.3	-0.7	0.6
2015-16	EDM	22	66	17	19	36					3.1	0.7	0.0	3.7

Only 22 years old, Nail Yakupov is one of the most exciting players to watch on the Oilers. That can be a good thing and a bad thing. The Russian winger drove former bench boss Dallas Eakins crazy with his inability to play within the system, but a midseason coaching change saw the 2012 first-overall pick receive more freedom, and he consequently produced more points. We should temper any excitement about his second half, though, despite Yakupov finally displaying his incredible offensive instincts. The underlying statistics are still worrisome, especially when you factor in his well-known lack of backchecking. With yet another new coach—one pegged to be around for a while (former San Jose bench boss Todd McLellan)—this could be a make or break year for Yakupov.

DEFENSEMEN

Keith Aulie						D							Free Agent	
Season	Team	Age	GP	G	A	Pts	+/-	ESP/60	AdjCF%	iCF/60	OGVT	DGVT	SGVT	GVT
2012-13	TBL	23	45	2	5	7	1	0.77	46.5%	8.2	0.6	1.1	0.0	1.7
2013-14	TBL	24	15	0	1	1	-3	0.43	42.1%	7.1	-0.2	-0.2	0.0	-0.4
2014-15	EDM	25	31	0	1	1	-3	0.14	43.4%	8.3	-1.4	1.1	-0.3	-0.5
2015-16	Free Agent	26	38	1	4	5					-0.6	1.3	0.0	0.7

Keith Aulie's season with the Oilers was not a productive one from an analytical—or any other—standpoint. He appeared in 31 games, recorded only one assist, and was last on the team in Corsi percentage. The massive six-foot-six, 220 pounder did rack up 66 penalty minutes (yay!), but the Oiler front office must have been hoping he would turn out to be a different player when they nabbed him from Tampa Bay. He remains an unrestricted free agent.

Brandon Davidson						D								EDM
Season	Team	Age	GP	G	A	Pts	+/-	ESP/60	AdjCF%	iCF/60	OGVT	DGVT	SGVT	GVT
2014-15	EDM	23	12	1	0	1	-5	0.36	44.0%	7.4	0.1	-0.4	0.0	-0.3
2015-16	EDM	24	29	2	5	7					0.4	0.6	0.0	1.0

24-year-old defenseman Brandon Davidson appeared in 55 games for the Barons along with getting into his first 12 NHL games, spread out between December and the end of the season. A conservative defenseman who is utilized on the penalty kill, he will likely start in the AHL again. There are plenty of one-year contracts for Oiler defensemen; Davidson is in contention for becoming one of them that gets re-signed for future seasons.

Mark Fayne						RD								EDM
Season	Team	Age	GP	G	A	Pts	+/-	ESP/60	AdjCF%	iCF/60	OGVT	DGVT	SGVT	GVT
2012-13	NJD	25	31	1	5	6	6	0.62	57.8%	9.4	0.5	3.8	0.0	4.3
2013-14	NJD	26	72	4	7	11	-5	0.51	55.4%	9.3	-0.8	5.4	0.0	4.7
2014-15	EDM	27	74	2	6	8	-21	0.32	45.2%	8.8	-1.7	2.4	0.0	0.7
2015-16	EDM	28	61	3	9	11					-0.3	3.0	0.0	2.7

Defensive defenseman Mark Fayne was brought over from New Jersey after almost four full seasons with the Devils. His largest role was on the penalty kill, where he spent almost 15% of his ice-time. Not surprisingly, in the first year of his four-year contract, the 27-year-old only put up eight points. It is safe to say he took on some of the toughest minutes and mitigated disaster as best he could, but with the addition of Andrej Sekera and prospect Darnell Nurse on the horizon, the Oilers hope Fayne will soon return to the role of a solid second-pairing defenseman.

Andrew Ference						LD								EDM
Season	Team	Age	GP	G	A	Pts	+/-	ESP/60	AdjCF%	iCF/60	OGVT	DGVT	SGVT	GVT
2012-13	BOS	33	48	4	9	13	9	0.88	53.2%	11.4	1.5	3.3	0.0	4.7
2013-14	EDM	34	71	3	15	18	-18	0.76	41.8%	6.5	0.9	3.1	0.0	4.1
2014-15	EDM	35	70	3	11	14	-17	0.66	44.2%	7.9	0.0	2.7	0.0	2.7
2015-16	EDM	36	55	3	10	13					0.4	2.5	0.0	2.9

Oilers captain Andrew Ference has been consistently over his head as a top-pairing defenseman. Once again, he played 70+ games, scored a few goals, faced tough competition, and put up very poor possession numbers. At age 36, his on-ice contributions have slipped, but he could transition into a serviceable bottom-pairing blueliner (until age hits really hard). While his value will not exist in goals or Corsi ratings, there is something to be said for adding experience and leadership with a budding squad. (Maybe.) With his contract up in two years, the broadcast booth may be the next stop for the bright defenseman.

Brad Hunt								LD					EDM
Season	Team	Age	GP	G	A	Pts	+/-	ESP/60	AdjCF%	iCF/60	OGVT	DGVT	SGVT	GVT
2013-14	EDM	25	3	0	0	0	-3	0.00	29.4%	3.4	-0.2	-0.4	0.0	-0.5
2014-15	EDM	26	11	1	2	3	-6	0.67	46.9%	10.6	-0.1	-0.1	0.0	-0.2
2015-16	EDM	27	29	2	7	9					0.5	0.8	0.0	1.4

While his time with the Oilers was short-lived, Brad Hunt did wonderful things in the AHL. The 27-year-old was second in the league in point production among defensemen, with 48 points in 57 games. Consequently, he was named an AHL first-team All-Star. His stellar offense will need to be coupled with stable defensive-mindedness for him to get regular NHL minutes. However, that may not be possible at his size and average speed.

Oscar Klefbom								LD					EDM
Season	Team	Age	GP	G	A	Pts	+/-	ESP/60	AdjCF%	iCF/60	OGVT	DGVT	SGVT	GVT
2013-14	EDM	20	17	1	2	3	-6	0.70	42.6%	6.8	0.1	-0.2	0.0	-0.2
2014-15	EDM	21	60	2	18	20	-21	0.91	49.1%	10.6	2.2	2.1	-0.3	4.0
2015-16	EDM	22	57	5	17	22					2.3	2.2	0.0	4.5

Oscar Klefbom was thrown into the fire in his first full season with the Oilers. The 21-year-old got significant time on the top defensive pairing with Justin Schultz, catching the eye of Edmonton's management and proving himself worthy of being part of the future. The big-framed Swede offered some passing skill to go along with his shutdown abilities. He ended the year a shade under 50% Corsi, which is impressive considering Edmonton was one of the poorer possession teams. As Klefbom continues to learn the NHL level, he will cut down on mistakes to become, at the very least, a solid second-pairing defender.

Martin Marincin								LD					TOR
Season	Team	Age	GP	G	A	Pts	+/-	ESP/60	AdjCF%	iCF/60	OGVT	DGVT	SGVT	GVT
2013-14	EDM	21	44	0	6	6	-2	0.33	46.0%	5.7	-1.1	2.0	0.0	0.9
2014-15	EDM	22	41	1	4	5	-4	0.44	47.8%	9.0	-0.2	1.4	0.6	1.8
2015-16	TOR	23	45	2	7	9					0.0	2.0	0.0	2.0

In his second season with Edmonton, Martin Marincin continued to put up surprisingly adequate possession numbers in a half-season of work on a team with an identity crisis on defense. He had two long spells with the Oilers, from mid-October to late November, and then from early February to the end of the season. The 22-year-old Slovakian didn't do much of anything offensively in his 18 minutes per game, but he was used as a second-unit defenseman when killing off penalties. There is potential in his game, but his time in Edmonton came to an end when he signed for the Maple Leafs in July.

David Musil — LD — EDM

Season	Team	Age	GP	G	A	Pts	+/-	ESP/60	AdjCF%	iCF/60	OGVT	DGVT	SGVT	GVT
2014-15	EDM	22	4	0	2	2	-2	1.64	44.4%	5.6	0.7	0.0	0.0	0.7
2015-16	EDM	23	26	2	6	8					0.8	0.8	0.0	1.6

Second rounder David Musil saw a glimpse of NHL life over his four games with the Oilers. The six-foot-four, 207-pound Czech is known as a slow but steady and defensive-minded defenseman—he recorded only 11 points in 65 AHL games for the Barons. Musil has been with the organization since 2011 and will need to take advantage of every opportunity put in front of him, as he is in the last year of his entry-level deal.

Nikita Nikitin — RD — EDM

Season	Team	Age	GP	G	A	Pts	+/-	ESP/60	AdjCF%	iCF/60	OGVT	DGVT	SGVT	GVT
2012-13	CBJ	26	38	3	6	9	2	0.65	46.4%	9.3	-0.2	2.5	0.0	2.3
2013-14	CBJ	27	66	2	13	15	9	0.88	50.0%	10.3	1.1	3.1	0.0	4.3
2014-15	EDM	28	42	4	6	10	-12	0.62	47.7%	10.2	0.3	1.2	0.0	1.5
2015-16	EDM	29	51	4	12	16					1.2	2.3	0.0	3.5

After a solid season with Columbus, Nikita Nikitin's time in Edmonton was a disappointment. His services were only available for half a season due to injury, and when he was on the ice, he was seen as a liability. The six-foot-three, 216-pound Russian was brought in to munch minutes and give stability to the defensive corps, but his cap hit of $4.5 million was not worth the value he contributed. At the time he was traded from the Blue Jackets, he was good for second-pairing puck-possession numbers, though his strength was getting pucks on net. However, even that skill was non-existent in his first year with the Oilers. Going forward, the best-case scenario for Nikitin seems to be on the third pairing.

Darnell Nurse — LD — EDM

Season	Team	Age	GP	G	A	Pts	+/-	ESP/60	AdjCF%	iCF/60	OGVT	DGVT	SGVT	GVT
2014-15	EDM	19	2	0	0	0	-2	0.00	53.5%	6.7	-0.3	0.0	0.0	-0.3
2015-16	EDM	20	25	2	5	7					0.3	0.8	0.0	1.1

With the youth movement of the forwards already in place, contrasted by a chaotic defense lacking consistency, young Darnell Nurse could soon turn into a marquee player for the Oilers. The seventh-overall pick from 2013 played the bulk of his season in the OHL with the powerhouse Sault Ste. Marie Greyhounds; he followed up an impressive 50-point, 64-game campaign in 2013-14 with 33 points in 36 games this past season. Nurse claims he is ready to be a blueline regular in Edmonton; the organization needs to decide when his time will come.

Jordan Oesterle — LD — EDM

Season	Team	Age	GP	G	A	Pts	+/-	ESP/60	AdjCF%	iCF/60	OGVT	DGVT	SGVT	GVT
2014-15	EDM	22	6	0	1	1	-4	0.73	48.1%	9.5	0.1	-0.4	0.0	-0.3
2015-16	EDM	23	26	2	5	7					0.5	0.6	0.0	1.1

Jordan Oesterle's first full season of pro hockey was a pleasant surprise for Oiler fans. While his only six NHL games came in late February and early March, he had been dazzling on the blue line in Oklahoma City. There, he netted eight goals and dished out 17 assists over 65 games on a young team full of conservative defensemen (aside from Brad Hunt). He proved he can make the jump from college to pro hockey, and is on track for an improved AHL season and more trips up to the big leagues when called upon.

Justin Schultz								RD						EDM
Season	Team	Age	GP	G	A	Pts	+/-	ESP/60	AdjCF%	iCF/60	OGVT	DGVT	SGVT	GVT
2012-13	EDM	22	48	8	19	27	-17	0.85	43.4%	8.4	4.8	-1.0	0.0	3.8
2013-14	EDM	23	74	11	22	33	-22	0.90	41.7%	6.6	4.2	-0.1	0.0	4.1
2014-15	EDM	24	81	6	25	31	-17	0.72	49.0%	8.2	1.6	3.5	-0.5	4.6
2015-16	EDM	25	71	7	24	32					2.7	3.2	0.0	6.0

After veteran Jeff Petry was moved at the trade deadline, Jeff Schultz handily led Oilers defensemen in ice-time—which is far from ideal. The offensive blueliner was able to show signs of the playmaking skill that drew interest from many teams after he left college for the NHL. Unfortunately, the defensive side of his game is still disastrous, showing no signs of improvement. The acquisition of Andrej Sekera will take some of the ice-time burden from him, but Schultz was only re-signed to a one-year deal for 2015-16. He needs to demonstrate that he belongs in the long-term plans of the Oilers.

GOALTENDERS

Richard Bachman								G						VAN
Season	Team	Age	GP	W	L	OT	GAA	Sv%	ESSV%	QS%	GGVT	DGVT	SGVT	GVT
2012-13	DAL	25	13	6	5	0	3.25	.885	.895	50.0%	-4.9	0.0	0.0	-4.9
2013-14	EDM	26	3	0	2	1	3.02	.916	.903	33.3%	0.4	-0.1	-0.9	-0.6
2014-15	EDM	27	7	3	2	0	2.84	.911	.938	75.0%	0.0	-0.1	0.5	0.4
2015-16	VAN	28	14					.914			1.3	-0.1	0.0	1.2

Hoping to ascend to the full-time backup role, Richard Bachman was unable to garner much more NHL playing time than in 2013-14; he spent the majority of his year in an Oklahoma City sweater—on the bench as an AHL backup. Instead, Laurent Brossoit took the OKC starting role for most of the season, but when Bachman was featured he was outstanding. He posted a 14-5-3 record with a .918 save percentage for the Barons, and aided them in their Calder Cup run. Similarly, when given a chance, Bachman was taking care of business in his NHL games, with a 3-2 record and a .911 save percentage. The five-foot-ten goalie is now a member of the Canucks, having rolled on down the highway as a free agent. You ain't seen nothing yet.

Laurent Brossoit								G						EDM
Season	Team	Age	GP	W	L	OT	GAA	Sv%	ESSV%	QS%	GGVT	DGVT	SGVT	GVT
2014-15	EDM	21	1	0	1	0	2.00	.961	.957	100.0%	2.1	-0.2	0.0	1.9
2015-16	EDM	22	14					.916			2.3	-0.2	0.0	2.2

Laurent Brossoit made an impressive NHL debut, turning away 49 of 51 shots in a 3-1 loss to Dallas in the Oilers' home finale. The 22-year-old featured prominently in the AHL for the Barons, registering an impressive .918 save percentage over the course of 53 games. He was a workhorse for Oklahoma City, and before his NHL debut, he had started 25 straight games. With the arrival of Cam Talbot and Anders Nilsson to Edmonton, Brossoit will likely spend another season in the same role, with the ability to pop up to the big club to gain further experience.

Tyler Bunz — G — Free Agent

Season	Team	Age	GP	W	L	OT	GAA	Sv%	ESSV%	QS%	GGVT	DGVT	SGVT	GVT
2014-15	EDM	22	1	0	0	0	9.00	.750	.750	0.0%	-1.6	0.0	0.0	-1.7
2015-16	Free Agent	23	11					.913			0.8	-0.1	0.0	0.7

A fifth-round pick of the Oilers in 2010, Tyler Bunz has spent most of his career in the ECHL putting up middling numbers. He was a surprise call-up in early April on an "emergency basis". In his only NHL playing time, he was called in to relieve Ben Scrivens against the Kings for the third period when the Oilers were down 5-1 (the game finished 8-2). He didn't get much time in Oklahoma City either, featuring in only two games.

Viktor Fasth — G — KHL

Season	Team	Age	GP	W	L	OT	GAA	Sv%	ESSV%	QS%	GGVT	DGVT	SGVT	GVT
2012-13	ANA	30	25	15	6	2	2.18	.921	.926	65.2%	8.4	0.2	0.1	8.7
2013-14	ANA, EDM	31	12	5	5	2	2.82	.903	.903	50.0%	-1.6	0.1	-1.6	-3.1
2014-15	EDM	32	26	6	15	3	3.41	.888	.896	37.5%	-12.8	-0.1	2.9	-10.1
2015-16	KHL	33	17					.908			-1.6	0.0	0.1	-1.5

Viktor Fasth hasn't reclaimed the form that he experienced early in his NHL career. After a .926 even-strength save percentage two years ago in Anaheim, that number plummeted to .896 in 26 games for the Oilers. There weren't any stretches of brilliance where fans could hope to claim the old Fasth had returned. He hasn't even recorded a shutout since April 2013. The 33-year-old saw his season and contract wind down with Edmonton, and now plays for CSKA Moscow of the KHL.

Ben Scrivens — G — EDM

Season	Team	Age	GP	W	L	OT	GAA	Sv%	ESSV%	QS%	GGVT	DGVT	SGVT	GVT
2012-13	TOR	26	20	7	9	0	2.69	.915	.920	58.8%	3.6	-0.5	0.0	3.1
2013-14	LAK, EDM	27	40	16	16	4	2.55	.922	.927	65.7%	13.5	-1.1	-1.1	11.3
2014-15	EDM	28	57	15	26	11	3.16	.890	.897	39.6%	-26.8	0.6	2.1	-24.0
2015-16	EDM	29	32					.909			-1.7	0.0	0.0	-1.7

Given his first shot to be the relied on as a starter, Ben Scrivens was one of the worst goaltenders in the NHL. Out of all goalies who played at least 20 games, Scrivens ranked 49th in save percentage (.890) and managed only a .897 even-strength save percentage. The former Maple Leaf could turn things around as a backup while playing behind an improved team. He had better.

Jack Ries

Florida Panthers

The Florida Panthers started their climb out of the cellar, finishing the year with 91 points, and showing significant progress with a new coach and exciting young roster. In terms of puck possession, this was the team's best season since 2006-07, with their 51.1 score-adjusted SAT% only the third time since 2005 the team has been over 50% on the season.

The 2014-15 team was surprisingly competitive considering their reliance on both players who haven't hit their prime and past-their-prime veterans. On average, NHL teams have nine players between the ages of 25 and 30. The Panthers, on the other hand, only had three skaters in that age group, with the rest of the players either younger than 25 or older than 30. Next year, Florida will have only five skaters between the ages of 25 and 30, which isn't exactly a lot more than three.

Can Florida win big?

Historically, the answer would be no. Looking at the Stanley Cup finalists from 2005-06 to the present, an average of 9.6 skaters aged between 25 and 30 dressed for at least one game during the team's playoff run, almost twice the number of mid-career veterans the Panthers currently have on their roster. Though it is possible that general manager Dale Tallon brings in more veterans at the trade deadline as he did with future Hall of Famer Jaromir Jagr in 2015, the team may be too much of a mix between young and old for them to make a legitimate run at the Cup.

But the team could surprise us. Aside from Dave Bolland, Shawn Thornton, and Derek Mackenzie, the majority of the skaters are either quality possession players (like Aleksander Barkov, Vincent Trocheck, and Brian Campbell), or players that can hold their own on a puck-possession heavyweight (like Willie Mitchell). Florida had several good stretches last season where they controlled the puck well and got solid goaltending from Roberto Luongo, consequently stringing together a series of wins.

If the Panthers are going to make the postseason in 2015-16, they must receive key performances from young and old – beyond what is usually expected from their age groups in the NHL. Examples of veterans meshing with youngsters can be found on the team already, with Brian Campbell helping blueline phenom Aaron Ekblad on the back end, and Jagr working with Barkov and Jonathan Huberdeau to create a *bona fide* first line for the Cats.

Campbell is one of the most criminally underrated defensemen in the NHL, as his knack for making smart plays out of his own zone and his smooth-skating abilities

PANTHERS IN A BOX

Last Season		
Goals For	206	25th
Goals Against	223	18th
GVT	-17	23rd
Points	91	20th
Playoffs	Did not make playoffs	

The Panthers, a solid team at even strength, got demolished on special teams, missing the playoffs for the ninth time in 10 years.

Three-Year Record		
GVT	-148	28th
Points	193	28th
Playoffs	0 Appearances, 0 Wins	

VUKOTA Projections		
Goals For	211	23rd
Goals Against	222	20th
GVT	-11	24th
Points	88	24th

Unless Florida can develop some offensive talent organically, they still don't have enough firepower to compete within their Conference.

Top Three Prospects
L. Crouse (F), M. Matheson (D), I. McCoshen (D)

have him consistently ranked as one of the top possession players in the league. This year, despite being 35 years old and playing with an 18-year-old who was making the jump directly from juniors to the NHL, Campbell led the Panthers in every score-adjusted relative possession metric (SAT%, USAT%, SCF%), and placed in the top 20 among defensemen who played at least 750 minutes.

The pairing was especially beneficial to the 2014 number-one overall pick, who had one of the best seasons in NHL history for an 18-year-old defenseman. His 39 points in 81 games was good enough for second among rookie blueliners, only behind 22-year-old John Klingberg of the Dallas Stars. The youngster's defensive play was also solid, both by the eye test and by possession numbers.

However, examining Campbell's past, and the way he elevated the play of Jason Garrison, Tom Gilbert, and several other defensemen, gives us pause to suspect that Ekblad may have looked better than he actually was. Sure enough, in 1,229 minutes with Campbell, Ekblad had a SAT% of 56.0, while in 171 minutes away from him—a small but not insignificant sample for a shot-based metric—his SAT% was a only 41.0.

That said, the relationship between Campbell and Ekblad wasn't all one-sided. Campbell's game does lack the ability to create quality shots, as his own shot has deteriorated over the years. The youngster has a cannon for a shot, and the veteran consistently defers to him when it comes to shooting the puck. And he is bound to get better. Most defensemen aren't ready to play big minutes until age 21 or 22 at the earliest, even if they are top picks.

Up front for the Panthers, Jagr takes the role of mentor for Barkov and Huberdeau, who flourished while playing with him and established themselves as the team's top line.

We have reached the point in Jagr's career where it seems like he is never going to retire, and he is just going to keep on playing and playing until his body literally quits on him. He is 43, but despite his age, he posted 47 points in 77 games (18 in 20 with the Panthers), with a relative score-adjusted SAT% of 5.6.

2013 second-overall pick Barkov and 2011 third-overall pick Huberdeau were having decent seasons up until Jagr arrived, but they really thrived under his tutelage—Barkov had 15 points in his 20 games, while Huberdeau had 21. Seeing the talented youngsters perform well is a treat for a fanbase that is used to their team drafting a different tier of players in the first round, like Rostislav Olesz, Keaton Ellerby, Kendall McArdle, and Petr Taticek.

Jagr continued to be Jagr while his young linemates seemed to take a step forward in their development. This interaction between veterans and rookies was easy to spot, as each time the line ended up on the bench, the two students would sit next to their teacher and soak in every word he had to say. Whatever he was telling them worked. In the 257 minutes the three forwards played together, they posted a SAT% of 55.3, and a 63.3% goals for. Though they got a share of puck luck, their possession numbers were still solid, and they have the makings of a good first line for Florida in 2015-16.

The team isn't ready to compete for a Stanley Cup yet and will need a few bounces to go their way if they want to make a serious run in the postseason. The Panthers are set up to make the 2016 playoffs, though, even if they won't go far in them. They have good possession numbers, a solid goaltender, and lots of young players who are only going to get better, even if they do have to rely on some old grizzled vets for now.

The combination of young and old in Florida is unique, but we may see more teams like this as the salary cap starts to create parity in the league – especially if this experiment works.

Shane O'Donnell

FLORIDA PANTHERS

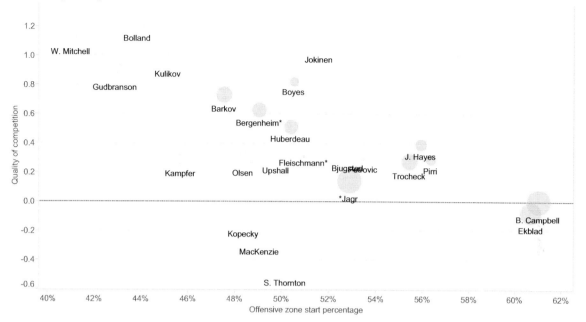

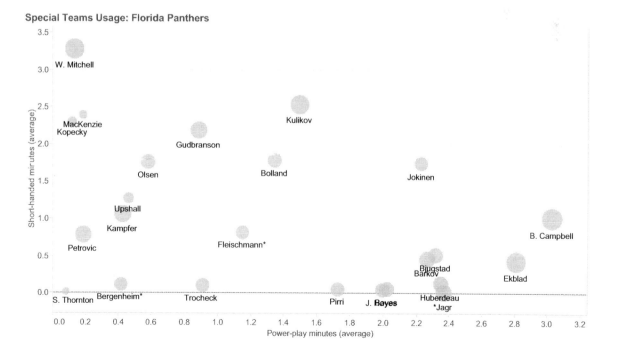

FLORIDA PANTHERS

Offensive Profile: Florida Panthers

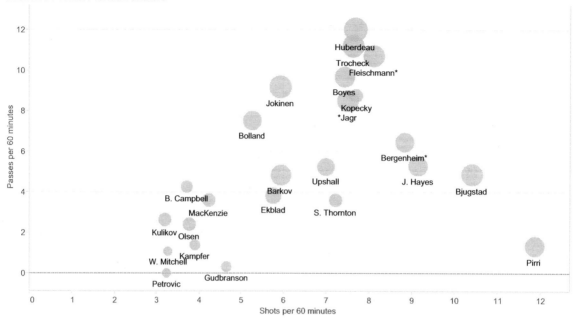

Cap Efficiency: Florida Panthers

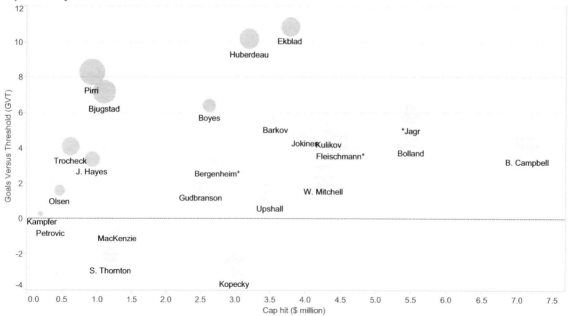

FLORIDA PANTHERS

FORWARDS

Aleksander Barkov — C — FLA

Season	Team	Age	GP	G	A	Pts	+/-	ESP/60	AdjCF%	iCF/60	OGVT	DGVT	SGVT	GVT
2013-14	FLA	18	54	8	16	24	-3	1.40	50.9%	8.4	0.6	1.6	-0.7	1.4
2014-15	FLA	19	71	16	20	36	-4	1.66	51.8%	9.5	4.1	1.6	-0.2	5.6
2015-16	FLA	20	66	17	24	41					4.3	1.9	0.0	6.1

Aleksander Barkov was having a decent age-19 season up until the legendary Jaromir Jagr was brought over in a trade with the floundering New Jersey Devils. After that, the 2013 second selection took off, cementing himself as the team's number-one center. The skilled Finn teamed up with Jagr and another of Florida's young guns, 2013 Calder Trophy winner Jonathan Huberdeau, to form a dominant line. Over the last 20 games, Barkov notched a promising 15 points. Add scoring touch to his size, skating, and tenacious defense and there is a chance Barkov could be considered a Bergeronesque two-way player within the next few years.

Nick Bjugstad — C — FLA

Season	Team	Age	GP	G	A	Pts	+/-	ESP/60	AdjCF%	iCF/60	OGVT	DGVT	SGVT	GVT
2012-13	FLA	20	11	1	0	1	-8	0.39	40.8%	7.1	-0.7	-0.4	0.0	-1.0
2013-14	FLA	21	76	16	22	38	-14	1.90	49.1%	14.2	3.8	1.8	0.4	6.0
2014-15	FLA	22	72	24	19	43	-7	1.88	49.9%	15.3	5.3	2.1	-0.2	7.2
2015-16	FLA	23	68	22	23	45					5.3	2.1	0.0	7.5

The Panthers have found their second-line center in six-foot-six Nick Bjugstad, who had a solid sophomore season, including 43 points in 72 games. Though there will be questions over his return to health after season-ending back surgery in March, his recent success should just be the tip of the iceberg as far as his talent is concerned. Not only does Bjugstad protect the puck with his size, but he has the ability to get close shots and beat NHL goalies. The Cats were wise to wrap up their big 23-year-old centerman with a six-year contract extension.

Dave Bolland — C — FLA

Season	Team	Age	GP	G	A	Pts	+/-	ESP/60	AdjCF%	iCF/60	OGVT	DGVT	SGVT	GVT
2012-13	CHI	26	35	7	7	14	-7	1.32	46.6%	7.9	0.0	0.2	0.0	0.2
2013-14	TOR	27	23	8	4	12	-1	1.85	44.2%	10.4	2.5	0.4	0.0	2.8
2014-15	FLA	28	53	6	17	23	4	1.45	49.4%	9.3	0.6	2.8	1.3	4.7
2015-16	FLA	29	53	9	16	25					1.7	2.0	0.1	3.8

A checking center on two Stanley Cup winners in Chicago, Dave Bolland had a season that wasn't as bad as expected, though he is still well below the Blackhawks version we all remember. Bolland was brought in by (ex-Chicago GM) Dale Tallon to be the team's shutdown center, a role that he is simply not fit for anymore. His underlying numbers weren't exactly terrible, but his production at five-on-five wasn't something that the team could be happy with. In his 53 games, his even-strength points per 60 minutes only ranked 251st out of 362 skaters (with 500+ minutes). The former London Knight is essentially a bottom-six player being paid the big bucks to bring intangibles to a team. It is a classic case of overpaying for the concept of a "proven winner".

Brad Boyes — RW — Free Agent

Season	Team	Age	GP	G	A	Pts	+/-	ESP/60	AdjCF%	iCF/60	OGVT	DGVT	SGVT	GVT
2012-13	NYI	30	48	10	25	35	-6	1.84	51.8%	12.7	4.4	0.9	-0.1	5.1
2013-14	FLA	31	78	21	15	36	-6	1.73	49.4%	13.7	2.5	2.6	2.5	7.7
2014-15	FLA	32	78	14	24	38	11	1.64	51.3%	12.1	3.5	3.0	-0.1	6.4
2015-16	Free Agent	33	65	14	20	34					3.0	2.2	0.0	5.3

Brad Boyes has bounced around the league, playing for San Jose, Boston, St. Louis, Buffalo, and the New York Islanders before ending up in Florida on a professional tryout contract in 2013. In his first year of that deal, he delivered what was expected of him, putting up a reasonable 38 points in 78 games for a player well into his thirties. Though the former Toronto draft choice was known for power-play success earlier in his career—as when he netted 43 goals for St. Louis in 2007-08—his even-strength play has picked up, his solid underlying numbers backed by a fringe top-six production rate. Simply put: Boyes turned out to be a steal.

Rocco Grimaldi — RW/C — FLA

Season	Team	Age	GP	G	A	Pts	+/-	ESP/60	AdjCF%	iCF/60	OGVT	DGVT	SGVT	GVT
2014-15	FLA	21	7	1	0	1	1	0.70	57.4%	18.1	0.0	0.2	0.0	0.3
2015-16	FLA	22	29	6	6	12					0.9	0.7	0.0	1.6

Rocco Grimaldi was tied with Martin St. Louis (prior to his retirement) for shortest man in the NHL, standing at a mere five-foot-six. He hasn't let that hold him back, though, having become one of Florida's more intriguing prospects with his game-changing offensive abilities. After a college career at North Dakota where he averaged about a point per game, the diminutive center turned pro and had a solid first AHL season, with 42 points in 64 games. In seven games with the big club, he was given highly-protected minutes, but showed some flashes of top-six potential. However, keep in mind that it is very difficult for players his size to be NHL contributors. Not everyone can be St. Louis.

Jimmy Hayes — RW — BOS

Season	Team	Age	GP	G	A	Pts	+/-	ESP/60	AdjCF%	iCF/60	OGVT	DGVT	SGVT	GVT
2012-13	CHI	23	10	1	3	4	0	1.73	45.3%	9.6	-0.1	0.1	0.0	0.0
2013-14	CHI, FLA	24	55	11	7	18	-5	1.57	45.6%	12.1	1.0	1.0	-0.6	1.4
2014-15	FLA	25	72	19	16	35	-4	1.53	51.3%	13.6	2.3	1.7	-0.5	3.4
2015-16	BOS	26	64	16	16	33					2.7	1.6	0.0	4.3

Big-bodied Jimmy Hayes demonstrated that he could be an effective third liner, scoring 19 goals and adding 16 assists in 72 games. The brother of the Rangers' Kevin Hayes, Jimmy does not quite bring the possession dominance of his bro as he simply lacks the puck skills and does not use his body as effectively. Moving on from Florida, if the Bruins expect Hayes to bring more than one-dimensional goal scoring—in the wake of Milan Lucic's departure—they will be disappointed.

Jonathan Huberdeau — C — FLA

Season	Team	Age	GP	G	A	Pts	+/-	ESP/60	AdjCF%	iCF/60	OGVT	DGVT	SGVT	GVT
2012-13	FLA	19	48	14	17	31	-15	1.89	49.4%	13.5	5.4	0.8	0.5	6.6
2013-14	FLA	20	69	9	19	28	-5	1.46	49.2%	9.8	1.4	1.9	0.2	3.5
2014-15	FLA	21	79	15	39	54	10	2.24	51.9%	12.1	7.6	3.4	-0.8	10.2
2015-16	FLA	22	72	18	34	52					6.3	2.8	0.0	9.1

Jonathan Huberdeau rebounded nicely in his third NHL season after experiencing a sophomore slump. This was great for fans to see, as the 2011 third-overall selection had shown flashes of top-end skill in his rookie season, culminating in being named the Calder Trophy winner. The Quebec native developed a knack for creating turnovers in the neutral zone, and had positive possession metrics, an improvement over last year, where he was consistently in the negative. If he continues to trend in the right direction, the partnership of Huberdeau and Barkov could be a force for years to come, and a cornerstone of the franchise.

Jaromir Jagr — RW — FLA

Season	Team	Age	GP	G	A	Pts	+/-	ESP/60	AdjCF%	iCF/60	OGVT	DGVT	SGVT	GVT
2012-13	DAL, BOS	40	45	16	19	35	-2	2.11	53.1%	13.4	4.8	0.3	0.5	5.6
2013-14	NJD	41	82	24	43	67	16	2.26	59.4%	14.4	9.7	5.4	-0.8	14.3
2014-15	NJD, FLA	42	77	17	30	47	-3	1.85	52.8%	12.8	4.2	2.3	-0.5	5.9
2015-16	FLA	43	65	12	24	36					3.0	1.9	0.0	4.9

Jaromir Jagr, the ageless wonder, added to his growing list of NHL teams when he was traded from the New Jersey Devils to the Panthers four days before the 2015 trade deadline. In Florida, Jagr had a revival. He had instant chemistry with Barkov and Huberdeau, averaging almost a point per game (18 points in 20 games). Though the 43-year-old obviously doesn't have the same jump in his step as he did 20+ years ago, he is savvy as hell and still impossible to get the puck away from. After Wayne Gretzky and Gordie Howe, there is a compelling argument that Jagr is the third-most-valuable forward of all time. By career GVT (378.5), he is well ahead of a pack of legends including Yzerman, Esposito, Messier, and Lemieux in providing value to his teams.

Jussi Jokinen — LW/C — FLA

Season	Team	Age	GP	G	A	Pts	+/-	ESP/60	AdjCF%	iCF/60	OGVT	DGVT	SGVT	GVT
2012-13	CAR, PIT	29	43	13	9	22	-5	1.78	52.5%	12.8	4.6	0.5	0.5	5.6
2013-14	PIT	30	81	21	36	57	12	1.99	55.4%	13.2	9.2	3.0	-0.7	11.5
2014-15	FLA	31	81	8	36	44	-2	2.03	50.6%	9.0	3.7	2.7	-1.4	5.0
2015-16	FLA	32	67	14	28	42					4.4	2.3	0.0	6.7

Out of the six free agents that Dale Tallon brought in during the offseason, Jussi Jokinen was the most productive, averaging over two points every 60 minutes of five-on-five play. The captain of the Finnish squad at the IIHF brings versatility as a center or wing who can play a third-line role or fill in on a top line if needed. Though his performance did decline throughout the year, it seems likely he will take some of the easier minutes as the young guns grow.

Corban Knight — C — FLA

Season	Team	Age	GP	G	A	Pts	+/-	ESP/60	AdjCF%	iCF/60	OGVT	DGVT	SGVT	GVT
2013-14	CGY	23	7	1	0	1	-1	1.12	42.3%	4.5	-0.4	0.1	0.6	0.3
2014-15	CGY	24	2	0	0	0	0	0.00	48.3%	17.3	0.0	0.0	-0.3	-0.3
2015-16	FLA	25	27	5	6	11					0.6	0.6	0.0	1.2

After a solid career at the University of North Dakota, including a 49-point senior season, Corban Knight has produced at a solid level in his first two AHL seasons, posting 80 points in 128 games. At six-foot-two and 200 pounds, the fifth rounder from 2009 has the size and willingness to play a bottom-six NHL role, but it is unclear whether he can keep up at the NHL pace or offer enough offense to be given a regular shot.

Tomas Kopecky — RW — Free Agent

Season	Team	Age	GP	G	A	Pts	+/-	ESP/60	AdjCF%	iCF/60	OGVT	DGVT	SGVT	GVT
2012-13	FLA	30	47	15	12	27	-8	1.58	45.8%	12.1	4.5	1.5	0.0	6.1
2013-14	FLA	31	49	4	8	12	0	1.06	50.9%	12.7	0.2	1.3	1.2	2.7
2014-15	FLA	32	64	2	6	8	-19	0.72	47.6%	15.0	-2.7	0.3	-0.3	-2.6
2015-16	Free Agent	33	51	5	7	12					-0.3	1.1	0.0	0.8

Two years removed from surprisingly leading the team in goals, Tomas Kopecky found himself playing exclusively on the fourth line. Though it is clear the Slovakian forward is not the player that he used to be, he still provided some value as a depth contributor. Florida's fourth line was at its best when it consisted of Kopecky, Derek Mackenzie, and Scottie Upshall. All three players are proven NHL forwards, a big upgrade from many bottom lines that are made up of grinders or call-ups.

Derek MacKenzie — C — FLA

Season	Team	Age	GP	G	A	Pts	+/-	ESP/60	AdjCF%	iCF/60	OGVT	DGVT	SGVT	GVT
2012-13	CBJ	31	43	3	5	8	1	1.26	41.2%	9.4	-0.4	1.6	0.0	1.2
2013-14	CBJ	32	71	9	9	18	0	1.36	49.6%	11.5	1.6	2.1	0.0	3.7
2014-15	FLA	33	82	5	6	11	-17	0.74	48.6%	8.0	-2.5	1.5	0.6	-0.4
2015-16	FLA	34	59	5	6	11					-0.7	1.4	0.0	0.8

Derek Mackenzie had a successful season by conventional standards, as his high-energy, grind-it-out style endeared the 33-year-old to fans and coaches alike. The long-time Blue Jacket averaged over 12 minutes per game, a career high, and punched the clock for all 82 games. The depth center experienced success when lining up with Tomas Kopecky and Scottie Upshall, so it will be up to the coaching staff to find Mackenzie some quality replacements at the fourth-line wings. He is not the type who can carry anyone.

Brandon Pirri — C — FLA

Season	Team	Age	GP	G	A	Pts	+/-	ESP/60	AdjCF%	iCF/60	OGVT	DGVT	SGVT	GVT
2012-13	CHI	21	1	0	0	0	0	0.00	49.9%	10.3	0.0	0.0	0.0	0.0
2013-14	CHI, FLA	22	49	13	12	25	6	2.02	51.2%	13.5	4.5	1.7	0.6	6.8
2014-15	FLA	23	49	22	2	24	6	1.60	51.9%	17.5	5.9	1.7	0.8	8.3
2015-16	FLA	24	51	18	11	29					4.3	1.6	0.0	5.9

FLORIDA PANTHERS

Brandon Pirri had one of the weirdest stat lines the NHL has ever seen. Despite scoring 22 goals, he ended up with only 24 total points. First of all, it is unlikely that the 2009 second rounder replicates his 0.45 goals-per-game pace, as he benefitted from a lofty 15.6 shooting percentage. However, he does have one of the highest shot-attempt rates in the NHL (27th among skaters with 500+ minutes), so he should at least match his goal production from 2013-14, especially if he plays the full season. At other levels (NCAA and AHL), and in other seasons, the one-time single-season RPI Engineer had significantly more assists than goals—all the more reason to conclude that it was a one-time fluky season.

Shawn Thornton — LW — FLA

Season	Team	Age	GP	G	A	Pts	+/-	ESP/60	AdjCF%	iCF/60	OGVT	DGVT	SGVT	GVT
2012-13	BOS	35	45	3	4	7	1	1.15	50.2%	16.6	-0.1	0.6	0.0	0.4
2013-14	BOS	36	64	5	3	8	3	0.86	49.9%	16.4	-0.5	1.0	0.0	0.5
2014-15	FLA	37	46	1	4	5	-13	0.69	49.0%	11.4	-1.8	-0.3	0.0	-2.1
2015-16	FLA	38	45	3	4	7					-0.5	0.6	0.0	0.1

The league has changed drastically over the last 10 years, meaning players like Shawn Thornton no longer find themselves as useful as they used to be. In the past, the two-time Stanley Cup champion (Ducks and Bruins) would have been effective in a fourth-line role by dispensing toughness and "policing" the opposition. However, the enforcer role has all but died out, with bare-knuckle brawls no longer common in NHL games. Consequently, players like Thornton now drag their team down, contributing little in terms of production or possession. The best place for Thornton is the press box, so he can continue to be a positive locker-room presence without hurting the team's on-ice performance.

Vincent Trocheck — C — FLA

Season	Team	Age	GP	G	A	Pts	+/-	ESP/60	AdjCF%	iCF/60	OGVT	DGVT	SGVT	GVT
2013-14	FLA	20	20	5	3	8	-11	1.28	49.1%	11.7	-0.1	-0.2	0.6	0.3
2014-15	FLA	21	50	7	15	22	9	1.94	53.3%	12.1	2.1	2.5	-0.4	4.1
2015-16	FLA	22	55	12	18	29					2.7	1.9	0.0	4.6

Vincent Trocheck is one of the Florida's most intriguing prospects. As a third-round pick, he has more to prove than players like Huberdeau or Barkov in order to receive top-six or top-nine minutes, but his hands and vision will give him a good shot at showing he belongs. The former Saginaw Spirit captain was second on the Panthers in five-on-five scoring and the top Corsi-percentage forward. The Pittsburgh native is a natural center, but might have to adapt to playing wing with Barkov and Bjugstad taking up the top two spots. However, he could serve as a versatile forward, shifting between third-line center and top-six wing.

Scottie Upshall — RW — Free Agent

Season	Team	Age	GP	G	A	Pts	+/-	ESP/60	AdjCF%	iCF/60	OGVT	DGVT	SGVT	GVT
2012-13	FLA	29	27	4	1	5	-8	0.78	45.6%	13.6	0.1	0.0	0.0	0.1
2013-14	FLA	30	76	15	22	37	1	1.81	50.2%	13.8	4.7	2.6	-0.3	7.0
2014-15	FLA	31	63	8	7	15	-8	1.22	50.4%	13.1	-0.2	2.0	-0.3	1.5
2015-16	Free Agent	32	59	10	12	22					1.5	1.8	0.0	3.3

Scottie Upshall, the 2002 sixth-overall pick, represents a paradoxical group: high draft-pick busts who end up having solid careers. Upshall was an 80-point, 100-PIM player in his draft year, leading Nashville to believe he would become a power forward. Instead, he topped out at 37 points and was never much more than a third liner. Injuries also took their toll, as the Alberta native couldn't exceed 70 games played until 2013-14. Still, a long NHL career is admirable – though Upshall's may be nearing the end.

Garrett Wilson						LW						FLA
Season	Team	Age	GP	G	A	Pts	+/-	ESP/60	AdjCF%	iCF/60	OGVT	DGVT	SGVT	GVT
2013-14	FLA	22	3	0	0	0	-1	0.00	44.0%	7.7	-0.2	-0.1	0.0	-0.2
2014-15	FLA	23	2	0	0	0	-2	0.00	45.8%	25.2	-0.3	-0.1	0.0	-0.4
2015-16	FLA	24	26	5	6	11					0.6	0.5	0.0	1.1

Prospects often just need an opportunity to showcase their skill, and this is exactly what happened with Garrett Wilson in 2014-15. The 23-year-old got consistent top-six AHL ice-time after Quinton Howden went down with an injury. Consequently, he managed to score 23 goals and add 15 assists over 71 games. Though that total isn't the most impressive, it earned Wilson a two-game NHL cameo, where he looked solid. It is unlikely that the 2011 OHL champion (with Owen Sound) has potential to be anything besides a fourth liner but he will have the opportunity to compete for a roster spot out of training camp.

DEFENSEMEN

Jesse Blacker						RD						FLA
Season	Team	Age	GP	G	A	Pts	+/-	ESP/60	AdjCF%	iCF/60	OGVT	DGVT	SGVT	GVT
2014-15	ANA	23	1	0	0	0	-2	0.00	12.9%	0.0	-0.1	-0.3	0.0	-0.4
2015-16	DAL	24	24	2	5	7					0.4	0.7	0.0	1.0

Jesse Blacker played just one game for the Ducks and it didn't go so well. The 24-year-old blueliner was a -2 plus/minus and was on the ice for 11 shot attempts against and just two shot attempts for in less than seven minutes on the ice. You can only go up from there! The second-round pick of the Leafs in 2009 showed some potential early on in his pro career with the Toronto Marlies, scoring 16 points in 58 games in his first full AHL season. However, he has not built on that start. Touted as an offensive-minded defender, Blacker has simply never proven he can be above average on the offensive end. With poor defensive skills, Blacker does not project to have an NHL future.

Brian Campbell						LD						FLA
Season	Team	Age	GP	G	A	Pts	+/-	ESP/60	AdjCF%	iCF/60	OGVT	DGVT	SGVT	GVT
2012-13	FLA	33	48	8	19	27	-22	0.61	49.8%	5.3	4.5	0.3	0.0	4.9
2013-14	FLA	34	82	7	30	37	-6	0.80	50.9%	6.4	3.3	3.3	0.0	6.6
2014-15	FLA	35	82	3	24	27	4	0.57	54.2%	5.9	0.6	3.9	-0.3	4.3
2015-16	FLA	36	64	5	20	25					1.7	3.4	0.0	5.1

Brian Campbell continued his iron-man streak for the Panthers, as he was one of only two players who played in all 82 contests. In total, he now has laced up for 304 consecutive games and has been an asset for his team in nearly every one of them. The former Sabre has experienced some decline in his play, but overall, was still a top-20 defenseman at five-on-five in terms of possession. The under-the-radar value Campbell brought to the Panthers was as the defensive partner of star rookie Aaron Ekblad, the 2014 first-overall pick. The 2010 Stanley

Cup champion provided a calming presence for the youngster and relieved some of the puck-handling pressure for the Calder Trophy winner.

Aaron Ekblad — RD — FLA

Season	Team	Age	GP	G	A	Pts	+/-	ESP/60	AdjCF%	iCF/60	OGVT	DGVT	SGVT	GVT
2014-15	FLA	18	81	12	27	39	12	1.04	53.4%	10.3	6.3	4.9	-0.3	10.9
2015-16	FLA	19	76	12	32	44					6.4	4.4	0.0	10.8

Phil Housley and Bobby Orr are the only two defensemen in NHL history to have better 18-year-old seasons than Aaron Ekblad. Though the former OHL standout played with underrated veteran Brian Campbell—who has a knack for making his partners look better than they are—the man-child produced at a nearly unprecedented level for a player of his age and showed plenty of poise along the way. Is it too soon to project him as the next Duncan Keith or Drew Doughty caliber defenseman? Maybe. But Ekblad's draft status, maturity, and skillset suggest it won't be long before he is considered a top-of-the-league defender. The only question is how much he will grow from here.

Erik Gudbranson — RD — FLA

Season	Team	Age	GP	G	A	Pts	+/-	ESP/60	AdjCF%	iCF/60	OGVT	DGVT	SGVT	GVT
2012-13	FLA	20	32	0	4	4	-22	0.34	46.1%	8.8	-0.9	-1.0	0.0	-1.9
2013-14	FLA	21	65	3	6	9	-7	0.49	49.2%	11.0	-0.9	2.0	0.0	1.0
2014-15	FLA	22	76	4	9	13	-4	0.46	49.0%	9.7	-1.3	3.4	-0.3	1.9
2015-16	FLA	23	65	4	11	15					0.1	3.2	0.0	3.3

Though he hasn't lived up to the expectations of a former third-overall pick, six-foot-five Eric Gudbranson has turned into a modestly effective defensive defenseman for the Panthers. Still struggling with his puck skills, the Ottawa native reminds us of how difficult it can be to project big, athletic blueliners at the top of the draft. At 23, another year of development should be good for the former Kingston Frontenac, and though he won't "wow" with his production, he should be a useful piece for the Panthers.

Steven Kampfer — RD — FLA

Season	Team	Age	GP	G	A	Pts	+/-	ESP/60	AdjCF%	iCF/60	OGVT	DGVT	SGVT	GVT
2014-15	FLA	26	25	2	2	4	-4	0.46	47.8%	9.3	0.0	0.3	0.0	0.3
2015-16	FLA	27	36	2	6	9					0.5	1.1	0.0	1.5

When the New York Rangers decided to keep Anthony Duclair up on their pro roster at the beginning of the 2014-15 season, they needed to open up space in their organization to stay within the 50-contract limit. As a result, they made a trade with the Panthers, sending big AHLer Andrew Yogan along with Steven Kampfer to Florida in exchange for AAAA journeyman Joey Crabb. The Cats certainly won that deal: the 26-year-old Kampfer made his first NHL appearance since 2011-12, and acquitted himself as a solid depth option for head coach Gerard Gallant. The team liked Kampfer so much, in fact, that they signed him to a two-year deal near the end of the season. Kampfer is a good depth defenseman, who can provide solid play on the third pairing.

Dmitry Kulikov — LD — FLA

Season	Team	Age	GP	G	A	Pts	+/-	ESP/60	AdjCF%	iCF/60	OGVT	DGVT	SGVT	GVT
2012-13	FLA	22	34	3	7	10	-5	0.41	47.8%	7.9	0.4	1.7	0.0	2.1
2013-14	FLA	23	81	8	11	19	-26	0.55	49.6%	7.3	-0.3	0.6	-0.8	-0.5
2014-15	FLA	24	73	3	19	22	0	0.71	50.7%	6.6	1.3	4.0	-0.3	5.0
2015-16	FLA	25	66	5	17	21					1.3	3.1	0.0	4.3

Though his offensive game hasn't developed in the way that many had hoped, Dmitry Kulikov has become a solid two-way defenseman. The Russian blueliner may have had a slightly negative Relative Corsi, but he also received the toughest minutes on the team with the Campbell-Ekblad pairing receiving easier ice-time. If the team wants to give Kulikov a benchmark to strive for, it is his game against Dallas at the end of the season. After getting into a fight, Kulikov would score a goal and make a beautiful assist to help the team pick up a point in an overtime loss. In that contest, his offense was on full display, but his defensive play wasn't compromised—exactly what the team should want from their former first-round pick.

Willie Mitchell — LD — FLA

Season	Team	Age	GP	G	A	Pts	+/-	ESP/60	AdjCF%	iCF/60	OGVT	DGVT	SGVT	GVT
2013-14	LAK	36	76	1	11	12	14	0.47	56.1%	7.9	-1.9	7.1	0.0	5.2
2014-15	FLA	37	66	3	5	8	1	0.35	50.3%	9.0	-1.8	4.6	-0.3	2.5
2015-16	FLA	38	58	2	9	11					-0.5	3.8	0.0	3.3

After winning two Stanley Cups with the Kings, Willie Mitchell signed a two-year deal with the Panthers to help the young, developing team, while collecting a check for more than most contenders were interested in paying. The former Clarkson Golden Knight performed his leadership role to perfection after being named the team's captain, even taking in Aaron Ekblad and being a father figure to him throughout the season. On the ice, he can still play. The hope for next year is that Mitchell continues to take on some of the more difficult assignments, allowing other players to flourish offensively.

Shane O'Brien — LD — ANA

Season	Team	Age	GP	G	A	Pts	+/-	ESP/60	AdjCF%	iCF/60	OGVT	DGVT	SGVT	GVT
2012-13	COL	29	28	0	4	4	0	0.57	51.4%	7.9	-0.4	0.9	0.0	0.5
2013-14	CGY	30	45	0	3	3	-8	0.36	42.6%	6.5	-1.3	0.8	0.0	-0.6
2014-15	FLA	31	9	0	1	1	-4	0.52	42.2%	2.1	-0.3	-0.2	0.0	-0.4
2015-16	ANA	32	33	1	4	5					-0.3	0.9	0.0	0.5

During the summer of 2014, long-time NHL defenseman Dale Tallon decided that his team needed defensive depth, bringing Shane O'Brien into camp on a PTO. The 31-year-old defenseman was eventually signed to a two-way contract, and he suited up for the Cats for nine contests, getting onto the scoreboard with an assist. O'Brien didn't fare well at even strength, but he is a big body who filled his role perfectly. Going forward, O'Brien could stick around the AHL, and if injuries strike, be promoted for a handful of games. Asking him to do more is risky, as he is really not capable of playing in a full-time NHL role. We will see if Bob Murray and the Anaheim Ducks agree with that assessment.

FLORIDA PANTHERS

Dylan Olsen — LD — FLA

Season	Team	Age	GP	G	A	Pts	+/-	ESP/60	AdjCF%	iCF/60	OGVT	DGVT	SGVT	GVT
2013-14	FLA	22	44	3	9	12	-3	1.09	48.7%	8.8	1.3	1.6	0.0	2.8
2014-15	FLA	23	44	2	6	8	-7	0.70	48.6%	7.9	-0.2	1.2	0.6	1.6
2015-16	FLA	24	46	3	9	12					0.7	1.9	0.0	2.6

Dylan Olsen was brought over to the Panthers in a trade with the Blackhawks, who had given up on the big defenseman after he failed to develop over three seasons with the organization. During his first season in Florida, he had some success alongside Erik Gudbranson, but his second season with the Panthers did not bring about the same results. Olsen got caved in at even strength, and was eventually sent back down to San Antonio. At this point, it is unlikely that he returns to the NHL as anything besides an injury call-up.

Alex Petrovic — RD — FLA

Season	Team	Age	GP	G	A	Pts	+/-	ESP/60	AdjCF%	iCF/60	OGVT	DGVT	SGVT	GVT
2012-13	FLA	20	6	0	0	0	-8	0.00	47.6%	7.8	-0.5	-0.7	0.0	-1.2
2013-14	FLA	21	7	0	1	1	3	0.74	42.3%	7.9	-0.2	0.8	0.0	0.7
2014-15	FLA	22	33	0	3	3	-4	0.36	47.6%	6.6	-0.8	0.6	0.0	-0.3
2015-16	FLA	23	39	1	5	7					-0.2	1.4	0.0	1.2

Alex Petrovic has been a solid defensive prospect for a number of years. After playing almost 150 AHL games, he finally made the jump to the NHL and stuck. Though he only managed three points in 33 games and was at the bottom end of the spectrum for many relative possession metrics, the large D-man has some upside at as a bottom-pairing guy. He will have to fight for a spot on the NHL roster, but some progress could turn him into a low-end regular.

GOALTENDERS

Dan Ellis — G — WSH

Season	Team	Age	GP	W	L	OT	GAA	Sv%	ESSV%	QS%	GGVT	DGVT	SGVT	GVT
2012-13	CAR	32	19	6	8	2	3.13	.906	.920	43.8%	-0.5	-0.7	-0.2	-1.4
2013-14	DAL, FLA	33	20	5	11	0	3.62	.879	.879	25.0%	-12.8	0.0	0.8	-12.0
2014-15	FLA	34	8	4	3	1	2.35	.914	.920	50.0%	0.9	0.2	0.7	1.8
2015-16	WSH	35	15					.909			-0.9	0.0	0.1	-0.8

Dan Ellis is a classic journeyman goaltender. He has bounced around from team to team, playing for Dallas, Nashville, Tampa Bay, Anaheim, and Carolina before making his way to south Florida. He played most of the season in the AHL, but was called into action after both Luongo and Montoya went down with injury. During that stretch, he provided solid play, with a .914 save percentage. Asking much more than fill-in duty as a backup from Ellis, at this point, would be too much.

Roberto Luongo — G — FLA

Season	Team	Age	GP	W	L	OT	GAA	Sv%	ESSV%	QS%	GGVT	DGVT	SGVT	GVT
2012-13	VAN	33	20	9	6	3	2.56	.907	.920	61.1%	0.7	0.2	0.0	0.8
2013-14	VAN, FLA	34	56	25	23	7	2.40	.919	.925	57.1%	13.6	0.0	0.8	14.4
2014-15	FLA	35	61	28	19	12	2.35	.921	.932	59.0%	16.5	-0.2	1.3	17.7
2015-16	FLA	36	45					.917			8.2	0.0	0.2	8.5

FLORIDA PANTHERS

Roberto Luongo had a successful first season back in Florida after finally—finally—being traded from Vancouver at the 2014 deadline—the longest ongoing drama in hockey. "Bobby Lu" gave the Cats something that they hadn't had for a while: solid goaltending. From 2012-2014, the team had a league-worst .893 save percentage. Contrast that with 2014-15, when the team was tied for 12th with a .912 mark. Florida's defense has to be given some credit, as their improved roster clearly made life easier on netminders than in the recent past. That said, it was still great for the team to have a solid presence on the back end, and though the two-time Olympic gold medalist is 36, he should continue providing solid to above-average goaltending for the next couple of years.

Al Montoya — G — FLA

Season	Team	Age	GP	W	L	OT	GAA	Sv%	ESSV%	QS%	GGVT	DGVT	SGVT	GVT
2012-13	WPG	27	7	3	1	0	2.91	.899	.909	40.0%	-1.3	0.0	0.0	-1.2
2013-14	WPG	28	28	13	8	3	2.30	.920	.925	59.1%	7.5	0.2	-1.3	6.3
2014-15	FLA	29	20	6	7	2	3.01	.892	.895	53.8%	-6.7	0.2	-1.9	-8.3
2015-16	FLA	30	20					.911			0.1	0.0	-0.3	-0.2

There was a lot of interest in how Al Montoya would perform in his first season in south Florida, as he is the first Cuban American to play in the NHL, and would hopefully help the team expand its audience by appealing to Hispanic fans in the area. Unfortunately, the sixth-overall pick for the Rangers in 2004 had a poor year, with a sub-.900 save percentage, a big reason why the team struggled to win games without Luongo in net. Obviously, the backup isn't going to provide the same level of play as the starter, but Montoya needs to better if the Cats want to rest Luongo without taking it on the chin in the standings.

Shane O'Donnell

Los Angeles Kings

The inevitability of age and inconsistency finally caught up with the Los Angeles Kings. Yes, they were a team that always seemed to dig a hole for themselves before clawing back into the playoffs. Yes, they always seemed to save their best for the stretch run and the postseason. Unfortunately, this time around, the Kings were unable to get out of the hole that they dug in the middle third of the season. It may come as a surprise, but they were still one of the better teams in the league despite the standings.

Why did they miss the playoffs?

Los Angeles were absent from the playoffs for the first time in five seasons. Ignominiously, they became the first defending champions to miss the postseason since the 2006-07 Carolina Hurricanes. But from an analysis of their advanced stats, it is obvious they were playing a winning game.

The Kings were yet again a top-five possession team with a solid defense. They had shifts in personnel, and their fair share of inconsistent performances to deal with, but overall, the team did not look much different from previous years. Better shootout and overtime results would have put the Kings right back in the thick of it come late April and May.

There were subtle differences from previous years. For instance, the Kings fared poorly in close games. Although no stalwarts in one-goal contests in previous years, Los Angeles held an abysmal 13-9-15 record in one-goal games in 2014-15 compared to their 21-14-8 record in 2013-14. In particular, individual performances in one-goal games were telling. Key players like Marian Gaborik, Jeff Carter, Drew Doughty, Anze Kopitar, Justin Williams, and Dustin Brown all saw dips in Fenwick percentages in close games (tied or within one goal). Kopitar went from 62.2 to a 57.7, Gaborik dropped from 67.7 to a 61.9, and Doughty, the Kings franchise defenseman, dipped from 59.0 down to 54.5. The Kings were simply not as good when it came to protecting one-goal leads, fighting back from one-goal deficits, or playing in tie games.

The poor close-game play may have simply been indicative of the Kings not being quite as good as they were in the past, despite some overall numbers indicating they were still a top dog.

Will they bounce back?

While the Kings have loads of elite talent, they also have some toxic contracts. There is the debacle of Mike Richards, the limbo of Slava Voynov, and the hefty price tags of players like Dustin Brown, that have left the

KINGS IN A BOX

Last Season

Goals For	220	20th
Goals Against	205	7th
GVT	15	14th
Points	95	18th
Playoffs	Did not make playoffs	

The Kings came out of the gate slowly, and finished two points shy of the playoffs.

Three-Year Record

GVT	62	9th
Points	254	9th
Playoffs	2 Appearances, 25 Wins, 1 Cup	

VUKOTA Projection

Goals For	223	13th
Goals Against	210	2nd
GVT	13	8th
Points	96	8th

Los Angeles won the Stanley Cup 16 months ago, but with Voynov gone they will be good, not great.

Top Three Prospects

A. Kempe (F), N. Shore (F), M. Mersch (F)

Kings with little more than a few million in cap space and a lot of work to be done. They are in a position where promoting from within and expanding player roles from within might be the most reasonable option. Do they have the horses for that, though? Some numbers would suggest yes, other numbers would suggest no.

L.A. possesses several young players ready to break out, or who have already broken out. Tyler Toffoli, Tanner Pearson, and Brayden McNabb all look like solid NHL players, and their numbers place them near the top of several analytics categories. Toffoli ranked second amongst King forwards in GVT while McNabb was third amongst King defensemen. If Pearson had not suffered a season-ending ankle injury, he may have landed toward the top.

Where there are talented youngsters who could become the next core of role players, there is also a questionable group of youngish, mid-career veterans in Brown, Trevor Lewis, Kyle Clifford, Jordan Nolan, and Dwight King who may not be able to bring what they once did to the lineup. With the departures of Jarret Stoll, Justin Williams, and (it seems) Mike Richards, someone has to fill in. Lewis is coming off his best statistical season, logging highs in points, goals, Corsi for, and shooting percentage. His short-lived, yet impressive time on the Kings top line with Kopitar and Gaborik suggested that there may be more to the Utah native than a simple defensive specialist. Others do not show quite the same promise. Nolan and Clifford appear to be no more than fourth-line grinders.

The biggest gap is in the decline of Brown and the lack of a suitable replacement. That means Nick Shore will have the task of stepping in as the Kings third-line center. Two-way superstar Kopitar managed nearly a goal less per 60 minutes with Brown (1.73) versus without Brown (2.72), not a good sign. The L.A captain managed 51.7 Corsi for and 47.7 Goals for percentages away from Kopitar.

The Kings will have the rely more than ever on their top six. Carter and Kopitar form one of the NHL's most formidable offensive-defensive one-two punches down the middle. The Kings had eight players in the top 20 in even-strength Corsi for percentage, and four within the top 40 in Corsi for per 60 minute rate. With a still-productive Gaborik and burgeoning young talents like Pearson and Toffoli rounding out the top six, it is hard to be too downtrodden. Jake Muzzin and Doughty remain an elite defensive tandem, McNabb has shown some promise, and 2012 Conn Smythe winner Jonathan Quick continues to be a top-10 goaltender (depending on the time of the year, that is) who earns his team plenty of points. They may not have the depth or money they had in previous years, but the Kings still project as a postseason competitor for the near future. Bouncing back to co-dynasty status with the Blackhawks, however, is going to be difficult.

The modern-day NHL is cyclical. Up periods eventually make way for down periods, and the Kings may be approaching a down period. However, with a little bit of savvy, some shrewd roster management, a few unexpected player performances, and maybe even a rookie contributor or two (Jordan Weal?), it may turn out like the Chicago's "down period" of 2010-2012. That little bit of a transition period seems to be working out pretty well for the Hawks these days. Chicago was able to move out players who would normally be overpaid while ushering in the next wave of young guns. Can L.A. be as savvy? We shall see.

Jason Lewis

LOS ANGELES KINGS

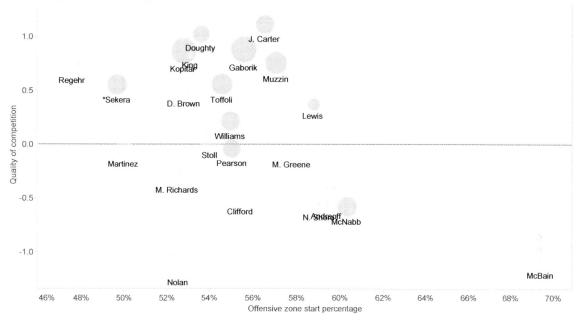

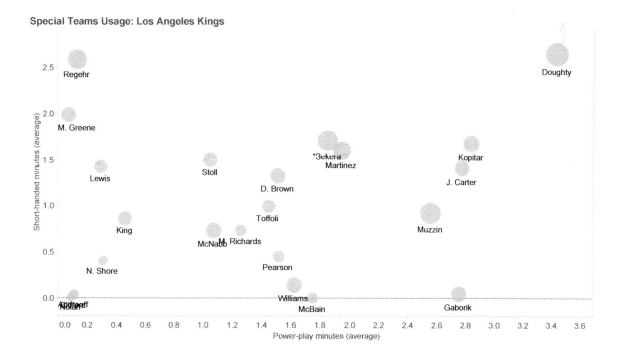

LOS ANGELES KINGS

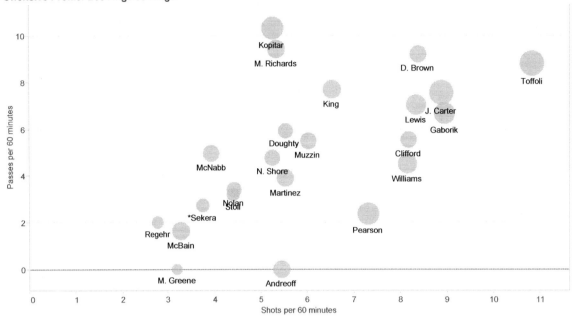

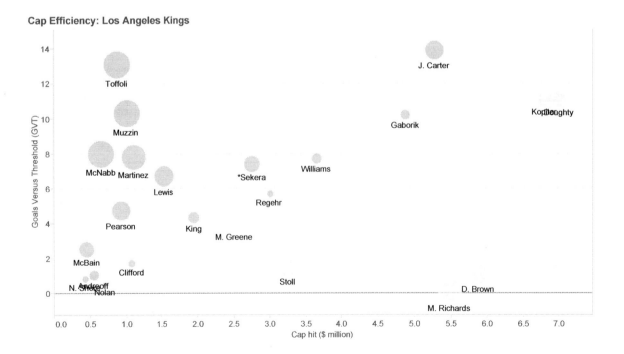

LOS ANGELES KINGS

FORWARDS

Andy Andreoff							C/LW							LAK
Season	Team	Age	GP	G	A	Pts	+/-	ESP/60	AdjCF%	iCF/60	OGVT	DGVT	SGVT	GVT
2014-15	LAK	23	18	2	1	3	1	1.18	46.6%	10.6	0.6	0.4	0.0	1.0
2015-16	LAK	24	34	6	6	12					0.9	0.8	0.0	1.7

Andy Andreoff was put in an awkward position for 2014-15. His play in the AHL warranted an opportunity at the Los Angeles bottom six, but the gritty center's waiver exemption status was void. As a result, he was relegated to just 18 games on an inconsistent basis due to the Kings not wanting to risk placing him on waivers and losing him. Further, his possession metrics did not help his case for staying in the lineup: the former Oshawa General finished as the worst possession forward on the Kings. That said, Andreoff had fairly good faceoff numbers and ended the year looking more comfortable with the NHL game than at the beginning.

Dustin Brown							RW							LAK
Season	Team	Age	GP	G	A	Pts	+/-	ESP/60	AdjCF%	iCF/60	OGVT	DGVT	SGVT	GVT
2012-13	LAK	28	46	18	11	29	6	1.36	60.3%	17.3	4.1	2.4	0.5	7.0
2013-14	LAK	29	79	15	12	27	7	1.32	58.6%	17.6	-0.3	3.3	0.0	3.0
2014-15	LAK	30	82	11	16	27	-17	1.12	55.2%	16.1	-0.2	1.5	0.0	1.3
2015-16	LAK	31	66	13	15	27					1.7	2.0	0.0	3.7

Dustin Brown had his worst statistical season to date. Rookie year notwithstanding, the L.A. captain logged a career low in goals and points with just 11 and 27 in 82 games. However, some of that can be attributed to bad luck—the 30-year-old forward had a 5.8% shooting percentage, nearly half his career average. Overall, he was putting up similar possession numbers and playing a very similar game to his last three seasons. The two-time Cup winner has seen far less time alongside Anze Kopitar on the top line the last two seasons, which is definitely hurting him—he totaled just 311 even-strength minutes alongside #11. A hard-checking playing style could also be contributing to an early decline, making a significant bounceback an unsure thing.

Jeff Carter							C							LAK
Season	Team	Age	GP	G	A	Pts	+/-	ESP/60	AdjCF%	iCF/60	OGVT	DGVT	SGVT	GVT
2012-13	LAK	28	48	26	7	33	0	2.10	56.0%	18.6	5.8	2.3	1.0	9.0
2013-14	LAK	29	72	27	23	50	8	2.06	57.2%	20.7	6.1	3.9	-0.1	9.9
2014-15	LAK	30	82	28	34	62	7	2.39	57.0%	17.0	9.8	4.8	-0.6	13.9
2015-16	LAK	31	75	26	32	58					7.7	3.3	0.0	10.9

Jeff Carter was the straw that stirred the L.A. Kings offensive drink, second on the team with 62 points while leading the squad with 28 goals. With Tyler Toffoli, he formed one of the more formidable scoring duos in the Western Conference. It would have been a monster offensive year for the former Flyer had he scored more than 10 power-play points. It is rare for a player to switch positions or change their game mid-prime, but Carter became a go-to penalty killer and moved back to center, performing well in the faceoff circle. If the Kings improve their power play, the six-foot-four freakish skater will see his stats jump.

Kyle Clifford — LW — LAK

Season	Team	Age	GP	G	A	Pts	+/-	ESP/60	AdjCF%	iCF/60	OGVT	DGVT	SGVT	GVT
2012-13	LAK	21	48	7	7	14	1	1.77	54.6%	13.1	1.2	1.5	0.0	2.7
2013-14	LAK	22	71	3	5	8	6	0.70	54.4%	11.3	-2.0	2.2	0.0	0.2
2014-15	LAK	23	80	6	9	15	5	1.06	54.6%	13.5	-1.0	2.7	0.0	1.7
2015-16	LAK	24	63	7	8	15					-0.5	2.1	0.0	1.6

It is hard to expect anything more out of Kyle Clifford than a fourth-line energy player. While offensive numbers are probably the last thing you want to look at, he did contribute at a decent per 60 minute rate for the role. The more positive thing about the 2009 second rounder is that he is not a huge liability defensively. Plus, he remains on the positive end of the Relative Corsi percentages when compared to his teammates. Regardless, he remains barely above a replacement-level grind-line forward.

Marian Gaborik — RW/LW — LAK

Season	Team	Age	GP	G	A	Pts	+/-	ESP/60	AdjCF%	iCF/60	OGVT	DGVT	SGVT	GVT
2012-13	NYR, CBJ	30	47	12	15	27	-3	1.46	52.3%	15.7	2.6	0.8	-0.9	2.5
2013-14	CBJ, LAK	31	41	11	19	30	7	2.38	54.8%	14.5	4.1	1.8	0.9	6.9
2014-15	LAK	32	69	27	20	47	7	1.79	59.9%	14.0	6.7	3.1	0.4	10.2
2015-16	LAK	33	64	20	22	43					5.2	2.2	0.0	7.5

Marian Gaborik remained relatively healthy—there is something to be said for that, given his early career woes—and productive. His speed, consistency, and all-together intelligent play in the attacking zone helped a fairly stunted offensive team. On a squad of notorious hot and cold scorers, the Slovak sniper never went more than six games without finding the back of the net. His net-front presence was key to his success, as his shot rate in the slot at even strength was 3.14 shots per 60 minutes higher than league average. In addition, the 32-year-old finished at around 20-22% in the slot, two to three percent higher than league average. When on ice, the Kings had their highest scoring chances for percentage (57%). When healthy, Gaborik is a massive cog in the L.A Kings offense, their most consistent scorer game to game.

Dwight King — LW — LAK

Season	Team	Age	GP	G	A	Pts	+/-	ESP/60	AdjCF%	iCF/60	OGVT	DGVT	SGVT	GVT
2012-13	LAK	23	47	4	6	10	-3	1.03	55.1%	10.6	-0.5	0.9	0.0	0.4
2013-14	LAK	24	77	15	15	30	16	1.59	59.0%	10.4	1.7	5.1	0.6	7.4
2014-15	LAK	25	81	13	13	26	-3	1.36	55.0%	10.7	1.4	3.2	-0.3	4.3
2015-16	LAK	26	68	13	15	28					1.9	2.8	0.0	4.7

While Dwight King draws the ire of a portion of the L.A. Kings faithful, he was solid yet again for what he brings to the table. As a cheap top-nine forward, King plays the role of complementary winger well. He is not the most skilled player, but his size and willingness to disrupt play in front of the net works well with the Kings' system of "heavy" forechecking and cycling. It is also hard to argue with roughly 30 points per season for less than $2.0 million AAV. The big forward is consistent, if anything: his individual Corsi, Fenwick, zone starts, and shooting numbers were nearly identical from 2013-14 to 2014-15. Late last season, he flourished alongside Toffoli and Carter. If you can get past his low-flash, low-skill game, he is a fairly effective and useful winger.

Anze Kopitar — C — LAK

Season	Team	Age	GP	G	A	Pts	+/-	ESP/60	AdjCF%	iCF/60	OGVT	DGVT	SGVT	GVT
2012-13	LAK	25	47	10	32	42	14	2.05	61.9%	11.5	6.2	3.7	0.5	10.4
2013-14	LAK	26	82	29	41	70	34	2.22	61.3%	12.1	10.8	7.9	1.7	20.4
2014-15	LAK	27	79	16	48	64	-2	2.04	59.7%	9.9	8.6	3.8	-1.2	11.1
2015-16	LAK	28	74	20	42	62					7.8	3.6	0.0	11.4

Anze Kopitar had a somewhat curious season. Like many Kings, he experienced lows in his offensive game. The eyesore of his stat column came in goals, managing only 16 over the 82-game season. It is hard to be upset with the Slovenian, though, as he remains one of the premier shutdown centers in the league—he gets no breaks when it comes to zone starts or quality of competition. He was the third-best center in the league in Relative Corsi percentage (750+ minutes). His offensive numbers were a run of bad luck.

Trevor Lewis — RW/C — LAK

Season	Team	Age	GP	G	A	Pts	+/-	ESP/60	AdjCF%	iCF/60	OGVT	DGVT	SGVT	GVT
2012-13	LAK	25	48	5	9	14	5	1.19	55.3%	13.4	0.3	3.0	0.0	3.3
2013-14	LAK	26	73	6	5	11	-1	0.74	53.8%	13.4	-1.3	3.0	-0.3	1.4
2014-15	LAK	27	73	9	16	25	8	1.59	57.2%	14.0	3.4	3.6	-0.3	6.7
2015-16	LAK	28	61	10	13	23					1.8	2.5	0.0	4.3

You could argue that Trevor Lewis is miscast on the Kings' bottom lines as the Utah native had an outstanding year in offensive and possession stats. The 27-year-old played stretches on the top line with Kopitar and Gaborik—and unlike Dustin Brown, it did not hurt the overall possession or goal numbers of his teammates. The former Des Moines Buccaneer has had a career as a defensive specialist, but last season, he showed there may be more to him in the right situation.

Jordan Nolan — RW — LAK

Season	Team	Age	GP	G	A	Pts	+/-	ESP/60	AdjCF%	iCF/60	OGVT	DGVT	SGVT	GVT
2012-13	LAK	23	44	2	4	6	-5	0.98	48.9%	7.0	-1.2	0.6	0.0	-0.5
2013-14	LAK	24	64	6	4	10	-1	1.05	53.8%	10.7	0.4	1.1	0.0	1.6
2014-15	LAK	25	60	6	3	9	-6	0.91	49.6%	9.1	-0.3	0.8	0.0	0.5
2015-16	LAK	26	52	6	5	11					-0.2	1.0	0.0	0.8

On the surface, Jordan Nolan looks to be barely above a replacement-level fourth-line grinder. However, he shows progression and flashes of a greater game at times—with emphasis on "at times". The reality is that his possession stats are ugly—barely above replacement level—yet the 25-year-old does show a softness of hands in shooting, passing, and puck handling that suggest more potential. He was briefly elevated to a top-nine role in 2014-15 and has moved away from his original enforcer role. It is a stretch given his poor possession stats, but the Kings may be looking to press Nolan into a more prominent role in the future.

Tanner Pearson — LW/RW — LAK

Season	Team	Age	GP	G	A	Pts	+/-	ESP/60	AdjCF%	iCF/60	OGVT	DGVT	SGVT	GVT
2013-14	LAK	21	25	3	4	7	2	1.43	56.3%	14.1	0.0	0.8	0.0	0.9
2014-15	LAK	22	42	12	4	16	14	1.89	55.7%	14.2	1.8	2.9	0.0	4.7
2015-16	LAK	23	52	12	12	24					2.1	2.1	0.0	4.2

While many analysts hinged on the loss of Slava Voynov as the insurmountable absence for the Kings, Tanner Pearson was actually the biggest loss. Everyone remembers the blistering (and unsustainable) start from the rookie, who at one point led the NHL in scoring. While his season did come back down to earth, the 2012 first rounder was still scoring and producing at a rate comparable to Tyler Toffoli. His season-ending injury took 20-25 goals out of an already low-scoring lineup. Expect the young forward to be just as effective when he returns to the L.A. top six.

Mike Richards — C — Free Agent

Season	Team	Age	GP	G	A	Pts	+/-	ESP/60	AdjCF%	iCF/60	OGVT	DGVT	SGVT	GVT
2012-13	LAK	27	48	12	20	32	-8	1.71	54.0%	10.4	4.1	1.1	0.5	5.6
2013-14	LAK	28	82	11	30	41	-6	1.57	55.1%	11.8	2.0	2.7	-1.3	3.4
2014-15	LAK	29	53	5	11	16	-10	1.29	51.5%	10.2	-0.5	1.0	-0.3	0.2
2015-16	Free Agent	30	57	8	15	24					1.1	1.5	0.0	2.5

The Kings won the Mike Richards trade simply by raising two Cups, but his years as a shutdown center have taken their toll. The decline came quickly as he tumbled to a fourth-line caliber center with a top-six salary. Questions were also raised about his fitness by management, and he did look a step slow defensively almost the entire season. We may have gotten a hint as to why with his off-ice issue, but it is hard to conclusively connect the dots. The Kings appeared to be in a no-win situation with Richards under contract through 2020 and recapture penalties in place.

Nick Shore — C — LAK

Season	Team	Age	GP	G	A	Pts	+/-	ESP/60	AdjCF%	iCF/60	OGVT	DGVT	SGVT	GVT
2014-15	LAK	22	34	1	6	7	0	1.02	54.5%	9.7	0.1	0.7	0.0	0.8
2015-16	LAK	23	41	5	9	14					0.6	1.1	0.0	1.7

Nick Shore blew the doors off the AHL to start 2014-15. A surprise performer, the 22-year-old University of Denver grad forced the Kings' hand to give him a shot at the NHL. While it is hard to look at his solitary goal and meager seven points over the 34-game stint, he morphed into a fairly responsible center—he had the lowest goals-against per 60 minutes at even strength amongst Kings centers. He also grew as the season progressed, with a 49.4 Corsi for percentage in his first 17 games climbing to 55.0 in his final 17 games. In addition, he ended the season as the Kings best faceoff man, which gives promise to him slotting into a third-line center role.

Jarret Stoll — C — NYR

Season	Team	Age	GP	G	A	Pts	+/-	ESP/60	AdjCF%	iCF/60	OGVT	DGVT	SGVT	GVT
2012-13	LAK	30	48	7	11	18	1	1.08	54.9%	9.1	1.6	2.7	-0.3	4.0
2013-14	LAK	31	78	8	19	27	9	1.38	56.6%	10.9	0.3	4.2	-0.6	3.9
2014-15	LAK	32	73	6	11	17	3	0.70	51.4%	7.5	-2.2	4.0	-0.3	1.5
2015-16	NYR	33	62	7	11	18					-0.4	2.6	0.0	2.1

Jarret Stoll had a major downturn to go along with Mike Richards' slide. The same center depth that was key in Los Angeles' Cup runs saw decline in almost every major statistical category, including Stoll's once-coveted faceoff ability. (Though, is one season the beginning of a trend, or an anomaly?) His other stats? Opposing goals against were up while he was on the ice, and he experienced lows in his individual shot rate, Corsi, Fenwick, points, assists, and goals. He also saw less time on the power play and on the penalty kill and led the team in minor penalties. Nevertheless, Stoll slots in as a low-risk role player on the Rangers for 2015-16.

Tyler Toffoli								RW/C						LAK
Season	Team	Age	GP	G	A	Pts	+/-	ESP/60	AdjCF%	iCF/60	OGVT	DGVT	SGVT	GVT
2012-13	LAK	20	10	2	3	5	3	1.73	53.1%	19.5	0.9	0.5	0.0	1.4
2013-14	LAK	21	62	12	17	29	21	2.15	61.2%	17.4	4.3	3.5	-0.3	7.5
2014-15	LAK	22	76	23	26	49	25	2.47	58.0%	19.2	8.6	5.5	-1.1	13.1
2015-16	LAK	23	72	22	26	48					6.6	3.8	-0.1	10.3

What sophomore slump? Tyler Toffoli had a terrific second year with 23 goals and 49 points, ranking third on the team in both. However, despite his high level of play, head coach Darryl Sutter held Toffoli's minutes in check—he averaged just 14:35 per game, with about 12 minutes at even strength. Still, he put up monster per 60 minute rates. At five-on-five, Toffoli was 12th overall in the league in points per 60 minutes, 15th in assists, and 38th in goals. If he proves worthy of increased ice-time, Toffoli could become a star—and a major success story for Kings' amateur scouting, given that he was nabbed with the 47th pick in the 2010 NHL Entry Draft.

David Van Der Gulik								LW/RW						Free Agent
Season	Team	Age	GP	G	A	Pts	+/-	ESP/60	AdjCF%	iCF/60	OGVT	DGVT	SGVT	GVT
2012-13	COL	29	9	0	2	2	2	1.72	58.1%	13.5	-0.1	0.6	0.0	0.5
2013-14	COL	30	2	0	0	0	0	0.00	52.5%	26.6	0.0	0.0	0.0	0.0
2014-15	LAK	31	1	0	0	0	0	0.00	58.6%	10.5	0.0	0.0	0.0	0.0
2015-16	Free Agent	32	24	4	5	8					0.5	0.5	0.0	1.0

What can you say about David Van Der Gulik? His one game and five minutes of ice-time with the Kings was as momentous as you could possibly imagine. Like Adam Cracknell, the 31-year-old vet was brought in during the offseason to presumably pressure the Kings bottom-line forwards. Although he made the team out of camp, his tenure was short lived. He has had mild success in the past as a bottom liner, but the former Av lacked the size and aggression to hang with the likes of Jordan Nolan and Kyle Clifford.

Justin Williams								RW						WSH
Season	Team	Age	GP	G	A	Pts	+/-	ESP/60	AdjCF%	iCF/60	OGVT	DGVT	SGVT	GVT
2012-13	LAK	31	48	11	22	33	15	2.32	63.6%	18.1	5.4	3.1	-0.3	8.1
2013-14	LAK	32	82	19	24	43	14	1.88	61.1%	17.2	4.8	4.2	-0.2	8.8
2014-15	LAK	33	81	18	23	41	8	1.48	57.8%	13.6	4.6	3.4	-0.3	7.7
2015-16	WSH	34	68	16	22	39					4.2	2.7	0.0	6.9

There is no doubting the importance of Justin Williams in the annals of Kings history. "Stick," as he is referred to by his teammates, will forever be remembered for his Conn Smythe Trophy winning performance in the 2014 postseason. However, age-related decline may be creeping in—eventually, it is inevitable. Several of the key categories which have endeared #14 to the stat guys and the Kings faithful alike were down. His Corsi for per 60 minutes dipped and his shots per 60 minutes were down—while his five-on-five shooting percentage hit a career high. Still, he has been a key L.A. Kings figure, and his loss may create a hole in an already thin group of wingers. Given his age and trends, parting may not be the worst idea though, even if it hurts.

LOS ANGELES KINGS

DEFENSEMEN

Drew Doughty								RD						LAK
Season	Team	Age	GP	G	A	Pts	+/-	ESP/60	AdjCF%	iCF/60	OGVT	DGVT	SGVT	GVT
2012-13	LAK	23	48	6	16	22	4	0.71	58.3%	11.5	2.4	4.7	-0.3	6.9
2013-14	LAK	24	78	10	27	37	17	0.80	58.9%	11.5	3.3	7.5	-0.3	10.5
2014-15	LAK	25	82	7	39	46	3	0.89	56.7%	11.3	4.9	6.5	-0.3	11.1
2015-16	LAK	26	79	10	35	45					5.4	5.8	0.0	11.1

If big minutes are needed, Drew Doughty is there to supply them. Not only did the 25-year-old D-man give the Kings a whopping 29 minutes per night, but he did so while playing excellent hockey in all zones and situations. With dominant possession numbers, Doughty and partner Jake Muzzin were the best play-driving pair in the NHL. While his 46 points did not compare to the production of his fellow Norris finalists Subban and Karlsson, Doughty arguably played against the more difficult matchups—head coach Darryl Sutter leaned on the former Guelph Storm defenseman in every situation and against the toughest opponents.

Matt Greene								RD						LAK
Season	Team	Age	GP	G	A	Pts	+/-	ESP/60	AdjCF%	iCF/60	OGVT	DGVT	SGVT	GVT
2012-13	LAK	29	5	0	1	1	-1	0.93	42.5%	4.7	0.1	0.0	0.0	0.1
2013-14	LAK	30	38	2	4	6	6	0.73	57.9%	10.3	0.3	3.6	0.0	3.9
2014-15	LAK	31	82	3	6	9	1	0.48	55.0%	9.3	-1.3	5.0	0.0	3.7
2015-16	LAK	32	64	2	8	10					-0.5	3.8	0.0	3.4

Matt Greene had been a very serviceable third-pairing defenseman for L.A. However, time catches up quicker with the grinders. Due to the Kings' personnel issues, he spent significant time spent with each of Martinez, McNabb, and Muzzin, which may have disrupted the rhythm of the normally reliable defenseman. "Greener" did, however, lead the league in one key category for the third consecutive year: blood loss from the face per 60 minutes.

Alec Martinez								LD						LAK
Season	Team	Age	GP	G	A	Pts	+/-	ESP/60	AdjCF%	iCF/60	OGVT	DGVT	SGVT	GVT
2012-13	LAK	25	27	1	4	5	-2	0.63	59.8%	9.3	0.5	1.0	0.0	1.5
2013-14	LAK	26	61	11	11	22	17	1.04	57.6%	12.1	4.7	4.8	0.0	9.5
2014-15	LAK	27	56	6	16	22	9	1.18	53.1%	11.5	3.7	4.1	0.0	7.8
2015-16	LAK	28	60	7	18	25					3.4	3.5	0.0	6.9

Alec Martinez had his season hindered by a concussion, but he was a valuable depth defenseman when healthy. His offensive numbers and point pace were some of the best on the Kings blueline. Without injury, he was looking at a 30-35 point season. The 2014 Stanley Cup Final hero has good vision coming out of the defensive zone on the breakout and gets shots through from the point. Turnovers and soft plays can still be an issue, but recognizing his value, GM Dean Lombardi and the Kings invested in Martinez long term.

Jamie McBain — RD — LAK

Season	Team	Age	GP	G	A	Pts	+/-	ESP/60	AdjCF%	iCF/60	OGVT	DGVT	SGVT	GVT
2012-13	CAR	24	40	1	7	8	0	0.74	52.0%	7.7	0.1	1.1	0.0	1.2
2013-14	BUF	25	69	6	11	17	-13	0.58	39.4%	7.7	0.6	1.2	0.0	1.8
2014-15	LAK	26	26	3	6	9	4	1.27	53.9%	8.5	1.0	1.6	0.0	2.5
2015-16	LAK	27	49	4	12	16					1.2	2.1	0.0	3.3

For an on-the-fly patch job to a beleaguered Kings defense, Jamie McBain didn't hurt the team. The recent Sabre (never a good thing for the resume) dressed for 26 games and received extremely protected ice-time. The University of Wisconsin product is an offensively-gifted defenseman who drives coaches insane with egregious defensive errors and disappointing point production despite his skill.

Brayden McNabb — LD — LAK

Season	Team	Age	GP	G	A	Pts	+/-	ESP/60	AdjCF%	iCF/60	OGVT	DGVT	SGVT	GVT
2013-14	BUF	22	12	0	0	0	1	0.00	43.6%	8.0	-0.7	0.4	0.0	-0.3
2014-15	LAK	23	71	2	22	24	11	1.14	57.7%	10.1	3.5	4.5	0.0	8.0
2015-16	LAK	24	62	4	16	20					2.0	3.4	0.0	5.5

Darryl Sutter is notoriously hard on young players. Last season, 23-year-old Brayden McNabb ran the gamut when it came to his usage under the curmudgeon bench boss. So despite going from first-pairing minutes to the press box within a span of three or four games, McNabb had a very promising season overall. His physical play and developing defensive poise eased the doubt in the minds of many fans who were unfamiliar with the former Sabres prospect. When he was paired with Andrej Sekera in the stretch run, the duo was perhaps the best and most cohesive pairing the Kings had all season. While the offensive instincts and booming slap shot he displayed with the WHL's Kootenay Ice remain relatively untapped, he should see plenty more opportunity moving forward to apply those skills with L.A.

Jake Muzzin — LD — LAK

Season	Team	Age	GP	G	A	Pts	+/-	ESP/60	AdjCF%	iCF/60	OGVT	DGVT	SGVT	GVT
2012-13	LAK	23	45	7	9	16	16	0.77	63.5%	10.8	2.9	3.9	0.0	6.8
2013-14	LAK	24	76	5	19	24	8	0.93	61.6%	14.7	2.5	4.2	0.0	6.7
2014-15	LAK	25	76	10	31	41	-4	1.07	58.4%	11.8	6.9	3.5	0.0	10.3
2015-16	LAK	26	69	9	28	37					5.4	3.7	0.0	9.1

Jake Muzzin has been one of the best possession defensemen in the league for several years running. The biggest question was whether his stats were inflated by playing with Doughty, but he has proven that notion to be false, dragging the numbers of inferior defensemen upward. He took a big step in the right direction in the form of production by posting a career year in goals, assists, and points. He more than tripled his power-play point production from 2013-14 as well. With elite numbers and two Cups, when will the 26-year-old get the recognition he deserves?

Robyn Regehr — LD — Retired

Season	Team	Age	GP	G	A	Pts	+/-	ESP/60	AdjCF%	iCF/60	OGVT	DGVT	SGVT	GVT
2012-13	BUF, LAK	32	41	0	4	4	-4	0.36	43.5%	5.6	-1.3	1.0	0.0	-0.3
2013-14	LAK	33	79	3	11	14	6	0.66	54.0%	7.4	-0.2	6.0	0.0	5.8
2014-15	LAK	34	67	3	10	13	10	0.61	52.2%	6.6	0.4	5.3	0.0	5.7
2015-16	Retired	35	59	3	10	13					0.4	3.8	0.0	4.1

Sutter leaned heavily on veteran defenseman Robyn Regehr—very familiar to him from Regehr's prime years in Calgary—which turned out to be a mistake by the Cup-winning coach. While Regehr is a hard-nosed, intelligent defender, his days as a shutdown man were long gone. Team shot rates against at even strength with versus without him were negative across the board. He drove down the Corsi for per 60 rate and drove up the Corsi against per 60 rate of almost every defender. On numerous occasions, Regehr was paired with Doughty—which consequently separated the Kings' best pairing of Muzzin-Doughty. He was also held in the lineup over Brayden McNabb and received the most difficult quality of competition minutes on the team. At age 35, Regehr will hang up the skates and forever close the "Tunnel of Doom".

Jeff Schultz — LD — LAK

Season	Team	Age	GP	G	A	Pts	+/-	ESP/60	AdjCF%	iCF/60	OGVT	DGVT	SGVT	GVT
2012-13	WSH	26	26	0	3	3	-6	0.54	47.1%	6.3	-0.5	-0.4	0.0	-0.9
2014-15	LAK	28	9	0	1	1	1	0.44	54.5%	6.7	-0.1	0.6	0.0	0.4
2015-16	LAK	29	27	1	5	6					0.3	1.1	0.0	1.3

The Kings needed Jeff Schultz sparingly in 2014-15, but they did need him. The lanky, plodding defenseman was part of just nine NHL games, but he did win an AHL Calder Cup in Manchester. In those nine games, he was given very little in terms of tough minutes and probably won't see much NHL action from here on out. But Kings fans can always remember his admirable fill-in work during the playoffs when they won the Cup.

Andrej Sekera — LD — EDM

Season	Team	Age	GP	G	A	Pts	+/-	ESP/60	AdjCF%	iCF/60	OGVT	DGVT	SGVT	GVT
2012-13	BUF	26	37	2	10	12	-2	0.98	43.2%	5.9	1.5	1.1	0.0	2.5
2013-14	CAR	27	74	11	33	44	4	1.23	51.2%	9.6	8.3	5.7	0.0	14.0
2014-15	CAR, LAK	28	73	3	20	23	-3	0.71	54.3%	9.5	0.7	6.7	0.0	7.4
2015-16	EDM	29	66	5	21	25					2.1	4.7	0.0	6.8

The Kings were in need of a legitimate top-three defenseman all the way up until the trade deadline when they landed Andrej Sekera. While Sekera struggled in his first few games matched up with Robyn Regehr, the Slovak found his form when paired with fellow ex-Sabre Brayden McNabb. While his partner was not Justin Faulk, McNabb and Sekera were fantastic. They were the best possession pairing for the Kings for a stretch of 10-12 games back in early- to mid-March. Teams simply could not score against them. In their 125 even-strength minutes together, they held a phenomenal 0.48 goals-against per 60 minutes rate coupled with an 80.0 goals-for percentage. Edmonton was criticized for spending big on Sekera as a free agent, but he has long been one of the most underappreciated all-around blueliners in the league. The Oilers will get their money's worth.

LOS ANGELES KINGS

Slava Voynov — RD — LAK

Season	Team	Age	GP	G	A	Pts	+/-	ESP/60	AdjCF%	iCF/60	OGVT	DGVT	SGVT	GVT
2012-13	LAK	22	48	6	19	25	5	1.15	54.4%	10.7	4.4	3.7	0.0	8.1
2013-14	LAK	23	82	4	30	34	6	0.88	55.6%	10.3	4.2	4.6	0.0	8.8
2014-15	LAK	24	6	0	2	2	0	0.00	45.2%	9.0	0.3	0.2	0.0	0.4
2015-16	LAK	25	48	4	14	18					1.9	2.4	0.0	4.3

After signing a six-year deal with Los Angeles in 2013, Slava Voynov hit a backslide the following season. Before he was able to rectify his downturn, he was involved in an off-ice domestic abuse case which held him out of the lineup for nearly the entirety of the year. His future with the Kings and in the NHL remains in question—the Kings could have used his 20+ minutes per night in 2014-15. His absence put the squeeze on his teammates, requiring several to play career highs in time on ice.

GOALTENDERS

Martin Jones — G — SJS

Season	Team	Age	GP	W	L	OT	GAA	Sv%	ESSV%	QS%	GGVT	DGVT	SGVT	GVT
2013-14	LAK	23	19	12	6	0	1.81	.934	.949	77.8%	11.2	0.3	3.3	14.9
2014-15	LAK	24	15	4	5	2	2.25	.906	.915	45.5%	-0.8	0.7	0.7	0.6
2015-16	SJS	25	25					.919			6.6	0.4	0.3	7.3

All you ask of an NHL backup is to come in and play well when given the opportunity to do so. In his understandably limited 15 appearances as Jonathan Quick's backup, Martin Jones was a mixed bag. Although he posted three shutouts on the season in his 11 starts, he also had seven starts where he posted sub-.910 save percentages. Granted, Jones does show promise as a quality goaltender, given his size and calm demeanor. In 2015-16, he will get a chance to prove himself against the Kings as netminder for the rival San Jose Sharks.

Jonathan Quick — G — LAK

Season	Team	Age	GP	W	L	OT	GAA	Sv%	ESSV%	QS%	GGVT	DGVT	SGVT	GVT
2012-13	LAK	26	37	18	13	4	2.45	.902	.910	61.1%	-2.8	1.3	-1.7	-3.2
2013-14	LAK	27	49	27	17	4	2.07	.915	.929	57.1%	8.7	2.3	2.5	13.5
2014-15	LAK	28	72	36	22	13	2.24	.918	.926	59.2%	13.1	1.7	-2.5	12.3
2015-16	LAK	29	54					.915			7.3	1.2	-0.1	8.4

You could have divided Jonathan Quick's 2014-15 season into thirds. In chronological order, he was outstanding, incredibly bad, and good. The Connecticut native finished up the year with a respectable .933 adjusted save percentage, good enough for ninth overall. That is hard to believe, when you factor in the 21-game stretch from December 6 to February 1 when he only managed an .884 save percentage. However, his start was great (.939). This seems to be his M.O., though: the 2012 Conn Smythe winner is wildly inconsistent, going from world beater to backup quality at a moment's notice. He always seems to latch it down when it matters the most, like down the stretch in 2014-15. His outstanding athleticism and acrobatics make him an exciting, mercurial talent.

Jason Lewis

Minnesota Wild

The Minnesota Wild had one of the stranger 2014-15 seasons in the National Hockey League. They opened as the league's possession powerhouse, posting a league-best 56.9% score-adjusted Corsi through November 15. It looked as if the team had come of age and that the big goaltending question mark was going to be settled. Young netminder Darcy Kuemper started on fire, not allowing a single goal in the season's first 164 minutes, following it up with a .923 adjusted save percentage through November 3.

Then, the bottom fell out. By January 15, the Wild were on a six-game losing streak, they had not won two in a row since November 20, and they had two goaltenders among the league's 10 worst—combining for a .895 even-strength save percentage, the worst mark in the NHL.

Unlikely trade target, unlikely hero

Minnesota's playoff probability had sunk to the low single digits when they decided to make a change, trading a third-round pick for backup goaltender Devan Dubnyk of the Arizona Coyotes—who had played so poorly in Edmonton in 2013-14 that it nearly cost him his NHL career. Of all the goaltenders speculated to be available at that moment, Dubnyk seemed a decidedly odd choice for GM Chuck Fletcher to target. Dubnyk's career numbers weren't bad, but he was coming off a career-worst season where he recorded a .902 even-strength save percentage, was traded twice, and finished the season as a "black ace" for the Montreal Canadiens after playing for their AHL club in Hamilton to end the regular season.

Incredibly, Dubnyk led the Wild on a 28-9-3 run from January 15 to the end of the season—and he started 39 of those 40 games. Minnesota had the NHL's best record from the All-Star break onward, playing their way from obscurity into the top wild-card position in the Western Conference.

The constant through the season was that even when they struggled, the team suppressed shot attempts well, at 52.9 Corsi against per 60 minutes for the season. The rate was consistent: Minnesota had a 52.2 Corsi against per 60 minutes through January 14 and a 52.8 Corsi against per 60 minutes afterward.

The big difference was in their Corsi for. When their goaltending tanked, the team played more conservatively, with defensemen activating in the offensive zone less frequently, and the team dumping into the offensive zone just to get it further away from their own net. That led to a loss of some of the aggressive-

WILD IN A BOX

Last Season

Goals For	231	14th
Goals Against	201	t-4th
GVT	30	7th
Points	100	t-11th
Playoffs	Lost Conference Semifinal	

The Wild were out of the playoffs at Christmas when the emergence of Dubnyk propelled them to 100 points and a first-round victory over the Blues.

Three-Year Record

GVT	26	12th
Points	253	10th
Playoffs	3 Appearances, 11 Wins	

VUKOTA Projections

Goals For	221	18th
Goals Against	219	14th
GVT	2	17th
Points	92	17th

No goaltender can maintain a 93.6% save percentage, but the Wild have enough talent to make the playoffs again.

Top Three Prospects

M. Reilly (D), A. Tuch (F), J. Eriksson Ek (F)

ness that marked their early-season play. Consequently, their 57.7 Corsi for per 60 minutes through January 14 fell to a 51.2 Corsi for per 60 minutes afterward.

In effect, Minnesota provided a unique case study on just how much teams rely on strong goaltending. Despite their shot-attempt numbers dropping steeply after January 15, that is when they made an incredible run to get back into the playoffs, largely on the back of their new netminder's .940 even-strength save percentage.

Dubnyk's run was incredible, but we shouldn't assume that he will match career-best numbers going forward. In the same way that teams overreacted to his single poor season, we shouldn't overreact to his single otherworldy season.

Since the start of 2009-10, when he debuted in the NHL, Dubnyk has a .922 even-strength save percentage. Among goaltenders who have played at least 82 games in that timeframe, he ranks 27th. The players closest to that level of performance are guys like Mike Smith, Cam Ward, Marc-Andre Fleury, Jhonas Enroth, James Reimer, and Miikka Kiprusoff, goaltenders that have had streaks of very good play offset by stretches of very mediocre play. Over his career, Dubnyk is neither the goaltender who nearly played himself out of the league in 2013-14 nor the incredible Vezina finalist we saw this past season.

The good news for the Wild is that he may now be a better goaltender than his career average, in no small part thanks to the confidence instilled in him by goaltending coach—goaltending guru—Sean Burke in Arizona. Burke had Dubnyk simplifying his game, focusing on lateral movement. Dubnyk also tweaked his game over the summer while working with Steve Valiquette, incorporating "Head Trajectory" into his style. The results we have seen since these small adjustments and the restoration of his confidence give reason to believe that Dubnyk could play a touch above his career average in coming seasons.

Of course, shot suppression and team defense also played a pivotal role in the Dubnyk's hot streak. It is not just a goaltender that takes a team through a 40-game stretch without ever losing two in a row. Which is why it is impressive that the very day that Dubnyk arrived, the Wild took off.

Yeo gets their attention

It was big news on January 7 when head coach Mike Yeo went on a profanity-laden tirade during practice, then broke his stick over the boards before exiting the ice; the video went viral. Days later, as losses continued to mount, the assumption was that Yeo hadn't reached his team. But the subsequent run the Wild went on is hard evidence that he did. There was an instant shift when Dubnyk arrived, due in no small part because of a coach who had his team ready to turn the corner despite the incredible frustration surrounding its goaltending.

That said, the goaltending situation still has a few question marks. Early on, the Wild played Kuemper to the point where he is no longer eligible to be sent to the AHL without going through waivers. It is not clear what the Wild would have done without him, since veteran Niklas Backstrom's numbers were far worse, but it was clear by the end of January that Kuemper would benefit from development time in Iowa. That may no longer be an option.

While there are questions about Yeo's player usage—benching depth possession kingpin Justin Fontaine in January or keeping Ryan Suter on the top power-play unit despite season-long struggles—he has continued to do a nice job of developing the franchise's young talent.

With questions lingering about the divide between young and old players on the team—the Wild are one of only two teams whose top-five highest-paid players are all over 30—many of the team's young players took huge strides forward. One of the best surprises was Jason Zucker, who shored up his defensive game while tallying 1.57 goals per 60 minutes, second in the NHL to only Rick Nash.

The success of young players like Zucker, Nino Niederreiter, Matt Dumba, Marco Scandella, Jonas Brodin, Jared Spurgeon, Christian Folin, and Mikael Granlund—though the team is still hoping for bigger steps forward from the former ninth overall draft pick—is a huge part of the team's success. The steps taken by these players helps ensure that the pieces that are improving for the Wild—positive possession for the first time in quite a while—can continue into future seasons.

Dustin Nelson

MINNESOTA WILD

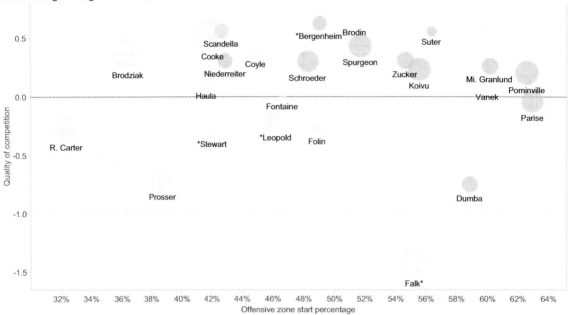

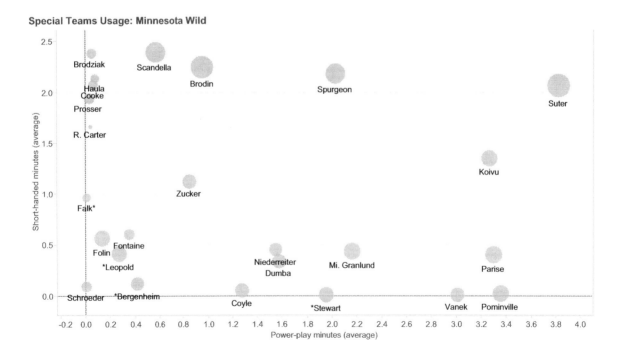

MINNESOTA WILD

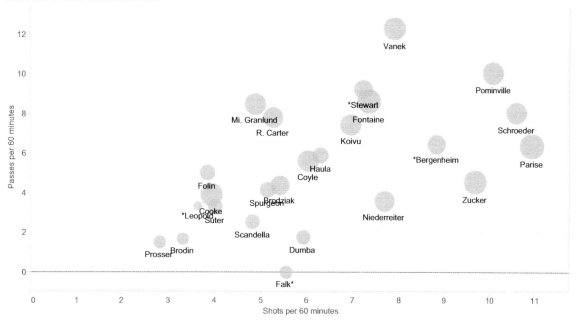

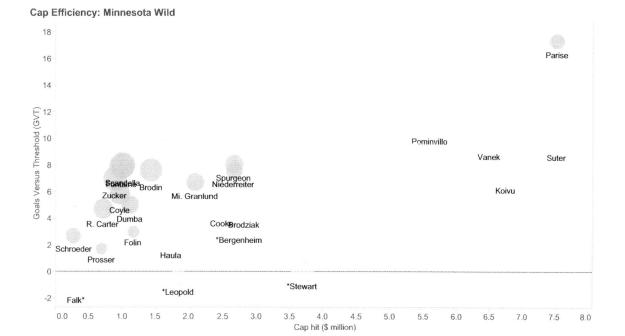

MINNESOTA WILD

FORWARDS

Sean Bergenheim — LW — Free Agent

Season	Team	Age	GP	G	A	Pts	+/-	ESP/60	AdjCF%	iCF/60	OGVT	DGVT	SGVT	GVT
2013-14	FLA	29	62	16	13	29	-16	1.75	53.4%	18.1	2.8	1.0	0.0	3.9
2014-15	FLA, MIN	30	56	9	10	19	-2	1.45	53.6%	15.5	1.1	1.5	0.6	3.2
2015-16	Free Agent	31	54	10	12	22					1.4	1.3	0.0	2.7

Consistently a quality, 20-point-per-year depth winger, Sean Bergenheim fell out of favor on an up-and-coming Panthers team, who traded him to the Wild. After arriving in Minnesota, things did not go well. He notched just one point in 17 games and appeared in only three postseason games. The Finnish forward has been known for his high shot rate, but with the Wild, he only put 25 shots on goal between the regular season and playoffs. Before his bad stretch in Minnesota, Bergenheim had terrific Corsi numbers and solid five-on-five scoring stats with Florida. However, his poor play on a legitimate contender will be what is remembered most, meaning he may have a tough time finding consistent NHL work.

Kyle Brodziak — C — STL

Season	Team	Age	GP	G	A	Pts	+/-	ESP/60	AdjCF%	iCF/60	OGVT	DGVT	SGVT	GVT
2012-13	MIN	28	48	8	4	12	-18	0.79	48.9%	10.9	-2.8	1.3	0.0	-1.5
2013-14	MIN	29	81	8	16	24	0	1.21	43.8%	11.4	-0.4	3.5	0.0	3.1
2014-15	MIN	30	73	9	11	20	-6	1.47	44.6%	10.2	0.3	3.9	0.0	4.2
2015-16	STL	31	63	8	11	19					0.0	2.4	0.0	2.4

There was a time when Kyle Brodziak was an effective depth player for the Wild, but those days may be over. Often used for defensive zone faceoffs, the one-time Oiler struggled to slow down opponents, giving up the most shot attempts per 60 minutes at five-on-five of any regular Wild forward. The offensive production of the veteran center has been in steady decline since posting 44 points in 2011-12, in part due to his shift to a fourth-line role. With 19 even-strength points, though, there is still some remnant of the good old days left.

Ryan Carter — C — MIN

Season	Team	Age	GP	G	A	Pts	+/-	ESP/60	AdjCF%	iCF/60	OGVT	DGVT	SGVT	GVT
2012-13	NJD	29	44	6	9	15	-2	1.36	54.8%	10.5	1.0	2.4	0.0	3.4
2013-14	NJD	30	62	7	3	10	-6	0.85	51.6%	10.5	-0.2	1.4	0.0	1.2
2014-15	MIN	31	53	3	10	13	3	1.62	47.0%	10.8	1.2	3.5	0.0	4.7
2015-16	MIN	32	51	5	8	14					0.4	2.0	0.0	2.4

Ryan Carter started his career in Minnesota with a bang, posting two goals and seven assists in his first 15 games. Unfortunately, over the next 38 games, he delivered just one goal and three assists. Overall, his season wasn't great. He posted a negative Relative Corsi (third worst among Wild regulars) for the fourth straight season, the seventh in his eight NHL seasons. The former Minnesota State Maverick is a role player, but he wasn't able to fill the available role successfully, and found himself scratched for nine of 10 playoff games.

Matt Cooke — LW — Free Agent

Season	Team	Age	GP	G	A	Pts	+/-	ESP/60	AdjCF%	iCF/60	OGVT	DGVT	SGVT	GVT
2012-13	PIT	34	48	8	13	21	-2	2.11	45.5%	10.4	3.1	1.5	0.0	4.7
2013-14	MIN	35	82	10	18	28	8	1.37	45.0%	9.7	1.6	4.3	0.0	5.9
2014-15	MIN	36	29	4	6	10	0	1.98	43.1%	8.6	1.2	3.0	0.0	4.1
2015-16	Free Agent	37	53	6	12	18					0.8	2.4	0.0	3.2

Matt Cooke entered the season coming off a solid campaign that ended in controversy, after he received a postseason suspension for a knee-on-knee hit against Colorado's talented young defender Tyson Barrie. Last season, the 2009 Stanley Cup winner played just eight games before getting injured himself, and struggled visibly after returning in December. He then left 19 games later to have sports hernia surgery, unable to return until the season's final two weeks. In other words, there are mitigating factors to why his boxcar numbers plummeted. At age 37, there may not be much in the tank for Cooke, who will be remembered more for his dirty hits than his play, which is unfortunate because he was a terrific role player throughout his career, including on that Penguins championship squad.

Charlie Coyle — RW/C — MIN

Season	Team	Age	GP	G	A	Pts	+/-	ESP/60	AdjCF%	iCF/60	OGVT	DGVT	SGVT	GVT
2012-13	MIN	20	37	8	6	14	3	1.52	55.7%	9.5	2.2	1.6	0.0	3.8
2013-14	MIN	21	70	12	18	30	-7	1.57	48.8%	11.2	-0.3	2.5	-0.2	2.0
2014-15	MIN	22	82	11	24	35	13	1.77	51.0%	10.6	2.9	3.2	-0.3	5.8
2015-16	MIN	23	69	13	21	34					2.2	2.4	0.0	4.7

At age 23, the Wild are ready for Charlie Coyle to deliver, and they showed it financially by signing him to a five-year, $3.2 million per year extension. However, he didn't quite deliver, in a hit-and-miss season. The 2010 Sharks first rounder started at wing before making his way to center, the position where the Wild want him on a more permanent basis. The good signs? His even-strength production was up. But his all-around game was disappointing. At six-foot-three, 220 pounds, GM Chuck Fletcher and head coach Mike Yeo want Coyle to be a force in the middle to be reckoned with. As of yet, he has not turned into that type of power forward.

Justin Fontaine — RW — MIN

Season	Team	Age	GP	G	A	Pts	+/-	ESP/60	AdjCF%	iCF/60	OGVT	DGVT	SGVT	GVT
2013-14	MIN	26	66	13	8	21	6	1.53	46.2%	10.3	2.6	2.5	0.6	5.7
2014-15	MIN	27	71	9	22	31	13	2.23	51.2%	13.4	5.0	3.2	-0.3	7.9
2015-16	MIN	28	65	13	21	34					3.7	2.5	0.0	6.3

Undrafted winger Justin Fontaine quietly became an indispensable piece of the Wild's defensive game this season. Despite a few somewhat inexplicable scratches, he made just about everyone he played with better. Fontaine bounced around the lineup, getting 10+ minutes with 12 different linemates, and 48+ minutes with 10 of them. The point production of the University of Minnesota-Duluth grad increased nicely this season as well, moving from 18 even-strength points to 28, darn good value for a player making $1 million.

Mikael Granlund — C — MIN

Season	Team	Age	GP	G	A	Pts	+/-	ESP/60	AdjCF%	iCF/60	OGVT	DGVT	SGVT	GVT
2012-13	MIN	20	27	2	6	8	-4	1.17	41.4%	9.7	-0.1	0.4	0.0	0.3
2013-14	MIN	21	63	8	33	41	-3	1.93	48.6%	9.0	3.2	2.3	-0.6	4.9
2014-15	MIN	22	68	8	31	39	17	1.79	53.2%	9.4	3.6	3.3	-0.3	6.7
2015-16	MIN	23	65	12	29	42					4.1	2.8	0.0	6.9

Mikael Granlund was not the dynamic player that we saw emerge at the 2014 Sochi Olympics, as the former ninth-overall draft pick managed just 39 points. That is lower than expected, especially considering that he spent almost the entire season on a line with Parise and Pominville. The five-foot-ten Finnish forward may have had a good Corsi number, but not enough of those shots came from his stick. Of the 998 shot attempts that took place with him on the ice, only 154 were his. That was just 15.4% of the total attempts, an even smaller portion than the previous season. It is also the lowest rate among Wild forwards, and only higher than defensemen Ryan Suter, Jonas Brodin, and Nate Prosser. Even as a playmaker at heart, Granlund will need to get more pucks on net in order to keep being considered a top-six forward.

Tyler Graovac — C — MIN

Season	Team	Age	GP	G	A	Pts	+/-	ESP/60	AdjCF%	iCF/60	OGVT	DGVT	SGVT	GVT
2014-15	MIN	21	3	0	0	0	0	0.00	41.5%	12.8	-0.1	0.0	0.0	0.0
2015-16	MIN	22	26	5	6	11					0.7	0.6	0.0	1.3

Making his NHL debut, versatile six-foot-five center Tyler Graovac saw action in three games. The 2011 seventh rounder is a strong forward with scoring upside and an ability to kill penalties. On the minor-league level, Graovac led the Iowa Wild with 21 goals and 25 assists through 73 games, the first player in Iowa history to cross the 20-goal mark. The former Ottawa 67s alternate captain provides a developing depth option for a team that isn't particularly strong down the middle.

Erik Haula — C/LW — MIN

Season	Team	Age	GP	G	A	Pts	+/-	ESP/60	AdjCF%	iCF/60	OGVT	DGVT	SGVT	GVT
2013-14	MIN	22	46	6	9	15	14	2.04	48.1%	11.7	2.1	2.7	0.0	4.8
2014-15	MIN	23	72	7	7	14	-7	1.01	49.1%	11.8	-0.3	2.2	0.0	1.9
2015-16	MIN	24	64	11	11	22					1.1	2.3	0.0	3.3

Erik Haula gave the Wild a surprise rookie year, producing 15 points in 46 games. Yet he was disappointing in his second year, only pulling in 14 points through 72 games. He didn't even earn a postseason appearance until injury necessitated it in the second round. With that big swing, we probably haven't seen the kind of player the University of Minnesota product is going to be. The native of Pori, Finland is smart, with great speed and a knack for killing penalties. Turning his speed into more consistent five-on-five production will be required in order to keep an NHL slot.

Mikko Koivu — C — MIN

Season	Team	Age	GP	G	A	Pts	+/-	ESP/60	AdjCF%	iCF/60	OGVT	DGVT	SGVT	GVT
2012-13	MIN	29	48	11	26	37	2	1.87	55.7%	14.4	4.8	2.8	0.7	8.3
2013-14	MIN	30	65	11	43	54	0	1.95	55.6%	12.4	5.6	3.2	1.4	10.2
2014-15	MIN	31	80	14	34	48	2	1.69	55.1%	11.0	3.8	3.1	0.4	7.4
2015-16	MIN	32	68	14	31	45					4.1	2.4	0.1	6.6

Wild captain Mikko Koivu continued his offensive decline. His power-play production dropped off a cliff this season, despite a top unit that also featured Thomas Vanek, Zach Parise, Jason Pominville, and Ryan Suter. Despite the slip in scoring, his defensive game was still on point. At a $6.8 million cap hit through 2018, there are concerns that his offensive game will continue to slide, making the contract an albatross. "Mike Birch" also disappeared in the postseason. For the second time in three years, he failed to register a postseason point at even strength.

Nino Niederreiter — RW — MIN

Season	Team	Age	GP	G	A	Pts	+/-	ESP/60	AdjCF%	iCF/60	OGVT	DGVT	SGVT	GVT
2013-14	MIN	21	81	14	22	36	12	1.75	50.2%	11.6	3.2	4.0	0.3	7.5
2014-15	MIN	22	80	24	13	37	2	1.67	52.9%	13.9	5.9	1.9	-0.3	7.6
2015-16	MIN	23	69	19	18	38					4.4	2.1	0.0	6.5

Nino Niederreiter started to deliver on the promise he exhibited late in the 2013-14 season. With 24 goals and a big frame, he continued to prove the Islanders wrong for jettisoning him. At midseason, he was pushed down the lineup and had his minutes limited by Mike Yeo, but nevertheless, he bounced back to finish one point ahead of his previous year's total. While the fifth-overall pick from 2010 set a career high in goals, it took an exceptionally high 16.1% shooting percentage to do so. If his goal production dips, he will be turn into a below-average top-six winger.

Zach Parise — LW — MIN

Season	Team	Age	GP	G	A	Pts	+/-	ESP/60	AdjCF%	iCF/60	OGVT	DGVT	SGVT	GVT
2012-13	MIN	28	48	18	20	38	2	1.98	55.5%	14.9	5.8	2.5	0.7	9.0
2013-14	MIN	29	67	29	27	56	10	1.95	55.3%	14.9	9.4	4.0	0.5	13.9
2014-15	MIN	30	74	33	29	62	21	2.41	53.7%	16.9	13.5	3.6	0.2	17.3
2015-16	MIN	31	69	28	32	60					9.5	2.7	0.0	12.2

Following his 2013-14 season, the second straight under 2.0 even-strength points per 60 minutes, there was some concern over how productive Zach Parise would remain as he ages, but he had a very productive season in 2014-15, topping 30 goals for the first time since leaving the Devils. Further, the two-way winger continued to be a dominant puck-possession force, using his dogged work ethic combined with elite hockey IQ to win battles, track opponents down from behind, and anticipate plays. While his overall game is still one of the best in the NHL, it appears his days of scoring 80+ points are over for the veteran American winger.

Jason Pominville — RW — MIN

Season	Team	Age	GP	G	A	Pts	+/-	ESP/60	AdjCF%	iCF/60	OGVT	DGVT	SGVT	GVT
2012-13	BUF, MIN	30	47	14	20	34	1	2.05	47.0%	13.3	2.6	1.6	0.9	5.1
2013-14	MIN	31	82	30	30	60	3	2.09	52.7%	13.2	8.6	3.6	-0.7	11.5
2014-15	MIN	32	82	18	36	54	9	1.96	54.4%	15.4	6.8	2.6	1.0	10.4
2015-16	MIN	33	70	20	30	49					6.0	2.4	0.0	8.4

After posting the third 30-goal season of his career in 2013-14, Jason Pominville's 18 markers may seem disappointing. However, the speedy winger experienced some bad luck, shooting 7.1%, down from 13.3% the previous year. "Pommer" took a scant eight penalty minutes, but that wasn't due to lack of effort: the former Sabres captain uses quickness and strong stickwork to frustrate opponents and gain possession. While he may be on the downside of his prime, the 33-year-old Pominville doesn't have a lot of hard miles on his body, which should allow him to continue being productive into his mid-thirties.

Jordan Schroeder — C/RW — MIN

Season	Team	Age	GP	G	A	Pts	+/-	ESP/60	AdjCF%	iCF/60	OGVT	DGVT	SGVT	GVT
2012-13	VAN	22	31	3	6	9	0	1.38	52.6%	7.5	-0.5	0.4	-0.1	-0.2
2013-14	VAN	23	25	3	3	6	-7	1.10	50.9%	9.2	-0.3	0.1	-0.3	-0.5
2014-15	MIN	24	25	3	5	8	9	1.78	55.0%	14.7	1.4	1.3	0.0	2.7
2015-16	MIN	25	38	6	8	14					1.0	1.2	0.0	2.2

An undersized forward from the University of Minnesota, Jordan Schroeder has never quite been able to make the cut as a regular NHLer, taking on fill-in duty in each of the last three seasons. After a strong showing in Iowa, where he scored 28 points in 35 games, Schroeder filled in his reserve role nicely with Minnesota, adding a handful of points and an 80% goals-for percentage over 25 games. Clearly, that heady percentage will drift back to the mean as he receives more ice-time, but a 53.9% Corsi suggests he was doing something right. After his quality stretch of hockey, we may see the Wild give the 2009 first-round pick more opportunity.

Chris Stewart — RW — ANA

Season	Team	Age	GP	G	A	Pts	+/-	ESP/60	AdjCF%	iCF/60	OGVT	DGVT	SGVT	GVT
2012-13	STL	25	48	18	18	36	0	2.23	48.9%	11.6	4.6	1.9	0.7	7.3
2013-14	STL, BUF	26	63	15	11	26	0	1.62	48.3%	13.5	2.3	1.3	-0.8	2.7
2014-15	BUF, MIN	27	81	14	22	36	-26	1.38	38.1%	10.0	0.5	0.2	-0.5	0.2
2015-16	ANA	28	65	11	17	29					1.1	0.9	0.0	1.9

Going into the season, Chris Stewart declared that the Buffalo Sabres would not be the worst team in hockey. Needless to say, he was wrong. Further, the former Av and Blue hit hard times in the Queen City. Not only did the six-foot-two, 231-pound power forward fail to score goals like he has in the past, but his defensive shortcomings and lack of consistent effort were on display. He was even a healthy scratch at one point. The Wild got some offense out of him after a deadline-day deal, but there can be no delusions about what Stewart is any more: a third-line winger who cannot be relied on for top-six minutes. He may very well flourish in Anaheim, with the pressure on Corey Perry and Ryan Getzlaf.

Brett Sutter — LW/C — MIN

Season	Team	Age	GP	G	A	Pts	+/-	ESP/60	AdjCF%	iCF/60	OGVT	DGVT	SGVT	GVT
2012-13	CAR	25	3	0	0	0	-1	0.00	42.8%	8.3	-0.2	-0.1	0.0	-0.2
2013-14	CAR	26	17	1	1	2	-4	1.00	46.9%	12.0	-0.4	0.0	0.0	-0.5
2014-15	MIN	27	6	0	3	3	1	3.53	43.9%	12.2	0.4	0.5	0.0	0.9
2015-16	MIN	28	29	4	7	11					0.7	0.8	0.0	1.5

A move from the Hurricanes organization to the Wild didn't provide the fresh start Brett Sutter might have been hoping for. Brandon's cousin found his way into six games and was pretty effective in limited minutes, posting a trio of assists and his highest average ice-time since 2009-10. Unfortunately, in Iowa, his 29 points in 71 games did very little to entice anyone to play him regularly in the NHL.

Thomas Vanek — LW — MIN

Season	Team	Age	GP	G	A	Pts	+/-	ESP/60	AdjCF%	iCF/60	OGVT	DGVT	SGVT	GVT
2012-13	BUF	28	38	20	21	41	-1	2.76	45.3%	15.5	7.6	0.2	1.0	8.7
2013-14	BUF, NYI, MTL	29	78	27	41	68	7	2.50	45.7%	15.1	11.0	4.0	0.4	15.4
2014-15	MIN	30	80	21	31	52	-6	1.99	47.9%	11.7	8.3	0.8	0.6	9.7
2015-16	MIN	31	66	18	30	48					5.9	1.5	0.0	7.4

One of the most heavily scrutinized players in the NHL, Thomas Vanek frustrated Wild fans the same way he frustrated Canadiens fans and Sabres fans before them. The fifth pick of the famed 2003 draft has incredible hands and scoring skill around the net and is an underrated playmaker, but his dreadfully slow skating and inconsistent efforts cause fans and coaches to tear their hair out when his scoring goes cold. Back in the days of 40 goals and a point-per-game, the defensive issues could be overlooked, but if he isn't adding more than his so-so 52 points, the Austrian winger isn't bringing much value.

Stephane Veilleux — LW — Free Agent

Season	Team	Age	GP	G	A	Pts	+/-	ESP/60	AdjCF%	iCF/60	OGVT	DGVT	SGVT	GVT
2013-14	MIN	32	34	3	0	3	-2	0.73	41.4%	10.6	-0.6	0.6	0.0	0.0
2014-15	MIN	33	12	1	1	2	0	1.56	52.4%	8.5	0.0	0.7	0.0	0.7
2015-16	Free Agent	34	34	4	4	8					0.1	0.9	0.0	1.0

Mike Yeo often talks about the energy "Steve" brings to the team. Unfortunately, it didn't translate into much while Stephane Veilleux was on the ice. His 93.9 PDO might be part of the reason, but low PDO is a trend for him, having only surpassed a breakeven 100 PDO once in his 10-year career, in 2006-07. He simply isn't a player who can drive play and dictate the flow on a depth line. Veilleux isn't a bad leader for the Iowa Wild, but the Minnesota Wild will continue to have better options among cusp AHL players.

Jason Zucker — LW — MIN

Season	Team	Age	GP	G	A	Pts	+/-	ESP/60	AdjCF%	iCF/60	OGVT	DGVT	SGVT	GVT
2012-13	MIN	20	20	4	1	5	4	1.37	46.7%	15.4	0.3	1.0	0.0	1.3
2013-14	MIN	21	21	4	1	5	2	0.71	42.7%	15.3	0.0	0.8	0.0	0.7
2014-15	MIN	22	51	21	5	26	-9	2.16	54.4%	16.3	5.0	2.0	0.0	7.0
2015-16	MIN	23	56	18	11	29					3.4	1.7	0.0	5.1

What a bizarre season it was for the Wild's second-round pick from 2010. Jason Zucker became one of the NHL's best five-on-five goal scorers, putting 17 pucks in the back of the net at even strength, the same number as Evgeni Malkin, and one behind Ryan Getzlaf. You might think that would make him one of the most exciting young players in the league at age 22, but Zucker only had five assists. In 98 career NHL games, somehow he has managed just nine helpers. As odd as those numbers might be, the Wild will be willing to overlook the lack of setup passes as long as he keeps putting up goals and strong Corsi Percentages, like he did last season (54.1%).

DEFENSEMEN

Keith Ballard							LD						Free Agent	
Season	Team	Age	GP	G	A	Pts	+/-	ESP/60	AdjCF%	iCF/60	OGVT	DGVT	SGVT	GVT
2012-13	VAN	30	36	0	2	2	-2	0.24	51.9%	7.7	-0.9	0.8	0.0	0.0
2013-14	MIN	31	45	2	7	9	-7	0.76	45.5%	7.0	-0.3	1.3	0.0	1.0
2014-15	MIN	32	14	0	1	1	-3	0.38	44.7%	3.3	-0.6	-0.1	0.0	-0.8
2015-16	Free Agent	33	35	1	5	6					-0.3	1.1	0.0	0.8

32-year-old defenseman Keith Ballard suffered a serious concussion on December 9 when the Islanders' Matt Martin drove his face into the boards in a frightening collision. Given Ballard's history of concussions, the hit may put his hockey future into question. Prior to that misfortune, the Baudette, Minnesota native may have been the team's best option on the left side of the third defensive pairing, though that is not saying much with their dearth of lefties outside the top four. With just five goals over the last five seasons, his production has stagnated and the ex-Canuck is not driving play in any fashion, either.

Stu Bickel							RD						Free Agent	
Season	Team	Age	GP	G	A	Pts	+/-	ESP/60	AdjCF%	iCF/60	OGVT	DGVT	SGVT	GVT
2012-13	NYR	26	16	0	0	0	-2	0.00	36.0%	3.6	-0.4	-0.1	0.0	-0.5
2014-15	MIN	28	9	0	1	1	1	1.23	36.8%	6.3	0.1	0.2	0.0	0.3
2015-16	Free Agent	29	27	1	4	5					0.2	0.9	0.0	1.1

Mike Yeo seemed to like one thing that Stu Bickel offered: a perceived ability to play both wing and defense. The team kept him in the pressbox, believing he could step in for either an injured forward or defenseman, instead of sitting two players in the stands while potentially stifling the development of a player the team had more invested in (not to mention gaining a modest cap savings). The veteran of three NHL seasons found his way into nine games, garnering a less-than-impressive 37.7% Corsi. The six-foot-four journeyman managed a total of 10 hits and drew just a single penalty while clocking in a whopping average of five minutes per game. Even if Bickel could be justified as a versatile player (he is below replacement level at both positions), it was clear from his paltry ice-time that the coaching staff didn't trust him.

Jonathon Blum — RD — MIN

Season	Team	Age	GP	G	A	Pts	+/-	ESP/60	AdjCF%	iCF/60	OGVT	DGVT	SGVT	GVT
2012-13	NSH	23	35	1	6	7	-1	0.92	45.3%	5.8	0.6	1.5	0.0	2.1
2013-14	MIN	24	15	0	1	1	-1	0.36	53.9%	8.3	-0.3	0.2	0.0	-0.1
2014-15	MIN	25	4	0	1	1	-3	1.57	53.1%	5.8	0.1	-0.4	0.0	-0.3
2015-16	MIN	26	27	2	5	6					0.3	0.7	0.0	1.0

Despite coming to Minnesota as a touted young defenseman with an offensive predisposition, Jonathon Blum hasn't found his way into Mike Yeo's favor. After lacing up for 15 games in his first year with the Wild, he played just four games this season, always getting less than 12 minutes of ice-time. That said, Nashville's 2007 first-round pick did manage to show his offensive prowess at AHL Iowa, where he finished tied for second in points with 12 goals and 25 assists. Not feeling the love in North America, Blum sailed away to Russia, to play for Admiral Vladivostock.

Jonas Brodin — LD — MIN

Season	Team	Age	GP	G	A	Pts	+/-	ESP/60	AdjCF%	iCF/60	OGVT	DGVT	SGVT	GVT
2012-13	MIN	19	45	2	9	11	3	0.60	51.7%	6.2	0.4	3.5	0.0	3.9
2013-14	MIN	20	79	8	11	19	0	0.45	46.9%	5.5	0.3	5.0	0.0	5.3
2014-15	MIN	21	71	3	14	17	21	0.56	51.1%	6.6	0.1	7.5	0.0	7.6
2015-16	MIN	22	70	4	15	19					0.2	5.1	0.0	5.4

Youngster Jonas Brodin continued to prove that he is an unrecognized prodigy in his own zone. Offensively, his game still has a ways to go, though, taking a step back from last season's eight goals, potting just three on a 3.2% shooting percentage. The six-foot-one Swede ranked second among team defensemen with a 25.6 shots against per 60 minutes. Brodin is young and his offensive game should continue to develop, but his ability to shut down the opposition is already impressive, not least of all because he is just 22 with three solid seasons behind him already.

Matt Dumba — RD — MIN

Season	Team	Age	GP	G	A	Pts	+/-	ESP/60	AdjCF%	iCF/60	OGVT	DGVT	SGVT	GVT
2013-14	MIN	19	13	1	1	2	-5	0.00	54.9%	10.3	0.4	-0.4	0.0	0.0
2014-15	MIN	20	58	8	8	16	13	0.79	53.2%	11.1	2.2	2.7	0.0	5.0
2015-16	MIN	21	58	7	16	22					2.7	2.5	0.0	5.1

2012 seventh-overall selection Matt Dumba had a patchy start to the season. The process was there, but the results weren't consistent enough for Minnesota to keep him when he was seeing limited minutes with no power-play time. In those first 20 games, the Regina, Saskatchewan native grabbed three assists and a goal. He then spent almost two months playing for AHL Iowa before returning to the NHL, where he scored seven goals and five assists in 38 games after his stay in minors, plus two power-play goals and a pair of assists in 10 playoff games. The former Red Deer Rebel will be just 21 years old at the start of the season; he has a bright future as an offensively-gifted defender.

Christian Folin									RD					MIN
Season	Team	Age	GP	G	A	Pts	+/-	ESP/60	AdjCF%	iCF/60	OGVT	DGVT	SGVT	GVT
2013-14	MIN	22	1	0	1	1	3	4.05	26.1%	0.0	0.2	0.6	0.0	0.7
2014-15	MIN	23	40	2	8	10	3	0.93	50.4%	8.5	1.1	2.0	0.0	3.0
2015-16	MIN	24	46	3	11	14					1.2	2.2	0.0	3.4

Christian Folin came out of college as a hot free-agent commodity, and proved it wasn't all hype in his rookie year. Though the UMass-Lowell product didn't become a standout, he displayed some offensive prowess and developed well, showing signs that he could become an impactful defenseman for the Wild. The six-foot-three blueliner found his way into 40 games, posting a 50.1 Corsi-against per 60 minutes, the best mark on the team among defensemen.

Jordan Leopold									LD					Free Agent
Season	Team	Age	GP	G	A	Pts	+/-	ESP/60	AdjCF%	iCF/60	OGVT	DGVT	SGVT	GVT
2012-13	BUF, STL	32	39	2	8	10	-8	0.56	48.5%	8.2	0.9	0.3	0.0	1.1
2013-14	STL	33	27	1	5	6	1	0.62	53.9%	9.7	0.6	0.6	0.0	1.3
2014-15	STL, CBJ, MIN	34	43	1	3	4	-6	0.29	45.1%	6.4	-0.5	0.1	0.0	-0.5
2015-16	Free Agent	35	40	1	5	5					-0.6	1.0	0.0	0.4

Jordan Leopold finished the season with the Minnesota Wild, his third team of the 2014-15 campaign. The 2002 NCAA champion, as captain of the Minnesota Gophers, was moved out of St. Louis, where he was expendable on a deep blue line, to Columbus, where he failed to carve out a space for himself. A trade deadline move saw him head to his home state, due to the Wild's dearth of left-shooting defensemen outside of the top four—after Keith Ballard was injured in early December, they couldn't find a reliable solution there. Leopold earned his spot through adequate play, which put him above Nate Prosser in the pecking order. The former Flame, Av, Panther, Penguin, Sabre, Blue, and Blue Jacket remains a serviceable defenseman, but is unlikely to be more an a cusp player who sees a significant number of healthy scratches.

Nate Prosser									RD					MIN
Season	Team	Age	GP	G	A	Pts	+/-	ESP/60	AdjCF%	iCF/60	OGVT	DGVT	SGVT	GVT
2012-13	MIN	26	17	0	0	0	4	0.00	47.3%	4.9	-0.5	1.0	0.0	0.5
2013-14	MIN	27	53	2	6	8	2	0.53	47.1%	7.0	-0.3	2.9	0.0	2.6
2014-15	MIN	28	63	2	5	7	-1	0.62	47.9%	6.5	-0.7	2.4	0.0	1.7
2015-16	MIN	29	54	2	6	8					-0.5	2.4	0.0	1.9

Nate Prosser and the Wild couldn't come to terms on a contract over the summer, with Minnesota wanting the deal to be two-way. Prosser ultimately signed a two-way deal with St. Louis, got waived before the season started, and the Wild claimed him on the contract they originally desired. The undrafted defenseman was on the fringes of the third pairing until Keith Ballard's season-ending injury opened up a spot playing his off-hand side, which he held until the Wild acquired Jordan Leopold at the trade deadline. Maybe Minnesota would have been better off picking up someone other than Prosser, as the 28-year-old was toward the bottom of the club in nearly statistical category.

Marco Scandella — LD — MIN

Season	Team	Age	GP	G	A	Pts	+/-	ESP/60	AdjCF%	iCF/60	OGVT	DGVT	SGVT	GVT
2012-13	MIN	22	6	1	0	1	-1	0.75	45.4%	9.8	0.0	0.3	0.0	0.3
2013-14	MIN	23	76	3	14	17	10	0.81	49.1%	8.7	0.6	5.8	0.0	6.5
2014-15	MIN	24	64	11	12	23	8	0.85	52.4%	11.3	4.2	3.8	0.0	8.0
2015-16	MIN	25	68	7	18	25					2.8	4.1	0.0	6.9

This season was a coming out party for Marco Scandella's booming slapshot, scoring 11 goals on the year, including two overtime game winners, and two more in the postseason. "Marco Goal-o" also proved to be reliable defensively, with Yeo utilizing him against tough opposition. He also led team defensemen on the penalty kill. Pleased to see how well he has developed since his first season in 2011-12, Minnesota signed Scandella to a long-term deal through 2020 at a reasonable $4 million cap hit.

Jared Spurgeon — RD — MIN

Season	Team	Age	GP	G	A	Pts	+/-	ESP/60	AdjCF%	iCF/60	OGVT	DGVT	SGVT	GVT
2012-13	MIN	23	39	5	10	15	1	0.72	50.2%	7.6	1.7	2.4	0.0	4.1
2013-14	MIN	24	67	5	21	26	15	0.92	51.8%	8.2	2.0	6.9	0.0	8.9
2014-15	MIN	25	66	9	16	25	3	0.94	54.1%	10.6	3.6	4.5	0.0	8.1
2015-16	MIN	26	66	7	21	28					3.2	4.2	0.0	7.4

Jared Spurgeon may have been Minnesota's best all-around defenseman this season. Though he is one of the smallest defenders in the NHL, he managed to create offense, setting a career-high in goals with nine. The 2008 sixth-round selection of the Islanders has exceptional ability with the puck, often darting between defenders and creating space for himself to make plays. The puck skills of the Edmonton native make up for what he lacks in stature at five-foot-nine, 176 pounds. At that size, it is rare for a defenseman to do enough on the defensive end to make up for the physical element required, but Spurgeon is clever enough with the use of his stick and smarts to survive.

Ryan Suter — LD — MIN

Season	Team	Age	GP	G	A	Pts	+/-	ESP/60	AdjCF%	iCF/60	OGVT	DGVT	SGVT	GVT
2012-13	MIN	27	48	4	28	32	2	0.99	49.0%	7.1	4.9	4.2	0.0	9.1
2013-14	MIN	28	82	8	35	43	15	0.79	48.5%	7.1	3.8	8.1	0.0	11.9
2014-15	MIN	29	77	2	36	38	7	0.87	51.8%	8.6	3.2	6.6	0.0	9.8
2015-16	MIN	30	71	6	28	34					3.2	5.0	0.0	8.2

Ryan Suter has an incredible ability to play huge minutes at a very high level; he led the NHL in ice-time at 29:03 per game. Nevertheless, the debate over the long-time Predator is whether he is worthy of a huge contract and All-Star status. While his Relative Corsi over the past three seasons is basically breakeven, opponents have only scored 1.90 goals against per 60 minutes with him on the ice, which is in the top 50 among defenders, despite the grueling minutes he is playing. Adding in his production on the power play and huge penalty-killing ice-time, the 2010 Olympic silver medalist is deserving of being considered a number-one defenseman, even though he may be a shade below the elites.

MINNESOTA WILD

GOALTENDERS

Niklas Backstrom							G						MIN
Season	Team	Age	GP	W	L	OT	GAA	Sv%	ESSV%	QS%	GGVT	DGVT	SGVT	GVT
2012-13	MIN	34	42	24	15	3	2.48	.909	.914	51.2%	0.8	0.8	-2.1	-0.5
2013-14	MIN	35	21	5	11	2	3.02	.899	.910	42.1%	-4.7	0.0	-1.0	-5.7
2014-15	MIN	36	19	5	7	3	3.04	.887	.889	14.3%	-8.5	0.5	-0.2	-8.3
2015-16	MIN	37	15					.907			-1.9	0.1	-0.1	-2.0

Despite having one year remaining on his three-year deal, we may have seen the last of Niklas Backstrom in the NHL. Coming off an injury-shortened season in 2013-14 that ended with sports-hernia surgery, it is hard to see how he finds his way into more games with Minnesota or another franchise. With a paltry .886 even-strength save percentage on the season, the 37-year-old netminder had the league's worst save percentage for a goalie who played at least nine games. Over the last handful of seasons, he has frequently been injured—likely the reason he wasn't given a compliance buyout—and his numbers have been well under par.

John Curry							G						Free Agent
Season	Team	Age	GP	W	L	OT	GAA	Sv%	ESSV%	QS%	GGVT	DGVT	SGVT	GVT
2013-14	MIN	29	2	1	0	0	3.00	.930	.975	100.0%	0.9	-0.2	0.0	0.7
2014-15	MIN	30	2	0	0	1	4.17	.800	.810	0.0%	-2.3	0.1	0.0	-2.2
2015-16	Free Agent	31	11					.913			0.7	0.0	0.0	0.7

The journeyman goaltender John Curry provided stability for the Wild's AHL affiliate, giving them 41 games and a .917 save percentage. That has been his M.O. since entering pro hockey back in 2007-08 after a stellar career at Boston University. At five-foot-eleven, the 31-year-old does not have typical NHL goaltender size or athleticism, but he has had a fair amount of success all over the minors, from the Las Vegas Wranglers, to the Wheeling Nailers, to the Orlando Solar Bears, to the Hamburg Freezers, and on and on. While Curry has only seen a handful of big-league games in his time, it has been quite the journey. There is something to be said for that.

Devan Dubnyk							G						MIN
Season	Team	Age	GP	W	L	OT	GAA	Sv%	ESSV%	QS%	GGVT	DGVT	SGVT	GVT
2012-13	EDM	26	38	14	16	6	2.57	.920	.922	54.1%	13.5	-1.3	-1.6	10.5
2013-14	EDM, NSH	27	34	11	18	3	3.43	.891	.898	35.5%	-14.1	-0.5	-0.7	-15.3
2014-15	ARI, MIN	28	58	36	14	4	2.07	.929	.934	67.3%	27.0	0.2	0.7	27.9
2015-16	MIN	29	45					.914			4.2	0.0	0.0	4.1

Having spent time with Edmonton, Nashville, Montreal, and Arizona since October 2013, before getting traded to a desperate Wild team in January 2015, Devan Dubnyk had literally played himself out of the NHL by the end of the 2013-14 season based on a disastrous stretch of games. After joining Minnesota, he played in 39 of 40 regular-season games, didn't lose two straight until the second round of the playoffs, and posted a .936 save percentage en route to earning himself both Vezina and Masterton nominations. While the six-foot-six, 209-pound netminder was out-of-this-world good for the Wild, it wasn't Dubnyk's first stretch of playing very well, making it unclear whether he can perform as a top goalie for an extended period of time. Regardless, Minnesota went all-in, signing the former Kamloops Blazer to a contract through 2021.

Josh Harding — G — Retired

Season	Team	Age	GP	W	L	OT	GAA	Sv%	ESSV%	QS%	GGVT	DGVT	SGVT	GVT
2012-13	MIN	28	5	1	1	0	3.24	.863	.864	33.3%	-2.7	0.2	0.00	-2.5
2013-14	MIN	29	29	18	7	3	1.65	.933	.940	80.8%	14.5	1.3	-0.3	15.5
2015-16	Retired	25	26					.913			1.4	0.2	-0.1	1.5

Josh Harding, diagnosed with multiple sclerosis in 2013, was an inspirational story, bouncing back as one of the league's best goaltenders through the first half of the 2013-14 season before being sidelined following a change in his medication. Harding looked like a real option to be Minnesota's starter this season, before a disagreement in camp saw him kick a wall and break his foot. That further sidelined him for a good portion of the start of the season, and once recovered, had him reporting to the Iowa Wild of the AHL. In his first start, he set a franchise record for saves in a game (this would later be broken, because Iowa was terrible). In his next start, he had to leave another impressive performance due to dehydration, which was related to his multiple sclerosis. He missed the reminder of the season.

Darcy Kuemper — G — MIN

Season	Team	Age	GP	W	L	OT	GAA	Sv%	ESSV%	QS%	GGVT	DGVT	SGVT	GVT
2012-13	MIN	22	6	1	2	0	2.08	.916	.915	66.7%	0.9	0.2	0.0	1.1
2013-14	MIN	23	26	12	8	4	2.43	.915	.932	52.0%	3.2	0.3	0.0	3.5
2014-15	MIN	24	31	14	12	2	2.6	.905	.911	57.1%	-2.6	0.6	-1.3	-3.4
2015-16	MIN	25	26					.913			1.4	0.2	-0.1	1.5

Darcy Kuemper entered the season as the heir apparent, with Niklas Backstrom coming off season-ending surgery and Josh Harding's health in question. The Saskatoon native opened the season with a bang, not allowing a goal in the first 164:02. However, the honeymoon ended quickly, with Kuemper ultimately finishing the season with a paltry .907 even-strength save percentage. For the Wild, playing him past the point where he required waivers to go to the AHL hurt both the team and the 24-year-old goaltender's development; it will have lasting effects on the roster, though it was difficult to avoid. The six-foot-five, 205-pound goalie wasn't ready for the spotlight this season, and once Dubnyk arrived, Kuemper only got one start through 40 games. He is penciled into the backup role for 2015-16, and will be in a position where he can develop as much as possible.

Dustin Nelson

Montreal Canadiens

Any summary of the 2014-15 NHL season for the Montreal Canadiens needs to begin with a discussion about Carey Price.

In terms of intangibles, outside observers can only speculate, but there was evidence that he contributed significantly to the team through leadership, consistency, and emotional stability. In terms of league recognition, he was the big winner on awards night, taking home three major individual awards: Price was voted by his peers as the league's Most Valuable Player, winning the Ted Lindsay Award; 27 out of 30 general managers selected him as the top goalie, the Vezina Trophy winner; he also accomplished the rare feat of being the seventh goalie to ever win the Hart Trophy as the league's Most Valuable Player (and the third to do so as a member of the Canadiens). And he didn't just win the latter award—he dominated the voting, earning 139 out of a possible 157 first-place votes.

More importantly, in terms of raw numbers, Price had a statistical season for the ages, leading the league in wins (44), goals-against average (1.96), and save percentage (.933); he finished second with an impressive nine shutouts.

His performance was nothing short of dominant. So it raises the question: was it the best goaltending performance in Canadiens history? Of course, that would be an easier question to answer if he had put up the same numbers with the less-storied Columbus Blue Jackets or the Winnipeg Jets instead, but the greatest franchise in NHL history has witnessed many noteworthy goaltenders and legendary performances. In order to make the claim that Price's season was the best, he would have to top goalies who backstopped the team to a Stanley Cup. Finishing second overall with 110 points is impressive, but a second-round playoff exit likely disqualifies him from consideration for some folks.

Still, there is one notable franchise record that Price now holds. Up until this past season, the mark for regular season wins by a Habs goalie was 42, a number matched by Ken Dryden (1975-76) and Jacques Plante, twice (1955-56 and 1961-62). This season, Price did two better, winning a total of 44 games.

Much has been written about how wins are an inadequate measure of a goaltender's performance. Quality Starts, created by Rob Vollman, is a metric that counts the number of games a goalie starts and finishes with a save percentage above league average, and it is often held up as a better metric of individual success. Applying Quality Starts to the 2014-15 season, Price would actually finish second to Braden

CANADIENS IN A BOX

Last Season		
Goals For	221	t-18th
Goals Against	189	t-1st
GVT	32	6th
Points	110	2nd
Playoffs	Lost Conference Semifinal	

Carey Price carried an ordinary team to first in the Atlantic Division.

Three-Year Record		
GVT	66	8th
Points	273	6th
Playoffs	3 Appearances, 17 Wins	

VUKOTA Projections		
Goals For	210	25th
Goals Against	208	1st
GVT	2	19th
Points	92	19th

There is nowhere to go but down for the Habs, who will fall back to the middle of the pack.

Top Three Prospects
N. Scherbak (F), M. De La Rose (F), M. McCarron (F)

Comparing the four highest goalie Win totals in Canadiens history

Name	Season	W	L	T	OTL	Pts	Win %
Ken Dryden	1975-76	42	10	8	-	92	.767
Jacques Plante	1955-56	42	12	10	-	94	.734
Carey Price	2014-15	44	16	-	6	94	.712
Jacques Plante	1961-62	42	14	14	-	98	.700

Holtby (44 to 43, although in six fewer games played). Other starters (with at least 27 GP) with comparable Quality Start percentages to Price's 65.2% are Holtby (61.1%), Corey Crawford (68.4%), Devan Dubnyk (67.3%), Henrik Lundqvist (65.2%), and Pekka Rinne (67.2%).

Suddenly, Price's individual performance doesn't look so dominant, finishing second in Quality Starts and tied for fourth in Quality Start percentage. Also, if you were wondering who else received the other first-place Vezina votes, they were split between three goalies. All three of them finished with an equal or greater Quality Start percentage than Price.

Other analytical measures can be used to argue which goaltender had the better team and/or defense playing in front of them, but like it or not, the statistics community will always struggle to trump the simplicity of wins and losses. Certainly a goaltender's skill is among the primary determining factors in winning and losing, but any goalie will tell you that they rely heavily on the team that is in front of them. Long before the goalie has a chance to stop the puck, he relies on his teammates to remove scoring threats, intercept passes, and clear sight lines. Price said as much when he gave his team the credit during one of his many acceptance speeches at the 2015 NHL Awards night. Still, it isn't simply a matter of saying that Price's 44 wins is bigger and therefore better than Plante and Dryden's 42 wins. A fuller look at their seasons can be found in the chart on this page.

Price's numbers become less impressive in terms of points earned and win percentage. In addition, Plante and Dryden accomplished their feats in the era before overtime losses were worth a point. If we assume that half of those ties would result in overtime or shootout wins, their respective win totals would jump to 47, 49, and 46, all of which would eclipse Price's 44. The alternative would be to adjust Price's record to reflect the previous point system. Four of his 44 wins and two of his six overtime losses came via the shootout. Translating them instead to ties, and the remaining overtime losses to regular losses, would give Price an adjusted record of 40-20-6. That record would still give him 86 points and a winning percentage of .652, a significant accomplishment, but not one for the franchise record books.

However, the reality of goaltending in 2014-15 is that it simply does not compare well to the past. Not only have the pad sizes, game styles, competition, and rules all changed, but the way the league keeps its standings has as well. We can only compare Price to his peers – and by that comparison, he was easily the best of the best in 2014-15.

William Loewen

MONTREAL CANADIENS

Even-Strength Usage: Montreal Canadiens

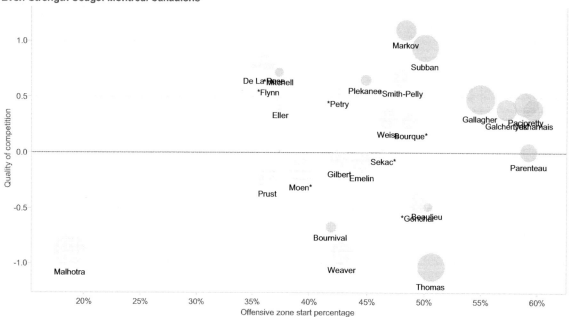

Special Teams Usage: Montreal Canadiens

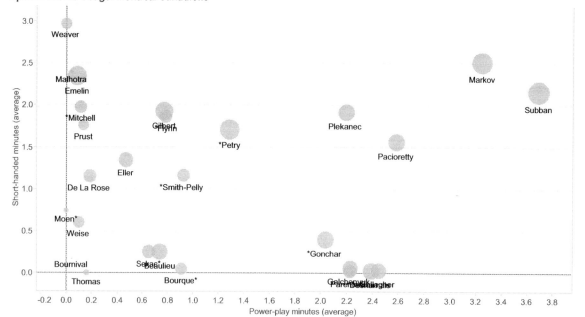

MONTREAL CANADIENS

Offensive Profile: Montreal Canadiens

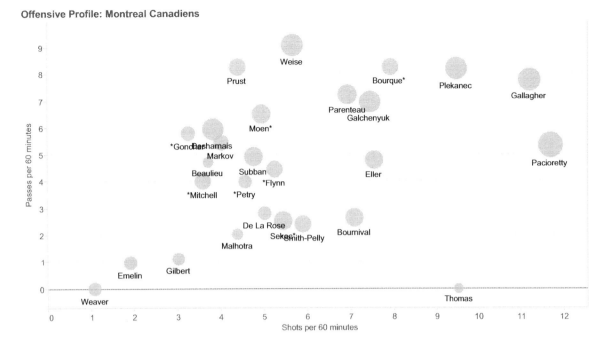

Cap Efficiency: Montreal Canadiens

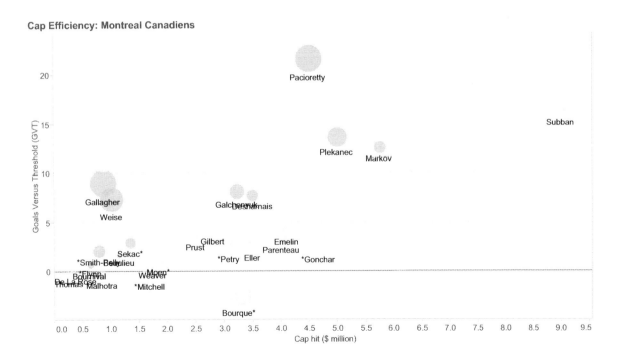

MONTREAL CANADIENS

FORWARDS

Sven Andrighetto							LW/C						MTL
Season	Team	Age	GP	G	A	Pts	+/-	ESP/60	AdjCF%	iCF/60	OGVT	DGVT	SGVT	GVT
2014-15	MTL	21	12	2	1	3	0	1.91	46.1%	11.2	-0.3	0.2	0.0	-0.2
2015-16	MTL	22	32	6	7	13					0.6	0.7	0.0	1.3

One player hoping to find a spot in the new, less size-and-grit-focused NHL is Sven Andrighetto, who has slowly moved his way up the pro ranks to the point where he should be ready for full-time duty. The five-foot-ten forward has averaged a healthy 0.72 points per game at the AHL level, following it up with a top-six even-strength production rate, albeit in limited minutes. His possession metrics are also promising, and given that the Swiss forward is only 22 years old, he may not have hit his ultimate ceiling yet. The former Rouyn-Noranda Huskie may still shift back and forth between the majors and minors in 2015-16, but expect him to make the full-time jump soon.

Michael Bournival							LW							MTL
Season	Team	Age	GP	G	A	Pts	+/-	ESP/60	AdjCF%	iCF/60	OGVT	DGVT	SGVT	GVT
2013-14	MTL	21	60	7	7	14	-6	1.17	44.3%	11.8	0.6	0.9	0.0	1.5
2014-15	MTL	22	29	3	2	5	3	1.35	49.0%	12.8	-0.5	0.8	0.0	0.3
2015-16	MTL	23	48	7	8	15					0.0	1.2	0.0	1.2

A Quebec native, Michael Bournival played his junior hockey in the province for the Shawinigian Cataractes before being drafted by Colorado in the third round in 2010. The Canadiens acquired the defensive forward at a low price, and he has since made himself a valuable prospect within the organization. While he saw a good deal of playing time in 2013-14, Bournival had trouble finding his way into the lineup and was plagued by injuries that limited him to 41 total games between the AHL and NHL levels. Given Montreal's lack of depth, Bournival's continued development is encouraging—the 23-year-old should compete for a bottom-six spot in 2015-16.

Drayson Bowman							LW							Free Agent
Season	Team	Age	GP	G	A	Pts	+/-	ESP/60	AdjCF%	iCF/60	OGVT	DGVT	SGVT	GVT
2012-13	CAR	23	37	3	2	5	-7	0.74	51.1%	15.8	-1.1	0.2	0.0	-0.9
2013-14	CAR	24	70	4	8	12	-2	1.07	45.0%	12.8	-0.9	1.5	0.0	0.6
2014-15	MTL	25	3	0	0	0	0	0.00	30.5%	2.8	-0.3	0.1	0.0	-0.2
2015-16	Free Agent	26	40	5	7	11					0.0	1.0	0.0	1.1

Drayson Bowman dressed for three games with Montreal after being invited to training camp on a PTO and playing his way to a contract. The vast majority of Bowman's season was spent in the familiar confines of the AHL, where he has played for Carolina affiliates since 2009-10. There, the 26-year-old forward totaled a modest 33 points in 62 games. At this stage in his career, Bowman can fill the role of an organizational reserve—an injury call-up—given his replacement-level play.

Jacob de la Rose							LW/C							MTL
Season	Team	Age	GP	G	A	Pts	+/-	ESP/60	AdjCF%	iCF/60	OGVT	DGVT	SGVT	GVT
2014-15	MTL	19	33	4	2	6	-5	0.73	44.8%	9.3	-0.3	0.2	0.0	-0.1
2015-16	MTL	20	45	6	5	11					-1.1	0.7	0.0	-0.4

MONTREAL CANADIENS

As a big, physical, defensive power forward, Jacob de la Rose fit right into what head coach Michel Therrien was looking for in Montreal. Consequently, the 19-year-old found himself getting consistent time in the lineup from February until the end of the season. The Swedish forward could probably use some more AHL seasoning, though, as his production did not match his coach's love. With an improved offensive game, de la Rose could become serviceable player at the NHL level.

David Desharnais									C						MTL
Season	Team	Age	GP	G	A	Pts	+/-	ESP/60	AdjCF%	iCF/60	OGVT	DGVT	SGVT	GVT
2012-13	MTL	26	48	10	18	28	-2	1.95	58.3%	8.4	2.6	1.0	0.5	4.0
2013-14	MTL	27	79	16	36	52	11	1.95	50.4%	7.2	6.2	2.6	2.5	11.2
2014-15	MTL	28	82	14	34	48	22	1.82	50.8%	7.4	3.8	3.6	0.4	7.7
2015-16	MTL	29	69	13	29	41					3.3	2.4	0.1	5.9

David Desharnais is a great success story, as the diminutive forward went undrafted after four solid QMJHL seasons, and then worked his way from the ECHL all the way up to the NHL over the course of four seasons. Since then, he has been a productive player for the Canadiens, averaging 0.62 points per game in 339 NHL games. He has spent most of his time on the team's first line, next to Max Pacioretty. As Pacioretty is a shoot-first player, while Desharnais is a pass-first player, the complementary duo was productive throughout the season—though the argument can be made that Pacioretty carried Desharnais, especially in terms of possession. The 29-year-old has seen his production decline over the years, and as such, the small center might not be the best choice for handling first-line minutes anymore.

Gabriel Dumont									C						MTL
Season	Team	Age	GP	G	A	Pts	+/-	ESP/60	AdjCF%	iCF/60	OGVT	DGVT	SGVT	GVT
2012-13	MTL	22	10	1	2	3	1	1.93	61.4%	18.2	0.7	0.3	0.0	1.0
2013-14	MTL	23	2	0	0	0	0	0.00	33.9%	4.9	0.0	0.0	0.0	0.0
2014-15	MTL	24	3	0	0	0	-1	0.00	45.3%	10.6	-0.2	-0.1	0.0	-0.2
2015-16	MTL	25	25	4	5	9					0.5	0.5	0.0	1.1

At age 25, Gabriel Dumont's window to become a consistent player at the NHL level is closing. He put up a solid 45 points in 66 AHL games during the 2014-15 season, and still has limited NHL potential, but it is unlikely that he gets himself onto the NHL roster to start the 2015-16 season. If injuries start to take their toll on the Canadiens, look for the five-foot-ten forward to make an appearance as a depth call-up.

Lars Eller									C						MTL
Season	Team	Age	GP	G	A	Pts	+/-	ESP/60	AdjCF%	iCF/60	OGVT	DGVT	SGVT	GVT
2012-13	MTL	23	46	8	22	30	8	2.58	50.6%	14.5	5.2	2.7	0.2	8.1
2013-14	MTL	24	77	12	14	26	-15	1.22	48.4%	12.5	0.4	1.1	1.5	3.0
2014-15	MTL	25	77	15	12	27	-6	1.31	47.8%	13.1	1.6	1.8	-0.5	2.8
2015-16	MTL	26	65	14	15	29					2.0	1.7	0.0	3.7

Lars Eller hasn't exactly been put in a situation to succeed while in Montreal, as he has been given tough defensive usage but linemates incapable of helping him carry the load. As a result, the 26-year-old has shown lesser production than he is likely capable of—though the Canadiens would certainly be worse off without the Danish pivot on the team's third line. With the two centers ahead of him on the depth chart both in the declining stages of their careers, it will be interesting to see if Eller's role increases, and if it does, how he produces in that new role.

Brian Flynn — RW/C — MTL

Season	Team	Age	GP	G	A	Pts	+/-	ESP/60	AdjCF%	iCF/60	OGVT	DGVT	SGVT	GVT
2012-13	BUF	24	26	6	5	11	6	1.76	47.4%	12.2	2.1	1.2	0.0	3.3
2013-14	BUF	25	79	6	7	13	-10	0.76	39.9%	8.5	-1.8	2.4	0.0	0.6
2014-15	BUF, MTL	26	63	5	12	17	-5	1.09	36.5%	8.9	-2.4	1.8	1.2	0.7
2015-16	MTL	27	59	5	11	17					-0.9	1.7	0.1	0.9

When the 2015 trade deadline came around, general manager Marc Bergevin looked to the Buffalo Sabres for depth forwards. One such player that they acquired was Brian Flynn, who would fail to put up any points in nine regular season matches. The 26-year-old forward did come through with three points in six playoff games, though, demonstrating he may have some worth as a speedy, penalty-killing fourth liner. But clearly, don't expect too many goals or assists.

Alex Galchenyuk — LW/C — MTL

Season	Team	Age	GP	G	A	Pts	+/-	ESP/60	AdjCF%	iCF/60	OGVT	DGVT	SGVT	GVT
2012-13	MTL	18	48	9	18	27	14	2.88	51.8%	13.9	4.6	2.5	0.2	7.2
2013-14	MTL	19	65	13	18	31	-12	1.57	47.8%	11.5	2.9	-0.1	-0.8	2.0
2014-15	MTL	20	80	20	26	46	8	1.80	50.8%	12.5	5.3	2.2	0.6	8.1
2015-16	MTL	21	72	20	28	48					5.2	1.8	0.0	7.0

The third-overall selection in 2012, Alex Galchenyuk has had a tentative start to his NHL career, as he has been somewhat successful at a young age, but hasn't been doing it at his natural position. A natural center, Galchenyuk has spent most of his NHL career up to this point on the wing. While he is valuable to the Canadiens anywhere, he would be more capable of controlling the puck and driving play at center. Someday, the Habs may be lauded for their patience, even if fans have been frustrated watching their 21-year-old uber-talent play a secondary role.

Brendan Gallagher — RW — MTL

Season	Team	Age	GP	G	A	Pts	+/-	ESP/60	AdjCF%	iCF/60	OGVT	DGVT	SGVT	GVT
2012-13	MTL	20	44	15	13	28	10	2.85	58.3%	21.0	4.8	2.1	0.2	7.1
2013-14	MTL	21	81	19	22	41	4	1.76	52.2%	18.6	2.8	1.7	-0.8	3.7
2014-15	MTL	22	82	24	23	47	18	2.02	53.4%	20.1	6.0	3.2	-0.2	9.0
2015-16	MTL	23	73	23	25	47					5.5	2.6	0.0	8.0

While he has been criticized for being spunky and gritty, 23-year-old Brendan Gallagher has turned into an effective top-six forward. Not only does he excel in possession metrics because of his ability to win battles and dog opponents for the puck, but the five-foot-nine winger has the capability to distribute the puck as a passer and get pucks on net from all angles as a shooter. Gallagher only trailed Max Pacioretty in even-strength shots and goals for the Habs. The Edmonton native also has a unique ability to get underneath the skin of opponents by occasionally stretching the rules, away from the play. Under contract through 2021 with a cap hit under $4 million, Montreal got a bargain for one of their key pieces.

Manny Malhotra — C — Free Agent

Season	Team	Age	GP	G	A	Pts	+/-	ESP/60	AdjCF%	iCF/60	OGVT	DGVT	SGVT	GVT
2012-13	VAN	32	9	0	0	0	-3	0.00	44.1%	4.8	-0.8	0.3	0.0	-0.5
2013-14	CAR	33	69	7	6	13	0	1.06	41.3%	6.9	-0.3	2.6	0.0	2.3
2014-15	MTL	34	58	1	3	4	-6	0.49	35.6%	9.2	-2.2	1.7	0.0	-0.4
2015-16	Free Agent	35	50	3	5	8					-0.8	1.5	0.0	0.7

Famous in analytical circles for being the first player truly buried in zone starts, by Vancouver coach Alain Vigneault, dropping from 45.3% to a mere 25.0% from 2009-10 to 2010-11—underheard of, before the days of Dallas Eakins and his 2014-15 fourth lines. Vigneault actually took Malhotra as low as 13.2% in 2011-12; this past year in Montreal, he was at 18.3%. Why the skewed utilization? To take advantage of still-elite faceoff skills (59.3%), defusing an offensive zone opportunity for the opposition, and also to allow the opposite, offensively-favorable usage for gifted scorers like the Sedin twins. The problem is, at age 35, the seventh-overall selection from 1998 gets absolutely crushed in possession nowadays, and that is no longer against top-six competition. Teams would be better off discovering the next Malhotra.

Torrey Mitchell — C — MTL

Season	Team	Age	GP	G	A	Pts	+/-	ESP/60	AdjCF%	iCF/60	OGVT	DGVT	SGVT	GVT
2012-13	MIN	27	45	4	4	8	-8	1.16	45.3%	9.7	-0.2	1.0	0.0	0.8
2013-14	MIN, BUF	28	67	2	8	10	-3	0.99	46.0%	8.4	-1.8	1.8	0.0	0.0
2014-15	BUF, MTL	29	65	6	8	14	-8	1.07	38.4%	6.9	-1.8	1.6	0.0	-0.2
2015-16	MTL	30	55	4	9	13					-0.9	1.5	0.0	0.6

Being traded from the last place Buffalo to the division-leading Montreal Canadiens was great for Torrey Mitchell, who made the most of his time, getting re-signed by the Canadiens to a three-year deal at the end of the season. Similar to his Buffalo-to-Montreal counterpart, Brian Flynn, Mitchell didn't produce for the Habs during the regular season, but had a solid postseason performing in depth roles. He can still skate, add a few goals here and there, and play a strong defensive game.

Max Pacioretty — LW — MTL

Season	Team	Age	GP	G	A	Pts	+/-	ESP/60	AdjCF%	iCF/60	OGVT	DGVT	SGVT	GVT
2012-13	MTL	24	44	15	24	39	8	2.76	60.8%	23.5	7.5	1.9	0.0	9.4
2013-14	MTL	25	73	39	21	60	8	2.39	51.6%	20.6	12.3	3.1	-0.3	15.1
2014-15	MTL	26	80	37	30	67	38	2.51	51.5%	21.8	13.7	7.0	1.0	21.6
2015-16	MTL	27	79	34	33	66					10.4	3.9	0.0	14.3

Max Pacioretty has cemented himself as a statistically elite power forward. While playing on the team's top line, he netted 37 goals, good for fifth in the league. One of his most impressive skills is getting shots on net from all areas and angles on the ice. In terms of shot-attempt generation, the 26-year-old Connecticut native had the fifth highest rate in the league. Only Alex Ovechkin, Rick Nash, James Neal, and Vladimir Tarasenko kept up a higher pace. Despite high-end numbers, even posting an incredible 67% goals-for at even strength, the US Olympian is still not considered the overall dominant player that would put him among the truly elite.

Pierre-Alexandre Parenteau							RW/LW						TOR
Season	Team	Age	GP	G	A	Pts	+/-	ESP/60	AdjCF%	iCF/60	OGVT	DGVT	SGVT	GVT
2012-13	COL	29	48	18	25	43	-11	2.31	48.4%	10.0	6.3	0.2	1.5	8.1
2013-14	COL	30	55	14	19	33	3	2.28	50.0%	10.3	4.2	1.1	-0.2	5.0
2014-15	MTL	31	56	8	14	22	0	1.51	50.2%	12.5	0.9	1.0	1.7	3.6
2015-16	TOR	32	52	10	15	24					1.8	1.2	0.1	3.0

P.A. Parenteau is the type of player who does things a bit differently, looks bad because of it, and is never quite given the credit he deserves for playing as well as he does. After a successful season in Colorado, John Tavares' former Islanders linemate was traded to the Canadiens for a replacement-level Danny Briere. While in Montreal, the 32-year-old long-time AHLer consistently found himself in the press box while players like Brandon Prust and Dale Weise stayed in the lineup. Parenteau joined a group of signings in Toronto that will likely be shipped off at the trade deadline for draft picks.

Tomas Plekanec							C						MTL
Season	Team	Age	GP	G	A	Pts	+/-	ESP/60	AdjCF%	iCF/60	OGVT	DGVT	SGVT	GVT
2012-13	MTL	30	47	14	19	33	3	1.63	52.8%	17.2	5.1	2.1	-0.6	6.6
2013-14	MTL	31	81	20	23	43	11	1.49	45.7%	15.1	5.7	5.4	-0.6	10.5
2014-15	MTL	32	82	26	34	60	8	1.95	49.1%	14.5	9.8	4.6	-0.8	13.6
2015-16	MTL	33	72	20	27	47					5.6	3.0	0.0	8.5

Tomas Plekanec had a great year by conventional statistics, as he put up his highest point totals since 2009-10. The Czech centerman has been incredibly consistent through the back end of his prime, scoring between 0.53 and 0.74 points per game over the last five years. He showed no sign of slowing down at 32, but one has to wonder if Montreal has a succession plan for Plekanec at top center. The two-time Czech Olympian received more ice-time than any other forward on the Habs, which is far from ideal for a post-prime player with average second-line talent.

Brandon Prust							LW/RW						VAN
Season	Team	Age	GP	G	A	Pts	+/-	ESP/60	AdjCF%	iCF/60	OGVT	DGVT	SGVT	GVT
2012-13	MTL	28	38	5	9	14	11	1.96	51.7%	8.2	1.6	2.5	0.0	4.1
2013-14	MTL	29	52	6	7	13	-1	1.17	42.8%	6.6	0.1	1.7	0.0	1.9
2014-15	MTL	30	82	4	14	18	6	1.12	45.7%	8.2	-0.1	3.5	0.0	3.4
2015-16	VAN	31	64	5	11	16					-0.4	2.1	0.0	1.7

Brandon Prust is the perfect example of the "grit" player that NHL coaches and executives love, despite their ineffectiveness on the ice. Prust actually produces goals and assists at a decent rate, but his possession numbers are terrible, and at the age of 32, the Ontario native isn't going to be getting much better. The former Flame and Ranger was shipped off to Vancouver during the offseason in exchange for underachieving power forward Zach Kassian.

Devante Smith-Pelly — RW — MTL

Season	Team	Age	GP	G	A	Pts	+/-	ESP/60	AdjCF%	iCF/60	OGVT	DGVT	SGVT	GVT
2012-13	ANA	20	7	0	0	0	-4	0.00	39.1%	5.1	-1.0	-0.1	0.0	-1.2
2013-14	ANA	21	19	2	8	10	5	2.69	44.4%	10.9	1.8	0.8	0.6	3.2
2014-15	ANA, MTL	22	74	6	14	20	-1	1.13	47.2%	10.5	0.1	2.3	-0.3	2.1
2015-16	MTL	23	61	7	14	21					0.3	1.7	0.0	2.1

Devante Smith-Pelly was brought to Montreal via a trade that saw teams swap disappointing prospects. Jiri Sekac, who only totaled 16 points in 50 games, was shipped to Anaheim, while Smith-Pelly, who netted 17 points in 54 games, ended up with the Habs. Though it is too early to tell who won the trade, Sekac performed much better in Anaheim than he did in Montreal, while Smith-Pelly continued to be a bit of a disappointment. The 22-year-old forward got trounced at even strength and didn't exactly rack up the points, either. This may be a make or break year to find out if former Mississauga St. Michael's Major will turn into a powerful top-six forward or end up being a frustrating bottom sixer.

Eric Tangradi — LW — DET

Season	Team	Age	GP	G	A	Pts	+/-	ESP/60	AdjCF%	iCF/60	OGVT	DGVT	SGVT	GVT
2012-13	PIT, WPG	23	41	1	3	4	-2	0.59	50.5%	12.2	-1.2	0.4	0.0	-0.8
2013-14	WPG	24	55	3	3	6	-6	0.77	53.3%	11.5	-1.2	0.1	0.0	-1.0
2014-15	MTL	25	7	0	0	0	-3	0.00	41.7%	8.7	-0.5	-0.2	0.0	-0.7
2015-16	DET	26	36	4	4	8					-0.2	0.5	0.0	0.3

As a theoretically bruising power forward, Eric Tangradi has found a bit of playing time in a fourth-line role. He has had to adapt to an energy role in the NHL, as he had long played a (middling) finesse game for a big athletic guy. As a case in point, he has only managed to put up 15 points in 143 career games, a mindbogglingly low total for a solid contributor at other levels. The 25-year-old forward only played seven games with Montreal, spending the rest of the season with the Hamilton Bulldogs. He was not brought back to the team, and instead signed a contract with Detroit, his fourth organization since 2013.

Christian Thomas — RW — MTL

Season	Team	Age	GP	G	A	Pts	+/-	ESP/60	AdjCF%	iCF/60	OGVT	DGVT	SGVT	GVT
2012-13	NYR	20	1	0	0	0	0	0.00	33.2%	10.7	0.0	0.0	0.0	0.0
2013-14	MTL	21	2	0	0	0	-1	0.00	27.2%	11.9	-0.1	-0.1	0.0	-0.2
2014-15	MTL	22	18	1	0	1	-2	0.37	56.5%	17.0	-0.3	0.0	0.0	-0.3
2015-16	MTL	23	31	5	4	9					0.3	0.6	0.0	0.9

Son of former NHLer Steve, Christian Thomas is mostly known as an AHL goal scorer. In his limited NHL experience (21 games over the past two seasons), he has only managed one point. Moreover, it is not as if the 23-year-old is tearing up the minors. In 185 AHL games, he has only managed 86 points. That type of production usually doesn't portend NHL success. Being an undersized skill player does not either, though the league is seeing more and more as goons go out of style. Thomas has puck skills and good possession numbers in his limited minutes, but unless he can produce more, he won't see the NHL regularly.

Dale Weise — RW — MTL

Season	Team	Age	GP	G	A	Pts	+/-	ESP/60	AdjCF%	iCF/60	OGVT	DGVT	SGVT	GVT
2012-13	VAN	24	40	3	3	6	-7	1.05	44.5%	8.9	-0.3	0.4	0.0	0.1
2013-14	VAN, MTL	25	61	6	10	16	3	1.80	44.7%	7.7	1.6	1.9	0.0	3.5
2014-15	MTL	26	79	10	19	29	21	1.92	45.7%	10.1	3.3	4.0	0.0	7.3
2015-16	MTL	27	65	10	16	25					1.6	2.6	0.0	4.1

Dale Weise is an unusual fourth-line player in that he is ineffective defensively and gets consistently caved in at even strength, yet somehow manages to put up an impressive amount of points. One theory is that he likes to completely desert his team during the breakout, which leads to scoring chances on the rare occasion that his team manages to get the puck out of the zone. Whatever the explanation, his production plus a grit factor are why he has a roster spot on an NHL team.

DEFENSEMEN

Bryan Allen — LD — Free Agent

Season	Team	Age	GP	G	A	Pts	+/-	ESP/60	AdjCF%	iCF/60	OGVT	DGVT	SGVT	GVT
2012-13	ANA	32	41	0	6	6	1	0.52	45.5%	7.6	-0.7	1.7	0.0	0.9
2013-14	ANA	33	68	0	10	10	20	0.52	50.6%	7.9	-1.0	5.0	0.0	4.0
2014-15	ANA, MTL	34	11	0	2	2	-2	0.76	51.7%	11.0	0.0	0.1	0.0	0.1
2015-16	Free Agent	35	41	1	6	7					-0.2	1.9	0.0	1.7

Bryan Allen was acquired by general manager Marc Bergevin from Anaheim early in the season, as the team desperately needed defensive depth, and had an extra forward in Rene Bourque who just wasn't producing anymore. At the age of 35, it is rather clear that Allen is in the downswing of his career. Coming down with the flu midway through the season didn't help his cause, either. In the end, the 1998 fourth-overall pick (Vancouver) played more games in the AHL than he did in the NHL.

Nathan Beaulieu — LD — MTL

Season	Team	Age	GP	G	A	Pts	+/-	ESP/60	AdjCF%	iCF/60	OGVT	DGVT	SGVT	GVT
2012-13	MTL	20	6	0	2	2	5	1.53	55.9%	10.0	0.2	1.0	0.0	1.2
2013-14	MTL	21	17	0	2	2	6	0.58	47.1%	10.2	-0.1	1.1	0.0	1.1
2014-15	MTL	22	64	1	8	9	6	0.45	49.0%	8.2	-0.1	1.8	0.0	1.7
2015-16	MTL	23	55	2	8	10					0.0	2.2	0.0	2.2

Nathan Beaulieu has been a highly-regarded prospect for the Canadiens ever since he was made the 17th-overall selection in the 2011 NHL Entry Draft. However, his first couple of seasons in Montreal haven't exactly gone as planned. The offensively-minded defenseman has had trouble escaping Michel Therrien's doghouse, and as a result, either spends his nights in the pressbox, in the AHL, or on the third pairing. The lack of ice-time results in his lack of offensive production, and nine points in 64 NHL games is a far cry from the two points per game pace Beaulieu once had in junior hockey. However, the potential is still there for the defensively-questionable 22-year-old.

Alexei Emelin — LD — MTL

Season	Team	Age	GP	G	A	Pts	+/-	ESP/60	AdjCF%	iCF/60	OGVT	DGVT	SGVT	GVT
2012-13	MTL	26	38	3	9	12	2	1.09	53.0%	9.5	4.1	0.1	0.0	4.3
2013-14	MTL	27	59	3	14	17	-1	0.84	44.7%	7.3	1.8	2.9	0.0	4.8
2014-15	MTL	28	68	3	11	14	5	0.71	45.7%	5.8	0.4	4.1	0.0	4.4
2015-16	MTL	29	59	2	11	13					0.1	2.9	0.0	3.0

Alexei Emelin perfectly fits the stereotype of a defensive defenseman who is unable to break the puck out of his defensive zone, resulting in his team constantly getting hemmed in and giving up a large amount of shot attempts while he is on the ice. His score-adjusted shot-attempt percentage was the lowest of any Habs defenseman who played at least 20 games. As the Canadiens become more numbers-savvy, it wouldn't be surprising to see them move on from Emelin in favor of a better puck handler.

Tom Gilbert — RD — MTL

Season	Team	Age	GP	G	A	Pts	+/-	ESP/60	AdjCF%	iCF/60	OGVT	DGVT	SGVT	GVT
2012-13	MIN	29	43	3	10	13	-11	0.77	49.4%	6.9	0.8	1.4	0.0	2.2
2013-14	FLA	30	73	3	25	28	-5	0.99	50.2%	6.8	2.8	2.9	0.0	5.6
2014-15	MTL	31	72	4	8	12	10	0.60	45.9%	6.7	-0.6	4.6	0.0	4.0
2015-16	MTL	32	61	4	14	18					0.9	3.3	0.0	4.2

After playing most of the 2013-14 season with Brian Campbell—who is known for making his teammates look better than they actually are—Tom Gilbert inked a two-year contract with Montreal, and as expected, he didn't show the high quality of play that he achieved next to Campbell. The lightweight defender is very good at moving the puck and making a good first pass, but he can struggle defensively and offers little other than passing skill. Gilbert should be a cautionary tale of calling players "underrated" simply based on Corsi.

Sergei Gonchar — LD — PIT

Season	Team	Age	GP	G	A	Pts	+/-	ESP/60	AdjCF%	iCF/60	OGVT	DGVT	SGVT	GVT
2012-13	OTT	38	45	3	24	27	4	1.11	53.5%	9.3	4.8	1.9	0.0	6.7
2013-14	DAL	39	76	2	20	22	-12	0.42	49.2%	8.4	1.0	-0.4	0.0	0.6
2014-15	DAL, MTL	40	48	1	13	14	6	0.82	46.4%	7.2	1.2	1.7	0.0	2.9
2015-16	PIT	41	47	2	11	13					0.8	1.5	0.0	2.4

There are only 16 defensemen in NHL history to score more than 800 regular-season points, and Sergei Gonchar is one of them. That makes it weird to say that he is not an NHL-caliber player, though at the age of 41, it is obvious that the Russian defenseman is not the player he was in his prime. Gonchar seems to think that he has still got some gas in the tank, as he accepted a PTO with the Pittsburgh Penguins. The Pens are light on defensive depth, but there are certainly better options than Gonchar still available, so it will be interesting to see if the veteran defenseman can play his way into a contract. He does have a good rapport with Evgeni Malkin, if he can stick on the merit of remaining skill.

Andrei Markov — LD — MTL

Season	Team	Age	GP	G	A	Pts	+/-	ESP/60	AdjCF%	iCF/60	OGVT	DGVT	SGVT	GVT
2012-13	MTL	34	48	10	20	30	-9	0.51	53.0%	7.7	5.6	0.6	0.0	6.2
2013-14	MTL	35	81	7	36	43	12	0.85	49.5%	7.2	4.6	5.7	0.6	11.0
2014-15	MTL	36	81	10	40	50	22	0.93	50.7%	9.7	7.0	5.9	-0.3	12.6
2015-16	MTL	37	67	7	28	34					3.9	4.1	0.0	7.9

While Andrei Markov is no longer the player he used to be, the 37-year-old defenseman remains arguably the second best on the Canadiens, behind P.K. Subban. The Russian defenseman still has exceptional offensive skill, producing at a good-enough rate at five-on-five to be considered a legit top-pairing defenseman. Where he really stands out is on the power play, where his points per 60 minutes was second among defensemen who played at least 250 minutes. Given his age, it is possible that Markov will start to decline soon. His role may need to get reduced, but he is still going to be a valuable piece on Montreal's back end.

Greg Pateryn — RD — MTL

Season	Team	Age	GP	G	A	Pts	+/-	ESP/60	AdjCF%	iCF/60	OGVT	DGVT	SGVT	GVT
2012-13	MTL	22	3	0	0	0	0	0.00	51.6%	4.1	-0.1	0.0	0.0	-0.1
2014-15	MTL	24	17	0	0	0	0	0.00	52.4%	6.1	-0.9	0.4	0.0	-0.5
2015-16	MTL	25	34	1	6	7					-0.1	1.2	0.0	1.1

In limited time, Greg Pateryn flashed some capability of being a solid depth NHLer. He doesn't do any one thing spectacularly, but does a lot of things at an average level including adding a plus shot from the point. The former Michigan D-man failed to post points in his regular-season time with the Habs, but as been a point producer at the AHL level, scoring 15 goals for the Hamilton in 2013-14. Draft status has pushed some other Montreal prospects up to the NHL ahead of him, but if the opportunity arises, he may not only see ice-time, but play his way into being a regular.

Jeff Petry — RD — MTL

Season	Team	Age	GP	G	A	Pts	+/-	ESP/60	AdjCF%	iCF/60	OGVT	DGVT	SGVT	GVT
2012-13	EDM	25	48	3	9	12	1	0.77	44.7%	9.0	1.0	2.2	0.0	3.2
2013-14	EDM	26	80	7	10	17	-22	0.64	45.7%	8.1	0.5	2.9	0.0	3.4
2014-15	EDM, MTL	27	78	7	15	22	-28	0.72	46.8%	10.1	2.1	0.7	-0.3	2.6
2015-16	MTL	28	63	4	13	18					0.9	1.9	0.0	2.8

Jeff Petry had a shaky start to his time in Montreal, but he clearly impressed general manager Marc Bergevin with his postseason play. The 28-year-old defenseman signed a six-year contract with the Canadiens during the offseason, and will likely feature in the team's top four for the near future. Petry's contract is a good example of how teams are evaluating defensemen these days. He is a possession-driving, intelligent defender. You won't get booming hits or 50 points, but you will have the puck with him on the ice more than the other team. Finally, we are seeing NHL clubs put the emphasis on this talent that it deserves.

P.K. Subban — RD — MTL

Season	Team	Age	GP	G	A	Pts	+/-	ESP/60	AdjCF%	iCF/60	OGVT	DGVT	SGVT	GVT
2012-13	MTL	23	42	11	27	38	12	1.00	57.1%	10.7	9.4	3.1	0.0	12.5
2013-14	MTL	24	82	10	43	53	-4	1.14	50.0%	8.1	7.6	1.9	0.0	9.5
2014-15	MTL	25	82	15	45	60	21	1.40	51.9%	9.0	10.8	5.8	-0.3	16.3
2015-16	MTL	26	76	12	40	52					8.0	4.2	0.0	12.1

One of the NHL's most polarizing players, P.K. Subban found his name in the mix once again for the Norris Trophy—and statistically, he had a case just as good as Erik Karlsson. You have to wonder if the criticism about his defensive game is because of one type of old-school bias or another, because all the statistical evidence screams that his "risk taking" is justified. Subban's size, power, skating, shot, and puck skills are amongst the best in the league. The Canadiens defense corps is already lacking behind their top pairing, so Subban is constantly asked to put them on his back—which he does really, really well.

Jarred Tinordi — LD — MTL

Season	Team	Age	GP	G	A	Pts	+/-	ESP/60	AdjCF%	iCF/60	OGVT	DGVT	SGVT	GVT
2012-13	MTL	20	8	0	2	2	5	1.39	64.4%	8.5	0.3	0.9	0.0	1.2
2013-14	MTL	21	22	0	2	2	-2	0.45	51.8%	7.3	-0.6	0.8	0.0	0.2
2014-15	MTL	22	13	0	2	2	-5	0.79	49.9%	6.2	0.1	-0.6	0.0	-0.4
2015-16	MTL	23	31	1	5	6					0.1	0.7	0.0	0.8

Though Montreal already has a young, talented defender on their roster, they have another ready to make the jump in Jarred Tinordi, who put up 36 points in 44 AHL games. For his size, the 2010 first rounder's skating ability is very impressive, but his decision making is not always up to the level of his other talents. Heading into 2015-16, the Minnesota native will be looking to compete for a roster spot, though it will be tough for him to beat out Greg Pateryn, Nathan Beaulieu, or Tom Gilbert.

Mike Weaver — RD — Free Agent

Season	Team	Age	GP	G	A	Pts	+/-	ESP/60	AdjCF%	iCF/60	OGVT	DGVT	SGVT	GVT
2012-13	FLA	34	27	1	8	9	-3	1.20	46.0%	5.4	1.6	1.4	0.0	3.0
2013-14	FLA, MTL	35	72	1	12	13	0	0.70	48.5%	5.9	0.1	2.9	0.0	3.0
2014-15	MTL	36	31	0	4	4	0	0.69	44.5%	5.6	0.6	1.4	0.0	0.8
2015-16	Free Agent	37	45	1	6	7					-0.4	2.0	0.0	1.6

Mike Weaver joins the long list of players who were effective until Father Time caught up with them. The 36-year-old had a long, successful run with Florida before joining the Canadiens at the end of the 2013-14 campaign. A good playoff performace earned the diminutive shot blocker a further contract, but he struggled to stay in Montreal's lineup and was not brought back to the team at the end of the season.

GOALTENDERS

Carey Price								G					MTL
Season	Team	Age	GP	W	L	OT	GAA	Sv%	ESSV%	QS%	GGVT	DGVT	SGVT	GVT
2012-13	MTL	25	39	21	13	4	2.59	.905	.920	55.3%	-0.8	0.5	0.7	0.5
2013-14	MTL	26	59	34	20	5	2.32	.927	.934	64.4%	28.0	-1.2	0.2	27.0
2014-15	MTL	27	66	44	16	6	1.96	.933	.942	65.2%	39.7	-0.1	2.3	42.0
2015-16	MTL	28	64					.921			20.5	-0.2	0.3	20.6

We could very simply state that Carey Price won the Vezina Trophy with one of the highest save percentages the league has ever seen, but that wouldn't be doing the season he had justice. The Montreal Canadiens ranked only 22nd in score-adjusted SAT%, but through Price's brilliance, they managed to finish the season in second place with 110 points. It was impossible to beat the 27-year-old goaltender if he got a clean look at the puck, as his low-danger save percentage was an insane .984. His high-danger save percentage was an equally impressive .865, and his overall adjusted save percentage was the best among goaltenders who played at least 60 games. You can't do much better, and the Canadiens needed every ounce of his greatness to be a contender.

Dustin Tokarski								G					MTL
Season	Team	Age	GP	W	L	OT	GAA	Sv%	ESSV%	QS%	GGVT	DGVT	SGVT	GVT
2013-14	MTL	24	3	2	0	0	1.84	.946	.944	100.0%	2.9	-0.1	-0.1	2.7
2014-15	MTL	25	17	6	6	4	2.75	.910	.910	50.0%	0.1	-0.2	-1.9	-2.0
2015-16	MTL	26	20					.913			1.5	-0.2	-0.2	1.0

Being Carey Price's backup isn't a great spot if you want to play much, but Dustin Tokarski has made the best of it. The 25-year-old netminder has provided reliable goaltending when called upon, in very limited duty. Tokarski was thrust into the national spotlight during the 2014 playoffs when Price went down with a Chris Kreider-induced injury, and though the Habs ended up losing that series, it wasn't the fault of Tokarski. His potential probably isn't any higher than that of a career backup, but finding a solid one isn't always easy. The Habs will hang onto him if they can.

Shane O'Donnell

Nashville Predators

After an offseason that saw the ouster of (very) long-time head coach Barry Trotz and a major trade for scorer James Neal, the Nashville Predators defied critics by finishing with 104 points and securing second place in the Central Division behind only the St. Louis Blues. Unlike some hot seasons in their past, this success had less to do with top-notch goaltending and more to do with the Predators simply outplaying, outshooting, and outscoring their opponents.

No team exceeded expectations to the same extent as Nashville—not even the Cinderella-story Calgary Flames. Quite simply, the Predators were legitimately and sustainably the sixth-best team in the NHL, and definitely not a bottom-tier team that got lucky.

The credit goes primarily to one man: general manager David Poile.

GM of the Year

Poile began his NHL front-office career as assistant GM of the old Atlanta Flames in 1977, five years into the franchise's existence. He remained in that position until 1982, when he left to take the reins of a 1974 expansion team, the Washington Capitals, where he remained for 15 years.

Days into his tenure in Washington, he rejuvenated the franchise with the famous 1982 preseason trade of Rick Green and Ryan Walter to the Montreal Canadiens for Brian Engblom, Doug Jarvis, Rod Langway, and Craig Laughlin. Later, Poile parlayed Engblom along with Ken Houston to steal Larry Murphy from Los Angeles.

All together, those four players formed the nucleus of an outstanding Washington lineup, an expansion team that had never qualified for the playoffs prior to his arrival, and then missed just once after Poile arrived—in his final season.

Poile's tremendous experience with expansion teams continued when he arrived in Nashville, this time on day one. Since their debut, the Predators have posted the best winning percentage of any of the nine modern expansion teams. Even though the Predators haven't enjoyed the same success in the playoffs as the others, most of these teams would gladly trade places with Nashville (see table, next page).

What is his secret? Poile's success in Nashville didn't occur by virtue of having an open wallet to sign big-name free agents, nor by tanking to the bottom of the league. It was a result of making tough decisions to keep this team as competitive as possible every season, on a limited budget.

So what did Poile do last summer that was so special? It was the culmination of good long-term drafting and develop-

PREDATORS IN A BOX

Last Season

Goals For	232	13th
Goals Against	208	8th
GVT	24	9th
Points	104	6th
Playoffs	Lost Conference Quarterfinal	

Nashville bounced back from two bad seasons to reclaim their spot among the Western elite.

Three-Year Record

GVT	-30	22nd
Points	233	20th
Playoffs	1 Appearance, 2 Wins	

VUKOTA Projection

Goals For	228	9th
Goals Against	221	18th
GVT	6	14th
Points	94	14th

Who are the real Predators? The 88-point weaklings from 2013-14, or the 104-point gorillas of 2014-15? The truth lies somewhere in between.

Top Three Prospects

K. Fiala (F), J. Vesey (F), V. Kamenev (F)

Modern expansion teams - regular season and playoff success

Franchise	Seasons	Win %	Playoffs	Series wins
Nashville	16	.539	8	2
Minnesota	14	.538	6	4
Anaheim	21	.534	11	14
San Jose	23	.526	17	14
Ottawa	22	.517	15	9
Florida	21	.484	4	3
Atlanta/Winnipeg	15	.470	2	0
Tampa Bay	22	.469	8	10
Columbus	14	.467	2	0

ment, complemented by four key moves: the adoption of analytics, the right coach selection, shrewd trades, and the correct usage of the free-agent process to acquire undervalued assets.

To begin, he hired a darn good coach. While there aren't a lot of statistics to measure coaches, the one that does exist ranked Peter Laviolette sixth among active coaches, going into last season.

Nashville: controlling play in 2014-15

Season	Possession
2007-08	49.8%
2008-09	49.7%
2009-10	51.2%
2010-11	48.5%
2011-12	47.3%
2012-13	48.2%
2013-14	50.1%
2014-15	53.2%

This system, which was introduced on our website back in 2009 and further explained in the first *Hockey Abstract*, ranks coaches based on how their teams have historically performed relative to expectations. Given that coaches who begin the season ranked in the bottom half have proven three times more likely to get fired, and given that the average preseason ranking of a coach in the final four is sixth, Laviolette's success was a lot more than just a lucky guess. Teams that invest in great coaching staffs have consistently outperformed those who have gambled.

Of course, Laviolette would have struggled without an upgraded roster. One of Nashville's other historic weaknesses has been its scoring line. Poile used the free-agency period to identify and acquire value-priced veteran Mike Ribeiro, along with Derek Roy and Anton Volchenkov, for a combined sum of just $3.1 million.

While they didn't have much cap space at stake if he had flopped, Ribeiro did turn out to be the perfect scoring-line complement to rookie Filip Forsberg, who Poile had acquired from the Washington Capitals at the 2013 trade-deadline steal for Martin Erat and Michael Latta. The most important addition was Neal, who Poile acquired from Pittsburgh for Patric Hornqvist and Nick Spaling.

Finally, the Predators had a scoring line!

Blue line

Not many teams have done a better job rebuilding their blue line through the draft than the Predators. Anaheim, Minnesota, and New Jersey have all been transitioning to their own promising collections of talented young defensemen, but just look at Nashville's top-six defensemen in the table below. Each of them was drafted by the organization (or signed as an undrafted free agent); overall, they will carry a cap hit of just $19.3 million. That gives Poile enormous cap freedom with the remaining roster spots.

Nashville's reasonably-priced, home-grown defense corps

Defenseman	Cap hit ($M)	Acquired	Year
Shea Weber	$7.9	Draft	2003
Roman Josi	$4.0	Draft	2008
Seth Jones	$3.2	Draft	2013
Ryan Ellis	$2.5	Draft	2009
Mattias Ekholm	$1.0	Draft	2009
Victor Bartley	$0.7	UFA	2011

So far, Roman Josi is the most pleasant surprise of the bunch. His 28 goals and 95 points over the past two seasons rank fifth and ninth among NHL defensemen. For the second year in a row, he played over 26 minutes per night on the top pairing with Shea Weber. As the team's Even-Strength Usage Chart demonstrates, the duo had one of the league's toughest assignments—perhaps excessively so, given their disappointing possession numbers.

There are a lot of theories about Weber's low possession numbers. Perhaps it is the tough minutes, maybe he is having difficulty with controlled zone exits, maybe he gets too much ice-time with defensive-minded possession sinkholes like Paul Gaustad, or maybe the rest of the team is improving around him so his numbers aren't as strong in relative terms. Most likely, it is a combination of all of these factors.

Mediocre possession aside, Weber is still a dominant physical force and consistent power-play producer. Poile's decision to keep him rather than allowing him to go to Philadelphia on an offer sheet will be questioned, but the former second rounder has been a huge part of the Preds being competitive, especially last season.

What to do with Weber?

Whatever the problem is, Weber is due a salary of $14.0 million in 2015-16, the highest in the league—more than even the new, front-loaded deals signed by Chicago's Patrick Kane and Jonathan Toews. In retrospect, should Poile have matched the offer sheet the Flyers extended to Weber back in the summer of 2012?

One school of thought is that it would be crazy to let a player of Weber's talents and credentials go, except in exchange for a player of equal impact. History has repeatedly proven this conventional wisdom as a general rule, but this particular case is interesting.

Letting Weber sign with the Flyers would have resulted in Nashville receiving Philadelphia's next four first-round draft choices. That is hardly trivial! The Flyers have picked 11th, 17th, and seventh overall since that offer sheet. In 2009, Nashville got Ellis 11th overall, the same year Nazem Kadri went seventh, and David Rundblad went 17th. Add in one more first-round choice, and that is the sort of package the Predators would be working with a few years down the line.

In terms of more immediate help, it was rumored that there were repeated attempts at a trade that included various combinations of Matt Read, Andrej Meszaros, Sean Couturier, Brayden Schenn, James van Riemsdyk, and multiple first-round draft selections. Players like Read, Couturier, and van Riemsdyk had the potential to be exceptional in Nashville, whose lone remaining weakness is a lack of forwards who can play tough minutes—Mike Fisher notwithstanding.

Of course, the two teams never agreed on a deal, Poile matched the offer sheet, and now the 30-year-old Weber will carry a huge $7.9 million cap hit until he is 41. As great as he is, Weber will inevitably, eventually decline. At some point, that same cap space could be used on one or more players that could contribute just as much as Weber, if not more. Add in a good shutdown forward, and some prospects down the line, and it wasn't crazy for Poile to have given this matter such careful consideration.

In the end, it is impossible to know if a deal would have made sense or not. There is no telling how well Weber will withstand Father Time, and we can only guess at what kind of return the Predators would have gotten, and how any draft picks would have turned out. What we do know is that Poile made one of many difficult decisions, and has continued to improve this organization one move at a time, to the point where it should be a legitimate playoff contender for years to come.

What to expect this year

Despite their great success, the Predators did close last season on a slide. They were 8-13-4 in the final third, including six straight losses down the stretch. Rinne posted just a .901 save percentage over those 25 games, and the team's shooting percentage fell. Furthermore, given this little love note we wrote about David Poile...the likeliest outcome is that this team will crash and burn, and that he will get fired.

But consider how Nashville pushed Chicago to the limit in the opening round of the playoffs. The Predators outscored the Blackhawks 21-19, and double and triple overtimes were required to best them in Game 1 and Game 4. This is a team that can compete with the league's elite, and has all the pieces required to continue to do so for years to come.

Rob Vollman

NASHVILLE PREDATORS

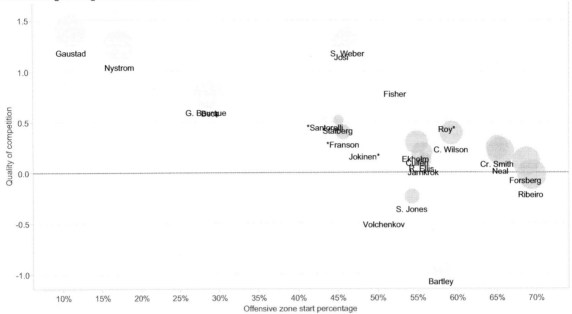

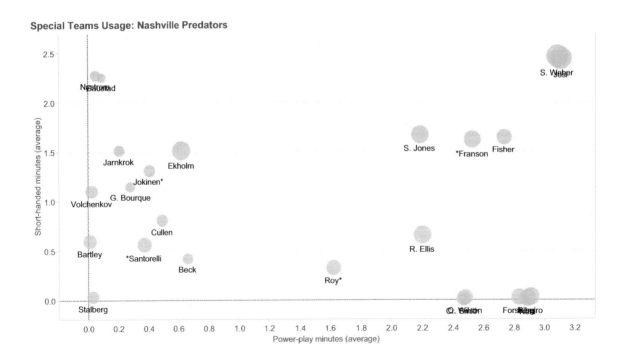

NASHVILLE PREDATORS

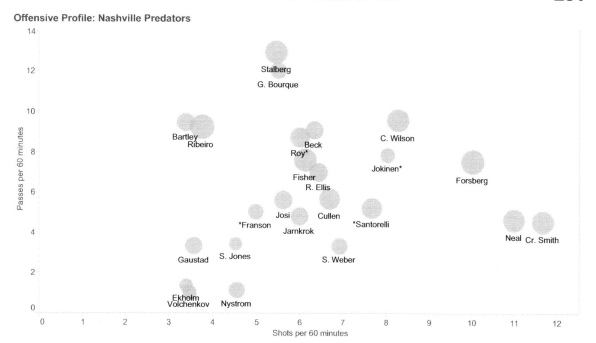

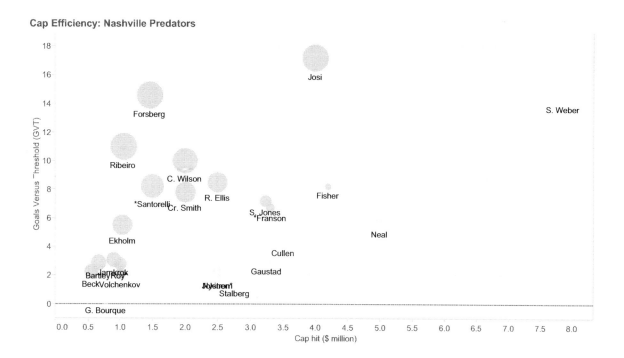

NASHVILLE PREDATORS

FORWARDS

Viktor Arvidsson				LW/RW									NSH
Season	Team	Age	GP	G	A	Pts	+/-	ESP/60	AdjCF%	iCF/60	OGVT	DGVT	SGVT	GVT
2014-15	NSH	21	6	0	0	0	0	0.00	49.5%	17.4	-0.3	0.1	0.0	-0.2
2015-16	NSH	22	28	5	6	10					0.5	0.6	0.0	1.1

Viktor Arvidsson got his first taste of NHL action, playing six games at the end of the season. A former SHL champion in his native Sweden, the 2014 fourth rounder spent the majority of the season with the Milwaukee Admirals, tallying a solid 22 goals and 33 assists through 70 AHL games. However, at five-foot-nine, the diminutive winger will have a tough time cracking an NHL top six unless his AHL production takes a further step forward.

Taylor Beck				RW										TOR
Season	Team	Age	GP	G	A	Pts	+/-	ESP/60	AdjCF%	iCF/60	OGVT	DGVT	SGVT	GVT
2012-13	NSH	21	16	3	4	7	0	1.32	47.8%	14.6	-0.1	0.9	-0.3	0.5
2013-14	NSH	22	7	0	0	0	-2	0.00	53.6%	8.8	-0.3	-0.1	-0.3	-0.7
2014-15	NSH	23	62	8	8	16	-4	1.25	47.3%	11.9	1.1	1.2	0.0	2.3
2015-16	TOR	24	53	8	8	16					0.4	1.1	0.0	1.5

Taylor Beck was one of several depth forwards spending time on Nashville's bottom line who was given absolutely abysmal zone starts, emblematic of anyone who played with Paul Gaustad—the old Manny Malhotra treatment in Vancouver. All four players in Nashville who spent significant time on the fourth line ranked in the bottom 11 league-wide for relative offensive zone starts. That limited what the 23-year-old winger could accomplish in his first full NHL season. Considering the big change from an AHL top-six forward to a defensive role in the NHL, Beck was solid at even strength. He may show more offensive talent if he gets more and more favorable ice-time in Toronto.

Gabriel Bourque				LW										NSH
Season	Team	Age	GP	G	A	Pts	+/-	ESP/60	AdjCF%	iCF/60	OGVT	DGVT	SGVT	GVT
2012-13	NSH	22	34	11	5	16	6	1.52	47.5%	10.2	1.5	2.2	-0.1	3.7
2013-14	NSH	23	74	9	17	26	-5	1.61	51.7%	11.4	0.4	2.7	-0.8	2.2
2014-15	NSH	24	69	3	10	13	-13	1.07	48.8%	9.5	-0.5	0.6	0.0	0.1
2015-16	NSH	25	57	7	11	18					0.1	1.3	0.0	1.4

24-year-old Gabriel Bourque had a strange year, taking a step back from previous seasons of top-nine rates to fourth-line type scoring, in part due to seeing a lot of defensive-zone minutes. His offensive production also dropped because of a surprisingly low even-strength on-ice shooting percentage, 2.9%. It would not be unexpected to see his underlying and conventional numbers rise next season.

Rich Clune — LW — TOR

Season	Team	Age	GP	G	A	Pts	+/-	ESP/60	AdjCF%	iCF/60	OGVT	DGVT	SGVT	GVT
2012-13	NSH	25	47	4	5	9	3	1.24	45.8%	10.2	0.0	1.6	0.0	1.6
2013-14	NSH	26	58	3	4	7	-7	0.88	47.5%	6.5	-0.9	0.5	0.0	-0.4
2014-15	NSH	27	1	0	0	0	0	0.00	13.5%	0.0	0.0	0.0	0.0	0.0
2015-16	TOR	28	36	4	4	8					-0.1	0.6	0.0	0.5

In a season where enforcers saw fewer jobs available and less ice-time allotted, Rich Clune's opportunities were understandably limited. He played in just one NHL game, following a season where he had suited up for 58 games with Nashville. His offensive production and defensive abilities aren't at a level where he is going to get a ton of ice-time. The Toronto native is headed to the Maple Leafs organization, but it is hard to see how a player like this fits into the NHL any longer.

Matt Cullen — C — PIT

Season	Team	Age	GP	G	A	Pts	+/-	ESP/60	AdjCF%	iCF/60	OGVT	DGVT	SGVT	GVT
2012-13	MIN	36	42	7	20	27	9	2.61	48.8%	12.5	3.1	3.4	1.5	8.0
2013-14	NSH	37	77	10	29	39	4	1.83	50.2%	11.5	3.1	3.3	-0.8	5.6
2014-15	NSH	38	62	7	18	25	8	1.74	53.8%	12.2	1.9	2.6	-0.2	4.4
2015-16	PIT	39	58	8	17	25					1.7	1.9	0.0	3.6

38-year-old center Matt Cullen continued to provide utility in 2014-15, winning 54% of his faceoffs and coming out better than breakeven in possession. However, age finally caught up with his scoring totals. While it isn't falling off the chart, the dip came while getting the lowest ice-time of his career and a majority of offensive zone starts for the first time since 2009-10, both of which further emphasize his decline. Still, as a veteran depth player, the Penguins will find him more effective than the hapless AHL crew they have been running out on the fourth line. Cullen can no longer be a shutdown center, but he can still outplay the grinders of the league.

Kevin Fiala — LW/RW — NSH

Season	Team	Age	GP	G	A	Pts	+/-	ESP/60	AdjCF%	iCF/60	OGVT	DGVT	SGVT	GVT
2014-15	NSH	18	1	0	0	0	-1	0.00	47.9%	15.0	-0.1	-0.1	0.0	-0.2
2015-16	NSH	19	26	5	6	11					0.6	0.4	0.0	1.0

Kevin Fiala made his NHL debut just months after being drafted 11th overall. He laced up for just one game before finishing the year playing in Sweden's SHL, and eventually scoring 11 goals and nine assists in 33 games with the AHL's Milwaukee Admirals. The five-foot-ten Swiss winger is an immensely talented player who will have a solid shot at making the NHL squad in 2015-16. The one thing that may get in the way is that the Predators already have a number of offensively gifted players they need to keep away from the tough minutes. So Fiala may have to start in the AHL before getting his full-time shot.

Mike Fisher — C — NSH

Season	Team	Age	GP	G	A	Pts	+/-	ESP/60	AdjCF%	iCF/60	OGVT	DGVT	SGVT	GVT
2012-13	NSH	32	38	10	11	21	6	1.55	46.0%	11.8	2.5	2.0	-0.6	3.9
2013-14	NSH	33	75	20	29	49	-4	1.96	46.1%	10.8	5.0	3.6	-0.3	8.3
2014-15	NSH	34	59	19	20	39	4	2.03	52.0%	11.3	5.2	3.0	0.0	8.2
2015-16	NSH	35	63	16	22	37					3.7	2.3	0.0	6.0

35-year-old Mike Fisher continues defy the kind of decline we are used to seeing in forwards during their mid-thirties. A veteran of 14 NHL seasons, the long-time Senator scored at two points per 60 minutes, his best mark since 2006-07, though certainly aided by getting positive relative zone starts for the first time in his career. Injuries have become an ongoing concern, but his on-ice offensive production has been excellent at 60.9 Corsi for per 60 minutes, the second best in his career. It is no surprise the two-way centerman was re-signed for two more seasons.

Filip Forsberg — RW/LW — NSH

Season	Team	Age	GP	G	A	Pts	+/-	ESP/60	AdjCF%	iCF/60	OGVT	DGVT	SGVT	GVT
2012-13	NSH	18	5	0	1	1	-5	0.89	43.3%	18.1	-0.3	-0.3	0.0	-0.6
2013-14	NSH	19	13	1	4	5	-8	0.49	46.3%	15.2	0.1	-0.5	-0.3	-0.7
2014-15	NSH	20	82	26	37	63	15	2.22	56.9%	19.7	10.5	3.6	0.5	14.6
2015-16	NSH	21	78	31	42	72					11.5	2.9	0.0	14.4

In his 20-year-old rookie season, Filip Forsberg broke out to become the player the Predators hoped he would be when they fleeced the Capitals to acquire him for declining veteran Martin Erat, a ham sandwich, and a bag of pucks. His 2.22 even-strength points per 60 minutes was the best in the lineup, as were his 26 goals and 63 points. The successful Swedish international (two silver medals and a gold medal in his WJC career) even came through in the playoffs with six points over six games, in a valiant effort against Chicago in the first round. Forsberg showed he is the total package offensively, with the ability to score, pass, and create room for himself with nifty puck skills. Put a green arrow on the 11th overall pick from 2012 because he is trending up. The only question is his ceiling as an all-around player. Could he develop into a true top center? It seems possible.

Paul Gaustad — C — NSH

Season	Team	Age	GP	G	A	Pts	+/-	ESP/60	AdjCF%	iCF/60	OGVT	DGVT	SGVT	GVT
2012-13	NSH	30	23	2	3	5	-1	1.06	45.7%	10.7	0.0	0.7	0.0	0.8
2013-14	NSH	31	75	10	11	21	-6	1.49	44.4%	7.1	0.9	3.4	0.0	4.3
2014-15	NSH	32	73	4	10	14	7	1.14	42.9%	8.2	-0.2	3.4	0.0	3.2
2015-16	NSH	33	59	5	9	14					-0.4	2.1	0.0	1.7

Paul Gaustad's one clear asset, throughout his career, has been his consistently elite faceoff percentage, a typically excellent 56.4% in 2014-15. He was regularly sent out for defensive zone faceoffs by new head coach Peter Laviolette to win the draw and get off the ice—the usual. The six-foot-five long-time Sabre took 744 defensive zone draws while just taking 74 in the offensive zone and 274 in the neutral zone. With zone starts that bad, his poor stats need to at least be taken in context, like the sixth-worst Corsi mark in the league. As Gaustad ages and the Preds build up some better forward talent, they may want to reconsider his role.

Calle Jarnkrok — C — NSH

Season	Team	Age	GP	G	A	Pts	+/-	ESP/60	AdjCF%	iCF/60	OGVT	DGVT	SGVT	GVT
2013-14	NSH	22	12	2	7	9	7	3.18	53.2%	8.4	1.6	1.1	0.0	2.7
2014-15	NSH	23	74	7	11	18	2	1.24	54.3%	12.7	0.1	3.0	0.0	3.1
2015-16	NSH	24	65	10	16	26					1.1	2.4	0.0	3.5

In his first full NHL season, Calle Jarnkrok provided depth scoring with a solid 1.24 points per 60 minutes in third- and fourth-line ice-time. Particularly impressive was his defensive ability, showing the capability to perform at a high level as a role player. The 24-year-old Swedish center has a lot to prove, but he should be a valuable piece of the team going forward, as a number of Nashville's other youngsters can create opportunities on offense, but don't exhibit a defensive mindset. Jarnkrok could eventually supplant Gaustad in the tough-minute role if he can at least take his 46.2% faceoff percentage to north of 50%.

James Neal — RW — NSH

Season	Team	Age	GP	G	A	Pts	+/-	ESP/60	AdjCF%	iCF/60	OGVT	DGVT	SGVT	GVT
2012-13	PIT	25	40	21	15	36	5	2.23	54.9%	19.4	8.3	0.5	1.0	9.9
2013-14	PIT	26	59	27	34	61	15	2.44	56.0%	22.4	11.9	2.7	-1.1	13.5
2014-15	NSH	27	67	23	14	37	12	1.95	56.7%	21.8	2.9	3.1	-0.2	5.9
2015-16	NSH	28	68	24	23	47					5.9	2.4	0.0	8.3

In his first time away from Pittsburgh's dangerous top lines in four-plus seasons, James Neal took a step back in terms of his production, falling towards a fringe top-six level away from Malkin and Crosby. Still, Neal did what Neal does: put a ton of shots on net and score goals, though the Predators were probably looking for more than 23 markers in 67 games from the former 40-goal man. While he may bounce back in terms of scoring, another is issue cropping up: the former Star has not played a full season since 2011-12 due to injuries and suspensions. Will he be worth the trouble, the inconsistency, and the lack of defensive ability if he is sitting out one-fourth or more of the year, especially as he heads into the tail end of his prime?

Eric Nystrom — LW — NSH

Season	Team	Age	GP	G	A	Pts	+/-	ESP/60	AdjCF%	iCF/60	OGVT	DGVT	SGVT	GVT
2012-13	DAL	29	48	7	4	11	-3	1.08	45.5%	10.4	-1.0	1.6	0.0	0.6
2013-14	NSH	30	79	15	6	21	-25	1.17	46.2%	12.0	0.6	2.0	0.0	1.4
2014-15	NSH	31	60	7	5	12	0	1.01	44.0%	8.7	-0.3	2.4	0.0	2.1
2015-16	NSH	32	58	8	7	15					0.2	1.8	0.0	1.9

Eric Nystrom is a fringe fourth-line player. His -11.0% Relative Corsi was seventh worst in the league. It is surprising that the 32-year-old forward has continued to find work despite never producing more than 21 points. His failures are as much on him being a first-round bust as they are on Laviolette, who continued to give him defensive zone minutes. Or just minutes in general. Without quality defensive skill or scoring talent, it is hard figure out why NHL teams keep signing such an ineffective player. Or is it? Cough, pedigree, cough.

Mike Ribeiro — C — NSH

Season	Team	Age	GP	G	A	Pts	+/-	ESP/60	AdjCF%	iCF/60	OGVT	DGVT	SGVT	GVT
2012-13	WSH	32	48	13	36	49	-4	1.93	45.2%	7.3	8.9	-0.1	-0.6	8.3
2013-14	PHX	33	80	16	31	47	-13	1.65	52.5%	7.2	3.7	1.3	-0.8	4.2
2014-15	NSH	34	82	15	47	62	11	2.31	56.9%	6.6	7.5	3.5	0.0	11.0
2015-16	NSH	35	68	13	33	46					4.6	2.2	0.0	6.8

Entering the year, Mike Ribeiro was contending with a couple rough seasons and some ugly legal troubles. While the allegations didn't subside, Ribeiro was given a one-year "prove-it" contract with Nashville, under which he performed very well on the offensive side of the ice. Starting nearly seven out of 10 faceoffs in the offensive zone was proof of smart usage by his coach. And keeping him out of the D-zone was not only important because of his shortcomings, but also because of a hideous 43.2% faceoff percentage. The only mistake in deployment was that he took more faceoffs than anyone else on the team.

Miikka Salomaki — LW/C — NSH

Season	Team	Age	GP	G	A	Pts	+/-	ESP/60	AdjCF%	iCF/60	OGVT	DGVT	SGVT	GVT
2014-15	NSH	21	1	1	0	1	1	6.06	71.0%	23.3	0.4	0.1	0.0	0.5
2015-16	NSH	22	26	6	6	12					1.1	0.6	0.0	1.7

Miikka Salomaki couldn't ask for his lone game to have gone any better, scoring a goal against Dallas on January 9 in his big-league debut. While the 21-year-old did not see any more NHL action, there is a good chance it won't be his only career game. The 2011 second rounder has had decent scoring success in the AHL since coming over from Finland, with 68 points in 113 games for the Milwaukee Admirals. With a reputation as a two-way, complementary winger, Salomaki could earn a bottom-six slot and hope to work his way up from there.

Mike Santorelli — C/RW — ANA

Season	Team	Age	GP	G	A	Pts	+/-	ESP/60	CF%	iCF/60	OGVT	DGVT	SGVT	GVT
2012-13	FLA, WPG	27	34	2	2	4	-12	0.61	49.5%	12.2	-1.5	-0.3	0.7	-1.0
2013-14	VAN	28	49	10	18	28	9	2.06	51.0%	13.3	3.6	3.6	-0.5	6.7
2014-15	TOR, NSH	29	79	12	21	33	0	1.64	47.0%	11.9	4.1	2.1	2.0	8.2
2015-16	ANA	30	64	11	21	32					2.8	2.3	0.1	5.2

Back in 2010-11, with Florida, you might have believed Mike Santorelli would turn into a quality second- or third-line center who could score 40+ points. However, he fell off the map until re-emerging two seasons ago. As a top sixer for Toronto, he produced—but once again, only on a bad team where he was in over his head getting top minutes. Acquired at the deadline by GM David Poile, the Vancouver-born Northern Michigan product provided little to the lineup.

Craig Smith — C — NSH

Season	Team	Age	GP	G	A	Pts	+/-	ESP/60	AdjCF%	iCF/60	OGVT	DGVT	SGVT	GVT
2012-13	NSH	23	44	4	8	12	-11	0.57	44.2%	12.4	-1.2	0.3	2.0	1.1
2013-14	NSH	24	79	24	28	52	16	2.23	50.0%	17.3	9.6	4.2	-1.3	12.5
2014-15	NSH	25	82	23	21	44	11	1.93	55.5%	19.0	5.0	3.4	-0.6	7.8
2015-16	NSH	26	73	24	26	50					6.6	3.0	-0.1	9.5

Madison, Wisconsin native Craig Smith already had something of a breakout in 2013-14, but last season cemented his status as an effective attacker worthy of consistent top-six consideration. He was among the NHL's most effective offensive players at generating shot attempts and being on the ice for goals by his club. The only argument against his success is that he may have been buoyed by strong linemates—which the Predators have lacked for quite a while until now. With more offensive skill, Smith's game is rounding out, and that is something Nashville waited a long time for.

Viktor Stalberg							LW						NYR
Season	Team	Age	GP	G	A	Pts	+/-	ESP/60	AdjCF%	iCF/60	OGVT	DGVT	SGVT	GVT
2012-13	CHI	26	47	9	14	23	16	2.26	56.9%	19.2	3.8	1.8	0.0	5.7
2013-14	NSH	27	70	8	10	18	-14	1.25	48.7%	13.5	0.2	0.6	0.0	0.9
2014-15	NSH	28	25	2	8	10	0	2.03	52.5%	10.5	1.1	0.7	0.0	1.7
2015-16	NYR	29	47	7	12	19					1.4	1.1	0.0	2.5

The Predators saw something in Viktor Stalberg's game while he was in Chicago that they wanted. Unfortunately, he was never able to give them the same type of production as when he was a Blackhawk. Playing alongside Toews and Hossa for big minutes in his UFA year helped. However, in Nashville, the Gothenburg native struggled with injuries and was waived, sent to the AHL twice, and ultimately bought out over the summer. He played in only 25 NHL games, the fewest of his career, while averaging just under 12 minutes of ice-time. It became clear he was a one-year wonder, but could probably improve someone's fourth line over, say, Tanner Glass.

Colin Wilson							C						NSH
Season	Team	Age	GP	G	A	Pts	+/-	ESP/60	AdjCF%	iCF/60	OGVT	DGVT	SGVT	GVT
2012-13	NSH	23	25	7	12	19	1	2.20	50.2%	9.1	3.2	1.1	-0.6	3.8
2013-14	NSH	24	81	11	22	33	-1	1.52	48.3%	9.5	2.1	2.5	-0.3	4.3
2014-15	NSH	25	77	20	22	42	19	1.99	55.6%	13.5	6.0	3.9	0.0	10.0
2015-16	NSH	26	69	19	22	41					4.9	2.6	0.0	7.5

In his sixth season in Nashville, 25-year-old Colin Wilson hit the 20-goal mark for the first time in his career. Wilson proved that he could be an offensive force, potentially poised to continue the growth of his offensive game. Should we expect him to be among the league's elite opportunity creators? Not necessarily, but his production proves that he shouldn't be ignored. On the defensive side, there is still work to do for the seventh-overall pick from 2008, but with the amount of offense he created last season, Wilson was a good example of the cliche that the best defense is a good offense.

DEFENSEMEN

Victor Bartley — LD — NSH

Season	Team	Age	GP	G	A	Pts	+/-	ESP/60	AdjCF%	iCF/60	OGVT	DGVT	SGVT	GVT
2012-13	NSH	24	24	0	7	7	2	0.99	45.6%	6.0	0.9	1.7	0.0	2.6
2013-14	NSH	25	50	1	5	6	0	0.52	44.6%	4.2	-0.6	2.5	0.0	1.8
2014-15	NSH	26	37	0	10	10	1	1.26	49.4%	7.9	1.2	1.7	0.0	2.9
2015-16	NSH	27	45	2	8	10					0.2	1.9	0.0	2.1

Ottawa-born Victor Bartley remained on the margins of the NHL in his age-26 season, appearing in 37 games for the Preds. It is not going to get easier for him, as a number of young defensemen in Nashville are coming of age and producing both offensively and defensively. Still, there is an intriguing element to the former Regina Pats captain, as he has tallied decent AHL scoring totals as well as 10 even-strength assists in his limited NHL time.

Anthony Bitetto — LD — NSH

Season	Team	Age	GP	G	A	Pts	+/-	ESP/60	AdjCF%	iCF/60	OGVT	DGVT	SGVT	GVT
2014-15	NSH	24	7	0	0	0	-1	0.00	48.9%	4.9	-0.2	0.0	0.0	-0.3
2015-16	NSH	25	27	2	5	6					0.2	0.8	0.0	1.0

Anthony Bitetto made his big-league debut, skating in seven games for the Predators. However, the 25-year-old Northeastern product has a tough job ahead of him if he wants to get regular NHL time despite intriguing AHL point totals—66 in his last 143 games. The six-foot-two, 201-pound blueliner is behind one of the deeper defensive groups in the league, and after spending three full seasons in the AHL after a couple years of playing Hockey East, he is no longer a budding young prospect.

Mattias Ekholm — LD — NSH

Season	Team	Age	GP	G	A	Pts	+/-	ESP/60	AdjCF%	iCF/60	OGVT	DGVT	SGVT	GVT
2012-13	NSH	22	1	0	0	0	-1	0.00	64.4%	3.9	-0.1	-0.1	0.0	-0.2
2013-14	NSH	23	62	1	8	9	-8	0.51	50.0%	7.3	-1.2	2.1	-0.3	0.6
2014-15	NSH	24	80	7	11	18	12	0.71	56.5%	7.8	0.7	4.8	0.0	5.5
2015-16	NSH	25	69	4	13	18					0.5	3.7	0.0	4.2

Mattias Ekholm was one of a handful of young defenders in Nashville who stepped up in a big way. The six-foot-three, 205-pound Swede showed an offensive element to his game that wasn't there previously. However, the question is whether Ekholm suddenly got better, or he was just lucky to be paired with Ryan Ellis? When Ekholm was with Ellis, the two tilted the ice in Nashville's favor to the tune of 56.8% Corsi, while the Swedish defenseman only managed a 51.7% Corsi without his main partner. Was it just great chemistry? It is hard not to lean toward Ellis' tremendous talent being the main difference.

Ryan Ellis — RD — NSH

Season	Team	Age	GP	G	A	Pts	+/-	ESP/60	AdjCF%	iCF/60	OGVT	DGVT	SGVT	GVT
2012-13	NSH	21	32	2	4	6	-2	0.52	49.5%	7.9	0.0	1.2	-0.3	1.0
2013-14	NSH	22	80	6	21	27	9	1.11	50.1%	9.3	3.5	4.1	0.6	8.2
2014-15	NSH	23	58	9	18	27	8	1.35	55.8%	9.6	5.8	3.1	-0.4	8.5
2015-16	NSH	24	65	8	22	30					4.4	3.4	0.0	7.8

Ryan Ellis' game continued to grow as he developed toward the highly-skilled defenseman the Predators envisioned when the five-foot-ten blueliner was selected 11th overall in 2009, after producing an amazing 89 points in 57 games in his draft-eligible season. Last year, Ellis posted a career-high mark in points per 60 minutes (1.4) while averaging 19 minutes of ice-time, also a personal best. Those improvements were driven by quality play, and not external factors, as Nashville has plenty of others worthy of playing time. Consequently, Ellis was finally given more responsibility on special teams, with over two minutes per game on the power play and a touch of shorthanded ice-time as well. At a $2.5 million cap hit, you won't find a better deal anywhere.

Cody Franson — RD — BUF

Season	Team	Age	GP	G	A	Pts	+/-	ESP/60	AdjCF%	iCF/60	OGVT	DGVT	SGVT	GVT
2012-13	TOR	25	45	4	25	29	4	1.42	46.4%	7.3	5.6	0.1	-0.3	5.4
2013-14	TOR	26	79	5	28	33	-20	0.71	44.4%	8.7	4.1	-1.6	0.0	2.6
2014-15	TOR, NSH	27	78	7	29	36	-7	0.94	49.6%	9.2	4.7	2.0	0.0	6.7
2015-16	BUF	28	62	5	23	28					2.9	1.8	0.0	4.7

Cody Franson had a good start to his year in Toronto, but simply floundered in his return to Nashville. For whatever reason, the quality puck-handler did not fit in amongst a talented blueline group. Still, he finished with his sixth straight season of positive relative possession. As a six-foot-five defenseman who is not fleet of foot or physical, it is harder to convince NHL GMs of his value. Yes, he has issues in his own zone and will disappoint if you are hoping for the next Shea Weber, but he is usually on the right side of the puck and can score from the point at a higher rate than most. Franson will have a good shot to prove himself on what should be a quickly improving Sabres squad.

Seth Jones — RD — NSH

Season	Team	Age	GP	G	A	Pts	+/-	ESP/60	AdjCF%	iCF/60	OGVT	DGVT	SGVT	GVT
2013-14	NSH	19	77	6	19	25	-23	0.78	49.0%	8.8	2.3	0.6	-0.3	2.6
2014-15	NSH	20	82	8	19	27	3	0.68	54.2%	9.2	3.5	3.7	0.0	7.2
2015-16	NSH	21	69	7	22	30					3.5	2.6	0.0	6.1

It is easy to forget that Seth Jones is just 20 years old when you watch him play. His natural gifts are obvious when he takes one stride to gain full speed with the puck and rockets a tape-to-tape pass. After a solid age-19 year, the son of former NBAer Popeye Jones didn't fall prey to the mythical sophomore slump, producing offense at about the same rate as his rookie season, but notably improving his underlying numbers: his score-adjusted Corsi for per 60 minutes rose from 51.5 to 58.1, while his score-adjusted Corsi against per 60 minutes fell from 53.9 to 49.4. If the 2013 fourth-overall selection continues to grow, he is on track to be one of the league's best young defenders.

Roman Josi — LD — NSH

Season	Team	Age	GP	G	A	Pts	+/-	ESP/60	AdjCF%	iCF/60	OGVT	DGVT	SGVT	GVT
2012-13	NSH	22	48	5	13	18	-7	0.70	45.4%	8.6	0.9	2.7	-0.3	3.3
2013-14	NSH	23	72	13	27	40	-2	1.08	48.6%	8.8	6.8	5.1	1.0	12.9
2014-15	NSH	24	81	15	40	55	15	1.31	50.4%	10.5	10.7	6.6	-0.2	17.2
2015-16	NSH	25	79	13	37	50					7.8	5.1	0.0	12.8

Roman Josi unseated Shea Weber as the team's top scoring defenseman, with 15 goals and 40 assists. The six-foot-two Swiss blueliner not only played the most even-strength minutes of his career at 20, but hit a career-high in points per 60 minutes as well. His role with the team grew as he has turned into the all-around defenseman Nashville had hoped could complement Weber. While the team captain is known for his shot and toughness, Josi can effectively move the puck with a clean first pass and set up shooters in the offensive zone. The combo is so good that allowing Ryan Suter to move on to huge money with the Wild back in the summer of 2012 looks like it has worked out just fine.

Joe Piskula — LD — ANA

Season	Team	Age	GP	G	A	Pts	+/-	ESP/60	AdjCF%	iCF/60	OGVT	DGVT	SGVT	GVT
2013-14	NSH	29	2	0	0	0	1	0.00	63.5%	10.1	-0.1	0.2	0.0	0.1
2014-15	NSH	30	1	0	0	0	-1	0.00	54.0%	13.5	0.0	0.0	0.0	0.0
2015-16	ANA	31	23	1	4	6					0.3	0.8	0.0	1.1

Lifetime AHLer Joe Piskula appeared in just one game for the Predators, marking his 13th NHL game over a 10-year pro career. The University of Wisconsin product has played a classic minor-league role as a consistent professional who sets an example for younger players. Unfortunately, with subpar skating ability and little offensive talent, an AHL leader is his ceiling.

Anton Volchenkov — RD

Season	Team	Age	GP	G	A	Pts	+/-	ESP/60	AdjCF%	iCF/60	OGVT	DGVT	SGVT	GVT
2012-13	NJD	30	37	1	4	5	-1	0.62	55.2%	9.0	0.0	3.3	0.0	3.3
2013-14	NJD	31	56	0	8	8	3	0.58	55.7%	9.2	-0.5	5.6	0.0	5.1
2014-15	NSH	32	46	0	7	7	4	0.76	52.1%	8.5	-0.2	2.3	0.0	2.1
2015-16	Free Agent	33	47	1	7	8					-0.1	2.5	0.0	2.5

At one time, Anton Volchenkov was a force, but no longer. His 13 minutes of ice-time per game was the lowest since 2004. With plenty of savvy and the ability to still throw a hit at the right time, his impact was more about giving the younger defensemen a reliable veteran on the bench than it was about the team's overall performance. Can the 33-year-old Russian still play a positive role on a contender? Possibly, but his numbers across the board screamed that he has to be given protected minutes, won't post much on the scoreboard, or positively affect the possession game. A few years ago, someone would have paid him for three or four more years. (Cough, New Jersey.) Teams are smartening up, which means Volchenkov will have a tough time finding a job.

Shea Weber								RD						NSH
Season	Team	Age	GP	G	A	Pts	+/-	ESP/60	AdjCF%	iCF/60	OGVT	DGVT	SGVT	GVT
2012-13	NSH	27	48	9	19	28	-2	0.98	44.9%	9.3	4.8	3.1	0.0	7.8
2013-14	NSH	28	79	23	33	56	-2	1.08	48.0%	9.7	12.0	5.6	0.0	17.6
2014-15	NSH	29	78	15	30	45	15	1.07	50.7%	11.6	7.9	6.5	0.0	14.4
2015-16	NSH	30	76	13	35	48					7.7	5.1	0.0	12.8

Shea Weber's age-29 campaign invigorated debate over whether the intimidating six-foot-four defender is in decline. It was the first time in three seasons he didn't lead the team in points and the first time since the 2007-08 season where he wasn't the highest-scoring defender. Flying in the face of that assessment is that his 1.07 even-strength points per 60 minutes was his best mark since 2010-11, which he managed while absorbing the worst zone starts of his career. In that light, Weber's 51% score-adjusted Corsi percentage is the best overall possession mark he has had since 2010-11. So, what is happening? It is a little of Column A and a little of Column B. The Predators made changes to their roster and hired a new head coach to become a more offensive team, which meant even more reliance defensively on Weber, who is considered the toughest man not named Chara in defending the front of the net.

GOALTENDERS

Carter Hutton								G						NSH
Season	Team	Age	GP	G	A	Pts	+/-	ESP/60	AdjCF%	iCF/60	OGVT	DGVT	SGVT	GVT
2012-13	CHI	27	1	0	1	0	3.05	.893	.870	0.0%	-0.4	0.0	0.0	-0.3
2013-14	NSH	28	40	20	11	4	2.62	.910	.918	47.1%	0.0	0.4	0.9	1.3
2014-15	NSH	29	18	6	7	4	2.61	.902	.909	41.2%	-2.8	0.5	-2.2	-4.5
2015-16	NSH	30	23					.911			-0.2	0.2	-0.2	-0.2

Sitting behind the frequent Vezina finalist, there isn't a lot of work to be had when Pekka Rinne is healthy. However, Carter Hutton got in 40 games during the 2013-14 campaign when Rinne missed most of the season, but he played just 18 last year, posting a poor .902 even-strength save percentage. Stating the obvious, it seems like Hutton's opportunities will be limited with Nashville. Throw in the fact that the UMass-Lowell alum will turn 30 before New Year's.

Marek Mazanec								G						NSH
Season	Team	Age	GP	W	L	OT	GAA	Sv%	ESSV%	QS%	GGVT	DGVT	SGVT	GVT
2013-14	NSH	22	25	8	10	4	2.80	.902	.904	50.0%	-4.3	0.3	-1.6	-5.6
2014-15	NSH	23	2	0	1	0	2.26	.915	.947	100.0%	0.2	0.1	0.0	0.3
2015-16	NSH	24	17					.910			-0.5	0.0	-0.1	-0.6

Marek Mazanec made a solid first impression with the Predators organization in 2013-14, performing fairly well in his first pro season in North America, posting a .914 AHL save percentage and a .902 NHL save percentage in limited duty. However, the 23-year-old Czech netminder did not show much in terms of improvement from his first year to his second, seeing a worrying dip in his AHL save percentage to .900. With franchise goalie Pekka Rinne in place, the Predators can give this six-foot-four goalie time to develop.

Pekka Rinne								G					NSH
Season	Team	Age	GP	G	A	Pts	+/-	ESP/60	AdjCF%	iCF/60	OGVT	DGVT	SGVT	GVT
2012-13	NSH	30	43	15	16	8	2.43	.910	.927	57.1%	2.4	0.8	-2.0	1.2
2013-14	NSH	31	24	10	10	3	2.77	.902	.901	54.2%	-3.8	0.4	-1.6	-5.1
2014-15	NSH	32	64	41	17	6	2.18	.923	.932	67.2%	19.4	0.9	0.4	20.8
2015-16	NSH	33	47					.914			4.4	0.5	-0.1	4.9

After a frustrating 2013-14 season, which included a hip surgery that sidelined him for longer than expected, Pekka Rinne bounced back nicely. He finished fifth among regular NHL goaltenders in even-strength save percentage. His .852 high-danger save percentage was the second best of his career and ranked 13th among regular netminders. The two-time SM-Liiga champion wasn't Carey Price, but he was consistent, weathering 64 games and certainly among the handful of top goaltenders, earning his third Vezina Trophy finalist nod.

Dustin Nelson

New Jersey Devils

In 2014-15, the New Jersey Devils did what many teams would do during a bad season: fire the head coach. They parted ways with Peter DeBoer in late December. Then, true to their way of doing things their way, replaced him with two former Devils assistants, Adam Oates and Scott Stevens. Oates would run the offense and power play; Stevens would run the defense and penalty kill. General manager Lou Lamoriello also was behind the bench, presumably to motivate players. Not surprisingly, the Devils landed in the lottery.

Typically, when a team names an interim head coach, there is a possibility that the interim tag will be removed. Heading into this offseason, one of the questions the team had to answer was whether to name Oates, Stevens, or someone else as head coach. However, a surprising development interjected itself into the process: Lou Lamoriello elected to step away from the general manager position (and even more unexpectedly, he moved on to the Toronto Maple Leafs as GM over the summer). With former Pittsburgh GM Ray Shero named as the franchise's first new general manager since 1987, the Devils officially kicked off what is likely to be a painful rebuild. Shero's first act was to hire Wilkes-Barre Scranton Penguins coach John Hynes—answering the coaching question.

New Jersey media and fans will quickly move along to the next steps of the Devils' rebuild. They will have to draft well, move out older players, and make savvy signings in order to get the club back to contention.

But let us not move too quickly away from Lou's final act: his Three-Headed Monster bench-boss plan was unlike anything done before. It deserves a closer look. Could it be a one-time thing? Could it be attempted again by other clubs?

On the surface, the Devils record did improve. Under DeBoer, the Devils were 12-17-6. Under the co-coaches—as Oates and Stevens were referred to by Lamoriello—the Devils went 20-19-8. They still missed the playoffs by 20 points, and even if we were to project the improved record under the co-coaches out to 82 games, New Jersey would still have missed the postseason. Overall, that speaks to the roster, of course. But as far as the coaching, despite the improvement, the underlying numbers at five-on-five tell a far different tale that strongly recommends against the Oates-Stevens duo (see table, next page).

Under DeBoer, the team's Corsi percentage was 49.6%, a bottom-10 percentage, but still close to breaking even. For comparison, the New

DEVILS IN A BOX

Last Season

Goals For	181	28th
Goals Against	216	t-14th
GVT	-35	25th
Points	78	25th
Playoffs	Did not make playoffs	

Schneider was the only bright spot in what was an otherwise forgettable season for the Devils.

Three-Year Record

GVT	-63	24th
Points	214	24th
Playoffs	0 Appearances, 0 Wins	

VUKOTA Projections

Goals For	192	29th
Goals Against	219	15th
GVT	-28	28th
Points	82	28th

The Devils have very little high-end talent, and it will take time to accumulate more. It will be another painful year in New Jersey.

Top Three Prospects

P. Zacha (F), S. Santini (D), R. Kujawinski (F)

Devils performance under DeBoer and Oates/Stevens		
Stat (five-on-five)	DeBoer (through 12/26)	Oates and Stevens (after 12/26)
Corsi for %	49.6%	45.3%
On-ice shooting %	6.7%	7.6%
Save percentage	.931	.938
Shots for per 60 minutes	25.8	23.2
Shots against per 60 minutes	28.5	29.0
Save percentage (Schneider)	.929	.939

York Rangers finished the season at 49.5%.

While it is clear that losing the likes of Ilya Kovalchuk and Zach Parise ended New Jersey's chances to return to the Stanley Cup final anytime soon, DeBoer did try to form his team around their lone strength: goaltending. Despite a struggling top pair of centers in Adam Henrique and Travis Zajac and a young defensive corps, the team's even-strength shots against per 60 minutes rate was around the league median, at 28.5. Their on-ice save percentage was one of the best in the league at .931.

It was the only chance they had to compete.

That chance dipped significantly when DeBoer was axed. The Devils' Corsi percentage tanked from a nearly breakeven 49.6% to 45.3%, comparable to the possession-challenged Maple Leafs. It was such a drop that it was noticeable even to those who are not inclined to use such stats. In five-on-five play, shots for—which was already low—cratered to roughly 23 shots per 60 minutes. Shots against—which was middle-of-the-road with DeBoer—nudged up to 29 per 60 minutes. In other words, the offense got worse under Oates, the defense gave up more shots under Stevens, and the team as a whole was getting licked in possession night in and night out. Other factors could be at play like injuries and quality of opponents, but the evidence hints that the Oates-Stevens combo used tactics that made things worse.

If they were worse, how did the Devils manage to improve their record? The answer is simple: Cory Schneider. DeBoer rode the former Canuck's 1B netminder hard, with 20 straight starts to begin the season. His even-strength save percentage was a very good .928, but we know now from many studies that playing back-to-backs can have a significant effect on save percentage over the long run. The co-coaches stuck with the same plan, receiving even better results (.939). Since the club didn't score more goals than under DeBoer (essentially steady at 1.7 to 1.8 per game at even strength), goaltending was the key reason why the record was better after the coaching switch — not anything the co-coaches put into place. Sadly, Schneider had one of the best seasons a goaltender could have...and it was wasted on the 2014-15 Devils.

With interim head coaches, the general idea is to keep him (or them, in this case) around if there is evidence the team has played better. The record was better under Oates and Stevens, but anyone who looked at the underlying stats—or saw the games—realized neither co-coach improved the team's play. While a coach cannot turn scrubs into All Stars, they can move a team onto a path towards improvement.

Outside of goaltending, the Devils absolutely need a rebuild in talent. But that means more than new players—it means a new set of ideas from a different set of eyes. One of Shero's first moves for that rebuild was to say "thanks, but no thanks" to Oates and Stevens as a head-coach combo. It didn't work this time, but give Lou credit for trying something new. Maybe someday we will see it again.

John Fischer

NEW JERSEY DEVILS

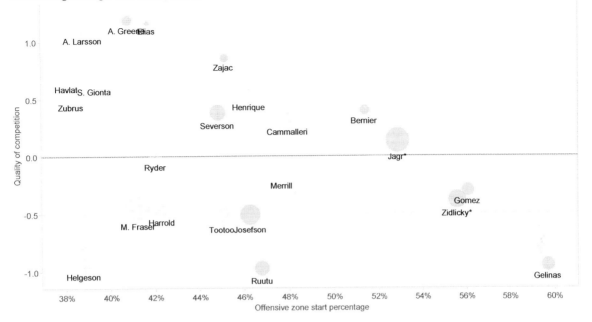

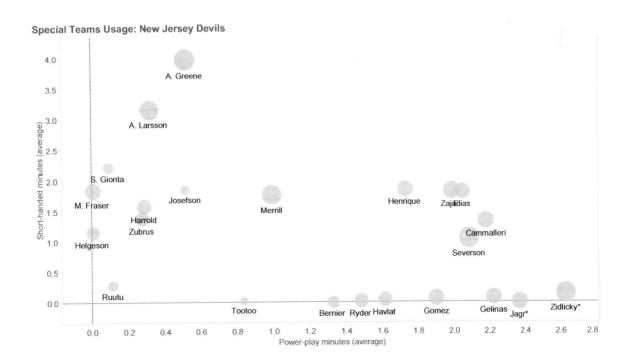

NEW JERSEY DEVILS

Offensive Profile: New Jersey Devils

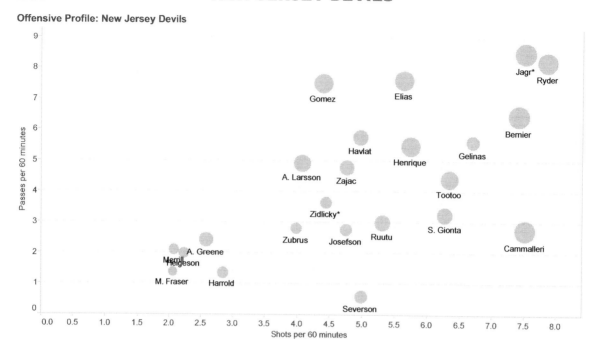

Cap Efficiency: New Jersey Devils

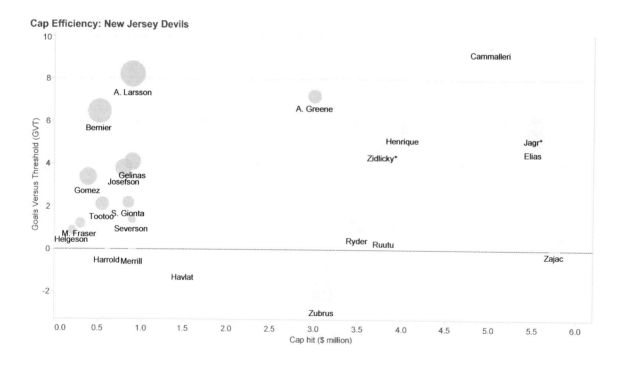

NEW JERSEY DEVILS

FORWARDS

Steve Bernier — RW — Free Agent

Season	Team	Age	GP	G	A	Pts	+/-	ESP/60	AdjCF%	iCF/60	OGVT	DGVT	SGVT	GVT
2012-13	NJD	27	47	8	7	15	-7	1.19	53.5%	11.8	-0.1	1.3	0.0	1.2
2013-14	NJD	28	78	3	9	12	-15	0.74	53.4%	10.0	-3.5	0.9	0.0	-2.6
2014-15	NJD	29	67	16	16	32	2	1.85	47.7%	11.0	4.3	2.2	0.0	6.5
2015-16	Free Agent	30	60	11	14	25					1.9	1.7	0.0	3.6

Steve Bernier has been a mainstay of the Devils' fourth line since 2011-12. However, this season, due to injury and poor play by others, Bernier received opportunities to play up the depth chart, and was a regular on the power play. Consequently, the 30-year-old turned in one of his best seasons. The 2003 first rounder set a career high in goals (16), and he tied for second with Henrique for five-on-five goals (10) and points (22). His shooting percentage jumped from an ice cold 2.9% to a blazing hot 15%. Bernier was getting the benefit of more bounces, but he was utilized well, often lining up with Gomez and Henrique. While a 47.5% Corsi is not good, a 1.1% Relative Corsi suggests he was not an anchor. For someone close to being out of the league not too long ago, this season was a triumph.

Reid Boucher — LW — NJD

Season	Team	Age	GP	G	A	Pts	+/-	ESP/60	AdjCF%	iCF/60	OGVT	DGVT	SGVT	GVT
2013-14	NJD	20	23	2	5	7	2	1.76	57.1%	13.2	0.5	0.9	0.3	1.8
2014-15	NJD	21	11	1	0	1	-4	0.49	50.1%	17.5	-0.7	0.0	-0.3	-1.0
2015-16	NJD	22	34	6	7	13					0.6	0.8	0.0	1.3

Corey Pronman once noted that Reid Boucher has a NHL-level shot – and that's it. As New Jersey continued to struggle to score, there was increased interest to see the former 62-goal scorer from Sarnia in the NHL. Alas, when he was called up, he and his NHL-level shot were not readily apparent. In 11 appearances, Boucher took 20 shots and scored only once. While possession was actually above 50% when he was on the ice, that is mitigated by very favorable zone starts to go with limited minutes. What is concerning is that in the AHL, Boucher put up a meager 15 goals and 15 assists to go with 172 shots. This does not suggest the 22-year-old is destined become a pro scorer. There is still time to develop, but hopes should be tempered.

Damien Brunner — RW — Swiss

Season	Team	Age	GP	G	A	Pts	+/-	ESP/60	AdjCF%	iCF/60	OGVT	DGVT	SGVT	GVT
2012-13	DET	26	44	12	14	26	-6	1.73	53.8%	18.7	1.5	0.6	-0.4	1.6
2013-14	NJD	27	60	11	14	25	-11	1.22	53.5%	14.3	1.6	1.1	-0.5	2.2
2014-15	NJD	28	17	2	5	7	-1	0.85	51.1%	11.9	0.6	0.1	-0.3	0.5
2015-16	Swiss	29	43	8	11	19					1.6	0.9	0.0	2.5

The Devils signed Damien Brunner to a two-year deal after a tryout in the summer of 2013. The first year went badly. He was expected to add speed and shots from the right wing position. Unfortunately, Brunner generally did not contribute except in flashes. The second year did not go any better. The Swiss winger never fit in with a Devils team that both requires forwards to play defense and tends to chip and chase pucks on offense. After failing to find a trade partner, the Devils put Brunner on unconditional waivers in December, which he cleared. Brunner returned home to Switzerland, where he plays for HC Lugano.

Mike Cammalleri							LW						NJD
Season	Team	Age	GP	G	A	Pts	+/-	ESP/60	AdjCF%	iCF/60	OGVT	DGVT	SGVT	GVT
2012-13	CGY	30	44	13	19	32	-15	1.60	47.1%	13.2	5.2	0.0	-0.3	4.9
2013-14	CGY	31	63	26	19	45	-13	1.80	50.0%	14.4	7.7	2.0	0.1	9.8
2014-15	NJD	32	68	27	15	42	2	1.73	45.2%	11.6	7.1	2.6	-0.2	9.5
2015-16	NJD	33	63	21	18	39					5.1	1.9	0.0	7.0

The Devils signed Mike Cammalleri to a large five-year deal with the intention that he would be a leader in offensive production. Cammalleri led the team in goals (27), shots (157), and power-play goals (9). So far, so good. However, there is reason to be concerned for the long term. The former King, Flame, Canadien, and Flame was not a consistent shooter; he varied between taking a lot of shots in a game and taking only one in others. The five-foot-nine winger also suffered some minor injuries that limited him to 68 games, something that has been a constant in his career. He was also one of the team's poorer possession players. Last but not least, Cammalleri shot at 17.3%, the highest of his career, a sign of getting more than his share of favorable bounces. At the end of the day, a rebuilding team doesn't need a pricey soon-to-be-fading veteran scorer.

Ryane Clowe							LW						Retired
Season	Team	Age	GP	G	A	Pts	+/-	ESP/60	AdjCF%	iCF/60	OGVT	DGVT	SGVT	GVT
2012-13	SJS, NYR	30	40	3	16	19	1	1.58	53.7%	15.5	0.5	1.3	-0.9	0.9
2013-14	NJD	31	43	7	19	26	-10	1.80	52.5%	9.7	1.8	1.1	-1.4	1.5
2014-15	NJD	32	13	1	3	4	-1	1.43	46.6%	7.9	-0.7	0.3	0.0	-0.4
2015-16	Retired	33	38	6	11	17					0.9	0.9	0.0	1.8

Last season, Ryane Clowe suffered from two concussions, which limited him to 13 appearances. In St. Louis on November 6, he got hit in the face by a stick, struck by an elbow to the head, and then took a hit to the side of the head. The first two resulted in stitches, the third led to a 14-second shift that would turn out to be his last of the season…and the last of his career. After his sixth concussion in three seasons, the long-time Shark decided to hang up his skates and step away from the game.

Patrik Elias							C/LW						NJD
Season	Team	Age	GP	G	A	Pts	+/-	ESP/60	AdjCF%	iCF/60	OGVT	DGVT	SGVT	GVT
2012-13	NJD	36	48	14	22	36	5	1.94	58.9%	13.3	7.4	3.0	-0.7	9.7
2013-14	NJD	37	65	18	35	53	-4	2.04	54.7%	10.5	7.1	5.2	-2.2	10.0
2014-15	NJD	38	69	13	21	34	-20	1.45	47.7%	9.0	2.6	1.3	1.3	5.3
2015-16	NJD	39	59	11	20	31					2.7	1.8	0.0	4.5

Patrik Elias has been a foundational player for the Devils since 2000. However, time is taking its toll on the 39-year-old. He still played a significant role for the team: tough competition at even strength, like Travis Zajac, and plenty of minutes in all situations. Yet, Elias was not as effective as he was even two seasons ago. For the first time in his career, Elias was a sub-50% Corsi player. Though it was one of the better percentages on the team, it still speaks to his decline. Though his even-strength points per 60 rate remained at a top-nine level, it was below 2.00 ESP/60 for the first time since the late 1990s. The four-time Czech Olympian also suffered from back spasms, limiting his availability. Given his age and decline, he is sadly no longer the foundational player the team has leaned on for so long.

Stephen Gionta — C/RW — NJD

Season	Team	Age	GP	G	A	Pts	+/-	ESP/60	AdjCF%	iCF/60	OGVT	DGVT	SGVT	GVT
2012-13	NJD	29	48	4	10	14	2	1.45	49.8%	8.7	0.3	3.4	0.0	3.7
2013-14	NJD	30	66	4	7	11	-8	0.86	50.6%	10.5	-1.0	3.3	0.0	2.3
2014-15	NJD	31	61	5	8	13	4	0.99	47.9%	10.9	-0.5	2.7	0.0	2.2
2015-16	NJD	32	54	6	8	14					0.1	2.1	0.0	2.2

Past seasons saw Stephen Gionta as a mainstay on the fourth line. Whether as a winger or a center, he could be counted on to accomplish basic tasks, help out on the penalty kill, and be a thorn in the opposition's side. In 2014-15, the former Albany Devils captain got to play a little more often, in somewhat bigger roles. His possession stats were not hideous (at least by the standards of this Devils squad). Gionta still displayed the same traits that have cemented his spot in the league. The five-foot-seven forward is too focused on the puck defensively, which gets him into trouble at times. Offensively, he does not provide much: his five goals were a career high.

Scott Gomez — C — Free Agent

Season	Team	Age	GP	G	A	Pts	+/-	ESP/60	AdjCF%	iCF/60	OGVT	DGVT	SGVT	GVT
2012-13	SJS	33	39	2	13	15	-10	0.95	52.0%	11.0	0.3	0.0	0.0	0.3
2013-14	FLA	34	46	2	10	12	-11	1.11	45.4%	8.2	-0.6	0.3	0.0	-0.3
2014-15	NJD	35	58	7	27	34	-10	1.42	47.0%	6.8	2.2	1.1	0.2	3.4
2015-16	Free Agent	36	51	7	18	25					1.6	1.1	0.0	2.8

In the summer of 2014, no one really wanted Scott Gomez. His prior three seasons were disappointing to the point where it looked like his time in the NHL was up. However, New Jersey gave him a tryout. He didn't make the team, but was told to stick around. When the mumps hit the Devils hard in early December, he was signed out of necessity. Consequently, Gomez demonstrated he still had game. Sure, his speed was diminished and his defensive play wasn't as good as once was, but his passing and vision were present as if he never left New Jersey. It helped he wasn't asked to play a dump-and-chase style. For a player seemingly on the outs, 34 points in 58 games was a shockingly pleasant surprise for a team lacking in offense. The Devils will move on, but the hope is that Gomez's NHL career will, too.

Martin Havlat — RW/LW — Free Agent

Season	Team	Age	GP	G	A	Pts	+/-	ESP/60	AdjCF%	ICF/60	OGVT	DGVT	SGVT	GVT
2012-13	SJS	31	40	8	10	18	7	1.57	52.5%	14.2	2.7	1.8	0.0	4.5
2013-14	SJS	32	48	12	10	22	14	1.95	51.1%	10.5	3.6	2.4	-0.3	5.8
2014-15	NJD	33	40	5	9	14	-11	0.91	45.3%	8.3	-0.6	0.2	-0.3	-0.7
2015-16	Free Agent	34	44	7	10	17					1.0	1.0	0.0	2.0

New Jersey signed Martin Havlat in the hopes he could add much-needed offense at wing; GM Lou Lamoriello inked the oft-injured winger to a one-year deal in case it did not work out. It certainly did not. Under all coaching staffs in New Jersey, Havlat was initially lined up with Patrik Elias. That meant shifts against difficult competition that were not always starting on offense. This lasted until the coaches realized opponents enjoyed his shifts. However, moving Havlat away from Elias did not help much, as his lack of a defensive game resulted in poor possession stats. His meager production did not justify significant minutes, either. Eventually, Havlat became a regular scratch. The flashes of offense he provided were too few and far between to keep him active on an offensively-challenged roster.

Adam Henrique — C/LW — NJD

Season	Team	Age	GP	G	A	Pts	+/-	ESP/60	AdjCF%	iCF/60	OGVT	DGVT	SGVT	GVT
2012-13	NJD	22	42	11	5	16	-3	0.92	56.3%	10.1	0.2	3.0	-0.6	2.6
2013-14	NJD	23	77	25	18	43	3	1.47	53.2%	9.5	5.6	6.0	-1.4	10.2
2014-15	NJD	24	75	16	27	43	-6	1.47	45.9%	10.5	3.1	3.1	-0.5	5.7
2015-16	NJD	25	71	18	24	43					4.0	3.0	0.0	7.0

Adam Henrique was used all over the lineup. Sometimes out of necessity and sometimes out of trying to find a workable combination, Henrique had shifts at center and left wing on second and third lines, as well as shifts as a first-line winger. Henrique also played plenty on the penalty kill, but curiously, not the power play. By season's end, his level of competition was about average, which makes his -1.2% Relative Corsi look rather poor. While the 2012 Calder Trophy finalist ended up leading the Devils in points, his performances fluctuated between playing like the top-six forward the team thinks he is and being entirely invisible. At the end of the day, the 25-year-old is essentially a complementary player. He has good speed, he is responsible in his own end, and his shot is not bad. He just cannot drive play or carry lesser teammates.

Jacob Josefson — C — NJD

Season	Team	Age	GP	G	A	Pts	+/-	ESP/60	AdjCF%	iCF/60	OGVT	DGVT	SGVT	GVT
2012-13	NJD	21	22	1	2	3	-10	0.78	51.4%	9.5	-1.0	0.5	-0.3	-0.7
2013-14	NJD	22	27	1	2	3	0	0.50	49.5%	8.8	-1.1	1.1	0.6	0.6
2014-15	NJD	23	62	6	5	11	0	0.58	50.6%	9.6	-0.8	2.2	2.3	3.8
2015-16	NJD	24	54	6	7	13					-0.5	2.0	0.1	1.6

2009 first-round draft pick Jacob Josefson finally played at least half of an NHL season after three campaigns of setbacks by injuries and healthy scratches. That began to happen in 2014-15, too, as Josefson was scratched early on due to a groin injury and illness. Still, the six-foot, 190-pound Swede managed to appear in 62 games, a big deal given the uneven start of his NHL career. So is being one of the few Devils to have Corsi above 50% while playing a regular shift, albeit against weak competition. The Djurgardens product tends to not shoot when he has the opportunity, he struggles when the play gets physical, and he is not so good at setting others up. However, as Josefson has proved useful on penalty kills and in the shootout, he is a least a bit more than just a guy.

Stefan Matteau — LW — NJD

Season	Team	Age	GP	G	A	Pts	+/-	ESP/60	AdjCF%	iCF/60	OGVT	DGVT	SGVT	GVT
2012-13	NJD	18	17	1	2	3	-1	1.15	51.7%	10.6	-0.2	0.5	0.0	0.4
2014-15	NJD	20	7	1	0	1	0	0.72	38.9%	8.6	0.4	0.1	0.0	0.4
2015-16	NJD	21	28	5	6	11					0.9	0.6	0.0	1.5

When Stefan Matteau was drafted by the Devils in 2012, the expectation was that he would become an NHL player, albeited limited to a bottom-six role. The fairly large and physical Matteau could be an energy player with some actual skill. After an early NHL debut in 2012-13 and unimpressive numbers in the AHL, Matteau demonstrated this potential in a few games with New Jersey in 2014-15. When lined up with Zajac and Cammalleri, his hard skating had purpose and he was useful on offense. However, when he was separated from those two or forced to play defense, he was a non-factor. Matteau is only 21, so there is plenty of time left to develop.

Tuomo Ruutu							LW						
Season	Team	Age	GP	G	A	Pts	+/-	ESP/60	AdjCF%	iCF/60	OGVT	DGVT	SGVT	GVT
2012-13	CAR	29	17	4	5	9	-6	2.29	51.8%	13.9	1.4	-0.1	0.0	1.3
2013-14	CAR, NJD	30	76	8	16	24	-18	1.30	51.6%	10.8	-1.0	1.0	-0.3	-0.3
2014-15	NJD	31	77	7	6	13	-3	0.97	49.2%	9.1	0.0	1.4	-0.3	1.1
2015-16	NJD	32	57	6	8	14					-0.1	1.2	0.0	1.1

In March 2014, the Devils acquired Tuomo Ruutu from Carolina. He ended up playing prime minutes with top forwards, looking like a younger Dainius Zubrus in 2013-14; you wouldn't know it from the 2014-15 season. While the older Zubrus continued to decline, the younger Ruutu's usefulness fell off the proverbial cliff. He was constantly used on the fourth line, averaging less than 11 minutes per game. The lack of ice-time undercut his meager production (13 points, less than a shot per game). On the plus side, the long-time Hurricane put up nearly even possession marks, but he played so little and against weak competition, that it is not worth much.

Michael Ryder							RW						Free Agent	
Season	Team	Age	GP	G	A	Pts	+/-	ESP/60	AdjCF%	iCF/60	OGVT	DGVT	SGVT	GVT
2012-13	DAL, MTL	32	46	16	19	35	2	1.80	52.4%	13.1	5.8	0.7	-0.3	6.2
2013-14	NJD	33	82	18	16	34	-6	1.37	53.6%	12.5	2.6	2.2	-0.6	4.3
2014-15	NJD	34	47	6	13	19	-1	1.67	46.8%	13.2	-0.1	1.5	-0.3	1.2
2015-16	Free Agent	35	57	10	14	24					1.5	1.6	0.0	3.1

The 2013-14 season featured Michael Ryder suffering from an epic cold streak that lasted 23 games. At least he stayed in the lineup. Under former bench boss Peter DeBoer, Ryder continued to receive 14-16 minutes per game in the hopes that he would score enough to justify his inclusion. Six goals on 89 shots did not fulfill that hope. The lesson: if Ryder is not shooting and scoring, then he provides very little to a team. The two-time Canadien was often a ghost in his own end, and possession swooned when he was on the ice. When DeBoer was shown the door and the co-coaches came in, Ryder played his way out of the lineup and into the pressbox by the end of January, with only a handful of games of spot duty afterwards. He was not missed.

Tim Sestito							C							KHL
Season	Team	Age	GP	G	A	Pts	+/-	ESP/60	AdjCF%	iCF/60	OGVT	DGVT	SGVT	GVT
2012-13	NJD	28	6	0	0	0	1	0.00	53.1%	12.3	-0.3	0.2	0.0	-0.1
2013-14	NJD	29	16	0	3	3	1	1.36	52.5%	8.5	-0.1	0.5	0.0	0.4
2014-15	NJD	30	15	0	2	2	-1	1.00	45.1%	7.7	-0.8	0.4	0.0	-0.3
2015-16	KHL	31	30	3	5	9					0.1	0.7	0.0	0.9

Last year, we summed up Tim Sestito with a football term: he is "just a guy." That is, he is just in the lineup when a body is needed. This is still true. Sestito brings almost no offense to the table, little on defense, and not much in between. The former Plymouth Whaler is not even a significant scorer on the low-scoring Albany team. In fact, Sestito is close to setting a dubious NHL record, eight games shy of the all-time mark for most games played by a forward without scoring one career NHL goal (108). It would immediately become the most notable fact about Tim Sestito's NHL career. Unfortunately, he is suiting up for Dinamo Riga of the KHL in 2015-16, so the record will have to wait.

Mike Sislo — RW — NJD

Season	Team	Age	GP	G	A	Pts	+/-	ESP/60	AdjCF%	iCF/60	OGVT	DGVT	SGVT	GVT
2013-14	NJD	25	14	0	0	0	-1	0.00	60.9%	15.0	-0.4	0.1	-0.3	-0.6
2014-15	NJD	26	10	0	1	1	-2	0.55	46.4%	10.2	-0.4	0.0	0.0	-0.4
2015-16	NJD	27	30	5	6	10					0.4	0.6	0.0	1.0

When injuries struck, Mike Sislo returned to New Jersey again as a spot replacement. The 27-year-old winger would finally earn his first NHL point among his 10 appearances, a primary assist on a Zidlicky goal in a 3-4 loss at St. Louis. As a call-up, the free agent out of New Hampshire was held to fourth-line duty. He did receive a surprising number of defensive zone faceoffs; that his on-ice possession was not horrid is a silver lining. That said, Sislo is only an extra body on the NHL level. He makes more of an impact in the AHL, as he did this season with 20 goals and 20 assists. That may not seem impressive, but it was good enough to put him third among Albany players in scoring.

Jordin Tootoo — RW — NJD

Season	Team	Age	GP	G	A	Pts	+/-	ESP/60	AdjCF%	iCF/60	OGVT	DGVT	SGVT	GVT
2012-13	DET	29	42	3	5	8	0	1.11	47.9%	12.4	0.2	0.8	0.0	1.0
2013-14	DET	30	11	0	1	1	-3	0.78	52.8%	15.7	-0.6	-0.1	0.0	-0.7
2014-15	NJD	31	68	10	5	15	1	1.29	44.1%	10.1	0.3	1.8	0.0	2.1
2015-16	NJD	32	55	8	6	14					0.2	1.4	0.0	1.6

A training camp invitee, Jordin Tootoo would earn a spot as the team's designated "tough guy". However, the long-time Predator and recent Red Wing did not fight all that much (eight majors), and surprisingly, he would get a more significant role in February. Tootoo lined up with Zajac and Cammalleri for several weeks. He even became a power-play regular. The five-foot-nine, 196 pounder was always more than just a pair of fists, and he tried to justify the promotion. With 10 goals, the most he has scored since 2007-08, he absolutely tried, though he was in over his head more often than not. Tootoo's skating remained choppy, he added nothing on defense, and he was a possession anchor. Yet, his occasional sparks—goals or hits—made him easy to cheer on.

Joe Whitney — LW/RW — NYI

Season	Team	Age	GP	G	A	Pts	+/-	ESP/60	AdjCF%	iCF/60	OGVT	DGVT	SGVT	GVT
2013-14	NJD	25	1	0	0	0	0	0.00	42.3%	0.0	0.0	0.0	0.0	0.0
2014-15	NJD	26	4	1	0	1	-1	2.19	32.9%	4.5	-0.2	0.1	0.0	-0.1
2015-16	NYI	27	28	5	6	11					0.6	0.6	0.0	1.2

When Joe Whitney made his season debut—his second-ever NHL game—he only played eight minutes. Some fans thought he got a raw deal. He got another chance and didn't make the most of it. In four appearances, Whitney took one shot on net, the shot somehow went in the net, and then he spent the rest of his ice-time behind the play and looking lost on defense. At five-foot-six, 170 pounds, and 27 years old, Whitney is not fast or skilled enough to warrant more minutes unless his team needs a body. He is great in the AHL, though, having led Albany in scoring for another season. He moves onto the Islanders' minor-league affiliate in Bridgeport in 2015-16.

Travis Zajac — C — NJD

Season	Team	Age	GP	G	A	Pts	+/-	ESP/60	AdjCF%	iCF/60	OGVT	DGVT	SGVT	GVT
2012-13	NJD	27	48	7	13	20	-5	1.28	56.7%	9.5	0.0	2.0	-0.3	1.7
2013-14	NJD	28	80	18	30	48	3	1.57	58.6%	10.4	3.0	7.2	-1.7	8.5
2014-15	NJD	29	74	11	14	25	-3	0.85	47.2%	7.9	-1.8	2.9	-0.5	0.6
2015-16	NJD	30	69	13	18	30					1.1	2.9	0.0	4.0

The good news is that Travis Zajac took on the toughest competition and his possession stats were not awful. Given the heavy minutes, and that his linemates usually included at least one defensively-questionable player (e.g. Tootoo or Jagr), it shows that Zajac can handle that piece of a first-line role. Unfortunately, Zajac was horrid offensively. 11 goals, 14 assists, and 117 shots is simply not acceptable for the amount of money and minutes he is receiving. It became ever clearer that Zajac is not a driver of production or offense, though he remains a top-six forward in that he can play against the other team's best. The six-foot-three center needs to play with others who can provide the offense, to squeeze more value out of his significant contract.

Dainius Zubrus — RW/C — NJD

Season	Team	Age	GP	G	A	Pts	+/-	ESP/60	AdjCF%	iCF/60	OGVT	DGVT	SGVT	GVT
2012-13	NJD	34	22	2	7	9	-3	1.37	54.1%	6.8	0.5	1.2	0.0	1.8
2013-14	NJD	35	82	13	13	26	1	1.27	54.2%	8.7	-0.8	5.8	-0.3	4.7
2014-15	NJD	36	74	4	6	10	-9	0.50	46.1%	6.1	-4.3	2.1	0.0	-2.1
2015-16	NJD	37	61	6	7	13					-1.0	2.1	0.0	1.0

The "Lithuanian Freight Train" was not running at full speed in 2014-15. Given that Dainius Zubrus has been in the NHL since he was drafted in 1996, his six-foot-five, 225-pound frame has a lot of mileage on it. The wear started to show in 2013-14, and it became dreadfully obvious this past season. Zubrus was never a production powerhouse, but this season was rough. While his shooting percentage hit a career low of 5.4%, his shots per game rate dipped below one, also a career low. The former Flyer, Canadien, Capital, and Sabre did not even win a lot of board battles despite his size and battle-tested experience. He was once a useful, versatile complementary winger. He was sadly now an albatross among the team's forwards. Incoming GM Ray Shero agreed, and the Devils bought out his remaining contract.

DEFENSEMEN

Mark Fraser — LD — Free Agent

Season	Team	Age	GP	G	A	Pts	+/-	ESP/60	AdjCF%	iCF/60	OGVT	DGVT	SGVT	GVT
2012-13	TOR	26	45	0	8	8	18	0.72	45.4%	8.0	-0.3	4.0	0.0	3.7
2013-14	TOR, EDM	27	42	1	1	2	-15	0.22	41.6%	3.9	-1.4	-0.8	0.0	-2.2
2014-15	NJD	28	34	0	4	4	2	0.37	41.2%	5.8	-0.6	1.8	0.0	1.2
2015-16	Free Agent	29	40	1	4	5					-0.5	1.4	0.0	0.9

In November, the Albany Devils signed former Oiler, Leaf, and…Devil Mark Fraser as additional depth and experience for their blueline. In early January, New Jersey signed Fraser in response to a rash of injuries on defense. Fraser is an acceptable option as a seventh or eighth defenseman in an organization's depth chart. However, he came on when the Devils' season was essentially lost, becoming a regular on the third pairing alongside youngster Eric Gelinas. There is not much to say about Fraser: he is a physical defenseman, evidenced by leading Devils defensemen with 55 penalty minutes; he is not good in his own end; he is even worse at anything on offense. In 34 games, he ended up with the team's lowest Corsi percentage. Clearly, he was not effective even with limited minutes.

Eric Gelinas — LD — NJD

Season	Team	Age	GP	G	A	Pts	+/-	ESP/60	AdjCF%	iCF/60	OGVT	DGVT	SGVT	GVT
2012-13	NJD	21	1	0	0	0	-1	0.00	54.8%	11.5	0.0	0.0	0.0	0.0
2013-14	NJD	22	60	7	22	29	-3	0.83	52.8%	11.9	4.7	2.5	0.0	7.2
2014-15	NJD	23	61	6	13	19	-2	0.69	48.4%	12.6	2.0	2.1	0.0	4.1
2015-16	NJD	24	58	6	18	24					3.0	2.6	0.0	5.6

If nothing else, Eric Gelinas has a fantastic shot. His slapshot is powerful: woe to any non-goalie who blocks it. His wristshot is good as well. Possession went decently when he was on the ice. However, that was with about 60% offensive zone starts, playing low-level competition, and it does not speak to Gelinas' other issues—which is mostly everything else. A 10-foot pass from Gelinas to an open teammate is not guaranteed to hit its mark. He cannot lead a breakout or handle the back "1" in the 1-3-1 power-play formation, despite repeated attempts. When the play gets physical, the six-foot-four, 216-pound Gelinas becomes invisible. He is also easy to knock off the puck despite his large frame. He is also a slow skater, so his poor defensive positioning becomes a bigger issue. But at least his shot is fantastic.

Andy Greene — RD — NJD

Season	Team	Age	GP	G	A	Pts	+/-	ESP/60	AdjCF%	iCF/60	OGVT	DGVT	SGVT	GVT
2012-13	NJD	30	48	4	12	16	12	0.60	55.0%	8.2	1.5	7.3	0.0	8.8
2013-14	NJD	31	82	8	24	32	3	0.67	56.6%	9.9	3.1	9.8	0.0	12.9
2014-15	NJD	32	82	3	19	22	1	0.77	48.1%	7.7	0.8	6.4	0.0	7.2
2015-16	NJD	33	69	4	18	22					1.5	5.1	0.0	6.6

Andy Greene was the iron man of the team, taking on significant, tough minutes night-in, night-out for all 82 games. He probably missed Mark Fayne, but the dropoff to being paired with Damon Severson and Adam Larsson was not that large. The former Miami Redhawks captain finished third among Devils defensemen in points, a bit of a feat given that he was not at all featured on the power play. He also tried his best to stay out of the box, as his 20 penalty minutes were the fewest among regulars. Greene was not as much of a boss as he was in 2013-14, but he handled a lot of difficult minutes well. That carries its own value on a rebuilding blueline.

Peter Harrold — RD/RW — STL

Season	Team	Age	GP	G	A	Pts	+/-	ESP/60	AdjCF%	iCF/60	OGVT	DGVT	SGVT	GVT
2012-13	NJD	29	23	2	3	5	-8	0.34	60.4%	8.7	0.3	0.1	0.0	0.3
2013-14	NJD	30	33	0	4	4	-2	0.44	55.2%	6.9	-0.6	1.4	0.0	0.8
2014-15	NJD	31	43	3	2	5	-10	0.52	43.4%	6.0	-0.7	0.6	0.0	-0.1
2015-16	STL	32	42	2	6	8					-0.1	1.4	0.0	1.3

Peter Harrold proved to be a solid depth player in 2013-14. This season, he proved to just be a depth player. The nine-year veteran is good enough to not get demolished, and he has the confidence to have the puck on his stick. It is just that it tends to be an adventure when he does have the puck. When he doesn't, his lack of size and speed puts him at a disadvantage. That said, he is willing to do what it takes to stay on the ice, even playing wing on the fourth line for a few games. The 2005 NCAA champion with Boston College could still be a viable seventh or eighth defenseman in a deeper organization, but that would be all.

Seth Helgeson — LD — NJD

Season	Team	Age	GP	G	A	Pts	+/-	ESP/60	AdjCF%	iCF/60	OGVT	DGVT	SGVT	GVT
2014-15	NJD	24	22	0	2	2	4	0.44	44.4%	6.1	-0.7	1.5	0.0	0.9
2015-16	NJD	25	36	1	6	7					-0.2	1.7	0.0	1.5

In the fourth round of the 2009 NHL Entry Draft, the Devils selected Seth Helgeson out of Sioux City in the USHL. After four years at the University of Minnesota and a full season in Albany, Helgeson made his NHL debut. When drafted, his size was a clear asset. Helgeson is six-foot-four and 215 pounds, and he knows how to use it. However, he has displayed very limited production at every level. In 22 appearances with New Jersey, Helgeson was on good behavior with only 18 penalty minutes. Yet, his lack of speed, lack of offensive talent, and relative inexperience meant his usage had to be limited. In another era, his skillset would be perfectly fine. In this one, he is unlikely to be more than a fill-in.

Raman Hrabarenka — RD — NJD

Season	Team	Age	GP	G	A	Pts	+/-	ESP/60	AdjCF%	iCF/60	OGVT	DGVT	SGVT	GVT
2014-15	NJD	22	1	0	0	0	1	0.00	51.1%	0.0	0.0	0.0	0.0	0.0
2015-16	NJD	23	25	2	5	7					0.4	0.8	0.0	1.2

Initially signed by Albany as an undrafted free agent in 2012, big Raman Hrabarenka made his NHL debut late in the 2014-15 season. While he did not make much of a mark at first, someone in New Jersey felt the six-foot-five Belarussian had enough potential to warrant an NHL contract in 2013. In the following two seasons, Hrabarenka displayed signs of an offensive game by way of putting up 20+ points and averaging over a shot per game in two AHL seasons. Injuries have limited his time; in fact, a broken jaw prevented an earlier call-up. Hrabarenka really did not do much in his lone NHL game, but the organization clearly thinks he is a part of the blueline's future depth.

Adam Larsson — LD — NJD

Season	Team	Age	GP	G	A	Pts	+/-	ESP/60	AdjCF%	iCF/60	OGVT	DGVT	SGVT	GVT
2012-13	NJD	20	37	0	6	6	4	0.58	51.3%	6.4	-0.4	4.1	0.0	3.7
2013-14	NJD	21	26	1	2	3	-1	0.42	55.7%	7.3	-0.3	1.1	-0.3	0.5
2014-15	NJD	22	64	3	21	24	2	1.13	46.9%	9.1	4.0	4.2	0.0	8.2
2015-16	NJD	23	60	5	17	21					2.5	3.2	0.0	5.8

After three seasons of potential and not playing a lot, Adam Larsson had a sort-of breakout season. Following an initial scratching, Larsson finally looked like a defenseman who figured it out. He became a player who did not take a hit or three every other shift, was not so tentative on the puck, and defended as if he had tunnel vision. As a result, Larsson performed better in his own end and he fired away more often on offense. Then he got the mumps. When Larsson returned, he was slotted next to Greene for the rest of the season—after Severson was hurt—and demonstrated these improvements again, which garnered plenty of attention. It appears the 2011 fourth-overall pick is living up to his initial potential.

Jon Merrill — LD — NJD

Season	Team	Age	GP	G	A	Pts	+/-	ESP/60	AdjCF%	iCF/60	OGVT	DGVT	SGVT	GVT
2013-14	NJD	21	52	2	9	11	-3	0.61	53.8%	7.4	0.1	2.6	0.0	2.7
2014-15	NJD	22	66	2	12	14	-14	0.46	45.4%	5.1	-1.6	1.4	0.0	-0.1
2015-16	NJD	23	58	3	12	15					-0.4	2.5	0.0	2.1

In 2013-14, Jon Merrill appeared to show signs of turning into a solid defender. Unfortunately, last season, Merrill was inconsistent. His role on the team was not. Under two coaching regimes, the Michigan Wolverine was consistently on the second pairing, averaging about 20 minutes per game. However, the eye test showed, for example, that he could win a puck to deny a rebound shot opportunity on one shift, but then skate the puck unforced into a forechecker on the next. The range was that wide. On top of that, he averaged less than a shot per game, which further suggests his offensive skills will not make up for everything else. What will he become? He is going to have to figure it soon, as he enters his NHL third season.

Bryce Salvador — LD — Retired

Season	Team	Age	GP	G	A	Pts	+/-	ESP/60	AdjCF%	iCF/60	OGVT	DGVT	SGVT	GVT
2012-13	NJD	36	39	0	2	2	-12	0.17	49.2%	7.0	-1.6	2.3	0.0	0.7
2013-14	NJD	37	40	1	3	4	-2	0.37	50.8%	6.4	-1.4	3.7	0.0	2.3
2014-15	NJD	38	15	0	2	2	-5	0.55	46.5%	7.4	-0.5	0.7	0.0	0.1
2015-16	Retired	39	34	1	5	6					-0.3	1.7	0.0	1.5

Bryce Salvador started the season as the Devils captain. He ended the season as the captain but unable to play. In fact, he only appeared in 15 games. After the season ended, it was revealed Salvador suffered from a bulging disc in his back and nerve damage that hurt his right hip and leg. With that in mind, it was a minor miracle he played at all. It would also partially explain how bad he was in those 15 games. His -7.7% Relative Corsi says a lot: whenever he was on the ice, the opposition enjoyed attacking. The long-time Blue was also featured on a penalty kill that got blown up early in the season. Not coincidentally, the PK got better when Salvador was not on the ice. With the age, injuries, and the poor performance, the 39-year-old called it a career in September.

Damon Severson — RD — NJD

Season	Team	Age	GP	G	A	Pts	+/-	ESP/60	AdjCF%	iCF/60	OGVT	DGVT	SGVT	GVT
2014-15	NJD	20	51	5	12	17	-13	0.62	50.2%	10.3	0.6	1.1	-0.3	1.4
2015-16	NJD	21	55	6	16	22					1.7	2.2	0.0	3.9

One of the knocks on Peter DeBoer was a perception that he did not like playing young players. It was never really true; 20-year-old Damon Severson lining up with Andy Greene from the start of the season obliterated that perception. Further, he did rather well next to Greene from October through December. Impressively, Severson made the jump from Kelowna to New Jersey and won matchups against the opposition's best skaters more often than not. Alas, the good times got an abrupt break when Severson fractured his ankle in December. The 2012 second rounder would return in March, in a different role with different coaches. From playing 22-23 minutes per night with Greene to playing 19-20 minutes per night with Merrill, Severson still displayed the signs of a bright future. He was the only Devils defenseman with positive possession stats in 2014-15.

GOALTENDERS

Scott Clemmensen							G							Retired
Season	Team	Age	GP	W	L	OT	GAA	Sv%	ESSV%	QS%	GGVT	DGVT	SGVT	GVT
2012-13	FLA	35	19	3	7	2	3.67	.874	.879	27.3%	-11.8	0.0	0.0	-11.8
2013-14	FLA	36	17	6	7	1	3.09	.896	.921	50.0%	-4.8	0.0	-1.7	-6.4
2014-15	NJD	37	3	0	0	1	4.71	.852	.897	0.0%	-2.6	0.0	-0.7	-3.4
2015-16	Retired	38	11					.908			-1.2	-0.1	-0.2	-1.5

Last summer, Scott Clemmensen was signed as insurance: to be a veteran backup to Schneider in case Kinkaid could not handle the role. Kinkaid showed that he could be the backup, so Clemmensen spent most of 2014-15 in the AHL. He did start one NHL contest, though. After Schneider got the call for the team's first 20 games, Clemmensen got a start in Calgary. Fans were reminded of his "happy feet" in the crease and how he looked out of control yet somehow was in control. The ex-Panther was close to earning a win, but the Flames would make a comeback which ended in a shootout loss. If only Jaromir Jagr ate the puck behind the net instead of giving it away with 10 seconds left. Not that it would have kept Clemmensen in the league, but it would have been a nice departing gift.

Keith Kinkaid							G							NJD
Season	Team	Age	GP	W	L	OT	GAA	Sv%	ESSV%	QS%	GGVT	DGVT	SGVT	GVT
2012-13	NJD	23	1	0	0	0	2.31	.923	.917	0.0%	0.2	0.0	0.0	0.2
2014-15	NJD	25	19	6	5	4	2.59	.915	.933	53.8%	2.2	-0.1	-0.4	1.7
2015-16	NJD	26	21					.914			2.0	-0.1	-0.1	1.8

The Devils signed Keith Kinkaid right out of Union College in 2011. He quickly became the starting goaltender for the Albany Devils until this past season. While his AHL save percentages were not amazing, management decided to give him a legitimate shot at the backup role behind Schneider. After two fill-in performances, Kinkaid got his first start: a trial by fire against Chicago where he faced 39 shots, conceded only two goals, and endured a shootout loss. That game set the mood for what the former Dutchman would provide: nothing particularly flashy, just a goalie with solid fundamentals and positioning who could handle a maelstrom of shots. While a .915 overall save percentage is not exceptional, Kinkaid did show in the majority of his 19 appearances that he can adequately fill in for Schneider. The Devils agreed by signing him to a two-year contract extension shortly after the 2014-15 campaign ended.

Cory Schneider							G							NJD
Season	Team	Age	GP	W	L	OT	GAA	Sv%	ESSV%	QS%	GGVT	DGVT	SGVT	GVT
2012-13	VAN	26	30	17	9	4	2.11	.927	.931	70.0%	14.6	-0.2	0.4	14.9
2013-14	NJD	27	45	16	15	12	1.97	.921	.918	65.1%	11.8	2.1	-3.4	10.5
2014-15	NJD	28	69	26	31	9	2.26	.925	.933	60.3%	27.1	-0.6	-0.5	26.0
2015-16	NJD	29	56					.917			11.2	0.3	-0.2	11.3

Before the season, the main question surrounding Cory Schneider as Devils' starting goaltender was whether he could appear in a majority of games and still provide his usual quality level of performance. It was a fair question. Schneider may have posted very good save percentages, but he had set a career high in 2013-14 with a modest 45 appearances while still sharing time with Martin Brodeur. One season and nearly 70 games later, Schneider answered said question emphatically with an excellent .925 save percentage. The long-time Canucks backup proved that an excellent goaltender can make up for many poor team performances, as he often dragged the Devils lineup to results they didn't earn. He was undoubtedly the team MVP in 2014-15, and one of the best goaltenders in NHL.

John Fischer

New York Islanders

Since 2005, the New York Islanders have been doormats in the Eastern Conference more often than not. If they made the playoffs, they snuck in as a lower seed. All of that changed in 2014-15. While most Islanders fans were not pleased with the first-round exit, New York was a legitimately good team. In fact, it was the team's first season with over 100 points since 1983-84. They even held first place in a tightly-contested Metropolitan Division for several weeks. The team's Corsi for percentage was the fifth best in the league, evidence that they were controlling the game along with getting results. No doubt, it was a successful season.

However, the goal is not for a team to have just one good season, it is to be good for as many seasons as possible. Last summer, general manager Garth Snow had one the best offseasons of any team executive in recent memory. Snow correctly identified team needs, and then—get this—made moves to address all of them. And in 2014-15, those moves worked out for the most part, leading to a great season. Snow should be lauded for this achievement—a timely achievement, as the team prepares to enter a new era and a new building in Brooklyn.

While the Islanders have a young roster, it is now on Snow to maintain success. In the NHL, that does not mean keep doing what you have been doing, but to identify what did and did not go well for the team and to make the appropriate decisions. Snow had one great offseason in 2014, but does it mean that he knows what he is doing?

While the Islanders were successful in the standings, they were not so successful in net. Despite signing Jaroslav Halak to replace the sputtering Evgeni Nabokov, the Islanders finished 27th in even-strength save percentage. Likewise, the Isles were 26th in overall save percentage. That is an obvious area that needs improvement. However, Halak was not really the problem. While his .914 save percentage was nothing to write home about, his .922 even-strength save percentage was acceptable. And as Halak has had better seasons, it is reasonable to think he will improve from those levels. The issue was with the backup goaltenders. Chad Johnson posted up a horrible .899 in all situations over 19 games. Snow moved Johnson for Michal Neuvirth, whom the Sabres were happy to move... for playing too well. Neuvirth only made five appearances with the Isles, giving up 14 goals for a save percentage of .881. Neuvirth has been better in the past than that small sample, but he has never posted a save percentage above .914, except for his

ISLANDERS IN A BOX

Last Season

Goals For	252	t-3rd
Goals Against	230	22nd
GVT	22	11th
Points	101	t-8th
Playoffs	Lost Conference Quarterfinal	

After an endless rebuild, the Islanders posted their best season in over a decade, marred only by a first-round loss to Washington.

Three-Year Record

GVT	-20	20th
Points	235	18th
Playoffs	1 Appearance, 3 Wins	

VUKOTA Projections

Goals For	236	4th
Goals Against	219	13th
GVT	17	3rd
Points	97	3rd

New York should match last season's result. The real question is: can they win their first playoff series since 1993?

Top Three Prospects

M. Dal Colle (F), M. Barzal (F), R. Pulock (D)

.918 with Buffalo in 2014-15. He is certainly not a slam dunk for the backup position, for taking pressure off Halak and strengthening the team.

Somewhat related to that, one of the biggest flaws of the 2014-15 Islanders was their special teams. Their power play had an average conversion rate in the regular season…but a goose egg in the postseason. Their penalty-kill success rate was near the bottom all season long. At five-on-five, the Islanders were a top possession team and had one of the lower shots-against per 60 minute rates in the league. However, when shorthanded, the goalies just got beaten more and the shots-against per 60 minutes rate ballooned to the top third of the league (the bad third). It does not appear to be the personnel as a whole, as they demonstrated the offensive talent to control play at even strength and their defense has been strong at five-on-five as well. Unless it is a fundamental coaching system issue, you could see the Isles' special teams bouncing back in a big way.

With pieces in place, Snow needs to be careful not to fall in love with this roster. While the team is certainly young and can improve, Snow will need to consider the future in terms of cap and roster space. The salary cap doesn't appear to be heading northward as it once was. New York has done a solid job of inking three of the top four on defense, Travis Hamonic, Nick Leddy, and Johnny Boychuk. Locking up 23-year-old Leddy for seven years was smart. However, locking up 31-year-old Boychuk—coming off a career year—for seven years (and more money!) was not so smart. Calvin de Haan may be the next to get a long-term deal, but that would be it for a while. At forward, New York will have to worry about six forwards becoming free agents after next season, including Kyle Okposo and Ryan Strome. Snow must leave cap space available to retain who he wants to keep around—especially Okposo, as he will command a lot of attention if he gets to free agency. As good as this team is now, the Islanders still have to account for players getting old, ineffective, or hurt, along with upgrading as prospects emerge. That requires flexibility; locking the team to this roster prevents that.

We are confident the Islanders will be a playoff team in 2015-16, and if they shore up a few leaks, they could be contending for the Eastern Conference title. The big question—one that Snow's actions going forward will determine—is whether they have a large or small window of opportunity. From their long rebuild, there are still prospects on the way, like fifth-overall pick Michael Dal Colle, but the time is nigh to win. Now, prospects and picks can be considered trade assets. The Islanders should become big-time buyers at the deadline—not a team that merely looks for a backup goalie. This is finally the window that the team lost and lost and lost to build up to. Snow can't pick now to be shy, especially in John Tavares' prime years.

John Fischer

NEW YORK ISLANDERS

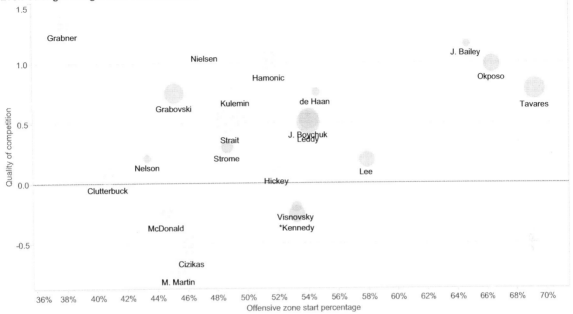

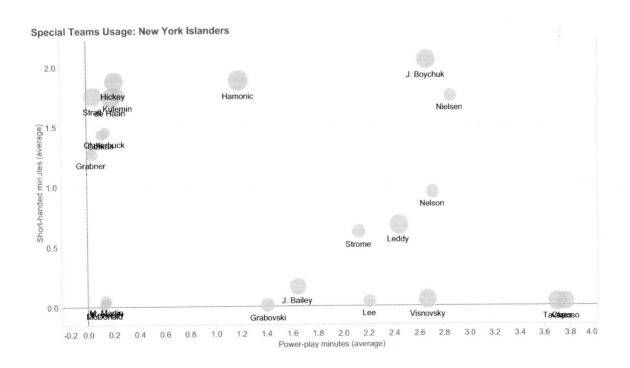

NEW YORK ISLANDERS

Offensive Profile: New York Islanders

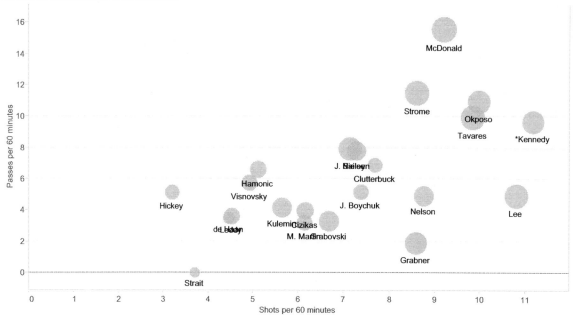

Cap Efficiency: New York Islanders

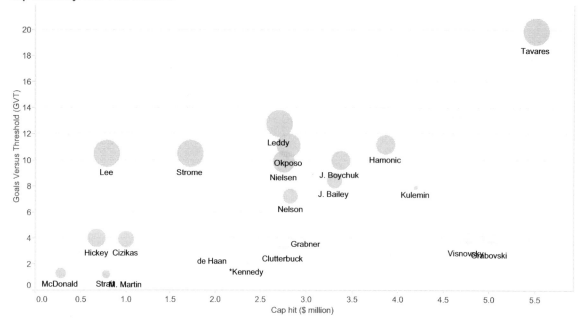

NEW YORK ISLANDERS

FORWARDS

Josh Bailey — LW/C — NYI

Season	Team	Age	GP	G	A	Pts	+/-	ESP/60	AdjCF%	iCF/60	OGVT	DGVT	SGVT	GVT
2012-13	NYI	23	38	11	8	19	7	1.89	49.8%	12.4	4.0	1.9	0.5	6.5
2013-14	NYI	24	77	8	30	38	-8	1.61	52.0%	9.6	3.2	2.1	-0.2	5.0
2014-15	NYI	25	70	15	26	41	3	2.12	53.4%	13.9	5.6	2.8	0.1	8.4
2015-16	NYI	26	65	15	27	42					4.8	2.3	0.0	7.1

Often-criticized Islanders forward Josh Bailey enjoyed a nice offensive season, setting a career high in points. The first-round pick from 2008 was juggled throughout the lineup for most of the season, but settled in nicely on the first line. His defensive awareness and positive possession numbers helped bring some balance to the top unit. During the team's brief postseason stint, Bailey was second on the team in points, with two goals and three assists. With more young talent on the way in the organization, this could very well end up being a "prove it" year for the intelligent and versatile complementary forward. Possessing a $3.3 million cap hit through 2017-18, he will have to secure a permanent top-nine spot to be worth it.

Eric Boulton — LW — Free Agent

Season	Team	Age	GP	G	A	Pts	+/-	ESP/60	AdjCF%	iCF/60	OGVT	DGVT	SGVT	GVT
2012-13	NYI	36	15	0	0	0	-4	0.00	46.1%	9.7	-0.7	-0.2	0.0	-0.9
2013-14	NYI	37	23	2	2	4	0	1.65	35.6%	11.6	0.5	0.4	0.0	0.9
2014-15	NYI	38	10	2	0	2	-1	1.67	45.9%	11.1	0.7	0.0	0.0	0.7
2015-16	Free Agent	39	29	4	4	8					0.6	0.5	0.0	1.0

Sure, Eric Boulton has provided toughness and depth, but overall, he does not bring much to an NHL club. Fourth liners are expected to contribute on the penalty kill and add the occasional offense, which Boulton has failed to do on a consistent basis. The Islanders have kept him around due to his locker-room presence, but that is hardly worth the roster spot. At age 39, it will be almost impossible for Boulton to find a regular opportunity at the highest level anymore. Give him credit for sacrificing his body over a long career, lacing 'em up for 648 NHL games.

Casey Cizikas — C/RW — NYI

Season	Team	Age	GP	G	A	Pts	+/-	ESP/60	AdjCF%	iCF/60	OGVT	DGVT	SGVT	GVT
2012-13	NYI	21	45	6	9	15	0	1.86	48.5%	10.5	1.4	1.5	0.0	2.9
2013-14	NYI	22	80	6	10	16	-12	0.84	44.2%	8.6	-0.4	1.7	0.6	1.9
2014-15	NYI	23	70	9	9	18	-2	1.17	50.4%	11.6	2.0	1.9	0.0	3.9
2015-16	NYI	24	60	9	10	19					0.8	1.7	0.0	2.5

Casey Cizikas was one of the few Islanders who had a set role all season long, lining up in the fourth-line center position. Considering he was given a merry-go-round of linemates and limited minutes, the Isles' fourth-round pick in 2009 provided solid production. The penalty kill was not a strong point of the Islanders for most of the season, but when the unit finally got its act together, Cizikas was right in the middle of it. The Toronto native should be locked into the same roles for 2015-16.

Cal Clutterbuck — RW — NYI

Season	Team	Age	GP	G	A	Pts	+/-	ESP/60	AdjCF%	iCF/60	OGVT	DGVT	SGVT	GVT
2012-13	MIN	25	42	4	6	10	-5	1.07	48.3%	15.8	0.3	1.4	0.0	1.7
2013-14	NYI	26	73	12	7	19	-9	1.10	48.1%	15.3	1.1	1.9	-0.3	2.7
2014-15	NYI	27	76	7	9	16	1	0.85	51.6%	14.0	0.7	2.3	0.4	3.3
2015-16	NYI	28	61	10	10	20					1.2	1.9	0.0	3.1

Islanders fans may still be scratching their heads at the deal that sent now-productive Nino Niederreiter to Minnesota for Cal Clutterbuck, as the hard-nosed veteran has offered very little value since being acquired. The five-foot-eleven, 216-pound winger posted the lowest points per 60 minutes of any forward on the team and had a sub-50% goals-for percentage despite playing on one of the best even-strength scoring teams in the NHL. The former Oshawa General will always be lauded for his toughness—he laid out 343 hits—but he offered very little beyond "energy." That certainly isn't worth a $2.8 million cap hit.

Michael Grabner — LW/RW — TOR

Season	Team	Age	GP	G	A	Pts	+/-	ESP/60	AdjCF%	iCF/60	OGVT	DGVT	SGVT	GVT
2012-13	NYI	25	45	16	5	21	4	1.90	49.6%	15.8	4.8	2.5	0.0	7.3
2013-14	NYI	26	64	12	14	26	-10	1.82	50.0%	13.9	2.9	2.0	0.0	5.0
2014-15	NYI	27	34	8	5	13	4	1.97	51.2%	16.9	2.7	1.6	0.0	4.3
2015-16	TOR	28	50	11	12	24					2.7	1.8	0.0	4.5

Michael Grabner's season was simply ruined by injuries. The lightning-fast left winger had trouble staying on the ice for an extended period of time, and therefore had trouble establishing any sort of rhythm throughout the regular season. When healthy, Grabner has proven to be a useful third-line player and effective penalty killer. However, as the Islanders have had the opportunity to break in a lot of young talent, the six-foot-one Austrian was pushed out of the mix for a permanent lineup spot. The underappreciated Grabner was finally shipped out of town in September, to add an additional element of speed to the Maple Leafs.

Mikhail Grabovski — C — NYI

Season	Team	Age	GP	G	A	Pts	+/-	ESP/60	AdjCF%	iCF/60	OGVT	DGVT	SGVT	GVT
2012-13	TOR	28	48	9	7	16	-10	1.17	44.7%	14.1	0.2	-0.9	-0.6	-1.3
2013-14	WSH	29	58	13	22	35	6	1.96	50.8%	8.8	4.8	1.8	1.1	7.6
2014-15	NYI	30	51	9	10	19	3	1.65	56.7%	14.5	2.6	1.6	-0.3	4.0
2015-16	NYI	31	51	10	14	24					2.3	1.5	0.0	3.8

Mikhail Grabovski's regular season was limited to just 51 games due to injury. The long-time Maple Leaf historically has been a positive possession player, but he had trouble finding a permanent role with the constant rotation of line combinations. The harshly-scrutinized Belrussian forward may not have posted huge offensive numbers, but was strong at five-on-five, scoring eight goals and nine assists at even strength. When healthy, Grabovski can have a positive impact on his teammates and play in all phases of the game. If he can stay on the ice, his tough-to-play-against style and ability to handle defensive assignments will allow the Isles' offensive dynamos to flourish.

NEW YORK ISLANDERS

Tyler Kennedy — RW — Free Agent

Season	Team	Age	GP	G	A	Pts	+/-	ESP/60	AdjCF%	iCF/60	OGVT	DGVT	SGVT	GVT
2012-13	PIT	26	46	6	5	11	-6	0.92	50.6%	18.0	-0.2	-0.2	0.0	-0.4
2013-14	SJS	27	67	4	13	17	-10	1.19	53.8%	19.6	-1.0	0.9	0.0	0.0
2014-15	SJS, NYI	28	38	6	8	14	-2	2.01	53.1%	19.3	1.6	1.0	-0.3	2.3
2015-16	Free Agent	29	49	7	11	18					1.0	1.1	0.0	2.1

Tyler Kennedy has always been a bit of an anomaly, analytically. He was famously ranked as one of the top forwards in the NHL a number of years ago, highlighting loopholes in certain analytics, and their common-sense application. Since leaving Pittsburgh, Kennedy's numbers point to being an effective bottom-six forward, but coaches continue to be disappointed in his overall performance. The undersized winger is among league leaders in shots attempts per 60 minutes, but he consistently shoots in the seven-percent range, which means he is not much of an offensive threat despite some nice-looking Corsi numbers. The trick in his utilization is to make sure he is not taking shots that more skilled linemates should be taking. In other words, a team would be nuts to put him in a top-six role.

Nikolay Kulemin — RW — NYI

Season	Team	Age	GP	G	A	Pts	+/-	ESP/60	AdjCF%	iCF/60	OGVT	DGVT	SGVT	GVT
2012-13	TOR	26	48	7	16	23	-5	2.03	41.5%	10.5	1.3	3.0	-0.6	3.7
2013-14	TOR	27	70	9	11	20	-4	1.26	40.4%	8.6	0.9	1.4	0.0	2.3
2014-15	NYI	28	82	15	16	31	7	1.54	52.7%	11.1	4.6	3.5	-0.3	7.9
2015-16	NYI	29	66	12	15	27					2.4	2.2	0.0	4.5

Magnitogorsk native Nikolay Kulemin can fill a third-line winger role to perfection, but do not expect much more than that. The long-time Leaf spent some time on the Islanders' top line in 2014-15, but could not keep up offensively. Once Kulemin settled into a third-line role, he was a productive player at both ends of the rink. At this point, it is highly unlikely Kulemin will have another 30-goal season (achieved once, in 2010-11) where he shoots 17.3%, but you would think he should be able to tally 15-20 goals on a consistent basis (achieved in four of his seven seasons, but in only one of the last four) and make a positive impact on the puck-possession game. For that alone, he was a smart signing by Garth Snow.

Anders Lee — C — NYI

Season	Team	Age	GP	G	A	Pts	+/-	ESP/60	AdjCF%	iCF/60	OGVT	DGVT	SGVT	GVT
2012-13	NYI	22	2	1	1	2	-3	7.32	51.0%	14.7	0.4	-0.2	0.0	0.2
2013-14	NYI	23	22	9	5	14	3	2.52	54.7%	16.7	3.0	1.0	-0.3	3.8
2014-15	NYI	24	76	25	16	41	9	2.27	54.6%	16.6	7.4	3.1	0.0	10.5
2015-16	NYI	25	69	23	20	44					6.0	2.4	0.0	8.4

After not initially making the varsity club out of training camp, Anders Lee proved to the Isles' management that he should have been there all along, by scoring 25 goals. This season, the young power forward will get a chance to compete for a spot on the left side of John Tavares, which could be a huge boost to his offensive statistics. He can provide a skilled net-front presence, as Matt Moulson once did—Moulson also benefited from riding shotgun with the team's franchise player. In 2014-15, Lee's regular season success did not carry over to the postseason, which caused head coach Jack Capuano to scratch him for the first time. Lee had no bitter feelings, and inked a four-year extension with the club. He could be set up for a monster season.

Matt Martin — RW/LW — NYI

Season	Team	Age	GP	G	A	Pts	+/-	ESP/60	AdjCF%	iCF/60	OGVT	DGVT	SGVT	GVT
2012-13	NYI	23	48	4	7	11	-2	1.24	47.2%	12.1	-0.4	1.7	0.0	1.3
2013-14	NYI	24	79	8	6	14	-11	0.98	44.3%	12.0	-1.1	1.4	-0.3	0.0
2014-15	NYI	25	78	8	6	14	-4	0.97	51.9%	9.7	-0.5	1.4	0.0	0.9
2015-16	NYI	26	62	7	7	14					-0.5	1.4	0.0	0.9

The coaches and front office will argue that Matt Martin's effect on a game goes beyond the stat sheet. His intention to hit the opponent rather than get the puck leads to very little in terms of offensive output or puck possession. There is, however, something to be said about toughness and character on the fourth line, when a few points are mixed in—which they were with the power forward's 14 even-strength points. Still, there may be diminishing room in the modern NHL for the six-foot-three, 216-pound winger's skilled tough-guy role. Also, with strong organizational depth at forward, Martin could be fighting for consistent playing time, maybe no longer a lock for a permanent lineup spot.

Colin McDonald — RW — PHI

Season	Team	Age	GP	G	A	Pts	+/-	ESP/60	AdjCF%	iCF/60	OGVT	DGVT	SGVT	GVT
2012-13	NYI	28	45	7	10	17	-1	1.92	50.0%	14.8	2.0	1.3	0.0	3.3
2013-14	NYI	29	70	8	10	18	-22	1.31	46.9%	11.2	-0.7	0.2	0.6	0.2
2014-15	NYI	30	18	2	6	8	-3	2.57	51.5%	15.7	1.0	0.2	0.0	1.3
2015-16	PHI	31	44	7	10	17					0.9	0.9	0.0	1.8

An alternate captain in Bridgeport, Colin McDonald provided valuable leadership at the AHL level, but on the ice, his performance—despite 35 points in 40 games—apparently did not warrant more than 18 games with the improving varsity club. That said, in his limited NHL played time, he did provide a boost for the fourth line. In only 184 minutes of ice-time, the Princeton grad tallied eight points. Signing with the reloading Flyers in the offseason, the 31-year-old veteran should once again split time between the AHL and NHL levels.

Kael Mouillierat — LW/C — PIT

Season	Team	Age	GP	G	A	Pts	+/-	ESP/60	AdjCF%	iCF/60	OGVT	DGVT	SGVT	GVT
2014-15	NYI	27	6	1	1	2	-3	2.31	45.2%	4.7	0.1	-0.1	0.0	0.0
2015-16	PIT	28	28	5	7	12					0.8	0.5	0.0	1.3

Minnesota State-Mankato standout Kael Mouillierat has carved out a nice pro career as an AHL scorer after initially being forced to start in the ECHL with the Idaho Steelheads back in 2009-10. Over the past three AHL seasons, Mouillerat has an impressive 145 points in 179 games between St. John's and Bridgeport. After years in the minors, the 27-year-old was finally given his chance to play in the NHL for eight games. While he does not have the high-end skill or skating ability to play regularly, a chance for limited NHL duty may open the door to more opportunities in the future.

Brock Nelson — C — NYI

Season	Team	Age	GP	G	A	Pts	+/-	ESP/60	AdjCF%	iCF/60	OGVT	DGVT	SGVT	GVT
2013-14	NYI	22	72	14	12	26	-10	1.37	53.0%	15.2	1.7	1.6	1.5	4.8
2014-15	NYI	23	82	20	22	42	6	1.62	53.8%	14.2	4.9	2.8	-0.5	7.2
2015-16	NYI	24	73	21	23	44					4.8	2.3	0.0	7.1

NEW YORK ISLANDERS

NHL sophomore Brock Nelson started the season on fire, tallying 10 goals in his first 20 games. Unfortunately, in his remaining 62 contests, he only netted 10 more. Consistency was a problem for the 23-year-old, as he disappeared for long stretches during the regular season. However, the Isles had to be pleased with the 16-point jump from his rookie campaign. The North Dakota product may not be the fastest skater, but he has high-end finishing skill, and a long reach to protect the puck. As he is expected to be a major part of the future, management will be patient as he continues to grow as an all-around player.

Frans Nielsen — C — NYI

Season	Team	Age	GP	G	A	Pts	+/-	ESP/60	AdjCF%	iCF/60	OGVT	DGVT	SGVT	GVT
2012-13	NYI	28	48	6	23	29	-3	1.67	46.8%	11.8	4.4	2.1	-0.4	6.1
2013-14	NYI	29	80	25	33	58	-11	2.06	49.9%	11.9	9.3	2.7	2.9	14.9
2014-15	NYI	30	78	14	29	43	8	1.41	53.1%	15.4	5.0	3.6	1.2	9.9
2015-16	NYI	31	67	16	27	43					4.7	2.5	0.1	7.3

While every baseball team carries a utility player, the Islanders have Frans Nielsen. The Danish center spends time on the penalty kill, the first power-play unit, and centers the second line. Though a repeat of his 58-point season from two years ago was not expected, nor another 15.1% shooting percentage, more was desired from the versatile forward, overall. A nagging ankle injury limited him down the stretch, but the New York will want more going forward. Entering the final year of a four-year contract, Nielsen is the type of player every successful team would like to have. However, one factor that may ding his future value is the league's change to three-on-three overtime, as Nielsen is one of the NHL's all-time best shootout scorers—the marginalized alternative.

Kyle Okposo — RW — NYI

Season	Team	Age	GP	G	A	Pts	+/-	ESP/60	AdjCF%	iCF/60	OGVT	DGVT	SGVT	GVT
2012-13	NYI	24	48	4	20	24	-2	1.71	50.7%	12.6	1.2	1.5	0.0	2.7
2013-14	NYI	25	71	27	42	69	-9	2.80	49.1%	14.2	10.8	2.7	0.9	14.4
2014-15	NYI	26	60	18	33	51	-8	2.09	54.7%	16.8	8.3	1.0	1.8	11.1
2015-16	NYI	27	64	22	35	57					8.0	2.0	0.1	10.0

Two years ago, Kyle Okposo enjoyed a dream season, but a devastating eye injury prevented a repeat performance, at least of the boxcar stats. Okposo's personal shooting percentage dipped from 13.8% in the breakout campaign, down to 9.5%. Despite the uphill battle and some struggles to return to form, the St. Paul native was still able to tally a strong 51 points in 60 games. As an upcoming free agent, the Islanders will have to ask themselves whether their 27-year-old is worth investing in long term or if his success has been due to his supremely talented centerman. Okposo's pedigree as a top-10 draft pick and his skillset as a speedy playmaker may suggest he is worth paying.

Ryan Strome — C/RW — NYI

Season	Team	Age	GP	G	A	Pts	+/-	ESP/60	AdjCF%	iCF/60	OGVT	DGVT	SGVT	GVT
2013-14	NYI	20	37	7	11	18	-1	1.38	52.3%	14.5	1.8	0.8	0.0	2.7
2014-15	NYI	21	81	17	33	50	23	2.40	54.1%	13.9	6.4	5.2	-1.1	10.5
2015-16	NYI	22	78	22	35	57					7.0	3.5	0.0	10.4

Ryan Strome had the opportunity to experience practically every forward role in 2014-15. Whether it was first-line wing, fourth-line center, playing the point on the power play, or killing penalties, Strome was literally used in all situations. During the four-on-four overtime sessions throughout the regular season and during the playoffs, the fifth-overall selection from 2011 saw plenty of ice-time with John Tavares. Strome had a relatively low 9.5% shooting percentage, but should get more opportunities next year playing on the top line. It was a very productive 50-point season for Strome in his first full-time NHL action; the gifted passer has only hit the tip of the iceberg with his talent.

John Tavares								C					NYI
Season	Team	Age	GP	G	A	Pts	+/-	ESP/60	AdjCF%	iCF/60	OGVT	DGVT	SGVT	GVT
2012-13	NYI	22	48	28	19	47	-2	2.25	53.2%	15.2	10.4	1.5	0.7	12.5
2013-14	NYI	23	59	24	42	66	-6	2.46	48.6%	13.9	11.7	2.2	-1.3	12.5
2014-15	NYI	24	82	38	48	86	5	2.33	55.2%	15.8	16.9	3.3	-0.3	19.9
2015-16	NYI	25	79	36	51	87					13.9	3.0	0.0	16.8

Despite fluctuating lineups constantly changing the Islanders' first line, John Tavares managed to tally 86 points, one point shy of winning the Art Ross Trophy. A deeper Islanders roster gave head coach Jack Capuano the ability to utilize the 2009 first-overall pick in the attacking zone more often. Consequently, Tavares had the highest offensive zone deployment of his career, with a 69.2% offensive zone start percentage. That allowed the Islanders captain to be on the attack as much as possible, which translated into one of his best offensive years. Just entering his prime years, don't be surprised if Tavares takes home a bunch of hardware at the next NHL awards ceremony or two.

Harry Zolnierczyk								LW					
Season	Team	Age	GP	G	A	Pts	+/-	ESP/60	AdjCF%	iCF/60	OGVT	DGVT	SGVT	GVT
2012-13	PHI	25	7	0	1	1	0	1.17	41.2%	11.7	0.0	0.1	0.0	0.1
2013-14	PIT	26	13	2	0	2	0	0.91	43.7%	8.8	0.4	0.2	0.0	0.5
2014-15	NYI	27	2	0	0	0	-1	0.00	52.0%	6.0	-0.1	0.0	0.0	-0.2
2015-16	ANA	28	27	4	5	9					0.5	0.5	0.0	1.1

Several teams have put some hope in "Harry Z" that he could be a fourth liner who adds some toughness and a little bit of offense. However, Zolnierczyk has been more likely to offer suspensions than goals. In 59 career NHL games, he has only managed to put five pucks in the back of the net. The Brown University grad has made a reputation for himself as a dirty player in the AHL and NHL, which could limit his future opportunities. Still, the scrappy 27-year-old winger produced at a solid AHL level for Bridgeport, scoring 44 points in 60 games.

DEFENSEMEN

Johnny Boychuk								RD					NYI
Season	Team	Age	GP	G	A	Pts	+/-	ESP/60	AdjCF%	iCF/60	OGVT	DGVT	SGVT	GVT
2012-13	BOS	28	44	1	5	6	5	0.46	54.6%	11.3	-1.3	2.8	0.0	1.5
2013-14	BOS	29	75	5	18	23	31	0.89	56.3%	12.0	1.9	6.6	0.0	8.5
2014-15	NYI	30	72	9	26	35	15	0.93	56.1%	13.7	5.3	4.7	0.0	10.0
2015-16	NYI	31	66	7	24	31					3.8	4.2	0.0	8.0

The Islanders acquired Johnny Boychuk and Nick Leddy within minutes of each other, right before the start of the season; the two will now be forever linked. Boychuk provided much-needed veteran leadership and a monster right-handed shot to the Islanders blueline. After living in the shadow of Zdeno Chara in Boston, "Johnny Rocket" proved that there was a lot more to his game than some expected, as he was one of the NHL's best possession defensemen on top of tallying 15 points on the man advantage without consistently playing on either of the Islanders' power-play units. With the Edmonton native signed long term, Capuano did an excellent job of managing his ice-time, limiting him to under 22 minutes per game on average. While Travis Hamonic is expected to do the heavy lifting on the backend, Boychuk certainly carries his fair share of the burden.

Calvin de Haan							LD						NYI
Season	Team	Age	GP	G	A	Pts	+/-	ESP/60	AdjCF%	iCF/60	OGVT	DGVT	SGVT	GVT
2013-14	NYI	22	51	3	13	16	-7	0.84	51.9%	8.2	1.8	1.9	0.0	3.7
2014-15	NYI	23	65	1	11	12	3	0.54	53.7%	10.9	-0.3	3.1	0.0	2.8
2015-16	NYI	24	58	3	13	16					0.8	2.7	0.0	3.5

To the disappointment of Isles' management, Calvin de Haan's strong rookie season did not carry over to his sophomore year. The left-shooting defenseman turned the puck over far too often in his own zone, which forced Capuano to scratch him late in the season. However, the 23-year-old did not have it easy in his second year. He was partnered with Travis Hamonic more often than not, drawing the opponents' toughest matchups. His calm temperament on the ice is a good complement to the emotional Hamonic, but de Haan will have to elevate his game if he wants to remain in the top four. His impressive offensive numbers from Canadian junior hockey have not translated to the NHL yet—they didn't translate to the AHL—but maybe in his third season, he finally puts it all together.

Matt Donovan							LD						BUF
Season	Team	Age	GP	G	A	Pts	+/-	ESP/60	AdjCF%	iCF/60	OGVT	DGVT	SGVT	GVT
2013-14	NYI	23	52	2	14	16	-9	0.74	53.2%	9.6	1.3	1.3	0.0	2.6
2014-15	NYI	24	12	0	3	3	4	0.92	47.6%	9.1	0.3	1.0	0.0	1.3
2015-16	BUF	25	41	3	10	12					0.9	1.8	0.0	2.6

Matt Donovan got caught in a numbers game and was designated as a healthy scratch for most of the season, only appearing in 12 regular-season and two postseason matches. During his pro career, the 25-year-old Oklahoma native has demonstrated the capability to be an offensive producer, scoring 19 points in 67 career NHL games and 119 points in 180 AHL games. Tim Murray and the Sabres picked up the University of Denver product in the offseason, placing a bet on Donovan's dormant upside. However, with the September signing of Cody Franson in Buffalo, he may be forced into the pressbox or an AHL role once again.

Travis Hamonic							RD						NYI
Season	Team	Age	GP	G	A	Pts	+/-	ESP/60	AdjCF%	iCF/60	OGVT	DGVT	SGVT	GVT
2012-13	NYI	22	48	3	7	10	-8	0.40	47.1%	10.7	-0.5	2.6	0.0	2.2
2013-14	NYI	23	69	3	15	18	2	0.63	49.6%	10.6	0.3	4.8	0.0	5.1
2014-15	NYI	24	71	5	28	33	15	1.13	51.4%	11.6	6.2	5.0	0.0	11.2
2015-16	NYI	25	66	7	22	29					3.8	4.1	0.0	7.9

With Boychuk and Leddy now on the team and inked to long-term extensions, Travis Hamonic may never get the credit he deserves on the Islanders blueline. On paper, the newcomers might be the top pairing, but Hamonic always draws the toughest matchups. Locked up long term to a team-friendly contract, the Manitoba native will continue to contribute in all three zones. His offensive numbers have not been quite as high as expected, but if Calvin de Haan can take the next step, Hamonic could be in line for another productive season.

Thomas Hickey — LD — NYI

Season	Team	Age	GP	G	A	Pts	+/-	ESP/60	AdjCF%	iCF/60	OGVT	DGVT	SGVT	GVT
2012-13	NYI	23	39	1	3	4	9	0.39	56.6%	9.4	-0.8	3.0	0.0	2.3
2013-14	NYI	24	82	4	18	22	5	0.88	49.9%	9.1	2.8	5.1	-0.3	7.6
2014-15	NYI	25	81	2	20	22	-12	0.88	52.6%	7.6	2.1	1.8	0.0	4.0
2015-16	NYI	26	65	4	15	19					1.5	2.8	0.0	4.3

Six-foot, 190-pound Thomas Hickey will always have trouble matching up against the bigger, more powerful forwards, especially when paired with a finesse defenseman like Lubomir Visnovsky. That said, the former Seattle Thunderbird and Manchester Monarch has proven to be a durable defenseman and a silent leader throughout his tenure with the Islanders, with his hockey IQ making him the perfect partner for an up-and-coming defenseman. While he has become a nice role player on a very good team, most around the league will consider Hickey at least a mild disappointment because of his draft status as fourth-overall pick in 2007.

Nick Leddy — RD — NYI

Season	Team	Age	GP	G	A	Pts	+/-	ESP/60	AdjCF%	iCF/60	OGVT	DGVT	SGVT	GVT
2012-13	CHI	21	48	6	12	18	15	0.85	56.5%	7.4	3.4	2.4	-0.3	5.5
2013-14	CHI	22	82	7	24	31	10	1.07	57.7%	9.3	5.3	2.8	0.0	8.1
2014-15	NYI	23	78	10	27	37	18	1.07	56.4%	8.4	7.6	5.2	0.0	12.8
2015-16	NYI	24	70	8	26	34					5.1	3.6	0.0	8.7

Smooth-skating Nick Leddy never had the chance to display all of his skills in Chicago, mostly playing limited third-pairing minutes under Joel Quenneville, but as soon as the Islanders acquired him, his role drastically changed. The 2009 first rounder slid in right next to Johnny Boychuk to form the top pairing. Leddy has always had the ability to provide tremendous stretch and outlet passes to help his team exit the defensive zone and enter the offensive zone, but he was finally given the chance to show his impact on possession and scoring with New York. In his first season on The Island, he notched an excellent 10 goals and 37 points, but there is plenty of room for improvement, especially if he can find his way onto the top power-play unit. Capuano encourages his defensemen to jump up in the play, so look for Leddy to continue taking advantage of this opportunity.

Griffin Reinhart — LD — EDM

Season	Team	Age	GP	G	A	Pts	+/-	ESP/60	AdjCF%	iCF/60	OGVT	DGVT	SGVT	GVT
2014-15	NYI	20	8	0	1	1	1	0.55	45.9%	6.1	-0.2	0.5	0.0	0.3
2015-16	EDM	21	29	2	5	7					0.1	1.0	0.0	1.1

Highly-touted prospect Griffin Reinhart was never able to impress the Islanders front office enough for him to earn a full-time NHL role. After a disappointing season at the AHL level in Bridgeport, New York was able to trade the first-year pro while he still had value. A change of scenery could help the 2012 fourth-overall draft choice, as he looks to make a name for himself in Edmonton, where they have long needed defensive talent. That said, the Oilers may need to see more offensive production and use of his six-foot-four frame before Reinhart gets a regular shot with the varsity squad.

Brian Strait — LD — NYI

Season	Team	Age	GP	G	A	Pts	+/-	ESP/60	AdjCF%	iCF/60	OGVT	DGVT	SGVT	GVT
2012-13	NYI	24	19	0	4	4	4	0.81	50.8%	5.8	-0.1	1.5	0.0	1.4
2013-14	NYI	25	47	3	6	9	-14	0.67	43.6%	6.4	0.2	0.8	0.0	1.0
2014-15	NYI	26	52	2	5	7	-1	0.42	47.1%	7.8	-0.9	2.1	0.0	1.2
2015-16	NYI	27	50	2	8	10					-0.3	1.9	0.0	1.6

No matter which metric you use, there is no possible way to say Brian Strait had a productive season. However, in the small sample of the playoffs, he played his best hockey, providing a reliable presence on the blueline during the New York's heart-wrenching seven-game loss to Washington. Last year, the Islanders did not have a clear-cut NHL-ready defenseman knocking on the door to push Strait out of a job, but this year things will be different. With Ryan Pulock and Scott Mayfield making their cases, Strait will have to play his A-game to earn his minutes, or he may find himself looking for a new team.

Lubomir Visnovsky — LD — CHI

Season	Team	Age	GP	G	A	Pts	+/-	ESP/60	AdjCF%	iCF/60	OGVT	DGVT	SGVT	GVT
2012-13	NYI	36	35	3	11	14	12	0.55	56.9%	10.2	1.3	3.1	0.0	4.4
2013-14	NYI	37	24	3	8	11	-1	0.61	53.5%	7.2	1.5	0.8	0.0	2.3
2014-15	NYI	38	53	5	15	20	-3	1.01	55.4%	9.6	2.8	1.3	0.0	4.1
2015-16	CHI	39	47	4	15	19					2.2	1.9	0.0	4.1

If Lubomir Visnovsky were in his prime when advanced stats became mainstream, he would have been viewed as a more important piece to an NHL roster. The issue with Visnovsky has never been his on-ice play, but whether the Slovakian defenseman could endure the grind of an NHL regular season. This past season, the 38-year-old was able to tally 20 points in only 53 regular-season games, a contribution many teams would like to get from their defenseman, but he suffered a serious concussion in the playoffs. His absence proved costly to the Islanders' up-tempo system and power play. Despite the long history of concussions, Stan Bowman and the Blackhawks rolled the dice on bringing the veteran offensive blueliner to Chicago.

GOALTENDERS

Jaroslav Halak — G — NYI

Season	Team	Age	GP	W	L	OT	GAA	Sv%	ESSV%	QS%	GGVT	DGVT	SGVT	GVT
2012-13	STL	27	16	6	5	1	2.14	.899	.911	40.0%	-1.6	1.1	0.0	-0.6
2013-14	STL, WSH	28	52	29	13	7	2.25	.921	.926	62.0%	14.9	0.5	-1.6	13.8
2014-15	NYI	29	59	38	17	4	2.43	.914	.922	61.0%	5.0	0.9	0.0	5.9
2015-16	NYI	30	46					.915			6.3	0.4	-0.1	6.6

Another solid acquisition by Snow, Jaroslav Halak set a new career high, taking the crease for 59 games as the undisputed starter. The Slovakian goaltender posted a roughly league-average .914 save percentage, but his performance was probably better than the numbers indicate, considering the Islanders' high-tempo system. Fatigue has been a problem in the past, but the former Habs and Blues netminder believed a new workout regimen allowed him to stay physically prepared for the entire season. If the previously-fragile veteran remains healthy, he should expect to play approximately the same number of games in 2015-16. Islanders' fans might think Halak played in too many contests, but they have not had a number-one starting goaltender for quite some time.

Chad Johnson — G — BUF

Season	Team	Age	GP	W	L	OT	GAA	Sv%	ESSV%	QS%	GGVT	DGVT	SGVT	GVT
2012-13	PHX	26	4	2	0	2	1.21	.954	.979	100.0%	4.4	0.1	0.1	4.5
2013-14	BOS	27	27	17	4	3	2.10	.925	.932	73.9%	9.9	0.4	-0.3	9.9
2014-15	NYI	28	19	8	8	1	3.08	.889	.904	41.2%	-8.6	0.3	0.4	-7.9
2015-16	BUF	29	22					.913			1.5	0.2	0.0	1.6

After a strong season for Chad Johnson in Boston as the backup netminder, Islanders general manager Garth Snow thought he would be able to bring stability to the crease as a strong backup. Johnson did anything but that for the blue and orange. In 19 games between the pipes, he had a 3.08 goals-against average and a troubling .889 save percentage. His poor performance on Long Island forced the team to make a move at the deadline to bring in a more established backup.

Michal Neuvirth — G — PHI

Season	Team	Age	GP	W	L	OT	GAA	Sv%	ESSV%	QS%	GGVT	DGVT	SGVT	GVT
2012-13	WSH	24	13	4	5	2	2.74	.910	.917	58.3%	1.0	-0.2	0.0	0.8
2013-14	WSH, BUF	25	15	4	8	2	2.78	.921	.923	69.2%	5.0	-0.8	0.1	4.3
2014-15	BUF, NYI	26	32	7	20	4	2.98	.914	.926	46.9%	3.2	-1.5	-3.2	-1.5
2015-16	PHI	27	27					.914			2.5	-0.9	-0.4	1.2

Michal Neuvirth was acquired at the trade deadline to prevent the team from overworking starter Jaroslav Halak, and to provide a better alternative than Chad Johnson. Neuvirth had been terrific as the number-one goalie for half the season in Buffalo, putting up a solid .918 save percentage in 27 games for the worst team in hockey. Neuvirth ended up starting five games for New York, winning just one with an ugly .881 save percentage in the small sample. Once considered the future of the Capitals, the Czech goaltender seems destined to be a backup now. He signed with Philadelphia in the offseason, where he will be behind the Flyers' number one, Steve Mason.

Kevin Poulin — G

Season	Team	Age	GP	W	L	OT	GAA	Sv%	ESSV%	QS%	GGVT	DGVT	SGVT	GVT
2012-13	NYI	22	5	1	3	0	3.02	.893	.906	50.0%	-1.5	0.0	0.0	-1.4
2013-14	NYI	23	28	11	16	1	3.29	.891	.900	34.6%	-12.1	-0.2	1.0	-11.3
2014-15	NYI	24	1	0	0	1	2.77	.885	.909	0.0%	-0.5	0.1	-0.1	-0.6
2015-16	NYI	25	16					.907			-1.9	0.0	0.0	-2.0

Considering his performance, it is surprising Kevin Poulin has received 50 NHL games during his career. Since turning pro, he has been nothing more than an average AHL goalie and well below-average NHLer. In his starts, the 2008 fifth-round pick has a .899 save percentage, which might have been acceptable in 1982. In his only start of 2014-15, Poulin allowed an inexplicable comeback by the NHL's worst team, the Buffalo Sabres, giving up three goals in the third period. It is safe to say he won't be seeing more than emergency duty going forward.

Scott Charles

New York Rangers

When analysts make broad, sweeping conclusions, there are almost always exceptions. For example: if you break down goaltenders' numbers since the 2005-06 lockout, you will find that most "franchise goaltenders" are not worth their high cap hit. Often, their performance can be replaced by trading for another team's quality backup or signing a free agent for lesser dollars.

However, in the case of Henrik Lundqvist, he is worth every single penny the New York Rangers have paid him. The seventh-round pick from 2000 has set the bar for modern goaltending, repeating his elite-level performance year after year, which has been extremely difficult for hundreds of other goalies since Lundqvist entered the league in 2005-06.

If you start by breaking down the greatness of "King Henrik" in a broad sense, he has made the Rangers a legitimate contender every year of his career. Some editions of the Blueshirts were stronger than others, but only during one season did he win fewer than 50% of the games he started: in 2009-10, he lost 10 overtime or shootout games, a stroke of bad luck more than anything else.

The 2006 Olympic gold-medal winner for Sweden has been a Vezina Trophy finalist five times and has never dipped below league average in save percentage during a single season or even seen a goals-against average higher than 2.43. Lundqvist's durability has also been remarkable—until last year, when he suffered a bizarre throat injury after being hit with a puck. He has played more than 70 games four times, and suited up for 43 of 48 games during the lockout-shortened season in 2012-13.

And we haven't even gotten to his absurd playoff numbers. Much has been made of Lundqvist's incredible record when facing elimination, but his overall numbers show he can always be counted on to give the Rangers a chance to reach the Cup Final—even if they don't put enough pucks in the net to get there. In 111 playoff games, he has a .923 save percentage and 64.3% quality start percentage (basically, the percentage of games where a goalie registers a save percentage above league average).

So, breaking news, Henrik Lundqvist is great. But the question is how much longer he will be the NHL's top goalie? And can the Rangers take advantage before an eventual, inevitable decline?

Multiple studies have found the same information about the goalie aging curve: that NHL netminders, on the whole, begin to see a drop in per-

RANGERS IN A BOX

Last Season

Goals For	252	t-3rd
Goals Against	192	3rd
GVT	60	1st
Points	113	1st
Playoffs	Lost Conference Final	

With some offensive flair and the most consistent goalie in the NHL, the Rangers were regular-season champions and Cup semifinalists.

Three-Year Record

GVT	103	4th
Points	265	7th
Playoffs	3 Appearances, 29 Wins	

VUKOTA Projections

Goals For	226	11th
Goals Against	217	11th
GVT	9	11th
Points	95	11th

As long as Lundqvist is around, the Blueshirts will contend, but can they get over the top finally?

Top Three Prospects

P. Buchnevich (F), B. Skjei (D), A. Tambellini (F)

formance between the ages of 32 and 35. Lundqvist is entering his age-33 season. Using common sense, you might say that King Henrik is not your average netminder and has a good chance to extend his prime beyond that of a normal player. While that might be true, the Rangers must plan according to the norm instead of hoping to buck the trend—they must do everything possible to win within the next several years before they lose their superstar player, either literally or effectively.

Questionable contracts are not so

The Rangers made sure to keep one of their core top-six forwards by re-signing Derek Stepan to a contract extension through 2021 with a cap hit of $6.5 million. The 25-year-old center continued to produce at a number-two center level, posting 16 goals and 39 assists in 68 games. His Corsi numbers have bounced up and down, and the former Wisconsin Badger still struggles in the faceoff circle, but he is considered a strong two-way player. While Stepan's cap hit is only $375,000 off of elite two-way center Patrice Bergeron and $200,000 behind future Hall of Fame center Nicklas Backstrom (older contracts, mind you), the Rangers were in a position to ensure they would not lose their former second-round pick under any circumstance.

The "win-now" mentality was in play when New York wrapped up Mats Zuccarello to a long-term contract as well. They may have given the five-foot-seven playmaker a contract extended farther in the future than many analysts would have expected—a $4.5 million cap hit through 2019—but they signed him through their winning window and were able to keep his cap hit lower via a longer contract.

The contract most worthy of criticism is that of defenseman Dan Girardi. While he is known to be the yang to elite defender Ryan McDonough's ying, Girardi only managed a 46.2 Corsi percentage overall. The pairing of McDonagh and Girardi had a 47.3 Corsi percentage and a 51.2 goals-for percentage. However, when McDonagh was away from Girardi, his numbers skyrocketed, to a 53.3 Corsi percentage and 66.7 goals-for percentage. These are not numbers that advocate for the McDonagh-Girardi pairing, or for Girardi period. Once a solid stay-at-home blueliner, it appears the 31-year-old has already started to fade, which is bad news for New York as he is under contract at a $5.5 million cap hit through 2020.

That said, if the Rangers had elected a less-risky, bigger-money, short-term deal for Girardi, they would have been in a more precarious position in re-signing Stepan, and young impact forwards Chris Kreider and Kevin Hayes next summer.

Despite moves to create as much cap room as possible, the Blueshirts experienced a significant cap casualty in speedy winger Carl Hagelin, who the Rangers sent to Anaheim for forward Emerson Etem, who will only cost $850,000 in cap.

Prospects and Nash

Hockey Prospectus ranks the Rangers' system 24th in the NHL, down significantly after the trade of a first-round pick and emerging prospect Anthony Duclair for offensive defenseman Keith Yandle, who will be an unrestricted free agent after this season. Oscar Lindberg, selected 57th overall in 2011, may be the only prospect in the system who will be ready to make an impact within the next year or two.

With the system weakened, Rangers management has been forced to restock via cheap free agents. They made low-risk pickups of Viktor Stalberg and Jarret Stoll, both of whom wore out their welcome in their previous homes. It would not be a surprise to see the Rangers use more draft picks at the trade deadline to add upcoming free agents for a playoff run. They will continue to damage their future outlook by doing so, but that is the necessary approach.

Considering the Rangers only have a few more years left of Lundqvist's prime, you might think they would not accept any phone calls about top-notch forward Rick Nash. However, the 2002 first-overall pick carries a $7.8 million cap hit and has only managed eight playoff goals in 44 games over the past two postseasons. Considering Nash netted 42 goals in 2014-15, the return would be significant. Making a rebuild move while in "win-now" mode is tricky, but it may be smart to move on before Nash's prime runs out as well.

One thing is clear: when analyzing moves by the Rangers, their window to win should always be considered. Some contracts may appear to be questionable in a vacuum, but are solely aimed at getting the most out of their roster as long as future Hall of Famer Henrik Lundqvist is still at his best.

Matthew Coller

NEW YORK RANGERS

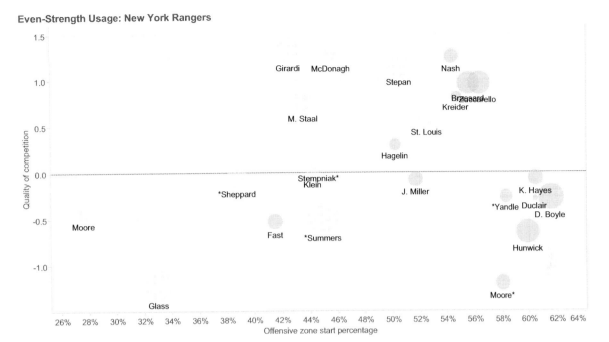

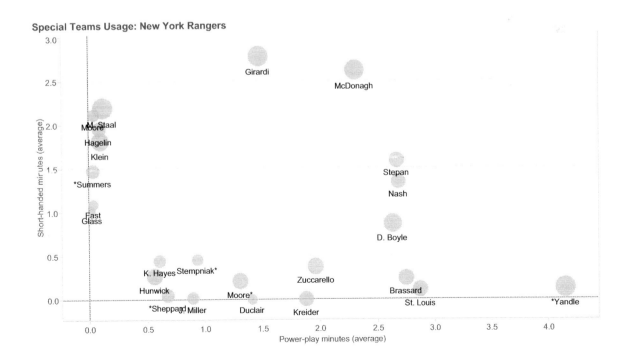

NEW YORK RANGERS

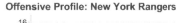

Offensive Profile: New York Rangers

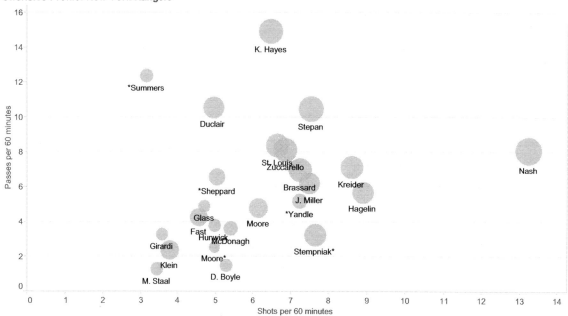

Cap Efficiency: New York Rangers

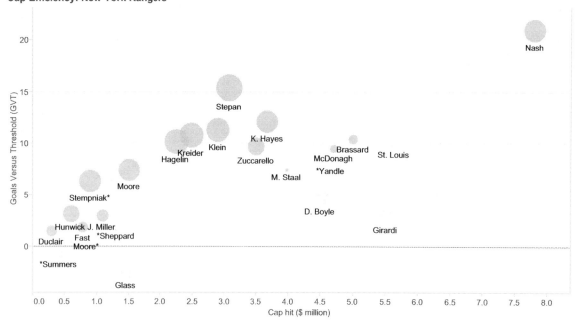

FORWARDS

Ryan Bourque — C/LW — NYR

Season	Team	Age	GP	G	A	Pts	+/-	ESP/60	AdjCF%	iCF/60	OGVT	DGVT	SGVT	GVT
2014-15	NYR	23	1	0	0	0	-1	0.00	69.8%	14.0	0.0	0.0	0.0	0.0
2015-16	NYR	24	26	5	6	11					0.8	0.5	0.0	1.3

It took some time, but Ryan Bourque finally received a taste of the NHL. After three straight seasons in the minors, the 2009 third-round pick was given 11 minutes in the Rangers last regular-season game. It was not much, but it was a start. Bourque was also recalled to be a spare for their playoff run, though he didn't see any action. Chris Bourque's younger brother sort of "broke out" on the AHL level in 2013-14 with 21 goals and 37 points for Hartford, but he only managed 12 goals and 32 points in 2014-15. At five-foot-nine and lacking in top-end speed and skill, it will be a tough road for the 24-year-old to earn the team's trust as a bottom-six forward, Hall of Fame father or not.

Derick Brassard — C — NYR

Season	Team	Age	GP	G	A	Pts	+/-	ESP/60	AdjCF%	iCF/60	OGVT	DGVT	SGVT	GVT
2012-13	CBJ, NYR	25	47	12	17	29	1	1.68	49.7%	11.1	3.3	1.0	0.2	4.5
2013-14	NYR	26	81	18	27	45	2	1.51	53.6%	11.2	5.2	2.2	-0.3	7.1
2014-15	NYR	27	80	19	41	60	9	2.19	53.2%	11.2	8.8	1.6	0.0	10.4
2015-16	NYR	28	70	20	33	54					6.9	2.2	0.0	9.1

Glen Sather took a risk in handing Derick Brassard a five-year, $25 million contract. However, early results point to the deal paying off for both sides. Brassard set a career highs in goals (19) and assists (41), he finished second on the Rangers in points (60), led the team in power-play points (18), and led the Rangers in playoff goals (9) and points (16). He also led Rangers forwards in Corsi percentage during the regular season (52.4%) and in the playoffs (53.2%). Although he received plenty of favorable zone starts, Brassard posted those figures against some of the toughest competition the Rangers faced. The 28-year-old has matured significantly, playing a more consistent 200-foot game than he ever did in Columbus.

Jesper Fast — RW — NYR

Season	Team	Age	GP	G	A	Pts	+/-	ESP/60	AdjCF%	iCF/60	OGVT	DGVT	SGVT	GVT
2013-14	NYR	22	11	0	0	0	-5	0.00	58.0%	7.9	-1.0	0.1	0.0	-0.9
2014-15	NYR	23	58	6	8	14	-1	1.26	51.6%	8.6	1.0	0.9	0.0	1.9
2015-16	NYR	24	57	8	11	19					0.3	1.2	0.0	1.4

Jesper Fast settled into a bottom-six role, averaging less than 12 minutes per game for 58 games. The Nassjo, Sweden native displayed some speed and enough skill to have a positive offensive impact, scoring six goals and eight assists. In the postseason, Fast kicked it up a notch, with three goals, three assists, and a bump in ice-time to over 14 minutes per game. The 23-year-old winger made enough of an impression to be rewarded with a two-year deal worth $1.9 million. Now the question is whether he can build on his postseason performance to turn into a viable third-line option or more.

Tanner Glass — LW — NYR

Season	Team	Age	GP	G	A	Pts	+/-	ESP/60	AdjCF%	iCF/60	OGVT	DGVT	SGVT	GVT
2012-13	PIT	29	48	1	1	2	-11	0.14	43.9%	8.0	-2.9	-0.2	0.0	-3.1
2013-14	PIT	30	67	4	9	13	-8	1.15	39.9%	8.1	-0.1	1.6	0.0	1.5
2014-15	NYR	31	66	1	5	6	-12	0.59	44.2%	8.0	-2.5	0.2	0.0	-2.3
2015-16	NYR	32	53	2	4	7					-1.8	0.8	0.0	-1.0

In Pittsburgh, Tanner Glass was a hit machine that opponents loved to play against because they often had the puck. In a puzzling move, Glen Sather decided the Rangers needed this element on a three-year contract. Head coach Alain Vigneault took it one step further by playing Glass in 66 regular-season and 19 playoff games, at less than 35% offensive zone starts. Not surprising to anyone who has witnessed Glass play (who doesn't work for an NHL team) the puck tended to stay in New York's end when he was out there. His Corsi in the playoffs was a team-low 45.0% after a second-worst 43.3% in the regular season. Yes, he was the team leader in penalty minutes and hits, but in our opinion, those aren't positives. Ranger fans will continue to be frustrated by his presence for two more seasons.

Carl Hagelin — LW — ANA

Season	Team	Age	GP	G	A	Pts	+/-	ESP/60	AdjCF%	iCF/60	OGVT	DGVT	SGVT	GVT
2012-13	NYR	24	48	10	14	24	10	1.85	55.2%	16.0	2.8	2.9	-0.3	5.4
2013-14	NYR	25	72	17	16	33	8	1.95	54.5%	14.0	4.7	4.2	0.0	8.8
2014-15	NYR	26	82	17	18	35	18	1.83	51.5%	16.5	5.4	4.8	0.0	10.2
2015-16	ANA	27	70	16	19	35					3.5	2.9	0.0	6.3

For four seasons, Carl Hagelin was a speedy, penalty-killing winger who also played well for the Rangers at even strength. While he set a career high in shots (185), frequently playing with Kevin Hayes, his production remained modest at 17 goals and 18 assists, plus only two goals and three assists in the postseason (though without a boost from power-play time). Still, the 27-year-old Swede is a smart player who often came through with key goals. To the chagrin of many Rangers fans, he became a cap casualty and was dealt to Anaheim primarily to make room for Stepan's new contract. Hagelin will fit in perfectly with the blazing fast tempo of the Ducks.

Kevin Hayes — C/LW — NYR

Season	Team	Age	GP	G	A	Pts	+/-	ESP/60	AdjCF%	iCF/60	OGVT	DGVT	SGVT	GVT
2014-15	NYR	22	79	17	28	45	15	2.47	52.0%	10.6	9.8	2.6	-0.3	12.1
2015-16	NYR	23	69	18	30	48					6.7	1.9	0.0	8.6

The New Jersey Devils traded a first-round pick in 2010 to Atlanta as part of the Ilya Kovalchuk deal. That pick was traded to Chicago as part of a package to bring Dustin Byfuglien to the Thrashers. The Blackhawks used this pick on Kevin Hayes at 24th overall. When they were unable to sign him by the deadline of August 15, 2014, it opened the door for the Rangers to sign the large, talented forward. Hayes' first impression in New York was an impressive one, posting the second highest five-on-five scoring rate on the team, only behind Rick Nash. The big center/winger is only 23 years old and has a bright future ahead, after a winding road to the NHL.

Carl Klingberg — LW/RW — KHL

Season	Team	Age	GP	G	A	Pts	+/-	ESP/60	AdjCF%	iCF/60	OGVT	DGVT	SGVT	GVT
2013-14	WPG	22	3	1	0	1	2	2.25	46.2%	13.7	0.3	0.2	0.0	0.5
2014-15	WPG	23	2	0	0	0	-1	0.00	48.8%	0.0	-0.2	-0.1	0.0	-0.2
2015-16	KHL	24	25	4	5	10					0.6	0.5	0.0	1.2

Since coming over from Sweden, Carl Klingberg has been a solid AHL player. The six-foot-three, 205-pound left winger has played in over 60 games in the minors every year since 2011-12, and has scored double-digit goals each season, including 17 last year. Despite adding to the St. John's team while with the Winnipeg organization and the Hartford club after being acquired in a deal that sent Lee Stempniak to the Jets, Klingberg has only skated in 12 NHL games and potted one goal. While his scoring totals are decent for the AHL level, the Swedish forward has not done enough to show he can put pucks in the net at the NHL level. The "power forward" label he was given when selected in the second round in 2009 has never come to fruition.

Chris Kreider — LW — NYR

Season	Team	Age	GP	G	A	Pts	+/-	ESP/60	AdjCF%	iCF/60	OGVT	DGVT	SGVT	GVT
2012-13	NYR	21	23	2	1	3	-1	0.83	40.3%	8.2	-0.7	0.4	-0.3	-0.6
2013-14	NYR	22	66	17	20	37	14	1.68	55.3%	12.7	5.0	3.0	0.0	8.1
2014-15	NYR	23	80	21	25	46	24	2.06	51.4%	14.5	7.8	3.0	0.0	10.8
2015-16	NYR	24	70	21	25	46					5.9	2.3	0.0	8.2

Chris Kreider has lots of fans in New York because of his exciting combination of size, quickness, aggressiveness, and skill. His 2014-15 campaign earned him a few more fans as he improved his totals in goals, assists, and shots over the previous season. Kreider got more ice-time in the playoffs than in the regular season and scored an impressive seven playoff goals. He even harnessed his natural aggressiveness, reducing his penalty differential to nearly zero. A restricted free agent at the end of 2015-16, Kreider has become increasingly important to the Rangers. It seems no question he is a main piece of their future plans.

Oscar Lindberg — C/LW — NYR

Season	Team	Age	GP	G	A	Pts	+/-	ESP/60	AdjCF%	iCF/60	OGVT	DGVT	SGVT	GVT
2014-15	NYR	23	1	0	0	0	0	0.00	62.4%	22.0	0.0	0.0	0.0	0.0
2015-16	NYR	24	26	5	6	11					0.8	0.0	0.0	1.3

The Rangers acquired Oscar Lindberg in exchange for Ethan Werek in 2011. It has been onwards and upwards for the six-foot-one, 194-pound Swede since then. He broke out in 2012-13 with Skelleftea AIK, scoring 42 points in 55 games and 12 points in 13 playoff games, which led to his earning the Stefan Liv Trophy as SHL playoff MVP. He then moved to North America and became a featured player in Hartford. Lindberg had a good 2013-14 (18 goals and 44 points in 75 AHL games) and a better 2014-15 (28 goals and 58 points in 75 AHL games). Due to Rick Nash getting a fever, he made his NHL debut on February 24, playing eight minutes. While he didn't do much, he did earn a two-year, one-way deal on the strength of his AHL play and promising development there. That suggests he could push for a roster spot in 2015-16.

Ryan Malone								LW						Retired
Season	Team	Age	GP	G	A	Pts	+/-	ESP/60	AdjCF%	iCF/60	OGVT	DGVT	SGVT	GVT
2012-13	TBL	33	24	6	2	8	-3	1.21	42.1%	9.3	-0.4	0.0	0.0	-0.4
2013-14	TBL	34	57	5	10	15	-7	1.21	51.4%	12.0	-0.5	0.6	-0.3	-0.2
2014-15	NYR	35	6	0	0	0	-4	0.00	56.6%	7.3	-0.9	-0.4	0.0	-1.2
2015-16	Retired	36	36	4	6	10					0.1	0.5	0.0	0.6

The Rangers signed aging power forward Ryan Malone in hopes he could provide some cheap offense, physical play, and veteran presence. While he made the team out of training camp, a storybook career rejuvenation did not happen. The 35-year-old only appeared with the Blueshirts early in the season and in limited minutes, tallying no goals, no points, and six shots in six games. He was sent down to Hartford, where he only posted only 10 points in 24 games. In February 2015, the team placed Malone on unconditional waivers with the intention of terminating his contract. It turned out to be a sad ending to a solid NHL career.

J.T. Miller								C/LW						NYR
Season	Team	Age	GP	G	A	Pts	+/-	ESP/60	AdjCF%	iCF/60	OGVT	DGVT	SGVT	GVT
2012-13	NYR	19	26	2	2	4	-7	0.39	49.5%	13.8	-1.8	-0.1	0.2	-1.6
2013-14	NYR	20	30	3	3	6	-6	0.75	51.1%	13.0	-0.5	-0.1	0.0	-0.6
2014-15	NYR	21	58	10	13	23	5	1.76	52.1%	12.8	2.2	1.1	-0.3	3.0
2015-16	NYR	22	58	10	17	27					1.8	1.4	0.0	3.2

While he still played in 18 early-season games with Hartford, J.T. Miller turned the corner to full-time NHL duty. The 2011 first-round pick appeared in 58 games with the Blueshirts. While his conventional stats didn't impress, Miller's game had evolved. He literally played up and down the lineup, and at both center and wing, improving the possession stats of whichever line he was placed with. Lapses in judgement and effort, once commonplace, were rare. Miller is an underrated contributor to the Rangers—as was Carl Hagelin. It would be a shame to lose another talented homegrown RFA for a second summer in a row, but Kreider and Hayes will no doubt be prioritized over Miller.

Dominic Moore								C						NYR
Season	Team	Age	GP	G	A	Pts	+/-	ESP/60	AdjCF%	iCF/60	OGVT	DGVT	SGVT	GVT
2013-14	NYR	33	73	6	12	18	0	1.24	48.9%	10.9	0.5	3.0	0.3	3.8
2014-15	NYR	34	82	10	17	27	5	1.51	48.6%	12.0	3.5	4.2	-0.3	7.4
2015-16	NYR	35	62	7	13	20					0.8	2.0	0.0	2.8

Head coach Alain Vigneault primarily uses Dominic Moore as a defensive specialist, in the old Manny Malhotra and Brian Boyle role. Moore received an astoundingly-low 27.6% offensive zone start percentage in the regular season and 30.7% in the playoffs—not surprising, as his elite faceoff percentage (54.5%) was in stark contrast to his faceoff-challenged brethren in New York (who were all below 49%). While he did not face tough competition at even strength, he matched up against the top players on the penalty kill and provided quality results. Moore led all Ranger forwards in average shorthanded ice-time. If that wasn't enough, his possession stats weren't too low given his utilization. He also posted his most productive season since 2010-11.

NEW YORK RANGERS

Chris Mueller								C/RW						ANA
Season	Team	Age	GP	G	A	Pts	+/-	ESP/60	AdjCF%	iCF/60	OGVT	DGVT	SGVT	GVT
2012-13	NSH	26	18	2	3	5	-4	1.62	43.3%	9.5	-0.1	0.4	0.0	0.3
2013-14	DAL	27	9	0	0	0	-2	0.00	46.8%	10.6	-0.4	0.0	0.0	-0.4
2014-15	NYR	28	7	1	1	2	-1	1.00	47.5%	8.9	-0.4	-0.1	0.0	-0.6
2015-16	ANA	29	27	4	5	9					0.3	0.5	0.0	0.7

Chris Mueller has gotten several call-ups to the NHL, but he has primarily spent his career toiling in the AHL. The 28-year-old was signed by the Rangers to add some center depth. He ended up making seven appearances on New York's fourth line early in the season, even scoring a goal and contributing an assist. However, after November 5, Mueller spent the rest of the year with Hartford, where he produced 14 goals and 40 points in 64 games, finishing fifth on the team in scoring. While not bad, it was a downgrade from past seasons in Milwaukee and Texas. Mueller isn't skilled enough to command scoring-line minutes, he is not good enough defensively to make it on a bottom-six role, and he is too old to really develop as a player. He is what he is, and now, he is a Duck for 2015-16.

Rick Nash								RW/LW						NYR
Season	Team	Age	GP	G	A	Pts	+/-	ESP/60	AdjCF%	iCF/60	OGVT	DGVT	SGVT	GVT
2012-13	NYR	28	44	21	21	42	16	2.68	55.6%	18.2	8.8	2.8	0.4	12.0
2013-14	NYR	29	65	26	13	39	10	1.84	54.2%	21.9	6.5	3.0	-1.1	8.4
2014-15	NYR	30	79	42	27	69	29	2.94	51.6%	22.5	16.1	4.4	0.4	21.0
2015-16	NYR	31	75	29	30	59					9.0	3.0	0.0	12.0

After a tough 2013-14 campaign, Rick Nash bounced back in a big way. His 42 goals scored were third in the entire NHL, trailing Steven Stamkos by one. His stick was rather warm in the regular season at a 13.8% shooting percentage, a recent high for him. However, in the playoffs, his results were disappointing again. The small sample size argument is harder and harder to make, as Nash has played 60 postseason games in his career now, while only managing 10 goals. The Rangers are in a tough spot, as they might like to move Nash's $7.8 million cap hit for youth, but they also need his regular-season goal scoring.

James Sheppard								LW/C						Free Agent
Season	Team	Age	GP	G	A	Pts	+/-	ESP/60	AdjCF%	iCF/60	OGVT	DGVT	SGVT	GVT
2012-13	SJS	24	32	1	3	4	-9	0.66	49.9%	10.5	-2.0	0.0	-0.3	-2.3
2013-14	SJS	25	67	4	16	20	3	1.43	53.8%	10.9	1.0	1.7	-0.3	2.5
2014-15	SJS, NYR	26	71	7	11	18	-4	1.15	47.2%	9.2	0.5	1.4	-0.3	1.6
2015-16	Free Agent	27	58	6	12	18					0.1	1.5	0.0	1.6

The Rangers acquired James Sheppard for a fourth-round pick at the trade deadline. With San Jose, Sheppard was depth winger who chipped in some offense and had solid possession numbers. In New York, he was a fourth liner for 14 regular-season and 13 playoff games. He chipped in three goals, one assist, and 23 shots across all 27 games. While he received a lot of defensive zone starts, he featured a team-low 36.9% Corsi in the regular season and a second-worst 45.5% Corsi in the playoffs against weak competition. It is true his linemates (aka Tanner Glass) were a major factor in those poor stats, but in any case, the Blueshirts can find a better fit. Really, just hanging onto Lee Stempniak would have been the best course of action.

NEW YORK RANGERS

Martin St. Louis — RW — Retired

Season	Team	Age	GP	G	A	Pts	+/-	ESP/60	AdjCF%	iCF/60	OGVT	DGVT	SGVT	GVT
2012-13	TBL	37	48	17	43	60	0	2.84	47.0%	10.4	11.0	0.9	-0.3	11.6
2013-14	TBL, NYR	38	81	30	39	69	13	2.07	50.6%	12.5	12.2	4.0	-0.2	16.0
2014-15	NYR	39	74	21	31	52	12	2.17	48.7%	9.4	8.2	1.6	0.1	9.9
2015-16	Retired	40	63	15	25	40					4.2	1.5	0.0	5.8

For a good portion of the season, Martin St. Louis appeared to have plenty left in the tank. While his production and shooting sagged from last year, St. Louis still finished fourth on the Rangers in points, recording a 20-goal season for the 11th time, and averaging over 17 minutes per game. Not bad for a 39-year-old. However, come playoff time, it became obvious that the end was near for the future Hall of Famer. St. Louis decided to call it a career in July.

Derek Stepan — C — NYR

Season	Team	Age	GP	G	A	Pts	+/-	ESP/60	AdjCF%	iCF/60	OGVT	DGVT	SGVT	GVT
2012-13	NYR	22	48	18	26	44	25	2.35	55.1%	13.6	8.3	4.2	0.2	12.7
2013-14	NYR	23	82	17	40	57	12	1.86	53.1%	13.3	8.1	4.4	0.0	12.6
2014-15	NYR	24	68	16	39	55	26	2.54	47.5%	12.4	10.1	4.6	0.7	15.4
2015-16	NYR	25	70	20	38	58					7.9	3.2	0.1	11.1

The Rangers showed they fully believe in Derek Stepan as a top-two center when they signed him to a six-year, $39 million contract in July. The second-round pick from 2008 timed his contract talks well, as he was coming off his best offensive season, setting a career high in points per game. The 2010 WJC gold medalist and Team USA captain was heavily leaned on, leading Rangers forwards in average ice-time while playing in all situations and against tough competition. While his scoring numbers yielded good results under that usage, his Corsi numbers slipped, which may suggest he is a little overmatched against the East's top lines. Still, 25-year-old, top-two centers are hard to find, and the Rangers made sure to keep their good one around.

Mats Zuccarello — LW — NYR

Season	Team	Age	GP	G	A	Pts	+/-	ESP/60	AdjCF%	iCF/60	OGVT	DGVT	SGVT	GVT
2012-13	NYR	25	15	3	5	8	10	1.71	59.6%	11.9	0.8	1.5	0.2	2.5
2013-14	NYR	26	77	19	40	59	11	2.29	53.9%	11.9	10.5	3.2	0.7	14.3
2014-15	NYR	27	78	15	34	49	17	2.22	53.4%	12.6	6.2	2.7	0.8	9.7
2015-16	NYR	28	69	16	32	48					5.7	2.6	0.1	8.5

Mats Zuccarello was again one of the top forwards for the Rangers during the regular season, but he suffered a scary head injury in the playoffs that proved costly to the Blueshirts. As a terrific even-strength player, the diminutive 27-year-old Norwegian winger ranked fourth in even-strength scoring on the Rangers and first in Corsi percentage. At five-foot-seven (maybe), his work ethic, skating skill, and clever approach have allowed him to not only succeed on the scoresheet, but as a 200-foot player as well. The Rangers will need their spark-plug back to 100%, or they will struggle to replace his production and hockey IQ.

NEW YORK RANGERS

DEFENSEMEN

Conor Allen — LD — NSH

Season	Team	Age	GP	G	A	Pts	+/-	ESP/60	AdjCF%	iCF/60	OGVT	DGVT	SGVT	GVT
2013-14	NYR	23	3	0	0	0	-1	0.00	49.8%	9.8	-0.1	-0.1	0.0	-0.2
2014-15	NYR	24	4	0	0	0	-1	0.00	55.8%	4.6	-0.2	-0.1	0.0	-0.3
2015-16	NSH	25	26	2	5	6					0.3	0.8	0.0	1.0

Two years ago, Conor Allen was signed out of UMass-Amherst by New York, making his NHL debut with a three-game call-up back in 2013-14. Last season was similar, as he received four games with the Rangers, limited to an average of 12 minutes per contest. In Hartford, he was far from limited. The 24-year-old played a key role on defense for the Wolf Pack, leading the blueline in goals (11) and points (34), while finishing second to McIlrath in penalty minutes (113). However, the logjam of organizational defensemen drove the Rangers to not qualify the pending restricted free agent. As an unrestricted free agent, Nashville signed Allen to a one-year, two-way deal. Expect him to be a featured player on the Milwaukee Admirals.

Dan Boyle — RD — NYR

Season	Team	Age	GP	G	A	Pts	+/-	ESP/60	AdjCF%	iCF/60	OGVT	DGVT	SGVT	GVT
2012-13	SJS	36	46	7	13	20	3	0.43	55.3%	10.9	2.6	2.9	-0.4	5.1
2013-14	SJS	37	75	12	24	36	-8	0.83	53.7%	8.7	5.9	0.5	-0.5	6.0
2014-15	NYR	38	65	9	11	20	18	0.66	54.0%	8.7	2.2	2.8	-0.3	4.8
2015-16	NYR	39	56	6	18	24					3.1	2.0	0.0	5.1

It is not uncommon for a contending team to add a veteran player in the hopes of providing that proverbial "final piece of the puzzle". With that in mind, the Rangers signed 38-year old Dan Boyle to a two-year, $9 million deal. Boyle's career has been all about creating offense and helping to push the play forward. While his production has dropped, 20 regular-season points and 10 playoff points from a player his age is solid. Still, his skills have diminished and his cap hit is a bit of an albatross for a team with very little cap room. The Rangers will hope he has something left in the tank in his second season in New York.

Dan Girardi — RD — NYR

Season	Team	Age	GP	G	A	Pts	+/-	ESP/60	AdjCF%	iCF/60	OGVT	DGVT	SGVT	GVT
2012-13	NYR	28	46	2	12	14	-1	0.77	50.5%	9.3	0.9	2.4	0.0	3.3
2013-14	NYR	29	81	5	19	24	6	0.75	49.9%	7.0	0.7	6.5	0.0	7.2
2014-15	NYR	30	82	4	16	20	12	0.64	46.9%	6.7	-0.9	4.2	0.0	3.4
2015-16	NYR	31	66	4	16	20					0.3	4.0	0.0	4.2

Dan Girardi kicked off his six-year, $33 million contract with an ugly statistical season. For getting paid $7 million in salary, he provided as many points as Marc Staal, despite averaging over 22 minutes of ice-time, including power-play time while getting to line up with star defenseman Ryan McDonagh at even strength. While McDonagh struggled slightly with difficult competition and zone starts, Girardi struggled mightily. The Rangers alternate captain posted the lowest Corsi percentage (45.9%) and Relative Corsi (-5.4%) among all regular Rangers defenders. In the postseason, Girardi's contributed fewer points and still got rolled in possession. While he is still lauded for his defensive shutdown skills, the numbers suggest Girardi is not worthy of a top-pairing slot.

Matt Hunwick — LD — TOR

Season	Team	Age	GP	G	A	Pts	+/-	ESP/60	AdjCF%	iCF/60	OGVT	DGVT	SGVT	GVT
2012-13	COL	27	43	0	6	6	4	0.47	47.0%	7.7	-1.6	3.0	0.0	1.4
2013-14	COL	28	1	0	0	0	0	0.00	49.7%	9.9	-0.1	0.0	0.0	-0.1
2014-15	NYR	29	55	2	9	11	17	0.66	53.7%	9.6	0.3	2.9	0.0	3.2
2015-16	TOR	30	52	3	10	12					0.3	2.6	0.0	2.8

The Rangers picked up Matt Hunwick in the hopes that he could be their seventh defenseman. For a big chunk of the season, the former Bruin and Av ended up splitting the job down the middle with John Moore, with each player often dressing for a string of games until a weak showing gave the other guy an opportunity. Eventually, Moore was shipped out, Yandle acquired, and Klein injured, which shuffled the deck a bit. Overall, Hunwick appeared in 55 regular-season games and six playoff games, and performed admirably as the Rangers sixth defenseman (on the nights he was in the lineup). At even strength, he mainly faced lower-line players, and did well in those matchups. His 52.9% Corsi on the season was one of the better ones in New York, and his 51.6% in the postseason was not too shabby either. Hunwick did his job in New York. Now, he will likely do the same in Toronto.

Kevin Klein — RD — NYR

Season	Team	Age	GP	G	A	Pts	+/-	ESP/60	AdjCF%	iCF/60	OGVT	DGVT	SGVT	GVT
2012-13	NSH	28	47	3	11	14	-1	1.02	45.4%	8.8	2.0	3.2	0.0	5.2
2013-14	NSH, NYR	29	77	2	7	9	-7	0.45	46.2%	7.7	-1.3	2.7	0.0	1.4
2014-15	NYR	30	65	9	17	26	24	1.45	50.6%	9.8	5.5	5.8	0.0	11.3
2015-16	NYR	31	62	4	15	20					1.8	3.5	0.0	5.3

The Rangers acquired Kevin Klein from Nashville in 2013-14, playing him for 15 minutes per game. In 2014-15, Alain Vigneault and his coaches saw it fit to give more minutes to Klein. The 2003 second rounder ended up being paired predominantly with Marc Staal, with a jump in ice-time to more than 18 minutes per game. Riding some crazy percentages, he even set a career high in goals and points. While his production improved, Klein may have been a little over his head on a top-four pairing. In the postseason, Klein got hammered for a 46.5% Corsi and -4.7% Relative Corsi.

Michael Kostka — RD — OTT

Season	Team	Age	GP	G	A	Pts	+/-	ESP/60	AdjCF%	iCF/60	OGVT	DGVT	SGVT	GVT
2012-13	TOR	27	35	0	8	8	-7	0.28	47.2%	9.3	-0.2	-0.6	0.0	-0.7
2013-14	CHI, TBL	28	28	4	7	11	10	1.68	53.0%	11.8	2.3	2.2	0.3	4.9
2014-15	NYR	29	7	0	1	1	1	0.59	52.3%	6.3	-0.3	0.3	0.0	0.1
2015-16	OTT	30	33	2	7	10					0.8	1.5	0.0	2.3

After being picked up on waivers by Tampa Bay in 2013-14, Mike Kostka signed with the Rangers, the fourth organization of his career. He spent the majority of his time in Hartford, where he put up 30 points and led the defense with 109 shots. Kostka would also suit up for seven games with New York. He contributed an assist and seven shots, while averaging less than 16 minutes per game, but did put up a good 52.6% Corsi. Alas, the 30-year-old defender has moved on, signing with his fifth organization, the Ottawa Senators, where he will either be an excellent AHLer or fringe NHLer.

Ryan McDonagh — LD — NYR

Season	Team	Age	GP	G	A	Pts	+/-	ESP/60	AdjCF%	iCF/60	OGVT	DGVT	SGVT	GVT
2012-13	NYR	23	47	4	15	19	13	1.03	54.2%	10.2	3.3	4.7	0.0	8.1
2013-14	NYR	24	77	14	29	43	11	1.05	51.0%	9.2	7.8	7.1	0.0	15.0
2014-15	NYR	25	71	8	25	33	23	0.84	50.0%	9.5	4.6	4.9	0.0	9.5
2015-16	NYR	26	71	9	29	38					5.1	4.4	0.0	9.5

Ryan McDonagh continues in his role as leader of the Rangers' defense and one of the best and most consistent blueliners in the NHL. Once again, he led team defensemen in ice-time, shots, and points. Once again, he played significant minutes in all situations. Once again, he received the toughest minutes and most unfavorable zone starts at even strength. The latter point explains some less-than-great underlying numbers. If the 26-year-old had a better partner or some relief, the stats would better reflect how outstanding he is at his job—something the Rangers faithful have known for the past few seasons.

Dylan McIlrath — RD — NYR

Season	Team	Age	GP	G	A	Pts	+/-	ESP/60	AdjCF%	iCF/60	OGVT	DGVT	SGVT	GVT
2013-14	NYR	21	2	0	0	0	-1	0.00	56.8%	7.0	-0.1	-0.1	0.0	-0.2
2014-15	NYR	22	1	0	0	0	0	0.00	65.2%	0.0	0.0	0.2	0.0	0.1
2015-16	NYR	23	25	2	5	7					0.4	0.9	0.0	1.2

Big Dylan McIlrath's 2014-15 campaign was similar to his 2013-14 campaign. He spent the vast majority of his season with Hartford, then racked up penalty minutes and hits in a cameo with the Rangers. McIlrath played all of 8:02 with the NHL team, managing to get posterized (along with Mike Kostka, while Tanner Glass watched) by Vladimir Tarasenko on one of the goals of the year. Normally, a young defenseman getting limited time on a team loaded with experienced players at this position is no cause for alarm. However, the 2010 first rounder is now 23 years old. If he can't make it in New York soon, like in 2015-16, you wonder if he will. There are other defenders in the system who may have passed him on the depth chart. In fact, other Hartford defenders got more minutes in call-ups than McIlrath last season. That does not bode well for his future.

Marc Staal — LD — NYR

Season	Team	Age	GP	G	A	Pts	+/-	ESP/60	AdjCF%	iCF/60	OGVT	DGVT	SGVT	GVT
2012-13	NYR	25	21	2	9	11	4	1.13	50.5%	8.1	1.8	1.7	0.0	3.5
2013-14	NYR	26	72	3	11	14	-1	0.55	55.0%	9.2	-0.2	3.5	0.0	3.3
2014-15	NYR	27	80	5	15	20	18	0.72	48.2%	7.8	1.9	5.4	0.0	7.4
2015-16	NYR	28	65	3	13	16					0.4	3.4	0.0	3.8

The Rangers tended to use their top-two defensive pairings equally against the opposition's top-six forwards. This did not bode well for the run of play, however, as Marc Staal struggled to keep the puck in the Rangers' end. Whereas he broke even in 2013-14 in terms of possession, last season, his Corsi was 46.7%, the second lowest among regular Rangers defensemen. While it may not have been the season Staal wanted, the good news is that he was able to stay healthy for the second full season in a row, playing 152 of the last 164 regular-season games. The six-foot-four defenseman is still only 28 years old, so it seems likely his possession numbers will return to being solid in the future.

NEW YORK RANGERS

Chris Summers — LD — NYR

Season	Team	Age	GP	G	A	Pts	+/-	ESP/60	AdjCF%	iCF/60	OGVT	DGVT	SGVT	GVT
2012-13	PHX	24	6	0	0	0	-3	0.00	40.1%	7.7	-0.4	-0.3	0.0	-0.7
2013-14	PHX	25	18	2	1	3	0	0.76	44.6%	6.9	0.5	0.6	0.0	1.1
2014-15	ARI, NYR	26	20	0	3	3	-12	0.71	40.2%	7.1	-0.1	-0.8	0.0	-0.8
2015-16	NYR	27	31	2	5	7					0.2	0.6	0.0	0.8

Chris Summers was acquired by New York as part of the Keith Yandle deal. Summers is a veteran tweener. He had been good enough to warrant call-ups to Arizona for the last five seasons, putting 64 NHL games under his belt before the trade. However, he has not been good enough to stick around. Such is the case with his brief time in New York. While he averaged just over 17 minutes in three games, he did not make his mark. His time with Hartford was limited to thirteen games, and he did not dress for their playoff run.

Keith Yandle — LD — NYR

Season	Team	Age	GP	G	A	Pts	+/-	ESP/60	AdjCF%	iCF/60	OGVT	DGVT	SGVT	GVT
2012-13	PHX	26	48	10	20	30	4	1.34	52.5%	13.5	6.4	1.4	0.0	7.9
2013-14	PHX	27	82	8	45	53	-23	0.82	51.0%	13.6	7.2	1.0	0.0	8.2
2014-15	ARI, NYR	28	84	6	46	52	-26	0.88	48.6%	13.3	7.9	0.4	0.0	8.2
2015-16	NYR	29	67	8	33	40					5.3	2.2	0.0	7.5

Glen Sather made a big trade to bring in Keith Yandle, who was one of the Coyotes' best players for years, eating up loads of minutes while producing points at an elite level for blueliners. The 29-year-old is a terrific skater, passer, and playmaker with tremendous vision, especially on the power play. He ranked in the top 20 in power-play points per 60 minutes despite playing a big chunk of the season on the second-worst team in hockey. With one more year left on his contract, the Rangers are in a tricky situation. They are cap strapped, which means it would make sense to trade him now, but the Blueshirts also want to win now.

GOALTENDERS

Henrik Lundqvist — G — NYR

Season	Team	Age	GP	W	L	OT	GAA	Sv%	ESSV%	QS%	GGVT	DGVT	SGVT	GVT
2012-13	NYR	30	43	24	16	3	2.05	.926	.937	65.1%	19.1	0.5	2.4	22.0
2013-14	NYR	31	63	33	24	5	2.36	.920	.926	59.7%	16.3	0.3	-0.6	15.9
2014-15	NYR	32	46	30	13	3	2.25	.922	.933	65.2%	14.1	0.3	-0.8	13.6
2015-16	NYR	33	48					.917			9.8	0.2	-0.1	9.9

There are very few goaltenders who are worth taking up more than 10% of their team's total salary cap space, but Henrik Lundqvist is one of them. The future Hall of Famer has done something only a select number of goalies have done in this era: be consistently great. Since 2008-09, "King Henrik" has posted save percentages above .920. He has also managed save percentages over .927 in the playoffs for four straight years. At age 32, he did not show any signs of slowing down, especially when the postseason came around. Statistically, goalies start to drop off around his age, but the 2006 Olympic gold medalist and 2014 Olympic silver medalist is not your average netminder. The question is whether the Rangers will be able to put together another deep playoff run during his remaining years in The Big Apple.

Mackenzie Skapski — G — NYR

Season	Team	Age	GP	W	L	OT	GAA	Sv%	ESSV%	QS%	GGVT	DGVT	SGVT	GVT
2014-15	NYR	20	2	2	0	0	0.50	.978	.971	100.0%	2.6	0.1	0.0	2.8
2015-16	NYR	21	15					.916			2.5	0.0	0.0	2.6

Rookie goaltender Mackenzie Skapski—great name—was used as a specialist in 2014-15. His mission, should he choose to accept it: beat the Buffalo Sabres. Skapski started two games for the Rangers, both against the lowly Sabres, and he defeated them both times, allowing just one goal on 45 shots. The two games allowed the 20-year-old prospect to dip his toe into NHL waters without facing a high-caliber offense. At AHL Hartford, he performed well in limited duty, posting a .914 save percentage. It will be several years before Skapski is truly ready for the NHL, but Rangers management is high on his potential.

Cam Talbot — G — EDM

Season	Team	Age	GP	W	L	OT	GAA	Sv%	ESSV%	QS%	GGVT	DGVT	SGVT	GVT
2013-14	NYR	26	21	12	6	1	1.64	.941	.940	84.2%	14.9	0.5	0.0	15.4
2014-15	NYR	27	36	21	9	4	2.21	.926	.931	52.9%	13.8	0.0	-1.5	12.3
2015-16	EDM	28	40					.919			10.4	0.1	-0.1	10.4

Don't ever let anyone tell you that luck isn't part of success in hockey. After years and years of perfect health, Henrik Lundqvist suffered a bizarre throat injury, opening up the door for Cam Talbot to take the reins. As the starter, the 27-year-old took off, starting 34 games, posting five shutouts, and a terrific .926 save percentage. His performance made him one of the hottest trade targets in the offseason. The Oilers acquired the former University of Alabama-Huntsville product, and will plug him in as their number-one starter.

John Fischer

Ottawa Senators

The Ottawa Senators rewrote their regular-season script in February without telling anyone else. Not considered favorites to play in the postseason, the Sens achieved the improbable by clinching a playoff spot after trailing by 14 points in the regular-season standings. During their historic 23-4-4 run over the final 31 games, the team received help from an AHL goalie with less than impressive minor-league numbers (Andrew Hammond), a rookie drafted in the sixth round (Mark Stone), and their assistant turned head coach (Dave Cameron).

MacLean to Cameron

When head coach Paul MacLean was dismissed in early December 2014, the team had an 11-11-5 record but was only 23rd in even-strength Corsi for (47.7). Puck possession was a major problem while goal-scoring efficiency and goaltending were not an issue, as team shooting percentage (7.1%) and save percentage (.931)—combining for a 100.2 PDO—did not deviate much from the league averages.

After Cameron became the bench boss, puck possession was emphasized, with even-strength Corsi for improving to 51.4%, to the top half of the league. The new head coach implemented a more aggressive system that put a premium on skating and gave younger, more offensively-minded players extra ice-time. However, considering the outstanding goaltending from Hammond and MVP-caliber play from Stone, how much of the team's success can be credited to Cameron?

Regardless of who is behind the bench, missing a key defenseman can hurt a team's performance. Lost in all of the excitement surrounding the rookies rising to sudden stardom was the return of Marc Methot, who sat out for significant time due to injury.

In the first 24 games without Methot—under MacLean—the Sens recorded a lousy 47.2% Corsi. The rugged defenseman briefly returned for two games but ended back on the injured reserve for about a month. During that time, Ottawa posted a 50.9% Corsi under the new coach which further improved to a 51.9% Corsi when Methot returned to the ice.

While an injury can hurt a team, sometimes it can work the other way around. Injuries to two of Ottawa's worst possession players benefited the Sens during the Cameron period. Under MacLean, tough guy Chris Neil was fourth worst on the team in Corsi, while gritty Zack Smith ranked last among team forwards (43.9%). Neil was out for extended periods of time while Smith was limited to 12 games during Cameron's tenure. Even when they were healthy, Cam-

SENATORS IN A BOX

Last Season

Goals For	238	9th
Goals Against	215	13th
GVT	23	10th
Points	99	t-13th
Playoffs	Lost Conference Quarterfinal	

The second-half emergence of goaltender Andrew Hammond turned a lost season into a minor miracle, even if they were eliminated in the first round.

Three-Year Record

GVT	6	14th
Points	243	14th
Playoffs	2 Appearances, 7 Wins	

VUKOTA Projections

Goals For	230	7th
Goals Against	224	25th
GVT	5	15th
Points	93	15th

This was, at various points last year, one of the worst teams in the league and one of the best. Ottawa will need more of the latter to make the playoffs again.

Top Three Prospects

T. Chabot (D), M. Puempel (F), N. Paul (F)

eron allocated reduced ice-time to them, 10:46 to 7:46 for Neil and 13:14 to 9:03 for Smith.

Likewise, Cameron cut the minutes of certain other veterans. Newly-signed center David Legwand, who was projected to be a top-nine center at the beginning of the season, went from 16:26 to 12:52 while long-time Senator Chris Phillips dropped from 22:28 minutes to 18:00 minutes. The two older veterans had been the worst on the team in Relative Corsi under MacLean's watch and ended up as frequent healthy scratches in 2014-15.

Ice-time changes for the two skaters were not enough for Cameron. He also deployed them differently: Phillips and Legwand started faceoffs in the offensive zone more often at even strength. The shift in zone starts benefited Legwand—who was deployed more defensively by MacLean—with his Relative Corsi increasing from -4.4 to 0.8.

Distributing ice-time is a zero-sum game. When one player loses minutes, another player gains. Cameron gave younger skaters Stone, Mike Hoffman, and Patrick Wiercioch at least a minute extra of ice-time on average. In Stone's case, he took full advantage of the 28% increase from 14:16 to 18:11—the rookie led the team with 3.18 points per 60 minutes, a rate that was good for eighth in the NHL.

A few players, like Bobby Ryan and Erik Condra, saw little change in ice-time but were deployed more often in the zone that suited their skills. As a former 30-goal scorer, Ryan started more frequently in the offensive zone, while increasing his even-strength production from 1.42 to 2.23 points per hour. Under Mac-Lean, he had started slightly more in the defensive zone. Condra took on more defensive responsibilities, starting twice as often in the defensive zone. Regardless of the tougher assignment, his Relative Corsi remained essentially unchanged.

To Cameron, salary and team loyalty did not matter as much as playing ability. MacLean relied more on highly-paid skaters whereas Cameron relied more on skaters with better possession numbers. Average ice-time per game and player salary correlated more closely for MacLean (a correlation coefficient of 0.65) than Cameron (0.51). And no, causation is not implied (see charts, this page).

The Hamburglar

Aside from player movement up and down or in and out the lineup, goaltending was a key factor in the post-All-Star-break surge. From October through December under MacLean, veteran Craig Anderson, appearing in 17 out of 27 games, posted a .940 even-strength save percentage. His quality goaltending continued into the Cameron era, with Anderson stopping 93.4% of even-strength shots. When Anderson and backup Robin Lehner were out with injuries in mid-

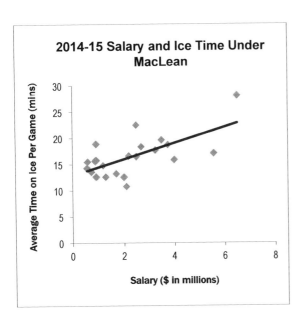

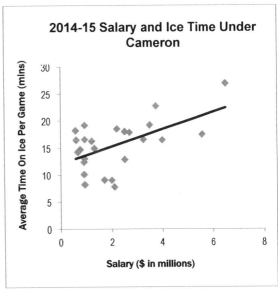

February, Binghamton Senator Andrew Hammond took over the net...for good. Hammond played in 24 of the final 28 regular-season games, stopping 94.1% of even-strength shots. The Senators won 20 out of the 24 games with the "Hamburglar" in net.

However, among all of positive the adjustments, Cameron may have had a lapse in judgement in his goalie decision-making. When Anderson returned from injury—with the Sens undefeated in regulation with Hammond in net—Cameron started Anderson for two games. Although the former Av played well enough, the Sens lost in the second one. Then, Cameron returned to Hammond, who continued to give the team spectacular goaltending until the team clinched a playoff berth.

While Cameron altered the game strategy from his predecessor and had control over who to play and when to play them, he had some outside factors work in his favor. The return of Methot was a boost to a fragile defensive corps. The rise of the rookie Stone to stardom gave the team a boost on offense. And the superb goaltending of Hammond provided the team with an excellent chance to win every night. However, these factors should not diminish the work of Cameron, who certainly had a role in helping the Senators turn their season around.

Wesley Chu

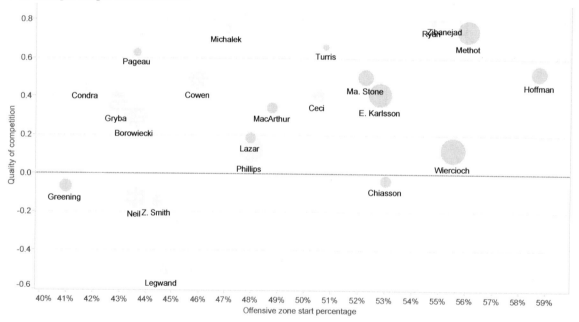

OTTAWA SENATORS

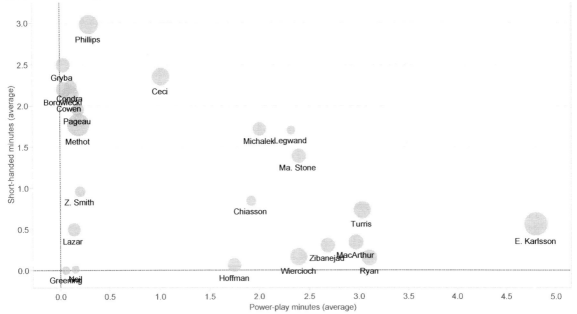

Special Teams Usage: Ottawa Senators

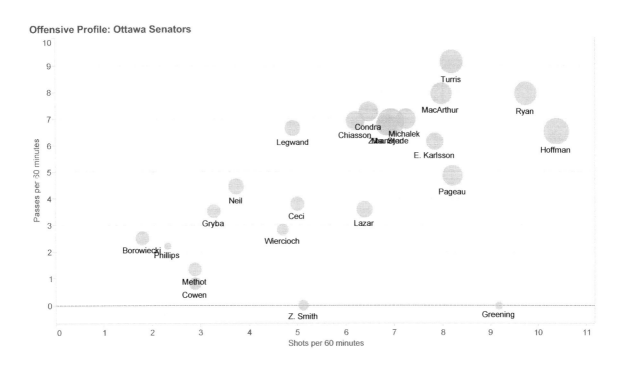

Offensive Profile: Ottawa Senators

Cap Efficiency: Ottawa Senators

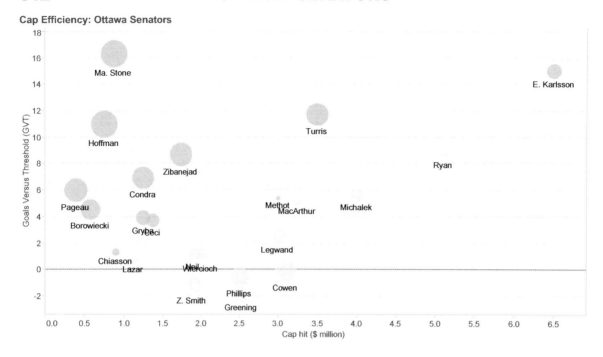

FORWARDS

Alex Chiasson														RW										OTT
Season	Team	Age	GP	G	A	Pts	+/-	ESP/60	AdjCF%	iCF/60	OGVT	DGVT	SGVT	GVT
2012-13	DAL	22	7	6	1	7	3	4.12	43.6%	11.8	2.3	0.4	0.0	2.8
2013-14	DAL	23	79	13	22	35	-21	1.49	49.4%	12.7	0.8	0.0	-0.5	0.3
2014-15	OTT	24	76	11	15	26	-5	1.41	51.1%	10.2	1.3	0.6	-0.5	1.3
2015-16	OTT	25	62	12	16	27					1.5	0.8	0.0	2.3

In the July 1, 2014 trade of Jason Spezza to Dallas, Alex Chiasson was the main piece acquired by Ottawa. During his first season as a Senator, the power forward produced top-nine offense as he did with the Stars, despite being relegated to the fourth line as the season went on. In the earlier days of his playing career, after being drafted 38th overall in 2009, Chiasson spent three seasons with Boston University, scoring 99 points in 108 games. Besides scoring, in the classic power forward mold, the six-foot-four, 216-pound winger can drop the gloves. Case in point: Chiasson received an instigator, a fighting major, and a misconduct in a December game against Pittsburgh when he responded to a hit on teammate Kyle Turris.

Erik Condra — RW — TBL

Season	Team	Age	GP	G	A	Pts	+/-	ESP/60	AdjCF%	iCF/60	OGVT	DGVT	SGVT	GVT
2012-13	OTT	26	48	4	8	12	3	1.36	56.0%	13.3	-0.1	3.5	0.0	3.4
2013-14	OTT	27	76	6	10	16	0	1.20	53.5%	13.6	0.6	2.1	-0.3	2.4
2014-15	OTT	28	68	9	14	23	13	1.53	51.2%	12.0	2.8	4.0	0.0	6.9
2015-16	TBL	29	61	9	13	22					1.4	2.5	0.0	3.9

Giving up on a play is not something Erik Condra does. As a testament to that trait, the penalty-killing specialist led team forwards with 0.78 blocked shots per game. His hard work and dedication was already recognized as a college player at Notre Dame, exemplified by his Terry Flanagan Memorial Award in 2009. However, all of that hard work did not seem to be enough to keep him from being a regular healthy scratch in late 2014 when Paul MacLean was head coach. Condra fared well despite a high percentage of defensive-zone starts: 2011 Calder Cup champion did not appear to be affected much, managing roughly breakeven possession. He is the type of player who is trusted to defend a one-goal lead in the last minute.

Colin Greening — LW — OTT

Season	Team	Age	GP	G	A	Pts	+/-	ESP/60	AdjCF%	iCF/60	OGVT	DGVT	SGVT	GVT
2012-13	OTT	26	47	8	11	19	5	1.48	53.9%	13.0	0.7	1.4	0.0	2.1
2013-14	OTT	27	76	6	11	17	-15	0.91	50.7%	11.0	-1.4	-0.2	0.0	-1.5
2014-15	OTT	28	26	1	0	1	-5	0.24	51.2%	14.5	-1.2	-0.2	-0.3	-1.6
2015-16	OTT	29	45	5	5	10					-0.3	0.5	0.0	0.2

Colin Greening had a very disappointing season. The former Cornell forward was relegated to Binghamton for nearly a month and was scratched for most of the time with Ottawa, appearing in only 26 games. Further, he played just under 10 minutes per game, his lowest seasonal average. When he did hit the ice, the three-time ECAC Second-Team All-Star was buried in the defensive zone for faceoffs more than any other Senator. Since his best offensive season in 2011-12, when he recorded 37 points on 184 shots in a full 82 games, his points-per-game rate and average ice-time has dropped each season.

Mike Hoffman — LW — OTT

Season	Team	Age	GP	G	A	Pts	+/-	ESP/60	AdjCF%	iCF/60	OGVT	DGVT	SGVT	GVT
2012-13	OTT	23	3	0	0	0	-1	0.00	50.6%	18.0	-0.2	-0.1	0.0	-0.3
2013-14	OTT	24	25	3	3	6	-2	0.66	55.0%	20.0	-0.1	-0.2	0.0	-0.3
2014-15	OTT	25	79	27	21	48	16	2.68	51.8%	18.8	9.6	2.5	-1.1	11.0
2015-16	OTT	26	69	23	23	47					6.8	1.9	-0.1	8.7

As a 25-year-old rookie, Mike Hoffman led the 2014-15 Senators with 8.8 shots and 1.43 even-strength goals per 60 minutes. A noticeably quick skater, the 2009 fifth-round selection had previously been named to the First All-Star Team twice in the QMJHL and once in the AHL. Without the puck, Hoffman needs to become more effective at defending in his own end. However, the six-foot forward did excel at stealing the puck from his opponents, ranking second on the team with 3.3 takeaways per 60 minutes.

Curtis Lazar — C/RW — OTT

Season	Team	Age	GP	G	A	Pts	+/-	ESP/60	AdjCF%	iCF/60	OGVT	DGVT	SGVT	GVT
2014-15	OTT	19	67	6	9	15	1	1.10	51.1%	11.7	-1.2	1.9	0.0	0.7
2015-16	OTT	20	61	8	11	19					-0.7	1.8	0.0	1.1

A two-way forward, Curtis Lazar was loaned to the Canadian National Junior team in December, where he would chip in nine points over seven games. In his last three WHL seasons with the Edmonton Oil Kings, Lazar had improved his point production from 0.49 to 0.85 to 1.31 points per game. Although his NHL output was sparse, the 2014 Memorial Cup winner did not look out of place on the ice for a rookie. As long as the he continues to work hard at both ends of the rink, Lazar will receive more ice-time and "bigger" minutes.

David Legwand — C — BUF

Season	Team	Age	GP	G	A	Pts	+/-	ESP/60	AdjCF%	iCF/60	OGVT	DGVT	SGVT	GVT
2012-13	NSH	32	48	12	13	25	-6	1.71	45.7%	8.2	1.6	2.0	-0.4	3.2
2013-14	NSH, DET	33	83	14	37	51	-17	1.65	49.2%	9.2	4.0	1.0	-0.5	4.5
2014-15	OTT	34	80	9	18	27	1	0.99	50.0%	8.5	0.9	1.9	-0.3	2.5
2015-16	BUF	35	61	8	17	25					1.1	1.3	0.0	2.4

Senators GM Bryan Murray signed David Legwand in the summer of 2014 to take some pressure off of young centers Mika Zibanejad and Kyle Turris. The long-time first-line center of the Predators started on the second line to begin the season, but was eventually demoted to the third and fourth lines, performing more of a shutdown role. His 14 minutes of ice-time was the lowest since his rookie season. The 34-year-old played in his 1,000th game in December. Although he has a history of injuries earlier in his career, the two-way center has missed only four games since 2011-12.

Clarke MacArthur — LW — OTT

Season	Team	Age	GP	G	A	Pts	+/-	ESP/60	AdjCF%	iCF/60	OGVT	DGVT	SGVT	GVT
2012-13	TOR	27	40	8	12	20	3	1.81	50.0%	12.2	3.2	0.3	-0.6	3.0
2013-14	OTT	28	79	24	31	55	12	2.07	54.0%	11.0	9.4	2.5	-0.6	11.4
2014-15	OTT	29	62	16	20	36	-6	1.84	50.6%	12.1	5.3	0.1	-0.3	5.1
2015-16	OTT	30	61	18	23	40					5.1	1.2	0.0	6.2

After a productive 2013-14, Clarke MacArthur took a step backward. Generally, he has missed few games because of injuries, but this time, he sat out for 18 games with a concussion. Fortunately, the one-time Sabre did not take long to start scoring again, tallying 10 points in the nine remaining games. The three-time 20-goal scorer is an underrated puck-possession player. Over the past five years with the Sens and Leafs, MacArthur has held a positive Relative Corsi every year. Given the raise he will be getting from his new five-year contract extension, MacArthur will be expected to continue playing top-line minutes.

Milan Michalek — RW/LW — OTT

Season	Team	Age	GP	G	A	Pts	+/-	ESP/60	AdjCF%	iCF/60	OGVT	DGVT	SGVT	GVT
2012-13	OTT	28	23	4	10	14	8	2.00	56.2%	18.0	1.3	1.0	-0.3	2.0
2013-14	OTT	29	82	17	22	39	-25	1.66	51.5%	12.6	0.8	-0.6	-1.3	-1.2
2014-15	OTT	30	66	13	21	34	3	1.65	49.6%	13.6	3.6	1.7	0.4	5.6
2015-16	OTT	31	62	14	19	33					2.8	1.3	0.0	4.0

A centerpiece of the Dany Heatley swap in 2010, Milan Michalek has been somewhat disappointing in a Sens uniform. He has had only one season of 40+ points since the trade. As a Senator, Michalek scored 0.56 points per game over 380 games, after recording 0.68 points per game over 317 games with the Sharks. Injuries are also a concern for the scoring winger. The 2013-14 season was the first in which he played all 82 games. The speedy winger can be streaky, scoring goals in clusters, and he can protect the puck reasonably well with his large frame. Due to competition from MacArthur and Hoffman on the left wing, Michalek received his lowest average ice-time since his rookie season.

Chris Neil							RW						OTT
Season	Team	Age	GP	G	A	Pts	+/-	ESP/60	AdjCF%	iCF/60	OGVT	DGVT	SGVT	GVT
2012-13	OTT	33	48	4	8	12	0	0.91	54.6%	12.6	-1.5	0.5	0.0	-1.1
2013-14	OTT	34	76	8	6	14	-10	0.92	50.4%	11.1	-1.1	-0.4	0.0	-1.5
2014-15	OTT	35	38	4	3	7	5	0.99	45.6%	7.6	0.3	0.9	0.0	1.1
2015-16	OTT	36	48	5	5	10					-0.2	0.7	0.0	0.5

Known for being a "character" guy who can irritate his opponents, Chris Neil saw his penalty differential per 60 minutes drop from -16 in 2013-14 to zero last season, meaning he showed a lot more discipline in not giving Ottawa opponents additional power plays. Not surprisingly, the physical winger ranked fifth in the league with 22.3 hits per 60 minutes, among regular skaters. His rough-and-tough play often leads to injuries, and it may have caught up to him last season, when he appeared in only 38 games, his lowest number ever. The 35-year-old also averaged less than 10 minutes of ice-time per game for the first time since 2003-04.

Jean-Gabriel Pageau							C						OTT
Season	Team	Age	GP	G	A	Pts	+/-	ESP/60	AdjCF%	iCF/60	OGVT	DGVT	SGVT	GVT
2012-13	OTT	20	9	2	2	4	3	2.52	60.5%	14.9	1.2	0.4	0.0	1.6
2013-14	OTT	21	28	2	0	2	-5	0.50	51.4%	13.5	-0.8	0.1	0.0	-0.7
2014-15	OTT	22	50	10	9	19	4	1.69	52.5%	13.0	3.7	2.3	0.0	6.0
2015-16	OTT	23	51	10	10	20					1.7	1.7	0.0	3.5

For a small guy, Jean-Gabriel Pageau acts like a physical forward, ranking third on the team with 15.2 hits per 60 minutes, though you can question just how punishing those hits are. Despite the kinetic play, Pageau leads the team in penalty differential per 60 minutes (1.1), drawing significantly more penalties than he takes. The former Gatineau Olympique, who scored 175 points in 175 games in the QMJHL, played 14 minutes per game last season in more of a defensive and energy role. When he was drafted, comparisons of him to Daniel Briere and Claude Giroux were already being made, a bit prematurely.

Shane Prince							LW/C						OTT
Season	Team	Age	GP	G	A	Pts	+/-	ESP/60	AdjCF%	iCF/60	OGVT	DGVT	SGVT	GVT
2014-15	OTT	22	2	0	1	1	1	2.86	59.9%	15.7	0.2	0.1	0.0	0.3
2015-16	OTT	23	26	5	7	12					1.0	0.6	0.0	1.6

The playmaker presently known as (Shane) Prince had a fantastic season in the AHL, firing off 193 shots in 72 games; he led the Binghamton Senators and placed sixth in the league with 65 points. The former Ottawa 67 has progressed well, recording 0.54, 0.70, and 0.90 points per game over the last three AHL seasons. In his last two OHL campaigns, he averaged 1.49 and 1.58 points per game. His two-game trial late in the season may be an indication that the 23-year-old is close to NHL-ready.

Matt Puempel						LW							OTT
Season	Team	Age	GP	G	A	Pts	+/-	ESP/60	AdjCF%	iCF/60	OGVT	DGVT	SGVT	GVT
2014-15	OTT	21	13	2	1	3	6	1.73	54.9%	15.4	0.3	0.7	0.0	1.1
2015-16	OTT	22	33	6	7	13					0.9	1.0	0.0	1.9

Matt Puempel has been hampered by injuries for quite some time. The natural goal scorer was limited to 13 NHL games because he sustained an injury during a March match. With Binghamton, he was third on the team with 2.9 shots per game, behind only Pageau and Eddie Shore Award winner Chris Wideman. Although the 2011 first-round pick had a solid AHL season with 32 points in 51 games last season, he had previously scored 30 goals in 74 AHL games in 2013-14.

Bobby Ryan						RW/LW							OTT
Season	Team	Age	GP	G	A	Pts	+/-	ESP/60	AdjCF%	iCF/60	OGVT	DGVT	SGVT	GVT
2012-13	ANA	25	46	11	19	30	3	2.15	48.7%	14.6	3.4	1.1	0.2	4.6
2013-14	OTT	26	70	23	25	48	7	2.36	50.5%	16.9	8.7	1.0	-1.1	8.6
2014-15	OTT	27	78	18	36	54	5	2.17	49.5%	14.7	7.5	1.2	0.0	8.7
2015-16	OTT	28	68	21	31	52					6.9	1.8	0.0	8.7

Expectations were high for 2005 second-overall pick Bobby Ryan when he arrived in Ottawa from Anaheim via trade in the summer of 2013, but as a Senator, the four-time 30-goal scorer has yet to deliver a season of even 25 goals. The drop in goal scoring was not from a lack of effort as he has fired 8.1 pucks on net per 60 minutes of five-on-five play. However, his 10.3% shooting in 2013-14 and 8.0% in 2014-15 while in Ottawa has lagged his career rate of 11.8%. Therefore, you would think that Ryan is due for a bounceback in the goal department next season, unless he has forgotten how to hit the back of the net.

Zack Smith						C							OTT
Season	Team	Age	GP	G	A	Pts	+/-	ESP/60	AdjCF%	iCF/60	OGVT	DGVT	SGVT	GVT
2012-13	OTT	24	48	4	11	15	-9	1.16	53.7%	14.2	-0.3	-0.1	-0.3	-0.6
2013-14	OTT	25	82	13	9	22	-9	1.02	50.0%	12.1	0.8	0.8	0.0	1.5
2014-15	OTT	26	37	2	1	3	-8	0.45	46.9%	9.1	-1.0	-0.2	0.0	-1.2
2015-16	OTT	27	51	7	6	13					0.0	0.7	0.0	0.7

As his ice-time dropped from 15:31 to 12:01 last season, Zack Smith interestingly saw his penalty minutes per game fall from 1.35 to 0.49, his lowest rate since 2004-05 in the WHL. In the past, the checking forward's aggressiveness and attempts to irritate opponents could turn into taking needless penalties. However, at even strength in 2014-15, Smith drew more penalties than he took, at a net penalty rate of 0.5 per 60 minutes. Like Condra, Smith specializes in killing penalties, but that skill might not be enough for him to be playing regularly as he was a healthy scratch multiple times.

Mark Stone — RW — OTT

Season	Team	Age	GP	G	A	Pts	+/-	ESP/60	AdjCF%	iCF/60	OGVT	DGVT	SGVT	GVT
2012-13	OTT	20	4	0	0	0	-1	0.00	53.7%	8.7	-0.4	0.0	0.0	-0.5
2013-14	OTT	21	19	4	4	8	5	1.73	58.4%	15.0	1.1	0.6	0.0	1.7
2014-15	OTT	22	80	26	38	64	21	2.83	51.7%	11.5	12.5	3.4	0.4	16.3
2015-16	OTT	23	72	23	38	61					9.0	2.8	0.0	11.8

Mark Stone broke out in a big way in 2015. Since January of that year, the 2010 sixth-round draft pick recorded a league-high of 3.08 even-strength points per 60 minutes. In addition, the former Brandon Wheat King tied for the league lead in rookie scoring as well. While Stone may be known for his offense, he is excellent at stealing the puck as well, leading the league with 4.3 takeaways per 60 minutes (although take this very subjective stat with a major dose of salt). In junior, Stone was an offensive force, scoring 123 points in his last 66 games. In 2013-14, Stone registered 41 points in 37 AHL games. Clearly, scoring was not an issue for him, but skating was considered to be one of his weaknesses on draft day, and it certainly can be a valid concern at the highest level. However, he has made noticeable improvements in that area since his first NHL game in 2012. One lingering concern for Stone is his injury history, even prior to the wrist injury he suffered in the playoffs.

Kyle Turris — C — OTT

Season	Team	Age	GP	G	A	Pts	+/-	ESP/60	AdjCF%	iCF/60	OGVT	DGVT	SGVT	GVT
2012-13	OTT	23	48	12	17	29	6	1.62	52.7%	15.1	3.1	2.8	-0.1	5.8
2013-14	OTT	24	82	26	32	58	22	2.06	52.5%	15.3	10.0	3.8	1.3	15.1
2014-15	OTT	25	82	24	40	64	5	2.23	50.4%	14.7	10.7	1.6	-0.5	11.7
2015-16	OTT	26	72	25	36	60					8.5	2.3	0.0	10.8

Following the departure of long-time number-one center Jason Spezza, Kyle Turris fared well in his first season taking on that role, reaching 60 points for the first time. Behind only Stone, the 2007 third-overall pick ranked second on the team with 0.82 primary assists per 60 minutes at even strength. Since he was acquired from Phoenix, Turris has consistently improved his points-per-game rates, from 0.59 to 0.60 to 0.71 to 0.78, over the last four seasons. Although he is sometimes labeled as a two-way forward, the team experiences an increase in shot volume toward their own goal when Turris is on the ice. The 2008 World Junior Championship gold medalist has missed only six career games due to injury, all in a Coyotes uniform.

Mika Zibanejad — C — OTT

Season	Team	Age	GP	G	A	Pts	+/-	ESP/60	AdjCF%	iCF/60	OGVT	DGVT	SGVT	GVT
2012-13	OTT	19	42	7	13	20	9	1.97	53.7%	15.0	1.6	1.3	0.2	3.1
2013-14	OTT	20	69	16	17	33	-15	1.81	53.1%	15.7	4.3	-0.9	1.0	4.3
2014-15	OTT	21	80	20	26	46	0	1.78	49.8%	12.0	6.2	0.8	1.8	8.7
2015-16	OTT	22	67	20	28	48					6.2	1.2	0.1	7.5

Mika Zibanejad saw more than a two-minute increase ice-time per game in 2014-15, one reason for his increased output. The 21-year-old from Stockholm, Sweden also found success on the second line with Hoffman and Ryan, showing flashes of his offensive skill, especially his wicked shot; at the Senators' skills competition in 2013-14, he broke the team record with a 106 mile-per-hour slapper. To create more opportunities on the attack, Zibanejad should fire the puck a lot more—his season high is 153 shots—and take advantage of his six-foot-two, 211-pound frame to protect the puck.

DEFENSEMEN

Mark Borowiecki — LD — OTT

Season	Team	Age	GP	G	A	Pts	+/-	ESP/60	AdjCF%	iCF/60	OGVT	DGVT	SGVT	GVT
2012-13	OTT	23	6	0	0	0	1	0.00	53.1%	3.7	-0.3	0.2	0.0	-0.1
2013-14	OTT	24	13	1	0	1	-2	0.42	46.2%	5.9	0.0	-0.2	0.0	-0.2
2014-15	OTT	25	63	1	10	11	15	0.77	46.8%	5.3	0.6	3.9	0.0	4.5
2015-16	OTT	26	56	1	7	9					-0.4	2.6	0.0	2.2

Physical depth defenseman Mark Borowiecki accumulated 100+ penalty minutes in three AHL seasons, and the streak continued into the NHL. Known for fighting, the former Clarkson captain committed fewer minor infractions as the season progressed, taking only five minor penalties in the 2015 portion of the season compared to his 16 minors in late 2014. His physical play comes with a price, though: 16 games missed recovering from injury. "Boro" also led the team with 1.62 blocked shots per game.

Cody Ceci — RD — OTT

Season	Team	Age	GP	G	A	Pts	+/-	ESP/60	AdjCF%	iCF/60	OGVT	DGVT	SGVT	GVT
2013-14	OTT	20	49	3	6	9	-5	0.79	50.9%	12.2	0.0	0.0	0.0	0.1
2014-15	OTT	21	81	5	16	21	-4	0.79	49.0%	9.9	1.9	1.8	0.0	3.7
2015-16	OTT	22	66	6	17	24					2.3	2.3	0.0	4.5

Cody Ceci finished his first full NHL season, clocking in 19 minutes per game, an increase of about two minutes from the previous season. In December 2013, the former Ottawa 67 had been recalled on an emergency basis; he impressed the coaching staff and has retained a spot on the main roster ever since. In 30 AHL games, the six-foot-two, 209-pound rearguard had registered 21 points and fired 70 shots on goal. Known for his offensive prowess from back in his OHL days, Ceci takes few penalties, chalking up only 20 PIMs in 130 NHL games.

Jared Cowen — LD — OTT

Season	Team	Age	GP	G	A	Pts	+/-	ESP/60	AdjCF%	iCF/60	OGVT	DGVT	SGVT	GVT
2012-13	OTT	21	7	1	0	1	1	0.51	56.7%	9.0	0.3	0.4	0.0	0.7
2013-14	OTT	22	68	6	9	15	0	0.71	50.9%	6.3	1.1	2.1	0.0	3.2
2014-15	OTT	23	54	3	6	9	-11	0.63	48.3%	7.1	-0.6	0.5	0.0	-0.1
2015-16	OTT	24	55	3	10	13					0.3	1.8	0.0	2.1

A scratch for 22 games, Jared Cowen was also suspended for three games. However, given his history, it was a surprise that the towering shutdown defenseman did not miss any games to injury in 2014-15. The ninth-overall pick from 2010 was named to the WHL First All-Star Team in 2010-11 when he averaged 0.83 points per game for the Spokane Chiefs. Offense may not be his speciality at the pro level, but he will have to step up his physical game to compete with Borowiecki and Gryba, who both seemed to have passed the more highly-touted Cowen on the depth chart.

Eric Gryba — RD — EDM

Season	Team	Age	GP	G	A	Pts	+/-	ESP/60	AdjCF%	iCF/60	OGVT	DGVT	SGVT	GVT
2012-13	OTT	24	33	2	4	6	-3	0.61	48.4%	9.6	0.0	0.9	0.0	1.0
2013-14	OTT	25	57	2	9	11	9	0.73	51.0%	9.1	0.8	2.6	0.0	3.3
2014-15	OTT	26	75	0	12	12	11	0.73	47.6%	9.1	-0.2	4.1	0.0	3.9
2015-16	EDM	27	61	2	9	11					-0.2	3.0	0.0	2.7

A physical defenseman, Eric Gryba has toned down his penalty taking at the NHL level with a mere 187 PIMs in 165 games, well down from 305 PIMs in 183 AHL games. When he is not serving time in the sin bin, the 2006 third-round selection is relied on to defend during the penalty kill, averaging of 2:30 minutes per game in shorthanded situations, second on the team to veteran Chris Phillips. Overall, his playing time has decreased over the past three seasons from 20:16, to 17:31, to 15:39.

Erik Karlsson — RD — OTT

Season	Team	Age	GP	G	A	Pts	+/-	ESP/60	AdjCF%	iCF/60	OGVT	DGVT	SGVT	GVT
2012-13	OTT	22	17	6	8	14	8	1.52	59.4%	21.9	3.9	1.7	0.0	5.7
2013-14	OTT	23	82	20	54	74	-15	1.47	54.4%	14.9	17.3	-1.2	0.3	16.4
2014-15	OTT	24	82	21	45	66	7	1.20	52.7%	14.6	13.8	1.4	-0.2	15.0
2015-16	OTT	25	77	19	49	68					12.4	2.5	0.0	14.8

Erik Karlsson set season highs with 292 shots on goal and 27:15 minutes per game. It was the fourth consecutive season in which the elite defender recorded at least 0.80 points per game and the second consecutive season of 20+ goals. Out of all league defensemen, "EK65" ranked 10th with 1.74 takeaways per 60 minutes. The 2012 and 2015 Norris Trophy winner has improved his defensive play over the years and has added a physical edge lately, but he will continue to be known for his smooth, quick skating, tremendous stickhandling ability, and vision.

Marc Methot — LD — OTT

Season	Team	Age	GP	G	A	Pts	+/-	ESP/60	AdjCF%	iCF/60	OGVT	DGVT	SGVT	GVT
2012-13	OTT	27	47	2	9	11	2	0.68	52.8%	6.1	0.1	4.0	0.0	4.0
2013-14	OTT	28	75	6	17	23	0	0.87	52.1%	8.0	2.9	2.1	0.0	4.9
2014-15	OTT	29	45	1	10	11	22	0.71	54.5%	5.5	0.7	4.6	0.0	5.4
2015-16	OTT	30	56	3	13	16					1.1	3.2	0.0	4.2

The list of injuries over Marc Methot's career lengthened last season. However, when he was on the ice, the defensive defenseman had an impressively low 38.5 Fenwick-against per 60 minutes, best among regular skaters on the team. The statistic was his best seasonal number as a Senator. His offensive abilities may be limited, but he is able to successfully exit the defending zone without turning it over, whether by carrying the puck or making a smart pass. For a six-foot-three, 230-pound defenseman, Methot can move well.

Chris Phillips — LD — OTT

Season	Team	Age	GP	G	A	Pts	+/-	ESP/60	AdjCF%	iCF/60	OGVT	DGVT	SGVT	GVT
2012-13	OTT	34	48	5	9	14	-5	0.99	52.2%	10.1	1.0	2.6	0.0	3.6
2013-14	OTT	35	70	1	14	15	-12	0.41	51.0%	8.2	-0.8	0.0	0.0	-0.8
2014-15	OTT	36	36	0	3	3	0	0.19	44.7%	6.5	-1.6	0.9	0.0	-0.6
2015-16	OTT	37	44	1	7	8					-0.4	1.4	0.0	1.0

OTTAWA SENATORS

Typically a fairly durable defenseman, 36-year-old Chris Phillips was unexpectedly limited to 36 games due to injury. The stay-at-home defender who was once taken first overall in the 1996 NHL Entry Draft ranked last on the team in possession; he has been a negative possession player since 2009-10. Although his defensive play may have deteriorated, he is still a leader with experience who can mentor the many youngsters on the team. The Calgary native has played mostly second-pairing minutes in his 1,179-game career, but with the emergence of Borowiecki and Gryba, his time as a Senator, and probably NHLer, may be running out.

Patrick Wiercioch — LD — OTT

Season	Team	Age	GP	G	A	Pts	+/-	ESP/60	AdjCF%	iCF/60	OGVT	DGVT	SGVT	GVT
2012-13	OTT	22	42	5	14	19	9	0.97	57.8%	11.7	3.3	1.5	-0.3	4.5
2013-14	OTT	23	53	4	19	23	-1	0.93	52.6%	12.3	4.2	-0.2	-0.3	3.7
2014-15	OTT	24	56	3	10	13	3	0.55	54.4%	8.6	0.3	0.7	0.0	1.0
2015-16	OTT	25	53	5	15	20					2.2	1.4	0.0	3.6

As a point-producing defenseman, Patrick Wiercioch took a bit of a step back offensively despite an increase in ice-time from 16 to 18 minutes. Likewise, his shot rate went down from 6.4 to 4.5 shots per 60 minutes. And yet, his Corsi percentage was still best on the team. The former WCHA First-Team All-Star at Denver led Ottawa with a 5.2% Relative Corsi, and has held a positive rating in that possession-proxy category every season. Entering his fourth NHL season, the 25-year-old puck-moving defenseman may still have more to show.

GOALTENDERS

Craig Anderson — G — OTT

Season	Team	Age	GP	W	L	OT	GAA	Sv%	ESSV%	QS%	GGVT	DGVT	SGVT	GVT
2012-13	OTT	31	24	12	9	2	1.69	.941	.943	66.7%	19.9	0.0	-1.5	18.3
2013-14	OTT	32	53	25	16	8	3.00	.911	.925	50.0%	3.7	-2.2	-0.2	1.3
2014-15	OTT	33	35	14	13	8	2.49	.923	.930	54.3%	12.9	-1.1	0.0	11.8
2015-16	OTT	34	36					.917			6.6	-0.7	0.0	5.8

In October 2014, Craig Anderson held Ottawa's number-one goaltending role. An injury to his hand in February gave minor-leaguer Andrew Hammond an opportunity to take over the starting duties, and he did. Boy, did he. "Andy" found himself in the backup role for the rest of the season. Over the years, Anderson's durability has continued to be an issue: in every season as a Senator, he has missed at least five games. The injuries have not seemed to affect the quality of his goaltending, though. In five seasons with Ottawa, Anderson has provided excellent goaltending, stopping an above-average percentage of even-strength shots (.929), ranking sixth among NHL goaltenders who played at least 150 games from the time when Anderson first donned his Senators jersey. The former OHL Goaltender of the Year may not be considered an elite goalie in this league, but he has the ability to "steal" games.

Chris Driedger — G — OTT

Season	Team	Age	GP	W	L	OT	GAA	Sv%	ESSV%	QS%	GGVT	DGVT	SGVT	GVT
2014-15	OTT	20	1	0	0	0	0.00	1.000	1.000	--	0.8	0.0	0.0	0.8
2015-16	OTT	21	13					.915			1.8	0.0	0.0	1.7

In his first NHL appearance, former Calgary Hitman Chris Driedger stopped all 10 shots he faced against the Rangers in late March after Andrew Hammond was pulled. For most of the season, Driedger split time between Ottawa's minor-league affiliates. He was the number-one goalie for the ECHL's Evansville Icemen, stopping only 88.5% of shots in 40 games as a rookie. In the AHL, the 2012 third-round pick fared better, with a .923 save percentage in eight games with Binghamton. Back in his junior years, his save percentage improved each year in four WHL seasons from .881 all the way up to .918 All in all, the 21-year-old still has plenty of time to prove himself at the pro level, especially if he keeps progressing.

Andrew Hammond — G — OTT

Season	Team	Age	GP	W	L	OT	GAA	Sv%	ESSV%	QS%	GGVT	DGVT	SGVT	GVT
2013-14	OTT	25	1	0	0	0	0.00	1.000	1.000	--	0.9	0.1	0.0	0.9
2014-15	OTT	26	24	20	1	2	1.79	.941	.943	78.3%	18.6	-0.2	0.2	18.6
2015-16	OTT	27	36					.919			9.4	-0.1	0.1	9.4

Last season was completely unexpected for Andrew Hammond. "The Hamburglar" was called up from Binghamton, where he had an unsightly .898 save percentage in 25 games, to big-league Ottawa, to fill in the breach for Anderson and Lehner. He took full advantage of the opportunity, with an unprecedented transformation. Hammond went 20-1-2 in 23 starts while leading the Senators' charge to make the playoffs from way down in the standings. Out of the NHL goalies who played at least 20 games in 2014-15, the six-foot-one netminder was ranked third in even-strength save percentage. Hammond is often composed (an image of the *MAD Magazine* character Alfred E. Neuman, whose catchphrase is "What, me worry?" appears on the side of his mask), but his rebound control can be a bit concerning. He will never replicate the magic of last season, but the undrafted netminder proved, at the very least, that he can be a very capable NHL goalie.

Robin Lehner — G — BUF

Season	Team	Age	GP	W	L	OT	GAA	Sv%	ESSV%	QS%	GGVT	DGVT	SGVT	GVT
2012-13	OTT	21	12	5	3	4	2.20	.936	.935	83.3%	10.5	-0.7	-1.9	7.8
2013-14	OTT	22	36	12	15	6	3.06	.913	.915	63.3%	4.8	-2.0	-0.4	2.4
2014-15	OTT	23	25	9	12	3	3.02	.905	.914	45.8%	-3.1	-0.6	0.2	-3.5
2015-16	BUF	24	26					.913			2.1	-0.6	-0.1	1.4

An unfortunate collision with Clarke MacArthur in February forced Robin Lehner to sit out with a concussion for the rest of the season. Prior to that incident, Ottawa's goalie of the future posted a .909 save percentage, a notch down from a solid .913 rate in 2013-14. Along those lines, Lehner's career even-strength save percentage of .917 ranks roughly in the middle of 114 goalies. He may have average statistics, but the six-foot-three Swede has the ability to step up his game when it matters. The feisty netminder backstopped the Binghamton Senators to a Calder Cup title, while winning the Jack A. Butterfield Trophy as MVP of the 2011 AHL playoffs.

Wesley Chu

Philadelphia Flyers

A failed 2014-15 campaign saw the Philadelphia Flyers finish with just 84 points and miss the playoffs for the second time in three seasons, a stretch of futility that had not occurred in more than 20 mostly competitive years. The failure was the result of several reactionary moves and hasty free-agent signings due to a mantra of "win now and by any means necessary" that not only financially hampered the franchise, but has now forced the team to engage in a rebuild for the next couple of seasons. New general manager Ron Hextall has been given the keys to the franchise to complete the arduous task of escaping cap hell and building up the team through shrewd trades and the draft.

What have you done for me lately?

The downfall of the Flyers is rooted in more than just bad signings. Impatience with young players led to the departures of forward James van Riemsdyk and goaltender Sergei Bobrovsky in June 2012. Van Riemsdyk's poor season—partially hampered by injuries—led to his exit. He was traded to Toronto for Luke Schenn, a return that both at the time and today is considered underwhelming. JVR has been one of the Leafs most consistent scorers while Schenn has been a middle-of-the-road second-pairing defenseman, at best.

Bobrovsky was one of the NHL's best rookies in 2010-11, a major reason Philadelphia was a postseason favorite. Unfortunately, a disappointing playoff performance led the Flyers to go all-in on enigmatic veteran Ilya Bryzgalov, inking him to a massive nine-year, $51 million contract. After struggling to adjust to the backup role behind Bryzgalov, "Bob" was dealt to Columbus for a chance at a new start in the Arch City. There, Bobrovsky not only flourished, but was dominant for the Blue Jackets *en route* to a Vezina Trophy. Meanwhile, the Flyers ended up buying out the floundering Bryzgalov.

Impatience cost the Flyers two Olympians in the matter of hours. While the renaissance of new netminder Steve Mason has helped fans swallow the loss of Bobrovsky, the carousel of first-line wingers with Claude Giroux and Jakub Voracek could have been filled by a more seasoned van Riemsdyk. Given the 57 goals "JVR" has tallied in the last two seasons with Toronto—and the pass-first mindset of Giroux and Voracek—the 26-year-old forward may have ultimately found success in that role.

Breaking the bank on the blue line

Since the loss of franchise defenseman Chris Pronger to post-concussion symptoms four years ago, the Flyers have tried

FLYERS IN A BOX

Last Season

Goals For	215	22nd
Goals Against	234	24th
GVT	-19	24th
Points	84	24th
Playoffs	Did not make playoffs	

Having the league's third-worst penalty killing doomed the Flyers to the bottom third of the Eastern Conference.

Three-Year Record

GVT	-26	21st
Points	227	22nd
Playoffs	1 Appearance, 3 Wins	

VUKOTA Projections

Goals For	221	16th
Goals Against	222	19th
GVT	-1	21st
Points	91	21st

Giroux and Voracek will still be awesome, but without more depth, Philadelphia will not be a playoff team.

Top Three Prospects

I. Provorov (D), T. Konecny (F), S. Laughton (F)

to fill that void via free agency and trades. However, the majority of all their blueline transactions have been regrettable—not only because the additions have been worth less than they are being paid, but also because they were thrust into improper roles. While Nicklas Grossmann, Nick Schultz, Andrew MacDonald, and even Luke Schenn could work in the right situation and with the proper usage, handing all of them significant ice-time is far from ideal. They would all be #5 or #6 defensemen on a majority of playoff rosters but they have cap hits commensurate to players with better production.

For the past several years, the Flyers have tied up more money in their defense than most of the league with little bang for their buck to show for it.

Cap hits of Flyers defensemen, season start 2011-12 to 2015-16

Season	Cap Hit, defensemen	Rank	% of Cap	Rank
2015-16	$24.6 million	7	34.7%	10
2014-15	$25.5 million	3	36.9%	3
2013-14	$24.7 million	3	40.2%	2
2012-13	$31.6 million	1	45.1%	1
2011-12	$33.1 million	1	51.6%	1

The cap space committed to the defense corps should produce much better results. Former GM Paul Holmgren's inefficient cap management of defensemen has hindered the team's ability to build through free agency. Hextall was finally able to shed several contracts this past summer, including the dead contract of Pronger. As the table shows, Hextall has been able to cut spending and allocate cap space more efficiently. By the end of next season, the Flyers should have enough room to start making a splash in free agency again, as the league is accustomed to seeing from Philadelphia.

Replenished prospect pool

Being forced into a rebuild has been a blessing in disguise for Philadelphia's farm system, which is more stocked with NHL prospects than it has been for 10+ years. With the Flyers used to competing year-to-year, draft picks and prospects had been used as assets to acquire players at the trade deadline. But now, thanks to being a seller in trades and selecting towards the top of the drafts, Philadelphia's defense should soon be a force again.

Prospects such as Sam Morin, Robert Hagg, Shayne Gostisbehere, Travis Sanheim, and 2015 first-round pick Ivan Provorov all make up one of the deepest defensive prospect pools in the league. The fact that the Flyers were able to replenish their farm system this quickly after being rated the worst in the league just a few years ago gives fans a reason to believe the post-Holmgren era of mediocrity may be brief, if said prospects turn out as hoped. That is always a big if.

The process will have to play out quickly if the Flyers are going to compete. Otherwise, the sands in the hourglass will simply run from defensemen to forwards if Philadelphia doesn't manage a turnaround while cornerstones Giroux and Voracek are in their primes. Hextall and the front office have begun to right the ship, but the Flyers have a long, long way to go before they are ready to be Broad Street Bullies again.

Erik Yost

PHILADELPHIA FLYERS

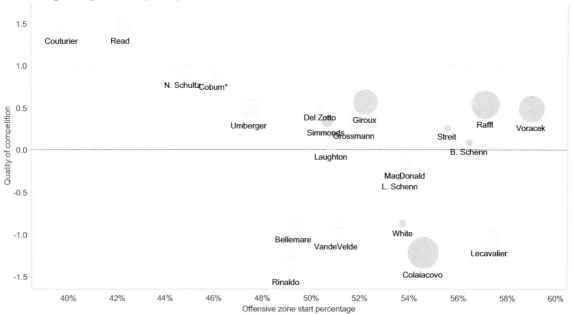

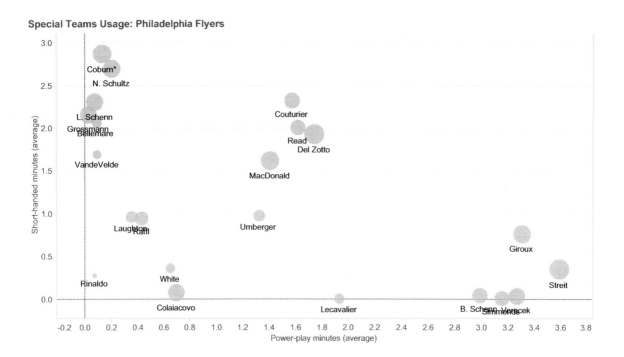

PHILADELPHIA FLYERS

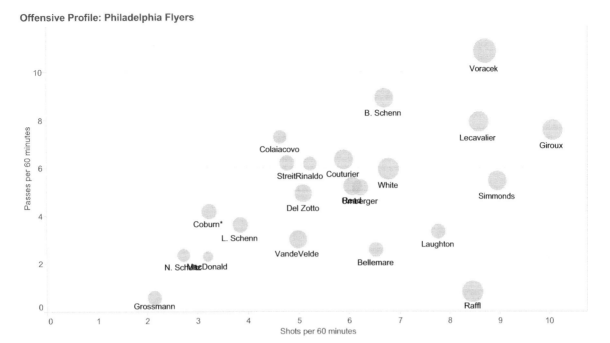

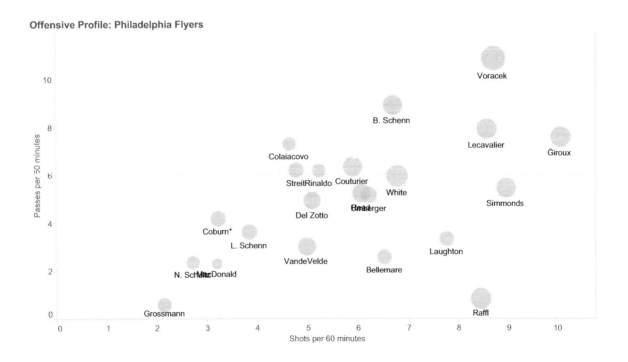

PHILADELPHIA FLYERS

FORWARDS

Jason Akeson — RW — BUF

Season	Team	Age	GP	G	A	Pts	+/-	ESP/60	AdjCF%	iCF/60	OGVT	DGVT	SGVT	GVT
2012-13	PHI	22	1	1	0	1	2	4.85	51.8%	15.7	0.5	0.0	0.0	0.5
2013-14	PHI	23	1	0	1	1	1	4.89	61.4%	13.2	0.1	0.1	-0.3	-0.1
2014-15	PHI	24	13	0	0	0	-1	0.00	37.2%	11.5	-0.6	0.1	0.0	-0.5
2015-16	BUF	25	29	4	5	9					0.3	0.6	0.0	0.9

After a surprising showing in the 2014 playoffs, Jason Akeson was hoping to compete for a regular role with the Flyers. Despite playing with the big-league club for the season's opening month, Akeson failed to make any notable impact, as he averaged around eight minutes per game, putting up horrific possession numbers. As a result, the team sent him back to Lehigh Valley, where he had very good production. It appears that the Ontario native is a classic AAAA player: a top player in the minors, but not quite good enough for the big leagues. With an already massive logjam at forward for the Flyers, Akeson's time with the franchise was at an end. He will look for a fresh start in Western New York as he signed a one-year, two-way deal with the Buffalo Sabres

Pierre-Edouard Bellemare — C/LW — PHI

Season	Team	Age	GP	G	A	Pts	+/-	ESP/60	AdjCF%	iCF/60	OGVT	DGVT	SGVT	GVT
2014-15	PHI	29	81	6	6	12	-3	0.83	46.0%	13.2	-2.4	2.2	0.0	-0.3
2015-16	PHI	30	66	8	7	15					-1.2	2.0	0.0	0.8

With a name equally as tough to pronounce as it is to spell, Pierre-Edouard Bellemare's path to the NHL was an arduous one. After spending his entire career playing in Sweden, Bellemare finally got his NHL opportunity when he was signed in the offseason by Philadelphia. With training camp his only guarantee, the Frenchman not only made the opening roster, but was a productive fourth liner and a mainstay on the penalty kill. While his underlying possession numbers were far from adequate, Bellemare did chip in 12 points and drew four times as many penalties as he took. The 29-year-old made a strong enough impression with the Flyers in his rookie season to earn himself a two-year contract extension.

Nick Cousins — C — PHI

Season	Team	Age	GP	G	A	Pts	+/-	ESP/60	AdjCF%	iCF/60	OGVT	DGVT	SGVT	GVT
2014-15	PHI	21	11	0	0	0	1	0.00	47.3%	5.6	-0.8	0.3	0.6	0.1
2015-16	PHI	22	30	4	5	9					0.0	0.8	0.0	0.8

The season's final month marked the NHL debut of 2011 third-round pick Nick Cousins. The 21-year-old agitator had a strong sophomore season with the Lehigh Valley Phantoms, as he put up 64 points in 72 games, earning himself a call-up. The former Soo Greyhound saw time on the third line for the Flyers, playing some strong hockey despite not putting up any points in his 11 games with the team. However, with both Ryan White and Chris VandeVelde re-upping and Vinny Lecavalier still on the roster, it appears Cousins will be back with the Phantoms for the start of the 2015-16 campaign, where he will have to earn his way back to the Flyers.

Sean Couturier — C — PHI

Season	Team	Age	GP	G	A	Pts	+/-	ESP/60	AdjCF%	iCF/60	OGVT	DGVT	SGVT	GVT
2012-13	PHI	20	46	4	11	15	-8	1.21	48.6%	10.9	0.0	3.6	0.0	3.6
2013-14	PHI	21	82	13	26	39	1	1.58	49.4%	11.8	3.4	5.5	-0.5	8.4
2014-15	PHI	22	82	15	22	37	4	1.46	48.0%	11.1	2.6	4.1	-1.2	5.4
2015-16	PHI	23	72	16	22	37					3.1	3.3	-0.1	6.3

While opinions among hockey pundits regarding Sean Couturier are divided, most can agree that the 23-year-old has developed into one of the elite defensive forwards in the game. Consistently skating against the top competition and buried in his defensive zone, it is baffling that some harp on Couturier's inconsistent offensive production considering his usage on a defensively inept team. That said, the former QMJHL scoring leader still tallied 15 goals, all while being tethered to R.J. Umberger for most of the year. With more favorable deployment, "Coots" could easily become a 45-50 point producer.

Claude Giroux — C/RW — PHI

Season	Team	Age	GP	G	A	Pts	+/-	ESP/60	AdjCF%	iCF/60	OGVT	DGVT	SGVT	GVT
2012-13	PHI	24	48	13	35	48	-7	2.06	50.6%	14.4	7.4	1.3	0.7	9.4
2013-14	PHI	25	82	28	58	86	7	2.28	53.1%	13.9	15.8	3.0	1.3	20.1
2014-15	PHI	26	81	25	48	73	-3	1.62	52.4%	17.1	11.0	2.6	-2.3	11.3
2015-16	PHI	27	74	28	45	73					10.6	2.7	0.0	13.3

Finishing as a top-10 scorer in the NHL would be a career highlight for most players, but for Claude Giroux, it was considered a quiet season. While 2014-15 was the first time in four years that the Flyers captain finished at under a point-per-game scoring rate, he still was among the best in the league and one of its most deadly power-play scorers; his 37 power-play points were tops in the NHL. It has been business as usual for the Ontario native, as he has amassed 376 points over the last five seasons, ahead of the likes of Evgeni Malkin and Alex Ovechkin. The former Hart Trophy nominee continues to be a dominant possession player, and his production with fellow All-Star Jakub Voracek makes them one of the most formidable duos in hockey.

Blair Jones — C — VAN

Season	Team	Age	GP	G	A	Pts	+/-	ESP/60	AdjCF%	iCF/60	OGVT	DGVT	SGVT	GVT
2012-13	CGY	26	15	0	1	1	-6	0.40	44.3%	12.6	-0.7	-0.2	-0.3	-1.2
2013-14	CGY	27	14	2	0	2	0	0.43	43.6%	11.7	0.2	0.5	-0.3	0.3
2014-15	PHI	28	4	0	0	0	-4	0.00	34.1%	5.6	-0.5	-0.2	0.0	-0.8
2015-16	VAN	29	27	4	5	8					0.3	0.5	0.0	0.8

Signed away from the Calgary organization in the offseason, the Flyers hoped Blair Jones would provide organizational depth, and scoring for the Lehigh Valley Phantoms. Injuries put a damper on his campaign, but he was still productive for the Phantoms with 21 points in 33 AHL games. The former Tampa Bay Lightning draft pick earned a forgettable four-game stint with the team early in the season and was sent back down after some poor play. The "Blair Jones Project" will make its way to British Columbia next, as Jones signed on with the Vancouver Canucks organization for 2015-16.

Scott Laughton — C — PHI

Season	Team	Age	GP	G	A	Pts	+/-	ESP/60	AdjCF%	iCF/60	OGVT	DGVT	SGVT	GVT
2012-13	PHI	18	5	0	0	0	0	0.00	42.0%	16.5	-0.1	0.3	0.0	0.1
2014-15	PHI	20	31	2	4	6	-1	0.85	45.5%	14.6	-1.0	0.8	-0.3	-0.5
2015-16	PHI	21	42	6	8	14					0.2	1.1	0.0	1.3

Scott Laughton finally got a full season of professional hockey under his belt after splitting time between Lehigh Valley and Philadelphia. The 2012 first-round pick really flourished in the AHL and quickly made an impact for the Phantoms, enough so that he was given a call-up by the Flyers in December. He suffered a concussion during his 31-game stint with the orange and black, perhaps why he looked out of place at times, registering only six points. With the season outlook looking grim and Laughton's minutes dwindling, the Flyers chose to send him back to the minors for further seasoning and regular ice-time. Laughton will challenge for a roster spot in the fall, as he did show flashes of production before he got injured.

Vincent Lecavalier — C/LW — PHI

Season	Team	Age	GP	G	A	Pts	+/-	ESP/60	AdjCF%	iCF/60	OGVT	DGVT	SGVT	GVT
2012-13	TBL	32	39	10	22	32	-5	2.42	45.5%	10.3	4.3	-0.1	0.0	4.2
2013-14	PHI	33	69	20	17	37	-16	1.64	45.4%	11.5	5.8	-0.5	-0.5	4.8
2014-15	PHI	34	57	8	12	20	-7	1.57	46.3%	13.3	0.6	1.0	-1.1	0.5
2015-16	PHI	35	53	10	12	23					1.9	0.9	-0.1	2.7

Vincent Lecavalier was hoping to rediscover his All-Star ability from seasons past, looking to rebound from a disappointing start to his Flyers career. Instead, Lecavalier turned in his worst statistical season as a professional as he struggled to find a place in the lineup, mostly playing on the fourth line with sporadic appearances on the power play. The 1998 first-overall draft choice and 2004 Stanley Cup champion continued to be a poor possession player despite favorable zone starts, and he saw his minutes drop to under 13 per game. With the Flyers in a midst of a rebuild, you would figure that Lecavalier's days in Philly would be numbered, but he remains on the roster.

Michael Raffl — LW/RW/C — PHI

Season	Team	Age	GP	G	A	Pts	+/-	ESP/60	AdjCF%	iCF/60	OGVT	DGVT	SGVT	GVT
2013-14	PHI	25	68	9	13	22	2	1.75	52.6%	13.5	2.2	2.3	0.0	4.6
2014-15	PHI	26	67	21	7	28	6	1.74	54.8%	14.3	3.4	3.3	0.0	6.7
2015-16	PHI	27	67	18	14	32					3.3	2.5	0.0	5.7

After a solid NHL debut in 2013-14, many wondered where Michael Raffl would ultimately wind up in the lineup after having success on all four lines. Last season, he was the third wheel to the dynamic first-line duo of Giroux and Voracek. Playing on the first line paid dividends on the scoresheet, as he potted 21 goals, partly thanks to an inflated 15.7% shooting percentage. But where he really flourished was in possession: his Corsi hovered around 55%, as every player had a better shot differential with him on the ice. A mainstay of Austria's World and Olympic teams, Raffl's versatility on the roster may make him more valuable to the Flyers beyond the scoring line, but the coaching staff no doubt has the confidence in the left winger to slide into that role at any given moment.

Matt Read — RW — PHI

Season	Team	Age	GP	G	A	Pts	+/-	ESP/60	AdjCF%	iCF/60	OGVT	DGVT	SGVT	GVT
2012-13	PHI	26	42	11	13	24	1	2.13	47.2%	10.8	4.0	1.9	-0.1	5.8
2013-14	PHI	27	75	22	18	40	-4	1.92	50.2%	14.0	6.6	4.0	-0.8	9.8
2014-15	PHI	28	80	8	22	30	-4	1.29	46.7%	11.3	0.2	2.9	-1.3	1.8
2015-16	PHI	29	67	13	19	32					2.5	2.5	-0.1	4.9

It was a rough season for Matt Read, as he struggled to find his usually reliable scoring touch while facing some of the opposition's top players on a nightly basis. A career 15% shooter coming into the year, the Calgary native converted on just 5.6% of his shots, resulting in a career-low eight goals despite playing 80 games for the first time. Making matters worse, his 1.8 GVT was terrible considering the top-six minutes he received. Even so, "Reader" still remains one of the most versatile skaters on the Flyers given his ability to play in all situations. Fortunately for the speedy winger, his scoring rate should progress closer to his career norms. A bounceback season of 18-20 goals would not be surprising at all.

Zac Rinaldo — LW — BOS

Season	Team	Age	GP	G	A	Pts	+/-	ESP/60	AdjCF%	iCF/60	OGVT	DGVT	SGVT	GVT
2012-13	PHI	22	32	3	2	5	-7	1.13	40.8%	5.5	-0.2	-0.2	0.0	-0.3
2013-14	PHI	23	67	2	2	4	-13	0.50	46.9%	13.6	-2.7	0.1	0.0	-2.5
2014-15	PHI	24	58	1	5	6	-9	0.72	44.0%	8.8	-2.3	0.4	0.0	-1.9
2015-16	BOS	25	51	3	4	6					-1.7	0.8	0.0	-0.9

There was a point in time when Zac Rinaldo showed glimpses of being a serviceable bottom-six player with a knack for agitation, drawing penalties, and even perhaps killing penalties. Instead, the former third-round pick drew the agitation of opposing fanbases—and his own—with his play in 2014-15. Rinaldo was the worst possession player on the team, turning in a -11.8 Relative Corsi, and led the team in penalty minutes for the umpteenth time. The Mississauga, Ontario native was also suspended eight games for a devastating hit on Penguins star defenseman Kris Letang. When you are suspended, or in the box for nearly as many minutes as you are on the ice, your value in the league is minimal at best. With Rinaldo unlikely to change his style of play, his act wore thin (even) in Philadelphia. Stunningly, the Flyers were able to purge a future third-round pick from the Bruins for his "gritty" services.

Brayden Schenn — C — PHI

Season	Team	Age	GP	G	A	Pts	+/-	ESP/60	AdjCF%	iCF/60	OGVT	DGVT	SGVT	GVT
2012-13	PHI	21	47	8	18	26	-8	1.56	48.0%	10.8	3.0	0.2	-0.3	2.9
2013-14	PHI	22	82	20	21	41	0	1.75	48.0%	14.0	6.1	1.1	0.3	7.6
2014-15	PHI	23	82	18	29	47	-5	1.46	49.4%	10.5	5.3	1.3	-0.8	5.8
2015-16	PHI	24	68	18	25	43					5.1	1.6	0.0	6.7

Despite setting a career high in points, Brayden Schenn continues to be the subject of hypothetical trade talks and overall fan frustration due to high expectations in development. Schenn has yet to truly settle into a permanent role, thanks in part to being repeatedly switched back and forth between center and wing. While his even-strength scoring was at its lowest since his rookie year despite very favorable zone starts, the Saskatoon native was a bright spot on the power play as he helped fill the void left by Scott Hartnell's departure. Just 24 years old, the 2009 fifth-overall pick still has time to put the pieces of his game together and make himself part of the Flyers' long-term plans.

Wayne Simmonds — RW — PHI

Season	Team	Age	GP	G	A	Pts	+/-	ESP/60	AdjCF%	iCF/60	OGVT	DGVT	SGVT	GVT
2012-13	PHI	24	45	15	17	32	-7	1.72	47.8%	14.0	6.1	0.0	-0.3	5.9
2013-14	PHI	25	82	29	31	60	-4	1.98	48.7%	13.7	9.8	0.2	-0.3	9.7
2014-15	PHI	26	75	28	22	50	-5	1.52	50.2%	14.0	6.7	1.4	1.7	9.8
2015-16	PHI	27	68	25	25	50					6.6	1.4	0.0	8.0

A *bona fide* fan favorite in Philadelphia, Wayne Simmonds again put together a strong, productive season for the Flyers, mainly due to his prowess on the power play. Furthermore, "Simmer" was a positive possession player and cut his penalty minutes down almost in half. However, despite his potency on the man advantage, Simmonds proved to be inconsistent at even strength, a big reason why his ESP/60 rate dropped to below top-six expectations. That said, "Wayne-Train" was on his way to breaking the 30-goal plateau for the first time when a late-season ankle injury cost him the opportunity. If Simmonds can find consistency at even strength, he can flirt with 60 points on a regular basis.

Petr Straka — RW/LW — PHI

Season	Team	Age	GP	G	A	Pts	+/-	ESP/60	AdjCF%	iCF/60	OGVT	DGVT	SGVT	GVT
2014-15	PHI	22	3	0	2	2	1	4.23	59.5%	10.8	0.3	0.2	0.0	0.5
2015-16	PHI	23	27	5	8	13					1.0	0.7	0.0	1.7

Once hailed as a dark horse to make the Flyers a year ago, Petr Straka needed some AHL seasoning after signing with the organization in 2013 as a free agent. Straka was a solid producer for the Phantoms the last two seasons, and despite facing several injuries, he played well enough to earn a midseason debut in Philadelphia. The Czech native notched two assists in three games, had some outstanding possession metrics, and made a strong impression overall. Despite having some upside, Straka faces an uphill battle to become a Flyers regular due his injury history and the depth in front of him at the forward position.

R.J. Umberger — LW — PHI

Season	Team	Age	GP	G	A	Pts	+/-	ESP/60	AdjCF%	iCF/60	OGVT	DGVT	SGVT	GVT
2012-13	CBJ	30	48	8	10	18	3	1.10	44.3%	11.8	-0.5	1.4	0.0	0.9
2013-14	CBJ	31	74	18	16	34	-3	1.25	47.1%	10.7	3.3	1.8	0.0	5.1
2014-15	PHI	32	67	9	6	15	-9	1.01	46.0%	12.4	-0.9	1.2	0.0	0.3
2015-16	PHI	33	57	10	9	19					0.8	1.3	0.0	2.1

Most fans and pundits were flabbergasted at the Flyers for their acquisition of R.J. Umberger from Columbus for fan favorite Scott Hartnell. Yes, Umberger had a memorable playoff run with Philadelphia back in 2008, but recent seasons have not been kind to Pittsburgh native. Injuries and persistent slumping derailed most of his 2014-15 campaign, as he turned in his most unproductive season. Umberger's play was barely above replacement level, as he was constantly bounced around the lineup, even spending time in the pressbox before requiring season-ending surgery. Still owed $9 million over the next two seasons, GM Ron Hextall may be forced to cut his losses sooner than later with the former Ohio State Buckeye.

PHILADELPHIA FLYERS

Chris VandeVelde — C — PHI

Season	Team	Age	GP	G	A	Pts	+/-	ESP/60	AdjCF%	iCF/60	OGVT	DGVT	SGVT	GVT
2012-13	EDM	25	11	0	0	0	-3	0.00	36.4%	7.8	-0.3	0.1	0.0	-0.2
2013-14	PHI	26	18	0	1	1	-3	0.00	44.1%	8.7	-0.8	0.0	0.0	-0.8
2014-15	PHI	27	72	9	6	15	-6	1.26	46.3%	9.7	-0.5	1.6	0.0	1.1
2015-16	PHI	28	57	7	7	14					-0.2	1.4	0.0	1.1

A fringe NHL player for most of his career, Chris VandeVelde earned a return to the Flyers after a positive stint with the team a year ago. However, no one could foresee VandeVelde being a mainstay on the checking line for most of 2014-15. After starting the season with affiliate Lehigh Valley, the Minnesota native was an early recall and went on to lace them up for 72 games, scoring nine goals while once again contributing on the penalty kill. VandeVelde was re-signed by the Flyers early in free agency, reuniting him with his former collegiate coach at North Dakota, Dave Hakstol.

Jakub Voracek — RW/LW — PHI

Season	Team	Age	GP	G	A	Pts	+/-	ESP/60	AdjCF%	iCF/60	OGVT	DGVT	SGVT	GVT
2012-13	PHI	23	48	22	24	46	-7	2.66	53.3%	11.5	9.3	0.4	0.0	9.7
2013-14	PHI	24	82	23	39	62	11	2.06	55.0%	15.7	9.5	1.8	-0.3	11.0
2014-15	PHI	25	82	22	59	81	1	2.30	53.1%	13.5	13.4	2.7	1.2	17.3
2015-16	PHI	26	72	25	46	70					10.3	2.6	0.1	12.9

Perhaps the most valuable skater for the Flyers in 2014-15, Jakub Voracek took another step forward in establishing himself as one of the league's better players. Voracek set a career high in scoring, finding himself in the thick of the Art Ross Trophy race for much of the season. The Czech Olympian set himself apart on the man advantage, registering 32 points at a rate of 6.65 power-play points per 60 minutes. The scoring winger was exemplary possession-wise as well, as his ability to generate zone entries and drive play was the main reason that his Relative Corsi was best among all Flyers. With his 17.3 GVT a full six points higher than his closest teammate, Voracek is no doubt one of the cornerstones of the franchise today.

Ryan White — C/RW — PHI

Season	Team	Age	GP	G	A	Pts	+/-	ESP/60	AdjCF%	iCF/60	OGVT	DGVT	SGVT	GVT
2012-13	MTL	24	26	1	0	1	1	0.28	40.1%	10.2	-1.0	0.8	0.0	-0.2
2013-14	MTL	25	52	2	4	6	-8	0.88	38.5%	10.7	-1.9	1.4	0.0	-0.5
2014-15	PHI	26	34	6	6	12	4	1.81	50.2%	10.5	1.8	1.3	0.0	3.1
2015-16	PHI	27	45	7	8	15					0.9	1.4	0.0	2.2

More known as a faceoff specialist during his time with the Montreal organization, Ryan White was a depth signing when he joined the Flyers on a one-year, two-way contract in the offseason. After spending the first half of the season in Lehigh Valley, White was called up in late January and turned out to be one of Philadelphia's most solid players in the second half. The former Calgary Hitman tallied 12 points in 34 games after entering with just 17 points in 151 games. White solidified the third line as he turned in top-six scoring production with the minutes he was given. White could flirt with 25 points given regular minutes in a full season of play. He re-upped with the Flyers on a two-year pact.

PHILADELPHIA FLYERS

DEFENSEMEN

Mark Alt							RD						PHI
Season	Team	Age	GP	G	A	Pts	+/-	ESP/60	AdjCF%	iCF/60	OGVT	DGVT	SGVT	GVT
2014-15	PHI	23	1	0	0	0	-1	0.00	67.9%	35.7	-0.1	-0.1	0.0	-0.2
2015-16	PHI	24	25	2	5	7					0.4	0.8	0.0	1.1

Mark Alt made his NHL debut and lone appearance with the Flyers in a 3-2 loss to San Jose. He registered just under 10 minutes of ice-time but was one of the best possession players of the game. Originally a 2010 second-round pick of the Carolina Hurricanes, he spent three seasons at the University of Minnesota before signing an entry-level deal with the Flyers. With the team's reloaded defensive prospect pool, Alt's chances to make the NHL regularly with the Flyers seem unlikely. Fun fact: his father John was a two-time Pro Bowl lineman for the Kansas City Chiefs.

Carlo Colaiacovo							LD							BUF
Season	Team	Age	GP	G	A	Pts	+/-	ESP/60	AdjCF%	iCF/60	OGVT	DGVT	SGVT	GVT
2012-13	DET	29	6	0	1	1	-4	0.00	56.0%	14.6	-0.2	-0.2	0.0	-0.5
2013-14	STL	30	25	1	3	4	-4	0.52	52.8%	7.3	0.0	-0.1	0.0	-0.1
2014-15	PHI	31	33	2	6	8	0	0.69	54.8%	11.6	1.3	0.8	0.0	2.1
2015-16	BUF	32	37	2	7	10					0.9	1.1	0.0	2.0

Signed as a depth defensemen in the offseason, Carlo Colaiacovo was a very serviceable player for the Flyers. Slowed by injuries in recent years, the former St. Louis Blue made quality plays in his own zone, helped generate chances, and was effective at driving possession. Colaiacovo deserved to play more games than some of his teammates due to his effectiveness and it was curious why he wasn't given more opportunities: he only dressed for 31 games. He likely would have earned another chance with the Flyers if the team wasn't hampered with contracts on the defensive side. The rejuvenated play of the 2001 first-round pick helped earned him a one-year deal with the Sabres.

Michael Del Zotto							LD							PHI
Season	Team	Age	GP	G	A	Pts	+/-	ESP/60	AdjCF%	iCF/60	OGVT	DGVT	SGVT	GVT
2012-13	NYR	22	46	3	18	21	6	0.84	49.7%	10.1	3.0	2.5	0.0	5.5
2013-14	NYR, NSH	23	67	3	13	16	-9	0.63	50.3%	9.7	0.3	1.2	0.0	1.5
2014-15	PHI	24	64	10	22	32	-5	1.18	48.1%	9.2	6.1	2.9	0.0	8.9
2015-16	PHI	25	62	7	20	27					3.7	2.7	0.0	6.3

Unsure of his fortunes just a month from the start of training camp, Michael Del Zotto was able to find a home with the Flyers after the indefinite loss of Kimmo Timonen. The former Blueshirt's offensive touch from the blueline was a big boost to the team's underwhelming play at even strength. Among their defensemen, Del Zotto was the top even-strength scorer, and second in ice-time at 21 minutes per game. His production makes it even more puzzling that he was scratched 11 times in December by former head coach Craig Berube. Del Zotto agreed to a new deal with Philadelphia in the offseason.

Shayne Gostisbehere — LD — PHI

Season	Team	Age	GP	G	A	Pts	+/-	ESP/60	AdjCF%	iCF/60	OGVT	DGVT	SGVT	GVT
2014-15	PHI	21	2	0	0	0	-2	0.00	34.1%	16.9	-0.1	-0.2	0.0	-0.3
2015-16	PHI	22	25	2	5	7					0.4	0.7	0.0	1.1

Shayne Gostisbehere became a household name when he powered Union College to a National Championship victory in of all places, his future home of Philadelphia. "Ghost" was a third-round draft pick in 2012 and developed into one of the most dynamic collegiate players as a do-it-all defenseman. The lightning-fast Gostisbehere made his NHL debut rather quickly thanks to some early-season injuries. In two games, his play was passable, like most young players in their first career appearances. Unfortunately, the Florida native's season was cut short after tearing his ACL in early November, and he missed the rest of the season. Gostisbehere will look to prove his health and ultimately compete for a roster spot.

Nicklas Grossmann — LD — ARI

Season	Team	Age	GP	G	A	Pts	+/-	ESP/60	AdjCF%	iCF/60	OGVT	DGVT	SGVT	GVT
2012-13	PHI	27	30	1	3	4	-1	0.53	47.0%	6.9	-0.1	2.4	0.0	2.3
2013-14	PHI	28	78	1	13	14	-6	0.61	47.5%	8.2	-0.4	3.8	0.0	3.4
2014-15	PHI	29	68	5	9	14	8	0.80	46.4%	5.7	1.5	4.0	0.0	5.5
2015-16	ARI	30	60	3	10	13					0.5	3.1	0.0	3.6

The clock is running out for stay-at-home defensemen to have a prominent role in the NHL, and that does not bode well for Nicklas Grossmann. At six-foot-four and 230 pounds, his size and snarl normally puts him near the top in hits and blocks, but his underlying numbers paint a different picture. His -8.7 Relative Corsi was the worst amongst Flyers' defensemen by far, as he is just not very good in his own end, and an anchor to his teammates. Although he matched his career-best goal total with five, Grossmann is just too vulnerable on an already-dismal blueline. With a cap hit of $3.5 million and one year left on his contract, Ron Hextall was able to deal away Grossmann and the contract of NHL Hall of Famer Chris Pronger in a creative deal with the Coyotes for perennially underachieving center Sam Gagner.

Radko Gudas — RD — PHI

Season	Team	Age	GP	G	A	Pts	+/-	ESP/60	AdjCF%	iCF/60	OGVT	DGVT	SGVT	GVT
2012-13	TBL	22	22	2	3	5	3	0.85	53.2%	9.6	0.6	0.9	0.0	1.5
2013-14	TBL	23	73	3	19	22	2	0.89	49.8%	11.5	2.2	3.1	0.0	5.3
2014-15	TBL	24	31	2	3	5	-5	0.60	53.3%	15.5	0.1	0.0	0.0	0.1
2015-16	PHI	25	51	4	11	15					1.3	1.8	0.0	3.2

Radko Gudas worked his way into being a regular in the Lightning lineup in 2013-14, playing 73 games, but lost that consistent spot when Tampa Bay made upgrades to their blueline with the acquisitions of Anton Stralman and Jason Garrison. While the physical Czech defenseman has more offensive talent than some bottom-pair bruisers, his lack of mobility did not match the tempo in which the Lightning wanted to play. He has been a negative Relative goals-for percentage and Relative Corsi percentage player since being moved up to the NHL, giving credence to Steve Yzerman's decision to move him.

Oliver Lauridsen							LD						Sweden
Season	Team	Age	GP	G	A	Pts	+/-	ESP/60	AdjCF%	iCF/60	OGVT	DGVT	SGVT	GVT
2012-13	PHI	23	15	2	1	3	0	0.84	46.4%	8.3	0.4	0.3	0.0	0.8
2014-15	PHI	25	1	0	0	0	-1	0.00	55.3%	18.2	-0.1	-0.1	0.0	-0.2
2015-16	Sweden	26	24	2	5	6					0.3	0.8	0.0	1.1

Oliver Lauridsen made his return to the Flyers nearly two years after an impressive 15-game stint in 2013. Lauridsen had been a regular with the Phantoms in the interim, mostly seeing time on their second pairing, racking up 152 penalty minutes in 75 AHL games. The "Great Dane" only appeared in one game for Philadelphia, and nearly totaled as many penalty minutes as he did overall ice-time. Lauridsen opted to leave the NHL and sign with Frolunda of the Swedish Hockey League for the 2015-16 season.

Andrew MacDonald							LD						PHI
Season	Team	Age	GP	G	A	Pts	+/-	ESP/60	AdjCF%	iCF/60	OGVT	DGVT	SGVT	GVT
2012-13	NYI	26	48	3	9	12	-2	0.59	46.9%	5.9	0.2	3.1	0.0	3.3
2013-14	NYI, PHI	27	82	4	24	28	-22	0.60	43.8%	6.3	0.5	1.9	0.0	2.3
2014-15	PHI	28	58	2	10	12	-5	0.43	48.7%	7.1	-0.3	1.7	0.0	1.4
2015-16	PHI	29	57	3	13	15					0.3	2.3	0.0	2.5

Being labeled as a "buyer beware" by some experts due to his overusage and poor possession numbers with the Islanders did not stop the Flyers from trading for Andrew MacDonald and promptly signing him to a six-year, $30 million contract in late 2013-14. Skeptics were proven right, as MacDonald did not remotely come close to living up to his money value in 2014-15. Poor neutral zone defending from the former Moncton Wildcat allowed opponents to bullrush the offensive zone with ease and usually left the Flyers on their heels deep in their own end. His inconsistent play even led to his being healthy scratched for a stretch in February. Injuries also forced MacDonald to miss almost a third of the season. His overpayment makes him nearly impossible to move off the roster for the next couple of seasons, leaving the front office and fans alike feeling buyer's remorse.

Brandon Manning							LD						PHI
Season	Team	Age	GP	G	A	Pts	+/-	ESP/60	AdjCF%	iCF/60	OGVT	DGVT	SGVT	GVT
2012-13	PHI	22	6	0	2	2	4	1.36	43.8%	6.2	0.3	0.7	0.0	1.1
2014-15	PHI	24	11	0	3	3	3	1.14	49.5%	8.1	0.6	0.7	0.0	1.3
2015-16	PHI	25	29	2	6	8					0.7	1.1	0.0	1.8

Brandon Manning returned for an 11-game stint with the Flyers late in 2014-15, in his first appearance with the orange and black since 2013. Manning was a quality offensive defenseman with Lehigh Valley, earning an AHL All-Star appearance as he put up 11 goals and 32 assists. With the Flyers, he saw more than 17 minutes of ice-time and was a positive possession player. The former captain of the then-Chilliwack Bruins made enough of an impression to re-sign with Philadelphia on a one-year deal, ensuring that Manning will at least be given an opportunity to make the team in training camp.

Luke Schenn							RD						PHI
Season	Team	Age	GP	G	A	Pts	+/-	ESP/60	AdjCF%	iCF/60	OGVT	DGVT	SGVT	GVT
2012-13	PHI	23	47	3	8	11	3	0.75	50.3%	10.2	0.7	4.0	0.0	4.7
2013-14	PHI	24	79	4	8	12	0	0.58	47.8%	9.6	-0.1	2.6	0.0	2.6
2014-15	PHI	25	58	3	11	14	-2	0.92	50.4%	9.8	0.7	2.9	0.0	3.6
2015-16	PHI	26	60	4	12	15					0.8	2.9	0.0	3.6

While Luke Schenn has shown flashes of top-four potential, the former Maple Leaf has not been able to live up to the expectations as the return in the trade for James van Riemsdyk. Brayden's big brother entered the season looking to bounce back from a forgettable 2013-14 campaign and find the form he had early in his career. Schenn was somewhat adequate, seeing his possession numbers out of the red and his penalties down. Despite appearing in only 58 games, the 25-year-old still finished among the top 50 in hits. The big blueliner has his most important season as a professional coming up, looking to prove his worth to not just the Flyers, but to the entire league as he enters the final year of his contract.

Nick Schultz							LD						PHI
Season	Team	Age	GP	G	A	Pts	+/-	ESP/60	AdjCF%	iCF/60	OGVT	DGVT	SGVT	GVT
2012-13	EDM	30	48	1	8	9	-13	0.70	45.8%	5.3	-0.1	0.0	0.0	-0.1
2013-14	EDM, CBJ	31	69	0	5	5	-13	0.25	41.1%	4.4	-1.9	1.4	0.0	-0.4
2014-15	PHI	32	80	2	13	15	2	0.65	47.3%	6.8	0.1	3.9	0.0	4.0
2015-16	PHI	33	59	2	8	10					-0.4	2.6	0.0	2.3

Brought in by the Flyers during the offseason with the intention of adding depth to their defensive corps, Nick Schultz surprised many by turning in his most consistent season in years. Injuries and poor play by the defense thrust Schultz into the regular lineup, registering about 19 minutes of ice-time and playing at least 80 games for the first time in five seasons. Despite his passable play, Schultz still took more than three times as many penalties as he drew and his possession numbers were laughable. Naturally, the Flyers rewarded him with a two-year extension at a $2.3 million annual cap hit, a curious decision considering the team's always-fragile cap situation and the overall uncertainty of his ability to repeat the performance.

Mark Streit							LD						PHI
Season	Team	Age	GP	G	A	Pts	+/-	ESP/60	AdjCF%	iCF/60	OGVT	DGVT	SGVT	GVT
2012-13	NYI	35	48	6	21	27	-14	1.10	49.5%	8.0	4.3	0.0	0.0	4.3
2013-14	PHI	36	82	10	34	44	3	1.21	50.4%	7.3	8.7	2.4	0.0	11.1
2014-15	PHI	37	81	9	43	52	-8	0.88	49.3%	7.6	8.0	1.9	0.0	9.9
2015-16	PHI	38	62	7	28	35					5.2	2.4	0.0	7.6

Even though the loss of Kimmo Timonen was crushing both offensively and defensively, the play of Mark Streit helped recoup those losses as he settled in as the Flyers' top defenseman by default. The Swiss Olympian went on to have his best statistical season since his 2008-09 campaign with Montreal. Streit quarterbacked one of the top power-play units in the league; his 5.47 power-play points per 60 minutes was amongst the NHL's best, and his 9.9 GVT was in the upper echelon of NHL defensemen. With the departures of Timonen and Braydon Coburn, Streit enters next season as the team's clear number-one defenseman—unfortunately more of a testament to the state of the Philadelphia blueline rather than to his level of play.

GOALTENDERS

Ray Emery — G — Free Agent

Season	Team	Age	GP	W	L	OT	GAA	Sv%	ESSV%	QS%	GGVT	DGVT	SGVT	GVT
2012-13	CHI	30	21	17	1	0	1.94	.922	.927	68.4%	5.8	0.8	0.9	7.4
2013-14	PHI	31	28	9	12	2	2.96	.903	.920	57.1%	-2.7	-0.3	-2.5	-5.5
2014-15	PHI	32	31	10	11	7	3.06	.894	.913	52.0%	-9.3	0.1	-1.6	-10.8
2015-16	Free Agent	33	18					.906			-3.1	-0.1	-0.4	-3.6

After providing some sound relief for an injured Steve Mason in the 2014 playoffs, Ray Emery's services were retained for another season. However, "Razor" was inconsistent in his 31 appearances as he struggled to find his form. His sub-.900 save percentage and poor lateral movement, due years of hip problems, coupled with a below-par defense in front of him was the writing on the wall. The Flyers chose to go with the younger Michal Neuvirth to back up Mason for 2015-16.

Steve Mason — G — PHI

Season	Team	Age	GP	W	L	OT	GAA	Sv%	ESSV%	QS%	GGVT	DGVT	SGVT	GVT
2012-13	CBJ, PHI	24	20	7	8	1	2.59	.916	.911	41.2%	4.4	-0.4	0.0	4.0
2013-14	PHI	25	61	33	18	7	2.50	.917	.923	58.3%	14.3	-0.5	-0.8	13.1
2014-15	PHI	26	51	18	18	11	2.25	.928	.940	60.4%	22.9	-0.8	-3.5	18.6
2015-16	PHI	27	48					.918			11.4	-0.4	-0.3	10.7

While last season as a whole was a disappointment for the Flyers, for Steve Mason, it was a massive success. Under a microscope since his arrival in Philadelphia at the end of the 2012-13 season, Mason produced his best season as a professional. The former Calder Trophy winner finally showed some consistency in goal on his way to a .928 save percentage and a spectacular .940 even-strength save percentage—the best in the NHL. Despite missing three weeks with a lower-body injury, Mason still appeared in 51 games and was a workhorse due to unreliable backup play. At a $4.1 million dollar cap hit, Mason is in the bottom third of NHL starting goalies in that regard, making him one of the more valuable players at his position. For once, it appears that goaltending is the least of worries for the Flyers.

Rob Zepp — G — Free Agent

Season	Team	Age	GP	W	L	OT	GAA	Sv%	ESSV%	QS%	GGVT	DGVT	SGVT	GVT
2014-15	PHI	33	10	5	2	0	2.89	.888	.894	33.3%	-3.9	0.3	0.5	-3.0
2015-16	Free Agent	34	15					.912			0.4	0.1	0.1	0.6

A long-time journeyman who bounced back from the minors and overseas multiple times, Rob Zepp made his long-awaited NHL debut in 2014-15. In his first game, against the Winnipeg Jets, the German goaltender made 25 saves as the Flyers were able to "win one for the Zepper" in a 4-3 comeback win in overtime. With the victory, Zepp became the oldest netminder in nearly 90 years to win in his debut, at the ripe old age of 33. Overall, he appeared in seven contests before returning back to Lehigh Valley. It was a feel-good story for the organization in what was a real bad year.

Erik Yost

Pittsburgh Penguins

The 2014-15 season brought sweeping changes to the Pittsburgh Penguins. The long-time management and coaching duo of Ray Shero and Dan Bylsma were relieved from their positions, replaced by former Hurricanes general manager Jim Rutherford and first-time NHL head coach Mike Johnston.

After the somewhat curious selection of Rutherford to lead the front office—well-regarded AGM Jason Botterill was considered a more progressive choice—the hiring process received further criticism: upper management left Bylsma "twisting in the wind" for a month after Shero's removal, possibly to deter him from immediately moving to another franchise. Further, during the search to replace Bylsma, Rutherford publicly claimed Pittsburgh had their man for the job. The problem was the man they chose—Willie Desjardins—embarrassingly elected to coach the Vancouver Canucks instead. The end result was a perception that Pittsburgh had to "settle" for Mike Johnston.

The good news for Pittsburgh fans was that they "settled" on a coach who valued puck possession and a modern approach the game, leading to tangible improvements for the team. Last season, Pittsburgh was the third-best score-adjusted Fenwick team (53.9%), a big step forward from their 2013-14 edition, which very literally ranked a middle-of-the-road 16th (50.0%).

The reason for the jump in possession was the style Johnston brought to the club, making major changes in how the Penguins formulated their attack. While there is no denying that Bylsma's teams frequently had success on the possession front, his style leaned more in the direction of a dump-and-chase mentality. Bylsma teams were also known for getting the puck out of the zone as quickly as possible while stretching forwards to the far blue line for chip-ins.

Under Johnston, Pittsburgh improved their puck-support game by incorporating more 10-15 foot passes rather than the longer stretch passes that often flat-footed the receiver, assuming the pass connected in the first place. The objective changed from pushing the puck north in a hurry to moving the puck up the ice with possession even if it took a bit longer to accomplish. This led to the Pens skating the puck with speed through the neutral zone, resulting in more controlled defensive zone exits as well as more controlled offensive zone entries. Why is that important? Because teams that control their zone exits and entries are teams that control the game.

The change in tactics had a positive impact on the possession front for nearly

PENGUINS IN A BOX

Last Season

Goals For	221	t-18th
Goals Against	210	t-9th
GVT	11	16th
Points	98	15th
Playoffs	Lost Conference Quarterfinal	

Pittsburgh was the best team in the league until Christmas...and then the wheels fell off.

Three-Year Record

GVT	99	5th
Points	279	4th
Playoffs	3 Appearances, 16 Wins	

VUKOTA Projections

Goals For	237	3rd
Goals Against	223	21st
GVT	14	7th
Points	96	7th

If the 2013-14 Penguins show up this season, they will be a threat. If the 2014-15 Penguins come to play, there will be golf in April.

Top Three Prospects

D. Pouliot (D), A. Clendening (D), D. Sprong (F)

every player on the roster in both 2013-14 and 2014-15, from highly-skilled players like Sidney Crosby, Evgeni Malkin, and Kris Letang to more deliberate lower-line players who perennially struggled with possession, like Brandon Sutter, Rob Scuderi, and Craig Adams.

Score-adjusted Fenwick, 2013-14 and 2014-15

Player	2013-14	2014-15	Change
Beau Bennett	55.1%	55.0%	-0.1%
Sidney Crosby	54.0%	56.0%	+2.0%
Chris Kunitz	53.4%	56.7%	+3.3%
Evgeni Malkin	52.8%	54.3%	+1.5%
Paul Martin	52.3%	53.8%	+1.5%
Simon Despres	51.9%	52.8%	+0.9%
Olli Maatta	51.7%	51.5%	-0.2%
Kris Letang	50.4%	56.0%	+5.6%
Robert Bortuzzo	46.6%	52.2%	+5.6%
Brandon Sutter	44.8%	50.7%	+5.9%
Rob Scuderi	44.7%	51.6%	+6.9%
Craig Adams	43.5%	48.9%	+5.4%
Zach Sill	34.9%	45.0%	+10.1%
Team overall	50.0%	53.9%	+3.9%

So if possession was a strength and goaltender Marc-Andre Fleury performed as an above-average starter, what went wrong for the Penguins in 2014-15? The same issue which has plagued the franchise since winning the Stanley Cup in 2009: injuries. Since 2008-09, Pittsburgh has led the league in man-games lost, very problematic in a hard-cap salary system. When teams are hit hard by injuries, they are limited in their ability to replace those players due to cap space.

Not all man-games lost are created equal. Unfortunately, Pittsburgh has suffered injuries to many key players over the course of time. While soft-tissue injuries are a part of the normal wear and tear of NHL hockey, the Penguins have been on the wrong end of non-hockey-related injuries for the past several seasons. For instance, Pittsburgh suffered from a mumps outbreak which sidelined Crosby, Olli Maatta, Beau Bennett, Steve Downie, and Thomas Greiss. Then, Maatta not only reinjured his surgically-repaired shoulder, but was diagnosed with thyroid cancer early in the season. Letang has been sidelined by multiple concussions, not to mention the stroke suffered late in 2013-14. Crosby famously missed chunks of two seasons with a concussion, followed up with a broken jaw from a wayward Brooks Orpik slapshot. Blood clots essentially put an end to goaltender Tomas Vokoun's career; they also cost Pascal Dupuis his 2014-15 season after he had rebounded from an ACL tear. Most of these ailments fall outside the realm of what is considered normal and preventable. The unfortunate string of bad luck has impacted Pittsburgh's ability to compete at a high level.

Man-games lost, Pittsburgh vs. Cup finalists

Season	Pittsburgh	East finalist	West finalist
2009-10	182	205 (PHI)	219 (CHI)
2010-11	350	105 (BOS)	360 (VAN)
2011-12	359	245 (NJD)	168 (LAK)
2012-13	82	51 (BOS)	94 (CHI)
2013-14	529	122 (NYR)	100 (LAK)
2014-15	343	168 (TBL)	158 (CHI)
Average	353	149	183

There is a correlation between man-games lost and the recent run of Stanley Cup winners. Since Pittsburgh's 2009 championship, the three teams that have won the Stanley Cup—Chicago, Los Angeles, Boston—rank no lower than fourth in man-games lost. The one season where Pittsburgh was able to keep their injury numbers in check was the shortened 2012-13 campaign—the only time the Penguins were able to make a return to the Conference Final.

As the possession metrics indicated, Pittsburgh showed signs of being a top-level team under Johnston—despite an eighth-place finish in the East and a first-round exit against the Rangers. Rutherford needs to continue to improve the depth which surrounds their core of Crosby, Malkin, and Letang—high-scoring Phil Kessel is an intriguing addition, but the departure of top-pairing defenseman Paul Martin adds a major question mark on the blue line—but even if he is successful, it won't matter if the team continues to be hurt all the time. If the Penguins cannot stay healthy, they are unlikely to return to glory days. The bad luck has to end at some point, right?

Ryan Wilson

PITTSBURGH PENGUINS

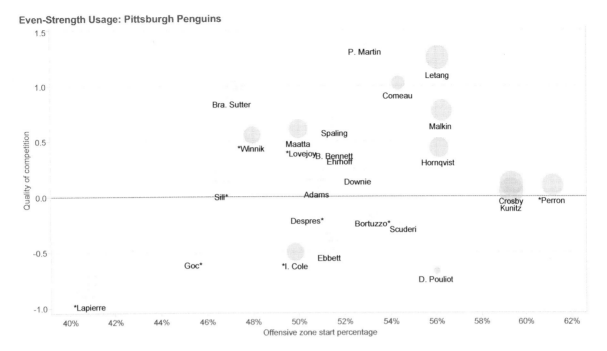

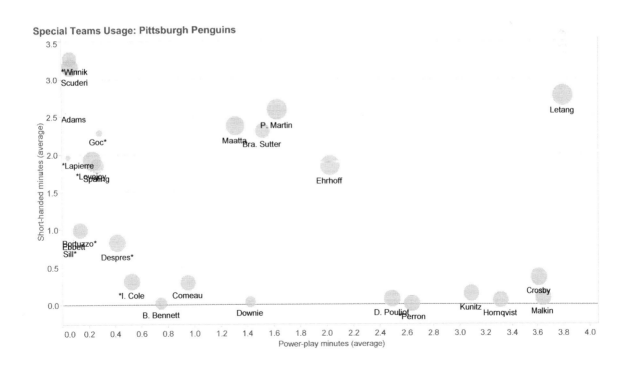

PITTSBURGH PENGUINS

Offensive Profile: Pittsburgh Penguins

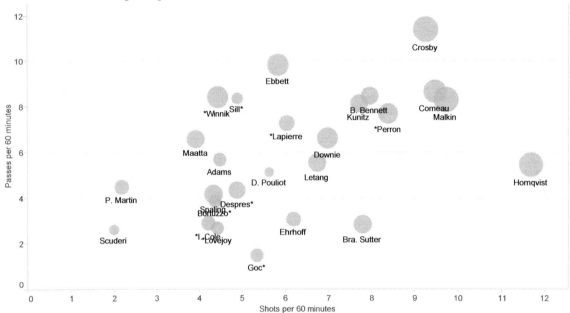

Cap Efficiency: Pittsburgh Penguins

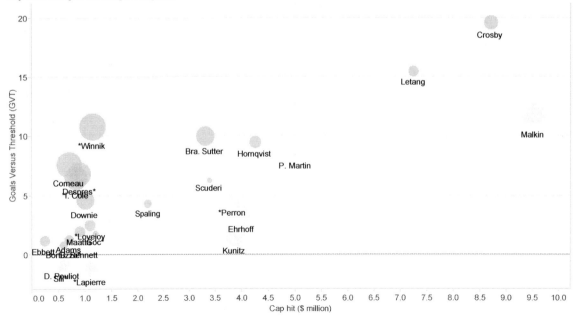

FORWARDS

Craig Adams								RW						Free Agent
Season	Team	Age	GP	G	A	Pts	+/-	ESP/60	AdjCF%	iCF/60	OGVT	DGVT	SGVT	GVT
2012-13	PIT	35	48	3	6	9	-1	1.18	44.5%	9.6	0.0	1.1	0.0	1.1
2013-14	PIT	36	82	5	6	11	-16	0.86	41.9%	9.3	-3.0	4.1	0.0	1.0
2014-15	PIT	37	70	1	6	7	-1	0.72	48.9%	8.3	-2.1	3.4	0.0	1.3
2015-16	Free Agent	38	57	3	5	7					-1.2	2.1	0.0	0.9

It was a record-breaking year for Craig Adams. Over the past few seasons, the Harvard graduate compiled a streak of 319 consecutive games played which concluded on December 18. The streak broke Ron Shock's previous mark of 313 consecutive games played, to set Pittsburgh's all-time record. While playing in 319 consecutive games is an incredible feat for a player in a fast, demanding, physical sport like hockey, it is more incredible that both the coaching staff and management actively kept him in the lineup for so long; the 37-year-old bottom-line grinder only registered 57 points during the streak. With his foot speed in clear decline, Adams no longer thrives in the role he is best known for, penalty killing.

Beau Bennett								LW/RW						PIT
Season	Team	Age	GP	G	A	Pts	+/-	ESP/60	AdjCF%	iCF/60	OGVT	DGVT	SGVT	GVT
2012-13	PIT	21	26	3	11	14	7	1.95	48.4%	10.5	1.8	0.8	0.0	2.5
2013-14	PIT	22	21	3	4	7	-2	1.59	58.4%	10.0	0.2	0.3	-0.3	0.2
2014-15	PIT	23	49	4	8	12	-1	1.25	53.5%	13.5	-0.2	1.1	-0.3	0.6
2015-16	PIT	24	48	7	10	17					0.6	1.3	0.0	1.9

The story of Beau Bennett's career to this point has been injuries. Unfortunately, 2014-15 was no exception. The six-foot-two Californian started his offseason by successfully rehabbing a wrist injury and came to training camp looking solid. However, a knee injury suffered at the end of camp caused him to miss the first 13 games of the year. Later in the season, he injured his other knee while also contracting mumps during that recovery. When Bennett is healthy—knock on wood—he has proven to be a very good possession player when given talented linemates. The problem is that the University of Denver product spent most of the season skating alongside less-skilled teammates, which put an artificial ceiling on his potential. Bennett will need to stay healthy and contribute in 2015-16, or he may find himself in another organization.

Blake Comeau								LW						COL
Season	Team	Age	GP	G	A	Pts	+/-	ESP/60	AdjCF%	iCF/60	OGVT	DGVT	SGVT	GVT
2012-13	CGY, CBJ	26	42	6	6	12	-4	1.45	48.6%	11.5	1.0	1.3	0.0	2.3
2013-14	CBJ	27	61	5	11	16	-2	1.37	53.4%	16.2	0.1	1.3	0.0	1.4
2014-15	PIT	28	61	16	15	31	6	2.10	53.8%	17.5	5.1	2.6	0.0	7.6
2015-16	COL	29	58	13	14	27					2.7	1.8	0.0	4.5

One of the multiple one-year deals that new general manager Jim Rutherford handed out last summer was to Blake Comeau. His $700,000 investment paid dividends. Originally signed as bottom-six help, Comeau found himself playing on a line with all-world center Evgeni Malkin, resulting in the former Islander, Flame, and Blue Jacket potting 16 goals, the same total as his previous three seasons combined. However, a midseason wrist injury caused Comeau to miss time and impacted his ability to finish. His goal-scoring ability was literally cut in half. Before the injury, he averaged 0.34 goals per game; that number dropped to 0.17 post-injury. Even in the diminished capacity, Comeau was a very good signing for Pittsburgh.

Sidney Crosby								C					PIT
Season	Team	Age	GP	G	A	Pts	+/-	ESP/60	AdjCF%	iCF/60	OGVT	DGVT	SGVT	GVT
2012-13	PIT	25	36	15	41	56	26	4.05	57.4%	15.6	12.0	2.7	1.0	15.7
2013-14	PIT	26	80	36	68	104	18	2.88	53.6%	13.4	21.6	4.1	0.4	26.1
2014-15	PIT	27	77	28	56	84	5	2.58	56.6%	14.3	15.7	1.8	2.0	19.6
2015-16	PIT	28	73	30	52	81					12.9	2.5	0.1	15.6

Sidney Crosby was his usual self in 2014-15. Despite some claiming it was a "down year," he led the league with 1.09 points per game, missing out on another Art Ross Trophy by three points. The Cole Harbor, Nova Scotia native continued to dominate play at even strength, to the tune of a 56.1% score-adjusted Fenwick. Crosby did see a sizable dip in his raw point totals, going from 104 points in 2013-14 (the league's only 100-point scorer; in fact, the league's only 90-point scorer) to 84 in 2014-15. The state of the league's officiating is one variable at play, but his ice-time is another. Crosby played 19:58 under new head coach Mike Johnston, a full two minutes less than the 21:58 he saw under Dan Bylsma. Crosby finished his year winning gold at the World Championships for Team Canada. By doing so, he joined the quadruple-gold club: winning the Stanley Cup, Olympics, World Juniors, and the World Championships. He is the only player ever to win those events along with earning both the Art Ross and Hart Trophies.

Steve Downie								RW/LW					ARI
Season	Team	Age	GP	G	A	Pts	+/-	ESP/60	AdjCF%	iCF/60	OGVT	DGVT	SGVT	GVT
2012-13	COL	25	2	0	1	1	1	3.90	47.3%	15.0	0.2	0.1	0.0	0.3
2013-14	COL, PHI	26	62	4	20	24	1	1.41	50.7%	10.9	0.0	0.9	0.0	1.0
2014-15	PIT	27	72	14	14	28	2	1.75	49.9%	11.2	3.5	1.4	-0.3	4.6
2015-16	ARI	28	61	10	15	25					1.7	1.3	0.0	2.9

One of the more emotional players in the NHL, Steve Downie was Pittsburgh's version of Dr. Jeckyll and Mr. Hyde. On one hand, you have a player who is able to put up a fringe top-six level of 1.75 even-strength points per 60 minutes, and on the other hand, you have a player who led the league in minor penalties with 49. The problem with signing a player like Downie is that you never know which guy is going to show up on any given shift. Given this unpredictability, it is no wonder that he was only able to land a one-year deal worth $1.1 million with struggling Arizona.

Pascal Dupuis								RW					PIT
Season	Team	Age	GP	G	A	Pts	+/-	ESP/60	AdjCF%	iCF/60	OGVT	DGVT	SGVT	GVT
2012-13	PIT	33	48	20	18	38	31	2.88	53.2%	19.8	7.9	4.1	-0.3	11.7
2013-14	PIT	34	39	7	13	20	6	1.99	54.9%	15.8	2.2	2.7	-0.3	4.7
2014-15	PIT	35	16	6	5	11	2	2.07	57.1%	15.9	2.0	0.9	0.0	2.9
2015-16	PIT	36	39	8	11	19					2.0	1.4	0.0	3.3

Pascal Dupuis is just the latest Pittsburgh player to suffer from a fluke season-ending health ailment. In November, Dupuis was diagnosed with a blood clot in his lung that effectively ended his 2014-15 season. The Penguins missed Dupuis' on-ice contributions, which included an impressive 2.07 even-strength points per 60 minutes in the 16 games which he was able to suit up for. It was not just Dupuis' hockey ability Pittsburgh missed, but the off-the-ice persona he brings to the room. The 14-year veteran is known as one of the more important character guys in the Pittsburgh locker room. With a clean bill of health, the former Thrasher will be welcomed back with open arms in 2015-16.

Andrew Ebbett							LW						Swiss
Season	Team	Age	GP	G	A	Pts	+/-	ESP/60	AdjCF%	iCF/60	OGVT	DGVT	SGVT	GVT
2012-13	VAN	29	28	1	5	6	-1	1.17	43.2%	8.7	-0.3	0.9	0.0	0.6
2013-14	PIT	30	9	0	1	1	-4	0.66	41.1%	10.8	-0.4	-0.2	0.0	-0.6
2014-15	PIT	31	24	1	5	6	1	1.86	48.3%	10.8	0.3	0.9	0.0	1.2
2015-16	Swiss	32	34	4	7	11					0.5	0.9	0.0	1.4

These days, Andrew Ebbett is best served providing depth to an organization's AHL team. At the NHL level, Teemu Selanne's one-time linemate has been a low-impact fourth-line player in recent years. The five-foot-nine Michigan grad has played 224 career games for six NHL teams, including the 24 games he contributed in 2014-15. His past big-league experience makes him an ideal candidate for promotion from the AHL when injuries hit.

Bobby Farnham							RW							PIT
Season	Team	Age	GP	G	A	Pts	+/-	ESP/60	AdjCF%	iCF/60	OGVT	DGVT	SGVT	GVT
2014-15	PIT	25	11	0	0	0	0	0.00	44.6%	9.2	-0.5	0.1	0.0	-0.4
2015-16	PIT	26	30	4	5	9					0.2	0.6	0.0	0.8

A fan favorite in Wilkes-Barre/Scranton, Bobby Farnham is a human tornado. His style of play brings tons of energy and has him flying all over the ice. Alas, working hard is not the same as working smart, and his hard work did not translate to positive possession metrics at the NHL level. His energy does, however, lead to drawing penalties. The five-foot-ten mini-wrecking ball drew 3.0 penalties per 60 minutes in 2014-15, a team best for Pittsburgh.

Patric Hornqvist							RW/LW							PIT
Season	Team	Age	GP	G	A	Pts	+/-	ESP/60	AdjCF%	iCF/60	OGVT	DGVT	SGVT	GVT
2012-13	NSH	26	24	4	10	14	-1	1.30	49.8%	16.9	1.7	0.6	-0.3	2.0
2013-14	NSH	27	76	22	31	53	1	2.04	50.7%	18.3	7.4	2.8	-0.3	9.9
2014-15	PIT	28	64	25	26	51	12	2.36	55.7%	19.1	7.9	1.9	-0.3	9.5
2015-16	PIT	29	68	25	28	53					7.2	2.2	0.0	9.4

Patric Hornqvist, the shot-volume machine from Sweden, was acquired in the blockbuster trade that saw former 40-goal scorer James Neal move on to Nashville, after management had soured on the former Star. Hornqvist paced the team with 3.4 shots per game while flanking either Crosby or Malkin. His propensity to fire the puck was rewarded with 25 goals, despite missing 18 games due to injury. Hornqvist's nose for the net was also a welcome addition for the Penguins, who were looking for more of a netfront presence to complement the two star centers. His 0.80 points per game was a career best. Staying healthy may be the only thing keeping the 2005 seventh rounder from achieving his second-career 30-goal season.

Chris Kunitz — LW — PIT

Season	Team	Age	GP	G	A	Pts	+/-	ESP/60	AdjCF%	iCF/60	OGVT	DGVT	SGVT	GVT
2012-13	PIT	33	48	22	30	52	30	3.20	55.5%	13.2	11.5	3.1	0.0	14.5
2013-14	PIT	34	78	35	33	68	25	2.31	52.9%	14.0	11.9	4.1	0.3	16.4
2014-15	PIT	35	74	17	23	40	2	1.27	57.4%	13.3	1.4	0.8	-0.5	1.7
2015-16	PIT	36	65	17	22	39					3.6	1.6	0.0	5.2

Over the years, Chris Kunitz has been one of the most reliable players on Pittsburgh's roster. The trusty sidekick of Sidney Crosby has shown a consistent ability to score goals on the top line. Last season started off at status quo, with Kunitz notching 15 goals in his first 41 games. Things then inexplicably fell apart in the goal-scoring department. The Ferris State graduate finished the year finding the back of the net only twice in the final 32 games. If goal scoring does not rebound for Kunitz in the future, he can continue to be productive by leaning on his team-leading 56.4% score-adjusted Fenwick. However, the 2014 Olympic gold medalist will be 36 years old when 2015-16 rolls around, so we have probably already seen the best of what he can offer.

Maxim Lapierre — C — SHL

Season	Team	Age	GP	G	A	Pts	+/-	ESP/60	AdjCF%	iCF/60	OGVT	DGVT	SGVT	GVT
2012-13	VAN	27	48	4	6	10	-6	1.15	43.1%	9.8	-0.5	1.6	0.7	1.8
2013-14	STL	28	71	9	6	15	-3	1.31	46.1%	11.6	0.4	2.2	-0.3	2.4
2014-15	STL, PIT	29	80	2	9	11	-15	0.95	44.7%	10.8	-2.8	1.6	0.0	-1.2
2015-16	SHL	30	60	4	7	10					-1.4	1.5	0.0	0.2

Max Lapierre was acquired by Rutherford in a midseason deal that saw Marcel Goc shipped off to St. Louis in a hockey trade of centermen. The thinking behind the move was for Pittsburgh to acquire a player who could harass the opposition while providing grit. What they received was a penalty-killing specialist who struggles to keep up at even strength. Consequently, Lapierre had only two points in 35 regular-season games while being a liability on the possession front. His 45.6% score-adjusted Fenwick was troubling, considering he was sheltered by his coach from the best that other teams had to offer. Targeting Lapierre via trade would not qualify as a statistically-progressive move by the analytics-touting front office.

Evgeni Malkin — C/RW — PIT

Season	Team	Age	GP	G	A	Pts	+/-	ESP/60	AdjCF%	iCF/60	OGVT	DGVT	SGVT	GVT
2012-13	PIT	26	31	9	24	33	5	1.91	57.8%	16.0	6.2	0.5	0.2	6.9
2013-14	PIT	27	60	23	49	72	10	2.72	53.7%	11.8	13.7	2.5	1.2	17.5
2014-15	PIT	28	69	28	42	70	-2	2.51	56.0%	15.5	11.8	0.7	-0.7	11.7
2015-16	PIT	29	67	26	39	65					9.4	1.8	0.0	11.2

When Evgeni Malkin is on his game, very few players in the world can match his brilliance. The problem is that he can only achieve this brilliance when he is on the ice. To that point, Malkin has only hit the 70-game mark in four out of eight non-lockout seasons. When "the Russian Lemieux" was on the ice in 2014-15, he was an impact player: he led all Pittsburgh players with an awesome 2.51 even-strength points per 60 minutes. Surprisingly, one area where Malkin can improve is on the power play. Over his first four seasons in the league, he averaged 15 power-play goals per year, while the last four non-lockout seasons saw that average drop to 8.25, nearly half. Despite that anomaly, "Geno Machino" still has many good years left and will remain one of the best players on the planet for the foreseeable future.

Jayson Megna — LW/C — NYR

Season	Team	Age	GP	G	A	Pts	+/-	ESP/60	AdjCF%	iCF/60	OGVT	DGVT	SGVT	GVT
2013-14	PIT	23	36	5	4	9	1	1.45	46.0%	10.2	0.6	0.8	0.0	1.4
2014-15	PIT	24	12	0	1	1	-2	0.48	44.4%	10.2	-0.6	0.2	0.0	-0.4
2015-16	NYR	25	37	6	7	12					0.3	0.9	0.0	1.2

Known as "Megnatron" by some, Jayson Megna had been given multiple chances to crack Pittsburgh's roster, but had not done much with those opportunities. The native of Fort Lauderdale, Florida is a fast skater with good size, but it has not translated to the NHL. Poor possession and minimal offense has tainted his time in Pittsburgh, leading to other minor-league options being tapped for promotions in his stead. Megna has taken the situation in stride, performing at a high level in the AHL. He led Wilkes-Barre/Scranton with 26 goals scored in 2014-15.

David Perron — LW/RW — PIT

Season	Team	Age	GP	G	A	Pts	+/-	ESP/60	AdjCF%	iCF/60	OGVT	DGVT	SGVT	GVT
2012-13	STL	24	48	10	15	25	0	1.61	53.0%	9.7	2.3	2.2	0.2	4.8
2013-14	EDM	25	78	28	29	57	-16	2.09	44.6%	14.7	9.1	1.1	0.7	10.9
2014-15	EDM, PIT	26	81	17	24	41	-25	1.62	54.2%	12.9	2.8	0.4	1.4	4.6
2015-16	PIT	27	68	18	24	42					4.3	1.2	0.1	5.6

Immediately after being traded away from Edmonton to Pittsburgh, it looked like David Perron had shackles taken off of him. The Sherbrooke, Quebec native scored nine goals and 13 points in his first 16 games with the Penguins. His super-slick hands and ability to battle in the corners with tenacity proved to be a positive match with superstar center Sidney Crosby. However, as the season progressed, Perron's numbers regressed. He only had two assists in Pittsburgh's final 17 games of the season, playoffs included. One explanation could be the fact that he was playing with a broken rib to close out the campaign. However, the injury did not negatively impact his possession game: Perron had an amazing score-adjusted Fenwick of 57.4% with Pittsburgh. (Although that might lead you to believe the Crosby guy is pretty good.)

Bryan Rust — RW/LW — PIT

Season	Team	Age	GP	G	A	Pts	+/-	ESP/60	AdjCF%	iCF/60	OGVT	DGVT	SGVT	GVT
2014-15	PIT	22	14	1	1	2	-3	0.74	50.9%	16.5	-0.9	0.0	0.0	-1.0
2015-16	PIT	23	32	6	6	12					0.4	0.6	0.0	1.0

Bryan Rust is a 2010 third-round pick out of Notre Dame who saw 14 games of NHL action in his first full professional season. He scored his first and only big-league goal in his second career game. Rust was returned to Wilkes-Barre/Scranton to make room for waiver acquisition Marc Arcobello, and he did not see any more time at the NHL level. Rust had solid possession numbers over his run in Pittsburgh, hinting he could be a candidate for cheap fourth-line help in 2015-16.

Nick Spaling — LW/C — TOR

Season	Team	Age	GP	G	A	Pts	+/-	ESP/60	AdjCF%	iCF/60	OGVT	DGVT	SGVT	GVT
2012-13	NSH	24	47	9	4	13	-10	0.94	40.9%	9.3	0.1	1.2	0.0	1.3
2013-14	NSH	25	71	13	19	32	2	1.59	45.5%	7.8	3.1	3.6	0.0	6.6
2014-15	PIT	26	82	9	18	27	-2	1.45	52.3%	9.1	0.5	3.8	0.0	4.3
2015-16	TOR	27	68	11	18	28					1.4	2.8	0.0	4.2

Pittsburgh acquired Nick Spaling in the James Neal trade at the 2014 NHL Entry Draft. The hope was that Spaling would improve Pittsburgh's ailing bottom-six forward depth. The change of scenery did wonders for Spaling's possession percentage, as his score-adjusted Fenwick jumped from 45.8% in 2013-14 all the way up to 52.8%. Yet while his raw possession percentage improved, he remained a negative relative possession player. It could be argued that his $2.2 million salary is higher than the value Pittsburgh gets in return. Pittsburgh is a cap-ceiling team, so it is important where they allocate money for depth players. Every cent counts, and Spaling's production could likely be replaced by a player making a third of his salary. The Penguins agreed, shipping him off to Toronto in the blockbuster Phil Kessel deal.

Brandon Sutter — C/RW — VAN

Season	Team	Age	GP	G	A	Pts	+/-	ESP/60	AdjCF%	iCF/60	OGVT	DGVT	SGVT	GVT
2012-13	PIT	23	48	11	8	19	3	1.41	43.6%	12.0	2.9	1.4	0.0	4.3
2013-14	PIT	24	81	13	13	26	-9	1.08	43.5%	11.5	2.3	3.5	1.2	7.0
2014-15	PIT	25	80	21	12	33	6	1.33	49.9%	12.9	4.9	5.2	-0.2	10.0
2015-16	VAN	26	70	18	15	33					3.5	3.3	0.0	6.8

Brandon Sutter was one of the more polarizing players with Pittsburgh's fanbase. Some pointed to his 21 goals scored in 2014-15, claiming it justified his $3.3 million salary, while others highlighted his below-average possession metrics as a reason for his being overvalued. The goals are nice, but his inability to drive possession throughout his Pittsburgh tenure consistently forced Crosby into more difficult usage. Since his arrival, Sutter's Fenwick-for percentage has been a paltry 46.6%. The Penguins needed more from Sutter, who was sent to Vancouver in an exchange that saw young center Nick Bonino and unproven defenseman Adam Clendening come to the Steel City.

Dominik Uher — C/LW — PIT

Season	Team	Age	GP	G	A	Pts	+/-	ESP/60	AdjCF%	iCF/60	OGVT	DGVT	SGVT	GVT
2014-15	PIT	22	2	0	0	0	-1	0.00	40.7%	0.0	-0.2	-0.1	0.0	-0.2
2015-16	PIT	23	26	5	6	10					0.7	0.5	0.0	1.2

Former Spokane Chief Dominik Uher was able to generate quality offense in the WHL. During his last two seasons with Spokane, the Czech native was a point-per-game player, 128 points in 128 games played. Since joining the AHL, he has been unable to recreate that offensive touch to say the least: with Wilkes-Barre/Scranton, he only has 30 points in 121 games. In an organization that desperately needs cheap forward depth, Uher remains an emergency call-up when the injury bug bites hard.

PITTSBURGH PENGUINS

Scott Wilson — LW/C — PIT

Season	Team	Age	GP	G	A	Pts	+/-	ESP/60	AdjCF%	iCF/60	OGVT	DGVT	SGVT	GVT
2014-15	PIT	22	1	0	0	0	0	0.00	23.7%	0.0	0.0	0.0	0.0	0.0
2015-16	PIT	23	27	4	6	10					0.3	0.6	0.0	0.9

Scott Wilson's NHL debut was over just as quickly as it started. He was injured in his first career game after playing only 4:21. The UMass-Lowell product did not play in another regular-season game for Pittsburgh in 2014-15, but he did find himself in three playoff games against the New York Rangers. Wilson has upside as a player who can provide some depth on the fourth line at a low cost. He could be Craig Adams' replacement.

Daniel Winnik — LW — TOR

Season	Team	Age	GP	G	A	Pts	+/-	ESP/60	AdjCF%	iCF/60	OGVT	DGVT	SGVT	GVT
2012-13	ANA	27	48	6	13	19	13	1.68	50.0%	11.8	1.8	3.3	0.0	5.1
2013-14	ANA	28	76	6	24	30	6	1.61	48.8%	11.8	3.2	2.9	0.0	6.1
2014-15	TOR, PIT	29	79	9	25	34	23	1.88	50.1%	8.9	4.7	6.1	0.0	10.8
2015-16	TOR	30	65	8	20	28					1.9	3.0	0.0	5.0

In what has become an annual tradition in Pittsburgh, the Penguins found themselves needing additional forward depth at the trade deadline. Enter: Daniel Winnik. Acquiring Winnik from Toronto came at the cost of second- and fourth-round picks. On its own, dealing away a second-round pick does not seem like a big deal. However, when you consider Pittsburgh's prospect pool was already limited due to prior deadline deals, and Winnik was entering free agency, you can see why Pittsburgh lacks impact players on entry-level contracts. The former Coyote, Av, Shark, and Duck was a productive possession player in the regular season for Pittsburgh, but he had the team's worst possession metrics in the playoffs. The key for the Penguins, moving forward, will be to acquire players like Winnik in free agency before they have to trade assets for them. Indeed, Winnik returned to his hometown of Toronto in the offseason, signing a two-year deal. See? That's how it is done.

DEFENSEMEN

Taylor Chorney — LD — WSH

Season	Team	Age	GP	G	A	Pts	+/-	ESP/60	AdjCF%	iCF/60	OGVT	DGVT	SGVT	GVT
2014-15	PIT	27	7	0	0	0	-1	0.00	53.6%	0.5	-0.2	-0.1	0.0	-0.2
2015-16	WSH	28	28	1	4	5					-0.1	0.8	0.0	0.7

Taylor Chorney has 68 NHL games played on his resume, earning that time with three different NHL franchises, Edmonton, St. Louis, and Pittsburgh. The 27-year-old Thunder Bay, Ontario native was able to earn some time in Pittsburgh after injuries decimated their defense corps. Chorney played in seven regular-season contests towards the end of the season, and all five playoff games. The Shattuck St. Mary's product is a nice depth player to stash in the AHL in case the big club needs to call on some quality reserves.

Ian Cole — LD — PIT

Season	Team	Age	GP	G	A	Pts	+/-	ESP/60	AdjCF%	iCF/60	OGVT	DGVT	SGVT	GVT
2012-13	STL	23	15	0	1	1	-4	0.23	52.5%	6.9	-0.7	0.3	0.0	-0.4
2013-14	STL	24	46	3	8	11	15	0.83	50.5%	9.5	1.8	3.2	0.0	5.0
2014-15	STL, PIT	25	74	5	12	17	14	0.86	54.8%	9.0	2.8	3.7	0.0	6.5
2015-16	PIT	26	63	4	12	16					1.6	3.0	0.0	4.6

After falling out of favor with St. Louis, Ian Cole was swapped at the deadline for physical third-pairing defenseman Robert Bortuzzo. Cole immediately found success with his new team, registering eight points in his first 20 games. In comparison, Cole had nine points in 54 games with St. Louis. Boxcar offense was not his only contribution; his possession game was excellent as well, with a 58.2% score-adjusted Fenwick after the trade. So far, the change of scenery has worked out well for both team and player.

Brian Dumoulin — LD — PIT

Season	Team	Age	GP	G	A	Pts	+/-	ESP/60	AdjCF%	iCF/60	OGVT	DGVT	SGVT	GVT
2013-14	PIT	22	6	0	1	1	1	0.65	44.0%	6.5	-0.2	0.6	0.0	0.4
2014-15	PIT	23	8	1	0	1	0	0.52	42.6%	2.4	-0.2	0.3	0.0	0.1
2015-16	PIT	24	31	2	5	7					-0.1	1.3	0.0	1.2

Six-foot-four Brian Dumoulin is another young defenseman in Pittsburgh's system whose NHL career has been postponed because of the volume of veteran defensemen in front of him. Dumoulin appeared in eight games during the regular season, notching his first career goal. Dumoulin struggled possession-wise, though. The good news is that the sample was small and his skating, puck skills, and size should lead to better success in the future.

Christian Ehrhoff — LD — LAK

Season	Team	Age	GP	G	A	Pts	+/-	ESP/60	AdjCF%	iCF/60	OGVT	DGVT	SGVT	GVT
2012-13	BUF	30	47	5	17	22	6	0.84	49.5%	9.9	2.0	1.8	0.0	3.8
2013-14	BUF	31	79	6	27	33	-27	0.77	44.2%	9.8	1.2	2.3	0.0	3.5
2014-15	PIT	32	49	3	11	14	8	0.82	51.9%	12.2	0.2	3.1	0.0	3.4
2015-16	LAK	33	58	5	18	23					1.8	3.3	0.0	5.1

Christian Ehrhoff was billed as one of the better unrestricted free agent signings of last summer. Pittsburgh was able to sign the German international to a very cap-friendly, one-year, $4.0 million deal—made possible by the enormous buyout Ehrhoff received from Buffalo. While the signing cannot be considered a mistake by the Penguins, it did not work out as planned. Ehrhoff was injured throughout the season, only skating in 49 regular-season games, while missing all five playoff contests. When healthy, Ehrhoff was not utilized on the man advantage, which could help explain his career-low 14 points. His perceived value may have taken a hit in 2014-15, but he is a productive puck-moving defenseman that can help a contending team. The Kings are betting on exactly that, having inked the long-time Shark over the summer.

Scott Harrington — LD — TOR

Season	Team	Age	GP	G	A	Pts	+/-	ESP/60	AdjCF%	iCF/60	OGVT	DGVT	SGVT	GVT
2014-15	PIT	21	10	0	0	0	-10	0.00	52.0%	6.6	-0.9	-1.1	0.0	-2.0
2015-16	TOR	22	27	2	4	6					-0.1	0.3	0.0	0.2

PITTSBURGH PENGUINS 349

A 2011 second-round pick from the London Knights, Scott Harrington was lost in a numbers game. Harrington has received multiple promotions to the NHL roster, but a majority of those opportunities had him sitting in the pressbox as the seventh defenseman. He played the first 10 games of his NHL career in 2014-15 and did not look out of place. Perhaps he will receive more of an opportunity in Toronto, as the Maple Leafs acquired the six-foot-two blueliner in the Phil Kessel deal.

Kris Letang							RD						PIT
Season	Team	Age	GP	G	A	Pts	+/-	ESP/60	AdjCF%	iCF/60	OGVT	DGVT	SGVT	GVT
2012-13	PIT	25	35	5	33	38	16	2.28	55.9%	11.9	8.6	2.5	0.0	11.1
2013-14	PIT	26	37	11	11	22	-8	0.88	49.7%	11.4	4.6	0.6	0.0	5.2
2014-15	PIT	27	69	11	43	54	12	1.33	56.3%	13.3	9.2	5.9	0.4	15.5
2015-16	PIT	28	71	12	36	48					7.4	4.8	0.0	12.1

One could argue that smooth-skating Kris Letang was having his finest season as an NHL defenseman before it was derailed by a season-ending concussion. He tied a career high with 11 goals and set a new personal best with 54 points while playing in only 69 games. Aside from scoring, Letang's ability to drive possession is what makes him one of the best defensemen in the league. When the former Val d'Or Foreurs captain is on the ice, Pittsburgh had an amazing 55.6% Fenwick, compared to 51.4% otherwise. At this point in his career, Letang is a proven number-one defenseman. The only thing holding him back is his health, which has included a stroke and multiple concussions in recent years.

Ben Lovejoy							RD						PIT
Season	Team	Age	GP	G	A	Pts	+/-	ESP/60	AdjCF%	iCF/60	OGVT	DGVT	SGVT	GVT
2012-13	PIT, ANA	28	35	0	10	10	4	0.62	51.1%	9.4	0.5	1.8	0.0	2.3
2013-14	ANA	29	78	5	13	18	21	0.76	48.8%	9.3	2.5	4.2	0.0	6.7
2014-15	ANA, PIT	30	60	2	12	14	-4	0.69	52.0%	9.4	1.3	1.2	0.0	2.5
2015-16	PIT	31	56	3	12	15					1.2	2.1	0.0	3.3

"The Reverend" was moved by Anaheim at the trade deadline, returning to the team with which he began his NHL career. Ben Lovejoy was brought back to the squad for his experience, locker-room presence, and to contribute bottom-pairing minutes. However, the plan blew up on Pittsburgh when injuries hit. Lovejoy was forced out of his element and into a top-pairing role late in the season and into the playoffs. Worst of all, the Penguins paid a premium to acquire Lovejoy, as promising puck-moving defenseman Simon Despres was the player traded to Anaheim. The trade has a high probability of looking bad for the Rutherford regime down the road.

Olli Maatta							LD						PIT
Season	Team	Age	GP	G	A	Pts	+/-	ESP/60	AdjCF%	iCF/60	OGVT	DGVT	SGVT	GVT
2013-14	PIT	19	78	9	20	29	8	1.05	51.2%	9.9	5.2	3.9	0.0	9.1
2014-15	PIT	20	20	1	8	9	1	1.23	52.1%	8.2	1.1	0.9	0.0	2.0
2015-16	PIT	21	53	5	17	22					2.7	2.5	0.0	5.2

20-year-old Olli Maatta had a year to forget. His season consisted of being diagnosed with thyroid cancer, contracting mumps, and having his surgically-repaired shoulder require additional surgery. Any one of those misfortunes would make for a rough year, let alone all three. Maatta's absence in the lineup was felt by Pittsburgh after his surprise top-four contribution in 2013-14. Even with all the things that went wrong in 2014-15, the

Jyvaskyla, Finland native still projects as a top-pairing defenseman that will help anchor Pittsburgh's defense corps for years to come.

Paul Martin — LD — SJS

Season	Team	Age	GP	G	A	Pts	+/-	ESP/60	AdjCF%	iCF/60	OGVT	DGVT	SGVT	GVT
2012-13	PIT	31	34	6	17	23	14	1.30	51.4%	7.0	4.8	2.5	0.0	7.3
2013-14	PIT	32	39	3	12	15	-4	0.49	50.1%	7.1	0.4	1.8	0.0	2.2
2014-15	PIT	33	74	3	17	20	17	0.83	53.6%	5.9	0.8	7.6	0.0	8.4
2015-16	SJS	34	63	3	16	19					1.0	4.4	0.0	5.4

As steady as they come, Paul Martin continued to play his quietly effective brand of hockey. Martin is not a great skater, he does not have a great shot, and he does not possess great size, but none of that prevents him from succeeding on the ice. He is extremely smart and has the puck skills to execute the game at a higher level. His ability to move the puck makes life easier for the talented forwards on the team. However, at 34 years of age, you have to wonder how much the US Olympian has left in the tank as a high-end, top-four defenseman. San Jose is determined to find out, as the Sharks inked the long-time Devil to a four-year deal in the offseason.

Derrick Pouliot — LD — PIT

Season	Team	Age	GP	G	A	Pts	+/-	ESP/60	AdjCF%	iCF/60	OGVT	DGVT	SGVT	GVT
2014-15	PIT	20	34	2	5	7	-11	0.35	53.0%	9.4	0.3	-0.8	-0.3	-0.8
2015-16	PIT	21	40	4	9	12					1.0	0.5	0.0	1.6

Derrick Pouliot, the highly-skilled eighth-overall pick from 2012, wasted no time in making his mark in the NHL. The 2014 CHL Defenseman of the Year scored his first NHL goal on his very first shot in the league. Pouliot had offseason shoulder surgery that caused him to begin the campaign in Wilkes-Barre/Scranton, but his fine AHL play earned him a permanent spot on the NHL roster. His transition to the NHL was made easier by the fact that his former coach with the Portland Winter Hawks was Mike Johnston, now Pittsburgh's bench boss. Pouliot's vision, puck skills, and skating make him a prime candidate to be an impact player on the team's top-four defense in the near future.

Rob Scuderi — LD — PIT

Season	Team	Age	GP	G	A	Pts	+/-	ESP/60	AdjCF%	iCF/60	OGVT	DGVT	SGVT	GVT
2012-13	LAK	34	48	1	11	12	-6	0.75	51.8%	4.9	0.1	4.1	0.0	4.2
2013-14	PIT	35	53	0	4	4	-8	0.28	44.2%	3.4	-2.4	3.2	0.0	0.7
2014-15	PIT	36	82	1	9	10	9	0.41	51.7%	5.3	-1.4	7.7	0.0	6.3
2015-16	PIT	37	61	1	7	8					-1.3	4.2	0.0	2.9

Rob Scuderi bounced back from an injury-riddled 2013-14 season, playing all 82 contests in 2014-15. With a clean bill of health, Scuderi improved his score-adjusted Fenwick from a woeful 44.7% in 2013-14 to a respectable 51.6%—although, one could argue that the possession hike was team driven, as Scuderi was still a negative relative possession player. Scuderi is often given accolades for his penalty killing, but he ranked 158th among 163 NHL defensemen in Fenwick against per 60 shorthanded minutes at an eye-popping 90.1. Scuderi is losing more foot speed with each passing season, making it really hard to justify his $3.4 million salary.

GOALTENDERS

Marc-Andre Fleury — G — PIT

Season	Team	Age	GP	W	L	OT	GAA	Sv%	ESSV%	QS%	GGVT	DGVT	SGVT	GVT
2012-13	PIT	28	33	23	8	0	2.39	.916	.927	45.2%	7.3	0.1	0.7	8.1
2013-14	PIT	29	64	39	18	5	2.37	.915	.917	57.8%	9.8	1.1	3.4	14.3
2014-15	PIT	30	64	34	20	9	2.32	.920	.925	54.7%	17.9	0.1	-2.1	15.9
2015-16	PIT	31	50					.916			8.9	0.3	0.0	9.2

Pittsburgh's main netminder has taken a lot of deserved criticism over the years, but in 2014-15, he earned praise. Marc-Andre Fleury's fine .925 even-strength save percentage in the regular season was followed up with a .936 mark in the postseason. "Flower" used to rely on athleticism to make saves, but the past two seasons under goaltender coach Mike Bales saw him adjust to a more positionally-based and quiet style of play. The result has been more consistency, and his best high-danger save percentage since 2007-08. Fleury's four-year, $23 million contract extension kicks in at the start of 2015-16. Pittsburgh will need him to continue performing at the same level to make it a worthwhile investment.

Thomas Greiss — G — NYI

Season	Team	Age	GP	W	L	OT	GAA	Sv%	ESSV%	QS%	GGVT	DGVT	SGVT	GVT
2012-13	SJS	26	6	1	4	0	2.53	.915	.918	60.0%	1.0	-0.1	0.0	0.9
2013-14	PHX	27	25	10	8	5	2.29	.920	.932	65.0%	6.1	0.2	2.1	8.5
2014-15	PIT	28	20	9	6	3	2.59	.908	.910	50.0%	0.0	0.2	-0.2	0.0
2015-16	NYI	29	24					.915			3.5	0.1	0.1	3.7

German-born Thomas Greiss has bounced around from team to team in a backup role. At each stop, he has provided solid play at a low cost. Last season with Pittsburgh was no exception, providing an insurance policy for Marc-Andre Fleury at the bargain price of $1 million. With a growing sample size of successful play, perhaps the time has come for a team to take a chance on Greiss as a full-time starter. However, he likely will not receive that opportunity in his new home in Brooklyn, where he will support Jaroslav Halak.

Jeff Zatkoff — G — PIT

Season	Team	Age	GP	W	L	OT	GAA	Sv%	ESSV%	QS%	GGVT	DGVT	SGVT	GVT
2013-14	PIT	26	20	12	6	2	2.61	.912	.916	55.6%	1.6	0.0	-0.6	0.9
2014-15	PIT	27	1	0	1	0	1.62	.941	.938	0.0%	0.5	0.0	0.0	0.5
2015-16	PIT	28	18					.914			2.0	0.0	-0.1	1.9

After starting 18 games as Fleury's backup in 2013-14, Jeff Zatkoff found himself back at Wilkes-Barre/Scranton. He did not start any games for Pittsburgh, and only saw 37 minutes of action coming off the bench. Things did not get any better in the AHL, where Zatkoff lost his starting job to upstart Matt Murray. With Murray playing at a high level, and second-round pick Tristan Jarry ready to start his professional career, Zatkoff is in danger of tumbling down the organization ladder.

Ryan Wilson

St. Louis Blues

Brian Elliott is not a name synonymous with elite goaltending. At the beginning of his NHL career, Elliott was not a very good netminder for the Ottawa Senators, stopping a dismal 90.3% of shots in 130 games, nor was he spectacular with the Colorado Avalanche after being acquired at the 2011 trade deadline. But when he joined the St. Louis Blues, Elliott's game appeared to turn around in an instant. He was named to the All-Star Game in his very first season with the Blues; he posted an eye-popping .940 save percentage. However, for the next two seasons, Elliott continued to be utilized primarily in the backup role behind Jaroslav Halak and then Ryan Miller.

Starting the 2014-15 season, Elliott and up-and-comer Jake Allen were to battle for starts, which generated some mixed reactions among Blues fans. Although Elliott had been able to fill in when the starting goalie (Halak, or Pascal Leclaire back with the Senators) was out with an extended injury, he was not widely considered as starting goaltender material. So why did he perform like a number-one goalie again last season? Part of Elliott's success with the Blues can be traced back to when a new head coach was hired four years ago.

Before Ken Hitchcock took over the Blues bench on November 6, 2011, the team had recorded six wins in 13 games to begin the season and showed no signs of improving on an 11th-place finish in the Western Conference. But when Hitchcock became the new bench boss, the results were immediate. In his first 10 games as head coach, Hitch led St. Louis to an impressive 7-1-2 record. The Blues went on to finish the season first in their division and second in the conference. After four seasons with the 1967 expansion team, the former Cup-winning coach had registered an excellent 62.3% winning rate, and had helped to steer the team into the playoffs every year.

Hitchcock's reputation as one of the best coaches of the post-lockout era stems from his airtight defensive system, which applies very aggressive forechecking. The implementation and execution of the system helped lower the Blues' Fenwick against (unblocked shot attempts against) per 60 minutes of five-on-five play from 38.1 in 2009-10 to 36 in 2010-11, a 5.5% reduction. During short-handed play, the statistic decreased by 8.1% from 70.6 to 64.9.

The Blues system has continued to work very well over the years. Under Hitchcock, the team's seasonal average of Fenwick against per 60 five-on-five minutes is 35.7 and for short-handed situations, it is 62.9. Post-Hitchcock, St. Louis is one of five teams to hold the 10 lowest numbers of unblocked shot attempts against per 60 minutes in a single season.

BLUES IN A BOX

Last Season

Goals For	248	5th
Goals Against	201	t-4th
GVT	47	3rd
Points	109	t-3rd
Playoffs	Lost Conference Quarterfinal	

The Blues followed another excellent regular season with another first-round disappointment. They have only won one series in the last decade.

Three-Year Record

GVT	118	2nd
Points	280	3rd
Playoffs	3 Appearances, 6 Wins	

VUKOTA Projections

Goals For	227	10th
Goals Against	212	4th
GVT	16	5th
Points	97	5th

St. Louis will challenge for the Western Conference crown again, but nobody will care unless they make some noise in May.

Top Three Prospects

R. Fabbri (F), I. Barbashev (F), J. Schmaltz (D)

While the system seems set up for goaltenders to face less rubber, good possession players should get some credit for reducing shot attempts against, too. Prior to his departure Assistant GM and Director of Amateur Scouting Jarmo Kekalainen helped St. Louis draft cornerstone pieces in Alex Pietrangelo, T.J. Oshie, David Backes, Vladimir Tarasenko, Jaden Schwartz, and others, all key elements of the team's core.

Elliott has had the privilege of backstopping great players, but another factor in his success with St. Louis is the team's ability to minimize shots in the slot and in low slot, a combined area War-On-Ice.com calls the "high-danger zone". The popular statistics website collects data on "high-danger saves" and "high-danger goals", which can be added together to create "high-danger shots". Shots from the high-danger zone have a better chance of going in the net than from any other area. The number of high-danger shots per 60 minutes of even-strength play faced by Elliott decreased from 7.95 under non-Hitchcock coached teams to 6.60 under the Hitchcock-coached team. On average, that is roughly one less scoring opportunity from the slot per game (see chart).

The former ninth-round pick is not the only netminder to benefit from the system. All Blues goaltenders—with the exception of Allen who has played during the Hitchcock era only—saw fewer scoring opportunities from the slot per 60 five-on-five minutes with Hitch behind the bench. Both Halak and Elliott, who played the vast majority of the games, stopped shots at a higher rate. In Elliott's case, his even-strength save percentage increased by nearly two percentage points.

Before his time with St. Louis, Elliott experienced some ups and downs. In his first season as the regular backup with Ottawa, he posted a solid .921 five-on-five save percentage. However, his performance appeared to deteriorate once he was put in the spotlight. In 2009-10, when Elliott assumed the role of starter from the injured Pascal Leclaire, he only managed to stop an unimpressive 90.3% of five-on-five shots. The next season, he was dealt to Colorado at the trade deadline, where he posted a mediocre .912 five-on-five save percentage—an increase from his abominal .898 with the Sens.

Elliott's first season in a Blues uniform was terrific. He led the league with a .942 five-on-five save percentage. In 2012-13, he took a step backward, however, stopping pucks at a 92.3% rate (a nearly 2% drop), ranking 20th out of 31 goaltenders with at least 1,000 minutes played. The next season, his five-on-five save percentage was approximately the same, but he improved his standing among his peers, ranking 31st out of 55.

Under the St. Louis/Hitchcock system, Elliott proved to be a more-than-capable "1B" goalie. Entering the 2014-15 season, the Jennings Trophy winner held a very respectable .930 even-strength save percentage with Hitchcock's Blues, which ranked eighth among goaltenders who played 2,500 minutes. In particular, Elliott performed well on very close-range scoring opportunities, ranking sixth out of 38 goaltenders who played 3,000 minutes in high-danger save percentage (.853).

In 2014-15, when Elliott split duties with Allen, the 30-year-old improved again. He appeared in 46 games, registering a .926 five-on-five save percentage, a value that placed him 15th out of 29 goaltenders with at least 40 games played. Elliott's workload increased from the season before, and would have been even more if he had not been injured for 14 games..

The senior Blues goalkeeper is signed for another two seasons at the bargain cap hit of $2.5 million per season. He has played very well for St. Louis, appearing in the All-Star Game and posting even-strength save percentages of .940, .927, .923, and .926 over the past four seasons. Although he did not play in more than 35 games in any of the first three St. Louis seasons, with the additional workload and some help from the coach and teammates in 2014-15, Elliott performed up to the expectations of a number-one goalie.

Wesley Chu

Goaltender	Before Hitchcock			Under Hitchcock		
	Games	ESSV%	High-danger shots/60 mins	Games	ESSV%	High-danger shots/60 mins
Brian Elliott	148	.909	7.95	132	.928	6.60
Jake Allen	N/A	N/A	N/A	52	.916	7.50
Jaroslav Halak	159	.921	8.79	95	.931	7.14
Ryan Miller	387	.923	8.83	19	.914	6.31
Martin Brodeur	392	.920	7.20	7	.920	6.34

ST. LOUIS BLUES

Even-Strength Usage: St. Louis Blues

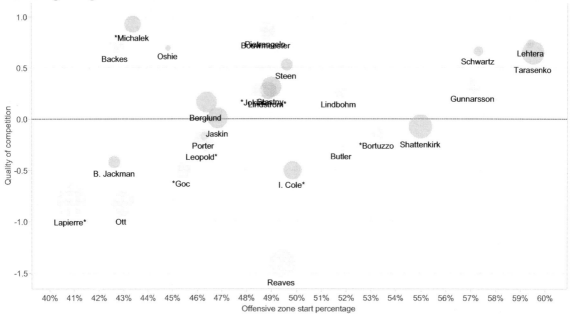

Special Teams Usage: St. Louis Blues

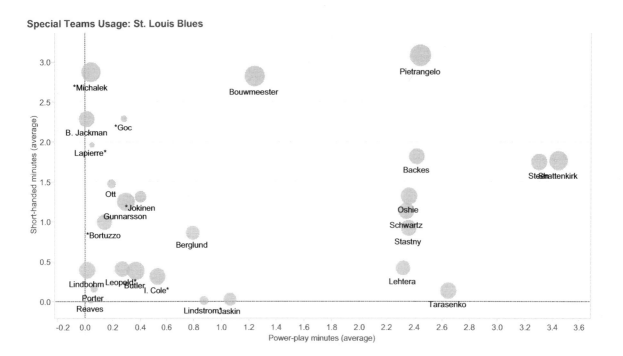

ST. LOUIS BLUES

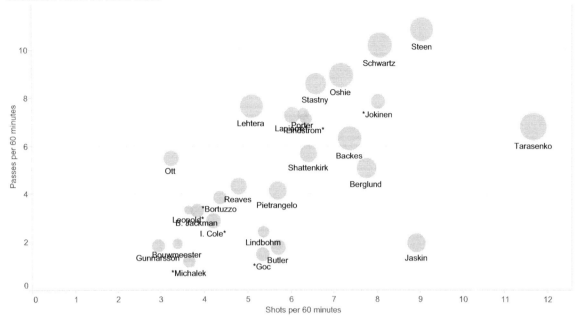

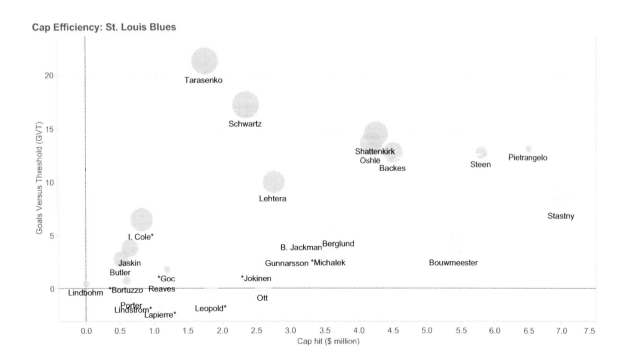

FORWARDS

David Backes								C					STL
Season	Team	Age	GP	G	A	Pts	+/-	ESP/60	AdjCF%	iCF/60	OGVT	DGVT	SGVT	GVT
2012-13	STL	28	48	6	22	28	5	1.76	52.5%	11.2	1.8	3.5	0.0	5.3
2013-14	STL	29	74	27	30	57	14	2.22	56.3%	11.9	9.8	5.2	0.0	15.0
2014-15	STL	30	80	26	32	58	7	2.19	50.4%	12.6	8.1	4.5	0.0	12.7
2015-16	STL	31	73	22	28	50					5.8	3.2	0.0	9.0

Place David Backes at either end of the rink and he will not disappoint. The two-way forward, year after year, has had steady offensive production and made for a tough defensive matchup for opponents. This was the fifth season in which he recorded at least 50 points and 100 penalty minutes, a rare combination. The hard-nosed forward hardly fights, but his aggressiveness led to him dishing out 1,899 hits in eight seasons and can sometimes cause him to take needless penalties. But when he was on the ice, Blues goaltenders could thank him for blocking 87 shots, a number that ranked fourth among forwards. Despite his rugged style of play, Backes has been very durable over his NHL career, missing only 25 games due to injury. Still, there are a lot of miles on his body, leaving the Blues in a tough spot when he becomes an unrestricted free agent next season.

Patrik Berglund								C/LW					STL
Season	Team	Age	GP	G	A	Pts	+/-	ESP/60	AdjCF%	iCF/60	OGVT	DGVT	SGVT	GVT
2012-13	STL	24	48	17	8	25	-2	1.62	49.0%	9.3	2.4	2.4	-0.3	4.4
2013-14	STL	25	78	14	18	32	10	1.64	55.1%	12.6	2.9	4.3	-0.3	7.0
2014-15	STL	26	77	12	15	27	-2	1.57	55.1%	13.2	2.3	3.0	0.0	5.3
2015-16	STL	27	66	14	17	30					2.7	2.7	0.0	5.4

After being phased out of a scoring role in favor of Jori Lehtera, Patrik Berglund tried to make the best of the situation. The offensively-skilled forward was taken off the power play, causing his ice-time to slip from 16:10 in 2013-14 to 14:34 per game, which may explain his lowest point total to date (not counting the shortened 2012-13 season). He was still able to produce 24 even-strength points. A former first-round pick, the 26-year-old has not been more productive than in his rookie season when he recorded 1.9 even-strength points per 60 minutes. "Bergy" will likely have to settle for third-line duties again, though it would make sense to move his $3.7 million cap hit if head coach Ken Hitchcock doesn't plan on giving his six-foot-three forward a bigger role.

Colin Fraser								C					Germany
Season	Team	Age	GP	G	A	Pts	+/-	ESP/60	AdjCF%	iCF/60	OGVT	DGVT	SGVT	GVT
2012-13	LAK	27	34	2	5	7	-4	1.43	51.3%	7.9	-0.3	0.7	0.0	0.4
2013-14	LAK	28	33	0	2	2	-4	0.44	51.7%	8.5	-1.0	0.2	0.0	-0.8
2014-15	STL	29	1	0	0	0	-1	0.00	19.9%	13.1	-0.1	-0.1	0.0	-0.2
2015-16	Germany	30	30	3	4	8					0.1	0.5	0.0	0.6

Colin Fraser saw a total of 4:42 of NHL ice-time last season while spending the rest of his time—59 games—with the AHL club. There, he scored 17 points and collected 67 penalty minutes. As a gritty role player, the 30-year-old has accumulated 290 penalty minutes in 359 NHL games and averaged 8.1 hits per 60 minutes. In the AHL, he was penalized more, with 559 minutes in 289 games. At the beginning of the Blackhawks' dynasty, the third-round selection from 2003 was a fairly effective depth player, producing as many as 19 points. Without any scoring touch to speak of since then, he has best been used in very limited duty ; he heads to Europe to play in 2015-16.

Marcel Goc							C						Germany
Season	Team	Age	GP	G	A	Pts	+/-	ESP/60	AdjCF%	iCF/60	OGVT	DGVT	SGVT	GVT
2012-13	FLA	29	42	9	10	19	-6	1.29	47.8%	11.7	1.8	1.5	0.0	3.3
2013-14	FLA, PIT	30	74	11	14	25	-7	1.41	49.6%	11.7	1.2	2.8	-0.3	3.7
2014-15	PIT, STL	31	74	3	6	9	-3	0.71	50.9%	10.4	-1.5	3.3	0.0	1.8
2015-16	Germany	32	58	4	7	11					-0.9	2.0	0.0	1.1

In Florida, Marcel Goc had established himself as a quality third-line center, adding occasional offense and playing a solid game at both ends of the ice. However, in back-to-back years with better teams, things have not quite worked out. The 2001 first-round pick saw a significant drop in ice-time after being traded to Pittsburgh, then limited ice-time in St. Louis after being moved by the Pens. While he can still be effective in the faceoff circle, it appears the days of Goc providing strong bottom-six play are over, as he scored just nine points and only put 77 shots on goal.

Dmitrij Jaskin							RW						STL
Season	Team	Age	GP	G	A	Pts	+/-	ESP/60	AdjCF%	iCF/60	OGVT	DGVT	SGVT	GVT
2012-13	STL	19	2	0	0	0	-1	0.00	71.9%	7.5	-0.2	0.0	0.0	-0.2
2013-14	STL	20	18	1	1	2	-3	0.67	51.2%	11.5	-0.4	0.0	0.0	-0.4
2014-15	STL	21	54	13	5	18	7	1.35	55.9%	15.2	2.3	1.7	-0.3	3.8
2015-16	STL	22	55	12	9	22					1.6	1.6	0.0	3.2

Although he started last season on the NHL second line, 2011 second-round pick Dmitrij Jaskin split time between the Blues and Chicago Wolves. In 60 AHL career games, he scored 44 points. In the NHL, his on-ice shot attempt statistics were strong, in part because Hitchcock gave his young winger minutes with Paul Stastny. Jaskin has a physical side to his game too, hitting his opponents 12.8 times per 60 minutes of five-on-five play. His minor-league days are likely over, as he found a permanent spot on the main roster partway through 2014-15. There are questions about his quickness and consistent efforts, but Jaskin is in a great situation to succeed.

Olli Jokinen							C						Free Agent
Season	Team	Age	GP	G	A	Pts	+/-	ESP/60	AdjCF%	iCF/60	OGVT	DGVT	SGVT	GVT
2012-13	WPG	34	45	7	7	14	-19	1.17	49.0%	12.4	-1.8	-0.7	-0.6	-3.0
2013-14	WPG	35	82	18	25	43	-8	1.74	49.0%	12.4	5.3	1.3	0.4	7.0
2014-15	NSH, TOR, STL	36	62	4	6	10	6	0.84	51.7%	14.0	-0.2	2.6	-0.3	2.1
2015-16	Free Agent	37	56	7	11	17					0.9	1.6	0.0	2.5

Olli Jokinen was moved from Nashville to Toronto after complaining about his role. The veteran scorer wanted to play center, but was put at wing, causing him to demand a trade. The Maple Leafs flipped him to a contender, who also did not see much left in the tank for the 36-year-old. The two-time 80+ point producer is not much of an offensive force anymore. As his ice-time has dropped, his production has decreased considerably from 0.52 to 0.16 points per game from the previous season. Despite playing in only six career playoff games, the 1997 third-overall pick has had a long career. In the active skaters category, Jokinen is ranked eighth all-time in games played (1,231) and in shots on goal (3,343).

Jori Lehtera — C/LW — STL

Season	Team	Age	GP	G	A	Pts	+/-	ESP/60	AdjCF%	iCF/60	OGVT	DGVT	SGVT	GVT
2014-15	STL	27	75	14	30	44	21	2.08	52.8%	8.6	5.5	3.9	0.6	10.0
2015-16	STL	28	71	16	32	48					5.3	2.9	0.1	8.3

Before his NHL debut, Jori Lehtera spent four seasons in the KHL, amassing 153 points in 178 games. A former KHL linemate of Blues phenom Vladimir Tarasenko, Lehtera played in his first NHL season as a 27-year-old with his old teammate. When on the ice together, the pair were unstoppable, posting a ridiculous 67.6% goals-for percentage. The third-round pick from 2008 has a decent shot, scoring 11 even-strength goals, but he only put 77 shots on net. Smartly, he was more willing to setup Tarasenko than take his own shot. That is a darn good way to rack up assists. It appears the Blues' patience in bringing Lehtera over to North America is paying off.

T.J. Oshie — RW — WSH

Season	Team	Age	GP	G	A	Pts	+/-	ESP/60	AdjCF%	iCF/60	OGVT	DGVT	SGVT	GVT
2012-13	STL	26	30	7	13	20	-5	1.07	50.3%	11.9	2.2	1.5	0.7	4.5
2013-14	STL	27	79	21	39	60	19	2.20	55.3%	10.7	9.1	5.6	4.6	19.3
2014-15	STL	28	72	19	36	55	17	2.31	52.2%	12.9	8.1	4.6	0.9	13.6
2015-16	WSH	29	71	19	33	52					6.3	3.3	0.1	9.7

After avoiding serious injuries in 2013-14, T.J. Oshie suffered a concussion in 2014-15. The three-time 50+ point scorer continued to put up terrific even-strength production, ranking second to Tarasenko in points per 60 minutes. That said, the Blues have been frustrated by the US Olympian's performances come playoff time. While he adds solid defensive play and work ethic when he isn't scoring, the five-foot-eleven forward has been a ghost in the postseason with just nine points in 30 career games. He will get plenty of opportunities to prove the Blues wrong as he heads to a stacked Capitals team.

Steve Ott — LW — STL

Season	Team	Age	GP	G	A	Pts	+/-	ESP/60	AdjCF%	iCF/60	OGVT	DGVT	SGVT	GVT
2012-13	BUF	30	48	9	15	24	3	1.70	39.7%	8.7	3.1	1.3	-0.1	4.3
2013-14	BUF, STL	31	82	9	14	23	-38	0.77	42.9%	8.1	-3.1	0.9	0.9	-1.2
2014-15	STL	32	78	3	9	12	-8	0.93	48.0%	7.9	-1.5	2.0	0.0	0.5
2015-16	STL	33	59	3	8	11					-1.4	1.4	0.0	-0.1

Steve Ott used to be an effective agitator, the key words being "used to". Over his career, the former Star scored 1.28 even-strength points per 60 minutes while adding the occasional fight and killing penalties. But his skating has slowed significantly and he has become a possession liability. With St. Louis, he received approximately eight minutes less of ice-time compared to his days with Buffalo a year before. As his minutes dropped, his scoring rate, number of shots, and penalty minutes have decreased as well.

Magnus Paajarvi — LW — STL

Season	Team	Age	GP	G	A	Pts	+/-	ESP/60	AdjCF%	iCF/60	OGVT	DGVT	SGVT	GVT
2012-13	EDM	21	42	9	7	16	-1	1.51	43.9%	11.5	1.6	0.9	0.0	2.5
2013-14	STL	22	55	6	6	12	-6	1.30	54.1%	11.6	0.2	0.8	-0.3	0.7
2014-15	STL	23	10	0	1	1	-2	0.00	53.8%	8.8	-0.5	-0.1	0.0	-0.6
2015-16	STL	24	38	5	6	12					0.3	0.8	0.0	1.0

ST. LOUIS BLUES

After being scratched for most of the first few months, Magnus Paajarvi was sent to the AHL. In 10 contests with the Blues, he played an average of 10 minutes per game and had just nine shots in total, but he did have a decent season with the Wolves, where he notched 29 points on 86 shots over 36 games. The 24-year-old has the talent to succeed at the NHL level, but has not shown enough of it to warrant a regular spot in the lineup. In the St. Louis organization, Paajarvi will need a breakout season or to improve his two-way play to have a better chance at reclaiming an NHL role since other promising prospects have passed him on the depth chart.

Chris Porter								LW						PHI
Season	Team	Age	GP	G	A	Pts	+/-	ESP/60	AdjCF%	iCF/60	OGVT	DGVT	SGVT	GVT
2012-13	STL	28	29	2	6	8	5	1.56	50.6%	12.6	0.6	1.8	0.0	2.4
2013-14	STL	29	22	0	1	1	-3	0.28	47.7%	10.3	-1.1	0.2	0.0	-0.8
2014-15	STL	30	24	1	1	2	-3	0.54	52.7%	11.8	-0.6	0.1	0.0	-0.6
2015-16	PHI	31	34	4	5	9					0.0	0.8	0.0	0.8

Missing 20 games with a leg injury plus healthy scratches limited Chris Porter to 24 games. Although he has been known for hitting, the 2003 ninth-round draft pick has added some sneaky value throughout his career, drawing more penalties than takes. In the AHL, he seems to be far less disciplined, compiling 310 minutes in 322 games. The 31-year-old former North Dakota captain continues to be a hardworking depth forward, who will add very little on offense and require extremely limited and protected minutes.

Ty Rattie								RW						STL
Season	Team	Age	GP	G	A	Pts	+/-	ESP/60	AdjCF%	iCF/60	OGVT	DGVT	SGVT	GVT
2013-14	STL	20	2	0	0	0	-2	0.00	45.2%	16.4	-0.2	-0.1	0.0	-0.4
2014-15	STL	21	11	0	2	2	0	1.29	53.1%	11.3	0.1	0.1	0.0	0.2
2015-16	STL	22	30	5	7	11					0.7	0.6	0.0	1.3

One of St. Louis' top prospects, Ty Rattie may finally be ready to be an NHL regular. He improved on his AHL scoring rate from 0.67 points per game in 2013-14 to 0.71 in 2014-15. His shooting rate also went up from 2.9 to 3.3 shots per game. Although he has yet to prove it at the highest level, the 22-year-old has always been a scorer going back to his days of posting 95 points in 76 games with the Portland Winter Hawks. A bit undersized, Rattie is quick and has tremendous offensive creativity. Will he be able to keep up on both ends of the ice under a Hitchcock system? That has yet to be seen.

Ryan Reaves								RW						STL
Season	Team	Age	GP	G	A	Pts	+/-	ESP/60	AdjCF%	iCF/60	OGVT	DGVT	SGVT	GVT
2012-13	STL	25	43	4	2	6	3	1.13	52.2%	6.6	0.2	1.1	0.0	1.3
2013-14	STL	26	63	2	6	8	-1	0.90	46.9%	6.9	-1.5	0.9	0.0	-0.6
2014-15	STL	27	81	6	6	12	-3	1.05	46.4%	8.2	-0.1	0.9	0.0	0.8
2015-16	STL	28	60	4	5	9					-1.1	1.2	0.0	0.1

Since he first entered the NHL, Ryan Reaves is second in hits per 60 minutes (24.6) in the league, behind only Zac Rinaldo. He is a big, tough, physical player who will take plenty of penalties and add very little on the scoreboard. For whatever reason, Hitchcock seems believe his tough-guy fourth liner is effective in an "energy" role because he was dressed for every game except for one. With the worst Relative Corsi on the Blues, we will have to agree to disagree with Hitchcock on that decision.

Jaden Schwartz — LW — STL

Season	Team	Age	GP	G	A	Pts	+/-	ESP/60	AdjCF%	iCF/60	OGVT	DGVT	SGVT	GVT
2012-13	STL	20	45	7	6	13	-4	1.44	51.5%	9.1	0.2	1.2	0.0	1.4
2013-14	STL	21	80	25	31	56	28	2.27	57.2%	13.0	10.4	6.3	-0.3	16.4
2014-15	STL	22	75	28	35	63	13	2.44	52.9%	13.2	13.3	3.8	0.0	17.2
2015-16	STL	23	72	26	34	61					9.3	3.3	0.0	12.6

With some assistance from breakout star and linemate Vladimir Tarasenko, Jaden Schwartz has had his best season yet, reaching career highs in goals, assists, and points. He is a quick, aggressive forward who is very skilled at tracking down pucks for his talented teammates. Schwartz's playoff production, like many of Blues forwards, has been lackluster. In 18 postseason games, he has just seven points, an unacceptable rate for a key top-six forward on a competing team.

Paul Stastny — C — STL

Season	Team	Age	GP	G	A	Pts	+/-	ESP/60	AdjCF%	iCF/60	OGVT	DGVT	SGVT	GVT
2012-13	COL	27	40	9	15	24	-7	1.44	46.0%	11.1	2.8	0.3	0.0	3.1
2013-14	COL	28	71	25	35	60	9	2.41	50.6%	11.6	10.9	2.0	0.0	12.9
2014-15	STL	29	74	16	30	46	5	1.75	54.6%	10.2	6.4	2.0	0.0	8.4
2015-16	STL	30	64	18	27	45					5.8	1.8	0.0	7.5

In his first season with St. Louis, Paul Stastny was not relied on to be the main pivot, surprising for a player the Blues paid a $7 million cap hit for in the offseason. Usually when you sign a huge contract, your ice-time goes up. Not for Stastny, whose average ice-time per game was marginally down to 17:37 minutes from 18:23 minutes with the Avalanche. Except for 2013-14, when he was entering the final year of his contract, Stastny has not recorded 60+ points since 2009-10.

Alexander Steen — LW — STL

Season	Team	Age	GP	G	A	Pts	+/-	ESP/60	AdjCF%	iCF/60	OGVT	DGVT	SGVT	GVT
2012-13	STL	28	40	8	19	27	5	1.82	55.0%	16.9	9.2	1.0	1.8	12.0
2013-14	STL	29	68	33	29	62	17	2.46	57.5%	17.5	11.6	4.3	1.6	17.5
2014-15	STL	30	74	24	40	64	8	2.17	53.4%	14.8	9.1	4.4	-0.9	12.7
2015-16	STL	31	72	24	34	59					7.6	3.0	0.0	10.7

Perhaps one of the most underappreciated forwards in the league, Alexander Steen continues to log big-time minutes on the Blues' top line. In one year, his shooting percentage went down from 15.6% to 10.8%, closer to his career average of 10.6%. Steen's shooting percentage may have regressed to the mean, but he reached career highs in assists, points, and shots (223). The former Maple Leaf's offensive effort has always had big peaks and valleys. In one January game against Anaheim, he fired a season high of 11 shots. In five other games, he failed to register a single shot. On defense, Steen is good at slowing opponents and using his stick. He is considered a great penalty killer.

ST. LOUIS BLUES

Vladimir Tarasenko								RW						STL
Season	Team	Age	GP	G	A	Pts	+/-	ESP/60	AdjCF%	iCF/60	OGVT	DGVT	SGVT	GVT
2012-13	STL	21	38	8	11	19	1	1.91	58.0%	15.7	1.8	1.0	-0.6	2.2
2013-14	STL	22	64	21	22	43	20	2.60	58.9%	17.3	8.5	3.4	1.2	13.2
2014-15	STL	23	77	37	36	73	27	2.89	55.7%	22.4	15.5	4.2	1.5	21.3
2015-16	STL	24	74	34	36	70					11.8	3.1	0.1	15.0

In only his third season, Vladimir Tarasenko had a huge breakout in offensive production, placing 10th among league scoring leaders. Expectations were high for the 2010 first-round pick and he seems to have met them early in his career. The Russian winger is the total package offensively, with explosive skating, a wicked shot, and creativity that ranks among the elite of the NHL. Tarasenko's age-23 season likely set the standard for the quality that Blues fans will enjoy for years to come.

DEFENSEMEN

Robert Bortuzzo								RD						STL
Season	Team	Age	GP	G	A	Pts	+/-	ESP/60	AdjCF%	iCF/60	OGVT	DGVT	SGVT	GVT
2012-13	PIT	23	15	2	2	4	3	1.27	49.5%	7.9	0.8	0.6	0.0	1.4
2013-14	PIT	24	54	0	10	10	-3	0.71	46.0%	8.1	0.1	1.3	0.0	1.4
2014-15	PIT, STL	25	51	3	5	8	-9	0.67	53.8%	9.9	0.1	0.8	0.0	0.8
2015-16	STL	26	49	2	7	9					-0.1	1.5	0.0	1.4

Before being moved from Pittsburgh to St. Louis at the 2015 trade deadline, Robert Bortuzzo struggled to fit in with the Penguins. In 13 games with the Blues, the six-foot-four blueliner did not produce much offensively, but found a comfort level playing alongside veteran Barrett Jackman. The two posted a Corsi percentage over 60% while on ice together. Over the course of last season with both the Penguins and Blues, Bortuzzo missed games due to injuries, a suspension, and lineup decisions by coaches. The big defenseman's new life in St. Louis may act as a jump start to what was a sputtering career.

Jay Bouwmeester								LD						STL
Season	Team	Age	GP	G	A	Pts	+/-	ESP/60	AdjCF%	iCF/60	OGVT	DGVT	SGVT	GVT
2012-13	CGY, STL	29	47	7	15	22	-6	0.83	47.9%	8.2	3.6	3.7	0.0	7.3
2013-14	STL	30	82	4	33	37	26	1.02	54.5%	8.9	4.9	9.2	0.0	14.2
2014-15	STL	31	72	2	11	13	7	0.40	51.0%	7.4	-1.6	5.8	0.0	4.1
2015-16	STL	32	66	4	16	19					0.7	4.9	0.0	5.6

A once highly sought-after, smooth skating blueliner, Jay Bouwmeester is still a solid all-around defenseman, albeit not the above-average top-pairing blueliner as he once was. However, it seems Hitckcock has not quite caught onto that concept yet, as he played the 31-year-old next to terrific defenseman Alex Pietrangelo for 770 of his 1,252 minutes. Bouwmeester dragged down his mate, with Pietrangelo at 49.5% Corsi when they are together, but 52.1% when away from the former Flame and Panther. The Blues would be wise to ship out their veteran before he really falls off, or reduce his role.

Chris Butler — LD — STL

Season	Team	Age	GP	G	A	Pts	+/-	ESP/60	AdjCF%	iCF/60	OGVT	DGVT	SGVT	GVT
2012-13	CGY	26	44	1	7	8	-10	0.63	43.7%	6.7	0.2	0.9	0.0	1.0
2013-14	CGY	27	82	2	14	16	-23	0.64	41.9%	7.1	0.3	2.4	0.0	2.7
2014-15	STL	28	33	3	6	9	8	0.88	51.2%	9.2	0.2	2.5	0.0	2.8
2015-16	STL	29	54	4	12	15					0.8	2.8	0.0	3.6

Placed on waivers at the start of 2014-15, Chris Butler struggled to get regular playing time. Limited to 33 games, a significant drop from the 82 games he played with the Flames in the previous season, the 2005 fourth-round draft pick averaged three minutes less ice-time in a St. Louis uniform. He also appeared in 14 AHL games with the Chicago Wolves and was scratched numerous times when he was on the main roster. Although he can move the puck well, the 28-year-old is not much of an offensive threat at the NHL level, having scored only 84 points in 382 games.

Carl Gunnarsson — LD — STL

Season	Team	Age	GP	G	A	Pts	+/-	ESP/60	AdjCF%	iCF/60	OGVT	DGVT	SGVT	GVT
2012-13	TOR	26	37	1	14	15	5	1.36	45.3%	4.9	2.6	2.7	0.0	5.3
2013-14	TOR	27	80	3	14	17	12	0.74	39.9%	4.4	0.8	3.8	0.0	4.6
2014-15	STL	28	61	2	10	12	10	0.65	50.5%	6.2	-0.2	3.7	0.0	3.5
2015-16	STL	29	60	2	11	13					0.0	3.3	0.0	3.2

St. Louis acquired Carl Gunnarsson from the Leafs to serve as a top-four defender, though he isn't exactly fit for that role. While he does have decent puck skills, soft defensive zone coverage and mental mistakes have often led to Gunnarsson being pinned in his own end. However, his season may look better than it actually was because of an assignment next to Kevin Shattenkirk. When the two were together, they had an outstanding 69.0% goals-for percentage, but the former Leaf was 44.4% goals-for away from Shattenkirk. At best, Gunnarsson is a sixth or seventh defenseman, though the Blues seem to believe he is more.

Barret Jackman — LD — NSH

Season	Team	Age	GP	G	A	Pts	+/-	ESP/60	AdjCF%	iCF/60	OGVT	DGVT	SGVT	GVT
2012-13	STL	31	46	3	9	12	6	0.95	47.1%	6.5	0.6	5.3	0.0	6.0
2013-14	STL	32	79	3	12	15	11	0.73	53.5%	7.6	-0.1	7.2	0.0	7.1
2014-15	STL	33	80	2	13	15	3	0.72	53.7%	7.8	0.3	4.4	0.0	4.8
2015-16	NSH	34	62	3	11	13					0.2	3.6	0.0	3.8

Although his playing time has continued to decline every season since 2008-09, Barret Jackman is still a reliable defensive defenseman. Given that he started a high percentage of five-on-five faceoffs in his own end, the former Calder Trophy winner's possession stats are excellent. He managed to stay mostly injury-free, missing only eight games in the past four years. As he gets older, Jackman brings leadership skills, which come in handy for the Cup contending team during a long season.

Petteri Lindbohm — LD — STL

Season	Team	Age	GP	G	A	Pts	+/-	ESP/60	AdjCF%	iCF/60	OGVT	DGVT	SGVT	GVT
2014-15	STL	21	23	2	1	3	-1	0.52	51.3%	9.2	0.2	0.3	0.0	0.5
2015-16	STL	22	36	3	6	9					0.6	1.1	0.0	1.8

Defensive defenseman Petteri Lindbohm was called up and sent down to and from the Wolves numerous times in 2014-15. He may not provide much offensive production, but he did fire 120 shots in 53 AHL games. With St. Louis, the 21-year-old Helsinki native could use his body more since he was credited with only 26 hits in 23 games.

Zbynek Michalek								RD						ARI
Season	Team	Age	GP	G	A	Pts	+/-	ESP/60	AdjCF%	iCF/60	OGVT	DGVT	SGVT	GVT
2012-13	PHX	30	34	0	2	2	4	0.19	51.1%	8.7	-2.1	2.0	0.0	-0.1
2013-14	PHX	31	59	2	8	10	6	0.56	49.6%	9.0	0.0	3.6	0.0	3.5
2014-15	ARI, STL	32	68	4	8	12	-3	0.59	51.3%	9.0	-0.9	4.6	0.0	3.7
2015-16	ARI	33	57	2	9	11					-0.5	3.3	0.0	2.7

Shot blocking is what Zbynek Michalek does best. Last season, he blocked 160 shots in 68 games, including 30 in 15 games with the Blues. But blocking shots and simply being a shutdown defender can take a toll on the body. Like his brother Milan, Zbynek is susceptible to injuries; the last time he played at least 70 games in a season was in 2010-11. The former Minnesota Wild blueliner is not much of an offensive producer. Despite the few points he records, Michalek has a booming shot from the point that he tends to underutilize.

Alex Pietrangelo								RD						STL
Season	Team	Age	GP	G	A	Pts	+/-	ESP/60	AdjCF%	iCF/60	OGVT	DGVT	SGVT	GVT
2012-13	STL	22	47	5	19	24	0	1.13	52.2%	10.4	2.2	5.9	0.0	8.1
2013-14	STL	23	81	8	43	51	20	1.24	55.5%	12.4	8.7	8.9	0.0	17.6
2014-15	STL	24	81	7	39	46	-2	1.27	50.5%	11.0	7.6	5.5	0.0	13.1
2015-16	STL	25	77	10	34	44					6.3	5.4	0.0	11.7

An all-around defender, Alex Pietrangelo was relied on more for his defensive abilities in 2014-15. The increase in responsibilities in the Blues defensive zone may have affected his possession-proxy metrics, as his Relative Fenwick went from 1.5 to -2.4. The physical demands of being a top-pairing defender at both ends of the ice has surprisingly not made Pietrangelo more vulnerable to injuries. Since late 2010, he has missed a combined seven regular-season and playoff games.

Kevin Shattenkirk								RD						STL
Season	Team	Age	GP	G	A	Pts	+/-	ESP/60	AdjCF%	iCF/60	OGVT	DGVT	SGVT	GVT
2012-13	STL	23	48	5	18	23	2	1.04	55.1%	10.4	3.5	3.9	0.2	7.6
2013-14	STL	24	81	10	35	45	1	0.81	55.5%	11.8	7.6	2.2	1.0	10.7
2014-15	STL	25	56	8	36	44	19	1.17	55.2%	11.0	8.5	4.8	1.2	14.5
2015-16	STL	26	66	10	37	47					7.8	4.3	0.0	12.2

If it were not for an abdominal surgery that sidelined him for 25 games, Kevin Shattenkirk would have likely exceeded his career high in points. In 56 games, he led league defensemen with 2.09 points per 60 minutes and 1.71 assists per 60 minutes. Prior to his injury, Shattenkirk was very durable, missing only two games in three seasons. On the power play, his on-ice shooting percentage was 18%, an increase of nearly five percentage points from the previous season. As skilled as the skaters on the power-play unit are, there may still be some element of luck in that increase. A repeat of similar success for the power-play quarterback would be difficult.

ST. LOUIS BLUES

GOALTENDERS

Jake Allen							G							STL
Season	Team	Age	GP	W	L	OT	GAA	Sv%	ESSV%	QS%	GGVT	DGVT	SGVT	GVT
2012-13	STL	22	15	9	4	0	2.46	.905	.911	46.2%	-0.6	0.4	0.6	0.4
2014-15	STL	24	37	22	7	4	2.28	.913	.917	56.3%	3.4	1.0	2.3	6.7
2015-16	STL	25	35					.914			3.9	0.7	0.3	4.9

As the Blues goalie of the future, Jake Allen spent the entire last season in the NHL, playing backup to Brian Elliott. When Elliott missed 14 games due to an injury, the New Brunswick native split time filling in with former Devils netminder Martin Brodeur. Like Brodeur, Allen possesses some puck skills, which helped him collect two assists in 37 games. In 172 AHL games, Allen stopped 91.7% of shots on goal. While his 2014-15 even-strength save percentage of .917 was below average, the 25-year-old still has time to develop and is expected to slowly take on a heavier workload.

Martin Brodeur							G							Retired
Season	Team	Age	GP	W	L	OT	GAA	Sv%	ESSV%	QS%	GGVT	DGVT	SGVT	GVT
2012-13	NJD	40	29	13	9	7	2.22	.901	.919	55.2%	-2.2	1.8	-1.6	-2.0
2013-14	NJD	41	39	19	14	6	2.51	.901	.906	48.7%	-5.6	1.6	-2.6	-6.6
2014-15	STL	42	7	3	3	0	2.87	.899	.915	40.0%	-1.4	0.1	0.0	-1.3
2015-16	Retired	43	17					.910			-0.8	0.3	-0.2	-0.8

Former Devils franchise goaltender Martin Brodeur split starts with Jake Allen when Brian Elliott missed some games with an injury. Weeks later, he retired to be part of the Blues front office. The 42-year-old had a .912 career save percentage in 1,266 regular-season games and a playoff save rate of .919. The puck-handling master finished his career with three Stanley Cups, four Vezina Trophies, a Calder Trophy, three First All-Star Team honors, two goals, and 45 assists during the regular season, and a goal and 12 assists during the playoffs. The only accomplishment left for "Marty" is an induction to the Hockey Hall of Fame.

Brian Elliott							G							STL
Season	Team	Age	GP	W	L	OT	GAA	Sv%	ESSV%	QS%	GGVT	DGVT	SGVT	GVT
2012-13	STL	27	24	14	8	1	2.28	.907	.917	60.0%	0.2	1.0	-0.2	1.0
2013-14	STL	28	31	18	6	2	1.96	.922	.924	64.0%	8.7	1.1	0.3	10.1
2014-15	STL	29	46	26	14	3	2.26	.917	.925	57.8%	7.4	0.9	0.7	9.1
2015-16	STL	30	38					.916			6.0	0.6	0.1	6.8

With Halak and Miller gone, 2014-15 was an opportunity for Brian Elliott to take hold of the number-one job. The 2003 ninth-round pick played in 46 games, a career high with St. Louis, but he also missed 14 contests with an injury. While he had never previously gotten the chance to be their number one or gotten a shot to go deep in the playoffs, Elliott has been solid during regular seasons in St. Louis, with a .923 save percentage and only one season with a save rate of less than .915.

Wesley Chu

San Jose Sharks

The line between making the postseason and missing it was razor thin in 2014-15. The San Jose Sharks can surely attest to that. Both they and division rival Los Angeles suffered similar fates despite having playoff-worthy seasons. While some teams can exhibit clear evidence for their failings, you need more of a fine-toothed comb to describe what happened to San Jose. Consequently, they still have the players and the numbers to be a competitive team in 2015-16.

When we say that the differences were razor thin, they really were in terms of regular-season performance. There were no gross dips in performance or blatantly telling stats. It may come as a surprise to discover—maybe to Todd McLellan's chagrin—that they were a very similar team to the 2013-14 Sharks who were considered a Cup favorite heading into the playoffs.

Puck possession-wise, there wasn't much of a gap. San Jose's five-on-five Corsi from 2011-12 to 2014-15 has been strong and steady: 51.8%, 51.3%, 53.5%, 51.2%. Their PDO was the lowest it has been since 2007-2008, but not by any large margin (99.7 in 2013-14 and 99.1 in 2014-15). Sure, they had some bad puck luck, but it was not a major reason for them falling out of the race so late. Everything just took a small tick towards the negative, and that was all it took. Goals against were slightly up, goals for were slightly down, shots against were up, shots for were down. Even in close games they were bit worse off than 2013-14 (maybe their best chance at a title), but still just as good as in 2011-12 and 2012-13. Those were years in which the Sharks made the playoffs on the strength of 40+ win seasons (pro-rating the 2012-13 lockout-shortened season, of course). The smallest of details matter, as the only real differences were that the Sharks allowed the most scoring chances and high-danger chances against since 2009-2010, and they got less than stellar special teams play when it mattered. Those factors, coupled with goaltender Antti Niemi's continued mediocrity (though he was essentially no different from the 2013-14 Niemi at even strength), equaled coming up short in a talented Western Conference.

The decimals in difference between San Jose as a powerhouse and San Jose as summer golfers point us toward the potential for the Sharks to be a playoff team again in 2015-16. What happened to them and what caused their monumental collapse down the stretch could be attributed to just plain bad luck and key losses. The Sharks had an 80% chance of making the playoffs as of early February; what happened in the ensuing month was

SHARKS IN A BOX

Last Season
Goals For	228	17th
Goals Against	232	23rd
GVT	-4	20th
Points	89	t-22nd
Playoffs	Did not make playoffs	

The aging Sharks remain a strong possession team, but they missed the playoffs for the first time in the Joe Thornton era.

Three-Year Record
GVT	53	10th
Points	257	8th
Playoffs	2 Appearances, 11 Wins	

VUKOTA Projection
Goals For	230	6th
Goals Against	212	5th
GVT	18	2nd
Points	98	2nd

San Jose remains a team with elite top-end talent. They are likely to return to the playoff picture.

Top Three Prospects
T. Meier (F), J. Roy (D), J. Donski (F)

a decline of crazy proportions. Their probabilities dropped from 80% to almost 20% in a month, while they compiled a record of 13-16-3 from the start of February to season's end. Though the team actually got better goaltending in close games in the final 32 games of the regular season versus the first 50 games (.919 to .907 save percentage), it was offset by less scoring (2.3 versus 2.6 goals per game). Calgary's miraculous run coinciding with some key San Jose losses—to Arizona, Vancouver, Winnipeg, Los Angeles, and two to the Flames in the final two and a half months—ended up being the death knell for the Sharks. It was as much a matter of who they lost to as how many they lost—losing an unacceptable number of points to teams they were fighting with for playoff spots.

To make matters worse, San Jose had a penalty kill that was lacking (78.5%) when compared to 2013-14 team (84.9%). Especially down the stretch, the penalty kill went MIA, giving up 24 power-play goals in 32 games. That number, 24, was the same number they gave up in the 50 previous games! As coaches like to say, it is not how many you give up, but when you give them up. Of the 24 power-play goals against in the final 32 games, 15 of them came in a close or tied score.

While the shortcomings of 2014-15 were a perfect storm for disappointment, the Sharks still retain an outstanding group of players, several which rank at the higher end of most analytics and traditional stats. Joe Pavelski, Joe Thornton, Logan Couture, and Patrick Marleau are all very good hockey players—though concerns about Marleau's age plus sharp decline are valid. Pavelski and Thornton ranked in the top 20 of possession forwards, while Tomas Hertl and youngster Melker Karlsson landed inside the top 100. The Sharks also have a solid group of blueliners in Marc-Edouard Vlasic, Brendan Dillon, and now newcomer Paul Martin. The one question mark will be in goal, with the tandem of (former Kings' backup) Martin Jones and Alex Stalock slated to kick off the season. However, considering that the team had goaltending that rated in the bottom third of the league for the last two seasons, there is no reason to believe they could be significantly worse off.

San Jose fans can rest easier knowing that, in the least, there is new voice in the locker room with former Panthers and Devils bench boss Peter DeBoer. While McLellan proved to be a capable coach, a new voice and new message should be a good thing after these past few seasons of collapse.

Though the window of opportunity is closing year after year on this group, the Sharks should be right back in the mix for a playoff position barring an unexpected downturn or key injuries. None of their overall numbers suggest otherwise. They simply fell on the wrong side of some key results and failed to tighten down their special teams when it mattered.

Jason Lewis

SAN JOSE SHARKS

Even-Strength Usage: San Jose Sharks

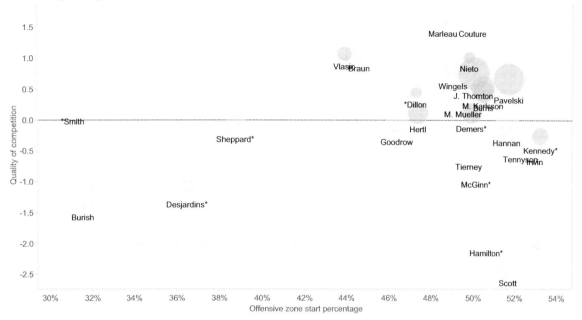

Special Teams Usage: San Jose Sharks

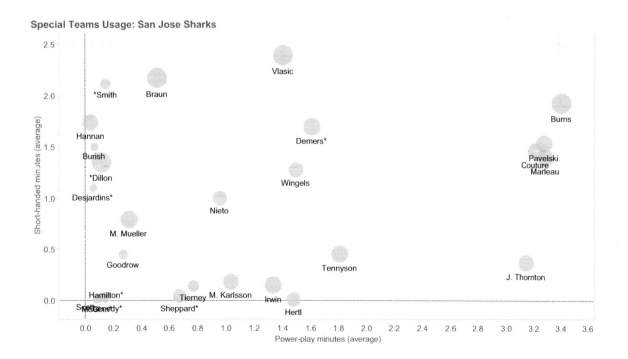

Offensive Profile: San Jose Sharks

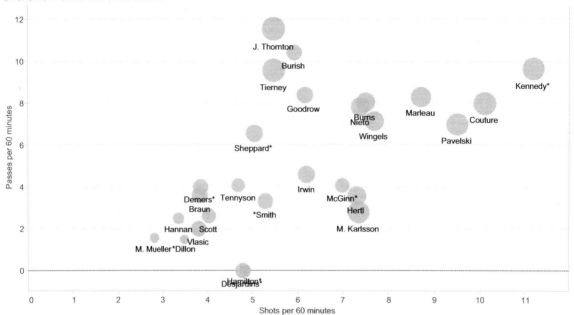

Cap Efficiency: San Jose Sharks

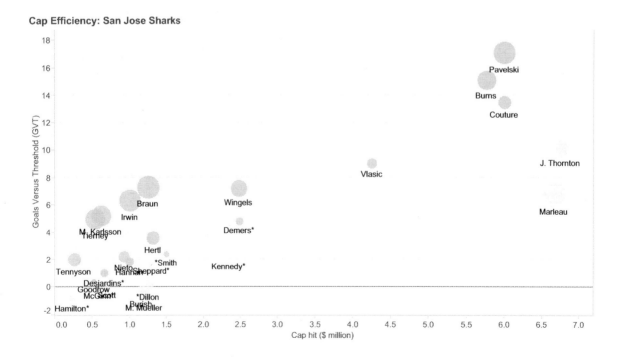

SAN JOSE SHARKS

FORWARDS

Mike Brown — RW/LW — SJS

Season	Team	Age	GP	G	A	Pts	+/-	ESP/60	AdjCF%	iCF/60	OGVT	DGVT	SGVT	GVT
2012-13	TOR, EDM	27	39	1	1	2	-7	0.42	40.3%	10.3	-1.6	0.0	0.0	-1.6
2013-14	EDM, SJS	28	56	2	3	5	-9	0.76	46.8%	11.6	-1.9	0.1	0.0	-1.8
2014-15	SJS	29	12	0	0	0	0	0.00	45.3%	14.8	-0.5	0.1	0.0	-0.3
2015-16	SJS	30	38	3	4	7					-0.5	0.7	0.0	0.2

Mike Brown's playing days are numbered, at least in the NHL. Traditional enforcers, as well as players who exclusively bring grit and compete level are being replaced by players who actually contribute to their club's point totals rather than PIM totals. When the five-foot-eleven, 205-pound winger was healthy—before suffering a broken right fibula—his 22 penalty minutes were his sole "contribution". Despite being paid a $1.3 million salary through the 2015-16 season, it should come as no surprise to see the former Leaf's playing time drop in favor of younger, faster teammates—upping San Jose's skill in lieu of pugnacity.

Adam Burish — C/RW — Free Agent

Season	Team	Age	GP	G	A	Pts	+/-	ESP/60	AdjCF%	iCF/60	OGVT	DGVT	SGVT	GVT
2012-13	SJS	29	46	1	2	3	-7	0.28	44.0%	10.1	-1.7	1.2	0.0	-0.4
2013-14	SJS	30	15	0	0	0	-4	0.00	54.4%	8.9	-1.1	0.2	0.0	-0.9
2014-15	SJS	31	20	1	2	3	-6	0.94	37.7%	10.4	-0.5	0.1	0.0	-0.4
2015-16	Free Agent	32	32	4	5	8					0.0	0.6	0.0	0.6

When Adam Burish signed with San Jose in 2012, he was expected to bring a strong veteran presence and gritty energy to a club that felt it was lacking in work ethic and will to win. However, the six-foot-one winger found it difficult to maintain a consistent spot in the lineup, eventually getting waived in November 2014 to clear space for younger talent after scratching out three points in 20 games. The 2006 NCAA champion—as captain of the Wisconsin Badgers—found a home with the AHL's Worcester Sharks, and eventually the AHL's Chicago Wolves, but was bought out of his remaining contract by San Jose over the summer.

Logan Couture — C — SJS

Season	Team	Age	GP	G	A	Pts	+/-	ESP/60	AdjCF%	iCF/60	OGVT	DGVT	SGVT	GVT
2012-13	SJS	23	48	21	16	37	7	2.13	52.5%	16.5	7.5	1.7	1.5	10.7
2013-14	SJS	24	65	23	31	54	21	2.41	54.8%	17.6	8.3	5.1	2.3	15.7
2014-15	SJS	25	82	27	40	67	-6	2.08	50.7%	17.7	9.9	3.0	0.5	13.5
2015-16	SJS	26	77	28	38	66					9.2	3.3	0.1	12.6

Logan Couture entered the league expected to be an offensive virtuoso, but he has evolved into an adaptable two-way player who also features great production. The 2007 ninth-overall selection finished second in points (67) behind Pavelski, and led the club in even-strength goals (18). Offensively, excellent puck management in the cycle, a deceptive release, and an evolving playmaking toolkit characterize Couture's game. In the other zones, "Cooch" assumes control with cerebral zone-exit passes, responsible play in the neutral zone, and deceptive stick work both on and off the puck. The former Ottawa 67 is in his prime at age 26 and will be expected to carry the team along with Pavleski, as the abilities of the aging Thornton and Marleau start to fade.

Barclay Goodrow							**RW/LW**						**SJS**
Season	Team	Age	GP	G	A	Pts	+/-	ESP/60	AdjCF%	iCF/60	OGVT	DGVT	SGVT	GVT
2014-15	SJS	21	60	4	8	12	-1	1.06	47.3%	11.8	-0.5	1.4	-0.5	0.4
2015-16	SJS	22	55	7	10	16					0.1	1.5	0.0	1.6

Barclay Goodrow had a surprising yet unremarkable rookie season. Entering training camp as an undrafted five-year OHL veteran, he cracked the Sharks opening lineup due to lingering injuries suffered by Tyler Kennedy, James Sheppard, and Raffi Torres. His agitating, high-energy, north-south playing style is exciting, similar to Tomas Hertl, Matt Nieto, and Chris Tierney. However, where his drafted counterparts excel in offensive decision-making and execution, Goodrow falters—he doesn't necessarily contribute to the bottom line. His 12 points and lowly 47.3% score-adjusted Corsi suggest he will develop into a utility third or fourth liner. The Sharks seem to have amassed a surplus of bottom-six forwards that will need vetting. Fortunately for Goodrow, his youth, speed, and slight offensive upside will play in his favor.

Micheal Haley							**C/LW**						**SJS**
Season	Team	Age	GP	G	A	Pts	+/-	ESP/60	AdjCF%	iCF/60	OGVT	DGVT	SGVT	GVT
2012-13	NYR	26	9	0	0	0	-1	0.00	35.7%	4.9	-0.3	0.0	0.0	-0.3
2014-15	SJS	28	4	0	0	0	-1	0.00	32.6%	3.4	-0.2	0.0	0.0	-0.2
2015-16	SJS	29	25	4	5	8					0.4	0.5	0.0	0.9

Micheal Haley is a replacement-level player who hasn't found a permanent NHL home over his nine-year career. He plays a rough and rugged game but is not much of a production artist at lower levels. In "the Woo", Haley recorded 31 points in 68 games—plus 100 penalty minutes. Unfortunately, he had managed only three points in 52 career games with the Islanders and Rangers before landing in San Jose. It should come as no surprise to see a player of Haley's caliber with a penchant for fighting standing in for John Scott—who was serving a four-game suspension—although what is remarkable is that Haley stands nearly a foot shorter than the man-mountain.

Eriah Hayes							**RW**						**STL**
Season	Team	Age	GP	G	A	Pts	+/-	ESP/60	AdjCF%	iCF/60	OGVT	DGVT	SGVT	GVT
2013-14	SJS	25	15	1	0	1	-2	0.51	51.0%	13.6	-0.4	0.0	0.0	-0.3
2014-15	SJS	26	4	0	0	0	-2	0.00	45.0%	15.7	-0.3	-0.1	0.0	-0.4
2015-16	STL	27	29	5	5	10					0.5	0.5	0.0	1.0

Eriah Hayes was another undrafted, college-signed player sitting in San Jose's reserves that had a proclivity for producing at the lower levels but struggled to find similar results in the professional ranks. In his first tour of duty with Worcester in 2013-14, the former Waterloo Black Hawk tallied an uninspiring 21 points in 59 games, and only improved that result by four points in as many games the following season. Although he does possess some qualities one would see in a typical power forward, the six-foot-four, 209-pound Hayes is nothing more than a replacement-level winger.

SAN JOSE SHARKS

Tomas Hertl							C/LW						SJS
Season	Team	Age	GP	G	A	Pts	+/-	ESP/60	AdjCF%	iCF/60	OGVT	DGVT	SGVT	GVT
2013-14	SJS	20	37	15	10	25	11	2.69	57.9%	17.5	5.2	2.1	-0.2	7.0
2014-15	SJS	21	82	13	18	31	-5	1.40	54.1%	14.2	2.3	2.0	-0.8	3.6
2015-16	SJS	22	71	19	22	40					4.6	2.2	-0.1	6.7

Coming off an electric rookie season that was inopportunely cut off, Tomas Hertl responded with an understated sophomore campaign. When drafted 17th overall in 2012, Hertl was projected as a consistent top-six scoring center, but was shuttled up and down Todd McLellan's lineup for the majority of the season before settling on the third line—though with a rotating cast of linemates. Since leaving Joe Thornton's side, Hertl's shots per 60 minutes dropped from 38.7 to 32.9, he received about one less shift per game, and his shooting percentage finished at 9.2%, a much more sustainable figure than last year's fluky 15.2%. Nevertheless, the young Czech has the raw offensive tools and stature to be a stable NHL goal scorer in time as he gradually finds a consistent role in San Jose.

Melker Karlsson							C/RW						SJS
Season	Team	Age	GP	G	A	Pts	+/-	ESP/60	AdjCF%	iCF/60	OGVT	DGVT	SGVT	GVT
2014-15	SJS	24	53	13	11	24	-3	1.83	54.4%	13.4	2.6	1.8	0.7	5.2
2015-16	SJS	25	57	15	16	31					3.4	1.8	0.0	5.2

Playing alongside Thornton and Pavelski is a pretty nice way to be ushered into the NHL, and like the few before him—think Jonathan Cheechoo and Devin Setoguchi—Melker Karlsson found instant success. Signed following San Jose's infamous playoff collapse to Los Angeles, the former SHLer performed well beyond expectations, tallying 13 goals and 24 assists while skating on the top line for the majority of his 56 games. The "Melk Man" did suffer through periodic droughts, as expected from a rookie forward. With his intensity and work ethic, he projects to be a middle-six forward.

Bryan Lerg							C/LW						SJS
Season	Team	Age	GP	G	A	Pts	+/-	ESP/60	AdjCF%	iCF/60	OGVT	DGVT	SGVT	GVT
2014-15	SJS	28	2	1	0	1	-1	2.59	60.9%	23.8	0.5	0.0	0.0	0.5
2015-16	SJS	29	26	6	6	12					1.2	0.6	0.0	1.7

29-year-old Worcester Sharks captain Bryan Lerg is a perennial AHLer who was finally rewarded with big-league playing time after eight years of minor-league service. The former Michigan State Spartan made his debut on April 9 and was rewarded once again by celebrating his first NHL goal. The journeyman depth forward has a history of great production at the AHL level and has a wealth of professional experience to draw upon, but there is no more than a minute likelihood he will be more than an occasional future call-up.

Patrick Marleau							LW/C						SJS
Season	Team	Age	GP	G	A	Pts	+/-	ESP/60	AdjCF%	iCF/60	OGVT	DGVT	SGVT	GVT
2012-13	SJS	33	48	17	14	31	-2	1.39	53.5%	15.2	3.7	2.4	0.7	6.9
2013-14	SJS	34	82	33	37	70	0	2.16	54.2%	16.4	10.5	4.7	1.3	16.5
2014-15	SJS	35	82	19	38	57	-17	1.62	50.7%	13.0	5.5	2.0	-0.7	6.8
2015-16	SJS	36	70	20	30	50					5.6	2.3	0.0	7.9

San Jose's all-time leading scorer, Patrick Marleau is a perennial workhorse, but he has begun to show his age. The Saskatchewan native endured his worst even-strength points per 60 minutes in a full season, lowest score-adjusted Corsi (50.7%), and a remarkably low shooting percentage (8.2%). At age 35, "Patty" was still deployed in San Jose's top shutdown trio with Logan Couture, which certainly has influence over his deflating performance, hinting to management of how he should be utilized in the future. Marleau has long been in discussion as trade bait despite his relatively consistent performance as a speedy scoring winger. His three-year, $20 million contract expires in 2018.

Matt Nieto							LW						SJS
Season	Team	Age	GP	G	A	Pts	+/-	ESP/60	AdjCF%	iCF/60	OGVT	DGVT	SGVT	GVT
2013-14	SJS	21	66	10	14	24	-4	1.44	52.7%	13.4	3.8	1.2	0.0	5.0
2014-15	SJS	22	72	10	17	27	-12	1.38	52.9%	12.6	0.5	2.0	-0.3	2.2
2015-16	SJS	23	65	14	19	33					2.9	2.0	0.0	4.9

Matt Nieto was primed for a role as a second-line scoring winger riding shotgun with Marleau and Couture, but the Long Beach, California native ended up bouncing around the lineup after periods of inconsistency. After finally finding a home on the third line with pesky center Chris Tierney, Nieto posted a reasonable 27 points in 72 games but registered a team-worst 3.3 goals-against per minutes 60. Marked by decent hockey sense and a diligent work ethic, a bottom-six role suits this agitating, high-energy player. However, San Jose possesses many young, small, speedy forwards with offensive upside, which makes Nieto—like the others—quite expendable.

Joe Pavelski							C/RW						SJS
Season	Team	Age	GP	G	A	Pts	+/-	ESP/60	AdjCF%	iCF/60	OGVT	DGVT	SGVT	GVT
2012-13	SJS	28	48	16	15	31	2	1.66	53.2%	14.2	4.3	2.6	-1.5	5.4
2013-14	SJS	29	82	41	38	79	23	2.28	57.4%	15.8	17.6	6.1	0.5	24.2
2014-15	SJS	30	82	37	33	70	12	1.86	56.9%	14.6	13.1	4.6	-0.6	17.1
2015-16	SJS	31	75	31	33	64					9.7	3.3	0.0	12.9

Joe Pavelski has quietly become an offensive anchor and all-around force in San Jose. Coming off another career year, the 205th-overall draft pick from 2003 led the Sharks in points (70), power-player goals (19), goals-for percentage (57%), and scoring-chances-for percentage (56%), the latter two adjusted for score effects. All of this despite regularly lining up against top competition in all situations. Although Pavelski played on a line that featured Joe Thornton's support and Melker Karlsson's eagerness, the versatile and relentless American is clearly at the peak of his career and has found a comfortable spot as natural leader on an otherwise identity-less Sharks club.

John Scott							LW						ARI
Season	Team	Age	GP	G	A	Pts	+/-	ESP/60	AdjCF%	iCF/60	OGVT	DGVT	SGVT	GVT
2012-13	BUF	30	34	0	0	0	-1	0.00	43.9%	7.5	-1.3	0.2	0.0	-1.2
2013-14	BUF	31	56	1	0	1	-12	0.16	38.5%	3.6	-3.5	-0.1	0.0	-3.6
2014-15	SJS	32	38	3	1	4	0	0.85	46.0%	8.5	-0.8	0.8	0.0	0.0
2015-16	ARI	33	43	3	2	5					-1.0	0.7	0.0	-0.3

John Scott is one of the last tried-and-true enforcers remaining in the National Hockey League who have not kept up with the game's paradigm shifts. However, recall early last season when the lumbering giant absolutely sniped a wristshot past Washington goaltender Braden Holtby? It not only amazed Sharks fans and hockey analysts, but indifferent spectators alike. "The big man can score!" they sang. Perhaps things were changing for the mammoth—he would adapt to the shifting environment and possibly even thrive in a world where speed and skill are king. But alas, in 38 games, Scott amassed 87 of something (and it wasn't points), and all optimism was exchanged for a dose of reality. Yet for reasons unknown to us, the legend of John Scott continues.

Ben Smith								RW						SJS
Season	Team	Age	GP	G	A	Pts	+/-	ESP/60	AdjCF%	iCF/60	OGVT	DGVT	SGVT	GVT
2012-13	CHI	24	1	1	0	1	1	3.96	48.5%	7.5	0.5	0.0	0.0	0.5
2013-14	CHI	25	75	14	12	26	3	1.73	51.9%	10.6	3.6	2.5	0.0	6.1
2014-15	CHI, SJS	26	80	7	7	14	2	0.97	50.2%	10.7	-0.5	2.8	0.0	2.4
2015-16	SJS	27	63	9	9	18					0.5	2.3	0.0	2.7

After a breakout season for Chicago in 2013-14 where he posted 26 points in 75 games, Ben Smith's encore was markedly less productive. This is likely explained by his shooting percentage dropping eight percentage points, and replacing skilled linemates Andrew Shaw and Brandon Saad with the likes of…John Scott and Mike Brown. The trade deadline acquisition has upside, but without any specific niche to his game, Smith is an average utility player who can provide some offense but ultimately relies on energy and tenacity over significant skill.

Daniil Tarasov								RW/LW						KHL
Season	Team	Age	GP	G	A	Pts	+/-	ESP/60	AdjCF%	iCF/60	OGVT	DGVT	SGVT	GVT
2014-15	SJS	23	5	0	1	1	2	1.67	54.6%	13.0	0.0	0.3	0.0	0.3
2015-16	KHL	24	28	5	7	11					0.8	0.7	0.0	1.5

Daniil Tarasov is a young, skilled, quick, productive Russian winger who has yet to make an impact at the NHL level despite impressive numbers in the minors. The six-foot, 185-pound former USHL star demonstrated offensive upside while playing in Worcester, but in five NHL games he produced one assist and had difficulty making any significant impact. Due to his inability to translate his skill and talent to the NHL (did he really get a chance?), the undrafted winger will return to his hometown to play for the HC Dynamo Moscow.

Joe Thornton								C						SJS
Season	Team	Age	GP	G	A	Pts	+/-	ESP/60	AdjCF%	iCF/60	OGVT	DGVT	SGVT	GVT
2012-13	SJS	33	48	7	33	40	6	1.63	54.6%	8.6	5.5	1.7	0.0	7.1
2013-14	SJS	34	82	11	65	76	20	2.75	59.1%	7.5	9.4	4.7	1.8	15.9
2014-15	SJS	35	78	16	49	65	-4	2.22	58.5%	10.1	8.4	2.5	-0.8	10.1
2015-16	SJS	36	68	14	38	53					5.7	2.3	0.1	8.1

Despite having the captaincy stripped away, receiving affirmation that San Jose wants to ice a younger club, and even publicly clashing with general manager Doug Wilson, Joe Thornton continues to produce. Polarizing "Jumbo Joe" finished his most recent campaign as 36th all-time in points, and second among active skaters behind the ageless Jaromir Jagr. The power center led his club with 2.7 points per 60 minutes in all situations while posting a 63.2% scoring-chances-for, despite being well past his peak at age 35. Few arguments suggest that Thornton should not be Hall-of-Famer regardless whether he ends up with a championship ring or not.

Although as the 2006 Hart Memorial Trophy winner jaunts towards retirement it doesn't seem like much will hold the wily veteran back.

Chris Tierney   C   SJS

Season	Team	Age	GP	G	A	Pts	+/-	ESP/60	AdjCF%	iCF/60	OGVT	DGVT	SGVT	GVT
2014-15	SJS	20	43	6	15	21	3	2.09	48.2%	10.4	3.4	1.5	0.0	4.9
2015-16	SJS	21	48	10	18	28					3.4	1.6	0.0	5.0

Drafting London Knights captain Chris Tierney 55th overall in 2013, the Sharks acquired an effective two-way centerman with excellent hockey sense and an ability to finish as well as create plays. After cracking the opening night roster, Tierney eventually found chemistry with Wingels and Nieto and finished the season with a highly-respectable 2.09 even-strength points per 60 minutes while shooting 12.5%. Although likely to lightly regress, the excellent north-south force justified he is an NHLer with staying power; Tierney will unquestionably start as San Jose's third-line center with excellent opportunity for growth.

Raffi Torres   LW

Season	Team	Age	GP	G	A	Pts	+/-	ESP/60	AdjCF%	iCF/60	OGVT	DGVT	SGVT	GVT
2012-13	SJS	30	39	7	11	18	0	2.15	50.9%	11.4	2.2	1.0	0.5	3.8
2013-14	SJS	31	5	3	2	5	4	6.57	52.4%	15.9	1.6	0.5	0.0	2.1
2015-16	SJS	32	7	2	2	4					0.7	0.3	0.1	1.1

Streaky winger Raffi Torres did not play a single game in 2014-15 due to a third season-ending knee injury. Having only appeared in five games over the past two years—posting an impressive five points in limited play—the punishing forward with a capricious past still seems to have some hockey left in him. Suspension and injury troubles aside, the two-time Stanley Cup finalist is a measure of consistency, posting a respectable 1.9 even-strength points per 60 minutes and a shooting percentage of 12.5% over 625 NHL games.

Tommy Wingels   RW   SJS

Season	Team	Age	GP	G	A	Pts	+/-	ESP/60	AdjCF%	iCF/60	OGVT	DGVT	SGVT	GVT
2012-13	SJS	24	42	5	8	13	-9	1.25	49.0%	11.1	-0.4	1.3	0.0	0.9
2013-14	SJS	25	77	16	22	38	11	1.72	53.8%	14.1	5.2	3.9	-0.3	8.8
2014-15	SJS	26	75	15	21	36	-7	1.46	48.8%	13.3	4.3	2.3	0.6	7.2
2015-16	SJS	27	65	16	21	36					4.1	2.4	0.0	6.5

Completing the first season of a three-year, $7.4 million contract, Tommy Wingels continued to demonstrate his utilitarian playing style. For a top-nine forward, his production was good but not great, though he makes up for offensive deficiencies with passionate play and an irritable confidence, registering the most hits among San Jose forwards (250). He continues to perform effectively in all situations, utilizing his deceptive shot. The 2008 sixth-round selection has found a comfortable home in between San Jose's second and third lines, valued as a versatile scoring winger.

DEFENSEMEN

Justin Braun							RD						SJS
Season	Team	Age	GP	G	A	Pts	+/-	ESP/60	AdjCF%	iCF/60	OGVT	DGVT	SGVT	GVT
2012-13	SJS	25	41	0	7	7	-5	0.55	51.0%	10.6	0.0	1.7	0.0	1.7
2013-14	SJS	26	82	4	13	17	19	0.66	55.4%	10.0	0.3	7.9	0.0	8.2
2014-15	SJS	27	70	1	22	23	8	0.98	50.9%	9.0	1.8	5.5	0.0	7.3
2015-16	SJS	28	67	4	17	21					1.5	4.7	0.0	6.2

Not a household name, Justin Braun is nevertheless a valuable top-pairing defenseman. Having signed a five-year, $19-million contract, he assumes some of the team's most challenging minutes for a relatively low cap hit, and does so quite successfully. Braun ranks third on San Jose in Corsi-against per 60 minutes, behind Olympic gold medalist Marc-Edouard Vlasic and the highly-sheltered Matt Irwin. However, Braun matches or bests Vlasic in regular season production, average ice-time, and shot suppression. The 2007 seventh rounder rarely makes a mistake—whether in his own end or not. He won't surprise you with flash and dynamism. On the contrary, his value is derived from an ability to play within expectations, making excellent zone-exit passes, tightly covering opponents at the blueline, and preventing shot attempts and scoring chances remarkably well.

Brent Burns							RD						SJS
Season	Team	Age	GP	G	A	Pts	+/-	ESP/60	AdjCF%	iCF/60	OGVT	DGVT	SGVT	GVT
2012-13	SJS	27	30	9	11	20	0	2.37	55.1%	17.0	3.3	1.1	-0.3	4.1
2013-14	SJS	28	69	22	26	48	26	2.21	58.0%	22.6	7.9	4.4	-0.6	11.8
2014-15	SJS	29	82	17	43	60	-9	1.41	53.5%	16.6	11.7	3.0	0.4	15.1
2015-16	SJS	30	74	14	40	54					9.4	3.7	0.0	13.1

When it was announced that Brent Burns would play the entirety of the 2014-15 NHL season on defense, many Sharks fans felt betrayed given his effectiveness as a power forward. However, the Bay Area faithful breathed a collective sigh of relief when "Burnsie" finished the regular season second in defenseman production while taking on 24 minutes per game. The former Minnesota Wild favorite is not without his defensive faults, though. His infamous "butt-check" regularly throws him out of position, and he is much more effective when using brute strength to rush the puck rather than making the first pass. Whether this performance on the blueline is sustainable remains to be seen, but Silicon Valley stalwarts need not fret because the reptile-loving, Wookie-lookalike, idiosyncratic All-Star has proven to be successful wherever he is deployed.

Brenden Dillon							LD						SJS
Season	Team	Age	GP	G	A	Pts	+/-	ESP/60	AdjCF%	iCF/60	OGVT	DGVT	SGVT	GVT
2012-13	DAL	22	48	3	5	8	1	0.54	50.7%	9.8	0.2	2.2	0.0	2.4
2013-14	DAL	23	80	6	11	17	9	0.61	51.3%	8.0	1.0	5.0	0.0	6.0
2014-15	DAL, SJS	24	80	2	8	10	-13	0.33	51.5%	10.6	-2.0	2.1	0.0	0.1
2015-16	SJS	25	65	2	9	11					-0.9	2.8	0.0	1.9

In an early-season acquisition, GM Doug Wilson brought in Brendan Dillon for his well-rounded, physical playing style in a "hockey trade" for the puck-moving Jason Demers. Dillon performed just as expected: he provided shutdown relief for the top pairing, Vlasic and Braun, and added physicality to a sparse defense corps, all while lining up alongside the aging Scott Hannan and green Mirco Mueller. The New Westminster, British Columbia native recorded a 51.7% score-adjusted Corsi-for percentage while deployed in heavy minutes, a testament to his defensive acumen. Although he likely will not be a significant point producer, his knack for consuming minutes against dangerous competition means he will be an NHL mainstay for years to come. He certainly has upside.

Taylor Fedun						RD							VAN
Season	Team	Age	GP	G	A	Pts	+/-	ESP/60	AdjCF%	iCF/60	OGVT	DGVT	SGVT	GVT
2013-14	EDM	25	4	2	0	2	-1	2.74	46.6%	13.6	0.6	0.1	0.0	0.7
2014-15	SJS	26	7	0	4	4	0	1.15	50.8%	11.8	1.3	0.0	0.0	1.3
2015-16	VAN	27	28	3	7	10					1.3	0.8	0.0	2.1

When Taylor Fedun did not receiving a qualifying offer from Edmonton following the 2013-14 season, San Jose scooped up the nimble puck-moving defenseman. Fedun is an energizing, defensively-responsible player with some scoring upside, although he has not proven it at the NHL level. He finished with 34 points with the AHL's Worcester Sharks, good for second among defensemen. Following a Vlasic injury, Fedun was called up late in the season and saw a healthy dose of third-pairing ice-time, recording a respectable four assists in seven games. Although he had suffered a significant injury over a year ago that slowed his development, Fedun now has an excellent opportunity to crack a sparse blueline in San Jose.

Scott Hannan						LD							Free Agent
Season	Team	Age	GP	G	A	Pts	+/-	ESP/60	AdjCF%	iCF/60	OGVT	DGVT	SGVT	GVT
2012-13	NSH, SJS	33	33	0	1	1	-14	0.11	45.4%	5.5	-2.1	0.1	0.0	-2.0
2013-14	SJS	34	56	3	9	12	1	0.75	51.3%	7.1	0.3	3.4	0.0	3.6
2014-15	SJS	35	58	2	5	7	0	0.50	47.5%	6.7	-0.9	2.8	0.0	1.8
2015-16	Free Agent	36	49	2	7	9					0.0	2.4	0.0	2.4

When Scott Hannan was offered a new contract in 2014, it was to provide some stability and mentorship for an inexperienced blueline, and consequently, he was often paired with younger partners like Matt Tennyson and Brenden Dillon. The 17-year veteran stay-at-home defenseman is a workhorse in every sense of the word, and is reasonably reliable, although starting to show signs of age. He posted a club-worst score-adjusted Corsi-for percentage among defensemen despite facing weak competition. Hannan does not possess the two-way acumen and puck-management skills that are so important for modern blueliners. Regardless, the former Kelowna Rocket is as intense and passionate as ever, which may warrant another contract in a lesser role in San Jose, or elsewhere in the league.

Matt Irwin						LD							BOS
Season	Team	Age	GP	G	A	Pts	+/-	ESP/60	AdjCF%	iCF/60	OGVT	DGVT	SGVT	GVT
2012-13	SJS	25	38	6	6	12	-1	0.64	54.7%	12.5	1.7	1.3	0.0	3.1
2013-14	SJS	26	62	2	17	19	5	0.76	51.5%	13.0	1.4	2.4	0.0	3.7
2014-15	SJS	27	53	8	11	19	3	1.17	51.8%	11.3	3.7	2.9	-0.3	6.3
2015-16	BOS	28	56	6	16	22					3.0	2.7	0.0	5.6

UMass product Matt Irwin signed with San Jose following his 2010 season and quickly demonstrated offensive value in Worcester before becoming a mainstay for San Jose in 2012. Since then, he has shown some improvement at the NHL level, sitting comfortably as a middle-of-the-road defenseman. This season, he posted a career-best 1.17 points per 60 minutes, but has been stagnant in his ability to drive possession numbers, especially as the most sheltered defenseman on the roster (by design, of course). The hope is that Irwin will step up and contribute offensively to a greater degree. At age 28, he will need to act fast or undoubtedly stay in limbo.

Mirco Mueller								LD						SJS
Season	Team	Age	GP	G	A	Pts	+/-	ESP/60	AdjCF%	iCF/60	OGVT	DGVT	SGVT	GVT
2014-15	SJS	19	39	1	3	4	-8	0.39	51.2%	6.6	-1.1	0.5	0.0	-0.6
2015-16	SJS	20	43	2	6	8					-0.4	1.3	0.0	1.0

More was expected from Mirco Mueller when the Swiss rookie secured a spot on the opening night roster. In 39 games, the six-foot-three defenseman posted roughly even possession numbers while averaging less than 17 minutes per game. Despite the positive signs, Mueller only managed a 40% goals-for percentage and a 54.0 Corsi-against per 60 minutes while playing alongside the bearded baron, Brent Burns—both measures adjusted for score and in the lower cohorts of San Jose defensemen. In addition, the lanky defender was prone to making questionable decisions with the puck and had difficulties managing opponents. After a season replete with injuries, inconsistent play, prolonged stints in the pressbox, and a mediocre World Juniors performance, the 2013 first-round draft pick will need to prove himself further.

Karl Stollery								LD						SJS
Season	Team	Age	GP	G	A	Pts	+/-	ESP/60	AdjCF%	iCF/60	OGVT	DGVT	SGVT	GVT
2013-14	COL	26	2	0	0	0	1	0.00	70.2%	9.6	-0.1	0.1	0.0	0.1
2014-15	COL, SJS	27	10	0	0	0	-1	0.00	56.5%	9.6	-0.5	0.4	0.0	0.0
2015-16	SJS	28	29	2	5	6					0.0	1.1	0.0	1.1

Camrose, Alberta native Karl Stollery is a solid puck-moving defenseman known for impressive AHL numbers and solid physicality considering his less-than-ideal size. The undrafted defender has a dozen NHL games under his belt since signing with Colorado as a free agent in 2013, but has registered no points. His proven ability to produce in the minors indicates he could be an occasional call-up, but expect him to spend the majority of his time with the team's new AHL affiliate, the San Jose Barracuda.

Matt Tennyson								RD						SJS
Season	Team	Age	GP	G	A	Pts	+/-	ESP/60	AdjCF%	iCF/60	OGVT	DGVT	SGVT	GVT
2012-13	SJS	22	4	0	2	2	2	1.93	56.8%	16.3	0.3	0.6	0.0	0.9
2014-15	SJS	24	27	2	6	8	0	0.73	46.7%	9.7	1.4	0.9	-0.3	2.0
2015-16	SJS	25	38	3	9	12					1.3	1.3	0.0	2.6

Another undrafted college free agent on San Jose's crowded roster, Matt Tennyson struggled to find his game. Touted as a natural offensive defenseman, and possessing the size and speed to become an NHL regular, Tennyson struggled against weaker competition and posted average possession numbers despite his cozy deployment. The Western Michigan product has yet to translate what was inspiring minor-league play to the bigs.

SAN JOSE SHARKS

Marc-Edouard Vlasic — LD — SJS

Season	Team	Age	GP	G	A	Pts	+/-	ESP/60	AdjCF%	iCF/60	OGVT	DGVT	SGVT	GVT
2012-13	SJS	25	48	3	4	7	5	0.48	54.0%	8.8	-1.0	3.9	0.0	3.0
2013-14	SJS	26	81	5	19	24	31	0.87	59.2%	13.0	2.7	9.3	0.0	12.1
2014-15	SJS	27	70	9	14	23	12	0.94	52.4%	9.3	2.6	6.4	0.0	9.0
2015-16	SJS	28	71	7	19	26						2.6	5.3	0.0	8.0

Marc-Edouard Vlasic has quietly become an elite defender, and is without question the anchor of San Jose's blueline. The new alternate captain is relied upon for his suffocating defensive play and ability to shut down the best opponents using a combination of mobile footwork, excellent stick position, and supreme puck management in all three zones. Although not outwardly physical or electrifying on offense like many top defenders in the league, the Olympic gold-medal-winning Quebecer effectively eats up big minutes while driving play.

GOALTENDERS

Troy Grosenick — G — SJS

Season	Team	Age	GP	W	L	OT	GAA	Sv%	ESSV%	QS%	GGVT	DGVT	SGVT	GVT
2014-15	SJS	25	2	1	1	0	1.53	.948	.945	50.0%	1.9	0.0	0.0	1.9
2015-16	SJS	26	14					.916			2.2	0.0	0.0	2.2

Former Union College starter Troy Grosenick made his debut on November 16, pitching a shutout against Carolina. The undrafted netminder was bombarded with 45 shots, singlehandedly defeating the Hurricanes using his athleticism, flash, and flair. He was rewarded with a second start the following night against the abysmal Buffalo Sabres, but this time, he recorded a loss after allowing three goals on 13 shots. The fluid, raw goaltender with a penchant for the spectacular save demonstrated that he still has a lot to learn in order to become an NHL regular. Fortunately, Grosenick has upside, which will allow him to compete against against the rest of the goaltending stable—Jones and Stalock—after signing a two-year, $1.2 million contract.

Antti Niemi — G — DAL

Season	Team	Age	GP	W	L	OT	GAA	Sv%	ESSV%	QS%	GGVT	DGVT	SGVT	GVT
2012-13	SJS	29	43	24	12	6	2.16	.924	.930	67.4%	17.0	0.2	2.2	19.4
2013-14	SJS	30	64	39	17	7	2.39	.913	.919	57.8%	4.0	1.6	-0.4	5.2
2014-15	SJS	31	61	31	23	7	2.59	.914	.922	52.5%	6.0	-0.2	2.2	8.1
2015-16	DAL	32	43					.914			4.1	0.3	0.2	4.6

After being between the pipes for a disastrous implosion in the 2014 Stanley Cup playoffs, 2010 Stanley Cup champion Antti Niemi rallied with a typically solid, NHL average-type season. "The Peninsula" is known for his focused demeanor, intense coverage of the crease, and remarkable reflexes, although he suffers from bouts of inconsistency and demonstrates difficulties managing the puck. However, when the Finnish netminder is well-positioned and has an opportunity to use his sound reflexes, he is a force in net.

Alex Stalock							G							SJS
Season	Team	Age	GP	W	L	OT	GAA	Sv%	ESSV%	QS%	GGVT	DGVT	SGVT	GVT
2012-13	SJS	25	2	0	0	1	2.86	.846	.818	0.0%	-0.6	0.1	0.0	-0.6
2013-14	SJS	26	24	12	5	2	1.87	.932	.934	72.2%	10.5	0.5	2.7	13.8
2014-15	SJS	27	22	8	9	2	2.62	.902	.914	52.6%	-3.5	0.6	-1.2	-4.1
2015-16	SJS	28	24					.915			3.5	0.3	0.0	3.9

Alex Stalock had an opportunity to dethrone Antti Niemi as the Sharks' *de facto* starter, but after opening the campaign with a shutout and matching Niemi's pace, the St. Paul, Minnesota native cooled down significantly. The six-foot, 190-pound goaltender did not improve on his spectacular 2013-14 season—on the contrary, his stats plummeted. The 2005 fourth rounder has mechanical issues and fumbles with certain fundamentals although he is athletic, flexible, and reactionary. The combination can result in Stalock making the improbable, big save at the expense of allowing the easy five-hole goal.

Benoit Roy

Tampa Bay Lightning

After a quick exit in the 2014 Stanley Cup playoffs, the Tampa Bay Lightning came into the 2014-15 season looking to prove they could be one of the top teams in the NHL. They succeeded, big time. The Lightning were runners up to the Chicago Blackhawks in the Stanley Cup Final after finishing the season second in score-adjusted Corsi percentage at five-on-five. The team's offense grew from very good to elite, with Steven Stamkos, Tyler Johnson, Nikita Kucherov, and Ondrej Palat leading the team to an NHL-best 260 goals.

Part of that impressive goal total was due to league-high 10.9% shooting (in all situations), a stat that tends to regress to the mean. Over the past five seasons, only one team (2009-10 Washington Capitals) had a higher shooting percentage over an 82-game season.

You may hear it said that regression is bound to occur, but there is reason to believe the Lightning will be able to rely on percentages—as well as possession—in order to remain one of the league's top offenses again next season, and into the near future. The roster that GM Steve Yzerman has built is set up to be a powerhouse for years to come, much like the Blackhawks.

Yzerman understood the modern state of hockey while building the Lightning: Tampa's possession dominance helps them get the puck on the stick of their best players. Starting from their defense, where they have possession heavyweights Victor Hedman and Anton Stralman, they are consistently able to get the puck out of their own zone, and force their opponents to make tough plays in order to get it back in. When their system works, their team speed creates numerous neutral-zone turnovers that allow them to enter the offensive zone with speed, and to create scoring chances.

Quick forwards such as Johnson and Kucherov allow the system work to near perfection, especially when paired with an excellent two-way player in Ondrej Palat. "The Triplets" were one of the league's best possession lines. All five were among the top 35 forwards (who played 750+ minutes) in score-adjusted SAT (over 55%).

Puck possession leads to the team's forwards getting more scoring chances than opposing forwards. However, what really separates Tampa from the rest of the league on offense is the number of forwards who have been capable of exceeding league average in shooting percentage.

The first and foremost is Steven Stamkos. In his seven-year NHL career, the Lightning captain has never finished with a shooting percentage

LIGHTNING IN A BOX

Last Season
Goals For	262	1st
Goals Against	211	t-11th
GVT	51	2nd
Points	108	5th
Playoffs	Lost Stanley Cup Final	

The emergence of a trio of young stars allowed the Lightning to surprise everyone, finishing just short of the Stanley Cup.

Three-Year Record
GVT	74	7th
Points	249	11th
Playoffs	2 Appearances, 14 Wins	

VUKOTA Projections
Goals For	235	5th
Goals Against	213	6th
GVT	22	1st
Points	99	1st

With a young lineup and the best offense in the league, Tampa Bay should be among the league's elite again.

Top Three Prospects
A. Vasilevsky (G), A. De Angelo (D), A. Erne (F)

below 12%, and since his rookie season, he has always topped 16%. The reason for this level of success seems to lie in his shot speed, a factor expected to affect shooting percentage (advanced video data, when it is available, is expected to support this conclusion). Stamkos has clocked shots at 104.5 mph, and even hit a 91-yard slapshot as part of a promotional stunt. With that type of rocket in his arsenal, it is no surprise the 2008 first-overall pick is consistently able to convert on his scoring chances, and remain among the league's leading goal scorers despite not matching the shot generation of his peers.

Even after Stamkos, the team has a number of players who profile well to have elevated shooting percentages—for instance, Kucherov and Johnson had shooting percentages over 14%. Both forwards are above-average skaters, and are good at getting themselves into open space where they can unleash their shots. Given the fact that they also play on a line separate from Stamkos, it also spreads the goal totals over the top lines.

Perhaps the most impressive part of Tampa's roster is that they are set up to succeed for a long time. The 18 players under the age of 26 who played at least one game for head coach Jon Cooper during the 2014-15 season scored an astounding 188 goals, 72% of the team's total.

The team that finished second in the league in goal differential had 72% of its offense come from players who can be expected to at least maintain their production level for the next three to four seasons—a fact that should be terrifying general managers across the league. To make matters worse for their opponents, the Lightning have an impressive array of prospects who can fill holes in their lineup when the veterans depart.

Andrei Vasilevskiy is considered one of the best goaltending prospects in the NHL right now. When Ben Bishop's contract runs out in 2017, the young Russian will be 23 and ready to take over the starting reins.

Defensemen Jason Garrison and Matt Carle are both 30, so when their performance starts to decline, Slater Koekkoek and Anthony DeAngelo will be ready to fill in their spots. Koekkoek had a solid AHL season at the age of 21, while DeAngelo tore up the OHL after being a 2014 first-round pick who slid down the draft board.

Centers Brian Boyle and Valtteri Filpulla are also in their thirties, but Vladislav Namestnikov, Cedric Paquette, and Brayden Point may be able to fill those slots. At wing, Adam Erne had 86 points in 60 games with the QMJHL's Quebec Remparts; he projects as a quality depth player.

It took a long time for the Lightning and their prospect system to start producing significant results, but the spectacular season in 2014-15 was just the beginning. Yzerman has laid out the blueprint for building a possession-dominant club. Expect to see many copycats going forward.

Shane O'Donnell

TAMPA BAY LIGHTNING

Even-Strength Usage: Tampa Bay Lightning

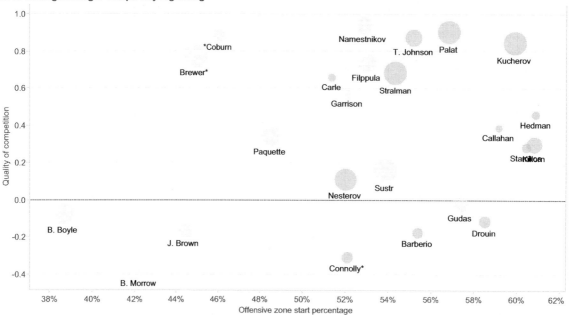

Special Teams Usage: Tampa Bay Lightning

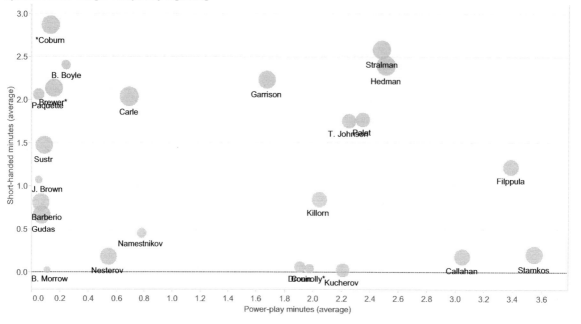

TAMPA BAY LIGHTNING

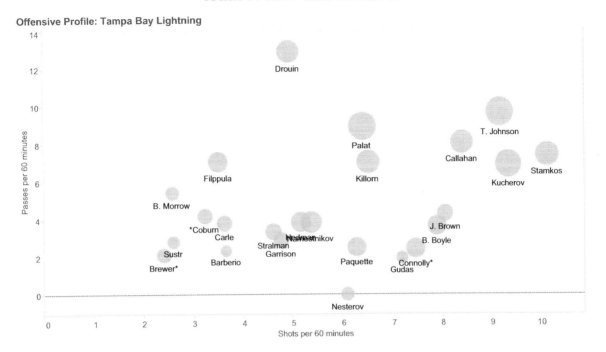

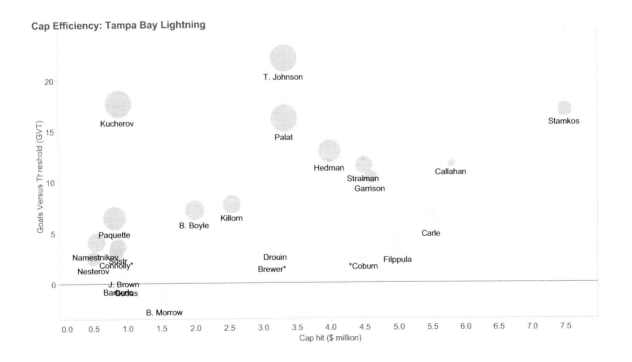

TAMPA BAY LIGHTNING

FORWARDS

Mike Angelidis — LW/C — TBL

Season	Team	Age	GP	G	A	Pts	+/-	ESP/60	AdjCF%	iCF/60	OGVT	DGVT	SGVT	GVT
2012-13	TBL	27	1	0	0	0	0	0.00	26.1%	7.7	0.0	0.1	0.0	0.1
2014-15	TBL	29	3	0	0	0	0	0.00	53.6%	0.0	-0.1	0.0	0.0	0.0
2015-16	TBL	30	24	4	5	8					0.5	0.5	0.0	1.0

At age 30, the NHL window for Mike Angelidis is essentially closed, and his value to a franchise is as an injury call-up. He played the vast majority of his season in the AHL, and was only up with the Bolts for three games. The Woodbridge, Ontario native fills an organizational role as captain of the AHL's Syracuse Crunch—since 2012-13—and a mentor for younger players. He was an alternate captain of the Calder Cup winner in 2012.

Carter Ashton — RW/LW — KHL

Season	Team	Age	GP	G	A	Pts	+/-	ESP/60	AdjCF%	iCF/60	OGVT	DGVT	SGVT	GVT
2013-14	TOR	22	32	0	3	3	1	0.91	44.5%	11.4	-0.5	0.4	0.0	-0.1
2014-15	TOR	23	7	0	0	0	-3	0.00	40.5%	10.1	-0.4	-0.2	0.0	-0.6
2015-16	KHL	29	25	4	5	8					0.3	0.4	0.0	0.8

After scoring 19 goals in 56 games in his first AHL season back in 2011-12, it seemed like the 29th-overall selection from 2009 was well on his way to becoming an NHL power forward. However, Carter Ashton did not build off his quality season, struggling mightily every time he was called up. In 54 NHL games, he has a grand total of three assists. The six-foot-three winger was big on talent but short on hockey IQ as he continued to frustrate coaches. Further, suspensions for PEDs did not help his cause. Ashton signed to play in the KHL this offseason.

Mike Blunden — RW/LW — TBL

Season	Team	Age	GP	G	A	Pts	+/-	ESP/60	AdjCF%	iCF/60	OGVT	DGVT	SGVT	GVT
2012-13	MTL	26	5	0	0	0	-1	0.00	46.2%	10.3	-0.4	0.1	0.0	-0.3
2013-14	MTL	27	7	0	0	0	-2	0.00	25.4%	5.8	-0.6	-0.1	0.0	-0.6
2014-15	TBL	28	2	0	0	0	-1	0.00	42.3%	3.2	-0.1	-0.1	0.0	-0.2
2015-16	TBL	29	25	4	5	8					0.3	0.4	0.0	0.8

Mike Blunden and Mike Angelidis are almost interchangeable, as both are big-bodied players who are past their prime, and only provide value to an NHL team as organizational depth. Blunden is 29 years old, and was initially drafted in the second round of 2005 by Chicago, before bouncing around to Columbus, Montreal, and finally, Tampa Bay. The six-foot-four, 216 pounder re-signed with the organization, slated to return to their Syracuse affiliate.

Brian Boyle — C — TBL

Season	Team	Age	GP	G	A	Pts	+/-	ESP/60	AdjCF%	iCF/60	OGVT	DGVT	SGVT	GVT
2012-13	NYR	28	38	2	3	5	-13	0.54	49.7%	12.7	-2.0	-0.1	0.0	-2.1
2013-14	NYR	29	82	6	12	18	1	0.98	47.3%	13.1	0.1	4.4	0.0	4.5
2014-15	TBL	30	82	15	9	24	3	1.49	51.0%	14.3	3.2	3.9	0.0	7.2
2015-16	TBL	31	65	9	10	19					0.3	2.3	0.0	2.6

Former Boston College captain Brian Boyle is one of the few NHL pivots that actually fulfill the role of a shutdown center, as he had some of the toughest minutes on the team but managed to perform better than expected in terms of possession. The six-foot-seven, 245-pound giant uses his size and skill to his advantage, making offense difficult for the opposition. Given that the Lightning have Tyler Johnson and Steven Stamkos as their #1 and #2 centers, having Boyle to impede the opposition's top lines allows the top two to concentrate on creating offense. The back-to-back Stanley Cup finalist is signed with Tampa through the 2016-17 season with a reasonable cap hit of $2 million per year.

J.T. Brown								**RW**						**TBL**
Season	Team	Age	GP	G	A	Pts	+/-	ESP/60	AdjCF%	iCF/60	OGVT	DGVT	SGVT	GVT
2013-14	TBL	23	63	4	15	19	-9	1.31	52.3%	14.4	0.0	0.9	0.0	0.9
2014-15	TBL	24	52	3	6	9	-2	1.09	51.3%	15.1	-0.4	1.2	0.0	0.7
2015-16	TBL	25	53	6	9	15					-0.6	1.1	0.0	0.5

J.T. Brown was signed out of the University of Minnesota-Duluth as an undrafted free agent back in 2012, and after having a solid year in the AHL, became a fixture in Tampa Bay's bottom six at the end of 2013-14, and for almost all of 2014-15. Most of his usage with Tampa has been in a defensive role, skating on the team's fourth line with Brian Boyle and Brenden Morrow. There, he added some speed and skill to one of the better shutdown lines in the league. The five-foot-ten Minnesotan may not have posted impressive point totals, but he did outperform his usage in terms of possession. At age 25, Brown should be in his prime. The former Waterloo Black Hawk does have top-six potential, so he has a chance to move up the lineup.

Ryan Callahan								**RW**						**TBL**
Season	Team	Age	GP	G	A	Pts	+/-	ESP/60	AdjCF%	iCF/60	OGVT	DGVT	SGVT	GVT
2012-13	NYR	27	45	16	15	31	9	1.69	51.8%	16.5	4.4	2.4	0.4	7.2
2013-14	NYR, TBL	28	65	17	19	36	1	1.43	50.9%	15.6	2.8	3.0	-0.8	5.0
2014-15	TBL	29	77	24	30	54	9	2.04	53.7%	13.3	9.4	1.8	0.4	11.7
2015-16	TBL	30	66	17	24	41					4.2	1.9	0.0	6.1

The fate of Ryan Callahan will forever be tied to the famous "captain-for-captain" swap that took place before the 2014 trade deadline, when Martin St. Louis (then the captain of the Tampa Bay Lightning) and Callahan (then the captain of the New York Rangers) were exchanged for one another after St. Louis requested a trade. Though Callahan isn't the captain in Tampa, he plays a prominent leadership role, and contributes on the ice. He was a better than breakeven possession player in 2014-15, and his power-play skills resulted in an overall 2.35 points per 60 minutes rate. Though he struggled in the playoffs, he is still one of the team's better forwards, especially on the man advantage. He will be hard pressed to maintain his level of play (and spot in the lineup) through 2020 (when his contract expires), but if he can, it will be safe to say that Tampa made out in the captain-for-captain trade.

Jonathan Drouin								**LW**						**TBL**
Season	Team	Age	GP	G	A	Pts	+/-	ESP/60	AdjCF%	iCF/60	OGVT	DGVT	SGVT	GVT
2014-15	TBL	19	70	4	28	32	3	1.98	54.3%	10.8	3.1	1.1	-0.5	3.7
2015-16	TBL	20	60	8	25	33					2.5	1.1	0.0	3.6

Jonathan Drouin was considered a Calder Trophy favorite before the season started, and though he certainly had the skill to win the NHL's rookie of the year award, a lack of ice-time severely limited his point totals and kept him off of the voters' radar. However, that doesn't mean his season was a failure, as the former Halifax Moosehead showcased the skill that got him drafted third overall back in 2013. He was fifth on the team in points per 60 minutes, and held his own in terms of possession. His absence from most of the playoffs is slightly perplexing, but one can guess head coach Jon Cooper had his reasons for keeping him out. At the tender age of 19, Drouin produced at a top-six level on one of the best teams in the league. He is going to be very good, for a very long time.

Valtteri Filppula — C/LW — TBL

Season	Team	Age	GP	G	A	Pts	+/-	ESP/60	AdjCF%	iCF/60	OGVT	DGVT	SGVT	GVT
2012-13	DET	28	41	9	8	17	-4	1.42	55.7%	11.6	1.5	1.3	-0.3	2.5
2013-14	TBL	29	75	25	33	58	5	1.96	52.8%	8.3	8.7	2.5	-0.1	11.1
2014-15	TBL	30	82	12	36	48	-14	1.57	51.3%	6.2	3.7	0.4	-0.3	3.9
2015-16	TBL	31	66	14	29	43					4.3	1.2	0.0	5.4

Valtteri Filppula's 2014-15 season is best explained in two pieces: First-line Valtteri Filppula, and third-line Valtteri Filppula. The two are very different, and make for an interesting study. First-line Valtteri Filppula is good. While playing with Steven Stamkos and Ryan Callahan on Tampa's first line, Filppula posted a shot-attempts percentage of 54.1%, and a goals-for percentage of 53.3%. However, take him away from the first line, and third-line Valtteri Filppula shows up. This Filppula struggled while playing with a mixture of Cedric Paquette, Alex Killorn, Brett Connolly, and Jonathan Drouin. This version's numbers? A 49.2% Corsi percentage, and a 41.1% goals-for percentage.

Tyler Johnson — C/RW — TBL

Season	Team	Age	GP	G	A	Pts	+/-	ESP/60	AdjCF%	iCF/60	OGVT	DGVT	SGVT	GVT
2012-13	TBL	22	14	3	3	6	3	2.40	49.1%	9.4	1.1	0.7	0.0	1.8
2013-14	TBL	23	82	24	26	50	23	1.75	51.4%	13.2	7.9	5.0	-0.6	12.3
2014-15	TBL	24	77	29	43	72	33	3.24	55.2%	16.6	15.4	6.8	0.0	22.1
2015-16	TBL	25	77	29	38	67					10.6	4.0	0.0	14.5

Undersized Tyler Johnson is part of one of the best one-two center combinations in the league, as opposing teams can either focus their attention on him, or on Steven Stamkos; good luck on keeping both of them in check. Though Johnson really put himself in the public eye with his playoff performance, he did amazing in the regular season as well. The 2010 World Junior goal medalist led all regular NHL skaters in even-strength points per 60 minutes, and at the tender age of 24, he is not set for a decline. That said, a lot of credit for Johnson's success does have to go to his linemates. While playing with Nikita Kucherov and Ondrej Palat, Johnson had a 57.4% Corsi. Away from them, it was only 47.8%.

Alex Killorn — C/LW — TBL

Season	Team	Age	GP	G	A	Pts	+/-	ESP/60	AdjCF%	iCF/60	OGVT	DGVT	SGVT	GVT
2012-13	TBL	23	38	7	12	19	-6	1.83	47.4%	13.3	3.1	0.4	0.0	3.5
2013-14	TBL	24	82	17	24	41	8	1.64	52.2%	13.2	3.4	3.0	-0.3	6.1
2014-15	TBL	25	71	15	23	38	8	2.05	55.4%	11.5	5.0	2.8	0.0	7.8
2015-16	TBL	26	68	18	25	43					5.0	2.3	0.0	7.3

TAMPA BAY LIGHTNING

Tampa Bay's forward depth seems to never end, with skilled players under the age of 25 just sort of showing up on the pro roster and earning themselves consistent ice-time. Alex Killorn, who played four years of college hockey and two years in the AHL before making the jump, is one of these forwards. The Harvard alum earned Jon Cooper's increasing trust as the season went on, and ended it as the forward who averaged the fifth-most ice-time per game. The six-foot-two forward deserves his top-six role; outside of the Triplets, he had the highest Relative Corsi of the team's forwards.

Nikita Kucherov								RW						TBL
Season	Team	Age	GP	G	A	Pts	+/-	ESP/60	AdjCF%	iCF/60	OGVT	DGVT	SGVT	GVT
2013-14	TBL	20	52	9	9	18	3	1.35	53.9%	15.4	2.3	1.2	0.4	3.9
2014-15	TBL	21	82	29	36	65	38	2.88	56.6%	15.1	12.4	4.9	0.4	17.7
2015-16	TBL	22	78	29	39	67					10.9	3.2	0.0	14.1

Nikita Kucherov is a bit of a steal from the 2011 NHL Entry Draft, as he was taken 58th overall, behind players like Lucas Lessio, Miikka Salomaki, and the immortal Tyler Biggs. Though he suffered from a low on-ice shooting percentage in 2013-14, he benefited from an elevated shooting percentage in 2014-15, consequently putting up 65 points on the season. Whether the totals can be repeated is up for discussion, but one thing about Kucherov's performance most likely won't change, his puck-possession dominance. While playing with Johnson and Palat for most of the year, the Russian forward controlled 56.0% of shot attempts at five-on-five.

Jonathan Marchessault								C/RW						TBL
Season	Team	Age	GP	G	A	Pts	+/-	ESP/60	AdjCF%	iCF/60	OGVT	DGVT	SGVT	GVT
2012-13	CBJ	22	2	0	0	0	-1	0.00	46.9%	2.2	-0.2	-0.1	0.0	-0.2
2014-15	TBL	24	2	1	0	1	1	2.69	45.1%	13.2	0.6	0.1	0.0	0.7
2015-16	TBL	25	26	5	5	10					0.6	0.6	0.0	1.2

As a smaller forward with an unconventional playing style, Jonathan Marchessault has had a tough path to professional hockey. He went undrafted after putting up good point totals in the QMJHL, and has only played in four NHL games despite averaging about a point per game in almost 300 AHL contests. Marchessault isn't a bad depth option for most teams, but for a team like Tampa Bay, who already has forwards like Jonathan Drouin, Cedric Paquette, J.T. Brown, and Vlasidislav Namestnikov in those depth roles, the former Connecticut Whale and Springfield Falcon may not be the best fit.

Brenden Morrow								LW						Free Agent
Season	Team	Age	GP	G	A	Pts	+/-	ESP/60	AdjCF%	iCF/60	OGVT	DGVT	SGVT	GVT
2012-13	DAL, PIT	33	44	12	13	25	-3	2.30	44.5%	8.7	3.7	0.3	0.0	4.0
2013-14	STL	34	71	13	12	25	1	1.40	49.1%	6.1	2.7	1.5	0.0	4.2
2014-15	TBL	35	70	3	5	8	-1	0.75	53.1%	5.5	-1.9	0.8	-0.3	-1.4
2015-16	Free Agent	36	54	4	5	9					-1.3	0.9	0.0	-0.5

Brenden Morrow had a mostly successful year alongside Brian Boyle, as the two played on the Bolts' fourth line and held their own possession-wise despite taking on some of the team's toughest minutes. At the age of 36, there are questions about how much Morrow has left in the tank. Re-signing him might help the team's shutdown line, but could also hinder the development of a prospect. The team lost Richard Panik to waivers at the beginning of 2014-15 due to a logjam of forwards.

Vladislav Namestnikov — C — TBL

Season	Team	Age	GP	G	A	Pts	+/-	ESP/60	AdjCF%	iCF/60	OGVT	DGVT	SGVT	GVT
2013-14	TBL	21	4	0	0	0	-1	0.00	49.8%	10.1	-0.2	0.0	0.0	-0.2
2014-15	TBL	22	43	9	7	16	1	1.81	50.1%	8.4	2.9	1.2	0.0	4.1
2015-16	TBL	23	50	9	11	20					1.2	1.1	0.0	2.3

Vladislav Namestnikov is yet another in Tampa's long list of skilled forward prospects under the age of 25. He started the year with the Lightning, was sent back down to the AHL—where he averaged a point per game—in December, and was called back up in March for the remainder of the regular season and the playoffs. Though the 22-year-old Russian played in a lower-line role for most of 2014-15, he has the potential to be a top-six forward.

Ondrej Palat — LW — TBL

Season	Team	Age	GP	G	A	Pts	+/-	ESP/60	AdjCF%	iCF/60	OGVT	DGVT	SGVT	GVT
2012-13	TBL	21	14	2	2	4	5	1.61	46.4%	10.2	0.4	0.8	0.0	1.2
2013-14	TBL	22	81	23	36	59	32	2.27	51.3%	12.3	9.7	5.9	-0.2	15.4
2014-15	TBL	23	75	16	47	63	31	3.00	56.9%	13.9	10.9	5.9	-0.5	16.2
2015-16	TBL	24	74	21	39	60					8.2	3.9	0.0	12.1

Ondrej Palat plays much bigger than his five-foot-eleven frame, providing the "Triplets" line with reliable two-way play. The Czech Olympian burst onto the scene in 2013-14, scoring 59 points in 81 games, receiving a surprise nomination for the Calder Trophy. He continued his strong two-way play in 2014-15, recording an impressive 63 points in 75 games and dominating possession alongside Johnson and Kucherov. His presence on the line adds a gritty element, and elevates the overall effectiveness of all three players.

Cedric Paquette — C — TBL

Season	Team	Age	GP	G	A	Pts	+/-	ESP/60	AdjCF%	iCF/60	OGVT	DGVT	SGVT	GVT
2013-14	TBL	20	2	0	1	1	1	2.12	36.2%	4.3	0.2	0.1	0.0	0.3
2014-15	TBL	21	64	12	7	19	4	1.39	52.0%	12.2	3.4	3.1	0.0	6.5
2015-16	TBL	22	63	12	10	22					0.8	1.7	0.0	2.5

21-year-old Cedric Paquette is already a mainstay on Tampa's roster, albeit in a lower-line role. Though he played with the Lightning for most of the year, Paquette probably would have been better served in the AHL. Given more time to develop, the 2012 fourth rounder could be Tampa's replacement for any number of their older forwards, such as Boyle or Morrow.

Steven Stamkos — C — TBL

Season	Team	Age	GP	G	A	Pts	+/-	ESP/60	AdjCF%	iCF/60	OGVT	DGVT	SGVT	GVT
2012-13	TBL	22	48	29	28	57	-4	2.78	49.1%	14.1	12.1	0.8	-0.6	12.3
2013-14	TBL	23	37	25	15	40	9	2.66	52.8%	14.9	9.1	1.9	0.6	11.6
2014-15	TBL	24	82	43	29	72	2	2.20	53.9%	16.6	16.7	1.1	-0.8	17.0
2015-16	TBL	25	75	36	36	72					12.3	1.9	0.0	14.2

Tampa Bay's captain is already one of the best goal scorers in the league, and at the age of 25, is right in his prime. Over the past 10 years, out of skaters who have played at least 1,000 minutes, Stamkos is second in goals per 60 minutes in all situations, behind only Alex Ovechkin. Thankfully for Stamkos, the Bolts understand how fortunate they are to have a superstar player like him on their team, and have surrounded him with lots of talent. Though his contract is up at the end of the 2015-16 season, it would be very surprising to see him sign anywhere else, especially if the Lightning look primed to make another run at the Stanley Cup.

DEFENSEMEN

Mark Barberio — LD — MTL

Season	Team	Age	GP	G	A	Pts	+/-	ESP/60	AdjCF%	iCF/60	OGVT	DGVT	SGVT	GVT
2012-13	TBL	22	2	0	0	0	-2	0.00	44.2%	6.1	-0.2	-0.3	0.0	-0.5
2013-14	TBL	23	49	5	5	10	10	0.79	53.4%	10.3	1.3	2.8	0.0	4.1
2014-15	TBL	24	52	1	6	7	-4	0.51	53.3%	8.5	-0.2	0.3	0.0	0.1
2015-16	MTL	25	49	3	8	10					0.4	1.5	0.0	2.0

After three seasons in the AHL, Mark Barberio made the jump to the NHL for good in 2013-14, bringing strong skating and passing skills from the back end. Last season, he played 52 games, but was a healthy scratch for a large portion of the playoffs. Nevertheless, his relative score-adjusted possession metrics were positive, helpful when regulars such as Andrej Sustr and Jason Garrison were in the negative. A restricted free agent at the end of the season, the Montreal native is heading back home to don the red jersey of the Habs.

Matthew Carle — RD — TBL

Season	Team	Age	GP	G	A	Pts	+/-	ESP/60	AdjCF%	iCF/60	OGVT	DGVT	SGVT	GVT
2012-13	TBL	28	48	5	17	22	1	1.14	45.5%	6.0	3.5	1.4	0.0	4.9
2013-14	TBL	29	82	2	29	31	11	0.95	48.3%	7.4	3.2	5.1	0.9	9.2
2014-15	TBL	30	59	4	14	18	12	0.97	53.9%	7.6	2.4	4.2	-0.3	6.3
2015-16	TBL	31	60	4	15	19					1.2	3.0	0.0	4.2

Though ex-Flyer Matt Carle isn't thought of as a shutdown defenseman, that is the role he played in 2014-15, taking on the toughest minutes on the Tampa Bay blueline while remaining an even relative possession player. The Alaska native will most likely perform in the same role for the team in 2015-16. Though he is 31 years old, his style of play shouldn't result in too much of a decline.

Braydon Coburn — LD — TBL

Season	Team	Age	GP	G	A	Pts	+/-	ESP/60	AdjCF%	iCF/60	OGVT	DGVT	SGVT	GVT
2012-13	PHI	27	33	1	4	5	-10	0.48	47.2%	9.0	-0.7	2.0	0.0	1.2
2013-14	PHI	28	82	5	12	17	-6	0.64	51.2%	9.8	0.0	5.4	0.0	5.3
2014-15	PHI, TBL	29	43	1	10	11	2	0.91	49.9%	9.1	0.5	2.8	0.0	3.2
2015-16	TBL	30	57	2	11	13					-0.2	2.7	0.0	2.5

Braydon Coburn is a perfect example of possession statistics not telling the whole story, as he performed well while playing with Philadelphia as a positive possession player, but worse with Tampa Bay, especially when looking at relative possession numbers. The Flyers were a team with lots of big, immobile defensemen, who weren't really counted on to break the puck out of the zone. The Lightning, on the other hand, were a team of mobile defensemen, and their system required the defense to skate the puck. Coburn, a big and slow defenseman, had trouble in the system. The eighth-overall pick from 2003 constantly got hemmed in his own zone, and had a relative USAT% under -10% in the 20+ games he played with the Bolts. The former Portland Winter Hawk is signed for one more season, but it wouldn't be shocking to see him moved.

Jason Garrison — LD — TBL

Season	Team	Age	GP	G	A	Pts	+/-	ESP/60	AdjCF%	iCF/60	OGVT	DGVT	SGVT	GVT
2012-13	VAN	28	47	8	8	16	18	0.75	54.2%	11.8	2.0	5.3	0.0	7.3
2013-14	VAN	29	81	7	26	33	-5	0.67	48.9%	9.7	3.8	3.6	0.0	7.3
2014-15	TBL	30	70	4	26	30	27	1.01	53.3%	10.4	3.8	6.6	0.0	10.4
2015-16	TBL	31	66	6	22	28					2.9	4.0	0.0	6.9

With the Panthers, Jason Garrison had experienced the "Brian Campbell effect": getting ice-time alongside Campbell makes a defenseman look better than they actually are. That, and 9.5% shooting leading to 16 goals in 2011-12, inflated his price in a contract year. This doesn't mean Garrison is terrible, though, and he is a solid top-four defenseman for the Bolts. He gets plenty of ice-time on special teams, and contributes there, while being a solid possession player at five-on-five.

Victor Hedman — LD — TBL

Season	Team	Age	GP	G	A	Pts	+/-	ESP/60	AdjCF%	iCF/60	OGVT	DGVT	SGVT	GVT
2012-13	TBL	22	44	4	16	20	1	1.34	47.3%	9.4	3.0	2.6	-0.1	5.5
2013-14	TBL	23	75	13	42	55	5	1.57	54.3%	12.5	12.2	3.9	-1.4	14.7
2014-15	TBL	24	59	10	28	38	12	1.54	54.4%	11.1	8.4	3.9	0.6	12.9
2015-16	TBL	25	68	10	32	42					7.0	3.6	0.0	10.6

Given his unique blend of size, speed, and strength, it is safe to assume that Victor Hedman is in fact a descendant of Thor, the Norse God of Thunder. There is no other way to explain the way he flies around the ice, while standing at six-foot-six…and the young Swede even plays for the Lightning! There are too many clues for us to not piece this together. Kidding aside, Hedman is one of the league's best young defensemen. The 2009 second-overall pick and countryman Anton Stralman are going to be a great top pairing for Tampa for the next four seasons. The two controlled 59.7% of shot attempts while playing together at five-on-five.

Slater Koekkoek — LD — TBL

Season	Team	Age	GP	G	A	Pts	+/-	ESP/60	AdjCF%	iCF/60	OGVT	DGVT	SGVT	GVT
2014-15	TBL	20	3	0	0	0	0	0.00	51.9%	10.3	0.0	0.0	0.0	0.0
2015-16	TBL	21	26	2	5	7					0.4	0.8	0.0	1.3

Besides having one of the best names in the league, Slater Koekkoek is one of Tampa's best defensive prospects. During his first pro season, the 10th overall pick from 2012 showed flashes of his offensive prowess, scoring 26 points in 72 AHL games. The 21-year-old still needs improvement in the defensive zone, but is a top-notch skater who will fit perfectly into the speedy Tampa Bay roster. At six-foot-two, 185 pounds, Koekkoek will have to balance his need to put on muscle to handle the NHL grind with the need to maintain his best tools: speed and mobility. There is a chance he could open the season with Tampa Bay, but they have no reason to push him.

Nikita Nesterov — LD — TBL

Season	Team	Age	GP	G	A	Pts	+/-	ESP/60	AdjCF%	iCF/60	OGVT	DGVT	SGVT	GVT
2014-15	TBL	21	27	2	5	7	6	0.72	55.2%	10.1	1.3	1.2	0.0	2.5
2015-16	TBL	22	45	4	12	15					1.4	2.0	0.0	3.3

Steve Yzerman's list of draft steals doesn't just have forwards on it. It has defensemen as well. Nikita Nesterov is one of those steals, having put up great possession numbers in the NHL despite getting snatched up in the fifth round of the 2011 NHL Entry Draft. The six-foot Chelyabinsk native had trouble gaining Jon Cooper's trust in 2014-15, but with aging defensemen such as Matt Carle, Jason Garrison, and Braydon Coburn starting to decline, it is likely that Nesterov will be getting more playing time in 2015-16. Nesterov saw the ice as a seventh defenseman in the late rounds of last year's playoffs, when Cooper decided to go with the unconventional 11 forwards and seven defensemen—it seemed to spark the team.

Anton Stralman — RD — TBL

Season	Team	Age	GP	G	A	Pts	+/-	ESP/60	AdjCF%	iCF/60	OGVT	DGVT	SGVT	GVT
2012-13	NYR	26	48	4	3	7	14	0.55	57.1%	10.4	-0.4	4.1	0.0	3.7
2013-14	NYR	27	81	1	12	13	9	0.55	56.5%	7.8	-1.5	5.6	0.0	4.1
2014-15	TBL	28	82	9	30	39	22	1.08	57.1%	10.4	5.4	6.2	0.0	11.6
2015-16	TBL	29	70	5	22	27					2.3	4.3	0.0	6.7

Anton Stralman has been bounced around from city to city in his NHL career, making stops in Toronto, Calgary, Columbus, and New York before finally ending up in Tampa. The puck-moving defenseman excelled for the Rangers in the 2014 Stanley Cup playoffs, but they felt that Dan Girardi was more important to their roster than Stralman; the Swedish blueliner left for Tampa, to a fairly lucrative contract. That contract has paid off for GM Steve Yzerman, as the 28-year-old has continued to possess the puck at an elite level. Though Stralman doesn't post amazing point totals, his possession metrics are superb, and it is clear that he helps win hockey games by doing the little things right.

Andrej Sustr — RD — TBL

Season	Team	Age	GP	G	A	Pts	+/-	ESP/60	AdjCF%	iCF/60	OGVT	DGVT	SGVT	GVT
2012-13	TBL	22	2	0	0	0	1	0.00	43.5%	7.6	-0.1	0.2	0.0	0.1
2013-14	TBL	23	43	1	7	8	3	0.58	51.2%	7.2	0.6	1.6	0.0	2.2
2014-15	TBL	24	72	0	13	13	10	0.62	50.6%	6.8	0.0	3.6	0.0	3.6
2015-16	TBL	25	61	2	9	11					-0.7	2.9	0.0	2.2

Standing at six-foot-eight and weighing in at 225 pounds, Andrej Sustr is one of the biggest players in the NHL. Though not overly physical, he can use his size to advantage, to prevent opposing forwards from entering the zone or from controlling the puck in the corners. Defense isn't Sustr's issue, but he fails to generate shot attempts on offense. Though he isn't a bad option as a depth blueliner, Tampa might be better off finding a player who is a bit better at moving the puck than the Czech goliath. That being said, he is only 25, and still has time to develop.

Luke Witkowski							RD						TBL
Season	Team	Age	GP	G	A	Pts	+/-	ESP/60	AdjCF%	iCF/60	OGVT	DGVT	SGVT	GVT
2014-15	TBL	24	16	0	0	0	0	0.00	51.6%	7.4	-0.8	0.2	0.0	-0.6
2015-16	TBL	25	31	1	4	6					-0.2	1.0	0.0	0.8

Coming from the same vein as Sustr, Luke Witkowski is a bigger defenseman (six-foot-two, 200 pounds) who may provide Tampa bottom-pairing minutes in the future. Witkowski got a taste of NHL action before finishing the season in the AHL, and he will be looking to prove himself at camp in the fall. At age 25, the Michigan native is nearing his prime, and is going to have to impress, sooner rather than later.

GOALTENDERS

Ben Bishop								G						TBL
Season	Team	Age	GP	W	L	OT	GAA	Sv%	ESSV%	QS%	GGVT	DGVT	SGVT	GVT
2012-13	OTT, TBL	26	22	11	9	1	2.67	.920	.927	66.7%	7.6	-1.0	2.3	9.0
2013-14	TBL	27	63	37	14	7	2.23	.924	.932	63.5%	23.2	0.1	3.0	26.4
2014-15	TBL	28	62	40	13	5	2.32	.916	.919	61.7%	9.7	1.1	-0.8	10.1
2015-16	TBL	29	52					.917			10.3	0.5	0.2	11.0

It has taken a while for Ben Bishop to live up to his potential as a starter after being drafted back in 2005 by the St. Louis Blues. Steve Yzerman seems to have a good grasp on Bishop's value, as the six-foot-seven goaltender is 29 and only signed for another two seasons. In those two years, Bishop should continue to give the Bolts some of the league's best goaltending, as he has for the previous two seasons. From 2013 to 2015, Bishop was sixth in the league in adjusted save percentage, in both all situations and at five-on-five.

Evgeni Nabokov								G						
Season	Team	Age	GP	W	L	OT	GAA	Sv%	ESSV%	QS%	GGVT	DGVT	SGVT	GVT
2012-13	NYI	37	41	23	11	7	2.50	.910	.916	53.7%	2.1	0.6	0.6	3.3
2013-14	NYI	38	40	15	14	8	2.74	.905	.915	43.6%	-3.3	0.3	-1.6	-4.7
2014-15	TBL	39	11	3	6	2	3.15	.882	.901	55.6%	-5.6	0.3	-1.3	-6.7
2015-16	SJS	40	17					.908			-1.5	0.1	-0.3	-1.7

For the fourth straight year, Evgeni Nabokov saw a decline in save percentage. The 39-year-old goaltender was in net for a rough ride with the Lightning, losing eight of 11 decisions. The long-time Sharks netminder showed that he is no longer fit for the NHL level with an .882 save percentage during that stretch. Tampa Bay quickly opted for an upgrade and waived Nabakov in early February. With 353 career wins and a solid .911 career save percentage, the ninth-round pick from 1994 will go down as a quality goaltender, but will always be remembered for coming up short in the postseason with great San Jose teams.

Andrei Vasilevskiy								G						
Season	Team	Age	GP	W	L	OT	GAA	Sv%	ESSV%	QS%	GGVT	DGVT	SGVT	GVT
2014-15	TBL	20	16	7	5	1	2.36	.918	.920	53.8%	3.1	0.1	0.0	3.2
2015-16	TBL	21	21					.914			2.3	0.0	0.0	2.4

Andrei Vasilevskiy earned the backup goaltender position at the age of 20, and has long been considered one of the league's best prospects at the netminder position. The young Russian is slotted to take over after Ben Bishop leaves, which could be after the latter's contract expires in two years. A solid .918 save percentage in the NHL as a 20-year-old is pretty impressive, though Vasilevskiy did only play in the small sample of 16 games. He also had a .923 save percentage in the KHL as a 19-year-old, as well as a .917 save percentage in the AHL before being called up to Tampa. If the Russian netminder continues on his development curve, he is going to end up becoming an elite NHL goaltender, giving the Bolts a great replacement for Bishop.

Shane O'Donnell

Toronto Maple Leafs

The Toronto Maple Leafs took a stick of dynamite to their front office and coaching staff following one of the worst stretches of hockey in recent memory. To start the season, the Leafs were 21-14-3 and one of the NHL's highest scoring teams. After January 1, they won just nine games. The collapse cost both head coach Randy Carlyle and general manager Dave Nonis their jobs and set into motion a complete overhaul of the franchise.

The Maple Leafs' renovation project began before 2014-15, when Toronto hired former NHL Director of Player Safety and Hall of Famer Brendan Shanahan as team president, but it kicked into full gear when the organization hired former Detroit Red Wings head coach Mike Babcock. They outpaid the Buffalo Sabres, commiting $50 million to grab Team Canada's coach.

It should not have been a huge surprise that one of the NHL's elite coaches would want to risk a rebuild project for a chance to become a hockey legend. With a Stanley Cup drought since 1967, any coach who can return the Leafs to glory will be lauded for a lifetime. What was surprising, however, was the hire of long-time New Jersey Devils GM Lou Lamoriello. The 72-year-old had recently been bumped from GM of the Devils to team president in favor of former Penguins GM Ray Shero. Now, he will help pilot a front office stacked with experience and a young, up-and-coming assistant GM in Kyle Dubas.

Most of the hockey world seems to be looking at the Leafs as a team with a huge mountain to climb before becoming competitive, but that may not be the reality. One thing that is ironic about hockey is just how much teams can benefit from ineptitude. Shanahan and his new crew of NHL legends are well aware that years of failure in Toronto have built up top-10 draft picks and formed an impressive prospect system—one that will play a huge role in returning the Leafs to prominence.

Winging it

There is a lot to be said about experience, leadership, and even culture when it comes to hockey, but each year, the thing that ultimately determines whether you raise the Cup is roster talent (and getting the most out of that talent). The Maple Leafs have young, raw talent to mold, starting with two very exciting wingers.

William Nylander has the potential to be the most offensively productive player of the 2014 NHL Entry Draft. The five-foot-eleven right winger has golden hands and offensive instincts that rank among the best

MAPLE LEAFS IN A BOX

Last Season
Goals For	211	24th
Goals Against	262	27th
GVT	-51	27th
Points	68	27th
Playoffs	Did not make playoffs	

Absolutely everything that could have gone wrong for the Leafs did, as they had their worst season over two decades.

Three-Year Record
GVT	-64	25th
Points	209	25th
Playoffs	1 Appearance, 3 Wins	

VUKOTA Projections
Goals For	210	24th
Goals Against	232	28th
GVT	-23	27th
Points	84	27th

Kessel is out, Babcock is in, and many new faces have been added. Toronto will be better, but expect a season of slow improvement.

Top Three Prospects
M. Marner (F), W. Nylander (F), C. Brown (F)

in the league. Eligible to play in the AHL at age 18, he did something few 18-year-olds can do: score at the pro level. He dangled and danced his way to 14 goals and 18 assists in 37 games with the Toronto Marlies and added three more points in five playoff games.

While his production at the AHL level is impressive, Nylander slipped in the draft because of concerns over whether he could play at both ends of the ice and whether he will be able to physically withstand the demands of the NHL with a slight frame.

And Nylander isn't the only slight-framed, offensively-dynamic winger that the Leafs will be centering their rebuild around. With the fourth-overall pick in the 2015 draft, they selected Mitch Marner, who has been a center in junior, but projects as a winger. Also at five-foot-eleven, and only 160 pounds, Marner is far from intimidating physically. His offensive gifts, on the other hand, may keep opponents up at night.

In the OHL, the Thornhill, Ontario native scored 44 goals and 82 assists in just 63 games for the London Knights in 2014-15. His quickness and innate ability to find holes in the defense shot him to the top of the draft boards; Marner solidified his position there by scoring nine goals in seven playoff games.

What sets Marner apart from Nylander is a skill set more fit to playing a 200-foot game. In juniors, he has been known as a hard worker and a relentless annoyance, battling for pucks despite his size and chasing opponents down from behind.

Both players have the talent to be centerpieces of the franchise. The reality is that draft picks outside the top three are hit or miss, even if they are eighth and fourth overall. Whether the Shanahan/Babcock/Lou combo becomes a success story will rely greatly on them being hits.

Franchise center

While Nylander and Marner could both become stars, one thing that has been proven in the NHL is that it is nearly impossible to win the Stanley Cup without a top-notch center. Jonathan Toews, Anze Kopitar, Patrice Bergeron, Sidney Crosby, and Pavel Datsyuk have raised Cups since the 2004-05 lockout. Unfortunately for Toronto's new brass, the next Toews is nowhere to be found in the prospect system. The Leafs decided to start their rebuild too late to get in on the Connor McDavid/Jack Eichel conversation.

That means the most likely scenario in the future is number-one center by committee, assuming Marner and Nylander develop where they are projected on the wing instead of in the middle.

Nazem Kadri will likely factor in the top two centers, though his results have been disappointing since posting 44 points in 48 games during the shortened 2012-13 season. Since then, he has managed only 89 points in 151 games and has faced the ire of coaches over his two-way game.

The flicker of hope for Kadri, the 2009 seventh-overall pick, to become the number-one center are his Corsi statistics. He boasts the best Relative Corsi on the Leafs over the past two seasons at +2.6%, though his Relative goals for is only +0.8%. Babcock will undoubtedly make Kadri's defensive game a focus. Still, he is a long shot to become a top center.

Will Toronto be low enough in the standings to have a shot at projected first-overall selection Auston Matthews? It seems possible, but the changing lottery rules have given 30th-place teams a lesser chance than ever of grabbing the number-one pick.

While it is hard to find the next great center, one factor on Shanahan's side is time. The Toronto media and fans have not been much for patience in the past, but they have bought into the long game in this case. And if the brain trust is able to find that center to go along with the talents they have accrued thus far, they will be a top contender for a long time.

Stephen Burtch

TORONTO MAPLE LEAFS

Even-Strength Usage: Toronto Maple Leafs

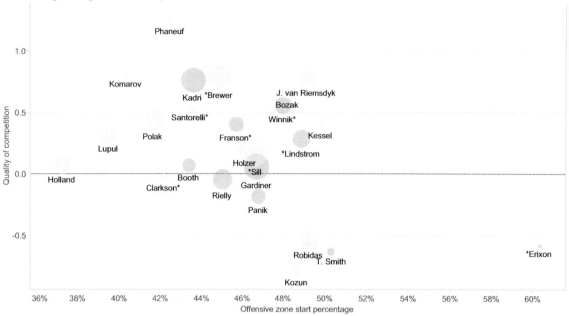

Special Teams Usage: Toronto Maple Leafs

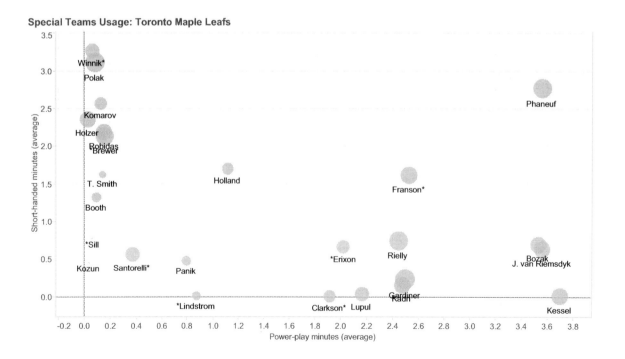

TORONTO MAPLE LEAFS

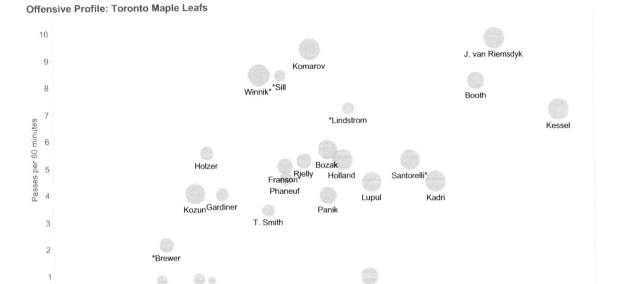

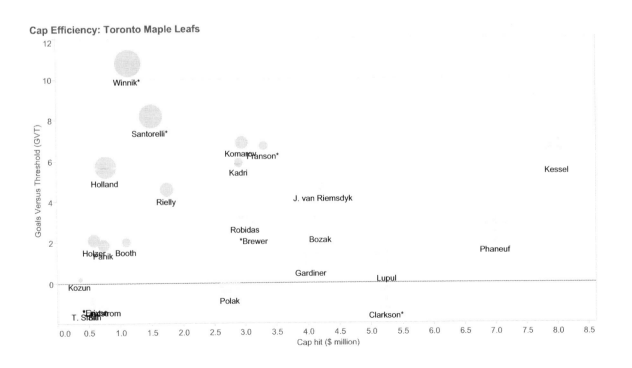

TORONTO MAPLE LEAFS

FORWARDS

Casey Bailey					C/RW								**TOR**
Season	Team	Age	GP	G	A	Pts	+/-	ESP/60	AdjCF%	iCF/60	OGVT	DGVT	SGVT	GVT
2014-15	TOR	23	6	1	0	1	1	1.12	49.4%	11.7	0.3	0.1	0.0	0.5
2015-16	TOR	24	28	6	6	11					1.0	0.6	0.0	1.6

Casey Bailey was signed towards the tail end of the season as an unrestricted free agent out of the NCAA ranks. He played six games before the Leafs season came to a merciful close, burning a year off of his two-year, entry-level contract in the process. The 23-year-old from Anchorage, Alaska finished his junior year at Penn State ranked 23rd in Division I with 1.08 points per game and tied for 10th with 0.59 goals per game. His play in college was noted for his solid positioning and dogged pressure on the forecheck down low, using his size well on the cycle with teammate and fellow Hobey Baker award nominee Thomas Holmstrom. Bailey has an accurate and heavy shot, being particularly fond of one timers from the faceoff dot. His size, at six-foot-three and 205 pounds, and history of physical play in the USHL and BCHL, suggest he will handle the NHL level once he adjusts to its size and speed. The Leafs are hoping he blossoms into a well-rounded power forward. The components are all there; the question is whether Bailey can put them together effectively.

Troy Bodie					RW								**Retired**
Season	Team	Age	GP	G	A	Pts	+/-	ESP/60	AdjCF%	iCF/60	OGVT	DGVT	SGVT	GVT
2013-14	TOR	28	47	3	7	10	6	1.48	42.6%	12.2	0.8	1.1	0.0	1.9
2014-15	TOR	29	5	0	0	0	0	0.00	48.7%	4.7	-0.1	0.0	0.0	-0.1
2015-16	Retired	30	34	4	6	10					0.5	0.8	0.0	1.3

Six-foot-five, 225-pound Troy Bodie is a physical fourth liner who contributes effectively from a possession standpoint. He lacks the puck skills to move much beyond that level, and is unlikely to last long term on any NHL roster as a result, but his defensive performance is above average and he skates very well for a man his size. In five games with the Leafs, Bodie averaged under five minutes per contest and picked up one five-minute fighting major. He generated one shot on goal and produced no points.

David Booth					LW								**Free Agent**
Season	Team	Age	GP	G	A	Pts	+/-	ESP/60	AdjCF%	iCF/60	OGVT	DGVT	SGVT	GVT
2012-13	VAN	28	12	1	2	3	-3	1.21	61.0%	17.4	-0.2	0.0	0.0	-0.2
2013-14	VAN	29	66	9	10	19	1	1.27	51.7%	15.5	0.8	2.1	-0.6	2.3
2014-15	TOR	30	59	7	6	13	-8	1.16	45.5%	15.0	1.4	0.6	0.0	2.0
2015-16	Free Agent	31	52	9	9	17					1.3	1.3	0.0	2.6

David Booth is a defensively-sound left winger whose concussion history and declining offense have combined to make him a marginal NHLer at the age of 31. He performed adequately as a fourth liner on a one-year contract with Toronto, after being bought out of his long-term deal by Vancouver. Booth suffered a broken foot in preseason and missed the first 21 games of the year, but eventually skated in 59 games for the Leafs. It took him a long while to get going, managing only three points through his first 35 games. He had one torrid 11-game stretch late in the year, producing five goals and nine points, before cooling off again as things wound down. Missing some additional time with concussion symptoms and a broken nose after a nasty collision with Anaheim's Sami Vatanen is obviously a cause for concern. His defensive performance was very solid overall, and he looked effective on the forecheck, but his extensive injury history will make it a challenge for him to find consistent work.

Tyler Bozak								C						TOR
Season	Team	Age	GP	G	A	Pts	+/-	ESP/60	AdjCF%	iCF/60	OGVT	DGVT	SGVT	GVT
2012-13	TOR	26	46	12	16	28	-1	1.50	46.1%	7.2	1.7	1.0	1.0	3.7
2013-14	TOR	27	58	19	30	49	2	2.42	42.6%	6.1	6.5	1.9	1.2	9.7
2014-15	TOR	28	82	23	26	49	-34	1.42	44.8%	7.2	3.8	-1.1	0.3	2.9
2015-16	TOR	29	68	20	28	48					4.9	0.8	0.0	5.7

For years, Tyler Bozak has been miscast as a top-line center by the Leafs. Attached at the hip to outgoing top scorer Phi Kessel, coaches have been infatuated with Bozak's skill on the draw and his knack for being in the general vicinity when exciting players do exciting things. His 53.2% faceoff percentage ranked a solid 23rd in the league, yet defensively, he had the second-worst rate of shot attempts against per 60 minutes of all full-time centers, trailing only Buffalo's Tyler Ennis. Offensively, he produced the sixth-fewest individual shot attempts among regular centers (139), and trailed teammates Winnik (157), Santorelli (208), and Kadri (253). Rumors have had the new Leafs management group looking to ship out Bozak's sizable $4.2 million cap hit, but with little interest being shown. If they hope to find any takers, they will need to accentuate the positives, such as his high shooting percentage, by sheltering his usage and limiting his negative defensive impacts.

Sam Carrick								C/RW						TOR
Season	Team	Age	GP	G	A	Pts	+/-	ESP/60	AdjCF%	iCF/60	OGVT	DGVT	SGVT	GVT
2014-15	TOR	22	16	1	1	2	1	1.19	45.4%	13.5	0.1	0.3	0.0	0.3
2015-16	TOR	23	33	5	6	11					0.6	0.7	0.0	1.4

Speedy, physical center Sam Carrick forechecks well and works hard defensively, but he is unlikely to develop into a top-six contributor. He produced two points in 16 games with the Leafs, in only six and a half minutes per game and has yet to break the 0.6 point per game threshold through two AHL seasons. The Leafs re-signed the 23-year-old to a one-year, two-way contract, to provide organizational depth.

Matt Frattin								RW						TOR
Season	Team	Age	GP	G	A	Pts	+/-	ESP/60	AdjCF%	iCF/60	OGVT	DGVT	SGVT	GVT
2012-13	TOR	24	25	7	6	13	6	2.47	48.6%	13.9	2.7	0.7	-0.3	3.1
2013-14	LAK, CBJ	25	44	2	5	7	-4	0.63	52.5%	11.5	-1.5	0.6	-0.3	-1.1
2014-15	TOR	26	9	0	0	0	0	0.00	46.3%	10.1	-0.2	0.0	0.0	-0.2
2015-16	TOR	27	35	4	5	9					0.0	0.7	0.0	0.7

Matt Frattin's second tenure as a Leafs prospect comes with far lower expectations than were placed upon him in his first time around. In 2014-15, he played 59 regular-season and five playoff games with the Marlies and another nine NHL games, in which he was hardly used. In an overtime loss to Detroit on October 18, he somehow managed to only play six shifts, for less than three minutes of ice-time. When he was in the AHL, he again provided a strong indication of why he was once considered a potential top-nine NHL winger by the L.A. Kings and Columbus Blue Jackets. His combined total of 29 goals and 54 points in 65 AHL regular-season and playoff games work out to 0.45 goals per game and 0.84 points per game, on 16.2% shooting. You would think that Frattin and his heavy shot will be given a legitimate shot at earning a spot on the NHL roster so the Leafs can reach a decision on whether or not he is worth keeping into the future.

Peter Holland								C					TOR
Season	Team	Age	GP	G	A	Pts	+/-	ESP/60	AdjCF%	iCF/60	OGVT	DGVT	SGVT	GVT
2012-13	ANA	21	21	3	2	5	4	1.05	47.2%	10.9	-0.1	0.8	0.0	0.7
2013-14	ANA, TOR	22	43	6	5	11	0	1.26	42.7%	9.3	0.5	0.6	0.0	1.1
2014-15	TOR	23	62	11	14	25	0	1.65	43.1%	10.3	3.1	2.5	0.1	5.7
2015-16	TOR	24	57	11	15	25					2.2	1.9	0.0	4.1

Slotting in as a middle-six center for Toronto, Peter Holland will need to see increase his even-strength production if he hopes to earn a decent RFA deal after his current contract expires. Much of this depends on who will play on Holland's wing. A reunion of the old line from his OHL team, the Guelph Storm, where Holland centered Richard Panik and Taylor Beck, looked like a possibility, but Beck was sent to the Islanders prior to training camp in the Michael Grabner acquisition. The trio had played together late in their final OHL season, when Beck led the team with 95 points in 62 games, Holland finished with 88 points in 67 games, and Panik produced 25 points in 24 games after being added from Belleville.

Nathan Horton								RW						TOR
Season	Team	Age	GP	G	A	Pts	+/-	ESP/60	AdjCF%	iCF/60	OGVT	DGVT	SGVT	GVT
2012-13	BOS	27	43	13	9	22	1	1.99	57.8%	16.0	0.9	0.8	-0.6	1.1
2013-14	CBJ	28	36	5	14	19	-3	1.89	53.1%	10.4	0.8	0.5	0.0	1.2
2015-16	TOR	29	16	3	6	9					0.4	0.2	-0.1	0.5

A devastating back injury has not only kept veteran winger Nathan Horton out of the lineup, but has put his career in jeopardy. The Blue Jackets signed him to a long-term contract, only to trade the contract and injured player to Toronto to get some bang for their buck (in David Clarkson). When Horton is healthy, he is a terrific player. The 29-year-old has a strong finishing touch and ability to use his body to gain scoring position. For whatever reason, the third-overall pick from 2003 was never a great power-play producer; otherwise, he would have had even higher totals. If he cannot return to the NHL, 421 points in 627 games will have made for a very good career.

Nazem Kadri								C						TOR
Season	Team	Age	GP	G	A	Pts	+/-	ESP/60	AdjCF%	iCF/60	OGVT	DGVT	SGVT	GVT
2012-13	TOR	22	48	18	26	44	15	3.29	47.9%	16.2	10.6	1.4	-1.4	10.6
2013-14	TOR	23	78	20	30	50	-11	1.66	44.4%	12.6	7.7	0.2	-0.3	7.6
2014-15	TOR	24	73	18	21	39	-7	1.70	48.9%	14.3	4.5	1.3	0.1	5.9
2015-16	TOR	25	66	20	25	45					5.5	1.6	0.0	7.1

Nazem Kadri drove play at an elite level, but unfortunately, his most skilled linemate, Joffrey Lupul, couldn't stay healthy (gasp!). Kadri's own production took a dip, as his 10.2% finishing rate was the lowest since his rookie season in 2010-11. But the possession numbers were good. When Kadri was paired with Winnik at even strength, the Leafs controlled 52.0% of shot attempts. When Kadri was paired with Joffrey Lupul, the Leafs controlled 53.2%. When Kadri was playing alongside both Lupul and Winnik, they miraculously controlled 60.6% of shot attempts and produced 60% of the goals. While that was in a small sample of just under 100 minutes, when you consider just how abysmal the Leafs possession results have been in recent seasons, it seems pretty remarkable. Expect the 2009 seventh-overall pick to see a much larger share of ice-time and offensive opportunity under new head coach Mike Babcock.

Phil Kessel								RW						PIT
Season	Team	Age	GP	G	A	Pts	+/-	ESP/60	AdjCF%	iCF/60	OGVT	DGVT	SGVT	GVT
2012-13	TOR	25	48	20	32	52	-3	2.35	46.8%	18.7	10.9	-0.8	-0.6	9.6
2013-14	TOR	26	82	37	43	80	-5	2.51	43.9%	17.3	16.4	1.4	-0.8	17.0
2014-15	TOR	27	82	25	36	61	-34	1.75	44.7%	17.0	8.6	-1.9	-0.3	6.4
2015-16	PIT	28	70	29	38	66					9.9	0.8	0.0	10.7

Phil Kessel had an abysmal season by his standards. Sure, by the standards of most other skaters, 25 goals and 61 points would have been deemed a success, but when a player scores 0.39+ goals per game for six consecutive years, he sets a standard that leads to expectations. So, when he only manages to produce 0.30 goals per game, it is a disappointment. The two-time US Olympian is a top-20 offensive talent. He finished in the top 10 in shots generated in each of the past six seasons, and his total (1,366) ranks only behind Alex Ovechkin (1,671); he tied Ryan Getzlaf for eighth with 379 points over that span. His trade to Pittsburgh is an obvious attempt to turn the page on the Brian Burke/Dave Nonis regime. The 2006 fifth-overall selection will provide Crosby and Malkin the elite sniper they have lacked since James Neal was shipped out last offseason.

Leo Komarov								LW/RW						TOR
Season	Team	Age	GP	G	A	Pts	+/-	ESP/60	AdjCF%	iCF/60	OGVT	DGVT	SGVT	GVT
2012-13	TOR	25	42	4	5	9	-1	1.08	46.5%	10.6	0.1	2.2	0.0	2.3
2014-15	TOR	27	62	8	18	26	0	1.77	45.6%	9.3	3.4	3.5	0.0	6.9
2015-16	TOR	28	57	10	18	28					2.7	2.6	0.0	5.3

Leo Komarov had a surprisingly effective season. Projected as a bottom-six grinder when he returned from the KHL, concern abounded regarding the heft of his cap hit. Many observers dismissed the fact that he had tied for the scoring lead of Dynamo Moscow as irrelevant. But Komarov's familiarity with the NHL bred confidence, and he handled the puck far more than in his first time in the league. His increased confidence also showed up in unexpected offensive production, as the 2014 Olympic bronze medalist fired home eight goals and produced 26 points in only 62 games, playing largely as a third liner. Of course, this came alongside his typically thorny, aggressive style of play that gets under opponents' skin so effectively. His defensive impacts are significant: he contributes to the penalty kill and again ranked among NHL's hit leaders. If Komarov can stay healthy and play a consistent third- or fourth-line role, he will help re-image the Leafs as a difficult to play against defensive group with some skill.

Brandon Kozun								RW						KHL
Season	Team	Age	GP	G	A	Pts	+/-	ESP/60	AdjCF%	iCF/60	OGVT	DGVT	SGVT	GVT
2014-15	TOR	24	20	2	2	4	-3	1.62	40.8%	5.7	-0.1	0.2	0.0	0.2
2015-16	KHL	25	35	5	7	12					0.5	0.7	0.0	1.2

Brandon Kozun is an excellent skating waterbug of a player who suffers some biases against his five-foot-eight, 168-pound stature. The most intriguing part of his AHL game, from the Leafs perspective, was his speed on the penalty kill when matched up with linemate Jerry D'Amigo. The two smallish forwards applied excellent pressure, contributed heavily to the Marlies improved shorthanded play in 2013-14. Kozun parlayed that defensive acumen into starting last season as a bottom-six NHL forward. In his 20-game stint with the Leafs, the former Calgary Hitman made a significant impact, helping to suppress shot attempts significantly. Unfortunately, he suffered a high-ankle sprain that knocked him out for six weeks after only his fifth game. He didn't get another prolonged stretch of play until late February, by which time the Leafs were in the midst of yet another downward spiral. Without a real opportunity to impress, Kozun has decided to try his luck overseas, inking a contract with Jokerit for 2015-16.

Josh Leivo						RW							TOR
Season	Team	Age	GP	G	A	Pts	+/-	ESP/60	AdjCF%	iCF/60	OGVT	DGVT	SGVT	GVT
2013-14	TOR	20	7	1	1	2	0	1.77	42.3%	5.8	0.4	0.1	0.0	0.5
2014-15	TOR	21	9	1	0	1	-1	0.88	50.9%	13.1	-0.3	0.1	0.0	-0.2
2015-16	TOR	22	30	5	6	11					0.6	0.6	0.0	1.3

Josh Leivo had a rough campaign. After showing much promise in his first year as a pro, including a seven-game cup of coffee with the big club, Leivo again joined the Leafs, for eight games in November. Unfortunately, he played very little and only generated one goal before being demoted. His second AHL season was marred by a shoulder separation in December that kept him out of action for 13 games. There, he also saw a significant decline in his shooting percentage, dropping from 15.8% to a pedestrian 8.6%, resulting in only 12 goals in 56 regular-season and playoff games combined. He closed out the season on a productive note, though, registering 12 points in his final 12 games of the regular season and playoffs.

Joakim Lindstrom						RW/LW							KHL
Season	Team	Age	GP	G	A	Pts	+/-	ESP/60	AdjCF%	iCF/60	OGVT	DGVT	SGVT	GVT
2014-15	STL, TOR	31	53	4	6	10	-15	0.57	50.6%	10.9	-0.3	-0.6	0.1	-0.9
2015-16	KHL	32	43	5	6	11					0.1	0.3	0.0	0.4

Joakim Lindstrom went from being a top-line winger who finished second in SHL scoring with Skelleftea in 2013-14, to a marginal fourth-line player with the contending Blues. One might have expected that the move to the far weaker Leafs would have led to an increase in opportunity for Lindstrom, but he actually averaged less ice-time. His 10 points in 53 games served as the writing on the wall with respect to his future opportunity. Lindstrom signed with SKA St. Petersburg, in what will be his second foray into the KHL.

Joffrey Lupul						RW							TOR
Season	Team	Age	GP	G	A	Pts	+/-	ESP/60	AdjCF%	iCF/60	OGVT	DGVT	SGVT	GVT
2012-13	TOR	29	16	11	7	18	8	4.18	43.7%	15.1	4.9	0.6	-0.3	5.3
2013-14	TOR	30	69	22	22	44	-15	1.74	41.9%	12.8	6.3	-0.4	3.3	9.3
2014-15	TOR	31	55	10	11	21	-10	1.48	42.8%	11.1	0.3	0.7	0.1	1.1
2015-16	TOR	32	55	13	16	29					2.5	1.0	0.1	3.6

Joffrey Lupul remains an elite offensive talent, but he is aging and continues to find himself in the infirmary on a consistent basis—making it challenging to justify his roster spot on a rebuilding team. Lupul hasn't dressed for a full NHL season since 2008-09 with Philadelphia. Since then, he has missed 175 of a possible 458 games, or 38% of them. Last season was no exception to this general trend, as Lupul sat out 27 games due to injury. When he did play, it was his least productive season since he was 23 with Edmonton. His offensive talents, his inadequate defensive performances, his injury history, his cap hit, and his age all combine to make for an unfortunate load the Leafs have to bear until his contract expires. They likely have their fingers crossed that he can stay healthy and contribute enough offense to lull another team into adding him via trade.

Greg McKegg								**C**						**FLA**
Season	Team	Age	GP	G	A	Pts	+/-	ESP/60	AdjCF%	iCF/60	OGVT	DGVT	SGVT	GVT
2013-14	TOR	21	1	0	0	0	0	0.00	100.0%	13.9	0.0	0.0	0.0	0.0
2014-15	TOR	22	3	0	0	0	0	0.00	31.3%	2.3	-0.1	0.0	0.0	-0.1
2015-16	FLA	23	26	5	6	10					0.7	0.6	0.0	1.2

Greg McKegg's promising AHL production from his second pro season declined by 10 points in year three, predominantly from a combination of injury issues and greater defensive expectations. The dropoff is sort of misleading, as McKegg's personal shot and goal-production rates increased by 29% and 22% over his sophomore season. The main decline came from a 43% dip in his assist rate, largely a finishing issue for Josh Leivo. Despite the decline, Florida saw enough in McKegg to trade the Leafs the rights to Zach Hyman for him; Hyman led the Michigan Wolverines with 54 points in 37 games played, the fourth-best scoring rate (1.46) in Division I, albeit skating alongside Detroit's top prospect Dylan Larkin.

Colton Orr								**RW**						**Free Agent**
Season	Team	Age	GP	G	A	Pts	+/-	ESP/60	AdjCF%	iCF/60	OGVT	DGVT	SGVT	GVT
2012-13	TOR	30	44	1	3	4	4	0.86	38.5%	5.2	-0.7	0.7	0.0	0.0
2013-14	TOR	31	54	0	0	0	-3	0.00	38.3%	5.7	-2.6	0.2	0.0	-2.4
2014-15	TOR	32	1	0	0	0	0	0.00	00.0%	0.0	0.0	0.0	0.0	0.0
2015-16	Free Agent	33	33	2	3	5					-0.6	0.5	0.0	-0.1

Colton Orr played a single-game swan song (sniff) against Montreal at the conclusion of the season, skating for 10 shifts and 6:06 of ice-time without registering any other recorded statistics; the Leafs generated zero shot attempts while surrendering five to the Habs. Without a contract, Orr, and his role on a team that is shifting towards a skill-based mentality, has been pushed aside. Entering his 12th season of professional hockey has to be considered a minor miracle for a player who generated 13 career goals and 28 career points in 477 NHL games. He will be greatly missed as a pugilist by many who follow the blue and white, but his roster spot can be put to much better use going forward.

Richard Panik								**RW**						**TOR**
Season	Team	Age	GP	G	A	Pts	+/-	ESP/60	AdjCF%	iCF/60	OGVT	DGVT	SGVT	GVT
2012-13	TBL	21	25	5	4	9	-2	1.60	48.5%	12.2	1.0	0.1	-0.3	0.9
2013-14	TBL	22	50	3	10	13	-9	0.95	48.9%	10.2	-0.8	0.2	-0.3	-0.9
2014-15	TOR	23	76	11	6	17	-8	1.14	46.2%	10.2	0.8	1.1	0.0	1.9
2015-16	TOR	24	60	9	9	18					0.5	1.2	0.0	1.7

Richard Panik was claimed off of waivers from Tampa Bay just before the 2014-15 season began. The Lightning were relatively happy with his development, but a numbers crunch and the fact he could not crack a championship-caliber roster meant he had to clear waivers for demotion to the AHL. By the time the final third of the season rolled around, it had become obvious to Leafs management that Panik's defensive skills and knack for scoring were useful, and his ice-time climbed accordingly. His 0.74 goals per 60 minutes was a pleasant bonus, and his impact on shot suppression was comparable to veteran contributors like Komarov, Winnik, and

Booth. He has offensive upside, plays with a physical edge, and under the right circumstances, could develop into a decent top-six forward.

Zach Sill — C — WSH

Season	Team	Age	GP	G	A	Pts	+/-	ESP/60	AdjCF%	iCF/60	OGVT	DGVT	SGVT	GVT
2013-14	PIT	25	20	0	0	0	-4	0.00	34.2%	8.4	-1.1	0.6	0.0	-0.5
2014-15	PIT, TOR	26	63	1	3	4	-5	0.50	45.2%	9.1	-1.9	0.8	0.0	-1.1
2015-16	WSH	27	53	2	3	5					-2.1	1.1	0.0	-1.0

Bought to the Leafs as part of the Daniel Winnik deadline move in 2014, Zach Sill is a rough-and-tumble physical presence in the lineup who skates well and is industrious in tight quarters and board battles. He is noteworthy as a decent-skating, solid forechecking presence, and is defensively reliable, though ineffective offensively. Sill signed a one-year contract with the Capitals, and may fill a bottom-six checking role for them.

Trevor Smith — C/LW — Swiss

Season	Team	Age	GP	G	A	Pts	+/-	ESP/60	AdjCF%	iCF/60	OGVT	DGVT	SGVT	GVT
2012-13	PIT	27	1	0	0	0	0	0.00	11.3%	0.0	0.0	0.0	0.0	0.0
2013-14	TOR	28	28	4	5	9	-3	1.77	40.4%	8.7	1.4	0.1	0.0	1.5
2014-15	TOR	29	54	2	3	5	-9	0.60	44.5%	9.1	-2.1	1.0	0.0	-1.1
2015-16	Swiss	30	47	4	6	10					-0.4	1.0	0.0	0.6

Trevor Smith is a prototypical AAAA player: he has excellent hands, a good shot he can get off quickly from virtually anywhere, but below-average skating and defensive play compared to most NHL center-ice men. Consequently, Smith has spent his NHL time as bottom-six filler, producing hardly any offense. Through 82 games with the Leafs across the last two seasons, he managed a sum total of six goals and 14 points. He did add value as a team leader with the Marlies, captaining the AHL side on a lengthy playoff run in 2014. Following the end of last season, Smith followed the trend of many older Leafs' fringe skaters, signing with an overseas squad; he will suit up for SC Bern in Switzerland.

James van Riemsdyk — LW — TOR

Season	Team	Age	GP	G	A	Pts	+/-	ESP/60	AdjCF%	iCF/60	OGVT	DGVT	SGVT	GVT
2012-13	TOR	23	48	18	14	32	-7	2.14	46.2%	15.5	4.3	-0.7	-0.6	3.0
2013-14	TOR	24	80	30	31	61	-9	1.91	44.0%	14.0	8.9	1.1	2.5	12.5
2014-15	TOR	25	82	27	29	56	-33	1.77	43.6%	14.9	7.7	-1.6	-1.3	4.8
2015-16	TOR	26	70	28	31	59					8.2	0.8	0.0	8.9

James van Riemsdyk has been developing into an elite offensive producer since his arrival from Philadelphia in the summer of 2012. Being granted first-line minutes alongside one of the top scoring talents in the world did wonders for his confidence, and helped push his offensive totals into the 30-goal and 30-assist range for the past two seasons. Having developed into his sizeable frame, "JVR" has learned to effectively use of his body position and good hands in tight to generate chances from the low slot at the extraordinarily high rate. Unfortunately, another side effect of being handed those prime minutes, with virtually no defensive responsibilities attached, has been the deterioration of his play in his own zone and on the backcheck. As he is only turning 26, and locked up for three more seasons at an affordable $4.3 million cap hit, the Leafs should be willing to invest

DEFENSEMEN

T.J. Brennan							LD						TOR
Season	Team	Age	GP	G	A	Pts	+/-	ESP/60	AdjCF%	iCF/60	OGVT	DGVT	SGVT	GVT
2012-13	BUF, FLA	23	29	3	7	10	-9	0.87	47.6%	10.3	1.5	-0.2	0.0	1.3
2014-15	TOR	25	6	0	1	1	-7	0.00	50.8%	10.6	-0.2	-0.8	0.0	-1.1
2015-16	TOR	26	25	2	5	7					0.3	0.4	0.0	0.7

T.J. Brennan deserves better than spending the rest of his professional hockey career as the top offensive defenseman in the AHL. The 31st-overall selection from 2007 has been a part of five NHL organizations. He was ready to start last season with the NY Islanders, but was included in the Nick Leddy trade, acquired to play with the Blackhawks before ever playing a game with the Isles. He was assigned to Rockford, and then was traded to the Leafs for Spencer Abbott in late February. Since 2012-13, Brennan has produced 51 goals and 159 points in 185 AHL games, for 0.28 goals and 0.86 points per game—great numbers for the capable puck handler with elite vision and shooting talent. Most questions about his play arise from how the six-foot, 214-pound rearguard defends. Yet, despite the fact that Brennan has made a positive impact on possession in all three of his NHL seasons, with no abnormally poor defensive showings, he languishes as if he were a fringe NHL talent—largely due to perceptions of his -16 rating in 46 contests. The longstanding bias against offensively-inclined, puck-moving defenders as if they are automatic defensive liabilities has had a negative impact on Brennan's NHL aspirations.

Eric Brewer							LD						Free Agent
Season	Team	Age	GP	G	A	Pts	+/-	ESP/60	AdjCF%	iCF/60	OGVT	DGVT	SGVT	GVT
2012-13	TBL	33	48	4	8	12	3	0.75	45.6%	8.7	1.1	2.4	0.0	3.5
2013-14	TBL	34	77	4	13	17	10	0.77	50.7%	9.0	1.9	4.2	0.0	6.2
2014-15	TBL, ANA, TOR	35	44	3	8	11	-5	0.83	43.9%	6.9	0.8	1.8	0.0	2.7
2015-16	Free Agent	36	50	2	9	12					0.6	2.3	0.0	2.8

Eric Brewer played his 1,000th NHL game on March 21, suiting up for the Leafs against Ottawa. He hasn't exceeded expectations in terms of possession since before 2005-06, and has clung to a role as a bottom-pairing defender for the past two years with Tampa Bay and Anaheim prior to joining Toronto. His peak performance came back with Edmonton from 2000-01 to 2003-04, including earning a spot on the Olympic roster for Team Canada in 2002. Brewer's influence in Toronto was mainly as a stopgap to ride out the tumultuous season.

Tim Erixon							LD						PIT
Season	Team	Age	GP	G	A	Pts	+/-	ESP/60	AdjCF%	iCF/60	OGVT	DGVT	SGVT	GVT
2012-13	CBJ	21	31	0	5	5	4	0.40	48.0%	6.2	-0.9	1.5	0.0	0.6
2013-14	CBJ	22	2	0	0	0	2	0.00	50.4%	6.3	-0.2	0.4	0.0	0.2
2014-15	CBJ, CHI, TOR	23	42	2	5	7	-7	0.23	47.2%	7.3	-0.3	-0.6	0.0	-0.9
2015-16	PIT	24	42	2	6	8					-0.3	0.7	0.0	0.4

Tim Erixon is another former top-prospect blueliner who is close to running out of opportunities to prove he belongs in the NHL. When he was claimed by the Leafs off of waivers from Chicago just prior to the trade deadline, Toronto became Erixon's fifth NHL organization before the age of 24. His brief 15-game showing with Toronto did little on the heels of eight games with Chicago to indicate that he is prepared for much more than a bottom-pairing role. He has produced two goals and 14 points in 93 career games, and his impacts on possession are relatively average. He has offensive potential, but has struggled to show enough of it to warrant promotion up an NHL depth chart. Erixon was included in the Phil Kessel trade; he may find more opportunity with the Penguins, given their cap constraints and needs on the blueline.

Jake Gardiner								**LD**						**TOR**
Season	Team	Age	GP	G	A	Pts	+/-	ESP/60	AdjCF%	iCF/60	OGVT	DGVT	SGVT	GVT
2012-13	TOR	22	12	0	4	4	0	0.56	49.7%	7.9	0.3	-0.1	0.0	0.2
2013-14	TOR	23	80	10	21	31	-3	0.78	45.7%	8.6	5.2	0.5	0.0	5.8
2014-15	TOR	24	79	4	20	24	-23	0.67	48.5%	8.3	2.4	-1.1	0.0	1.3
2015-16	TOR	25	63	6	19	25					2.9	1.1	0.0	4.0

Jake Gardiner never seems to satisfy an impatient fanbase that struggles with how to interpret defensive performance. Toronto has suffered so mightily from a defensive perspective during Gardiner's entire tenure that to almost any casual, and many non-casual observers, his performance has never lived up to billing. An obviously elite skater, Gardiner is an excellent passer who comes by his playmaking skillset from his fairly recent days as a forward. If you are looking for his "defensive impacts" to show up in measures such as hits, safe plays off the glass, or pucks in deep, you will be looking in vain. His ability to control play with the puck on his stick, and cover long distances to retrieve loose pucks are both exceptional, and it would likely surprise people to learn that he makes a vastly more significant contribution defensively in suppressing shot attempts than he does offensively generating them. It remains to be seen how new coach Mike Babcock will approach Gardiner, particularly as he often butted heads trying to rein in and restrict the play of a similar player, Brendan Smith, in Detroit. Gardiner's elite passing, skating, and defensive impacts all indicate that he has a significant future as a top-pairing defender.

Petter Granberg								**RD**						**TOR**
Season	Team	Age	GP	G	A	Pts	+/-	ESP/60	AdjCF%	iCF/60	OGVT	DGVT	SGVT	GVT
2013-14	TOR	21	1	0	0	0	0	0.00	18.5%	5.1	0.0	0.0	0.0	0.0
2014-15	TOR	22	7	0	0	0	1	0.00	41.1%	1.9	-0.2	0.5	0.0	0.2
2015-16	TOR	23	28	2	5	6					0.2	1.0	0.0	1.2

Petter Granberg was drafted with a reputation as a rugged, physically-punishing, shutdown defender. Following a debut season in North America that saw him produce a grand total of two goals and nine points in 88 regular- and post-season AHL games, plus a single NHL game, Granberg provided significantly more offense in his second season. Mostly playing alongside Stuart Percy in the Marlies' top four, Granberg produced one goal and 15 points in 53 AHL games. He also slotted in as the sixth defender for Sweden at the World Championships, behind a deep group of Oliver Ekman-Larsson, Mattias Ekholm, John Klingberg, Staffan Kronwall, and Oscar Klefblom. After an Achilles tendon injury while training in early June, his slim chance of starting in the NHL fell. He will be out until at least early October.

TORONTO MAPLE LEAFS

Andrew MacWilliam — LD — WPG

Season	Team	Age	GP	G	A	Pts	+/-	ESP/60	AdjCF%	iCF/60	OGVT	DGVT	SGVT	GVT
2014-15	TOR	24	12	0	2	2	-6	0.80	37.0%	4.7	0.2	-0.4	0.0	-0.2
2015-16	WPG	25	29	2	5	7					0.4	0.6	0.0	1.0

Andrew MacWilliam is a physically rugged defender in the classic "shutdown" mold, long on size, strength, intangibles, and grit, but short on puck skills and offensive ability. MacWilliam was originally drafted in the seventh round back in 2008, following it up with a four-year term at North Dakota, captaining the side in his senior year of 2012-13. A noted leader, he was named an alternate captain with the Marlies in his first full year of pro hockey. The six-foot-two, 230-pound rearguard was called up late in 2014-15, after trade deadline moves saw Korbinian Holzer and Cody Franson leave the club, freeing up room on the roster. In 12 games, MacWilliam recorded two assists to go along with 35 hits and seven blocked shots. His play fits the traditional (i.e. old-fashioned) view of how defenders are supposed to defend, but his possession impacts were negative at both ends of the ice.

Stuart Percy — LD — TOR

Season	Team	Age	GP	G	A	Pts	+/-	ESP/60	AdjCF%	iCF/60	OGVT	DGVT	SGVT	GVT
2014-15	TOR	21	9	0	3	3	-4	0.45	42.2%	7.2	0.1	-0.1	0.0	-0.1
2015-16	TOR	22	29	2	7	9					0.6	0.8	0.0	1.4

Stuart Percy made the Leafs out of training camp, showing a maturity and poise beyond his years, as he handled very difficult defensive assignments with aplomb in his early season showing. He was one of the five Leafs defenders that outperformed possession expectations at both the offensive and defensive ends, a select group including Rielly, Gardiner, Franson, and Brennan. Percy even found himself granted an solid opportunity on the power play, serving as a testament to his heads-up play and puck-distribution skills. Reportedly, when Percy was demoted in early November, he took it pretty hard, reflective of the fact that he had been successfully managing everything that had been thrown his way at the NHL level. His resulting disappointment may explain his lackluster offensive performance in the AHL for the remainder of the season, where he only produced 11 points in 43 regular-season games.

Dion Phaneuf — LD — TOR

Season	Team	Age	GP	G	A	Pts	+/-	ESP/60	AdjCF%	iCF/60	OGVT	DGVT	SGVT	GVT
2012-13	TOR	27	48	9	19	28	-4	0.80	42.4%	9.1	4.4	1.7	-0.3	5.8
2013-14	TOR	28	80	8	23	31	2	0.82	40.4%	9.8	3.0	2.2	0.0	5.1
2014-15	TOR	29	70	3	26	29	-11	0.64	44.3%	9.0	0.8	1.6	0.0	2.5
2015-16	TOR	30	64	6	22	28					2.2	2.9	0.0	5.1

Dion Phaneuf always appears to be the piece coaches think they can mold or fix. His physical attributes, pedigree, and NHL history all seem to work against this theory when it is put into practice. Since being cast as an offensive powerhouse in sheltered minutes in Calgary early in his career, Phaneuf never really developed a consistent defensive game. Since being dealt to Toronto, both Ron Wilson and Randy Carlyle felt Phaneuf was best utilized as the Leafs' premier shutdown defender. When partnered with a healthy and effective Carl Gunnarsson, there was a respite of one year for Phaneuf when the team's defense wasn't abysmal. Without Gunnarsson (or Franson) alongside him, virtually all available evidence indicates that the Leafs are one of the worst teams in the NHL defensively when Phaneuf is on the ice. Now, incoming head coach Mike Babcock is inclined to suggest he will solve the Phaneuf conundrum. Unlike the other coaches mentioned, Babcock does have a history of getting excellent results defensively from teams featuring defensive liabilities playing significant minutes. It will be interesting to see if he can work his magic with Phaneuf.

Roman Polak					**RD**								**TOR**
Season	Team	Age	GP	G	A	Pts	+/-	ESP/60	AdjCF%	iCF/60	OGVT	DGVT	SGVT	GVT
2012-13	STL	26	48	1	5	6	-2	0.46	50.3%	7.5	-0.9	3.6	0.0	2.7
2013-14	STL	27	72	4	9	13	3	0.72	49.7%	8.8	0.7	4.1	0.0	4.8
2014-15	TOR	28	56	5	4	9	-22	0.54	44.0%	7.1	-0.2	0.1	0.0	-0.1
2015-16	TOR	29	55	4	9	12					0.4	1.9	0.0	2.3

Roman Polak was a key offseason addition, brought in via trade from St. Louis for blueliner Carl Gunnarsson. The logic surrounding the Polak deal revolved around thinking that defense is best measured by physical plays such as hits and blocked shots. Unfortunately, those statistics are usually window dressing for ineffective defensive performances, and while not necessarily negatives, they often obscure accurate assessments. In Polak's case, he largely lived up to expectations defensively in his 56 games: he wasn't the main source of difficulty for the Leafs. He did block 128 shots, or 36.8% of all shot attempts when he was on the ice, the highest proportion of any regular Leafs defender. He also made his presence known through hits, landing 225, at a rate of 0.16 hits per shot attempt against, which ranked 13th amongst regular defenders in the league. Unfortunately, playing adequate defense while blocking a lot of shots and making hits didn't turn around the fortunes of the Leafs defensive unit.

Morgan Rielly					**LD**								**TOR**
Season	Team	Age	GP	G	A	Pts	+/-	ESP/60	AdjCF%	iCF/60	OGVT	DGVT	SGVT	GVT
2013-14	TOR	19	73	2	25	27	-13	0.79	43.8%	9.0	2.7	-0.8	0.0	1.9
2014-15	TOR	20	81	8	21	29	-16	0.86	46.9%	11.3	4.3	0.3	0.0	4.6
2015-16	TOR	21	66	8	23	31					4.1	1.6	0.0	5.7

Morgan Rielly has made consistent progress towards hopefully becoming a star contributor for the Leafs. His offensive impacts are significant, as his ability to push play out of the defensive zone and carry the puck up-ice is obviously elite. His passing and puck skills led to him setting up or generating his own shot attempts at a rate of 22.7 per 60 minutes, which ranked in the top 20 defenders, marginally ahead of the likes of Doughty, Boychuk, Hamilton, Carlson, and Yandle. Having just turned 21, the Leafs have every reason to believe that his performance at both ends of the ice will continue to develop significantly. Last season saw his ice-time jump by 28% and his shot total increase by 54%. Assuming he stays healthy, Rielly could potentially average over 24 minutes per game and produce over 40 points, entering discussion as one of the NHL's primetime defenders.

Stephane Robidas					**RD**								**TOR**
Season	Team	Age	GP	G	A	Pts	+/-	ESP/60	AdjCF%	iCF/60	OGVT	DGVT	SGVT	GVT
2012-13	DAL	35	48	1	12	13	2	0.66	48.2%	7.2	-0.4	2.4	0.0	2.0
2013-14	DAL, ANA	36	38	5	5	10	10	0.83	51.2%	10.1	0.8	2.8	0.0	3.6
2014-15	TOR	37	52	1	6	7	8	0.47	43.3%	6.5	-0.3	3.4	0.0	3.2
2015-16	TOR	38	46	2	7	9					0.1	2.5	0.0	2.6

Stephane Robidas was signed to a three-year, 35+ contract by Toronto during a bout of temporary insanity, in a deal that was widely criticized for its myopia. Very few NHL defenders are capable of playing at an elite level coming off injury as significant as breaking the same leg twice in the same year. It would be almost unimaginable to expect them to do so past the age of 35. Robidas played in 52 games with the Leafs and was granted a voice in the locker room as an alternate captain. His performance defensively was actually quite adequate in a bottom-pairing role. The problem is that he drastically underperformed expectations offensively, as the Leafs generated very little in the way of scoring chances with him present on the ice. Further, his decline in offensive performance is a trend that dates back three seasons, an aspect of his game that is unlikely to right itself as he ages further.

GOALTENDERS

Jonathan Bernier — G — TOR

Season	Team	Age	GP	W	L	OT	GAA	Sv%	ESSV%	QS%	GGVT	DGVT	SGVT	GVT
2012-13	LAK	24	14	9	3	1	1.88	.922	.932	75.0%	4.2	0.6	-1.5	3.3
2013-14	TOR	25	55	26	19	7	2.68	.923	.933	59.2%	19.2	-2.5	-1.0	15.7
2014-15	TOR	26	58	21	28	7	2.87	.912	.921	47.3%	4.1	-1.7	-2.8	-0.4
2015-16	TOR	27	41					.916			6.8	-1.1	-0.4	5.3

Jonathan Bernier had a season of reversion. One year after seeming to grasp the starter's role by the horns, his performance collapsed in the latter half, along with that of the rest of the team. His save percentage post All-Star Game was .911, and despite improved possession and lower shot totals from the squad in front of him, the ship never seemed to right itself for an extended period. The most disheartening aspect may be Bernier's Quality Start percentage over the past two seasons, ranking only 37th amongst regular goalies. Ironically, the goaltender in 36th place, is his battery-mate James Reimer, the man he is supposed to supplant; it remains to be seen if that oft-discussed outcome ever comes to fruition. If Bernier hopes to be paid as a top-end starter, some increased consistency would be a positive step.

James Reimer — G — TOR

Season	Team	Age	GP	W	L	OT	GAA	Sv%	ESSV%	QS%	GGVT	DGVT	SGVT	GVT
2012-13	TOR	24	33	19	8	5	2.46	.924	.924	51.6%	13.7	-1.0	-0.3	12.4
2013-14	TOR	25	36	12	16	1	3.29	.911	.923	46.9%	1.5	-2.0	0.4	-0.1
2014-15	TOR	26	35	9	16	1	3.16	.907	.914	44.4%	-2.3	-1.3	-0.4	-4.0
2015-16	TOR	27	25					.913			1.4	0.8	-0.1	0.5

James Reimer has never seemed to earn the respect and admiration of his team or the pundits. This despite the fact that the only time the Leafs have made it to the playoffs in the past decade, he was the starter, carrying the team to within one minute of eliminating the Boston Bruins in seven games. If it weren't for his concussion history and subsequent downturns in play, it seems unlikely that the debate around Reimer's performance would be at the point it has gotten to in recent seasons. It will be interesting to see how Mike Babcock deploys his goaltending tandem as the upcoming season progresses, and if Reimer earns a fairer shake in a 1A-1B system, rather than the outright backup he has been the past two years.

Stephen Burtch

Vancouver Canucks

Vancouver produced what was quite possibly the most average team iced in any season in recent memory—average goaltending, average scoring, average injuries, and that most average of results, a first-round playoff exit.

They were neither lucky nor unlucky in most of the usual categories—overtime and shootout records, team shooting and save percentage, record in one-goal games—all perfectly normal. To the pessimist, it was a humdrum body of bland hockey featuring mostly players somewhat past their prime, a prelude to a soft sunset and several years of mediocrity. To the optimist, it was an extraordinary display of ever-elusive consistency, with great depth, and without seemingly any glaring weaknesses, a platform on which a decisive general manager and head coach could work with confidence and options.

To get a handle on just how very average Vancouver was in 2014-2015, start with the foundation of all winning teams—the ability to generate and suppress shot attempts at five-on-five. The Canucks generated 0.88 shot attempts per five-on-five minute, 49th percentile among teams over the last eight years. Conversely, they allowed 0.90 shot attempts per five-on-five minute, 52nd percentile over the last eight years. As far as finishing, Vancouver had perfectly average five-on-five shooting, hitting the back of the net at exactly the league average of 7.7% of shots on goal.

On the other side of shots, the Canucks have been spoiled in goal in their recent history: the star veteran, Luongo, and the star understudy, Schneider, were embroiled in year after year of the *ur*-example of goalie controversy, with both providing stellar results. This was the first year with neither goalie around—oddly quiet. Although the heat and fury of controversy were diminished, so too were the saves, with Miller, Lack, and Markstrom recording a five-on-five save percentage of only .917, compared to a .923 league average.

After firebrand John Tortorella was fired in the offseason, the head coaching job was entrusted to Willie Desjardins, a long-time coach but never an NHL head coach. After the hot-headed approach of Tortorella, Desjardins applied a very steady hand—perhaps a shade too steady. The 2014 Calder Cup winning coach rolled four lines throughout the season and the playoffs, featuring one of the smallest gaps in five-on-five ice-time between first and fourth lines in the league.

The Canucks employ very few of the kind of very poor players who anchor the rosters of most teams, and dress those

CANUCKS IN A BOX

Last Season
Goals For	242	t-6th
Goals Against	222	17th
GVT	20	t-12th
Points	101	t-8th
Playoffs	Lost Conference Quarterfinal	

After missing the playoffs in 2014, Vancouver's offense bounced back and the team finished fifth in the West.

Three-Year Record
GVT	-1	16th
Points	243	15th
Playoffs	2 Appearances, 2 Wins	

VUKOTA Projection
Goals For	215	22nd
Goals Against	225	26th
GVT	-10	23rd
Points	88	23rd

The Sedins will be 35, Vrbata 34, Hamhuis 33, Edler 30. This is a team in decline, and 2014-15 was probably their last hurrah.

Top Three Prospects
J. McCann (F), B. Boeser (F), C. Cassels (F)

The very average Canucks, 2014-15

Stat	NHL rank
Shots for	12th
Shots against	14th
Sv% + Sh%	13th
Man-games lost	17th

few sparingly. However, the dropoff in skill from the Sedin twins to the bottom of the regular roster is still substantial. If the root of the unusually even-handed deployment is a rookie coach hewing too tightly to a conservative path, that approach may become less typical as Desjardins becomes more sure and aggressive. If, instead, it is a deliberate sheltering of the team's aging star players, it betokens rough seas ahead.

That said, the decline of the team's aging star players has been predicted many times before, and the past season was a stiff refutation to doom-and-gloomers. The Sedins were wizardly again, posting nearly a point per game while suppressing shots against better than all but a handful of players—all while missing a combined zero games and facing the opponents' top lines. In an enlightened era, the league might let them share a Selke Trophy. Freshly-acquired free agent Radim Vrbata scored alongside the Sedins at a healthy clip as hoped for, but the remainder of the roster was more stolid than stellar.

Looking to the past as a guide shows mixed portents. Based on five-on-five shot generation and suppression, two of the most similar teams to the past year's Canucks were the 2010-11 Rangers, who have since become perennial playoff contenders, and the 2011-12 Sabres, who have essentially burned their team to the ground since that time. Where the Canucks go from here depends very much on the willingness of the management and coaches to make the correct risky maneuvers.

If they act conservatively, turning over few players and making the consistently "safe" coaching choices, they may well find that the tide of the league will leave them behind in a very few years. If they assiduously winnow the well-understood but mediocre players from the roster in favor of unprovens, and decisively push their few but definite advantages, they may parlay a consistency that many teams would kill for into a strong, competitive team for the next several years.

Micah Blake McCurdy

Even-Strength Usage: Vancouver Canucks

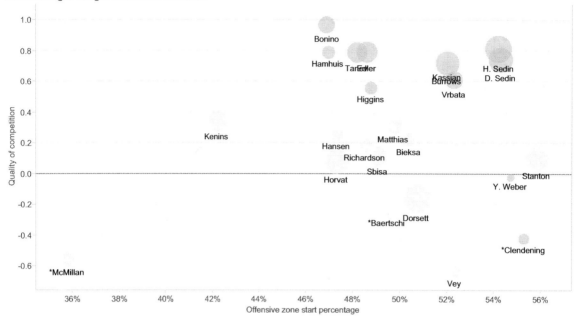

Special Teams Usage: Vancouver Canucks

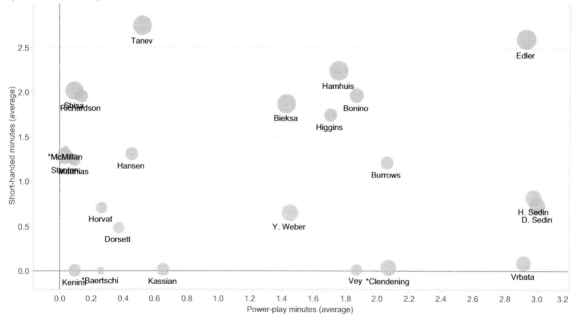

VANCOUVER CANUCKS

Offensive Profile: Vancouver Canucks

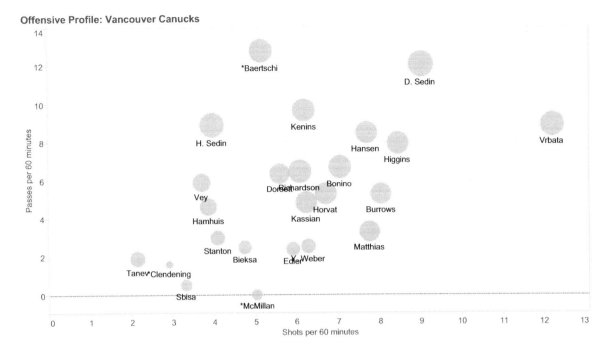

Cap Efficiency: Vancouver Canucks

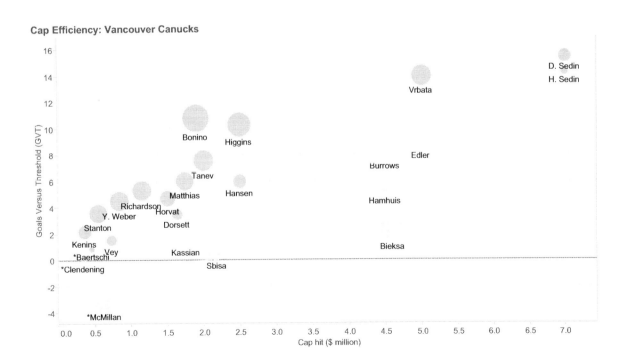

VANCOUVER CANUCKS

FORWARDS

Will Acton							C/LW						Free Agent
Season	Team	Age	GP	G	A	Pts	+/-	ESP/60	AdjCF%	iCF/60	OGVT	DGVT	SGVT	GVT
2013-14	EDM	26	30	3	2	5	-2	1.64	37.8%	11.1	0.3	1.3	0.0	1.6
2014-15	EDM	27	3	0	0	0	-2	0.00	40.4%	5.7	-0.5	0.0	0.0	-0.4
2015-16	Free Agent	28	34	5	6	11					0.3	0.9	0.0	1.2

Back in 2013-14, Will Acton was mostly paired with Luke Gazdic on the fourth line. Perhaps not too surprisingly, he failed to put up any encouraging possession stats over the course of his 30 games. Last season, the son of long-time journeyman Keith Acton (whose best output was 88 points as a third-year NHLer for the Habs, in 1981-82) appeared in just six games for Oklahoma City and three for Edmonton before getting traded to the Canucks' organization in late November. Acton's game is comprised mostly of physicality, defensive awareness, and faceoff ability.

Sven Baertschi							LW/RW							VAN
Season	Team	Age	GP	G	A	Pts	+/-	ESP/60	AdjCF%	iCF/60	OGVT	DGVT	SGVT	GVT
2012-13	CGY	20	20	3	7	10	0	2.56	47.2%	9.6	2.1	0.4	0.0	2.5
2013-14	CGY	21	26	2	9	11	-4	1.25	42.2%	9.0	0.4	0.5	-0.6	0.4
2014-15	CGY, VAN	22	18	2	4	6	-3	2.12	44.1%	8.1	0.8	0.1	0.0	0.9
2015-16	VAN	23	35	5	9	14					0.8	0.7	0.0	1.6

The Calgary Flames raised some eyebrows when they decided to trade promising youngster Sven Baertschi to Vancouver for a second-round pick. Though unproven in the NHL, the 2011 first rounder is a prospect of considerable skill. The five-foot-ten Swiss winger appeared in only three games for the Canucks at the very end of the season, playing around 30 minutes including a sniff on the power play. Baertschi still lingers on the edge of getting serious playing time. We will see if he fares better in the Canucks organization.

Nick Bonino							C							PIT
Season	Team	Age	GP	G	A	Pts	+/-	ESP/60	AdjCF%	iCF/60	OGVT	DGVT	SGVT	GVT
2012-13	ANA	24	27	5	8	13	-3	1.72	44.6%	10.2	1.4	0.2	1.0	2.6
2013-14	ANA	25	77	22	27	49	14	1.94	50.8%	11.5	8.1	2.8	0.4	11.3
2014-15	VAN	26	75	15	24	39	7	2.08	51.1%	11.9	6.2	4.5	0.2	10.8
2015-16	PIT	27	68	17	25	42					5.3	2.9	0.0	8.2

Nick Bonino, the centerpiece of the Kesler trade package, settled in smoothly in Vancouver, leading the team in shot attempts per 60 minutes while putting up nearly 40 points. Bonino's line was routinely buried in the defensive zone to allow the Sedins the choice minutes, but the Avon Old Farms product consistently pushed the puck up the ice despite playing the toughest competition of any on the team. The Hartford-born forward contributed on both special teams.

VANCOUVER CANUCKS

Alexandre Burrows								RW						VAN
Season	Team	Age	GP	G	A	Pts	+/-	ESP/60	AdjCF%	iCF/60	OGVT	DGVT	SGVT	GVT
2012-13	VAN	31	47	13	11	24	15	1.90	58.8%	15.1	2.0	4.0	-1.2	4.8
2013-14	VAN	32	49	5	10	15	-9	0.72	55.4%	14.7	-1.3	1.3	-0.5	-0.6
2014-15	VAN	33	70	18	15	33	0	1.69	52.7%	13.0	4.8	2.4	0.6	7.8
2015-16	VAN	34	60	13	15	28					2.6	1.8	0.0	4.4

Versatile winger Alex Burrows played substantially on the top line with the Sedins, but also with Bonino and Higgins, putting up excellent possession numbers with almost every teammate. His on-ice save percentage of 90% suggests that he was unlucky to be on the ice for so many goals against, yet his 33 points were nothing out of the ordinary, as he returned to a more typical individual shooting percentage of 12%, near his pre-slump mark. As far as defenders, he showed an unusually strong chemistry with Yannick Weber as well as Luca Sbisa.

Cory Conacher								LW						Swiss
Season	Team	Age	GP	G	A	Pts	+/-	ESP/60	AdjCF%	iCF/60	OGVT	DGVT	SGVT	GVT
2012-13	TBL, OTT	23	47	11	18	29	3	2.68	48.8%	10.4	4.4	1.1	0.0	5.5
2013-14	OTT, BUF	24	79	7	19	26	1	1.65	48.8%	9.5	0.7	1.3	-0.6	1.5
2014-15	NYI	25	15	1	2	3	-3	0.94	51.1%	10.0	-0.8	0.2	0.0	-0.6
2015-16	Swiss	26	47	6	11	17					0.4	1.1	0.0	1.5

Once part of the AHL's most dangerous tandem, Cory Conacher and Tyler Johnson dominated as linemates for the Syracuse Crunch. While Johnson has turned out to be a star with the Lightning, scoring 72 regular-season points plus 23 points in 26 playoff games, Conacher had a short flash in the pan in Tampa Bay before being traded to Ottawa for big goaltender Ben Bishop. Since putting up a head-turning 24 points in 35 games in 2012-13, the Canisius University grad only has 34 points in 106 games. The speedy winger does not have the skill to score at a top-six level, or the size—at five-foot-eight, 180 pounds—to play in the bottom six. He will likely struggle to find consistent NHL work.

Brandon Defazio								LW						BOS
Season	Team	Age	GP	G	A	Pts	+/-	ESP/60	AdjCF%	iCF/60	OGVT	DGVT	SGVT	GVT
2014-15	VAN	26	2	0	0	0	0	0.00	47.3%	19.6	0.0	0.0	0.0	0.0
2015-16	BOS	27	26	5	6	11					0.7	0.6	0.0	1.3

Brandon Defazio played a grand total of just over 10 minutes for the Canucks, to zero net effect, being on the ice for no goals for or against. The six-foot-one, 201-pound Clarkson graduate has modestly increased his minor-league numbers from 41 points in his first 137 games to 77 points in his last 151 games. He moves on to play for Providence in the Bruins organization.

Derek Dorsett								RW						VAN
Season	Team	Age	GP	G	A	Pts	+/-	ESP/60	AdjCF%	iCF/60	OGVT	DGVT	SGVT	GVT
2012-13	CBJ, NYR	26	24	3	6	9	-11	1.63	44.9%	9.2	-1.0	0.4	0.0	-0.6
2013-14	NYR	27	51	4	4	8	-1	0.93	49.8%	12.1	-0.3	1.4	0.0	1.2
2014-15	VAN	28	79	7	18	25	4	1.56	43.0%	10.9	1.6	2.0	0.0	3.5
2015-16	VAN	29	62	6	11	17					0.0	1.5	0.0	1.5

Tough winger Derek Dorsett was in the midst of the fray throughout the year, both taking and drawing minor penalties at a faster rate than any other regular forward. The long-time Blue Jacket fought 17 times, second in the league, and more than thrice as often as any other Canuck. As you might expect, the 2006 seventh-round selection played strictly under 15 minutes nightly although he dressed for all but three games. Unfortunately, he was the team's worst forward by shot metrics, by some margin. The Canucks clearly felt his physical play was necessary, though, inking him to a hefty extension at the end of the regular season.

Jannik Hansen							RW						VAN
Season	Team	Age	GP	G	A	Pts	+/-	ESP/60	AdjCF%	iCF/60	OGVT	DGVT	SGVT	GVT
2012-13	VAN	26	47	10	17	27	12	2.23	51.2%	14.0	2.7	2.8	-0.3	5.3
2013-14	VAN	27	71	11	9	20	-9	1.09	51.3%	11.1	-0.3	2.3	0.0	2.0
2014-15	VAN	28	81	16	17	33	-6	1.82	48.4%	13.6	4.2	1.8	0.0	6.0
2015-16	VAN	29	66	14	16	30					2.9	1.9	0.0	4.8

Jannik Hansen lined up mostly with Dorsett and Horvat, picking up even-strength minutes as the season moved along. Any suggestion that the Danish winger was being carried by Kesler should be well laid to rest after this season: his offensive contributions of 15 even-strength goals and the same number of assists were very handy considering his minutes. As the season wore along, he opened up his game, finishing at a shot-attempt tempo of nearly double that of the start of the campaign while improving his team's possession by five percentage points.

Chris Higgins							LW						VAN
Season	Team	Age	GP	G	A	Pts	+/-	ESP/60	AdjCF%	iCF/60	OGVT	DGVT	SGVT	GVT
2012-13	VAN	29	41	10	5	15	-4	1.61	49.3%	12.6	1.4	1.3	0.7	3.4
2013-14	VAN	30	78	17	22	39	-14	1.74	50.5%	15.1	2.6	3.8	-0.5	6.0
2014-15	VAN	31	77	12	24	36	8	1.96	50.9%	14.0	4.5	5.1	0.7	10.3
2015-16	VAN	32	67	14	21	35					3.3	3.1	0.0	6.4

Smithtown, Long Island's own Chris Higgins suited up for all but five games, despite his reputation as injury prone. The former Hab, Ranger, Flame, and Panther was a consistent contributor to the second line, with a boost in minutes when the Canucks trailed, and his 36 points were useful but perhaps a shade underwhelming. He drove possession moderately, although his defensive shot-suppression results suffered as the year wore on. The 2002 first rounder showed great chemistry with new acquisition Nick Bonino, with whom he played the bulk of his five-on-five minutes. Unusual for the Canucks, Higgins drew minor penalties three times as often as he took them, a more subtle but nevertheless substantial contribution.

Bo Horvat							C						VAN
Season	Team	Age	GP	G	A	Pts	+/-	ESP/60	AdjCF%	iCF/60	OGVT	DGVT	SGVT	GVT
2014-15	VAN	19	68	13	12	25	-8	1.88	45.0%	10.1	3.4	1.4	0.0	4.7
2015-16	VAN	20	63	15	18	33					3.7	1.6	0.0	5.3

Bo Horvat, the first-round pick for whom Cory Schneider was traded at the 2013 NHL Entry Draft, grew slowly but surely into a regular player. After missing the first 12 contests, he dressed for all but two of the rest, taking on more and more minutes as the season wore on, allowing head coach Willie Desjardins to roll four very even ice-time lines, as he strongly prefers to do. The former London Knight showed good chemistry with Ronalds Kenins, but his defensive/possession play was suspect, allowing shot attempts against more quickly than any other Canucks forward. That said, Horvat was somewhat unlucky to be graced with a .909 save percentage while on the ice. If that regresses—in a good way—as it should, and Bo can tighten up defensively, he should become a solid player, especially considering his respectable point generation for a youngster who doesn't receive time on the man advantage.

Nicklas Jensen — RW — VAN

Season	Team	Age	GP	G	A	Pts	+/-	ESP/60	AdjCF%	iCF/60	OGVT	DGVT	SGVT	GVT
2012-13	VAN	19	2	0	0	0	-1	0.00	48.9%	4.1	-0.2	-0.1	0.0	-0.2
2013-14	VAN	20	17	3	3	6	-1	1.28	56.5%	13.2	-0.3	0.6	0.3	0.6
2014-15	VAN	21	5	0	0	0	-1	0.00	49.4%	11.5	-0.4	0.0	0.0	-0.4
2015-16	VAN	22	30	5	6	11					0.5	0.7	0.0	1.2

Nicklas Jensen took a step backward, garnering less than half a point per game in Utica, where he spent most of the year, only earning five games up with the Canucks. The Danish/Canadian prospect played only 40 minutes at five-on-five in those five contests, mostly with Shawn Matthias and Brad Richardson, with virtually no special-teams time. Jensen put up no points, though his team shot a laughable 4% during his small sample of playing time, which is surely the sort of luck that will turn.

Zack Kassian — RW — MTL

Season	Team	Age	GP	G	A	Pts	+/-	ESP/60	AdjCF%	iCF/60	OGVT	DGVT	SGVT	GVT
2012-13	VAN	21	39	7	4	11	-7	1.02	48.9%	11.4	0.0	0.0	-0.1	-0.1
2013-14	VAN	22	73	14	15	29	-4	1.88	50.7%	10.5	2.7	2.4	-1.1	4.0
2014-15	VAN	23	42	10	6	16	-5	1.79	49.6%	10.1	1.2	0.2	0.0	1.4
2015-16	MTL	24	55	12	12	24					1.9	1.1	0.0	3.0

Ever since getting swapped for the slowly-deflating Cody Hodgson, Zack Kassian has been the subject of much ornery discussion. Some would prefer he play a regular top-nine shift, while others say he is not good enough to play much; the Canucks largely opted for the latter course, dressing the former Sabre and Amerk for half the games while giving him decent fourth-line minutes when he did play. Kassian was much more noticeable for his 81 penalty minutes than his 16 points, but although he has a reputation for undisciplined play, he draws penalties nearly as quickly as he takes them.

Ronalds Kenins — LW — VAN

Season	Team	Age	GP	G	A	Pts	+/-	ESP/60	AdjCF%	iCF/60	OGVT	DGVT	SGVT	GVT
2014-15	VAN	23	30	4	8	12	-2	1.97	47.1%	10.9	1.9	0.2	0.0	2.2
2015-16	VAN	24	42	8	13	21					2.2	1.0	0.0	3.2

Charismatic Latvian Ronalds Kenins led a charmed life, not really in the Canucks plans but somehow constantly in the lineup in the second half of the season as he filled in on the fourth line, playing nearly all of his minutes with Horvat and Hansen. His shot suppression faltered as the campaign ended, like most of the team, but he was strong in shots despite starting only 45% of his shifts in the offensive zone. The six-foot, 201-pound winger showed a worrying tendency to take around three penalties every five games, while drawing none whatsoever. If he can rein in some of that energy—akin to what Ryan Garbutt has done—he could provide some bottom-six value.

Shawn Matthias						LW/C							TOR
Season	Team	Age	GP	G	A	Pts	+/-	ESP/60	AdjCF%	iCF/60	OGVT	DGVT	SGVT	GVT
2012-13	FLA	24	48	14	7	21	-8	1.61	46.7%	13.7	2.3	1.7	-0.3	3.7
2013-14	FLA, VAN	25	77	12	11	23	-3	1.64	46.9%	12.4	2.4	2.7	0.0	5.0
2014-15	VAN	26	78	18	9	27	-3	1.63	47.3%	12.7	4.1	2.0	0.0	6.0
2015-16	TOR	27	64	14	12	26					2.4	1.7	0.0	4.2

In contrast to the hospital-ward blueline, the Canucks were quite healthy at center; Shawn Matthias was a fine example, missing only four games, none to injury. Deployed almost entirely at even strength and shorthanded, the athletically-gifted six-foot-three, 212-pound forward shot an unusually high 14% and contributed a handy 27 points from the third line, including a memorable hat trick—the only one of his career—at home to Boston. Although his possession numbers were roughly team-average, he was the opposite of consistent, alternating dismal performances with sparkling outings—his M.O. during his professional career.

Brandon McMillan						C/LW							Free Agent
Season	Team	Age	GP	G	A	Pts	+/-	ESP/60	AdjCF%	iCF/60	OGVT	DGVT	SGVT	GVT
2012-13	ANA	22	6	0	1	1	-1	1.27	43.6%	4.8	-0.1	0.1	0.0	0.0
2013-14	PHX	23	22	2	4	6	0	1.39	55.1%	11.7	0.1	0.7	0.0	0.8
2014-15	ARI, VAN	24	58	1	3	4	-19	0.46	45.7%	11.1	-3.4	0.2	0.0	-3.2
2015-16	Free Agent	25	49	3	5	8					-1.7	0.9	0.0	-0.8

Brandon McMillan appeared in only a handful of games, playing fourth-line minutes in all of them. Considering his very heavy defensive-zone deployment and playing over half his minutes with the likes of Derek Dorsett, he moved the puck up the ice after soaking up pressure surprisingly well. Scoring a playoff goal was perhaps the highlight of his season, but the former Duck and Coyote acquitted himself nicely and could easily work his way into regular bottom-line duty next year.

Brad Richardson						LW/C							ARI
Season	Team	Age	GP	G	A	Pts	+/-	ESP/60	AdjCF%	iCF/60	OGVT	DGVT	SGVT	GVT
2012-13	LAK	27	16	1	5	6	2	2.18	56.6%	16.9	0.9	0.6	0.0	1.4
2013-14	VAN	28	73	11	12	23	1	1.23	47.7%	10.3	0.2	4.1	0.0	4.3
2014-15	VAN	29	45	8	13	21	0	2.05	48.6%	11.5	2.5	2.8	0.0	5.3
2015-16	ARI	30	57	9	14	23					1.3	2.2	0.0	3.6

Veteran journeyman Brad Richardson played bottom-six minutes with a healthy dose of penalty-killing time until sidelined with a pair of injuries which took him out of the lineup for most of the second half. The Owen Sound product was given somewhat less heavily defensive usage than in years past, but still contributed a useful half a point per game on the wing. Moving from center to wing evidently did not hamper the Belleville native, although he took penalties at a worryingly high rate of well over one per 60 minutes, three times as often as he drew them—usually not a good sign for a post-prime player.

VANCOUVER CANUCKS

Daniel Sedin								LW						VAN
Season	Team	Age	GP	G	A	Pts	+/-	ESP/60	AdjCF%	iCF/60	OGVT	DGVT	SGVT	GVT
2012-13	VAN	32	47	12	28	40	12	2.34	62.2%	15.1	6.6	1.8	-0.3	8.1
2013-14	VAN	33	73	16	31	47	0	1.48	56.6%	13.4	4.8	2.9	-1.1	6.6
2014-15	VAN	34	82	20	56	76	5	2.55	53.3%	14.4	13.5	1.9	0.0	15.5
2015-16	VAN	35	69	19	38	58					7.6	2.1	0.0	9.8

The widely-circulated rumors of the imminent demise of the Sedins were shown to be false, as Daniel led the team in scoring once again at just under a point-per-game pace, all while playing 82 games, like his brother. Although favorably deployed in the offensive zone, on the power play, and when trailing by one—the better to maximize their extraordinary offensive skills—both twins allowed shot attempts against at a rate normally associated only with Selke winners. Daniel's on-ice save percentage of .906 suggests his goals against were a shade unlucky, and he took half as many penalties as he drew. Age comes for us all, but this year was a sparkling season for the future Hall of Famer.

Henrik Sedin								C						VAN
Season	Team	Age	GP	G	A	Pts	+/-	ESP/60	AdjCF%	iCF/60	OGVT	DGVT	SGVT	GVT
2012-13	VAN	32	48	11	34	45	19	2.48	61.4%	7.1	7.8	2.6	0.0	10.5
2013-14	VAN	33	70	11	39	50	3	1.69	55.4%	7.0	5.3	3.5	-0.6	8.3
2014-15	VAN	34	82	18	55	73	11	2.37	54.0%	6.3	11.7	2.6	0.0	14.3
2015-16	VAN	35	68	15	39	54					6.2	2.2	0.0	8.5

Vancouver captain Henrik Sedin put up another extraordinarily strong campaign as the best even-strength defensive forward on the team—slightly edging out his brother—all while recording nearly 0.9 points per game. His durability was again a feature, as he missed zero games. Henrik's game-to-game play was among the most consistent on the team, both in terms of possession, scoring, and ice-time, even with the now-typical carousel of right wingers. In addition to capable power-play performance, the 2006 Olympic gold medalist was sterling in penalty differential, drawing two minors for every one he committed.

Tom Sestito								LW						Free Agent
Season	Team	Age	GP	G	A	Pts	+/-	ESP/60	AdjCF%	iCF/60	OGVT	DGVT	SGVT	GVT
2012-13	PHI, VAN	25	30	3	0	3	-2	0.93	43.5%	7.6	-0.1	0.2	0.0	0.1
2013-14	VAN	26	77	5	4	9	-14	0.98	44.0%	5.2	-1.7	0.2	0.0	-1.5
2014-15	VAN	27	3	0	1	1	1	3.21	28.6%	6.6	0.2	0.1	0.0	0.3
2015-16	Free Agent	28	41	4	5	8					-0.4	0.6	0.0	0.2

Playing only three games, with the scarcest of minutes in them, Tom Sestito was a possession black hole, with the team 19 percentage points worse in shot-attempt share when he was on the ice versus when he was not. In those three games, Sestito marked his name on the scoresheet to the tune of one assist, a minor penalty, and a fighting major. The Canucks clearly had a change of heart, having dressed him for 77 games in 2013-14, and it appears now that his departure is one more example of the downward trend in enforcers across the league.

Linden Vey — C/RW — VAN

Season	Team	Age	GP	G	A	Pts	+/-	ESP/60	AdjCF%	iCF/60	OGVT	DGVT	SGVT	GVT
2013-14	LAK	22	18	0	5	5	0	1.03	52.1%	5.9	0.0	0.6	-0.3	0.3
2014-15	VAN	23	75	10	14	24	-3	1.28	47.8%	6.9	0.7	0.7	0.0	1.5
2015-16	VAN	24	63	10	15	25					0.9	1.2	0.0	2.1

A utility player, Linden (no relation to Trevor) Vey played his 11-12 minutes per night with all manner of players, never establishing himself with any particular linemates despite appearing in almost every game. His possession rates varied heavily depending on his line, and he put up only modest scoring numbers, with a point every three games or so. The former Medicine Hat Tiger and Manchester Monarch was deployed favorably in the offensive zone and was consistently given substantial power-play minutes, especially early in the season, so his lack of production must be furrowing some brows in the organization already.

Radim Vrbata — RW — VAN

Season	Team	Age	GP	G	A	Pts	+/-	ESP/60	AdjCF%	iCF/60	OGVT	DGVT	SGVT	GVT
2012-13	PHX	31	34	12	16	28	6	1.79	51.5%	15.3	5.1	1.0	-0.1	5.9
2013-14	PHX	32	80	20	31	51	-6	1.53	51.0%	18.3	5.9	2.2	1.1	9.1
2014-15	VAN	33	79	31	32	63	6	2.23	51.4%	17.9	12.3	1.6	0.2	14.0
2015-16	VAN	34	66	23	28	51					7.2	1.7	0.0	8.9

Long-time Coyote Radim Vrbata performed as well as expected when paired with the Sedin twins on the top line, producing 54% of the even-strength shot attempts with them, while allowing a scant 42 attempts per 60 minutes. His 31 goals led the squad by some distance: he may well be the ideal "winger for the Sedins" that has become such a fixation among the fanbase and the front office. Curiously, the Czech winger oscillated between heavy power-play deployment with no penalty killing for a handful of games, followed by the reverse, several times during the season. Perhaps the coaching staff is not quite certain where to best deploy his talents just yet.

DEFENSEMEN

Alex Biega — RD — VAN

Season	Team	Age	GP	G	A	Pts	+/-	ESP/60	AdjCF%	iCF/60	OGVT	DGVT	SGVT	GVT
2014-15	VAN	26	7	1	0	1	-2	0.56	43.2%	9.8	-0.1	-0.2	0.0	-0.3
2015-16	VAN	27	28	2	5	8					0.4	0.8	0.0	1.2

Former Harvard captain and MVP Alex Biega got an unexpected call-up for seven games during a rash of injuries. He was mostly unremarkable, though his lone point was a memorable game-winning goal against Minnesota. His poor shot totals were largely the result of one very poor game. It is hard to imagine Biega will play a large role in the Canucks future, but if he continues to play capably in Utica, he will surely receive more spot duty for the parent club when need arises.

Kevin Bieksa — RD — ANA

Season	Team	Age	GP	G	A	Pts	+/-	ESP/60	AdjCF%	iCF/60	OGVT	DGVT	SGVT	GVT
2012-13	VAN	31	36	6	6	12	6	0.84	50.7%	12.7	1.2	2.7	0.0	4.0
2013-14	VAN	32	76	4	20	24	-8	0.68	51.3%	11.7	1.2	4.2	0.0	5.4
2014-15	VAN	33	60	4	10	14	0	0.68	48.7%	10.0	0.2	2.1	0.0	2.3
2015-16	ANA	34	58	4	13	17					1.0	2.8	0.0	3.8

Famously sour-faced defender Kevin Bieksa skated for 17 minutes per night; he was given the bulk of the minutes protecting one-goal leads when the Canucks had them, playing the shutdown role more than any other defender. Perhaps as a consequence of this deployment, the Bowling Green product was the tempo leader of the team, with the most shot attempts per minute—for and against. Unfortunately, his scoring contribution fell, but his tendency to take nearly triple the minor penalties he draws continued.

Adam Clendening — RD — PIT

Season	Team	Age	GP	G	A	Pts	+/-	ESP/60	AdjCF%	iCF/60	OGVT	DGVT	SGVT	GVT
2014-15	CHI, VAN	22	21	1	3	4	2	0.20	50.1%	7.6	-0.5	0.5	0.0	0.0
2015-16	PIT	23	35	2	7	8					-0.1	1.2	0.0	1.1

Obtained from the Blackhawks in a midseason trade, Adam Clendening filled in on a banged-up blueline for 17 games, and acquitted himself admirably. He improved the possession stats of virtually everyone he played with, though he was given unusually favorable zone starts. He scored no goals himself, but the Canucks shot 10% with him on the ice; those numbers should move towards one another next season. The 2011 second rounder was kept carefully away from the high-leverage score states, receiving more minutes when leading or trailing by two or more, but as he gains more trust in the league, his deployment should normalize. The former Rockford IceHog will get a chance to earn that trust in the Pittsburgh organization in 2015-16.

Frank Corrado — RD — VAN

Season	Team	Age	GP	G	A	Pts	+/-	ESP/60	AdjCF%	iCF/60	OGVT	DGVT	SGVT	GVT
2012-13	VAN	19	3	0	0	0	-1	0.00	44.4%	11.9	0.0	0.0	0.0	0.0
2013-14	VAN	20	15	1	0	1	-2	0.34	47.6%	13.1	-0.5	0.4	0.0	0.0
2014-15	VAN	21	10	1	0	1	-7	0.40	46.8%	5.7	-0.1	-0.7	0.0	-0.8
2015-16	VAN	22	29	2	5	7					0.3	0.7	0.0	1.0

Former Sudbury Wolves captain Frank Corrado played only 10 games with third-pairing minutes, seeing hardly any power-play time and even fewer minutes on the penalty kill. Corrado was average defensively, and very up-and-down generating shot attempts in his scarce minutes, at times very poor and in other games dynamic. Expect to see more of him in 2015-16, in a slightly expanded role.

Alexander Edler — LD — VAN

Season	Team	Age	GP	G	A	Pts	+/-	ESP/60	AdjCF%	iCF/60	OGVT	DGVT	SGVT	GVT
2012-13	VAN	26	45	8	14	22	-5	0.88	52.0%	11.9	3.6	1.0	-1.1	3.5
2013-14	VAN	27	63	7	15	22	-39	0.52	52.0%	15.2	1.8	-1.5	-0.6	-0.2
2014-15	VAN	28	74	8	23	31	13	0.75	51.8%	10.8	2.9	5.7	0.0	8.6
2015-16	VAN	29	67	8	24	32					3.5	3.8	0.0	7.3

Calm Swedish rearguard Alexander Edler was the minutes-per-game leader of the Canucks, heavily deployed in all score and manpower situations. After a dire previous year when many said he was washed up, analytics suggested he would bounce back. In a modest way he did: his 31 points were the best on the blueline. His possession results were best on the team, save the top-line players, and he consistently ended his shifts further up the ice than he started them. Age will surely take its toll, and his penalty differential is beginning to become worrisome, but rumors of Edler's demise have been much exaggerated.

Dan Hamhuis — LD — VAN

Season	Team	Age	GP	G	A	Pts	+/-	ESP/60	AdjCF%	iCF/60	OGVT	DGVT	SGVT	GVT
2012-13	VAN	30	47	4	20	24	9	1.20	54.6%	9.8	4.4	4.3	0.0	8.7
2013-14	VAN	31	79	5	17	22	13	0.76	51.2%	10.5	1.0	8.9	0.0	10.0
2014-15	VAN	32	59	1	22	23	0	1.16	50.4%	8.5	2.4	3.0	0.0	5.5
2015-16	VAN	33	60	4	17	21					1.7	3.8	0.0	5.5

Dan Hamhuis, the pride of Smithers, British Columbia, played heavy minutes, especially after returning from a lengthy 23-game midseason injury. For a stretch, he frequently skated for nearly 45% of all five-on-five minutes, in addition to moderate power-play deployment and a regular turn on the penalty kill. The long-time Predator consistently put up well above team-average possession numbers despite unfavorable zone starts, and showed good chemistry with young forwards Horvat and Kenins. The 21 points don't hurt, either, and his comically low 1% shooting percentage can only go up.

Luca Sbisa — LD — VAN

Season	Team	Age	GP	G	A	Pts	+/-	ESP/60	AdjCF%	iCF/60	OGVT	DGVT	SGVT	GVT
2012-13	ANA	22	41	1	7	8	0	0.42	45.6%	7.4	-0.9	1.7	0.0	0.8
2013-14	ANA	23	30	1	5	6	0	0.77	48.9%	9.5	0.4	0.3	0.0	0.7
2014-15	VAN	24	76	3	8	11	-8	0.52	47.1%	7.7	-1.6	2.1	0.0	0.6
2015-16	VAN	25	62	3	10	13					-0.1	2.3	0.0	2.2

Newly-arrived from Anaheim in the Kesler deal, the Swiss defender that some fans have taken to calling "Pizza" had a quiet season offensively, putting up only 11 points while seeing little power-play time. Luca Sbisa gave up steadily more and more shot attempts per minute as the season wore on, with only slightly improved shot generation. His shooting percentage was under half of league average, though, which is almost certain to rise substantially. Perhaps that is part of what the Canucks had in mind when they signed him to a hefty contract extension at the end of the year.

Ryan Stanton — LD — WSH

Season	Team	Age	GP	G	A	Pts	+/-	ESP/60	AdjCF%	iCF/60	OGVT	DGVT	SGVT	GVT
2012-13	CHI	23	1	0	0	0	1	0.00	57.0%	6.9	0.0	0.0	0.0	0.0
2013-14	VAN	24	64	1	15	16	5	1.06	52.8%	9.4	1.7	3.8	0.0	5.5
2014-15	VAN	25	54	3	8	11	9	0.83	45.3%	7.9	1.0	2.6	0.0	3.6
2015-16	WSH	26	55	3	11	14					1.1	2.6	0.0	3.7

Ryan Stanton was the weakest possession defender who played serious quantities of hockey for Vancouver, though he received third-pairing minutes and was largely kept away from trailing situations, where the shot attempts come easiest. The Albertan blueliner took an average of one more minor penalty per 60 minutes than he drew despite being given the softest zone starts on the team. Add all of that to a scoring rate under 0.2 points per game and one starts to see why he was waived by the Blackhawks.

Christopher Tanev							RD						VAN
Season	Team	Age	GP	G	A	Pts	+/-	ESP/60	AdjCF%	iCF/60	OGVT	DGVT	SGVT	GVT
2012-13	VAN	23	38	2	5	7	4	0.71	52.2%	5.8	0.8	1.8	0.0	2.6
2013-14	VAN	24	64	6	11	17	12	0.86	51.4%	6.6	2.1	7.0	0.0	9.1
2014-15	VAN	25	70	2	18	20	8	0.87	52.0%	5.4	1.8	5.8	0.0	7.6
2015-16	VAN	26	65	4	16	20					1.5	4.6	0.0	6.1

Chris Tanev was rewarded for his steady play with a five-year, $22 million extension, and for good reason: the perennially cool performer is the rising tide that lifts all boats. Virtually every Canuck saw their share of the shot attempts increase when playing with the Toronto native, and he shone defensively. His personal five-on-five shot suppression was team best, and he and his constant partner Alex Edler formed the stingiest regular pairing. The one-time RIT Tiger shouldered nearly half of all the shorthanded minutes over the games in which he appeared. Maybe he really will start playing the game with a cigarette in his mouth.

Yannick Weber							RD						VAN
Season	Team	Age	GP	G	A	Pts	+/-	ESP/60	AdjCF%	iCF/60	OGVT	DGVT	SGVT	GVT
2012-13	MTL	24	6	0	2	2	-1	0.85	47.8%	7.8	0.4	0.0	0.0	0.4
2013-14	VAN	25	49	6	4	10	-7	0.61	49.3%	13.1	1.1	0.5	0.3	1.9
2014-15	VAN	26	65	11	10	21	4	0.80	50.0%	11.8	3.3	1.3	0.0	4.5
2015-16	VAN	27	57	7	14	21					2.4	1.7	0.0	4.1

Swiss international Yannick Weber received regular third-pairing minutes, and made the most of reasonably easy deployment, putting up 21 points. He showed good chemistry with forward Alex Burrows at five-on-five, and saw power-play minutes late in the year as well as some time on the penalty kill. Webber's possession metrics were steady early on, but he suffered at shot suppression as the season wore on, perhaps dealing with fatigue or an undisclosed injury.

GOALTENDERS

Eddie Lack							G						CAR
Season	Team	Age	GP	W	L	OT	GAA	Sv%	ESSV%	QS%	GGVT	DGVT	SGVT	GVT
2013-14	VAN	25	41	16	17	5	2.41	.912	.921	56.8%	3.1	0.9	3.4	7.4
2014-15	VAN	26	41	18	13	4	2.45	.921	.922	57.1%	11.8	-0.6	1.1	12.3
2015-16	CAR	27	39								7.8	0.1	0.3	8.2

Eddie Lack started the year as backup to Ryan Miller, who had been obtained in the offseason from St. Louis. However, not all backups are created equal, with Lack taking an unusually large portion of starts for a backup—around one in three—until taking over the starter's job when the former Sabre was injured late in the season. In the end, the perennially-smiling Swede played similar minutes to Miller, while putting up a fine .921 save percentage. Alas, the Canucks scored dramatically less frequently in front of him, with Vancouver taking "only" 57% of the available points in his decisions, compared to 64% for Miller, despite Lack's better save percentage.

Jacob Markstrom — G — VAN

Season	Team	Age	GP	W	L	OT	GAA	Sv%	ESSV%	QS%	GGVT	DGVT	SGVT	GVT
2012-13	FLA	22	23	8	14	1	3.22	.901	.912	43.5%	-4.0	-0.7	1.2	-3.6
2013-14	FLA, VAN	23	16	2	8	3	3.39	.873	.876	25.0%	-10.8	0.4	-1.6	-12.0
2014-15	VAN	24	3	1	1	0	3.08	.879	.879	50.0%	-0.8	0.1	0.0	-0.8
2015-16	VAN	25	12								-2.8	0.1	-0.2	-2.8

Jacob Markstrom played only one full game for the Canucks in 2014-15, called up while Ryan Miller was hurt, saving 24 of 25 shots on goal versus the Coyotes. The six-foot-four Swedish prospect saw less than half a period in each of two other games, coming in for Lack once and giving up three early to San Jose. It was only the smallest taste of the NHL, and it did not bear much resemblance to the dominant .935 save percentage that Markstrom put up for the Utica Comets in the AHL.

Ryan Miller — G — VAN

Season	Team	Age	GP	W	L	OT	GAA	Sv%	ESSV%	QS%	GGVT	DGVT	SGVT	GVT
2012-13	BUF	32	40	17	17	5	2.81	.915	.928	53.8%	9.0	-1.8	2.5	9.7
2013-14	BUF, STL	33	59	25	30	4	2.64	.918	.923	61.0%	15.0	-1.5	2.1	15.6
2014-15	VAN	34	45	29	15	1	2.53	.911	.913	55.6%	1.9	0.5	1.3	3.7
2015-16	VAN	35	38								5.3	-0.1	0.2	5.4

The storied career of US Olympian Ryan Miller is finely balanced after a variegated year in Vancouver. His .911 save percentage is well below that of his peak, and at the age of 34, his best years seem to be well behind him. His subpar performance was masked by consistently strong offensive numbers from the Canucks in his decisions. If decline from age hits hard next year, combined with slightly unlucky offensive numbers in front of him, public perception could fall very quickly indeed.

Micah Blake McCurdy

Washington Capitals

With 40 years in the National Hockey League and not a single Stanley Cup to show for it, defining a successful season is difficult for the Washington Capitals. Is it enough just to make the playoffs and put up a good showing? Is it enough to play hard, virtually as well as your opponent, but not quite come out on top in the end? Or has it been too many seasons without a championship for moral victories, requiring the team to capture the ultimate prize or be labeled a failure each season going forward?

An offseason following missing the playoffs (a feat that marks a team as irrelevant as a New Kids on the Block reunion tour, given the number and quality of teams that qualify for the NHL's postseason) the Capitals went on a changing spree. They added a new general manager, a new coach, a new coaching staff, a new system, and a bunch of new players. Based on that, you might think reaching the seventh game of the second round would be considered a success. And in many ways it was. But in one big important way, it very much wasn't.

The 2013-14 Capitals were a team with weak goaltending (weaker than it should have been given the personnel), an insufficiently deep defense, and a highly inflexible coach who was convinced his ways were the only ways. It wasn't that now-former head coach Adam Oates didn't have some good ideas for positive changes, it was that he was convinced he had a good idea to positively change everything. He changed Alex Ovechkin's position. It worked! He changed the team's power play. It worked! He changed just about every player's stick. Welcome to diminishing returns! He changed the style in which goalie Braden Holtby played—had played since his youth. This profoundly didn't work. He insisted on players lining up on their strong side whether they ever had before or not—with limited results, at best. He demanded defensemen pass the puck within five feet of receiving it rather than carry it, even though the defensive corps had been built around players with the skills to carry the puck. He refused to let his players block shots. He routinely played checking line players on the first line with superstar Alex Ovechkin. And when these ideas failed, he was never able to admit it, relent, and fix the new problem he had created. Instead, he kept butting his head into the same tree over and over and over again. For these and other slights to smart hockey, Oates was rightfully fired. And after 17 years without a Cup, so was GM George McPhee.

Enter new general manager Brian MacLellen. In his first offseason on the

CAPITALS IN A BOX

Last Season
Goals For	242	t-6th
Goals Against	203	6th
GVT	39	5th
Points	101	t-8th
Playoffs	Lost Conference Semifinal	

With strong offense, defense, and goaltending, the Capitals had one of the best seasons of the Ovechkin-Backstrom era.

Three-Year Record
GVT	53	11th
Points	248	13th
Playoffs	2 Appearances, 10 Wins	

VUKOTA Projections
Goals For	216	21st
Goals Against	215	10th
GVT	2	18th
Points	92	18th

The loss of Green will hurt, and Ovechkin will be 30 in September. This is still a good team, but the window of 105-point seasons and Cup contention has closed.

Top Three Prospects
J. Vrana (F), M. Bowey (D), R. Barber (F)

job, MacLellen hired a new head coach, a new analytics guy, and brought in several premiere free agents. GMBM's choice for head coach was Barry Trotz, the former Nashville Predators bench boss. Trotz proved himself to be more flexible than Oates ever was when he decided to not alter the way the Capitals played on the power play. He allowed Holtby to go back to the attacking style that had made him one of the best young goalies in the game. He let his defensemen carry the puck if they thought they could. He allowed Ovechkin to go back to left wing. He stopped playing Jay Beagle and Joey Crabb on a line with Ovechkin, which had been kind of like putting huge truck tires on your Ferrari. You don't want huge truck tires on your Ferrari. Also…congratulations on your Ferrari! (What do we mean?)

As part of the changes within the organization, MacLellan hired "Vic Ferrari", the former hockey blogger, to take over and spruce up the team's analytics department which had been lying fallow during the reign of George McPhee. Ferrari's real name is Tim Barnes, and it was he who did much of the pioneering work that determined the importance of possession and team shots, leading the charge in hockey's analytics revolution.

Under Trotz, the Capitals went from a negative possession team with a bad goalie situation living off of power-play opportunities to a positive possession team with a good goalie situation less-dependent-on but still able-to-capitalize-on power-play opportunities. They also made the playoffs, and in a very Capitals way, blew a three-games-to-one lead in the second round to the New York Rangers.

Despite the outcome, it was the process that should be encouraging to Capitals fans. The team improved on the ice and in the front office—at least with the addition of Barnes—though it remains to be seen whether MacLellen will truly embrace analytics. Team centerpiece Alex Ovechkin was once again a force, leading the league in goals while crushing opponents into the boards for funsies. With Braden Holtby, the team has found a franchise goalie for the first time since Olie Kolzig. The team's defense went from a liability to a strength with the additions of Brooks Orpik and Matt Nisakanen, and that is before the impending arrivals of Nate Schmidt and Connor Carrick, and further down the line, Madison Bowey.

This summer, the Caps went all-in by signing "Mr. Game 7" Justin Williams and trading for analytics-friendly winger T.J. Oshie. It should, once again, make them a Cup contender going into 2015-16. And if it works, we will remember this offseason as the one which got the franchise over the hump.

For now and the foreseeable future, this is MacLellan's team, this is Trotz's team, and this is Alex Ovechkin's team: the Capitals will go as far as those three take them. This past season, that was the second round of the playoffs. Was it a success? It is hard to say it wasn't, but for a team 40 years without a Cup to its name, it is equally hard to say it was.

Matthew Kory

WASHINGTON CAPITALS

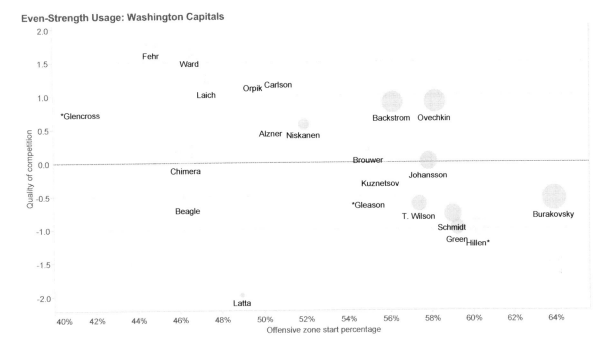

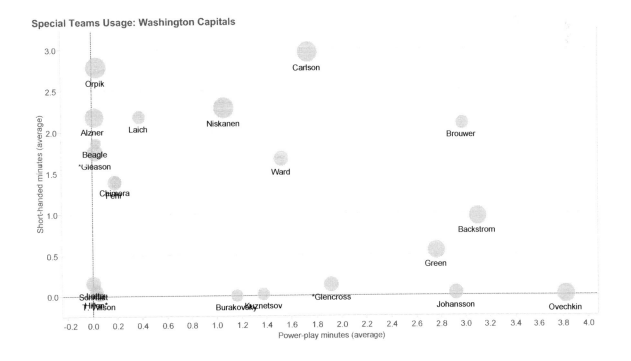

Offensive Profile: Washington Capitals

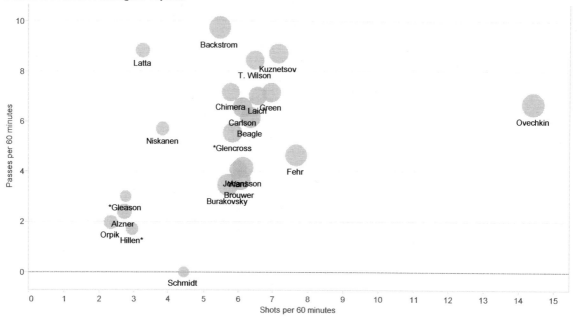

Cap Efficiency: Washington Capitals

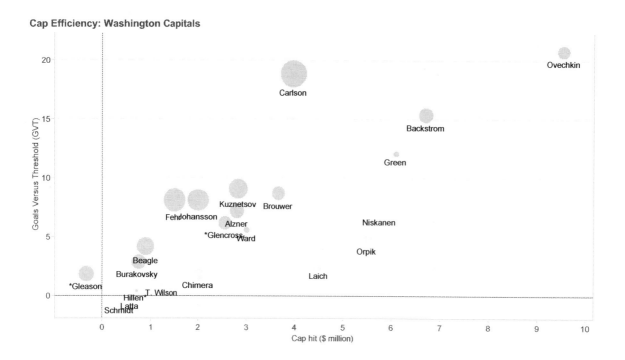

WASHINGTON CAPITALS

FORWARDS

Nicklas Backstrom — C — WSH

Season	Team	Age	GP	G	A	Pts	+/-	ESP/60	AdjCF%	iCF/60	OGVT	DGVT	SGVT	GVT
2012-13	WSH	25	48	8	40	48	8	2.53	51.5%	10.3	7.7	1.5	0.5	9.8
2013-14	WSH	26	82	18	61	79	-20	1.64	48.8%	11.5	11.9	0.1	1.4	13.5
2014-15	WSH	27	82	18	60	78	5	2.00	54.3%	9.6	12.3	3.1	0.0	15.4
2015-16	WSH	28	71	20	48	68					9.2	2.1	0.1	11.4

If a player is widely considered to be underrated, is that player still underrated? Since being drafted fourth overall in 2006, Nicklas Backstrom has quietly been one of the top centers in the game, year in and year out. Backstrom has more points than any other player from his draft class, which included Claude Giroux, Phil Kessel, and Jonathan Toews. But don't feel bad for Backstrom over his lack of notoriety. The unassuming Swede wouldn't have it any other way.

Jay Beagle — C — WSH

Season	Team	Age	GP	G	A	Pts	+/-	ESP/60	AdjCF%	iCF/60	OGVT	DGVT	SGVT	GVT
2012-13	WSH	27	48	2	6	8	-1	1.02	46.7%	11.6	-0.6	0.7	0.0	0.1
2013-14	WSH	28	62	4	5	9	-9	0.85	45.1%	9.3	-0.7	0.5	-0.3	-0.6
2014-15	WSH	29	62	10	10	20	6	1.68	51.1%	11.0	1.2	3.3	-0.3	4.2
2015-16	WSH	30	56	8	11	18					0.6	1.8	0.0	2.3

Jay Beagle is clearly a bottom sixer, yet the past three coaches in DC have puzzlingly given him extended stints in the top six, where he has done the impossible: turned Backstrom and Ovechkin into mediocre possession players. A solid fourth-line player and maybe a third liner in a pinch, any GM that overpays for Beagle should find himself in the doghouse. Woof.

Troy Brouwer — RW — STL

Season	Team	Age	GP	G	A	Pts	+/-	ESP/60	AdjCF%	iCF/60	OGVT	DGVT	SGVT	GVT
2012-13	WSH	27	47	19	14	33	-5	1.50	47.8%	11.7	5.7	-0.1	0.0	5.6
2013-14	WSH	28	82	25	18	43	-6	1.21	47.6%	11.8	4.4	1.6	0.1	6.2
2014-15	WSH	29	82	21	22	43	11	1.59	51.6%	10.5	4.7	3.0	0.4	8.7
2015-16	STL	30	68	16	19	35					2.9	2.0	0.0	4.9

A mainstay in the top six and on the first power-play unit, Troy Brouwer finished second on the team with 21 goals. But all of the underlying numbers suggest this is a third-line forward being propped up by superior linemates. An important contributor on the penalty kill as well, and proficient at the faceoff dot, Brouwer would be better served in a complementary role moving forward. It is not a knock on a seventh rounder who became a contributor to a Stanley Cup champion.

WASHINGTON CAPITALS

Chris Brown — C — WSH

Season	Team	Age	GP	G	A	Pts	+/-	ESP/60	AdjCF%	iCF/60	OGVT	DGVT	SGVT	GVT
2012-13	PHX	21	5	0	0	0	0	0.00	48.0%	18.7	-0.1	0.0	0.0	-0.1
2013-14	PHX, WSH	22	12	1	1	2	0	1.16	43.0%	10.3	0.2	0.1	0.0	0.3
2014-15	WSH	23	5	1	0	1	1	1.86	34.7%	7.3	0.3	0.2	0.0	0.4
2015-16	WSH	24	28	5	5	10					0.7	0.6	0.0	1.3

Acquired as part of the trade that sent Martin Erat to the Arizona Coyotes, Chris Brown has yet to receive an extended look in the nation's capital. However, this may be the year Brown gets a chance to stick in a depth role if he has a strong training camp. A 29-goal, 47-point campaign in the AHL for Portland in 2012-13 suggests he has the ability to score, but he has laced up for just 11 games over two seasons with the Capitals.

Andre Burakovsky — LW/C — WSH

Season	Team	Age	GP	G	A	Pts	+/-	ESP/60	AdjCF%	iCF/60	OGVT	DGVT	SGVT	GVT
2014-15	WSH	19	53	9	13	22	12	1.83	55.1%	12.6	0.8	2.4	-0.3	2.9
2015-16	WSH	20	59	12	16	28					1.2	2.0	0.0	3.2

All Andre Burakovsky did was lead all Caps forwards in Relative Corsi, shot attempts per 60, and scoring chances per 60. He also finished in the top three in points per 60, relative scoring chances, and individual shot attempts per 60. Oh, and he improved the Corsi percentage of seven of the nine forwards he skated 45+ minutes with. Yet, throughout the season, the six-foot-two Swede spent time as a healthy scratch, on the fourth line, and in the AHL. The Caps have a first-line player in the Austrian-born 2013 first rounder, but it is now up to them to deploy him as such.

Jason Chimera — LW — WSH

Season	Team	Age	GP	G	A	Pts	+/-	ESP/60	AdjCF%	iCF/60	OGVT	DGVT	SGVT	GVT
2012-13	WSH	33	47	3	11	14	-5	1.45	48.3%	14.2	0.0	0.4	0.0	0.3
2013-14	WSH	34	82	15	27	42	4	2.05	46.2%	12.8	4.6	3.5	-0.3	7.8
2014-15	WSH	35	77	7	12	19	-1	1.30	47.9%	11.5	0.0	2.1	-0.3	1.8
2015-16	WSH	36	62	9	15	24					1.4	1.9	0.0	3.3

Whoever had the video game controller in their hand when creating Jason Chimera pumped all of his attributes into speed and forgot to give him any hands. He is a speedy fourth-line forward at this point in his career, nothing more, although he did record his single-season career-best point total just two years ago. Though partially explicable due to less ice-time, Chimera's 1.25 shots per game was a precipitous drop from 2.05; it was his lowest-ever rate in anything approaching a full season. Watch out for age to hit hard.

Chris Conner — RW/LW — PHI

Season	Team	Age	GP	G	A	Pts	+/-	ESP/60	AdjCF%	iCF/60	OGVT	DGVT	SGVT	GVT
2012-13	PHX	29	12	1	1	2	3	0.90	48.4%	11.7	-0.1	0.5	0.0	0.4
2013-14	PIT	30	19	4	1	5	-3	1.38	37.7%	8.2	0.4	0.1	0.0	0.5
2014-15	WSH	31	2	0	0	0	1	0.00	62.8%	24.3	-0.2	0.1	0.0	0.0
2015-16	PHI	32	28	4	5	9					0.5	0.6	0.0	1.1

Chris Conner is a professional hockey player who appeared in two games for the Capitals in 2014-15. His tenure will be remembered by Washington fans quite fondly, to be sure. This season, he will ply his trade with the Flyers—or more realistically, with the Lehigh Valley Phantoms. The five-foot-seven Conner has not played for the same organization in consecutive seasons since 2010-11.

Eric Fehr								RW/C						PIT
Season	Team	Age	GP	G	A	Pts	+/-	ESP/60	AdjCF%	iCF/60	OGVT	DGVT	SGVT	GVT
2012-13	WSH	27	41	9	8	17	14	1.61	52.7%	15.4	2.1	2.1	0.0	4.1
2013-14	WSH	28	73	13	18	31	0	1.81	49.1%	13.3	3.7	2.2	1.3	7.2
2014-15	WSH	29	75	19	14	33	8	1.87	51.0%	13.7	4.6	3.6	-0.2	8.1
2015-16	PIT	30	65	15	16	30					3.1	2.3	0.0	5.4

A wing for much of his career, Eric Fehr has spent most of the past two seasons centering the third line. Some would argue this proves his versatility, nicely filling in on a team that is perennially shallow up the middle. Others would argue the team is wasting a legitimate top-six winger as a bottom-six center. Either way, Fehr continues to be a solid contributor who has found himself on the right side of 50% Corsi in all but one of his NHL seasons. He will contribute to the Penguins' oft-maligned depth-forward corps in 2015-16 after being acquired by Pittsburgh.

Stanislav Galiev								RW						WSH
Season	Team	Age	GP	G	A	Pts	+/-	ESP/60	AdjCF%	iCF/60	OGVT	DGVT	SGVT	GVT
2014-15	WSH	22	2	1	0	1	1	3.25	65.9%	12.7	0.5	0.0	0.0	0.5
2015-16	WSH	23	26	6	6	12					1.1	0.5	0.0	1.7

The Caps' third-round pick in 2010, Stanislav Galiev had failed to establish himself within the organization, with the 2014-15 season feeling like a make-or-break campaign for him. Galiev came through with 25 goals in the AHL, plus he appeared in two games with the Caps towards the end of the season, potting his first career goal in the big leagues. All indications are he will be given a chance to earn an NHL roster spot entering the 2015-16 campaign, possibly giving the Caps another dynamic Russian in their lineup.

Curtis Glencross								LW						Free Agent
Season	Team	Age	GP	G	A	Pts	+/-	ESP/60	AdjCF%	iCF/60	OGVT	DGVT	SGVT	GVT
2012-13	CGY	30	40	15	11	26	-8	1.98	48.4%	14.9	4.3	1.0	-0.3	5.0
2013-14	CGY	31	38	12	12	24	-11	1.72	42.4%	13.5	3.0	0.9	0.0	3.9
2014-15	CGY, WSH	32	71	13	22	35	2	1.49	45.3%	9.9	4.1	2.1	0.0	6.2
2015-16	Free Agent	33	59	10	17	27					2.0	1.3	0.0	3.2

The Caps decided to give up assets for an ostensibly redundant forward piece at the trade deadline. Consequently, by playoff time, Curtis Glencross found himself shuttling between the fourth line and the pressbox. One goal in 10 playoff appearances is not what Washington had in mind when they acquired the former Calgary Flame, though Glencross looks better by advanced stats than conventional ones.

Marcus Johansson — C/LW — WSH

Season	Team	Age	GP	G	A	Pts	+/-	ESP/60	AdjCF%	iCF/60	OGVT	DGVT	SGVT	GVT
2012-13	WSH	22	34	6	16	22	3	2.15	49.9%	6.9	2.7	1.0	0.0	3.7
2013-14	WSH	23	80	8	36	44	-21	1.21	47.8%	7.0	1.6	-0.8	-0.3	0.5
2014-15	WSH	24	82	20	27	47	6	1.73	54.0%	11.7	6.4	1.9	-0.3	8.1
2015-16	WSH	25	68	15	26	42					4.0	1.6	0.0	5.6

Drafted 24th overall in 2009, Marcus Johansson was far from a bust entering the season, but had yet to cement himself as a core player moving forward. Last season changed that, as the five-foot-eleven Swede easily surpassed his previous career high in goals of 14 with 20. The main difference in his game was that he shot the puck a lot more. Johansson's 11.9 individual shot attempts per 60 minutes was his first time north of 8.0 shot attempts per 60 minutes since his rookie season. His role on the first power-play unit should not be overlooked either, as Johansson is often Plan A on zone entries, drawing the opponent's attention away from the superstars, giving Ovechkin more space to get open on the initial setup.

Evgeny Kuznetsov — RW/C — WSH

Season	Team	Age	GP	G	A	Pts	+/-	ESP/60	AdjCF%	iCF/60	OGVT	DGVT	SGVT	GVT
2013-14	WSH	21	17	3	6	9	-2	1.71	43.3%	9.0	1.2	0.1	1.0	2.3
2014-15	WSH	22	80	11	26	37	10	1.51	49.8%	11.9	4.7	2.4	2.0	9.1
2015-16	WSH	23	69	16	27	42					4.9	2.3	0.1	7.3

By the end of his first full season in the NHL, Evgeny Kuznetsov appeared to have the second-line center job nailed down. Often dazzling with his skating, puck-handling, and passing skills, Kuznetsov looks like a potential star on the rise. But the underlying numbers give some pause. His Relative Corsi (-3.1%) ranked second worst among the regular forwards on the team, and he never seemed to find consistent chemistry with Johansson while the two were together on the second line.

Brooks Laich — C — WSH

Season	Team	Age	GP	G	A	Pts	+/-	ESP/60	AdjCF%	iCF/60	OGVT	DGVT	SGVT	GVT
2012-13	WSH	29	9	1	3	4	2	1.48	51.4%	12.2	0.4	0.4	0.0	0.8
2013-14	WSH	30	51	8	7	15	-7	0.90	47.2%	9.3	-0.8	1.7	1.2	2.1
2014-15	WSH	31	66	7	13	20	-2	1.35	50.4%	11.6	0.0	2.5	0.6	3.1
2015-16	WSH	32	58	8	11	18					0.1	1.8	0.0	2.0

While he is no longer worth the $4.5 million cap hit, Brooks Laich is still an effective player when he is healthy. Laich played the second-most minutes per game on the penalty kill among the team's forwards and managed to stay in the neighborhood of a 50% Corsi despite facing tough zone starts and competition. It was encouraging to see him appear in 66 games—the most he has dressed for since 2011-12.

Michael Latta — C — WSH

Season	Team	Age	GP	G	A	Pts	+/-	ESP/60	AdjCF%	iCF/60	OGVT	DGVT	SGVT	GVT
2013-14	WSH	22	17	1	3	4	0	2.14	48.1%	5.7	0.4	0.3	0.0	0.7
2014-15	WSH	23	53	0	6	6	4	0.82	51.8%	7.1	-1.1	1.2	-0.3	-0.2
2015-16	WSH	24	50	3	7	10					-1.2	1.2	0.0	-0.1

While his boxcar stats of zero goals and six assists might point to "fringe NHL player," Michael Latta could slot in as a bottom-six center moving forward. He goes to high traffic areas, sticks up for his teammates, and even shows the occasional finesse move in the offensive zone. If his on-ice shooting percentage of 4.5% normalizes a bit, his conventional stats will better reflect his abilities.

Liam O'Brien								C/LW						WSH
Season	Team	Age	GP	G	A	Pts	+/-	ESP/60	AdjCF%	iCF/60	OGVT	DGVT	SGVT	GVT
2014-15	WSH	20	13	1	1	2	4	1.22	54.9%	13.4	0.1	0.6	0.0	0.7
2015-16	WSH	21	32	5	6	11					0.7	0.9	0.0	1.6

One of the feelgood stories of the season, Liam O'Brien came out of nowhere in training camp, earning a spot on the opening-night roster. Despite the fact that he only stuck with the big club for 13 games, O'Brien quickly endeared himself to fans and teammates alike with his hard-nosed, no-nonsense style of play. After all, how can you not take a liking to a guy who taunted six-foot-eight John Scott by sticking out his tongue?

Alex Ovechkin								LW						WSH
Season	Team	Age	GP	G	A	Pts	+/-	ESP/60	AdjCF%	iCF/60	OGVT	DGVT	SGVT	GVT
2012-13	WSH	27	48	32	24	56	2	2.23	49.1%	22.3	12.9	0.7	1.5	15.1
2013-14	WSH	28	78	51	28	79	-35	1.94	49.0%	24.7	16.9	-2.3	-2.7	11.9
2014-15	WSH	29	81	53	28	81	10	2.11	54.0%	25.2	18.3	2.8	-0.4	20.8
2015-16	WSH	30	74	42	31	73					12.5	1.4	-0.1	13.8

If someone is convinced Alex Ovechkin is selfish or a "coach killer", they haven't been listening to any of his current or former NHL coaches and teammates. And if someone is not yet convinced he is one of the greatest goal scorers in the history of the NHL, nothing can be done to convince that person. But what might fly under the radar is how much Ovechkin does off the ice. The list includes donating a car to a hockey program for individuals with specials needs, befriending a young girl from said team, hosting multiple skates with youth organizations in the DC area, and supporting and making donations to seven orphanages in Russia. The list goes on. Ovechkin is a once in a generation talent who also happens to have a big heart. And remember that -35 plus/minus? A fluke that is in the rearview mirror.

Aaron Volpatti								LW						Free Agent
Season	Team	Age	GP	G	A	Pts	+/-	ESP/60	AdjCF%	iCF/60	OGVT	DGVT	SGVT	GVT
2012-13	VAN, WSH	27	33	1	1	2	-2	0.44	45.7%	9.5	-0.9	0.2	0.0	-0.7
2013-14	WSH	28	41	2	0	2	-3	0.40	39.9%	7.7	-1.0	0.1	0.0	-0.9
2014-15	WSH	29	2	0	0	0	0	0.00	49.7%	9.1	0.0	0.0	0.0	0.0
2015-16	Free Agent	30	32	3	4	7					0.0	0.5	0.0	0.5

Aaron Volpatti was a non-factor for the Caps in 2014-15, limited to two games, mainly due to injury, but also because he could not crack the lineup when healthy. The former Brown University captain has not scored more than two pro-level points in a season since 2010-11. He will be hard pressed to find an NHL job.

Joel Ward — RW — SJS

Season	Team	Age	GP	G	A	Pts	+/-	ESP/60	AdjCF%	iCF/60	OGVT	DGVT	SGVT	GVT
2012-13	WSH	32	39	8	12	20	7	2.06	50.2%	9.6	2.8	1.4	0.0	4.2
2013-14	WSH	33	82	24	25	49	7	2.17	47.1%	10.3	8.0	3.5	-0.3	11.3
2014-15	WSH	34	82	19	15	34	-4	1.23	50.7%	10.2	3.0	2.0	0.6	5.6
2015-16	SJS	35	65	15	18	33					3.2	1.8	0.0	5.0

At 35 years old, Joel Ward just keeps on ticking. In 2013-14, he set a career high with 24 goals, following it up with a solid 19 in 2014-15. The former University of Prince Edward Island star scored at a rate above his career shooting percentage for the third straight season. While puck luck is certainly a factor here, over the past two seasons, Ward has also somehow managed to more than triple the rate at which he attempts shots from the slot—he has improved with age. Ward should remain a good third-line forward for the next couple of seasons.

Tom Wilson — RW — WSH

Season	Team	Age	GP	G	A	Pts	+/-	ESP/60	AdjCF%	iCF/60	OGVT	DGVT	SGVT	GVT
2013-14	WSH	19	82	3	7	10	1	0.84	45.1%	8.9	-1.2	1.0	0.0	-0.2
2014-15	WSH	20	67	4	13	17	-1	1.40	52.7%	12.3	0.1	1.2	-0.3	1.0
2015-16	WSH	21	63	5	10	15					-1.1	1.2	0.0	0.0

Big Tom Wilson spent last season either playing limited minutes on the fourth line...or riding shotgun to Ovechkin and Backstrom on the first line. Would it be crazy to say that some playing time in the middle six might be best for his development? Given that he has already spent two seasons in the NHL, it can be easy to forget that Wilson is only entering his age-21 season. He has the size and tools to develop into an effective and disruptive force, but still has a lot left to learn and prove.

DEFENSEMEN

Karl Alzner — LD — WSH

Season	Team	Age	GP	G	A	Pts	+/-	ESP/60	AdjCF%	iCF/60	OGVT	DGVT	SGVT	GVT
2012-13	WSH	24	48	1	4	5	-6	0.34	49.1%	6.4	-1.7	0.3	0.0	-1.3
2013-14	WSH	25	82	2	16	18	-7	0.65	46.8%	8.4	0.6	3.0	0.0	3.6
2014-15	WSH	26	82	5	16	21	14	0.89	51.7%	7.1	2.8	4.8	-0.3	7.2
2015-16	WSH	27	67	4	14	19					1.4	3.2	0.0	4.5

The Caps' spending spree on defensemen during the 2014 offseason bumped veteran Karl Alzner down to the second defensive pair, where he settled in quite nicely next to recent ex-Penguin Matt Niskanen. Alzner appeared in every game for the fifth straight season, setting career highs in goals and points, while continuing to be a steadying presence on the penalty kill. With a very successful junior/minor-league career—2008 CHL defenseman of the year as captain of the Calgary Hitmen, captain of the 2008 WJC gold medal winning Team Canada squad, and a two-time Calder Cup champion—Alzner continues to set his sights on NHL glory, albeit as a solid player and not a star.

WASHINGTON CAPITALS

John Carlson — RD — WSH

Season	Team	Age	GP	G	A	Pts	+/-	ESP/60	AdjCF%	iCF/60	OGVT	DGVT	SGVT	GVT
2012-13	WSH	22	48	6	16	22	11	1.19	49.2%	10.3	3.7	2.7	0.0	6.3
2013-14	WSH	23	82	10	27	37	-3	0.58	46.7%	10.2	4.5	3.3	0.0	7.7
2014-15	WSH	24	82	12	43	55	11	1.51	51.9%	12.3	11.7	6.6	0.6	18.9
2015-16	WSH	25	75	11	35	46					7.2	4.7	0.0	11.9

John Carlson was an absolute horse for the Caps in 2014-15, playing on the first pairing alongside Brooks Orpik. He set career highs in goals, assists, and points, all while facing the top forwards on the opposing team. Not only did Carlson finish fifth among all NHL defensemen with 55 points, but his advanced stats were outstanding as well, with ridiculous numbers in even-strength scoring and Corsi, along with an elite GVT. Assuming his game continues to progress, he will garner serious Norris consideration in the years ahead.

Tim Gleason — LD — Free Agent

Season	Team	Age	GP	G	A	Pts	+/-	ESP/60	AdjCF%	iCF/60	OGVT	DGVT	SGVT	GVT
2012-13	CAR	29	42	0	9	9	-3	0.69	47.9%	8.0	0.1	1.7	0.0	1.8
2013-14	CAR, TOR	30	56	1	5	6	-21	0.44	41.8%	5.4	-1.0	-1.6	0.0	-2.7
2014-15	CAR, WSH	31	72	1	8	9	-13	0.52	49.3%	6.2	-1.3	3.3	0.0	1.9
2015-16	Free Agent	32	54	1	5	6					-1.5	1.7	0.0	0.2

Tim Gleason was brought in at the trade deadline to provide "protection" for Mike Green on the third defensive pair. A hard worker, often willing to pay the price with his body by blocking shots and doling out hits, the 2010 Olympic silver medalist is the epitome of the tough, stay-at-home defenseman who is a dying breed in a league that continues to put more and more value on puck-moving defensemen.

Mike Green — RD — DET

Season	Team	Age	GP	G	A	Pts	+/-	ESP/60	AdjCF%	iCF/60	OGVT	DGVT	SGVT	GVT
2012-13	WSH	27	35	12	14	26	-3	1.04	49.0%	11.2	6.6	-0.2	0.0	6.4
2013-14	WSH	28	70	9	29	38	-16	1.01	51.1%	11.8	6.2	-0.7	-0.3	5.3
2014-15	WSH	29	72	10	35	45	15	1.48	52.7%	12.3	9.1	3.3	-0.3	12.1
2015-16	DET	30	64	9	27	35					5.3	2.5	0.0	7.7

Since Alexander Semin left town, no player has been more polarizing among the Caps' fanbase than Mike Green. Even his critics generally recognize his ability to drive possession and create offense. But his defense gets a bad rap, likely due to the fact that his playing style can lead to glaring mistakes. Nonetheless, his 1.76 goals against per 60 minutes was best among all of the team's defensemen and 11th among all defenders who played 1,000+ five-on-five minutes. Signed by Detroit over the offseason, he will be playing for a different team after 10 seasons and 360 points in America's capital.

Matt Niskanen — RD — WSH

Season	Team	Age	GP	G	A	Pts	+/-	ESP/60	AdjCF%	iCF/60	OGVT	DGVT	SGVT	GVT
2012-13	PIT	26	40	4	10	14	4	1.05	52.3%	10.3	2.6	1.1	0.0	3.7
2013-14	PIT	27	81	10	36	46	33	1.31	54.1%	10.3	8.7	7.3	0.0	16.0
2014-15	WSH	28	82	4	27	31	7	0.77	52.5%	9.5	4.1	3.7	-0.3	7.5
2015-16	WSH	29	68	6	24	30					3.8	3.5	0.0	7.3

PDO regression and a drop in power-play time led to less impressive offensive totals from Matt Niskanen in the first year of a seven-year contract, but it was a successful season nonetheless. Considered a third-pairing guy before 2013-14 and putting up the numbers of a first-pairing defenseman in 2014-15, Niskanen should provide stability on Washington's second defensive pairing for years to come.

Steve Oleksy							RD						PIT
Season	Team	Age	GP	G	A	Pts	+/-	ESP/60	AdjCF%	iCF/60	OGVT	DGVT	SGVT	GVT
2012-13	WSH	26	28	1	8	9	9	1.24	51.9%	9.1	1.3	1.9	0.0	3.2
2013-14	WSH	27	33	2	8	10	7	1.35	46.4%	8.0	1.8	2.1	0.0	3.9
2014-15	WSH	28	1	0	0	0	-1	0.00	43.4%	9.5	-0.1	-0.1	0.0	-0.2
2015-16	PIT	29	32	2	6	8					0.7	1.2	0.0	2.0

Steven Oleksy, captain of the AHL's Hershey Bears, played in only one game for the Caps in 2014-15. But he is still on the team's radar. New head coach Barry Trotz noted Olesky's strong training camp, and he periodically spent time with the team as the—non-dressing—seventh defenseman. He is not a guy who you pencil in your opening-night lineup, but Oleksy has proven he can hold his own when the Caps' defensive depth needs to be called on.

Dmitry Orlov							LD						WSH
Season	Team	Age	GP	G	A	Pts	+/-	ESP/60	AdjCF%	iCF/60	OGVT	DGVT	SGVT	GVT
2012-13	WSH	21	5	0	1	1	5	0.86	52.4%	6.8	0.0	0.8	0.0	0.8
2013-14	WSH	22	54	3	8	11	-1	0.58	51.3%	7.3	0.0	1.5	-0.3	1.2
2015-16	WSH	23	16	1	2	3					0.0	0.5	-0.1	0.4

Because of a wrist injury, 2014-15 was a lost season for Dmitri Orlov. Despite his injury and his relatively slow progression from the farm to the big time, Orlov is still very much in the team's plans and is highly thought-of throughout the organization. Therefore, look for the 2011 WJC gold medalist to start next season on the Caps' third defensive pairing. A bit undersized as far as height, at five-foot-eleven, the Russian blueliner is nonetheless of sturdy build, coming in a 209 pounds. His 47 points in 79 AHL games are excellent for a defenseman.

Brooks Orpik							LD						WSH
Season	Team	Age	GP	G	A	Pts	+/-	ESP/60	AdjCF%	iCF/60	OGVT	DGVT	SGVT	GVT
2012-13	PIT	32	46	0	8	8	17	0.55	45.6%	5.0	-1.2	3.8	0.0	2.6
2013-14	PIT	33	72	2	11	13	-3	0.60	46.7%	5.8	-1.4	4.8	0.0	3.4
2014-15	WSH	34	78	0	19	19	5	0.77	50.5%	6.8	-1.3	5.8	0.6	5.2
2015-16	WSH	35	62	1	12	14					-0.7	4.2	0.0	3.5

The good news is that year one of Orpik's five-year deal went okay—better than many in analytics circles would have predicted. The long-time Penguin, two-time US Olympian, 2009 Stanley Cup champion, and 2001 NCAA champion regularly faced the opponent's top line and was asked to do the heavy lifting with frequent defensive zone draws. And yet, he was able to post a not terrible -2.4% Relative Corsi. The downside? Four years left at a cap hit of $5.5 million is far from ideal for a big, fairly immobile defenseman entering his age-35 season. Did Vic Ferrari sign off on this one?

WASHINGTON CAPITALS

Cameron Schilling — LD — CHI

Season	Team	Age	GP	G	A	Pts	+/-	ESP/60	AdjCF%	iCF/60	OGVT	DGVT	SGVT	GVT
2012-13	WSH	24	1	0	0	0	-1	0.00	32.3%	0.0	-0.1	-0.1	0.0	-0.2
2013-14	WSH	25	1	0	0	0	-2	0.00	33.7%	10.1	-0.1	-0.3	0.0	-0.3
2014-15	WSH	26	4	0	0	0	1	0.00	59.9%	8.4	-0.2	0.2	0.0	0.0
2015-16	CHI	27	25	1	4	6					0.2	0.8	0.0	1.1

Miami University of Ohio graduate Cameron Schilling appeared in four games in 2014-15, more than the single games he had gotten in the previous two seasons. With much of the defensive corps at the NHL level locked up long term, and plenty of help on the way in terms of prospects, it is tough to envision Schilling being more than a solid AHLer who could contribute in the case of an injury stack.

Nate Schmidt — LD — WSH

Season	Team	Age	GP	G	A	Pts	+/-	ESP/60	AdjCF%	iCF/60	OGVT	DGVT	SGVT	GVT
2013-14	WSH	22	29	2	4	6	4	0.69	50.1%	8.4	0.2	1.5	0.0	1.7
2014-15	WSH	23	39	1	3	4	-2	0.45	54.1%	9.7	-0.9	0.7	-0.3	-0.5
2015-16	WSH	24	37								0.8	-0.1	-0.3	0.5

Despite being armed with one of the best smiles in the league, Nate Schmidt is sometimes overlooked, given the blueline depth in Washington. But the undrafted University of Minnesota product has been great when given a chance in DC. Schmidt's +2.9% Relative Corsi and 53.9% Corsi led all Washington defensemen who appeared in at least five games. Smallish for an NHL defenseman at six foot, 194 pounds, maybe he just doesn't appear the part.

GOALTENDERS

Philipp Grubauer — G — WSH

Season	Team	Age	GP	W	L	OT	GAA	Sv%	ESSV%	QS%	GGVT	DGVT	SGVT	GVT
2012-13	WSH	21	2	0	1	0	3.57	.915	.947	0.0%	0.4	-0.2	0.0	0.2
2013-14	WSH	22	17	6	5	5	2.38	.925	.927	64.3%	6.6	-0.4	-0.7	5.5
2014-15	WSH	23	1	1	0	0	1.85	.920	.950	100.0%	0.3	0.1	-0.1	0.2
2015-16	WSH	24	17					.916			2.7	0.1	-0.1	2.5

Philipp Grubauer has nothing left to prove in the AHL, putting up save percentages of .919, .916, and .921 over 28, 28, and 49 games. The six-foot-one German netminder has honed his skills in Hershey over the past three seasons while Braden Holtby has put a stranglehold on the starting job in Washington. If Grubauer can play up to his capabilities in a backup role—with the veteran Holtby firmly entrenched ahead of him—he could find himself dealt to a team in need of a starter, much like Jonathan Bernier and Cory Schneider were in years past.

Braden Holtby — G — WSH

Season	Team	Age	GP	W	L	OT	GAA	Sv%	ESSV%	QS%	GGVT	DGVT	SGVT	GVT
2012-13	WSH	23	36	23	12	1	2.58	.920	.931	54.3%	12.2	-1.2	1.8	12.7
2013-14	WSH	24	48	23	15	4	2.85	.915	.928	60.0%	7.0	-1.7	-0.1	5.2
2014-15	WSH	25	73	41	20	10	2.22	.923	.929	61.1%	24.6	0.4	0.6	25.6
2015-16	WSH	26	62					.918			13.7	-0.2	0.1	13.6

Braden Holtby's performance this past season put him on the map around the league. Those who have followed him closely know that this is the arc his career has been following since entering the league—save for an uneven 2013-14 that many blame on head coach Adam Oates' unnecessarily tinkering with Holtby's game. Since 2010, his .930 five-on-five save percentage ranks sixth of the 51 goalies who have played 4,000+ minutes over that span. His career playoff save percentage of .936 is the best in the history of the NHL for any goalie who has appeared in 25 or more playoff games. That is pretty good.

Justin Peters								G						WSH
Season	Team	Age	GP	W	L	OT	GAA	Sv%	ESSV%	QS%	GGVT	DGVT	SGVT	GVT
2012-13	CAR	26	19	4	11	1	3.46	.891	.893	31.3%	-6.8	-0.4	0.0	-7.2
2013-14	CAR	27	21	7	9	4	2.50	.919	.921	60.0%	4.7	-0.1	-1.8	2.7
2014-15	WSH	28	12	3	6	1	3.25	.881	.892	11.1%	-6.9	0.2	-0.7	-7.4
2015-16	WSH	29	17					.910			-0.4	0.0	-0.2	-0.6

Partially due to his shaky play and partially due to Holtby's elite season, Justin Peters didn't see much action after signing a two-year deal prior to the season. The long-time Hurricanes backup only has a .901 career save percentage, just barely above the Mendoza line for goaltenders. With Grubauer knocking on the door from Hershey, Peters' role with the team is very much in doubt.

Pat Holden

Winnipeg Jets

A pessimist sees the difficulty in every opportunity; an optimist sees the opportunity in every difficulty."

-Winston Churchill

Prior to midseason 2014-15, Winnipeg Jets' GM Kevin Cheveldayoff might have been seen as a Churchillian pessimist. A study by former *Hockey Prospectus* author and *Illegal Curve* contributor Richard Pollock, looking at the trades consummated by "Chevy" since he was hired in June 2011 showed...a whole lot of nothing. In his first calendar year, the former Blackhawks AGM pulled the trigger on five deals, bringing in players who would total 44 games played while producing three points for the team. In fairness, he gave up even less. In his second calendar year, the GM swung four deals, bringing in three players who combined for 91 games and 10 points, all from the immortal Eric Tangradi. Year three saw the young GM trade in quantity for some quality. He engaged in only two exchanges, but the incoming players—Michael Frolik and Devin Setoguchi—combined for 238 games and 111 points.

Perhaps his reticence was because the only player of note he gave up in those three years, Johnny Oduya, earned a Stanley Cup ring in his first full season with his new team while enhancing his reputation as a true shutdown blueliner. Or maybe Cheveldayoff simply had a hard time finding a good fit. Consider that the Jets were never clearly a buyer nor a seller, and thus found themselves stuck in the murky middle during trade deadline season.

However, Cheveldayoff shed that gun-shy reputation in 2014-15, and then some. The Jets were involved in what could be considered the year's biggest trade, sending former fourth overall pick Evander Kane to Buffalo in a seven-player (plus a first-round pick) blockbuster, that in addition to a few other smaller trades.

First, the warm-up deal. With training camp barely over, Chevy warmed up his trading gun by sending Tangradi to Montreal for goaltending depth in Peter Budaj and minor-league winger Patrick Holland. On its face, not a significant trade, as neither player would get into a single game for Winnipeg, but an omen of what was in store. On December 18, shortly before the Christmas trade freeze, the Jets acquired blueliner Jay Harrison from Carolina for a sixth rounder.

Then, three weeks prior to the trade deadline, the Jets GM woke up. The groundwork would have been laid in the days and weeks prior, but on this date, he managed to leverage an asset that was of no

JETS IN A BOX

Last Season
Goals For	230	15th
Goals Against	210	t-9th
GVT	20	t-12th
Points	99	t-13th
Playoffs	Lost Conference Quarterfinal	

With improved defense and goaltending, the first winning season since their arrival in Winnipeg allowed the Jets to make an unexpected playoff appearance.

Three-Year Record
GVT	-6	18th
Points	234	19th
Playoffs	1 Appearance, 0 Wins	

VUKOTA Projection
Goals For	218	19th
Goals Against	223	24th
GVT	-5	22nd
Points	90	22nd

The Jets will still pay the price of being in a division with Chicago, St. Louis, Nashville, Minnesota, and Dallas. It will be a struggle to make the top eight again.

Top Four Prospects
N. Ehlers (F), J. Morrissey (D), K. Connor (F)

use to him on the ice, and that had been at the center of numerous off-ice distractions—Evander Kane—packaging him up with former first rounder Zach Bogosian and the rights to NCAA netminder Jason Kasdorf in a trade to Buffalo. In return for a single player who may have played a role on a team fighting for a postseason berth, the GM managed to secure the services of former Calder Trophy winner Tyler Myers, an expiring contract in winger Drew Stafford, two intriguing prospects in Joel Armia and Brendan Lemieux, and a 2015 first-round pick expected to fall in the latter third of the round.

That move, if Cheveldayoff had stopped there, would have been enough to remove the stigma of "non-trader" from his reputation. But having got the itch, he had to keep scratching. In the final week before the trade deadline, the Jets acquired additional offensive depth in two separate deals for wingers on expiring contracts, first getting Jiri Tlusty from Carolina for a third- and a conditional sixth-round pick. Later, Lee Stempniak was picked up from the Rangers, themselves a competing team, but one who needed to clear a little cap room for a later acquisition, in exchange for AHL winger Carl Klingberg.

Starting with the Harrison deal, the Jets found themselves firmly in a playoff position, but at great risk of falling aside due to a sudden and severe injury stack on the blue line. Bogosian and Toby Enstrom, half of their presumptive top four, were already on the injured reserve when they lost another 25% of their top four, Jacob Trouba, to the dreaded "upper body injury". Not helping matters was the fact that depth defender Grant Clitsome had only recently returned from his own sojourn to the IR. If ever there was a time to make a trade, this was it. Cheveldayoff found a trade partner in Carolina GM Ron Francis, who himself had yet to consummate an NHL trade, shoring up the Winnipeg back end. By the time Harrison suffered his own injury, the aforementioned legacy defense corps had all returned to action. More importantly, the Jets maintained their hold on a postseason slot for another month. Harrison's 1.4 GVT over 34 games may not sound like much, but the incumbent depth—guys like Paul Postma, Keaton Ellerby, and Julien Brouillette—combined for a meager 0.6 GVT in 44 games.

On February 11, the blueline was fully healthy. The Jets had 60 points, which saw them holding on to the fourth and final playoff spot in the Central Division, but only two points back of second and five out of first place. There were only two injuries keeping players out of the lineup. Depth winger Matt Halischuk was on the IR and approximately one month from returning. No big deal there, but on the other hand, the mercurial Evander Kane, recently labeled as a disruptive influence in the clubhouse due to an alleged incident involving teammate Dustin Byfuglien, track suits, and shower stalls, admitted that he had been dealing with a very painful and very limiting shoulder injury, and finally succumbed to surgery. He was expected to miss the remainder of the season.

Regardless of the trouble that seemed to follow him around like Olof's personal snowstorm, Kane was undoubtedly a talented offensive producer. His absence would have made it difficult for the Jets to maintain playoff position, of psychological importance as the club had yet to make a postseason appearance in the three seasons since moving to Manitoba. In this case, the Jets GM would have been excused for not doing anything. As much as the locker-room rumors made some believe that a Kane trade would be a foregone conclusion, as an injured player with a heavy contract, few foresaw a significant demand for his services.

Enter the Buffalo Sabres, the epitome of a non-competitive club. With less than nothing to play for in 2014-15, the Sabres could afford to let Kane sit on the injured reserve. For the promise of owning the services of the talented sniper for three future seasons, GM Tim Murray was all too happy to return a depreciating asset in Drew Stafford (along with his expiring contract), plus the aforementioned two prospects and a first rounder—as long as Winnipeg would also swap Myers, the talented, gargantuan blueliner who had fallen on hard times since a promising debut, for Bogosian, himself a former high draft pick who had stalled in his development.

As for the later deals for Tlusty and Stempniak, well, those were just for kicks. No longer in need of an injury replacement, Cheveldayoff had learned that trades could be made to simply upgrade the roster. Neither player moved the needle much, but they served to prove that the Jets can no longer be counted out of trade speculation and innuendo. After years of relative silence, Chevy demostrated that, when faced with a setback, he can see his way out of the gloomy difficulties and take advantage of opportunities as they present themselves.

Ryan Wagman

WINNIPEG JETS

441

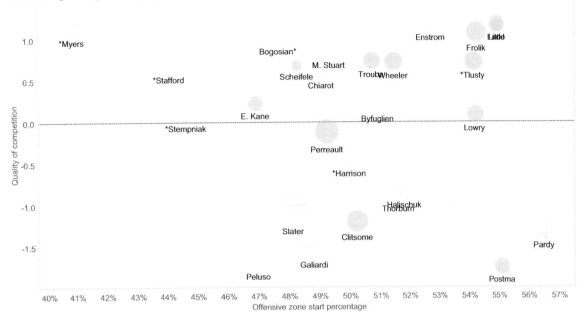

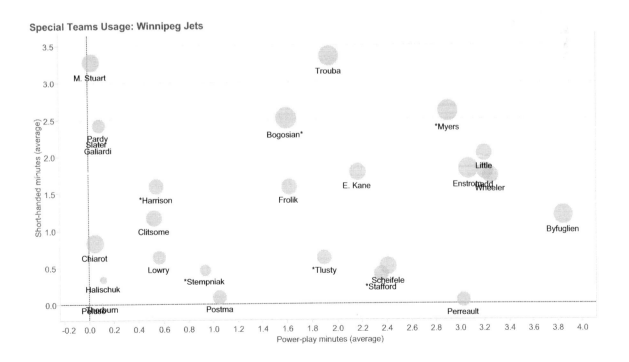

WINNIPEG JETS

Offensive Profile: Winnipeg Jets

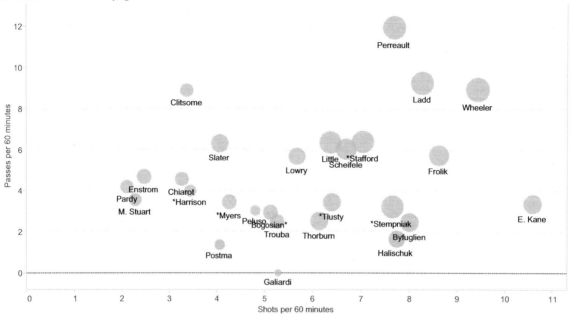

Cap Efficiency: Winnipeg Jets

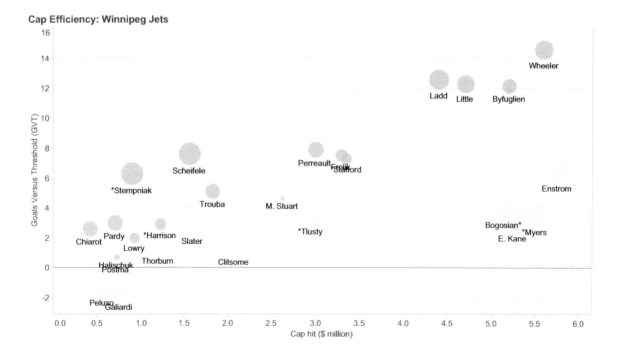

FORWARDS

Joel Armia								RW						WPG
Season	Team	Age	GP	G	A	Pts	+/-	ESP/60	AdjCF%	iCF/60	OGVT	DGVT	SGVT	GVT
2014-15	BUF	21	1	0	0	0	0	0.00	28.7%	0.0	0.0	0.0	0.0	0.0
2015-16	WPG	22	26	5	6	11					0.8	0.5	0.0	1.3

For Joel Armia, a change of scenery was not for the best. The tall Finnish winger was traded to Winnipeg as part of the deal that sent 2009 fourth-overall pick Evander Kane to Buffalo; the 21-year-old struggled after being moved. Buffalo's first-round pick in 2011 scored 25 points in 33 games with the Sabres AHL affiliate in Rochester, but had only eight in 21 games with Winnipeg's minor-league club. No need to panic yet, however, as the athletic forward has progressed a long ways since coming over from Finland to North America. Armia has great hands and creativity with the puck to go along with strong effort at both ends of the ice. The concern is whether he can bring consistent effort. Despite the late-season struggles, Armia should be in good position to see significant NHL time. He has star potential.

Andrew Copp								C						WPG
Season	Team	Age	GP	G	A	Pts	+/-	ESP/60	AdjCF%	iCF/60	OGVT	DGVT	SGVT	GVT
2014-15	WPG	20	1	0	1	1	2	4.86	50.3%	19.5	0.3	0.0	0.0	0.3
2015-16	WPG	21	26	5	7	12					1.1	0.6	0.0	1.7

After three strong seasons at University of Michigan, 21-year-old Andrew Copp decided to go pro, playing one game for the Jets. It turned out to be a nice debut as he notched an assist, put four shots on goal and was +2 in a 5-1 win over Calgary. At the NCAA level, he was nearly a point-per-game player, scoring 60 points in 69 games over the past two seasons in Ann Arbor. The fourth-round pick in 2013 is unlikely to repeat that type of production at the NHL level, but he has a strong two-way game and NHL frame at six-foot-two, 210 pounds.

Patrice Cormier								C/LW						WPG
Season	Team	Age	GP	G	A	Pts	+/-	ESP/60	AdjCF%	iCF/60	OGVT	DGVT	SGVT	GVT
2012-13	WPG	22	10	0	0	0	-3	0.00	53.6%	16.2	-0.5	-0.2	0.0	-0.7
2013-14	WPG	23	9	0	3	3	2	2.91	45.4%	7.6	0.5	0.3	0.0	0.8
2014-15	WPG	24	1	0	0	0	0	0.00	55.9%	0.0	0.0	0.0	0.0	0.0
2015-16	WPG	25	26	4	6	10					0.7	0.6	0.0	1.3

The last remaining piece still held by the organization from the Ilya Kovalchuk blockbuster of 2010—back when the Jets were known as the Atlanta Thrashers—Patrice Cormier seems destined to go the way of Niclas Bergfors, Johnny Oduya, and the first- and second-round picks that were subsequently dealt to Chicago in the Dustin Byfuglien deal. To understand the change in opinion as to Cormier's place in the system, note that he appeared in 21 games for the Thrashers in their final season in Atlanta. In his four seasons as a Jet, he has appeared in only 29 games combined.

Michael Frolik — RW/LW — CGY

Season	Team	Age	GP	G	A	Pts	+/-	ESP/60	AdjCF%	iCF/60	OGVT	DGVT	SGVT	GVT
2012-13	CHI	24	45	3	7	10	5	1.35	57.7%	19.5	-0.5	3.0	0.0	2.5
2013-14	WPG	25	81	15	27	42	8	2.01	52.7%	16.2	5.0	4.1	-0.6	8.5
2014-15	WPG	26	82	19	23	42	4	1.64	56.2%	16.8	4.9	2.7	0.0	7.5
2015-16	CGY	27	70	18	24	42					4.5	2.6	0.0	7.1

A standout penalty killer, Michael Frolik scored three shorthanded goals, the first three of his career, a culmination of above-average speed, instincts, and a strong wristshot. Recognizing the versatility of the Czech winger, head coach Paul Maurice also gave the 2006 top-10 draft pick his most ice-time on the man advantage since 2009-10, when Frolik was a sophomore on a dreadful Florida Panthers team. The 2013 Stanley Cup champion is also generally assigned to cover top-six forwards at even strength, adding additional gravitas to his positive possession numbers. In spite of the above, as well as top-end durability—Frolik has missed only four games over the past three seasons—he is a very easy player to overlook.

T.J. Galiardi — LW — Sweden

Season	Team	Age	GP	G	A	Pts	+/-	ESP/60	AdjCF%	iCF/60	OGVT	DGVT	SGVT	GVT
2012-13	SJS	24	36	5	9	14	1	1.60	51.3%	15.0	2.1	1.3	0.0	3.5
2013-14	CGY	25	62	4	13	17	-13	1.09	48.7%	12.3	-1.2	1.8	0.0	0.6
2014-15	WPG	26	38	1	0	1	-8	0.19	46.9%	9.0	-2.6	0.8	0.0	-1.8
2015-16	Sweden	27	47	4	6	10					-0.9	1.3	0.0	0.5

Getting the obvious out of the way first: T.J. Galiardi is not an especially good NHLer. He had a decent full season in 2009-10, but has been injured and ineffective ever since. This holds true whether we look at traditional metrics (240 GP, 26 G, 36 A, 62 Pts, -34) or advanced ones (-1.1% Relative Corsi). Now for some ephemera: Galiardi was the second T.J. drafted in the second round of the 2007 NHL Entry Draft, taken 24 picks after T.J. Brennan, but our T.J. has nearly as many career goals (44) as Brennan has games played (46). As mediocre as the Calgary native's career has been, only three others selected in that year and round have had more successful NHL careers. Another reminder that mediocrity is often a victory when it comes to the Draft.

Matt Halischuk — RW/LW — WPG

Season	Team	Age	GP	G	A	Pts	+/-	ESP/60	AdjCF%	iCF/60	OGVT	DGVT	SGVT	GVT
2012-13	NSH	24	36	5	6	11	1	1.67	43.9%	10.8	1.0	1.4	0.0	2.5
2013-14	WPG	25	46	5	5	10	-1	1.27	43.8%	11.3	0.3	1.0	0.0	1.3
2014-15	WPG	26	47	3	5	8	5	1.10	51.1%	11.7	-0.8	1.4	0.0	0.7
2015-16	WPG	27	46	6	7	13					0.2	1.3	0.0	1.5

Now 26 years old and unable to secure a full-time role in any given lineup for the third year running—like every year but one of his career—Matt Halischuk's 15-goal season with Nashville in 2011-12 is looking more and more like an unrepeatable high-water mark. In truth, he is just not that good. His career year was juiced—as they often are—by an uncharacteristic 15.6% shooting percentage, while he has connected on only 8.3% otherwise, over a career spanning 250 games.

Andrew Ladd — LW — WPG

Season	Team	Age	GP	G	A	Pts	+/-	ESP/60	AdjCF%	iCF/60	OVGT	DGVT	SGVT	GVT
2012-13	WPG	27	48	18	28	46	10	3.20	51.3%	14.6	8.2	3.1	0.5	11.7
2013-14	WPG	28	78	23	31	54	8	2.06	52.4%	14.1	7.1	4.2	2.5	13.8
2014-15	WPG	29	81	24	38	62	9	2.06	54.8%	13.9	9.8	3.7	-0.9	12.6
2015-16	WPG	30	73	22	33	55					6.9	2.8	0.0	9.7

One third of a great two-way first line in Winnipeg, captain Andrew Ladd excels at moving the puck in the right direction. With his plus hand-eye coordination and willing muscle, the two-time Stanley Cup winner is the practically perfect support player. A positive possession player in every season since turning 20, and never having scored less than 1.76 even-strength points per 60 minutes, Ladd has, in an understated way, lived up to his advance billing as the fourth-overall pick of the 2004 NHL Entry Draft. His consistent, above-average production, by both regular metrics as well as advanced ones, indicates that he should be a prime target in next summer's free agent market, if the Jets don't extend him first.

Bryan Little — C — WPG

Season	Team	Age	GP	G	A	Pts	+/-	ESP/60	AdjCF%	iCF/60	OGVT	DGVT	SGVT	GVT
2012-13	WPG	25	48	7	25	32	8	2.07	49.0%	9.3	2.0	2.8	-0.6	4.3
2013-14	WPG	26	82	23	41	64	8	2.18	52.5%	10.2	9.3	4.3	1.0	14.5
2014-15	WPG	27	70	24	28	52	8	1.93	54.5%	10.6	9.4	3.6	-0.6	12.3
2015-16	WPG	28	70	23	32	55					7.4	2.7	0.0	10.2

Bryan Little is emblematic of Thrashers/Jets history as being never good enough for the playoffs, but never bad enough to pick near the top of the draft—Evander Kane notwithstanding. One of many former Barrie Colts dotting the Jets roster, Little was a mid-first-round pick who has matured into a mid-tier top-six center. A positive possession player, with above-average Corsi-for marks in five of the past six seasons, he falls short of elite in that department. He has eclipsed 1.8 even-strength points per 60 minutes in each of the past three seasons, after falling short of that mark in three of his first four seasons, proving that he has risen to the level of *bona fide* top-six offensive contributor. All of which is to say that the Jets are happy to have Little on their roster, especially after taking his reasonable $4.7 million cap hit into consideration. But once in a while, they have to wish they had been a little worse in 2006 and drafted Jonathan Toews or Nicklas Backstrom instead.

Adam Lowry — C/LW — WPG

Season	Team	Age	GP	G	A	Pts	+/-	ESP/60	AdjCF%	iCF/60	OGVT	DGVT	SGVT	GVT
2014-15	WPG	21	80	11	12	23	1	1.14	55.3%	10.3	0.0	1.9	0.0	2.0
2015-16	WPG	22	69	13	16	29					1.5	1.9	0.0	3.4

For an organization that prefers to take its time when it comes to the development of prospects, it does seem a bit odd that they moved Adam Lowry up to the NHL after only one full season on the farm. Perhaps it was his NHL bloodlines, with father Dave having a track record of over 1,000 NHL games as well as ample high-level coaching experience, giving the Jets the confidence to break camp with young Adam. Maybe it is his large frame, complete with an extra-wide wingspan and the requisite physical game. Or just maybe it is the soft hands portending offensive upside. Or it could be that they just figured that all of those things would add up to a useful bottom-six forward who could hold his head above water in the possession game, while chipping in his share of offense and crashing his way through the league; Lowry led the Jets in hits (256) as a rookie.

Eric O'Dell						C/RW							OTT
Season	Team	Age	GP	G	A	Pts	+/-	ESP/60	AdjCF%	iCF/60	OGVT	DGVT	SGVT	GVT
2013-14	WPG	23	30	3	4	7	-2	1.50	51.1%	6.7	0.1	0.3	0.0	0.4
2014-15	WPG	24	11	0	1	1	0	0.75	59.2%	11.5	-0.3	0.2	0.0	-0.2
2015-16	OTT	25	35	5	7	12					0.3	0.7	0.0	1.1

Positive possession pointers are one thing, but when the points are in regression, that is another thing altogether. Such was the case for Eric O'Dell last season, as he could add only a single solitary helper in his 11 appearances with the Jets despite starting 72.7% of his non-neutral zone faceoffs in the offensive end. His 29 points in 37 AHL games were nice, but it still fell short of his previous two seasons, when he had accumulated 97 points in 101 games with St. John's. Moving on to Binghamton, O'Dell will try to become another success story to rise up from the affiliate to Ottawa.

Anthony Peluso						RW							WPG
Season	Team	Age	GP	G	A	Pts	+/-	ESP/60	AdjCF%	iCF/60	OGVT	DGVT	SGVT	GVT
2012-13	WPG	23	5	0	2	2	1	5.00	65.1%	10.0	0.3	0.2	0.0	0.5
2013-14	WPG	24	53	2	3	5	-5	0.99	45.9%	6.1	-1.5	0.2	-0.3	-1.6
2014-15	WPG	25	49	1	1	2	-3	0.42	50.8%	8.9	-2.1	0.5	0.0	-1.6
2015-16	WPG	26	45	3	3	5					-1.4	0.7	0.0	-0.6

By both rates and raw totals, the only Jet to spend as much time in the sin bin as Anthony Peluso (86 PIM) was "Big Buff". In many senses, it is kind of weird that the Jets had the success that they did while using a roster spot on a player as limited as the former waiver-wire pickup. Not a single skater who played in at least 40 games averaged as little as Peluso's 5:52 of ice-time per game. In fact, no one came within 90 seconds of that meager total. Other than literal bang for his buck—Peluso hits a lot of people (100 hits in 49 games)—the North York native does little to recommend bringing him back for another season.

Mathieu Perrault						C							WPG
Season	Team	Age	GP	G	A	Pts	+/-	ESP/60	AdjCF%	iCF/60	OGVT	DGVT	SGVT	GVT
2012-13	WSH	24	39	6	11	17	7	2.06	54.0%	11.9	2.3	1.2	0.0	3.5
2013-14	ANA	25	69	18	25	43	13	2.53	52.1%	12.0	8.3	1.9	-0.3	9.9
2014-15	WPG	26	62	18	23	41	7	2.13	57.0%	12.1	6.6	1.7	-0.4	7.9
2015-16	WPG	27	61	18	25	43					5.7	1.7	0.0	7.4

Perhaps the best free-agent value signing of last offseason, Matheiu Perreault picked up right where he left off with the Ducks. Although durability remains a concern, the 2006 sixth rounder is a world-class possession demon, with the best Relative Corsi among regular Jets in spite of being unprotected by Paul Maurice. Getting past his five-foot-ten stature, and the seemingly resultant injuries that have plagued his career (only once in seven professional seasons has he managed 70 games), the former Acadie-Bathurst Titan has scored in bunches wherever and whenever he has played. It seems to us that a team should want a very good player for 65 games rather than a mediocre one for 80 games.

Mark Scheifele								C						WPG
Season	Team	Age	GP	G	A	Pts	+/-	ESP/60	AdjCF%	iCF/60	OGVT	DGVT	SGVT	GVT
2012-13	WPG	19	4	0	0	0	0	0.00	49.7%	13.3	-0.8	0.0	0.0	-0.8
2013-14	WPG	20	63	13	21	34	9	1.99	48.3%	9.9	3.8	2.1	-0.3	5.6
2014-15	WPG	21	82	15	34	49	11	1.68	53.9%	11.7	4.9	3.2	-0.5	7.6
2015-16	*WPG*	*22*	*73*	*18*	*32*	*50*					*5.4*	*2.7*	*0.0*	*8.0*

While the offensive output has not moved much on a per-game basis, Mark Scheifele did take a huge step forward in his sophomore campaign. Playing most of the season at age 21, the former Barrie Colt turned his possession game around, raising his Corsi-for percentage from a subpar 48.6% to a well above-average 53%. Adding in additional context makes the feat even more impressive: the two-time WJC participant did all of this while also going from taking 52.5% of his non-neutral zone shifts in the offensive end down to 48.9%, and against improved opponents. A heady player with solid hands and skating ability, Scheifele should be an above-average number-two center for many years to come.

Jim Slater								C						Free Agent
Season	Team	Age	GP	G	A	Pts	+/-	ESP/60	AdjCF%	iCF/60	OGVT	DGVT	SGVT	GVT
2012-13	WPG	30	26	1	1	2	-3	0.54	48.3%	9.8	-1.0	0.9	0.0	-0.2
2013-14	WPG	31	27	1	1	2	-5	0.51	48.6%	7.6	-1.2	0.6	0.0	-0.6
2014-15	WPG	32	82	5	8	13	-4	1.28	47.0%	9.1	-0.4	2.5	0.0	2.2
2015-16	*Free Agent*	*33*	*59*	*4*	*6*	*10*					*-0.9*	*1.7*	*0.0*	*0.7*

A powerful skater with little subtlety to his game, Jim Slater played out the 2014-15 season as the longest-serving member of the Winni-lanta Jet-shers, having joined the organization as a back-end first-round pick in the 2002 NHL Entry Draft. A little trivia, as the pick was originally traded away by the Red Wings as part of the package for Dominik Hasek. A pending UFA, there was both good and bad in the Michigan State grad's potential final season with the only team he has ever known. On the positive side, he was healthy for the first time in years, setting a new career high in games played (all of them). On the other hand, he wasn't very good, at least at even strength. He couldn't score and his possession numbers were brutal, despite facing mostly fellow shlubs. Most of Slater's value comes on the penalty kill, as he was a first option for Winnipeg when down a man and on the draw, where he is among the best in hockey. There are worse ways to fill a fourth-line role.

Drew Stafford								RW						WPG
Season	Team	Age	GP	G	A	Pts	+/-	ESP/60	AdjCF%	iCF/60	OGVT	DGVT	SGVT	GVT
2012-13	BUF	27	46	6	12	18	-16	1.46	45.7%	13.6	-0.2	-0.7	0.5	-0.4
2013-14	BUF	28	70	16	18	34	-19	1.50	41.0%	13.4	1.5	2.2	0.0	3.7
2014-15	BUF, WPG	29	76	18	25	43	-12	1.90	40.8%	9.8	5.3	1.2	0.7	7.3
2015-16	*WPG*	*30*	*64*	*15*	*22*	*37*					*3.5*	*1.5*	*0.0*	*5.0*

After futzing along with Buffalo for a third straight year of bottom-six production, Drew Stafford was dealt to Winnipeg as the fourth wheel of the Kane-Myers-Bogosian deal. Rescued from the Western New York tire fire, the 13th-overall draft pick from 2004 rescued his numbers in turn. In the small sample of 26 games with the Jets, Stafford's even-strength production ranked above that of any but his rookie season. Much of that was fueled by his own 16.1% shooting percentage with Winnipeg, nearly 50% higher than his career rate—if you needed a concrete reason to believe the Milwaukee native did not reach a new standard as a 29-year-old. Re-signed in the offseason, Stafford was paid like a second liner but may quickly go back to producing like a third liner. Unfortunately for decision makers, salaries do not regress like the on-ice metrics do.

Lee Stempniak — RW — Free Agent

Season	Team	Age	GP	G	A	Pts	+/-	ESP/60	AdjCF%	iCF/60	OGVT	DGVT	SGVT	GVT
2012-13	CGY	29	47	9	23	32	2	1.96	49.2%	14.2	4.7	3.6	-0.3	8.0
2013-14	CGY, PIT	30	73	12	22	34	-16	1.35	46.8%	12.9	0.6	2.1	0.4	3.1
2014-15	NYR, WPG	31	71	15	13	28	8	2.01	51.6%	13.7	4.3	2.0	0.1	6.3
2015-16	Free Agent	32	61	11	15	26					2.0	1.7	0.0	3.7

Acquired at the deadline for AHL winger Carl Klingberg, Lee Stempniak finished out his one-year contract in style, putting up 10 points in 18 games for the Jets as they battled to secure their first playoff spot since moving "back" to Winnipeg. A solid possession player despite being buried in terms of zone starts for the past five seasons, the Buffalo native should have enough offensive talent, relative youth, and complementary possession skills to find an NHL home again for 2015-16. At least, that is what we think.

Chris Thorburn — RW — WPG

Season	Team	Age	GP	G	A	Pts	+/-	ESP/60	AdjCF%	iCF/60	OGVT	DGVT	SGVT	GVT
2012-13	WPG	29	42	2	2	4	-5	0.95	48.8%	6.8	-0.3	0.2	0.0	-0.1
2013-14	WPG	30	55	2	9	11	0	1.36	43.8%	6.3	-0.3	0.8	0.0	0.5
2014-15	WPG	31	81	7	7	14	-5	1.30	50.0%	12.0	0.2	0.8	0.0	1.0
2015-16	WPG	32	58	5	7	11					-0.4	1.0	0.0	0.6

You want to be kind, and commend this blue-collar-type winger for his steadiness and consistency. After all, it says a great deal about Chris Thorburn that he has scored between 11-19 points in each and every non-labor-shortened season of his career. That is seven seasons of reliable, replacement-level, fourth-line work, for those of you counting at home. And therein lies the rub. It is imminently replaceable. In spite of his low scoring totals, Thorburn is given very little time on the penalty kill, and tends to get shifts that have been trending more towards sheltered for each of the past four seasons, with his offensive zone start rate rising from 38.8% to 44% to 48.9%, and finally to 51.6% last year. Is he worth sheltering?

Jiri Tlusty — LW — Free Agent

Season	Team	Age	GP	G	A	Pts	+/-	ESP/60	AdjCF%	iCF/60	OGVT	DGVT	SGVT	GVT
2012-13	CAR	24	48	23	15	38	15	2.56	48.8%	13.3	9.5	2.8	-0.3	12.0
2013-14	CAR	25	68	16	14	30	2	1.82	50.8%	14.0	3.5	2.8	0.0	6.3
2014-15	CAR, WPG	26	72	14	17	31	-18	1.30	54.0%	12.1	1.7	1.8	-0.3	3.2
2015-16	Free Agent	27	62	12	16	28					1.6	1.7	0.0	3.3

Once upon a time, Jiri Tlusty was a highly coveted teenager, so highly thought of that the Maple Leafs used the 13th-overall pick of the 2006 draft to secure his rights. Six years and a trade to Carolina later, the Czech winger scored 23 goals in the labor-damaged 2012-13 season, on the strength of a surprise 19.7% shooting percentage. He has always had a good shot, but his rate hitting twine on 12.3% of his shots—as he has done for the other years of his career—is far more reflective of what to expect. Acquired by the Jets as the trade deadline approached to add some scoring depth for the middle six, Tlusty fizzled, lighting the lamp only once in 20 games. A pending UFA, the six-foot winger may be wearing a different uniform in October.

Blake Wheeler — RW — WPG

Season	Team	Age	GP	G	A	Pts	+/-	ESP/60	AdjCF%	iCF/60	OGVT	DGVT	SGVT	GVT
2012-13	WPG	26	48	19	22	41	-3	2.68	50.0%	15.2	6.6	1.2	0.2	8.0
2013-14	WPG	27	82	28	41	69	4	2.41	49.4%	15.8	12.8	2.4	-0.8	14.5
2014-15	WPG	28	79	26	35	61	26	2.28	55.3%	17.4	9.5	4.8	0.4	14.6
2015-16	WPG	29	75	26	35	61					8.3	3.0	0.0	11.3

Selected one spot after current linemate Andrew Ladd in the 2004 NHL Entry Draft, Blake Wheeler has magical hands that combined with his condor-like reach, make him an exceptional possession player and offensive threat whenever he has the puck. Acquired by the organization from Boston along with Mark Stuart in exchange for Boris Valabik and Rich Peverley in one of ex-GM Rick Dudley's finer moments, the former Golden Gopher has scored at a higher rate in every season with the Thrashers/Jets than in any season with Boston. As he nears age 30, and is owed $23.2 million over the next four years, the Jets will need Wheeler to continue at this production level to avoid dragging down what has typically been more of a floor team than a cap spender.

DEFENSEMEN

Julien Brouillette — LD — Sweden

Season	Team	Age	GP	G	A	Pts	+/-	ESP/60	AdjCF%	iCF/60	OGVT	DGVT	SGVT	GVT
2013-14	WSH	27	10	1	1	2	3	0.80	41.3%	6.5	0.2	0.7	0.0	0.8
2014-15	WPG	28	1	0	0	0	0	0.00	13.8%	0.0	0.0	0.0	0.0	0.0
2015-16	Sweden	29	27	2	5	7					0.4	1.0	0.0	1.4

Perseverance is admirable, but in some cases, ultimately futile. After debuting in his first NHL action at the age of 27 with the Capitals in 2013-14, Julien Brouillette could not return to those lofty heights last year with Winnipeg, playing less than 10 minutes in his only game of the year, an early January tilt against the Sharks. A veteran of six different AHL franchises, the proud alumnus of the Chicoutimi Saugeneens program is off to try his luck in Europe instead, with Karlskrona HK of the SHL.

Dustin Byfuglien — RD/RW — WPG

Season	Team	Age	GP	G	A	Pts	+/-	FSP/60	AdjCF%	iCF/60	OGVT	DGVT	SGVT	GVT
2012-13	WPG	27	43	8	20	28	-1	1.24	50.2%	13.1	5.4	1.6	-0.3	6.7
2013-14	WPG	28	78	20	36	56	-20	1.28	49.9%	13.6	11.7	0.0	-0.3	11.4
2014-15	WPG	29	69	18	27	45	5	1.33	53.3%	12.9	9.3	2.8	0.0	12.2
2015-16	WPG	30	70	14	34	48					8.1	2.8	0.0	10.8

So is Dustin Byfuglien a defenseman or a winger? The Jets seemed to answer that question more firmly last season, with "Big Buff" settling in on the blueline. Paired up most often with young Ben Chiarot when the rookie was healthy, the former Blackhawk was able to be activated more often than in the past, knowing there was a steady and responsible presence at his side to pick up for him. As a defender, Byfuglien is a veritable offensive weapon with a heavy slapshot from the point and a penchant for disruption. On the other hand, at least partially due to his extra-wide frame, he lacks in mobility, leaving him exposed to a quick transition game as a slow moving target. Maybe the best answer is to let him play both positions, depending on the matchups.

Ben Chiarot							LD						WPG
Season	Team	Age	GP	G	A	Pts	+/-	ESP/60	AdjCF%	iCF/60	OGVT	DGVT	SGVT	GVT
2013-14	WPG	22	1	0	0	0	-3	0.00	27.2%	0.0	-0.1	-0.4	0.0	-0.5
2014-15	WPG	23	40	2	6	8	5	0.74	54.3%	8.2	0.5	2.2	0.0	2.6
2015-16	WPG	24	46	3	9	12					0.5	2.0	0.0	2.4

After three and a half years on the farm, the Jets finally experienced enough injuries on the blueline that Ben Chiarot was afforded a serious opportunity to show what he had learned at St. John's. Even though he was not sheltered by head coach Paul Maurice, the former Guelph Storm defenseman held his own in third-pairing minutes. Not a flashy player, Chiarot is a capable puck-mover who is not shy about crashing and banging his big frame around the ice. While his ceiling is not far above what is already there, he has the makings of the type that could play to this level for a long time yet.

Grant Clitsome							LD						WPG
Season	Team	Age	GP	G	A	Pts	+/-	ESP/60	AdjCF%	iCF/60	OGVT	DGVT	SGVT	GVT
2012-13	WPG	27	44	4	12	16	10	1.09	50.5%	8.2	2.7	3.6	0.0	6.2
2013-14	WPG	28	32	2	10	12	-5	1.11	50.8%	8.2	1.5	0.6	0.0	2.1
2014-15	WPG	29	24	0	4	4	4	0.68	54.9%	8.5	0.2	1.0	0.0	1.2
2015-16	WPG	30	36	2	8	10					0.7	1.4	0.0	2.1

Although his season was cut short due to sustaining a back injury, 2004 ninth rounder Grant Clitsome should land on his feet once he recovers. A poor man's John-Michael Liles, the Clarkson grad is a solid possession player who can contribute decent offense from the third pairing. A free agent after next season, the Jets will find a willing taker if they don't want to keep him around.

Keaton Ellerby							LD						KHL
Season	Team	Age	GP	G	A	Pts	+/-	ESP/60	AdjCF%	iCF/60	OGVT	DGVT	SGVT	GVT
2012-13	FLA, LAK	24	44	0	3	3	3	0.32	52.8%	6.8	-1.0	2.1	0.0	1.1
2013-14	WPG	25	51	2	4	6	4	0.43	47.8%	7.1	-0.4	1.4	0.0	1.0
2014-15	WPG	26	1	0	1	1	-1	3.54	44.2%	3.4	0.3	0.0	0.0	0.3
2015-16	KHL	27	35	2	6	8					0.4	1.2	0.0	1.5

Before hiring Dale Tallon to begin the process of stockpiling their system with high-end, exciting young talent, the Florida Panthers would do silly things like use the 10th-overall pick in the amateur draft on big-bodied, bruising blueliners such as Keaton Ellerby. Eight years later, the former Kamloops Blazer is still big and bruising, but has never been able to put the rest of his game together. He has never finished a season of more than one single game played as a positive relative possession player and his career high of 12 points is now four years in the rearview mirror. His size and decent play at the AHL level will keep Ellerby drawing paychecks, but not so much that his children won't have to work.

Tobias Enstrom — LD — WPG

Season	Team	Age	GP	G	A	Pts	+/-	ESP/60	AdjCF%	iCF/60	OGVT	DGVT	SGVT	GVT
2012-13	WPG	28	22	4	11	15	-8	1.11	48.3%	4.8	2.4	0.0	0.0	2.4
2013-14	WPG	29	82	10	20	30	-9	0.67	50.2%	6.0	1.7	1.3	0.0	3.0
2014-15	WPG	30	60	4	19	23	13	0.86	51.9%	4.9	2.0	4.4	0.0	6.4
2015-16	WPG	31	61	5	19	23					1.7	3.2	0.0	4.8

For the fourth time in the past five seasons, Tobias Enstrom missed a significant chunk of the campaign due to injuries. Further, his scoring rate was not able to rebound from what had been a career worst showing on a per-game basis in 2013-14. To add fuel to a 30-year-old fire, Enstrom also saw a dip in possession metrics, with a -1.7% Relative Corsi marking his worst mark since 2007-08 with Atlanta. His season may have even looked worse were it not for a career-best 103.1 PDO, which is more than just a reflection of his favored zone start rate. By the postseason, the 2003 eighth-round selection looked diminished and limited on the ice. With another three years on a contract that carries a $5.8 million cap hit, the Jets have to hope that better luck with health—which is likely not a luck-based thing—will lead to a moderate rebound.

Jay Harrison — LD — WPG

Season	Team	Age	GP	G	A	Pts	+/-	ESP/60	AdjCF%	iCF/60	OGVT	DGVT	SGVT	GVT
2012-13	CAR	30	47	3	7	10	-10	0.67	49.5%	8.3	0.5	0.8	0.0	1.2
2013-14	CAR	31	68	4	11	15	-1	0.53	47.1%	10.2	0.8	2.4	0.0	3.1
2014-15	CAR, WPG	32	55	3	6	9	-1	0.55	50.6%	9.3	-0.1	3.0	0.0	2.9
2015-16	WPG	33	52	3	9	11					0.3	2.5	0.0	2.8

Big Jay Harrison passes the eye test. Unfortunately, he fails the nose test. That isn't so much to say that he stinks, but his production does carry an odd odor. He is huge, but doesn't really make his presence felt with punishing checks or otherwise perform wondrous feats of strength. He isn't a complete cipher on the offensive end, but has only once surpassed 15 points in his eight NHL seasons. In spite of favorable usage, both in terms of ample offensive zone starts and against a lower caliber of competition, his possession rates have been retrograde for his entire career. The Jets wisely, but futilely, made Harrison a healthy scratch throughout the short duration of their playoff "run".

Tyler Myers — RD — WPG

Season	Team	Age	GP	G	A	Pts	+/-	ESP/60	AdjCF%	iCF/60	OGVT	DGVT	SGVT	GVT
2012-13	BUF	22	39	3	5	8	-8	0.46	45.2%	6.4	-0.1	0.0	0.0	-0.1
2013-14	BUF	23	62	9	13	22	-26	0.74	42.9%	7.7	2.5	0.2	0.0	2.7
2014-15	BUF, WPG	24	71	7	21	28	-6	0.88	38.4%	6.6	1.4	2.2	0.0	3.6
2015-16	WPG	25	63	6	19	25					1.7	2.4	0.0	4.1

In the history of the "real-time stats" era—10 seasons—there has never been a team as across-the-board futile as the 2014-15 Buffalo Sabres. In fact, no other team had a Corsi-for percentage within 5% of their horrid 38%. So who do we blame? In all honestly, current tools cannot factor out everything to micro-analyze individual players at such extremes. Tyler Myers is a great example. Many pundits gleefully pointed fingers at Myers for failing to live up to his rookie-year promise, when he won the Calder Trophy. Forget for a moment that he had been buried over the past two seasons in terms of zone starts and generally played the oppositions' top lines, but he was clearly not as exciting as he once seemed to be. Before the trade to Winnipeg, Myers' Corsi percentage was 34.1%, even worse than his team as a whole. After crossing the border, his Corsi percentage jumped to

49.4%, albeit in a fraction of a season. Still not great, but suddenly the 2008 first rounder's other talents are not crushed by massive possession deficiencies. Ultimately, the smooth-skating six-foot-eight defender might be best served on a second pairing, not a first unit, but some of the criticisms should begin to subside, at least a bit.

Adam Pardy — LD — WPG

Season	Team	Age	GP	G	A	Pts	+/-	ESP/60	AdjCF%	iCF/60	OGVT	DGVT	SGVT	GVT
2012-13	BUF	28	17	0	4	4	4	0.92	44.0%	3.9	0.6	0.9	0.0	1.5
2013-14	WPG	29	60	0	6	6	4	0.45	53.3%	7.2	-1.1	1.9	0.0	0.8
2014-15	WPG	30	55	0	9	9	9	0.70	52.4%	6.8	-0.2	3.2	0.0	3.0
2015-16	WPG	31	50	1	7	9					-0.1	2.3	0.0	2.1

Watching the Jets on TV, the cameras only seem to spot Adam Pardy when the Jets are defending in their own zone. Once they are on the attack, the blueliner effectively disappears. We assume that he gets up there, but do we really know? In three of the past five seasons, the former Flame, Star, and Sabre has been a positive possession player. In one of the two other seasons, it was close enough to give Pardy the benefit of the doubt. The remaining negative season was spent with Buffalo. Consider us as sold on the Newfoundlander as a viable and valuable third-pairing defender.

Paul Postma — RD — WPG

Season	Team	Age	GP	G	A	Pts	+/-	ESP/60	AdjCF%	iCF/60	OGVT	DGVT	SGVT	GVT
2012-13	WPG	23	34	4	5	9	-5	0.66	52.6%	9.2	1.2	-0.3	0.0	1.0
2013-14	WPG	24	20	1	2	3	1	0.60	47.2%	8.3	0.3	0.6	0.0	0.9
2014-15	WPG	25	42	2	4	6	1	0.44	54.9%	10.6	-0.7	1.0	0.0	0.3
2015-16	WPG	26	44	2	7	9					0.1	1.6	0.0	1.7

As the Jets faced a serious injury stack on the blueline, Paul Postma was doubly victimized by the troubles. Technically not injured, Postma could not secure the trust of head coach Paul Maurice, and was electively scratched for 27 straight games from January 10 through March 12. The Red Deer, Alberta native returned on March 14 to log over 20 minutes for the first time in the season... and was promptly knocked out for the rest of the campaign with a lower body injury. A solid possession player, Postma has nonetheless been lapped on the depth chart by the emergence of Ben Chiarot and the anticipated arrival of stud prospect Josh Morrissey. A right-handed shot, the 2007 seventh rounder would be best served by a trade to a team with more need on the starboard side of its blueline.

Mark Stuart — LD — WPG

Season	Team	Age	GP	G	A	Pts	+/-	ESP/60	AdjCF%	iCF/60	OGVT	DGVT	SGVT	GVT
2012-13	WPG	28	42	2	2	4	5	0.40	48.8%	11.3	-0.4	2.4	0.0	2.0
2013-14	WPG	29	69	2	11	13	11	0.73	47.8%	8.1	0.1	5.9	0.0	6.0
2014-15	WPG	30	70	2	12	14	5	0.65	53.7%	8.1	0.5	4.2	0.0	4.6
2015-16	WPG	31	59	3	11	13					0.5	3.4	0.0	3.9

While Mark Stuart isn't a bad player per se, there is more than a little cognitive dissonance in noting that only two Jets currently have contracts that will expire after the stay-at-home blueliner's pact ends. He bangs a lot of opposition bodies and blocks a ton of shots—leading the team in the latter category. Add it all up, along with the suddenly crowded defense corps in Winnipeg and his reasonable cap hit of $2.6 million, and the Minnesotan makes for a very nice trade chip.

Jacob Trouba — RD — WPG

Season	Team	Age	GP	G	A	Pts	+/-	ESP/60	AdjCF%	iCF/60	OGVT	DGVT	SGVT	GVT
2013-14	WPG	19	65	10	19	29	4	1.32	48.8%	12.3	4.9	4.2	0.0	9.1
2014-15	WPG	20	65	7	15	22	2	0.82	55.6%	13.1	1.9	3.2	0.0	5.1
2015-16	WPG	21	66	8	22	30					3.5	3.6	0.0	7.1

A cursory glance at his boxcar stats gives the impression that Jacob Trouba, as talented as he is purported to be, regressed heavily in his sophomore campaign. Even though he played the same number of games, he had seven fewer points, a dropoff of nearly 25%. Thankfully, we have a variety of advanced metrics which suggest that the 2012 ninth-overall draft pick actually saw his game improve with experience. Although mitigated by an increase in offensive zone starts, his total usage pattern suggests that was due to his skills with the puck as opposed to a need to be sheltered. To wit, Maurice had Trouba lining up against top-six forwards and the 20-year-old responded by improving his possession metrics from a negative to significantly in the black. Throw in a good physical game and plus anticipation of the play as it unfolds in front of him, and Trouba is likely to develop into a top-pairing option—perhaps as soon as this year.

GOALTENDERS

Michael Hutchinson — G — WPG

Season	Team	Age	GP	W	L	OT	GAA	Sv%	ESSV%	QS%	GGVT	DGVT	SGVT	GVT
2013-14	WPG	23	3	2	1	0	1.64	.943	.958	100.0%	2.6	0.0	0.8	3.5
2014-15	WPG	24	38	21	10	5	2.39	.914	.924	58.3%	5.3	0.4	2.0	7.7
2015-16	WPG	25	37					.917			7.1	0.3	0.4	7.8

Emerging from seemingly out of nowhere, Michael Hutchinson nearly walked away with the starting netminder job in Winnipeg. Through the 2014 portion of the schedule, the former Bruins draft pick had a .937 save percentage, while his counterpart stopped only 91.1% of shots. Things got a little ugly for "Hutch" in February and March, though, and consequently, he rarely saw the ice down the stretch. Agile and with plus anticipation of the play, the tools are there for the 25-year-old to be the average goaltender that the Jets have been searching for since the Atlanta days. With one more year to go before he becomes a restricted free agent, Winnipeg should give the former Barrie Colt and London Knight a few more chances to wrest away the #1 mantle from an unconvincing Ondrej Pavelec.

Ondrej Pavelec — G — WPG

Season	Team	Age	GP	W	L	OT	GAA	Sv%	ESSV%	QS%	GGVT	DGVT	SGVT	GVT
2012-13	WPG	25	44	21	20	3	2.80	.905	.914	44.2%	-3.2	-0.1	1.2	-2.1
2013-14	WPG	26	57	22	26	7	3.01	.901	.908	47.4%	-10.2	-0.5	-0.3	-11.0
2014-15	WPG	27	50	22	16	8	2.28	.920	.927	50.0%	14.4	0.1	-2.4	12.1
2015-16	WPG	28	37					.912			0.8	-0.1	-0.3	0.5

Everyone deserves at least one chance for redemption, even goalies like Ondrej Pavelec, who have only reached the level of "roughly NHL average" in one of six previous seasons. Yes, he stank even when the sample size was very small. Thankfully for Pavelec and Winnipeg, the Czech netminder took advantage of his chance, performing roughly NHL average for much of the season and then turning it up a few notches when the Jets desperately needed a few wins in the last week of the season. The two-time Czech Olympian went nuts, pitching three consecutive shutouts to secure the team's first playoff berth since returning to Manitoba. Unfortunately, when the postseason began, the old Ondrej returned, with subpar performances in three of four games as they were swept by Anaheim. There is a fine line between being an athletic netminder and a desperate one; Ondrej Pavelec has made a career out of straddling that line.

Ryan Wagman

Fenwick vs. Estimated Possession from Play-by-Play

At the heart of analytics for any sport, the measure of effectiveness is how well you are doing with the data at your disposal. Even before the start of the 21st century, there were many ways to take the scarce information at hand and make good use of it to make valuable decisions on how to play, or how to run a team. While we are not on the same level as baseball, the NHL has been progressive with the data they store and share with the public. What we are doing with the data within the hockey community is fascinating. The "Summer of Analytics" wouldn't have occurred last year had creative minds not manipulated and presented the right data in creative ways to convey various discoveries.

Two stats at the public face of hockey analytics are Corsi and Fenwick (also called SAT and USAT on *NHL.com*). Their lasting presence and effectiveness is credited with their repeatability and correlation to future success. Further, they correlate well with puck possession, which one writer at *Hockey Prospectus* dubbed the "on-base percentage" of hockey, or rather hockey's gateway statistic that could lead to further understanding of how the game is played.

The intersection of these two ideas recently caused me to question what more can be extracted from the information we have at hand. Until tracking technology, such as SportsVU, makes its way to hockey and is provided to the general public, we will need to continue to make approximations for the stats that aren't tracked. Therefore, I created my own method to approximate possession based on the play-by-play data that the NHL provides for every game.

Play-by-play logs contain many more events than the average fan might expect. While Corsi and Fenwick consider only shot attempts, we have accurate timestamps that contain not only shot attempts, but takeaways and giveaways (subjective as they are), hits, faceoffs, and more. My program is set up to estimate possession by assigning the time between events to the teams based on which events occur. The less time there is between events, the better we can estimate who had the puck between those events.

Events recorded in the play-by-play log that have something to do with possession are **SHOT, MISS, BLOCK, GOAL, FAC, HIT, TAKE,** and **GIVE.** They are coded as follows:

SHOT, MISS, BLOCK, GOAL: The team that performed these events had the puck before these events.

FAC (faceoff): The winner of this event had the puck directly after the event.

HIT: The team that performed this event didn't have the puck before the event.

TAKE: The team that performed this event didn't have the puck before the event, but had the puck after the event.

GIVE: The team that performed this event had the puck before the event, but doesn't have the puck after the event.

For instance, suppose a game starts with a faceoff win for Team A, and the next event is a takeaway by Team B that occurs seven seconds after the faceoff. In this instance, Team A is credited with seven seconds of possession. While we are not entirely sure what else could have happened between those events, we can only use the information available to us to make approximations.

There are the awkward situations when successive events don't matchup so cleanly, when it is impossible to know how or when possession switched. As an example, if a faceoff win from Team A is followed by a shot on goal by Team B only six seconds later, we have no further information to estimate when the puck changed hands. For those situations (which occur less than 30% of all game time), the elapsed time is split in half and assigned to each team. Like any statistic, on a micro-level, these data points are not worth much. But after being teased out over longer periods of time, the signal starts to differentiate itself from the noise (see tables, this page).

When dealing with season-long results, this new method of calculating possession mirrors Fenwick values quite well. For all five-on-five situations when the game is close (within one goal for the first two periods, or tied in the third) the R2 value was 0.73 for 2013-14 and 0.67 for 2014-15, indicating a fairly strong correlation.

Using this method of estimating possession, we are able to compare it alongside scoring chances or other shot-based stats to determine which teams are keeping possession for possession's sake, or which teams are making the most of the time they handle the puck.

For example, we can study a team like the 2014-

Estimated possession percentage vs. Fenwick close											
2013-14						2014-15					
Team	With puck (seconds)	Without puck (seconds)	Estimated possession	Fenwick close	Difference	Team	With puck (seconds)	Without puck (seconds)	Estimated possession	Fenwick close	Difference
ANA	67006	67171	49.9%	50.2%	-0.3%	ANA	71775	70882	50.3%	51.5%	-1.2%
ARI	71833	73280	49.5%	49.9%	-0.4%	ARI	72529	76859	48.6%	46.3%	2.3%
BOS	76625	70805	52.0%	54.1%	-2.1%	BOS	83690	77459	51.9%	50.8%	1.1%
BUF	67515	83536	44.7%	40.9%	3.8%	BUF	66188	84609	43.9%	39.0%	4.9%
CAR	73000	75489	49.2%	48.1%	1.1%	CAR	75698	73273	50.8%	51.8%	-1.0%
CBJ	69759	71802	49.3%	50.7%	-1.4%	CBJ	65776	74055	47.0%	46.0%	1.0%
CGY	71565	79186	47.5%	47.3%	0.2%	CGY	70100	78947	47.0%	46.2%	0.8%
CHI	83168	66138	55.7%	55.2%	0.5%	CHI	82751	67299	55.1%	53.0%	2.1%
COL	70047	76081	47.9%	46.8%	1.1%	COL	71122	81042	46.7%	43.8%	2.9%
DAL	71503	68676	51.0%	51.8%	-0.8%	DAL	72564	68407	51.5%	52.3%	-0.8%
DET	78427	71294	52.4%	51.3%	1.1%	DET	80903	71564	53.1%	52.1%	1.0%
EDM	64158	69134	48.1%	43.6%	4.5%	EDM	73104	75767	49.1%	47.3%	1.8%
FLA	66863	66996	50.0%	49.6%	0.4%	FLA	77607	81596	48.7%	50.1%	-1.4%
LAK	74166	68560	52.0%	56.7%	-4.7%	LAK	71689	67554	51.5%	53.1%	-1.6%
MIN	73881	74380	49.8%	48.7%	1.1%	MIN	72799	70235	50.9%	52.0%	-1.1%
MTL	70145	70497	49.9%	48.4%	1.5%	MTL	78141	73283	51.6%	50.7%	0.9%
NJD	82134	75606	52.1%	53.9%	-1.8%	NJD	73067	76110	49.0%	47.0%	2.0%
NSH	69221	70625	49.5%	50.7%	-1.2%	NSH	78931	75954	51.0%	53.6%	-2.6%
NYI	72174	78921	47.8%	49.5%	-1.7%	NYI	78837	80003	49.6%	54.3%	-4.7%
NYR	74251	73506	50.3%	53.5%	-3.2%	NYR	72709	74114	49.5%	49.7%	-0.2%
OTT	75483	71860	51.2%	50.8%	0.4%	OTT	76845	79964	49.0%	47.8%	1.2%
PHI	66436	69555	48.9%	48.2%	0.7%	PHI	77496	77068	50.1%	48.6%	1.5%
PIT	73937	70712	51.1%	50.2%	0.9%	PIT	72515	69791	51.0%	53.8%	-2.8%
SJS	76030	69146	52.4%	54.6%	-2.2%	SJS	74741	73922	50.3%	51.5%	-1.2%
STL	69900	65413	51.7%	53.2%	-1.5%	STL	79850	75108	51.5%	52.3%	-0.8%
TBL	76855	73713	51.0%	51.7%	-0.7%	TBL	72073	66302	52.1%	53.7%	-1.6%
TOR	67529	76066	47.0%	41.6%	5.4%	TOR	64375	68085	48.6%	45.4%	3.2%
VAN	80004	76126	51.2%	52.2%	-1.0%	VAN	71661	69463	50.8%	50.7%	0.1%
WPG	75014	81704	47.9%	49.7%	-1.8%	WPG	73801	75632	49.4%	54.1%	-4.7%
WSH	73379	76030	49.1%	47.5%	1.6%	WSH	77442	76432	50.3%	51.8%	-1.5%

15 Winnipeg Jets, who were second in the league in Fenwick percentage at five-on-five in close situations, but were 20th by this Estimated Possession metric. Through these numbers, we can see that the Jets didn't spend a lot of time with the puck relative to other teams, but tended to take more shots than their opponents. My conclusion is that Winnipeg was careful on defense without the puck, as evidenced by their having the second-least goals allowed per 60 minutes in five-on-five close situations.

We can also look to the other end of the spectrum at a team like the 2014-15 Boston Bruins, who were fourth by Estimated Possession, but 16th in Fenwick close. The Bruins spent more time with the puck relative to their opponent while not getting as many shots off, plus they allowed their opponents minimal time with the puck yet relatively many shots against. My conclusion is their offensive playing style hinges on careful shot selection, or a slower, safer buildup of play.

We can gain more from further development of this method, as each event line in the play-by-play logs contains ample information. We can break down possession for different players, line combinations, game situations, on-ice locations, and the like. Estimated Possession is not a be-all, end-all statistic that renders other statistics less useful, but an additional tool we can use to help understand the game we love.

Jack Ries

Microstat Tracking 2.0: Passes

Passing to set up high-quality scoring chances

What do Jakub Voracek, Joe Thornton, Scott Gomez, Tyler Johnson, and Sidney Crosby all have in common? Of all players with 200+ even-strength minutes in 2014-15, they were the league's top-five passers in terms of setting up scoring chances. Through a tracking project that defines scoring-chance setups as a pass sent into the "home plate area" (from the goalposts to the faceoff dots to the top of the faceoff circle and across) and leading to a shot attempt, these players were the NHL leaders in most frequently setting up these dangerous shot attempts ("scoring chances") (see chart, this page).

To recap: two players traded away from the teams that drafted them, a player whose career was thought to be finished who only made a team through a tryout (not even signing a contract until December 1), an undrafted player who was a key piece of his team's run to the Stanley Cup Final, and the best player in the league.

A hockey player's passing ability can be measured by microstats, akin to earlier microstats like zone entries and zone exits. Microstats help find value where traditional metrics do not show there to be any, and help further explain why a good player has value or a poor player does not. Gomez, in particular, is the poster child for this type of microstat value player. In a league with an increasing focus on analytics, these underappreciated players are about exploiting market inefficiencies. With passing data unavailable except through tracking projects, this is a key inefficiency. Had detailed data been available at developmental levels, a team might have drafted Tyler Johnson. Properly identifying these skills before the player gets to the NHL can be a real advantage.

Looking at the top 10 players who generated scoring chances most frequently from passes, we see a similar, eclectic mix in players 6-10 as we did in the top five: three of the game's top centers, a seventh-round draft pick, and an aging veteran.

The list as a whole includes some of the game's best playmakers. But this is strictly a list of forwards. How can we use passing data to evaluate defensemen?

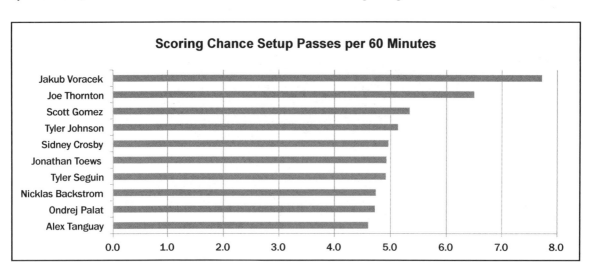

Passing to efficiently gain zone entries

"Puck-moving" defensemen are believed to offer greater value as they transition play from defense to offense more effectively than "defensive" defensemen. These generalized labels are in quotes because the benefit of having additional data is in finding new ways to quantify more of the game. With more data, we can assign a numerical value to the buzzwords we often hear (like "breakout pass" or "first pass"). This is true for "puck possession" and Corsi.

So, in looking at passes occuring in transition that lead to controlled zone entries (which we know are of great importance based on work spearheaded by *Hockey Prospectus 2012-13* contributor Eric Tulsky, now Hockey Analyst with the Carolina Hurricanes), we can quantify how many entry assists defensemen have. As teams break out of their zone, it is often a correctly-timed pass that allows for a clean zone entry. Which defensemen facilitate transition offense the best? Let's have a look (see chart, this page)

Of defensemen with over 200 minutes, Drew Doughty's transition passes led to controlled entries most frequently on a per-60 minute basis. From there, we have a mix of young and veteran defensemen, including some that are commonly thought of as puck movers and some that are not. What is intriguing is that there were two Pittsburgh Penguins defensemen in the top 10, suggesting a few things: 1) The Penguins breakout and neutral zone transition phases were largely successful; 2) Penguins forwards were especially adept at receiving a pass and continuing over the blueline with possession; and 3) the Penguins simply have a skilled group on the back end. Well, we should say had, with the trade of Simon Depres to Anaheim—where he was rightly promoted from a bottom-pairing to middle-pairing role. Kris Letang was just outside the top 10 defensemen.

Identifying undervalued players by highlighting new skillsets

As analytics become more prevalent in hockey and more accepted by those closest to the game, there is a hunger for new ways to analyze the game and evaluate players. Similar to zone exits and zone entries, quantifying puck movement and shot generation provide more metrics to explain more of what happens on the ice.

Currently, we use a player's individual shot attempts or individual scoring chances as a way to measure how much direct impact the player has on his team's offensive output. We can also take a macro approach, looking at how the team does when he is on the ice, represented by on-ice shot attempt totals. However, there is a gap that needs to be quantified.

Players like Scott Gomez and David Rundblad exist in this gap. Both players could be targeted by teams if they feel they are lacking in a specific area. In the case of Gomez, that is a pivot who excels at distributing the puck and creating scoring chances, especially within the offensive zone. In Rundblad's case, it is a defenseman who excels at making passes that generate offensive zone entries. Let's look at the context of these numbers within the entire season.

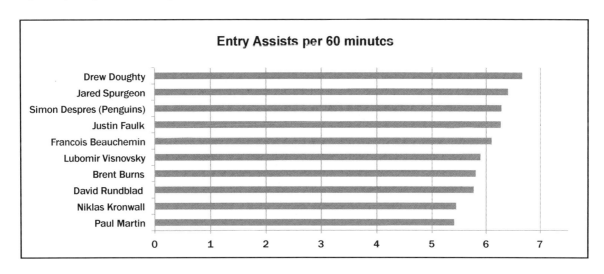

Gomez: His Corsi percentage (47.1%) was not flattering, especially once you consider the favorable relative zone starts (+14.3%) he received. However, the rate at which Gomez generated scoring chances leads us to believe that there is more quality to the team's offense with Gomez on the ice. The War on Ice website allows you to look at "high-danger" scoring chances when a player is on the ice versus when they are off the ice. The Devils received a 6% boost in quality when Gomez was on the ice. In fact, Gomez comes ahead in these types of chances (51.3%) compared to overall possession. In the context of the Devils' offense, Gomez was the point guard carrying the puck in and setting up teammates for quality chances. Without him, a poor offense became almost listless. If there is a team out there who feels their bottom-six wingers need someone to generate offense and provide depth scoring, they could likely pick up Gomez for next to nothing and be quite pleased with the signing. While his overall possession numbers aren't great, and he suffers from a reputation of defensive flaws, Gomez was quite literally the driving force behind the Devils coming out ahead in the highest quality chances. With the right coach and deployment, Gomez can still bring depth scoring to any team in the league.

Rundblad: Rundblad was also frequently deployed in the offensive zone (+18.3% relative zone starts). He took advantage, maintaining excellent possession, good for a 56.9% Corsi percentage. While many will point to that favorable deployment as a significant reason for his strong possession numbers, passing data shows that once the Blackhawks left the offensive zone, Rundblad was instrumental in completing passes to re-enter the zone. And since he didn't start all of his shifts in the offensive zone, Rundblad also made a strong contribution in transitioning out of Chicago's own end and through the neutral zone. The Blackhawks have him signed for the next two seasons at an inexpensive $1 million cap hit. They know their transition game won't fall off with him on the ice.

Do these players come with risks? Yes. But solid depth throughout the lineup is associated with teams that make playoff runs. Allowing those depth players to succeed depends on playing to their strengths and putting them in situations where they are not asked to do what they cannot. Being able to quantify different aspects of play can unearth these strengths and provide valuable insight into what a player can bring to a team.

We know Corsi and puck possession matter, but if a coach walked up to you and asked how to improve his team's Corsi numbers, how would you respond? It is in breaking the possession game down to its components where we can truly attempt to answer that question. It is in bridging the gap between the data the analytics community uses to evaluate players, and quantifying the components of possession that coaches preach to their players.

If a coach tells his GM they are having trouble breaking out of their zone and maintaining possession while entering the offensive zone, a player like Rundblad could be targeted to provide depth on the blue line, and to improve this phase of the game. If the coach feels that, inside the offensive zone, the team simply isn't generating enough quality chances, a player like Gomez could certainly help in that department. Having more of the game quantified can help in identifying players to improve specific aspects of the team.

Passing sequences leading to higher quality chances

Where to go from here? Moving from an isolated event like an entry assist or setting up a scoring chance, there is more work to be done on shot sequencing and various types of passing plays. In the chart below are the shooting percentages for a few shot sequences. Using passing data for the six teams whose entire 2014-15 season was tracked (Chicago, Florida, New Jersey, NY Islanders, NY Rangers, and Washington), we can isolate how effective they were at scoring goals based on specific shot sequences (see chart, next page).

The bottom three categories tell us the shooting percentage that these teams averaged for shots that did not come from a pass, shots that came from all passes, and shots preceded by multiple passes. You can quickly see the likelihood of a goal increases 0.8% if a shot was taken after a completed pass versus a shot that was not preceded by a pass. More importantly, the graph illustrates a 2.4% increase in shooting percentage if the shot was preceded by at least two passes. If a team is completing multiple passes prior to a shot attempt, this sustained offense can now be assigned a quantifiable value.

The remaining three categories—the most dangerous chances—are specific by either type of shot, location, or specific movement of the pass. Players with accurate one-timers can boost a team's shooting per-

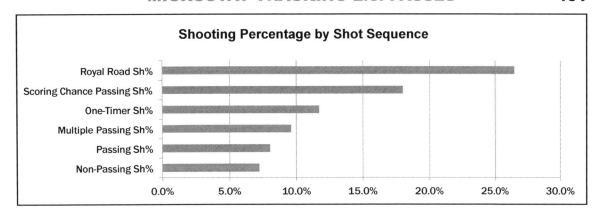

centage due to the higher percentage chance of that type of shot resulting in a goal. Passes sent into the scoring chance, or "home plate area", understandably result in a goal more often than other passes. Passes across the "Royal Road" (which former NHL goaltender Steve Valiquette coined as the line extending from the goal to the top of the faceoff circles), were the most dangerous, as these force the goalie to move laterally, opening up holes in his stance.

Conclusion

Passing microstats open up a number of new ways to evaluate players, allowing for more precise methods for GMs to pinpoint exactly what their team needs.

Sustained offense is what teams should strive to replicate. By quantifying more of the game and looking at how shot sequences originate, there is value to be found in certain players that we might otherwise overlook. This is an area of the game that cannot be ignored any longer.

Additional tracking projects that can provide even further detail will provide the next leap in hockey analysis. More importantly, these projects can provide context around isolated events (shot attempts, passing, zone exits, zone entries, and more) that offer deeper understanding of how events occur. Knowing a shot attempt occurred is relevant, but knowing how something occurred is far more important.

Ryan Stimson

Top 100 NHL Prospects

For the sixth edition of the *Hockey Prospectus*' "Top NHL Prospects", I was struck by the ephemeral nature of prospects. Simply put, a player's prospect lifetime is, by nature, a very short and wondrous thing. The player is drafted and suddenly elevated to the status of "great future hope" for his new team. Within two years, that player has either made it or is on the cusp of making it to the NHL, or he begins to dwindle in terms of expectations. A quick look at last year's list confirms this notion. Many of the repeat candidates are only one or two years removed from draft day. Those who are further removed have either already exhausted their prospect eligibility, or they have been surpassed by younger players who have not yet been afforded the opportunity in the best league in the world but have not had enough time pass by to disappoint fans and the punditry.

So this list is but a snapshot in time, taken at the conclusion of the 2014-15 season, of players in that sweet spot after being drafted or signed by an NHL team, but not yet fully graduated to the NHL and still in their ascendancy.

To retain eligibility for this list, position players cannot have played in 40 NHL games, while goalies are cut off at 25 games. Players over the age of 25 are also excluded from consideration. Ages listed are as of October 7, 2015.

Finally, this list would not have been possible without the diligent contributions of *Hockey Prospectus*' prospect team. While the history of *Hockey Prospectus*' prospect coverage has always been the work of one person—first, for many years, Corey Pronman, and last year, Leslie Treff—this past season, we have taken prospect coverage in an exciting new direction. With the understanding that four eyes are better than two, then 10 eyes must be even better. With that in mind, the prospect team expanded fivefold this year. Under the leadership of Ryan Wagman, who mostly covered the AHL and OHL, the team expanded to include Craig Smith (OHL/QMJHL), David McKnight (QMJHL), Benoit Roy (WHL), and Dennis Schellenberg (Europe). In addition to their home territories, each prospect team member also supplemented coverage with video analysis. This list is dotted throughout with the insight of all five prospect team members.

Without further ado, these are your Top 100 NHL Prospects.

Ryan Wagman

1 Connor McDavid, Center, Edmonton Oilers

2014-15 ranking: Ineligible **Age:** 18
Height: 6'1" **Weight:** 194 **Shoots:** Left
Statistics: 47 GP, 44 G, 76 A, 120 Pts (Erie, OHL)
First round, first overall, 2015

Everything has already been written about McDavid, and it is largely true. One of a handful of players ever granted exceptional status by the CHL, allowing him to begin his junior career one year early, the future #1 pivot in Edmonton is now ready to graduate. His blinding speed and incredible offensive vision make him the odds-on favorite to win the Calder this year. As many have said, this is the best prospect since Sidney Crosby.

2 Jack Eichel, Center, Buffalo Sabres

2014-15 ranking: Ineligible **Age:** 18
Height: 6'2" **Weight:** 196 **Shoots:** Right
Statistics: 40 GP, 26 G, 45 A, 71 Pts (Boston University, Hockey East)
First round, second overall, 2015

If it were not for the young man immediately preceding him on this list, it could also reasonably have been said that Eichel is the best prospect since Sidney Crosby. A sublime skater and stickhandler, the second pick of the draft plays with notable intensity and a responsible two-way game. Even on off-nights, he can turn the game on its head.

3. Teuvo Teravainen, Right Wing, Chicago Blackhawks

2014-15 ranking: 3   Age: 21
Height: 5'11"   Weight: 176   Shoots: Left
Statistics: 39 GP, 6 G, 19 A, 25 Pts (Rockford, AHL). 34 GP, 4 G, 5 A, 9 Pts (Chicago, NHL)
First round, 18th overall, 2012

Had the games-played cutoff for this list included the postseason, Teravainen would not be eligible. In fact, it was the past Stanley Cup playoffs where the creative Finn reminded the 17 teams which overlooked him on draft day in 2012 just how wrong they were. With the concern that his small frame might be diminished in the NHL, he excelled just when space became even more difficult to come by. He is ready to take the mantle as Chicago's second-line center.

4. Leon Draisaitl, Center, Edmonton Oilers

2014-15 ranking: 16 Age: 19
Height: 6'1"   Weight: 209   Shoots: Left
Statistics: 32 GP, 19 G, 34 A, 53 Pts (Kelowna, WHL). 37 GP, 2 G, 7 A, 9 Pts (Edmonton, NHL)
First round, third overall, 2014

As they had done so often in the recent past, the Oilers tried to rush Draisaitl to the NHL as an 18-year-old; the young German was in over his head. Sent back to the WHL with only a few games of prospect eligibility remaining, he reminded the world that his ascension is only a matter of when, not if. With great acceleration and an amazing shot release, he will team with McDavid to make Edmonton must-watch hockey again.

5. Dylan Larkin, Center, Detroit Red Wings

2014-15 ranking: 70 Age: 19
Height: 6'1"   Weight: 192   Shoots: Left
Statistics: 35 GP, 15 G, 32 A, 47 Pts (Michigan, Big 10)
First round, 15th overall, 2014

Leaving the University of Michigan after only a single season, Larkin will put the Red Wings' longstanding practice of lengthy AHL apprenticeships to the test. Between a star turn for the Team USA at the World Junior Championship and finishing 11th in NCAA scoring as a true freshman, the teenage power forward has an exemplary ability to rush the puck and create havoc near the opposing goal.

6. Sam Bennett, Center, Calgary Flames

2014-15 ranking: 9   Age: 19
Height: 6'1"   Weight: 181   Shoots: Left
Statistics: 11 GP, 11 G, 13 A, 24 Pts (Kingston, OHL)
First round, fourth overall, 2014

After raising eyebrows due to his inability to perform even a single pull-up at the 2014 NHL Combine, all was revealed after Bennett underwent shoulder surgery in early October. When he returned late in the season, he actually produced better than he ever had before, which continued to be the case after he joined the Flames for their playoff run. Quick and energetic, he is ready for a top-six NHL role.

7. Sam Reinhart, Center, Buffalo Sabres

2014-15 ranking: 2   Age: 19
Height: 6'1"   Weight: 190   Shoots: Right
Statistics: 47 GP, 19 G, 46 A, 65 Pts (Kootenay, WHL). 9 GP, 0 G, 1 A, 1 Pt (Buffalo, NHL)
First round, second overall, 2014

Whether or not he was ready for the NHL as an 18-year-old, the state of Buffalo hockey was so decrepit last year that it is better that Reinhart was given more time to develop with Kootenay. Reinhart excels as much with his hockey smarts as he does with his physical tools, allowing him to always be in the right place at the right time to make something happen. With the Sabres teardown now complete, expect there to be a place for him on the team.

8. Dylan Strome, Center, Arizona Coyotes

2014-15 ranking: Ineligible   Age: 18
Height: 6'3"   Weight: 185   Shoots: Left
Statistics: 68 GP, 45 G, 84 A, 129 Pts (Erie, OHL)
First round, third overall, 2015

Only by spending two thirds of his season on a roster with Connor McDavid can the OHL's leading scorer be overshadowed. It should not be forgotten that Strome put up most of his points playing on Erie's second line, away from his top-ranked teammate. Unfairly criticized for his skating, Strome is a highly intelligent pivot with the body to line up against shutdown lines and still come out on top.

9 Mitch Marner, Center, Toronto Maple Leafs

2014-15 ranking: Ineligible Age: 18
Height: 5'11" Weight: 161 Shoots: Right
Statistics: 63 GP, 44 G, 82 A, 126 Pts (London, OHL)
First round, fourth overall, 2015

One of the most dazzling puck handlers you are likely to find, the undersized Marner, who patterns his game after Patrick Kane and Doug Gilmour, two other vertically-challenged offensive dynamos, proved himself too good for the OHL as a 17-year-old. His intelligence and elusiveness will help him continue to produce once the opponents get bigger.

10 William Nylander, Center, Toronto Maple Leafs

2014-15 ranking: 14 Age: 19
Height: 5'11" Weight: 170 Shoots: Right
Statistics: 21 GP, 8 G, 12 A, 20 Pts (MODO, SHL). 37 GP, 14 G, 18 A, 32 Pts (Toronto, AHL)
First round, eighth overall, 2015

Nylander is another silky puck handler in the Toronto system. After a brief period of acclimation in the AHL, Nylander began to produce like few teenagers can in the pro circuit. While he still needs to work on strength and his game away from the puck, the son of former NHLer Michael Nylander is dynamic with the puck on his stick.

11 Max Domi, Left Wing/Center, Arizona Coyotes

2014-15 ranking: 37 Age: 20
Height: 5'10" Weight: 201 Shoots: Left
Statistics: 57 GP, 32 G, 70 A, 102 Pts (London, OHL)
First round, 12th overall, 2013

Although stocky like his father, famed pugilist Tie Domi, Max's game could not be more different. A plus-plus skater and puck handler, the former London Knight plays a power game, and is comfortable at any spot on the ice. While it is unclear whether he will play as a center or a winger as a pro, it is certain that he will do so as a top-six player.

12 Nikolaj Ehlers, Left Wing, Winnipeg Jets

2014-15 ranking: 52 Age: 19
Height: 6'0" Weight: 176 Shoots: Left
Statistics: 51 GP, 37 G, 63 A, 100 Pts (Halifax, QMJHL)
First round, ninth overall, 2014

Scoring four fewer points than in his draft-eligible year, it would be simplistic to view Ehlers' age-19 season as a mild disappointment although he played in 12 fewer games this time. A tremendous skater and puck mover in perpetual motion, Ehlers is a threat whenever his team gets possession. Despite his skinny frame, a move to the pro ranks should not change that.

13 Robby Fabbri, Right Wing, St. Louis Blues

2014-15 ranking: Not Ranked (NR) Age: 19
Height: 5'10" Weight: 170 Shoots: Left
Statistics: 30 GP, 25 G, 26 A, 51 Pts (Guelph, OHL)
First round, 21st overall, 2014

After narrowly missing the final cut to open the season as a member of the St. Louis Blues, Fabbri returned to Guelph to pick up where he left off in his thrilling draft-eligible season. An ill-timed high-ankle sprain at the WJC put him out of the lineup for a few months, and out of sorts upon his return, but the feisty skill game that took the Storm to the Memorial Cup tournament in 2014 is still very much in evidence.

14 Josh Morrissey, Defense, Winnipeg Jets

2014-15 ranking: 75 Age: 20
Height: 6'0" Weight: 185 Shoots: Left
Statistics: 47 GP, 13 G, 25 A, 38 Pts (Prince Albert/Kelowna, WHL)
First round, 13th overall, 2013

One of the keys to Canada's victory at the WJC, Morrissey next turned his sights to helping Kelowna, who he joined via trade, to the Memorial Cup final, where the Rockets fell short by a single game. As smooth a puck mover as you will find, Morrissey's game is aided greatly by his high panic threshold. Having also helped Winnipeg's AHL affiliate to the Calder Cup final at age 19, he has more big game experience than most rookies do.

TOP 100 NHL PROSPECTS

15 Mike Reilly, Defense, Minnesota Wild
2014-15 ranking: Not Ranked Age: 22
Height: 6'1" Weight: 183 Shoots: Left
Statistics: 39 GP, 6 G, 36 A, 42 Pts (University of Minnesota, Big 10)
Fourth round, 98th overall, 2011

After he left college, Reilly broke a lot of hearts in central Ohio when he spurned the Blue Jackets, who owned his rights until July. A confident puck handler with a heavy point shot and great vision for hidden passing lanes, the Minnesotan decided to stay in-state, signing as a free agent with the Wild, where he will compete for a spot in their regular blueline rotation.

16 Noah Hanifin, Defense, Carolina Hurricanes
2014-15 ranking: Ineligible Age: 18
Height: 6'2" Weight: 205 Shoots: Left
Statistics: 37 GP, 5 G, 18 A, 23 Pts (Boston College, Hockey East)
First round, fifth overall, 2015

The epitome of the puck-moving two-way defenseman, Hanifin has a very good chance to stick in the Hurricanes lineup as the rare 18-year-old NHL blueliner. Very aware of everything happening on the ice, he is never caught flatfooted and excels at transitions thanks to his top-end speed. Hanifin is too responsible to be considered an offensive blueliner but too dynamic to be considered a shutdown type.

17 Kevin Fiala, Left Wing, Nashville Predators
2014-15 ranking: 28 Age: 19
Height: 5'10" Weight: 187 Shoots: Left
Statistics: 20 GP, 5 G, 9 A, 14 Pts (HV71, SHL). 33 GP, 11 G, 9 A, 20 Pts (Milwaukee, AHL)
First round, 11th overall, 2014

An undersized winger with special puck-moving and passing skills, Fiala has demonstrated his vision and skating at the professional level on two continents before leaving his teen years. He also has enough jam to his game to make the Predators feel comfortable allowing him to get his feet wet as a third liner before graduating him to his more natural spot in the top six.

18 Michael Dal Colle, Left Wing, New York Islanders
2014-15 ranking: 24 Age: 19
Height: 6'2" Weight: 190 Shoots: Left
Statistics: 56 GP, 42 G, 51 A, 93 Pts (Oshawa, OHL)
First round, fifth overall, 2014

With the frame of a power forward and the game of a skill man, Dal Colle can be a man for all seasons. Playing with a chip on his shoulder after not making the Islanders out of camp and receiving a snub from Team Canada for the WJC, Dal Colle upped his offensive production from its already high perch and was one of the driving forces for the Memorial Cup champions from Oshawa. Expect Dal Colle to torture unsuspecting NHL netminders with his weapon of a wristshot this season.

19 Derrick Pouliot, Defense, Pittsburgh Penguins
2014-15 ranking: 30 Age: 21
Height: 6'0" Weight: 203 Shoots: Left
Statistics: 31 GP, 7 G, 17 A, 24 Pts (Wilkes-Barre/Scranton, AHL). 34 GP, 2 G, 5 A, 7 Pts (Pittsburgh, NHL)
First round, eighth overall, 2012

Derrick Pouliot narrowly missed our eligibility cut-off of 40 games and is all but certain to eclipse that mark by the close of October. With Christian Ehrhoff and Paul Martin departing Pittsburgh via free agency, primetime on the Pens' man advantage should be Pouliot's for the taking. He may need to be sheltered to an extent for now, but the former Winterhawk is a future power-play QB.

20 Mathew Barzal, Center, New York Islanders
2014-15 ranking: Ineligible Age: 18
Height: 6'0" Weight: 181 Shoots: Right
Statistics: 44 GP, 12 G, 45 A, 57 Pts (Seattle, WHL)
First round, 16th overall, 2015

As one of the top pure playmakers available in the 2015 draft, one of the surprises of the event was Barzal's fall to the middle of the first round, allowing the Islanders to trade their former fourth-overall pick for the right to select him. Were it not for the knee injury sustained mid-year, there is little reason to think the skilled puck carrier would have remained on the board for as long as he did.

21 Jimmy Vesey, Left Wing, Nashville Predators

2014-15 ranking: Not Ranked　　　　　Age: 22
Height: 6'1"　　　Weight: 194　　　Shoots: Right
Statistics: 37 GP, 22 G, 36 A, 58 Pts (Harvard, ECAC)
Third round, 66th overall, 2012

One of the most dynamic players in the collegiate ranks, the Predators spent the early offseason working Jimmy Vesey hard to get him signed to an entry-level contract, to avoid the type of situation that occurred between Mike Reilly and Columbus. A strong skater and above-average puck handler with a goal-scorer's shot, Vesey also has the muscle and drive to play in the dirty areas of the ice.

22 Darnell Nurse, Defense, Edmonton Oilers

2014-15 ranking: 7　Age: 20
Height: 6'4"　　　Weight: 205　　　Shoots: Left
Statistics: 36 GP, 10 G, 23 A, 33 Pts (Sault Ste. Marie, OHL)
First round, seventh overall, 2013

In spite of gaudy point totals for the Soo Greyhounds, Nurse projects as a shutdown defenseman at the highest level. The rangy blueliner has premium recovery speed, almost assuring an absence of clean breakaways while he is on the ice. One of the smartest moves by the Edmonton's former braintrust was to allow Nurse two extra seasons in the OHL, where he has advanced by leaps and bounds and is now ready for the pro game.

23 Ivan Provorov, Defense, Philadelphia Flyers

2014-15 ranking: Ineligible　　　　　Age: 18
Height: 6'1"　　　Weight: 201　　　Shoots: Left
Statistics: 60 GP, 15 G, 46 A, 61 Pts (Brandon, WHL)
First round, seventh overall, 2015

A mobile and decisive defenseman, Provorov blends the best tools of an offensive defenseman with the physicality and responsibility of a shutdown type. Mobile and owning a heavy shot, the young Russian is a patient player, secure in the knowledge that he has the ability to make the right play if he lets it develop naturally. Having played in North America since he was 14, there is no fear of the "Russian factor" with Provorov.

24 Pavel Buchnevich, Right Wing, New York Rangers

2014-15 ranking: 73　Age: 20
Height: 6'2"　　　Weight: 176　　　Shoots: Left
Statistics: 48 GP, 13 G, 17 A, 30 Pts (Severstal Cherepovets, KHL)
Third round, 75th overall, 2013

The KHL's leading 20-and-under scorer, Buchnevich is a very creative stickhandler, with a fantastic shot release. Although he will spend at least one more season overseas, the lanky winger has teased North American fans with his playmaking skills over the past two WJCs. As talented as he is, Buchnevich is unselfish and has no qualms about passing to a better positioned teammate.

25 Shea Theodore, Defense, Anaheim Ducks

2014-15 ranking: 63　Age: 20
Height: 6'2"　　　Weight: 182　　　Shoots: Left
Statistics: 43 GP, 13 G, 35 A, 48 Pts (Seattle, WHL)
First round, 26th overall, 2013

Like most 20-and-under players, Theodore could stand to put on some weight. That is about the extent of his weaknesses. An intelligent defender who reads the play well at both ends and contributes throughout the 200 feet of the rink, Theodore profiles as a strong #2 or #3 defenseman. His mobility is an asset in both directions and he is as likely to lead a two-on-one as he is to be the man back to break one up at the other end.

26 Mikko Rantanen, Left Wing, Colorado Avalanche

2014-15 ranking: Ineligible　　　　　Age: 18
Height: 6'4"　　　Weight: 212　　　Shoots: Left

Statistics: 56 GP, 9 G, 19 A, 28 Pts (TPS, Liiga)
First round, 10th overall, 2015

With 33% more points than the runner-up amongst 19-and-under scorers in the highest league in Finland, Rantanen was his country's most effective performer in an otherwise disappointing showing at the WJC. A confident stickhandler, he can weave past opposing defenders or bullrush through. His physicality will lead to many power plays for his team. Combined with a powerful wristshot, Rantanen was one of the more NHL-ready players in the 2015 draft.

27 Jakub Vrana, Right Wing, Washington Capitals

2014-15 ranking: 53   Age: 19
Height: 5'11"   Weight: 185   Shoots: Left
Statistics: 44 GP, 12 G, 12 A, 24 Pts (Linkoping, SHL)
First round, 13th overall, 2014

A versatile forward who can play on both wings, Vrana took a huge step forward last year, his first in the SHL. Owning a great release on a powerful wristshot, he is the type of player who excels at finding gaps in coverage to put that shot to use, or to find a more open teammate. After the Swedish season ended, he had a strong audition in the AHL, with 11 points in 13 regular season and playoff contests for Hershey.

28 Nick Ritchie, Left Wing, Anaheim Ducks

2014-15 ranking: 65   Age: 19
Height: 6'2"   Weight: 225   Shoots: Left
Statistics: 48 GP, 29 G, 33 A, 62 Pts (Peterborough/Sault Ste. Marie, OHL)
First round, 10th overall, 2014

A man-child on skates, Ritchie has surprisingly soft and dexterous hands for a player who makes his mark by driving the net. His exceptional stickhandling is aided by the long reach afforded to him by virtue of his sheer size. His regular season, interrupted by the WJC, injuries, and a trade, was topped by a fantastic postseason in which he scored 13 times in 14 games, reminding everyone of his above-average finishing skills headlined by a powerful wristshot.

29 Ivan Barbashev, Center, St. Louis Blues

2014-15 ranking: Not Ranked   Age: 19
Height: 6'1"   Weight: 190   Shoots: Left
Statistics: 57 GP, 45 G, 50 A, 95 Pts (Moncton, QMJHL)
Second round, 33rd overall, 2014

To go from the 33rd pick in 2014 to the 29th-best prospect in the sport in 2015 is an achievement borne on the back of a stellar season with Moncton as well as a star turn at the WJC for silver medalist Russia. Barbashev finished seventh in QMJHL scoring, third once we remove overagers from the equation. With a mixture of creative offensive flair and bulldog strength, the Blues have another dynamic talent to add to their already strong crew.

30 Marko Dano, Center, Chicago Blackhawks

2014-15 ranking: Not Ranked   Age: 20
Height: 6'0"   Weight: 198   Shoots: Left
Statistics: 39 GP, 11 G, 8 A, 19 Pts (Springfield, AHL). 35 GP, 8 G, 13 A, 21 Pts (Columbus, NHL)
First round, 27th overall, 2013

An important part of the return to Columbus in their offseason trade for Stanley Cup hero Brandon Saad, Dano actually produced more in his NHL debut than he had in similar time in the AHL. Now beginning to fill out his frame, the creative Slovakian forward packs a hard, accurate shot. His high energy level gives him a good chance to break into the always-competitive Chicago lineup in a bottom-six role as he bides his time for more prime opportunities.

31 Andrei Vasilevsky, Goaltender, Tampa Bay Lightning

2014-15 ranking: 10   Age: 21
Height: 6'3"   Weight: 201   Catches: Left
Statistics: 25 GP, 2.45 GAA, .917 Sv% (Syracuse, AHL). 16 GP, 2.36 GAA, .918 Sv% (Tampa Bay, NHL)
First round, 19th overall, 2012

Once again the top goaltending prospect in hockey, Vasilevsky took his first steps towards justifying the faith placed in him by taking over the backup goalie role from veteran Evgeni Nabokov at midseason. The Russian netminder has good size, strong legs, and very good lateral movement and rebound control. He is ready for a greater NHL role, which will be delayed by a few months due to a blood clot discovered in the summer.

32 Nikita Scherbak, Center, Montreal Canadiens

2014-15 ranking: 99   Age: 19
Height: 6'1"   Weight: 174   Shoots: Left
Statistics: 65 GP, 27 G, 55 A, 82 Pts (Everett, WHL)
First round, 26th overall, 2014

Whether playmaking or carrying the puck himself, Scherbak is an exciting offensive talent. While he has plenty of room for added muscle, the young Russian has enough strength to go through defenders when he is not going around them. He profiles as a puck-possession center who should find a spot on the second line once he rounds out his defensive game.

33 Kyle Connor, Center, Winnipeg Jets

2014-15 ranking: Ineligible   Age: 18
Height: 6'1"   Weight: 183   Shoots: Left
Statistics: 56 GP, 34 G, 46 A, 80 Pts (Youngstown, USHL)
First round, 17th overall, 2015

An excellent stickhandler and plus skater, Connor has the look of a primetime offensive contributor for the Jets once both parties decide that he has learned enough under Red Berenson in Ann Arbor. The feeling here is that Connor's tools will translate well from the USHL to the college game and beyond, although a move to left wing may be in the cards.

34 Ryan Pulock, Defense, New York Islanders

2014-15 ranking: 26   Age: 21
Height: 6'1"   Weight: 212   Shoots: Right
Statistics: 54 GP, 17 G, 12 A, 29 Pts (Bridgeport, AHL)
First round, 15th overall, 2013

Among the leading goal scorers of AHL defensemen, Pulock was a full two years younger than the next youngest blueliner above him on that list. Any perceived lack of mobility is more than made up for by his booming point shot. As the trade of Griffin Reinhart to Edmonton implies, the Islanders agree with that assessment and are clearing the way for Pulock to play in Brooklyn.

35 Zach Werenski, Defense, Columbus Blue Jackets

2014-15 ranking: Ineligible   Age: 18
Height: 6'2"   Weight: 206   Shoots: Left
Statistics: 35 GP, 9 G, 16 A, 25 Pts (Michigan, Big 10)
First round, eighth overall, 2015

A prototypical big and mobile blueliner, Werenski was the youngest defenseman in the NCAA last year, and by season's end, he was Michigan's number one rearguard. Calm under pressure with plus puck-moving abilities, his NHL ceiling is to fulfill a similar role with the Blue Jackets. However, more development time is necessary for him to reach those heights.

36 Timo Meier, Right Wing, San Jose Sharks

2014-15 ranking: Ineligible   Age: 18
Height: 6'1"   Weight: 209   Shoots: Left
Statistics: 61 GP, 44 G, 46 A, 90 Pts (Halifax, QMJHL)
First round, ninth overall, 2015

A bulldozer on skates, Meier has uncommon offensive skills for a player of his stature. While not a burner, he is quick for his size and very effective when he plays a north-south game. Much of his scoring is as the result of advanced hockey sense. His timing, whether for shooting or passing, can create seams for instant offense.

37 Jared McCann, Center, Vancouver Canucks

2014-15 ranking: Not Ranked   Age: 19
Height: 6'0"   Weight: 185   Shoots: Left
Statistics: 56 GP, 34 G, 47 A, 81 Pts (Sault Ste. Marie, OHL)
First round, 24th overall, 2014

Known for his responsible two-way game when drafted in the late first round by Vancouver, McCann took a few steps forward from an offensive production standpoint. While he has always had a tremendous shot—both wrist and slap—his sense of when and where to use it came to fruition, resulting in a big uptick in points. Expect him to represent Canada at the next WJC as he completes his amateur career.

38 Nick Merkley, Center, Arizona Coyotes

2014-15 ranking: Ineligible   Age: 19
Height: 5'11"   Weight: 190   Shoots: Right
Statistics: 72 GP, 20 G, 70 A, 90 Pts (Kelowna,

WHL)
First round, 30th overall, 2015

Merkley falling to the final pick of the first round was the surprise of the 2015 NHL Entry Draft. An elite playmaker with a non-stop motor, his point totals obscure the fact that he is an excellent defender who is surprisingly physical and a veritable weapon on the penalty kill. He also added 27 points in 19 playoff games as the Rockets won the WHL championship and nearly won the Memorial Cup.

39 Griffin Reinhart, Defense, Edmonton Oilers
2014-15 ranking: 15   Age: 21
Height: 6'3"   Weight: 216   Shoots: Left
Statistics: 59 GP, 7 G, 15 A, 22 Pts (Bridgeport, AHL)
First round, fourth overall, 2012

A heavy-set, physical defenseman who excels in his own end, Reinhart is coming off an underwhelming first professional season. While whispers of mobility issues followed him around at Bridgeport, potentially contributing to his trade to Edmonton, home of his junior exploits, a deeper look reveals a player in need of more careful coaching. Like brother Sam, listed above, Griffin succeeds as much due to smarts as to skills.

40 Oliver Bjorkstrand, Right Wing, Columbus Blue Jackets
2014-15 ranking: 15   Age: 20
Height: 6'0"   Weight: 174   Shoots: Right
Statistics: 59 GP, 63 G, 55 A, 118 Pts (Portland, WHL)
Third round, 89th overall, 2013

The WHL's leading scorer, with more than one goal scored per game, Bjorkstrand unsurprisingly knows what to do in the offensive end. He is knocked for a slight frame and for questions about his defensive skills, although the latter is unjust. When a player is so good at controlling the pace of play, his best defense is his great offense. The AHL presents a great test for the Danish highlight reel.

41 Travis Konecny, Center, Philadelphia Flyers
2014-15 ranking: Ineligible   Age: 18
Height: 5'10"   Weight: 176   Shoots: Right
Statistics: 60 GP, 29 G, 39 A, 68 Pts (Ottawa, OHL)
First round, 24th overall, 2015

A high-motor skater with great agility, Konecny's physical play belies his slight physique. There is some feeling that his rambunctious style may get in the way of increased offensive production, as his puck skills border on the sublime and there is no other plausible explanation for what are ultimately decent numbers. The Flyers traded up to select him, indicating that they also see the immense upside.

42 Anthony Mantha, Right Wing, Detroit Red Wings
2014-15 ranking: 38   Age: 21
Height: 6'5"   Weight: 205   Shoots: Left
Statistics: 62 GP, 15 G, 18 A, 33 Pts (Grand Rapids, AHL)
First round, 20th overall, 2013

Coming off consecutive 50-goal seasons in the QMJHL to score only 15 as a rookie professional had to rank as a disappointment for both Mantha and the Detroit organization. Between rumors of poor work ethic and poor marks for both skating and defensive zone play, the prospect still retains his core skillset which rotates around his whiplike wrist shot. Expect a big step up in a repeat engagement at Grand Rapids.

43 Brandon Gormley, Defense, Colorado Avalanche
2014-15 ranking: 20   Age: 23
Height: 6'1"   Weight: 187   Shoots: Left
Statistics: 23 GP, 3 G, 7 A, 10 Pts (Portland, AHL). 27 GP, 2 G, 2 A, 4 Pts (Arizona, NHL)
First round, 13th overall, 2010

On the verge of graduating out of prospecthood, Gormley should cement his place in the NHL before attrition lowers his profile. While he does not play a flashy game, the Moncton alumnus stays clam under pressure, with a solid game in his own end. The offense he produced as a junior has diminished as a pro, although his AHL numbers have been respectable. He should be ready to assume a steady spot on the third pairing with the Avalanche, who acquired him in trade this September.

44 Lawson Crouse, Left Wing, Florida Panthers
2014-15 ranking: Ineligible   Age: 18
Height: 6'4"   Weight: 212   Shoots: Left
Statistics: 56 GP, 29 G, 22 A, 51 Pts (Kingston, OHL)

First round, 11th overall, 2015

A large man with soft hands, defensive responsibility, and a mean streak, Crouse elicits visions of a front-line power forward when he is on his game. His strength is in the 95th percentile of all junior-aged players, while his skill level—though not as high—is still more than respectable, easily in the upper quartile. While there is an outside shot that Crouse makes the Panthers as an 18-year-old, his development would be assisted by one more season in Kingston.

45 Anthony De Angelo, Defense, Tampa Bay Lightning

2014-15 ranking: 98   Age: 19
Height: 5'10"   Weight: 176   Shoots: Right
Statistics: 55 GP, 25 G, 64 A, 89 Pts (Sarnia/Sault Ste. Marie, OHL)
First round, 19th overall, 2014

When considering De Angelo's gaudy point totals coming from the blueline, it is helpful to note that the numbers were not nearly as high before being traded from Windsor to the powerhouse Soo Greyhounds. An aggressive defenseman with plus gap control to help mitigate his small stature, De Angelo has almost mesmerizing patience with the puck in the offensive end. His straight-ahead speed will also help him make up for some unnecessary aggression.

46 Yevgeni Svechnikov, Left Wing, Detroit Red Wings

2014-15 ranking: Ineligible   Age: 18
Height: 6'2"   Weight: 201   Shoots: Left
Statistics: 55 GP, 32 G, 46 A, 78 Pts (Cape Breton, QMJHL)
First round, 19th overall, 2015

A prototypical Red Wings draftee, Svechnikov knows that the best method of defense is to maintain possession of the puck. This is something the Russian teenager can achieve through strength on the stick when puck handling as well as the necessary patience to hold on until a good opportunity arises. Big and rangy, Svechnikov has adapted quickly to the North American game and is no stranger to its physical aspects.

47 Madison Bowey, Defense, Washington Capitals

2014-15 ranking: 96   Age: 20
Height: 6'2"   Weight: 207   Shoots: Right
Statistics: 58 GP, 17 G, 43 A, 60 Pts (Kelowna, WHL)
Second round, 53rd overall, 2013

The defenseman factory that is Kelowna has produced another in their distinguished line. In spite of surpassing the point-per-game mark for the WHL champion Rockets, Bowey's best skill is his shot-blocking prowess. He may seem to be completely out of a play, but no sooner does the opposing skater rear back to shoot, than Bowey emerges from out of nowhere, sliding across the ice to nullify the shooting lane. He projects as a #2 or #3 blueliner on a good team.

48 Chris Bigras, Defense, Colorado Avalanche

2014-15 ranking: 105 Age: 20
Height: 6'1"   Weight: 194   Shoots: Left
Statistics: 62 GP, 20 G, 51 A, 71 Pts (Owen Sound, OHL)
Second round, 32nd overall, 2013

Bigras responded to a rough training camp with Colorado and a subpar start to his season (which led to his being passed over for selection to Canada's WJC squad despite being a feature player at age 19) by closing his OHL career with an offensive bang. Mobile with plus puck skills, a second-pairing future is still very much within reach, and considering the depth of the Avalanche system, sooner rather than later.

49 Scott Laughton, Center, Philadelphia Flyers

2014-15 ranking: 35   Age: 21
Height: 6'1"   Weight: 190   Shoots: Left
Statistics: 39 GP, 14 G, 13 A, 27 Pts (Lehigh Valley, AHL). 31 GP, 2 G, 4 A, 6 Pts (Philadelphia, NHL)
First round, 20th overall, 2012

While his fitful NHL experience showed that Laughton needed some time to develop in the AHL, his play on the farm justified his standing as one of the top prospects in the Flyers system. A responsible player with the ability to take over a shift with smart puck play and offensive instincts, Laughton should be ready to take over a middle-six center role in Philadelphia, with more tangible results to boot.

50 Pavel Zacha, Center, New Jersey Devils

2014-15 ranking: Ineligible Age: 18
Height: 6'3" Weight: 212 Shoots: Left
Statistics: 37 GP, 16 G, 18 A, 34 Pts (Sarnia, OHL)
First round, sixth overall, 2015

Those who like Zacha point to his obvious tools, including strong skating and an above-average shot. Those two attributes are coupled with his unmistakable physical acumen, as the Czech import is simply bigger and stronger than the vast majority of his peers at any level. They see a power forward with a two-way game. His detractors point to his point totals and wonder at what is missing that holds his numbers down. Between injuries, the WJC, and suspensions, there is more to his game than his production implies. Look for it to emerge this season.

51 Adrian Kempe, Center, Los Angeles Kings

2014-15 ranking: 93 Age: 19
Height: 6'2" Weight: 187 Shoots: Left
Statistics: 50 GP, 5 G, 12 A, 17 Pts (MODO, SHL)
First round, 29th overall, 2014

The pride of the L.A. Kings' system, Kempe is a natural finisher, in spite of his meager point totals while playing against men in Sweden. Between his plus speed and a sharp wristshot, the teenager will always be a threat to score when he is on the ice. Given more ice-time in the AHL than he received with MODO, that skillset will lead to increased production.

52 Thomas Chabot, Defense, Ottawa Senators

2014-15 ranking: Ineligible Age: 18
Height: 6'2" Weight: 181 Shoots: Left
Statistics: 66 GP, 12 G, 29 A, 41 Pts (Saint John, QMJHL)
First round, 18th overall, 2015

Among the strongest skating defensemen in last year's draft class, Chabot is very comfortable leading the rush into the opposing end. That said, he does not lack for knowledge of his defensive responsibilities. While he can stand to fill out more, the young blue-liner does not shy away from physical play. Expect to see more maturity from his game as he better learns when to take risks and when to be cautious.

53 Nicolas Petan, Center, Winnipeg Jets

2014-15 ranking: 81 Age: 20
Height: 5'9" Weight: 172 Shoots: Left
Statistics: 54 GP, 15 G, 74 A, 89 Pts (Portland, WHL)
Second round, 43rd overall, 2013

An elusive skater with a penchant for dangling, Petan can be a mesmerizing stickhandler when at his best. His assist-heavy stat line has become more and more pronounced since his draft year, a function of a decline in goals while his playmaking has remained steady. While his hands make him a threat in the offensive zone, his lack of size portends struggles in his own end.

54 Conor Hellebuyck, Goaltender, Winnipeg Jets

2014-15 ranking: Not Ranked Age: 22
Height: 6'4" Weight: 201 Catches: Left
Statistics: 58 GP, 2.51 GAA, .921 Sv% (St. John's, AHL)
Fifth round, 130th overall, 2012

A former winner of the Mike Richter Award given to the NCAA's best goaltender, Hellebuyck turned pro early and put together a strong rookie season for the Jets' AHL affiliate in St. John's. The UMass-Lowell alum combines prototypical netminder size with sound positioning and strong composure. He is also a workhorse, having played in five more games than any other AHL netminder.

55 Jansen Harkins, Center, Winnipeg Jets

2014-15 ranking: Ineligible Age: 18
Height: 6'1" Weight: 183 Shoots: Left
Statistics: 70 GP, 20 G, 59 A, 79 Pts (Prince George, WHL)
Second round, 47th overall, 2015

One of the steals of the 2015 draft, Harkins combines with Kyle Connor and Jack Roslovic to give the Jets an astounding influx of high-end talent. The Prince George pivot is a smart, two-way center, earning above-average grades in every facet of the game, but without any one area in which he truly excels. Harkins profiles as a solid second-line center at the next level, although he is not a player who would be served by leaving the WHL early.

56 Connor Brown, Right Wing, Toronto Maple Leafs

2014-15 ranking: Not Ranked   Age: 21
Height: 5'11"   Weight: 170   Shoots: Right
Statistics: 76 GP, 21 G, 40 A, 61 Pts (Toronto, AHL)
Sixth round, 156th overall, 2012

After leading the OHL in scoring as an overager, Brown led all AHL rookies in points, proving that his junior-level success went far beyond playing with Connor McDavid. The winger has an excellent shot and release which he combines with above-average vision in the offensive zone. Although undersized, Brown keeps his stick active in the neutral zone and has shown a penchant for forcing turnovers. He may be ready to contribute in the NHL.

57 Alex Tuch, Right Wing, Minnesota Wild

2014-15 ranking: 66   Age: 19
Height: 6'4"   Weight: 220   Shoots: Right
Statistics: 37 GP, 14 G, 14 A, 28 Pts (Boston College, Hockey East)
First round, 18th overall, 2014

A large man with plus puck skills, Tuch has prototypical power-forward size and style. Active in all three zones, Tuch can contribute both with the puck and without it. With the puck, the big winger can carry the biscuit across the lines and stickhandle his way out of potential trouble. Without the puck, he is a physical player who will punish the opponent who doesn't hear his approaching footsteps. If there is a weakness, it is in his skating, as his first-step quickness lacks.

58 Joel Eriksson Ek, Center, Minnesota Wild

2014-15 ranking: Ineligible   Age: 18
Height: 6'2"   Weight: 183   Shoots: Left
Statistics: 25 GP, 21 G, 11 A, 32 Pts (Farjestad J20, SuperElit). 34 GP, 4 G, 2 A, 6 Pts (Farjestad, SHL)
First round, 20th overall, 2015

A hard-nosed two-way center, Eriksson Ek has proven himself to be an effective player in all three zones. A North American style player, the Swedish teenager makes up for slightly subpar skating with a very strong shot that has allowed him to score nearly one goal per game in the Swedish junior ranks. He should stick with the men for good this year, playing heavier minutes in tougher situations before he is ready to cross the pond.

59 Adam Clendening, Defense, Pittsburgh Penguins

2014-15 ranking: Not Ranked   Age: 22 Height: 6'0"   Weight: 194   Shoots: Right
Statistics: 49 GP, 2 G, 16 A, 18 Pts (Rockford/Utica, AHL). 21 GP, 1 G, 3 A, 4 Pts (Chicago/Vancouver, NHL)
Second round, 36th overall, 2011

A smooth all-around defender, Clendening, played regularly with Vanouver in the NHL down the stretch, before the brain trust elected to use him for the AHL playoffs instead of the NHL variety. Although he has produced far better AHL numbers in past seasons, the totality of the Boston University alum's game should allow him to grow into a second-pairing defender over time. He may get the chance to continue that growth this year with Pittsburgh, who acquired him in July.

60 Jakub Zboril, Defense, Boston Bruins

2014-15 ranking: Ineligible   Age: 18
Height: 6'1"   Weight: 185   Shoots: Left
Statistics: 44 GP, 13 G, 20 A, 33 Pts (Saint John, QMJHL)
First round, 13th overall, 2015

Much like his junior teammate Chabot, Zboril is a mobile, physical blueliner who can hurt the opposition in all three zones, with and without the puck. A smart player who minimizes mental mistakes, he has all of the tools to eventually become a top-pairing defender. Chabot ranks higher on this list due to elite skating, although the Czech import has nothing to be ashamed of in that department.

61 Brock Boeser, Right Wing, Vancouver Canucks

2014-15 ranking: Ineligible   Age: 18
Height: 6'1"   Weight: 192   Shoots: Right
Statistics: 57 GP, 35 G, 33 A, 68 Pts (Waterloo, USHL)
First round, 23rd overall, 2015

Boeser is a pure goal scorer who tied for the USHL lead in that category. Electric in the offensive end and very strong on the puck, the North Dakota commit can be very hard to defend against. While his puck play borders on the elite, Boeser will need to show that same level of commitment in his own end at the NCAA level.

62 Calvin Pickard, Goaltender, Colorado Avalanche

2014-15 ranking: Not Ranked	Age: 23
Height: 6'1"	Weight: 198	Catches: Left
Statistics: 50 GP, 2.61 GAA, .917 Sv% (Lake Erie, AHL). 16 GP, 2.35 GAA, .932 Sv%
Second round, 49th overall, 2010

A fairly run-of-the-mill AHL netminder with strong prospect pedigree, Pickard was elevated to top prospect discussion after an NHL run in late December in which he carried the Avalanche during an injury to incumbent starter Semyon Varlamov. His high-danger save percentage (.884) was better than any other netminder with at least 600 minutes of even-strength ice time. Economical, but somewhat inconsistent, Pickard should receive many more NHL opportunities.

63 Cole Cassels, Center, Vancouver Canucks

2014-15 ranking: Not Ranked	Age: 20
Height: 6'1"	Weight: 183	Shoots: Right
Statistics: 54 GP, 30 G, 51 A, 81 Pts (Oshawa, OHL)
Third round, 85th overall, 2013

During last year's run through the OHL playoffs and to the Memorial Cup title, Cassels proved that he can play a disciplined game without having his defensive aptitude or physicality suffer, a previous question mark. He was the prime reason Oshawa was able to shut down Connor McDavid in the OHL final. The son of Andrew Cassels also brings a robust offensive game to the table, with above-average passing and finishing skills.

64 Daniel Sprong, Right Wing, Pittsburgh Penguins

2014-15 ranking: Ineligible	Age: 18
Height: 6'0"	Weight: 183	Shoots: Right
Statistics: 68 GP, 39 G, 49 A, 88 Pts (Charlottetown, QMJHL)
Second round, 46th overall, 2013

An agile skater and all-around offensive weapon, Sprong's hands suggest a monster ceiling in terms of point production. While his compete level and attention to detail in his own zone come into question, the excitement he can bring at the other end can only be matched by a few others on this list. While the risk of busting remains high, it is more than balanced by the boom potential.

65 Anthony Beauvillier, Left Wing, New York Islanders

2014-15 ranking: Ineligible	Age: 18
Height: 5'10"	Weight: 170	Shoots: Left
Statistics: 67 GP, 42 G, 52 A, 94 Pts (Shawinigan, QMJHL)
First round, 28th overall, 2013

An undersized offensive sparkplug, the dynamic Beauvillier ranked as the top-scoring 18-and-under player in the QMJHL. For teams like the Islanders, who could get past his short and lean frame, they see a high-end puck handler with tricky hands. He protects the puck well and needs only the bare minimum of space to get into shooting or passing position. He does not need to fill out much to remain a threat at higher levels.

66 Denis Guryanov, Right Wing, Dallas Stars

2014-15 ranking: Ineligible	Age: 18
Height: 6'2"	Weight: 190	Shoots: Left
Statistics: 23 GP, 15 G, 10 A, 25 Pts (Lada Togliatti, MHL)
First round, 12th overall, 2015

On a per-game basis, Guryanov was the top scoring threat in the Russian junior league. A sniper with soft hands, the winger projects as a front line scorer in North America who can find twine with both his slapshot and wristshot. While it is unknown when he will leave Russia, his game already fits the North American style, as he is physical, defensively responsible, and mobile. Although he may have been an overdraft at 12th, there is no question that Guryanov is a fine prospect.

67 Jeremy Roy, Defense, San Jose Sharks

2014-15 ranking: Ineligible	Age: 18
Height: 6'0"	Weight: 185	Shoots: Right
Statistics: 46 GP, 5 G, 38 A, 43 Pts (Sherbrooke, QMJHL)
First round, 12th overall, 2015

While unremarkable to look at, Roy's whole is greater than the sum of its parts, which tends to be the case with defensemen of high intelligence. As he lacks the size to be a crushing blueliner, he takes care of his own end through smart body positioning and timely stickchecks. The gap between Roy today and a second-pairing NHL blueliner is not too large.

68. Joonas Donskoi, Right Wing, San Jose Sharks

2014-15 ranking: Not Ranked Age: 23
Height: 6'0"   Weight: 187   Shoots: Right
Statistics: 58 GP, 19 G, 30 A, 49 Pts (Karpat, Liiga)
Fourth round, 99th overall, 2010

Unable to come to terms with the Panthers, who drafted him in 2010, Donskoi stayed home in Finland, slowly honing his game until he broke out last year to finish fifth in Liiga scoring. Possessing size, skill, and speed, Donskoi should be able to fit in a second-line role after he acclimates himself to the North American game. A stellar turn at the recent World Championships indicates that he is ready.

69. Josh Ho-Sang, Right Wing, New York Islanders

2014-15 ranking: Not Ranked Age: 19
Height: 6'0"   Weight: 170   Shoots: Right
Statistics: 60 GP, 17 G, 64 A, 81 Pts (Windsor/Niagara, OHL)
First round, 28th overall, 2014

One of the most creative stickhandlers not yet in the NHL, Ho-Sang stands out for the way he can carry the puck into the zone and proceed to create deadly scoring chances by skating himself into the clear, puck-handling through traffic, or finding an open teammate with an incisive pass. The knocks on Ho-Sang remain his commitment to defense and a personality that has rubbed more than a few hockey lifers the wrong way.

70. Jacob de la Rose, Center, Montreal Canadiens

2014-15 ranking: Not Ranked Age: 20
Height: 6'3"   Weight: 198   Shoots: Left
Statistics: 37 GP, 6 G, 5 A, 11 Pts (Hamilton, AHL). 33 GP, 4 G, 2 A, 6 Pts (Montreal, NHL)
Second round, 34th overall, 2013

While de la Rose has never impressed with his offensive production, he has always been among the youngest at his level, including last year, splitting his age-19 season between the AHL and NHL. The Swedish center is one of the better defensive forwards among eligible prospects, with enough speed, strength, and creativity to envision a productive third- or even second-line pivot once he gets fully acclimated to the North American game.

71. Julius Honka, Defense, Dallas Stars

2014-15 ranking: 90 Age: 19
Height: 5'10"   Weight: 181   Shoots: Right
Statistics: 68 GP, 8 G, 23 A, 31 Pts (Texas, AHL)
First round, 14th overall, 2014

Because of his above-average smarts and quickness, Honka's size will not prevent him from growing into a role as a second-pairing defender with first unit power-play duties. A decisive puck mover, he is more than comfortable carrying the load from his own zone into the offensive end. An excellent low slapshot is also a weapon, as it will lead to plenty of rebounds or tip opportunities for teammates. Having thrived as a teenager in the AHL, the NHL is not far off.

72. Jordan Schmaltz, Defense, St. Louis Blues

2014-15 ranking: Not Ranked Age: 21
Height: 6'2"   Weight: 192   Shoots: Right
Statistics: 42 GP, 4 G, 24 A, 28 Pts (North Dakota, NCHC)
First round, 25th overall, 2012

Another mobile two-way defender, Schmaltz was a reliable point man for North Dakota for three seasons. Owning a very hard shot, its general lack of accuracy tends to lead to assists rather than direct scoring opportunities. On the other hand, his gap control, trustworthy positioning, and smart passing help control the flow of the game and ensure that his team has a possession edge. Schmaltz will receive his first taste of professional hockey this season.

73. Vladislav Kamenev, Center, Nashville Predators

2014-15 ranking: 62 Age: 19
Height: 6'2"   Weight: 203   Shoots: Left
Statistics: 41 GP, 6 G, 4 A, 10 Pts (Metallurg Magnitogorsk, KHL)
Second round, 42nd overall, 2014

A large and skilled center, Kamenev's most notable traits are his passing abilities and sense of anticipation for where the puck will be and when it will be there. As with many teenagers playing in the KHL (or other senior European leagues) his numbers need to be taken with a grain of salt as he received very limited ice-time in Magnitogorsk. Now coming to North America and expected to spend time in the AHL, we will know much more about Kamenev next summer.

74 Michael McCarron, Right Wing, Montreal Canadiens

2014-15 ranking: Not Ranked Age: 20
Height: 6'6" Weight: 225 Shoots: Right
Statistics: 56 GP, 28 G, 40 A, 68 Pts (London/Oshawa, OHL)
First round, 25th overall, 2013

While McCarron will never be a plus skater, he has improved that facet—along with nearly every other part of his game—tremendously over the last calendar year. He always had the size, but last year, he put the pieces in place and became a better hockey player, better utilizing his plus wristshot and his off-puck play. McCarron has also lined up at center and may be tried there at the next level.

75 Brady Skjei, Defense, New York Rangers

2014-15 ranking: 71 Age: 21
Height: 6'3" Weight: 205 Shoots: Left
Statistics: 33 GP, 1 G, 9 A, 10 Pts (Minnesota, Big 10)
First round, 28th overall, 2012

The name of the game for Skjei is mobility. Not a flashy defender, the former Golden Gopher does his best work when transitioning the puck from his own end to the neutral zone. He is actually a decent stickhandler, which is aptly demonstrated when he feints to gain space to more safely execute his exit passes. The Rangers see a potential shutdown defenseman in the near future in Skjei, who has left school one year early to begin his pro career.

76 Riley Barber, Right Wing, Washington Capitals

2014-15 ranking: Not Ranked Age: 21
Height: 6'0" Weight: 198 Shoots: Right
Statistics: 38 GP, 20 G, 20 A, 40 Pts (Miami University, NCHC)
Sixth round, 167th overall, 2012

Another player who succeeds despite average-at-best skating, Barber more than gets by on what he has due to smarts, good positioning, and a deadly snapshot. After three seasons of consistent scoring at Miami University, including two star turns for the American squad at the WJC, Barber is ready for the pro game. His frame should be able to withstand the rigors inherent in the enhanced schedule, and his hands should allow him to continue to produce offensively.

77 Andreas Johnson, Left Wing, Toronto Maple Leafs

2014-15 ranking: Not Ranked Age: 21
Height: 5'10" Weight: 176 Shoots: Left
Statistics: 55 GP, 22 G, 13 A, 35 Pts (Frolunda, SHL)
Seventh round, 202nd overall, 2012

The top 21-and-under scorer in the SHL, Johnson is an undersized offensive dynamo. Between his skating, shooting, and puckhandling, he has the full breadth of tools you would want in a top-six player. Skilled at finding gaps in coverage to get himself open for passes, he will have to prove that he can do the same in the smaller rinks of North America. As he will return to Frolunda for another season, that question will remain unanswered for one more year.

78 Nick Shore, Center, Los Angeles Kings

2014-15 ranking: Not Ranked Age: 23
Height: 6'0" Weight: 190 Shoots: Right
Statistics: 38 GP, 20 G, 22 A, 42 Pts (Manchester, AHL). 34 GP, 1 G, 6 A, 7 Pts (Los Angeles, NHL)
Third round, 82nd overall, 2011

An intelligent two-way center, Shore spent half of his season up with the Kings, and the other half leading the Manchester Monarchs to the Calder Cup championship. The Denver alum is a strong reactive player with plus vision in the offensive end. Although his NHL production was poor, his possession numbers were strong enough to suggest more in the tank in his next go-round.

79 Sonny Milano, Left Wing, Columbus Blue Jackets

2014-15 ranking: 80 Age: 19
Height: 6'0" Weight: 190 Shoots: Left
Statistics: 50 GP, 22 G, 46 A, 68 Pts (Plymouth, OHL)
First round, 16th overall, 2014

From his draft year to his first post-draft season, the pros and cons on Milano have not changed. The USNDTP graduate is a great skater with elite puckhandling skills, but there remain questions about his game away from the puck. He has put on some weight since being selected, but will need a second OHL campaign to show that he has begun to round out his overall game.

80. Jake Virtanen, Left Wing, Vancouver Canucks
2014-15 ranking: 33   Age: 19
Height: 6'1"   Weight: 212   Shoots: Left
Statistics: 50 GP, 21 G, 31 A, 52 Pts (Calgary, WHL)
First round, sixth overall, 2014

All that separates Virtanen from being ranked 50 spots higher on this list is more consistent production befitting his skillset and prospect pedigree. Between his plus shot and aggressive physical game, Virtanen profiles as a top-six bruising winger who can score 20+ goals per season. He simply needs to show that he can be that player with more regularity. If he gets there, this ranking could look foolish.

81. Malcolm Subban, Goaltender, Boston Bruins
2014-15 ranking: 29   Age: 21
Height: 6'1"   Weight: 187   Catches: Left
Statistics: 35 GP, 2.44 GAA, .921 Sv% (Providence, AHL)
First round, 24th overall, 2012

Appropriate for the middle brother among three drafted players, one of whom is among the best handful of defenders in the game, Subban is a highly athletic netminder. He displays excellent lateral agility and fares well in one-on-one situations. His second pro season was a virtual carbon copy of the first, although he would prefer to forget his one-game NHL cameo in which he surrendered three goals on six shots before being removed. Subban is favored to begin the season as Tuukka Rask's backup in Boston.

82. Kerby Rychel, Left Wing, Columbus Blue Jackets
2014-15 ranking: Not Ranked   Age: 21
Height: 6'1"   Weight: 203   Shoots: Left
Statistics: 51 GP, 12 G, 21 A, 33 Pts (Springfield, AHL)
First round, 19th overall, 2013

Kerby Rychel, the son of "hockey boxer" Warren Rychel, had a reasonably successful rookie pro season, spent largely in the AHL. While he can play with the toughness his father demonstrated, the younger Rychel is more of a skill player, albeit one who makes his mark in the dirty areas. While he could not score as he did in the OHL, when we consider that Springfield was one of the AHL's lowest scoring teams, Rychel's 33 points look pretty good.

83. Iiro Pakarinen, Right Wing, Edmonton Oilers
2014-15 ranking: Not Ranked   Age: 24
Height: 6'1"   Weight: 194   Shoots: Right
Statistics: 39 GP, 17 G, 11 A, 28 Pts (Oklahoma City, AHL). 17 GP, 1 G, 2 A, 3 Pts (Edmonton, NHL)
Seventh round, 184th overall, 2011

Like Joonas Donskoi above, Pakarinen was a former draft pick of the Panthers who never came to terms with his first organization. In this case, Pakarinen failed to stick out in two Liiga seasons after being drafted. Once he had gained free agency, he exploded with HIFK and signed as a free agent with Edmonton. A strong skater with a good shot, Pakarinen will quickly become a favorite of the analytic set as he loves nothing more than shooting the puck.

84. Samuel Morin, Defense, Philadelphia Flyers
2014-15 ranking: 77   Age: 20
Height: 6'7"   Weight: 225   Shoots: Left
Statistics: 38 GP, 5 G, 27 A, 33 Pts (Rimouski, QMJHL)
First round, 11th overall, 2013

After starting his season off on the wrong foot, breaking his jaw in his fifth game for Rimouski, Morin stood out for more than just his fantastic height and attendant wingspan after returning. Very mobile for a big man, he makes strong first passes, with the ability to stretch out defenses on occasion. He also owns a hard slot shot. While not always as physical as his natural gifts might allow, Morin is physical enough that opponents are always aware of his presence.

85. Matt Murray, Goaltender, Pittsburgh Penguins
2014-15 ranking: Not Ranked   Age: 21
Height: 6'4"   Weight: 179   Catches: Left
Statistics: 40 GP, 1.58 GAA, .941 Sv% (Wilkes-Barre/Scranton, AHL)
Third round, 83rd overall, 2012

Drafted as an underperforming collection of tools in 2012, Murray exploded in his rookie pro season with Wilkes-Barre/Scranton, leading the circuit in both GAA and save percentage, and winning awards for rookie of the year and goalie of the year. Tall and lanky, Murray is a calm goaltender who exhibits steady feet in the crease. He made waves by breaking the AHL record for longest shutout streak with a run of 304 minutes, 11 seconds, spanning parts of six games.

86 Adam Erne, Left Wing, Tampa Bay Lightning

2014-15 ranking: Not Ranked Age: 20
Height: 6'1" Weight: 218 Shoots: Left
Statistics: 60 GP, 41 G, 45 A, 86 Pts (Quebec, QMJHL)
Second round, 33rd overall, 2013

The leading goal scorer of the QMJHL playoffs, Erne is a high energy player who combines extreme tenacity with high-level puck skills. A strong defensive forward, he sells out for shot blocks and has been a primary penalty killer throughout his career. The Connecticut native is also dangerous with the puck, with quick hands and solid moves, and he is able to beat the goalie with both his wristshot and his backhander.

87 Nikolai Goldobin, Right Wing, San Jose Sharks

2014-15 ranking: Not Ranked Age: 20
Height: 6'0" Weight: 185 Shoots: Left
Statistics: 38 GP, 11 G, 10 A, 21 Pts (HIFK, Liiga)
First round, 27th overall, 2014

An elite puck artist, Goldobin can handle his way through a minefield and unleash very creative passing plays to create offense. A good skater as well, the Russian-born winger left his OHL team to play against men in Finland. The knock on him remains an extreme lack of commitment on defense. He is expected to play in North America this year, most likely in the AHL.

88 Anthony Duclair, Right Wing, Arizona Coyotes

2014-15 ranking: Sleeper Age: 20
Height: 5'11" Weight: 185 Shoots: Left
Statistics: 26 GP, 15 G, 19 A, 34 Pts (Quebec, QMJHL). 18 GP, 1 G, 6 A, 7 Pts (NY Rangers, NHL)
Third round, 80th overall, 2013

A key component of last season's Keith Yandle trade to the Rangers, Duclair overcame the disappointment of his demotion from Broadway back to the Q by helping lead the Remparts to the QMJHL final. Duclair has fantastic breakout speed and a very heavy shot. He can beat any defender to the outside and knows how to finish his rushes. The downside is inconsistent play away from the puck, and a propensity to streakiness.

89 Jake McCabe, Defense, Buffalo Sabres

2014-15 ranking: Not Ranked Age: 21
Height: 6'1" Weight: 205 Shoots: Left
Statistics: 57 GP, 5 G, 24 A, 29 Pts (Rochester, AHL)
Second round, 44th overall, 2012

A smooth-skating blueliner, McCabe impressed in his rookie season with a moribund Rochester squad in the AHL. The former Wisconsin Badger captained the US team to the WJC gold medal in 2013. McCabe projects as a steady, reliable second-pairing type who can munch up ice-time. He has a strong chance to break camp with the Sabres as soon as this season.

90 Emile Poirier, Right Wing, Calgary Flames

2014-15 ranking: 43 Age: 20
Height: 6'1" Weight: 183 Shoots: Left
Statistics: 55 GP, 19 G, 23 A, 42 Pts (Adirondack, AHL)
First round, 22nd overall, 2013

A highly competitive offensive winger, Poirier had a very strong rookie season with Adirondack, suggesting that his scoring prowess in the Q has made the transition to the pro game. The former Olympique does a good job of maintaining puck possession and is not easy to play against. He could use more AHL seasoning, but is not too far removed from being able to contribute points on a third line in the NHL.

91 Teemu Pulkkinen, Left Wing, Detroit Red Wings

2014-15 ranking: Not Ranked Age: 23
Height: 5'10" Weight: 198 Shoots: Left
Statistics: 46 GP, 34 G, 27 A, 61 Pts (Grand Rapids, AHL). 31 GP, 5 G, 3 A, 8 Pts (Detroit, NHL)
Fourth round, 111th overall, 2010

After posting 130 points in 170 games over his final three years in Finland, Pulkkinen has produced over a point per game in his first two AHL seasons. That he is an offensive force is without question, with his nose for the puck, quick release, and preternatural ability to find holes in the coverage to pounce in. The reason a player with these numbers is not a top-20 prospect is that there remain legitimate questions about whether he has enough strength or effort level to produce in the NHL.

92 Brian Dumoulin, Defense, Pittsburgh Penguins
2014-15 ranking: 57   **Age:** 24
Height: 6'4"   **Weight:** 209   **Shoots:** Left
Statistics: 62 GP, 4 G, 29 A, 33 Pts (Wilkes-Barre/Scranton, AHL)
Second round, 51st overall, 2009

Part of the package Pittsburgh received in the Jordan Staal trade, Dumoulin has a level of vision and patience that suggest a competent two-way NHL blueliner is waiting to emerge. Part of what has held him back has been opportunity. Large, but not overly physical, the Boston College product should finally receive his well-deserved chance as the Penguins have cleared out some of the veterans above him on the depth chart as well as one or two of his direct competitors.

93 Mirco Mueller, Defense, San Jose Sharks
2014-15 ranking: 68   **Age:** 20
Height: 6'3"   **Weight:** 205   **Shoots:** Left
Statistics: 39 GP, 1 G, 3 A, 4 Pts (San Jose, NHL)
First round, 18th overall, 2014

Only by the slimmest of margins is Mueller still eligible for this list. Had San Jose not released him to play for Switzerland during the WJC, he would not have been here at all. A late-season hand injury cemented it. Justifiably sheltered as a teenage NHLer, he did reasonably well with the opportunities afforded him. The Swiss rearguard projects as a solid stay-at-home blueliner with a mature, if not overly physical game.

94 Jack Roslovic, C/RW
Winnipeg Jets
2014-15 ranking: Ineligible   **Age:** 18
Height: 6'1"   **Weight:** 187   **Shoots:** Right
Statistics: 65 GP, 27 G, 52 A, 79 Pts (USNTDP, USHL)
First round, 25th overall, 2015

An energetic, three-zone forward with an omnipresent motor, Roslovic impressed most as a junior with his smarts. Usually utilized as the supporting winger on the first line, his versatile style of play makes him an ideal wingman who can fit in seamlessly with more dynamic players. Between his situational awareness, incisive passing skills, and effective forechecking, the Miami University commit makes those around him better.

95 Mike Matheson, Defense, Florida Panthers
2014-15 ranking: 79   **Age:** 21
Height: 6'2"   **Weight:** 194   **Shoots:** Left
Statistics: 38 GP, 3 G, 22 A, 25 Pts (Boston College, Hockey East)
First round, 23rd overall, 2012

A very physical defender, Matheson recently turned pro after three seasons at Boston College. Although his first-step quickness is questionable, his top speed is more than enough to play at the next level. He can also weave in and out of traffic as the situation demands, demonstrating average or better puck-handling skills. With his strong slapper, he should also receive some power-play time.

96 Tyler Bertuzzi, Left Wing, Detroit Red Wings
2014-15 ranking: Not Ranked   **Age:** 20
Height: 6'0"   **Weight:** 192   **Shoots:** Left
Statistics: 68 GP, 43 G, 55 A, 98 Pts (Guelph, OHL)
Second round, 58th overall, 2013

A very aggressive, physical player—much like uncle Todd—Bertuzzi greatly improved his discipline in his final OHL season. Still a big hitter who lives and dies in the dirty areas around the net, he has done better in straddling the fine line between aggravation and indiscipline. Between his well above-average wristshot and high-level hockey smarts, Bertuzzi could have a nice career. With 12 points in 14 AHL playoff games shortly after his OHL career ended, it has certainly gotten started on the right foot.

97 Justin Bailey, Center, Buffalo Sabres
2014-15 ranking: Not Ranked   **Age:** 20

Height: 6'3" Weight: 194 Shoots: Right
Statistics: 57 GP, 34 G, 35 A, 69 Pts (Kitchener/Sault Ste. Marie, OHL)
Second round, 52nd overall, 2013

Bailey, the son of a longtime NFLer, combines elements of both physical and a finesse games in one versatile package. Big bodied and committed to the forecheck, he also is surprisingly quick, with good puck-protection and puck-handling skills. The package still lacks some refinement, as he needs to improve his reads of the play in front of him. If it all comes together, we are looking at a front-line power forward.

98 Brett Ritchie, Right Wing, Dallas Stars
2014-15 ranking: 23 Age: 22
Height: 6'3" Weight: 220 Shoots: Right
Statistics: 33 GP, 14 G, 7 A, 21 Pts (Texas, AHL). 31 GP, 6 G, 3 A, 9 Pts (Dallas, NHL)
Second round, 44th overall, 2011

Like younger brother Nick, Brett Ritchie is a wide-bodied power forward whose physical gifts alone are enough to make him dangerous in the home plate area of the offensive end. He has the hands and shot to become a 20-goal scorer in the NHL, but he seems more primed to get his start as a fourth-line grinder, more immediately plausible with the offseason trade of Ryan Garbutt to Chicago.

99 Matt Puempel, Left Wing, Ottawa Senators
2014-15 ranking: Not Ranked Age: 22
Height: 6'0" Weight: 196 Shoots: Left
Statistics: 51 GP, 12 G, 20 A, 32 Pts (Binghamton, AHL). 13 GP, 2 G, 1 A, 3 Pts (Ottawa, NHL)
First round, 24th overall, 2011

A hard worker with good hands, Puempel may not have lived up to his advanced billing as a first-round pick in 2011, but he has developed enough in the AHL to have legitimately staked a claim to a fourth-line role in the NHL to start next season. While most casual observers do not get excited by fourth-line pluggers, Puempel has enough offensive talents to put up above-average production numbers from that depth role.

100 Travis Sanheim, Defense, Philadelphia Flyers
2014-15 ranking: Not Ranked Age: 19
Height: 6'3" Weight: 183 Shoots: Left
Statistics: 67 GP, 15 G, 50 A, 65 Pts (Calgary, WHL)
First round, 17th overall, 2015

A fast skater who plays a heads-up, responsible two-way style, Sanheim's game took several step forwards in his draft-plus-one year with the WHL's Calgary Hitmen. He still needs to fill out a lanky frame, but he does not shy away from physical play, regularly going into the corners to battle for loose pucks. An average-at-best point shot will prevent him from being a power-play weapon, but he has enough offensive sense to be a suitable second option.

Top 100 NHL Prospects - Summary

Rank	Name	Position	Team	Rank	Name	Position	Team
1	Connor McDavid	C	EDM	12	Nikolaj Ehlers	LW	WPG
2	Jack Eichel	C	BUF	13	Robby Fabbri	RW	STL
3	Teuvo Teravainen	RW	CHI	14	Josh Morrissey	D	WPG
4	Leon Draisaitl	C	EDM	15	Mike Reilly	D	MIN
5	Dylan Larkin	C	DET	16	Noah Hanifin	D	CAR
6	Sam Bennett	C	CGY	17	Kevin Fiala	LW	NSH
7	Sam Reinhart	C	BUF	18	Michael Dal Colle	LW	NYI
8	Dylan Strome	C	ARI	19	Derrick Pouliot	D	PIT
9	Mitch Marner	C	TOR	20	Mathew Barzal	C	NYI
10	William Nylander	C	TOR	21	Jimmy Vesey	LW	NSH
11	Max Domi	LW/C	ARI	22	Darnell Nurse	D	EDM

Top 100 NHL Prospects - Summary

Rank	Name	Position	Team	Rank	Name	Position	Team
23	Ivan Provorov	D	PHI	62	Calvin Pickard	G	COL
24	Pavel Buchnevich	RW	NYR	63	Cole Cassels	C	VAN
25	Shea Theodore	D	ANA	64	Daniel Sprong	RW	PIT
26	Mikko Rantanen	LW	COL	65	Anthony Beauvillier	LW	NYI
27	Jakub Vrana	RW	WSH	66	Denis Guryanov	RW	DAL
28	Nick Ritchie	LW	ANA	67	Jeremy Roy	D	SJS
29	Ivan Barbashev	C	STL	68	Joonas Donskoi	RW	SJS
30	Marko Dano	C	CHI	69	Josh Ho-Sang	RW	NYI
31	Andrei Vasilevsky	G	TBL	70	Jacob de la Rose	C	MTL
32	Nikita Scherbak	C	MTL	71	Julius Honka	D	DAL
33	Kyle Connor	C	WPG	72	Jordan Schmaltz	D	STL
34	Ryan Pulock	D	NYI	73	Vladislav Kamenev	C	NSH
35	Zach Werenski	D	CBJ	74	Michael McCarron	RW	MTL
36	Timo Meier	RW	SJS	75	Brady Skjei	D	NYR
37	Jared McCann	C	VAN	76	Riley Barber	RW	WSH
38	Nick Merkeley	C	ARI	77	Andreas Johnson	LW	TOR
39	Griffin Reinhart	D	EDM	78	Nick Shore	C	LAK
40	Oliver Bjorkstrand	RW	CBJ	79	Sonny Milano	LW	CBJ
41	Travis Konecny	C	PHI	80	Jake Virtanen	LW	VAN
42	Anthony Mantha	RW	DET	81	Malcolm Subban	G	BOS
43	Brandon Gormley	D	ARI	82	Kerby Rychel	LW	CBJ
44	Lawson Crouse	LW	FLA	83	Iiro Pakarinen	RW	EDM
45	Anthony De Angelo	D	TBL	84	Samuel Morin	D	PHI
46	Yevgeni Svechnikov	LW	DET	85	Matt Murray	G	PIT
47	Madison Bowey	D	WSH	86	Adam Erne	LW	TBL
48	Chris Bigras	D	COL	87	Nikolai Goldobin	RW	SJS
49	Scott Laughton	C	PHI	88	Anthony Duclair	RW	ARI
50	Pavel Zacha	C	NJD	89	Jake McCabe	D	BUF
51	Adrian Kempe	C	LAK	90	Emile Poirier	RW	CGY
52	Thomas Chabot	D	OTT	91	Teemu Pulkkinen	LW	DET
53	Nicolas Petan	C	WPG	92	Brian Dumoulin	D	PIT
54	Conor Hellebuyck	G	WPG	93	Mirco Mueller	D	SJS
55	Jansen Harkins	C	WPG	94	Jack Roslovic	C/RW	WPG
56	Connor Brown	RW	TOR	95	Mike Matheson	D	FLA
57	Alex Tuch	RW	MIN	96	Tyler Bertuzzi	LW	DET
58	Joel Eriksson Ek	C	MIN	97	Justin Bailey	C	BUF
59	Adam Clendening	D	VAN	98	Brett Ritchie	RW	DAL
60	Jakub Zboril	D	BOS	99	Matt Puempel	LW	OTT
61	Brock Boeser	RW	VAN	100	Travis Sanheim	D	PHI

Something for everyone
The top player for every organization outside of the Top 100 NHL Prospect list.

Team	Name	Position	Most recent team	Team	Name	Position	Most recent team
ANA	Nicolas Kerdiles	LW	Norfolk (AHL)	MTL	Noah Juulsen	D	Everett (WHL)
ARI	Brendan Perlini	LW	Niagara (OHL)	NSH	Yakov Trenin	LW	Gatineau (QMJHL)
BOS	Seth Griffith	C/RW	Providence (AHL)/Boston (NHL)	NJD	Steve Santini	D	Boston College (Hockey East)
BUF	Hudson Fasching	RW	Minnesota (Big 10)	NYI	Mitch Vande Sompel	D	Oshawa (OHL)
CGY	Morgan Klimchuk	LW	Regina/Brandon (WHL)	NYR	Adam Tambellini	C	Calgary (WHL)
CAR	Lucas Wallmark	C	Lulea (SHL)	OTT	Nick Paul	C	North Bay (OHL)
CHI	Artemy Panarin	LW	St. Petersburg (KHL)	PHI	Robert Hagg	D	Lehigh Valley (AHL)
COL	Connor Bleakley	C	Red Deer (WHL)	PIT	Tristan Jarry	G	Edmonton (WHL)
CBJ	William Karlsson	C	Norfolk/Springfield (AHL)	SJS	Taylor Doherty	D	Worcester (AHL)
DAL	Jason Dickinson	LW	Guelph (OHL)	STL	Vince Dunn	D	Niagara (OHL)
DET	Landon Ferraro	RW	Grand Rapids (AHL)	TBL	Mitchell Stephens	C	Saginaw (OHL)
EDM	Joey LaLeggia	D	Denver (NCHC)	TOR	Brendan Leipsic	C	Milwaukee/Toronto (AHL)
FLA	Kyle Rau	C	Minnesota (Big 10)	VAN	Thatcher Demko	G	Boston College (Hockey East)
LAK	Michael Mersch	LW	Manchester (AHL)	WSH	Ilya Samsonov	G	Stalnye Lisy Magnitogorsk (MHL)
MIN	Christoph Bertschy	C	Bern (NLA)	WPG	Chase De Leo	C	Portland (WHL)

Player Tables

NHL All-Time Career Leaders

Best 50 forwards (all-time, regular season)

Rank	Name	Season	GP	G	A	Pts	+/-	OGVT	DGVT	GVT
1	Wayne Gretzky	1979-1999	1487	894	1963	2857	518	444.2	70.0	514.2
2	Gordie Howe	1949-1980	1609	766	981	1747	87	329.8	127.2	457.0
3	**Jaromir Jagr**	**1990-2015**	**1550**	**722**	**1080**	**1802**	**291**	**323.6**	**64.0**	**384.5**
4	Steve Yzerman	1983-2006	1514	692	1063	1755	185	250.5	86.3	337.1
5	Phil Esposito	1963-1981	1282	717	873	1590	197	276.5	57.8	334.3
6	Mark Messier	1979-2004	1756	694	1193	1887	210	256.4	73.6	329.9
7	Mario Lemieux	1984-2006	915	690	1033	1723	115	292.3	35.3	326.8
8	Jean Beliveau	1950-1971	1125	507	712	1219	67	236.5	81.7	318.2
9	Joe Sakic	1988-2009	1378	625	1016	1641	30	265.4	51.5	317.2
10	Marcel Dionne	1971-1989	1348	731	1040	1771	28	253.0	56.3	309.3
11	Teemu Selanne	1992-2014	1451	684	773	1457	95	257.5	45.6	304.7
12	Stan Mikita	1958-1980	1394	541	926	1467	159	215.9	79.8	295.6
13	Red Kelly	1949-1967	1197	270	517	787	0	169.6	113.1	282.7
14	Brett Hull	1985-2006	1269	741	650	1391	23	236.8	41.7	278.5
15	Bobby Hull	1957-1980	1063	610	560	1170	105	206.1	70.1	276.2
16	Mats Sundin	1990-2009	1346	564	785	1349	73	221.8	50.5	274.4
17	Mike Modano	1988-2011	1499	561	813	1374	114	203.5	69.4	271.2
18	Ron Francis	1981-2004	1731	549	1249	1798	-10	200.4	70.4	270.7
19	Alex Delvecchio	1950-1974	1549	456	825	1281	33	173.8	94.2	268.0
20	Brendan Shanahan	1987-2009	1524	656	698	1354	151	215.4	51.0	267.0
21	Mark Recchi	1988-2011	1652	577	956	1533	0	218.1	50.1	266.1
22	Guy Lafleur	1971-1991	1126	560	793	1353	453	207.8	55.6	263.4
23	**Marian Hossa**	**1997-2015**	**1172**	**486**	**570**	**1056**	**228**	**209.2**	**54.5**	**262.7**
24	Pierre Turgeon	1987-2007	1294	515	812	1327	139	204.5	57.3	261.5
25	**Jarome Iginla**	**1995-2015**	**1392**	**589**	**637**	**1226**	**82**	**207.8**	**53.1**	**259.0**
26	Sergei Fedorov	1990-2009	1248	483	696	1179	261	194.3	64.0	257.0
27	Jean Ratelle	1960-1981	1281	491	776	1267	299	192.3	63.4	255.7
28	**Joe Thornton**	**1997-2015**	**1285**	**358**	**901**	**1259**	**174**	**193.1**	**61.0**	**254.4**
29	Frank Mahovlich	1956-1974	1181	533	570	1103	173	179.7	70.1	249.8
30	Luc Robitaille	1986-2006	1431	668	726	1394	72	211.1	35.8	247.6
31	Daniel Alfredsson	1995-2014	1246	444	713	1157	155	195.9	50.3	245.4
32	Norm Ullman	1955-1975	1410	490	739	1229	40	168.6	74.5	243.2
33	Bryan Trottier	1975-1994	1279	524	901	1425	452	176.5	65.6	242.1
34	John Bucyk	1955-1978	1540	556	813	1369	146	194.8	47.0	241.8
35	Bobby Clarke	1969-1984	1144	358	852	1210	506	160.2	81.1	241.3
36	Jeremy Roenick	1988-2009	1363	513	703	1216	153	171.5	63.5	236.8
37	**Patrik Elias**	**1995-2015**	**1224**	**406**	**611**	**1017**	**167**	**163.0**	**71.9**	**236.6**
38	Henri Richard	1955-1975	1256	358	688	1046	126	161.2	74.4	235.6
39	Doug Gilmour	1983-2003	1474	450	964	1414	132	157.3	76.8	234.1
40	Joe Nieuwendyk	1986-2007	1257	564	562	1126	155	180.8	47.3	227.3
41	Adam Oates	1985-2004	1337	341	1079	1420	35	160.7	64.7	225.4
42	Jari Kurri	1980-1998	1251	601	797	1398	298	179.1	45.7	224.8
43	Bernie Geoffrion	1950-1968	883	393	429	822	1	160.1	64.7	224.8
44	Mike Bossy	1977-1987	752	573	553	1126	381	185.6	34.4	220.0
45	Keith Tkachuk	1991-2010	1201	538	527	1065	33	170.3	44.6	214.1
46	Theoren Fleury	1988-2003	1084	455	633	1088	145	163.5	50.1	213.6
47	Alexander Mogilny	1989-2006	990	473	559	1032	81	178.0	34.7	211.8
48	Dave Andreychuk	1982-2006	1639	640	698	1338	38	156.5	55.0	211.5
49	Rod Brind'Amour	1988-2010	1484	452	732	1184	-39	145.6	64.6	210.7
50	Mike Gartner	1979-1998	1432	708	627	1335	67	152.6	55.9	208.6

Best 50 defensemen (all-time, regular season)

Rank	Name	Season	GP	G	A	Pts	+/-	OGVT	DGVT	GVT
1	Raymond Bourque	1979-2001	1612	410	1169	1579	528	266.8	194.4	461.2
2	Nicklas Lidstrom	1991-2012	1564	264	878	1142	450	229.4	124.2	353.6
3	Al MacInnis	1981-2004	1416	340	934	1274	373	232.1	113.5	345.6
4	Paul Coffey	1980-2001	1409	396	1135	1531	294	263.7	62.5	326.2
5	Bobby Orr	1966-1979	657	270	645	915	597	226.1	92.0	318.1
6	Larry Murphy	1980-2001	1615	287	929	1216	200	177.4	105.9	283.3
7	Scott Stevens	1982-2004	1635	196	712	908	393	109.3	172.7	282.1
8	Larry Robinson	1972-1992	1384	208	750	958	730	126.5	150.8	277.3
9	Denis Potvin	1973-1988	1060	310	742	1052	460	175.4	97.3	272.7
10	Chris Chelios	1983-2010	1651	185	763	948	350	112.0	158.7	270.7
11	Phil Housley	1982-2003	1495	338	894	1232	-53	199.7	66.9	266.6
12	Brad Park	1968-1985	1113	213	683	896	358	138.5	118.5	256.9
13	Brian Leetch	1987-2006	1205	247	781	1028	25	181.9	65.6	247.5
14	Chris Pronger	1993-2012	1167	157	541	698	183	126.5	96.3	222.0
15	Sergei Zubov	1992-2009	1068	152	619	771	148	143.1	75.1	220.3
16	Scott Niedermayer	1991-2010	1263	172	568	740	167	129.4	86.9	215.8
17	**Sergei Gonchar**	**1994-2015**	**1301**	**220**	**591**	**811**	**33**	**162.9**	**51.9**	**214.5**
18	Doug Harvey	1949-1969	1023	81	435	516	11	101.6	105.2	206.8
19	Tim Horton	1949-1974	1446	115	403	518	81	66.7	132.3	199.0
20	Mathieu Schneider	1987-2010	1289	223	520	743	66	127.3	68.8	197.0
21	Mark Howe	1979-1995	929	197	545	742	400	105.9	86.4	192.4
22	Rob Blake	1989-2010	1270	240	537	777	-4	143.9	46.1	190.0
23	Steve Duchesne	1986-2002	1113	227	525	752	88	124.4	62.9	187.3
24	Gary Suter	1985-2002	1145	203	641	844	126	123.9	61.3	185.1
25	Kevin Hatcher	1984-2001	1157	227	450	677	-27	92.9	86.8	179.8
26	Eric Desjardins	1988-2006	1143	136	439	575	198	81.4	95.5	176.9
27	Guy Lapointe	1968-1984	884	171	451	622	329	99.7	73.6	173.3
28	Borje Salming	1973-1990	1148	150	637	787	175	93.3	78.0	171.2
29	Pierre Pilote	1955-1969	890	80	418	498	-3	92.1	75.0	167.1
30	**Zdeno Chara**	**1997-2015**	**1195**	**169**	**369**	**538**	**188**	**94.9**	**71.7**	**166.2**
31	Teppo Numminen	1988-2009	1372	117	520	637	56	83.3	79.3	162.6
32	Bill Gadsby	1949-1966	1090	113	408	521	0	100.5	61.9	162.4
33	Doug Wilson	1977-1993	1024	237	590	827	53	110.0	51.9	162.0
34	Roman Hamrlik	1992-2013	1395	155	483	638	-49	95.2	64.7	159.9
35	Brian Rafalski	1999-2011	833	79	436	515	178	94.5	63.1	157.6
36	James Patrick	1983-2004	1280	149	490	639	104	79.4	77.0	156.3
37	Reed Larson	1976-1990	904	222	463	685	-127	90.5	61.6	152.1
38	Serge Savard	1966-1983	1040	106	333	439	460	46.8	104.6	151.5
39	**Dan Boyle**	**1998-2015**	**1019**	**153**	**428**	**581**	**-5**	**104.9**	**46.4**	**149.5**
40	Wade Redden	1996-2013	1023	109	348	457	160	80.2	67.4	147.6
41	Marcel Pronovost	1949-1970	1206	88	257	345	3	46.1	101.2	147.3
42	Carol Vadnais	1966-1983	1087	169	418	587	-62	77.3	68.9	146.2
43	Allan Stanley	1949-1969	1204	98	325	423	2	63.4	81.6	145.0
44	Bryan McCabe	1995-2011	1135	145	383	528	34	92.2	52.7	144.8
45	Calle Johansson	1987-2004	1109	119	416	535	57	64.0	78.2	142.3
46	Glen Wesley	1987-2008	1457	128	409	537	66	42.7	99.2	141.9
47	**Kimmo Timonen**	**1998-2015**	**1108**	**117**	**454**	**571**	**35**	**98.5**	**42.6**	**140.5**
48	Sandis Ozolinsh	1992-2008	875	167	397	564	-44	109.3	31.1	140.4
49	**Lubomir Visnovsky**	**2000-2015**	**883**	**128**	**367**	**495**	**40**	**91.2**	**44.5**	**136.0**
50	Tomas Kaberle	1998-2013	984	87	476	563	17	101.0	33.0	134.8

Best 25 goaltenders (all-time, regular season)

Rank	Name	Season	GP	GAA	GA	SA	SV%	GGVT	DGVT	GVT
1	Patrick Roy	1984-2003	1004.1	253	2546	28353	910	418.1	9.4	427.5
2	Tony Esposito	1968-1984	876.4	292	2563	27299	906	424.6	-5.3	419.3
3	Dominik Hasek	1990-2008	714.1	220	1572	20220	922	406.6	0.6	405.3
4	Jacques Plante	1952-1973	825.2	237	1964	24666	920	332.8	11.1	343.8
5	Glenn Hall	1952-1971	889.4	249	2222	26845	917	304.0	9.0	313.0
6	**Roberto Luongo**	**1999-2015**	**827.4**	**249**	**2067**	**25558**	**919**	**329.6**	**-18.9**	**311.8**
7	**Martin Brodeur**	**1991-2015**	**1240.9**	**224**	**2781**	**31709**	**912**	**247.5**	**45.5**	**297.3**
8	Bernie Parent	1965-1979	585.9	254	1493	17576	915	290.6	2.2	292.8
9	Ken Dryden	1970-1979	389.2	223	870	11092	921	262.6	8.2	270.8
10	Ed Belfour	1988-2007	928.4	249	2317	24751	906	248.4	17.4	264.2
11	**Henrik Lundqvist**	**2005-2015**	**610.4**	**226**	**1381**	**17398**	**920**	**219.8**	**6.5**	**246.7**
12	Johnny Bower	1953-1970	531.5	252	1340	17174	921	245.1	-5.6	239.5
13	John Vanbiesbrouck	1981-2002	841.5	297	2503	24708	898	233.7	-0.4	233.3
14	Terry Sawchuk	1949-1970	954.9	250	2389	27262	912	214.6	14.7	229.3
15	Billy Smith	1971-1989	640.6	317	2031	19273	894	228.4	0.1	228.5
16	Curtis Joseph	1989-2009	901.1	279	2516	26795	906	218.2	-8.6	212.3
17	Tomas Vokoun	1996-2013	661.7	255	1688	20313	916	219.0	-12.2	205.4
18	Gump Worsley	1952-1974	837.4	287	2407	27859	913	214.9	-19.6	195.3
19	Glenn Resch	1973-1987	538	327	1761	16151	890	189.9	0.6	190.5
20	Dan Bouchard	1972-1986	632.1	326	2061	18725	889	166.7	4.0	170.8
21	Andy Moog	1980-1998	669.3	313	2097	19327	891	158.2	5.6	163.8
22	Sean Burke	1987-2007	774.3	295	2290	23299	901	175.4	-11.4	160.3
23	Tim Thomas	2002-2014	407.6	251	1027	12822	919	155.9	-7.5	158.5
24	Kelly Hrudey	1983-1998	634.9	342	2174	20328	893	166.4	-14.4	152.1
25	Rogie Vachon	1966-1982	771.6	299	2310	22198	895	133.2	14.7	147.9

Best 20 offensive forwards (all-time, regular season)

Rank	Name	Season	GP	G	A	Pts	+/-	OGVT	DGVT	GVT
1	Wayne Gretzky	1979-1999	1487	894	1963	2857	518	444.2	70.0	514.2
2	Gordie Howe	1949-1980	1609	766	981	1747	87	329.8	127.2	457.0
3	**Jaromir Jagr**	**1990-2015**	**1550**	**722**	**1080**	**1802**	**291**	**323.6**	**64.0**	**384.5**
4	Mario Lemieux	1984-2006	915	690	1033	1723	115	292.3	35.3	326.8
5	Phil Esposito	1963-1981	1282	717	873	1590	197	276.5	57.8	334.3
6	Joe Sakic	1988-2009	1378	625	1016	1641	30	265.4	51.5	317.2
7	Teemu Selanne	1992-2014	1451	684	773	1457	95	257.5	45.6	304.7
8	Mark Messier	1979-2004	1756	694	1193	1887	210	256.4	73.6	329.9
9	Marcel Dionne	1971-1989	1348	731	1040	1771	28	253.0	56.3	309.3
10	Steve Yzerman	1983-2006	1514	692	1063	1755	185	250.5	86.3	337.1
11	Brett Hull	1985-2006	1269	741	650	1391	23	236.8	41.7	278.5
12	Jean Beliveau	1950-1971	1125	507	712	1219	67	236.5	81.7	318.2
13	Mats Sundin	1990-2009	1346	564	785	1349	73	221.8	50.5	274.4
14	Mark Recchi	1988-2011	1652	577	956	1533	0	218.1	50.1	266.1
15	Stan Mikita	1958-1980	1394	541	926	1467	159	215.9	79.8	295.6
16	Brendan Shanahan	1987-2009	1524	656	698	1354	151	215.4	51.0	267.0
17	Luc Robitaille	1986-2006	1431	668	726	1394	72	211.1	35.8	247.6
18	**Marian Hossa**	**1997-2015**	**1172**	**486**	**570**	**1056**	**228**	**209.2**	**54.5**	**262.7**
19	Guy Lafleur	1971-1991	1126	560	793	1353	453	207.8	55.6	263.4
20	**Jarome Iginla**	**1995-2015**	**1392**	**589**	**637**	**1226**	**82**	**207.8**	**53.1**	**259.0**

Best 20 offensive defensemen (all-time, regular season)

Rank	Name	Season	GP	G	A	Pts	+/-	OGVT	DGVT	GVT
1	Raymond Bourque	1979-2001	1612	410	1169	1579	528	266.8	194.4	461.2
2	Paul Coffey	1980-2001	1409	396	1135	1531	294	263.7	62.5	326.2
3	Al MacInnis	1981-2004	1416	340	934	1274	373	232.1	113.5	345.6
4	Nicklas Lidstrom	1991-2012	1564	264	878	1142	450	229.4	124.2	353.6
5	Bobby Orr	1966-1979	657	270	645	915	597	226.1	92.0	318.1
6	Phil Housley	1982-2003	1495	338	894	1232	-53	199.7	66.9	266.6
7	Brian Leetch	1987-2006	1205	247	781	1028	25	181.9	65.6	247.5
8	Larry Murphy	1980-2001	1615	287	929	1216	200	177.4	105.9	283.3
9	Denis Potvin	1973-1988	1060	310	742	1052	460	175.4	97.3	272.7
10	**Sergei Gonchar**	**1994-2015**	**1301**	**220**	**591**	**811**	**33**	**162.9**	**51.9**	**214.5**
11	Rob Blake	1989-2010	1270	240	537	777	-4	143.9	46.1	190.0
12	Sergei Zubov	1992-2009	1068	152	619	771	148	143.1	75.1	220.3
13	Brad Park	1968-1985	1113	213	683	896	358	138.5	118.5	256.9
14	Scott Niedermayer	1991-2010	1263	172	568	740	167	129.4	86.9	215.8
15	Mathieu Schneider	1987-2010	1289	223	520	743	66	127.3	68.8	197.0
16	Larry Robinson	1972-1992	1384	208	750	958	730	126.5	150.8	277.3
17	Chris Pronger	1993-2012	1167	157	541	698	183	126.5	96.3	222.0
18	Steve Duchesne	1986-2002	1113	227	525	752	88	124.4	62.9	187.3
19	Gary Suter	1985-2002	1145	203	641	844	126	123.9	61.3	185.1
20	Chris Chelios	1983-2010	1651	185	763	948	350	112.0	158.7	270.7

Best 20 defensive forwards (all-time, regular season)

Rank	Name	Season	GP	G	A	Pts	+/-	OGVT	DGVT	GVT
1	Gordie Howe	1949-1980	1609	766	981	1747	87	329.8	127.2	457.0
2	Red Kelly	1949-1967	1197	270	517	787	0	169.6	113.1	282.7
3	Craig Ramsay	1971-1985	1070	252	420	672	328	65.5	98.1	163.6
4	Guy Carbonneau	1980-2000	1318	260	403	663	186	43.4	95.8	139.1
5	Alex Delvecchio	1950-1974	1549	456	825	1281	33	173.8	94.2	268.0
6	Steve Yzerman	1983-2006	1514	692	1063	1755	185	250.5	86.3	337.1
7	Jean Beliveau	1950-1971	1125	507	712	1219	67	236.5	81.7	318.2
8	Bobby Clarke	1969-1984	1144	358	852	1210	506	160.2	81.1	241.3
9	Stan Mikita	1958-1980	1394	541	926	1467	159	215.9	79.8	295.6
10	Don Luce	1969-1982	894	225	329	554	197	63.4	78.8	142.3
11	Doug Gilmour	1983-2003	1474	450	964	1414	132	157.3	76.8	234.1
12	Norm Ullman	1955-1975	1410	490	739	1229	40	168.6	74.5	243.2
13	Henri Richard	1955-1975	1256	358	688	1046	126	161.2	74.4	235.6
14	Mark Messier	1979-2004	1756	694	1193	1887	210	256.4	73.6	329.9
15	Kelly Miller	1984-1999	1057	181	282	463	71	16.6	73.6	90.2
16	**Patrik Elias**	**1995-2015**	**1224**	**406**	**611**	**1017**	**167**	**163.0**	**71.9**	**236.6**
17	Bob Gainey	1973-1989	1160	239	262	501	196	16.9	70.8	87.7
18	Ed Westfall	1961-1979	1226	231	394	625	149	37.5	70.7	108.2
19	Ron Francis	1981-2004	1731	549	1249	1798	-10	200.4	70.4	270.7
20	Bobby Hull	1957-1980	1063	610	560	1170	105	206.1	70.1	276.2

Best 20 defensive defensemen (all-time, regular season)

Rank	Name	Season	GP	G	A	Pts	+/-	OGVT	DGVT	GVT
1	Raymond Bourque	1979-2001	1612	410	1169	1579	528	266.8	194.4	461.2
2	Scott Stevens	1982-2004	1635	196	712	908	393	109.3	172.7	282.1
3	Chris Chelios	1983-2010	1651	185	763	948	350	112.0	158.7	270.7
4	Larry Robinson	1972-1992	1384	208	750	958	730	126.5	150.8	277.3
5	Tim Horton	1949-1974	1446	115	403	518	81	66.7	132.3	199.0
6	Nicklas Lidstrom	1991-2012	1564	264	878	1142	450	229.4	124.2	353.6
7	Brad Park	1968-1985	1113	213	683	896	358	138.5	118.5	256.9
8	Al MacInnis	1981-2004	1416	340	934	1274	373	232.1	113.5	345.6
9	Terry Harper	1962-1981	1066	35	221	256	169	0.4	107.3	107.7
10	Larry Murphy	1980-2001	1615	287	929	1216	200	177.4	105.9	283.3
11	Doug Harvey	1949-1969	1023	81	435	516	11	101.6	105.2	206.8
12	Serge Savard	1966-1983	1040	106	333	439	460	46.8	104.6	151.5
13	Rod Langway	1978-1993	994	51	278	329	277	16.1	102.9	119.0
14	Brad McCrimmon	1979-1997	1222	81	322	403	444	21.5	101.5	123.0
15	Craig Ludwig	1982-1999	1256	38	184	222	79	-16.3	101.5	85.2
16	Marcel Pronovost	1949-1970	1206	88	257	345	3	46.1	101.2	147.3
17	Glen Wesley	1987-2008	1457	128	409	537	66	42.7	99.2	141.9
18	Bill Hajt	1973-1987	854	42	202	244	321	5.7	98.7	104.4
19	Jean-Guy Talbot	1954-1971	1056	43	242	285	1	23.6	97.5	121.0
20	Denis Potvin	1973-1988	1060	310	742	1052	460	175.4	97.3	272.7

Best 20 forwards (all-time, playoffs)

Rank	Name	Season	GP	G	A	Pts	+/-	OGVT	DGVT	GVT
1	Wayne Gretzky	1979-1999	208	122	260	382	67	101.7	11.3	113.0
2	Mark Messier	1979-2004	236	109	186	295	42	74.3	10.5	84.8
3	Peter Forsberg	1994-2011	151	64	107	171	54	58.6	11.2	69.7
4	Joe Sakic	1988-2009	172	84	104	188	-2	63.8	4.9	68.6
5	Jari Kurri	1980-1998	200	106	127	233	73	55.8	11.4	67.2
6	**Jaromir Jagr**	**1990-2015**	**201**	**78**	**121**	**199**	**32**	**57.5**	**9.5**	**67.0**
7	Brett Hull	1985-2006	202	103	87	190	13	56.1	9.5	65.6
8	Jean Beliveau	1950-1971	162	79	97	176	0	54.2	8.5	62.7
9	Sergei Fedorov	1990-2009	183	52	124	176	38	49.5	13.2	62.6
10	Steve Yzerman	1983-2006	196	70	115	185	-11	51.5	9.3	60.8
11	Glenn Anderson	1980-1996	225	93	121	214	63	45.8	11.6	57.5
12	Mario Lemieux	1984-2006	107	76	96	172	20	52.6	4.7	57.3
13	Doug Gilmour	1983-2003	182	60	128	188	27	44.7	10.0	54.7
14	Gordie Howe	1949-1980	131	59	88	147	0	49.1	5.3	54.4
15	Mike Modano	1988-2011	176	58	88	146	0	41.4	8.9	50.3
16	Claude Lemieux	1983-2009	234	80	78	158	42	35.8	14.1	49.9
17	Brendan Shanahan	1987-2009	184	60	74	134	31	35.2	11.8	47.0
18	Mike Bossy	1977-1987	129	85	75	160	3	39.7	7.1	46.8
19	**Patrik Elias**	**1995-2015**	**159**	**44**	**80**	**124**	**15**	**37.3**	**9.4**	**46.7**
20	**Marian Hossa**	**1997-2015**	**193**	**49**	**95**	**144**	**29**	**36.6**	**10.1**	**46.7**

Best 20 defensemen (all-time, playoffs)

Rank	Name	Season	GP	G	A	Pts	+/-	OGVT	DGVT	GVT
1	Nicklas Lidstrom	1991-2012	263	54	129	183	61	58.1	31.3	89.4
2	Paul Coffey	1980-2001	194	59	137	196	42	52.5	14.7	67.1
3	Raymond Bourque	1979-2001	214	41	139	180	5	46.2	18.7	64.8
4	Chris Chelios	1983-2010	266	31	113	144	48	30.2	29.1	59.3
5	Al MacInnis	1981-2004	177	39	121	160	12	45.3	13.4	58.7
6	Larry Murphy	1980-2001	215	37	115	152	29	37.3	18.9	56.2
7	Larry Robinson	1972-1992	227	28	116	144	27	30.1	25.0	55.2
8	Denis Potvin	1973-1988	185	56	108	164	-17	41.2	13.7	54.9
9	Chris Pronger	1993-2012	173	26	95	121	40	36.9	16.5	53.4
10	Sergei Zubov	1992-2009	164	24	93	117	28	34.9	16.8	51.7
11	Scott Stevens	1982-2004	233	26	92	118	48	25.8	25.0	50.8
12	Brian Rafalski	1999-2011	165	29	71	100	42	31.8	16.9	48.6
13	Brad Park	1968-1985	161	35	90	125	-8	31.5	15.2	46.7
14	Scott Niedermayer	1991-2010	202	25	73	98	20	26.1	18.7	44.8
15	Brian Leetch	1987-2006	95	28	69	97	2	31.3	7.0	38.2
16	Bobby Orr	1966-1979	74	26	66	92	0	29.2	6.3	35.4
17	**Sergei Gonchar**	**1994-2015**	**141**	**22**	**68**	**90**	**3**	**26.1**	**9.1**	**35.1**
18	Sandis Ozolinsh	1992-2008	137	23	67	90	-10	27.0	6.2	33.1
19	Eric Desjardins	1988-2006	168	23	57	80	16	18.7	13.4	32.2
20	Doug Harvey	1949-1969	130	8	63	71	0	18.5	11.9	30.4

Best 20 goaltenders (all-time, playoffs)

Rank	Name	Season	GP	GAA	GA	SA	SV%	GGVT
1	Patrick Roy	1984-2003	253.5	230	584	7149	918	117.7
2	Ed Belfour	1988-2007	165.8	216	359	4476	919	70.4
3	**Martin Brodeur**	**1991-2015**	**209**	**201**	**421**	**5186**	**918**	**60.3**
4	Billy Smith	1971-1989	127.5	272	348	3663	904	59.5
5	Ken Dryden	1970-1979	114.1	240	274	3239	915	57.4
6	Dominik Hasek	1990-2008	122	201	246	3283	925	56.3
7	Jacques Plante	1952-1973	110.9	213	237	3081	923	49.4
8	Curtis Joseph	1989-2009	135.1	242	327	3927	916	42.6
9	**Henrik Lundqvist**	**2005-2015**	**114**	**222**	**253**	**3292**	**923**	**33.9**
10	Grant Fuhr	1981-2000	147.2	292	430	4210	897	33.5
11	John Vanbiesbrouck	1981-2002	66.2	267	177	2073	914	31.8
12	Johnny Bower	1953-1970	73	246	180	2374	924	31.3
13	Bernie Parent	1965-1979	71.7	242	174	2080	916	31.1
14	**Jonathan Quick**	**2007-2015**	**75.1**	**223**	**168**	**2180**	**922**	**28.2**
15	Tim Thomas	2002-2014	49.9	212	106	1527	930	28.1
16	**Tuukka Rask**	**2007-2015**	**49.8**	**208**	**104**	**1487**	**930**	**27.9**
17	Ken Wregget	1983-2000	55.7	287	160	1796	910	25.5
18	Tom Barrasso	1983-2003	115.9	301	349	3569	902	24.9
19	Kirk McLean	1985-2001	69.8	283	198	2134	907	24.7
20	Chris Osgood	1993-2011	118.4	210	249	2948	915	24.2

Leaders since 2005-06

Best 50 forwards (since 2005-06, regular season)

Rank	Name	Season	GP	G	A	Pts	+/-	OGVT	DGVT	GVT
1	Alexander Ovechkin	2005-2015	760	475	420	895	57	190.7	18.9	206.9
2	Sidney Crosby	2005-2015	627	302	551	853	129	163.4	25.3	195.6
3	Pavel Datsyuk	2005-2015	678	245	470	715	220	125.6	40.1	172.5
4	Joe Thornton	2005-2015	776	198	640	838	149	121.4	43.4	165.0
5	Marian Hossa	2005-2015	705	298	368	666	164	127.1	38.4	164.7
6	Jarome Iginla	2005-2015	766	339	384	723	59	126.2	25.6	149.9
7	Evgeni Malkin	2006-2015	587	268	434	702	56	133.0	14.7	149.9
8	Martin St. Louis	2005-2015	770	282	492	774	-1	124.1	26.8	147.9
9	Daniel Sedin	2005-2015	746	266	464	730	153	123.5	28.4	147.8
10	Henrik Zetterberg	2005-2015	696	259	440	699	138	119.2	33.1	147.4
11	Henrik Sedin	2005-2015	774	167	602	769	175	110.8	31.8	141.4
12	Jonathan Toews	2007-2015	565	223	283	506	171	91.1	34.7	137.6
13	Zach Parise	2005-2015	691	274	292	566	90	88.5	40.4	137.0
14	Eric Staal	2005-2015	765	301	410	711	-48	116.8	21.9	137.0
15	Patrick Marleau	2005-2015	771	303	358	661	3	102.4	32.2	134.6
16	Corey Perry	2005-2015	722	296	306	602	92	103.4	28.9	134.4
17	Ryan Getzlaf	2005-2015	710	208	470	678	124	102.0	31.6	133.5
18	Rick Nash	2005-2015	708	320	281	601	46	100.6	27.4	131.3
19	Jason Spezza	2005-2015	657	239	434	673	28	112.4	16.5	131.2
20	Anze Kopitar	2006-2015	683	218	392	610	45	88.5	39.1	130.9
21	Ilya Kovalchuk	2005-2013	589	309	302	611	-63	110.1	16.3	129.5
22	Thomas Vanek	2005-2015	743	298	310	608	35	106.8	16.9	126.1
23	Patrick Kane	2007-2015	576	205	352	557	51	97.8	19.3	123.8
24	Dany Heatley	2005-2015	679	292	318	610	73	100.9	22.8	119.1
25	Daniel Alfredsson	2005-2014	617	225	364	589	101	95.9	23.4	118.6
26	Patrik Elias	2005-2015	666	199	359	558	27	77.8	39.0	118.5
27	Nicklas Backstrom	2007-2015	577	145	427	572	79	96.4	19.8	118.2
28	Marian Gaborik	2005-2015	584	278	265	543	87	93.2	24.9	116.6
29	Joe Pavelski	2006-2015	643	228	257	485	76	79.9	31.8	115.2
30	Steven Stamkos	2008-2015	492	276	222	498	2	103.7	12.1	112.5
31	Jason Pominville	2005-2015	751	237	342	579	53	86.2	23.8	112.2
32	Patrick Sharp	2005-2015	701	244	275	519	83	86.5	26.5	110.9
33	Brad Richards	2005-2015	732	204	423	627	-59	86.5	21.1	110.6
34	Jeff Carter	2005-2015	718	283	239	522	54	86.8	25.1	109.4
35	Alexander Semin	2006-2015	583	228	263	491	72	89.3	20.9	109.1
36	Vincent Lecavalier	2005-2015	696	265	339	604	-75	95.0	17.8	107.8
37	Mike Ribeiro	2005-2015	750	183	433	616	4	81.1	24.3	106.3
38	Teemu Selanne	2005-2014	572	232	274	506	62	87.0	16.9	105.5
39	Patrice Bergeron	2005-2015	669	190	321	511	105	75.0	27.7	102.5
40	Chris Kunitz	2005-2015	712	224	281	505	153	69.5	26.6	98.1
41	Alex Tanguay	2005-2015	639	167	339	506	42	71.2	22.1	95.7
42	Claude Giroux	2007-2015	496	144	305	449	22	76.9	16.8	94.8
43	Phil Kessel	2006-2015	668	247	273	520	-74	87.3	9.7	94.4
44	Michael Cammalleri	2005-2015	678	249	272	521	-54	79.5	16.2	93.5
45	Ray Whitney	2005-2014	630	180	349	529	6	80.0	14.3	93.4
46	Tomas Plekanec	2005-2015	759	202	297	499	40	65.5	32.6	93.2
47	Mikko Koivu	2005-2015	681	144	356	500	28	56.6	28.7	92.7
48	Jaromir Jagr	2005-2015	523	185	308	493	84	72.6	22.8	92.3
49	Alexander Steen	2005-2015	679	180	249	429	43	60.7	26.5	89.6
50	Derek Roy	2005-2015	689	180	325	505	37	71.8	18.9	89.6

Best 50 defensemen (since 2005-06, regular season)

Rank	Name	Season	GP	G	A	Pts	+/-	OGVT	DGVT	GVT
1	Nicklas Lidstrom	2005-2012	548	91	325	416	173	85.8	42.3	128.1
2	Zdeno Chara	2005-2015	736	128	278	406	157	75.2	45.1	119.9
3	Duncan Keith	2005-2015	766	75	340	415	137	64.9	54.7	119.6
4	Shea Weber	2005-2015	685	146	246	392	55	74.7	39.5	113.9
5	Dan Boyle	2005-2015	694	116	314	430	-5	77.2	31.2	106.7
6	Brian Campbell	2005-2015	753	67	348	415	40	65.4	34.9	100.0
7	Lubomir Visnovsky	2005-2015	615	101	281	382	19	70.9	28.1	99.3
8	Mike Green	2005-2015	575	113	247	360	58	76.2	20.0	94.0
9	Brent Seabrook	2005-2015	763	71	247	318	108	44.4	48.3	93.3
10	Andrei Markov	2005-2015	579	78	302	380	48	68.4	24.2	92.9
11	Dion Phaneuf	2005-2015	750	117	283	400	-6	66.8	27.7	92.5
12	Brent Burns	2005-2015	679	113	229	342	14	55.4	34.9	90.8
13	Niklas Kronwall	2005-2015	654	70	265	335	37	53.2	36.7	89.7
14	Ryan Suter	2005-2015	749	52	299	351	67	42.0	46.9	88.9
15	Kimmo Timonen	2005-2015	694	62	313	375	58	62.5	26.2	88.1
16	Brian Rafalski	2005-2011	456	49	259	308	82	56.3	31.8	88.1
17	Mark Streit	2005-2015	654	84	300	384	-58	68.0	17.6	83.9
18	Christian Ehrhoff	2005-2015	700	71	244	315	55	40.4	41.5	81.9
19	Sergei Gonchar	2005-2015	632	72	314	386	-24	68.9	13.1	81.6
20	Chris Pronger	2005-2012	445	63	235	298	58	57.1	23.8	80.1
21	Jay Bouwmeester	2005-2015	775	72	249	321	17	40.8	39.1	79.0
22	Dennis Wideman	2005-2015	707	92	257	349	-57	51.5	27.6	78.5
23	Matt Carle	2005-2015	660	43	230	273	79	38.9	38.2	77.8
24	Drew Doughty	2008-2015	524	66	201	267	38	34.9	43.3	77.5
25	Dan Hamhuis	2005-2015	734	45	219	264	95	29.3	47.1	76.5
26	Kris Letang	2006-2015	491	66	219	285	46	49.1	24.7	74.8
27	Dustin Byfuglien	2005-2015	597	134	210	344	-41	59.8	16.8	74.5
28	Tomas Kaberle	2005-2013	541	46	293	339	-40	58.7	14.9	74.3
29	Paul Martin	2005-2015	627	37	211	248	88	25.4	47.9	73.3
30	Erik Karlsson	2009-2015	397	84	219	303	-20	66.6	6.5	73.1
31	Mark Giordano	2005-2015	510	66	179	245	38	37.7	34.0	71.7
32	Alex Pietrangelo	2008-2015	386	44	174	218	43	36.8	34.4	70.9
33	Marek Zidlicky	2005-2015	701	71	277	348	-53	50.7	21.7	70.7
34	John-Michael Liles	2005-2015	640	71	239	310	-42	49.2	20.8	70.4
35	Marc-Edouard Vlasic	2006-2015	670	39	148	187	110	13.5	56.8	70.1
36	Keith Yandle	2006-2015	579	67	255	322	-28	52.0	16.1	67.5
37	Trevor Daley	2005-2015	729	66	159	225	12	22.4	43.1	65.5
38	Michal Rozsival	2005-2015	653	48	180	228	80	26.3	39.3	64.8
39	Bryan McCabe	2005-2011	427	69	189	258	-3	49.2	13.8	63.0
40	Joe Corvo	2005-2014	586	79	194	273	16	45.2	16.5	61.7
41	Scott Niedermayer	2005-2010	371	60	204	264	-5	52.7	9.5	61.6
42	James Wisniewski	2005-2015	551	53	221	274	-22	42.6	18.0	60.9
43	Alexander Edler	2006-2015	568	66	193	259	2	37.9	23.0	59.8
44	Andy Greene	2006-2015	559	31	140	171	7	11.5	48.1	59.6
45	Alex Goligoski	2007-2015	480	50	190	240	47	36.1	23.5	59.3
46	Sami Salo	2005-2014	530	64	150	214	77	30.7	27.7	58.4
47	Andrej Meszaros	2005-2015	645	63	175	238	25	34.1	24.2	58.0
48	Fedor Tyutin	2005-2015	717	51	190	241	-18	21.8	35.3	57.4
49	Kevin Bieksa	2005-2015	597	56	185	241	22	32.0	26.1	57.3
50	P.K. Subban	2009-2015	366	57	170	227	31	39.5	18.6	57.1

Best 25 goaltenders (since 2005-06, regular season)

Rank	Name	Season	GP	GAA	GA	SA	SV%	GGVT	DGVT	GVT
1	Henrik Lundqvist	2005-2015	610.4	226	1381	17398	.920	219.8	6.5	246.7
2	Roberto Luongo	2005-2015	580.2	243	1414	17356	.918	206.2	-3.7	203.6
3	Tomas Vokoun	2005-2013	401.5	255	1026	13003	.921	177.7	-11.3	165.1
4	Tim Thomas	2005-2014	403.9	251	1016	12704	.920	155.6	-7.4	158.4
5	Ryan Miller	2005-2015	570.6	257	1468	17406	.915	145.8	-5.6	150.1
6	Carey Price	2007-2015	427.5	243	1041	12899	.919	137.0	-3.7	139.7
7	Tuukka Rask	2007-2015	254.1	216	550	7463	.926	112.1	0.6	117.2
8	Marc-Andre Fleury	2005-2015	550.5	255	1404	15966	.912	100.1	1.8	116.8
9	Pekka Rinne	2005-2015	366	235	862	10635	.918	97.9	2.8	106.6
10	Martin Brodeur	2005-2015	515.6	234	1208	13829	.912	82.9	15.6	102.8
11	Miikka Kiprusoff	2005-2013	524.7	251	1322	15052	.912	106.3	3.8	99.7
12	Kari Lehtonen	2005-2015	486.7	270	1318	15201	.913	98.7	-8.6	98.8
13	Jonathan Quick	2007-2015	396.8	227	902	10651	.915	76.5	10.3	89.8
14	Craig Anderson	2005-2015	357.6	270	966	11572	.916	98.9	-10.3	87.7
15	Jonas Hiller	2007-2015	354.2	248	881	10568	.916	84.1	-1.0	83.4
16	Cory Schneider	2008-2015	199.7	216	433	5804	.925	85.7	0.5	82.7
17	Jaroslav Halak	2006-2015	318.5	238	760	9156	.916	76.9	2.6	80.6
18	Antti Niemi	2008-2015	328.4	239	786	9337	.915	54.2	4.4	70.6
19	Semyon Varlamov	2008-2015	257.8	254	657	8010	.917	64.7	-3.9	67.0
20	Ilya Bryzgalov	2005-2015	441.1	257	1138	12971	.912	76.1	0.2	66.8
21	Jimmy Howard	2005-2015	326.6	241	790	9363	.915	64.9	2.4	66.5
22	Jean-Sebastien Giguere	2005-2014	333.3	256	855	9699	.911	73.4	0.4	64.5
23	Niklas Backstrom	2006-2015	387.6	248	962	11283	.914	79.3	1.9	63.6
24	Sergei Bobrovsky	2010-2015	218	250	547	6711	.918	59.6	-3.1	60.7
25	Corey Crawford	2005-2015	257	233	601	7203	.916	46.1	4.3	57.0

Best 20 offensive forwards (since 2005-06, regular season)

Rank	Name	Season	GP	G	A	Pts	+/-	OGVT	DGVT	GVT
1	Alexander Ovechkin	2005-2015	760	475	420	895	57	190.7	18.9	206.9
2	Sidney Crosby	2005-2015	627	302	551	853	129	163.4	25.3	195.6
3	Evgeni Malkin	2006-2015	587	268	434	702	56	133.0	14.7	149.9
4	Marian Hossa	2005-2015	705	298	368	666	164	127.1	38.4	164.7
5	Jarome Iginla	2005-2015	766	339	384	723	59	126.2	25.6	149.9
6	Pavel Datsyuk	2005-2015	678	245	470	715	220	125.6	40.1	172.5
7	Martin St. Louis	2005-2015	770	282	492	774	-1	124.1	26.8	147.9
8	Daniel Sedin	2005-2015	746	266	464	730	153	123.5	28.4	147.8
9	Joe Thornton	2005-2015	776	198	640	838	149	121.4	43.4	165.0
10	Henrik Zetterberg	2005-2015	696	259	440	699	138	119.2	33.1	147.4
11	Eric Staal	2005-2015	765	301	410	711	-48	116.8	21.9	137.0
12	Jason Spezza	2005-2015	657	239	434	673	28	112.4	16.5	131.2
13	Henrik Sedin	2005-2015	774	167	602	769	175	110.8	31.8	141.4
14	Ilya Kovalchuk	2005-2013	589	309	302	611	-63	110.1	16.3	129.5
15	Thomas Vanek	2005-2015	743	298	310	608	35	106.8	16.9	126.1
16	Steven Stamkos	2008-2015	492	276	222	498	2	103.7	12.1	112.5
17	Corey Perry	2005-2015	722	296	306	602	92	103.4	28.9	134.4
18	Patrick Marleau	2005-2015	771	303	358	661	3	102.4	32.2	134.6
19	Ryan Getzlaf	2005-2015	710	208	470	678	124	102.0	31.6	133.5
20	Dany Heatley	2005-2015	679	292	318	610	73	100.9	22.8	119.1

Best 20 offensive defensemen (since 2005-06, regular season)

Rank	Name	Season	GP	G	A	Pts	+/-	OGVT	DGVT	GVT
1	Nicklas Lidstrom	2005-2012	548	91	325	416	173	85.8	42.3	128.1
2	Dan Boyle	2005-2015	694	116	314	430	-5	77.2	31.2	106.7
3	Mike Green	2005-2015	575	113	247	360	58	76.2	20.0	94.0
4	Zdeno Chara	2005-2015	736	128	278	406	157	75.2	45.1	119.9
5	Shea Weber	2005-2015	685	146	246	392	55	74.7	39.5	113.9
6	Lubomir Visnovsky	2005-2015	615	101	281	382	19	70.9	28.1	99.3
7	Sergei Gonchar	2005-2015	632	72	314	386	-24	68.9	13.1	81.6
8	Andrei Markov	2005-2015	579	78	302	380	48	68.4	24.2	92.9
9	Mark Streit	2005-2015	654	84	300	384	-58	68.0	17.6	83.9
10	Dion Phaneuf	2005-2015	750	117	283	400	-6	66.8	27.7	92.5
11	Erik Karlsson	2009-2015	397	84	219	303	-20	66.6	6.5	73.1
12	Brian Campbell	2005-2015	753	67	348	415	40	65.4	34.9	100.0
13	Duncan Keith	2005-2015	766	75	340	415	137	64.9	54.7	119.6
14	Kimmo Timonen	2005-2015	694	62	313	375	58	62.5	26.2	88.1
15	Dustin Byfuglien	2005-2015	597	134	210	344	-41	59.8	16.8	74.5
16	Tomas Kaberle	2005-2013	541	46	293	339	-40	58.7	14.9	74.3
17	Chris Pronger	2005-2012	445	63	235	298	58	57.1	23.8	80.1
18	Brian Rafalski	2005-2011	456	49	259	308	82	56.3	31.8	88.1
19	Brent Burns	2005-2015	679	113	229	342	14	55.4	34.9	90.8
20	Niklas Kronwall	2005-2015	654	70	265	335	37	53.2	36.7	89.7

Best 20 defensive forwards (since 2005-06, regular season)

Rank	Name	Season	GP	G	A	Pts	+/-	OGVT	DGVT	GVT
1	Joe Thornton	2005-2015	776	198	640	838	149	121.4	43.4	165.0
2	Zach Parise	2005-2015	691	274	292	566	90	88.5	40.4	137.0
3	Pavel Datsyuk	2005-2015	678	245	470	715	220	125.6	40.1	172.5
4	Anze Kopitar	2006-2015	683	218	392	610	45	88.5	39.1	130.9
5	Patrik Elias	2005-2015	666	199	359	558	27	77.8	39.0	118.5
6	Marian Hossa	2005-2015	705	298	368	666	164	127.1	38.4	164.7
7	Travis Zajac	2006-2015	625	127	221	348	31	25.5	34.9	58.1
8	Jonathan Toews	2007-2015	565	223	283	506	171	91.1	34.7	137.6
9	Alexandre Burrows	2005-2015	688	175	167	342	122	41.9	34.7	78.4
10	Henrik Zetterberg	2005-2015	696	259	440	699	138	119.2	33.1	147.4
11	Tomas Plekanec	2005-2015	759	202	297	499	40	65.5	32.6	93.2
12	David Backes	2006-2015	648	185	230	415	61	53.9	32.4	85.2
13	Patrick Marleau	2005-2015	771	303	358	661	3	102.4	32.2	134.6
14	Henrik Sedin	2005-2015	774	167	602	769	175	110.8	31.8	141.4
15	Joe Pavelski	2006-2015	643	228	257	485	76	79.9	31.8	115.2
16	Ryan Getzlaf	2005-2015	710	208	470	678	124	102.0	31.6	133.5
17	Matt Cooke	2005-2016	667	109	150	259	35	23.5	30.2	53.7
18	Jarret Stoll	2005-2015	720	130	227	357	-2	27.0	29.2	59.6
19	Chris Kelly	2005-2015	736	116	159	275	55	22.0	29.1	50.5
20	Corey Perry	2005-2015	722	296	306	602	92	103.4	28.9	134.4

Best 20 defensive defensemen (since 2005-06, regular season)

Rank	Name	Season	GP	G	A	Pts	+/-	OGVT	DGVT	GVT
1	Marc-Edouard Vlasic	2006-2015	670	39	148	187	110	13.5	56.8	70.1
2	Willie Mitchell	2005-2015	619	26	95	121	107	-3.0	55.1	51.8
3	Duncan Keith	2005-2015	766	75	340	415	137	64.9	54.7	119.6
4	Barret Jackman	2005-2015	705	24	135	159	31	2.1	53.4	55.5
5	Brent Seabrook	2005-2015	763	71	247	318	108	44.4	48.3	93.3
6	Andy Greene	2006-2015	559	31	140	171	7	11.5	48.1	59.6
7	Paul Martin	2005-2015	627	37	211	248	88	25.4	47.9	73.3
8	Rob Scuderi	2005-2015	707	7	90	97	16	-15.7	47.8	32.1
9	Dan Hamhuis	2005-2015	734	45	219	264	95	29.3	47.1	76.5
10	Ryan Suter	2005-2015	749	52	299	351	67	42.0	46.9	88.9
11	Anton Volchenkov	2005-2015	620	15	99	114	75	-1.5	46.2	44.7
12	Brooks Orpik	2005-2015	696	12	129	141	78	-5.6	46.2	41.2
13	Robyn Regehr	2005-2015	726	24	121	145	58	-0.7	45.5	44.8
14	Zdeno Chara	2005-2015	736	128	278	406	157	75.2	45.1	119.9
15	Daniel Girardi	2006-2015	651	40	158	198	28	12.6	43.8	56.4
16	Drew Doughty	2008-2015	524	66	201	267	38	34.9	43.3	77.5
17	Trevor Daley	2005-2015	729	66	159	225	12	22.4	43.1	65.5
18	Nicklas Lidstrom	2005-2012	548	91	325	416	173	85.8	42.3	128.1
19	Christian Ehrhoff	2005-2015	700	71	244	315	55	40.4	41.5	81.9
20	Stephane Robidas	2005-2015	680	44	168	212	22	16.1	41.3	57.0

Best 20 shootout skaters (since 2005-06)

Rank	Name	Season	Goals	Shots	SGVT
1	Frans Nielsen	2006-2015	38	72	12.6
2	Jonathan Toews	2007-2015	40	80	11.8
3	T.J. Oshie	2008-2015	31	58	10.6
4	Vyacheslav Kozlov	2005-2010	27	46	9.4
5	Erik Christensen	2005-2012	29	55	9.4
6	Brad Boyes	2005-2015	39	87	9.0
7	Zach Parise	2005-2015	39	89	8.1
8	Radim Vrbata	2005-2015	37	87	7.8
9	Mikko Koivu	2005-2015	38	89	7.4
10	Sidney Crosby	2005-2015	31	71	6.9
11	Pavel Datsyuk	2005-2015	38	91	6.8
12	Patrick Kane	2007-2015	36	87	6.7
13	Ales Kotalik	2005-2011	22	44	5.9
14	Jakob Silfverberg	2011-2015	14	23	5.8
15	Jussi Jokinen	2005-2015	35	88	4.9
16	Tyler Seguin	2010-2015	18	38	4.8
17	Mike Santorelli	2008-2015	16	34	4.5
18	David Desharnais	2009-2015	17	37	4.4
19	Michal Handzus	2005-2014	19	42	4.3
20	Milan Hejduk	2005-2013	25	60	4.3

Best 20 shootout goaltenders (since 2005-06)

Rank	Name	Season	Goals	Shots	SGVT
1	Henrik Lundqvist	2005-2015	82	327	20.3
2	Marc-Andre Fleury	2005-2015	59	237	14.8
3	Antti Niemi	2008-2015	55	214	12.0
4	Tim Thomas	2005-2014	64	234	10.2
5	Ryan Miller	2005-2015	81	284	9.9
6	Johan Hedberg	2005-2013	32	129	8.7
7	Kari Lehtonen	2005-2015	63	228	8.7
8	Mathieu Garon	2005-2013	27	109	7.6
9	Corey Crawford	2005-2015	44	158	6.6
10	Carey Price	2007-2015	51	178	6.5
11	Marc Denis	2005-2009	6	41	6.2
12	Semyon Varlamov	2008-2015	33	127	6.2
13	Rick DiPietro	2005-2013	34	126	6.1
14	Pekka Rinne	2005-2015	58	200	5.9
15	Johan Holmqvist	2006-2008	5	37	5.9
16	Jhonas Enroth	2009-2015	17	70	4.7
17	Tuukka Rask	2007-2015	46	160	4.6
18	Eddie Lack	2013-2015	7	39	4.5
19	Martin Brodeur	2005-2015	75	244	4.3
20	Sergei Bobrovsky	2010-2015	28	102	4.1

Best 20 forwards (since 2005-06, playoffs)

Rank	Name	Season	GP	G	A	Pts	+/-	OGVT	DGVT	GVT
1	Henrik Zetterberg	2005-2015	115	52	61	113	43	35.8	9.1	44.9
2	Sidney Crosby	2005-2015	100	43	75	118	13	36.6	5.2	41.8
3	Evgeni Malkin	2006-2015	101	42	69	111	7	34.0	4.6	38.6
4	Daniel Briere	2005-2015	118	51	62	113	-6	34.7	3.4	38.1
5	Pavel Datsyuk	2005-2015	114	39	62	101	33	29.7	8.1	37.8
6	Patrick Kane	2007-2015	115	48	66	114	7	33.1	4.4	37.5
7	Marian Hossa	2005-2015	142	36	74	110	32	26.2	7.8	34.0
8	Jonathan Toews	2007-2015	116	38	62	100	16	25.7	5.6	31.3
9	Johan Franzen	2005-2015	106	42	39	81	27	23.1	7.2	30.3
10	Ryan Getzlaf	2005-2015	97	27	67	94	5	26.6	3.2	29.8
11	Justin Williams	2005-2015	95	28	43	71	32	19.0	7.8	26.8
12	David Krejci	2006-2015	90	28	47	75	28	20.4	6.2	26.6
13	Corey Perry	2005-2015	90	32	42	74	8	20.8	3.3	24.2
14	Patrick Sharp	2005-2015	116	42	38	80	9	19.7	4.4	24.1
15	Alexander Ovechkin	2005-2015	72	36	34	70	6	21.0	2.9	23.9
16	Mike Richards	2005-2015	121	26	58	84	-9	19.7	4.1	23.8
17	Claude Giroux	2007-2015	57	23	38	61	15	19.1	4.3	23.3
18	Jeff Carter	2005-2015	108	35	35	70	-1	18.5	4.4	22.8
19	Patrick Marleau	2005-2015	96	41	31	72	-10	19.0	3.6	22.6
20	Joe Thornton	2005-2015	97	18	64	82	-17	19.0	3.2	22.2

Best 20 defensemen (since 2005-06, playoffs)

Rank	Name	Season	GP	G	A	Pts	+/-	OGVT	DGVT	GVT
1	Nicklas Lidstrom	2005-2012	95	20	47	67	30	21.0	10.6	31.5
2	Chris Pronger	2005-2012	88	16	54	70	25	21.2	8.4	29.6
3	Duncan Keith	2005-2015	115	15	59	74	35	19.0	10.2	29.3
4	Brian Rafalski	2005-2011	83	15	42	57	22	16.8	7.3	24.1
5	Kris Letang	2006-2015	93	15	38	53	4	14.6	7.1	21.8
6	Brent Seabrook	2005-2015	111	19	38	57	13	13.6	7.2	20.7
7	Zdeno Chara	2005-2015	103	13	35	48	25	11.4	9.1	20.5
8	Dan Boyle	2005-2015	92	15	48	63	-17	16.2	3.9	20.1
9	Drew Doughty	2008-2015	73	15	32	47	3	14.2	5.9	20.1
10	Sergei Gonchar	2005-2015	83	8	46	54	-1	14.1	5.4	19.4
11	Niklas Kronwall	2005-2015	103	5	41	46	23	9.4	9.4	18.8
12	Brian Campbell	2005-2015	97	9	34	43	9	9.7	7.5	17.2
13	Brad Stuart	2005-2015	96	7	22	29	28	4.4	9.3	13.7
14	P.K. Subban	2009-2015	55	11	27	38	1	10.5	3.1	13.6
15	Paul Martin	2005-2015	80	4	34	38	2	8.2	5.3	13.4
16	Francois Beauchemin	2005-2015	97	10	29	39	4	8.3	5.0	13.3
17	Scott Niedermayer	2005-2010	56	0	26	34	1	9.8	3.3	13.1
18	Viatcheslav Voynov	2011-2015	61	9	16	25	15	6.4	6.4	12.8
19	Ryan McDonagh	2010-2015	81	8	26	34	4	6.4	5.4	11.8
20	Johnny Boychuk	2007-2015	83	13	15	28	17	5.4	6.4	11.8

Best 20 goaltenders (since 2005-06, playoffs)

Rank	Name	Season	GP	GAA	GA	SA	SV%	GGVT
1	Henrik Lundqvist	2005-2015	114.0	222	253	3292	.923	33.9
2	Jonathan Quick	2007-2014	75.1	223	168	2180	.922	28.2
3	Tim Thomas	2005-2014	49.9	212	106	1527	.930	28.1
4	Tuukka Rask	2007-2014	49.8	208	104	1487	.930	27.9
5	Dwayne Roloson	2005-2012	35.7	240	86	1159	.925	21.7
6	Chris Osgood	2005-2011	42.8	180	77	1067	.927	20.3
7	Mike Smith	2006-2014	36.0	191	69	1076	.935	17.6
8	Roberto Luongo	2005-2014	19.1	188	36	650	.944	17.4
9	Jonas Hiller	2007-2014	63.1	248	157	1911	.917	16.9
10	Cam Ward	2005-2014	26.8	234	63	941	.933	15.6
11	Corey Crawford	2005-2014	79.1	223	177	2239	.920	15.0
12	Ryan Miller	2005-2014	29.8	235	70	1000	.930	14.3
13	Marty Turco	2005-2012	40.4	237	96	1160	.917	14.3
14	Jaroslav Halak	2006-2014	58.7	248	146	1709	.914	12.7
15	Jimmy Howard	2005-2014	33.0	209	69	876	.921	11.9
16	Craig Anderson	2005-2014	27.2	238	65	855	.923	11.7
17	Martin Brodeur	2005-2014	44.7	255	114	1392	.918	9.7
18	Braden Holtby	2010-2014	59.0	238	141	1662	.915	8.9
19	Semyon Varlamov	2008-2014	25.7	257	66	773	.914	5.7
20	Cristobal Huet	2005-2010	16.4	267	44	535	.917	5.6

Best players of 2014-15

Best 50 forwards (2014-15, regular season)

Rank	Name	Team(s)	GP	G	A	Pts	+/-	OGVT	DGVT	SGVT	GVT
1	Tyler Johnson	TBL	77	29	43	72	33	15.4	6.8	0.0	22.1
2	Max Pacioretty	MTL	80	37	30	67	38	13.7	7.0	1.0	21.6
3	Jamie Benn	DAL	82	35	52	87	1	18.5	3.1	0.0	21.5
4	Vladimir Tarasenko	STL	77	37	36	73	27	15.5	4.2	1.5	21.3
5	Rick Nash	NYR	79	42	27	69	29	16.1	4.4	0.4	21.0
6	Alex Ovechkin	WSH	81	53	28	81	10	18.3	2.8	-0.4	20.8
7	Tyler Seguin	DAL	71	37	40	77	-1	17.7	1.2	1.6	20.5
8	John Tavares	NYI	82	38	48	86	5	16.9	3.3	-0.3	19.9
9	Sidney Crosby	PIT	77	28	56	84	5	15.7	1.8	2.0	19.6
10	Jonathan Toews	CHI	81	28	38	66	30	11.0	5.8	2.1	18.9
11	Jiri Hudler	CGY	78	31	45	76	17	14.0	4.3	0.2	18.5
12	Nikita Kucherov	TBL	82	29	36	65	38	12.9	4.9	0.4	18.2
13	Jakub Voracek	PHI	82	22	59	81	1	13.4	2.7	1.2	17.3
14	Zach Parise	MIN	74	33	29	62	21	13.5	3.6	0.2	17.2
15	Jaden Schwartz	STL	75	28	35	63	13	13.3	3.8	0.0	17.2
16	Joe Pavelski	SJS	82	37	33	70	12	13.1	4.6	-0.6	17.1
17	Steven Stamkos	TBL	82	43	29	72	2	16.7	1.1	-0.8	17.0
18	Nick Foligno	CBJ	79	31	42	73	16	14.5	3.4	-1.1	16.8
19	Pavel Datsyuk	DET	63	26	39	65	12	13.8	3.3	-0.3	16.8
20	Mark Stone	OTT	80	26	38	64	21	12.5	3.4	0.4	16.3
21	Patrick Kane	CHI	61	27	37	64	10	11.4	2.2	2.7	16.3
22	Ondrej Palat	TBL	75	16	47	63	31	10.9	5.9	-0.5	16.2
23	Ryan Getzlaf	ANA	77	25	45	70	15	12.0	4.6	-0.5	16.1
24	Daniel Sedin	VAN	82	20	56	76	5	13.5	1.9	0.0	15.5
25	Derek Stepan	NYR	68	16	39	55	26	10.1	4.6	0.7	15.4
26	Nicklas Backstrom	WSH	82	18	60	78	5	12.3	3.1	0.0	15.4
27	Ryan Johansen	CBJ	82	26	45	71	-6	10.7	2.0	2.4	15.2
28	Marian Hossa	CHI	82	22	39	61	17	9.4	5.9	-0.3	15.0
29	Corey Perry	ANA	67	33	22	55	13	11.5	3.0	0.3	14.7
30	Filip Forsberg	NSH	82	26	37	63	15	10.5	3.6	0.5	14.6
31	Blake Wheeler	WPG	79	26	35	61	26	9.5	4.8	0.4	14.6
32	Henrik Sedin	VAN	82	18	55	73	11	11.7	2.6	0.0	14.3
33	Tomas Tatar	DET	82	29	27	56	6	11.5	2.5	0.3	14.3
34	Radim Vrbata	VAN	79	31	32	63	6	12.3	1.6	0.2	14.0
35	Jakob Silfverberg	ANA	81	13	26	39	15	5.4	4.1	4.5	14.0
36	Sean Monahan	CGY	81	31	31	62	8	10.1	3.7	0.2	14.0
37	Jeff Carter	LAK	82	28	34	62	7	9.8	4.8	-0.6	13.9
38	Tomas Plekanec	MTL	82	26	34	60	8	9.8	4.6	-0.8	13.6
39	T.J. Oshie	STL	72	19	36	55	17	8.1	4.6	0.9	13.6
40	Logan Couture	SJS	82	27	40	67	-6	9.9	3.0	0.5	13.5
41	Tyler Toffoli	LAK	76	23	26	49	25	8.6	5.5	-1.1	13.1
42	Jarome Iginla	COL	82	29	30	59	0	10.4	1.7	1.0	13.0
43	Gustav Nyquist	DET	82	27	27	54	-11	8.7	0.9	3.4	13.0
44	John Gaudreau	CGY	80	24	40	64	11	8.9	3.7	0.2	12.8
45	David Backes	STL	80	26	32	58	7	8.1	4.5	0.0	12.7
46	Alex Steen	STL	74	24	40	64	8	9.1	4.4	-0.9	12.7
47	Andrew Ladd	WPG	81	24	38	62	9	9.7	3.7	-0.9	12.6
48	Bryan Little	WPG	70	24	28	52	8	9.3	3.6	-0.6	12.3
49	Kevin Hayes	NYR	79	17	28	45	15	9.8	2.6	-0.3	12.1
50	Matt Duchene	COL	82	21	34	55	3	8.3	2.0	1.6	11.9

Best 50 defensemen (2014-15, regular season)

Rank	Name	Team(s)	GP	G	A	Pts	+/-	OGVT	DGVT	SGVT	GVT
1	John Carlson	WSH	82	12	43	55	11	11.7	6.6	0.6	18.9
2	Roman Josi	NSH	81	15	40	55	15	10.7	6.6	-0.2	17.2
3	P.K. Subban	MTL	82	15	45	60	21	10.8	5.8	-0.3	16.3
4	Mark Giordano	CGY	61	11	37	48	13	10.4	5.4	0.0	15.7
5	Kris Letang	PIT	69	11	43	54	12	9.2	5.9	0.4	15.5
6	Brent Burns	SJS	82	17	43	60	-9	11.7	3.0	0.4	15.1
7	Erik Karlsson	OTT	82	21	45	66	7	13.8	1.4	-0.2	15.0
8	Dennis Wideman	CGY	80	15	41	56	6	10.6	4.3	0.0	14.9
9	Justin Faulk	CAR	82	15	34	49	-19	8.3	6.3	0.0	14.6
10	Kevin Shattenkirk	STL	56	8	36	44	19	8.5	4.8	1.2	14.5
11	Shea Weber	NSH	78	15	30	45	15	7.9	6.5	0.0	14.4
12	T.J. Brodie	CGY	81	11	30	41	15	6.9	6.8	0.0	13.7
13	Alex Pietrangelo	STL	81	7	39	46	-2	7.6	5.5	0.0	13.1
14	Victor Hedman	TBL	59	10	28	38	12	8.4	3.9	0.6	12.9
15	Nick Leddy	NYI	78	10	27	37	18	7.6	5.2	0.0	12.8
16	Andrei Markov	MTL	81	10	40	50	22	7.0	5.9	-0.3	12.6
17	Duncan Keith	CHI	80	10	35	45	12	6.5	5.8	0.0	12.3
18	Dustin Byfuglien	WPG	69	18	27	45	5	9.3	2.8	0.0	12.2
19	Mike Green	WSH	72	10	35	45	15	9.1	3.3	-0.3	12.1
20	Hampus Lindholm	ANA	78	7	27	34	25	5.1	6.8	0.0	12.0
21	Anton Stralman	TBL	82	9	30	39	22	5.4	6.2	0.0	11.6
22	Kevin Klein	NYR	65	9	17	26	24	5.5	5.8	0.0	11.3
23	Travis Hamonic	NYI	71	5	28	33	15	6.2	5.0	0.0	11.2
24	Drew Doughty	LAK	82	7	39	46	3	4.9	6.5	-0.3	11.1
25	Aaron Ekblad	FLA	81	12	27	39	12	6.3	4.9	-0.3	10.9
26	Niklas Kronwall	DET	80	9	35	44	-4	6.3	4.8	-0.5	10.5
27	Jason Garrison	TBL	70	4	26	30	27	3.8	6.6	0.0	10.4
28	Jake Muzzin	LAK	76	10	31	41	-4	6.9	3.5	0.0	10.4
29	Oliver Ekman-Larsson	ARI	82	23	20	43	-18	7.9	3.0	-0.5	10.3
30	Danny DeKeyser	DET	80	2	29	31	11	4.1	6.1	0.0	10.3
31	Tyson Barrie	COL	80	12	41	53	5	9.4	1.5	-0.5	10.3
32	John Klingberg	DAL	65	11	29	40	5	8.7	2.0	-0.5	10.2
33	Sami Vatanen	ANA	67	12	25	37	5	6.4	3.1	0.6	10.1
34	Johnny Boychuk	NYI	72	9	26	35	15	5.3	4.7	0.0	10.1
35	Torey Krug	BOS	78	12	27	39	12	6.9	3.8	-0.7	10.0
36	Mark Streit	PHI	81	9	43	52	-8	8.0	1.9	0.0	9.9
37	Ryan Suter	MIN	77	2	36	38	7	3.2	6.6	0.0	9.8
38	Ryan McDonagh	NYR	71	8	25	33	23	4.6	4.9	0.0	9.5
39	Dougie Hamilton	BOS	72	10	32	42	-2	6.8	2.8	-0.3	9.3
40	Francois Beauchemin	ANA	64	11	12	23	17	4.2	5.0	0.0	9.3
41	Trevor Daley	DAL	68	16	22	38	-13	7.8	1.5	-0.3	9.1
42	Alex Goligoski	DAL	81	4	32	36	0	4.7	4.4	0.0	9.0
43	Marc-Edouard Vlasic	SJS	70	9	14	23	12	2.6	6.4	0.0	9.0
44	Michael Del Zotto	PHI	64	10	22	32	-5	6.1	2.9	0.0	8.9
45	Niklas Hjalmarsson	CHI	82	3	16	19	25	1.2	7.5	0.0	8.8
46	Kris Russell	CGY	79	4	30	34	18	2.2	6.4	0.0	8.6
47	David Savard	CBJ	82	11	25	36	0	5.8	2.8	0.0	8.6
48	Alexander Edler	VAN	74	8	23	31	13	2.9	5.7	0.0	8.6
49	Ryan Ellis	NSH	58	9	18	27	8	5.8	3.1	-0.4	8.5
50	Paul Martin	PIT	74	3	17	20	17	0.8	7.6	0.0	8.4

Best 25 goaltenders (2014-15, regular season)

Rank	Name	Team(s)	GP	GAA	GA	SA	SV%	GGVT	DGVT	SGVT	GVT
1	Carey Price	MTL	66.3	196	130	1953	.933	39.7	-0.1	2.3	42.0
2	Devan Dubnyk	MIN, ARI	55.5	207	115	1625	.929	27.0	0.2	0.2	27.4
3	Cory Schneider	NJD	65.4	226	148	1982	.925	27.1	-0.6	-0.5	26.0
4	Braden Holtby	WSH	70.8	221	157	2044	.923	24.6	0.4	0.6	25.6
5	Tuukka Rask	BOS	67.7	230	156	2011	.922	21.5	-0.2	2.4	23.7
6	Corey Crawford	CHI	55.6	226	126	1661	.924	18.8	0.0	2.4	21.2
7	Pekka Rinne	NSH	64.2	218	140	1807	.922	19.4	0.9	0.4	20.8
8	Steve Mason	PHI	48.1	224	108	1490	.927	22.9	-0.8	-3.5	18.6
9	Andrew Hammond	OTT	23.5	178	42	707	.940	18.6	-0.2	0.2	18.6
10	Roberto Luongo	FLA	58.8	234	138	1743	.920	16.5	-0.2	1.3	17.7
11	Sergei Bobrovsky	CBJ	49.9	268	134	1632	.917	12.8	-1.8	6.1	17.1
12	Marc-Andre Fleury	PIT	62.9	231	146	1831	.920	17.9	0.1	-2.1	15.9
13	Semyon Varlamov	COL	55.1	255	141	1791	.921	16.7	-1.5	-0.1	15.1
14	Henrik Lundqvist	NYR	45.7	225	103	1329	.922	14.1	0.3	-0.8	13.6
15	Cam Talbot	NYR	34.9	220	77	1038	.925	13.8	0.0	-1.5	12.3
16	Eddie Lack	VAN	38.7	245	95	1201	.920	11.8	-0.6	1.1	12.3
17	Jonathan Quick	LAK	69.7	223	156	1896	.917	13.1	1.7	-2.5	12.3
18	Ondrej Pavelec	WPG	47.3	228	108	1353	.920	14.4	0.1	-2.4	12.1
19	Craig Anderson	OTT	34.9	249	87	1134	.923	12.9	-1.1	0.0	11.8
20	Scott Darling	CHI	13.9	194	27	419	.935	8.8	0.0	1.9	10.6
21	Ben Bishop	TBL	58.7	231	136	1620	.916	9.7	1.1	-0.8	10.1
22	Brian Elliott	STL	42.4	226	96	1150	.916	7.4	0.9	0.7	9.1
23	Calvin Pickard	COL	14.9	234	35	511	.931	9.1	-0.6	-0.1	8.3
24	Antti Niemi	SJS	59.8	259	155	1811	.914	6.0	-0.2	2.2	8.1
25	Michael Hutchinson	WPG	35.6	238	85	986	.913	5.3	0.4	2.0	7.7

Best 20 offensive forwards (2014-15, regular season)

Rank	Name	Team(s)	GP	G	A	Pts	+/-	OGVT	DGVT	SGVT	GVT
1	Jamie Benn	DAL	82	35	52	87	1	18.5	3.1	0.0	21.5
2	Alex Ovechkin	WSH	81	53	28	81	10	18.3	2.8	-0.4	20.8
3	Tyler Seguin	DAL	71	37	40	77	-1	17.7	1.2	1.6	20.5
4	John Tavares	NYI	82	38	48	86	5	16.9	3.3	-0.3	19.9
5	Steven Stamkos	TBL	82	43	29	72	2	16.7	1.1	-0.8	17.0
6	Rick Nash	NYR	79	42	27	69	29	16.1	4.4	0.4	21.0
7	Sidney Crosby	PIT	77	28	56	84	5	15.7	1.8	2.0	19.6
8	Vladimir Tarasenko	STL	77	37	36	73	27	15.5	4.2	1.5	21.3
9	Tyler Johnson	TBL	77	29	43	72	33	15.4	6.8	0.0	22.1
10	Nick Foligno	CBJ	79	31	42	73	16	14.5	3.4	-1.1	16.8
11	Jiri Hudler	CGY	78	31	45	76	17	14.0	4.3	0.2	18.5
12	Pavel Datsyuk	DET	63	26	39	65	12	13.8	3.3	-0.3	16.8
13	Max Pacioretty	MTL	80	37	30	67	38	13.7	7.0	1.0	21.6
14	Zach Parise	MIN	74	33	29	62	21	13.5	3.6	0.2	17.2
15	Daniel Sedin	VAN	82	20	56	76	5	13.5	1.9	0.0	15.5
16	Jakub Voracek	PHI	82	22	59	81	1	13.4	2.7	1.2	17.3
17	Jaden Schwartz	STL	75	28	35	63	13	13.3	3.8	0.0	17.2
18	Joe Pavelski	SJS	82	37	33	70	12	13.1	4.6	-0.6	17.1
19	Nikita Kucherov	TBL	82	29	36	65	38	12.9	4.9	0.4	18.2
20	Mark Stone	OTT	80	26	38	64	21	12.5	3.4	0.4	16.3

Best 20 offensive defensemen (2014-15, regular season)

Rank	Name	Team(s)	GP	G	A	Pts	+/-	OGVT	DGVT	SGVT	GVT
1	Erik Karlsson	OTT	82	21	45	66	7	13.8	1.4	-0.2	15.0
2	John Carlson	WSH	82	12	43	55	11	11.7	6.6	0.6	18.9
3	Brent Burns	SJS	82	17	43	60	-9	11.7	3.0	0.4	15.1
4	P.K. Subban	MTL	82	15	45	60	21	10.8	5.8	-0.3	16.3
5	Roman Josi	NSH	81	15	40	55	15	10.7	6.6	-0.2	17.2
6	Dennis Wideman	CGY	80	15	41	56	6	10.6	4.3	0.0	14.9
7	Mark Giordano	CGY	61	11	37	48	13	10.4	5.4	0.0	15.7
8	Tyson Barrie	COL	80	12	41	53	5	9.4	1.5	-0.5	10.3
9	Dustin Byfuglien	WPG	69	18	27	45	5	9.3	2.8	0.0	12.2
10	Kris Letang	PIT	69	11	43	54	12	9.2	5.9	0.4	15.5
11	Mike Green	WSH	72	10	35	45	15	9.1	3.3	-0.3	12.1
12	John Klingberg	DAL	65	11	29	40	5	8.7	2.0	-0.5	10.2
13	Kevin Shattenkirk	STL	56	8	36	44	19	8.5	4.8	1.2	14.5
14	Victor Hedman	TBL	59	10	28	38	12	8.4	3.9	0.6	12.9
15	Justin Faulk	CAR	82	15	34	49	-19	8.3	6.3	0.0	14.6
16	Mark Streit	PHI	81	9	43	52	-8	8.0	1.9	0.0	9.9
17	Shea Weber	NSH	78	15	30	45	15	7.9	6.5	0.0	14.4
18	Oliver Ekman-Larsson	ARI	82	23	20	43	-18	7.9	3.0	-0.5	10.3
19	Keith Yandle	NYR, ARI	84	6	46	52	-26	7.9	0.4	0.0	8.2
20	Trevor Daley	DAL	68	16	22	38	-13	7.8	1.5	-0.3	9.1

Best 20 defensive forwards (2014-15, regular season)

Rank	Name	Team(s)	GP	G	A	Pts	+/-	OGVT	DGVT	SGVT	GVT
1	Max Pacioretty	MTL	80	37	30	67	38	13.7	7.0	1.0	21.6
2	Jay McClement	CAR	82	7	14	21	-7	-2.3	6.9	-0.3	4.4
3	Tyler Johnson	TBL	77	29	43	72	33	15.4	6.8	0.0	22.1
4	Daniel Winnik	PIT, TOR	79	9	25	34	23	4.7	6.1	0.0	10.8
5	Ondrej Palat	TBL	75	16	47	63	31	10.9	5.9	-0.5	16.2
6	Marian Hossa	CHI	82	22	39	61	17	9.4	5.9	-0.3	15.0
7	Jonathan Toews	CHI	81	28	38	66	30	11.0	5.8	2.1	18.9
8	Tyler Toffoli	LAK	76	23	26	49	25	8.6	5.5	-1.1	13.1
9	Luke Glendening	DET	82	12	6	18	5	0.2	5.3	0.0	5.4
10	Ryan Strome	NYI	81	17	33	50	23	6.4	5.2	-1.1	10.5
11	Brandon Sutter	PIT	80	21	12	33	6	4.9	5.2	-0.2	10.0
12	Chris Higgins	VAN	77	12	24	36	8	4.5	5.1	0.7	10.3
13	Nikita Kucherov	TBL	82	29	36	65	38	12.9	4.9	0.4	18.2
14	Jeff Carter	LAK	82	28	34	62	7	9.8	4.8	-0.6	13.9
15	Blake Wheeler	WPG	79	26	35	61	26	9.5	4.8	0.4	14.6
16	Carl Hagelin	NYR	82	17	18	35	18	5.4	4.8	0.0	10.2
17	Maxime Talbot	BOS, COL	81	5	13	18	-1	-1.8	4.8	0.6	3.7
18	Lance Bouma	CGY	78	16	18	34	10	5.1	4.7	0.0	9.8
19	Joe Pavelski	SJS	82	37	33	70	12	13.1	4.6	-0.6	17.1
20	Ryan Getzlaf	ANA	77	25	45	70	15	12.0	4.6	-0.5	16.1

Best 20 defensive defensemen (2014-15, regular season)

Rank	Name	Team(s)	GP	G	A	Pts	+/-	OGVT	DGVT	SGVT	GVT
1	Rob Scuderi	PIT	82	1	9	10	9	-1.4	7.7	0.0	6.3
2	Paul Martin	PIT	74	3	17	20	17	0.8	7.6	0.0	8.4
3	Niklas Hjalmarsson	CHI	82	3	16	19	25	1.2	7.5	0.0	8.8
4	Jonas Brodin	MIN	71	3	14	17	21	0.1	7.5	0.0	7.6
5	T.J. Brodie	CGY	81	11	30	41	15	6.9	6.8	0.0	13.7
6	Hampus Lindholm	ANA	78	7	27	34	25	5.1	6.8	0.0	12.0
7	Andrej Sekera	LAK, CAR	73	3	20	23	-3	0.7	6.7	0.0	7.4
8	John Carlson	WSH	82	12	43	55	11	11.7	6.6	0.6	18.9
9	Roman Josi	NSH	81	15	40	55	15	10.7	6.6	-0.2	17.2
10	Jason Garrison	TBL	70	4	26	30	27	3.8	6.6	0.0	10.4
11	Ryan Suter	MIN	77	2	36	38	7	3.2	6.6	0.0	9.8
12	Shea Weber	NSH	78	15	30	45	15	7.9	6.5	0.0	14.4
13	Drew Doughty	LAK	82	7	39	46	3	4.9	6.5	-0.3	11.1
14	Marc-Edouard Vlasic	SJS	70	9	14	23	12	2.6	6.4	0.0	9.0
15	Kris Russell	CGY	79	4	30	34	18	2.2	6.4	0.0	8.6
16	Andy Greene	NJD	82	3	19	22	1	0.8	6.4	0.0	7.2
17	Justin Faulk	CAR	82	15	34	49	-19	8.3	6.3	0.0	14.6
18	Anton Stralman	TBL	82	9	30	39	22	5.4	6.2	0.0	11.6
19	Ron Hainsey	CAR	81	2	8	10	-14	-2.8	6.2	0.0	3.4
20	Danny DeKeyser	DET	80	2	29	31	11	4.1	6.1	0.0	10.3

Best 20 forwards (2014-15, playoffs)

Rank	Name	Team(s)	GP	G	A	Pts	+/-	OGVT	DGVT	GVT
1	Tyler Johnson	TBL	26	13	10	23	7	6.6	1.0	7.6
2	Nikita Kucherov	TBL	26	10	12	22	7	5.6	1.0	6.6
3	Patrick Kane	CHI	23	11	12	23	7	6.1	0.4	6.5
4	Corey Perry	ANA	16	10	8	18	6	5.2	0.5	5.7
5	Jonathan Toews	CHI	23	10	11	21	7	5.2	0.4	5.6
6	Ryan Getzlaf	ANA	16	2	18	20	6	4.5	0.5	5.0
7	Derick Brassard	NYR	19	9	7	16	9	3.8	1.1	4.9
8	Jakob Silfverberg	ANA	16	4	14	18	6	4.1	0.5	4.6
9	Alex Killorn	TBL	26	9	9	18	3	3.8	0.5	4.3
10	Steven Stamkos	TBL	26	7	11	18	2	3.4	0.4	3.8
11	Ondrej Palat	TBL	26	8	8	16	5	2.9	0.8	3.6
12	Rick Nash	NYR	19	5	9	14	8	2.3	1.0	3.3
13	Zach Parise	MIN	10	4	6	10	0	3.0	0.2	3.3
14	Marian Hossa	CHI	23	4	13	17	7	2.5	0.4	2.9
15	Ryan Kesler	ANA	16	7	6	13	2	2.8	0.0	2.8
16	Vladimir Tarasenko	STL	6	6	1	7	-4	2.7	-0.3	2.4
17	Filip Forsberg	NSH	6	4	2	6	1	2.3	0.1	2.4
18	Patrick Maroon	ANA	16	7	4	11	4	2.1	0.2	2.3
19	John Gaudreau	CGY	11	4	5	9	-2	2.2	-0.2	2.0
20	Colin Wilson	NSH	6	5	0	5	-1	2.1	-0.2	1.9

Best 10 defensemen (2014-15, playoffs)

Rank	Name	Team(s)	GP	G	A	Pts	+/-	OGVT	DGVT	GVT
1	Duncan Keith	CHI	23	3	18	21	16	5.5	1.3	6.7
2	Victor Hedman	TBL	26	1	13	14	11	2.4	1.6	4.0
3	Kevin Shattenkirk	STL	6	0	8	8	2	2.3	0.6	2.9
4	Sami Vatanen	ANA	16	3	8	11	5	2.5	0.4	2.8
5	Keith Yandle	NYR	19	2	9	11	7	1.9	0.9	2.8
6	Brent Seabrook	CHI	23	7	4	11	5	2.4	-0.1	2.3
7	Cam Fowler	ANA	16	2	8	10	5	1.9	0.4	2.3
8	Hampus Lindholm	ANA	16	2	8	10	2	1.9	0.0	1.9
9	Ryan McDonagh	NYR	19	3	6	9	2	1.4	0.3	1.7
10	P.K. Subban	MTL	12	1	7	8	1	1.6	0.0	1.6

Best 5 goaltenders (2014-15, playoffs)

Rank	Name	Team(s)	GP	GAA	GA	SA	SV%	GGVT	DGVT	GVT
1	Braden Holtby	WSH	13.4	171	23	412	.944	8.7	0.0	8.7
2	Craig Anderson	OTT	4.1	97	4	142	.971	6.6	0.0	6.6
3	Henrik Lundqvist	NYR	19.4	210	41	570	.928	3.6	0.0	3.6
4	Scott Darling	CHI	4.8	227	11	171	.935	2.3	0.0	2.3
5	Corey Crawford	CHI	20.4	230	47	616	.923	1.4	0.0	1.4

PLAYER TABLES

VUKOTA Projections for 2015-16

Top 20 projected goal-scorers, 2015-16 VUKOTA

Rank	Name	Pos	Team	GP	G	A	Pts	OGVT	DVGT	SGVT	PIM	GVT
1	Alex Ovechkin	F	WSH	73.7	41.9	31.4	73.3	12.5	1.4	-0.1	46.3	13.8
2	Tyler Seguin	F	DAL	71.9	37.2	45.0	82.2	14.6	2.3	0.1	22.8	17.0
3	John Tavares	F	NYI	79.2	36.3	50.7	87.0	13.9	3.0	0.0	44.5	16.8
4	Steven Stamkos	F	TBL	74.5	36.2	35.7	71.9	12.3	1.9	0.0	46.9	14.2
5	Jamie Benn	F	DAL	78.1	34.8	48.8	83.6	13.9	3.1	0.0	57.1	17.0
6	Max Pacioretty	F	MTL	79.0	34.0	32.5	66.4	10.4	3.9	0.0	41.5	14.3
7	Vladimir Tarasenko	F	STL	74.4	33.9	35.7	69.7	11.8	3.1	0.1	29.0	15.0
8	Corey Perry	F	ANA	72.9	31.4	33.9	65.3	10.7	2.5	0.0	60.6	13.2
9	Joe Pavelski	F	SJS	74.8	31.0	33.1	64.1	9.7	3.3	0.0	29.0	12.9
10	Filip Forsberg	F	NSH	78.1	30.9	41.5	72.3	11.5	2.9	0.0	27.7	14.4
11	Sidney Crosby	F	PIT	72.6	29.5	51.6	81.1	12.9	2.5	0.1	38.2	15.6
12	Rick Nash	F	NYR	74.5	29.3	29.8	59.1	9.0	3.0	0.0	32.2	12.0
13	Phil Kessel	F	PIT	69.9	28.7	37.5	66.3	9.9	0.8	0.0	23.1	10.7
14	Tyler Johnson	F	TBL	76.7	28.7	38.4	67.1	10.6	4.0	0.0	34.9	14.5
15	Nikita Kucherov	F	TBL	78.2	28.7	38.5	67.1	10.9	3.2	0.0	36.2	14.1
16	Sean Monahan	F	CGY	76.1	28.5	30.4	58.9	8.1	2.3	0.0	13.9	10.5
17	Patrick Kane	F	CHI	67.5	28.3	40.7	69.0	11.0	2.3	0.1	17.8	13.4
18	Claude Giroux	F	PHI	73.9	28.1	44.6	72.7	10.6	2.7	0.0	34.6	13.3
19	Logan Couture	F	SJS	76.6	28.1	37.7	65.7	9.2	3.3	0.1	18.6	12.6
20	Zach Parise	F	MIN	69.3	28.0	32.4	60.4	9.5	2.7	0.0	35.2	12.2

Top 20 projected assist-scorers, 2015-16 VUKOTA

Rank	Name	Pos	Team	GP	G	A	Pts	OGVT	DVGT	SGVT	PIM	GVT
1	Sidney Crosby	F	PIT	72.6	29.5	51.6	81.1	12.9	2.5	0.1	38.2	15.6
2	John Tavares	F	NYI	79.2	36.3	50.7	87.0	13.9	3.0	0.0	44.5	16.8
3	Erik Karlsson	D	OTT	77.2	18.5	49.0	67.5	12.4	2.5	0.0	38.5	14.8
4	Ryan Getzlaf	F	ANA	73.5	24.9	48.9	73.8	11.0	3.2	0.0	43.4	14.3
5	Jamie Benn	F	DAL	78.1	34.8	48.8	83.6	13.9	3.1	0.0	57.1	17.0
6	Nicklas Backstrom	F	WSH	70.8	20.0	47.7	67.6	9.2	2.1	0.1	32.1	11.4
7	Jakub Voracek	F	PHI	72.3	24.8	45.5	70.3	10.3	2.6	0.1	51.3	12.9
8	Tyler Seguin	F	DAL	71.9	37.2	45.0	82.2	14.6	2.3	0.1	22.8	17.0
9	Claude Giroux	F	PHI	73.9	28.1	44.6	72.7	10.6	2.7	0.0	34.6	13.3
10	John Gaudreau	F	CGY	76.8	27.5	42.4	69.9	10.0	2.7	0.0	20.0	12.7
11	Anze Kopitar	F	LAK	73.5	20.0	41.9	61.9	7.8	3.6	0.0	16.9	11.4
12	Filip Forsberg	F	NSH	78.1	30.9	41.5	72.3	11.5	2.9	0.0	27.7	14.4
13	Patrick Kane	F	CHI	67.5	28.3	40.7	69.0	11.0	2.3	0.1	17.8	13.4
14	P.K. Subban	D	MTL	76.1	12.0	40.4	52.4	8.0	4.2	0.0	69.4	12.1
15	Brent Burns	D	SJS	73.6	14.1	40.3	54.4	9.4	3.7	0.0	52.8	13.1
16	Ryan Johansen	F	CBJ	73.6	27.4	40.0	67.4	9.9	2.4	0.1	35.8	12.4
17	Jonathan Toews	F	CHI	76.7	27.1	39.5	66.5	9.6	3.7	0.1	33.2	13.4
18	Henrik Sedin	F	VAN	67.8	14.8	39.2	53.9	6.2	2.2	0.0	20.8	8.5
19	Evgeni Malkin	F	PIT	66.6	25.5	39.1	64.6	9.4	1.8	0.0	50.6	11.2
20	Ondrej Palat	F	TBL	74.0	21.4	38.9	60.3	8.2	3.9	0.0	26.6	12.1

Top 20 projected point-scorers, 2015-16 VUKOTA

Rank	Name	Pos	Team	GP	G	A	Pts	OGVT	DVGT	SGVT	PIM	GVT
1	John Tavares	F	NYI	79.2	36.3	50.7	87.0	13.9	3.0	0.0	44.5	16.8
2	Jamie Benn	F	DAL	78.1	34.8	48.8	83.6	13.9	3.1	0.0	57.1	17.0
3	Tyler Seguin	F	DAL	71.9	37.2	45.0	82.2	14.6	2.3	0.1	22.8	17.0
4	Sidney Crosby	F	PIT	72.6	29.5	51.6	81.1	12.9	2.5	0.1	38.2	15.6
5	Ryan Getzlaf	F	ANA	73.5	24.9	48.9	73.8	11.0	3.2	0.0	43.4	14.3
6	Alex Ovechkin	F	WSH	73.7	41.9	31.4	73.3	12.5	1.4	-0.1	46.3	13.8
7	Claude Giroux	F	PHI	73.9	28.1	44.6	72.7	10.6	2.7	0.0	34.6	13.3
8	Filip Forsberg	F	NSH	78.1	30.9	41.5	72.3	11.5	2.9	0.0	27.7	14.4
9	Steven Stamkos	F	TBL	74.5	36.2	35.7	71.9	12.3	1.9	0.0	46.9	14.2
10	Jakub Voracek	F	PHI	72.3	24.8	45.5	70.3	10.3	2.6	0.1	51.3	12.9
11	John Gaudreau	F	CGY	76.8	27.5	42.4	69.9	10.0	2.7	0.0	20.0	12.7
12	Vladimir Tarasenko	F	STL	74.4	33.9	35.7	69.7	11.8	3.1	0.1	29.0	15.0
13	Patrick Kane	F	CHI	67.5	28.3	40.7	69.0	11.0	2.3	0.1	17.8	13.4
14	Nicklas Backstrom	F	WSH	70.8	20.0	47.7	67.6	9.2	2.1	0.1	32.1	11.4
15	Erik Karlsson	D	OTT	77.2	18.5	49.0	67.5	12.4	2.5	0.0	38.5	14.8
16	Ryan Johansen	F	CBJ	73.6	27.4	40.0	67.4	9.9	2.4	0.1	35.8	12.4
17	Tyler Johnson	F	TBL	76.7	28.7	38.4	67.1	10.6	4.0	0.0	34.9	14.5
18	Nikita Kucherov	F	TBL	78.2	28.7	38.5	67.1	10.9	3.2	0.0	36.2	14.1
19	Jonathan Toews	F	CHI	76.7	27.1	39.5	66.5	9.6	3.7	0.1	33.2	13.4
20	Max Pacioretty	F	MTL	79.0	34.0	32.5	66.4	10.4	3.9	0.0	41.5	14.3

Top 10 projected defensemen goal-scorers, 2015-16 VUKOTA

Rank	Name	Pos	Team	GP	G	A	Pts	OGVT	DVGT	SGVT	PIM	GVT
1	Erik Karlsson	D	OTT	77.2	18.5	49.0	67.5	12.4	2.5	0.0	38.5	14.8
2	Oliver Ekman-Larsson	D	ARI	77.8	15.7	33.7	49.4	7.8	3.7	-0.1	48.3	11.4
3	Brent Burns	D	SJS	73.6	14.1	40.3	54.4	9.4	3.7	0.0	52.8	13.1
4	Dustin Byfuglien	D	WPG	69.6	13.7	33.9	47.6	8.1	2.8	0.0	90.8	10.8
5	Shea Weber	D	NSH	75.7	13.1	35.0	48.1	7.7	5.1	0.0	59.1	12.8
6	Roman Josi	D	NSH	79.0	13.0	37.3	50.4	7.8	5.1	0.0	27.9	12.8
7	P.K. Subban	D	MTL	76.1	12.0	40.4	52.4	8.0	4.2	0.0	69.4	12.1
8	Justin Faulk	D	CAR	78.0	12.0	34.8	46.8	6.7	5.3	0.0	35.4	11.9
9	Torey Krug	D	BOS	73.2	11.8	30.4	42.3	6.9	3.5	0.0	30.1	10.4
10	Aaron Ekblad	D	FLA	76.0	11.7	31.8	43.5	6.4	4.4	0.0	34.4	10.8

Top 10 projected defensemen assist-scorers, 2015-16 VUKOTA

Rank	Name	Pos	Team	GP	G	A	Pts	OGVT	DVGT	SGVT	PIM	GVT
1	Erik Karlsson	D	OTT	77.2	18.5	49.0	67.5	12.4	2.5	0.0	38.5	14.8
2	P.K. Subban	D	MTL	76.1	12.0	40.4	52.4	8.0	4.2	0.0	69.4	12.1
3	Brent Burns	D	SJS	73.6	14.1	40.3	54.4	9.4	3.7	0.0	52.8	13.1
4	Roman Josi	D	NSH	79.0	13.0	37.3	50.4	7.8	5.1	0.0	27.9	12.8
5	Kevin Shattenkirk	D	STL	66.3	9.9	36.9	46.8	7.8	4.3	0.0	42.7	12.2
6	Kris Letang	D	PIT	70.7	11.6	36.2	47.7	7.4	4.8	0.0	62.2	12.1
7	Duncan Keith	D	CHI	71.7	9.3	35.6	45.0	6.9	4.6	0.0	17.6	11.4
8	Shea Weber	D	NSH	75.7	13.1	35.0	48.1	7.7	5.1	0.0	59.1	12.8
9	John Carlson	D	WSH	75.3	11.0	34.9	45.9	7.2	4.7	0.0	26.8	11.9
10	Justin Faulk	D	CAR	78.0	12.0	34.8	46.8	6.7	5.3	0.0	35.4	11.9

Top 10 projected defensemen point-scorers, 2015-16 VUKOTA

Rank	Name	Pos	Team	GP	G	A	Pts	OGVT	DVGT	SGVT	PIM	GVT
1	Erik Karlsson	D	OTT	77.2	18.5	49.0	67.5	12.4	2.5	0.0	38.5	14.8
2	Brent Burns	D	SJS	73.6	14.1	40.3	54.4	9.4	3.7	0.0	52.8	13.1
3	P.K. Subban	D	MTL	76.1	12.0	40.4	52.4	8.0	4.2	0.0	69.4	12.1
4	Roman Josi	D	NSH	79.0	13.0	37.3	50.4	7.8	5.1	0.0	27.9	12.8
5	Oliver Ekman-Larsson	D	ARI	77.8	15.7	33.7	49.4	7.8	3.7	-0.1	48.3	11.4
6	Shea Weber	D	NSH	75.7	13.1	35.0	48.1	7.7	5.1	0.0	59.1	12.8
7	Kris Letang	D	PIT	70.7	11.6	36.2	47.7	7.4	4.8	0.0	62.2	12.1
8	Dustin Byfuglien	D	WPG	69.6	13.7	33.9	47.6	8.1	2.8	0.0	90.8	10.8
9	Justin Faulk	D	CAR	78.0	12.0	34.8	46.8	6.7	5.3	0.0	35.4	11.9
10	Kevin Shattenkirk	D	STL	66.3	9.9	36.9	46.8	7.8	4.3	0.0	42.7	12.2

Top 20 projected offensive GVT 2015-16 VUKOTA

Rank	Name	Pos	Team	GP	G	A	Pts	OGVT	DVGT	SGVT	PIM	GVT
1	Tyler Seguin	F	DAL	71.9	37.2	45.0	82.2	14.6	2.3	0.1	22.8	17.0
2	John Tavares	F	NYI	79.2	36.3	50.7	87.0	13.9	3.0	0.0	44.5	16.8
3	Jamie Benn	F	DAL	78.1	34.8	48.8	83.6	13.9	3.1	0.0	57.1	17.0
4	Sidney Crosby	F	PIT	72.6	29.5	51.6	81.1	12.9	2.5	0.1	38.2	15.6
5	Alex Ovechkin	F	WSH	73.7	41.9	31.4	73.3	12.5	1.4	-0.1	46.3	13.8
6	Erik Karlsson	D	OTT	77.2	18.5	49.0	67.5	12.4	2.5	0.0	38.5	14.8
7	Steven Stamkos	F	TBL	74.5	36.2	35.7	71.9	12.3	1.9	0.0	46.9	14.2
8	Vladimir Tarasenko	F	STL	74.4	33.9	35.7	69.7	11.8	3.1	0.1	29.0	15.0
9	Filip Forsberg	F	NSH	78.1	30.9	41.5	72.3	11.5	2.9	0.0	27.7	14.4
10	Patrick Kane	F	CHI	67.5	28.3	40.7	69.0	11.0	2.3	0.1	17.8	13.4
11	Ryan Getzlaf	F	ANA	73.5	24.9	48.9	73.8	11.0	3.2	0.0	43.4	14.3
12	Nikita Kucherov	F	TBL	78.2	28.7	38.5	67.1	10.9	3.2	0.0	36.2	14.1
13	Corey Perry	F	ANA	72.9	31.4	33.9	65.3	10.7	2.5	0.0	60.6	13.2
14	Claude Giroux	F	PHI	73.9	28.1	44.6	72.7	10.6	2.7	0.0	34.6	13.3
15	Tyler Johnson	F	TBL	76.7	28.7	38.4	67.1	10.6	4.0	0.0	34.9	14.5
16	Max Pacioretty	F	MTL	79.0	34.0	32.5	66.4	10.4	3.9	0.0	41.5	14.3
17	Jakub Voracek	F	PHI	72.3	24.8	45.5	70.3	10.3	2.6	0.1	51.3	12.9
18	John Gaudreau	F	CGY	76.8	27.5	42.4	69.9	10.0	2.7	0.0	20.0	12.7
19	Ryan Johansen	F	CBJ	73.6	27.4	40.0	67.4	9.9	2.4	0.1	35.8	12.4
20	Phil Kessel	F	PIT	69.9	28.7	37.5	66.3	9.9	0.8	0.0	23.1	10.7

Top 20 projected defensive GVT 2015-16 VUKOTA

Rank	Name	Pos	Team	GP	G	A	Pts	OGVT	DVGT	SGVT	PIM	GVT
1	Drew Doughty	D	LAK	79.1	9.9	34.5	44.5	5.4	5.8	0.0	53.4	11.1
2	Alex Pietrangelo	D	STL	76.5	9.5	34.4	43.9	6.3	5.4	0.0	28.2	11.7
3	Marc-Edouard Vlasic	D	SJS	70.9	6.5	19.1	25.6	2.6	5.3	0.0	32.4	8.0
4	Justin Faulk	D	CAR	78.0	12.0	34.8	46.8	6.7	5.3	0.0	35.4	11.9
5	Jonas Brodin	D	MIN	69.8	4.0	15.3	19.2	0.2	5.1	0.0	18.4	5.4
6	Shea Weber	D	NSH	75.7	13.1	35.0	48.1	7.7	5.1	0.0	59.1	12.8
7	Andy Greene	D	NJD	68.5	4.2	18.0	22.2	1.5	5.1	0.0	20.2	6.6
8	Roman Josi	D	NSH	79.0	13.0	37.3	50.4	7.8	5.1	0.0	27.9	12.8
9	Ryan Suter	D	MIN	70.5	5.8	28.0	33.8	3.2	5.0	0.0	28.8	8.2
10	T.J. Brodie	D	CGY	74.6	8.0	27.3	35.3	4.5	5.0	0.0	25.2	9.4
11	Jay Bouwmeester	D	STL	66.0	3.5	15.7	19.1	0.7	4.9	0.0	21.8	5.6
12	Kris Letang	D	PIT	70.7	11.6	36.2	47.7	7.4	4.8	0.0	62.2	12.1
13	Andrej Sekera	D	EDM	66.3	4.6	20.9	25.4	2.1	4.7	0.0	14.5	6.8
14	John Carlson	D	WSH	75.3	11.0	34.9	45.9	7.2	4.7	0.0	26.8	11.9
15	Justin Braun	D	SJS	66.6	3.9	17.0	20.9	1.5	4.7	0.0	37.9	6.2
16	Chris Tanev	D	VAN	65.0	3.6	16.2	19.8	1.5	4.6	0.0	15.5	6.1
17	Duncan Keith	D	CHI	71.7	9.3	35.6	45.0	6.9	4.6	0.0	17.6	11.4
18	Hampus Lindholm	D	ANA	73.6	7.7	27.4	35.2	4.2	4.6	0.0	31.9	8.8
19	Paul Martin	D	SJS	62.8	3.1	16.1	19.2	1.0	4.4	0.0	17.1	5.4
20	Aaron Ekblad	D	FLA	76.0	11.7	31.8	43.5	6.4	4.4	0.0	34.4	10.8

Top 20 projected PIM 2015-16 VUKOTA

Rank	Name	Pos	Team	GP	G	A	Pts	OGVT	DVGT	SGVT	PIM	GVT
1	Steve Downie	F	ARI	60.9	10.0	14.8	24.8	1.7	1.3	0.0	154.7	2.9
2	Tom Wilson	F	WSH	62.7	5.1	9.7	14.8	-1.1	1.2	0.0	150.1	0.0
3	Antoine Roussel	F	DAL	66.0	11.9	13.3	25.3	1.9	1.7	0.0	134.7	3.6
4	Derek Dorsett	F	VAN	62.1	6.1	11.1	17.2	0.0	1.5	0.0	131.2	1.5
5	Cody McLeod	F	COL	61.2	5.8	4.7	10.6	-0.7	1.4	0.0	128.7	0.7
6	Brandon Prust	F	VAN	63.7	5.1	11.0	16.1	-0.4	2.1	0.0	113.5	1.7
7	Zac Rinaldo	F	BOS	51.3	2.6	3.6	6.2	-1.7	0.8	0.0	97.3	-0.9
8	Mark Borowiecki	D	OTT	56.1	1.4	7.3	8.6	-0.4	2.6	0.0	94.6	2.2
9	Tom Sestito	F	PIT	40.8	3.6	4.5	8.0	-0.4	0.6	0.0	92.5	0.2
10	Zack Kassian	F	MTL	55.1	12.0	11.8	23.8	1.9	1.1	0.0	91.6	3.0
11	Chris Neil	F	OTT	47.7	4.9	4.7	9.6	-0.2	0.7	0.0	91.3	0.5
12	Dustin Byfuglien	D	WPG	69.6	13.7	33.9	47.6	8.1	2.8	0.0	90.8	10.8
13	Ryan Reaves	F	STL	59.5	4.3	4.8	9.1	-1.1	1.2	0.0	89.2	0.1
14	Dion Phaneuf	D	TOR	63.9	5.7	22.3	28.0	2.2	2.9	0.0	86.0	5.1
15	Matt Martin	F	NYI	61.5	7.4	6.5	14.0	-0.5	1.4	0.0	85.1	0.9
16	Jared Boll	F	CBJ	52.0	1.2	2.2	3.4	-2.2	0.3	0.0	84.0	-1.9
17	Brandon Bollig	F	CGY	56.1	4.2	4.0	8.2	-1.5	0.9	0.0	83.7	-0.7
18	David Backes	F	STL	73.4	21.6	28.3	50.0	5.8	3.2	0.0	82.4	9.0
19	John Scott	F	ARI	42.9	2.9	2.2	5.0	-1.0	0.7	0.0	80.6	-0.3
20	Radko Gudas	D	PHI	50.9	4.0	10.9	14.9	1.3	1.8	0.0	78.3	3.2

Top 20 projected goaltenders, 2015-16 VUKOTA

Rank	Name	Pos	Team	GP	SV%	GGVT	DVGT	SGVT	GVT
1	Carey Price	G	MTL	64.0	.921	20.5	-0.2	0.3	20.6
2	Tuukka Rask	G	BOS	61.0	.920	18.0	0.1	0.4	18.5
3	Sergei Bobrovsky	G	CBJ	48.6	.920	14.2	-0.5	0.6	14.3
4	Semyon Varlamov	G	COL	51.7	.920	14.9	-0.9	0.0	14.1
5	Braden Holtby	G	WSH	61.8	.918	13.7	-0.2	0.1	13.6
6	Cory Schneider	G	NJD	55.8	.917	11.2	0.3	-0.2	11.3
7	Ben Bishop	G	TBL	51.6	.917	10.3	0.5	0.2	11.0
8	Steve Mason	G	PHI	48.1	.918	11.4	-0.4	-0.3	10.7
9	Cam Talbot	G	EDM	39.5	.919	10.4	0.1	-0.1	10.4
10	Corey Crawford	G	CHI	48.9	.917	9.3	0.4	0.2	9.9
11	Henrik Lundqvist	G	NYR	47.6	.917	9.8	0.2	-0.1	9.9
12	Andrew Hammond	G	OTT	35.9	.919	9.4	-0.1	0.1	9.4
13	Marc-Andre Fleury	G	PIT	50.4	.916	8.9	0.3	0.0	9.2
14	Roberto Luongo	G	FLA	44.9	.917	8.2	0.0	0.2	8.5
15	Jonathan Quick	G	LAK	53.9	.915	7.3	1.2	-0.1	8.4
16	Eddie Lack	G	CAR	38.6	.917	7.8	0.1	0.3	8.2
17	Scott Darling	G	CHI	28.7	.919	7.6	0.0	0.3	8.0
18	Michael Hutchinson	G	WPG	36.8	.917	7.1	0.3	0.4	7.8
19	Martin Jones	G	SJS	25.0	.919	6.6	0.4	0.3	7.3
20	Brian Elliott	G	STL	38.0	.916	6.0	0.6	0.1	6.8

Top 50 projected GVT, 2015-16 VUKOTA

Rank	Name	Pos	Team	GP	G	A	Pts	SV%	OGGVT	DVGT	SGVT	PIM	GVT
1	Carey Price	G	MTL	64.0				.921	20.5	-0.2	0.3		20.6
2	Tuukka Rask	G	BOS	61.0				.920	18.0	0.1	0.4		18.5
3	Tyler Seguin	F	DAL	71.9	37.2	45.0	82.2		14.6	2.3	0.1	22.8	17.0
4	Jamie Benn	F	DAL	78.1	34.8	48.8	83.6		13.9	3.1	0.0	57.1	17.0
5	John Tavares	F	NYI	79.2	36.3	50.7	87.0		13.9	3.0	0.0	44.5	16.8
6	Sidney Crosby	F	PIT	72.6	29.5	51.6	81.1		12.9	2.5	0.1	38.2	15.6
7	Vladimir Tarasenko	F	STL	74.4	33.9	35.7	69.7		11.8	3.1	0.1	29.0	15.0
8	Erik Karlsson	D	OTT	77.2	18.5	49.0	67.5		12.4	2.5	0.0	38.5	14.8
9	Tyler Johnson	F	TBL	76.7	28.7	38.4	67.1		10.6	4.0	0.0	34.9	14.5
10	Filip Forsberg	F	NSH	78.1	30.9	41.5	72.3		11.5	2.9	0.0	27.7	14.4
11	Max Pacioretty	F	MTL	79.0	34.0	32.5	66.4		10.4	3.9	0.0	41.5	14.3
12	Ryan Getzlaf	F	ANA	73.5	24.9	48.9	73.8		11.0	3.2	0.0	43.4	14.3
13	Sergei Bobrovsky	G	CBJ	48.6				.920	14.2	-0.5	0.6		14.3
14	Steven Stamkos	F	TBL	74.5	36.2	35.7	71.9		12.3	1.9	0.0	46.9	14.2
15	Semyon Varlamov	G	COL	51.7				.920	14.9	-0.9	0.0		14.1
16	Nikita Kucherov	F	TBL	78.2	28.7	38.5	67.1		10.9	3.2	0.0	36.2	14.1
17	Alex Ovechkin	F	WSH	73.7	41.9	31.4	73.3		12.5	1.4	-0.1	46.3	13.8
18	Braden Holtby	G	WSH	61.8				.918	13.7	-0.2	0.1		13.6
19	Patrick Kane	F	CHI	67.5	28.3	40.7	69.0		11.0	2.3	0.1	17.8	13.4
20	Jonathan Toews	F	CHI	76.7	27.1	39.5	66.5		9.6	3.7	0.1	33.2	13.4
21	Claude Giroux	F	PHI	73.9	28.1	44.6	72.7		10.6	2.7	0.0	34.6	13.3
22	Corey Perry	F	ANA	72.9	31.4	33.9	65.3		10.7	2.5	0.0	60.6	13.2
23	Brent Burns	D	SJS	73.6	14.1	40.3	54.4		9.4	3.7	0.0	52.8	13.1
24	Jakub Voracek	F	PHI	72.3	24.8	45.5	70.3		10.3	2.6	0.1	51.3	12.9
25	Joe Pavelski	F	SJS	74.8	31.0	33.1	64.1		9.7	3.3	0.0	29.0	12.9
26	Roman Josi	D	NSH	79.0	13.0	37.3	50.4		7.8	5.1	0.0	27.9	12.8
27	Shea Weber	D	NSH	75.7	13.1	35.0	48.1		7.7	5.1	0.0	59.1	12.8
28	John Gaudreau	F	CGY	76.8	27.5	42.4	69.9		10.0	2.7	0.0	20.0	12.7
29	Logan Couture	F	SJS	76.6	28.1	37.7	65.7		9.2	3.3	0.1	18.6	12.6
30	Jaden Schwartz	F	STL	72.3	26.1	34.4	60.5		9.3	3.3	0.0	21.4	12.6
31	Ryan Johansen	F	CBJ	73.6	27.4	40.0	67.4		9.9	2.4	0.1	35.8	12.4
32	Zach Parise	F	MIN	69.3	28.0	32.4	60.4		9.5	2.7	0.0	35.2	12.2
33	Kevin Shattenkirk	D	STL	66.3	9.9	36.9	46.8		7.8	4.3	0.0	42.7	12.2
34	Kris Letang	D	PIT	70.7	11.6	36.2	47.7		7.4	4.8	0.0	62.2	12.1
35	Ondrej Palat	F	TBL	74.0	21.4	38.9	60.3		8.2	3.9	0.0	26.6	12.1
36	P.K. Subban	D	MTL	76.1	12.0	40.4	52.4		8.0	4.2	0.0	69.4	12.1
37	Rick Nash	F	NYR	74.5	29.3	29.8	59.1		9.0	3.0	0.0	32.2	12.0
38	Justin Faulk	D	CAR	78.0	12.0	34.8	46.8		6.7	5.3	0.0	35.4	11.9
39	John Carlson	D	WSH	75.3	11.0	34.9	45.9		7.2	4.7	0.0	26.8	11.9
40	Mark Stone	F	OTT	71.6	23.4	37.5	61.0		9.0	2.8	0.0	15.9	11.8
41	Mark Giordano	D	CGY	64.5	10.4	32.1	42.5		7.4	4.4	0.0	43.4	11.7
42	Alex Pietrangelo	D	STL	76.5	9.5	34.4	43.9		6.3	5.4	0.0	28.2	11.7
43	Matt Duchene	F	COL	71.8	24.1	38.0	62.1		9.1	2.4	0.1	16.4	11.7
44	Duncan Keith	D	CHI	71.7	9.3	35.6	45.0		6.9	4.6	0.0	17.6	11.4
45	Oliver Ekman-Larsson	D	ARI	77.8	15.7	33.7	49.4		7.8	3.7	-0.1	48.3	11.4
46	Anze Kopitar	F	LAK	73.5	20.0	41.9	61.9		7.8	3.6	0.0	16.9	11.4
47	Nicklas Backstrom	F	WSH	70.8	20.0	47.7	67.6		9.2	2.1	0.1	32.1	11.4
48	Nick Foligno	F	CBJ	71.5	25.4	34.5	59.9		8.8	2.5	0.0	55.5	11.3
49	Blake Wheeler	F	WPG	75.0	25.5	35.0	60.5		8.3	3.0	0.0	57.6	11.3
50	Cory Schneider	G	NJD	55.8				.917	11.2	0.3	-0.2		11.3

Biographies

Tom Awad

Tom Awad likes numbers more than anything else on Earth. He started tabulating hockey statistics by hand at age 11 while watching Montreal Canadiens games in his parents' basement. His Eureka moment was when he came across a friend's copy of *Total Baseball* and discovered Pete Palmer's Linear Weights. He immediately designed something similar for hockey and tested it by transcribing the full statistics of the 1995-96 season by hand. GVT was born. Tom may be best known for GVT, but over the years he has performed statistical analysis of the draft, shot quality, player usage, goaltending, and much more. He developed the VUKOTA projection system which was found by David Staples of the *Edmonton Journal* to be the most accurate of seven systems for two consecutive seasons. He is a founding member of *Hockey Prospectus* and his analysis has also been published in *ESPN Insider*, *Arctic Ice Hockey*, Montreal's *Journal Metro*, and *Rob Vollman's Hockey Abstract*. When not analyzing hockey numbers, Tom can often be found analyzing other numbers in his job as an Electrical Engineer in Montreal, or discussing mathematics, physics, or the relative merits of Sauron and Unicron with his children David, 9, and Karina, 7. His wife Marisa (age redacted) sadly does not share his love of numbers, but nobody's perfect.

Steven Burtch

Stephen Burtch has been working with and writing about hockey analytics since the 2004-05 lockout. He began with a Leafs focus at the now defunct *Leafs.HockeyAnalysis.com* before joining *Pension Plan Puppets* at SB Nation in 2010. He has also written for *NHLNumbers* and *Hockey Prospectus* and became one of the lead hockey analytics writers for *Sportsnet.ca* in 2014. He has delivered feature presentations on usage adjustment of possession statistics (dCorsi) at the 2014 Pittsburgh Hockey Analytics Conference and measuring coaching impacts at the 2014 Ottawa Hockey Analytics Conference. He can be found flooding people's timelines with Nazem Kadri and Cody Franson stats on Twitter via @steveburtch when he isn't teaching high school math students in Toronto or hanging out with his wife, two children, and Boston terrier.

Matt Cane

As a Sens fan living in Toronto, Matt Cane has come to rely on statistics as a defense against the constant insistence of friends, coworkers, and random strangers that this year will really be different for the Maple Leafs. His work to date has focused on tackling hockey's biggest questions, like whether an AHL team could actually beat the 2014-15 Buffalo Sabres. Matt's articles are available on *Hockey Prospectus* and at his website, *Puck++*. When he's not splitting his laptop screen between a Gamecenter window and a spreadsheet, Matt can be found flailing helplessly in net for his ball hockey team or willing the Blue Jays to finally end their 21-year playoff drought.

BIOGRAPHIES

Scott Charles

Scott Charles is a graduate from SUNY College at Old Westbury with a BS in Finance. He had no intention of joining the sports-media world until one day he started working for the legendary Stan Fischler. During his time with Stan, Scott was the lead reporter covering both the New York Islanders and New York Rangers. He would collaborate with other staff members to research, organize, and edit columns for *The Fischler Report*. At practices and games, Scott would conduct extensive interviews with players, coaches, team executives, league officials, and national journalists. After working with Stan for a year, Scott moved on to work with *Islanders Insight*, *Blueshirts Bulletin*, and WLIE SportsTalkNY. Scott can also be heard on *The Shutdown Pair* podcast on *AlongTheBoards.com*. You can follow him on Twitter @Scottmcharles.

Wesley Chu

Wesley Chu joined *Hockey Prospectus* in 2015 as a contributor. With an education background in Statistics, during his spare time, he can usually be found applying statistical and predictive analytics methods to the sticks and skates game. His proudest hockey moment may be when, in one season, his fantasy team finished third overall among all public ESPN roto teams. Poolies can find his fantasy hockey work at *Today's Slapshot*. As for physically playing the sport, his highest level is pond hockey.

Matthew Coller

Matthew Coller is managing editor of *Hockey Prospectus*, produces and hosts *Hockey Prospectus Radio*, and works as a producer for WGR SportsRadio 550 in Buffalo. He has worked to bring analytics to the mainstream in Buffalo, where fans will now focus on Jack Eichel's Corsi rating. Matthew believes that Dominic Hasek was the best goalie of all time and that mascots falling down on the ice is the best thing in sports.

John Fischer

John Fischer founded and ran *In Lou We Trust* from October 2006 to July 2015. Due to monumental changes to the Devils organization, it will be officially renamed *All About the Jersey* in September. It's a new name, but with the same purpose: a blog all about the New Jersey Devils. It'll still be about the third-best one on the internet and John will still run it. When he's not doing that and working a day job, he can be regularly seen and heard in Section 1 at The Rock for Devils games, Section 133 for the Red Bulls, Section 109 for Rutgers football, and anywhere in his vicinity as he is not a quiet person. John thanks God, his parents, his brother Jim, James Mirtle, Tyler Bleszinski, Timo Seppa, and all of the readers for making all of this possible. Between the site and this book, they are testaments that people do want hockey analysis - even if it's not favorable.

Lucas Friesen

Lucas Friesen is a fourth year Bachelor of Sport Management student at Brock University, who first came across hockey analytics as an additional way to look at the game. With further research and projects, he became interested in exploring the new realm of hockey statistics. Moving forward, Lucas looks to take on projects and studies that focus on the economics of hockey, both on and off the ice, along with the analysis of team statistics on a year-to-year basis.

Sam Hitchcock

Sam Hitchcock frequently publishes articles analyzing National Hockey League trends, teams, and players for *Hockey Prospectus* and *intelligenthockey.com*. He has contributed to *ESPN Insider* and *NBC SportsWorld*. Aside from watching as much hockey as human possible, and loving every second of it, his other loves include his alma mater and buffalo wings. He strongly believes that statistics are an important tool in the toolbox and that our understanding of players and teams, in the thousands a little sequences in each game, should be fluid and evolving. Hockey is the greatest sport on earth, and it is perfectly acceptable to find unrestrained excitement in the discussion and viewing of the sport.

BIOGRAPHIES

Pat Holden
Pat Holden writes regularly for the Caps' blog *Russian Machine Never Breaks* and has also contributed to *The Washington Post* and *ESPN.com*. As the son of a math teacher, Pat has numbers in his genes. Pat and numbers grew distant during his apathetic teenage years, but their relationship was rekindled when he needed quantifiable rebukes to criticisms of Mike Green and Alex Semin. You can find Pat on Twitter @pfholden where he is likely defending the latest whipping boy of the Caps' fanbase.

Matthew Kory
Matthew Kory is a sports writer. He has sports-written at many different online locales, most prominently *Baseball Prospectus*, *Sports on Earth*, *Vice*, *FanGraphs*, and uh...probably others as well. He has also contributed at *Hockey Prospectus* no matter how many press releases Matthew Coller issues denying it. He's also also written multiple chapters for *Baseball Prospectus 2013*, an actual book made of real honest-to-goodness paper. He lives with his wife, twin boys, cat, and graying hair in Portland, Oregon, where he watches the Washington Capitals gradually destroy his sense of humor from afar.

Jason Lewis
Jason Lewis is a product of mid- to early-90's Southern California hockey culture—a culture that allowed him to grow up on legends like Bob Miller, Wayne Gretzky, Paul Kariya, Teemu Selanne, Luc Robitaille, and the mustache of Charlie Huddy. With around 4+ years of hockey writing experience and over 25 of watching it, there is evidence that he makes at least some sense (arguable). He also survived the 2006-07 season of Yutaka Fukufuji, Barry Brust, and Dan Cloutier and lived to tell about it. When not knee deep in statistics (nerd), Jason writes over at *HockeyBuzz* about the Los Angeles Kings and at *Hockey's Future* on the Los Angeles Kings and Anaheim Ducks. He can be found on Twitter (@SirJDL) where he posts an excess of graphs, makes way too many *Seinfeld* and *It's Always Sunny in Philadelphia* references, and continues his ardent defense of Jake Muzzin as a class defenseman. Scouts also say he has wicked good hockey sense, but needs to work on his skating and defensive zone coverage.

William Loewen
William Loewen grew up in a large family, where sharing and fairness were strictly enforced, so now as an adult he focuses most of his analytical energy on studying league parity. He dreams of a day when the NHL will award the same number of points after each game. He has a degree from the University of Waterloo and currently lives with his family in Okotoks, Alberta.

Micah Blake McCurdy
Micah Blake McCurdy has a variety of math degrees from a handful of continents and a taste for visual representations of abstract ideas. He lives in Halifax, where he was a school-truant teenager some while ago; these days he works full time doing freelance hockey analysis and visualizations. He reads the same story to his toddler every naptime and is trying to teach his baby not to steal his glasses. He pours his spare time into his website, *hockeyviz.com*, and playing games with his friends.

Dustin Nelson
Dustin Nelson is a writer whose work has appeared at *Hockey Prospectus*, *Rotowire*, *The Hockey Writers*, *Hockey Wilderness*, and elsewhere. He's also written for *Electric Literature*, *The Rumpus*, *InDigest*, *JSTOR Daily*, *Prefix Magazine*, and *Tiny Mix Tapes*. He sure likes writing. And look! He has a book coming out in Fall 2015. He lives in New York City, but still says Minnesota is home.

Shane O'Donnell
Shane O'Donnell is a student at the University of Central Florida, where he is majoring in statistics and sociology while playing for the schools ACHA DII ice hockey team. Besides writing for *Hockey Prospectus*, he also contributes to *Litter Box Cats* and *Today's Slapshot*. Twitter: @shane1342o.

Jack Ries

Jack Ries is an occasional data scraper and writer for *Hockey Prospectus,* and when he has to be a functioning member of society, he works at a software company in Minneapolis. A 2011 graduate of Saint John's University (MN) with a Mathematics degree, he, like many others of his generation, cites *Moneyball* as the spark to his statistics-oriented thinking. Outside of that, you may be lucky enough to spot him trying to card count in a shady late-night backroom blackjack game or at the pub at 7am watching his beloved Arsenal figure out ever more impressive ways to do just enough to keep his fandom. He's not much of a tweetsman, but if he ever decides to get Twitter-fingers, you can follow @JackRies.

Benoit Roy

Benoit is a Calgary-based prospect analyst for *Hockey Prospectus* who focuses on providing WHL player reports. Originally from beautiful Sudbury, Ontario, Benoit has worked for the Western Hockey League in player development, has scouted for ISS Hockey, and was a jack-of-all-hockey-related-trades for his alma mater, the Laurentian Voyageurs. He is also a regular contributor to the ground-breaking NHL Pass-Tracking Project spearheaded by Ryan Stimson. An unfortunate Sharks fan, Benoit has learned to ignore the playoffs and firmly believes that any-and-all success in the NHL is dictated by regular-season performance, exclusively.

JH Schroeder

JH Schroeder fell in love with hockey at an early age playing on the rural ponds of Vermont. While a lack of foot speed meant an early end to his competitive career, he has remained active in the game coaching a variety of age groups from mini mites to college. Currently, he works as Video Scout for Baseball Information Solutions, which allows him to stay up to date on cutting edge sports analytics.

Ryan Schwepfinger

Ryan Schwepfinger returns to lend a hand with editing a third consecutive Hockey Prospectus annual. Previously managing editor of *Hockey Prospectus,* this is the fourth year that Schwepfinger has been involved with *Hockey Prospectus* in some capacity. He considers himself fortunate to be involved with sports statistics and information on a daily basis, as he works in communications for Major League Soccer's Columbus Crew SC. Formerly of the USHL's Youngstown Phantoms as well as the Philadelphia Flyers and New York Rangers, he also considers himself fortunate to continue to have involvement with the fine folks at *Hockey Prospectus*, even though his career has taken him away from the game. Last year, in these very pages, he boasted that this book has helped him finish third or better in his highly-competitive home fantasy hockey league for seven straight seasons—make it eight, and make it three career titles, as the trophy currently on his fireplace mantle proves.

Timo Seppa

A founding author of *Hockey Prospectus* in 2009—most notably, with Tom Awad and Rob Vollman—Timo Seppa followed Andrew Rothstein as managing editor in 2010 before becoming editor-in-chief in 2013. He has been editor of all of Hockey Prospectus' six annual books, a long-time contributor to *ESPN Insider*, and guest on NHL Network Radio's *The War Room*. His amazing streak of picking the correct winner and number of games in five straight Cup Finals is over. Starting in 2012-13, he has consulted for two very successful NHL teams and advised a prominent NCAA program—making on-ice impacts in each case, he would like to think. As a hockey outsider, "He coached the coaches" is the compliment he is most proud of.

BIOGRAPHIES

Ryan Stimson

Ryan Stimson created and manages an ambitious project to track passing in the NHL. Similar to zone exit and zone entry projects, this involves hours of data collection and offers new ways to better and more precisely quantify the game. Entering his third season managing this project, Ryan hopes to have enough volunteers to exceed last season's mark of 500 games. Ryan believes not enough people have thanked him and demands more hero worship. He started writing at *In Lou We Trust* when fellow *Hockey Prospectus* writer John Fischer appeared to him in a dream and said, "Someone should track passes". Like another *Hockey Prospectus* writer who shares his namesake, Ryan hails from the booming metropolis of Rochester, New York: home to fading industry giants and plates of food called garbage. Twitter: @RK_Stimp

Robert Vollman

For a man who was once known for making jokes about him, Rob Vollman has ironically become the Chris Chelios of *Hockey Prospectus* - the grizzled old veteran that continues to find ways to keep up with the all the youngsters. Best known for innovations like Player Usage Charts and Quality Starts, Rob can now be found wandering from one hockey analytics conference to the next, bitterly complaining about having "peaked too soon" to cash in on the front-office hiring frenzy. Rob's work can be found...well, everywhere.

Ryan Wagman

Ryan Wagman leads the prospect coverage for *Hockey Prospectus* after a few years on the transaction beat. Recently transplanted from his native Toronto to Chicago, he will miss the easy access to OHL action. On the bright side, he will love the newfound access to the USHL and NCAA. No matter the venue or the level of hockey, his wife and daughter will have to find something else to do when Ryan is at the game.

Ryan Wilson

Ryan Wilson is the lead blogger for the Pittsburgh Penguins at *Hockeybuzz* as well as co-host of the *Hockey Hurts* podcast. This is the second year that Ryan has contributed to the *Hockey Prospectus* annual. When taking a break from the blogging life, he utilizes his Master's degree in education to teach Physical Education and Health to the youth of Western New York. Not only does Ryan actually watch the games, he played Division III college hockey for SUNY Brockport many moons ago. Ryan also has 11 years of experience as a varsity high school hockey coach, and you can sometimes hear him grumbling about how the high school season is too small of a sample size for Corsi to be useful.

Erik Yost

Erik Yost is thrilled to be part of the Hockey Prospectus annual for a third consecutive edition. The 26-year-old has been covering hockey regularly now for more than two years, credentialed for both NHL and AHL games. Erik currently writes for the blog *Pattison Ave* in addition to his contributions to *Hockey Prospectus*. When Erik is not thinking about hockey, the Ohio State alum is living in South Jersey, praising Ron Hextall, and preparing to return to school for his Masters degree in the upcoming months. Twitter: @ErikYost_

Glossary

Adjusted Corsi For %

AdjCF% adjusts Corsi For percentage for quality of teammates, quality of competition, zone start percentage, and score state in an attempt to find a player's individual contribution to Corsi.

Adjusted Goals For %

AdjGF% adds shot quality factors to AdjCF% in an attempt to find a player's individual contribution to goal differential.

AHL

American Hockey League. A professional minor league commonly used as a feeder league for NHL clubs, as all AHL teams are affiliated with an NHL team.

Art Ross Trophy

The award given to the player who leads the NHL in points scored for a given season.

Assist

An assist can be attributed to one or two players on a goal. They are awarded to the players touching the puck before the goal scorer, provided they contributed to the goal-scoring play, with some discretion given to the scorekeeper of the game in question.

Bill Masterton Memorial Trophy

The award given annually to the player who best exemplifies perseverance, sportsmanship, and dedication to the game of hockey.

Blocks/60

A rate statistic showing the number of blocked shots a player recorded per 60 minutes of ice time.

Bottom pairing

Typically refers to the fifth- and sixth-best defensemen on a squad. Most teams play three sets of defensemen in a game, hence the "bottom pairing" label for the third set. The term can be used to describe a player's role on the team, often noticeable in their ice time or talent level.

Bottom six

Typically, forwards are considered "bottom six" if they play on the third or fourth lines. The term can be used to describe a player's role on the team—both in ice time and responsibilities, or their talent level.

C

An abbreviation for the Center position.

Calder Trophy

The annual award given "to the player selected as the most proficient in his first year of competition in the National Hockey League." It is commonly referred to as the Rookie of the Year award. To be eligible, a player must be 26 years old or younger, and have played less than 25 games in any NHL season, or no more than six games in each of two or more seasons.

Cap Efficiency Chart

A graphical representation of a player's total contributions on the ice versus his cost against the salary cap. The x-axis represents his previous season's cap hit in millions of dollars, while the y-axis represents his previous season's GVT. The bubble size represents Goals Versus Salary, with shaded bubbles being players performing above their cap hit and white bubbles performing below their cap hit.

Cap hit
The value of a player's contract that is recorded against the salary cap. Regardless of salary variation from year to year of the contract, under the current CBA, the cap hit is calculated as the total value of the contract divided by the term of the contract.

CBA
An abbreviation for Collective Bargaining Agreement. Refers to the agreement between the NHL and the players association (NHLPA) which governs the salary cap, player contracts, discipline, etc. The current CBA will run through September 15, 2022, with a mutual option to terminate two years earlier.

Close-game Fenwick
A close game is defined as a game within a single goal in the first two periods or tied in the third period or overtime. Close-game Fenwick is considered one the best measures of team possession ability, and a good predictor of future success.

Comparable
A player with similar, and era-normalized, statistics.

Conn Smythe Trophy
The award given to the player judged most valuable to his team in each year's Stanley Cup playoffs. It is based on the entire postseason, not just the final game or series, as in some other sports.

Core Age (team)
The sum of each skater's GVT multiplied by age on a team, divided by the team GVT. It is a better measure of the average age of a team, weighting the best players the most.

Corsi
A statistic originally invented by Jim Corsi, who was the goaltender coach for the Buffalo Sabres. Corsi is essentially a plus-minus statistic that measures shot attempts. A player receives a plus for any shot attempt (on net, missed, or blocked) that his team directs at the opponent's net, and a minus for any shot attempt against his own net. A proxy for possession.

Corsi QoC
A measure of competition quality using Corsi as its basis. While a slight improvement on goal-based measures, the scale can be hard to decipher based on the quality of teams faced throughout the year.

Corsi Rel QoC
A measure of competition quality using Relative Corsi as its basis. It is less luck-driven than QualComp and more universal than Corsi QoC because it is based on a relative metric. The most statistically sound quality of competition metric commonly used.

D
The abbreviation for Defenseman.

DGVT
Defensive Goals Versus Threshold. This stat measures a player's worth, in goals, primarily at shot suppression. It also rewards players for shorthanded play.

Do-It-All Index
A top-level measurement of a player's versatility based on their ability to exceed the league average in 10 separate offensive and defensive statistics.

ESP/60
Even strength points per 60 minutes. A commonly used statistic measuring the rate of points a player scores per 60 minutes of even strength ice time. 1.80 ESP/60 is considered the common benchmark, but the cutoff has been slightly lower over the past few seasons.

ESSV%
Even strength save percentage. Many analysts prefer to measure goaltenders using only their even strength shot-stopping since there is less year-to-year variation and less luck involved.

ESTOI
Even strength time on ice is a measure of the ice time a player averages per game in even strength situations.

Fenwick
Another possession metric, originally devised by Matt Fenwick of the *Battle of Alberta* blog. Fenwick follows the same concept as Corsi, but doesn't include blocked shots. Fenwick is considered to have better predictive value for future goal differential than Corsi. The removal of blocked shots is also valuable since blocked shots are a proven skill worthy of being separated.

FO%
Faceoff percentage. The ratio of faceoffs that a player has won. Any rate better than 55% is considered elite.

Frank J. Selke Trophy
The award given yearly to the forward in the NHL who best demonstrates defensive skill.

G
Commonly used abbreviation for goal, but also for Goaltender when referring to positions.

GA
Abbreviation for Goals Against. This is the total goals given up by a team or by a goaltender.

GAA
Goals Against Average is a commonly-used statistic to measure the average number of goals a goaltender gives up per game, measured in 60 minute increments. It is similar to ERA in baseball, and just as poor at representing goaltender talent since it is extremely dependent on the team in front of the goalie. Most analysts consider this statistic obsolete and of little use.

GD
Abbreviation for Goal Differential. It represents the difference between the number of goals a team scores minus the number of goals conceded. Goal differential is commonly used as a better measure of team talent than win-loss record in the absence of possession metrics. Equal to overall GVT for teams.

GF
Abbreviation for Goals For. This is the total goals scored by a team, commonly paired with Goals Against to show a team's Goal Differential.

Giveaway
A form of turnover in which the player makes an unforced error that results in giving the puck up to the opposition. It can be unreliable as a statistic since the definition is subjective and individual rink scorers show significant differences in the way they record them.

GP
Abbreviation for Games Played.

GVS
Goals Versus Salary. A measure of a player's value in goals relative to the average return on the same cap space. The formula is GVT - 3 x (Cap Hit - League Minimum Salary). League minimum salary is close to 0.5.

GVT (Individual)
Goals Versus Threshold. Developed by Tom Awad of Hockey Prospectus, GVT measures a player's worth in comparison to a typical fringe NHL player. GVT has two major advantages over most metrics: it is measured in goals, which are easily equated to wins, and it is capable of comparing players across multiple positions and multiple eras. GVT is the summation of OGVT, GGVT, DGVT, and SGVT.

GVT (Team)
Goals Versus Threshold for a team is equal to the team's goal differential. By definition Team GVT = sum of Player GVT - Replacement Level (which GVT defines as 1.5 goals per game or 123 goals per season).

Hart Memorial Trophy
The award given annually to the NHL player judged by the sportswriters to be most valuable to their team during the NHL's regular season.

Heavy lifting
Refers to difficult roles that certain players are placed in, with significantly tougher quality of competition and zone starts that skew towards the defensive end of the rink. Synonym for "tough minutes."

Hits/60
A rate statistic showing the number of hits a player delivers per 60 minutes of ice time. While interesting, it has very little predictive value on goals scored or goals prevented.

Hobey Baker Award
An annual award presented to the NCAA hockey player considered the most outstanding throughout all affiliated conferences. As the award qualifications also include academic achievements, the statistically best players are occasionally overlooked.

Jack Adams Trophy
The annual award given to the NHL coach judged to have contributed most to his team's success.

James Norris Memorial Trophy
The award given on a yearly basis to the defenseman who shows the best all-around ability in the NHL.

Junior
Players aged 15-20 are commonly referred to as "junior" players given that they are eligible to play major junior hockey in the Canadian Hockey League (CHL) or other junior leagues.

KHL
The Kontinental Hockey League was formed in 2008 as the top professional hockey league in Russia. The league also contains teams from seven other eastern European countries. The NHL and KHL have an agreement to honor the contracts from the other league in order to avoid poaching of players under contract, Alexander Radulov notwithstanding.

Lady Byng Memorial Trophy
The award given to the NHL player who best exhibited sportsmanship and gentlemanly play combined with a high standard of playing ability in a given season.

LD
Abbreviation for Left Defenseman, merely indicating the side of the ice the player generally occupies. NHL players are typically listed as Defensemen, without identifying which side they generally play on, but several European leagues make the distinction.

Lockout (of 2004-05)
When the owners and the players association reached an impasse during negotiations after the 2003-04 season, the owners locked the players out. An entire season was lost, but the NHL emerged as a salary cap league, which has helped smaller market clubs achieve financial stability in most of the league's locales.

Lockout (of 2012-13)
Owners once again locked players out at the beginning of 2012-13, with games not resuming until January 19, 2013. An abbreviated 48-game schedule was played, the same length as for the 1994-95 season.

LW
The abbreviation for the Left Wing position.

Maurice "Rocket" Richard Trophy
The award given to the NHL player who scores the most goals during a given regular season.

Moneypuck player
An undervalued player.

Net Penalties/60
The difference between the penalties a players draws and the penalties a player takes. This difference is recorded as a rate per 60 minutes of ice time. Net Penalties per 60 gives insight into which players are giving their teams extra power play opportunities. Net Penalties/60 tends to be higher for forwards and lower (often negative) for defensemen, given their roles on the ice.

Offensive Profile Chart
A graphical representation of the players on a team, showing who are the shooters and who are the playmakers. Shots per 60 minutes is shown on the x-axis, and (estimated) passes leading to shots per 60 minutes is shown on the y-axis, with the bubble size indicating ESP/60 over a 0.50 threshold.

OGVT
Offensive Goals Versus Threshold is the portion of GVT measuring a player's ability to generate goals. OGVT measures a player's contribution to goal creation. It weights goals as more important than assists.

GLOSSARY

OHL

The Ontario Hockey League is part of the CHL, which comprises all three of Canada's top-tier junior hockey leagues. Although most participating teams are located in Ontario, a handful are based out of cities south of the US/Canada border, such as the Plymouth Whalers.

On-ice save percentage

The save percentage of the team (at even strength) when a particular player is on the ice. It is used to help determine whether a player has had exceptionally poor or good luck, which may have influenced his other statistics.

On-ice shooting percentage

The shooting percentage of the entire team when a particular player is on the ice (at even strength). This metric can be used to look for underlying reasons why a player's assist totals have moved considerably or to determine the general amount of luck a player has had relative to his career average.

Passes

Created by Rob Vollman, it is an estimate of the number of passes that lead to shots.

PDO

Created by Vic Ferrari, PDO is the sum of a player's on-ice save percentage and on-ice shooting percentage. PDO is an excellent way to measure "puck luck" or good fortune as it regresses heavily to the mean of 100 (sometimes shown as 1000). For example, a player with a PDO of 103.4 is likely to see his luck drop next year, affecting his plus-minus or point totals. A player with a PDO of 97.1 will likely have a "bounce-back" year purely by getting a few more bounces to go his way.

PIM

Abbreviation for penalty minutes. Not a particularly useful statistic in measuring discipline, because it doesn't differentiate between penalties that put the other team on the power play and offsetting penalties like fighting majors or misconduct penalties which do not lead to power play situations.

Player Usage Chart

A graphical representation of how players on a team are being used at even strength, with offensive zone starts on the x-axis, quality of competition on the y-axis, and the bubble size and shade indicating possession skills (Relative Corsi).

Plus/minus

A traditional hockey statistic used to show the team's goal differential when a particular player is on the ice. The theory seems to makes sense, but in reality it is heavily driven by luck, quality of teammates, and other situational factors. Commonly misused as a defensive statistic.

Possession

A term used to describe how well a team directs play at the opposition net. At the moment, the best commonly-used proxies for possession are Corsi and Fenwick. Possession is important to hockey analysts because it has a very high correlation with winning and predicting future performance of a team.

PPP/60

A rate stat that measures the number of points a player records per 60 minutes of power play time. Even strength and power play rates are split out to give better insight into which situations a player excels at. Much more liable to fluctuate than ESP/60 based on much less playing time involved, it is better to observe a player's PPP/60 over several seasons.

PPSV%

Power play save percentage is the save rate a goaltender records on the man advantage.

PPTOI

The average time on ice a player spends per game in man advantage situations.

President's Trophy

The award given to the team that finishes the regular season with the most points.

Primary assist
Since up to two assists can be assigned per goal in the NHL, the primary assist (A1) is awarded to the player who touched the puck directly before the goal-scorer. Primary assists are considered to be generally less luck driven than secondary assists.

QualComp
A measure of competition quality using relative plus/minus as its basis. A number higher than 0 indicates a higher than average level of competition. One drawback to QualComp is that it is goal based, incorporating more puck luck than Corsi-based methods.

QMJHL
The Quebec Major Junior Hockey League is part of the CHL, which comprises all three of Canada's top-tier junior hockey leagues. While the majority of franchises are based in Quebec, Canada's Maritime provinces are also represented, such as the recent Memorial Cup winning Halifax Mooseheads.

QS
A Quality Start is a measure of whether a goaltender "gave his team a chance to win." In order to record a quality start, the goalie record a save percentage over league average (currently .917), or between .885 and .917 while allowing less than three goals. The reason Quality Starts are so important is that teams win 77.5% of the games in which their goalie records a Quality Start. The threshold for a QS changes with fluctuating league save rates.

QS%
Quality Start Percentage shows the ratio of a goaltender's games in which they recorded a quality start. A quality start rate of 60% is considered elite, while anything below 40% is quite poor.

Regression to the mean
A statistical term that refers to the phenomenon of statistical measures returning to their average value over time. For example, if Player A's career shooting percentage is 8.5% and he shot 11.3% last season, he will likely *regress* closer to 8.5% the following year. It can have either a positive and negative implication depending on the situation.

RD
Abbreviation for Right Defenseman, merely indicating the side of the ice the player generally occupies. NHL players are typically listed as Defensemen, without identifying which side they generally play on, but several European leagues make the distinction.

Relative Corsi
A player's Corsi value in comparison to his teammates. Relative Corsi is expressed as the player's Corsi minus the team Corsi rate. A positive value indicates a player who is better than the team average and a negative number is a player who is worse than the team average.

Relative Plus/Minus (RPM)
A player's Plus/Minus adjusted for team goal differential and goaltending. Relative plus/minus subtracts 80% of his team's expected goal differential (since the player is one of five skaters on the ice) from a player's plus/minus, and adjusts goals against by his team's save percentage.

Replacement level
The level of performance of an easily-obtainable player, such as an AHL call-up. Many statistics (such as GVT) express the value of players as value over replacement level.

R^2
A statistical term showing the degree of correlation between two variables. It is typically expressed in a percentage, indicating the amount of variation in Variable A that can be explained by Variable B.

RW
The abbreviation for the Right Wing position.

Salary cap
The maximum amount a team can spend on player salaries each year. The values for each player's contract include their annual salary and their signing bonus, split over the number of years the contract is signed for. Governed by the CBA, it is set at $64.3 million for the 2013-14 season.

GLOSSARY

Salary floor

The minimum amount a team must spend on player salaries each year. The values for each player's contract include their annual salary and their signing bonus, split over the number of years the contract is signed for. Governed by the CBA, it is set at $44 million for 2013-14.

Save percentage

The percentage of shots on goal that a goalie prevents from going in his team's net.

Scoring chance

Scoring chances are generally defined as shots taken from within the arc that extends from the crease, through the faceoff dots and to the top of the circles. They add a shot quality factor to shot-based possession proxies, but at the expense of sample size. Also, individual recording of scoring chances tends to be subjective.

Score effects

The skewing effect teams either sitting on or chasing a lead have on statistics, most notably shots.

Second assist

Since up to two assists can be assigned per goal in the NHL, the secondary assist (A2) is awarded to the player who touched the puck two players before the goal scorer. Secondary assists are considered to be more luck driven than primary assists.

SGVT

Shootout Goals Versus Threshold is a measure of a skater's or goaltender's value in the shootout. It is based on the player's ability to score or prevent goals in the shootout versus a league-average player in the same situation.

Sheltered minutes

A term referring to the type of ice time a player is given by his coach. Players given "sheltered minutes" are generally matched up against easy competition and/or given a very high offensive zone start ratio.

SHL

The rebranded name for the Swedish Hockey League, formerly the Swedish Elite League (SEL) or the Elitserien. The highest level of professional hockey in Sweden, it is considered one of the two best non-NHL leagues in the world, along with the KHL.

Shooting percentage

The percentage of shots on goal (by a team or player) that go in the net. It does not take missed shots into consideration.

SHSV%

Shorthanded save percentage is merely the save percentage of a team or player while in a shorthanded situation. Save percentages while shorthanded are generally much lower than those at even strength. SHSV% is considered quite volatile from year-to-year due to small sample size.

SHTOI

The time on ice per game that a player spends in shorthanded situations.

Shot quality

The combined impact of the timing, type, circumstances, and location of a shot, sometimes together with the shooter's skill.

Shutdown

An elite defensive player or duo who is good at shutting down opposition scoring—as in shutdown defenseman, a shutdown pairing, or a shutdown forward.

SM-Liiga

The top professional hockey league in Finland. Occasionally referred to as the Finnish Elite League, SM-Liiga translates to "Finnish Championship League".

Snepsts System

A projection system created by Rob Vollman, based on searching historical data for players the same age with similar era-adjusted statistics (comparables) as a player's past few seasons, and averaging their future performance. Also useful for establishing minimum and maximum scoring expectations based on historical precedent.

SOG
The abbreviation for Shots On Goal.

Special Teams Usage Chart
A graphical representation of the ice time players on a team are receiving in different manpower situations. Average power play minutes per game are shown on the x-axis, average shorthanded minutes per game are shown on the y-axis, and the bubble size indicates average even strength ice time over a 10-minute threshold.

Takeaway
A form of turnover in which the player takes the puck from the opposition, rather than gaining possession through an opposition error. It can be unreliable as a statistic since the definition is subjective and individual rink scorers show significant differences in the way they record them.

Ted Lindsay Award
Formerly known as the Lester B. Pearson Trophy, the Ted Lindsay Award is awarded to the player judged by his peers (other active players) as the most outstanding player of a given season.

TOI
The abbreviation for time on ice. Typically represented in minutes:seconds per game.

Top four
Typically refers to a squad's best four defensemen. On most teams, the top four defensemen shoulder the majority of the ice time among defensemen. The term can be used to describe a player's role on the team, or their talent level.

Top six
Typically refers to a squad's first two lines of forwards. These lines are usually counted on to provide the bulk of the scoring for most teams. The term can be used to describe a player's role on the team, or their talent level.

Top nine
Typically refers to a squad's first three lines of forwards. The top nine forwards generally play the bulk of the minutes on most teams. The term can be used to describe a player's role on the team, or their talent level.

Top pairing
Refers to the top two defensemen on a team. These two players are typically relied on to play against the opposition's best offensive players. The term can be used to describe a player's role on the team, or their talent level.

Total offense
Shots plus (estimated) passes leading to shots, a stat created by Rob Vollman.

Tough minutes
Refers to difficult roles that certain players are placed in, with significantly tougher quality of competition and zone starts that skew towards the defensive end of the rink.

Translations
Converting a player's scoring data from other leagues to an NHL equivalent, using scoring changes of those who made the move previously as a basis. For example, an AHL translation would be what a player would score in the NHL, based on what happened to previous AHL players with similar statistics when they went to the NHL.

UFO%
An advanced faceoff metric created by Timo Seppa, Ultimate Faceoff Percentage is calculated from even strength, non-empty net situation, road faceoffs only, and adjusted for strength of competition.

USHL

The United States Hockey League is a junior-level league located entirely in the midwestern United States, which includes the United States National Team Development Program of 18-and-unders as one of their teams. The league is seen as a viable alternative to the CHL to many junior-aged players who wish to retain NCAA eligibility, which would be lost after one game played for any CHL team, due to the stipends those leagues provide their players.

Vezina Trophy

The award given to the goaltender judged to be the best in the NHL in a given season.

VUKOTA

Hockey Prospectus' proprietary projection system, based on the GVT metric and created by Tom Awad.

WHL

The Western Hockey League is part of the CHL, which comprises all three of Canada's top-tier junior hockey leagues. The WHL consists of teams located in Western Canada and the upper Northwest of the United States.

William M. Jennings Trophy

The award given annually to the goaltenders of the team with the lowest combined GAA in the NHL. To be eligible for the honor, the goaltenders need to have played in at least 25 games for that team.

World Junior Hockey Championship

Officially, the IIHF World Under 20 Championship, it is the annual international Under-20 ice hockey tournament held in late December and early January. It usually showcases the best junior-aged prospects in the world as well as potential top picks for the upcoming draft.

WOWY

With or Without You is a style of analysis used to determine which players benefit the most from their linemates and which players are driving play.

Zone entries

Statistics built around looking at the efficiencies of players and teams moving the puck into the offensive zone, pioneered in part by Eric Tulsky.

Zone exits

Statistics built around looking at the efficiencies of players and teams moving the puck out of the defensive zone, pioneered in part by Corey Sznajder.

Zone Start% (OZ% or ZS%)

A ratio showing the percentage of a player's non-neutral-zone shifts that were started in the offensive zone. Zone starts use faceoffs as a proxy for all shifts. Players with a OZ% higher than 54% could be considered sheltered or deployed offensively while players with ZS% south of 46% can be considered to be deployed defensively or doing the "heavy lifting".

Appendix

Mat Clark								RD						COL
Season	Team	Age	GP	G	A	Pts	+/-	ESP/60	AdjCF%	iCF/60	OGVT	DGVT	SGVT	GVT
2014-15	ANA	24	7	0	1	1	2	0.73	44.3%	5.2	0.0	0.4	0.0	0.4
2015-16	COL	25	27	2	5	6					0.3	1.0	0.0	1.3

Known as a big hitter and defensive defenseman for a good Brampton Battalion team in junior, six-foot-three Mat Clark was drafted in the second round of 2009 by Anaheim. You might be able to guess how this story goes. While averaging more than a PIM per game at the AHL level since 2010, Clark has managed only 0.16 points per game. Plus, he has played in nine NHL games, tallying an assist.

Adam Cracknell								RW						VAN
Season	Team	Age	GP	G	A	Pts	+/-	ESP/60	AdjCF%	iCF/60	OGVT	DGVT	SGVT	GVT
2012-13	STL	27	20	2	4	6	3	2.09	56.9%	13.8	0.9	0.8	0.0	1.7
2013-14	STL	28	19	0	2	2	0	0.79	50.5%	11.5	-0.9	0.3	0.0	-0.6
2014-15	CBJ	29	17	0	1	1	-8	0.38	39.1%	10.0	-1.1	-0.4	0.0	-1.5
2015-16	VAN	30	31	3	5	8					-0.1	0.5	0.0	0.4

A ninth-round pick by Calgary, from back in 2004, when there were as many as nine rounds, Adam Cracknell has pieced together a full 82 games of NHL hockey...over five seasons. His stat line for that "season"? 6 goals, 11 assists, 17 points, -3, 14 PIM. Cracknell is probably better than a lot of fourth liners who have gotten more playing time. Release the Cracknell!

Michael Sgarbossa								C						ANA
Season	Team	Age	GP	G	A	Pts	+/-	ESP/60	AdjCF%	iCF/60	OGVT	DGVT	SGVT	GVT
2012-13	COL	20	6	0	0	0	-3	0.00	41.4%	8.5	-0.4	-0.2	0.0	-0.6
2014-15	COL	22	3	0	1	1	0	2.82	39.2%	13.9	-0.3	0.1	0.0	-0.2
2015-16	ANA	23	26	4	6	10					0.5	0.6	0.0	1.1

An AHL All-Star in his first and best minor-league season of 2012-13, undrafted Michael Sgarbossa hasn't managed to get more than a couple of peeks at the big-league level. In his final year of junior hockey, the five-foot-eleven, 181-pound center tallied an impressive-looking 102 points in 66 games for Sudbury. It doesn't mean that much as an older player, though.

Index

Abdelkader, Justin, 162
Acton, Will, 414
Adam, Luke, 130
Adams, Craig, 341
Agozzino, Andrew, 113
Akeson, Jason, 326
Allen, Bryan, 242
Allen, Conor, 303
Allen, Jake, 364
Alt, Mark, 332
Alzner, Karl, 434
Andersen, Frederik, 14
Anderson, Craig, 320
Anderson, Josh, 130
Andersson, Joakim, 162
Andreoff, Andy, 207
Andrighetto, Sven, 236
Angelidis, Mike, 384
Anisimov, Artem, 130
Arcobello, Mark, 20
Armia, Joel, 443
Arvidsson, Viktor, 252
Ashton, Carter, 384
Atkinson, Cam, 131
Aulie, Keith, 184
Bachman, Richard, 187

Backes, David, 352
Backlund, Mikael, 66
Backstrom, Nicklas, 429
Backstrom, Niklas, 230
Baertschi, Sven, 414
Bailey, Casey, 3989
Bailey, Josh, 283
Bailey, Justin, 478
Ballard, Keith, 226
Barbashev, Ivan, 467
Barber, Riley, 475
Barberio, Mark, 389
Barkov, Aleksander, 193
Barrie, Tyson, 120
Bartkowski, Matt, 42
Bartley, Victor, 258
Barzal, Mathew, 465
Baun, Kyle, 98
Beagle, Jay, 429
Beauchemin, Francois, 11
Beaulieu, Nathan, 242
Beauvillier, Anthony, 473
Beck, Taylor, 252
Beleskey, Matt, 5
Bellemare, Pierre-Edouard, 326
Bellemore, Brett, 88

Benn, Jamie, 148
Benn, Jordie, 153
Bennett, Beau, 341
Bennett, Sam, 66, 463
Benoit, Andre, 56
Bergenheim, Sean, 220
Bergeron, Patrice, 35
Berglund, Patrik, 352
Bernier, Jonathan, 409
Bernier, Steve, 267
Berra, Reto, 124
Bertuzzi, Tyler, 478
Bickel, Stu, 226
Bickell, Bryan, 98
Biega, Alex, 420
Biega, Danny, 88
Bieksa, Kevin, 421
Bigras, Chris, 470
Bishop, Ben, 392
Bitetto, Anthony, 258
Bjorkstrand, Oliver, 469
Bjugstad, Nick, 193
Blacker, Jesse, 198
Blum, Jonathon, 227
Blunden, Mike, 384
Bobrovsky, Sergei, 141

Bodie, Troy, 398
Boedker, Mikkel, 20
Boeser, Brock, 472
Bogosian, Zach, 57
Bolduc, Alexandre, 20
Boll, Jared, 131
Bolland, Dave, 193
Bollig, Brandon, 66
Bonino, Nick, 414
Booth, David, 398
Bordeleau, Patrick, 114
Borowiecki, Mark, 318
Bortuzzo, Robert, 361
Boucher, Reid, 267
Boulton, Eric, 283
Bouma, Lance, 67
Bournival, Michael, 236
Bourque, Gabriel, 252
Bourque, Rene, 131
Bourque, Ryan, 297
Bouwmeester, Jay, 361
Bowey, Madison, 470
Bowman, Drayson, 236
Boychuk, Johnny, 288
Boychuk, Zach, 82
Boyes, Brad, 194
Boyle, Brian, 384
Boyle, Dan, 303
Bozak, Tyler, 399
Brassard, Derick, 297

Braun, Justin, 375
Brennan, T.J., 405
Brewer, Eric, 405
Briere, Daniel, 114
Brodeur, Martin, 364
Brodie, T.J., 73
Brodin, Jonas, 227
Brodziak, Kyle, 220
Brossoit, Laurent, 187
Brouillette, Julien, 449
Brouwer, Troy, 429
Brown, Chris, 430
Brown, Connor, 471
Brown, Dustin, 207
Brown, J.T., 385
Brown, Mike, 369
Brown, Patrick, 82
Brunner, Damien, 267
Bryzgalov, Ilya, 14
Buchnevich, Pavel, 466
Bunz, Tyler, 188
Burakovsky, Andre, 430
Burish, Adam, 369
Burns, Brent, 375
Burrows, Alexandre, 415
Butler, Chris, 362
Byfuglien, Dustin, 449
Byron, Paul, 67
Callahan, Ryan, 385
Calvert, Matt, 132

Cammalleri, Mike, 268
Campbell, Andrew, 27
Campbell, Brian, 198
Campbell, Gregory, 35
Carcillo, Daniel, 98
Carey, Paul, 35
Carle, Matthew, 389
Carlson, John, 435
Caron, Jordan, 114
Carrick, Sam, 399
Carter, Jeff, 207
Carter, Ryan, 220
Cassels, Cole, 473
Ceci, Cody, 318
Chabot, Thomas, 471
Chaput, Michael, 132
Chara, Zdeno, 42
Chiarot, Ben, 450
Chiasson, Alex, 312
Chimera, Jason, 430
Chipchura, Kyle, 21
Chorney, Taylor, 347
Cizikas, Casey, 283
Clark, Mat, 520
Clarkson, David, 132
Cleary, Daniel, 162
Clemmensen, Scott, 277
Clendening, Adam, 421, 472
Cliche, Marc-Andre, 115
Clifford, Kyle, 208

INDEX

Clitsome, Grant, 450
Clowe, Ryane, 268
Clune, Rich, 253
Clutterbuck, Cal, 284
Coburn, Braydon, 389
Cogliano, Andrew, 5
Colaiacovo, Carlo, 332
Colborne, Joe, 67
Cole, Erik, 163
Cole, Ian, 348
Collins, Sean, 133
Comeau, Blake, 341
Conacher, Cory, 415
Condra, Erik, 313
Connauton, Kevin, 138
Conner, Chris, 430
Connolly, Brett, 36
Connor, Kyle, 468
Cooke, Matt, 221
Copp, Andrew, 443
Cormier, Patrice, 443
Corrado, Frank, 421
Cousins, Nick, 326
Couture, Logan, 369
Couturier, Sean, 327
Cowen, Jared, 318
Coyle, Charlie, 221
Cracknell, Adam, 520
Craig, Ryan, 133
Crawford, Corey, 107

Crombeen, B.J., 21
Crosby, Sidney, 342
Crouse, Lawson, 469
Cullen, Matt, 253
Cumiskey, Kyle, 104
Cunningham, Craig, 21
Curry, John, 230
Dahlbeck, Klas, 27
Dal Colle, Michael, 465
Daley, Trevor, 154
Dalpe, Zac, 51
D'Amigo, Jerry, 51
Danault, Phillip, 99
Dano, Marko, 133, 467
Darling, Scott, 107
Datsyuk, Pavel, 163
Davidson, Brandon, 184
de Haan, Calvin, 289
De La Rose, Jacob, 236, 474
DeAngelo, Anthony, 470
DeFazio, Brandon, 415
DeKeyser, Danny, 167
Del Zotto, Michael, 332
Demers, Jason, 154
Desharnais, David, 237
Desjardins, Andrew, 99
Deslauriers, Nicolas, 51
Despres, Simon, 11
Diaz, Raphael, 73
Dillon, Brenden, 375

Dini, Max, 464
Doan, Shane, 22
Domingue, Louis, 29
Donovan, Matt, 289
Donski, Joonas, 474
Dorsett, Derek, 415
Doughty, Drew, 212
Downie, Steve, 342
Draisaitl, Leon, 177, 463
Driedger, Chris, 320
Drouin, Jonathan, 385
Dubinsky, Brandon, 134
Dubnyk, Devan, 230
Duchene, Matt, 115
Duclair, Anthony, 22, 477
Dumba, Matt, 227
Dumont, Gabriel, 237
Dumoulin, Brian, 348, 478
Dupuis, Pascal, 342
Dwyer, Patrick, 82
Eakin, Cody, 148
Eaves, Patrick, 148
Ebbett, Andrew, 343
Eberle, Jordan, 177
Edler, Alexander, 421
Ehlers, Nikolaj, 464
Ehrhoff, Christian, 348
Eichel, Jack, 462
Ekblad, Aaron, 199
Ekholm, Mattias, 258

INDEX

Ekman-Larsson, Oliver, 27
Elias, Patrik, 268
Eller, Lars, 237
Ellerby, Keaton, 450
Elliott, Brian, 364
Elliott, Stefan, 121
Ellis, Dan, 201
Ellis, Matt, 51
Ellis, Ryan, 259
Emelin, Alexei, 243
Emery, Ray, 336
Engelland, Deryk, 73
Ennis, Tyler, 52
Enroth, Jhonas, 156
Enstrom, Toby, 451
Erat, Martin, 22
Ericsson, Jonathan, 168
Eriksson Ek, Joel, 472
Eriksson, Loui, 36
Erixon, Tim, 405
Erne, Adam, 477
Etem, Emerson, 5
Everberg, Dennis, 115
Fabbri, Robby, 464
Falk, Justin, 138
Farnham, Bobby, 343
Fast, Jesper, 297
Fasth, Viktor, 188
Faulk, Justin, 88
Fayne, Mark, 184

Fedun, Taylor, 376
Fehr, Eric, 431
Ference, Andrew, 184
Ferland, Micheal, 67
Ferlin, Brian, 36
Ferraro, Landon, 163
Fiala, Kevin, 253, 465
Fiddler, Vernon, 149
Filppula, Valtteri, 386
Fisher, Mike, 254
Fistric, Mark, 11
Fleischmann, Tomas, 6
Fleury, Marc-Andre, 351
Flynn, Brian, 238
Foligno, Marcus, 52
Foligno, Nick, 134
Folin, Christian, 228
Fontaine, Justin, 221
Forsberg, Anton, 141
Forsberg, Filip, 254
Fowler, Cam, 12
Franson, Cody, 259
Franzen, Johan, 164
Fraser, Colin, 352
Fraser, Mark, 273
Fraser, Matt, 178
Frattin, Matt, 399
Friberg, Max, 6
Frolik, Michael, 444
Gaborik, Marian, 208

Gagne, Simon, 37
Gagner, Sam, 22
Galchenyuk, Alex, 238
Galiardi, T.J., 444
Galiev, Stanislav, 431
Gallagher, Brendan, 238
Garbutt, Ryan, 149
Gardiner, Jake, 406
Garrison, Jason, 390
Gaudet, Tyler, 23
Gaudreau, Johnny, 68
Gaustad, Paul, 254
Gazdic, Luke, 178
Gelinas, Eric, 274
Gerbe, Nathan, 83
Getzlaf, Ryan, 6
Gibbons, Brian, 134
Gibson, John, 14
Gilbert, Tom, 243
Gionta, Brian, 52
Gionta, Stephen, 269
Giordano, Mark, 74
Girardi, Dan, 303
Girgensons, Zemgus, 53
Giroux, Claude, 327
Glass, Tanner, 298
Gleason, Tim, 435
Glencross, Curtis, 431
Glendening, Luke, 164
Goc, Marcel, 357

INDEX

Goldobin, Nikolai, 477
Goligoski, Alex, 154
Goloubef, Cody, 139
Gomez, Scott, 269
Gonchar, Sergei, 243
Goodrow, Barclay, 370
Gordon, Boyd, 178
Gorges, Josh, 57
Gormley, Brandon, 28, 469
Gostisbehere, Shayne, 333
Grabner, Michael, 284
Grabovski, Mikhail, 284
Granberg, Petter, 406
Granlund, Markus, 68
Granlund, Mikael, 222
Graovac, Tyler, 222
Green, Mike, 435
Greene, Andy, 274
Greene, Matt, 212
Greening, Colin, 313
Greiss, Thomas, 351
Griffith, Seth, 37
Grigorenko, Mikhail, 53
Grimaldi, Rocco, 194
Grosenick, Troy, 378
Grossmann, Nicklas, 333
Grubauer, Philipp, 437
Gryba, Eric, 319
Gudas, Radko, 333
Gudbranson, Erik, 199

Guenin, Nate, 121
Gunnarsson, Carl, 362
Guryanov, Denis, 473
Gustavsson, Jonas, 171
Hackett, Matt, 60
Hagelin, Carl, 298
Hainsey, Ron, 89
Halak, Jaroslav, 291
Haley, Micheal, 370
Halischuk, Matt, 444
Hall, Taylor, 179
Hamhuis, Dan, 422
Hamilton, Curtis, 179
Hamilton, Dougie, 42
Hamilton, Freddie, 116
Hamilton, Ryan, 179
Hammond, Andrew, 321
Hamonic, Travis, 289
Hanifin, Noah, 465
Hannan, Scott, 376
Hansen, Jannik, 416
Hanzal, Martin, 23
Harding, Josh, 231
Harkins, Jansen, 471
Harrington, Scott, 348
Harrison, Jay, 451
Harrold, Peter, 274
Hartman, Ryan, 99
Hartnell, Scott, 135
Haula, Erik, 222

Havlat, Martin, 269
Hayes, Eriah, 370
Hayes, Jimmy, 194
Hayes, Kevin, 298
Heatley, Dany, 7
Hedman, Victor, 390
Hejda, Jan, 121
Helgeson, Seth, 275
Hellebuyck, Conor, 471
Helm, Darren, 164
Hemsky, Ales, 149
Hendricks, Matt, 179
Henrique, Adam, 270
Hertl, Tomas, 371
Hickey, Thomas, 290
Higgins, Chris, 416
Hillen, Jack, 89
Hiller, Jonas, 76
Hishon, Joey, 116
Hjalmarsson, Niklas, 104
Hodgman, Justin, 23
Hodgson, Cody, 53
Hoffman, Mike, 313
Holden, Nick, 122
Holland, Peter, 400
Holtby, Braden, 437
Holzer, Korbinian, 12
Honka, Julius, 474
Horcoff, Shawn, 150
Hornqvist, Patric, 343

Horton, Nathan, 400
Horvat, Bo, 416
Ho-Sang, Josh, 474
Hossa, Marian, 99
Howard, Jimmy, 171
Hrabarenka, Raman, 275
Huberdeau, Jonathan, 195
Hudler, Jiri, 69
Hunt, Brad, 185
Hunwick, Matt, 304
Hutchinson, Michael, 453
Hutton, Carter, 261
Iginla, Jarome, 116
Irwin, Matt, 376
Jackman, Barret, 362
Jackman, Tim, 7
Jagr, Jaromir, 195
Jarnkrok, Calle, 255
Jaskin, Dmitrij, 357
Jenner, Boone, 135
Jensen, Nicklas, 417
Joensuu, Jesse, 180
Johansen, Ryan, 135
Johansson, Marcus, 432
Johnson, Andreas, 475
Johnson, Chad, 292
Johnson, Erik, 122
Johnson, Jack, 139
Johnson, Tyler, 386
Jokinen, Jussi, 195

Jokinen, Olli, 357
Jokipakka, Jyrki, 155
Jones, Blair, 327
Jones, David, 69
Jones, Martin, 215
Jones, Seth, 259
Jooris, Josh, 69
Jordan, Michal, 89
Josefson, Jacob, 270
Josi, Roman, 260
Jurco, Tomas, 165
Kadri, Nazem, 400
Kaleta, Patrick, 54
Kamenev, Vladislav, 474
Kampfer, Steven, 199
Kane, Evander, 54
Kane, Patrick, 100
Karlsson, Erik, 319
Karlsson, Melker, 371
Karlsson, William, 136
Kassian, Zack, 417
Keith, Duncan, 104
Kelly, Chris, 37
Kempe, Adrian, 471
Kenins, Ronalds, 417
Kennedy, Tyler, 285
Kesler, Ryan, 7
Kessel, Phil, 401
Khokhlachev, Alex, 38
Khudobin, Anton, 91

Killorn, Alex, 386
Kindl, Jakub, 168
King, Dwight, 208
Kinkaid, Keith, 277
Klefbom, Oscar, 185
Klein, Kevin, 304
Klingberg, Carl, 299
Klingberg, John, 155
Klinkhammer, Rob, 180
Knight, Corban, 196
Koekkoek, Slater, 390
Koivu, Mikko, 223
Komarov, Leo, 401
Konecny, Travis, 469
Kopecky, Tomas, 196
Kopitar, Anze, 209
Korpikoski, Lauri, 24
Kostka, Michael, 304
Kozun, Brandon, 401
Kreider, Chris, 299
Krejci, David, 38
Kronwall, Niklas, 168
Krug, Torey, 43
Kruger, Marcus, 100
Kucherov, Nikita, 387
Kuemper, Darcy, 231
Kulak, Brett, 74
Kulemin, Nikolay, 285
Kulikov, Dmitry, 200
Kunitz, Chris, 344

INDEX

Kuznetsov, Evgeny, 432
LaBarbera, Jason, 14
Lack, Eddie, 423
Ladd, Andrew, 445
Laich, Brooks, 432
Lander, Anton, 180
Landeskog, Gabriel, 117
Lapierre, Maxim, 344
Larkin, Dylan, 463
Larsson, Adam, 275
Larsson, Johan, 54
Lashoff, Brian, 169
Latta, Michael, 432
Laughton, Scott, 328, 470
Lauridsen, Oliver, 334
Lazar, Curtis, 314
Lecavalier, Vincent, 328
Leddy, Nick, 290
Lee, Anders, 285
Legwand, David, 314
Lehner, Robin, 321
Lehtera, Jori, 358
Lehtonen, Kari, 156
Leivo, Josh, 402
Leopold, Jordan, 228
Lerg, Bryan, 371
Lessio, Lucas, 24
Letang, Kris, 349
Letestu, Mark, 136
Lewis, Trevor, 209

Liles, John-Michael, 90
Lindback, Anders, 60
Lindberg, Oscar, 299
Lindblad, Matt, 38
Lindbohm, Petteri, 362
Lindholm, Elias, 83
Lindholm, Hampus, 12
Lindstrom, Joakim, 402
Little, Bryan, 445
Lovejoy, Ben, 349
Lowe, Keegan, 90
Lowry, Adam, 445
Lucic, Milan, 39
Lundqvist, Henrik, 306
Luongo, Roberto, 201
Lupul, Joffrey, 402
Maatta, Olli, 349
MacArthur, Clarke, 314
MacDonald, Andrew, 334
MacKenzie, Derek, 196
MacKinnon, Nathan, 117
MacWilliam, Andrew, 407
Makarov, Andrey, 61
Malhotra, Manny, 239
Malkin, Evgeni, 344
Malone, Brad, 83
Malone, Ryan, 300
Manning, Brandon, 334
Manson, Josh, 12
Mantha, Anthony, 469

Marchand, Brad, 39
Marchenko, Alexey, 169
Marchessault, Jonathan, 387
Marincin, Martin, 185
Markov, Andrei, 244
Markstrom, Jacob, 424
Marleau, Patrick, 371
Marner, Mitch, 464
Maroon, Patrick, 8
Martin, Matt, 286
Martin, Paul, 350
Martinez, Alec, 212
Martinook, Jordan, 24
Mason, Steve, 336
Matheson, Mike, 478
Matteau, Stefan, 270
Matthias, Shawn, 418
Mazanec, Marek, 261
McBain, Jamie, 213
McCabe, Jake, 57, 477
McCann, Jared, 468
McCarron, Michael, 475
McClement, Jay, 84
McCollum, Tom, 171
McCormick, Cody, 55
McDavid, Connor, 462
McDonagh, Ryan, 305
McDonald, Colin, 286
McElhinney, Curtis, 142
McGinn, Jamie, 117

INDEX

McGinn, Tye, 25
McGrattan, Brian, 70
McIlrath, Dylan, 305
McKegg, Greg, 403
McKenna, Mike, 30
McKenzie, Curtis, 150
McLeod, Cody, 118
McMillan, Brandon, 418
McNabb, Brayden, 213
McQuaid, Adam, 43
Megna, Jayson, 345
Meier, Timo, 468
Merkeley, Nick, 468
Merrill, Jon, 276
Meszaros, Andrej, 58
Methot, Marc, 319
Michalek, Milan, 314
Michalek, Zbynek, 363
Milano, Sonny, 475
Miller, Andrew, 181
Miller, Drew, 165
Miller, J.T., 300
Miller, Kevan, 43
Miller, Ryan, 424
Mitchell, John, 118
Mitchell, Torrey, 239
Mitchell, Willie, 200
Moen, Travis, 150
Monahan, Sean, 70
Montoya, Al, 201

Moore, Dominic, 300
Moore, John, 28
Morin, Jeremy, 136
Morin, Samuel, 476
Morin, Travis, 151
Morrissey, Josh, 464
Morrow, Brenden, 387
Morrow, Joe, 44
Moss, David, 25
Mouillierat, Kael, 286
Moulson, Matt, 55
Mrazek, Petr, 172
Mueller, Chris, 301
Mueller, Mirco, 377, 478
Murphy, Connor, 28
Murphy, Ryan, 90
Murray, Matt, 476
Murray, Ryan, 139
Musil, David, 186
Muzzin, Jake, 213
Myers, Tyler, 451
Nabokov, Evgeni, 392
Namestnikov, Vladislav, 388
Nash, Rick, 301
Nash, Riley, 84
Neal, James, 255
Neil, Chris, 315
Nelson, Brock, 286
Nemeth, Patrik, 155
Nesterov, Nikita, 391

Nestrasil, Andrej, 84
Neuvirth, Michal, 292
Nichushkin, Valeri, 151
Niederreiter, Nino, 223
Nielsen, Frans, 287
Niemi, Antti, 378
Nieto, Matt, 372
Nikitin, Nikita, 186
Niskanen, Matt, 435
Noesen, Stefan, 8
Nolan, Jordan, 209
Nordstrom, Joakim, 100
Nugent-Hopkins, Ryan, 181
Nurse, Darnell, 186, 466
Nylander, William, 464
Nyquist, Gustav, 165
Nystrom, Eric, 255
O'Brien, Liam, 433
O'Brien, Shane, 200
O'Dell, Eric, 446
Oduya, Johnny, 105
Oesterle, Jordan, 186
Okposo, Kyle, 287
Oleksiak, Jamie, 156
Oleksy, Steve, 436
Olsen, Dylan, 201
O'Reilly, Ryan, 118
Orlov, Dmitry, 436
Orpik, Brooks, 436
Orr, Colton, 403

INDEX

Ortio, Joni, 77
Oshie, T.J., 358
Ott, Steve, 358
Ouellet, Xavier, 169
Ovechkin, Alex, 443
Paajarvi, Magnus, 358
Pacioretty, Max, 239
Pageau, Jean-Gabriel, 315
Paille, Daniel, 39
Pakarinen, Iiro, 181, 476
Palat, Ondrej, 388
Paliotta, Michael, 105
Palmieri, Kyle, 8
Panik, Richard, 403
Paquette, Cedric, 388
Pardy, Adam, 452
Parenteau, P-A, 240
Parise, Zach, 223
Pastrnak, David, 40
Pateryn, Greg, 244
Pavelec, Ondrej, 453
Pavelski, Joe, 372
Pearson, Tanner, 209
Peluso, Anthony, 446
Percy, Stuart, 407
Perreault, Mathieu, 446
Perron, David, 345
Perry, Corey, 9
Petan, Nicolas, 471
Peters, Justin, 438

Petrovic, Alex, 201
Petry, Jeff, 244
Peverley, Rich, 151
Phaneuf, Dion, 407
Phillips, Chris, 319
Pickard, Calvin, 124, 473
Pietrangelo, Alex, 363
Pinizzotto, Steven, 181
Pirri, Brandon, 196
Piskula, Joe, 260
Pitlick, Tyler, 182
Plekanec, Tomas, 240
Poirier, Emile, 70, 477
Polak, Roman, 408
Pominville, Jason, 224
Porter, Chris, 359
Postma, Paul, 452
Potter, Corey, 74
Poulin, Kevin, 292
Pouliot, Benoit, 182
Pouliot, Derrick, 350, 465
Price, Carey, 246
Prince, Shane, 315
Prosser, Nate, 228
Prout, Dalton, 140
Provorov, Ivan, 466
Prust, Brandon, 240
Puempel, Matt, 316, 479
Pulkkinen, Teemu, 166, 477
Pulock, Ryan, 468

Purcell, Teddy, 182
Pysyk, Mark, 58
Quick, Jonathan, 215
Quincey, Kyle, 170
r Tanev, Christoph, 423
Raanta, Antti, 107
Raffl, Michael, 328
Rakell, Rickard, 9
Ramage, John, 74
Ramo, Karri, 77
Ranford, Brendan, 151
Rantanen, Mikko, 466
Rask, Tuukka, 45
Rask, Victor, 85
Rattie, Ty, 359
Raymond, Mason, 71
Read, Matt, 329
Reaves, Ryan, 359
Redmond, Zach, 122
Reese, Dylan, 28
Regehr, Robyn, 214
Regin, Peter, 101
Reilly, Mike, 465
Reimer, James, 409
Reinhart, Griffin, 290, 469
Reinhart, Max, 71
Reinhart, Sam, 55, 463
Rendulic, Borna, 119
Ribeiro, Mike, 256
Richards, Brad, 101

Richards, Mike, 210
Richardson, Brad, 418
Rieder, Tobias, 25
Rielly, Morgan, 408
Rinaldo, Zac, 329
Rinne, Pekka, 262
Rissanen, Rasmus, 91
Ristolainen, Rasmus, 58
Ritchie, Brett, 152, 479
Ritchie, Nick, 467
Robak, Colby, 13
Robidas, Stephane, 408
Robins, Bobby, 40
Roslovic, Jack, 478
Roussel, Antoine, 152
Roy, Derek, 183
Roy, Jeremy, 473
Rozsival, Michal, 105
Ruhwedel, Chad, 59
Rundblad, David, 105
Russell, Kris, 75
Rust, Bryan, 345
Ruutu, Tuomo, 271
Ryan, Bobby, 316
Rychel, Kerby, 136, 476
Ryder, Michael, 271
Rynnas, Jussi, 157
Saad, Brandon, 101
Salomaki, Miikka, 256
Salvador, Bryce, 276

Samuelsson, Henrik, 25
Samuelsson, Philip, 29
Sanheim, Travis, 479
Santorelli, Mike, 256
Savard, David, 140
Sbisa, Luca, 422
Scandella, Marco, 229
Sceviour, Colton, 152
Schaller, Tim, 56
Scheifele, Mark, 447
Schenn, Brayden, 329
Schenn, Luke, 335
Scherbak, Nikita, 468
Schilling, Cameron, 437
Schlemko, David, 75
Schmaltz, Jordan, 474
Schmidt, Nate, 437
Schneider, Cory, 277
Schroeder, Jordan, 224
Schultz, Jeff, 214
Schultz, Justin, 187
Schultz, Nick, 335
Schwartz, Jaden, 360
Scott, John, 372
Scrivens, Ben, 188
Scuderi, Rob, 350
Seabrook, Brent, 106
Sedin, Daniel, 419
Sedin, Henrik, 419
Seguin, Tyler, 153

Seidenberg, Dennis, 44
Sekac, Jiri, 9
Sekera, Andrej, 214
Semin, Alexander, 85
Sestito, Tim, 271
Sestito, Tom, 419
Setoguchi, Devin, 71
Severson, Damon, 276
Sgarbossa, Michael, 520
Sharp, Patrick, 102
Shattenkirk, Kevin, 363
Shaw, Andrew, 102
Sheahan, Riley, 166
Sheppard, James, 301
Shinnimin, Brendan, 26
Shore, Drew, 72
Shore, Nick, 210, 475
Shugg, Justin, 85
Siemens, Duncan, 123
Silfverberg, Jakob, 10
Sill, Zach, 404
Simmonds, Wayne, 330
Sislo, Mike, 272
Skapski, Mackenzie, 307
Skille, Jack, 137
Skinner, Jeff, 86
Skjei, Brady, 475
Slater, Jim, 447
Smid, Ladislav, 75
Smith, Ben, 373

INDEX

Smith, Brendan, 170
Smith, Colin, 119
Smith, Craig, 256
Smith, Mike, 30
Smith, Reilly, 40
Smith, Trevor, 404
Smith, Zack, 316
Smith-Pelly, Devante, 241
Soderberg, Carl, 41
Spaling, Nick, 346
Spezza, Jason, 153
Spooner, Ryan, 41
Sprong, Daniel, 473
Spurgeon, Jared, 229
St. Denis, Frederic, 140
St. Louis, Martin, 302
Staal, Eric, 86
Staal, Jordan, 86
Staal, Marc, 305
Stafford, Drew, 447
Stajan, Matt, 72
Stalberg, Viktor, 257
Stalock, Alex, 378
Stamkos, Steven, 388
Stanton, Ryan, 422
Stastny, Paul, 360
Steen, Alexander, 360
Stempniak, Lee, 448
Stepan, Derek, 302
Stewart, Chris, 224

Stoll, Jarret, 210
Stollery, Karl, 377
Stone, Mark, 317
Stone, Michael, 29
Stoner, Clayton, 13
Strachan, Tyson, 59
Strait, Brian, 291
Straka, Petr, 330
Stralman, Anton, 391
Street, Ben, 119
Streit, Mark, 335
Strome, Dylan, 463
Strome, Ryan, 287
Stuart, Brad, 123
Stuart, Mark, 452
Subban, Malcolm, 45, 476
Subban, P.K., 245
Summers, Chris, 306
Sustr, Andrej, 391
Suter, Ryan, 229
Sutter, Brandon, 346
Sutter, Brett, 225
Sutter, Brody, 87
Svechnikov, Yevgeni, 470
Svedberg, Niklas, 46
Szwarz, Jordan, 26
Talbot, Cam, 307
Talbot, Max, 41
Tangradi, Eric, 241
Tanguay, Alex, 119

Tarasenko, Vladimir, 361
Tarasov, Daniil, 373
Tatar, Tomas, 166
Tavares, John, 288
Tennyson, Matt, 377
Teravainen, Teuvo, 102, 463
Terry, Chris, 87
Theodore, Shea, 466
Thomas, Christian, 241
Thompson, Nate, 10
Thorburn, Chris, 448
Thornton, Joe, 373
Thornton, Shawn, 197
Tierney, Chris, 374
Timonen, Kimmo, 106
Tinordi, Jarred, 245
Tlusty, Jiri, 448
Toews, Jonathan, 103
Toffoli, Tyler, 211
Tokarski, Dustin, 246
Tootoo, Jordin, 272
Torres, Raffi, 374
Trocheck, Vincent, 197
Tropp, Corey, 137
Trotman, Zach, 44
Trouba, Jacob, 453
Tuch, Alex, 472
Turris, Kyle, 317
Tyrell, Dana, 137
Tyutin, Fedor, 141

Uher, Dominik, 346
Umberger, R.J., 330
Upshall, Scottie, 197
Van Der Gulik, David, 211
van Riemsdyk, James, 404
van Riemsdyk, Trevor, 106
VandeVelde, Chris, 331
Vanek, Thomas, 225
Varlamov, Semyon, 124
Varone, Philip, 56
Vasilevskiy, Andrei, 392, 467
Vatanen, Sami, 13
Veilleux, Stephane, 225
Vermette, Antoine, 103
Versteeg, Kris, 103
Vesey, Jimmy, 466
Vey, Linden, 420
Vincour, Tomas, 120
Virtanen, Jake, 476
Visnovsky, Lubomir, 291
Vitale, Joe, 26
Vlasic, Marc-Edouard, 378
Volchenkov, Anton, 260
Volpatti, Aaron, 433
Voracek, Jakub, 331

Voynov, Slava, 215
Vrana, Jakub, 467
Vrbata, Radim, 420
Wagner, Chris, 10
Ward, Cam, 91
Ward, Joel, 434
Warsofsky, David, 45
Weaver, Mike, 245
Weber, Mike, 59
Weber, Shea, 261
Weber, Yannick, 423
Weise, Dale, 242
Weiss, Stephen, 167
Wennberg, Alexander, 138
Werenski, Zach, 468
Wheeler, Blake, 449
White, Ryan, 331
Whitney, Joe, 272
Wideman, Dennis, 76
Wiercioch, Patrick, 320
Williams, Justin, 211
Wilson, Colin, 257
Wilson, Garrett, 198
Wilson, Ryan, 123
Wilson, Scott, 347

Wilson, Tom, 434
Winchester, Jesse, 120
Wingels, Tommy, 374
Winnik, Daniel, 347
Wisniewski, James, 14
Witkowski, Luke, 392
Wolf, David, 72
Woods, Brendan, 87
Wotherspoon, Tyler, 76
Yakimov, Bogdan, 183
Yakupov, Nail, 183
Yandle, Keith, 306
Zacha, Pavel, 470
Zadorov, Nikita, 60
Zajac, Travis, 273
Zatkoff, Jeff, 351
Zboril, Jakub, 472
Zepp, Rob, 336
Zetterberg, Henrik, 167
Zibanejad, Mika, 317
Zidlicky, Marek, 170
Zolnierczyk, Harry, 288
Zubrus, Dainius, 273
Zuccarello, Mats, 302
Zucker, Jason, 225

Made in the USA
Lexington, KY
05 October 2015